America

Past and Present

America

Past and Present

Volume II Since 1865
Seventh Edition

ROBERT A. DIVINE
University of Texas

T. H. BREEN
Northwestern University

GEORGE M. FREDRICKSON
Stanford University

R. HAL WILLIAMS
Southern Methodist University

ARIELA J. GROSS
University of Southern California

H. W. BRANDS
Texas A&M University

PEARSON
Longman

New York   San Francisco   Boston
London   Toronto   Sydney   Tokyo   Singapore   Madrid
Mexico City   Munich   Paris   Cape Town   Hong Kong   Montreal

Vice President and Publisher: Priscilla McGeehon
Development Manager: Betty Slack
Development Editor: Karen Helfrich
Executive Marketing Manager: Sue Westmoreland
Media Editor: Patrick McCarthy
Supplements Editor: Kristi Olson
Production Manager: Douglas Bell
Project Coordination, Text Design, and Electronic Page Makeup: Elm Street Publishing Services, Inc.
Senior Design Manager/Cover Designer: Nancy Danahy
Cover and Frontispiece Image: Native Quilter's Gathering Quilt. Made by Native Quilter's gathering participants
    in East Lansing, Michigan. Courtesy of Michigan State University Museum, photographed by Doug Elbing.
Art Studio: Maps.com and Burmar Technical Corporation
Photo Research: Photosearch, Inc.
Senior Manufacturing Buyer: Alfred C. Dorsey
Printer and Binder: Quebecor World/Versailles
Cover Printer: The Lehigh Press, Inc.

For permission to use copyrighted material, grateful acknowledgment is made to the following copyright holders
and to those on pp. C1–C3, which are hereby made part of this copyright page.

Text credits: p. 529, Arthur Miller, *The Price*. New York, New York: Viking Penguin, 1968; p. 868, from "I Have
a Dream" by Martin Luther King, Jr. Copyright © 1963 by Martin Luther King, Jr., copyright renewed © 1991 by
Coretta Scott King. Reprinted by arrangement with the Heirs to the Estate of Martin Luther King, Jr.,
c/o Writer's House, Inc. as agent for the proprietor.

Library of Congress Cataloging-in-Publication Data

America, past and present / Robert A. Divine . . . [et al.].—7th ed.
    p. cm.
Includes bibliographical references and index.
ISBN 0-321-18309-6 (set)—ISBN 0-321-18308-8 (v. 1)—ISBN
0-321-18307-X (v. 2)
  1. United States—History.   I. Divine, Robert A.
E178.1.A4894 2004
973—dc22

                                                                2003026058

Please visit our website at http://www.ablongman.com/divine

ISBN 0-321-18309-6 (Complete Edition)
ISBN 0-321-18308-8 (Volume I)
ISBN 0-321-18307-X (Volume II)
ISBN 0-321-24380-3 (Advanced Placement Edition)

1 2 3 4 5 6 7 8 9 10—QWV—07 06 05 04

Brief Contents

Detailed Contents vii

Maps xiii

Figures and Tables xv

Features xvii

Preface xix

Supplements xxiii

Acknowledgments xxvii

About the Authors xxxi

CHAPTER 16
The Agony of Reconstruction 450

CHAPTER 17
The West:
Exploiting an Empire 480

CHAPTER 18
The Industrial Society 510

CHAPTER 19
Toward an Urban Society,
1877–1900 538

CHAPTER 20
Political Realignments
in the 1890s 572

CHAPTER 21
Toward Empire 600

CHAPTER 22
The Progressive Era 626

CHAPTER 23
From Roosevelt to Wilson in the
Age of Progressivism 654

CHAPTER 24
The Nation at War 688

CHAPTER 25
Transition to Modern America 718

CHAPTER 26
Franklin D. Roosevelt and
the New Deal 748

CHAPTER 27
America and the World,
1921–1945 776

CHAPTER 28
The Onset of the Cold War 806

CHAPTER 29
Affluence and Anxiety 836

CHAPTER 30
The Turbulent Sixties 856

CHAPTER 31
A Crisis in Confidence,
1969–1980 892

CHAPTER 32
The Republican Resurgence,
1980–1992 926

CHAPTER 33
America in Flux 960

Appendix A-1

Glossary G-1

Credits C-1

Index I-1

Detailed Contents

Maps   xiii

Figures and Tables   xv

Features   xvii

Preface   xix

Supplements   xxiii

Acknowledgments   xxvii

About the Authors   xxxi

CHAPTER 16
The Agony of Reconstruction   450

Robert Smalls and Black Politicians during Reconstruction   451

The President versus Congress   452
    Wartime Reconstruction   453
    Andrew Johnson at the Helm   453
    Congress Takes the Initiative   456
    Congressional Reconstruction Plan Enacted   457
    The Impeachment Crisis   458

Reconstructing Southern Society   460
    Reorganizing Land and Labor   460
    Black Codes: A New Name for Slavery?   462
    Republican Rule in the South   462
    Claiming Public and Private Rights   464

Retreat from Reconstruction   466
    Rise of the Money Question   466
    Final Efforts of Reconstruction   466
    A Reign of Terror Against Blacks   467
    Spoilsmen versus Reformers   469

Reunion and the New South   471
    The Compromise of 1877   471
    "Redeeming" a New South   472
    The Rise of Jim Crow   473

Conclusion: Henry McNeal Turner and the "Unfinished Revolution"   475

Feature Essay
Changing Views of Reconstruction   476

CHAPTER 17
The West: Exploiting an Empire   480

Lean Bear's Changing West   481

Beyond the Frontier   482

Crushing the Native Americans   483
    Life of the Plains Indians   483
    "As Long as Waters Run": Searching for an Indian Policy   485
    Final Battles on the Plains   486
    The End of Tribal Life   487

Settlement of the West   491
    Men and Women on the Overland Trail   492
    Land for the Taking   493
    Territorial Government   495
    The Spanish-Speaking Southwest   495

The Bonanza West   496
    The Mining Bonanza   496
    Gold from the Roots Up: The Cattle Bonanza   499
    Sodbusters on the Plains: The Farming Bonanza   502
    New Farming Methods   503
    Discontent on the Farm   505
    The Final Fling   506

Conclusion: The Meaning of the West   507

Feature Essay
Blacks in Blue: The Buffalo Soldiers in the West   488

CHAPTER 18
The Industrial Society   510

A Machine Culture   511

Industrial Development   512

An Empire on Rails   512
    "Emblem of Motion and Power"   513
    Building the Empire   514
    Linking the Nation via Trunk Lines   515
    Rails Across the Continent   516
    Problems of Growth   518

An Industrial Empire   519
    Carnegie and Steel   519
    Rockefeller and Oil   521
    The Business of Invention   522

The Sellers   525

The Wage Earners   529
    Working Men, Working Women, Working Children   529
    Culture of Work   531
    Labor Unions   531
    Labor Unrest   533

Conclusion: Industrialization's Benefits and Costs   536

Feature Essay
Chicago's "Second Nature"   526

CHAPTER 19

Toward an Urban Society, 1877–1900   538

The Overcrowded City   539

The Lure of the City   540
  Skyscrapers and Suburbs   540
  Tenements and the Problems of Overcrowding   541
  Strangers in a New Land   543
  Immigrants and the City   547
  The House That Tweed Built   548

Social and Cultural Change, 1877–1900   550
  Manners and Mores   551
  Leisure and Entertainment   552
  Changes in Family Life   554
  Changing Views: A Growing Assertiveness Among Women   554
  Educating the Masses   555
  Higher Education   557

The Stirrings of Reform   560
  Progress and Poverty   560
  New Currents in Social Thought   560
  The Settlement Houses   562
  A Crisis in Social Welfare   564

Conclusion: The Pluralistic Society   565

Feature Essay
Ellis Island: Isle of Hope, Isle of Tears   544

Law and Society
Plessy v. Ferguson: The Shaping of Jim Crow   567

CHAPTER 20

Political Realignments in the 1890s   572

Hardship and Heartache   573

Politics of Stalemate   574
  The Party Deadlock   575
  Experiments in the States   576
  Reestablishing Presidential Power   576

Republicans in Power: The Billion-Dollar Congress   578
  Tariffs, Trusts, and Silver   578
  The 1890 Elections   579

The Rise of the Populist Movement   579
  The Farm Problem   580
  The Fast-Growing Farmers' Alliance   581
  The People's Party   582

The Crisis of the Depression   583
  The Panic of 1893   583
  Coxey's Army and the Pullman Strike   584
  The Miners of the Midwest   585
  A Beleaguered President   587
  Breaking the Party Deadlock   587

Changing Attitudes   588
  "Everybody Works But Father"   588
  Changing Themes in Literature   589

The Presidential Election of 1896   591
  The Mystique of Silver   591

The Republicans and Gold   594
The Democrats and Silver   594
Campaign and Election   595

The McKinley Administration   596

Conclusion: A Decade's Dramatic Changes   598

Feature Essay
The Wonderful Wizard of Oz   592

CHAPTER 21

Toward Empire   600

Roosevelt and the Rough Riders   601

America Looks Outward   602
  Catching the Spirit of Empire   602
  Reasons for Expansion   603
  Foreign Policy Approaches, 1867–1900   606
  The Lure of Hawaii and Samoa   608
  The New Navy   610

War with Spain   611
  A War for Principle   611
  "A Splendid Little War"   613
  "Smoked Yankees"   615
  The Course of the War   616

Acquisition of Empire   617
  The Treaty of Paris Debate   619
  Guerrilla Warfare in the Philippines   620
  Governing the Empire   622
  The Open Door   623

Conclusion: Outcome of the War with Spain   624

Feature Essay
Americans by the Numbers: The 1890 Census   604

CHAPTER 22

The Progressive Era   626

Muckrakers Call for Reform   627

The Changing Face of Industrialism   628
  The Innovative Model T   629
  The Burgeoning Trusts   630
  Managing the Machines   631

Society's Masses   633
  Better Times on the Farm   633
  Women and Children at Work   634
  The Niagara Movement and the NAACP   635
  "I Hear the Whistle": Immigrants in the Labor Force   639

Conflict in the Workplace   641
  Organizing Labor   642
  Working with Workers   644
  Amoskeag   644

A New Urban Culture   645
  Production and Consumption   645
  Living and Dying in an Urban Nation   646
  Popular Pastimes   647
  Experimentation in the Arts   649

Conclusion: A Ferment of Discovery and Reform   650

Feature Essay
Margaret Sanger and the Birth Control Movement   636

CHAPTER 23
From Roosevelt to Wilson in the Age of Progressivism   654

The Republicans Split   655

The Spirit of Progressivism   656
  The Rise of the Professions   657
  The Social-Justice Movement   658
  The Purity Crusade   659
  Woman Suffrage, Women's Rights   660
  A Ferment of Ideas: Challenging the Status Quo   662

Reform in the Cities and States   663
  Interest Groups and the Decline of Popular Politics   663
  Reform in the Cities   664
  Action in the States   665

The Republican Roosevelt   667
  Busting the Trusts   667
  "Square Deal" in the Coalfields   668

Roosevelt Progressivism at Its Height   669
  Regulating the Railroads   669
  Cleaning Up Food and Drugs   669
  Conserving the Land   671

The Ordeal of William Howard Taft   672
  Party Insurgency   673
  The Ballinger-Pinchot Affair   673
  Taft Alienates the Progressives   673
  Differing Philosophies in the Election of 1912   675

Woodrow Wilson's New Freedom   676
  The New Freedom in Action   676
  Wilson Moves Toward the New Nationalism   678

Conclusion: The Fruits of Progressivism   682

Feature Essay
Madam C.J. Walker: African American Business
  Pioneer   680

⚖ *Law and Society*
Muller v. *Oregon:* Expanding the Definition of Acceptable
  Evidence   684

CHAPTER 24
The Nation at War   688

The Sinking of the Lusitania   689

A New World Power   690
  "I Took the Canal Zone"   691
  The Roosevelt Corollary   692
  Ventures in the Far East   693
  Taft and Dollar Diplomacy   693

Foreign Policy Under Wilson   694
  Conducting Moral Diplomacy   694
  Troubles Across the Border   694

Toward War   696
  The Neutrality Policy   696
  Freedom of the Seas   697
  The U-Boat Threat   698
  "He Kept Us Out of War"   699
  The Final Months of Peace   700

Over There   701
  Mobilization   701
  War in the Trenches   702

Over Here   706
  The Conquest of Convictions   706
  A Bureaucratic War   708
  Labor in the War   709

The Treaty of Versailles   712
  A Peace at Paris   712
  Rejection in the Senate   715

Conclusion: Postwar Disillusionment   716

Feature Essay
Measuring the Mind   704

CHAPTER 25
Transition to Modern America   718

Wheels for the Millions   719

The Second Industrial Revolution   720
  The Automobile Industry   720
  Patterns of Economic Growth   720
  Economic Weaknesses   722

City Life in the Jazz Age   723
  Women and the Family   724
  The Roaring Twenties   726
  The Flowering of the Arts   727

The Rural Counterattack   732
  The Fear of Radicalism   732
  Prohibition   734
  The Ku Klux Klan   735
  Immigration Restriction   736
  The Fundamentalist Challenge   737

Politics of the 1920s   737
  Harding, Coolidge, and Hoover   737
  Republican Policies   738
  The Divided Democrats   739
  The Election of 1928   740

Conclusion: The Old and the New   741

Feature Essay
Marcus Garvey: Racial Redemption and Black Nationalism   730

⚖ *Law and Society*
The Scopes "Monkey" Trial: Contesting Cultural Differences   743

CHAPTER 26
Franklin D. Roosevelt and the New Deal   748

The Struggle Against Despair   749

The Great Depression   750
  The Great Crash   750
  Effect of the Depression   752

Fighting the Depression   754
  Hoover and Voluntarism   754
  The Emergence of Roosevelt   754
  The Hundred Days   755
  Roosevelt and Recovery   757
  Roosevelt and Relief   759

Roosevelt and Reform   761
  Challenges to FDR   762
  Social Security   762
  Labor Legislation   763

Impact of the New Deal   764
  Rise of Organized Labor   764
  The New Deal Record on Help to Minorities   766
  Women at Work   767

End of the New Deal   768
  The Election of 1936   768
  The Supreme Court Fight   769
  The New Deal in Decline   773

Conclusion: The New Deal and American Life   774

Feature Essay
Eleanor Roosevelt and the Quest for Social Justice   770

CHAPTER 27
America and the World, 1921–1945   776

A Pact Without Power   777

Retreat, Reversal, and Rivalry   778
  Retreat in Europe   778
  Cooperation in Latin America   779
  Rivalry in Asia   780

Isolationism   780
  The Lure of Pacifism and Neutrality   781
  War in Europe   783

The Road to War   784
  From Neutrality to Undeclared War   784
  Showdown in the Pacific   786

Turning the Tide Against the Axis   788
  Wartime Partnerships   788
  Halting the German Blitz   790
  Checking Japan in the Pacific   791

The Home Front   792
  The Arsenal of Democracy   792
  A Nation on the Move   794
  Win-the-War Politics   797

Victory   798
  War Aims and Wartime Diplomacy   798
  Triumph and Tragedy in the Pacific   802

Conclusion: The Transforming Power of War   804

Feature Essay
The Face of the Holocaust   800

CHAPTER 28
The Onset of the Cold War   806

The Potsdam Summit   807

The Cold War Begins   808
  The Division of Europe   808
  Withholding Economic Aid   810
  The Atomic Dilemma   810

Containment   811
  The Truman Doctrine   811
  The Marshall Plan   812
  The Western Military Alliance   813
  The Berlin Blockade   814

The Cold War Expands   815
  The Military Dimension   815
  The Cold War in Asia   816
  The Korean War   817

The Cold War at Home   819
  Truman's Troubles   819
  Truman Vindicated   822
  The Loyalty Issue   823
  McCarthyism in Action   824
  The Republicans in Power   825

Eisenhower Wages the Cold War   827
  Entanglement in Indochina   829
  Containing China   830
  Turmoil in the Middle East   830
  Covert Actions   831
  Waging Peace   831

Conclusion: The Continuing Cold War   833

Feature Essay
The "Lost Sheep" of the Korean War   820

CHAPTER 29
Affluence and Anxiety   836

Levittown: The Flight to the Suburbs   837

The Postwar Boom   839
  Postwar Prosperity   839
  Life in the Suburbs   840

The Good Life?   841
  Areas of Greatest Growth   841
  Critics of the Consumer Society   842
  The Reaction to *Sputnik*   846

Farewell to Reform   847
  Truman and the Fair Deal   847
  Eisenhower's Modern Republicanism   848

The Struggle over Civil Rights   849
  Civil Rights as a Political Issue   850
  Desegregating the Schools   850
  The Beginnings of Black Activism   852

Conclusion: Restoring National Confidence   854

Feature Essay
Rise of a New Idiom in Modern Painting: Abstract Expressionism   844

CHAPTER 30
The Turbulent Sixties   856

Kennedy versus Nixon: The First Televised Presidential Candidate Debate   857

Kennedy Intensifies the Cold War   859
    Flexible Response   859
    Crisis over Berlin   859
    Containment in Southeast Asia   860
    Containing Castro: The Bay of Pigs Fiasco   861
    Containing Castro: The Cuban Missile Crisis   861

The New Frontier at Home   864
    The Congressional Obstacle   865
    Economic Advance   865
    Moving Slowly on Civil Rights   866
    "I Have a Dream"   867
    The Supreme Court and Reform   868

"Let Us Continue"   869
    Johnson in Action   870
    The Election of 1964   871
    The Triumph of Reform   872

Johnson Escalates the Vietnam War   876
    The Vietnam Dilemma   876
    Escalation   877
    Stalemate   878

Years of Turmoil   880
    The Student Revolt   880
    Protesting the Vietnam War   881
    The Cultural Revolution   882
    "Black Power"   882
    Ethnic Nationalism   884
    Women's Liberation   884

The Return of Richard Nixon   885
    Vietnam Undermines Lyndon Johnson   885
    The Democrats Divide   886
    The Republican Resurgence   888

Conclusion: The End of an Era   889

Feature Essay
Unintended Consequences: The Second Great Migration   874

CHAPTER 31
A Crisis in Confidence, 1969–1980   892

The Watergate Break-in   893

Nixon in Power   895
    Reshaping the Great Society   895
    Nixonomics   896
    Building a Republican Majority   897
    In Search of Détente   897
    Ending the Vietnam War   898

The Crisis of Democracy   899
    The Election of 1972   899
    The Watergate Scandal   900

Energy and the Economy   901
    The October War   901

The Oil Shocks   902
    The Search for an Energy Policy   903
    The Great Inflation   904
    The Shifting American Economy   904

Private Lives—Public Issues   905
    The Changing American Family   908
    Gains and Setbacks for Women   908
    The Gay Liberation Movement   910

Politics after Watergate   912
    The Ford Administration   912
    The 1976 Campaign   913
    Disenchantment with Carter   913

From Détente to Renewed Cold War   914
    Retreat in Asia   914
    Accommodation in Latin America   915
    The Quest for Peace in the Middle East   916
    The Cold War Resumes   917

Conclusion: A Failed Presidency   918

Feature Essay
Three Mile Island and Chernobyl: The Promise and Peril of Nuclear Power   906

Law and Society
Roe v. *Wade:* The Struggle over Women's Reproductive Rights   920

CHAPTER 32
The Republican Resurgence, 1980–1992   926

Reagan and the Rise of Conservatism   927

Reagan in Power   929
    The Reagan Victory   929
    Cutting Spending and Taxes   930
    Limiting the Role of Government   931

Reaganomics   933
    Recession and Recovery   933
    The Growing Deficit   933
    The Rich Grow Richer   936
    Reagan Affirmed   938

Reagan and the World   939
    Challenging the "Evil Empire"   939
    Turmoil in the Middle East   940
    Confrontation in Central America   941
    Trading Arms for Hostages   942
    Reagan the Peacemaker   943

Social Dilemmas   944
    The AIDS Epidemic   944
    The War on Drugs   946

Passing the Torch to Bush   947
    The Changing Palace Guard   947
    The Election of 1988   948
    Bush's Domestic Agenda   949
    The End of the Cold War   950
    Waging Peace   952

Conclusion: Republican Economic Woes   954

Feature Essay
The Christian Right   934

⚖ *Law and Society*
Bakke v. *Regents of the University of California:* The Question of Affirmative Action   956

CHAPTER 33
America in Flux   960

The Buck Starts Here   961

The Changing American Population   963
  A People on the Move   963
  The Revival of Immigration   964
  The Surging Hispanics   965
  Advance and Retreat for African Americans   966
  Americans from Asia and the Middle East   967
  Melting Pot or Multiethnic Diversity?   968

Democratic Revival   969
  The Election of 1992   969
  Economic Recovery   970
  President versus Congress   971
  Contract with America   973
  The Clinton Rebound   974

Clinton and the World   976
  Global Tensions in the Post–Cold War Era   976
  Intervening in Somalia and Haiti   977
  Halting Civil War in Bosnia   978
  Saving Kosovo   979

The End of the Century   980
  From Deficit to Surplus   980
  Violence in the 1990s   980
  Shadow on the White House   982

The New Millennium   984
  The Disputed Election of 2000   984
  Bush's Domestic Agenda   986
  Terrorism: Attack and Counterattack   990
  The New American Empire?   993

Conclusion: The American Century?   996

Feature Essay
The Dot.com Boom and Bust   988

APPENDIX   A-1

The Declaration of Independence   A-3

The Articles of Confederation   A-5

The Constitution of the United States of America   A-9

Amendments to the Constitution   A-14

Presidential Elections   A-18

Political and Physical Map of the United States   A-24

Political Map of the World   A-26

Glossary G-1

Credits C-1

Index I-1

Maps

PAGE

458 Reconstruction
472 Election of 1876
482 Physiographic Map of the United States
485 Native Americans in the West: Major Battles and Reservations
498 Mining Regions of the West
501 Cattle Trails
505 Agricultural Land Use in the 1880s
514 Federal Land Grants to the Railroads as of 1871
517 Railroads, 1870 and 1890
534 Labor Strikes, 1870–1890
546 Foreign-born Population, 1890
577 Election of 1888
583 Election of 1892
596 Election of 1896
609 Hawaiian Islands
616 Spanish-American War: Pacific Theater
617 Spanish-American War: Caribbean Theater
619 American Empire, 1900
621 World Colonial Empires, 1900
633 Irrigation and Conservation in the West to 1917
661 Woman Suffrage Before 1920
671 National Parks and Forests
676 Election of 1912
691 The Panama Canal Zone
695 Activities of the United States in the Caribbean, 1898–1930s
700 Election of 1916
702 European Alliances and Battlefronts, 1914–1917
703 The Western Front: U.S. Participation, 1918
711 African American Migration Northward, 1910–1920

PAGE

714 Europe After the Treaty of Versailles, 1919
740 Election of 1928
755 Election of 1932
757 The Tennessee Valley Authority
792 World War II in the Pacific
796 Japanese American Internment Camps
799 World War II in Europe and North Africa
809 Europe After World War II
813 Marshall Plan Aid to Europe, 1948–1952
818 The Korean War, 1950–1953
822 Election of 1948
849 The Interstate Highway System
858 Election of 1960
873 African American Voter Registration Before and After Passage of the Voting Rights Act of 1965
877 Southeast Asia and the Vietnam War
888 Election of 1968
899 Election of 1972
910 Voting on the Equal Rights Amendment
930 Election of 1980
941 Trouble Spots in the Middle East
942 Trouble Spots in Central America and the Caribbean
952 The End of the Cold War
963 Population Shifts, 1970–2000
970 Election of 1992
975 Election of 1996
978 The Breakup of Yugoslavia/Civil War in Bosnia
985 Election of 2000
A-24 Political and Physical Map of the United States
A-26 Political Map of the World

Figures and Tables

FIGURES

PAGE

515 Railroad Construction, 1830–1920

519 International Steel Production, 1880–1914

523 Patents Issued, by Decade, 1850–1899

543 Immigration to the United States, 1870–1900

550 Urban and Rural Population, 1870–1900

580 Selected Commodity Prices

630 Business Consolidations (Mergers), 1895–1905

639 Immigration to the United States, 1900–1920 (by area of origin)

640 Mexican Immigration to the United States, 1900–1920

642 Labor Union Membership, 1897–1920

664 Voter Participation in Presidential Elections, 1876–1920

PAGE

701 U.S. Losses to the German Submarine Campaign, 1916–1918

751 U.S. Unemployment, 1929–1942

754 Bank Failures, 1929–1933

839 Birthrate, 1940–1970

875 The Second Great Migration: A Theoretical Example

878 U.S. Troop Levels in Vietnam

902 The Oil Shocks: Price Increases of Crude Oil and Gasoline, 1973–1985

908 Types of Households in the United States, 2000

936 U.S. Budget Deficits, 1980–1997

937 Share of Aggregate Household Income by Quintiles, 1975–1995

TABLES

PAGE

457 Reconstruction Amendments, 1865–1870

466 The Election of 1868

470 The Election of 1872

475 Supreme Court Decisions Affecting Black Civil Rights, 1875–1900

577 The Election of 1880

577 The Election of 1884

597 The Election of 1900

669 The Election of 1904

672 The Election of 1908

713 Woodrow Wilson's Fourteen Points, 1918: Success and Failure in Implementation

716 The Election of 1920

740 The Election of 1924

PAGE

755 Presidential Voting in Chicago by Ethnic Groups, 1924–1932 (percentage Democratic)

769 The Election of 1936

772 Major New Deal Legislation and Agencies

785 The Election of 1940

798 The Election of 1944

826 The Election of 1952

849 The Election of 1956

872 The Election of 1964

875 Region of Birth of Foreign Born, 2000

913 The Election of 1976

939 The Election of 1984

948 The Election of 1988

Features

FEATURE ESSAYS

PAGE

476 Changing Views of Reconstruction
488 Blacks in Blue: The Buffalo Soldiers in the West
526 Chicago's "Second Nature"
544 Ellis Island: Isle of Hope, Isle of Tears
592 The Wonderful Wizard of Oz
604 Americans by the Numbers: The 1890 Census
636 Margaret Sanger and the Birth Control Movement
680 Madam C.J. Walker: African American Business Pioneer
704 Measuring the Mind
730 Marcus Garvey: Racial Redemption and Black Nationalism

PAGE

770 Eleanor Roosevelt and the Quest for Social Justice
800 The Face of the Holocaust
820 The "Lost Sheep" of the Korean War
844 Rise of a New Idiom in Modern Painting: Abstract Expressionism
874 Unintended Consequences: The Second Great Migration
906 Three Mile Island and Chernobyl: The Promise and Peril of Nuclear Power
934 The Christian Right
988 The Dot.com Boom and Bust

LAW AND SOCIETY ESSAYS

PAGE

567 *Plessy* v. *Ferguson:* The Shaping of Jim Crow
684 *Muller* v. *Oregon:* Expanding the Definition of Acceptable Evidence
743 The Scopes "Monkey" Trial: Contesting Cultural Differences

PAGE

920 *Roe* v. *Wade:* The Struggle Over Women's Reproductive Rights
956 *Bakke* v. *Regents of the University of California:* The Question of Affirmative Action

A LOOK AT THE PAST

PAGE

469 Cartoon "Worse Than Slavery"
500 Cowboy Clothing
504 Barbed Wire
524 Cash Register
525 Typewriter
549 Toy Bank
575 Ballot Box
603 Trade Card
618 Cartoon "School Begins"
646 Sears Catalog
670 Patent Medicine
697 Sheet Music Cover
721 Glenwood Stove Ad
723 Radio

PAGE

756 Jefferson Monument
759 FSA Photos
789 Service Stars
794 Ration Stamps
832 Fallout Shelter
840 Western-Themed Toys
882 Army Fatigue Jacket
883 Woodstock Brochure
901 Locking Gas Cap
945 AIDS Brochure
949 Christian Right Bumper Sticker
984 Handheld Computer
990 Patriotic Symbols

Preface

The seventh edition of *America Past and Present* is a major revision that strives to achieve the shared goal of the previous editions: to present a clear, relevant, and balanced history of the United States as an unfolding story of national development, from the days of the earliest inhabitants to the present. We emphasize the story because we strongly believe in the value of historical narrative in providing a vivid sense of the past. In each chapter, we seek to blend the excitement and drama of the American experience with insights about the social, economic, and cultural issues that underlie it.

REVISIONS FOR THE SEVENTH EDITION

In this edition, we have reviewed each chapter carefully to take account of recent scholarly work, to offer new perspectives, and to sharpen the analysis and the prose. In many cases, we have adopted the suggestions offered by those who used the previous editions in their classrooms.

Throughout this edition, as in previous editions, we pay particular attention to the roles that women and minority groups have played in the development of American society and the American nation. These people appear throughout the text, not as witnesses to the historical narrative but as principal actors in its evolution. New and expanded material in this edition includes the following:

- Chapter 1, ecological transformation and the impact of the environment on human encounters during the contact era.
- Chapter 6, new opening vignette highlighting the search for balance between public morality and private freedom in the new republic; additional coverage of treaties and western lands after the Revolutionary War.
- Chapter 7, scientific debate and the spirit of nationalism in the post–revolutionary era.
- Chapter 9, expanded discussion of treaties negotiated with Great Britain following the War of 1812.
- Chapter 11, revised and reorganized to enhance and emphasize coverage of the lives and lifestyles of slaves and their experience of slavery.

- Chapter 12, expanded discussion of black abolitionists and women's right reformers.
- Chapter 16, restructured and revised to devote greater attention to lives of former slaves during Reconstruction; includes new sections on Black Codes and Jim Crow laws.
- Chapter 17, new opening vignette exploring a Native American's experience of conquest and exploitation of the American West.
- Chapter 26, new opening vignette highlighting personal experiences of hardship during the Great Depression; revised discussion of the stock market crash of 1929.
- Chapter 29, expanded discussion of early civil rights leaders.
- Chapter 31, shifts in the labor movement in the 1970s, including the rise of public employee unions; the changing American family at the turn of the century.
- Chapter 33, revised and restructured to concentrate on the shifting economy of the 1990s to the present and the role of government policy in shaping American economy; updated with new discussion of foreign policy and homeland defense post–September 11, including new sections on the war on terrorism and war in Iraq.

APPROACH AND THEMES

As the title suggests, our book is a blend of the traditional and the new. The strong narrative emphasis and chronological organization are traditional; the incorporation of the many fresh insights that historians have gained from social sciences in the past quarter century is new. We have used significant incidents and episodes to reflect the dilemmas, the choices, and the decisions made by the people as well as by their leaders. After discussion of the colonial period, most of the chapters examine shorter time periods, usually about a decade, permitting us to view major political and public events as points of reference and orientation around which social themes are integrated. This approach gives unity and direction to the text.

In recounting the story of the American past, we see a nation in flux. The early Africans and Europeans developed complex agrarian folkways that blended Old World customs and New World experiences; as cultural identities evolved, the idea of political independence became more acceptable. People who had been subjects of the British crown created a system of government that challenged later Americans to work out the full implications of theories of social and economic equality.

The growing sectional rift between the North and South, revolving around divergent models of economic growth and conflicting social values, culminated in civil war. In the post–Civil War period, the development of a more industrialized economy severely tested the values of an agrarian society, engendering a Populist reform movement. In the early twentieth century, Progressive reformers sought to infuse the industrial order with social justice. World War I demonstrated the extent of American power in the world. The Great Depression and World War II tested the resiliency of the maturing American nation. The Cold War ushered in an era of crises, foreign and domestic, that revealed both the strengths and the weaknesses of modern America. Although the Cold War ended with the break-up of the Soviet Union in the early 1990s, new threats to world peace in Africa, the Balkans, and the Middle East, and attacks on the World Trade Center and the Pentagon on September 11, 2001, led to the war on terrorism rather than to a new era of peace and tranquility.

Our story of American history goes beyond the major events that have helped to shape the nation—the wars fought, the presidents elected, the legislation enacted, the treaties signed. The impact of change on human lives adds a vital dimension to our understanding of history. How did the American Revolution affect the lives of ordinary citizens? What was it like for both blacks and whites to live in a plantation society? How did the shift from an agrarian to an industrial economy affect both men and women? What impact has technology, in the form of the automobile and the computer, had on patterns of life in the twentieth century? Our narrative explores these issues as well.

Our commitment is not to any particular ideology or point of view; rather, we hope to challenge our readers to rediscover the fascination of the American past and reach their own conclusions about its significance in their lives. At the same time, we have not avoided controversial issues; instead, we have tried to offer reasoned judgments on such morally charged subjects as the nature of slavery and the advent of nuclear weapons. We believe that while history rarely repeats itself, the story of the American past is relevant to the problems and dilemmas facing the nation today, and we have therefore sought to

stress themes and ideas that continue to shape our national culture.

STRUCTURE AND FEATURES

The structure and features of the book are intended to stimulate student interest and to reinforce learning. Each chapter begins with a vignette that introduces the chapter themes and previews the topics to be discussed. The chapter chronology serves as a summary of the key events covered in the chapter. The recommended readings and suggested Web sites at the end of each chapter are sources students can consult for further information on many topics. The feature essay in each chapter offers an examination of a high-interest topic related to the chapters themes and topics. Key terms, highlighted in boldface type in the chapter text, are defined in the new end-of-text glossary, pp. G1–G13.

Feature Essays

There are eight new "Feature Essays" in the seventh edition, four of them focusing on aspects of peoples' relationships with and impact on the natural world throughout American history. The new essays are:

- Chapter 7, "Defense of Superiority: Science in the Service of Nationalism in the Early Republic"
- Chapter 8, "Barbary Pirates and American Captives: The Nation's First Hostage Crisis"
- Chapter 9, "Confronting New Land"
- Chapter 11, "Harriet Jacobs and Maria Norcom: Women of Southern Households"
- Chapter 18, "Chicago's 'Second Nature'"
- Chapter 19, "Ellis Island: Isle of Hope, Isle of Tears"
- Chapter 31, "Three Mile Island and Chernobyl: The Promise and Peril of Nuclear Power"
- Chapter 33, "The Dot.com Boom and Bust"

Law and Society Essays

Nine "Law and Society" essays appear in the text. Each of these essays focuses on a significant legal case or legal problem in American history and includes a discussion of the background of the case, excerpts from the trial transcript or other relevant primary source material, and coverage of the case in the news media of the period. The introductory section establishes the context for the case and the concluding paragraphs of each essay invite students to explore the legal contest from the perspective of social/cultural historians. New discussion questions are included to spark class discussion. The seventh edition includes two new "Law and Society" essays:

- Chapter 12, "The Legal Rights of Married Women: Reforming the Law of Coverture"
- Chapter 25, "The Scopes "Monkey" Trial: Contesting Cultural Differences"

Visual Program

The extensive full-color map program has been improved with several new and revised maps. Each map includes a caption to help students identify the purpose and significance of the map. New charts, graphs, and tables—many with a capsulized format for convenient review of factual information—relate to social and economic change. The rich, full-color illustration program, bearing directly on the narrative, advances and expands the themes, provides elaboration and contrast, tells more of the story, and generally adds another dimension of learning. "Look at the Past" photographs are illustrations of artifacts that present students with a material record of America's past. Captions invite them to consider the historical signifi-

cance of the artifacts and make connections with similar materials they encounter today.

AUTHOR RESPONSIBILITY

Although this book is a joint effort, each author took primary responsibility for writing one section. T. H. Breen contributed the first eight chapters, going from the earliest Native American period to the second decade of the nineteenth century. George M. Fredrickson wrote Chapters 9 through 16, carrying the narrative through the Reconstruction era. Ariela J. Gross revised Chapters 11 and 16 and contributed the Law and Society feature in Chapter 12. R. Hal Williams was responsible for Chapters 17 through 24, focusing on the industrial transformation, urbanization, and the events culminating in World War I. The final nine chapters, bringing the story through the Great Depression, World War II, and the Cold War and its aftermath, were the work of H. W. Brands, especially Chapters 25 through 27, and Robert A. Divine, primarily Chapters 28 through 33. Each contributor reviewed and revised the work of his or her colleagues and helped shape the material into its final form.

Supplements

For Qualified College Adopters: Instructor Supplements

Instructor's Resource Manual

Prepared by James Walsh of Central Connecticut State University, each chapter of this resource manual contains interpretive essays, anecdotes and references to biographical or primary sources, and a comprehensive summary of the text. ISBN: 0-321-21724-1.

Test Bank

Prepared by Denise Wright of University of Georgia, this test bank contains over 1,200 multiple-choice, true/false, matching, and completion questions. ISBN: 0-321-21721-7.

TestGen-EQ Computerized Testing System

This flexible, easy-to-master computerized test bank on a dual-platform CD includes all of the items in the printed test bank and allows instructors to select specific questions, edit existing questions, and add their own items to create exams. Tests can be printed in several different fonts and formats and can include figures such as graphs and tables. ISBN: 0-321-21720-9.

History Digital Media Archive CD-ROM

The Digital Media Archive CD-ROM contains electronic images and interactive and static maps, along with media elements such as video. These media assets are fully customizable and ready for classroom presentation or easy downloading into your PowerPoint™ presentations or any other presentation software. ISBN: 0-321-14976-9.

Digital Media Archive, Updated Second Edition

Now on two CD-ROMs and with added content, this encyclopedic collection contains dozens of narrated vignettes and videos as well as hundreds of photos and illustrations ready for use in your own PowerPoint™ presentations, course web sites, or on-line courses. Free to qualified college adopters.

Companion Web Site, www.ablongman.com/divine

Instructors can take advantage of the Companion Web Site that supports this text. The instructor section of the Web site includes teaching links and links to downloadable versions of all print supplements.

PowerPoint™ Presentations

These presentations contain an average of 15 PowerPoint™ slides for each chapter. These slides may include key points and terms for a lecture on the chapter as well as four-color slides of all maps, graphs, and charts within a particular chapter. The presentations are available for download at www.ablongman.com/suppscentral.

CourseCompass™, www.ablongman.com/coursecompass

Combines the strength of the content from *America Past and Present,* Seventh Edition, with state-of-the-art eLearning tools. CourseCompass™ is an easy-to-use on-line course management system that allows professors to tailor content and functionality to meet individual course needs. Every CourseCompass™ course includes a range of pre-loaded content—all designed to help students master core course objectives. Organized by era, CourseCompass™ allows you to access maps, map exercises, and primary sources as well as test questions from the print test bank and the full text of several of our best-selling supplements. The *America Past and Present* CourseCompass™ site is available at no additional charge for students whose professor has requested that a student Access Kit be bundled with the text.

BlackBoard and WebCT

Longman's extensive American history content is available in these two major course management platforms: BlackBoard and WebCT. All quickly and easily customizable for use with *America Past and Present,* Seventh Edition, the content includes multiple primary sources, maps, and map exercises. Book-specific testing is simply uploaded.

The History Place Premium Web Site, www.ushistoryplace.com

Available at no additional cost when requested as a bundle component by the professor, the site offers extraordinary breadth and depth, featuring unmatched interactive maps, timelines, and activities; hundreds of source documents, images, and audio clips; and much more.

Comprehensive American History Transparency Set

This collection includes more than 200 four-color American history map transparencies on subjects ranging from the first Native Americans to the end of the Cold War, covering wars, social trends, elections, immigration, and demographics. ISBN: 0-673-97211-9.

Text-specific Transparency Set

A set of four-color transparency acetates showing maps from the text. ISBN: 0-321-21719-5.

Video Lecture Launchers

Prepared by Mark Newman, University of Illinois at Chicago, these video lecture launchers (each two to five minutes in duration) cover key issues in American history from 1877 to the present. The launchers are accompanied by an Instructor's Manual. ISBN: 0-321-01869-9.

For Students

Multimedia Edition CD-ROM for *America Past and Present*, Seventh Edition

This unique CD-ROM takes students beyond the printed page, offering them a complete multimedia learning experience. It contains the full annotatable textbook on CD-ROM, with contextually placed media—audio, video, interactive maps, photos, figures, Web links, and practice tests—that link students to additional content directly related to key concepts in the text. The CD also contains the Study Guide, map workbooks, a primary source reader, and more than a dozen supplementary books most often assigned in American history courses. Free to qualified college adopters when packaged with the text. ISBN: 0-321-23474-4.

Study Guide and Practice Tests

Prepared by Jennifer Lynn Gross of Jacksonville State University and John Walker Davis of University of Georgia. Each of the two-volume study guides begins with an introductory essay, "Skills for Studying and Learning History." Each chapter contains a summary, learning objectives, identification list, map exercises, glossary, and multiple-choice, completion, and essay questions, and new critical thinking exercises involving primary sources. Volume One: ISBN: 0-321-21286-X; Volume Two: ISBN: 0-321-21722-5.

Longman American History Atlas

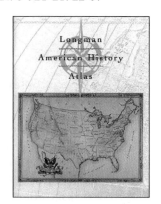

A four-color reference tool and visual guide to American history that includes almost 100 maps and covers the full scope of history. Atlas overhead transparencies available to qualified college adopters. $3.00 when bundled. ISBN: 0-321-00486-8.

Mapping America: A Guide to Historical Geography, Second Edition

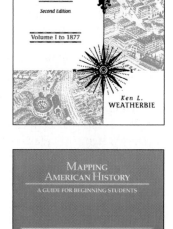

A two-volume workbook by Ken L. Weatherbie, Del Mar College, that presents the basic geography of the United States and helps students place the history of the United States into spatial perspective. Free to qualified college adopters when bundled. Volume One: ISBN: 0-321-00487-6; Volume Two: ISBN: 0-321-00488-4.

Mapping American History

A workbook created by Gerald A. Danzer for use in conjunction with *Discovering American History Through Maps and Views* and designed to teach students to interpret and analyze cartographic materials as historical documents. Free to qualified college adopters when bundled. ISBN: 0-673-53768-4.

Companion Web Site for *America Past and Present,* Seventh Edition, www.ablongman.com/divine

The Companion Web Site provides a wealth of resources for students using the text. Students can access chapter summaries, interactive practice test questions, and Web links for every chapter. The Web site is a comprehensive on-line study guide for students.

Research Navigator Guide

This guidebook includes exercises and tips on how to use the Internet. It also includes an access code for Research Navigator™—the easiest way for students to start a research assignment or research paper. Research Navigator™ is composed of three exclusive databases of credible and reliable source material including EBSCO's ContentSelect™ Academic Journal Database, New York Times Search by Subject Archive, and "Best of the Web" Link Library. This comprehensive site also includes a detailed help section. ISBN: 0-205-40838-9.

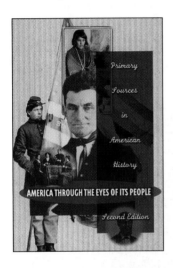

America Through the Eyes of Its People, Second Edition

A comprehensive anthology that makes primary sources widely available in an inexpensive format, balancing social and political history and providing up-to-date narrative material. Free to qualified college adopters when bundled. ISBN: 0-673-97738-2.

Sources of the African American Past, Second Edition

Edited by Roy Finkenbine, University of Detroit at Mercy, this collection of primary sources covers key themes in the African American experience from the West African background to the present. Balanced between political and social history, it offers a vivid snapshot of the lives of African Americans in different historical periods and includes documents representing women and different regions of the United States. Available to qualified college adopters at a minimum cost when bundled with the text. ISBN: 0-321-16216-1.

Women and the National Experience, Second Edition

Edited by Ellen Skinner, Pace University, this primary source reader contains both classic and unusual documents describing the history of women in the United States. The documents provide dramatic evidence that outspoken women attained a public voice and participated in the development of national events and policies long before they could vote. Chronologically organized and balanced between social and political history, this reader offers a striking picture of the lives of women across American history. Available to qualified college adopters at a minimum cost when bundled with the text. ISBN: 0-321-00555-4.

Reading the American West

Edited by Mitchel Roth, Sam Houston State University, this primary source reader uses letters, diary excerpts, speeches, interviews, and newspaper articles to let students experience how historians research and how history is written. Every document is accompanied by a contextual headnote and study questions. The book is divided into chapters with extensive introductions. Available to qualified college adopters at a minimum cost when bundled with the text. ISBN: 0-321-04409-6.

A Short Guide to Writing About History, Fifth Edition

Richard Marius, Harvard University, Melvin E. Page Eastern Tennessee University. This engaging and practical text helps students get beyond merely compiling dates and facts; it teaches them how to incorporate their own ideas into their papers and to tell a story about history that interests them and their peers. Covering both brief essays and the documented resource paper, the text explores the writing and researching processes, different modes of historical writing including argument, and concludes with guidelines for improving style. ISBN: 0-321-22716-6.

Constructing the American Past, Fifth Edition

Compiled and edited by Elliot Gorn and Randy Roberts of Purdue University, this popular two-volume reader consists of a variety of primary sources, grouped around central themes in American history. Each chapter focuses on a particular problem in American history, providing students with several points of view from which to examine the historical evidence. Introductions and study questions prompt students to participate in interpreting the past and challenge them to understand the problems in relation to the big picture of American history. Volume One ISBN: 0-321-21642-3; Volume Two ISBN: 0-321-21641-5.

From These Beginnings: A Biographical Approach to American History, Seventh Edition

Written by Roderick Nash of the University of California, Santa Barbara, and Gregory Graves of California State University, Northridge, this collection of biographical essays takes a look at the lives of famous men and women whose contributions helped create a nation and a society. Each biography offers students a uniquely personal and provocative glimpse into the lives of these Americans and shows how their experiences are linked to historical events. Volume One ISBN: 0-321-21640-7; Volume Two ISBN: 0-321-21639-3.

American Experiences: Readings in American History, Sixth Edition

This two-volume collection of secondary readings, compiled and edited by Randy Roberts of Purdue University and James Olson of Sam Houston State University, contains articles that emphasize social history in order to illuminate important aspects of America's past. *American Experiences* addresses the complexity and richness of the nation's past by focusing on the people themselves—how they coped with, adjusted to, or rebelled against America. The readings examine people as they worked and played, fought and loved, lived and died. Volume One ISBN: 0-321-21644-X; Volume Two ISBN: 0-321-21643-1.

American History in a Box

This unique primary source reader offers students the opportunity to experience written documents, visual materials, material culture artifacts, and maps in order to learn firsthand what history is and what historians actually do. It was written and put together by Julie Roy Jeffrey and Peter Frederick; Volume One (to 1877) ISBN: 0-321-30005-2; Volume Two (since 1865) ISBN: 0-321-03006-0.

The History Place Premium Web Site, www.ushistoryplace.com

Available at no additional cost when requested as a bundle component by the professor, the site is a continually updated American history Web site of extraordinary breadth and depth, which features unmatched interactive maps, timelines, and activities; hundreds of source documents, images, and audio clips; and much more.

The Library of American Biography Series

Each of the interpretative biographies in this series focuses on a figure whose actions and ideas significantly influenced the course of American history and national life. Brief and inexpensive, they are ideal for any American history survey course. Available to qualified college adopters at a discount when bundled with this text.

Penguin Books

The partnership between Penguin-Putnam USA and Longman Publishers offers students a discount on many titles when you bundle them with any Longman survey. Among these include

- Frederick Douglass, *Narrative of the Life of Frederick Douglass*
- L. Jesse Lemisch (Editor), *Benjamin Franklin: The Autobiography & Other Writings*
- Upton Sinclair, *The Jungle*
- Harriet Beecher Stowe, *Uncle Tom's Cabin*

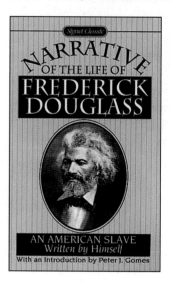

Acknowledgments

The authors acknowledge with special gratitude the contribution of Professor Jeanne Whitney of Salisbury State University for her work in selecting many of the featured "Look at the Past" illustrations and writing the informative and thought-provoking captions to accompany these photos. We are also most grateful to our consultants and reviewers whose thoughtful and constructive work contributed greatly to this edition. Their many helpful suggestions led to significant improvements in the final product.

Elizabeth Ansnes, *San Jose State University*
Donald Scott Barton, *East Central University*
Chad Berry, *Maryville College*
Kent Blaser, *Wayne State College*
Eric J. Bolsterli, *University of Texas at Arlington*
Kathleen S. Carter, *High Point University*
Yvonne Sutton Cornelius, *Nashville State Community College*
Edward R. Crowther, *Adams State University*
Roger P. Davis, *University of Nebraska at Kearney*
Patricia Norred Derr, *Kutztown University*
Wallace Hettle, *University of Northern Iowa*
Virginia G. Jelatis, *Western Illinois University*
Sandra Wagner-Wright, *University of Hawaii at Hilo*

This book owes much to the many conscientious historians who reviewed previous editions and offered valuable suggestions that led to many improvements in the text. We acknowledge with gratitude the contributions of the following:

Frank W. Abbott, *University of Houston*
Joseph L. Adams, *St. Louis Community College at Meramec*
Frank Alduino, *Anne Arundel Community College*
Kenneth G. Alfers, *Mountain View College*
Thomas Archdeacon, *University of Wisconsin*
James Axtell, *College of William and Mary*
Kenneth R. Bain, *Northwestern University*
James Banks, *Cuyahoga Community College*
Lois W. Banner, *Hamilton College*
David Bernstein, *California State University, Long Beach*
James D. Border, *Berkshire Community College*
Alexander O. Boulton, *Villa Julie College*
Mary C. Brennan, *Ohio State University*
Blanche Brick, *Blinn College*
Daniel Patrick Brown, *Moorpark College*
Thomas Camfield, *Sam Houston State University*
Clayborne Carson, *Stanford University*
Kathleen S. Carter, *High Point University*
Raphael Cassimere, Jr., *University of New Orleans*
Francis Coan, *Central Connecticut State University*
Charles L. Cohen, *University of Wisconsin*
Jerald Combs, *San Francisco State University*
John Cooper, *University of Wisconsin*
Nancy F. Cott, *Yale University*
Virginia Crane, *University of Wisconsin, Oshkosh*
James C. Curtis, *University of Delaware*
Bruce J. Dierenfield, *Canisius College*
Charles Douglass, *Florida Community College at Jacksonville*
Thomas Dublin, *State University of New York at Binghamton*
Perry R. Duis, *University of Illinois at Chicago*
Richard Ellis, *State University of New York at Buffalo*
John P. Farr, *Chattanooga State Technical Community College*
James E. Fell, Jr., *University of Colorado, Denver*
Eric Foner, *Columbia University*
Stephen Foster, *Northern Illinois University*
William W. Freehling, *Johns Hopkins University*
Fred E. Freidel, *Bellevue Community College*
Richard Frey, *Southern Oregon State College*
Gary W. Gallagher, *Pennsylvania State University*
Sara E. Gallaway, *Oxnard College*
Don R. Gerlach, *University of Akron*
August W. Giebelhaus, *Georgia Institute of Technology*
Louis S. Gomolak, *Southwest Texas State University*
Lewis L. Gould, *University of Texas*

Lawrence Grear, *Langston University*

Richard C. Haney, *University of Wisconsin, Whitewater*

George Harrison, *Jones County Junior College*

Edward F. Hass, *Wright State University*

Tim Heinrichs, *Bellevue Community College*

Mary Ann Heiss, *Kent State University*

Kenneth E. Hendrickson, *Sam Houston State University*

Sondra Herman, *De Anza Community College*

Anne Hickling, *San Jose City College*

James Hollingsworth, *Pasco-Hernando Community College*

Ranford Hopkins, *Moorpark College*

Brian Hosmer, *University of Delaware*

John R. Howe, *University of Minnesota*

Nathan I. Huggins, *Harvard University*

Susan Hult, *Houston Community College*

James A. Hurst, *Northwest Missouri State University*

Wallace S. Hutcheon, *Northern Virginia Community College*

Robert M. Ireland, *University of Kentucky*

Carol E. Jenson, *University of Wisconsin, La Crosse*

Juli A. Jones, *St. Charles County Community College*

Robert R. Jones, *University of Southwestern Louisiana*

John Kelley, *Shawnee State Community College*

Richard S. Kirkendall, *University of Washington*

I. E. Kirkpatrick, *Tyler Junior College*

Fred Koestler, *Tarleton State University*

Lawrence F. Kohl, *University of Alabama*

Steven Lawson, *Rutgers University*

Edward Lee, *Winthrop University*

Kathy Long, *Chattanooga State Technical Community College*

Henry Louis, *Kansas City Kansas Community College*

Warren Mackey, *Chattanooga State Technical Community College*

Thomas R. Mandeville, *Clinton Community College*

Karen Marcotte, *Palo Alto College*

Herbert F. Margulies, *University of Hawaii*

Myron Marty, *National Endowment for the Humanities*

Robert C. McMath, Jr., *Georgia Institute of Technology*

T. Ronald Melton, *Brewton-Parker College*

James H. Merrell, *Vassar College*

Joseph C. Miller, *University of Virginia*

William G. Morris, *Midland College*

Harmon Mothershead, *Northwest Missouri State University*

Timothy Moy, *University of New Mexico*

Peter Murray, *Methodist College*

John M. Murrin, *Princeton University*

John K. Nelson, *University of North Carolina*

Roger L. Nichols, *University of Arizona*

Elizabeth R. Osborne, *Indiana University–Purdue University at Indianapolis*

Elliot Pasternack, *Middlesex County College*

J'Nell L. Pate, *Tarrant County Junior College*

Michael Perman, *University of Illinois, Chicago*

Charles A. Pilant, *Cumberland College*

Nora Ramirez, *San Antonio Community College*

Marlette Rebhorn, *Austin Community College*

Douglas W. Richmond, *University of Texas, Arlington*

Andrew W. Robertson, *Louisiana State University*

David Sandoval, *University of Southern Colorado*

Howard Schonberger, *University of Maine*

Ingrid Winther Scobie, *Texas Women's University*

Rebecca S. Shoemaker, *Indiana State University*

Kathryn Kish Sklar, *State University of New York at Binghamton*

Allan Spetter, *Wright State University*

Cherry L. Spruill, *Indiana University–Purdue University at Indianapolis*

Mark J. Stegmaier, *Cameron University*

George G. Suggs, Jr., *Southeast Missouri State University*

H. Micheal Tarver, *McNeese State University*

Paul F. Taylor, *Augusta College*

Michael E. Thompson, *South Seattle Community College*

George Torok, *El Paso Community College*

Clyde D. Tyson, *Niagara County Community College*

Nancy C. Unger, *San Francisco State University*

Richard Vanderpool, *Umpqua Community College*

Donna L. VanRaaphorst, *Cuyahoga Community College*

Russell Veeder, *Dickinson State University*

Daniel C. Vogt, *Jackson State University*

Forrest A. Walker, *Eastern New Mexico State University*

James P. Walsh, *Central Connecticut State University*

Ronald Walters, *Johns Hopkins University*

Marli Weiner, *University of Maine*

Frank Wetta, *Galveston Community College*

James C. Williams, *De Anza College*

James M. Woods, *Georgia Southern University*

David Yancey, *San Jose City College*

Rosemarie Zagarri, *Catholic University*

Robert F. Zeidel, *University of Wisconsin, Stout*

The staff at Longman continued its generous support and assistance for our efforts. We thank Acquisitions Editor Ashley Dodge for her attention, support, and thoughtful guidance throughout this revision; Development Manager Betty Slack and Development Editor Karen Helfrich, who helped us augment and enhance the appeal of the text; and Executive Marketing Manager Sue Westmoreland, who worked zealously to convey the message and vision of the authors to the Longman sales force and to the marketplace. Production Manager Douglas Bell, Cover Design Manager/Cover Designer Nancy Danahy, and Project Editor Heather Johnson and the staff at Elm Street Publishing Services put the finishing touches on this new edition and deftly guided it through the many phases of production.

Finally, each author received aid and encouragement from many colleagues, friends, and family members. Bob Divine extends special thanks to Mitch Lerner for research assistance and editorial suggestions. T. H. Breen thanks Bradley S. Schlager, Seth Cotlar, Timothy Hall, Christopher Hodson, and Patrick Griffin for their help with this edition. George Fredrickson acknowledges with gratitude the research and assistance of Jared Farmer. Hal Williams extends thanks to Carole S. Cohen, Jacqueline Bradley, Lisa R. Henry, and Susan Harper-Bisso for their help with revisions for this edition. Ariela Gross extends thanks to Lori Martinez, John Acevedo, and especially Stephen Andrews for invaluable help with this edition.

The Authors

ROBERT A. DIVINE

Robert A. Divine, George W. Littlefield Professor Emeritus in American History at the University of Texas at Austin, received his Ph.D. from Yale University in 1954. A specialist in American diplomatic history, he taught from 1954 to 1996 at the University of
Texas, where he was honored by both the student association and the graduate school for teaching excellence. His extensive published work includes *The Illusion of Neutrality* (1962); *Second Chance: The Triumph of Internationalism in America During World War II* (1967); and *Blowing on the Wind* (1978). His most recent work is *Perpetual War for Perpetual Peace* (2000), a comparative analysis of twentieth-century American wars. He is also the author of *Eisenhower and the Cold War* (1981) and editor of three volumes of essays on the presidency of Lyndon Johnson. His book, *The Sputnik Challenge* (1993), won the Eugene E. Emme Astronautical Literature Award for 1993. He has been a fellow at the Center for Advanced Study in the Behavioral Sciences and has given the Albert Shaw Lectures in Diplomatic History at Johns Hopkins University.

T. H. BREEN

T. H. Breen, William Smith Mason Professor of American History at Northwestern University, received his Ph.D. from Yale University in 1968. He has taught at Northwestern since 1970. Breen's major books include *The Character of the Good Ruler: A Study of Puritan*
Political Ideas in New England (1974); *Puritans and Adventurers: Change and Persistence in Early America* (1980); *Tobacco Culture: The Mentality of the Great Tidewater Planters on the Eve of Revolution* (1985); and, with Stephen Innes of the University of Virginia, *"Myne Owne Ground": Race and Freedom on Virginia's Eastern Shore* (1980). His *Imagining the Past* (1989) won the 1990

Historic Preservation Book Award. His most recent book is *Common Goods: Revolutionary Markets on the Eve of American Independence* (2003). In addition to receiving several awards for outstanding teaching at Northwestern, Breen has been the recipient of research grants from the American Council of Learned Societies, the Guggenheim Foundation, the Institute for Advanced Study (Princeton), the National Humanities Center, and the Huntington Library. For his article "Narrative of Commercial Life: Consumption, Ideology, and Community on the Eve of the American Revolution," which appeared in the July 1993 issue of *William and Mary Quarterly*, Breen received an award from the National Society, Daughters of Colonial Wars, for best article published in the quarterly in 1993 and the Douglass Adair Memorial Prize for best article published in the quarterly during the 1988–1993 period. He has served as the Fowler Hamilton Fellow at Christ Church, Oxford University (1987–1988), the Pitt Professor of American History and Institutions, Cambridge University (1990–1991), and the Harmsworth Professor of American History at Oxford University (2000–2001). He is currently working on an opera based on an essay he wrote on the wrongful execution of an African American in 1768.

GEORGE M. FREDRICKSON

George M. Fredrickson is Edgar E. Robinson Professor Emeritus of United States History at Stanford University. He is the author or editor of several books, including *The Inner Civil War* (1965), *The Black Image in the White Mind* (1971), and *White Supremacy:*
A Comparative Study in American and South African History (1981), which won both the Ralph Waldo Emerson Award from Phi Beta Kappa and the Merle Curti Award from the Organization of American Historians. His most recent books are *Black Liberation: A Comparative History of Black Ideologies in the United States and South Africa* (1995); *The Comparative Imagination: Racism, Nationalism, and Social Movements* (1997); and *Racism: A Short History* (2002). He received

his A.B. and Ph.D. from Harvard and has been the recipient of a Guggenheim Fellowship, two National Endowment for the Humanities Senior Fellowships, and a fellowship from the Center for Advanced Studies in the Behavioral Sciences. Before coming to Stanford in 1984, he taught at Northwestern. He has also served as Fulbright lecturer in American History at Moscow University and as the Harmsworth Professor of American History at Oxford. He served as president of the Organization of American Historians in 1997–1998.

R. HAL WILLIAMS

R. Hal Williams is professor of history at Southern Methodist University. He received his A.B. from Princeton University in 1963 and his Ph.D. from Yale University in 1968. His books include *The Democratic Party and California Politics, 1880–1896* (1973); *Years of Decision: American Politics in the 1890s* (1978); and *The Manhattan Project: A Documentary Introduction to the Atomic Age* (1990). A specialist in American political history, he taught at Yale University from 1968 to 1975 and came to SMU in 1975 as chair of the Department of History. From 1980 to 1988, he served as dean of Dedman College, the school of humanities and sciences, at SMU. In 1980, he was a visiting professor at University College, Oxford University. Williams has received grants from the American Philosophical Society and the National Endowment for the Humanities, and he has served on the Texas Committee for the Humanities. He is currently working on a biography of James G. Blaine, the late-nineteenth-century speaker of the House, secretary of state, and Republican presidential candidate.

ARIELA J. GROSS

Ariela J. Gross is professor of law and history at the University of Southern California. She received her B.A. from Harvard University, her J.D. from Stanford Law School, and her Ph.D. from Stanford University. She is the author of *Double Character: Slavery and Mastery in the Antebellum Southern Courtroom* (2000) and numerous law review articles and book chapters. Her current work in progress, a history of racial identity on trial in the United States to be published by Farrar, Straus & Giroux, is supported by fellowships from the Guggenheim Foundation, the National Endowment for the Humanities, and the American Council for Learned Societies.

H. W. BRANDS

H. W. Brands is University Distinguished Professor and Melbern G. Glasscock Chair in American History at Texas A&M University, where he has taught since 1987. He is the author of numerous works of history and international affairs, including *The Devil We Knew: Americans and the Cold War* (1993), *What America Owes the World: The Struggle for the Soul of Foreign Policy* (1998), *Into the Labyrinth: The United States and the Middle East* (1994), *The Reckless Decade: America in the 1890s* (1995), *TR: The Last Romantic* (a biography of Theodore Roosevelt) (1997), *The First American: The Life and Times of Benjamin Franklin* (2000), *The Strange Death of American Liberalism* (2001), *The Age of Gold: The California Gold Rush and the New American Dream* (2002), and *Woodrow Wilson* (2003). His writing has received critical and popular acclaim; *The First American* was a finalist for the Pulitzer Prize and a national bestseller. He lectures frequently across North America and in Europe. His essays and reviews have appeared in the *New York Times*, the *Wall Street Journal*, the *Washington Post*, the *Los Angeles Times*, and *Atlantic Monthly*. He is a regular guest on radio and television, and has participated in several historical documentary films.

America

Past and Present

The First Vote, *drawn by A. H. Ward for* Harper's Weekly, *November 16, 1867.* ❖

The Agony of Reconstruction

$\mathcal{R}$obert Smalls and Black Politicians During Reconstruction

During the Reconstruction period immediately following the Civil War, African Americans struggled to become equal citizens of a democratic republic. They produced a number of remarkable leaders who showed that blacks were as capable as other Americans of voting, holding office, and legislating for a complex and rapidly changing society. Among these leaders was Robert Smalls of South Carolina. Although virtually forgotten by the time of his death in 1915, Smalls was perhaps the most famous and widely respected southern black leader of the Civil War and Reconstruction era. His career reveals some of the main features of the African American experience during that crucial period.

Born a slave in 1839, Smalls had a white father whose identity has never been clearly established. But his white ancestry apparently gained him some advantages, and as a young man he was allowed to live and work independently, hiring his own time from a master who may have been his half brother. Smalls worked as a sailor and trained himself to be a pilot in Charleston Harbor.

When the Union navy blockaded Charleston in 1862, Smalls, who was then working on a Confederate steamship called the *Planter,* saw a chance to win his freedom in a particularly dramatic way. At three o'clock in the morning on May 13, 1862, when the white officers of the *Planter* were ashore, he took command of the vessel and its slave crew, sailed it out of the heavily fortified harbor, and surrendered it to the Union navy. Smalls immediately became a hero to those antislavery Northerners who were seeking evidence that the slaves were willing and able to serve the Union. The *Planter* was turned into a Union army transport, and Smalls was made its captain after being commissioned as an officer. During the remainder of the war, he rendered conspicuous and gallant service as captain and pilot of Union vessels off the coast of South Carolina.

Like a number of other African Americans who had fought valiantly for the Union, Smalls went on to a distinguished political career during Reconstruction, serving in the South Carolina constitutional convention, in the state legislature, and for several terms in the U.S. Congress. He was also a shrewd businessman and became the owner of extensive properties in Beaufort, South Carolina, and its vicinity. (His first purchase was the house of his former master, where he had spent his early years as a slave.) As the leading citizen of Beaufort during Reconstruction and for some years thereafter, he acted like many successful white Americans, combining the acquisition of wealth with the exercise of political power.

The electoral organization Smalls established resembled in some ways the well-oiled "machines" being established in northern towns and cities. It was so effective that he was able to control local government and get himself elected to Congress even after the election of 1876 had placed the state under the control of white conservatives bent on depriving blacks of political power. Organized mob violence defeated him in 1878, but he bounced back to win by decision of Congress a contested congressional election in 1880. He did not leave the House of Representatives for good until 1886, when he lost another contested election that had to be decided by Congress. It revealed the

OUTLINE
✦✦✦

The President Versus Congress

Reconstructing Southern Society

Retreat from Reconstruction

Reunion and the New South

Conclusion: Henry McNeal Turner and the "Unfinished Revolution"

FEATURE ESSAY
✦✦✦

Changing Views of Reconstruction

With the help of several black crewmen, Robert Smalls—then twenty-three years old—commandeered the Planter, *a Confederate steamship used to transport guns and ammunition, and surrendered it to the Union vessel, U.S.S.* Onward. *Smalls provided distinguished service to the Union during the Civil War and after the war went on to become a successful politician and businessman.* ❖

changing mood of the country that his white challenger was seated despite evidence of violence and intimidation against black voters.

In their efforts to defeat him, Smalls's white opponents frequently charged that he had a hand in the corruption that was allegedly rampant in South Carolina during Reconstruction. But careful historical investigation shows that he was, by the standards of the time, an honest and responsible public servant. In the South Carolina convention of 1868 and later in the state legislature, he was a conspicuous champion of free and compulsory public education. In Congress, he fought for the enactment and enforcement of federal civil rights laws. Not especially radical on social questions, he sometimes bent over backward to accommodate what he regarded as the legitimate interests and sensibilities of South Carolina whites. Like other middle-class black political leaders in Reconstruction-era South Carolina, he can perhaps be faulted in hindsight for not doing more to help poor blacks gain access to land of their own. But in 1875, he sponsored congressional legislation that opened for purchase at low prices the land in his own district that had been confiscated by the federal government during the war. As a result, blacks were able to buy most of it, and they soon owned three-fourths of the land in Beaufort and its vicinity.

Robert Smalls spent the later years of his life as U.S. collector of customs for the port of Beaufort, a beneficiary of the patronage that the Republican party continued to provide for a few loyal southern blacks. But the loss of real political clout for Smalls and men like him was one of the tragic consequences of the fall of Reconstruction.

FOR A BRIEF PERIOD OF YEARS, black politicians such as Robert Smalls exercised more power in the South than they would for another century. A series of political developments on the national and regional stage made Reconstruction "an unfinished revolution," promising but not delivering true equality for newly freed African Americans. National party politics, shifting priorities among Northern Republicans, white Southerners' commitment to white supremacy, backed by legal restrictions, as well as massive extra-legal violence against blacks, all combined to stifle the promise of Reconstruction.

Yet the Reconstruction Era also saw major transformations in American society in the wake of the Civil War—new ways of organizing labor and family life, new institutions within and outside of the government, and new ideologies regarding the role of institutions and government in social and economic life. Many of the changes begun during Reconstruction laid the groundwork for later revolutions in American life.

THE PRESIDENT VERSUS CONGRESS

The problem of how to reconstruct the Union in the wake of the South's military defeat was one of the most difficult and perplexing challenges ever faced by American policymakers. The Constitution provided no firm guidelines, for the framers had not anticipated a division of the country into warring sections. After emancipation became a northern war aim, the problem was compounded by a new issue: How far should the federal government go to secure freedom and civil rights for four million former slaves?

The debate that evolved led to a major political crisis. Advocates of a minimal Reconstruction policy favored quick restoration of the Union with no protection for the freed slaves beyond the prohibition of slavery. Proponents of a more radical policy wanted readmission of the southern states to be dependent on guarantees that "loyal" men would displace the Confederate elite in positions of power and that blacks would acquire basic rights of American citizenship. The White House favored the minimal approach, whereas Congress came to endorse the more radical and thoroughgoing form of Reconstruction. The resulting struggle between Congress and the chief executive was the most serious clash between two branches of government in the nation's history.

Wartime Reconstruction

Tension between the president and Congress over how to reconstruct the Union began during the war. Occupied mainly with achieving victory, Lincoln never set forth a final and comprehensive plan for bringing rebellious states back into the fold. But he did take initiatives that indicated he favored a lenient and conciliatory policy toward Southerners who would give up the struggle and repudiate slavery. In December 1863, he issued a Proclamation of Amnesty and Reconstruction, which offered a full pardon to all Southerners (with the exception of certain classes of Confederate leaders) who would take an oath of allegiance to the Union and acknowledge the legality of emancipation. This **Ten Percent Plan** provided that once 10 percent or more of the voting population of any occupied state had taken the oath, they were authorized to set up a loyal government. By 1864, Louisiana and Arkansas, states that were wholly or partially occupied by Union troops, had established Unionist governments. Lincoln's policy was meant to shorten the war. First, he hoped to weaken the southern cause by making it easy for disillusioned or lukewarm Confederates to switch sides. Second, he hoped to further his emancipation policy by insisting that the new governments abolish slavery

Congress was unhappy with the president's Reconstruction experiments and in 1864 refused to seat the Unionists elected to the House and Senate from Louisiana and Arkansas. A minority of congressional Republicans—the strongly antislavery **Radical Republicans**—favored protection for black rights (especially black male suffrage) as a precondition for the readmission of southern states. But a larger group of Congressional moderates opposed Lincoln's plan, not on the basis of black rights but because they did not trust the repentant Confederates who would play a major role in the new governments. They feared that the old ruling class would return to power and cheat the North of the full fruits of its impending victory.

Congress also believed the president was exceeding his authority by using executive powers to restore the Union. Lincoln operated on the theory that secession, being illegal, did not place the Confederate states outside the Union in a constitutional sense. Since individuals and not states had defied federal authority, the president could use his pardoning power to certify a loyal electorate, which could then function as the legitimate state government.

The dominant view in Congress, on the other hand, was that the southern states had forfeited their place in the Union and that it was up to Congress to decide when and how they would be readmitted. The most popular justification for congressional responsibility was based on the clause of the Constitution providing that "the United States shall guarantee to every State in this Union a Republican Form of Government." By seceding, Radicals argued, the Confederate states had ceased to be republican, and Congress had to set the conditions to be met before they could be readmitted.

After refusing to recognize Lincoln's 10 percent governments, Congress passed a Reconstruction bill of its own in July 1864. Known as the **Wade-Davis Bill**, this legislation required that 50 percent of the voters take an oath of future loyalty before the restoration process could begin. Once this had occurred, those who could swear they had never willingly supported the Confederacy could vote in an election for delegates to a constitutional convention. The bill in its final form did not require black suffrage, but it did give federal courts the power to enforce emancipation. Faced with this attempt to nullify his own program, Lincoln exercised a pocket veto by refusing to sign the bill before Congress adjourned. He justified his action by announcing that he did not want to be committed to any single Reconstruction plan. The sponsors of the bill responded with an angry manifesto, and Lincoln's relations with Congress reached their low.

Congress and the president remained stalemated on the Reconstruction issue for the rest of the war. During his last months in office, however, Lincoln showed some willingness to compromise. He persisted in his efforts to obtain full recognition for the governments he had nurtured in Louisiana and Arkansas but seemed receptive to the setting of other conditions—perhaps including black suffrage—for readmission of those states where wartime conditions had prevented execution of his plan. However, he died without clarifying his intentions, leaving historians to speculate whether his quarrel with Congress would have worsened or been resolved. Given Lincoln's past record of political flexibility, the best bet is that he would have come to terms with the majority of his party.

Andrew Johnson at the Helm

Andrew Johnson, the man suddenly made president by an assassin's bullet, attempted to put the Union back together on his own authority in 1865. But his policies eventually set him at odds with Congress and the Republican party and provoked the most serious crisis in the history of relations between the executive and legislative branches of the federal government.

Johnson's background shaped his approach to Reconstruction. Born in dire poverty in North Carolina, he migrated as a young man to eastern Tennessee, where he made his living as a tailor. Lacking

In this cartoon, President Andrew Johnson (left) and Thaddeus Stevens, the Radical Republican Congressman from Pennsylvania, are depicted as train engineers in a deadlock on the tracks. Indeed, neither Johnson nor Stevens would give way on his plans for Reconstruction. ❖

formal schooling, he did not learn to read and write until adult life. Entering politics as a Jacksonian Democrat, he became known as an effective stump speaker. His railing against the planter aristocracy made him the spokesman for Tennessee's nonslaveholding whites and the most successful politician in the state. He advanced from state legislator to congressman to governor and in 1857 was elected to the U.S. Senate.

When Tennessee seceded in 1861, Johnson was the only senator from a Confederate state who remained loyal to the Union and continued to serve in Washington. But his Unionism and defense of the common people did not include antislavery sentiments. Nor was he friendly to blacks. While campaigning in Tennessee, he had objected only to the fact that slaveholding was the privilege of a wealthy minority. He revealed his attitude when he wished that "every head of family in the United States had one slave to take the drudgery and menial service off his family."

During the war, while acting as military governor of Tennessee, Johnson endorsed Lincoln's emancipation policy and carried it into effect. But he viewed it primarily as a means of destroying the power of the

hated planter class rather than as a recognition of black humanity. He was chosen as Lincoln's running mate in 1864 because it was thought that a pro-administration Democrat, who was a southern Unionist in the bargain, would strengthen the ticket. No one expected Johnson to succeed to the presidency; it is one of the strange accidents of American history that a southern Democrat, a fervent white supremacist, came to preside over a Republican administration immediately after the Civil War.

Some Radical Republicans initially welcomed Johnson's ascent to the nation's highest office. Their hopes make sense in the light of Johnson's record of fierce loyalty to the Union and his apparent agreement with the Radicals that ex-Confederates should be severely treated. More than Lincoln, who had spoken of "malice toward none and charity for all," Johnson seemed likely to punish southern "traitors" and prevent them from regaining political influence. Only gradually did the deep disagreement between the president and the Republican Congressional majority become evident.

The Reconstruction policy that Johnson initiated on May 29, 1865, created some uneasiness among the Radicals, but most Republicans were willing to give it a chance. Johnson placed North Carolina and eventually other states under appointed provisional governors chosen mostly from among prominent southern politicians who had opposed the secession movement and had rendered no conspicuous service to the Confederacy. The governors were responsible for calling constitutional conventions and ensuring that only "loyal" whites were permitted to vote for delegates. Participation required taking the oath of allegiance that Lincoln had prescribed earlier. Once again, Confederate leaders and former officeholders who had participated in the rebellion were excluded. To regain their political and property rights, those in the exempted categories had to apply for individual presidential pardons. Johnson made one significant addition to the list of the excluded: all those possessing taxable property exceeding $20,000 in value. In this fashion, he sought to prevent his longtime adversaries—the wealthy planters—from participating in the Reconstruction of southern state governments.

Once the conventions met, Johnson urged them to do three things: Declare the ordinances of secession illegal, repudiate the Confederate debt, and ratify the **Thirteenth Amendment** abolishing slavery. After governments had been reestablished under constitutions meeting these conditions, the president assumed that the Reconstruction process would be complete and that the ex-Confederate states could regain their full rights under the Constitution.

The results of the conventions, which were dominated by prewar Unionists and representatives of backcountry yeoman farmers, were satisfactory to the president but troubling to many congressional Republicans. Rather than quickly accepting Johnson's recommendations, delegates in several states approved them begrudgingly or with qualifications. Furthermore, all the resulting constitutions limited suffrage to whites, disappointing the large number of Northerners who hoped, as Lincoln had, that at least some African Americans—perhaps those who were educated or had served in the Union army—would be given the vote. Johnson on the whole seemed eager to give southern white majorities a free hand in determining the civil and political status of the freed slaves.

Republican uneasiness turned to disillusionment and anger when the state legislatures elected under the new constitutions proceeded to pass **Black Codes** subjecting former slaves to a variety of special regulations and restrictions on their freedom. Especially troubling were vagrancy and apprenticeship laws that forced African Americans to work and denied them a free choice of employers. Blacks in some states were also prevented from testifying in court on the same basis as

whites and were subject to a separate penal code. To Radicals, the Black Codes looked suspiciously like slavery under a new guise. More upsetting to northern public opinion in general, a number of prominent ex-Confederate leaders were elected to Congress in the fall of 1865.

Johnson himself was partly responsible for this turn of events. Despite his lifelong feud with the planter class, he was generous in granting pardons to members of the old elite who came to him, hat in hand, and asked for them. When former Confederate Vice President Alexander Stephens and other proscribed ex-rebels were elected to Congress although they had not been pardoned, Johnson granted them special amnesty so they could serve.

The growing rift between the president and Congress came into the open in December, when the House and Senate refused to seat the recently elected southern delegation. Instead of endorsing Johnson's work and recognizing the state governments he had called into being, Congress established a joint committee, chaired by Senator William Pitt Fessenden of

"Slavery Is Dead?" asks this 1866 cartoon by Thomas Nast. To the cartoonist, the Emancipation Proclamation of 1863 and the North's victory in the Civil War meant little difference to the treatment of the freed slaves in the South. Freed slaves convicted of crimes often endured the same punishments as had slaves—sale, as depicted in the left panel of the cartoon, or beatings, as shown on the right. ❖

Maine, to review Reconstruction policy and set further conditions for readmission of the seceded states.

Congress Takes the Initiative

The struggle over how to reconstruct the Union ended with Congress doing the job of setting policy all over again. The clash between Johnson and Congress was a matter of principle and could not be reconciled. President Johnson, an heir of the Democratic states' rights tradition, wanted to restore the prewar federal system as quickly as possible and without change except that states would not have the right to legalize slavery or to secede.

Most Republicans wanted firm guarantees that the old southern ruling class would not regain regional power and national influence by devising new ways to subjugate blacks. They favored a Reconstruction policy that would give the federal government authority to limit the political role of ex-Confederates and provide some protection for black citizenship.

Republican leaders—with the exception of a few extreme Radicals such as Charles Sumner—lacked any firm conviction that blacks were inherently equal to whites. They did believe, however, that in a modern democratic state, all citizens must have the same basic rights and opportunities, regardless of natural abilities. Principle coincided easily with political expediency; southern blacks, whatever their alleged short-comings, were likely to be loyal to the Republican party that had emancipated them. They could be used, if necessary, to counteract the influence of resurgent ex-Confederates, thus preventing the Democrats from returning to national dominance through control of the South.

The disagreement between the president and Congress became irreconcilable in early 1866, when Johnson vetoed two bills that had passed with overwhelming Republican support. The first extended the life of the **Freedmen's Bureau**—a temporary agency set up to aid the former slaves by providing relief, education, legal help, and assistance in obtaining land or employment. The second was a civil rights bill meant to nullify the Black Codes and guarantee to freedmen "full and equal benefit of all laws and proceedings for the security of person and property as is enjoyed by white citizens."

Johnson's vetoes shocked moderate Republicans who had expected the president to accept the relatively modest measures as a way of heading off more radical proposals, such as black suffrage and a prolonged denial of political rights to ex-Confederates. Presidential opposition to policies that represented the bare minimum of Republican demands on the South alienated moderates in the party and ensured a wide opposition to Johnson's plan of Reconstruction. Johnson suc-

ceeded in blocking the Freedmen's Bureau bill, although a modified version later passed. But the Civil Rights Act won the two-thirds majority necessary to override his veto, signifying that the president was now hopelessly at odds with most of the congressmen from what was supposed to be his own party. Never before had Congress overridden a presidential veto.

Johnson soon revealed that he intended to abandon the Republicans and place himself at the head of a new conservative party uniting the small minority of Republicans who supported him with a reviving Democratic party that was rallying behind his Reconstruction policy. In preparation for the elections of 1866, Johnson helped found the National Union movement to promote his plan to readmit the southern states to the Union without further qualifications. A National Union convention meeting in Philadelphia in August 1866 called for the election to Congress of men who endorsed the presidential plan for Reconstruction.

Meanwhile, the Republican majority on Capitol Hill, fearing that Johnson would not enforce civil rights legislation or that the courts would declare such federal laws unconstitutional, passed the **Fourteenth Amendment.** This, perhaps the most important of all the constitutional amendments, gave the federal government responsibility for guaranteeing equal rights under the law to all Americans. Section 1 defined national citizenship for the first time as extending to "all persons born or naturalized in the United States." The states were prohibited from abridging the rights of American citizens and could not "deprive any person of life, liberty, or property, without due process of law; nor deny to any person . . . equal protection of the laws."

The other sections of the amendment were important in the context of the time but had fewer long-term implications. Section 2 sought to penalize the South for denying voting rights to black men by reducing the congressional representation of any state that formally deprived a portion of its male citizens of the right to vote. Section 3 denied federal office to those who had taken an oath of office to support the U.S. Constitution and then had supported the Confederacy, and Section 4 repudiated the Confederate debt. The amendment was sent to the states with the understanding that Southerners would have no chance of being readmitted to Congress unless their states ratified it.

The congressional elections of 1866 served as a referendum on the Fourteenth Amendment. Johnson opposed the amendment on the grounds that it created a "centralized" government and denied states the right to manage their own affairs; he also counseled southern state legislatures to reject it, and all except Tennessee followed his advice. But the president's case for state autonomy was weakened by the publicity resulting from bloody race riots in New Orleans and Memphis. These and other reported atrocities against blacks made it clear that the existing southern state governments were failing abysmally to protect the "life, liberty, or property" of the ex-slaves.

Johnson further weakened his cause by taking the stump on behalf of candidates who supported his policies. In his notorious "swing around the circle," he toured the nation, slandering his opponents in crude language and engaging in undignified exchanges with hecklers. Enraged by southern inflexibility and the antics of a president who acted as if he were still campaigning in the backwoods of Tennessee, northern voters repudiated the administration. The Republican majority in Congress increased to a solid two-thirds in both houses, and the Radical wing of the party gained strength at the expense of moderates and conservatives.

Among the most influential of the Radical Republicans was Congressman Thaddeus Stevens of Pennsylvania. He advocated seizing land from southern planters and distributing it among the freed slaves. ❖

Congressional Reconstruction Plan Enacted

Congress was now in a position to implement its own plan of Reconstruction. In 1867 and 1868, it passed a series of acts that nullified the president's initiatives and reorganized the South on a new basis. Generally referred to as **Radical Reconstruction,** the measures actually represented a compromise between genuine Radicals and more moderate elements within the party.

Consistent Radicals such as Senator Charles Sumner of Massachusetts and Congressmen Thaddeus Stevens of Pennsylvania and George Julian of Indiana wanted to reshape southern society before readmitting ex-Confederates to the Union. Their program of "regeneration before Reconstruction" required an extended period of military rule, confiscation and redis-

tribution of large landholdings among the freedmen, and federal aid for schools to educate blacks and whites for citizenship. But the majority of Republican congressmen found such a program unacceptable because it broke too sharply with American traditions of federalism and regard for property rights and might mean that decades would pass before the Union was back in working order.

The First Reconstruction Act, passed over Johnson's veto on March 2, 1867, did place the South under the rule of the army by reorganizing the region into five military districts. But military rule would last for only a short time. Subsequent acts of 1867 and 1868 opened the way for the quick readmission of any state that framed and ratified a new constitution providing for black suffrage. Ex-Confederates

RECONSTRUCTION AMENDMENTS, 1865–1870

Amendment	Main Provisions	Congressional Passage (2/3 majority in each house required)	Ratification Process (3/4 of all states required, including ex-Confederate states)
13	Slavery prohibited in United States	January 1865	December 1865 (27 states, including 8 southern states)
14	National citizenship; State representation in Congress reduced proportionally to number of voters disfranchised; Former Confederates denied right to hold office; Confederate debt repudiated	June 1866	Rejected by 12 southern and border states, February 1867; Radicals make readmission of southern states hinge on ratification; ratified July 1868
15	Denial of franchise because of race, color, or past servitude explicitly prohibited	February 1869	Ratification required for readmission of Virginia, Texas, Mississippi, Georgia; ratified March 1870

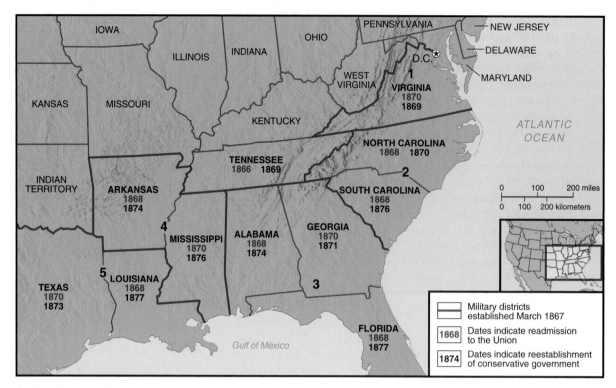

RECONSTRUCTION   *During the Reconstruction era, the southern state governments passed through three phases: control by white ex-Confederates; domination by Republican legislators, both white and black; and, finally, the regain of control by conservative white Democrats.* ❖

disqualified from holding federal office under the Fourteenth Amendment were prohibited from voting for delegates to the constitutional conventions or in the elections to ratify the conventions' work. Since blacks were allowed to participate in this process, Republicans thought they had found a way to ensure that "loyal" men would dominate the new governments. Radical Reconstruction was based on the dubious assumption that once blacks had the vote, they would have the power to protect themselves against white supremacists' efforts to deny them their rights. The Reconstruction Acts thus signaled a retreat from the true Radical position that a sustained use of federal authority was needed to complete the transition from slavery to freedom and prevent the resurgence of the South's old ruling class. (Troops were used in the South after 1868, but only in a very limited and sporadic way.) The majority of Republicans were unwilling to embrace centralized government and an extended period of military rule over civilians, and even Radicals such as Thaddeus Stevens supported the compromise as the best that could be achieved. Yet a genuine spirit of democratic idealism did give legitimacy and fervor to the cause of black male suffrage. Enabling people who were so poor and downtrodden to have access to the ballot box was a bold

and innovative application of the principle of government by the consent of the governed. The problem was finding a way to enforce equal suffrage under conditions then existing in the postwar South.

The Impeachment Crisis

The first obstacle to enforcement of congressional Reconstruction was resistance from the White House. Johnson thoroughly disapproved of the new policy and sought to thwart the will of Congress by administering the plan in his own obstructive fashion. He immediately began to dismiss officeholders who sympathized with Radical Reconstruction, and he countermanded the orders of generals in charge of southern military districts who were zealous in their enforcement of the new legislation. Some Radical generals were transferred and replaced by conservative Democrats. Congress responded by passing laws designed to limit presidential authority over Reconstruction matters. One of the measures was the Tenure of Office Act, requiring Senate approval for the removal of cabinet officers and other officials whose appointment had needed the consent of the Senate. Another measure—a rider to an army appropriations bill—sought to limit Johnson's authority to issue orders to military commanders.

Johnson objected vigorously to the restrictions on the grounds that they violated the constitutional doctrine of the separation of powers. When it became clear that the president was resolute in fighting for his powers and using them to resist the establishment of Radical regimes in the southern states, some congressmen began to call for his impeachment. A preliminary effort foundered in 1867, but when Johnson tried to discharge Secretary of War Edwin Stanton—the only Radical in the cabinet—and persisted in his efforts despite the disapproval of the Senate, the pro-impeachment forces gained in strength.

In January 1868, Johnson ordered General Grant, who already commanded the army, to replace Stanton as head of the War Department. But Grant had his eye on the Republican presidential nomination and refused to defy Congress. Johnson subsequently appointed General Lorenzo Thomas, who agreed to serve. Faced with this apparent violation of the Tenure of Office Act, the House voted overwhelmingly to impeach the president on February 24, and he was placed on trial before the Senate.

Because seven Republican senators broke with the party leadership and voted for acquittal, the effort to convict Johnson and remove him from office fell one vote short of the necessary two-thirds. This outcome resulted in part from a skillful defense. Attorneys for the president argued for a narrow interpretation of the constitutional provision that a president could be impeached only for "high crimes and misdemeanors," asserting that this referred only to indictable offenses. Responding to the charge that Johnson had deliberately violated the Tenure of Office Act, the defense contended that the law did not apply to the removal of Stanton because he had been appointed by Lincoln, not Johnson.

The prosecution countered with a different interpretation of the Tenure of Office Act, but the core of their case was that Johnson had abused the powers of his office in an effort to sabotage the congressional Reconstruction policy. Obstructing the will of the legislative branch, they claimed, was sufficient grounds for conviction even if no crime had been committed. The Republicans who broke ranks to vote for acquittal could not endorse such a broad view of the impeachment power. They feared that removal of a president for essentially political reasons would threaten the constitutional balance of powers and open the way to legislative supremacy over the executive. In addition, the man who would have succeeded Johnson— Senator Benjamin Wade of Ohio, the president pro tem of the Senate—was unpopular with conservative Republicans because of his radical position on labor and currency questions.

Andrew Johnson's successful defense against conviction in his impeachment case centered on his invocation of the Constitution to defend his presidential rights and powers. Impeached in 1868, Johnson escaped conviction by a single vote. ❖

Although Johnson's acquittal by the narrowest of margins protected the American presidency from congressional domination, the impeachment episode helped create an impression in the public mind that the Radicals were ready to turn the Constitution to their own use to gain their objectives. Conservatives were again alarmed when Congress took action in 1868 to deny the Supreme Court's appellate jurisdiction in cases involving the military arrest and imprisonment of anti-Reconstruction activists in the South. But the evidence of congressional ruthlessness and illegality is not as strong as most historians used to think. Modern legal scholars have found merit in the Radicals' claim that their actions did not violate the Constitution.

Failure to remove Johnson from office was an embarrassment to congressional Republicans, but the episode did ensure that Reconstruction in the South would proceed as the majority in Congress intended. During the trial, Johnson helped influence the verdict by pledging to enforce the Reconstruction Acts, and he held to this promise during his remaining months in office. Unable to depose the president, the Radicals had at least succeeded in neutralizing his opposition to their program.

RECONSTRUCTING SOUTHERN SOCIETY

The Civil War left the South devastated, demoralized, and destitute. Slavery was dead, but what this meant for future relationships between whites and blacks was still in doubt. The overwhelming majority of southern whites wanted to keep blacks adrift between slavery and freedom—without rights, in a status resembling that of the "free Negroes" of the Old South. Blacks sought to be independent of their former masters and viewed the acquisition of land, education, and the vote as the best means of achieving this goal. The thousands of Northerners who went south after the war for materialistic or humanitarian reasons hoped to extend Yankee "civilization" to what they viewed as an unenlightened and barbarous region. For most of them, this reformation required the aid of the freedmen; not enough southern whites were willing to accept the new order and embrace northern middle-class values.

The struggle of these groups to achieve their conflicting goals bred chaos, violence, and instability. Unsettled conditions created many opportunities for corruption, crime, and terrorism. This was scarcely an ideal setting for an experiment in interracial democracy, but one was attempted nonetheless. Its success depended on massive and sustained support from the federal government. To the extent that this was forthcoming, progressive reform could be achieved. When it faltered, the forces of reaction and white supremacy were unleashed.

Reorganizing Land and Labor

The Civil War scarred the southern landscape and wrecked its economy. One devastated area—central South Carolina—looked to an 1865 observer "like a broad black streak of ruin and desolation—the fences are gone; lonesome smokestacks, surrounded by dark heaps of ashes and cinders, marking the spots where human habitations had stood; the fields all along the roads widely overgrown with weeds, with here and there a sickly patch of cotton or corn cultivated by negro squatters." Other areas through which the armies had passed were similarly ravaged. Several major cities—including Atlanta, Columbia, and Richmond—were gutted by fire. Most factories were dismantled or destroyed, and long stretches of railroad were torn up.

Physical ruin would not have been so disastrous if investment capital had been available for rebuilding. But the substantial wealth represented by Confederate currency and bonds had melted away, and emancipation of the slaves had divested the propertied classes of their most valuable and productive assets. According to some estimates, the South's per capita wealth in 1865 was only about half what it had been in 1860.

Recovery could not even begin until a new labor system replaced slavery. It was widely assumed in both the North and the South that southern prosperity would continue to depend on cotton and that the plantation was the most efficient unit for producing the crop. Hindering efforts to rebuild the plantation economy were lack of capital, the deep-rooted belief of southern whites that blacks would work only under compulsion, and the freedmen's resistance to labor conditions that recalled slavery.

Blacks strongly preferred to determine their own economic relationships, and for a time they had reason to hope the federal government would support their ambitions. The freed slaves were placed in a precarious position and were, in effect, fighting a two-front war. Although they were grateful for the federal aid in ending slavery, freed slaves often had ideas about freedom that contradicted the plans of their northern allies. Many ex-slaves wanted to hold on to the family-based communal work methods that they utilized during slavery. Freed slaves in areas of South Carolina, for example, attempted to maintain the family task system rather than adopting the individual piecework system pushed by northern capitalists. Many ex-slaves opposed plans to turn them into wage laborers who produced exclusively for a market. Finally, freed slaves often wanted to stay on the land their families had spent generations farming rather than move elsewhere to assume plots of land as individual farmers.

While not guaranteeing all of the freed slaves' hopes for economic self-determination, the northern military attempted to establish a new economic base for the freed men and women. General Sherman, hampered by the huge numbers of black fugitives that followed his army on its famous march, issued an order in January 1865 that set aside the islands and coastal areas of Georgia and South Carolina for exclusive black occupancy on 40-acre plots. Furthermore, the Freedmen's Bureau, as one of its many responsibilities, was given control of hundreds of thousands of acres of abandoned or confiscated land and was authorized to make 40-acre grants to black settlers for three-year periods, after which they would have the option to buy at low prices. By June 1865, forty thousand black farmers were at work on 300,000 acres of what they thought would be their own land.

But for most of them the dream of "forty acres and a mule," or some other arrangement that would give them control of their land and labor, was not to be realized. President Johnson pardoned the owners of most of the land consigned to the ex-slaves by Sherman and the Freedmen's Bureau, and proposals for an effective program of land confiscation and redistribution failed to get through Congress. Among the considerations prompting most congressmen to oppose land reform were a tenderness for property rights, fear of sapping the freedmen's initiative by giving them something they allegedly had not earned, and the desire to restore cotton production as quickly as possible to increase agricultural exports and stabilize the economy. Consequently, most blacks in physical possession of small farms failed to acquire title, and the mass of freedmen were left with little or no prospect of becoming landowners. Recalling the plight of southern blacks in 1865, an ex-slave later wrote that "they were set free without a dollar, without a foot of land, and without the wherewithal to get the next meal even."

Despite their poverty and landlessness, ex-slaves were reluctant to settle down and commit themselves to wage labor for their former masters. Many took to the road, hoping to find something better. Some were still expecting grants of land, but others were simply trying to increase their bargaining power. One freedman later recalled that an important part of being free was that, "we could move around [and] change bosses." As the end of 1865 approached, many freedmen had still not signed up for the coming season; anxious planters feared that blacks were plotting to seize land by force. Within a few weeks, however, most holdouts signed for the best terms they could get.

One common form of agricultural employment in 1866 was a contract labor system. Under this system, workers committed themselves for a year in return for fixed wages, a substantial portion of which was withheld until after the harvest. Since many planters were inclined to drive hard bargains, abuse their workers, or cheat them at the end of the year, the Freedmen's Bureau assumed the role of reviewing the contracts and enforcing them. But bureau officials had differing notions of what it meant to protect African Americans from exploitation. Some stood up strongly for the rights of the freedmen; others served as allies of the planters, rounding up available workers, coercing them to sign contracts for low wages, and then helping keep them in line.

The bureau's influence waned after 1867 (it was phased out completely by 1869), and the experiment with contract wage labor was abandoned. Growing up

alongside the contract system and eventually displacing it was an alternative capital-labor relationship—**sharecropping.** First in small groups known as "squads" and later as individual families, blacks worked a piece of land independently for a fixed share of the crop, usually one-half. The advantage of this arrangement for credit-starved landlords was that it did not require much expenditure in advance of the harvest. The system also forced the tenant to share the risks of crop failure or a fall in cotton prices. These considerations loomed larger after disastrous harvests in 1866 and 1867.

African Americans initially viewed sharecropping as a step up from wage labor in the direction of landownership. But during the 1870s, this form of tenancy evolved into a new kind of servitude. Croppers had to live on credit until their cotton was sold, and planters or merchants seized the chance to "provision" them at high prices and exorbitant rates of interest. Creditors were entitled to deduct what was owed to them out of the tenant's share of the crop, and this left most sharecroppers with no net profit at the end of the year—more often than not with a debt that had to be worked off in subsequent years. Various methods, legal

The Civil War brought emancipation to slaves, but the sharecropping system kept many of them economically bound to their employers. At the end of a year the sharecropper tenants might owe most—or all—of what they had made to their landlord. Here a sharecropping family poses in front of their cabin. Ex-slaves often built their living quarters near woods in order to have a ready supply of fuel for heating and cooking. The cabin's chimney lists away from the house so that it can be easily pushed away from the living quarters should it catch fire. ❖

and extralegal, were eventually devised in an effort to bind indebted tenants to a single landlord for extended periods, but considerable movement was still possible.

Black Codes: A New Name for Slavery?

While landless African Americans in the countryside were being reduced to economic dependence, those in towns and cities found themselves living in an increasingly segregated society. The Black Codes of 1865 attempted to require separation of the races in public places and facilities; when most of the codes were overturned by federal authorities as violations of the Civil Rights Act of 1866, the same end was often achieved through private initiative and community pressure. In some cities, blacks successfully resisted being consigned to separate streetcars by appealing to the military during the period when it exercised authority or by organizing boycotts. But they found it almost impossible to gain admittance to most hotels, restaurants, and other privately owned establishments catering to whites. Although separate black, or "Jim Crow," cars were not yet the rule on railroads, African Americans were often denied first-class accommodations. After 1868, black-supported Republican governments passed civil rights acts requiring equal access to public facilities, but little effort was made to enforce the legislation.

The Black Codes had other onerous provisions meant to control African Americans and return them to quasi-slavery. Most codes even made black unemployment a crime, which meant blacks had to make long-term contracts with white employers or be arrested for vagrancy. Others limited the rights of African Americans to own property or engage in occupations other than those of servant or laborer. The codes were set aside by the actions of Congress, the military, and the Freedmen's Bureau, but vagrancy laws remained in force across the South.

Furthermore, private violence and discrimination against blacks continued on a massive scale unchecked by state authorities. Hundreds, perhaps thousands, of blacks were murdered by whites in 1865–1866, and few of the perpetrators were brought to justice. The imposition of military rule in 1867 was designed in part to protect former slaves from such violence and intimidation, but the task was beyond the capacity of the few thousand troops stationed in the South. When new constitutions were approved and states readmitted to the Union under the congressional plan in 1868, the problem became more severe. White opponents of Radical Reconstruction adopted systematic terrorism and organized mob violence to keep blacks away from the polls.

The freed slaves, in the face of opposition from both their Democratic enemies and some of their Republican allies, tried to defend themselves by organizing their own militia groups for protection and to assert their political rights. However, the militia groups were not powerful enough to overcome the growing power of the anti-Republican forces. Also, the military presence was progressively reduced, leaving the new Republican regimes to fight a losing battle against armed white supremacists. In the words of historian William Gillette, "there was simply no federal force large enough to give heart to black Republicans or to bridle southern white violence."

Republican Rule in the South

Hastily organized in 1867, the southern Republican party dominated the constitution making of 1868 and the regimes that came out of it. The party was an attempted coalition of three social groups (which varied in their relative strength from state to state). One was the same class that was becoming the backbone of the Republican party in the North—businessmen with an interest in enlisting government aid for private enterprise. Many Republicans of this stripe were recent arrivals from the North—the so-called **carpetbaggers**—but some were scalawags, former Whig planters or merchants who were born in the South or had immigrated to the region before the war and now saw a chance to realize their dreams for commercial and industrial development.

Poor white farmers, especially those from upland areas where Unionist sentiment had been strong during the Civil War, were a second element in the original coalition. These owners of small farms expected the party to favor their interests at the expense of the wealthy landowners and to come to their aid with special legislation when—as was often the case in this period of economic upheaval—they faced the loss of their homesteads to creditors. Newly enfranchised blacks were the third group to which the Republicans appealed. Blacks formed the vast majority of the Republican rank and file in most states and were concerned mainly with education, civil rights, and landownership.

Under the best of conditions, these coalitions would have been difficult to maintain. Each group had its own distinct goals and did not fully support the aims of the other segments. White yeomen, for example, had a deeply rooted resistance to black equality. And for how long could one expect essentially conservative businessmen to support costly measures for the elevation or relief of the lower classes of either race? In some states, astute Democratic politicians exploited these divisions by appealing to disaffected white Republicans.

But during the relatively brief period when they were in power in the South—varying from one to nine years depending on the state—the Republicans chalked up some notable achievements. They established (on paper at least) the South's first adequate systems of public education, democratized state and local government, and appropriated funds for an enormous expansion of public services and responsibilities.

As important as these social and political reforms were, they took second place to the Republicans' major effort—to foster economic development and restore southern prosperity by subsidizing the construction of railroads and other internal improvements. But the policy of aiding railroads turned out to be disastrous, even though it addressed the region's real economic needs and was initially very popular. Extravagance, corruption, and routes laid out in response to local political pressure rather than on sound economic grounds made for an increasing burden of public debt and taxation.

The policy did not produce the promised payoff of efficient, cheap transportation. Subsidized railroads frequently went bankrupt, leaving the taxpayers holding the bag. When the Panic of 1873 brought many southern state governments to the verge of bankruptcy, and railroad building came to an end, it was clear the Republicans' "gospel of prosperity" through state aid to private enterprise had failed miserably. Their political opponents, many of whom had originally favored such policies, now saw an opportunity to take advantage of the situation by charging that Republicans had ruined the southern economy.

In general, the Radical regimes failed to conduct public business honestly and efficiently. Embezzlement of public funds and bribery of state lawmakers or officials were common occurrences. State debts and tax burdens rose enormously, mainly because governments had undertaken heavy new responsibilities, but partly because of waste and graft. The situation varied from state to state; ruling cliques in Louisiana and South Carolina were guilty of much wrongdoing, yet Mississippi had a relatively honest and frugal regime.

Furthermore, southern corruption was not exceptional, nor was it a special result of the extension of suffrage to uneducated African Americans, as critics of Radical Reconstruction have claimed. It was part of a national pattern during an era when private interests considered buying government favors to be a part of the cost of doing business, and many politicians expected to profit by obliging them.

Blacks bore only a limited responsibility for the dishonesty of the Radical governments. Although sixteen African Americans served in Congress—two in the Senate—between 1869 and 1880, only in South Carolina did blacks constitute a majority of even one house of the state legislature. Furthermore, no black governors were elected during Reconstruction (although Pinkney B. S. Pinchback served for a time as acting governor of Louisiana). The biggest grafters were opportunistic whites. Some of the most notorious were carpetbaggers, but others were native Southerners. Businessmen offering bribes included members of the prewar gentry who were staunch opponents of Radical programs. Some black legislators went with the tide and accepted "loans" from those

On either side of Frederick Douglass on this poster are two African American heroes of the Reconstruction era. Senator Blanche K. Bruce of Mississippi, on the left, was the first African American to be elected to a full term in the U.S. Senate. Senator Hiram R. Revels, also representing Mississippi, was elected to the U.S. Senate in 1870 to fill the seat previously occupied by Confederate President Jefferson Davis. ❖

railroad lobbyists who would pay most for their votes, but the same men could usually be depended on to vote the will of their constituents on civil rights or educational issues.

If blacks served or supported corrupt and wasteful regimes, it was because the alternative was dire. Although the Democrats, or Conservatives as they called themselves in some states, made sporadic efforts to attract African American voters, it was clear that if they won control, they would attempt to strip blacks of their civil and political rights. But opponents of Radical Reconstruction were able to capitalize on racial prejudice and persuade many Americans that "good government" was synonymous with white supremacy.

Contrary to myth, the small number of African Americans elected to state or national office during Reconstruction demonstrated on the average more integrity and competence than their white counterparts. Most were fairly well educated, having been free Negroes or unusually privileged slaves before the war. Among the most capable were Robert Smalls (whose career was described earlier); Blanche K. Bruce of Mississippi, elected to the U.S. Senate in 1874 after rising to deserved prominence in the Republican party of his home state; Congressman Robert Brown Elliott of South Carolina, an adroit politician who was also a consistent champion of civil rights; and Congressman James T. Rapier of Alabama, who stirred Congress and the nation in 1873 with his eloquent appeals for federal aid to southern education and new laws to enforce equal rights for African Americans.

Claiming Public and Private Rights

As important as party politics to the changing political culture of the Reconstruction South were the ways that freed slaves claimed rights for themselves. They did so not only in negotiations with employers and in public meetings and convention halls, but also through the institutions they created, and perhaps most important, the households they formed.

As one black corporal in the Union Army told an audience of ex-slaves, "The Marriage covenant is at the foundation of all our rights. In slavery we could not have *legalized* marriage: *now* we have it . . . and we shall be established as a people." Through marriage, historian Laura Edwards tells us, African Americans claimed citizenship. Freedmen hoped that marriage would allow them to take on the rights that accrued to the independent head of a household, not only political rights, but the right to control the labor of wives and children for the first time.

Many states' Black Codes included apprenticeship provisions, providing for freed children to be apprenticed by courts to some white person (with preference given to former masters) if their parents were paupers, unemployed, of "bad character," or even simply if it were found to be "better for the habits and comfort of a child." Ex-slaves struggled to win their children back from what often amounted to re-enslavement for arbitrary reasons. Freedpeople challenged the apprenticeship system in county courts, and through the Freedmen's Bureau. As one group of petitioners from Maryland asserted, "Our homes are invaded and our little ones seized at the family fireside."

While many former slaves lined up eagerly to formalize their marriages, many also retained their own definitions of marriage and defied the efforts of the Freedmen's Bureau to use the marriage relation as a disciplinary tool. Perhaps as many as 50 percent of ex-slaves chose not to marry legally, and whites criticized them heavily for it. African American leaders worried about this refusal to follow white norms. The Army cor-

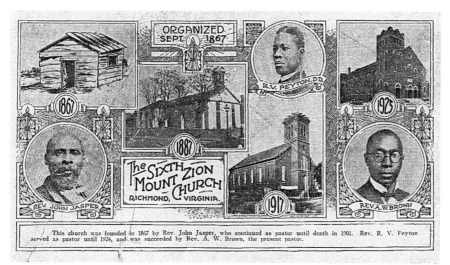

As slaves, many blacks attended white churches and listened to sermons preached by white ministers. After the Civil War and the end of slavery, African Americans joined or founded black churches, such as the Sixth Mount Zion Baptist Church of Richmond, Virginia. This postcard of the church's history includes a photograph of its founding pastor, John Jasper. ❖

A Freedmen's school, one of the more successful endeavors supported by the Freedmen's Bureau. The bureau, working with teachers from northern abolitionist and missionary societies, founded thousands of schools for freed slaves and poor whites. ❖

poral who had described marriage as "the foundation of all our rights" urged his audience: "Let us conduct ourselves worthy of such a blessing—and all the people will respect us." Yet many poor blacks continued to recognize as husband and wife people who cared for and supported one another without benefit of legal sanction. The new legal system punished couples who deviated from the legal norm through laws against bastardy, adultery, and fornication. Furthermore, the Freedmen's Bureau made the marriage of freedpeople a priority because, as historian Noralee Frankel explained, "The agency's overriding concern was keeping blacks from depending on the federal government for economic assistance." Once married, the husband became legally responsible for his family's support.

Some ex-slaves used institutions formerly closed to them like the courts to assert rights against white people as well as other blacks, suing over domestic violence, child support, assault, and debt. Freed women sued their husbands for desertion and alimony in order to enlist the Freedman's Bureau to help them claim property from men. Other ex-slaves mobilized kin networks and other community resources to make claims on property and family.

Immediately after the war, freedpeople flocked to create institutions that had been denied to them under slavery: churches, fraternal and benevolent associations, political organizations, and schools. Many joined all-black denominations such as the African

Methodist Episcopal church, which provided freedom from white dominance and a more congenial style of worship. Black women formed all-black chapters of organizations such as the Women's Christian Temperance Union, and their own women's clubs to oppose lynching and work for "uplift" in the black community.

A top priority for most ex-slaves was the opportunity to educate their children; the first schools for freedpeople were all-black institutions established by the Freedmen's Bureau and various northern missionary societies. At the time, having been denied all education during the antebellum period, most blacks viewed separate schooling as an opportunity rather than as a form of discrimination. However, these schools were precursors to the segregated public school systems first instituted by Republican governments. Only in city schools of New Orleans and at the University of South Carolina were there serious attempts during Reconstruction to bring white and black students together in the same classrooms.

In a variety of ways, African American men and women during Reconstruction claimed freedom in the "private" realm as well as the public sphere, by claiming rights to their own families and building their own institutions. They did so in the face of the vigorous efforts of their former masters as well as the new government agencies to control their private lives and shape their new identities as husbands, wives, and citizens.

RETREAT FROM RECONSTRUCTION

The era of Reconstruction began coming to an end almost before it got started. Although it was only a scant three years from the end of the Civil War, the impeachment crisis of 1868 represented the high point of popular interest in Reconstruction issues. That year, Ulysses S. Grant was elected president. Many historians blame Grant for the corruption of his administration and for the inconsistency and failure of his southern policy. He had neither the vision nor the sense of duty to tackle the difficult challenges the nation faced. From 1868 on, political issues other than southern Reconstruction moved to the forefront of national politics, and the plight of African Americans in the South receded in white consciousness.

Rise of the Money Question

In the years immediately following the Civil War, another issue already competing for public attention was the money question: whether to allow "greenbacks"—paper money issued during the war—to continue to circulate or to return to "sound" or "hard" money, meaning gold or silver. Supporters of paper money, known as **greenbackers,** were strongest in the credit-hungry West and among expansion-minded manufacturers. Defenders of hard money were mostly the commercial and financial interests in the East; they received crucial support from intellectuals who regarded government-sponsored inflation as immoral or contrary to the natural laws of classical economics.

In 1868, the money question surged briefly to the forefront of national politics. Faced with a business recession blamed on the Johnson administration's policy of contracting the currency, Congress voted to stop the retirement of greenbacks. The Democratic party, responding to Midwestern pressure, included in its platform for the 1868 national election a plan calling for the redemption of much of the Civil War debt in greenbacks rather than gold. Yet they nominated for president a sound-money supporter, so that the greenback question never became an issue in the 1868 presidential campaign. Grant, already a popular general, won the election handily with the help of the Republican-dominated Southern states.

In 1869 and 1870, a Republican-controlled Congress passed laws that assured payment in gold to most bondholders but eased the burden of the huge Civil War debt by exchanging bonds that were soon coming due for those that would not be payable for ten, fifteen, or thirty years. In this way, the public credit was protected.

Still unresolved, however, was the problem of what to do about the $356 million in greenbacks that

THE ELECTION OF 1868

Candidate	Party	Popular Vote	Electoral Vote[*]
Grant	Republican	3,013,421	214
Seymour	Democratic	2,706,829	80
Not voted[*]			23

[*]Unreconstructed states did not participate in the election.

remained in circulation. Hard-money proponents wanted to retire them quickly; inflationists thought more should be issued to stimulate the economy. The Grant administration followed the middle course of allowing the greenbacks to float until economic expansion would bring them to a par with gold, thus permitting a painless return to specie payments. But the Panic of 1873, which brought much of the economy to its knees, led to a revival of agitation to inflate the currency. Debt-ridden farmers, who would be the backbone of the greenback movement for years to come, now joined the soft-money clamor for the first time.

Responding to the money and credit crunch, Congress moved in 1874 to authorize a modest issue of new greenbacks. But Grant, influenced by the opinions of hard-money financiers, vetoed the bill. In 1875, Congress, led by Senator John Sherman of Ohio, enacted the Specie Resumption Act, which provided for a limited reduction of greenbacks leading to full resumption of specie payments by January 1, 1879. Its action was widely interpreted as deflation in the midst of depression. Farmers and workers, who were already suffering acutely from deflation, reacted with dismay and anger.

The Democratic Party could not capitalize adequately on these sentiments because of the influence of its own hard-money faction, and in 1876 an independent Greenback party entered the national political arena. The party's nominee for president, Peter Cooper, received an insignificant number of votes, but in 1878 the Greenback Labor party polled more than a million votes and elected fourteen congressmen. The Greenbackers were able to keep the money issue alive into the following decade.

Final Efforts of Reconstruction

The Republican effort to make equal rights for blacks the law of the land culminated in the **Fifteenth Amendment.** Passed by Congress in 1869 and ratified by the states in 1870, the amendment prohibited any state from denying a male citizen the right to vote because of race, color, or previous condition of servitude. A more radical version, requiring universal manhood suffrage, was rejected partly because it departed too sharply from traditional views of federal-state rela-

Shown seated at the table are feminist leaders Elizabeth Cady Stanton and Susan B. Anthony. They and their adherents split with Lucy Stone (right) and her followers over the Fifteenth Amendment and its failure to extend the vote to women. ❖

tions. States therefore could still limit the suffrage by imposing literacy tests, property qualifications, or poll taxes allegedly applying to all racial groups; such devices would eventually be used to strip southern blacks of the right to vote. But the makers of the amendment did not foresee this result. They believed their action would prevent future Congresses or southern constitutional conventions from repealing or nullifying the provisions for black male suffrage included in the Reconstruction Acts. A secondary aim was to enfranchise African Americans in those northern states that still denied them the vote.

Many feminists were bitterly disappointed that the amendment did not extend the vote to women as well as freedmen. A militant wing of the women's rights movement, led by Elizabeth Cady Stanton and Susan B. Anthony, was so angered that the Constitution was being amended in a way that, in effect, made gender a qualification for voting that they campaigned against ratification of the Fifteenth Amendment. Another group of feminists led by Lucy Stone supported the amendment on the grounds that this was "the Negro's hour" and that women could afford to wait a few years for the vote. This disagreement divided the woman suffrage movement for a generation to come.

The Grant administration was charged with enforcing the amendment and protecting black men's voting rights in the reconstructed states. Since survival of the Republican regimes depended on African American support, political partisanship dictated federal action, even though the North's emotional and ideological commitment to black citizenship was waning.

A Reign of Terror Against Blacks

Between 1868 and 1872, the main threat to southern Republican regimes came from the **Ku Klux Klan** and other secret societies bent on restoring white supremacy by intimidating blacks who sought to exercise their political rights. First organized in Tennessee in 1866, the Klan spread rapidly to other states, adopting increasingly lawless and brutal tactics. A grassroots vigilante movement and not a centralized conspiracy, the Klan thrived on local initiative and gained support from whites of all social classes. Its secrecy, decentralization, popular support, and utter ruthlessness made it very difficult to suppress. As soon as blacks had been granted the right to vote, hooded "night riders" began to visit the cabins of those who were known to be active Republicans; some victims were only threatened, but others were whipped or even murdered. One black Georgian related a typical incident: "They broke my door open, took me out of bed, took me to the woods and whipped me three hours or more and left me for dead. They said to me, 'Do you think you will vote for another damned radical ticket?'"

Such methods were first used effectively in the presidential election of 1868. Grant lost in Louisiana and Georgia mainly because the Klan—or the Knights of the White Camellia, as the Louisiana variant was called—launched a reign of terror to prevent prospective black voters from exercising their rights. In Louisiana, political violence claimed more than a thousand lives, and in Arkansas, which Grant managed to carry, more than two hundred Republicans, including a congressman, were assassinated.

Thereafter, Klan terrorism was directed mainly at Republican state governments. Virtual insurrections broke out in Arkansas, Tennessee, North Carolina, and parts of South Carolina. Republican governors called out the state militia to fight the Klan, but only the Arkansas militia succeeded in bringing it to heel. In Tennessee, North Carolina, and Georgia, Klan activities helped undermine Republican control, thus allowing the Democrats to come to power in all of these states by 1870.

This 1868 photograph shows typical regalia of members of the Ku Klux Klan, a secret white supremacist organization. Before elections, hooded Klansmen terrorized African Americans to discourage them from voting. ❖

Faced with the violent overthrow of the southern Republican Party, Congress and the Grant administration were forced to act. A series of laws passed in 1870–1871 sought to enforce the Fifteenth Amendment by providing federal protection for black suffrage and authorizing use of the army against the Klan. The **Force acts,** also known as the Ku Klux Klan acts, made interference with voting rights a federal crime and established provisions for government supervision of elections. In addition, the legislation empowered the president to call out troops and suspend the writ of habeas corpus to quell insurrection. In 1871–1872, thousands of suspected Klansmen were arrested by the military or U.S. marshals, and the writ was suspended in nine counties of South Carolina that had been virtually taken over by the secret order. Although most of the accused Klansmen were never brought to trial, were acquitted, or received suspended sentences, the enforcement effort was vigorous enough to put a damper on hooded terrorism and ensure relatively fair and peaceful elections in 1872.

A heavy black turnout in these elections enabled the Republicans to hold on to power in most states of the Deep South, despite efforts of the Democratic-Conservative opposition to cut into the Republican vote by taking moderate positions on racial and economic issues. This setback prompted the Democratic-Conservatives to make a significant change in their strategy and ideology. No longer did they try to take votes away from the Republicans by proclaiming support for black suffrage and government aid to business. Instead they began to appeal openly to white supremacy and to the traditional Democratic and agrarian hostility to government promotion of economic development. Consequently, they were able to bring back to the polls a portion of the white electorate, mostly small farmers, who had not been turning out because they were alienated by the leadership's apparent concessions to Yankee ideas.

This new and more effective electoral strategy dovetailed with a resurgence of violence meant to reduce Republican, especially black Republican, voting. The new reign of terror differed from the previously discussed Klan episode; its agents no longer wore masks but acted quite openly. They were effective because the northern public was increasingly disenchanted with federal intervention on behalf of what were widely viewed as corrupt and tottering Republican regimes. Grant used force in the South for the last time in 1874 when an overt paramilitary organization in Louisiana, known as the White League, tried to overthrow a Republican government accused of stealing an election. When another unofficial militia in Mississippi instigated a series of bloody race riots prior to the state elections of 1875, Grant refused the governor's request for federal troops. As a result, black

✦ A Look at the Past ✦

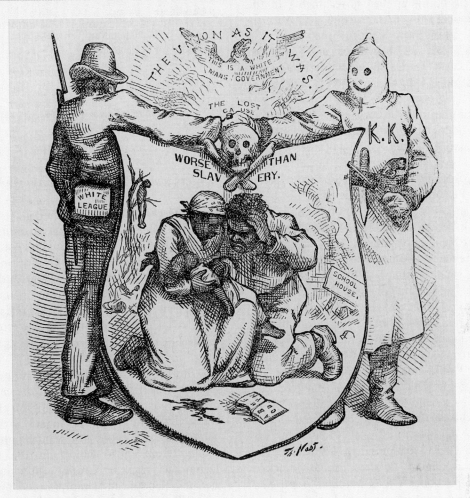

Cartoon "Worse Than Slavery"

Political cartoonist Thomas Nast offered his commentary on and critique of contemporary events through his cartoons in *Harper's Weekly,* a popular magazine that had a circulation of over 100,000 readers. This Nast cartoon, "Worse Than Slavery," appeared in the magazine on October 24, 1874. Carefully examine the individuals and items depicted in the cartoon. Note that the phrase near the top of the drawing, "This is a white man's government," is a quotation from the 1868 Democratic Party platform. According to the cartoon, what conditions or events are "worse than slavery"? What view of Reconstruction policy does the cartoonist appear to be expressing?

voters were successfully intimidated—one county registered only seven Republican votes where there had been a black majority of two thousand—and Mississippi fell to the Democratic-Conservatives. According to one account, Grant decided to withhold troops because he had been warned that intervention might cost the Republicans the crucial state of Ohio in the same off-year elections.

By 1876, Republicans held on to only three southern states: South Carolina, Louisiana, and Florida. Partly because of Grant's hesitant and inconsistent use of presidential power, but mainly because the northern electorate would no longer tolerate military action to sustain Republican governments and black voting rights, Radical Reconstruction was falling into total eclipse.

Spoilsmen Versus Reformers

One reason Grant found it increasingly difficult to take strong action to protect southern Republicans was the bad odor surrounding his stewardship of the federal government and the Republican Party. Reformers charged that a corrupt national administration was propping up bad governments in the South for personal and partisan advantage. An apparent case in point was Grant's intervention in Louisiana in 1872 on behalf of an ill-reputed Republican faction headed by his wife's brother-in-law, who controlled federal patronage as collector of customs in New Orleans.

The Republican party in the Grant era was losing the idealism and high purpose associated with the crusade against slavery. By the beginning of the 1870s, the men who had been the conscience of the party—old-line radicals such as Thaddeus Stevens, Charles Sumner, and Benjamin Wade—were either dead, out of office, or at odds with the administration. New leaders of a different stamp, whom historians have dubbed "spoilsmen" or "politicos," were taking their place. When he made common cause with hard-boiled manipulators such as senators Roscoe Conkling of New York and James G. Blaine of Maine, Grant lost credibility with reform-minded Republicans.

During Grant's first administration, an aura of scandal surrounded the White House but did not directly implicate the president. In 1869, the financial buccaneer Jay Gould enlisted the aid of a brother-in-law of Grant to further his fantastic scheme to corner the gold market. Gould failed in the attempt, but he did manage to save himself and come away with a huge profit.

Grant's first-term vice president, Schuyler Colfax of Indiana, was directly involved in the notorious Crédit Mobilier scandal. Crédit Mobilier was a construction company that actually served as a fraudulent device for siphoning off profits that should have gone to the stockholders of the Union Pacific Railroad, which was the beneficiary of massive federal land grants. In order to forestall government inquiry into this arrangement, Crédit Mobilier stock was distributed to influential congressmen, including Colfax (who was speaker of the House before he was elected vice president). The whole business came to light just before the campaign of 1872.

Republicans who could not tolerate such corruption or had other grievances against the administration broke with Grant in 1872 and formed a third party committed to "honest government" and "reconciliation" between the North and the South. Led initially by high-minded reformers such as Senator Carl Schurz of Missouri, the Liberal Republicans endorsed reform of the civil service to curb the corruption-breeding patronage system and advocated laissez-faire economic policies—which meant low tariffs, an end to government subsidies for railroads, and hard money. Despite their rhetoric of idealism

THE ELECTION OF 1872

Candidate	Party	Popular Vote	Electoral Vote[*]
Grant	Republican	3,598,235	286
Greeley	Democratic and Liberal Republican	2,834,761	Greeley died before the electoral college voted.

[*]Out of a total of 366 electoral votes. Greeley's votes were divided among the four minor candidates.

and reform, the Liberal Republicans were extremely conservative in their notions of what government should do to assure justice for blacks and other underprivileged Americans.

The Liberal Republicans' national convention nominated Horace Greeley, editor of the respected New York *Tribune*. This was a curious and divisive choice, since Greeley was at odds with the founders of the movement on the tariff question and was indifferent to civil service reform. The Democrats also nominated Greeley, mainly because he promised to end Radical Reconstruction by restoring "self-government" to the South.

But the journalist turned out to be a poor campaigner who failed to inspire enthusiasm from life-long supporters of either party. Most Republicans stuck with Grant, despite the corruption issue, because they still could not stomach the idea of ex-rebels returning to power in the South. Many Democrats, recalling Greeley's previous record as a staunch Republican, simply stayed away from the polls. The result was a decisive victory for Grant, whose 56 percent of the popular vote was the highest percentage won by any candidate between Andrew Jackson and Theodore Roosevelt.

Grant's second administration seemed to bear out the reformers' worst suspicions about corruption in high places. In 1875, the public learned that federal revenue officials had conspired with distillers to defraud the government of millions of dollars in liquor taxes. Grant's private secretary, Orville E. Babcock, was indicted as a member of the "Whiskey Ring" and was saved from conviction only by the president's personal intercession. The next year, Grant's secretary of war, William E. Belknap, was impeached by the House after an investigation revealed he had taken bribes for the sale of Indian trading posts. He avoided conviction in the Senate only by resigning from office before his trial. Grant fought hard to protect Belknap, to the point of participating in what a later generation might call a cover-up.

There is no evidence that Grant profited personally from any of the misdeeds of his subordinates. Yet

In this Puck *cartoon, U. S. Grant clutches the Whiskey and Navy rings and supports an assortment of bosses, profiteers, and scandals associated with the Grant administration.* ❖

he is not entirely without blame for the corruption in his administration. He failed to take firm action against the malefactors, and, even after their guilt had been clearly established, he sometimes tried to shield them from justice. Ulysses S. Grant was the only president between Jackson and Wilson to serve two full and consecutive terms. But unlike other chief executives so favored by the electorate, Grant is commonly regarded as a failure. Although the problems he faced would have challenged any president, the shame of Grant's administration was that he made loyalty to old friends a higher priority than civil rights or sound economic principles.

REUNION AND THE NEW SOUTH

Congressional Reconstruction prolonged the sense of sectional division and conflict for a dozen years after the guns had fallen silent. Its final liquidation in 1877 opened the way to a reconciliation of North and South. But the costs of reunion were high for less privileged groups in the South. The civil and political rights of African Americans, left unprotected, were

progressively and relentlessly stripped away by white supremacist regimes. Lower-class whites saw their interests sacrificed to those of capitalists and landlords. Despite the rhetoric hailing a prosperous "New South," the region remained poor and open to exploitation by northern business interests.

The Compromise of 1877

The election of 1876 pitted Rutherford B. Hayes of Ohio, a Republican governor untainted by the scandals of the Grant era, against Governor Samuel J. Tilden of New York, a Democratic reformer who had battled against Tammany Hall and the Tweed Ring. Honest government was apparently the electorate's highest priority. When the returns came in, Tilden had clearly won the popular vote and seemed likely to win a narrow victory in the electoral college. But the result was placed in doubt when the returns from the three southern states still controlled by the Republicans— South Carolina, Florida, and Louisiana—were contested. If Hayes were to be awarded these three states, plus one contested electoral vote in Oregon, Republican strategists realized, he would triumph in the electoral college by a single vote.

The outcome of the election remained undecided for months, plunging the nation into a major political crisis. To resolve the impasse, Congress appointed a special electoral commission of fifteen members to determine who would receive the votes of the disputed states. Originally composed of seven Democrats, seven Republicans, and an independent, the commission fell under Republican control when the independent member resigned to run for the Senate and a Republican was appointed to take his place. The commission split along party lines and voted eight to seven to award Hayes all of the disputed votes. But this decision still had to be ratified by both houses of Congress. The Republican-dominated Senate readily approved it, but the Democrats in the House planned a filibuster to delay the final counting of the electoral votes until after inauguration day. If the filibuster succeeded, neither candidate would have a majority and, as provided in the Constitution, the election would be decided by the House, where the Democrats controlled enough states to elect Tilden.

To ensure Hayes's election, Republican leaders negotiated secretly with conservative southern Democrats, some of whom seemed willing to abandon the filibuster if the last troops were withdrawn and home rule restored to the South. Eventually an informal bargain was struck, which historians have dubbed the **Compromise of 1877**. What precisely was agreed to and by whom remains a matter of dispute; but one

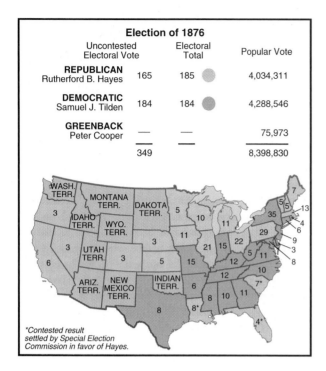

Election of 1876

	Uncontested Electoral Vote	Electoral Total		Popular Vote
REPUBLICAN Rutherford B. Hayes	165	185		4,034,311
DEMOCRATIC Samuel J. Tilden	184	184		4,288,546
GREENBACK Peter Cooper	—	—		75,973
		349		8,398,830

*Contested result settled by Special Election Commission in favor of Hayes.

thing at least was understood by both sides: Hayes would be president and southern blacks would be abandoned to their fate. In a sense, Hayes did not concede anything, because he had already decided to end federal support for the crumbling Radical regimes. But southern negotiators were heartened by firm assurances that this would indeed be the policy. Some also were influenced by vaguer promises involving federal support for southern railroads and internal improvements.

With southern Democratic acquiescence, the filibuster was broken, and Hayes took the oath of office. He immediately ordered the army not to resist a Democratic takeover of state governments in South Carolina and Louisiana. Thus fell the last of the Radical governments, and the entire South was firmly under the control of white Democrats. The trauma of the war and Reconstruction had destroyed the chances for a renewal of two-party competition among white Southerners.

Northern Republicans soon reverted to denouncing the South for its suppression of black suffrage. But this "waving of the bloody shirt," which also served as a reminder of the war and northern casualties, quickly degenerated into a campaign ritual aimed at northern voters who could still be moved by sectional antagonism.

"Redeeming" a New South

The men who came to power after Radical Reconstruction fell in one southern state after another

are usually referred to as the **Redeemers.** They had differing backgrounds and previous loyalties. Some were members of the Old South's ruling planter class who had warmly supported secession and now sought to reestablish the old order with as few changes as possible. Others, of middle-class origin or outlook, favored commercial and industrial interests over agrarian groups and called for a New South committed to diversified economic development. A third group were professional politicians bending with the prevailing winds, such as Joseph E. Brown of Georgia, who had been a secessionist, a wartime governor, and a leading scalawag Republican before becoming a Democratic Redeemer.

Although historians have tried to assign the Redeemers a single coherent ideology or view of the world and have debated whether it was Old South agrarianism or New South industrialism they endorsed, these leaders can perhaps best be understood as power brokers mediating among the dominant interest groups of the South in ways that served their own political advantage. In many ways, the "rings" that they established on the state and county level were analogous to the political machines developing at the same time in northern cities. (See the Feature Essay, "Changing Views of Reconstruction," pp. 476–477.)

Redeemers did, however, agree on and endorse two basic principles: laissez-faire and white supremacy. Laissez-faire—the notion that government should be limited and should not intervene openly and directly in the economy—could unite planters, frustrated at seeing direct state support going to businessmen, and capitalist promoters who had come to realize that low taxes and freedom from government regulation were even more advantageous than state subsidies. It soon became clear that the Redeemers responded only to privileged and entrenched interest groups, especially landlords, merchants, and industrialists, and offered little or nothing to tenants, small farmers, and working people. As industrialization began to gather steam in the 1880s, Democratic regimes became increasingly accommodating to manufacturing interests and hospitable to agents of northern capital who were gaining control of the South's transportation system and its extractive industries.

White supremacy was the principal rallying cry that brought the Redeemers to power in the first place. Once in office, they found they could stay there by charging that opponents of ruling Democratic cliques were trying to divide "the white man's party" and open the way for a return to "black domination." Appeals to racism could also deflect attention from the economic grievances of groups without political clout.

The new governments were more economical than those of Reconstruction, mainly because they cut back

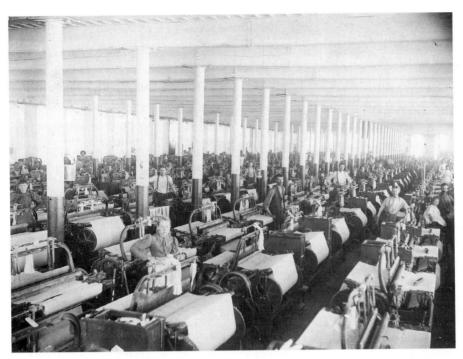

The growing industrialization that was characteristic of the New South is evident in this photograph of a South Carolina cotton mill. Steam power and the abundance of cheap coal in the Appalachians helped shift the textile industry from the North to the South. ❖

drastically on appropriations for schools and other needed public services. But they were scarcely more honest—embezzlement of funds and bribery of officials continued to occur to an alarming extent. Louisiana, for example, suffered for decades from the flagrant corruption associated with a state-chartered lottery.

The Redeemer regimes of the late 1870s and 1880s badly neglected the interests of small white farmers. Whites, as well as blacks, were suffering from the notorious crop lien system, which gave local merchants who advanced credit at high rates of interest during the growing season the right to take possession of the harvested crop on terms that buried farmers deeper and deeper in debt. As a result, increasing numbers of whites lost title to their homesteads and were reduced to tenancy. When a depression of world cotton prices added to the burden of a ruinous credit system, agrarian protesters began to challenge the ruling elite, first through the Southern Farmers' Alliance of the late 1880s and then by supporting its political descendant—the Populist party of the 1890s (see Chapter 20).

The Rise of Jim Crow

African Americans bore the greatest hardships imposed by the new order. From 1876 through the first decade of the twentieth century, Southern states imposed a series of restrictions on black civil rights known as **Jim Crow laws.** While segregation and dis-

franchisement began as informal arrangements, they culminated in a legal regime of separation and exclusion that took firm hold in the 1890s.

The rise of Jim Crow in the political arena was especially bitter for Southern blacks who realized that only political power could ensure other rights. The Redeemers promised, as part of the understanding that led to the end of federal intervention in 1877, that they would respect the rights of blacks as set forth in the Fourteenth and Fifteenth Amendments. Governor Wade Hampton of South Carolina was especially vocal in pledging that African Americans would not be reduced to second-class citizenship by the new regimes. But when blacks tried to vote Republican in the "redeemed" states, they encountered renewed violence and intimidation. "Bulldozing" African American voters remained common practice in state elections during the late 1870s and early 1880s; those blacks who withstood the threat of losing their jobs or being evicted from tenant farms if they voted for the party of Lincoln were visited at night and literally whipped into line. The message was clear: Vote Democratic, or vote not at all.

Furthermore, white Democrats now controlled the electoral machinery and were able to manipulate the black vote by stuffing ballot boxes, discarding unwanted votes, or reporting fraudulent totals. Some states also imposed complicated new voting requirements to discourage black participation. Full-scale disfranchisement did not occur until literacy tests and other legalized obstacles to voting were imposed in the period from 1890 to 1910, but by that time, less formal and comprehensive methods had already made a mockery of the Fifteenth Amendment.

Nevertheless, blacks continued to vote freely in some localities until the 1890s; a few districts, like the one Robert Smalls represented, even elected black Republicans to Congress during the immediate post-Reconstruction period. The last of these, Representative George H. White of North Carolina, served until 1901. His farewell address eloquently conveyed the agony of southern blacks in the era of Jim Crow (strict segregation):

These parting words are in behalf of an outraged, heart-broken, bruised, and bleeding but God-fearing people, faithful, industrious, loyal people—rising people, full of potential force. . . . The only apology that I have to make for the earnestness with which I have spoken is that I am pleading for the life, the liberty, the future happiness, and manhood suffrage of one-eighth of the entire population of the United States.

The dark night of racism that fell on the South after Reconstruction seemed to unleash all the baser impulses of human nature. Between 1889 and 1899, an average of 187 blacks were lynched every year for alleged offenses against white supremacy. The protection of Southern white womanhood became the rally-

CHRONOLOGY

1863	Lincoln sets forth 10 percent Reconstruction plan
1864	Wade-Davis Bill passes Congress but is pocket vetoed by Lincoln
1865	Johnson moves to reconstruct the South on his own initiative ❖ Congress refuses to seat representatives and senators elected from states reestablished under presidential plan (December)
1866	Johnson vetoes Freedmen's Bureau Bill (February) ❖ Johnson vetoes Civil Rights Act; it passes over his veto (April) ❖ Congress passes Fourteenth Amendment (June) ❖ Republicans increase their congressional majority in the fall elections
1867	First Reconstruction Act is passed over Johnson's veto (March)
1868	Johnson is impeached; he avoids conviction by one vote (February–May) ❖ Southern blacks vote and serve in constitutional conventions ❖ Grant wins presidential election, defeating Horatio Seymour
1869	Congress passes Fifteenth Amendment, granting African Americans the right to vote
1870–1871	Congress passes Ku Klux Klan Acts to protect black voting rights in the South
1872	Grant reelected president, defeating Horace Greeley, candidate of Liberal Republicans and Democrats
1873	Financial panic plunges nation into depression
1875	Congress passes Specie Resumption Act ❖ "Whiskey Ring" scandal exposed
1876–1877	Disputed presidential election resolved in favor of Republican Hayes over Democrat Tilden
1877	Compromise of 1877 ends military intervention in the South and causes fall of the last Radical governments

Perhaps no event better expresses the cruel and barbaric nature of the racism and white supremacy that swept the South after Reconstruction than lynching. Although lynchings were not confined to the South, most occurred there and African American men were the most frequent victims. Here two men lean out of a barn window above a black man who is about to be hanged. Others below prepare to set on fire the pile of hay at the victim's feet. Lynchings were often public events, drawing huge crowds to watch the victim's agonizing death. ❖

ing cry for many lynch mobs, as African American men were accused, often with little or no evidence, of raping white women.

Those convicted of petty crimes against property were often little better off; many were condemned to be leased out to private contractors whose brutality rivaled that of the most sadistic slaveholders. The convict-lease system enabled entrepreneurs, such as mine owners and extractors of forest products, to rent prisoners from the state and treat them as they saw fit. Unlike slaveowners, they suffered no loss when a

SUPREME COURT DECISIONS AFFECTING BLACK CIVIL RIGHTS, 1875–1900

Case	Effects of Court's Decisions
Hall v. *DeCuir* (1878)	Struck down Louisiana law prohibiting racial discrimination by "common carriers" (railroads, steamboats, buses). Declared the law a "burden" on interstate commerce, over which states had no authority.
United States v. *Harris* (1882)	Declared federal laws to punish crimes such as murder and assault unconstitutional. Declared such crimes to be the sole concern of local government. Ignored the frequent racial motivation behind such crimes in the South.
Civil Rights Cases (1883)	Struck down Civil Rights Act of 1875. Declared that Congress may not legislate on civil rights unless a state passes a discriminatory law. Declared the Fourteenth Amendment silent on racial discrimination by private citizens.
Plessy v. *Ferguson* (1896)	Upheld Louisiana statute requiring "separate but equal" accommodations on railroads. Declared that segregation is *not* necessarily discrimination.
Williams v. *Mississippi* (1898)	Upheld state law requiring a literacy test to qualify for voting. Refused to find any implication of racial discrimination in the law, although it permitted illiterate whites to vote if they "understood" the Constitution. Using such laws, southern states rapidly disfranchised blacks.

forced laborer died from overwork. (Annual mortality rates in the convict camps ranged as high as 25 percent.) Even after convict leasing was banned in some states, blacks continued into the twentieth century to work on chain gangs and prison plantations such as the notorious Parchman Farm in Mississippi. Parchman Farm resembled a slave plantation more than a prison: Chained men picked cotton from sunup to sundown, constantly under the threat of being shot or whipped by "a leather strap, three feet long and six inches wide, known as 'Black Annie,' which hung from the driver's belt."

Finally, the dignity of blacks was cruelly affronted by the wave of segregation laws passed around the turn of the century, which served to remind them constantly that they were deemed unfit to associate with whites on any basis that implied equality. To some extent, the segregation laws were a white reaction to the refusal of many blacks to submit to voluntary segregation of railroads, streetcars, and other public facilities. On railroads, for example, elite free women of color had been accustomed to riding in the first-class ladies car; being relegated to the "smoking car" with men who were often drinking and gambling put them in physical danger of molestation.

The North and the federal government did little or nothing to stem the tide of racial oppression in the South. The high point of legislation came in 1875, when Congress passed a Civil Rights Act with far-reaching provisions to protect public and private discrimination on the basis of race. The Supreme Court invalidated the 1875 Act just eight years later, in an opinion that scolded the former slaves that "there must be some stage" when they "cease to be the special favorite of the laws." A series of Supreme Court decisions between 1878 and 1898

gutted the Reconstruction amendments and the legislation passed to enforce them, leaving blacks virtually defenseless against political and social discrimination.

CONCLUSION: HENRY MCNEAL TURNER AND THE "UNFINISHED REVOLUTION"

The career of Henry McNeal Turner sums up the bitter side of the black experience in the South during and after Reconstruction. Born free in South Carolina in 1834, Turner became a minister of the African Methodist Episcopal (AME) Church just before the outbreak of the Civil War. During the war, he recruited African Americans for the Union army and later served as chaplain for black troops. After the fighting was over, he went to Georgia to work for the Freedmen's Bureau but encountered racial discrimination from white Bureau officers and left government service for church work and Reconstruction politics. Elected to the 1867 Georgia constitutional convention and to the state legislature in 1868, he was one of a number of black clergymen who assumed leadership roles among the freedmen. But whites won control of the Georgia legislature and expelled all the black members. Turner's reaction was an angry speech in which he proclaimed that white men were never to be trusted. As the inhabitant of a state in which blacks never gained the degree of power that they achieved in some other parts of the South, Turner was one of the first black leaders to see the failure of Reconstruction as the betrayal of African American hopes for citizenship.

Becoming a bishop of the AME Church in 1880, Turner emerged as the late nineteenth century's

CHANGING VIEWS OF RECONSTRUCTION

A central issue of Reconstruction was the place of blacks in American life after slavery. Changing attitudes on this question strongly influenced later representations of the Reconstruction era, whether in historical writing or in the popular media. Indeed, what later generations imagined had happened in the South in the years immediately after the Civil War is a fairly reliable index of how they viewed black-white relations in their own time.

In the early twentieth century, when white supremacists were in control in the South and northern public opinion was learning to tolerate southern policies of rigid segregation and disfranchisement of blacks, historians played a major role in rationalizing the new order in southern race relations. According to historians such as Professor John W. Burgess of Columbia University, writing in 1902, Reconstruction governments represented an unholy alliance of corrupt northern carpetbaggers seeking to profit at the expense of the "prostrate South"; southern white opportunists of mean origins, known as "scalawags"; and black demagogues who sought power by putting false and dangerous aspirations for equality into the heads of newly freed slaves. What made this orgy of misrule possible, said Burgess, was the colossal blunder that Congress made when it extended the vote to "ignorant and vicious" blacks. In the eyes of Burgess and a whole school of historians, Reconstruction was "the most soul-sickening spectacle that Americans have ever been called upon to behold . . . here was government by the most ignorant and vicious part of the population for the vulgar, materialistic, brutal benefit of the governing set."

In 1915, the most ambitious film yet made by the fledgling American movie industry—D. W. Griffith's *Birth of a Nation*—popularized this image of Reconstruction and made its racism more lurid and explicit. To underscore the message of this technically brilliant film, words flashed on the screen describing Reconstruction as a callous attempt to "put the white South under the heel of the black South." In the film, leering blacks carry signs advocating interracial marriage. Mainly responsible for this state of affairs is a vengeful Congressman meant to represent Thaddeus Stevens, who hatches a devilish plot to oppress and humiliate the white South. One famous scene portrays the South Carolina state legislature as a mob of grinning barefoot blacks, carousing at the taxpayers' expense. The film's melodramatic plot features the suicide of one southern white maiden to escape the embraces of a black pursuer and the Ku Klux Klan's epic rescue of another damsel from a forced marriage to a mulatto politician.

Birth of a Nation's depiction of the Klan as saving white civilization from bestial blacks inspired vigorous protests from the recently founded National Association for the Advancement of Colored People (NAACP), and censors in a few northern cities deleted some of the more blatantly racist scenes. But President Woodrow Wilson endorsed the film. "My only regret is that it is all so terribly true," he is reported to have said. Most white moviegoers seemed to agree with the president rather than with the NAACP. Millions of Americans saw and applauded this cinematic triumph.

During the period between 1915 and the 1940s, most historians echoed the judgment of *Birth of a Nation* that efforts to enforce equal rights for blacks after the Civil War had been a grave mistake. One popular work of that era was *The Tragic Era,* and another summed up Reconstruction as "the blackout of honest government." The biases of mainstream historiography served to justify the Jim Crow system of the South by portraying blacks as unqualified for citizenship.

A few black historians of the 1920s and 1930s advanced the contrary view that Reconstruction was a noble effort to achieve a color-blind democracy, which failed because of the strength of white racism and conservative economic interests. The most powerful example of this early revisionism was W. E. B. DuBois's *Black Reconstruction in America* (1935).

During the 1950s and 1960s, another image of Reconstruction emerged. The majority of historians writing about the era finally rejected the exaggerations, distortions, and racist assumptions of the traditional view. The triumph of "revisionism" was evident in 1965 when Kenneth M. Stampp published his *Era of Reconstruction.* As influential northern opinion shifted from tolerance of segregation to support for the black struggle for equality in the South, a more favorable view of earlier efforts on behalf of civil rights became acceptable. White liberal historians like Stampp concentrated on rehabilitating the Radical Republicans by stressing their idealism, while black scholars like John Hope Franklin highlighted the constructive policies and positive achievements of the much maligned black leaders of the Reconstruction South. Previous moral judgments thus tended to be

reversed; white and black Republicans became the heroes, and the southern whites who resisted and eventually overthrew Reconstruction became the villains. The analogy between these earlier adversaries and the civil rights activists and southern segregationists of the 1960s was clear.

During the 1970s and early 1980s, a "postrevisionism" began to develop. As it became apparent that the dream of equality for blacks was still unrealized, historians responded to the changing perceptions and complex crosscurrents of black-white relations in their own time by taking another look at Reconstruction. They found, among other things, that those in charge of efforts to make blacks equal citizens in the late 1860s had views that were quite moderate by the standards of the post–civil rights era of the 1970s and early 1980s. Radical Reconstruction no longer seemed very radical. The reputations of carpetbag-

gers and upper-class scalawags went down again as historians emphasized their opportunism and probusiness economic policies at the expense of social justice. Black politicians, too, came in for critical reassessment. It was argued that many worked more for their own interests as members of a black middle class than for the kinds of policies—such as land reform—that would have met the vital needs of their impoverished constituents.

Eric Foner's widely acclaimed *Reconstruction: America's Unfinished Revolution, 1863–1877* (1998) reemphasized some of the achievements of Radical rule in the South. Reflecting the new trend toward "history from the bottom up," its heroes were local black activists rather than white Radicals or even the black elite. But Foner and W. E. B. DuBois, historians who have argued that Reconstruction was a noble and inspiring effort to achieve racial democ-

racy, have had to acknowledge that it failed to prevent the restoration of a brutally oppressive form of white supremacy after the "Redemption" of the 1870s. Was that failure due primarily to the deep-seated racism that drove the white South to carry on a guerrilla war against black participation in politics and also prevented many white Republicans from identifying fully with the cause of black equality? Or did it result from the gulf between the economic interests of those in charge of implementing and managing Reconstruction and the poor people of the South who were supposed to be its beneficiaries? As historians debate this unresolved issue, they should be aware that policymakers and sociologists are currently engaged in similar debates about the relative significance of "race" and "class" as explanations for the persistence of black disadvantage in the United States.

leading proponent of black emigration to Africa. Because he believed that white Americans were so deeply prejudiced against blacks that they would never grant them equal rights, Turner became an early advocate of black nationalism and a total separation of the races. Emigration became a popular movement among southern blacks, who were especially hard hit by terror and oppression just after the end of Reconstruction. Still, a majority of blacks in the nation as a whole and even in Turner's own church refused to give up on the hope of eventual equality on American soil. But Bishop Turner's anger and despair were the understandable responses of a proud man to the way that he and his fellow African Americans had been treated in the post–Civil War period.

By the late 1880s, the wounds of the Civil War were healing, and white Americans were seized by the spirit of sectional reconciliation. Union and Confederate veterans were tenting together and celebrating their common Americanism. "Reunion" was becoming a cultural as well as political reality. But whites could come back together only because Northerners had tacitly agreed to give Southerners a free hand in their efforts to reduce blacks to a new form of servitude. The "outraged, heart-broken,

Henry McNeal Turner, who was born in freedom, became a bishop of the African Methodist Episcopal Church and was elected to the Georgia legislature. ✦

bruised, and bleeding" African Americans of the South paid the heaviest price for sectional reunion. Reconstruction remained, in the words of historian Eric Foner, an "unfinished revolution." It would be another century before African Americans rose up once more to demand full civil and political rights.

RECOMMENDED READING

The best one-volume account of Reconstruction is Eric Foner, *Reconstruction: America's Unfinished Revolution* (1988). Two excellent short surveys are Kenneth M. Stampp, *The Era of Reconstruction, 1865–1877* (1965), and John Hope Franklin, *Reconstruction: After the Civil War* (1961). Both were early efforts to synthesize modern "revisionist" interpretations. W. E. B. DuBois, *Black Reconstruction in America, 1860–1880* (1935), remains brilliant and provocative. On the politics of Reconstruction, see Stephen David Kantrowitz, *Ben Tillman and the Reconstruction of White Supremacy* (2001), Laura F. Edwards, *Gendered Strife and Confusion: The Political Culture of Reconstruction* (1997), J. Morgan Kousser and James M. McPherson, eds., *Region, Race, and Reconstruction: Essays in Honor of C. Vann Woodward* (1982), and Eric Foner, *Nothing But Freedom: Emancipation and Its Legacy* (1983).

Leon F. Litwack, *Been in the Storm So Long: The Aftermath of Slavery* (1979), provides a moving portrayal of the black experience of emancipation. On changing society and family life during Reconstruction, see Noralee Frankel, *Freedom's Women: Black Women and Families in Reconstruction Era Mississippi* (1999), Dylan Penningroth, *Claiming Kin and Property: African American Life Before and After Emancipation* (2003), and Amy Dru Stanley, *From Bondage to Contract: Wage Labor, Marriage, and the Market in the Age of Slave Emancipation* (1998). On what freedom meant in economic terms, see Gerald David Jaynes, *Branches Without Roots: Genesis of the Black Working Class in the American South, 1862–1882* (1986). A work that focuses on ex-slaves' attempts to create their own economic order is Julie Saville, *The Work of Reconstruction: Free Slave to Wage Laborer in South Carolina, 1860–1870* (1994). The best overview of the postwar southern economy is Gavin Wright, *Old South, New South* (1986). On the end of Reconstruction, see David W. Blight, *Race and Reunion: The Civil War in American Memory* (2000). On the character of the post-Reconstruction South, see the classic work by C. Vann Woodward, *Origins of the New South, 1877–1913* (1951) and Edward Ayers, *The Promise of the New South* (1992).

For a list of additional titles related to this chapter's topics, please see http://www.ablongman.com/divine.

SUGGESTED WEB SITES

Diary and Letters of Rutherford B. Hayes

http://www.ohiohistory.org/onlinedoc/hayes/index.cfm
The Rutherford B. Hayes Presidential Center in Fremont, Ohio, maintains this searchable database of Hayes's writings.

Images of African Americans from the Nineteenth Century

http://digital.nypl.org/schomburg/images_aa19/
The New York Public Library-Schomburg Center for Research in Black Culture site contains numerous visuals.

Freedmen and Southern Society Project (University of Maryland-College Park)

http://www.inform.umd.edu/ARHU/Depts/History/Freedman/home.html
This site contains a chronology and sample documents from several print collections or primary sources about emancipation and freedom in the 1860s.

Andrew Johnson

http://www.whitehouse.gov/WH/glimpse/presidents/html/aj17.html
White House history of Johnson.

Ulysses S. Grant

http://www.whitehouse.gov/WH/glimpse/presidents/html/ug18.html
White House history of Grant.

History of the Suffrage Movement

http://www.rochester.edu/SBA
This site includes a chronology, important texts relating to women's suffrage, and biographical information about Susan B. Anthony and Elizabeth Cady Stanton.

Charles M. Russell, *Cowboy Camp During Roundup, ca. 1885–1887. Artist Charles Russell here documents the cowboys' activities during the annual spring roundup. Before setting off on the long trek to drive cattle to market, the cowboys had to rope and break in horses that might have gone a little wild over the winter.* ❖

The West:
Exploiting an Empire

Lean Bear's Changing West

In 1863, federal Indian agents took a delegation of Cheyenne, Arapaho, Comanche, Kiowa, and Plains Apache to visit the eastern United States, hoping to impress them with the power of the white man. The visitors were, in fact, impressed. In New York City, they stared at the tall buildings and crowded streets, so different from the wide-open plains with which they were accustomed. They visited the museum of the great showman Phineas T. Barnum, who in turn put them on display; they even saw a hippopotamus.

In Washington, they met with President Abraham Lincoln. Lean Bear, a Cheyenne chief, assured Lincoln that Indians wanted peace but worried about the numbers of white people who were pouring into their country. Lincoln swore friendship, said the Indians would be better off if they began to farm, and promised he would do his best to keep the peace. But, he said, smiling at Lean Bear, "You know it is not always possible for any father to have his children do precisely as he wishes them to do."

Lean Bear, who had children of his own, understood what Lincoln had had to say in Washington, at least in a way. Just a year later, back on his own lands, he watched as federal troops, Lincoln's "children," approached his camp. Wearing a peace medal that Lincoln had given him, Lean Bear rode slowly toward the troops to once again offer his friendship. When he was twenty yards away, they opened fire, then rode closer and fired again and again into his fallen body.

As Lean Bear had feared, in the last three decades of the nineteenth century, a flood of settlers ventured into the vast lands across the Mississippi River. Prospectors searched for "pay dirt," railroads crisscrossed the continent, eastern and foreign capitalists invested in cattle and land bonanzas, and farmers took up the promise of free western lands. In 1867, Horace Greeley, editor of the New York *Tribune*, told New York City's unemployed: "If you strike off into the broad, free West, and make yourself a farm from Uncle Sam's generous domain, you will crowd nobody, starve nobody, and neither you nor your children need evermore beg for something to do."

With the end of the Civil War, white Americans again claimed a special destiny to expand across the continent. In the process, they crushed the culture of the Native Americans and ignored the contributions of people of other races, such as the Chinese miners and laborers and the Mexican herdsmen. As millions moved west, the states of Colorado, Washington, Montana, the Dakotas, Idaho, Wyoming, and Utah were carved out of the lands across the Mississippi. At the turn of the century, only Arizona, New Mexico, and Oklahoma remained as territories.

The West became a great colonial empire, harnessed to eastern capital and tied increasingly to national and international markets. Its raw materials, sent east by wagon, train, and ship, helped fuel eastern factories. Western economies relied heavily on the federal government, which subsidized their railroads, distributed their land, and spent

OUTLINE

Beyond the Frontier

Crushing the Native Americans

Settlement of the West

The Bonanza West

Conclusion: The Meaning of the West

FEATURE ESSAY

Blacks in Blue: The Buffalo Soldiers in the West

481

millions of dollars for the upkeep of soldiers and Indians.

By the 1890s, the West of the lands beyond the Mississippi had undergone substantial change. In place of buffalo and unfenced vistas, there were cities and towns, health resorts, homesteads, sheep ranches, and, in the arid regions, the beginnings of the irrigated agri- culture that would reshape the West in the twentieth century. Ghost towns, abandoned farms, and the scars in the earth left by miners and farmers spoke to the less favorable side of settlement. As the new century dawned, the West had become a place of conquest and exploitation, as well as a mythic land of cowboys and quick fortunes.

BEYOND THE FRONTIER

The line of white settlement had reached the edge of the Missouri timber country by 1840. Beyond lay an enormous land of rolling prairies, parched deserts, and rugged, majestic mountains. Emerging from the tim- ber country, travelers first encountered the Great Plains—treeless, nearly flat, an endless "sea of grassy hillocks" extending from the Mississippi River to the Rocky Mountains. The Prairie Plains, the eastern part of the region, enjoyed rich soil and good rainfall; it in- cluded parts of present-day Wisconsin, Minnesota, the Dakotas, Nebraska, Kansas, Oklahoma, and Texas. To the west—covering Montana, Wyoming, Colorado,

New Mexico, and Arizona—were the High Plains, rough, semiarid, rising gently to the foothills of the Rocky Mountains.

Running from Alaska to central New Mexico, the Rockies presented a formidable barrier. There were valuable beaver in the streams and gold near Pikes Peak. But most travelers hurried through the northern passes, emerging in the desolate basin of present-day southern Idaho and Utah. Native Americans lived there—the Ute, Paiute, Bannock, and Shoshone tribes—surviving in the harsh environment by digging for roots and gathering seeds and berries. On the west, the lofty Coast Ranges— the Cascades and Sierra Nevada—held back rainfall; be- yond were the temperate lands of the Pacific Coast.

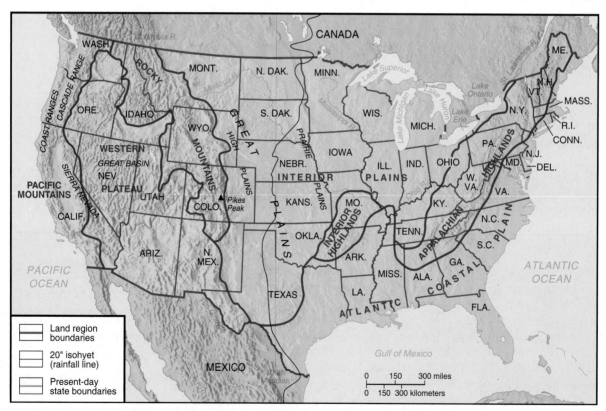

PHYSIOGRAPHIC MAP OF THE UNITED STATES   *In the Great Plains and Rocky Mountains, the topography, altitudes, crops, and climate—especially the lack of rain west of the rainfall line shown here—led to changes in a mode of settlement that had been essentially uniform from the Atlantic Coast through Kentucky, Ohio, and Missouri. The rectangular land surveys and quarter-section lots that were traditional before could not accommodate Great Plains conditions.* ❖

Early explorers like Zebulon Pike thought the country beyond the Mississippi was uninhabitable, fit only, Pike said, for "wandering and uncivilized aborigines." Mapmakers agreed; between 1825 and 1860, American maps showed this land as "The Great American Desert." As a result, settlement paused on the edge of the Plains, and most early settlers headed directly for California and Oregon.

Few rivers cut through the Plains; those that did raged in the winter and trickled in the summer. Rainfall usually did not reach 15 inches a year, not enough to support extensive agriculture. There was little lumber for homes and fences, and the tools of eastern settlement—the cast-iron plow, the boat, and the ax—were virtually useless on the tough and treeless Plains soil. "East of the Mississippi," historian Walter Prescott Webb noted, "civilization stood on three legs—land, water, and timber; west of the Mississippi not one but two of these legs were withdrawn—water and timber—and civilization was left on one leg—land."

Hot winds seared the Plains in summer, and northers, blizzards, and hailstorms froze them in winter. Wildlife roamed in profusion. Antelope shared the open prairies with wolves, coyote, and millions of jackrabbits and prairie dogs. The American bison, better known as the buffalo, grazed in enormous herds from Mexico to Canada. In 1865, perhaps fifteen million buffalo lived on the Plains, so many they seemed like "leaves in a forest" to an early observer. A single herd sighted in 1871 had four million head.

CRUSHING THE NATIVE AMERICANS

When Greeley urged New Yorkers to move West and "crowd nobody," he—like almost all white Americans—ignored the fact that large numbers of people already lived there. At the close of the Civil War, Native Americans inhabited nearly half the United States. By 1880, they had been driven onto smaller and smaller reservations and were no longer an independent people. A decade later, even their culture had crumbled under the impact of white domination.

In 1865, nearly a quarter million Native Americans lived in the western half of the country. Tribes such as the Winnebago, Menominee, Cherokee, and Chippewa were resettled there, forced out of their eastern lands by advancing white settlement. Other tribes were native to the region. In the Southwest there were the Pueblo groups, including the Hopi, Zuni, and Rio Grande Pueblos. Peaceful farmers and herders, they had built up complex traditions around a settled way of life.

The Pueblo groups were cultivators of corn. They lived on the subdesert plateau of present-day western New Mexico and eastern Arizona. Harassed by powerful neighboring tribes, they built communal houses of adobe brick on high mesas or in cracks in the cliffs. More nomadic were the Camp Dwellers, the Jicarilla Apache and Navajo who roamed eastern New Mexico and western Texas. Blending elements of the Plains and Plateau environments, they lived in tepees or mud huts, grew some crops to supplement their hunting, and moved readily from place to place. The Navajo herded sheep and produced beautiful ornamental silver, baskets, and blankets. Fierce fighters, Apache horsemen were feared by whites and fellow Indians across the southwestern Plains.

Farther west were the tribes that inhabited present-day California. Divided into many small bands, they eked out a difficult existence living on roots, grubs, berries, acorns, and small game. In the Pacific Northwest, where fish and forest animals made life easier, the Klamath, Chinook, Yurok, and Shasta tribes developed a rich civilization. They built plank houses and canoes, worked extensively in wood, and evolved a complex social and political organization. Settled and determined, they resisted the invasion of the whites.

By the 1870s, most of these tribes had been destroyed or beaten into submission. The powerful Ute, crushed in 1855, ceded most of their Utah lands to the United States and settled on a small reservation near Great Salt Lake. The Navajo and Apache fought back fiercely, but between 1865 and 1873 they too were confined to reservations. The Native Americans of California succumbed to the contagious diseases carried by whites during the Gold Rush of 1849. Miners burned their villages, and by 1880, fewer than twenty thousand Indians lived in California.

Life of the Plains Indians

In the mid-nineteenth century, nearly two-thirds of the Native Americans lived on the Great Plains. The Plains tribes included the Sioux of present-day Minnesota and the Dakotas; the Blackfoot of Idaho and Montana; the Cheyenne, Crow, and Arapaho of the central Plains; the Pawnee of western Nebraska; and the Kiowa, Apache, and Comanche of present-day Texas and New Mexico.

Nomadic and warlike, the Plains Indians depended on the buffalo and horse. The modern horse, first brought by Spanish explorers in the 1500s, spread north from Mexico onto the Plains, and by the 1700s the Plains Indians' way of life had changed. The Plains tribes gave up farming almost entirely and hunted the buffalo, ranging widely over the rolling plains. The men became superb warriors and horsemen, among the best light cavalry in the world.

After the buffalo was killed, women skinned the hide, cut up the meat, and then cured the hide, as shown in the painting Halcyon Days *by George Catlin. Women also decorated the tepees and preserved the meat by drying it in the sun.* ❖

Equipped with stout wooden bows 3 feet or less in length, Plains Indians were fierce warriors. Hiding their bodies behind their racing ponies, they drove deadly arrows clear through buffalo. Against white troops or settlers, the skillful Comanche rode three hundred yards and shot twenty arrows in the time it took a soldier to load his firearm once. The introduction of the new Colt six-shooters during the 1850s gave government troops a rapid-fire weapon but did not entirely offset the Indians' advantage.

Migratory in culture, the Plains Indians formed tribes of several thousand people but lived in smaller bands of three to five hundred. The Comanche, who numbered perhaps seven thousand, had thirteen bands with such names as Burnt Meat, Making Bags While Moving, and Those Who Move Often. Each band was governed by a chief and a council of elder men, and Indians of the same tribe transferred freely from band to band. Bands acted independently, making it difficult for the U.S. government to deal with the fragmented tribes.

The bands followed and lived off the buffalo. Buffalo provided food, clothing, and shelter; the Indians, unlike later white hunters, used every part of the animal. The meat was dried or "jerked" in the hot Plains air. The skins made tepees, blankets, and robes. Buffalo bones became knives; tendons were made into bowstrings; horns and hooves were boiled into

glue. Buffalo "chips"—dried manure—were burned as fuel. All in all, the buffalo was "a galloping department store."

Warfare between tribes usually took the form of brief raids and skirmishes. Plains Indians fought few prolonged wars and rarely coveted territory. Most conflicts involved only a few warriors intent on stealing horses or "counting coup"—touching an enemy's body with the hand or a special stick. Tribes developed a fierce and trained warrior class, recognized for achievements in battle. Speaking different languages, Native Americans of various tribes were nevertheless able to communicate with one another through a highly developed sign language.

The Plains tribes divided labor tasks according to gender. Men hunted, traded, supervised ceremonial activities, and cleared ground for planting. They usually held the positions of authority, such as chief or medicine man. Women were responsible for child rearing and artistic activity. They also performed the camp work, grew vegetables, prepared buffalo meat and hides, and gathered berries and roots. In most tribes, women played an important role in political, economic, and religious activities. Among the Navajo and Zuni, kinship descended from the mother's side, and Navajo women were in charge of most of the family's property. In tribes such as the Sioux, there was little difference in status. Men were respected for hunting and war, women for their artistic skills with quill and paint.

"As Long as Waters Run": Searching for an Indian Policy

Before the Civil War, Americans used the land west of the Mississippi as "one big reservation." The government named the area "Indian Country," moved eastern tribes there with firm treaty guarantees, and in 1834 passed the Indian Intercourse Act, which prohibited any white person from entering Indian country without a license.

The situation changed in the 1850s. Wagon trains wound their way to California and Oregon, miners pushed into western goldfields, and there was talk of a transcontinental railroad. To clear the way for settlement, the federal government in 1851 abandoned "One Big Reservation" in favor of a new policy of concentration. For the first time, it assigned definite boundaries to each tribe. The Sioux, for example, were given the Dakota country north of the Platte River, the Crow a large area near the Powder River, and the Cheyenne and Arapaho the Colorado foothills between the North Platte and Arkansas rivers for "as long as waters run and the grass shall grow."

The concentration policy lasted only a few years. Accustomed to hunting widely for buffalo, many Native Americans refused to stay within their assigned areas. White settlers poured into Indian lands, then called on the government to protect them. Indians were pushed out of Kansas and Nebraska in the 1850s, even as white reformers fought to hold those territories open for free blacks. In 1859, gold miners moved into the Pikes Peak country, touching off warfare with the Cheyenne and Arapaho.

In 1864, tired of the fighting, the two tribes asked for peace. Certain that the war was over, Chief Black Kettle led his seven hundred followers to camp on Sand Creek in southeastern Colorado. Early on the morning of November 29, 1864, a group of Colorado militia led by Colonel John M. Chivington attacked the sleeping group. "Kill and scalp all, big and little," Chivington told his men. "Nits make lice." Black Kettle tried to stop the ambush, raising first an American flag and then a white flag. Neither worked. The Native

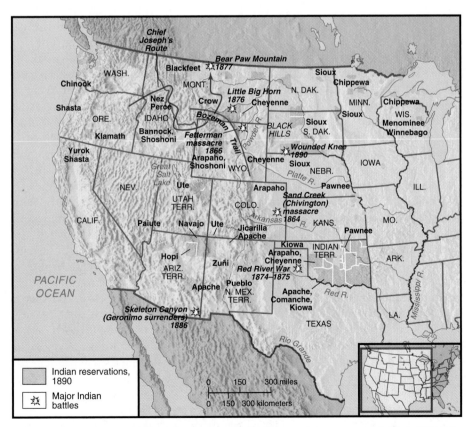

NATIVE AMERICANS IN THE WEST: MAJOR BATTLES AND RESERVATIONS
"They made us many promises, more than I remember, but they never kept but one; they promised to take our land, and they took it." So said Red Cloud of the Oglala Sioux, summarizing Native American–white relations in the 1870s. ❖

American men, women, and children were clubbed, stabbed, and scalped.

The Chivington massacre set off angry protests in Colorado and the East. Congress appointed an investigating committee, and the government concluded a treaty with the Cheyenne and Arapaho, condemning "the gross and wanton outrages." Still, the two tribes were forced to surrender their Sand Creek reservation in exchange for lands elsewhere. The Kiowa and Comanche were also ousted from areas they had been granted "forever" only a few years before. As the Sioux chief Spotted Tail said, "Why does not the Great Father put his red children on wheels so that he can move them as he will?"

Before long, the powerful Sioux were on the warpath in the great Sioux War of 1865–1867. Once again, an invasion of gold miners touched off the war, which flared even more intensely when the federal government announced plans to connect the various mining towns by building the Bozeman Trail through the heart of the Sioux hunting grounds in Montana. Red Cloud, the Sioux chief, determined to stop the trail. In December 1866, pursued by an army column under Captain William J. Fetterman, he lured the incautious Fetterman deep into the wilderness, ambushed him, and wiped out all eighty-two soldiers in his command.

The Fetterman massacre, coming so soon after the Chivington massacre, sparked a public debate over the nation's Indian policy. Like the policy itself, the debate reflected differing white views of the Native Americans. In the East, some reform, humanitarian, and church groups wanted a humane peace policy, directed toward educating and "civilizing" the tribes. Many white people, in the East and West, questioned this approach, convinced that Native Americans were savages unfit for civilization. Westerners, of course, had some reason to fear Indian attacks, and the fears often fed on wild rumors of scalped settlers and besieged forts. As a result, Westerners in general favored firm control over the Native Americans, including swift punishment of any who rebelled.

In 1867, the peace advocates won the debate. Halting construction on the Bozeman Trail, Congress created a Peace Commission of four civilians and three generals to end the Sioux War and eliminate permanently the causes of Indian wars. Setting out for the West, the Peace Commissioners agreed that only one policy offered a permanent solution: a policy of "small reservations" to isolate the Native Americans on distant lands, teach them to farm, and gradually "civilize" them.

The commissioners chose two areas to hold all the Plains Indians. Fifty-four thousand Native Americans on the northern Plains would be moved north of the Black Hills in Dakota Territory, far from prospective white settlement. On the southern Plains, eighty-six thousand Native Americans would be moved into present-day Oklahoma, a region also considered difficult to farm and unattractive to whites. In both areas, tribes would be assigned specific reservations where government agents could supervise them.

The Kiowa, Comanche, Cheyenne, and Arapaho agreed to the plan in 1867, the Sioux in 1868. The policy was extended beyond the Plains, and the Ute, Shoshone, Bannock, Navajo, and Apache tribes also accepted small reservations. "We have now selected and provided reservations for all, off the great road," an army commander wrote. "All who cling to their old hunting-grounds are hostile and will remain so till killed off."

Final Battles on the Plains

Few Native Americans settled peacefully into life on the new reservations. The reservation system not only changed their age-old customs; it chained them in a situation of poverty and isolation. Soon, young warriors and minor chiefs denounced the treaties and drifted back to the open countryside. In late 1868, warfare broke out again, and it took more than a decade of violence to beat the Indians into submission. The Kiowa and Comanche rampaged through the Texas Panhandle, looting and killing, until the U.S. Army—including the feared "buffalo soldiers," African American cavalrymen on the western frontier—crushed them in the Red River War of 1874–1875 and ended warfare in the Southwest. (See the Feature Essay, "Blacks in Blue: The Buffalo Soldiers in the West," pp. 488–489.)

On the northern Plains, fighting resulted from the Black Hills Gold Rush of 1875. As prospectors tramped across Native American hunting grounds, the Sioux gathered to stop them. They were led by Rain-in-the-Face, the great war chief Crazy Horse, and the famous medicine man Sitting Bull. The army sent several columns of troops after the Indians, but one, under flamboyant Lieutenant Colonel George Armstrong Custer, pushed recklessly ahead, eager to claim the victory. On the morning of June 25, 1876, thinking he had a small band of Native Americans surrounded in their village on the banks of the Little Bighorn River in Montana, Custer divided his column and took 265 men toward it. Instead of finding a small band, he discovered he had stumbled on the main Sioux camp with 2500 warriors. It was the largest Native American army ever assembled in the United States.

By midafternoon it was over; Custer and his men were dead. Custer was largely responsible for the loss, but "Custer's Last Stand," set in blazing headlines across the country, set off a nationwide demand for revenge. Within a few months, the Sioux were surrounded and

This pictogram by Oglala Sioux Amos Bad Heart Bull is a Native American version of the battle of the Little Bighorn, also known as Custer's Last Stand. ❖

beaten, three thousand of them surrendering in October 1876. Sitting Bull and a few followers who had fled to Canada gave up in 1881.

The Sioux War ended the major Indian warfare in the West, but occasional outbreaks occurred for several years thereafter. In 1877, the Nez Percé tribe of Oregon, a people who had warmly welcomed Lewis and Clark in 1805, rebelled against government policy. Hoping to reach Canada, Chief Joseph led the tribe on a courageous flight lasting 75 days and covering 1321 miles. They defeated the pursuing army at every turn but then ran out of food, horses, and ammunition. Surrendering, they were sent to barren lands in the Indian Country of Oklahoma, and there, most of them died from disease.

In 1890, the Teton Sioux of South Dakota, bitter and starving, became restless. Many of them turned to the **Ghost Dances,** a set of dances and rites that grew from a vision of a Paiute messiah named Wovoka. Performance of the dances, Wovoka said, would bring back Native American lands and would cause the whites to disappear. All Native Americans would reunite, the earth would be covered with dust, and a new earth would come upon the old. The vanished buffalo would return in great herds.

The army intervened to stop the dancing, touching off violence that killed Sitting Bull and a number of other warriors. Frightened Native Americans fled southwest to join other Ghost Dancers under the aging chief Big Foot. Moving quickly, troops of the Seventh Cavalry, Custer's old regiment, caught up with Big Foot's band and took them to the army camp on Wounded Knee Creek in South Dakota. A Native American, it is thought, fired the first shot, returned by the army's new machine guns. Firing a shell a second, they shredded tepees and people. In the infamous **Wounded Knee Massacre,** about two hundred men, women, and children were killed in the snow.

The End of Tribal Life

The final step in Indian policy came in the 1870s and 1880s. Some reformers had long argued against segregating the Native Americans on reservations, urging instead that the nation assimilate them individually into white culture. These "assimilationists" wanted to use education, land policy, and federal law to eradicate tribal society.

Congress began to adopt the policy in 1871 when it ended the practice of treaty making with Native American tribes. Since tribes were no longer separate nations, they lost many of their political and judicial functions, and the power of the chiefs was weakened. In 1882, Congress created a Court of Indian Offenses

BLACKS IN BLUE

The Buffalo Soldiers in the West

On Saturday afternoons, youngsters used to sit in darkened movie theaters and cheer the victories of the U.S. Cavalry over the Indians. Typically, the Indians were about to capture a wagon train when army bugles suddenly sounded. Then the blue-coated cavalry charged over the hill. Few in the theaters cheered for the Indians; fewer still noticed the absence of black faces among the charging cavalry. But in fact, more than two thousand African American cavalrymen served on the western frontier between 1867 and 1890. Known as the buffalo soldiers, they made up one-fifth of the U.S. Cavalry.

Black troops were first used on a large scale during the Civil War. Organized in segregated units, with white officers, they fought with distinction. Nearly 180,000 blacks served in the Union army; 34,000 of them

died. When the war ended in 1865, Congress for the first time authorized black troops to serve in the regular peacetime army. In addition to infantry, it created two cavalry regiments—the Ninth and Tenth, which became known as the famous buffalo soldiers.

Like other black regiments, the Ninth and Tenth Cavalry had white officers who took special examinations before they could serve. The chaplains were assigned not only to preach but to teach reading, writing, and arithmetic. The food was poor; racism was widespread. The army stocked the first black units with worn-out horses, a serious matter to men whose lives depended on the speed and stamina of their mounts. "Since our first mount in 1867 this regiment has received nothing but broken down horses and repaired equipment," an officer said in 1870.

Many white officers refused to serve with black troops. George Armstrong Custer, the handsome "boy general," turned down a position in the Ninth and joined the new Seventh Cavalry, headed for disaster at Little Bighorn. The *Army and Navy Journal* carried ads that told a similar story:

A FIRST LIEUTENANT
OF INFANTRY
(white)
Stationed at a
very desirable post
in the Department of the South
desires a transfer with
an officer of the same grade
on equal terms
if in a white regiment
but if in a colored regiment
a reasonable bonus
would be expected.

Although they were not, in fact, treated as well as the white soldiers in their regiments, many African American cavalrymen such as those pictured here were probably drawn into service by hard-sell recruitment posters such as the one shown on the facing page. ❖

ATTENTION! INDIAN FIGHTERS

Having been authorized by the Governor to raise a Company of 100 day

U. S. VOL CAVALRY!

For immediate service against hostile Indians. I call upon all who wish to engage in such service to call at my office and enroll their names immediately.

Pay and Rations the same as other U. S. Volunteer Cavalry.

Parties furnishing their own horses will receive 40c per day, and rations for the same, while in the service.
The Company will also be entitled to all horses and other plunder taken from the Indians.

Office first door East of Recorder's Office.
HAL SAYR.

Central City, Aug. 13, '64.

There was no shortage of black troops for the officers to lead. Blacks enlisted because the army offered some advancement in a closed society. It also paid $13 a month, plus room and board.

In 1867, the Ninth and Tenth Cavalry were posted to the West, where they remained for two decades. Under Colonel Benjamin H. Grierson, a Civil War hero, the Tenth went to Fort Riley, Kansas; the regiment arrived in the midst of a great Indian war. The Kiowa, Comanche, Cheyenne, Arapaho, and Sioux were on the warpath. Troopers of the Tenth defended farms, stages, trains, and work crews building railroad tracks to the West. Cornered by a band of Cheyenne, they beat back the attack and won a new name. They had been known as the "brunettes" or "Africans," but the Cheyenne now called them the buffalo soldiers, a name that soon applied to all African American soldiers in the West.

From 1868 to 1874, the Tenth served on the Kansas frontier. The dull winter days were filled with drills and scouting parties outside the post. In spring and summer, the good weather brought forth new forays. Indian bands raided farms and ranches and stampeded cattle herds on the way north from Texas. They struck and then melted back into the reservations.

The Ninth Cavalry also had a difficult job. Commanded by Colonel Edward Hatch, who had served with Grierson in the Civil War, it was stationed in West Texas and along the Rio Grande. The summers were so hot that men collapsed with sunstroke, the winters so cold that water froze in canteens. Native Americans from outside the area frequently raided it. From the north, Kiowa and Comanche warriors rode down the Great Comanche War Trail; Kickapoos crossed the Rio Grande from Mexico. Gangs of Mexican bandits and restless Civil War veterans roamed and plundered at will.

From 1874 to 1875, the Ninth fought in the great Red River War, in which the Kiowa and Comanche, fed up with conditions on the reservations, revolted against Grant's peace policy. Marching, fighting, then marching again, the soldiers harried and wore out the Indians, who finally surrendered in the spring of 1875. Herded into a new and desolate reservation, the Mescalero Apache of New Mexico took to the warpath in 1877 and again in 1879. Each time, it took a year of grueling warfare to effect their surrender. In 1886, black cavalrymen surrounded and captured the famous Apache chief Geronimo. In that and other campaigns, several buffalo soldiers won the Congressional Medal of Honor.

Black troops hunted Big Foot and his band before the slaughter at Wounded Knee in 1890 (see p. 487), and they served in many of the West's most famous Indian battles. While one-third of all army recruits deserted between 1865 and 1890, the Ninth and Tenth Cavalry had few desertions. In 1880, the Tenth had the fewest desertions of any regiment in the country.

It was ironic that in the West, black men fought red men to benefit white men. Once the Indian wars ended, the buffalo soldiers worked to keep illegal settlers out of Indian or government land; much of the land was later opened to settlement. Both regiments saw action in the Spanish-American War, the Ninth at San Juan Hill, the Tenth in the fighting around Santiago. Unlike white veterans of the same campaigns, the old buffalo soldiers were forgotten in retirement, although some of them had the satisfaction of settling on the western lands they had done so much to pacify.

Tom Torlino, a Navajo Indian, photographed before and after his "assimilation." Torlino attended the Carlisle Indian School in Pennsylvania. ❖

to try Native Americans who broke government rules, and soon thereafter it made them answerable in regular courts for certain crimes.

While Congress worked to break down the tribes, educators trained young Native Americans to adjust to white culture. In 1879, fifty Pawnee, Kiowa, and Cheyenne youths were brought east to the new Carlisle Indian School in Carlisle, Pennsylvania. Other Native American schools soon opened, including the Haskell Institute in Kansas and numerous day schools on the western reservations. The schools taught students to fix machines and farm; they forced young Indians to trim their long hair and made them speak English, banned the wearing of tribal paint or clothes, and forbade tribal ceremonies and dances. "Kill the Indian and save the man," said Richard H. Pratt, the army officer who founded the Carlisle School.

Land ownership was the final and most important link in the new policy. Native Americans who owned land, it was thought, would become responsible, self-reliant citizens. Deciding to give each Native American a farm, Congress in 1887 passed the **Dawes Severalty Act,** the most important legal development in Indian-white relations in more than three centuries.

Aiming to end tribal life, the Dawes Act divided tribal lands into small plots for distribution among members of the tribe. Each family head received 160 acres, single adults 80 acres, and children 40 acres. Once the land was distributed, any surplus was sold to white settlers, with the profits going to Native American schools. To keep the Indians' land from falling into the hands of speculators, the federal government held it in trust for twenty-five years. Finally, American citizenship was granted to Native Americans

who accepted their land, lived apart from the tribe, and "adopted the habits of civilized life."

Through the Dawes Act, 47 million acres of land were distributed to Native Americans and their families. There were another 90 million acres in the reservations, and these lands, often the most fertile, were sold to white settlers. Speculators evaded the twenty-five-year rule, leasing rather than purchasing the land from the Native Americans. Many Native Americans knew little about farming. Their tools were rudimentary, and in the culture of the Plains Indians, men had not ordinarily participated in farming. In 1934, the government returned to the idea of tribal land ownership, but by then 138 million acres of Indian land had shrunk to 48 million acres, half of which was barren.

The final blow to tribal life came not in the Dawes Act but in the virtual extermination of the buffalo, the Plains Indians' chief resource and the basis for their unique way of life. The killing began in the 1860s as the transcontinental railroads pushed west, and it stepped up as settlers found they could harm the Indians by harming the buffalo. "Kill every buffalo you can," an army officer said. "Every buffalo dead is an Indian gone." Then, in 1871, a Pennsylvania tannery discovered that buffalo hides made valuable leather. Professional hunters such as William F. "Buffalo Bill" Cody swarmed across the Plains, killing millions of the beasts.

Between 1872 and 1874, professional hunters slaughtered three million buffalo a year. In a frontier form of a factory system, riflemen, skinners, and transport wagons pushed through the vast herds, which shrank steadily behind them. A good hunter killed a hundred buffalo a day. Skinners took off the hides, removed the tongue, hump, and tallow, and left the rest. "I have seen their bodies so thick after being skinned," a hunter said, "that they would look like logs where a hurricane had passed through a forest."

By 1883, the buffalo were almost gone. When the government set out to produce the famous "buffalo nickel," the designer had to go to the Bronx Zoo in New York City to find a buffalo.

By 1900, there were only 250,000 Native Americans in the country. (There were 600,000 within the limits of the present-day United States in 1800, and more than 5 million in 1492, when Columbus first set foot in the New World.) Most of the Indians lived on reservations. Many lived in poverty. Alcoholism and unemployment were growing problems, and Native Americans, no longer able to live off the buffalo, became wards of the state. They lost their cultural distinctiveness. Once possessors of the entire continent, they had been crowded into smaller and smaller areas, overwhelmed by the demand to become settled, literate, and English-speaking. "Except for the internment of the West Coast Japanese during World War II," said historian Roger L. Nichols, "Indian removal is the only example of large-scale government-enforced migration in American history. For the Japanese, the move was temporary; for the Indians it was not."

Even as the Native Americans lost their identity, they entered the romantic folklore of the West. Dime novels, snapped up by readers young and old, told tales of Indian fighting on the Plains. "Buffalo Bill" Cody turned it all into a profitable business. Beginning in 1883, his Wild West Show ran for more than three decades, playing to millions of viewers in the United States, Canada, and Europe. It featured Plains Indians chasing buffalo, performing a war dance, and attacking a settler's cabin. In 1885, Sitting Bull himself, victor over Custer at the battle of Little Bighorn, performed in the show.

SETTLEMENT OF THE WEST

Between 1870 and 1900, white—and some African, Hispanic, and Asian—Americans settled the enormous total of 430 million acres west of the Mississippi; they took over more land than had been occupied by Americans in all the years before 1870.

People moved West for many reasons. Some sought adventure; others wanted to escape the drab routine of factory or city life. Many moved to California for their health. The Mormons settled Utah to escape religious persecution. Others followed the mining camps, the advancing railroads, and the farming and cattle frontier.

Whatever the specific reason, most people moved West to better their lot. On the whole, their timing was good, for as the nation's population grew, so did demand for the livestock and the agricultural, mineral, and lumber products of the expanding West. Contrary to older historical views, the West did not act as a major "safety valve," an outlet for social and economic tensions. The poor and unemployed did not have the means to move there and establish farms. "Moreover," as Douglass C. North, an economic historian, said, "most people moved West in good times . . . in periods of rising prices, of expanding demand,

Huge buffalo herds grazing along railroads in the West frequently blocked the path of passing trains. Passengers often killed for sport, shooting at the beasts with no intention of using or removing the animal carcasses, glad to know that they were harming the Native Americans by destroying their most important reserve. ❖

when the prospects for making money from this new land looked brightest; and this aspect characterized the whole pattern of settlement."

Men and Women on the Overland Trail

The first movement west aimed not for the nearby Plains but for California and Oregon on the continent's far shore. It started in the **Gold Rush of 1849** to California, and in the next three decades perhaps as many as half a million individuals made the long journey over the **Overland Trail** leading west. Some walked; others rode horses alone or in small groups. About half joined great caravans, numbering 150 wagons or more, that inched across the two thousand miles between the Missouri River and the Pacific Coast.

More often than not, men made the decision to make the crossing, but, except for the stampedes to the mines, migration usually turned out to be a family affair. Wives were consulted, though in some cases they had little real choice. They could either go along or live alone at home. While many women regretted leaving family and friends, they agreed to the trip, sometimes as eagerly as the men. "With good courage and not one sigh of regret I mounted my pony," Lydia Rudd said. "I would not be left behind," said Luzena Wilson, whose husband ached to join the Gold Rush to California. "I thought where he could go I could, and where I went I could take my two little toddling babies." Like the Wilsons, the majority of people traveled in family groups, including in-laws, grandchildren, aunts, and uncles. As one historian said, "The quest for something new would take place in the context of the very familiar."

Individuals and wagon trains set out from various points along the Missouri River. Leaving in the spring and traveling through the summer, they hoped to reach their destination before the first snowfall. During April, travelers gradually assembled in spring camp just across the Missouri River, waiting for the new grass to ripen into forage. They packed and repacked the wagons and elected the trains' leaders, who would set the line of march, look for water and campsites, and impose discipline. Some trains adopted detailed rules, fearing a lapse into savagery in the wild lands across the Missouri. "Every man to carry with him a Bible and other religious books, as we hope not to degenerate into a state of barbarism," one agreement said.

Setting out in early May, travelers divided the enormous route into manageable portions. The first leg of the journey followed the Platte River west to Fort Kearney in central Nebraska Territory, a distance of about three hundred miles. The land was even, with good supplies of wood, grass, and water. From a distance, the white-topped wagons seemed driven by a common force, but, in fact, internal discipline broke down almost immediately. Arguments erupted over the pace of the march, the choice of campsites, the number of guards to post, whether to rest or push on. Elected leaders quit; new ones were chosen. Every train was filled with individualists, and as the son of one train captain said, "If you think it's any snap to run a wagon train of 66 wagons with every man in the train having a different idea of what is the best thing to do, all I can say is that some day you ought to try it."

Men, women, and children had different tasks on the trail. Men concerned themselves almost entirely with hunting buffalo and antelope, guard duty, and transportation. They rose at 4 A.M. to hitch the wagons, and after breakfast began the day's march. At noon, they stopped and set the teams to graze. After the midday meal, the march continued until sunset. Then, while the men relaxed, the women fixed dinner and the next day's lunch, and the children kindled the fires, brought water to camp, and searched for wood or other fuel. Walking fifteen miles a day, in searing heat and mountain cold, travelers were exhausted by late afternoon. "We can all, as soon as we stop, lie down on the grass or anywhere and be asleep in less than no time almost," Rebecca Ketcham, an Oregon-bound emigrant, reported.

For women, the trail was lonely, and they worked to exhaustion. Before long, some adjusted their clothing to the harsh conditions, adopting the new bloomer pants, shortening their skirts, or wearing regular "wash dresses"—so called because they had shorter hemlines that did not drag on the wet ground on washday. Other women continued to wear their long dresses, thinking bloomers "indecent." Both men and women carried firearms in case of Indian attacks, but most emigrants saw few Indians en route.

What they often did see was trash, miles of it, for the wagon trains were an early example of the impact of migration and settlement on the western environment. On the Oregon and other trails, travelers sidestepped mounds of garbage, tin cans, furniture, cooking stoves, kegs, tools, and clothing, all discarded by people who had passed through before. Along a forty-mile trail in the Nevada desert, a migrant tallied two thousand abandoned wagons. On some trails, animals and people stirred up so much dust that drivers wore goggles to protect their eyes.

The first stage of the journey was deceptively easy, and travelers usually reached Fort Kearney by late May. The second leg led another 300 miles up the Platte River to Fort Laramie on the eastern edge of Wyoming Territory. The heat of June had dried the grass, and there was no wood. Anxious to beat the

The migration westward on the overland trail was long and difficult. In this photograph from the 1870s, a caravan of covered wagons stretches as far as the eye can see. Emigrants often chose oxen to pull the wagons because oxen were strong, less expensive than horses, and they could survive on a diet of prairie grasses. ❖

early snowfalls, travelers rested a day or two at the fort, then hurried on to South Pass, 280 miles to the west, the best route through the forbidding Rockies. The land was barren. It was now mid-July, but the mountain nights were so cold that ice formed in the water buckets.

Beyond South Pass, some emigrants turned south to the Mormon settlements on the Great Salt Lake, but most headed 340 miles north to Fort Hall on the Snake River in Idaho. It took another three months to cover the remaining 800 miles. California-bound travelers followed the Humboldt River through the summer heat of Nevada. Well into September, they began the final arduous push: first, a 55-mile stretch of desert; then 70 difficult miles up the eastern slopes of the Sierra Nevada, laboriously hoisting wagons over massive outcrops of rock; and finally the last 100 miles down the western slopes to the welcome sight of California's Central Valley in October.

Under the best of conditions the trip took six months, sixteen hours a day, dawn to dusk, of hard, grueling labor. Walking halfway across the continent was no easy task, and it provided a never-to-be-forgotten experience for those who did it. The wagon trains, carrying the dreams of thousands of individuals, reproduced society in small focus: individualistic, hopeful, mobile, divided by age and gender roles, apprehensive, yet willing to strike out for the distant and new.

Land for the Taking

As railroads pushed west in the 1870s and 1880s, locomotive trains replaced wagon trains, but the shift was gradual, and until the end of the century, emigrants often combined both modes of travel. Into the 1890s, travelers could be seen making their way across the West by any available means. Early railroad transportation was expensive, and the average farm family could not afford to buy tickets and ship supplies. Many Europeans traveled by rail to designated outfitting places and then proceeded West with wagons and oxen.

Traffic flowed in all directions, belying the image of a simple "westward" movement. Many people did go west, of course, but others, such as migrants from Mexico, became westerners by moving north, and Asian Americans moved eastward from the Pacific Coast. Whatever their route, they all ended up in the meeting ground of cultures that formed the modern West.

Why did they come? "The motive that induced us to part with the pleasant associations and the dear friends of our childhood days," explained Phoebe Judson, an early emigrant, "was to obtain from the government of the United States a grant of land that 'Uncle Sam' had promised to give to the head of each family who settled in this new country." A popular camp song reflected the same motive:

Come along, come along—don't be alarmed,
Uncle Sam is rich enough to give us all a farm.

Uncle Sam owned about one billion acres of land in the 1860s, much of it mountain and desert land unsuited for agriculture. By 1900, the various land laws had distributed half of it. Between 1862 and 1890, the government gave away 48 million acres under the **Homestead Act of 1862,** sold about 100 million acres to private citizens and corporations, granted 128 million acres to railroad companies to tempt them to build across the unsettled West, and sold huge tracts to the states.

The Homestead Act of 1862, a law of great significance, gave 160 acres of land to anyone who would pay a $10 registration fee and pledge to live on it and cultivate it for five years. The offer set off a mass migration of land-hungry Europeans, dazzled by a country that gave its land away. Americans also seized on the act's provisions, and between 1862 and 1900, nearly 600,000 families claimed free homesteads under it.

Yet the Homestead Act did not work as Congress had hoped. Few farmers and laborers had the cash to move to the frontier, buy farm equipment, and wait out the year or two before the farm became self-supporting. Tailored to the timber and water conditions of the East, the act did not work as well in the semiarid West. In the fertile valleys of the Mississippi, 160 acres provided a generous farm. A farmer on the Great Plains needed either a larger farm for dry farming or a smaller one for irrigation.

The Timber Culture Act of 1873 attempted to adjust the Homestead Act to western conditions. It allowed homesteaders to claim an additional 160 acres if they planted trees on a quarter of it within four years. A successful act, it distributed 10 million acres of land, encouraged needed forestation, and enabled homesteaders to expand their farms to a workable size. Cattle ranchers lobbied for another law, the Desert Land Act of 1877, which allowed individuals to obtain 640 acres in the arid states for $1.25 an acre, provided they irrigated part of it within three years. The act invited fraud. Irrigation sometimes meant a bucket of water dumped on the ground, and ranchers used their hired hands to claim large tracts. More than 2.6 million acres of land were distributed, much of it fraudulently.

The Timber and Stone Act of 1878 applied only to lands "unfit for cultivation" and valuable chiefly for timber or stone. It permitted anyone in California, Nevada, Oregon, and Washington to buy up to 160 acres of forest land for $2.50 an acre. Like ranchers, lumber companies used employees to file false claims. Company agents rounded up seamen on the water-

Railroad companies distributed elaborately illustrated brochures and broadsides to lure people to the West, where they could settle on land owned by the railroads, such as the 3 million acres in Nebraska advertised in this Union Pacific poster. ✦

front, marched them to the land office to file their claims, took them to a notary public to sign over the claims to the company, and then marched them back to the waterfront for payment in beer or cash. By 1900, 3.6 million acres of rich forest land had been claimed under the measure.

Speculators made ingenious use of the land laws. Sending agents in advance of settlement, they moved along choice river bottoms or irrigable areas, accumulating large holdings to be held for high prices. In the arid West, where control of water meant control of the surrounding land, shrewd ranchers plotted their holdings accordingly. In Colorado, one cattleman, John F. Iliff, owned only 105 small parcels of land, but by placing them around the few water holes, he effectively dominated an empire stretching over 6000 square miles.

Water, in fact, became a dominant western issue, since aside from the Pacific Northwest, northern California, parts of the Rocky Mountain West, and the eastern half of the Great Plains, much of the trans-Mississippi West was arid, receiving less than 20 inches of rainfall annually. People speculated in water as if it were gold and planned great irrigation systems in Utah, eastern Colorado, and California's Central Valley to "make the desert bloom." A sign in Modesto, California, read "Water, Wealth, Contentment, Health."

Irrigators received a major boost in 1902 when the **National Reclamation Act (Newlands Act)** set aside most of the proceeds from the sale of public lands in sixteen western states to finance irrigation projects in the arid states. Over the next decades, dams, canals, and irrigation systems channeled water into dry areas, creating a "hydraulic" society that was rich in crops and cities (such as Los Angeles and Phoenix), but ever thirstier and in danger of outrunning the precious water on which it all depended.

As beneficiaries of the government's policy of land grants for railway construction, the railroad companies were the West's largest landowners. Eager to have immigrants settle on the land they owned near the railroad right-of-way, and eager to boost their freight and passenger business, the companies sent agents to the East and Europe. Attractive brochures touted life in the West. The Union Pacific called the rocky Platte Valley in Nebraska "a flowery meadow of great fertility, clothed in nutritious grasses."

Railroad lines set up land departments and bureaus of immigration. The land departments priced the land, arranged credit terms, and even gave free farming courses to immigrants. The bureaus of immigration employed agents in Europe, met immigrants at eastern seaports, and ran special cars for land seekers heading west.

Half a billion acres of western land were given or sold to speculators and corporations. At the same time, only 600,000 homestead patents were issued, covering 80 million acres. Thus, only one acre in every nine initially went to individual pioneers, the intended beneficiaries of the nation's largesse. Two-thirds of all homestead claimants before 1890 failed in their efforts to farm their new land.

Territorial Government

As new areas of the West opened, they were organized as territories under the control of Congress and the president. The territorial system started with the famous Northwest Ordinance of 1787, which established the rules by which territories became states. Washington ran the territories like "a passive group of colonial mandates." The president appointed the governor and judges in each territory; Congress detailed their duties, set their budgets, and

oversaw their activities. Territorial officials had almost absolute power over the territories.

Until they obtained statehood, then, the territories depended on the federal government for their existence. They became an important part of the patronage system, as sources of jobs for deserving politicians.

The national political parties, especially the Republicans, funneled government funds into the territorial economies, and in areas such as Wyoming and the Dakotas, where resources were scarce, economic growth depended on this money. Many early settlers held patronage jobs or hoped for them, traded with government-supported Native Americans, sold supplies to army troops, and speculated in government lands.

In a large portion of the trans-Mississippi West, a generation grew up under territorial rule. Inevitably, these citizens developed distinct ideas about politics, government, and the economy.

The Spanish-Speaking Southwest

In the nineteenth century, almost all Spanish-speaking people in the United States lived in California, Arizona, New Mexico, Texas, and Colorado. Their numbers were small—California had only 8,086 Mexican residents in 1900—but the influence of their culture and institutions was large. In some respects,

In Invitation to the Dance by Theodore Gentilz, a young woman stands in the doorway of her San Antonio home to greet the group of caballeros riding up on their horses and making music on the violin and guitar. The caballeros' flared trousers, known as calzoneras, were well suited for riding and dancing. Note the distinctive architectural style of the white building at the left where a couple is dancing. ❖

the southwestern frontier was more Spanish American than Anglo-American.

Pushing northward from Mexico, the Spanish gradually established the present-day economic structure of the Southwest. They brought with them techniques of mining, stock raising, and irrigated farming. After winning independence in the 1820s, the Mexicans brought new laws and ranching methods as well as chaps and the burro. Both Spanish and Mexicans created the legal framework for distributing land and water, a precious resource in the Southwest. They gave large grants of land to communities for grazing, to individuals as rewards for service, and to the various Native American pueblos.

In Southern California, the Californios, descendants of the original colonizers, began after the 1860s to lose their once vast landholdings to drought and mortgages. Some turned to crime and became feared bandidos; others, such as José María Amador, lived in poverty and remembered better days:

> When I was but a little boy I drained the
>   chocolate pot,
> But now I am a poor man and am condemned
>   to slop.

In 1875, Romualdo Pacheco, an aristocratic native son, served as governor of California and then went on to Congress. But as the Californios died out, Mexican Americans continued the Spanish-Mexican influence. In 1880, one-fourth of the residents of Los Angeles County were Spanish speaking.

In New Mexico, Spanish-speaking citizens remained the majority ethnic group until the 1940s, and the Spanish Mexican culture dominated the territory. Contests over land grants became New Mexico's largest industry; lawyers who dealt in them amassed huge holdings. After 1888, *Las Gorras Blancas* ("The White Caps"), a secret organization of Spanish Americans, attacked the movement of Anglo ranchers into the Las Vegas community land grant. Armed and hooded, they cut down fences and scattered the stock of those they viewed as intruders.

Throughout the Southwest, the Spanish Mexican heritage gave a distinctive shape to society. Men headed the families and dominated economic life. Women had substantial economic rights (though few political ones), and they enjoyed a status their English American counterparts did not have. Wives kept full control of property acquired before their marriage; they also held half title to all property in a marriage, which later caused many southwestern states to pass community property laws.

In addition, the Spanish Mexican heritage fostered a modified economic caste system, a strong Roman Catholic influence, and the primary use of the Spanish language. Continuous immigration from Mexico kept language and cultural ties strong. Spanish names and customs spread, even among Anglos. David Starr Jordan, arriving from Indiana to become the first president of Stanford University in California, bestowed Spanish names on streets, houses, and a Stanford dormitory. Spanish was the region's first or second language. Confronted by Sheriff Pat Garrett in a darkened room, New Mexico's famous outlaw Billy the Kid died asking, "Quién es? Quién es?" ("Who is it? Who is it?").

THE BONANZA WEST

Between 1850 and 1900, wave after wave of newcomers swept across the trans-Mississippi West. There were riches for the taking, hidden in gold-washed streams, spread lushly over grass-covered prairies, or available in the gullible minds of greedy newcomers. The nineteenth-century West took shape in the search for mining, cattle, and land bonanzas that drew eager settlers from the East and around the world.

As with all bonanzas, the consequences in the West were uneven growth, boom-and-bust economic cycles, and wasted resources. Society seemed constantly in the making. People moved here and there, following river bottoms, gold strikes, railroad tracks, and other opportunities. "Instant cities" arose. San Francisco, Salt Lake City, and Denver were the most spectacular examples, but every cow town and mining camp witnessed similar phenomena of growth. Boston needed more than two centuries to attract one-third of a million people; San Francisco did the same in a little more than twenty years.

Many Westerners had left home to get rich quickly, and they adopted institutions that reflected that goal. As a contemporary poem said:

> Love to see the stir an' bustle
> In the busy town,
> Everybody on the hustle
> Saltin' profits down.
> Everybody got a wad a'
> Ready cash laid by;
> Ain't no flies on Colorado—
> Not a cussed fly.

In their lives, the West was an idea as well as a region, and the idea molded them as much as they molded it.

The Mining Bonanza

Mining was the first important magnet to attract people to the West. Many hoped to "strike it rich" in gold and silver, but at least half the newcomers had no intention of working in the mines. Instead, they pro-

Before the California Gold Rush of 1849, San Francisco was a sleepy little Spanish-Mexican village called Yerba Buena. Gold seekers turned it into a boomtown with an international population. Here, Spanish Mexican rancheros, white prospectors, Chinese laborers, and a top-hatted professional gambler mingle in a San Francisco saloon. ❖

vided food, clothing, and services to the thousands of miners. Leland Stanford and Collis P. Huntington, who later built the Central Pacific Railroad, set up a general store in Sacramento where they sold shovels and supplies. Stephen J. Field, later a prominent justice of the U.S. Supreme Court, followed the Gold Rush to California to practice law.

The California Gold Rush of 1849 began the mining boom and set the pattern for subsequent strikes in other regions. Individual prospectors made the first strikes, discovering pockets of gold along streams flowing westward from the Sierra Nevada. To get the gold, they used a simple process called **placer mining,** which required little skill, technology, or capital. A placer miner needed only a shovel, a washing pan, and a good claim. As the placers gave out, a great deal of gold remained, but it was locked in quartz or buried deep in the earth. Mining became an expensive business, far beyond the reach of the average miner.

Large corporations moved in to dig the deep shafts and finance costly equipment. Quartz mining required heavy rock crushers, mercury vats to dissolve the gold, and large retorts to recapture it. Eastern and European financiers assumed control, labor became unionized, and mining towns took on some of the characteristics of the industrial city. Individual prospectors meanwhile dashed on to the next find. Unlike other frontiers, the mining frontier moved from west to east, as the original California miners—the "yonder-siders," they were called—hurried eastward in search of the big strike.

In 1859, fresh strikes were made near Pikes Peak in Colorado and in the Carson River Valley of Nevada. News of both discoveries set off wild migrations—

100,000 miners were in Pikes Peak country by June 1859. The gold there quickly played out, but the Nevada find uncovered a thick bluish black ore that was almost pure silver and gold. A quick-witted drifter named Henry T. P. Comstock talked his way into partnership in the claim, and word of the **Comstock Lode**—with ore worth $3,876 a ton—flashed over the mountains.

Thousands of miners climbed the Sierra Nevada that summer. On the rough slopes of Davidson Mountain, they created Virginia City, the prototype of the tumultuous western mining town. Mark Twain was there and described the scene in *Roughing It* (1872): "The sidewalks swarmed with people. . . . Joy sat on every countenance, and there was a glad, almost fierce, intensity in every eye, that told of the money-getting schemes that were seething in every brain and the high hope that held sway in every heart."

The biggest strike was yet to come. In 1873, John W. Mackay and three partners formed a company to dig deep into the mountain, and at 1,167 feet they hit the Big Bonanza, a seam of gold and silver more than 54 feet wide. It was the richest discovery in the history of mining. Between 1859 and 1879, the Comstock Lode produced gold and silver worth $306 million. Most of it went to financiers and corporations. Mackay himself became the richest person in the world, earning (according to a European newspaper) $25 a minute, $5 a minute more than Czar Alexander II of Russia.

In the 1860s and 1870s, important strikes were made in Washington, Idaho, Nevada, Colorado, Montana, Arizona, and Dakota. Extremely mobile, miners flocked from strike to strike, and new camps

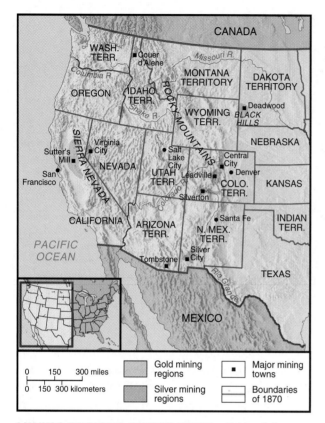

MINING REGIONS OF THE WEST *Gold and silver mines dotted the West, drawing settlers and encouraging political organization in many areas.* ❖

opment process in the frontier experience. The farming frontier had developed naturally in a rural setting. On the mining frontier, the germ of a city—the camp—appeared almost simultaneously with the first "strike." Periodicals, the latest fashions, theaters, schools, literary clubs, and lending libraries came quickly to the camps, providing civilized refinements not available on other frontiers. Urbanization also created the need for municipal government, sanitation, and law enforcement.

Mining camps were governed by a simple democracy. Soon after a strike, the miners in the area met to organize a mining "district" and adopted rules governing behavior in it. Rules regulated the size and boundaries of claims, established procedures for settling disputes, and set penalties for crimes. Petty criminals were banished from the district; serious offenders were hanged. In the case of a major dispute, the whole camp gathered, chose legal counsel for both sides, and heard the evidence. If all else failed, miners formed secret vigilance committees to hang a few offenders as a lesson to the rest. Early visitors to the mining country were struck by the way miners, solitary and competitive, joined together, founded a camp, and created a society.

The camps were mostly male, made up of "men who can rough it" and a few "ladies of spirit and energy." In 1870, men outnumbered women in the mining districts by more than two to one; there were few children. Prostitutes followed the camps around the West, and a "respectable" woman was an object of curiosity. Four arrived in Nevada City in 1853, and one observed, "The men stand and gaze at us with mouth and eyes wide open, every time we go out." Some women worked claims, but more often they took jobs as cooks, housekeepers, and seamstresses—for wages considerably higher than in the East.

In most camps, between one-quarter and one-half of the population was foreign born. The lure of gold drew large numbers of Chinese, Chileans, Peruvians, Mexicans, French, Germans, and English. Experienced miners, the Latin Americans brought valuable mining techniques. At least six thousand Mexicans joined the California rush of 1849, and by 1852, there were twenty-five thousand Chinese in California. Painstaking, the Chinese profitably worked claims others had abandoned. In the 1860s, almost one-third of the miners in the West were Chinese.

Hostility often surfaced against foreign miners, particularly the French, Latin Americans, and Chinese. In 1850, California passed a Foreign Miners' Tax that charged foreign miners a $20 monthly licensing fee. As intended, it drove out Mexicans and other foreigners. Riots against Chinese laborers occurred in the 1870s and 1880s in Los Angeles, San Francisco, Seattle, Reno,

and mining towns sprang up overnight. "The miners of Idaho were like quicksilver," said Hubert Howe Bancroft, an early historian. "A mass of them dropped in any locality, broke up into individual globules, and ran off after any atom of gold in their vicinity. They stayed nowhere longer than the gold attracted them."

The final fling came in the Black Hills rush of 1874 to 1876. The army had tried to keep miners out of the area, the heart of the Sioux hunting grounds, and even sent a scientific party under Colonel George Armstrong Custer to disprove the rumors of gold and stop the miners' invasion. Instead, Custer found gold all over the hills, and the rush was on. Miners, gamblers, desperadoes, and prostitutes flocked to Deadwood, the most lawless of all the mining camps. There, Martha Jane Canary—a crack shot who, as Calamity Jane, won fame as a scout and teamster—fell in love with "Wild Bill" Hickok. Hickok himself—a western legend who had tamed Kansas cow towns, killed an unknown number of men, and toured in Buffalo Bill's Wild West Show—died in Deadwood, shot in the back of the head. Hickok was 39 years old.

Towns such as Deadwood, in the Dakota Territory; Virginia City, Nevada; Leadville, Colorado; and Tombstone, Arizona, demonstrated a new devel-

and Denver. Responding to pressure, Congress passed the Chinese Exclusion Act of 1882, which suspended immigration of Chinese laborers for ten years. The number of Chinese in the United States fell drastically.

By the 1890s, the early mining bonanza was over. All told, the western mines contributed billions of dollars to the economy. They had helped finance the Civil War and provided needed capital for industrialization. The vast boost in silver production from the Comstock Lode changed the relative value of gold and silver, the base of American currency. Bitter disputes over the currency affected politics and led to the famous "battle of the standards" in the presidential election of 1896 (see Chapter 20).

The mining frontier populated portions of the West and sped its process of political organization. Nevada, Idaho, and Montana were granted early statehood because of mining. Merchants, editors, lawyers, and ministers moved with the advancing frontier, establishing permanent settlements. Women in the mining camps helped to foster family life and raised the moral tone by campaigning against drinking, gambling, and prostitution. But not all the effects of the mining boom were positive. The industry also left behind painful scars in the form of invaded Indian reservations, pitted hills, and lonely ghost towns.

Photographer John C. H. Grabill documented frontier life in Colorado, the Dakota territory, and Wyoming. This 1889 photograph shows three men placer mining at a camp in Rockerville, South Dakota. ❖

Gold from the Roots Up: The Cattle Bonanza

"There's gold from the grass roots down," said California Joe, a guide in the gold districts of Dakota in the 1870s, "but there's more gold from the grass roots up." Ranchers began to recognize the potential of the vast grasslands of the West. The Plains were covered with buffalo or grama grass, a wiry variety with short, hard stems. Cattle thrived on it.

For twenty years after 1865, cattle ranching dominated the "open range," a vast fenceless area extending from the Texas Panhandle north into Canada. The techniques of the business came from Mexico. Long before American cowboys moved herds north, their Mexican counterparts, the *vaqueros,* developed the essential techniques of branding, roundups, and roping. The cattle themselves, the famous Texas longhorns,

also came from Mexico. Spreading over the grasslands of southern Texas, the longhorns multiplied rapidly. Although their meat was coarse and stringy, they fed a nation hungry for beef at the end of the Civil War.

The problem was getting the beef to eastern markets, and Joseph G. McCoy, a livestock shipper from Illinois, solved it. Looking for a way to market Texas beef, McCoy conceived the idea of taking the cattle to railheads in Kansas. He talked first with the president of the Missouri Pacific, who ordered him out of his office, and then with the head of the Kansas Pacific, who laughed at the idea. The persistent McCoy finally signed a contract in 1867 with the Hannibal and St. Joseph Railroad. Searching for an appropriate rail junction, he settled on the sleepy Kansas town of Abilene, "a very small, dead place," he remembered, with about a dozen log huts and one nearly bankrupt saloon.

In September 1867, McCoy shipped the first train of twenty cars of longhorn cattle. By the end of the year, a thousand carloads had followed, all headed for Chicago markets. In 1870, 300,000 head of Texas cattle reached Abilene, followed the next year—the peak year—by 700,000 head. The Alamo Saloon, crowded with tired cowboys at the end of the drive, now employed seventy-five bartenders, working three 8-hour shifts.

The profits were enormous. Drivers bought cheap Texas steers for $4 a head and sold them for $30 or $40 a head at the northern railhead. The most famous trail

❖ A Look at the Past ❖

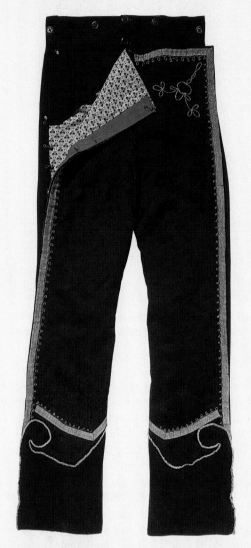

Cowboy Clothing

Cowboys hold a special place in American mythology, representing rugged individuals able to survive in the wilderness. They symbolize another element of our nation's history: the variety of people who formed the country. African Americans, Mexican Americans, Anglo-Americans, and others rode the plains. The clothes cowboys wore during the mid-nineteenth century, such as these wool caballeros pants trimmed with gold braid and with flared legs that button down the sides, show the cultural mixing that took place in the West and how people adapted to the demands of the environment. By the end of the nineteenth century, cowboy heroes, such as those in Buffalo Bill's Wild West Show, no longer wore serapes, sashes, short jackets, or pants such as these that shared Spanish and Mexican origins. What does the change in cowboy fashion suggest about attitudes toward Mexicans? Why would it matter that cowboy heroes wore clothes that reflected Anglo origins, rather than Mexican?

was the Chisholm, running from southern Texas through Oklahoma Territory to Ellsworth and Abilene, Kansas, on the Kansas Pacific Railroad. Dodge City, Kansas, became the prime shipping center between 1875 and 1879.

Cowboys pushed steers northward in herds of two to three thousand. Novels and films have portrayed the cowboys as white, but at least a quarter of them were black, and possibly another quarter were Mexicans. A typical crew on the trail north might have eight men, half of them black or Mexican. Most of the trail bosses were white; they earned about $125 a month. James "Jim" Perry, a renowned black cowboy who worked for more than twenty years as a rider, roper, and cook for the XIT ranch, said, "If it weren't for my damned old black face, I'd have been a boss long ago."

Like miners, cattlemen lived beyond the formal reach of the law and so established their own. Before each drive, Charles Goodnight drew up rules governing behavior on the trail. A cowboy who shot another was hanged on the spot. Ranchers adopted rules for cattle ownership, branding, roundups, and drives, and they formed associations to enforce them. The Wyoming Stock Growers' Association, the largest and most formidable, had four hundred members owning two million cattle; its reach extended well beyond Wyoming into Colorado, Nebraska, Montana, and the Dakotas. Throughout this vast territory, the "laws" of the association were often the law of the land.

Hollywood images to the contrary, there was little violence in the booming cow towns. The number of homicides in a year never topped five in any town, and in many years no one was killed. Doc Holliday and William B. "Bat" Masterson never killed anyone. John Wesley Hardin, a legendary teenaged gunman, shot only one man, firing blindly through a hotel room wall to stop him from snoring. Famous western sheriffs had everyday duties. Wild Bill Hickok served as Abilene's street commissioner, and the Wichita city council made its lawmen, including Wyatt Earp, repair streets and sidewalks before each cattle season.

By 1880, more than six million cattle had been driven to northern markets. But the era of the great cattle drive was ending. Farmers were planting wheat on the old buffalo ranges; barbed wire, a recent invention, cut across the trails and divided up the big ranches. Mechanical improvements in slaughtering, refrigerated transportation, and cold storage modernized the industry. Ranchers bred the Texas longhorns with heavier Hereford and Angus bulls, and as the new breeds proved profitable, more and more ranches opened on the northern ranges.

By the mid-1880s, some 4.5 million cattle grazed the High Plains, reminding people of the once great herds of buffalo. Stories of vast profits circulated,

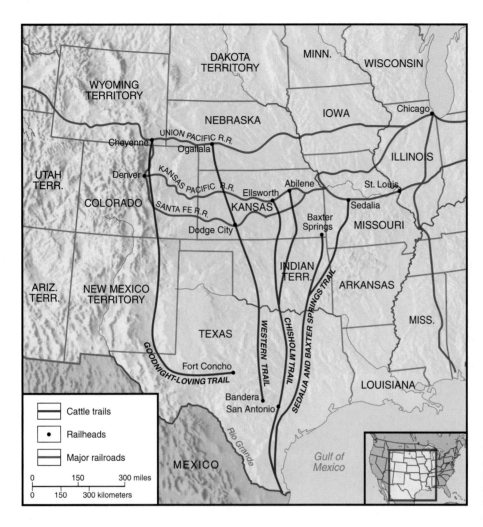

CATTLE TRAILS *Cattle raised in Texas were driven along the cattle trails to the northern railheads, and trains carried them to market.* ❖

attracting outside capital. Large investments transformed ranching into big business, often controlled by absentee owners and subject to new problems.

By 1885, experienced cattle ranchers were growing alarmed. A presidential order that year forced them out of the Indian Territory in Oklahoma, adding 200,000 cattle to the overcrowded northern ranges. The winter of 1885 to 1886 was cold, and the following summer was one of the hottest on record. Water holes dried up; the grass turned brown. Beef prices fell.

The winter of 1886–1887 was one of the worst in western history. Temperatures dropped to 45 degrees below zero, and cattle that once would have saved themselves by drifting ahead of the storms came up against the new barbed wire fences. Herds jammed together, pawing the frozen ground or stripping bark from trees in search of food. Cattle died by the tens of thousands. In the spring of 1887, when the snows thawed, ranchers found stacks of carcasses piled up against the fences.

The melting snows did, however, produce a lush crop of grass for the survivors. The cattle business

recovered, but it took different directions. Outside capital, so plentiful in the boom years, dried up. Ranchers began fencing their lands, reducing their herds, and growing hay for winter food. To the dismay of cowboys, mowing machines and hay rakes became as important as chuck wagons and branding irons. "I tell you times have changed," one cowboy said sadly.

The last roundup on the northern ranges took place in 1905. Ranches grew smaller, and some ranchers, at first in the scrub country of the Southwest, then on the Plains themselves, switched to raising sheep. By 1900, there were nearly thirty-eight million sheep west of the Missouri River, far more than there were cattle. In Montana, there were six or seven sheep for each cow, and even Wyoming, the great center of the northern ranches, had more sheep than cows.

Ranchers and sheepherders fought bitterly to control the grazing lands, but they had one problem in common: the troubles ahead. Homesteaders, armed with barbed wire and new strains of wheat, were pushing onto the Plains, and the day of the open range was over.

In the late 1800s, cowboys drove enormous herds of cattle on trails north out of Texas to railheads, where the cattle could be transported by railroad car to major markets such as Chicago. As suggested by this panoramic view of life on the trail, it was no easy task to control two to three thousand steers and the work generally required a crew of several men. ❖

Sodbusters on the Plains: The Farming Bonanza

Like miners and cattle ranchers, millions of farmers moved into the West in the decades after 1870 to seek crop bonanzas and new ways of life. Some realized their dreams; many fought just to survive.

Said a folksong from Greer County, Oklahoma:

Hurrah for Greer County! The land of the free,
The land of the bedbug, grasshopper, and flea;
I'll sing of its praises, I'll tell of its fame,
While starving to death on my government claim.

Between 1870 and 1900, farmers cultivated more land than ever before in American history. They peopled the Plains from Dakota to Texas, pushed the Indians out of their last sanctuary in Oklahoma, and poured into the basins and foothills of the Rockies. By 1900, the western half of the nation contained almost 30 percent of the population, compared to less than 1 percent just a half century earlier.

Unlike mining, farm settlement often followed predictable patterns, taking population from states east of the settlement line and moving gradually westward. Crossing the Mississippi, farmers settled first in western Iowa, Minnesota, Nebraska, Kansas, Texas, and South Dakota. The movement slumped during the depression of the 1870s, but then a new wave of optimism carried thousands more west. Several years of above average rainfall convinced farmers that the Dakotas, western Nebraska and Kansas, and eastern Colorado were the "rain belt of the Plains." Between 1870 and 1900, the population on the Plains tripled.

In some areas, the newcomers were blacks who had fled the South, fed up with beatings and murders, crop liens, and the Black Codes that institutionalized their subordinate status. In 1879, about six thousand African Americans known as the **Exodusters** left their homes in Louisiana, Mississippi, and Texas to establish new and freer lives in Kansas, the home of John Brown and the Free-Soil campaigns of the 1850s. Once there, they farmed or worked as laborers; women worked in the fields alongside the men or cleaned houses and took in washing to make ends meet. All told, the Exodusters homesteaded 20,000 acres of land, and though they met prejudice, it was not as extreme as they had known at home. "I asked my wife did she know the ground she stands on," said John Solomon Lewis, a Louisianan, soon after arriving. "She said, 'No!' I said it is free ground; and she cried like a child for joy."

Other African Americans moved to Oklahoma, thinking they might establish the first African American state. Whether headed for Oklahoma or Kansas, they picked up and moved in sizable groups that were based on family units; they took with them the customs they had known, and in their new homes they were able, for the first time, to have some measure of self-government.

For blacks and whites alike, farming on the Plains presented new problems. There was little surface water, and wells ranged between 50 and 500 feet deep. Well drillers charged up to $2 a foot. Taking advantage of the steady Plains winds, windmills brought the water to the surface, but they too were expensive, and until 1900, many farmers could not afford them. Lumber for homes and fences was also scarce. Some settlers imported it from distant Wisconsin, but a single homestead of 160 acres cost $1000 to fence, an amount few could pay.

Unable to afford wood, farmers often started out in dreary sod houses. Cut into 3-foot sections, the thick prairie sod was laid like brick, with space left for two windows and a door. Since glass was scarce, cloth hung over the windows; a blanket was hung from the ceiling to make two rooms. Sod houses were small, provided little light and air, and were impossible to keep clean. When it rained, water seeped through the roof. Yet a sod house cost only $2.78 to build.

Outside, the Plains environment sorely tested the men and women who moved there. Neighbors were distant; the land stretched on as far as the eye could see. Always the wind blew. "As long as I live I'll never see such a lonely country," a woman said of the Texas Plains; a Nebraska woman said, "These unbounded prairies have such an air of desolation—and the stillness is very oppressive."

In the winters, savage storms swept the open grasslands. Ice caked on the cattle until their heads were too heavy to hold up. Summertime temperatures stayed near 110 degrees for weeks at a time. Fearsome rainstorms, building in the summer's heat, beat down the young corn and wheat. The summers also brought grasshoppers, arriving without warning, flying in clouds so huge they shut out the sun. The grasshoppers ate everything in sight: crops, clothing, mosquito netting, tree bark, even plow handles. In the summer of 1874, they devastated the whole Plains from Texas to the Dakotas, eating everything "but the mortgage," as one farmer said.

New Farming Methods

Farmers adopted new techniques to meet conditions on the Plains. For one thing, they needed cheap and effective fencing material, and in 1874, Joseph F. Glidden, a farmer from De Kalb, Illinois, provided it with the invention of barbed wire. By 1883, his factory was turning out 600 miles of barbed wire every day, and farmers were buying it faster than it could be produced.

Dry farming, a new technique, helped compensate for the lack of rainfall. By plowing furrows 12 to 14 inches deep and creating a dust mulch to fill the furrow, farmers loosened the soil and slowed evaporation. Wheat farmers imported European varieties of plants that could withstand the harsh Plains winters. Hard-kerneled varieties such as Turkey red wheat from Russia required new milling methods, developed during the 1870s. By 1881, Minneapolis, St. Louis, and Kansas City had become milling centers for the rich "new process" flour.

Disappointed with the failures of Reconstruction and fearful of the violence that surrounded them, many southern blacks migrated to Kansas in the 1870s and 1880s. Comparing their trek to the biblical story of the Israelites' exodus from Egypt, they became known as "Exodusters." ❖

❖ A Look at the Past ❖

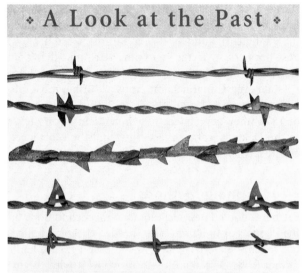

Barbed Wire

Barbed wire forever altered land use in the West. Perfected in 1874, barbed wire made effective, economical fencing. Reflecting its importance to western farmers, barbed wire soon came in hundreds of varieties, including decorative versions. Most variations performed equally well, however, making so many designs unnecessary. Why do you think so many types existed?

Farm technology changed long before the Civil War, but later developments improved it. In 1877, James Oliver of Indiana patented a chilled-iron plow with a smooth-surfaced moldboard that did not clog in the thick prairie soils. The spring-tooth harrow (1869) sped soil preparation; the grain drill (1874) opened furrows and scientifically fed seed into the ground. The lister (1880) dug a deep furrow, planted corn at the bottom, and covered the seed—all in one operation.

The first baling press was built in 1866, and the hay loader was patented in 1876. The first successful harvester, the cord binder (1878), cut and tied bundles of grain, enabling two men and a team of horses to harvest 20 acres of wheat a day. Invented earlier, threshers grew larger; employing as many as nine men and ten horses, one machine could thresh 300 bushels of grain a day.

In 1890, more than nine hundred corporations manufactured farm machinery. Scientific agriculture flourished under new discoveries linking soil minerals and plant growth. Samuel Johnson of Yale University published *How Crops Grow* (1868) and *How Crops Feed* (1870), and one of his students pioneered work on nitrogen, the base of many modern fertilizers. The Hatch Act, passed in 1887, supported agricultural experiment stations that spread the discoveries among farmers. Four years later, the stations employed more than 450 persons and distributed more than 300 published reports annually to some 350,000 readers.

In the late 1870s, huge **bonanza farms** rose, run by the new machinery and financed with outside capital. Oliver Dalrymple, the most famous of the bonanza farmers, headed an experiment in North Dakota's Red River Valley in 1875, then moved on to manage the Grandin Bonanza of 61,000 acres, five times the size of Manhattan Island. Dalrymple hired armies of workers, bought machinery by the carload, and planted on a scale that dazzled the West.

The bonanza farms—thanks to their size and machinery—captured the country's imagination. Using 200 pairs of harrows, 155 binders, and 16 threshers, Dalrymple produced 600,000 bushels of wheat in 1881. He and other bonanza managers profited from the economies of scale, buying materials at wholesale prices and receiving rebates from the railroads. Then a period of drought began. Rainfall dropped between 1885 and 1890, and the large-scale growers found it hard to compete with smaller farmers who diversified their crops and cultivated more intensively. Many of the large bonanzas slowly disintegrated, and Dalrymple himself went bankrupt in 1896.

A work crew on the Dalrymple farm in the Red River Valley gathers grain wired into bundles by self-binding harvesters. In 1877, Dalrymple used a hundred workers to harvest his 4000 acres of wheat; by 1884, the number of harvesters employed on the farm had increased to a thousand. ❖

Discontent on the Farm

Touring the South in the 1860s, Oliver H. Kelley, a clerk in the Department of Agriculture, was struck by the drabness of rural life. In 1867, he founded the **National Grange of the Patrons of Husbandry,** known simply as the Grange. The Grange provided social, cultural, and educational activities for its members. Its constitution banned involvement in politics, but Grangers often ignored the rules and supported railroad regulation and other measures.

The Grange grew rapidly during the depression of the 1870s, and by 1875, it had more than 800,000 members in 20,000 local Granges. Most were in the Midwest and South. The Granges set up cooperative stores, grain elevators, warehouses, insurance companies, and farm machinery factories. Many failed, but in the meantime the organization made its mark. Picking up where the Grange left off, farm-oriented groups

such as the Farmers' Alliance, with branches in both South and West, began to attract followers.

Like the cattle boom, the farming boom ended sharply after 1887. A severe drought that year cut harvests, and other droughts followed in 1889 and 1894. Thousands of new farmers were wiped out on the western Plains. Between 1888 and 1892, more than half the population of western Kansas left. Farmers grew angry and restless. They complained about declining crop prices, rising railroad rates, and heavy mortgages.

Although many farmers were unhappy, the peopling of the West in those years transformed American agriculture. The states beyond the Mississippi became the garden land of the nation. California sent fruit, wine, and wheat to eastern markets. Under the Mormons, Utah flourished with irrigation. Texas beef stocked the country's tables, and vast wheat fields, stretching to the horizon, covered Minnesota, the

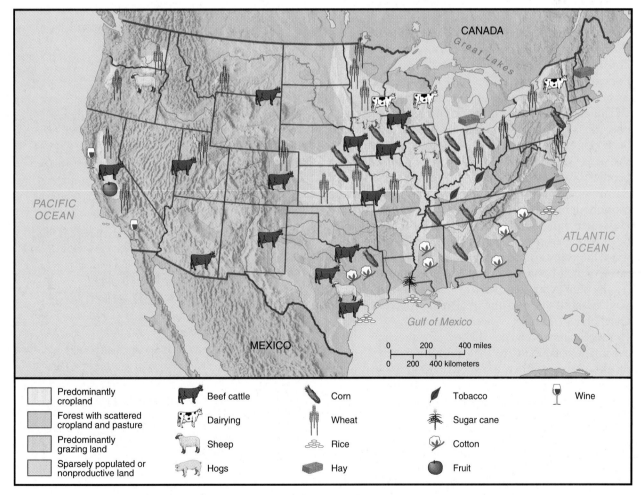

AGRICULTURAL LAND USE IN THE 1880s   *New farming technology and new crops enabled more and more land to be put to productive use.* ❖

Dakotas, Montana, and eastern Colorado. All produced more than Americans could consume. By 1890, American farmers were exporting large amounts of wheat and other crops.

Farmers became more commercial and scientific. They needed to know more and work harder. Mail-order houses and rural free delivery diminished their isolation and tied them ever closer to the national future. "This is a new age to the farmer," said a statistician in the Department of Agriculture in 1889. "He is now, more than ever before, a citizen of the world."

The Final Fling

As the West filled in with people, pressure mounted on the president and Congress to open the last Indian territory, Oklahoma, to settlers. In March 1889, Congress acted and forced the Creek and Seminole tribes, who had been moved into Oklahoma in the 1820s, to surrender their rights to the land. With arrangements complete, President Benjamin Harrison announced the opening of the Oklahoma District as of noon, April 22, 1889.

Preparations were feverish all along the frontier. "From all the West," historian Ray Allen Billington noted, "the homeless, the speculators, the adventurers, flocked to the still forbidden land." On the morning of April 22, nearly a hundred thousand people lined the Oklahoma borders; "for miles on end horsemen, wagons, hacks, carriages, bicycles, and a host of vehicles beggaring description stood wheel to wheel awaiting the signal." Fifteen Santa Fe trains were jammed with people from platform to roof.

At noon, the starting flag dropped. Bugles and cannon signaled the opening of the "last" territory. Horsemen lunged forward; overloaded wagons collided and overturned. The trains steamed slowly forward, forced by army troops to keep a pace that would not give their passengers an undue advantage.

By sunset that day, settlers claimed twelve thousand homesteads, and the 1.92 million acres of the Oklahoma District were officially settled. Homesteaders threw up shelters for the night. By evening, Oklahoma City, that morning merely a spot on the prairie with cottonwoods and grass, had ten thousand people; Guthrie to the north had fifteen thousand. Speculators swiftly erected pay toilets, and drinking water cost as much as a beer.

The "Boomers" (those who waited for the signal) and "Sooners" (those who had jumped the gun) reflected the speed of western settlement. "Creation!" a character in Edna Ferber's novel *Cimarron* declared. "Hell! That took six days. This was done in one. It was History made in an hour—and I helped make it."

CHRONOLOGY

1849	Gold Rush to California
1859	More gold and silver discoveries in Colorado and Nevada
1862	Congress passes Homestead Act encouraging western settlement
1864	Nevada admitted to the Union ❖ Colonel John Chivington leads massacre of Indians at Sand Creek, Colorado
1865–1867	Sioux War against white miners and U.S. Army
1866	"Long drive" of cattle touches off cattle bonanzas
1867	Horace Greeley urges Easterners to "Go West, young man" ❖ National Grange of the Patrons of Husbandry (the Grange) founded to enrich farmers' lives
1867–1868	Policy of "small reservations" for Indians adopted
1873	Congress passes Timber Culture Act ❖ Big bonanza discovered on the Comstock Lode in Nevada
1874	Joseph F. Glidden invents barbed wire ❖ Discovery of gold in Dakota Territory sets off Black Hills Gold Rush
1876	Colorado admitted to the Union ❖ Custer and his men defeated and killed by the Sioux at battle of the Little Bighorn (June)
1883	Museum expedition discovers fewer than two hundred buffalo in the West
1886–1887	Severe drought and winter damage cattle and farming bonanzas
1887	Congress passes Dawes Severalty Act, making Indians individual landowners ❖ Hatch Act provides funds for establishment of agricultural experiment stations
1889	Washington, Montana, and the Dakotas admitted to the Union ❖ Oklahoma Territory opened to settlement
1890	Idaho and Wyoming admitted to the Union ❖ Teton Sioux massacred at battle of Wounded Knee, South Dakota (December)
1893	Young historian Frederick Jackson Turner analyzes closing of the frontier
1902	Congress passes National Reclamation Act (the Newlands Act)

CONCLUSION: THE MEANING OF THE WEST

Between the Civil War and 1900, the West witnessed one of the greatest migrations in history. With the Native Americans driven into smaller and smaller areas, farms, ranches, mines, and cities took over the vast lands from the Mississippi to the Pacific. The 1890 census noted that for the first time in the country's history, "there can hardly be said to be a frontier line." Picking up the theme, Frederick Jackson Turner, a young history instructor at the University of Wisconsin, examined its importance in an influential 1893 paper, "The Significance of the Frontier in American History."

"The existence of an area of free land," Turner wrote, "its continuous recession, and the advance of American settlement westward, explain American development." It shaped customs and character; gave rise to independence, self-confidence, and individualism; and fostered invention and adaptation. Historians have substantially modified **Turner's thesis** by pointing to frontier conservatism and imitativeness, the influence of varying racial groups, and the persistence of European ideas and institutions. Most recently, they have shown that family and community loomed as large as individualism on the frontier; men, women, and children played very much the same roles as they had back home.

Rejecting Turner almost completely, a group of "new Western historians" has advanced a different and complex view of the West, and one with few heroes and heroines. Emphasizing the region's racial and ethnic diversity, these historians stress the role of women as well as men, trace struggles between economic interests instead of fights between gunslingers, and question the impact of development on the environment. White English-speaking Americans, they suggest, could be said to have conquered the West rather than settled it.

The West, in this view, was not settled by a wave of white migrants moving west across the continent (Turner's "frontier") but by a set of waves—Anglo, Mexican American, African American, Asian American, and others—moving in many directions and interacting with each other and with Native American cultures to produce the modern West. Nor did western history end in 1890 as Turner would have it. Instead, migration, development, and economic exploitation continued into the twentieth century, illustrated in the fact that the number of people who moved to the West after 1900 far exceeded those who had moved there before.

In both the nineteenth and twentieth centuries, there can be no doubt that the image of the frontier and the West influenced American development. Western lands attracted European, Latin American, and Asian immigrants, adding to the society's talent and diversity. The mines, forests, and farms of the West fueled the economy, sent raw materials to eastern factories, and fed the growing cities. Though defeated in warfare, the Native Americans and Mexicans influenced art, architecture, law, and western folklore. The West was the first American empire, and it had a profound impact on the American mind and imagination.

RECOMMENDED READING

The best traditional account of the movement west is Ray Allen Billington, *Westward Expansion* (1967), which also has a first-rate bibliography. Walter Prescott Webb, *The Great Plains* (1931), offers a fascinating analysis of development on the Plains.

For examples of the work of "new Western historians," see Donald Worster, *Rivers of Empire* (1985), a powerful study of the "hydraulic" society, and his *Under Western Skies: Nature and History in the American West* (1992); William Cronon, *Nature's Metropolis: Chicago and the Great West* (1991), a provocative analysis of the relationship of Chicago and the West; Patricia Nelson Limerick, *The Legacy of Conquest* (1987); and Richard White, *"It's Your Misfortune and None of My Own": A History of the American West* (1991).

More recent authors have taken fresh and stimulating looks at older or ignored questions. Robert R. Dykstra, *The Cattle Towns* (1968), examines five Kansas cattle towns, with interesting results. Elliott West discusses the Plains in *The Contested Plains: Indians, Goldseekers, and the Rush to Colorado* (1998). Gregory Nobles, *American Frontiers: Cultural Encounters and Continental Conquest* (1997), is an engaging synthesis of frontier history.

There are a number of insightful recent studies of the environment, including Andrew C. Isenberg, *The Destruction of the Bison: An Environmental History, 1750–1920* (2000), Shepard Krech III, *The Ecological Indian: Myth and History* (1999), Karl Jacoby, *Crimes Against Nature: Squatters, Poachers, Thieves, and the Hidden History of American Conservation* (2001), and Dan L. Flores, *The Natural West: Environmental History in the Great Plains and Rocky Mountains* (2001). Susan Lee Johnson, *Roaring Camp: The Social World of the California Gold Rush* (2000), is a fascinating examination of the gold camps.

On the Native Americans, there are a number of valuable works, including R. Douglas Hurt's excellent *Indian

Agriculture in America (1987), Janet A. McDonnell, *The Dispossession of the American Indian, 1887–1934* (1991), Robert A. Trennert, Jr., *The Phoenix Indian School* (1988), Scott Riney, *The Rapid City Indian School, 1898–1933* (1999), Paul H. Carlson, *The Plains Indians* (1998), and John William Sayer, *Ghost Dancing the Law: The Wounded Knee Trials* (1997).

Nell Irvin Painter, *Exodusters: Black Migration to Kansas After Reconstruction* (1976), tells the story of the Exodusters, as Monroe Lee Billington does for New Mexico's *Buffalo Soldiers, 1866–1900* (1991). Also see Frank N. Schubert, *Buffalo Soldiers, Braves, and the Brass* (1993).

Julie Roy Jeffrey, *Frontier Women: The Trans-Mississippi West* (1979), Joanna L. Stratton, *Pioneer Women: Voices from the Kansas Frontier* (1981), and Deena J. González, *Refusing the Favor: The Spanish-Mexican Women of Santa Fe, 1820–1880* (1999), are perceptive works on a neglected topic. John Mack Faragher, *Women and Men on the Overland Trail* (1979), and John Phillip Reid, *Law for the Elephant* (1980), examine relationships on the trails west.

For a list of additional titles related to this chapter's topics, please see http://www.ablongman.com/divine.

SUGGESTED WEB SITES

Indian Affairs: Laws and Treaties, compiled and edited by Charles J. Kappler (1904)

http://digital.library.okstate.edu/kappler
This digitized text at Oklahoma State University includes preremoval treaties with the Five Civilized Tribes and other tribes.

Native American Documents Project

http://www.csusm.edu/projects/nadp/nadp.htm
California State University at San Marcos has several digital documents relating to Native Americans on this site.

Geronimo

http://odur.let.rug.nl/~usa/B/geronimo/geronixx.htm
This site contains biographical and autobiographical information about the famous Native American who resisted European American domination.

National Museum of the American Indian

http://www.si.edu/nmai
The Smithsonian Institution maintains this site, providing information about the museum. The museum is dedicated to everything about Native Americans.

The Northern Great Plains, 1880–1920: Photographs from the Fred Hultstrand and F. A. Pazandak Photograph Collections

http://memory.loc.gov/ammem/award97/ndfahtml/ngphome.html
This American Memory site from the Library of Congress contains "two collections from the Institute for Regional Studies at North Dakota State University" with "900 photographs of rural and small town life at the turn of the century." Included are "images of sod homes and the people who built them; images of farms and the machinery that made them prosper; and

images of one-room schools and the children that were educated in them."

On the Trail in Kansas

http://www.kancoll.org/galtrl.htm
This Kansas Collection site holds several good primary sources with images concerning the Oregon trail and America's early movement westward.

"California as I Saw It": First-Person Narratives of California's Early Years, 1849–1900

http://memory.loc.gov/ammem/cbhtml/cbhome.html
This site is a part of the American Memory series and contains "full texts and illustrations of 190 works documenting the formative era of California's history through eyewitness accounts." It covers the Gold Rush, the interaction of various groups, and the settling of the region.

Home on the Range/Cowboy Heritage

http://history.cc.ukans.edu/heritage/old_west/cowboy.html
This site tells the history of the cattle trails and towns such as Dodge City, with useful text, links, documents, and maps.

The Evolution of the Conservation Movement, 1850–1920

http://memory.loc.gov/ammem/amrvhtml/conshome.html
This American Memory site brings together scores of primary sources and photographs about "the historical formation and cultural foundations of the movement to conserve and protect America's natural heritage."

Heroes and Villains in Kansas

http://www.kancoll.org/galhero.htm
The Kansas Collection Gallery of both famous and little-known people who made up the history of the state.

The Corliss engine, a "mechanical marvel" at the Centennial Exposition, was a prime example of the giantism so admired by the public. ❖

The Industrial Society

_A_ Machine Culture

In 1876, Americans celebrated their first century of independence. Survivors of a recent civil war, they observed the centenary proudly and rather self-consciously, in song and speech, and above all in a grand Centennial Exposition held in Philadelphia, Pennsylvania.

Spread over 13 acres, the exposition focused more on the present than the past. Fairgoers strolled through exhibits of life in colonial times, then hurried off to see the main attractions: machines, inventions, and products of the new industrial era. They saw linoleum, a new, easy-to-clean floor covering. For the first time, they tasted root beer, supplied by a young druggist named Charles Hires, and the exotic banana, wrapped in foil and selling for a dime. They saw their first bicycle, an awkward high-wheeled contraption with solid tires.

A Japanese pavilion generated widespread interest in the culture of Japan. There was also a women's building, the first ever in a major exposition. Inside were displayed paintings and sculpture by women artists, along with rows of textile machinery staffed by female operators.

In the entire exposition, machinery was the focus, and Machinery Hall was the most popular building. Here were the products of an ever improving civilization. Long lines of the curious waited to see the telephone, Alexander Graham Bell's new device. ("My God, it talks!" the emperor of Brazil exclaimed.) Thomas A. Edison displayed several recent inventions, while nearby, whirring machines turned out bricks, chewing tobacco, and other products. Fairgoers saw the first public display of the typewriter, Elisha Otis's new elevator, and the Westinghouse railroad air brake.

But above all, they crowded around the mighty Corliss engine, the focal point of the exposition. A giant steam engine, it dwarfed everything else in Machinery Hall, its twin vertical cylinders towering almost four stories in the air. Alone, it supplied power for the eight thousand other machines, large and small, on the exposition grounds. Poorly designed, the Corliss was soon obsolete, but for the moment it captured the nation's imagination. It symbolized swift movement toward an industrial and urban society. John Greenleaf Whittier, the aging rural poet, likened it to the snake in the Garden of Eden and refused to see it.

AS WHITTIER FEARED, the United States was fast becoming an industrial society. Developments earlier in the century laid the basis, but the most spectacular advances in industrialization came during the three decades after the Civil War. At the start of the war, the country lagged well behind industrializing nations such as Great Britain, France, and Germany. By 1900, it had vaulted far into the lead, with a manufacturing output that exceeded the _combined_ output of its three European rivals. Over the same years, cities grew, technology advanced, and farm production rose. Developments in manufacturing, mining, agriculture, transportation, and communications changed society.

OUTLINE
❖❖❖

Industrial Development

An Empire on Rails

An Industrial Empire

The Sellers

The Wage Earners

Conclusion: Industrialization's Benefits

FEATURE ESSAY
❖❖❖

Chicago's "Second Nature"

In this change, railroads, steel, oil, and other industries, all shaped by the hands of labor, played a leading role. Many Americans eagerly welcomed the new directions. William Dean Howells, a leading novelist, visited the Centennial Exposition and stood in awe before the Corliss. Comparing it to the paintings and sculpture on display, Howells preferred the machine: "It is in these things of iron and steel," he said, "that the national genius most freely speaks."

INDUSTRIAL DEVELOPMENT

American industry owed its remarkable growth to several considerations. It fed on an abundance of natural resources: coal, iron, timber, petroleum, waterpower. An iron manufacturer likened the nation to "a gigantic bowl filled with treasure." Labor was also abundant, drawn from American farm families and the hosts of European immigrants who flocked to American mines, cities, and factories. Nearly eight million immigrants arrived in the 1870s and 1880s; another fifteen million came between 1890 and 1914—large figures for a nation whose total population in 1900 was about seventy-six million people.

The burgeoning population led to expanded markets, which new devices such as the telegraph and telephone helped to exploit. The swiftly growing urban populations devoured goods, and the railroads, spreading pell-mell across the land, linked the cities together and opened a national market. Within its boundaries, the United States had the largest free-trade market in the world, while tariff barriers partially protected its producers from outside competition.

Expansive market and labor conditions buoyed the confidence of investors, European and American, who provided large amounts of capital. Technological progress, so remarkable in these years, doomed some older industries (tallow, for example) but increased productivity in others, such as the kerosene industry, and created entirely new industries as well. Through inventions such as the harvester and the combine, it also helped foster a firm agricultural base, on which industrialization depended.

Eager to promote economic growth, government at all levels—federal, state, and local—gave manufacturers money, land, and other resources. Other benefits, too, flowed from the American system of government: stability, commitment to the concept of private property, and, initially at least, a reluctance to regulate industrial activity. Unlike their European counterparts, American manufacturers faced few legal or social barriers, and their main domestic rivals, the southern planters, had lost political power in the Civil War.

In this atmosphere, entrepreneurs flourished. Taking steps crucial for industrialization, they organized, managed, and assumed the financial risks of the new enterprises. Admirers called them captains of industry; foes labeled them robber barons. To some degree, they were both—creative *and* acquisitive. If sometimes they seemed larger than life, it was because they dealt in concepts, distances, and quantities often unknown to earlier generations.

Industrial growth, it must be remembered, was neither a simple nor steady nor inevitable process. It involved human decisions and brought with it large social benefits and costs. Growth varied from industry to industry and from year to year. It was concentrated in the Northeast, where in 1890, more than 85 percent of America's manufactured goods originated. The more sparsely settled West provided raw materials, while the South, although making major gains in iron, textiles, and tobacco, had to rebuild after wartime devastation. In 1890, the industrial production of the entire South amounted in value to about half that of the state of New York.

Still, industrial development proceeded at an extraordinary pace. Between 1865 and 1914, the real gross national product—the total monetary value of all goods and services produced in a year, with prices held stable—grew at a rate of more than 4 percent a year, increasing about eightfold overall. As Robert Higgs, an economic historian, noted, "Never before had such rapid growth continued for so long."

AN EMPIRE ON RAILS

Genuine revolutions happen rarely, but a major one occurred in the nineteenth century: a revolution in transportation and communications. When the nineteenth century began, people traveled and communicated much as they had for centuries before; when it ended, the railroad, the telegraph, the telephone, and the oceangoing steamship had wrought enormous changes.

The steamship sliced in half the time of the Atlantic crossing and, not dependent on wind and tide, introduced new regularity in the movement of goods and passengers. The telegraph, flashing messages almost instantaneously along miles of wire (400,000 miles of it in the early 1880s), transformed communications, as did the telephone a little later. But the railroad worked the largest changes of all. Along with Bessemer steel, it was the most significant technical innovation of the century.

"Emblem of Motion and Power"

The railroad dramatically affected economic and social life. Economic growth would have occurred without it, of course; canals, inland steamboats, and the country's superb system of interior waterways already provided the outlines of an effective transportation network. But the railroad added significantly to the network and contributed advantages all its own.

Those advantages included more direct routes, greater speed, greater safety and comfort than other modes of land travel, more dependable schedules, a larger volume of traffic, and year-round service. A day's land travel on stagecoach or horseback might cover fifty miles. The railroad covered 50 miles in about an hour, 700 miles in a day. It went where canals and rivers did not go—directly to the loading platforms of great factories or across the arid West. As construction crews pushed tracks onward, vast areas of the continent opened for settlement.

Consequently, American railroads differed from European ones. In Europe, railroads were usually built between cities and towns that already existed; they carried mostly the same goods that earlier forms of transportation had. In the United States, they did that and more: they often created the very towns they then served, and they ended up carrying cattle from Texas, fruit from Florida, and other goods that had never been carried before.

Linking widely separated cities and villages, the railroad ended the relative isolation and self-sufficiency of the country's "island communities." It tied people together, brought in outside products, fostered greater interdependence, and encouraged economic specialization. Under its stimulus, Chicago supplied meat to the nation, Minneapolis supplied grain, and St. Louis, beer. For these and other communities, the railroad made possible a national market and in so doing pointed the way toward mass production and mass consumption, two of the hallmarks of twentieth-century society.

It also pointed the way toward later business development. The railroad, as Alfred D. Chandler, a historian of business, has written, was "the nation's first big business"; it worked out "the modern ways of finance, management, labor relations, competition, and government regulation."

A railroad corporation, far-flung and complex, was a new kind of business. It stretched over thousands of miles, employed thousands of people, dealt with countless customers, and required a scale of organization and decision making unknown in earlier business. Railroad managers never met most customers or even many employees; thus arose new problems in marketing and labor relations. Year by year, railroad companies consumed large quantities of iron, steel, coal, lumber, and glass, stimulating growth and employment in numerous industries.

No wonder, then, that the railroad captured so completely the country's imagination. Walt Whitman, a poet who celebrated American achievement, chanted the locomotive's praises:

Like no form of transportation before it, the railroad could meet the challenge presented by the varied topography of the land west of the Mississippi River—from the Great Plains to the vast deserts, from the deep gorges to the Rocky Mountains. ❖

Thy black cylindric body, golden brass and silvery steel,

. . . .

Thy great protruding head-light fix'd in front,

Thy long, pale, floating vapor-pennants, tinged with
  delicate purple,
The dense and murky clouds out-belching from thy
  smoke-stack,
Thy knitted frame, thy springs and valves, the
  tremulous twinkle of thy wheels,

Thy train of cars behind, obedient, merrily following,
Through gale or calm, now swift, now slack, yet
  steadily careening;
Type of the modern—emblem of motion and power—
  pulse of the continent,

. . . .

Fierce-throated beauty!

For nearly a hundred years—the railroad era lasted through the 1940s—children gathered at depots, paused in the fields to wave as the fast express flashed by, listened at night to far-off whistles, and wondered what lay down the tracks. They lived in a world grown smaller.

Building the Empire

When Lee surrendered at Appomattox in 1865, the country already had 35,000 miles of track, and much of the railroad system east of the Mississippi River was in place. Farther west, the rail network stood poised on the edge of settlement. Although southern railroads were in shambles from the war, the United States had nearly as much railroad track as the rest of the world.

After the Civil War, rail construction increased by leaps and bounds. From 35,000 miles in 1865, the network expanded to 93,000 miles in 1880; 166,000 in 1890; and 193,000 in 1900—more than in all Europe, including Russia. Mileage peaked at 254,037 miles in 1916, just before the industry began its long decline into the mid-twentieth century.

To build such an empire took vast amounts of capital—more than $4.5 billion by 1880, before even half of it was complete. American and European investors provided some of the money; government supplied the rest. In all, local governments gave railroad companies about $300 million, and state governments added $228 million more. The federal government loaned nearly $65 million to a half dozen western railroads and donated millions of acres of the public domain. Between 1850 and 1871, some eighty railroads received more than 170 million acres of land.

Almost 90 percent of the federal land grants lay in twenty states west of the Mississippi River. Federal land grants helped build 18,738 miles of track, less than 8 percent of the system. The land was frequently distant and difficult to market. Railroad companies

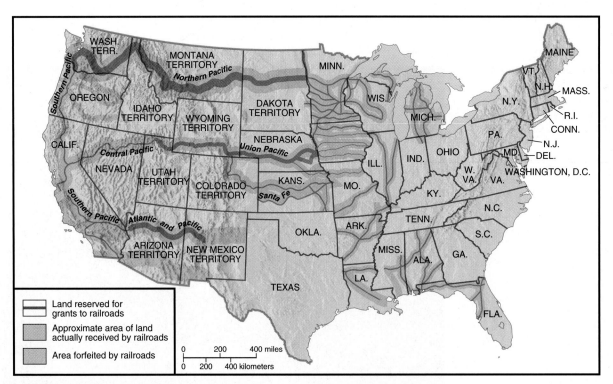

FEDERAL LAND GRANTS TO RAILROADS AS OF 1871   *Besides land, the government
provided loans of $16,000 for each mile built on level ground, $32,000 for each mile built on hilly
terrain, and $48,000 for each mile in high mountain country.* ❖

RAILROAD CONSTRUCTION, 1830–1920

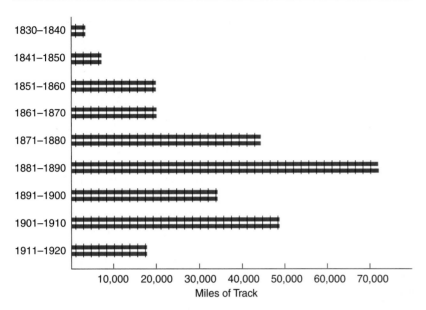

Source: U.S. Bureau of the Census, *Historical Statistics of the United States, Colonial Times to 1970*, Bicentennial Edition, Washington, D.C., 1975.

sometimes sold it to raise cash, but more often they used it as security for bonds or loans.

Beyond doubt, the grants of cash and land promoted waste and corruption. The companies built fast and wastefully, eager to collect the subsidies that went with each mile of track. Wanting quick profits, some owners formed separate construction companies to which they awarded lavish contracts. In this way, the notorious Crédit Mobilier, a construction company controlled by an inner ring on the Union Pacific, enriched its owners in the 1860s, while the Contract and Finance Company did the same on the Central Pacific. The Crédit Mobilier bribed congressmen and state legislators to avoid investigation of its activities. The grants also enabled railroads to build into territories that were pledged to the Indians, thus contributing to the wanton destruction of Indian life.

Yet, on balance, the grants probably worked more benefits than evils. As Congress had hoped, the grants were the lure for railroad building across the rugged, unsettled West, where it would be years before the railroads' revenues would repay their construction. Farmers, ranchers, and merchants poured into the newly opened areas, settling the country and boosting the value of government and private land nearby. The grants seemed necessary in a nation which, unlike Europe, expected private enterprise to build the railroads. In return for government aid, Congress required the railroads to carry government freight, troops, and mail at substantially reduced rates—resulting in savings to the government of almost $1 billion between 1850

and 1945. In no other cases of federal subsidies to carriers—canals, highways, and airlines—did Congress exact specific benefits in return.

Linking the Nation via Trunk Lines

The early railroads may seem to have linked different regions, but in fact they did not. Built with little regard for through traffic, they were designed more to protect local interests than to tap outside markets. Many extended less than fifty miles. To avoid cooperating with other lines, they adopted conflicting schedules, built separate depots, and above all, used different gauges. Gauges, the distance between the rails, ranged from 4 feet $8^1/_2$ inches, which became the standard gauge, to 6 feet. Without special equipment, trains of one gauge could not run on tracks of another.

The Civil War showed the value of fast long-distance transportation, and after 1865, railroad managers worked to provide it. In a burst of consolidation, the large companies swallowed the small; integrated rail networks became a reality. Railroads also adopted standard schedules, signals, and equipment and finally, in 1886, the standard gauge. In 1866, in a dramatic innovation to speed traffic, railroad companies introduced fast freight lines that pooled cars for service between cities.

In the Northeast, four great **trunk lines** took shape, all intended to link eastern seaports with the rich traffic of the Great Lakes and western rivers. Like a massive river system, trunk lines drew traffic from

Cornelius the "Commodore" Vanderbilt, in this cartoon of the "Modern Colossus of (Rail) Roads," is shown towering over his rail empire and pulling the strings to control its operations. In addition to the New York Central, Vanderbilt gained control of the Hudson River Railroad, the Lake Shore and Michigan Southern Railway, and the Canadian Southern Railway. ❖

dozens of tributaries (feeder lines) and carried it to major markets. The Baltimore and Ohio (B & O), which reached Chicago in 1874, was one; the Erie Railroad, which ran from New York to Chicago, was another. The Erie competed bitterly with the New York Central Railroad, the third trunk line, and its owner, Cornelius Vanderbilt—the "Commodore"—a crusty old multimillionaire from the shipping business.

Nearly seventy years old when he first entered railroading, Vanderbilt wasted no time. In 1867, he took over the New York Central and merged it with other lines to provide a track from New York City to Buffalo and Chicago. When he died in 1877, his Central operated more than 4500 miles of track.

J. Edgar Thomson and Thomas A. Scott built the fourth trunk line, the Pennsylvania Railroad, which initially ran from Philadelphia to Pittsburgh. Restless and energetic, they dreamed of a rail empire stretching

through the South and West. An aggressive business leader, Scott expanded the Pennsylvania system to Cincinnati, Indianapolis, St. Louis, and Chicago in 1869; New York City in 1871; and Baltimore and Washington soon thereafter.

In the war-damaged South, consolidation took longer. As Reconstruction waned, northern and European capital rebuilt and integrated the southern lines, especially during the 1880s, when rail construction in the South led the nation. By 1900, the South had five large systems linking its major cities and farming and industrial regions. Four decades after the secession crisis, these systems tied the South into a national transportation network.

Over that rail system, passengers and freight moved in relative speed, comfort, and safety. Automatic couplers (1867), air brakes (1869), refrigerator cars (1867), dining cars, heated cars, electric switches, and stronger locomotives transformed railroad service. George Pullman's lavish sleeping cars became popular. Handsome depots, such as New York's Grand Central and Washington's Union Station, were erected at major terminals. Passenger miles per year increased from 5 billion in 1870 to 16 billion in 1900.

In November 1883, the railroads even changed time. Ending the crazy quilt jumble of local times that caused scheduling difficulties, the American Railway Association divided the country into four time zones and adopted the modern system of standard time. Congress took thirty-five years longer; it adopted standard time in 1918, in the midst of World War I.

Rails Across the Continent

The dream of a transcontinental railroad, linking the Atlantic and Pacific oceans, stretched back many years but had always been lost to sectional quarrels over the route. In 1862 and 1864, with the South out of the picture, Congress moved to build the first transcontinental railroad. It chartered the Union Pacific Railroad Company to build westward from Nebraska and the Central Pacific Railroad Company to build eastward from the Pacific Coast. For each mile built, the two companies received from Congress 20 square miles of land in alternate sections along the track. For each mile, they also received a thirty-year loan of $16,000, $32,000, or $48,000, depending on the difficulty of the terrain over which they built.

Construction began simultaneously at Omaha and Sacramento in 1863, lagged during the war, and moved vigorously ahead after 1865. It became a race, each company vying for land, loans, and potential markets. General Grenville M. Dodge, a tough Union army veteran, served as construction chief for the Union Pacific, while Charles Crocker, a former Sacramento dry goods merchant, led the Central

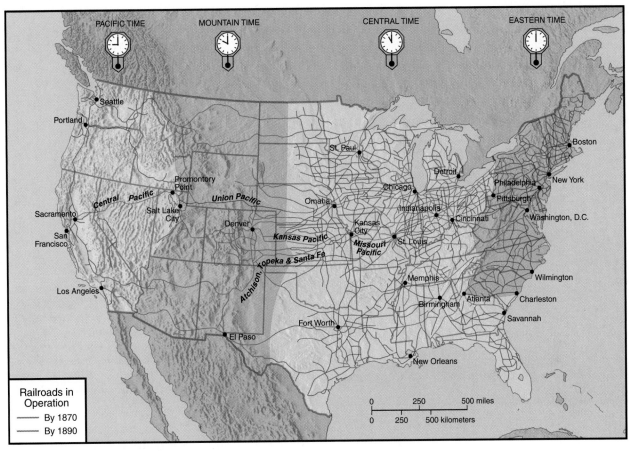

PACIFIC TIME   MOUNTAIN TIME   CENTRAL TIME   EASTERN TIME

Railroads in Operation
— By 1870
— By 1890

RAILROADS, 1870 AND 1890   *In the last quarter of the nineteenth century, railroads expanded into Texas, the far Southwest, and the Northwest, carrying settlers, businesses, and government to the far-flung areas.* ❖

Pacific crews. Dodge organized an army of ten thousand workers, many of them ex-soldiers and Irish immigrants. Pushing rapidly westward, he encountered frequent attacks from Native Americans defending their lands, but he had the advantage of building over flat prairie.

Crocker faced more trying conditions in the high Sierra Nevada along California's eastern border. After several experiments, he decided that Chinese laborers worked best, and he hired six thousand of them, most brought directly from China. "I built the Central Pacific," Crocker enjoyed boasting, but the Chinese crews in fact did the awesome work. Under the most difficult conditions, they dug, blasted, and pushed their way slowly east.

On May 10, 1869, the two lines met at Promontory, Utah, near the northern tip of the Great Salt Lake. Dodge's crews had built 1086 miles of track, Crocker's 689. The Union Pacific and Central Pacific presidents hammered in a golden spike (both missed it on the first try), and the dreamed-of connection was made. The telegraph flashed the news east and west, setting off wild celebrations. A photograph was taken, but it included

none of the Chinese who had worked so hard to build the road; they were all asked to step aside.

The transcontinental railroad symbolized American unity and progress. Along with the Suez Canal, completed the same year, it helped knit the world together. Bret Harte, the exuberant poet of the West, wrote of Promontory:

What was it the Engines said,
Pilots touching,—head to head
Facing on the single track,
Half a world behind each back?

Three more railroads reached the coast in 1883: the Northern Pacific, running from Minnesota to Oregon; the Atchison, Topeka, and Santa Fe, connecting Kansas City and Los Angeles; and the powerful Southern Pacific, running from San Francisco and Los Angeles to New Orleans. Ten years later James J. Hill's superbly built Great Northern Railway extended from Minneapolis–St. Paul to Seattle, Washington.

By the 1890s, business leaders talked comfortably of railroad systems stretching deep into South America and across the Bering Strait to Asia, Europe, and

After the last spike was hammered in at Promontory, Utah, the pilots of the two locomotives exchanged champagne toasts. The chief engineers of the two lines are seen shaking hands. Conspicuously absent from the photograph are the Chinese laborers who helped build the railroad. ❖

Africa. In an age of progress, anything seemed possible. "The American," said the *Chicago Tribune*, "intelligent and self-reliant, has banished forever the impossible from his philosophy."

Problems of Growth

Overbuilding during the 1870s and 1880s caused serious problems for the railroads. Lines paralleled each other, and where they did not, speculators such as Jay Gould often laid one down to force a rival line to buy it at inflated prices. While many managers worked to improve service, Gould and others bought and sold railroads like toys, watered their stock, and milked their assets. By 1885, almost one-third of railroad stock represented "water," that is, stock distributed in excess of the real value of the assets.

Competition was severe, and managers fought desperately for traffic. They offered special rates and favors: free passes for large shippers; low rates on bulk freight, carload lots, and long hauls; and, above all, rebates—secret, privately negotiated reductions below published rates. Fierce rate wars broke out frequently, convincing managers that ruthless competition helped no one. Rebates made more enemies than friends.

Managers such as Albert Fink, the brilliant vice president of the Louisville & Nashville, tried first to arrange pooling agreements, a way to control competition by sharing traffic. Fink directed the Eastern Trunk Line Association (1877), which divided westbound traffic among the four trunk lines. Similar associations pooled traffic in the South and West, but none survived the intense pressures of competition. Legally unenforceable, pools were handshake agreements among individuals who did not always keep their word. Customers grew adept at bargaining for rebates and other privileges, and railroads rarely felt able to refuse them. In the first six months of 1880, the New York Central alone granted six thousand special rates.

Failing to cooperate, railroad owners next tried to consolidate. Through purchase, lease, and merger, they gobbled up competitors and built "self-sustaining systems" that dominated entire regions. But many of the systems, expensive and unwieldy, collapsed in the Panic of 1893. By mid-1894, a quarter of the railroads were bankrupt. The victims of the panic included such legendary names as the Erie, B & O, Santa Fe, Northern Pacific, and Union Pacific.

Needing money, railroads turned naturally to bankers, who finally imposed order on the industry. J. Pierpont Morgan, head of the New York investment house of J. P. Morgan and Company, took the lead. Massively built, with eyes so piercing they seemed like the headlights of an onrushing train, Morgan was the most powerful figure in American finance. He liked efficiency, combination, and order. He disliked "wasteful" competition. In 1885, during a bruising rate war between the New York Central and the Pennsylvania, Morgan invited the combatants to a conference aboard his palatial steam yacht, *Corsair*. Cruising on Long Island Sound, he arranged a traffic-sharing agreement and collected a million-dollar fee. Bringing peace to an industry could be profitable. It also satisfied Morgan's passion for stability.

After 1893, Morgan and a few other bankers refinanced ailing railroads, and in the process they took control of the industry. Their methods were direct: Fixed costs and debt were ruthlessly cut, new stock was issued to provide capital, rates were stabilized, rebates and competition were eliminated, and control was vested in a "voting trust" of handpicked trustees. Between 1894 and 1898, Morgan reorganized—critics said "Morganized"—the Southern Railway, the Erie, the Northern Pacific, and the B & O. In addition, he took over a half dozen other important railroads. By 1900, he was a dominant figure in American railroading.

As the new century began, the railroads had pioneered the patterns followed by most other industries. Seven giant systems controlled nearly two-thirds of the mileage, and they in turn answered to a few investment banking firms such as the house of Morgan. For good and ill, a national transportation network, centralized and relatively efficient, was now in place.

AN INDUSTRIAL EMPIRE

The new industrial empire was based on a number of dramatic innovations, including steel, oil, and inventions of all kinds that transformed ordinary life. In this process, steel was as important as the railroads. Harder and more durable than other kinds of iron, steel wrought changes in manufacturing, agriculture, transportation, and architecture. It permitted construction of longer bridges, taller buildings, stronger railroad track, deadlier weapons, better plows, heavier machinery, and faster ships. Made in great furnaces by strong men, it symbolized the tough, often brutal nature of industrial society. From the 1870s onward, steel output became the worldwide accepted measure of industrial progress, and nations around the globe vied for leadership.

The Bessemer process, developed in the late 1850s by Henry Bessemer in England and independently by William Kelly in the United States, made increased steel production possible. Both Bessemer and Kelly discovered that a blast of air forced through molten iron burned off carbon and other impurities, resulting in steel of a more uniform and durable quality. The

discovery transformed the industry. While earlier methods produced amounts a person could lift, a Bessemer converter handled 5 tons of molten metal at a time. The mass production of steel was now possible.

Carnegie and Steel

Bessemer plants demanded extensive capital investment, abundant raw materials, and sophisticated production techniques. Using chemical and other processes, the plants required research departments, which became critical components of later American industries. Costly to build, they limited entry into the industry to the handful who could afford them.

Great steel districts arose in Pennsylvania, Ohio, and Alabama—in each case around large coal deposits that fueled the huge furnaces. Pittsburgh became the center of the industry, its giant mills employing thousands of workers. Output shot up. In 1874, the United States produced less than half the amount of pig iron produced in Great Britain. By 1890, it took the lead, and in 1900, it produced four times as much as Britain.

Iron ore abounded in the fabulous deposits near Lake Superior, the greatest deposits in the world. In the mines of the Mesabi Range in Minnesota, giant steam shovels loaded ore onto railroad cars for transport to ships on the Great Lakes. Powered lifts, self-loading devices, and other innovations sped the process. "By the turn of the century," historian Peter Temin noted,

INTERNATIONAL STEEL PRODUCTION, 1880–1914

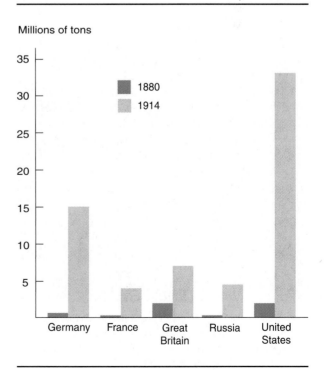

Millions of tons

"the transport of Lake ores had become an intricate ballet of large and complex machines."

Like the railroads, steel companies grew larger and larger. In 1880, only nine companies could produce more than 100,000 tons a year. By the early 1890s, several companies exceeded 250,000 tons, and two—including the great Carnegie Steel Company—produced more than 1 million tons a year. As operations expanded, managers needed more complex skills. Product development, marketing, and consumer preferences became important. Competition was fierce, and steel companies, like the railroads, tried secret agreements, pools, and consolidation. During the 1880s and 1890s, they moved toward **vertical integration,** a type of organization in which a single company owns and controls the entire process from the unearthing of the raw materials to the manufacture and sale of the finished product. Such companies combined coal and iron mines, transportation companies, blast furnaces, and rolling mills into integrated networks.

The machinery dwarfs the workers in this colored engraving of steel making using the Bessemer process at Andrew Carnegie's Pittsburgh steel works. Men worked twelve hours a day in the blazing heat and deafening roar of the machines. ❖

Andrew Carnegie emerged as the undisputed master of the industry. Born in Scotland, he came to the United States in 1848 at the age of 12. Settling near Pittsburgh, he went to work as a bobbin boy in a cotton mill, earning $1.20 a week. He soon took a job in a telegraph office, where in 1852 his hard work and skill caught the eye of Thomas A. Scott of the Pennsylvania Railroad. Starting as Scott's personal telegrapher, Carnegie spent a total of twelve years on the Pennsylvania, a training ground for company managers. By 1859, he had become a divisional superintendent. He was 24 years old.

Soon rich from shrewd investments, Carnegie plunged into the steel industry in 1872. On the Monongahela River south of Pittsburgh, he built the giant J. Edgar Thomson Steel Works, named after the president of the Pennsylvania Railroad, his biggest customer. With his warmth and salesmanship, he attracted able partners and subordinates such as Henry Clay Frick and Charles M. Schwab, whom he drove hard and paid well. Although he had written magazine articles defending the rights of workers, Carnegie kept the wages of the laborers in his mills low and disliked unions. With the help of Frick, he crushed a violent strike at his Homestead works in 1892 (see p. 535).

In 1878, he won the steel contract for the Brooklyn Bridge. During the next decade, as city building boomed, he converted the huge Homestead works near Pittsburgh to the manufacture of structural beams and angles, which went into the New York City elevated railway, the first skyscrapers, and the Washington Monument. Carnegie profits mounted: from $2 million in 1888 to $40 million in 1900. That year, Carnegie Steel alone produced more steel than Great Britain. Employing twenty thousand people, it was the largest industrial company in the world.

In 1901, Carnegie sold it. Believing that wealth brought social obligations, he wanted to devote his full time to philanthropy. He found a buyer in J. Pierpont Morgan, who in the late 1890s had put together several steel companies, including Federal Steel, Carnegie's chief rival. Carnegie Steel had blocked Morgan's well-known desire for control, and in mid-1900, when a war loomed between the two interests, Morgan decided to buy Carnegie out. In early January 1901, Morgan told Charles M. Schwab: "Go and find his price." Schwab cornered Carnegie on the golf course; Carnegie listened, and the next day he handed Schwab a note, scribbled in blunt pencil, asking almost a half billion dollars. Morgan glanced at it and said, "I accept this price."

Drawing other companies into the combination, Morgan on March 3, 1901, announced the creation of the United States Steel Corporation. The new firm was capitalized at $1.4 billion, the first billion-dollar company. It absorbed more than 200 other companies, employed 168,000 people, and produced 9 million tons of iron and steel a year. It controlled three-fifths of the country's steel business. Soon there were other giants, including Bethlehem Steel, Republic Steel, and National Steel. As the nineteenth century ended, steel products—rare just thirty years before—had altered the landscape. Huge firms, investment bankers, and professional managers dominated the industry.

Rockefeller and Oil

Petroleum worked comparable changes in the economic and social landscape, although mostly after 1900. Distilled into oil, it lubricated the machinery of the industrial age. There seemed little use for gasoline (the internal combustion engine had only just been developed), but kerosene, another major distillate, brought inexpensive illumination into almost every home. Whale oil, cottonseed oil, and even tallow candles were expensive to burn; consequently, many people went to bed at nightfall. Kerosene lamps opened the evenings to activity, altering the patterns of life.

Like other changes in these years, the oil boom happened with surprising speed. In the mid-1850s, petroleum was a bothersome, smelly fluid that occasionally rose to the surface of springs and streams. Clever entrepreneurs bottled it in patent medicines; a few scooped up enough to burn. Other entrepreneurs soon found that drilling reached pockets of oil beneath the earth. In 1859, Edwin L. Drake drilled the first oil well near Titusville in northwest Pennsylvania, and the "black gold" fever struck. Chemists soon discovered ways to transform petroleum into lubricating oil, grease, paint, wax, varnish, naphtha, and paraffin. Within a few years, there was a world market in oil.

At first, growth of the oil industry was chaotic. Early drillers and refiners produced for local markets, and since drilling wells and even erecting refineries cost little, competition flourished. Output fluctuated dramatically; prices rose and fell, with devastating effect. Refineries—usually a collection of wooden shacks and tanks—were centered in Cleveland and Pittsburgh, near the original oil-producing regions.

A young merchant from Cleveland named John D. Rockefeller imposed order on the industry. "I had an ambition to build," he later recalled, and beginning in 1863 at the age of 24, he built the Standard Oil Company, soon to become one of the titans of corporate business. Like Morgan, Rockefeller considered competition wasteful, small-scale enterprise inefficient, and consolidation the path of the future. Consolidation "revolutionized the way of doing business all over the world," he said. "The time was ripe for it. It had to come, though all we saw at the mo-

John D. Rockefeller, satirized in a 1901 Puck *cartoon, is enthroned on oil, the base of his empire; his crown is girded by other holdings.* ❖

ment was the need to save ourselves from wasteful conditions."

Methodically, Rockefeller absorbed or destroyed competitors in Cleveland and elsewhere. As ruthless in his methods as Carnegie, he lacked the steel master's spontaneous charm. He was distant and taciturn, a man of deep religious beliefs who taught Bible classes at Cleveland's Erie Street Baptist Church. Like Carnegie, he demanded efficiency, relentless cost cutting, and the latest technology. He attracted exceptional lieutenants—although, as one said, he could see farther ahead than any of them, "and then see around the corner."

"Nothing in haste, nothing ill-done," Rockefeller often said to himself. "Your future hangs on every day that passes." Paying careful attention to detail, he counted the stoppers in barrels, shortened barrel hoops to save metal, and, in one famous incident, reduced the number of drops of solder on kerosene cans from forty to thirty-nine. In large-scale production, Rockefeller realized, even small reductions meant huge savings. Research uncovered other ways of lowering costs and improving products, and Herman Frasch, a brilliant Standard chemist, solved problem after problem in the refining of oil.

In the end, Rockefeller triumphed over his competitors by marketing products of high quality at the lowest unit cost. But he employed other, less savory methods as well. He threatened rivals and bribed politicians. He employed spies to harass the customers of competing refiners. Above all, he extorted railroad rebates that lowered his transportation costs and undercut competitors. By 1879, he controlled 90 percent of the country's entire oil-refining capacity.

Vertically integrated, Standard Oil owned wells, timberlands, barrel and chemical plants, refineries, warehouses, pipelines, and fleets of tankers and oil cars. Its marketing organization served as the model for the industry. Standard exported oil to Asia, Africa, and South America; its 5-gallon kerosene tin, like Coca-Cola bottles and cans of a later era, was a familiar sight in the most distant parts of the world.

To manage it all, the company developed a new plan of business organization, the **trust,** which had profound significance for American business. In 1881, Samuel T. C. Dodd, Standard's attorney, set up the Standard Oil Trust, with a board of nine trustees empowered "to hold, control, and manage" all Standard's properties. Stockholders exchanged their stock for trust certificates, on which dividends were paid. On January 2, 1882, the first of the modern trusts was born. As Dodd intended, it immediately centralized control of Standard's far-flung empire.

Competition almost disappeared; profits soared. A trust movement swept the country as industries with similar problems—whiskey, lead, and sugar, among others—followed Standard's example. The word *trust* became synonymous with monopoly, amid vehement protests from the public. *Antitrust* became a watchword for a generation of reformers from the 1880s through the era of Woodrow Wilson. But Rockefeller's purpose had been *management* of a monopoly, not monopoly itself, which he had already achieved.

During the 1890s, Rockefeller helped pioneer another form of industrial consolidation, the holding company. Taking advantage of an 1889 New Jersey law that allowed companies to purchase other companies, he moved Standard Oil to New Jersey and bought up his own subsidiaries to form a holding company. The trust, he had learned, was somewhat cumbersome, and it was under attack in Congress and the courts. Holding companies offered the next step in industrial management. They were simply large-scale mergers, in which a central corporate organization purchased the stock of the member companies and established direct formal control.

Other companies followed suit, including American Sugar Refining, the Northern Securities Company, and the National Biscuit Company. Merger followed merger. By 1900, 1 percent of the nation's companies controlled more than one-third of its industrial production. A decade later, a congressional investigation showed that two individuals, Rockefeller and Morgan, between them controlled businesses worth more than $22 billion.

In 1897, Rockefeller retired with a fortune of nearly $900 million, but for Standard Oil and petroleum in general, the most expansive period was yet to come. The great oil pools of Texas and Oklahoma had not yet been discovered. Plastics and other oil-based synthetics were several decades in the future. There were only four usable automobiles in the country, and the day of the gasoline engine, automobile, and airplane lay just ahead.

The Business of Invention

"America has become known the world around as the home of invention," boasted the commissioner of patents in 1892. It had not always been so; until the last third of the nineteenth century, the country had imported most of its technology. Then an extraordinary group of inventors and tinkerers—"specialists in invention," Thomas A. Edison called them—began to study the world around them. Some of their inventions gave rise to new industries; a few actually changed the quality of life.

In the very act of inventing, Edison and others drew on a deeper "invention," a realization that people could mold nature to their own ends. They could create out of "first nature," as one environmental historian has noted, a "second nature," shaped as they wished. (See the Feature Essay, "Chicago's 'Second Nature,'" pp. 526–527.)

The number of patents issued to inventors reflected the trend. During the 1850s, fewer than 2,000 patents were issued each year. By the 1880s and 1890s, the figure reached more than 20,000 a year. Between 1790 and 1860, the U.S. Patent Office issued just 36,000 patents; in the decade of the 1890s alone, it issued more than 200,000.

Some of the inventions transformed communications. In 1866, Cyrus W. Field improved the transatlantic cable linking the telegraph networks of Europe and the United States. By the early 1870s, land and submarine cables ran to Brazil, Japan, and the China coast; in the next two decades, they reached Africa and spread across South America. Diplomats and business leaders could now "talk" to

PATENTS ISSUED, BY DECADE, 1850–1899

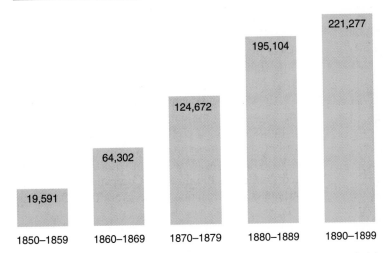

Source: U.S. Bureau of the Census, *Historical Statistics of the United States, Colonial Times to 1970*, Bicentennial Edition, Washington, D.C., 1975.

their counterparts in Berlin or Hong Kong. Even before the telephone, the cables quickened the pace of foreign affairs, revolutionized journalism, and allowed businesses to expand and centralize.

The typewriter (1867), stock ticker (1867), cash register (1879), calculating machine (1887), and adding machine (1888) helped business transactions. High-speed spindles, automatic looms, and electric sewing machines transformed the clothing industry, which for the first time in history turned out ready-made clothes for the masses. In 1890, the Census Bureau first used machines to sort and tabulate data on punched cards, a portent of a new era of information storage and processing.

In 1879, George Eastman patented a process for coating gelatin on photographic dry plates, which led to celluloid film and motion pictures. By 1888, he was marketing the Kodak camera, which weighed 35 ounces, took 100 exposures, and cost $25. Even though early Kodaks had to be returned to the factory, camera and all, for film developing, they revolutionized photography. Now almost anyone could snap a picture.

Other innovations changed the diet. There were new processes for flour, canned meat, vegetables, condensed milk, and even beer (from an offshoot of Louis Pasteur's discoveries about bacteria). Packaged cereals appeared on breakfast tables. Refrigerated railroad cars, ice-cooled, brought fresh fruit from Florida and California to all parts of the country. In the 1870s, Gustavus F. Swift, a Chicago meatpacker, hit on the idea of using the cars to distribute meat nationwide. Setting up "dissembly" factories to butcher meat (Henry Ford later copied them for his famous "assem-

bly" lines), he started an "era of cheap beef," as a newspaper said.

No innovation, however, rivaled the importance of the telephone and the use of electricity for light and power. The telephone was the work of Alexander Graham Bell, a shrewd and genial Scot who settled in Boston in 1871. Interested in the problems of the deaf, Bell experimented with ways to transmit speech electrically, and after several years he had developed electrified metal disks that, much like the human ear, converted sound waves to electrical impulses and back again. On March 10, 1876, he transmitted the first sentence over a telephone: "Mr. Watson, come here; I want you." Later that year, he exhibited the new device to excited crowds at the Centennial Exposition in Philadelphia.

In 1878—the year a telephone was installed in the White House—the first telephone exchange opened in New Haven, Connecticut. Fighting off competitors who challenged the patent, the young Bell Telephone Company dominated the growing industry. By 1895, there were about 310,000 phones; a decade later, there were 10 million—about one for every ten people. American Telephone and Telegraph Company, formed by the Bell interests in 1885, became another of the vast holding companies, consolidating more than a hundred local systems.

If the telephone dissolved communication barriers as old as the human race, Thomas Alva Edison, the "Wizard of Menlo Park," invented processes and products of comparable significance. Born in 1847, Edison had little formal education, although he was an avid reader. Like Carnegie, he went into the new field of

Electric-powered subway systems were an important development in urban mass transportation. The nation's first subway system opened in 1897 in Boston, Massachusetts, allowing commuters to avoid the delays of heavy street traffic via trains that ran on elevated and underground tracks. Here, train cars are shown as they descend into the subway at the Boston Public Garden. ❖

In 1879 came an even larger triumph, the incandescent lamp. Sir Joseph William Swan, an English inventor, had already experimented with the carbon filament, but Edison's task involved more than finding a durable filament. He set out to do nothing less than change light. A trial-and-error inventor, Edison tested sixteen hundred materials before producing, late in 1879, the carbon filament he wanted. Then he had to devise a complex system of conductors, meters, and generators by which electricity could be divided and distributed to homes and businesses.

With the financial backing of J. P. Morgan, he organized the Edison Illuminating Company and built the Pearl Street power station in New York City, the testing

telegraphy. Tinkering in his spare time, he made several important improvements, including a telegraph capable of sending four messages over a single wire. Gathering teams of specialists to work on specific problems, Edison built the first modern research laboratory at Menlo Park, New Jersey. It may have been his most important invention.

The laboratory, Edison promised, would turn out "a minor invention every ten days and a big thing every six months or so." In 1877, it turned out a big thing. Worried about a telephone's high cost, Edison set out to invent a "telephone repeater," which became the phonograph. Those unable to afford a phone, he thought, could record their voices for replay from a central telephone station. Using tin foil wrapped around a grooved, rotating cylinder, he shouted the verses of "Mary Had a Little Lamb" and then listened in awe as the machine played them back. "I was never so taken aback in all my life," he later said. "Everybody was astonished. I was always afraid of things that worked the first time."

In 1896, records made of hard rubber and shellac appeared on the market; the following year, a phonograph sold for $20. In 1904, someone had the idea of recording on both sides of the disk, and the phonograph record in its modern form was born. For the first time in history, people could listen again and again to a favorite symphony or piano solo. The phonograph made human experience repeatable in a way never before possible.

❖ A Look at the Past ❖

Cash Register

Mass-produced goods of every kind flooded markets at the turn of the century. Industrial productivity made the flood possible and consumer spending fueled production. Railroads and free mail delivery after 1896 brought factory-made goods even to consumers who lived in remote, rural locations. In cities, department stores transformed shopping into a pleasurable experience. By the 1880s retailers were investing in cash registers that tallied sales. Previously, merchants recorded sales by hand into daybooks and later, when closed for business, transcribed the sales into a ledger. This wooden model from 1890 registered sales with ceramic balls, which dropped into a labyrinth of tracks to mark daily totals. How did the cash register transform the act of selling goods? Why do you think merchants invested in them?

ground of the new apparatus. On September 4, 1882, as Morgan and others watched, Edison threw a switch and lit the house of Morgan, the stock exchange, the *New York Times,* and a number of other buildings. Amazed, a *Times* reporter marveled that writing stories in the office at night "seemed almost like writing in daylight." Power stations soon opened in Boston, Philadelphia, and Chicago. By 1900, there were 2774 stations, lighting some 2 million electric lights around the country. In a nation alive with light, the habits of centuries changed. A flick of the switch lit homes and factories at any hour of the day or night.

In a rare blunder, Edison based his system on low-voltage direct current, which could be transmitted only about two miles. George Westinghouse, the inventor of the railroad air brake, demonstrated the advantages of high-voltage alternating current for transmission over great distances. In 1886, he formed the Westinghouse Electric Company and with the inventor Nikola Tesla, a Hungarian immigrant, developed an alternating-current motor that could convert electricity into mechanical power. Electricity could light a lamp or illuminate a skyscraper, pull a streetcar or drive an entire railroad, run a sewing machine or power a mammoth assembly line. Transmitted easily over long distances, it freed factories and cities from location near water or coal. Electricity, in short, brought a revolution.

Taking advantage of the new devices, Frank J. Sprague, a young engineer, electrified the Richmond, Virginia, streetcar system in 1887. Other cities quickly followed. Electric-powered subway systems opened in Boston in 1897 and New York City in 1904. Overhead wires and third rails made urban transportation quieter, faster, and cleaner. Buried under pavement or strung from pole to pole, wires of every description—trolley, telephone, and power—marked the birth of the modern city.

THE SELLERS

The increased output of the industrial age alone was not enough to ensure huge profits. The products still had to be sold, and that gave rise to a new "science" of marketing. Some business leaders—such as Swift in meatpacking, James B. Duke in tobacco, and Rockefeller in oil—built extensive marketing organizations of their own. Others relied on retailers, merchandising techniques, and advertising, developing a host of methods to convince consumers to buy.

In 1867, businesses spent about $50 million on advertising; in 1900, they spent more than $500 million, and the figure was increasing rapidly. The first advertising agency, N. W. Ayer and Son, of Philadelphia, began to service businesses in the mid-1870s, and it was fol-

❖ A Look at the Past ❖

Typewriter

By the end of the nineteenth century, typewriters became increasingly common in offices. The earliest typewriters worked in a variety of ways and did not even have similar keyboards. By the 1890s, however, the keyboard used today had become standard. The standardized keyboard made it easier for people to learn to type, and also made it possible to type more quickly. The awkward arrangement on the keyboard intentionally slowed typists to prevent keys from jamming as a result of rapid typing. Even though typewriters did not work as quickly as typists could, they offered numerous advantages over pen and ink. What do typewriters suggest about business practices? How do you suppose they affected the amount of paper used in offices? How could typed and printed forms alter the pace of business?

lowed by numerous imitators. The rotary press (1875) churned out newspapers and introduced a new era in newspaper advertising. Woodcuts, halftones, and photoengraving added illustrations to catch the consumer's eye. Brand names became popular, and already Kellogg

Feature Essay

CHICAGO'S "SECOND NATURE"

Chicago's early boosters bragged that nature had given their city everything it needed to be great: a river running through it and a harbor on busy Lake Michigan. What the boosters did not say was that the river was short and shallow—"a sluggish, slimy stream, too lazy to cleanse itself," a visitor noted—or that sand often blocked the entrance to the harbor. To make Chicago work, humans would have to intrude upon nature to change the river and clear the harbor, creating out of "first nature" a "second nature," as environmental historian William Cronon put it.

They did just that. In remaking "first nature," government-financed engineers deepened the river and erected barriers to the sand. Then they turned to another of nature's challenges—the thick, cloying mud that plagued Chicago whenever it rained. Using muscle and jacks, they simply lifted the city a dozen feet out of the mud, producing "second nature" once again.

The city, now raised to working level, next turned to the railroads, the dazzling technological innovation that mastered nature to transform nineteenth-century life. Unlike rivers and canals, railroads could go virtually anywhere, and many of them wound up going to Chicago, which became the main terminal point for trains heading east and west. It was "natural" for them to do so, Chicagoans believed, and they certainly seemed right. By the early 1890s, one-twenty-fifth of all railroad mileage in the world terminated in Chicago.

They terminated there, in part, to drop off and pick up the city's most recent tinkering with nature, the pigs and cows destined to feed the country's growing population. A city that exuded life and growth, Chicago became filled with death, famed for "the Chicago style" of killing pigs. It was, said British writer Rudyard Kipling after visiting the city, a "death factory."

To organize the killing, the giant Union Stockyards opened on Christmas Day, 1865, built just south of the city on a marshy prairie prone to flooding. "Second nature" again took charge. Thirty miles of pipes drained the water from the prairie. The water, carrying with it waste from the stockyards, discharged into the Chicago River, which soon smelled horrific and carried disease. Within the stockyards, 10 miles of troughs dispersed corn and hay among 2000 pens, to feed at any one time 21,000 head of cattle, 75,000 pigs, and 22,000 sheep. Sidetracks allowed animals to be brought into the yards for slaughter and then carried the resulting products out to distant markets.

The river, meanwhile, grew increasingly polluted. Stockyard waste fermented on the bottom, producing large bubbles of methane gas that erupted on the grease-covered surface. Occasionally, the river caught fire. Chicago officials toyed with ways to solve the problem and settled on a most extraordinary idea: Reverse the flow of the river away from Lake Michigan into the Illinois River, a tributary of the Mississippi. Waters from the lake would flush the river and cleanse it—a happy solution for the people of

A view of Chicago's Union Stockyards in 1900. ❖

526

Chicago, but not so pleasant for those who lived along the Illinois. On a July day in 1871, Chicagoans lined the riverbanks to watch the engineering feat. Helped by pumps and channels, the river suddenly ran "upstream."

Problems remained in the stockyards, however, including how to kill so many animals and keep fresh the marketable remains. Gustavus F. Swift, a butcher from Boston, arrived in 1875 and provided an answer. Drawing on earlier experiments among meat packers in Cincinnati, he hit upon the idea of passing the pigs along on a chain between two lines of stationary workers, each of whom had a specific job in taking apart the carcass. One cut the throat, another made a slit down the body, a third used a saw to cut the breastbone, a fourth tore out the entrails. Others down the chain sliced and chopped.

Without fully knowing it, Swift and rival meat packers such as Philip D. Armour who adopted similar systems were introducing the methods of modern mass production. But instead of Henry Ford's Model T assembly lines, Swift's pigs passed through giant "disassembly" lines, in numbers previously unimagined. By the early 1870s, Chicago meat packers were processing well over a million pigs a year.

Killing in such quantities created a problem of its own. For as long as there had been pigs, killing and dressing them had been a seasonal event, confined by nature to the early winter, when cold temperatures would keep the meat from spoiling. While that system worked well with small numbers of pigs, the huge meat packing plants with their many employees could not stand idle for the rest of the year. Swift needed a way to keep the meat cold, and he found it in ice, cut in enormous quantities from area lakes and rivers and stored in insulated warehouses for use during the spring, summer, and fall.

By the 1880s, Swift was buying 450,000 tons of ice a year, and his packing plants never closed. Creating once again a "second nature," he had found a way to make winter last year-round.

He also found a way to carry winter with him. Ice preserved Chicago's slaughtered pigs, to be sure, but the meat still had to get to market, usually

Workers dressing beef carcasses for market at the Armour meat packing plant in Chicago. ❖

over very long distances. Again the solution was ice, this time carried on new-fangled refrigerated railroad cars, developed by Swift himself, who also established icehouses along the tracks so trains could restock the ice and replenish the cold.

Even the very pig itself had moved further and further from its own natural state. In the old days it had become ham, bacon, sausage, and lard, products still recognizable as parts of the original animal. By the 1880s that was no longer true. Dealing with a million pigs a year, Swift and other meat packers found ways to use every part of the animal. Their research laboratories discovered byproducts such as oleomargarine, shoes, fertilizer, buttons, soap, combs, and glue. Lathering up in the bath, few people thought of the pig as the source of their soap.

In a final twist to nature, even nature's skyline changed. Smoke poured from the stockyards, as did the odor of manure that, when the wind was right (or wrong), swept north across the

city. Ash from burning bones rained down on the city, "like black snow," one onlooker said. On some days it was hard even to see the river and the harbor. "See that cloud?" a character in a contemporary novel asked, pointing out the train window; "that's Chicago." "There is no sky now," another writer said.

A half-century later, the slaughterhouses had moved west to feedlots on the plains. Brokers on Chicago's Commodity Exchange still trade in hogs and pork belly futures, but those pigs will never see the old Union Stockyards, now a popular tourist attraction. Chicagoans have cleaned up their river; restaurants line the riverbanks and pleasure boats ply the waters.

In their time, the meat packers of Chicago transformed the diet of the United States and, in fact, the world. As early as 1912, Swift and Company had outlets in 400 cities on four continents and employed more than 30,000 people worldwide. The fresh meat products derived from Chicago's "second nature" fed people as never before.

was promising cornflake eaters "Genuine Joy, Genuine Appetite, Genuine Health and therefore Genuine Complexion."

Bringing producer and consumer together, nationwide advertising was the final link in the national market. From roadside signs to newspaper ads, it pervaded American life. "Do you know why we publish the *Ladies' Home Journal?*" the magazine's owner asked an audience of manufacturers. "The editor thinks it is for the benefit of American women. That is an illusion, but a very proper one for him to have. But I will tell you; the real reason, the publisher's reason, is to give you people who manufacture things that American women want and buy a chance to tell them about your products."

R. H. Macy in New York, John Wanamaker in Philadelphia, and Marshall Field in Chicago turned the department store into a national institution. There people could browse (a relatively new concept) and buy. Innovations in pricing, display, and advertising helped customers develop wants they did not know they had. In 1870, Wanamaker took out the first full-

page newspaper ad, and Macy, an aggressive advertiser, touted "goods suitable for the millionaire at prices in reach of the millions."

The "chain store"—an American term—spread across the country. The A & P grocery stores, begun in 1859, numbered sixty-seven by 1876, all marked by a familiar red-and-gold facade. By 1915, there were a thousand of them. In 1880, F. W. Woolworth, bored with the family farm, opened the first "Five and Ten Cent Store" in Utica, New York. He had fifty-nine stores in 1900, the year he adopted the bright red storefront and heaping counters to lure customers in and persuade them to buy.

In similar fashion, Sears, Roebuck and Montgomery Ward sold to rural customers through mail-order catalogs—a means of selling that depended on effective transportation and a high level of customer literacy. As a traveler for a dry goods firm, Aaron Montgomery Ward had seen an unfulfilled need of people in the rural West. He started the mail-order trend in 1872, with a one-sheet price list offered from

A cutaway view of the "bee-hive" headquarters of mail-order giant Montgomery Ward & Co. of Chicago. By the time Ward moved into this building in 1899, rival retailer Sears, Roebuck & Co. was challenging Ward's mail-order business. ❖

a Chicago loft. By 1884, he offered almost ten thousand items in a catalog of 240 pages.

Richard W. Sears also saw the possibilities in the mail-order business. Starting with watches and jewelry, he gradually expanded his list. In the early 1880s, he moved to Chicago and with Alvah C. Roebuck founded Sears, Roebuck and Company. Sears sold anything and everything, prospering in a business that relied on mutual faith between unseen customers and distant distributors. Sears catalogs, soon more than five hundred pages long, exploited four-color illustration and other new techniques. By the early 1900s, Sears distributed six million catalogs annually.

Advertising, brand names, chain stores, and mail-order houses brought Americans of all varieties into a national market. Even as the country grew, a certain homogeneity of goods bound it together, touching cities and farms, East and West, rich and poor. There was a common language of consumption. The market, some contemporaries thought, also bridged ethnic and other differences. A prominent English economist wrote in 1919, "Widely as the Scandinavians are separated from the Italians, and the native Americans from the Poles, in sentiment, in modes of living, and even in occupations, they are yet purchasers of nearly the same goods. . . . They buy similar clothes, furniture, and implements."

The theory had severe limits; ethnic and racial differences remained entrenched in the society. But Americans *had* become a community of consumers, surrounded by goods unavailable just a few decades before, and able to purchase them. They had learned to make, want, and buy. "Because you see the main thing today is—shopping," Arthur Miller, a twentieth-century playwright, said in *The Price:*

> Years ago a person, he was unhappy, didn't know what to do with himself—he'd go to church, start a revolution—something. Today you're unhappy? Can't figure it out? What is the salvation? Go shopping.

THE WAGE EARNERS

Although entrepreneurs were important, it was the labor of millions of men and women that built the new industrial society. In their individual stories, nearly all unrecorded, lay much of the achievement, drama, and pain of these years.

In a number of respects, their lot improved during the last quarter of the nineteenth century. Real wages rose, working conditions improved, and the workers' influence in national affairs increased. Between 1880 and 1914, wages of the average worker rose about $7 a year. Like others, workers also benefited from expanding health and educational services.

Working Men, Working Women, Working Children

Still, life for workers was not easy. Before 1900, most wage earners worked at least ten hours a day, six days a week. If skilled, they earned about 20 cents an hour; if unskilled, just half that. On average, workers earned between $400 and $500 a year. It took about $600 for a family of four to live decently. Construction workers, machinists, government employees, printers, clerical workers, and western miners made more than the average. Eastern coal miners, agricultural workers, garment workers, and unskilled factory hands made considerably less.

There were few holidays or vacations, and there was little respite from the grueling routine. Skilled workers could turn the system to their own ends—New York City cigar makers, for example, paid someone to read to them while they worked—but the unskilled seldom had such luxury. They were too easily replaced. "A bit of advice to you," said a guidebook for immigrant Jews in the 1890s: "do not take a moment's rest. Run, do, work, and keep your own good in mind."

Work was not only grueling; it was very dangerous. Safety standards were low, and accidents were common, more common in fact than in any other

Many children in the late nineteenth century grew up in the nation's factories, working long hours for low wages in often dangerous conditions. This young girl working as a spinner in a textile mill posed for photographer Lewis Hine. ❖

industrial nation in the world at that time. On the railroads, 1 in every 26 workers was injured and 1 in every 399 was killed each year. Thousands suffered from chronic illness, unknowing victims of dust, chemicals, and other pollutants. In the early 1900s, physician Alice Hamilton established a link between jobs and disease, but meanwhile, illness weakened or struck down many a breadwinner.

The breadwinner might be a woman or a child; both worked in increasing numbers. In 1870, about 15 percent of women over the age of 16 were employed for wages; in 1900, 20 percent (5.3 million women) were. Of 303 occupations listed in the 1900 census, women were represented in 296. The textile industry was their largest single employer. Between 1870 and 1900, the number of working children rose nearly 130 percent to 1.8 million. In 1900, 1 out of every 10 girls and 1 out of every 5 boys between the ages of 10 and 15 held jobs. In Paterson, New Jersey, an important industrial city, about half of all boys and girls aged 11 to 14 had jobs.

There were so many children in the labor force that when people spoke of child labor, they often meant boys and girls under the age of 14. Boys were paid little enough, but girls made even less. Girls, it was argued, were headed for marriage; those who worked were just doing so in order to help out their families. "We try to employ girls who are members of families," a box manufacturer said, "for we don't pay the girls a living wage in this trade."

Most working women were young and single. Many began working at 16 or 17, worked a half dozen years or so, married, and quit. In 1900, only 5 percent of all married women were employed outside the home, although African American women were an important exception. Among them, 25 percent of married women worked in 1900, usually on southern farms or as low-paid laundresses or domestic servants. As clerical work expanded, women learned new skills such as typing and stenography. Moving into formerly male occupations, they became secretaries, bookkeepers, typists, telephone operators, and clerks in the new department stores.

A few women—very few—became ministers, lawyers, and doctors. Arabella Mansfield, admitted to the Iowa bar in 1869, was the first woman lawyer in the country. But change was slow, and in the 1880s, some law schools still were refusing to admit women because they "had not the mentality to study law." Among women entering the professions, the overwhelming majority became nurses, schoolteachers, and librarians. In such professions, a process of "feminization" occurred: Women became a majority of the workers, a small number of men took the management roles, and most men left for other jobs, lowering the profession's status.

In most jobs, status and pay were divided unequally between men and women. Many of both sexes thought a woman's place was in the home, "queen of a little house—no matter how humble—where there are children rolling on the floor." When employed in factories, women tended to occupy jobs that were viewed as natural extensions of household activity. They made clothes and textiles, processed food, and made cigars, tobacco, and shoes. In the women's garment industry, which employed large numbers of women, they were the sewers and finishers, doing jobs that paid less; men were the higher-paid cutters and pressers.

In *The Long Day: The Story of a New York Working Girl as Told by Herself* (1906), the "working girl," a young schoolteacher, earned $2.50 a week, paid $1.00 for her room, and had $1.50 for food, clothes, transportation, and any social life. For breakfast, she had bread, butter, and coffee; for lunch, bread and butter;

A typing pool in the audit division of the Metropolitan Life Insurance Company, 1897. As demand for clerical workers grew, women took over many of the secretarial duties formerly performed by men. Despite their prominence in the workplace, however, the women were usually overseen by male supervisors. ❖

for dinner, potato soup, bread, and butter. In Pittsburgh, a worker in a pickle factory said of her day: "I have stood ten hours; I have fitted 1,300 corks; I have hauled and loaded 4,000 jars of pickles. My pay is seventy cents." Exhausted, such workers fell into bed at night and crawled out again at dawn to begin another "long day."

In general, adults earned more than children, the skilled more than the unskilled, native born more than foreign born, Protestants more than Catholics or Jews, and whites more than blacks and Asians. On average, women made a little more than half as much as men, according to contemporary estimates. In some cases, employers defended the differences—the foreign born, for example, might not speak English—but most simply reflected bias against race, creed, or gender. In the industrial society, white, native-born Protestant men—the bulk of the male population—reaped the greatest rewards.

Blacks labored on the fringes, usually in menial occupations. The last hired and first fired, they earned less than other workers at almost every level of skill. On the Pacific Coast, the Chinese—and later the Japanese—lived in enclaves and suffered periodic attacks of discrimination. In 1879, the Workingmen's party of California got a provision in the state constitution forbidding corporations to employ Chinese, and in 1882, Congress passed the **Chinese Exclusion Act,** prohibiting the immigration of Chinese workers for ten years.

Culture of Work

Among almost all groups, industrialization shattered age-old patterns, including work habits and the culture of work, as Herbert G. Gutman, a social historian, noted. It made people adapt "older work routines to new necessities and strained those wedded to premodern patterns of labor." Adaptation was difficult and often demeaning. Virtually everyone went through it, and newcomers repeated the experiences of those who came before.

Men and women fresh from farms were not accustomed to the factory's disciplines. Now they worked indoors rather than out, paced themselves to the clock rather than the movements of the sun, and followed the needs of the market rather than the natural rhythms of the seasons. They had supervisors and hierarchies and strict rules. Piecework determined wages, and always—as Morris Rosenfeld, a clothing presser, wrote—there was the relentless clock:

> The Clock in the workshop,—it rests not a moment;
> It points on, and ticks on: eternity-time;
> Once someone told me the clock had a meaning,
> In pointing and ticking had reason and rhyme.

> At times, when I listen, I hear the clock plainly;
> The reason of old—the old meaning—is gone!
> The maddening pendulum urges me forward
> To labor and still labor on.
> The tick of the clock is the boss in his anger.
> The face of the clock has the eyes of the foe.
> The clock—I shudder—Dost hear how it draws me?
> It calls me "Machine" and it cries [to] me "Sew"!

As industries grew larger, work became more impersonal. Machines displaced skilled artisans, and the unskilled tended the machines for employers they never saw. Workers picked up and left their jobs with startling frequency, and factories drew on a churning, highly mobile labor supply. Historian Stephan Thernstrom, who carefully studied the census records, found that only about half the people recorded in any census still lived in the same community ten years later. "The country had an enormous reservoir of restless and footloose men, who could be lured to new destinations when opportunity beckoned."

Thernstrom and others have also found substantial economic and social mobility. The rags-to-riches stories of Horatio Alger, had always said so, and careers of men such as Andrew Carnegie—the impoverished immigrant boy who made good—seemed to confirm it. The actual record was considerably more limited. Most business leaders in the period came from well-to-do or middle-class families of old American stock. Of 360 iron and steel barons in Pittsburgh, Carnegie's own city, only 5 fit the Carnegie characteristics, and one of those was Carnegie himself. Still, if few workers became steel magnates, many workers made major progress during their lifetimes. Thernstrom discovered that a quarter of the manual laborers rose to middle-class positions, and working-class children were even more likely to move up the ladder. In Boston, about half the Jewish immigrants rose from manual to middle-class jobs, and English, Irish, and Italian immigrants were not far behind.

The chance for advancement played a vital role in American industrial development. It gave workers hope, wedded them to the system, and tempered their response to the appeal of labor unions and working-class agitation. Very few workers rose from rags to riches, but a great many rose to better jobs and higher status.

Labor Unions

Weak throughout the nineteenth century, labor unions never included more than 2 percent of the total labor force or more than 10 percent of industrial workers. To many workers, unions seemed "foreign," radical, and out of step with the American tradition of individual advancement. Craft, ethnic, and other differences fragmented the labor force, and its extraordinary mobility made organization difficult. Employers opposed unions. "I have always had one rule," said an executive of U.S. Steel. "If a worker sticks up his head, hit it."

As the national economy emerged, however, national labor unions gradually took shape. The early unions often represented skilled workers in local areas, but in 1866, William H. Sylvis, a Pennsylvania iron molder, united several unions into a single national organization, the National Labor Union. Like many of the era's labor leaders, Sylvis sought long-range humanitarian reforms, such as the establishment of workers' cooperatives, rather than specific bread-and-butter goals. A talented propagandist, he attracted many members—some 640,000 by 1868—but he died in 1869, and the organization did not long survive him.

The year Sylvis died, Uriah S. Stephens and a group of Philadelphia garment workers founded a far more successful organization, the Noble and Holy Order of the Knights of Labor, known simply as the **Knights of Labor.** A secret fraternal order, it grew slowly through the 1870s, until Terence V. Powderly, the new Grand Master Workman elected in 1879, ended the secrecy and embarked on an aggressive recruitment program. Wanting to unite all labor, the Knights welcomed everyone who "toiled," regardless of skill, creed, sex, or color. Unlike most unions, it or-

ganized women workers, and at its peak, it had 60,000 black members.

Harking back to the Jacksonians, the Knights set the "producers" against monopoly and special privilege. As members they excluded only "nonproducers"—bankers, lawyers, liquor dealers, and gamblers. Since employers were "producers," they could join; and since workers and employers had common interests, the Knights maintained that workers should not strike. The order's platform included the eight-hour day and the abolition of child labor, but more often it focused on uplifting, utopian reform. Powderly, the eloquent and idealistic leader, spun dreams of a new era of harmony and cooperation. He wanted to sweep away trusts and end drunkenness. Workers should pool their resources, establish worker-run factories, railroads, and mines, and escape from the wage system. "The aim of the Knights of Labor—properly understood—is to make each man his own employer," Powderly said.

Membership grew steadily—from 42,000 in 1882 to 110,000 in 1885. In March 1885, ignoring Powderly's dislike of strikes, local Knights in St. Louis, Kansas City, and other cities won a victory against Jay Gould's Missouri Pacific Railroad, and membership soared. It soon reached almost 730,000, but neither Powderly nor the union's loose structure could handle the growth. In 1886, the wily Gould struck back, crushing the Knights on the Texas and Pacific Railroad. The defeat punctured the union's growth and revealed the ineffectiveness of its national leaders. Tens of thousands of unskilled laborers, who had recently rushed to join, deserted the ranks. The Haymarket Riot turned public sympathy against unions like the Knights. By 1890, the order had shrunk to 100,000 members, and a few years later, it was virtually defunct.

Even as the Knights waxed and waned, another organization emerged that was to endure. Founded in 1886, the **American Federation of Labor (AFL)** was a loose alliance of national craft unions. It organized only skilled workers along craft lines, avoided politics, and worked for specific practical objectives. "I

Women delegates at a national meeting of the Knights of Labor in 1886. Women belonged to separate associations affiliated with local all-male unions. ◆

have my own philosophy and my own dreams," said Samuel Gompers, the founder and longtime president, "but first and foremost I want to increase the working-man's welfare year by year."

Born in a London tenement in 1850, Gompers was a child of the union movement. Settling in New York, he worked as a cigar maker, took an active hand in union activities, and experimented for a time with socialism and working-class politics. As leader of the AFL, he adopted a pragmatic approach to labor's needs. Gompers accepted capitalism and did not argue for fundamental changes in it. For labor he wanted simply a recognized place within the system and a greater share of the rewards.

Unlike Powderly, Gompers and the AFL assumed that most workers would remain workers throughout their lives. The task, then, lay in improving lives in "practical" ways: higher wages, shorter hours, and better working conditions. The AFL offered some attractive assurances to employers. As a trade union, the AFL would use the strike and boycott, but only to achieve limited gains; if treated fairly, the organization would provide a stable labor force. The AFL would not oppose monopolies and trusts, as Gompers said, "so long as we obtain fair wages."

By the 1890s, the AFL was the most important labor group in the country, and Gompers, the guiding spirit, was its president, except for one year, until his death in 1924. Membership expanded from 140,000 in 1886, past 250,000 in 1892, to more than 1 million by 1901. The AFL then included almost one-third of the country's skilled workers. By 1914, it had more than 2 million members. The great majority of workers—skilled and unskilled—remained unorganized, but Gompers and the AFL had become a significant force in national life.

Few unions allowed women to join. The Knights of Labor had a Department of Woman's Work headed by Leonora M. Barry, a shrewd, enthusiastic organizer who established a dozen women's locals and investigated the condition of women's labor. The Knights welcomed housewives because they were "producers." The AFL either ignored or opposed women workers. Only two of its national affiliates—the Cigar Makers' Union and the Typographical Union—accepted women as members; others prohibited them outright, and Gompers himself often complained that women workers undercut the pay scales for men. Working conditions improved after 1900, but even then, unions were largely a man's world. In 1910, when there were 6.3 million women at work, only 125,000 of them were in unions.

The AFL did not expressly forbid black workers from joining, but member unions used high initiation fees, technical examinations, and other means to discourage black membership. The AFL's informal exclusion practices were, all in all, a sorry record, but Gompers defended his policy toward blacks, women, and the unskilled by pointing to the dangers that unions faced. Only by restricting membership, he argued, could the union succeed.

Labor Unrest

Workers used various means to adjust to the factory age. To the dismay of managers and "efficiency" experts, the employees often dictated the pace and quality of their work and set the tone of the workplace. Friends and relatives of newly arrived immigrants found jobs for them, taught them how to deal with factory conditions, and humanized the workplace.

Workers also formed their own institutions to deal with their jobs. Overcoming differences of race or ethnic origin, they often banded together to help each other. They joined social or fraternal organizations, and their unions did more than argue for higher

Violence and fires associated with the great railroad strike of 1877 destroyed railyards across the country. By the end of the strike, which lasted about two weeks, $10 million of railroad property had been reduced to rubble, and more than a hundred people had died. ❖

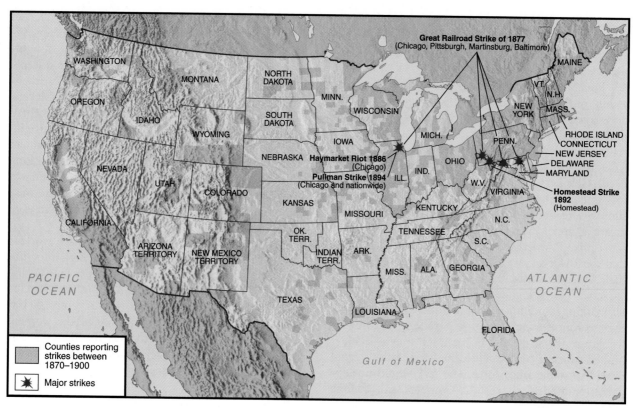

LABOR STRIKES, 1870–1890   *More than 14,000 strikes occurred in the 1880s and early 1890s, involving millions of workers.* ◆

wages. Unions offered companionship, news of job openings, and much needed insurance plans for sickness, accident, or death. Workers went to the union hall to play cards or pool, sing union songs, and hear older workers tell of past labor struggles. Unions provided food for sick members, and there were dances, picnics, and parades. "The night I joined the Cattle Butchers' Union," a young Lithuanian said, "I was led into the room by a negro member. With me were Bohemians, Germans and Poles. . . . We swore to be loyal to our union above everything else except the country, the city and the State—to be faithful to each other—to protect the women workers—to do our best to understand the history of the labor movement, and to do all we could to help it on."

Many employers believed in an "iron law of wages" in which supply and demand, not the welfare of their workers, dictated wages. "If I wanted boiler iron," a steelmaker said, "I would go out on the market and buy where I could get it the cheapest, and if I wanted to employ men I would do the same thing." Wanting a docile labor force, employers fired union members, hired scabs to replace strikers, and used a new weapon, the court injunction, to quell strikes.

The injunction, which forbade workers to interfere with their employers' business, was used to break the great Pullman strike of 1894, and the Supreme Court upheld use of the injunction in *In re Debs* (1895). Court decisions also affected the legal protection offered to workers. In *Holden* v. *Hardy* (1898), the Court upheld a law limiting working hours for miners because their work was dangerous and long hours might increase injuries. In *Lochner* v. *New York* (1905), however, it struck down a law limiting bakery workers to a sixty-hour week and ten-hour day. Because baking was safer than mining, the Court saw no need to interfere with the right of bakers to sell their labor freely. (For a case involving women workers, see "*Muller* v. *Oregon*: Expanding the Definition of Acceptable Evidence," pp. 684–687.)

As employers' attitudes hardened, strikes and violence broke out. The United States had the greatest number of violent confrontations between capital and labor in the industrial world. Between 1880 and 1900, there were more than 23,000 strikes involving 6.6 million workers. The great railroad strike of 1877 paralyzed railroads from West Virginia to California, resulted in the deaths of more than a hundred workers, and required federal troops to suppress it. Another outburst of labor unrest occurred during the mid-1880s; in 1886, the peak year, 610,000 workers were off the job because of strikes and lockouts.

The worst incident took place at Haymarket Square in Chicago, where workers had been campaigning for an eight-hour workday. In early May 1886, police, intervening in a strike at the McCormick Harvester works, shot and killed two workers. The next evening, May 4, labor leaders called a protest meeting at Haymarket Square near downtown Chicago. The meeting was peaceful, even a bit dull. About three thousand people were there; police ordered them to disperse, and someone threw a dynamite bomb that instantly killed one policeman and fatally wounded six others. Police fired into the crowd and killed four people.

The authorities never discovered who threw the bomb, but many Americans—not just business leaders—immediately labeled the incident the **Haymarket Riot** and demanded action against labor "radicalism." Cities strengthened their police forces and armories. In Chicago, donors helped to establish nearby Fort Sheridan and the Great Lakes Naval Training Station to curb social turmoil. Uncertain who threw the bomb, Chicago police rounded up eight anarchists, who were convicted of murder. Although there was no evidence of their guilt, four were hanged, one committed suicide, and three remained in jail until pardoned by the governor in 1893. Linking labor and anarchism in the public mind, the Haymarket Riot weakened the national labor movement.

Violence again broke out in the unsettled conditions of the 1890s. In 1892, federal troops crushed a strike of silver miners in the Coeur d'Alene district of Idaho. That same year, Carnegie and Henry Clay Frick, Carnegie's partner and manager, cut wages nearly 20 percent at the Homestead steel plant. The Amalgamated Iron and Steel Workers, an AFL affiliate, struck, and Frick responded by locking the workers out of the plant. The workers surrounded it, and Frick, furious, hired a small private army of Pinkerton detectives to drive them off. But alert workers spotted the detectives, pinned them down with gunfire, and forced them to surrender. Three detectives and ten workers died in the battle.

A few days later, the Pennsylvania governor ordered the state militia to impose peace at Homestead. On July 23, an anarchist named Alexander Berkman, who was not one of the strikers, walked into Frick's office and shot him twice, then stabbed him several times. Incredibly, Frick survived, watched the police take Berkman away, called in a doctor to bandage his wounds, and stayed in the office until closing time. "I do not think I shall die," he told reporters. "But if I do or not, the company will pursue the same policy and it will win." In late July, the Homestead works reopened under military guard, and in November the strikers gave up.

Events like the **Homestead Strike** troubled many Americans who wondered whether industrialization,

In the rioting that followed the bomb explosion in Haymarket Square in Chicago, seven police officers and four workers died and more than seventy officers were wounded, many of them by fellow police. August Spies, one of the anarchists convicted of murder and sent to the gallows, said at his trial, "Let the world know that in A.D. 1886, in the state of Illinois, eight men were sentenced to death because they believed in a better future; because they had not lost their faith in the ultimate victory of liberty and justice!" (Actually, seven of the agitators were sentenced to death, the eighth to imprisonment.) ❖

for all its benefits, might carry a heavy price in social up-heaval, class tensions, and even outright warfare. Most workers did not share in the immense profits of the industrial age, and as the nineteenth century came to a close, there were some who rebelled against the inequity.

CONCLUSION: INDUSTRIALIZATION'S BENEFITS AND COSTS

In the half century after the Civil War, the United States became an industrial nation—the leading one, in fact, in the world. On one hand, industrialization meant "progress," growth, world power, and in some sense, fulfillment of the American promise of abundance. National wealth grew from $16 billion in 1860 to $88 billion in 1900; wealth per capita more than doubled. For the bulk of the population, the standard of living—a particularly American concept—rose.

But industrialization also meant rapid change, social instability, exploitation of labor, and growing disparity in income between rich and poor. Industry flourished, but control rested in fewer and fewer hands. Maturing quickly, the young system became a new corporate capitalism: giant businesses, interlocking in ownership, managed by a new professional class, and selling an expanding variety of goods in an increasingly controlled market. As goods spread through the society, so did a sharpened, aggressive materialism. Workers felt the strains of the shift to a new social order.

In 1902, a well-to-do New Yorker named Bessie Van Vorst decided to see what it was like to work for a living in a factory. Disguising herself in coarse woolen clothes, a shabby felt hat, a cheap piece of fur, and an old shawl and gloves, she went to Pittsburgh and got a job in a canning factory. She worked ten hours a day, six days a week, including four hours on Saturday afternoons when she and the other women, on their hands and knees, scrubbed the tables, stands, and entire factory floor. For that she earned $4.20 a week, $3 of which went for food alone. "My hands are stiff," she said, "my thumbs almost blistered. . . . Cases are emptied and refilled; bottles are labeled, stamped and rolled away . . . and still there are

CHRONOLOGY

1859	First oil well drilled near Titusville, Pennsylvania
1866	William Sylvis establishes National Labor Union
1869	Transcontinental railroad completed at Promontory, Utah ❖ Knights of Labor organize
1876	Alexander Graham Bell invents the telephone ❖ Centennial Exposition held in Philadelphia
1877	Railroads cut workers' wages, leading to bloody and violent strike
1879	Thomas A. Edison invents the incandescent lamp
1882	Rockefeller's Standard Oil Company becomes nation's first trust ❖ Edison opens first electric generating station in New York
1883	Railroads introduce standard time zones
1886	Samuel Gompers founds American Federation of Labor (AFL) ❖ Labor protest erupts in violence in Haymarket Riot in Chicago ❖ Railroads adopt standard gauge
1892	Workers strike at Homestead steel plant in Pennsylvania
1893	Economic depression begins
1901	J. P. Morgan announces formation of U.S. Steel Corporation, nation's first billion-dollar company

more cases, more jars, more bottles. Oh! the monotony of it!" The noise around her was deafening; her head grew dazed and weary.

Van Vorst was lucky—when she tired of the life, she could go back to her home in New York. The working men and women around her were not so fortunate. They stayed on the factory floor and, by dint of their labor, created the new industrial society.

RECOMMENDED READING

Samuel P. Hays, *The Response to Industrialism: 1885–1914* (1957), is an influential interpretation of the period. Douglass C. North, *Growth and Welfare in the American Past: A New Economic History* (1966), is stimulating. David Montgomery, *The Fall of the House of Labor* (1987), is an outstanding study of labor in the period. Richard Franklin Bensel, *The Political Economy of American Industrialization, 1877–1900* (2000), and Charles Perrow, *Organizing America: Wealth, Power, and the Origins of Corporate Capitalism*

(2002), trace the underlying ideas of the new industrialization.

Alfred D. Chandler, *The Visible Hand: The Managerial Revolution in American Business* (1978), Olivier Zunz, *Making America Corporate, 1870–1920* (1990), and JoAnne Yates, *Control Through Communication: The Rise of System in American Management* (1989), are perceptive. The railroad empire is treated in John R. Stilgoe, *Metropolitan Corridor: Railroads and the American Scene* (1983), John

Hoyt Williams, *A Great and Shining Road: The Epic Story of the Transcontinental Railroad* (1988), and John F. Stover, *American Railroads* (1961); its legal implications in, James W. Ely, Jr., *Railroads and American Law* (2001), and Barbara Young Welke, *Recasting American Liberty: Gender, Race, Law, and the Railroad Revolution, 1865–1920* (2001). On the steel industry, see Peter Temin, *Iron and Steel in Nineteenth-Century America* (1964).

Two superb books by Sam Bass Warner, Jr., *Streetcar Suburbs: The Process of Growth in Boston, 1870–1900* (1962), and *The Urban Wilderness: A History of the American City* (1973), examine technology and city development. The wage earner is examined in Herbert G. Gutman, *Work, Culture, and Society in Industrializing America* (1976), and Joshua L. Rosenbloom, *Looking for Work, Searching for Workers: American Labor Markets during Industrialization* (2002). Two books by Stephan Thernstrom, *Poverty and Progress: Social Mobility in the Nineteenth-Century City* (1964) and *The Other Bostonians: Poverty and Progress in the American Metropolis, 1880–1970* (1973), examine mobility. Philip S. Foner, *Women and the American Labor Movement*, 2 vols. (1979), Susan E. Kennedy, *If All We Did Was to Weep at Home* (1979), Barbara Mayer Wertheimer, *We Were There: The Story of Working Women in America* (1977), and Alice Kessler-Harris, *Out to Work: A History of Wage-Earning Women in the United States* (1982), are excellent on the subject of women in the workplace.

For a list of additional titles related to this chapter's topics, please see http://www.ablongman.com/divine.

SUGGESTED WEB SITES

Alexander Graham Bell Family Papers at the Library of Congress

http://memory.loc.gov/ammem/bellhtml/bellhome.html

This site contains papers from 1862 to 1939, but includes a chronology, images, selected documents, and interpretive essays about Bell.

The Richest Man in the World: Andrew Carnegie

http://www.pbs.org/wgbh/amex/carnegie/

This American Experience/PBS site provides images and text about Carnegie's life and activities.

The Anarchy Archives at Pitzer University

http://dwardmac.pitzer.edu/Anarchist_Archives/archivehome.html

This archive includes classic anarchist texts, especially information about and graphics of the Haymarket Riot.

John D. Rockefeller and the Standard Oil Company

http://www.micheloud.com/FXM/SO/

This study with accompanying images by François Micheloud tells of the rise of Rockefeller and his mammoth company.

National Refinery Company

http://www.enarco.com/

This positive history of the company reflects the industrial changes of late-nineteenth-century America.

American Labor History

http://www.geocities.com/CollegePark/Quad/6460/AmLabHist/index.html

This site takes a general look at the history of labor in America.

Labor-Management Conflict in American History

http://www.history.ohio-state.edu/projects/laborconflict/

This Ohio State University site includes primary accounts of some of the major events in the history of labor-management conflict in the late nineteenth and early twentieth centuries.

Samuel Gompers Papers at the University of Maryland

http://www.history.umd.edu/Gompers/index.html

This site includes information about the papers project but also has a photo gallery, selected documents, and a brief history of the first president of the American Federation of Labor.

The Strike at Homestead

http://www.history.ohio-state.edu/projects/HomesteadStrike1892/

This site provides a collection of historical documents on the strike and reactions to it.

Chapter **19**

During the second half of the nineteenth century, cities of the Midwest drew people and businesses to America's heartland. Milwaukee, shown here in a photograph by William Henry Jackson, was a major center of German immigration. ❖

Toward an Urban Society, 1877–1900

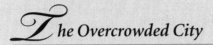The Overcrowded City

One day around 1900, Harriet Vittum, a settlement house worker in Chicago, went to the aid of a young Polish girl who lived in a nearby slum. The girl, aged 15, had discovered she was pregnant and had taken poison. An ambulance was on the way, and Vittum, told of the poisoning, rushed over to do what she could.

Quickly, she raced up the three flights of stairs to the floor where the girl and her family lived. Pushing open the door, she found the father, several male boarders, and two or three small boys asleep on the kitchen floor. In the next room, the mother was on the floor among several women boarders and one or two small children. Glancing out the window, Vittum saw the wall of another building so close she could reach out and touch it.

There was a third room; in it lay the 15-year-old girl, along with two more small children who were asleep. Looking at the scene, Vittum thought about the girl's life in the crowded tenement. Should she try to save her? Vittum asked herself. Should she even try to bring the girl back "to the misery and hopelessness of the life she was living in that awful place"?

The young girl died, and in later years, Vittum often told her story. It was easy to see why. The girl's life in the slum, the children on the floor, the need to take in boarders to make ends meet, the way the mother and father collapsed at the end of a workday that began long before sunup—all reflected the experiences of millions of people living in the nation's cities.

VITTUM AND PEOPLE LIKE HER were attempting to respond to the overwhelming challenges of the nation's burgeoning cities. People poured into cities in the last part of the nineteenth century, lured by glitter and excitement, by friends and relatives who were already there, and, above all, by the greater opportunities for jobs and higher wages. Between 1860 and 1910, the rural population of the United States almost doubled; the number of people living in cities increased sevenfold.

Little of the increase came from natural growth, since urban families had high rates of infant mortality, a declining fertility rate, and a high death rate from injury and disease. Many of the newcomers came from rural America, and many more came from Europe, Latin America, and Asia. In one of the most significant migrations in American history, thousands of African Americans began in the 1880s to move from the rural South to northern cities. By 1900, there were large black communities in New York, Baltimore, Chicago, Washington, D.C., and other cities. Yet to come was the even greater black migration during World War I.

OUTLINE

The Lure of the City

Social and Cultural Change, 1877–1900

The Stirrings of Reform

Conclusion: The Pluralistic Society

FEATURE ESSAY

Ellis Island: Isle of Hope, Isle of Tears

LAW AND SOCIETY

Plessy v. *Ferguson:* The Shaping of Jim Crow

Two major forces reshaped American society between 1870 and 1920. One was industrialization; the other was urbanization, the headlong rush of people from their rural roots into the modern urban environment. In these years, cities grew upward and outward, attracting millions of newcomers and influencing politics, education, entertainment, and family life. By 1920, they had become the center of American economic, social, and cultural life.

THE LURE OF THE CITY

William Allen White, later a famous journalist, reflected the country's fascination with the city. He left the small Kansas town of his boyhood in 1891 to go to what he called the "gilded metropolis" of Kansas City. White was 23 years old, and the experience affected him for the rest of his life. He rode the cable cars and used the brand-new telephone—"always with the consciousness that I was tampering with a miracle." He purchased a secondhand dress suit, listened to the music of a sixty-piece orchestra, attended plays, and heard James Whitcomb Riley recite poetry. "Life was certainly one round of joy in Kansas City," White said.

Between 1870 and 1900, the city—like the factory—became a symbol of a new America. Drawn from farms, small towns, and foreign lands, newcomers swelled the population of older cities and created new ones almost overnight. At the beginning of the Civil War, only one-sixth of the American people lived in cities of eight thousand people or more. By 1900, one-third did; by 1920, one-half. "We live in the age of great cities," wrote the Reverend Samuel Lane Loomis in 1887. "Each successive year finds a stronger and more irresistible current sweeping in towards the centers of life."

The current brought growth of an explosive sort. Thousands of years of history had produced only a handful of cities with more than a half million in population. In 1900, the United States had six such cities, including three—New York, Chicago, and Philadelphia—with populations greater than one million.

Skyscrapers and Suburbs

Like so many things in these years, the city was transformed by a revolution in technology. Beginning in the 1880s, the age of steel and glass produced the skyscraper; the streetcar produced the suburbs and new residential patterns.

On the eve of the change, American cities were a crowded jumble of small buildings. Church steeples stood out on the skyline, clearly visible above the roofs of factories and office buildings. Buildings were usually made of masonry, and since the massive walls had to support their own weight, they could be no taller than a dozen or so stories. Steel frames and girders ended that limitation and allowed buildings to soar higher and higher. "Curtain walls," which concealed the steel framework, were no longer load bearing; they

In 1900, Chicago was the most populated U.S. city after New York. The new skyscrapers allowed the city to expand upward, while the elevated rapid transit system enabled the city to sprawl outward into the suburbs. This photograph of Chicago by William Henry Jackson shows the busy sidewalks and elevated track at Wabash Avenue. ❖

were pierced by many windows that let in fresh air and light. Completed in 1885, the Home Insurance Building in Chicago was the country's first metal-frame structure.

To a group of talented Chicago architects, the new trends served as a springboard for innovative forms. The leaders of the movement were John Root and Louis H. Sullivan, both of whom were attracted by the chance to rebuild Chicago after the great fire of 1871. Noting that the fire had fed on fancy exterior ornamentation, Root developed a plain, stripped-down style, bold in mass and form—the keynotes of modern architecture. He had another important insight, too. In an age of business, Root thought, the office tower, more than a church or a government building, symbolized the society, and he designed office buildings that carried out, as he said, "the ideas of modern business life: simplicity, stability, breadth, dignity."

Sullivan had studied at the Massachusetts Institute of Technology (MIT) and in Paris before settling in Chicago. In 1886, at the age of 30, he began work on the Chicago Auditorium, one of the last great masonry buildings. "Then came the flash of imagination which saw the single thing," he later said. "The trick was turned; and there swiftly came into being something new under the sun." Sullivan's skyscrapers, that "flash of imagination," changed the urban skyline.

In the Wainwright Building in St. Louis (1890), the Schiller Building (1892) and the Carson, Pirie, and Scott department store (1899) in Chicago, and the Prudential Building in Buffalo (1895), Sullivan developed the new forms. Architects must discard "books, rules, precedents," he announced; responding to the new, they should design for a building's function. "Form follows function," Sullivan believed, and he passed the idea on to a talented disciple, Frank Lloyd Wright. The modern city should stretch to the sky. A skyscraper "must be every inch a proud and soaring thing, rising in sheer exaltation . . . from bottom to top."

Electric elevators, first used in 1871, carried passengers upward in the new skyscrapers. During the same years, streetcars, another innovation, carried the people outward to expanded boundaries that transformed urban life.

Cities were no longer largely "walking cities," confined to a radius of two or three miles, the distance an individual might walk. Streetcar systems extended the radius and changed the urban map. Cable lines, electric surface lines, and elevated rapid transit brought shoppers and workers into central business districts and sped them home again. Offering a modest five-cent fare with a free transfer, the mass transit systems fostered commuting and widely separated business and residential districts sprang up. The middle class moved farther and farther out to the leafy greenness of the suburbs.

As the middle class moved out of the cities, the immigrants and working class poured in. They took over the older brownstones, row houses, and workers' cottages, turning them, under the sheer weight of numbers, into the slums of the central city. In the cities of the past, classes and occupations had been thrown together; without streetcars and subways, there was no other choice. The streetcar city, sprawling and specialized, became a more fragmented and stratified society with middle-class residential rings surrounding a business and working-class core.

Tenements and the Problems of Overcrowding

In the shadow of the skyscrapers, grimy rows of tenements filled the central city. Exploring them in words and photographs, Jacob Riis described *How the Other Half Lives* (1890):

> Be a little careful, please! The hall is dark and you might stumble. . . . Here where the hall turns and dives into utter darkness is . . . a flight of stairs. You can feel your way, if you cannot see it. Close? Yes! What would you have? All the fresh air that enters these stairs comes from the hall-door that is forever slamming. . . . Here is a door. Listen! That short,

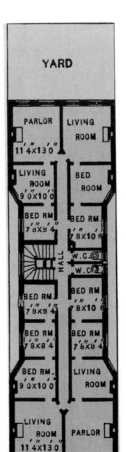

This 1879 dumbbell floor plan was meant to provide four apartments to a floor. However, a whole family might live in each room. Crowded, unsanitary conditions contributed to the spread of tuberculosis, the chief cause of death in the United States until 1909. ❖

The kitchen of a tenement apartment was often a multipurpose room. Here the tenement dwellers prepared and ate their meals; the room might also serve as a workroom, and it might be used as sleeping quarters for one or more members of the family. ❖

hacking cough, that tiny, helpless wail—what do they mean? . . . The child is dying of measles. With half a chance it might have lived; but it had none. That dark bedroom killed it.

Tenement houses on small city lots crowded people into cramped apartments. In the late 1870s, architect James E. Ware won a competition for tenement design with the "dumbbell tenement." Rising seven or eight stories in height, the dumbbell tenement packed about 30 four-room apartments on a lot only 25 by 100 feet. Between four and sixteen families lived on a floor; two toilets in the hall of each floor served their needs. Narrowed at the middle, the tenement resembled a giant dumbbell in shape. The indented middle created an air shaft between adjoining buildings that provided a little light and ventilation. In case of fire, it also carried flames from one story to the next, making the buildings notorious firetraps. In 1890, nearly half the dwellings in New York City were tenements.

That year, more than 1.4 million people lived on Manhattan Island, one of whose wards had a population density of 334,000 people per square mile. Many people lived in alleys and basements so dark they could not be photographed until flashlight photography was invented in 1887. Exploring the city, William

Dean Howells, the prominent author, inhaled "the stenches of the neglected street . . . [and] the yet fouler and dreadfuller poverty smell which breathes from the open doorways."

Howells smelled more than poverty. In the 1870s and 1880s, cities stank. One problem was horse manure, hundreds of tons of it a day in every city. Another was the privy, "a single one of which," said a leading authority on public health, "may render life in a whole neighborhood almost unendurable in the summer."

Baltimore smelled "like a billion polecats," recalled H. L. Mencken, who grew up there. Said one New York City resident, "The stench is something terrible." Another wrote that "the stink is enough to knock you down." In 1880, the Chicago *Times* said that a "solid stink" pervaded the city. "No other word expresses it so well as stink. A stench means something finite. Stink reaches the infinite and becomes sublime in the magnitude of odiousness." In 1892, one neighborhood of Chicago, covering one-third of a square mile, had only three bathtubs.

Cities dumped their wastes into the nearest body of water, then drew drinking water from the same site. Many built modern purified waterworks but could not keep pace with spiraling growth. In 1900, fewer than one in ten city dwellers drank filtered water. Factories, the pride of the era, polluted the urban air. At night, Pittsburgh looked and sounded like "Hell with the lid off," according to contemporary observers. Smoke poured from seventy-three glass factories, forty-one iron and steel mills, and twenty-nine oil refineries. The choking air helped prevent lung diseases and malaria—or so the city's advertising claimed.

Crime was another growing problem. The nation's homicide rate nearly tripled in the 1880s, much of the increase coming in the cities. Slum youths formed street gangs with names such as the Hayes Valley Gang in San Francisco and the Baxter Street Dudes, the Daybreak Boys, and the Alley Gang in New York. After remaining constant for many decades, the suicide rate rose steadily between 1870 and 1900, according to a study of Philadelphia. Alcoholism also rose, especially among men, though recent studies have shown that for working-class men, the urban saloon was as much a gathering spot as it was a place to drink. Nonetheless, a 1905 survey of Chicago counted as many saloons as grocery stores, meat markets, and dry goods stores combined.

Strangers in a New Land

While some of the new city dwellers came from farms and small towns, many more came from abroad. Most came from Europe, where unemployment, food shortages, and increasing threats of war sent millions fleeing across the Atlantic to make a fresh start. Often they knew someone already in the United States, a friend or relative who had written them about prospects for jobs and freer lives in a new land. Italians first came in large numbers to escape an 1887 cholera epidemic in southern Italy; tens of thousands of Jews sought refuge from the anti-Semitic massacres that swept Russia and czarist-ruled Poland after 1880.

All told, the immigration figures were staggering. Between 1877 and 1890, more than 6.3 million people entered the United States. In one year alone, 1882, almost 789,000 people came. By 1890, about 15 percent of the population, 9 million people, were foreign born. (See "Americans by the Numbers: The 1890 Census," pp. 604–605.)

Most newcomers were job seekers. Nearly two-thirds were males, and the majority were between the ages of 15 and 40. Most were unskilled laborers. Most settled on the eastern seaboard. In 1901, the Industrial Relocation Office was established to relieve overcrowding in the eastern cities; opening Galveston, Texas, as a port of entry, it attracted many Russian Jews to Texas and the Southwest. But most immigrants preferred the shorter, more familiar journey to New York. Entering through Ellis Island in New York harbor, as four in every ten immigrants did, most tended to

IMMIGRATION TO THE UNITED STATES, 1870–1900

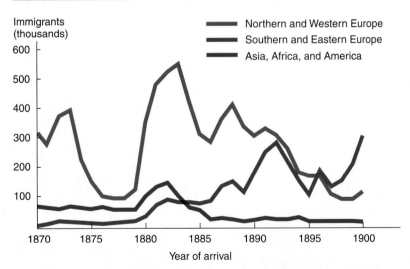

Note: For purposes of classification, "Northern and Western Europe" includes Great Britain, Ireland, Scandinavia, the Netherlands, Belgium, Luxembourg, Switzerland, France, and Germany. "Southern and Eastern Europe" includes Poland, Austria-Hungary, Russia and the Baltic States, Romania, Bulgaria, European Turkey, Italy, Spain, Portugal, and Greece. "Asia, Africa, and America" includes Asian Turkey, China, Japan, India, Canada, the Caribbean, Latin America, and all of Africa.

Source: U.S. Bureau of the Census, *Historical Statistics of the United States, Colonial Times to 1970,* Bicentennial Edition, Washington, DC, 1975.

ELLIS ISLAND

Isle of Hope, Isle of Tears

Ten years after he left Selo, his small Bulgarian village, for the United States, Michael Gurkin returned to tell of the wonders he had seen, including "buildings that scratched the sky," rooms in them that moved up and down, buttons that, pushed, lit a house or a street. Stoyan Christowe, 13, listened intently, caught up in the "Americamania," as he called it, that swept through his village. Soon he was on his way to the new land, his pockets stuffed with walnuts because he was too young to drink the farewell toast.

Unknowingly, he had joined a flood of people who were making their way to the United States. Between 1880 and 1920, a period of just forty years, the remarkable total of 23.5 million immigrants arrived in the country. They came from around the world, though mostly from Europe, driven from their homelands by economic, religious, or other troubles, lured across the ocean by the chance

for a better life. They entered the country through several ports, but by far the most—about seven out of every ten—landed in the city of New York.

Until 1892, they landed at a depot known as Castle Garden, a sprawling building on the tip of Manhattan Island. When it could no longer handle the flow, the entry site was moved to Ellis Island, a bank of sand and shells, close to the Statue of Liberty. Contractors erected a wooden structure, which opened in 1892 and burned down five years later. They then put up the current edifice, an imposing red brick building with triple-arch entrances and corner steeples. A small city, it had dormitories, a hospital, a post office, and showers that could bathe eight thousand people a day. It opened in 1900.

The change to Ellis Island represented more than just a shift in site. Entrance at Castle Garden had been fairly informal, since control over immigration still rested largely in the hands of the states. Officials merely registered newcomers, a process that took about thirty seconds.

In 1891, worried about the growing numbers of people who wanted in, Congress acted to bring immigration under federal control. Ellis Island was given tasks Castle Garden had never had, including mandates to keep out people some Americans considered undesirable. It became, one observer said, "the nearest earthly likeness to the Final Day of Judgement, when we have to prove our fitness to enter Heaven."

Many of those who sailed into the harbor, it should be remembered, never passed through the island at all. Arriving in first or second class, they had a fast on-board examination and went ashore, monied enough, it was assumed, not to become wards of the state. But those in third class—"steerage," as it was known—had a very different experience, and they faced it chock full of fear they would fail some test and be sent back home.

The day they docked, in 1910, Christowe and others washed thoroughly, hoping to look clean enough to pass inspection. Crowding the ship's rails, they gazed in wonder at the statue in the harbor, its arm lifted in the air. It was a saint, some guessed; Christopher Columbus, others said. It was a monument to freedom, Christowe was told, with Emma Lazarus's inviting poem at its base, "Give me your tired, your poor, Your huddled masses yearning to breathe free."

Once on the island, those huddled masses were under scrutiny from the moment they landed. Officials watched them climb the stairs, looking for heart problems or lameness.

A view of the landing station at Ellis Island in 1905, where millions of immigrants entered the country. ◆

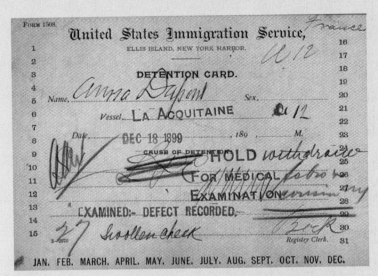

Ellis Island Detention Card for a French immigrant detained because of a "swollen cheek." ◈

Physicians administered the "six-second exam," checking quickly for disabilities or contagious diseases. If anything seemed out of sort, they put a chalk mark on the immigrant's coat calling for closer examination.

The next exam was the most feared of all: a doctor using a tailor's buttonhook to pull back eyelids to look for signs of diseases such as trachoma, a highly contagious bacterial eye infection that could lead to blindness. Most immigrants had never heard of trachoma, nor even knew they had the disease but it alone could strand them in the island's hospital or put them on a boat back home.

No one who went through the exam ever forgot it, as an immigrant poet wrote:

A stranger receives us
Harshly and asks: "And your health?"
He examines us. His look
Assesses us like dogs.

He studies in depth
Eyes and mouth. No doubt
That if he'd probed our hearts
He would have seen the wound.

Immigrants with chalk marks were herded to the left, while most went to the right, filing by a matron who searched the faces of women for evidence of "loose character." With so many languages among the arrivals, there were few written signs, and officials used metal barricades to guide

people along, "like puppets on conveyor-belts," Christowe later recalled.

Last there were the inspectors, seated behind desks, asking name, age, occupation, among dozens of other questions. On a busy day, the inspectors had two minutes to decide the fate of a newcomer. Those who "failed" went before a feared Board of Special Inquiry for final decision. For most immigrants the whole process took less than five hours; many others, held for proof of funds or further examination, spent days in the dormitories or hospital. Despite the harsh rumors, no more than 3 percent in a given year were turned away.

Still, it was becoming harder and harder to get in. People who feared the effect of immigrants on the nation clamored to keep them out. Some worried about the numbers of people who were arriving; others about disease or "radical" political views. Some did not like the shift in immigration after 1890 from largely Protestant northern and western Europe to Catholics, Jews, and others from southern and eastern Europe.

Reflecting such concerns, Congress passed laws to keep certain types of people out. In 1875, it prohibited the entrance of criminals and prostitutes. In 1882, it barred convicts and lunatics and excluded laborers from China, the first measure aimed directly at a racial group. In 1885, it banned the entry of laborers under

contract, imported by industries to work at low wages; in 1891, polygamists and people with "loathsome" diseases; in 1903, anarchists. In 1917, it passed, over Woodrow Wilson's veto, a literacy test that required immigrants to read a passage in their native tongue.

The great burst of immigration, halted during World War I, ended with the adoption of restrictive legislation in the 1920s. Ellis Island became more and more a detention center for "radicals" and other people awaiting deportation. Once the gateway to the United States, the famous island had become an exit.

Ellis Island closed in 1954 and in 1965, recognizing its historic importance, the government made it a national monument. It reopened in 1990 as a museum of American immigration, and is so popular it attracts more than two million tourists a year; many of whom retrace the footsteps of their own ancestors who had landed there. Stoyan Christowe's name is in the records. Starting with a miserable job in a railroad yard in St. Louis, he went to college, served in military intelligence during World War II, wrote several books, and became a member of the Vermont legislature.

His experience on Ellis Island blended into the nation's experience. More than 100 million Americans—about four in every ten—trace their ancestry to those who found a new home through its gates.

U.S. inspectors questioned and examined immigrants at Ellis Island. In this photograph from 1905, a woman is shown receiving an eye inspection. ◈

FOREIGN-BORN POPULATION, 1890 *Immigrants tended to settle in regions where jobs were relatively plentiful or conditions were similar to those they had left in their homelands. Cities of the northeast, Midwest, and West offered job opportunities, while land available for cultivation drew immigrant farmers to the plains and prairies of the nation's midsection.* ❖

crowd into northern and eastern cities, settling in areas where others of their nationality or religion lived. (See the Feature Essay, "Ellis Island: Isle of Hope, Isle of Tears," pp. 544–545.)

They were often dazzled by what they saw. They stared at electric lights, indoor plumbing, soda fountains, streetcars, plush train seats for all classes, ice cream, lemons, and bananas. Relatives whisked them off to buy new "American" clothes and showed them the teeming markets, department stores, and Woolworth's new five-and-ten stores. "It seemed quite advanced compared with our home in Khelm," said a Polish girl. "There was a sense of safety and hope that we had never felt in Poland."

Cities had increasingly large foreign-born populations. In 1900, four-fifths of Chicago's population was foreign born or of foreign-born parentage, two-thirds of Boston's, and one-half of Philadelphia's. New York City, where most immigrants arrived and many stayed, had more Italians than lived in Naples, more Germans than lived in Hamburg, and twice as many Irish as lived in Dublin. Four out of five New York City residents in 1890 were of foreign birth or foreign parentage.

Beginning in the 1880s, the sources of immigration shifted dramatically away from northern and western Europe, the chief source of immigration for more than two centuries. More and more immigrants came from southern and eastern Europe: Italy, Greece, Austria-Hungary, Poland, and Russia. Between 1880 and 1910, approximately 8.4 million people came from these lands. The **new immigrants** tended to be Catholics or Jews rather than Protestants. Like their predecessors, most were unskilled rather than skilled, and they often spoke "strange" languages. Most were poor and uneducated; sticking together in close-knit communities, they clung to their native customs, languages, and religions.

More than any previous group, the so-called new immigrants troubled the mainstream society. Could they be assimilated? Did they share "American" values? Such questions preoccupied groups like the American Protective Association, a midwestern anti-Catholic organization that expanded in the 1890s and worked to limit or end immigration. Sneering epithets became part of the national vocabulary: "wop" and "dago" for Italians; "bohunk" for Bohemians, Hungarians, and other Slavs; "greaseball" for Greeks; and "kike" for Jews. "You don't call . . . an Italian a white man?" a congressman asked a railroad construction boss in 1890. "No, sir," the boss replied. "An Italian is a Dago."

Anti-Catholicism and anti-Semitism flared up again, as they had in the 1850s. Edward A. Ross, a prominent sociologist, publicly decried "the lower class of Jews of Eastern Europe [who] reach here [as] moral cripples, their souls warped and dwarfed." In 1889, the head of the Fresh Air Fund, a program that sent New York City children on vacations to the suburbs, noted that "no one asked for Italian children." The Immigration Restriction League, founded in 1894, demanded a literacy test for immigrants from southern and eastern Europe. Congress passed such a law in 1896, but President Cleveland vetoed it.

Immigrants and the City

Industrial capitalism—the world of factories and foremen and grimy machines—tested the immigrants and placed an enormous strain on their families. Many immigrants came from peasant societies where life proceeded according to outdoor routine and age-old tradition. In their new city homes, they found both new freedoms and new confinements, a different language, and a novel set of customs and expectations. Historians have only recently begun to discover the remarkable ways in which they learned to adjust.

Like native-born families, most immigrant families were nuclear in structure—they consisted of two parents and their children. Though variations occurred from group to group, men and women occupied roles similar to those in native families: Men were wage earners, women were housekeepers and mothers.

Margaret Byington, who studied steelworkers' homes in Homestead in the early 1900s, learned that the father played a relatively small role in child rearing or managing the family's finances. "His part of the problem is to earn and hers to spend." In Chicago, social reformer Jane Addams discovered that immigrant women made it "a standard of domestic virtue that a man must not touch his pay envelope, but bring it home unopened to his wife."

Although patterns varied among ethnic groups, and between economic classes within ethnic groups, immigrants tended to marry within the group more than did the native born. In one New York community, only 2 percent of French Canadian and 7 percent of Irish workingmen married outside their ethnic group in 1880, compared to almost 40 percent of native-born workingmen. Immigrants also tended to marry at a later age than natives, and they tended to have more children, a fact that worried nativists opposed to immigration.

Immigrants shaped the city as much as it shaped them. Most of them tried to retain their traditional culture for themselves and their children while at the same time adapting to life in their new country. To do this, they spoke their native language, practiced their religious faith, read their own newspapers, and established special parochial or other schools. They observed traditional holidays and formed a myriad of social organizations to maintain ties among members of the group.

Immigrant associations—there were many of them in every city—offered fellowship in a strange land. They helped newcomers find jobs and homes; they provided important services such as unemployment insurance and health insurance. In a Massachusetts textile town, the Irish Benevolent Society said, "We visit our sick, and

In a Puck cartoon titled "Looking Backward," the shadows of their immigrant origins loom over the rich and powerful who wanted to deny the "new" immigrants from central and southern Europe admission to America. The caption on the cartoon reads, "They would close to the newcomer the bridge that carried them and their fathers over." ❖

The fiftieth-anniversary issue of the Illinois Staats Zeitung, the Chicago-area German-language newspaper with the largest circulation. There were more than twenty German-language newspapers distributed in Chicago in the 1890s. ❖

bury our dead." Some groups were no larger than a neighborhood; others spread nationwide. In 1914, the Deutsch-Amerikanischer Nationalbund, the largest of the associations, had more than two million members in dozens of cities and towns. Many women belonged to and participated in the work of the immigrant associations; in addition, there were groups exclusively for women, such as the Polish Women's Alliance, the Jednota Ceskyck Dam (Society of Czech Women), and the National Council of Jewish Women.

The Polish National Alliance (PNA), a typical immigrant association, was founded in 1880. Like other organizations, it helped new immigrants on their arrival, offered insurance plans, established libraries and museums, sponsored youth programs, fielded baseball teams, and organized trips back to Poland. Each year, the PNA published a sought-after calendar filled with Polish holidays, information, and proverbs. Extolling Poles' contributions to their new country, it erected monuments to distinguished Americans of Polish descent.

Every major city had dozens of foreign language newspapers, with circulations large and small. The first newspaper published in the Lithuanian language appeared in the United States, not in Lithuania. Eagerly read, the papers not only carried news of events in the homeland but also reported on local ethnic leaders, told readers how to vote and become citizens, and gave practical tips on adjusting to life in the United States. The Swedes, Poles, Czechs, and Germans established ethnic theaters that performed national plays and music. The most famous of these, the Yiddish (Jewish) Theater, started in the 1880s in New York City and lasted more than fifty years.

The church and the school were the most important institutions in every immigrant community. Eastern European Jews established synagogues and religious schools wherever they settled; they taught the Hebrew language and raised their children in a heritage they did not want to leave behind. Among such groups as the Irish and the Poles, the Roman Catholic church provided spiritual and educational guidance. In the parish schools, Polish priests and nuns taught Polish American children about Polish as well as American culture in the Polish language.

Church, school, and fraternal societies shaped the way in which immigrants adjusted to life in America. By preserving language, religion, and heritage, they also shaped the country itself.

The House That Tweed Built

Closely connected with explosive urban growth was the emergence of the powerful city political machine. As cities grew, lines of responsibility in city governments became hopelessly confused, increasing the opportunity for corruption and greed. Burgeoning populations required streets, buildings, and public services; immigrants needed even more services. In this situation, political party machines played an important role.

The machines traded services for votes. Loosely knit, they were headed by a strong, influential leader—the "boss"—who tied together a network of ward and precinct captains, each of whom looked after his local constituents. In New York, "Honest" John Kelly, Richard Croker, and Charles F. Murphy led Tammany Hall, the famous Democratic party organization that dominated city politics from the 1850s to the 1930s. Other bosses included "Hinky Dink" Kenna and "Bathhouse John" Coughlin in Chicago, James McManes in Philadelphia, and Christopher A. Buckley—the notorious "Blind Boss," who used an exceptional memory for voices to make up for failing eyesight—in San Francisco.

William M. Tweed, head of the famed Tweed Ring in New York, provided the model for them all. Nearly six feet tall, weighing almost three hundred pounds, Tweed rose through the ranks of Tammany Hall. He

❖ A Look at the Past ❖

Toy Bank

Political Boss William Tweed of Tammany Hall pockets money as a mechanical bank. This bank was first patented in the 1870s, after Tweed's fall from power in 1872, and it became a very popular model. While charming children with his moving hand and head that nodded thanks upon the deposit of a coin, the bank also satirized political machines, graft, and corruption. What does such a satirical toy suggest about attitudes toward political corruption at the time? Why do you think it was so popular?

served in turn as city alderman, member of Congress, and New York State assemblyman. A man of culture and warmth, he moved easily between the rough back alleys of New York and the parlors and clubs of the city's elite. Behind the scenes, he headed a ring that plundered New York for tens of millions of dollars.

The New York County Courthouse—"the house that Tweed built"—was his masterpiece. Nestled in City Hall Park in downtown Manhattan, the three-story structure was designed to cost $250,000, but the

bills ran a bit higher. Furniture, carpets, and window shades alone came to more than $5.5 million. Three tables and forty chairs cost the city $180,000. Tweed's own quarry supplied the marble; the plumber was paid almost $1.5 million for fixtures. Andrew Garvey, the "prince of plasterers," charged $500,000 for plaster-work, and then $1 million to repair the same work. His total bill came to $2,870,464.06. (The *New York Times* suggested that the six cents be donated to charity.) In the end, the building cost more than $13 million—and in 1872, when Tweed fell, it was still not finished.

The role of the political bosses can be overemphasized. Power structures in the turn-of-the-century city were complex, involving a host of people and institutions. Banks, real estate investors, insurance companies, architects, and engineers, among others, played roles in governing the city. Viewed in retrospect, many city governments were remarkably successful. With populations that in some cases doubled every decade, city governments provided water and sewer lines, built parks and playgrounds, and paved streets. When it was over, Boston had the world's largest public library and New York City had the Brooklyn Bridge and Central Park, two of the finest achievements in city planning and architecture of any era. By the 1890s, New York also had 660 miles of water lines, 464 miles of sewers, and 1800 miles of paved streets, far more than comparable cities in Europe.

Bosses, moreover, differed from city to city. Buckley stayed in power in San Francisco by keeping city tax rates low. "Honest" John Kelly earned his nickname serving as a watchdog over the New York City treasury. Tweed was one of the early backers of the Brooklyn Bridge. Some bosses were plainly corrupt; others believed in *honest graft*, a term Tammany's George Washington Plunkitt coined to describe "legitimate" profits made from advance knowledge of city projects.

Why did voters keep the bosses in power? The answers are complex, but two reasons were skillful political organization and the fact that immigrants and others made up the bosses' constituency. Most immigrants had little experience with democratic government and proved easy prey for well-oiled machines. For the most part, however, the bosses stayed in power because they paid attention to the needs of the least privileged city voters. They offered valued services in an era when neither government nor business lent a hand.

If an immigrant, tired and bewildered after the long crossing, came looking for a job, bosses like Tweed, Plunkitt, or Buckley found him one in city offices or local businesses. If a family's breadwinner died or was injured, the bosses donated food and clothing and saw to it that the family made it through the crisis. If the winter was particularly cold, they provided free coal to heat tenement apartments. They ran picnics for slum children on hot summer days and contributed to hospitals, orphanages, and dozens of worthy neighborhood causes.

Most bosses became wealthy; they were not Robin Hoods who took from the rich to give to the poor. They took for themselves as well. Reformers occasionally ousted them. Tweed fell from power in 1872, "Blind Boss" Buckley in 1891, Croker in 1894. But the reformers rarely stayed in power long. Drawn mainly from the middle and upper classes, they had little understanding of the needs of the poor. Before long, they returned to private concerns, and the bosses, who had known that they would all along, cheerily took power again.

"What tells in holdin' your grip on your district," the engaging Plunkitt once said, "is to go right down among the poor families and help them in the different ways they need help. . . . It's philanthropy, but it's politics, too—mighty good politics. . . . The poor are the most grateful people in the world."

SOCIAL AND CULTURAL CHANGE, 1877–1900

The rise of cities and industry between 1877 and the 1890s affected all aspects of American life. Mores changed; family ties loosened. Factories turned out consumer goods, and the newly invented cash register rang up record sales. Public and private educational systems burgeoned, illiteracy declined, life expectancy increased. While many people worked harder and harder just to survive, others found they had a greater amount of leisure time. The roles of women and children changed in a number of ways, and the family took on functions it had not had before. Thanks to advancing technology, news flashed quickly across the oceans, and for the first time in history, people read of the day's events in distant lands when they opened their daily newspapers.

"We are in a period," President Rutherford B. Hayes said in 1878, "when old questions are settled, and the new ones are not yet brought forward." Old questions—questions of racial, social and economic justice, and of federal-state relations—were not settled, but people wanted new directions. Political issues lost the sharp focus of the Civil War and Reconstruction. For men and women of middle age in 1877, the issues of the Union and slavery had been the overriding public concerns throughout their adult lives. Now, with the end of Reconstruction, it seemed time for new concerns.

In 1877, the country had 47 million people. In 1900, it had nearly 76 million. Nine-tenths of the population was white; just under one-tenth was black. There were 66,000 American Indians, 108,000

Chinese, and 148 Japanese. The bulk of the white population, most of whom were Protestant, came from the so-called Anglo-Saxon countries of northern Europe. WASPs—white Anglo-Saxon Protestants—were the dominant members of American society.

Though the rush to the cities was about to begin, most people of 1877 still lived on farms or in small towns. Their lives revolved around the farm, the church, and the general store. In 1880, nearly 75 percent of the population lived in communities of fewer than 2500 people. In 1900, in the midst of city growth, 60 percent still did. The average family in 1880 had three children, dramatically fewer than at the beginning of the century, and life expectancy was about 43 years. By 1900, it had risen to 47 years, a result of improved health care. For blacks and other minorities, who often lived in unsanitary rural areas, life expectancy was substantially lower: 33 years.

In small towns, houses were usually made of wooden shingles or clapboard, set back from unpaved streets. Life was quiet. Many homes had a front porch for summertime sitting. In the backyard there were numerous outbuildings, including one—at the end of a well-worn path—with a distinctive half moon carved in the door. There was a vegetable garden and often a chicken coop or cowshed; families—even in the cities—needed backyard produce to supplement their diets.

Meals tended to be heavy, and so did people. Even breakfast had several courses and could include steak, eggs, fish, potatoes, toast, and coffee. Food prices were

URBAN AND RURAL POPULATION, 1870–1900 (IN MILLIONS)

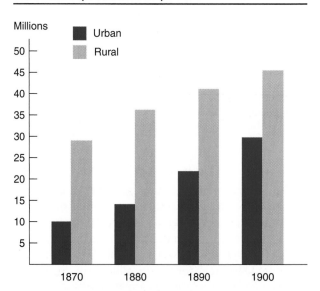

Source: U.S. Bureau of the Census, *Historical Statistics of the United States, Colonial Times to 1970,* Bicentennial Edition, Washington, DC, 1975.

low. Families ate fresh homegrown produce in the summer and "put up" their fruits and vegetables for the long winters. Toward the end of the century, eating habits changed. New packaged breakfast cereals became popular; fresh fruit and vegetables came in on fast trains from Florida and California, and commercially canned food became safer and cheaper. The newfangled icebox, cooled by blocks of ice, kept food fresher and added new treats such as ice cream.

Medical science was in the midst of a major revolution. Louis Pasteur's recent discovery that germs cause infection and disease created the new science of microbiology and led the way to the development of vaccines and other preventive measures. But tuberculosis, typhoid, diphtheria, and pneumonia—all now curable—were still the leading causes of death. Infant mortality declined between 1877 and 1900, but the decline was gradual; a great drop did not come until after 1920.

There were few hospitals and no hospital insurance. Most patients stayed at home, although medical practice, especially surgery, expanded rapidly. Once brutal and dangerous, surgery in these years became relatively safe and painless. Anesthetics—ether and chloroform—eliminated pain, and antiseptic practices helped prevent postoperative infections. Antiseptic practices at childbirth also cut down on puerperal fever, an infection that for centuries had killed many women and newborn infants. The new science of psychology began to explore the mind, hitherto uncharted. William James, a leading American psychologist and philosopher, laid the foundations of modern behavioral psychology, which stressed the importance of the environment on human development.

Manners and Mores

The code of Victorian morality, its name derived from the British queen who reigned throughout the period, set the tone for the era. The code prescribed strict standards of dress, manners, and sexual behavior. It was both obeyed and disobeyed, and it reflected the tensions of a generation that was undergoing a change in moral standards.

In 1877, children were to be seen and not heard. They spoke when spoken to, listened rather than chattered—or at least that was the rule. Older boys and girls were often chaperoned, although they could always find moments alone. They played post office and spin the bottle; they puffed cigarettes behind the barn. Journalist William Allen White recalled the high jinks of his boyhood. He and his friends smeared their naked bodies with mud and leaped out in full view of passengers on passing trains. Counterbalancing such youthful exuberance was strong pride in virtue and

Victorian fashion ideals for women emphasized elaborate, confining dress styles with a tiny waistline and full skirts that reached to the floor. Throughout the 1890s, as women began to participate in some of the new sports or go to work in factories, stores, or business offices, styles gradually became less restrictive. This 1900 cover of Ladies' Home Journal shows women wearing tailored jackets and simple pleated skirts hemmed above the ankle playing golf with men. ❖

self-control. "Thank heaven I am absolutely pure," Theodore Roosevelt, the future president, wrote in 1880 after proposing to Alice Lee. "I can tell Alice everything I have ever done."

Gentlemen of the middle class dressed in heavy black suits, derby hats, and white shirts with paper collars. Women wore tight corsets, long dark dresses, and black shoes reaching well above the ankles. As with so many things, styles changed dramatically toward the end of the century, spurred in part by new sporting fads such as golf, tennis, and bicycling, which required looser clothing. By the 1890s, a middle-class woman wore a tailored suit or a dark skirt and a blouse, called a shirtwaist, modeled after men's shirts. Her skirts still draped about the ankles, but more and more she removed or loosened the corset, the dread device that squeezed skin and internal organs into fashionable 18-inch waistlines.

Religious and patriotic values were strong. A center of community life, the church often set the tenor for family and social relationships. In the 1880s, eight out of ten church members were Protestants; most of the rest were Roman Catholics. Evangelists such as Dwight L. Moody (a former Chicago shoe salesman) and Ira B. Sankey (an organist and singer) conducted mass revival meetings across the country. Enormously successful, Moody preached to millions and sparked a spiritual awakening on American college campuses.

With slavery abolished, reformers turned their attention to new moral and political issues. One group, known as the **Mugwumps,** worked to end corruption in politics. Drawn mostly from the educated and upper class, they included Thomas Nast, the famous political cartoonist; George William Curtis, editor of *Harper's Weekly;* and E. L. Godkin, editor of the influential *Nation.* Other zealous reformers campaigned for prohibition of the sale of intoxicating liquors, hoping to end the social evils that stemmed from drunkenness. In 1874, women who advocated total abstinence from alcoholic beverages formed the **Women's Christian Temperance Union (WCTU).** Their leader, Frances E. Willard, served as president of the group from 1879 until her death in 1898. By then, the WCTU had 10,000 branches and 500,000 members.

In New York City, Anthony Comstock formed the Society for the Suppression of Vice, which supervised public morality. At his request, Congress passed the Comstock Law (1873) prohibiting the mailing or transporting of "obscene, lewd or lascivious" articles. The law was not successful; within a few years, Comstock reported finding 64,094 "articles for immoral use," 700 pounds of "lead moulds for making obscene matter," 202,679 obscene photographs, and 26 "obscene pictures, framed on walls of saloons."

Leisure and Entertainment

In the 1870s, people tended to rise early. On getting up, they washed from the pitcher and bowl in the bedroom, first breaking the layer of ice if it was winter. After dressing and eating, they went off to work and school. Without large refrigerators, housewives marketed almost daily. In the evening, families gathered in the "second parlor" or living room, where the children did their lessons, played games, sang around the piano, and listened to that day's verse from the Bible.

Popular games included cards, dominoes, backgammon, chess, and checkers. Many homes had a packet of "author cards" that required knowledge of books, authors, and noted quotations. The latest fad was the stereopticon or "magic lantern," which brought three-dimensional life to art, history, and

nature. Like author cards and other games, it was instructional as well as entertaining.

The newest outdoor game was croquet, so popular that candles were mounted on the wickets to allow play at night. Croquet was the first outdoor game designed for play by both sexes, and it frequently served as a setting for courtship. Early manuals advised girls how to assume attractive poses while hitting the ball. A popular song of the period told of a pair seated side by side:

> Mallets and balls unheeded lay . . .
> And I thought to myself, is that Croquet?

Sentimental ballads such as "Silver Threads Among the Gold" (1873) remained the most popular musical form, but the insistent syncopated rhythms of ragtime were being heard, reflecting the influence of the new urban culture. By the time the strains of Scott Joplin's "Maple Leaf Rag" (1899) popularized ragtime, critics complained that "a wave of vulgar, filthy and suggestive music has inundated the land." Classical music flour-

The Sells Brothers promised a world of entertainment to the patrons of their circus, which featured—according to this poster— an Australian aviary, an African aquarium, a Roman hippodrome, and an exhibit of trans-Pacific wild beasts. The principal act of the three-ring circus, however, promised to be the spectacular bareback riding of equestrienne Polly Lee. ❖

As early as 1866, Currier and Ives described baseball as the "American National Game." Although we can recognize some similarities between the game portrayed here and the modern game of baseball, there are also some notable differences. For example, the players depicted in the lithograph do not wear any protective gear: The batter wears no batting helmet, the catcher has no face mask or chest protector, and none of the players appear to wear a baseball glove. ❖

ished. The New England Conservatory (1867), the Cincinnati College of Music (1878), and the Metropolitan Opera (1883) were new sources of civic pride; New York, Boston, and Chicago launched first-rate symphony orchestras between 1878 and 1891.

In the hamlets and small towns of America, traveling circuses were enormously popular. Hamlin Garland, an author who grew up in small Iowa villages, recalled how the circus came "trailing clouds of glorified dust and filling our minds with the color of romance. . . . It brought to our ears the latest band pieces and taught us the popular songs. It furnished us with jokes. It relieved our dullness. It gave us something to talk about." Larger circuses, run by entrepreneurs such as P. T. Barnum and James A. Bailey, played the cities, but every town attracted its own smaller version.

Fairs, horse races, balloon ascensions, bicycle tournaments, and football and baseball contests attracted avid fans. The years between 1870 and 1900 saw the rise of organized spectator sports, a trend reflecting both the rise of the city and the new uses of leisure. Baseball's first professional team, the Cincinnati Red Stockings, appeared in 1869, and baseball soon became the preeminent national sport. Fans sang songs about it ("Take Me Out to the Ballgame"), wrote poems about it ("Casey at the Bat"), and made up riddles about it ("What has eighteen feet and catches flies?"). Modern rules were adopted. Umpires were designated to call balls and strikes; catchers wore masks and chest protectors and

moved closer to the plate instead of staying back to catch the ball on the bounce. Fielders had to catch the ball on the fly rather than on one bounce in their caps. By 1890, professional baseball teams were drawing crowds of sixty thousand daily. In 1901, the American League was organized, and two years later the Boston Red Sox beat the Pittsburgh Pirates in the first modern World Series.

In 1869, Princeton and Rutgers played the first intercollegiate football game. Soon, other schools picked up the sport, and by the early 1890s, crowds of fifty thousand or more attended the most popular contests. Basketball, invented in 1891, gained a large following. Boxing, a popular topic of conversation in saloons and schoolyards, was outlawed in most states. For a time, championship prizefights were held in secret, with news of the result spread rapidly by word of mouth. Matches were long and bloody, fought with bare knuckles until the invention in the 1880s of the 5-ounce boxing glove. John L. Sullivan, the "Boston Strong Boy" and the era's most popular champion, won the heavyweight title in 1889 in a brutal 75-round victory over the stubborn Jake Kilrain.

As gas and electric lights brightened the night, and streetcars crisscrossed city streets, leisure habits changed. Delighted with the new technology, people took advantage of an increasing variety of things to do. They stayed home less often. New York City's first electric sign—"Manhattan Beach Swept by Ocean

Breezes"—appeared in 1881, and people went out at night filling the streets on their way to the theater, vaudeville shows, and dance halls or just out for an evening stroll.

Changes in Family Life

Under the impact of industrialization and urbanization, family relationships were changing. On the farm, parents and children worked more or less together, and the family was a producing unit. In factories and offices, family members rarely worked together. In working-class families, mothers, fathers, and children separated at dawn and returned, ready for sleep, at dark. Morris Rosenfeld, a clothing presser lamenting that he was unable to spend more time with his son, wrote a poem titled "My Boy":

> I have a little boy at home,
> A pretty little son;
> I think sometimes the world is mine
> In him, my only one. . . .
>
> 'Ere dawn my labor drives me forth;
> Tis night when I am free;
> A stranger am I to my child;
> And stranger my child to me.

Working-class families of the late nineteenth century, like the family of the young Polish girl that Harriet Vittum saw, often lived in complex household units—taking in relatives and boarders to pay the rent. As many as one-third of all households contained people who were not members of the immediate family. Although driven apart by the daily routine, family ties among the working class tended to remain strong, cemented by the need to join forces in order to survive in the industrial economy.

The middle-class wife and children, however, became increasingly isolated from the world of work. Turning inward, the middle-class family became more self-contained. Older children spent more time in adolescence, and periods of formal schooling were lengthier. Families took in fewer apprentices and boarders. By the end of the century, most middle-class offspring continued to live with their parents into their late teens and their twenties, a larger proportion than today.

Fewer middle-class wives participated directly in their husbands' work. As a result, they and their children occupied what contemporaries called a "separate sphere of domesticity," set apart from the masculine sphere of income-producing work. The family home became a "walled garden," a place to retreat from the crass materialism of the outside world. Middle-class fathers began to move their families out of the city to the suburbs, commuting to work on the new streetcars and leaving wives and children at home and school.

The middle-class family had once functioned in part to transmit a craft or skill, arrange marriages, and offer care for dependent kin. Now, as these functions declined, the family took on new emotional and ideological responsibilities. In a society that worried about the weakening hold of other institutions, the family became more and more important as a means of social control. It also placed new burdens on wives.

"In the old days," said a woman in 1907, "a married woman was supposed to be a frump and a bore and a physical wreck. Now you are supposed to keep up intellectually, to look young and well and be fresh and bright and entertaining." Magazines such as the *Ladies' Home Journal,* which started in 1889, glorified motherhood and the home, but its articles and ads featured women as homebound, child-oriented consumers. While society's leaders spoke fondly of the value of homemaking, the status of housewives declined under the factory system, which emphasized money rewards and devalued household labor.

Underlying all these changes was one of the modern world's most important trends, a major decline in fertility rates that lasted from 1800 to 1939. Though blacks, immigrants, and rural dwellers continued to have more children than white native-born city dwellers, the trend affected all classes and races; among white women, the birthrate fell from seven in 1800 to just over four in 1880 to about three in 1900. People everywhere tended to marry later and have fewer children.

Since contraceptive devices were not yet widely used, the decline reflected abstinence and a conscious decision to postpone or limit families. Some women decided to devote greater attention to a smaller number of children, others to pursue their own careers. There was a marked increase in the number of young unmarried women working for wages or attending school, an increase in the number of women delaying marriage or not marrying at all, and a gradual decline in rates of illegitimacy and premarital pregnancy.

In large part, the decline in fertility stemmed from people's responses to the social and economic forces around them, the rise of cities and industry. In a host of individual decisions, they decided to have fewer children, and the result reshaped some of the fundamental attitudes and institutions of American society.

Changing Views: A Growing Assertiveness Among Women

In and out of the family, there was growing recognition of self-sufficient working women, employed in factory, telephone exchange, or business office, who were entering the workforce in increasing numbers. In

Female operators, called "hello girls," were hired to work telephone switchboards after it was discovered that male operators tended to argue too much with subscribers. As suggested by this photograph of operators working an early switchboard with a tangle of intersecting wires, it was a tough job that required patience. ❖

1880, 2.6 million women were gainfully employed; in 1890, 4 million. In 1882, the Census Bureau took the first census of working women; most were single and worked out of necessity rather than choice.

Many regarded this "new woman" as a corruption of the ideal vision of the American woman, in which man worshiped "a diviner self than his own," innocent, helpless, and good. Women were to be better than the world around them. They were brought up, said Ida Tarbell, a leading political reformer, "as if wrongdoing were impossible to them."

Views changed, albeit slowly. One important change occurred in the legal codes pertaining to women, particularly in the common law doctrine of *femme couverte.* Under that doctrine, wives were chattel of their husbands; they could not legally control their own earnings, property, or children unless they had drawn up a specific contract before marriage. By 1890, many states had substantially revised the doctrine to allow wives control of their earnings and inherited property. (See "The Legal Rights of Married Women: Reforming the Law of Coverture," pp. 354–357.) In cases of divorce, the new laws also

recognized women's rights to custody or joint custody of their children. Although divorce was still far from being socially acceptable, divorce rates more than doubled during the last third of the century. By 1905, one in twelve marriages was ending in divorce.

In the 1870s and 1880s, a growing number of women were asserting their own humanness. They fought for the vote, lobbied for equal pay, and sought self-fulfillment. The new interest in psychology and medicine strengthened their causes. Charlotte Perkins Gilman, author of *Women and Economics* (1898), joined other women in questioning the ideal of womanly "innocence," which, she argued, actually meant ignorance. In medical and popular literature, menstruation, sexual intercourse, and childbirth were becoming viewed as natural functions instead of taboo topics.

Edward Bliss Foote's *Plain Home Talk of Love, Marriage, and Parentage,* a best-seller that went through many editions between the 1880s and 1900, challenged Victorian notions that sexual intercourse was unhealthy and intended solely to produce children. In *Plain Facts for Old and Young* (1881), Dr. John H. Kellogg urged parents to recognize the early awakening of sexual feelings in their children. Still, such matters were avoided in many American homes. Rheta Childe Dorr, a journalist, remembered that when a girl reached the age of 14, new rules were introduced, "and when you asked for an explanation you met only embarrassed silence."

Women espoused causes with new fervor. Susan B. Anthony, a veteran of many reform campaigns, tried to vote in the 1872 presidential election and was fined $100, which she refused to pay. In 1890, she helped form the **National American Woman Suffrage Association** to work for the enfranchisement of women. On New York's Lower East Side, the Ladies Anti–Beef Trust Association, which formed to protest increases in the price of meat, established a boycott of butcher shops. When their demands were ignored, the women invaded the shops, poured kerosene on the meat, and set fire to it. "We don't riot," Rebecca Ablowitz told the judge. "But if all we did was to weep at home, nobody would notice it; so we have to do something to help ourselves."

Educating the Masses

Continuing a trend that stretched back a hundred years, childhood was becoming an even more distinct time of life. There was still only a vague concept of adolescence—the special nature of the teenage years—but the role of children was changing. Less and less were children perceived as "little adults," valued for the additional financial gain they might bring into the family. Now children were to grow and learn and be nurtured rather than rushed into adulthood.

As a result, schooling became more important, and American children came closer than ever before to universal education. By 1900, thirty-one states and territories (out of fifty-one) had enacted laws making school attendance compulsory, though most required attendance only until the age of 14. In 1870, there were only 160 public high schools; in 1900, there were 6000. In the same years, public school budgets rose from $63 million to $253 million; illiteracy declined from 20 percent to just over 10 percent of the population. Still, even as late as 1900, the average adult had only five years of schooling.

Educators saw the school as the primary means to train people for life and work in an industrializing society. Hence teachers focused on basic skills—reading and mathematics—and on values—obedience and attentiveness to the clock. Most schools had a highly structured curriculum, built around discipline and routine. In 1892, Joseph Rice, a pediatrician, toured twelve hundred classrooms in thirty-six cities. In a typical classroom, he reported, the atmosphere was "damp and chilly," the teacher strict. "The unkindly spirit of the teacher is strikingly apparent; the pupils being completely subjugated to her will, are silent and motionless." One teacher asked her pupils,

Schools, regarded primarily as training grounds for a life of work, stressed conformity and deportment—feet on the floor, hands folded and resting atop the desk. The teacher was drillmaster and disciplinarian as well as instructor. ❖

"How can you learn anything with your knees and toes out of order?"

Many children dropped out of school early, and not just to earn money. Helen Todd, a factory inspector in Chicago, found a group of young girls working in a hot, stuffy attic. When she asked why they were not in school, Tillie Isakowsky, who was 14, said, "School! School is de fiercest t'ing youse kin come up against. Factories ain't no cinch, but schools is worst." A few blocks away, Todd stumbled on a 13-year-old boy hiding in a basement. He cried when she said he would have to go to school, blurting that "they hits ye if yer don't learn, and they hits ye if ye whisper, and they hits ye if ye have string in yer pocket, and they hits ye if yer seat squeaks, and they hits ye if ye don't stan' up in time, and they hits ye if yer late, and they hits ye if ye ferget the page." Curious, Todd asked 500 children whether they would go to school or work in a factory if their families did not need the money—412 preferred the factory.

School began early; boys attended all day, but girls often stayed home after lunch, since it was thought they needed less in the way of learning. On the teacher's command, students stood and recited from *Webster's Spellers* and *McGuffey's Eclectic Readers*, the period's most popular textbooks. The work of William Holmes McGuffey, a professor of languages at Miami University in Ohio, *McGuffey's Eclectic Readers* had been in use since 1836; 100 million copies were sold in the last half of the nineteenth century. Nearly every child read them; they taught not only reading but also ethics, values, and religion. In the *Readers*, boys grew up to be heroes, girls to be mothers, and hard work always meant success:

> Shall birds, and bees, and ants, be wise,
>   While I my moments waste?
> O let me with the morning rise,
>   And to my duty haste.

The South lagged far behind in education. The average family size there was about twice as large as in the North, and a greater proportion of the population lived in isolated rural areas. State and local authorities mandated fewer weeks in the average school year, and many southern states refused to adopt compulsory education laws. Even more important was the effect of Southern Jim Crow laws, passed in the 1890s and after to keep African Americans from voting, serving on juries, and participating in other aspects of Southern life. Southerners used these laws to maintain separate school systems to segregate the races. Supported by the U.S. Supreme Court decision of 1896 in **Plessy v. Ferguson** (see "The Shaping of Jim Crow," pp. 567–570), segregated schooling added a devastating financial burden to education in the South.

North Carolina and Alabama mandated segregated schools in 1876, South Carolina and Louisiana in 1877, Mississippi in 1878, and Virginia in 1882. A series of Supreme Court decisions in the 1880s and 1890s upheld the concept of segregation. In the *Civil Rights Cases* (1883), the Court ruled that the Fourteenth Amendment barred state governments from discriminating on account of race but did not prevent private individuals or organizations from doing so. *Plessy* v. *Ferguson* (1896) established the doctrine of "separate but equal" and upheld a Louisiana law requiring different railroad cars for whites and blacks. The Court applied the doctrine directly to schools in *Cumming* v. *County Board of Education* (1899), which approved the creation of separate schools for whites, even if there were no comparable schools for blacks.

Southern school laws often implied that the schools would be "separate but equal," and they were often separate but rarely equal. Black schools were usually dilapidated, and black teachers were paid considerably less than white teachers. In 1890, only 35 percent of black children attended school in the South; 55 percent of white children did. That year nearly two-thirds of the country's black population was illiterate.

Educational techniques changed after the 1870s. Educators paid more attention to early elementary education, a trend that placed young children in school and helped the growing number of mothers who worked outside the home. The kindergarten movement, started in St. Louis in 1873, spread across the country. In kindergartens, 4- to 6-year-old children learned by playing, not by keeping their knees and toes in order. For older children, social reformers advocated "practical" courses in manual training and homemaking. "We are impatient with the schools which lay all stress on reading and writing," Jane Addams said, for "they fail to give the child any clew to the life about him."

For the first time, education became a field of university study. European theorists such as Johann Friedrich Herbart, a German educator, argued that learning occurred best in an atmosphere of freedom and confidence between teachers and pupils. Teacher training became increasingly professional. Only 10 normal schools, or teacher training institutions, existed in the United States before the Civil War. By 1900, there were 345, and one in every five elementary teachers had graduated from a professional school.

Higher Education

Nearly 150 new colleges and universities opened in the twenty years between 1880 and 1900. The Morrill Land Grant Act of 1862 gave large grants of land to the states for the establishment of colleges to teach "agriculture and the mechanic arts." The act fostered 69 "land-grant" institutions, including the great state universities of Wisconsin, California, Minnesota, and Illinois.

Private philanthropy, born of the large fortunes of the industrial age, also spurred growth in higher education. Leland Stanford gave $24 million to endow Stanford University on his California ranch, and John D. Rockefeller, founder of the Standard Oil Company, gave $34 million to found the University of Chicago. Other industrialists established Cornell (1865), Vanderbilt (1873), and Tulane (1884).

As colleges expanded, their function changed and their curriculum broadened. No longer did they exist primarily to train young men for the ministry. They moved away from the classical curriculum of rhetoric, mathematics, Latin, and Greek toward "reality and practicality," as President David Starr Jordan of Stanford University said. The Massachusetts Institute of Technology (MIT), founded in 1861, focused on science and engineering.

Influenced by the new German universities, which emphasized specialized research, Johns Hopkins University in Baltimore opened the nation's first separate graduate school in 1876. Under President Daniel Coit Gilman, Johns Hopkins stressed the seminar and laboratory as teaching tools, bringing together student and teacher in close association.

Charles W. Eliot, who became president of Harvard in 1869 at the age of 35, moved to end, as an admirer said, the "old fogyism" that marked the institution. Revising the curriculum, Eliot set up the elective system, in which students chose their own courses rather than following a rigidly prescribed curriculum. Lectures and discussions replaced rote recitation, and courses in the natural and social sciences, fine arts, and modern languages multiplied. In the 1890s, Eliot's Harvard moved to the forefront of educational innovation.

Women still had to fight for educational opportunities. Some formed study clubs, an important movement that spread rapidly between 1870 and 1900. Groups such as the Decatur (Illinois) Art Class, the Boston History Class, and the Barnesville (Georgia) Shakespeare Club aimed "to enlarge the mental horizon as well as the knowledge of our members." Club members read Virgil and Chaucer, studied history and architecture, and discussed women's rights. As the Monday Club of Mount Vernon, Ohio, put it:

In ancient days when Monday came
We used our clothes to rub,
And set them boiling on the stove,
And stir them with a club.
But, Oh, our Monday Club today

Is quite a different stick;
For we've abandoned household toils
And learned a better trick.

. . . .

And with it, just as Moses did,
We drive the waves apart,
And enter on the promised land
Of learning and of art.

Clubs sprang up almost everywhere there were women: in Caribou, Maine; Tyler, Texas; and Leadville, Colorado—as well as San Francisco, New York, and Boston. Although they were usually small, study clubs sparked a greater interest in education among women and their daughters and contributed to a rapid rise in the number of women entering college in the early 1900s.

Before the Civil War, only three private colleges admitted women to study with men. After the war, educational opportunities increased for women. A number of women's colleges opened, including Vassar (1865), Wellesley (1875), Smith (1875), Bryn Mawr (1885), Barnard (1889), and Radcliffe (1893). The land-grant colleges of the Midwest, open to women from the outset, spurred a nationwide trend toward coeducation, although some physicians, such as Harvard Medical School's Dr. Edward H. Clarke in his popular *Sex in Education* (1873), continued to argue that the strain of learning made women sterile. By 1900, women made up about 40 percent of college students, and four out of five colleges admitted them.

Fewer opportunities existed for African Americans and other minorities. Jane Stanford encouraged the Chinese who had worked on her husband's Central Pacific Railroad to apply to Stanford University, but her policy was unusual. Most colleges did not accept minority students, and only a few applied. W. E. B. Du Bois, the brilliant African American sociologist and civil rights leader, attended Harvard in the late 1880s but found the society of Harvard Yard closed against him. Disdained and disdainful, he "asked no fellowship of my fellow students." Chosen as one of the commencement speakers, Du Bois picked as his topic "Jefferson Davis," treating it, said an onlooker, with "an almost contemptuous fairness."

Black students turned to black colleges such as the Hampton Normal and Industrial Institute in Virginia and the Tuskegee Institute in Alabama. These colleges were often supported by whites who favored manual training for blacks. Booker T. Washington, an ex-slave, put into practice his educational ideas at Tuskegee, which opened in 1881. Washington began Tuskegee with limited funds, four run-down buildings, and only thirty students; by 1900, it was a model industrial and agricultural school. Spread over forty-six buildings, it offered instruction in thirty trades to fourteen hundred students.

A physics lecture at the University of Michigan in the late 1880s or early 1890s. The land-grant university admitted women, but seating in the lecture hall was segregated by gender—although not by race. Notice that both whites and African Americans are seated in the back rows of the men's section. ❖

Booker T. Washington, who served as the first president of Tuskegee Institute, advocated work efficiency and practical skills as keys to advancement for African Americans. Students like these at Tuskegee studied academic subjects and received training in trades and professions. ❖

Washington stressed patience, manual training, and hard work. "The wisest among my race understand," he said in a widely acclaimed speech at the Atlanta Exposition in 1895, "that the agitation of questions of social equality is the extremest folly." Blacks should focus on economic gains; they should go to school, learn skills, and work their way up the ladder. "No race," he said at Atlanta, "can prosper till it learns that there is as much dignity in tilling a field as in writing a poem. It is at the bottom of life we must begin, and not at the top." Southern whites should help out because they would then have "the most patient, faithful, law-abiding, and unresentful people that the world has seen."

Outlined most forcefully in Washington's speech in Atlanta, the philosophy became known as the Atlanta Compromise, and many whites and some blacks welcomed it. Acknowledging white domination, it called for slow progress through self-improvement, not through lawsuits or agitation. Rather than fighting for equal rights, blacks should acquire property and show they were worthy of their rights. But Washington did believe in black equality. Often secretive in his methods, he worked behind the scenes to organize black voters and lobby against harmful laws. In his own way, he bespoke a racial pride that contributed to the rise of black nationalism in the twentieth century.

Du Bois wanted a more aggressive strategy. Born in Massachusetts in 1868, the son of poor parents, he studied at Fisk University in Tennessee and the University of Berlin before he went to Harvard. Unable to find a teaching job in a white college, he took a low-paying research position at the University of Pennsylvania. He had no office but did not need one. Du Bois used the new discipline of sociology, which emphasized factual observation in the field, to study the condition of blacks.

Notebook in hand, he set out to examine crime in Philadelphia's black seventh ward. He interviewed five thousand people, mapped and classified neighborhoods, and produced *The Philadelphia Negro* (1898). The first study of the effect of urban life on blacks, it cited a wealth of statistics, all suggesting that crime in the ward stemmed not from inborn degeneracy but from the environment in which blacks lived. Change the environment, and people would change, too; education was a good way to go about it.

In *The Souls of Black Folk* (1903), Du Bois openly attacked Booker T. Washington and the philosophy of the Atlanta Compromise. He urged African Americans to aspire to professional careers, to fight for the restoration of their civil rights, and, wherever possible, to get a college education. Calling for integrated schools with equal opportunity for all, Du Bois urged blacks to educate their "talented tenth," a highly trained intellectual elite, to lead them.

Du Bois was not alone in promoting careers in the professions. Throughout higher education there was increased emphasis on professional training, particularly in medicine, dentistry, and law. Enrollments swelled, even as standards of admission tightened. The number of medical schools in the country rose from 75 in 1870 to 160 in 1900, and the number of medical students—including more and more women—almost tripled. Schools of nursing grew from only 15 in 1880 to 432 in 1900. Doctors, lawyers, and others became part of a growing middle class that shaped the concerns of the Progressive Era of the early twentieth century.

Although less than 5 percent of the college-age population attended college during the 1877–1890 period, the new trends had great impact. A generation of men and women encountered new ideas that changed their views of themselves and society. Courses never before offered, such as Philosophy II at Harvard, "The

Ethics of Social Reform," which students called "drainage, drunkenness, and divorce," heightened interest in social problems and the need for reform. Some graduating students burned with a desire to cure society's ills. "My life began . . . at Johns Hopkins University," Frederic C. Howe, an influential reformer, recalled. "I came alive, I felt a sense of responsibility to the world, I wanted to change things."

THE STIRRINGS OF REFORM

When Henry George, one of the era's leading reformers, asked a friend what could be done about the problem of political corruption in American cities, his friend replied: "Nothing! You and I can do nothing at all. . . . We can only wait for evolution. Perhaps in four or five thousand years evolution may have carried men beyond this state of things."

This stress on the slow pace of change reflected the doctrine of **social Darwinism,** based on the writings of English social philosopher Herbert Spencer. In several influential books, Spencer took the evolutionary theories of Charles Darwin and applied Darwinian principles of natural selection to society, combining biology and sociology in a theory of "social selection" that tried to explain human progress. Like animals, society evolved, slowly, by adapting to the environment. The "survival of the fittest"—a term that Spencer, not Darwin, invented—preserved the strong and weeded out the weak. "If they are sufficiently complete to live, they do live, and it is well they should live. If they are not sufficiently complete to live, they die, and it is best they should die."

Social Darwinism had a number of influential followers in the United States, including William Graham Sumner, a professor of political and social science at Yale University. One of the country's best known academic figures, Sumner was forceful and eloquent. In writings such as *What Social Classes Owe to Each Other* (1883) and "The Absurd Effort to Make the World Over" (1894), he argued that government action on behalf of the poor or weak interfered with evolution and sapped the species. Reform tampered with the laws of nature. "It is the greatest folly of which a man can be capable to sit down with a slate and pencil to plan out a new social world," Sumner said.

The influence of social Darwinism on American thinking has been exaggerated, but in the powerful hands of Sumner and others it did influence some journalists, ministers, and policymakers. Between 1877 and the 1890s, however, it came under increasing attack. In fields such as religion, economics, politics, literature, and law, thoughtful people raised questions about established conditions and suggested the need for reform.

Progress and Poverty

Read and reread, passed from hand to hand, Henry George's nationwide best-seller *Progress and Poverty* (1879) led the way to a more critical appraisal of American society in the 1880s and beyond. The book jolted traditional thought. "It was responsible," one historian has said, "for starting along new lines of thinking an amazing number of the men and women" who became leaders of reform.

Born in 1839, the child of a poor Philadelphia family, George had little formal schooling. As a boy he went to sea; he also worked as a prospector, printer, and journalist. Self-educated as an economist, he moved to San Francisco in the late 1850s and began to study "the fierce struggle of our civilized life." Disturbed by the depression of the 1870s and labor upheavals such as the great railroad strikes of 1877, George saw modern society—rich, complex, with material goods hitherto unknown—as sadly flawed.

"The present century," he wrote, "has been marked by a prodigious increase in wealth-producing power. . . . It was natural to expect, and it was expected, that . . . real poverty [would become] a thing of the past." Instead, he argued:

> it becomes no easier for the masses of our people to make a living. On the contrary, it is becoming harder. The wealthy class is becoming more wealthy; but the poorer class is becoming more dependent. The gulf between the employed and the employer is growing wider; social contrasts are becoming sharper; as liveried carriages appear, so do barefooted children.

George proposed a simple solution. Land, he thought, formed the basis of wealth, and a few people could grow wealthy just because the price of their land rose. Since the rise in price did not result from any effort on their part, it represented an "unearned increment," which, George argued, should be taxed for the good of society. A "single tax" on the increment, replacing all other taxes, would help equalize wealth and raise revenue to aid the poor. "Single-tax" clubs sprang up around the country, but George's solution, simplistic and unappealing, had much less impact than his analysis of the problem itself. He raised questions a generation of readers set out to answer.

New Currents in Social Thought

George's emphasis on deprivation in the environment excited a young country lawyer in Ashtabula, Ohio—Clarence Darrow. Unlike the social Darwinists, Darrow was sure that criminals were made and not born. They grew out of "the unjust condition of human life." In the mid-1880s, he left for Chicago and a forty-year career working to convince people that poverty lay at the root of crime. "There is no such thing as crime as the word is generally understood," he told a group of startled prisoners in the Cook County jail. "If every man, woman and child in the world had a chance to make a decent, fair, honest living there would be no jails and no lawyers and no courts."

As Darrow rejected the implications of social Darwinism, in similar fashion Richard T. Ely and a group of young economists poked holes in traditional economic thought. Fresh from graduate study in Germany, Ely in 1884 attacked classical economics for its dogmatism, simple faith in laissez-faire, and reliance on self-interest as a guide for human conduct. The "younger" economics, he said, must no longer be "a tool in the hands of the greedy and the avaricious for keeping down and oppressing the laboring classes. It does not acknowledge laissez-faire as an excuse for doing nothing while people starve."

Accepting a post at Johns Hopkins University, Ely assigned graduate students to study labor conditions in Baltimore and other cities; one of them, John R. Commons, went on to publish a massive four-volume study, *History of Labour in the United States.* In 1885, Ely led a small band of rebels in founding the American Economic Association, which linked economics to social problems and urged government intervention in economic affairs. Social critic Thorstein Veblen saw economic laws as a mask for human greed. In *The Theory of the Leisure Class* (1899), Veblen analyzed the "predatory wealth" and "conspicuous consumption" of the business class.

Edward Bellamy dreamed of a cooperative society in which poverty, greed, and crime no longer existed. A lawyer from western Massachusetts, Bellamy published *Looking Backward, 2000–1887,* in 1887 and became a national reform figure virtually overnight. The novel's protagonist, Julian West, falls asleep in 1887 and awakes in the year 2000. Wide-eyed, he finds himself in a socialist utopia: The government owns the means of production, and citizens share the material rewards. Cooperation, rather than competition, is the watchword.

The world of *Looking Backward* had limits; it was regimented, paternalistic, and filled with the gadgets and material concerns of Bellamy's own day. But it had a dramatic effect on many readers. The book sold at the rate of ten thousand copies a week, and its followers formed Nationalist Clubs to work for its objectives. By 1890, there were such clubs in twenty-seven states, all calling for the nationalization of public utilities and a wider distribution of wealth.

Walter Rauschenbusch, a young Baptist minister, read widely from the writings of Bellamy and George, along with the works of other social reformers. When he took his first church post in Hell's Kitchen, a blighted area of New York City, he soon discovered the weight of the slum environment. "One could hear," he said, "human virtue cracking and crushing all around." In the 1890s, Rauschenbusch became a professor at the Rochester Theological Seminary, and he began to expound on the responsibility of organized religion to advance social justice.

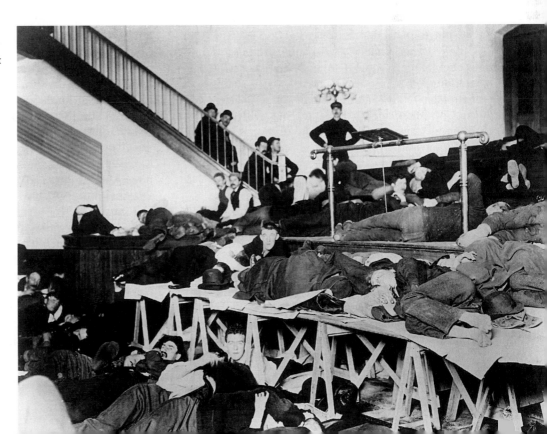

Men sleeping in crowded conditions at the Salvation Army headquarters in New York City, 1897. The Salvation Army's missions for the homeless ministered to the material and spiritual needs of the poor, unemployed, and outcast in the city's slums. ❖

Some Protestant sects stressed individual salvation and a better life in the next world, not in this one. Poverty was evidence of sinfulness; the poor had only themselves to blame. "God has intended the great to be great and the little to be little," said Henry Ward Beecher, the country's best known pastor. Wealth and destitution, suburbs and slums—all formed part of God's plan.

Challenging those traditional doctrines, a number of churches in the 1880s began establishing missions in the city slums. William Dwight Porter Bliss, an Episcopal clergyman, founded the Church of the Carpenter in a working-class district of Boston. Lewis M. Pease worked in the grim Five Points area of New York; Alexander Irvine, a Jewish missionary, lived in a flophouse in the Bowery. Irvine walked his skid row neighborhood every afternoon to lend a hand to those in need. Living among the poor and homeless, the urban missionaries grew impatient with religious doctrines that endorsed the status quo.

Many of the new trends were reflected in an emerging religious philosophy known as the **Social Gospel.** As the name suggests, the Social Gospel focused on society as well as individuals, on improving living conditions as well as saving souls. Sermons in Social Gospel churches called on church members to fulfill their social obligations, and adults met before and after the regular service to discuss social and economic problems. Children were excused from sermons, organized into age groups, and encouraged to make the church a center for social as well as religious activity. Soon churches included dining halls, gymnasiums, and even theaters.

The most active Social Gospel leader was Washington Gladden, a Congregational minister and prolific writer. Linking Christianity to the social and economic environment, Gladden spent a lifetime working for "social salvation." He saw Christianity as a fellowship of love and the church as a social agency. In *Applied Christianity* (1886) and other writings, he denounced competition, urged an "industrial partnership" between employers and employees, and called for efforts to help the poor.

The Settlement Houses

A growing number of social reformers living in the urban slums shared Gladden's concern. Like Tweed and Plunkitt, they appreciated the dependency of the poor; unlike them, they wanted to eradicate the conditions that underlay it. To do so, they formed **settlement houses** in the slums and went to live in them to experience the problems they were trying to solve.

Youthful, idealistic, and mostly middle class, these social workers took as their model Toynbee Hall, founded in 1884 in the slums of East London to provide community services. Stanton Coit, a moody and poetic graduate of Amherst College, was the first American to borrow the settlement house idea; in 1886, he opened the Neighborhood Guild on the Lower East Side of New York. The idea spread swiftly. By 1900, there were more than a hundred settlements in the country; five years later, there were more than two hundred, and by 1910, more than four hundred.

The settlements included Jane Addams's famous Hull House in Chicago (1889), Robert A. Woods's South End House in Boston (1892), and Lillian Wald's Henry Street Settlement in New York (1893). The reformers wanted to bridge the socioeconomic gap between rich and poor and to bring education, culture, and hope to the slums. They sought to create in the heart of the city the values and sense of community of small-town America. Of settlement workers, Wald said in *The House on Henry Street* (1915), "We were to live in a neighborhood . . . identify ourselves with it socially, and, in brief, contribute to it our citizenship."

Many of the settlement workers were women, some of them college graduates, who found that society had little use for their talents and energy. Jane Addams, a graduate of Rockford College in Illinois, opened Hull House on South Halsted Street in the heart of the Chicago slums. Twenty-nine years old, endowed with a forceful and winning personality, she intended "to share the lives of the poor" and humanize the industrial city. "American ideals," she said, "crumbled under the overpowering poverty of the overcrowded city."

Occupying an old, rundown house, Hull House stressed education, offering classes in elementary English and Shakespeare, lectures on ethics and the history of art, and courses in cooking, sewing, and manual skills. A pragmatist, Addams believed in investigating a problem and then doing something to solve it. Noting the lack of medical care in the area, she established an infant welfare clinic and free medical dispensary. Because the tenements lacked bathtubs, she installed showers in the basement of the house and built a bathhouse for the neighbors. Because there was no local library, she opened a reading room. Gradually, Hull House expanded to occupy a dozen buildings sprawling over more than a city block.

Like settlement workers in other cities, Addams and her colleagues studied the immigrants in nearby tenements. Laboriously, they identified the background of every family in a one-third-square-mile area around Hull House. Finding people of eighteen different nationalities, they taught them American history and the English language, yet Addams also

Jane Addams founded Chicago's Hull House in 1889. The settlement house provided recreational and day-care facilities; offered extension classes in academic, vocational, and artistic subjects; and, above all, sought to bring hope to poverty-stricken slum dwellers. ❖

OPENING OF
HULL=HOUSE
PLAY GROUND

Polk Street, Near Halsted

Saturday, May 1st, 1897,
AT 3 O'CLOCK, P. M.

"The air is warm, the skies are clear,
Birds and blossoms all are here,
Come old and young with spirits gay,
To welcome back the charming May."

MUSIC BY THE BRASS BAND

...Kindergarten Games---May Pole Dance...

ALL KINDS OF RACES

encouraged them—through folk festivals and art—to preserve their own heritage.

In Boston, Robert Woods of South End House focused on the problem of school dropouts. He offered manual training, formed clubs to get young people off the streets, and established a cheap restaurant where the hungry could eat. Lillian Wald, the daughter of a middle-class family and herself a graduate nurse, concentrated on providing health care for the poor. In 1898, the first Catholic-run settlement house opened in New York, and in 1900, Bronson House opened in Los Angeles to work in the Mexican American community.

Florence Kelley, an energetic graduate of Cornell University, taught night school one winter in Chicago. Watching children break under the burden of poverty, she devoted her life to the problem of child labor. Convinced of the need for political activism, she worked with Addams and others to push through the Illinois Factory Act of 1893, which mandated an eight-hour day for women in factories and for children under the age of 14.

The settlement house movement had its limits. Hull House, one of the best, attracted two thousand visitors a week, still just a fraction of the seventy thousand people who lived within six blocks. Immigrants sometimes resented the middle-class "strangers" who told them how to live. Dressed always in a brown suit and dark stockings, Harriet Vittum, the head resident of Chicago's Northwestern University Settlement (who told the story of the suicide victim at the beginning of this chapter), was known in the neighborhood as "the police lady in brown." She once stopped a dance because it was too wild, and then watched in disgust as the boys responded by "making vulgar sounds with their lips." Though her attempts to help were sincere, in private Vittum called the people she was trying to help "ignorant foreigners, who live in an atmosphere of low morals . . . surrounded by anarchy and crime."

Although Addams tried to offer a few programs for blacks, most white reformers did not, and after 1900, a number of black reformers opened their own settlements. Like the whites, they offered employment information, medical care, and recreational facilities, along with concerts, lectures, and other educational events. White and black, the settlement workers made important contributions to urban life.

A Crisis in Social Welfare

The depression of 1893 jarred the young settlement workers, many of whom had just begun their work. Addams and the Hull House workers helped form the Chicago Bureau of Charities to coordinate emergency relief. Kelley, recently appointed the chief factory inspector of Illinois, worked even harder to end child labor, and in 1899, she moved to New York City to head the National Consumers League, which marshaled the buying power of women to encourage employers to provide better working conditions.

In cities and towns across the country, traditional methods of helping the needy foundered in the crisis. Churches, Charity Organization Societies, and Community Chests did what they could, but their resources were limited, and they functioned on traditional lines. Many of them still tried to change rather than aid individual families, and people were often reluctant to call on them for help.

Gradually, a new class of professional social workers arose to fill the need. Unlike the church and charity volunteers, these social workers wanted not only to feed the poor but to study their condition and alleviate it. Revealingly, they called themselves "case workers" and daily collected data on the income, housing, jobs, health, and habits of the poor. Prowling tenement districts, they gathered information about the number of rooms, number of occupants, ventilation, and sanitation of the buildings, putting together a fund of useful data.

Studies of the poor popped up everywhere. Walter Wyckoff, a graduate of Princeton University, embarked in 1891 on what he called "an experiment in reality." For eighteen months, he worked as an unskilled laborer in jobs from Connecticut to California. "I am vastly ignorant of the labor problems and am trying to learn by experience," he said as he set out. After working as a ditchdigger, farmhand, and logger, Wyckoff summarized his findings in *The Workers* (1897), a book immediately hailed as a major contribution to sociology.

So many others followed Wyckoff's example that sometimes it seemed the observers outnumbered those being observed. W. E. B. Du Bois did his pioneering study of urban blacks; Lillian Pettengill took a job as a domestic servant to see "the ups and downs of this particular dog-life from the dog's end of the chain." Others became street beggars, miners, lumberjacks, and factory laborers. Bessie and Marie Van Vorst's *The Woman Who Toils: Being the Experiences of Two Gentlewomen as Factory Girls* (1903) studied female workers, as did Helen Campbell's *Women Wage-Earners: Their Past, Their Present and Their Future* (1893), which suggested that the conditions of factory employment prepared women mainly "for the hospital, the workhouse, and the prison."

CHRONOLOGY

1862	Morrill Land Grant gives land to states for establishment of colleges
1869	Rutgers and Princeton play in nation's first intercollegiate football game ❖ Cincinnati Red Stockings, baseball's first professional team, organized
1873	Comstock Law bans obscene articles from U.S. mail ❖ Nation's first kindergarten opens in St. Louis, Missouri
1874	Women's Christian Temperance Union formed to crusade against evils of liquor
1876	Johns Hopkins University opens first separate graduate school
1879	Henry George analyzes problems of urbanizing America in *Progress and Poverty* ❖ Salvation Army arrives in United States
1880	Polish National Alliance formed to help Polish immigrants adjust to life in America
1881	Booker T. Washington opens Tuskegee Institute in Alabama ❖ Dr. John H. Kellogg advises parents to teach their children about sex in *Plain Facts for Old and Young*
1883	Metropolitan Opera opens in New York
1885	Home Insurance Building, country's first metal-frame structure, erected in Chicago ❖ American Economic Association formed to advocate government intervention in economic affairs
1887	Edward Bellamy promotes idea of socialist utopia in *Looking Backward, 2000–1887*
1889	Jane Addams opens Hull House in Chicago
1890	National Woman Suffrage Association and the American Woman Suffrage Association, both formed in 1869, merge to consolidate the women's suffrage movement
1894	Immigration Restriction League formed to limit immigration from southern and eastern Europe
1896	Supreme Court decision in *Plessy* v. *Ferguson* establishes constitutionality of "separate but equal" facilities ❖ John Dewey's Laboratory School for testing and practice of new educational theory opens at University of Chicago

William T. Stead, a prominent British editor, visited the Chicago World's Fair in 1893 and stayed to examine the city. He roamed the flophouses and tenements and dropped in at Hull House to drink hot chocolate and talk over conditions with Jane Addams. Later he wrote an influential book, *If Christ Came to*

Chicago (1894), and in a series of mass meetings during 1893, he called for a civic revival. In response, Chicagoans formed the Civic Federation, a group of forty leaders who aimed to make Chicago "the best governed, the healthiest city in this country." Setting up task forces for philanthropy, moral improvement, and legislation, the new group helped spawn the National Civic Federation (1900), a nationwide organization devoted to reform of urban life.

CONCLUSION: THE PLURALISTIC SOCIETY

"The United States was born in the country and moved to the city," historian Richard Hofstadter said. Much of that movement occurred during the nineteenth century when the United States was the most rapidly urbanizing nation in the Western world. American cities bustled with energy; they absorbed millions of migrants who came from Europe and other distant and not-so-distant parts of the world. That migration, and the urban growth that accompanied it, reshaped American politics and culture.

By 1920, the census showed that, for the first time, most Americans lived in cities. By then, too, almost half the population was descended from people who had arrived after the American Revolution. As European, African, and Asian cultures met in the American city, a culturally pluralistic society emerged. Dozens of nationalities produced a culture whose members considered themselves Polish Americans, African Americans, and Irish Americans. The melting pot sometimes softened distinctions between the various groups, but it only partially blended them into a unified society.

"Ah, Vera," said a character in Israel Zangwill's popular play *The Melting Pot* (1908), "what is the glory of Rome and Jerusalem where all nations and races come to worship and look back, compared with the glory of America, where all races and nations come to labour and look forward!" Critics scorned the play as "romantic claptrap," and indeed it was. But the metaphor of the melting pot clearly depicted a new national image. In the decades after the 1870s a jumble of ethnic and racial groups struggled for a place in society.

That society, it is clear, experienced a crisis between 1870 and 1900. Together, the growth of cities and the rise of industrial capitalism brought jarring change, the exploitation of labor, ethnic and racial tensions, poverty—and, for a few, wealth beyond the imagination. At Homestead, Pullman, and a host of other places, there was open warfare between capital and labor. As reformers struggled to mediate the situation, they turned more and more to state and federal government to look after human welfare, a tendency the Supreme Court stoutly resisted. In the midst of the crisis, the depression of the 1890s struck, adding to the turmoil and straining American institutions. Tracing the changes wrought by waves of urbanization and industrialization, Henry George described the country as "the House of Have and the House of Want," almost in paraphrase of Lincoln's earlier metaphor of the "house divided." The question was, could this house, unlike that one, stand?

RECOMMENDED READING

On urban America, see Sam Bass Warner, Jr., *Streetcar Suburbs* (1962) and *The Urban Wilderness* (1972). William R. Taylor, *In Pursuit of Gotham: Culture and Commerce in New York* (1992), Eric H. Monkkonen, *America Becomes Urban* (1988), Sven Beckert, *The Monied Metropolis: New York City and the Consolidation of the American Bourgeoisie, 1850-1896* (2001), and David Schuyler, *The New Urban Landscape* (1986), are also valuable. See also two books by Jon C. Teaford: *The Unheralded Triumph: City Government in America, 1870–1900* (1984) and *City and Suburb: The Political Fragmentation of Metropolitan America, 1850–1970* (1979).

For family life, see Joseph Kett, *Rites of Passage: Adolescence in America* (1977), Elaine Tyler May, *Great Expectations: Marriage and Divorce in Post-Victorian America* (1980), Steven Mintz, *A Prison of Expectations: The Family in Victorian Culture* (1983), Stephen M. Frank, *Life With Father: Parenthood and Masculinity in the Nineteenth-Century American North* (1998), and Norma Basch, *In the Eyes of the Law: Women, Marriage, and Property in Nineteenth-Century New York* (1982). Karen Lystra, *Searching the Heart: Women, Men, and Romantic Love in Nineteenth-Century America* (1989), is valuable.

Urban reform is examined in Judith Ann Trolander, *Professionalism and Social Change: From the Settlement House Movement to Neighborhood Centers, 1886 to the Present* (1987), Shannon Jackson, *Lines of Activity: Performance, Historiography, Hull-House Domesticity* (2001), Allen F. Davis, *Spearheads for Reform: The Social Settlements and the Progressive Movement, 1890–1914* (1967), and *American Heroine: The Life and Legend of Jane Addams* (1973).

For a list of additional titles related to this chapter's topics, please see http://www.ablongman.com/divine.

SUGGESTED WEB SITES

The American Experience: America 1900

http://www.pbs.org/wgbh/amex/1900/

Companion to the PBS documentary, this site includes audio clips of respected historians on the economics, politics, and culture of 1900, a primary source database, a timeline of the year, downloadable software to compile a family tree, and other materials.

Touring Turn-of-the-Century America: Photographs from the Detroit Publishing Company, 1880–1920

http://memory.loc.gov/ammem/detroit/dethome.html

This Library of Congress collection has thousands of photographs from turn-of-the-century America.

World's Columbian Exposition: Idea, Experience, Aftermath

http://xroads.virginia.edu/~MA96/WCE/title.html

This site has a virtual tour of the fair, along with contemporary reactions and modern analysis.

United States History: The Gilded Age (1890) to World War I

http://www.emayzine.com/lectures/Gilded~1.htm

This site consists of a good overview essay of the era.

Frank Lloyd Wright

http://www.prairiestyles.com/wright.htm

This site provides information on Wright's life, work, and influence.

Chapter Three: American Socialists and Reformers

http://www.vineyard.net/vineyard/history/pdgech3.htm

This site includes a fine essay about Edward Bellamy and some of the movements and ideas he inspired.

Jane Addams Hull-House Museum

http://www.uic.edu/jaddams/hull/hull_house.html

This site offers information on Addams, her settlement house programs, and the neighborhoods they served.

African American Perspectives: Pamphlets from the Daniel A. P. Murray Collection, 1818–1907

http://memory.loc.gov/ammem/aap/aaphome.html

This collection includes writings of famous African Americans, including Frederick Douglass, Booker T. Washington, Ida B. Wells-Barnett, Benjamin W. Arnett, Alexander Crummel, and Emanuel Love.

PLESSY V. FERGUSON

The Shaping of Jim Crow

In a nation of laws, the interpretation of law can profoundly change people's lives. *Plessy* v. *Ferguson* (1896), one of the most important cases ever to reach the Supreme Court, changed the lives of millions of black and white Americans. Interpreting law in a way that lasted for more than a half century, it permitted the segregation of blacks in public facilities throughout the land.

Given the significance of the case, we know surprisingly little about Homer A. Plessy, the man who figured in it. He was young—we know that—and apparently worked as a carpenter in Louisiana. According to the court records, he was "seven-eighths Caucasian," which perhaps was a reason he was chosen to test the constitutionality of a Louisiana law requiring railroad companies to segregate whites and blacks on trains in the state. It seemed a good law to test. Louisiana's own constitution forbade such discrimination; so did the federal **Civil Rights Act of 1875,** which guaranteed blacks "full and equal enjoyment" of public conveyances.

Whatever the details of his life, Plessy lived in a post–Reconstruction South in which racism was widespread but segregation was not. Where segregation did exist, it usually was not enacted into law. During the 1870s and 1880s, blacks and whites often ate together, rode together, and worked together. "I can ride in first-class cars on the railroads and in the streets," a delighted black visitor wrote home from South Carolina in 1885. "I can stop in and drink a glass of soda and be more politely waited upon than in some parts of New England."

That situation changed near the end of the century. The courts often reflect trends in the society, and whites in both North and South in the 1890s had little enthusiasm for civil rights or racial equality. In addition, eco-

nomic depression heightened racial tensions, and the spread of colonial imperialism in Africa and Asia led to talk about "inferior" people, both at home and abroad. Beginning in the 1870s, the Supreme Court handed down a series of decisions that overturned much Reconstruction legislation, limited federal protection for blacks, and encouraged racial segregation.

In the *Slaughterhouse Cases* of 1873, the Supreme Court narrowed the scope of the Fourteenth Amendment protecting blacks; a decade later, in the *Civil Rights Cases* (1883), it said that Congress could not punish private individuals for acts of racial discrimination. Emboldened by such decisions, southern states passed many segregation laws, including laws requiring railroad companies to separate white and black riders. In the summer of 1890, Louisiana passed "An Act to promote the comfort of passengers" that made railroads in the state provide "equal but separate" cars "for the white and colored races."

Segregationists were delighted. "The Southern whites," a New Orleans newspaper said, had passed the law "in no spirit of hostility to the negroes," but to make sure that "the two races shall live separate and distinct from each other in all things, with separate schools, separate hotels, and separate cars."

New Orleans, more than most southern cities, had a group of talented African American leaders, educated, aggressive, and experienced in politics and the judicial system. Outraged by the new law, they thought first of boycotting the railroads that obeyed it but then decided to contest it in the courts. Led by Louis A. Martinet, a well-known lawyer and physician, and Rodolphe L. Desdunes, an important Reconstruction Republican, they formed the Citizens' Committee to Test the Constitutionality of the Separate Car Law, raised money for the cause, and enlisted the aid of Albion W. Tourgée of New York, a prominent white lawyer, novelist, and longtime crusader for African American rights.

Tourgée did not hesitate to join in the fight, for which he charged no fee. "Submission to such outrages," he angrily wrote his New Orleans friends, tends "only to their multiplication and exaggeration. It is by constant resistance to oppression that the race must ultimately win equality of right."

As a first step, Citizens' Committee members went to various railroad officials to ask for aid in establishing a case that could test the law. Disliking the cost of the extra cars the law forced them to buy, the officials were sympathetic but reluctant. One railroad already refused to enforce the law; officials on two other railroads said it was "a bad and mean one; they would like to get rid of it," but were afraid of public opinion. At last, the East Louisiana Railway agreed to help.

And so on June 7, 1892, to test the law, Homer A. Plessy boarded an East Louisiana Railway train in New Orleans for the 30-mile trip to Covington. He took a seat in the car reserved for whites, refused to move when a conductor asked him to, and was arrested by a detective who was standing by for the occasion. John H. Ferguson, a local judge, ruled against Plessy's argument that the law violated his rights, and Plessy appealed to the State Supreme Court, arguing that the law violated the "equal protection" clause of the Fourteenth Amendment to the Constitution. That Court, too, promptly ruled against him.

Delighted, Louisiana segregationists hoped, as one of their newspapers said, that the two decisions would knock some sense into "the silly negroes who are trying to fight this law. The sooner they drop their so-called 'crusade' against the 'Jim Crow Car,' and stop wasting their money in combating so well-established a principle—the right to separate the races in cars and elsewhere—the better for them."

It took three more years before the United States Supreme Court heard the case. Tourgée himself was pleased with the delay, hoping that time might improve racial feelings in the country and bring popular support

to his cause. Those hopes did not bear out, nor did his arguments before the Court.

In an unusual approach, Tourgée began by arguing that Homer A. Plessy, who was light-skinned in color, had been deprived of property without due process of law, contrary to the Fourteenth Amendment. Able to pass for white, he had been identified by the railroad conductor as black. He had been robbed, therefore, of his "property," Tourgée said, the sense of being white, and thus barred from association with white people, who in the United States controlled the avenues to advancement.

"Probably most white persons if given a choice," Tourgée argued, "would prefer death to life in the United States *as colored persons.* Under these conditions, is it possible to conclude that the *reputation of being white* is not property? Indeed, is it not the most valuable sort of property, being the master-key that unlocks the golden door of opportunity?"

The remainder of Tourgée's brief was straightforward, stressing the incompatibility of the separate car law with the intent of the Thirteenth and Fourteenth Amendments, the inequities it fostered, and its basis in claims of white superiority. Unless the Court stopped it now, enforced segregation would soon spread everywhere through life. "Why may [a law] not require all red-headed people to ride in a separate car? Why not require all colored people to walk on one side of the street and the whites on the other?" Why not houses of different color, or clothes, or carriages? Laws might make blacks and whites (or Protestants and Catholics, natives and foreign-born, or anyone else, for that matter) sit on opposite sides of a courtroom or use different playgrounds.

Deciding the case was simple, Tourgée concluded: "Suppose you, the members of the Court, were suddenly ordered into a Jim Crow car of your own. What humiliation, what rage would then fill the judicial mind!"

Finally, on May 18, 1896, the Court handed down its decision in *Plessy* v. *Ferguson.* By a vote of 7 to 1, it decided against Plessy. Upholding the doctrine of "separate but equal," it held that the Louisiana law did not violate Plessy's rights. It did not violate them, the Court said, because the law was "reasonable"; it had been passed "with reference to the established usages, customs and traditions of the people."

It was precisely those usages and customs—race prejudice, in short—that Tourgée had argued against. They were contrary to the Reconstruction amendments to the Constitution, he had argued, but the majority of the Court would have none of it. The authors of those amendments, they said, could not have meant to do away with racial distinctions or institute social equality; that simply could not be done. Laws did not create race prejudice, and they could not change it. Enforced segregation did not label anyone as inferior. "We consider," the Court said, "the underlying fallacy of the plaintiff's argument to consist in the assumption that the enforced separation of the two races stamps the colored race with a badge of inferiority. If this be so, it is not by reason of anything found in the act, but solely because the colored race chooses to put that construction upon it."

There was irony in the Court's vote. Justice Henry Billings Brown, a son of Massachusetts and Michigan, wrote the opinion for the majority, a measure of changing opinion in the North. The single dissenter in the case, Justice John Marshall Harlan of Kentucky, on the other hand, was not only from the South, he had once owned slaves. But accepting the changed requirements of the Reconstruction amendments, he became the "Great Dissenter" in a Court—and a country—fast fleeing its important responsibilities.

Dissenting in *Plessy,* he scoffed at the majority's reasoning. The Louisiana law, he said, was clearly prejudicial, designed to keep blacks from railroad cars occupied by whites, and as such was in clear conflict with both the Thirteenth and Fourteenth Amendments. It was "a badge of servitude," inconsistent with "the equality before the law established by the Constitution. It cannot be justified upon any legal grounds."

"Our Constitution is color-blind, and neither knows nor tolerates classes among citizens. In respect of civil rights, all citizens are equal before the law. The humblest is the peer of the most powerful. The law regards man as man, and takes no account of his surroundings or of his color when his civil rights as guaranteed by the supreme law of the land are involved."

"In my opinion," Harlan concluded, "the judgment this day rendered will, in time, prove to be quite as pernicious as the decision made by this tribunal in the *Dred Scott case.*"

It was.

After Plessy, Jim Crow laws spread swiftly through the South. More and more public conveyances, schools, and restaurants were segregated. Signs saying "Whites only" or "Colored" appeared on entrances and exits, restrooms and water fountains, waiting rooms, and even elevators. In 1905, Georgia passed the first law requiring separate public parks. In 1909, Mobile, Alabama, enacted a curfew requiring blacks to be off the streets by 10 P.M. In 1915, South Carolina forbade blacks and whites to work in the same rooms in textile factories. The Oklahoma legislature required separate telephone booths; New Orleans segregated white and black prostitutes.

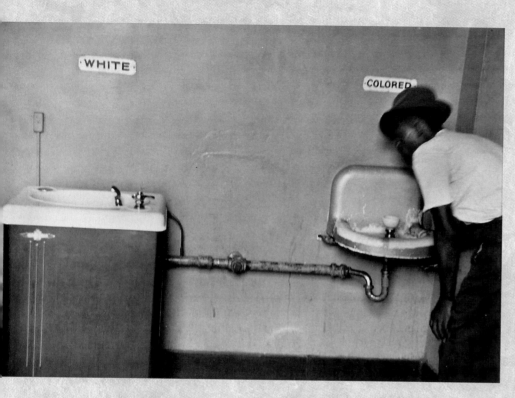

The Louisiana segregation law tested by Homer Plessy in 1892 was representative of a growing number of such laws passed in the 1880s and 1890s. *Plessy* v. *Ferguson* served to reinforce policies of racial segregation and eventually resulted in the institution of "separate but equal" facilities, which, like the ones shown here, were often not equal at all. ❖

Atlanta had separate Bibles for black witnesses in the city courts.

Harlan had, in general terms, predicted it all, in words still worth reading today: "The destinies of the two races, in this country, are indissolubly linked together, and the interests of both require that the common government of all shall not permit the seeds of race hate to be planted under the sanction of law. What can more certainly arouse race hate, what more certainly create and perpetuate a feeling of distrust between these races, than state enactments, which, in fact, proceed on the ground that colored citizens are so inferior and degraded that they cannot be allowed to sit in public coaches occupied by white citizens? That, as all will admit, is the real meaning of such legislation as was enacted in Louisiana."

Plessy v. *Ferguson* set a pattern of court-supported segregation that lasted sixty years. Generations of blacks and whites, children and adults alike, were deeply affected—sometimes traumatized—by it. The practice became a major focus of grievance in the growing movement for civil rights during the 1930s and 1940s.

"Justice," Tourgée had written in his original brief, "is pictured blind and her daughter, the Law, ought at least to be color-blind." Harlan had used the same word, "color-blind," a welcome concept to those fighting for civil rights in the 1890s. But history takes interesting and different turns, as does the law, and the word would come up again decades later, in arguments against affirmative action programs that helped African Americans get into colleges and professional schools. (See *Bakke* v. *Regents of the University of California,* pp. 956–959.)

Plessy, by then, was no more. At last, exactly fifty-eight years after the decision had been announced, on May 17, 1954, in the case of *Brown* v. *Board of Education of Topeka* (see Chapter 29), the Supreme Court reversed itself and overturned *Plessy.* Ruling that segregated schools are inherently unequal, the Court's stand toppled segregation of many kinds and changed lives once again.

Questions for Discussion

- What did the majority of the Supreme Court give as its reasons in deciding *Plessy* v. *Ferguson*? What do you think of these reasons? How do you think the majority reflected the climate of their times? What changes in public opinion have occurred since?

- Do you think Tourgée established an effective defense in arguing that the light-skinned Plessy had been deprived of his valuable property, "*the reputation of being white*"? Why or why not?

- What are some of the factors that contributed to increased segregation in the American South, and North, after 1890?

This campaign card from the 1896 presidential election predicts that Republican candidate William McKinley's protariff, protectionist policy will lead to prosperity and thriving industrialism while Democratic candidate William Jennings Bryan's free trade policy will lead to economic ruin. ❖

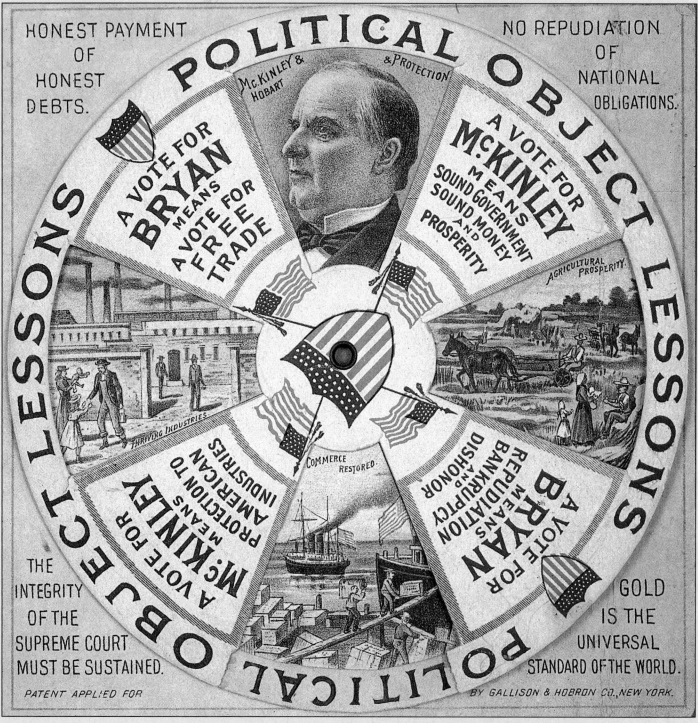

HONEST PAYMENT OF HONEST DEBTS.

NO REPUDIATION OF NATIONAL OBLIGATIONS.

POLITICAL OBJECT LESSONS

McKINLEY & HOBART & PROTECTION

A VOTE FOR BRYAN MEANS A VOTE FOR FREE TRADE

A VOTE FOR McKINLEY MEANS SOUND GOVERNMENT AND SOUND MONEY AND PROSPERITY

AGRICULTURAL PROSPERITY.

THRIVING INDUSTRIES

A VOTE FOR McKINLEY MEANS PROTECTION TO AMERICAN INDUSTRIES

COMMERCE RESTORED.

A VOTE FOR BRYAN MEANS REPUDIATION BANKRUPTCY AND DISHONOR

THE INTEGRITY OF THE SUPREME COURT MUST BE SUSTAINED.

GOLD IS THE UNIVERSAL STANDARD OF THE WORLD.

PATENT APPLIED FOR

BY GALLISON & HOBRON CO., NEW YORK.

Political Realignments in the 1890s

$\mathcal{H}$ardship and Heartache

In June 1894, Susan Orcutt, a young farm woman from western Kansas, sat down to write the governor of her state a letter. She was desperate. The nation was in the midst of a devastating economic depression, and, like thousands of other people, she had no money and nothing to eat. "I take my Pen In hand to let you know that we are Starving to death," she wrote. Hail had ruined the Orcutts' crops, and none of the household could find work. "My Husband went away to find work and came home last night and told me that we would have to Starve. [H]e has bin in ten countys and did not Get no work.... I havent had nothing to Eat today and It is three oclock[.]"

As bad as conditions were on the farms, they were no better in the cities. "There are thousands of homeless and starving men in the streets," reported a journalist in Chicago in the winter of 1893. "I have seen more misery in this last week than I ever saw in my life before." Charity societies and churches tried to help, but they could not handle the huge numbers of people who were in need. The records of the Massachusetts state medical examiner told a grim story:

> K.R., 29   Suicide by drowning
> Boston   October 2, 1896
> Out of work and despondent for a long while. Body found floating in the Charles [River].

> F.S., 29   Suicide by arsenic
> Boston   January 1, 1896
> Much depressed for several weeks. Loss of employment. At 7:50 A.M. Jan. 1, she called her father and told him she had taken poison and wished to die.

> L.M., 38   Hanging suicide
> E. Boston   October 15, 1895
> Had been out of work for several weeks and was very despondent. Wife went to market at about 11 A.M. and upon returning at about 12 P.M. found him hanging from bedroom door.... Slipped noose about his neck and [fell] forward upon it.

> R.N., 23   Suicide by bullet wound of brain
> Boston   June 22, 1896
> Out of work. Mentally depressed. About 3 P.M. June 21 shot himself in right temple.... Left a letter explaining that he killed himself to save others the trouble of caring for him.

Lasting until 1897, the depression was the decisive event of the decade. At its height, three million people were unemployed—fully 20 percent of the workforce. The human costs were enormous, even among the well-to-do. "They were for me years of simple Hell," shattering "my whole scheme of life," said Charles Francis Adams, Jr., the descendant of two American presidents. "I was sixty-three years old and a tired man when at last the effects of the 1893 convulsion wore themselves out."

OUTLINE
❖❖❖

Politics of Stalemate

Republicans in Power: The Billion-Dollar Congress

The Rise of the Populist Movement

The Crisis of the Depression

Changing Attitudes

The Presidential Election of 1896

The McKinley Administration

Conclusion: A Decade's Dramatic Changes

FEATURE ESSAY
❖❖❖

The Wonderful Wizard of Oz

LIKE THE GREAT DEPRESSION of the 1930s that gave rise to the New Deal, the depression of the 1890s had profound and lasting effects. Bringing to a head many of the tensions that had been building in the society, it increased rural hostility toward the cities, brought about a bitter fight over the currency, and changed people's thinking about government, unemployment, and reform. There were outbreaks of warfare between capital and labor; farmers demanded a fairer share of economic and social benefits; the "new" immigrants came under fresh attack. The depression of the 1890s changed the course of American history, as did another event of that decade: the war with Spain in 1898.

Under the cruel impact of the depression, ideas changed in many areas, including a stronger impulse toward reform, a larger role for the presidency, and a call for help from many farmers and laborers. One of the most important of these areas was politics. A realignment of the American political system, which had been developing since the end of Reconstruction, finally reached its fruition in the 1890s, establishing new patterns that gave rise to the Progressive Era and lasted well into the twentieth century.

POLITICS OF STALEMATE

Politics was a major fascination of the late nineteenth century, its mass entertainment and favorite sport. Political campaigns were events that involved the whole community, even though in most states men were the only ones who could vote. During the weeks leading up to an election, there were rallies, parades, picnics, and torchlight processions. Millions of Americans read party newspapers, listened to three-hour speeches by party leaders, and in elections turned out in enormous numbers to vote. In the six presidential elections from 1876 to 1896, an average of almost 79 percent of the electorate voted, a higher percentage than voted before or after.

White males made up the bulk of the electorate; until after the turn of the century, women could vote in national elections only in Wyoming, Utah, Idaho, and Colorado. The National Woman Suffrage Association early sued for the vote, but in 1875, the Supreme Court (*Minor* v. *Happersett*) upheld the power of the states to deny this right to women. On several occasions, Congress refused to pass a constitutional amendment for women's suffrage, and between 1870 and 1910, nearly a dozen states defeated referenda to grant women the vote.

Black men were another group kept from the polls. In 1877, Georgia adopted the poll tax to make voters pay an annual tax for the right to vote. The technique, aimed at impoverished blacks, was quickly copied across the South. In 1882, South Carolina adopted the "eight box" law, soon copied elsewhere, that required ballots for separate offices to be placed in separate boxes, a difficult task for illiterate voters.

In 1890, Mississippi required voters to be able to read and interpret the federal Constitution to the satisfaction of registration officials, all of them white. Such literacy tests, which the Supreme Court upheld in the case of *Williams* v. *Mississippi* (1898), excluded poor white voters as well as blacks. In 1898, Louisiana

A delegation of women's rights advocates addressed the judiciary committee of the House of Representatives to present their arguments in favor of woman suffrage. Reading the argument is Victoria Claflin Woodhull, one of the more radical activists in the women's movement. ❖

avoided the problem by adopting the famous "grand-father clause," which used a literacy test to disqualify black voters but permitted men who had failed the test to vote anyway if their fathers and grandfathers had voted before 1867—a time, of course, when no blacks could vote. The number of black voters decreased dramatically. In 1896, there were 130,334 registered black voters in Louisiana; in 1904, there were 1,342.

The Party Deadlock

The 1870s and 1880s were still dominated by the Civil War generation, the unusual group of people who rose to power in the turbulent 1850s. In both the North and South, they had ruled longer than most generations, with a consciousness that the war experience had set them apart. Five of the six presidents elected between 1865 and 1900 had served in the war, as had many civic, business, and religious leaders. In 1890, well over one million veterans of the Union army were still alive, and Confederate veterans numbered in the hundreds of thousands.

Party loyalties—rooted in Civil War traditions, ethnic and religious differences, and perhaps class distinctions—were remarkably strong. Voters clung to their old parties, shifts were infrequent, and there were relatively few "independent" voters. Although linked to the defeated Confederacy, the Democrats revived quickly after the war. In 1874, they gained control of the House of Representatives, which they maintained for all but four of the succeeding twenty years. The Democrats rested on a less sectional base than the Republicans. Identification with civil rights and military rule cut Republican strength in the South, but the Democratic party's principles of states' rights, decentralization, and limited government won supporters everywhere.

While Democrats wanted to keep government local and small, the Republicans pursued policies for the nation as a whole, in which government was an instrument to promote moral progress and material wealth. The Republicans passed the Homestead Act (1862), granted subsidies to the transcontinental railroads, and pushed other measures to encourage economic growth. They enacted legislation and constitutional amendments to protect civil rights. They advocated a high protective tariff as a tool of economic policy, to keep out foreign products while "infant industries" grew.

In national elections, sixteen states, mostly in New England and the North, consistently voted Republican; fourteen states, mostly in the South, consistently voted Democratic. Elections, therefore, depended on a handful of "doubtful" states, which could swing elections either way. These states—New York, New Jersey, Connecticut, Ohio, Indiana, and Illinois—received

✦ A Look at the Past ✦

Ballot Box

Until the 1890s, political parties printed their own ballots, which voters requested in order to cast a ballot. Voters revealed their political decisions simply by obtaining a ballot. Glass ballot boxes such as this one made it possible for others to witness that the voter actually cast the ballot. While today voters make their decisions and cast their votes privately, before 1890 voting was a visible, public act, and political intimidation could and did occur. Why would Americans use such a system? Why did they change to secret balloting at the end of the nineteenth century?

special attention at election time. Politicians lavished money and time on them; presidential candidates usually came from them. From 1868 to 1912, eight of the nine Republican presidential candidates and six of the seven Democratic candidates came from the "doubtful" states, especially New York and Ohio.

The two parties were evenly matched, and elections were closely fought. In three of the five presidential elections from 1876 to 1892, the victor won by less than 1 percent of the vote; in 1876 and 1888, the losing candidates actually had more popular votes than the winners but lost in the electoral college. Knowing that

A toy scale pitting the presidential candidates of 1888 (Harrison and Cleveland) against each other invites participation in determining the election outcome. More than a plaything, this scale symbolizes the high level of voter participation during the late nineteenth century when elections hung in balance until the last vote was counted. ❖

small mistakes could lose elections, politicians became extremely cautious. Only twice during these years did one party control both the presidency and the two houses of Congress—the Republicans in 1888 and the Democrats in 1892.

Historians once believed that political leaders accomplished little between 1877 and 1900, but those who saw few achievements were looking in the wrong location. With the impeachment of Andrew Johnson, the authority of the presidency dwindled in relation to congressional strength. For the first time in many years, attention shifted away from Washington itself. North and South, people who were weary of the centralization brought on by war and Reconstruction looked first to state and local governments to deal with the problems of an urban-industrial society.

Experiments in the States

Across the country, state bureaus and commissions were established to regulate the new industrial society. Many of the early commissions were formed to oversee the railroads, at the time the nation's largest businesses. People who shipped goods over the railroads, especially farmers and merchants, wanted to end the policies of rate discrimination and other harmful practices. In 1869, Massachusetts established the first commission to regulate the railroads; by 1900, twenty-eight states had taken such action.

Most of the early commissions were advisory in nature. They collected statistics and published reports on rates and practices—serving, one commissioner said, "as a sort of lens" to focus public attention. Impatient with the results, legislatures in the Midwest and on the Pacific Coast established commissions with greater power to fix rates, outlaw rebates, and investigate rate discrimination. These commissions, experimental in nature, served as models for later policy at the federal level.

Illinois had one of the most thoroughgoing provisions. Responding to local merchants who were upset with existing railroad rate policies, the Illinois state constitution of 1870 declared railroads to be public highways and authorized the legislature to pass laws establishing maximum rates and preventing rate discrimination. In the important case of *Munn* v. *Illinois* (1877), the Supreme Court upheld the Illinois legislation, declaring that private property "affected with the public interest . . . must submit to being controlled by the public for the common good."

But the Court soon weakened that judgment. In the *Wabash* case of 1886 (*Wabash, St. Louis, & Pacific Railway Co.* v. *Illinois*), it narrowed the *Munn* ruling and held that states could not regulate commerce extending beyond their borders. Only Congress could. The *Wabash* decision turned people's attention back to the federal government. It spurred Congress to pass the Interstate Commerce Act (1887), which created the **Interstate Commerce Commission (ICC)** to investigate and oversee railroad activities. The act outlawed rebates and pooling agreements, and the ICC became the prototype of the federal commissions that today regulate many parts of the economy.

Reestablishing Presidential Power

Johnson's impeachment, the scandals of the Grant administrations, and the controversy surrounding the 1876 election weakened the presidency. During the last two decades of the nineteenth century, presidents fought to reassert their authority, and by 1900, under William McKinley, they had succeeded to a remarkable degree. The late 1890s, in fact, marked the birth of the modern powerful presidency.

Rutherford B. Hayes entered the White House with his title clouded by the disputed election of 1876. Opponents called him "His Fraudulency" and "Rutherfraud B. Hayes," but soon he began to reassert the authority of the presidency. Hayes worked for reform in the civil service, placed well-known reformers in high offices, and, ordering the last troops out of South Carolina and Louisiana, ended military Reconstruction. He hoped to revive the Republican party in the South by persuading business-oriented

THE ELECTION OF 1880

Candidate	Party	Popular Vote	Electoral Vote
Garfield	Republican	4,446,158	214
Hancock	Democrat	4,444,260	155
Weaver	Greenback	305,997	0

THE ELECTION OF 1884

Candidate	Party	Popular Vote	Electoral Vote
Cleveland	Democrat	4,874,621	219
Blaine	Republican	4,848,936	182
Butler	Greenback	175,096	0
St. John	Prohibition	147,482	0

ex-Whigs to join a national party that would support their economic interests more effectively than the Democrats did. In this attempt, however, he failed. Committed to the gold standard—the only basis, Hayes thought, of a sound currency—in 1878 he vetoed a bill that called for the partial coinage of silver, but Congress passed this **Bland-Allison Silver Purchase Act** over his veto.

James A. Garfield, a Union army hero and long-time member of Congress, succeeded Hayes. Winning by a handful of votes in 1880, he took office energetically, determined to unite the Republican party (which had been split by personality differences and disagreement over policy toward the tariff and the South), lower the tariff to cut taxes, and assert American economic and strategic interests in Latin America. Ambitious and eloquent, Garfield had looked forward to the presidency, yet within a few weeks he said to friends, "My God! What is there in this place that a man should ever want to get into it?"

Office seekers, hordes of them, evoked Garfield's anguish. Each one wanted a government job, and each one thought nothing of cornering the president on every occasion. The problem of government jobs also provoked a bitter fight with the powerful senator from New York, Roscoe Conkling, who resented some of Garfield's choices. On the verge of victory over Conkling, Garfield planned to leave Washington on July 2, 1881, for a vacation in New England. Walking toward his train, he was shot in the back by Charles J. Guiteau, a deranged lawyer and disappointed office seeker. Suffering through the summer, Garfield died on September 19, 1881, and Vice President Chester A. Arthur—an ally of Senator Conkling—became president.

Arthur was a better president than many had expected. Deftly, he established his independence of Conkling. Conservative in outlook, he reversed Garfield's foreign policy initiatives in Latin America, but he approved the construction of the modern American navy. Arthur worked to lower the tariff, and in 1883, with his backing, Congress passed the **Pendleton Act** to reform the civil service. In part a reaction to Garfield's assassination, the act created a bipartisan Civil Service Commission to administer competitive examinations and appoint officeholders on the basis of merit. Initially, the act affected only about 14,000 of some 100,000 government offices, but it laid the basis for the later expansion of the civil service.

In the election of 1884, Grover Cleveland, the Democratic governor of New York, narrowly defeated Republican nominee, James G. Blaine, largely because of the continuing divisions in the Republican party. The first Democratic president since 1861, Cleveland was slow and ponderous, known for his honesty, stubbornness, and hard work. His term in the White House from 1885 to 1889 reflected the Democratic party's desire to curtail federal activities. Cleveland vetoed more than two-thirds of the bills presented to him, more than all his predecessors combined.

Forthright and sincere, he brought a new respectability to a Democratic party still tainted by its link with secession. Working long into the night, he reviewed veterans' pensions and civil service appointments. He continued Arthur's naval construction program and forced railroad, lumber, and cattle companies to surrender millions of acres of fraudulently occupied

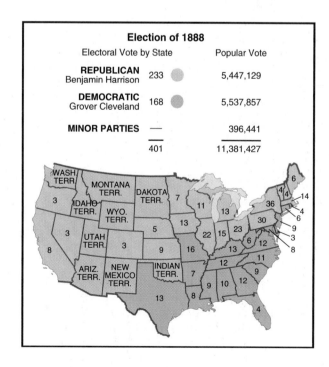

public domain. Late in 1887, he devoted his annual message to an attack on the tariff, "the vicious, inequitable, and illogical source of unnecessary taxation," and committed himself and the Democratic party to lowering the tariff.

The Republicans accused him of undermining American industries, and in 1888, they nominated for the presidency Benjamin Harrison, a defender of the tariff. Cleveland garnered ninety thousand more popular votes than Harrison but won the electoral votes of only two northern states and the South. Harrison won the rest of the North, most of the "doubtful" states, and the election.

REPUBLICANS IN POWER: THE BILLION-DOLLAR CONGRESS

Despite Harrison's narrow margin, the election of 1888 was the most sweeping victory for either party in almost twenty years; it gave the Republicans the presidency and both houses of Congress. The Republicans, it seemed, had broken the party stalemate and become the majority party in the country.

Democratic leaders hoped not, and, eager to embarrass the Republicans and block Republican-sponsored laws, the Democrats in Congress used minority tactics, especially the "disappearing quorum" rule, which let members of the House of Representatives join in debate but then refuse to answer the roll call to determine whether a quorum was present.

For two months, the Democrats used the rule to bring Congress to a halt. The Republicans grew angry and impatient. On January 29, 1890, they fell two votes short of a quorum, and speaker of the House Thomas B. Reed, a crusty veteran of Maine politics, made congressional history. "The Chair," he said, "directs the Clerk to record the following names of members present and refusing to vote." Democrats shouted "Czar! Czar!", a title that stuck to Reed for the rest of his life. Tumult continued for days, but in mid-February 1890, the Republicans adopted the Reed rules and proceeded to enact the party's program.

Tariffs, Trusts, and Silver

As if a dam had burst, law after law poured out of the Republican Congress during 1890. The Republicans passed the McKinley Tariff Act, which raised tariff duties about 4 percent, higher than ever before; it also included a novel reciprocity provision that allowed the president to lower duties if other countries did the same. In addition, the act used duties to promote new industries, such as tinplate for packaging the new "canned" foods appearing on grocery store shelves. A

Dependent Pensions Act granted pensions to Union army veterans and their widows and children. The pensions were modest—$6 to $12 a month—but the number of pensioners doubled by 1893, when nearly 1 million individuals received about $160 million in pensions.

With little debate, the Republicans and Democrats joined in passing the **Sherman Antitrust Act,** the first federal attempt to regulate big business. As the initial attempt to deal with the problem of trusts and industrial growth, the act shaped all later antitrust policy. It declared illegal "every contract, combination in the form of trust or otherwise, or conspiracy, in restraint of trade or commerce." Penalties for violation were stiff, including fines and imprisonment and the dissolution of guilty trusts. Experimental in nature, the act's terms were often vague and left precise interpretation to later experience and the courts.

One of the most important laws Congress passed, the Sherman Antitrust Act made the United States virtually the only industrial nation to regulate business combinations. It tried to harness big busi-

In this 1886 cartoon illustrating the silver standard versus gold standard controversy, Uncle Sam bicycles to national bankruptcy on an enormous silverite dollar. ❖

ness without harming it. Many members of Congress did not expect the new law to have much effect on businesses, and for a decade, in fact, it did not. The Justice Department rarely filed suit under it, and in the *United States* v. *E. C. Knight Co.* decision (1895), the first judicial interpretation of the law, the Supreme Court severely crippled it. Though the E. C. Knight Co. controlled 98 percent of all sugar refining in the country, the Court drew a sharp distinction between commerce and manufacturing, holding that the company, as a manufacturer, was not subject to the law. But judicial interpretations changed after the turn of the century, and the Sherman Antitrust Act gained fresh power.

Another measure, the **Sherman Silver Purchase Act,** tried to end the troublesome problem presented by silver. As one of the two most commonly used precious metals, silver had once played a large role in currencies around the world, but by the mid-1800s, it had slipped into disuse. With the discovery of the great bonanza mines in Nevada, American silver production quadrupled between 1870 and 1890, glutting the world market, lowering the price of silver, and persuading many European nations to demonetize silver in favor of the scarcer metal, gold. The United States kept a limited form of silver coinage with congressional passage of the Bland-Allison Act in 1878.

Support for silver coinage was especially strong in the South and West, where people thought it might inflate the currency, raise wages and crop prices, and challenge the power of the gold-oriented Northeast. Eager to avert the free coinage of silver, which would require the coinage of all silver presented at the U.S. mints, President Harrison and other Republican leaders pressed for a compromise that took shape in the Sherman Silver Purchase Act of 1890.

The act directed the Treasury to purchase 4.5 million ounces of silver a month and to issue legal tender in the form of Treasury notes in payment for it. The act was a compromise; it satisfied both sides. Opponents of silver were pleased that it did not include free coinage. Silverites, on the other hand, were delighted that the monthly purchases would buy up most of the country's silver production. The Treasury notes, moreover, could be cashed for either gold or silver at the bank, a gesture toward a true bimetallic system based on silver and gold.

As a final measure, Republicans in the House courageously passed a federal elections bill to protect the voting rights of blacks in the South. Although restrained in language and intent, it set off a storm of denunciation among the Democrats, who called it a "force bill" that would station army troops in the South. Because of the outcry, the bill failed in the Senate; it was

the last major effort until the 1950s to enforce the Fifteenth Amendment to the Constitution.

The 1890 Elections

The Republican Congress of 1890 was one of the most important Congresses in American history. It passed a record number of significant laws that helped shape later policy and asserted the authority of the federal government to a degree the country would not then accept. Sensing the public reaction, the Democrats labeled it the "Billion-Dollar Congress" for spending that much in appropriations and grants.

"This is a billion-dollar country," Speaker Reed replied, but the voters disagreed. The 1890 elections crushed the Republicans, who lost an extraordinary seventy-eight seats in the House. The elections also crushed Republicans in the Midwest, where, again enlarging government authority, they had passed state laws prohibiting the sale of alcoholic beverages, requiring the closing of businesses on Sunday, and mandating the use of English in the public and parochial schools. Roman Catholics, German Lutherans, and other groups resented such laws, which they saw as a direct attack on their religion and personal freedoms, and they angrily deserted the Republicans.

Political veterans went down to defeat, and new leaders vaulted into sudden prominence. Nebraska elected a Democratic governor for the first time in its history. The state of Iowa, once so staunchly Republican that a local leader had predicted that "Iowa will go Democratic when Hell goes Methodist," went Democratic in 1890.

THE RISE OF THE POPULIST MOVEMENT

The elections of 1890 drew attention to a fast-growing movement among farmers that soon came to be known far and wide as populism. The movement had begun rather quietly, in places distant from normal centers of attention, and for a time it went almost unnoticed in the press. But during the summer of 1890, wagonloads of farm families in the South and West converged on campgrounds and picnic areas to socialize and discuss common problems. They came by the thousands, weary of drought, mortgages, and low crop prices. At the campgrounds, they picnicked, talked, and listened to recruiters from an organization called the **National Farmers' Alliance and Industrial Union,** which promised unified action to solve agricultural problems.

Farmers were joining the Alliance at the rate of 1,000 a week; the Kansas Alliance alone claimed

130,000 members in 1890. The summer of 1890 became "that wonderful picnicking, speech-making Alliance summer," a time of fellowship and spirit long remembered by farmers.

The Farm Problem

Farm discontent was a worldwide phenomenon between 1870 and 1900. With the new means of transportation and communication, farmers everywhere were caught up in a complex international market they neither controlled nor entirely understood.

American farmers complained bitterly about declining prices for their products, rising railroad rates for shipping them, and burdensome mortgages. Some of their grievances were valid. Farm profits were certainly low; agriculture in general tends to produce low profits because of the ease of entry into the industry. The prices of farm commodities fell between 1865 and 1890—corn sold at sixty-three cents a bushel in 1881 and twenty-eight cents in 1890—but they did not fall as low as did other commodity prices. Despite the fact that farmers received less for their crops, their purchasing power actually increased.

Neither was the farmers' second grievance—rising railroad rates—entirely justified. Railroad rates actually fell during these years, benefiting shippers of all products. Farm mortgages, the farmers' third grievance, were common because many farmers mortgaged their property to expand their holdings or buy new farm machinery. While certainly burdensome, most mortgages did not bring hardship. They were often short, with a term of four years or less, after which farmers could renegotiate at new rates, and the new machinery the farmers bought enabled them to triple their output and increase their income.

The terms of the farm problem varied from area to area and year to year. New England farmers suffered from overworked land; farmers in western Kansas and Nebraska went broke in a severe drought that followed a period of unusual rainfall. Many southern farmers were trapped in the crop lien system that kept them in debt. They called it the "anaconda" system because of the way it coiled slowly and tightly around them.

A study of farms in the Midwest between 1860 and 1900 suggests that farm income rose substantially in the 1860s, fell during the devastating depression of the 1870s, rose in the 1880s, and remained roughly constant in the 1890s. There were also large variations in farm profits from county to county, again indicating the absence of clear nationwide patterns. Farmers who had good land close to railroad transportation did well; others did not.

Some farmers did have valid grievances, though many understandably tended to exaggerate them. More important, many farmers were sure their condition had declined, and this perception—as bitterly real as any actual fact—sparked a growing anger. Equally upsetting, everyone in the 1870s and 1880s seemed excited about factories, not farms. Farmers had become

SELECTED COMMODITY PRICES

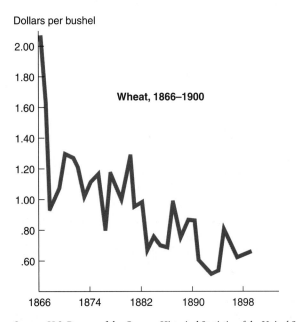

Dollars per bushel

Wheat, 1866–1900

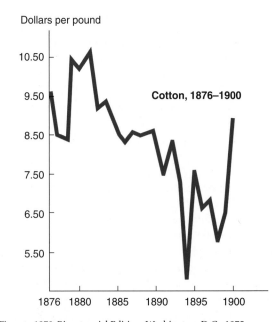

Dollars per pound

Cotton, 1876–1900

Source: U.S. Bureau of the Census, *Historical Statistics of the United States, Colonial Times to 1970,* Bicentennial Edition, Washington, D.C., 1975.

"hayseeds," a word that first appeared in 1889, and they watched their offspring leave for city lights and new careers. Books such as *The Spider and the Fly: or, Tricks, Traps, and Pitfalls of City Life by One Who Knows* (1873) warned against such a move, but still the children went. A literature of disillusionment emerged, most notably Hamlin Garland's *Son of the Middle Border* (1890) and *Main-Travelled Roads* (1891), which described the drabness of farm life.

The Fast-Growing Farmers' Alliance

Originally a social organization for farmers, the Grange lost many of its members as it turned more and more toward politics in the late 1870s. In its place, a multitude of farm societies sprang into existence. By the end of the 1880s, they had formed into two major organizations: the National Farmers' Alliance, located on the Plains west of the Mississippi and known as the Northwestern Alliance, and the Farmers' Alliance and Industrial Union, based in the South and known as the Southern Alliance.

The Southern Alliance began in Texas in 1875 but did not assume major proportions until Dr. Charles W. Macune, an energetic and farsighted person, took over the leadership in 1886. Rapidly expanding, the Alliance absorbed other agricultural societies. Its agents spread across the South, where farmers were fed up with crop liens, depleted lands, and sharecropping. They "seem like unto ripe fruit," an Alliance organizer said; "you can garner them by a gentle shake of the bush." In 1890, the Southern Alliance claimed more than a million members. It welcomed to membership the farmers' "natural friends"—country doctors, schoolteachers, preachers, and mechanics. It excluded lawyers, bankers, cotton merchants, and warehouse operators.

An effective organization, the Southern Alliance published a newspaper and distributed Alliance material to hundreds of local newspapers, and in five years it sent lecturers to forty-three states and territories where they spoke to two million farm families. It was "the most massive organizing drive by any citizen institution of nineteenth-century America." Like the Grange, the Alliance also established cooperative grain elevators, marketing associations, and retail stores—all designed to bring farmers together to make greater profits. Most of the projects were short-lived, but for a time, between 1886 and 1892, cooperative enterprises blossomed in the South.

Loosely affiliated with the Southern Alliance, a separate Colored Farmers' National Alliance and Cooperative Union enlisted black farmers in the South. Claiming more than 1 million members, it probably had closer to 250,000, but even that figure

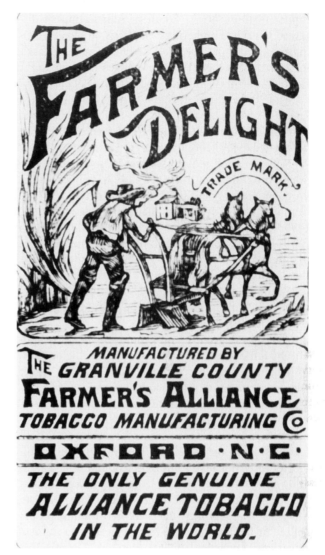

This advertisement for Farmer's Delight tobacco from the May 21, 1889, issue of the Progressive Farmer *is an example of the type of products sold through Alliance cooperatives. The Alliance organizations formed cooperatives in an effort to guarantee farmers greater profits by negotiating for better prices for farm products sold in bulk. Farmers could also avoid creditors' fees by buying goods through the cooperatives. However, failure to secure the credit necessary to finance the cooperatives and lack of management experience in operating them doomed the cooperative venture to failure.* ❖

was sizable in an era when "uppity" blacks faced not merely defeat, but death. In 1891, black cotton pickers struck for higher wages near Memphis, Tennessee. Led by Ben Patterson, a 30-year-old picker, they walked off several plantations, but a posse hunted them down and, following violence on both sides, lynched fifteen strikers, including Patterson. The abortive strike ended the Colored Farmers' Alliance.

On the Plains, the Northwestern Alliance, a smaller organization, was formed in 1880. Its objectives were similar to those of the Southern Alliance, but it disagreed with the Southerners' emphasis on secrecy, centralized control, and separate organizations for blacks. In 1889, the Southern Alliance changed its name to the National Farmers' Alliance and Industrial Union and persuaded the three strongest state alliances on the Plains—those in North Dakota, South Dakota, and Kansas—to join. Thereafter, the renamed organization dominated the Alliance movement.

The Alliance mainly sponsored social and economic programs, but it turned early to politics. In the West, its leaders rejected both the Republicans and Democrats and organized their own party; in June 1890, Kansas Alliance members formed the first major People's party. The Southern Alliance resisted the idea of a new party for fear it might divide the white vote, thus undercutting white supremacy. The Southerners instead followed leaders such as Benjamin F. Tillman of South Carolina, who wanted to capture control of the dominant Democratic party.

Thomas E. Watson and Leonidas L. Polk, two politically minded Southerners, reflected the high quality of Alliance leadership. Georgia-born, Watson was a talented orator and organizer; he urged Georgia farmers, black and white, to unite against their oppressors. The president of the National Farmers' Alliance, Polk believed in scientific farming and cooperative action. Jeremiah Simpson of Kansas, probably the most able of the western leaders, was reflective and well-read. A follower of reformer Henry George, he pushed for major social and economic change. Also from Kansas, Mary E. Lease—Mary Ellen to her friends, "Mary Yellin" to her opponents—helped head a movement remarkably open to female leadership. A captivating speaker, she made 160 speeches during the summer of 1890, calling on farmers to rise against Wall Street and the industrial East.

Meeting in Ocala, Florida, in 1890, the Alliance adopted the **Ocala Demands,** the platform the organization pushed as long as it existed. First and foremost, the demands called for the creation of a "sub-treasury system," which would allow farmers to store their crops in government warehouses. In return, they could claim Treasury notes for up to 80 percent of the local market value of the crop, a loan to be repaid when the crops were sold. Farmers could thus hold their crops for the best price. The Ocala Demands also urged the free coinage of silver, an end to protective tariffs and national banks, a federal income tax, the direct election of senators by voters instead of state legislatures, and tighter regulation of railroad companies.

The Alliance strategy worked well in the elections of 1890. In Kansas, the Alliance-related People's party, organized just a few months before, elected four congressmen and a U.S. senator. Across the South, the

Populist Mary E. Lease advised farmers to "raise less corn and more hell." She also said, "If one man has not enough to eat three times a day and another man has $25 million, that last man has something that belongs to the first." ❖

Alliance won victories based on the "Alliance yardstick," a demand that Democratic party candidates pledge support for Alliance measures. Alliance leaders claimed thirty-eight Alliance supporters elected to Congress, with at least a dozen more pledged to Alliance principles.

The People's Party

After the 1890 elections, Northern Alliance leaders urged the formation of a national third party to promote reform, although the Southerners remained reluctant, still hopeful of capturing control of the Democratic party. Plans for a new party were discussed at Alliance conventions in 1891 and the following year. In July 1892, a convention in Omaha, Nebraska, formed the new **People's (or Populist) party.** Southern Alliance leaders joined in, convinced now that there was no reason to cooperate with the Democrats who exploited Alliance popularity but failed to adopt its reforms.

In the South, some Populists had worked to unite black and white farmers. "They are in the ditch just like we are," a white Texas Populist said. Blacks and whites served on Populist election committees; they spoke from the same platforms, and they ran on the same tickets. Populist sheriffs called blacks for jury duty, an unheard-of practice in the close-of-the-century South. In 1892, a black Populist was threatened with lynching; he took refuge with Tom Watson, and two thousand white farmers, some of whom rode all night to get there, guarded Watson's house until the threat passed.

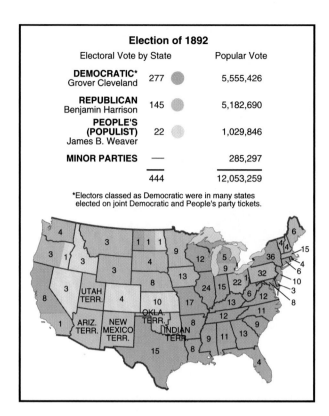

Election of 1892

	Electoral Vote by State		Popular Vote
DEMOCRATIC* Grover Cleveland	277		5,555,426
REPUBLICAN Benjamin Harrison	145		5,182,690
PEOPLE'S (POPULIST) James B. Weaver	22		1,029,846
MINOR PARTIES	—		285,297
	444		12,053,259

*Electors classed as Democratic were in many states elected on joint Democratic and People's party tickets.

Many of the delegates at the Omaha convention had planned to nominate Leonidas L. Polk for president, but he died suddenly in June, and the convention turned instead to James B. Weaver of Iowa, a former congressman, Union army general, and third-party candidate for president in 1880 (on the Greenback-Labor party ticket). As its platform, the People's party adopted many of the Ocala Demands.

Weaver waged an active campaign but with mixed results. He won 1,029,000 votes, the first third-party presidential candidate ever to attract more than a million. He carried Kansas, Idaho, Nevada, and Colorado, along with portions of North Dakota and Oregon, for a total of twenty-two electoral votes. The Populists elected governors in Kansas and North Dakota, ten congressmen, five senators, and about fifteen hundred members of state legislatures.

Despite the Populists' victories, the election brought disappointment. Southern Democrats used intimidation, fraud, and manipulation to hold down Populist votes. Weaver was held to less than a quarter of the vote in every southern state except Alabama. In most of the country, he lost heavily in urban areas, with the exception of some mining towns in the Far West. He also failed to win over most farmers. In no midwestern state except Kansas and North Dakota did he win as much as 5 percent of the vote.

In the election of 1892, many voters switched parties, but they tended to realign with the Democrats rather than the Populists, whose platform on silver and other issues had relatively little appeal among city dwellers or factory workers. Although the Populists did run candidates in the next three presidential elections, they had reached their peak in 1892. That year, Farmers' Alliance membership dropped for the second year in a row, and the organization, which was once the breeding ground of the People's party, was broken.

While it lived, the Alliance was one of the most powerful protest movements in American history. Catalyzing the feelings of hundreds of thousands of farmers, it attempted to solve specific economic problems while at the same time advancing a larger vision of harmony and community, in which people who cared about each other were rewarded for what they produced.

THE CRISIS OF THE DEPRESSION

It was economic crisis, however, not harmony and community, that dominated the last decade of the century. Responding to the heady forces of industrialization, the American economy had expanded too rapidly in the 1870s and 1880s. Railroads had overbuilt, gambling on future growth. Companies had grown beyond their markets; farms and businesses had borrowed heavily for expansion.

The Panic of 1893

The mood changed early in 1893. In mid-February, panic suddenly hit the New York stock market. In one day, investors dumped one million shares of a leading company, the Philadelphia and Reading Railroad, and it went bankrupt. Business investment dropped sharply in the railroad and construction industries, touching off the worst economic downturn to that point in the country's history.

Frightened, people hurriedly sold stocks and other assets to buy gold. The overwhelming demand depleted the gold reserve of the U.S. Treasury. Eroding almost daily, in March 1893, the Treasury's reserve slumped toward the $100 million mark, an amount that stood for the government's commitment to maintain the gold standard. On April 22, for the first time since the 1870s, the reserve fell below $100 million.

The news shattered business confidence—the stock market broke. On Wednesday, May 3, railroad and industrial stocks plummeted, and the next day, several major firms went bankrupt. When the market opened on Friday, crowds filled its galleries, anticipating a panic. Within minutes, leading stocks plunged to record lows, and there was pandemonium on the floor and in the streets outside. May 5, 1893, Wall Street's worst day until the Great Crash of 1929, became

Customers line up in front of the Farmers and Mechanics Bank in Minneapolis, Minnesota, in May 1893 to try to withdraw their savings. Many banks had loaned out most of their deposits and kept only a small portion of cash in reserve. When they could not meet depositors' demands for cash withdrawals, banks closed their doors. ❖

"Industrial Black Friday," "a day of terrible strain long remembered on the market."

Afterward, banks cut back on loans. Unable to get capital, businesses failed at an average rate of two dozen a day during the month of May. "The papers are full of failures—banks are breaking all over the country, and there is a tremendous contraction of credits and hoarding of money going on everywhere," an observer noted. On July 26, the Erie Railroad, one of the leading names in railroading history, failed.

August 1893 was the worst month. Across the country, factories and mines shut down. In Orange, New Jersey, Thomas A. Edison, the symbol of the country's ingenuity, laid off 240 employees at the Edison Phonograph Works. On August 15, the Northern Pacific Railroad went bankrupt; the Union Pacific and the Santa Fe soon followed. Some economists estimated unemployment at 2 million people, or nearly 15 percent of the labor force. During 1893, 15,000 business firms and more than 600 banks closed.

The year 1894 was even worse. The gross national product dropped again, and by midyear the number of unemployed stood at 3 million. One out of every five workers was unemployed. "Famine is in our midst," said the head of one city's relief committee. In the summer, a heat wave and drought struck the farm belt west of the Mississippi River, creating conditions unmatched until the devastating Dust Bowl of the 1930s. Corn withered in the fields. In the South, the price of cotton fell below five cents a pound, far under the break-even point.

People became restless and angry. As one newspaper said in 1896: "On every corner stands a man whose fortune in these dull times has made him an ugly critic of everything and everybody." There was even talk of revolution and bloodshed. "Everyone scolds," Henry Adams, the historian, wrote a British friend. "Everyone also knows what ought to be done. Everyone reviles everyone who does not agree with him, and everyone differs, or agrees only in contempt for everyone else. As far as I can see, everyone is right."

Coxey's Army and the Pullman Strike

Some of the unemployed wandered across the country—singly, in small groups, and in small armies. In February 1894, police ejected six hundred unemployed men who stormed the State House in Boston demanding relief. During 1894, there were some fourteen hundred strikes involving more than a half million workers.

On Easter Sunday 1894, an unusual "army" of perhaps three hundred people left Massillon, Ohio. At its head rode "General" Jacob S. Coxey, a mild-looking middle-aged businessman who wanted to put the nation's jobless to work building roads. Coxey wanted Congress to pass the Coxey Good Roads bill, which would authorize the printing of $500 million in paper money to finance road construction. His march to Washington—"a petition in boots," he called it—drew nationwide attention. Forty-three newspaper correspondents accompanied him, reporting every detail of the march.

Other armies sprang up around the country, and all headed for Washington to persuade the government to provide jobs on irrigation, road construction, or other projects. In the West, they commandeered freight trains and headed east. Coxey himself reached Washington on May 1, 1894, after a difficult, tiring

Jacob Coxey (left) and two of his associates in a police station lockup after their arrest for trespassing on the lawn surrounding the U.S. Capitol. On the fiftieth anniversary of his march to Washington, Coxey was permitted to finish the speech that had been interrupted by his arrest in 1894. ❖

march. Police were everywhere, lining the streets and blocking the approaches to the Capitol. Coxey made it to the foot of the Capitol steps, but before he could do anything, the police were on him. He and a companion were clubbed, then arrested for trespassing. A week later, Coxey was sentenced to twenty days in jail.

The armies melted away, but discontent did not. The great **Pullman strike**—one of the largest strikes in the country's history—began just a few days after Coxey's arrest when the employees of the Pullman Palace Car Company, living in a company town just outside Chicago (a town in which everything was owned and meted out by the company), struck to protest wage cuts, continuing high rents, and layoffs. On June 26, 1894, the American Railway Union (ARU) under Eugene V. Debs joined the strike by refusing to handle trains that carried Pullman sleeping cars.

Within hours, the strike paralyzed the western half of the nation. Grain and livestock could not reach markets. Factories shut down for lack of coal. The strike extended into twenty-seven states and territories, tying up the economy and renewing talk of class warfare. In Washington, President Grover Cleveland, who had been reelected to the presidency in 1892, decided to break the strike on the grounds that it obstructed delivery of the mail.

On July 2, he secured a court injunction against the ARU, and he ordered troops to Chicago. When they arrived on the morning of Independence Day, the city was peaceful. Before long, however, violence broke out, and mobs, composed mostly of nonstrikers, overturned freight cars, looted, and burned. Restoring order, the army occupied railroad yards in Illinois, California, and other places. By late July, the strike was over; Debs was jailed for violating the injunction. Many people applauded Cleveland's action, "nominally for the expedition of the mails," a newspaper said, but "really for the preservation of society."

The Pullman strike had far-reaching consequences for the development of the labor movement. Working people resented Cleveland's actions in the strike, particularly as it became apparent that he sided with the railroads. Upholding Debs's sentence in *In re Debs* (1895), the Supreme Court endorsed the use of the injunction in labor disputes, thus giving business and government an effective antilabor weapon that hindered union growth in the 1890s. The strike's failure catapulted Debs into prominence. During his time in jail, he turned to socialism, and after his release, he worked to build the Socialist party of America, which experienced some success after 1900.

The Miners of the Midwest

The plight of coal miners in the Midwest illustrated the personal and social impact of the depression. Even in the best of times, mining was a dirty and dangerous business. One miner in twelve died underground; one in three suffered injury. Mines routinely closed for as long as six months a year, and wages fell with the depression. An Illinois miner earned 97 cents a ton in 1889 and only 80 cents in 1896. A bituminous coal miner made $282 a year.

Midwestern mining was often a family occupation, passed down from father to son. It demanded delicate judgments about when to blast, where to follow a seam, and how to avoid rockfalls. Until 1890, English and Irish immigrants dominated the business. They migrated from mine to mine, and they nearly always lived in flimsy shacks owned by the company. Time and again the miners struck for higher wages—between 1887 and 1894, there were 116 major coal strikes in Illinois, 111 in Ohio.

After 1890, immigration from southern and eastern Europe, hitherto a trickle, became a flood. Italians, Lithuanians, Poles, Slovaks, Magyars, Russians, Bohemians, and Croatians came to the mines to find work. In three years, nearly one thousand Italians settled in Coal City, Illinois; they comprised more than one-third of the population. In other mining towns, Italian and Polish miners soon made up almost half the population.

A United Mine Workers certificate of membership illustrates some of the work undertaken by the brother members. The United Mine Workers of America was formed in Columbus, Ohio, in 1890 and sought to provide its members with a safe workplace and fair wages and benefits. Although the union pledged to seek ways to maintain peace between miners and their employers and to make strikes unnecessary, such means as arbitration and conciliation often failed and strikes did occur, many of them violent and destructive. ✦

As the depression deepened, tensions grew between miners and their employers and between "old" miners and the "new." Many "new" miners spoke no English, and often they were "birds of passage," transients who had come to the United States to make money to take back home. Lacking the skills handed down by the "old" miners, they were often blamed for accidents, and they worked longer hours for less pay. At many a tavern after work, "old" miners grumbled about the different-looking newcomers and considered ways to get rid of them.

In April 1894, a wave of wage reductions sparked an explosion of labor unrest in the mines. The United Mine Workers, a struggling union formed just four years earlier, called for a strike of bituminous coal miners, and on April 21, virtually all midwestern and Pennsylvania miners—some 170,000 in all—quit working. The flow of crucial coal slackened; cities faced blackouts; factories closed.

The violence that soon broke out followed a significant pattern. Over the years, the English and Irish miners had built up a set of unspoken understandings with their employers. The "new" miners had not, and they were more prone to violent action to win a strike. The depression hit them especially hard, frustrating their plans to earn money and return home. In many areas, anger and frustration turned the 1894 strikes into outright war.

For nearly two weeks in June 1894, fighting rocked the Illinois, Ohio, and Indiana coalfields. Mobs ignited mine shafts, dynamited coal trains, and defied state militias. While miners of all backgrounds participated in the violence, it often divided "old" miners and "new." In Spring Valley, Illinois, exiled Italian anarchists took over the strike leadership and incited rioting despite the opposition of the "old" miners. Elsewhere, a mine fired by arsonists burned because the "new" miners prevented the "old" ones from extinguishing the blaze.

Shocked by the violence, public opinion shifted against the strikers. The strike ended in a matter of weeks, but its effects lingered. English and Irish miners moved out into other jobs or up into supervisory positions. Jokes and songs poked cruel fun at the "new" immigrants, and the Pennsylvania and Illinois legislatures adopted laws to keep them out of the mines. Thousands of "old" miners voted Populist in 1894—the Populist platform called for restrictions on immigration—in one of the Populists' few successes that year. The United Mine Workers, dominated by the older miners, began in 1896 to urge Congress to stop the "demoralizing effects" of immigration.

Occurring at the same time, the Pullman strike pulled attention away from the crisis in the coalfields, yet the miners' strike involved three times as many workers and provided a revealing glimpse of the tensions within American society. The miners of the Midwest were the first large group of skilled workers seriously affected by the flood of immigrants from southern and eastern Europe. Buffeted by depression, they reflected the social and economic discord that permeated every industry.

A Beleaguered President

Building on the Democratic party's sweeping triumph in the midterm elections of 1890, Grover Cleveland decisively defeated the Populist candidate, James B. Weaver, and the incumbent president, Benjamin Harrison, in 1892. He won by nearly 400,000 votes, a large margin by the standards of the era, and the Democrats increased their strength in the cities and among working-class voters. For the first time since the 1850s, they controlled the White House and both branches of Congress.

The Democrats, it now seemed, had broken the party stalemate, but unfortunately for Cleveland, the Panic of 1893 struck almost as he took office. He was sure that he knew its cause. The Sherman Silver Purchase Act of 1890, he believed, had damaged business confidence, drained the Treasury's gold reserve, and caused the panic. The solution to the depression was equally simple: Repeal the act.

In June 1893, Cleveland summoned Congress into special session. India had just closed its mints to silver, and Mexico was now the only country in the world with free silver coinage. The silverites were on the defensive, although they pleaded for a compromise. Rejecting the pleas, Cleveland pushed the repeal bill through Congress, and on November 1, 1893, he signed it into law. Always sure of himself, he had staked everything on a single measure—a winning strategy if he succeeded, a devastating one if he did not.

Repeal of the Sherman Silver Purchase Act was probably a necessary action. It responded to the realities of international finance, reduced the flight of gold out of the country, and, over the long run, boosted business confidence. Unfortunately, it contracted the currency at a time when inflation might have helped.

It did not bring economic revival. The stock market remained listless, businesses continued to close, unemployment spread, and farm prices dropped. "We are hourly expecting the arrival of the benevolent man who is to pay ten cents a pound for cotton," a Virginia newspaper said.

The repeal battle of 1893, discrediting the conservative Cleveland Democrats who had dominated the party since the 1860s, reshaped the politics of the country. It confined the Democratic party largely to the South, helped the Republicans become the majority party in 1894, and strengthened the position of the silver Democrats in their bid for the presidency in 1896. It also focused national attention on the silver issue and thus intensified the silver sentiment Cleveland had intended to dampen. In the end, repeal did not even solve the Treasury's gold problem. By January 1894, the reserve had fallen to $65 million. A year later, it fell to $44.5 million.

In January 1894, Cleveland desperately resorted to a sale of $50 million in gold bonds to replenish the gold reserve. The following November, he again sold bonds, and in February 1895, arousing outrage among many, he agreed to a third bond sale that allowed financier J. Pierpont Morgan and other bankers to reap large profits. A fourth bond sale in January 1896 also failed to stop the drain on the reserve, although it further sharpened the silverites' hatred of President Cleveland.

Still another blow to the morale of the Democrats came in 1894, when they tried to fulfill their long-standing promise to reduce the tariff. Despite all their efforts, the Wilson-Gorman Tariff Act, passed by Congress in August 1894, contained only modest reductions in duties. It reduced the tariff on coal, iron ore, wool, and sugar, ended the McKinley Tariff Act's popular reciprocity agreements with other countries, and moved some duties higher than ever before. It also imposed a small income tax, a provision the Supreme Court overturned in 1895 (*Pollock* v. *Farmer's Loan and Trust Co.*). Very few Democrats, including Cleveland, were pleased with the measure, and the president let it become law without his signature.

Breaking the Party Deadlock

The Democrats were buried in the elections of 1894. Suffering the greatest defeat in congressional history, they lost 113 House seats, while the Republicans gained 117. In twenty-four states, not a single Democrat was elected to Congress. Only one Democrat (Boston's John F. Fitzgerald, the grandfather of President John F. Kennedy) came from all of New England. The Democrats even lost some of the "solid

South," and in the Midwest, a crucial battleground of the 1890s, the party was virtually destroyed.

Wooing labor and the unemployed, the Populists made striking inroads in parts of the South and West, yet their progress was far from enough. In a year in which thousands of voters switched parties, the People's party elected only four senators and four congressmen. Southern Democrats again used fraud and violence to keep the Populists' totals down. In the Midwest, the Populists won double the number of votes they had received in 1892, yet still attracted less than 7 percent of the vote. Across the country, the discontented tended to vote for the Republicans, not the Populists, a discouraging sign for the Populist party.

For millions of people, Grover Cleveland became a scapegoat for the country's economic ills. Fearing attack, he placed new police barracks on the White House grounds. The Democratic party split, and southern and western Democrats deserted him in droves. At Democratic conventions, Cleveland's name evoked jeers. "He is an old bag of beef," Democratic Congressman "Pitchfork" Ben Tillman told a South Carolina audience, "and I am going to go to Washington with a pitchfork and prod him in his old fat ribs."

The elections of 1894 marked the end of the party deadlock that had existed since the 1870s. The Democrats lost, the Populists gained somewhat, and the Republicans became the majority party in the country. In the midst of the depression, the Republican doctrines of activism and national authority, which voters had repudiated in the elections of 1890, became more attractive. This was a development of great significance, because as Americans became more accepting of the use of government power to regulate the economy and safeguard individual welfare, the way lay open to the reforms of the Progressive Era, the New Deal, and beyond.

CHANGING ATTITUDES

The depression, brutal and far-reaching, did more than shift political alignments. Across the country, it undermined traditional views and caused people to rethink older ideas about government, the economy, and society. As men and women concluded that established ideas had failed to deal with the depression, they looked for new ones. There was, the president of the University of Wisconsin said, "a general, all-pervasive, restless discontent with the results of current political and economic thought."

In prosperous times, Americans had thought of unemployment as the result of personal failure, affecting primarily the lazy and immoral. "Let us remember," a leading Protestant minister once said, "that

there is not a poor person in the United States who was not made poor by his own shortcomings." In the midst of depression, such views were harder to maintain, since everyone knew people who were both worthy and unemployed. Next door, a respected neighbor might be laid off; down the block, an entire factory might be shut down.

People debated issues they had long taken for granted. New and reinvigorated local institutions—discussion clubs, women's clubs, reform societies, university extension centers, church groups, farmers' societies—gave people a place to discuss alternatives to the existing order. Pressures for reform increased, and demand grew for government intervention to help the poor and unemployed.

"Everybody Works But Father"

Women and children had been entering the labor force for years, and the depression accelerated the trend. As husbands and fathers lost their jobs, more and more women and children went to work. Even as late as 1901, well after the depression had ended, a study of working-class families showed that more than half the principal breadwinners were out of work. So many women and children worked that in 1905 there was a popular song titled "Everybody Works But Father."

During the 1890s, the number of working women rose from 4 million to 5.3 million. Trying to make ends meet, they took in boarders and found jobs as laundresses, cleaners, or domestics. Where possible, they worked in offices and factories. Far more black urban women than white worked to supplement their husbands' meager earnings. In New York City in 1900, nearly 60 percent of all black women worked, compared to 27 percent of the foreign-born and 24 percent of native-born white women. Men still dominated business offices, but during the 1890s, more and more employers noted the relative cheapness of female labor. Women telegraph and telephone operators nearly tripled in number during the decade. Women worked as clerks in the new five-and-tens and department stores, and as nurses; in 1900, a half million were teachers. They increasingly entered office work as stenographers and typists, occupations in which they earned between $6.00 and $15.00 a week, compared to factory wages of $1.50 to $8.00 a week.

The depression also caused an increasing number of children to work. During the 1890s, the number of children employed in southern textile mills jumped more than 160 percent, and boys and girls under 16 years of age made up nearly one-third of the labor force of the mills. Youngsters of 8 and 9 years worked twelve hours a day for pitiful wages. In most cases,

Tiny children peddling newspapers and women domestics serving the rich—their meager earnings were desperately needed. ❖

however, children worked not in factories but in farming and city street trades such as peddling and shoe shining. In 1900, the South had more than half the child laborers in the nation.

Concerned about child labor, middle-class women in 1896 formed the League for the Protection of the Family, which called for compulsory education to get children out of factories and into classrooms. The Mothers Congress of 1896 gave rise to the National Congress of Parents and Teachers, the spawning ground of thousands of local Parent-Teacher Associations. The National Council of Women and the General Federation of Women's Clubs took up similar issues. By the end of the 1890s, the Federation had 150,000 members who worked for various civic reforms in the fields of child welfare, education, and sanitation.

Changing Themes in Literature

The depression also gave point to a growing movement in literature toward realism and naturalism. In the years after the Civil War, literature often reflected the mood of romanticism—sentimental and unrealistic. Walt Whitman called it "ornamental confectionary" and "copious dribble," but it remained popular through the end of the century.

The novels of Horatio Alger, which provided simple lessons about how to get ahead in business and life, continued to attract large numbers of readers. A failed New York minister, Alger published some 130 novels—with titles such as *Sink or Swim, Work and Win,* and *Struggling Upward*—which sold more than 20 million copies. They told of poor youngsters who made their way to the top through hard work, thrift, honesty, and luck. Louisa May Alcott's *Little Women* (1868–1869) related the daily lives of four girls in a New England family, Anna Sewell's *Black Beauty* (1877) charmed readers with the story of an abused horse that found a happy home, and Lew Wallace's *Ben Hur* (1880), one of the era's best-selling books, offered a sweeping epic of life in the Roman empire.

After the 1870s, however, a number of talented authors began to reject romanticism and escapism, turning instead to realism. Determined to portray life as it was, they studied local dialects, wrote regional stories, and emphasized the "true" relationships between people. In doing so, they reflected broader trends in the society, such as industrialism; evolutionary theory, which emphasized the effect of the environment on humans; and the new philosophy of pragmatism, which stressed the relativity of values.

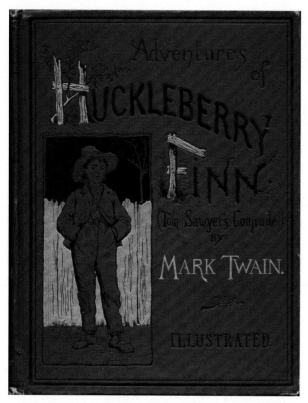

Mark Twain's novel Adventures of Huckleberry Finn, *published in the United States in 1885, was both popular and controversial. Banned by some public libraries shortly after its publication because of Twain's use of dialect and narration from the point of view of an unschooled boy in conflict with conventional society—both shocking by the cultural and literary standards of the day—the novel is still widely read today, and is still considered controversial by some for its portrayal of race relations in the antebellum South.* ❖

Regionalist authors such as Joel Chandler Harris and George Washington Cable depicted life in the South. Hamlin Garland described the grimness of life on the Great Plains, and Sarah Orne Jewett wrote about everyday life in rural New England. Another regionalist, Bret Harte, achieved fame with stories that portrayed the local color of the California mining camps, particularly in his popular tale "The Outcasts of Poker Flat."

Harte was joined by a more talented writer, Mark Twain, who became the country's most outstanding realist author. Growing up along the Mississippi River in Hannibal County, Missouri, the young Samuel Langhorne Clemens observed life around him with a humorous and skeptical eye. Adopting a pen name from the river term "mark twain" (two fathoms), he wrote a number of important works that drew on his own experiences. *Life on the Mississippi* (1883) described his career as a steamboat pilot. *The Adventures*

of *Tom Sawyer* (1876) and *The Adventures of Huckleberry Finn* (1884) gained international prominence. In these books, Twain used dialect and common speech instead of literary language, touching off a major change in American prose style.

William Dean Howells—after Twain, the country's most famous author—came more slowly to the realist approach. At first, he wrote about the happier sides of life, but then he grew worried about the impact of industrialization. *A Traveler from Altruria* (1894), a utopian novel, described an industrial society that consumed lives. The poem "Society" (1895), written in the midst of the depression, compared society to a splendid ball in which men and women danced on flowers covering the bodies of the poor:

> And now and then from out the dreadful floor
> An arm or brow was lifted from the rest,
> As if to strike in madness, or implore
> For mercy; and anon some suffering breast
> Heaved from the mass and sank; and as before
> The revellers above them thronged and prest.

Other writers, the naturalists, became impatient even with realism. Pushing Darwinian theory to its limits, they wrote of a world in which a cruel and merciless environment determined human fate. Often focusing on economic hardship, naturalist writers studied the poor, the lower classes, and the criminal mind; they brought to their writing the social worker's passion for direct and honest experience.

Stephen Crane spent a night in a seven-cent lodging house on the Bowery and in "An Experiment in Misery" captured the smells and sounds of the poor. Crane depicted the carnage of war in *The Red Badge of Courage* (1895) and the impact of poverty in *Maggie: A Girl of the Streets* (1893). His poetry suggested the unimportance of the individual in an uncaring world:

> A man said to the universe
> "Sir, I exist!"
> "However," replied the universe,
> "The fact has not created in me
> A sense of obligation."

Frank Norris assailed the power of big business in two dramatic novels, *The Octopus* (1901) and *The Pit* (1903), both the story of individual futility in the face of the heartless corporations. Norris's *McTeague* (1899) studied the disintegration of character under economic pressure. Jack London, another naturalist author, traced the power of nature over civilized society in novels such as *The Sea Wolf* (1904) and *The Call of the Wild* (1903), his classic tale of a sled dog that

A scene from Stephen Crane's novel Maggie: A Girl of the Streets. *Crane's tale painted a grim picture of life in the tenements of New York City's Bowery as it chronicled the story of slum child Maggie Johnson, victimized and trapped in her squalid, violent world.* ❖

preferred the difficult life of the wilderness to the world of human beings.

Theodore Dreiser, the foremost naturalist writer, grimly portrayed a dark world in which human beings were tossed about by forces beyond their understanding or control. "My own ambition," Dreiser said, "is to represent my world, to conform to the large, truthful lines of life." In his great novel *Sister Carrie* (1901), he followed a young farm girl who took a job in a Chicago shoe factory. He described the exhausting nature of factory work: "Her hands began to ache at the wrists and then in the fingers, and towards the last she seemed one mass of dull, complaining muscle, fixed in an eternal position, and performing a single mechanical movement."

Like other naturalists, Dreiser focused on environment and character. He thought writers should tell the truth about human affairs, not fabricate romance, and *Sister Carrie*, he said, was "not intended as a piece of literary craftsmanship, but was a picture of conditions."

THE PRESIDENTIAL ELECTION OF 1896

The election of 1896 was known as the "battle of the standards" because it focused primarily on the gold and silver standards of money. As an election, it was exciting and decisive. New voting patterns replaced old, a new majority party confirmed its control of the country, and national policy shifted to suit new realities.

The Mystique of Silver

Sentiment for free silver coinage grew swiftly after 1894, dominating the South and West, appearing even in the farming regions of New York and New England. Prosilver literature flooded the country. (See the Feature Essay, "The Wonderful Wizard of Oz," pp. 592–593.) Pamphlets issued by the millions argued silver's virtues.

People wanted quick solutions to the economic crisis. During 1896, unemployment shot up and farm income and prices fell to the lowest point in the decade. "I can remember back as far as 1858," an Iowa hardware dealer said in February 1896, "and I have never seen such hard times as these are." The silverites offered a solution, simple but compelling: the free and independent coinage of silver at the ratio of 16 ounces of silver to every ounce of gold. Free coinage meant that the U.S. mints would coin all the silver offered to them. Independent coinage meant that the country would coin silver regardless of the policies of other nations, nearly all of which were on the gold standard.

It is difficult now to understand the kind of faith the silverites placed in silver as a cure for the depression. But faith it was, and of a sort that some observers compared to religious fervor. Underlying it all was a belief in a quantity theory of money: The silverites believed the amount of money in circulation determined the level of activity in the economy. If money was short, that meant there was a limit on economic activity and ultimately a depression. If the government coined silver as well as gold, that meant more money in circulation, more business for everyone, and thus prosperity. Farm prices would rise; laborers would go back to work. As one silverite said, "It means the reopening of closed factories, the relighting of fires in darkened furnaces; it means hope instead of despair; comfort in place of suffering; life instead of death."

By 1896, silver was also a symbol. It had moral and patriotic dimensions—by going to a silver standard, the United States could assert its independence in the world—and it stood for a wide range of popular grievances. For many, it reflected rural values rather than urban ones, suggested a shift of power

THE WONDERFUL WIZARD OF OZ

A restless dreamer, Frank Baum tried his hand at several careers before he gained fame and fortune as a writer of children's literature. From 1888 to 1891, he ran a store and newspaper in South Dakota, where he experienced the desolation and grayness that accompanied agrarian discontent. An avid supporter of William Jennings Bryan in the "battle of the standards," Baum wrote what many interpret as an enduring allegory of the silver movement, *The Wonderful Wizard of Oz.* Published in April 1900, it was an immediate success.

The book opens with a grim description of Kansas:

> When Dorothy stood in the doorway and looked around, she could see nothing but the great gray prairie on every side. Not a tree nor a house broke the broad sweep of flat country that reached the edge of the sky in all directions. The sun had baked the plowed land into a gray mass, with little cracks running through it. Even the grass was not green, for the sun had burned the tops of the long blades until they were the same gray color to be seen everywhere. Once the house had been painted, but the sun blistered the paint and the rains washed it away, and now the house was as dull and gray as everything else.

Kansas had not always seemed that way. After 1854, when the Kansas-Nebraska Act opened to settlement its 50 million acres of grassland, people poured into the state to stake their claims. Many came from the hilly timbered country to the east, and breaking onto the prairie, they saw "a new world, reaching to the far horizon without break of trees or chimney stack; just sky and grass and grass and sky. . . . The hush was so loud. . . . The heavens seemed nearer than ever before and awe and beauty and majesty over all."

In later years, railroads crisscrossed the state, and advertisements touted the fertile soil. Land was plentiful, rainfall somehow seemed to increase each year, crop prices held at levels high enough to pay, new farming implements yielded larger crops, and property values increased.

Yet life on the prairie was never an easy matter. Flat, lonely, and windswept, the land affected people in ways that were hard to describe to the folks back East. When Aunt Em, Dorothy's aunt, came to Kansas to live, she was young and pretty, but the sun and wind soon changed her. "They had taken the sparkle from her eyes and left them a sober gray; they had taken the red from her cheeks and lips, and they were gray also." Like Aunt Em, Uncle Henry never laughed. "He worked hard from morning till night and did not know what joy was."

After 1887, a series of droughts struck Kansas, and as many as three out of four farms were mortgaged in some Kansas counties. Thousands of settlers like Aunt Em and Uncle Henry gave up and retraced their steps East; others trusted in the Farmers' Alliance and pinned their hopes on the free coinage of silver. While gold as a standard of currency symbolized the idle rich of the industrial Northeast, silver stood for the common folk. Added to the currency in the form of silver dollars, it meant more money, higher crop prices, and a return of prosperity.

Or so the supporters of silver coinage believed. In *The Wonderful Wizard of Oz,* read as an allegory, Dorothy (every person) is carried by a cyclone (a victory of the silver forces at the polls) from drought-stricken Kansas to a marvelous land of riches and witches. Unlike dry, gray Kansas, Oz is beautiful, with rippling brooks, stately trees, colorful flowers, and bright-feathered birds. On arrival, Dorothy disposes of one witch, the Wicked Witch of the East (the eastern

The Wicked Witch of the West. ❖

Dorothy (wearing silver, not ruby, slippers in the original version) and her friends prepare to "follow the yellow brick road." ❖

money power and those favoring gold), and frees the Munchkins (the common people) from servitude. To return to Kansas, she must first go to the Emerald City (the national capital, greenback-colored).

Dorothy wears magical silver slippers and follows the yellow brick road, thus achieving a proper relationship between the precious metals, silver and gold. Like many of her countrymen, she does not at first recognize the power of the silver slippers, but a kiss from the Good Witch of the North (Northern voters) protects her on the road. Dorothy meets the Scarecrow (the farmer), who has been told he has no brain but actually possesses great common sense (no "hick" or "hayseed," he); the Tin Woodman (the industrial worker), who fears he has become heartless but discovers the spirit of love and cooperation; and the Cowardly Lion (reformers, particularly William Jennings Bryan), who turns out not to be very cowardly at all.

When the four companions reach the Emerald City, they meet the "Great and Terrible" Wizard, who tells them that, to gain his help, they must destroy the Wicked Witch of the West (mortgage companies, heartless nature, and other things opposing progress there). Courageously, they set forth. Dorothy dissolves the witch with a bucket of water (what else for drought-ridden farmers?), but when they return to the Emerald City, they find that the great and powerful Wizard (the money power) is only a charlatan, a manipulator, whose power rests on myth and illusion. "'I thought Oz was a great Head,' said Dorothy. . . . 'And I thought Oz was a terrible Beast,' said the Tin Woodman. 'And I thought Oz was a Ball of Fire,' exclaimed the Lion. 'No; you are all wrong,' said the little man meekly. 'I have been making believe.'"

Dorothy unmasks the wizard, and with the help of Glinda, the Good Witch of the South (support for silver was strong in the South), uses the silver slippers to return home to Kansas. Sadly, the shoes are lost in flight. Back in Oz, the Scarecrow rules the Emerald City (the triumph of the farmers), and the Tin Woodman reigns in the West (industrialism moves West). *Oz* was a familiar abbreviation to those involved in the fight over the ratio of silver to gold—16 ounces to 1.

Baum wanted to write American fairy tales to "bear the stamp of our times and depict the progressive fairies of today." The land of Oz reflected his belief in the American values of freedom and independence, love of family, self-reliance, individualism, and sympathy for the underdog. *Oz,* he said in the original introduction, "aspires to being a modernized fairy tale, in which the wonderment and joy are retained and the heartaches and nightmares are left out."

The *Oz* stories have remained popular, and they still rest on many children's bookshelves. A 1939 film starring Judy Garland as Dorothy, with Ray Bolger as the Scarecrow, Jack Haley as the Tin Woodman, Bert Lahr as the Cowardly Lion, and Frank Morgan as the Wizard, was spectacularly successful. Released in the midst of another depression, the film included songs designed to escape hardship, as Dorothy once had, "somewhere over the rainbow."

away from the Northeast, and spoke for the down-trodden instead of the well-to-do. Silver represented the common people, as the vast literature of the movement showed.

William H. Harvey's *Coin's Financial School* (1894), the most popular of all silver pamphlets, had the eloquent Coin, a wise but unknown youth, tutoring famous people on the currency. Bankers, lawyers, and scholars came to argue for gold, but they left shaken, leaning toward silver. *Coin's Financial School* sold five thousand copies a day at its peak in 1895, with tens of thousands of copies distributed free by silver organizations. It "is being sold on every railroad train by the newsboys and at every cigar store," a Mississippi congressman said. "It is being read by almost everybody."

Silver was more than just a political or economic issue. It was a social movement, one of the largest in American history, but its life span turned out to be brief. As a mass phenomenon, it flourished between 1894 and 1896, then succumbed to electoral defeat, the return of prosperity, and the onset of fresh concerns. But in its time, the silver movement bespoke a national mood and won millions of followers.

The Republicans and Gold

Scenting victory over the discredited Democrats, numerous Republicans fought for the party's presidential nomination, including "Czar" Thomas B. Reed of the Billion-Dollar Congress. Reed picked up early support but suffered from his reputation for biting wit. William McKinley of Ohio, his chief rival, soon passed him in the race for the nomination.

Able, calm, and affable, McKinley had served in the Union army during the Civil War. In 1876, he won a seat in Congress, where he became the chief sponsor of the tariff act named for him. In the months before the 1896 national convention, Marcus A. Hanna, his campaign manager and trusted friend, built a powerful national organization that featured McKinley as "the advance agent of prosperity," an alluring slogan in a country beset with depression. When the convention met in June, McKinley had the nomination in hand, and he backed a platform that favored the gold standard against the free coinage of silver.

Republicans favoring silver proposed a prosilver platform, but the convention overwhelmingly defeated it. Twenty-three silverite Republicans, far fewer than prosilver forces had hoped, marched out of the convention hall. The remaining delegates waved handkerchiefs and flags and shouted "Good-bye" and "Put them out." Hanna stood on a chair screaming "Go! Go! Go!" William Jennings Bryan, who was

there as a special correspondent for a Nebraska newspaper, climbed on a desk to get a better view.

The Democrats and Silver

Silver, meanwhile, had captured large segments of the Democratic party in the South and West. Despite President Cleveland's opposition, more than twenty Democratic state platforms came out for free silver in 1894. Power in the party shifted to the South, where it remained for decades. The party's base narrowed; its outlook increasingly reflected southern views on silver, race, and other issues. In effect, the Democrats became a sectional—no longer a national—party.

The anti-Cleveland Democrats had their issue, but they lacked a leader. Out in Nebraska, Bryan saw the opportunity to take on that role. He was barely 36 years old and had relatively little political experience. But he had spent months wooing support, and he was a captivating public speaker—tall, slender, and handsome, with a resounding voice that, in an era without microphones, projected easily into every corner of an auditorium. Practicing at home before a mirror, he rehearsed his speeches again and again, as his wife, Mary, a bright, sharp, and politically astute woman, listened for errors.

From the outset of the 1896 Democratic convention, the silver Democrats were in charge, and they put together a platform that stunned the Cleveland wing of the party. It demanded the free coinage of silver, attacked Cleveland's actions in the Pullman strike, and censured his sales of gold bonds. On July 9, as delegates debated the platform, Bryan's moment came. Striding to the stage, he stood for an instant, a hand raised for silence, waiting for the applause to die down. He would not contend with the previous speakers, he began, for "this is not a contest between persons. The humblest citizen in all the land, when clad in the armor of a righteous cause, is stronger than all the hosts of error. I come to speak to you in defense of a cause as holy as the cause of liberty—the cause of humanity."

The delegates were captivated. Like a trained choir, they rose, cheered each point, and sat back to listen for more. Easterners, Bryan said, liked to praise businessmen but forgot that plain people—laborers, miners, and farmers—were businessmen, too. Shouts rang through the hall, and delegates pounded on chairs. Savoring each cheer, Bryan defended silver. Then came the famous closing: "Having behind us the producing masses of this nation and the world . . . we will answer their demand for a gold standard by saying to them: 'You shall not press down upon the brow of labor this crown of thorns, you shall not crucify mankind upon a cross of gold.'"

The religious symbolism in Bryan's "Cross of Gold" speech is satirized in this cartoon, but his stirring rhetoric captivated his audience and won him the Democratic presidential nomination for the election of 1896. ❖

The choice was unpleasant, and it shattered the People's party. Meeting late in July, the party's national convention nominated Bryan, but rather than accept the Democratic candidate for vice president, it named Tom Watson instead. The Populists' endorsement probably hurt Bryan as much as it helped. It won him relatively few votes, since many Populists would have voted for him anyway. It also identified him as a Populist, which he was not, allowing the Republicans to accuse him of heading a ragtag army of malcontents. The squabble over Watson seemed to prove that the Democratic-Populist alliance could never stay together long enough to govern.

In August 1896, Bryan set off on a campaign that became an American legend. Much of the conservative Democratic eastern press had deserted him, and he took his campaign directly to the voters, the first presidential candidate in history to do so in a systematic way. By his own count, Bryan traveled 18,009 miles, visited 27 states, and spoke 600 times to a total of some 3 million people. He built skillfully on a new "merchandising" style of campaign in which he worked to educate and persuade voters.

Bryan summoned voters to an older America: a land where farms were as important as factories, where the virtues of rural and religious life outweighed the doubtful lure of the city, where common people still ruled and opportunity existed for all. He drew on the Jeffersonian tradition of rural virtue, distrust of central authority, and abiding faith in the powers of human reason.

Urged to take the stump against Bryan, McKinley replied, "I might just as well put up a trapeze on my front lawn and compete with some professional athlete as go out speaking against Bryan." The Republican candidate let voters come to him. Railroads brought them by the thousands into McKinley's hometown of Canton, Ohio, and he spoke to them from his front porch. Through use of the press, he reached fully as many people as Bryan's more strenuous effort. Appealing to labor, immigrants, well-to-do farmers, businessmen, and the middle class, McKinley defended economic nationalism and the advancing urban-industrial society.

On election day, voter turnout was extraordinarily high, a measure of the intense interest. By nightfall, the

Bryan moved his fingers down his temples, suggesting blood trickling from his wounds. He ended with his arms outstretched as on a cross. Letting the silence hang, he dropped his arms, stepped back, then started to his seat. Suddenly, there was pandemonium. Delegates shouted and cheered. When the tumult subsided, they adopted the anti-Cleveland platform, and the next day, Bryan won the presidential nomination.

Campaign and Election

The Democratic convention presented the Populists with a dilemma. The People's party had staked everything on the assumption that neither major party would endorse silver. Now it faced a painful choice: Nominate an independent ticket and risk splitting the silverite forces, or nominate Bryan and give up its separate identity as a party.

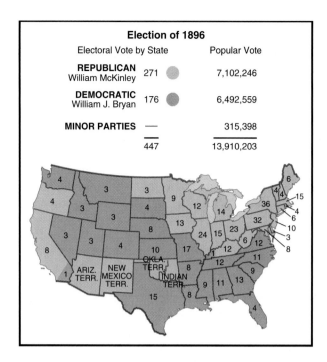

Election of 1896

	Electoral Vote by State		Popular Vote
REPUBLICAN William McKinley	271		7,102,246
DEMOCRATIC William J. Bryan	176		6,492,559
MINOR PARTIES	—		315,398
	447		13,910,203

CHRONOLOGY

1876	Mark Twain publishes *The Adventures of Tom Sawyer*
1877	Disputed election of 1876 results in awarding of presidency to Republican Rutherford B. Hayes
1880	Republican James A. Garfield elected president
1881	Garfield assassinated; Vice President Chester A. Arthur becomes president
1884	Democrat Grover Cleveland elected president, defeating Republican James G. Blaine
1887	Cleveland calls for lowering of tariff duties
1888	Republican Benjamin Harrison wins presidential election
1889	National Farmers' Alliance and Industrial Union formed to address problems of farmers
1890	Republican-dominated "Billion-Dollar" Congress enacts McKinley Tariff Act, Sherman Antitrust Act, and Sherman Silver Purchase Act ❖ Farmers' Alliance adopts the Ocala Demands
1892	Democrat Cleveland defeats Republican Harrison for presidency ❖ People's party formed
1893	Financial panic touches off depression lasting until 1897 ❖ Sherman Silver Purchase Act repealed ❖ World Columbian Exposition opens in Chicago
1894	Coxey's army marches on Washington ❖ Pullman employees strike
1896	Republican McKinley defeats William Jennings Bryan, Democratic and Populist candidate, in "battle of the standards"
1897	Gold discovered in Alaska ❖ Dingley Tariff Act raises tariff duties
1900	McKinley reelected, again defeating Bryan ❖ Gold Standard Act establishes gold as standard of currency
1901	McKinley assassinated; Vice President Theodore Roosevelt assumes presidency ❖ Naturalist writer Theodore Dreiser publishes *Sister Carrie*

outcome was clear: McKinley won 50 percent of the vote to Bryan's 46 percent. He won the Northeast and Midwest and carried four border states. In the cities, McKinley crushed Bryan.

The election struck down the Populists, whose totals sagged nearly everywhere. Many Populist proposals were later adopted under different leadership. The graduated income tax, crop loans to farmers, the secret ballot, and direct election of U.S. senators all were early Populist ideas. But the People's party never could win over a majority of the voters, and failing that, it vanished after 1896.

THE MCKINLEY ADMINISTRATION

The election of 1896 cemented the voter realignment of 1894 and initiated a generation of Republican rule. For more than three decades after 1896, with only a brief Democratic resurgence under Woodrow Wilson, the Republicans remained the country's majority party.

McKinley took office in 1897 under favorable circumstances. To everyone's relief, the economy had begun to revive. The stock market rose, factories once again churned out goods, and farmers prospered. Farm prices climbed sharply during 1897 on bumper crops of wheat, cotton, and corn. Discoveries of gold in Australia and Alaska—together with the development of a new cyanide process for extracting gold from ore—enlarged the world's gold supply, decreased its price, and inflated the currency as the silverites had hoped. For the first time since 1890, the 1897 Treasury statements showed a comfortable gold reserve.

McKinley and the Republicans basked in the glow. They became the party of progress and prosperity, an image that helped them win victories until another depression hit in the 1930s. McKinley's popularity soared. Open and accessible, in contrast to Cleveland's isolation, he rode the Washington streetcars, walked the streets, and enjoyed looking in department store

THE ELECTION OF 1900

Candidate	Party	Popular Vote	Electoral Vote
McKinley	Republican	7,218,039	292
Bryan	Democrat	6,358,345	155
Woolley	Prohibition	209,004	0
Debs	Socialist	86,935	0

windows. Cleveland's special police barracks vanished from the White House lawn. McKinley became the first president to ride in an automobile, reaching the speed of 18 miles an hour.

An activist president, he set the policies of the administration. Conscious of the limits of power, he maintained close ties with Congress and worked hard to educate the public on national choices and priorities. McKinley struck new relations with the press and traveled far more than previous presidents. In some ways, he began the modern presidency.

Shortly after taking office, he summoned Congress into special session to revise the tariff. In July 1897, the Dingley Tariff passed the House and Senate. It raised average tariff duties to a record level, and as the final burst of nineteenth-century protectionism, it caused trouble for the Republican party. By the end of the 1890s, consumers, critics, and the Republicans themselves were wondering if the tariff had outlived its usefulness in the maturing American economy.

From the 1860s to the 1890s, the Republicans had built their party on a pledge to *promote* economic growth through the use of state and national power. By 1900, with the industrial system firmly in place, the focus had shifted. The need to *regulate,* to control the effects of industrialism, became a central public concern of the new century. McKinley prodded the Republicans to meet that shift, but he died before his plans matured.

McKinley toyed with the idea of lowering the tariff, but one obstacle always stood in the way: The government needed revenue, and tariff duties were one of the few taxes the public would support. The Spanish-American War of 1898 persuaded people to accept greater federal power and, with it, new forms of taxation. In 1899, McKinley spoke of lowering tariff barriers in a world that technology had made smaller. "God and man have linked the nations together," he said in his last speech at Buffalo, New York, in 1901. "Isolation is no longer possible or desirable."

In 1898 and 1899, the McKinley administration focused on the war with Spain, the peace treaty that followed, and the dawning realization that the war had thrust the United States into a position of world power. In March 1900, Congress passed the **Gold Standard Act,** which declared gold the standard of currency and ended the silver controversy that had dominated the 1890s.

The presidential campaign of 1900 was a replay of the McKinley-Bryan fight of 1896. McKinley's running mate was Theodore Roosevelt, hero of the Spanish-American War and former governor of New York, who was nominated for vice president to capitalize on his popularity and, his enemies hoped, to sidetrack his political career into oblivion. Bryan stressed the issues of imperialism and the trusts; McKinley stressed his record at home and abroad. The result in 1900 was a landslide.

On September 6, 1901, a few months after his second inauguration, McKinley stood in a receiving line at the Pan-American Exposition in Buffalo. Leon Czolgosz, a 28-year-old unemployed laborer and anarchist, moved through the line and, reaching the

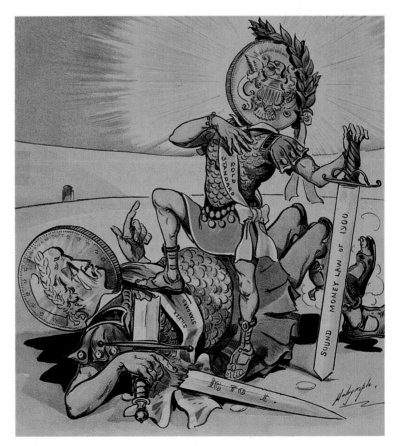

Gold triumphs over silver in this Puck *cartoon referring to the Gold Standard Act of 1900.* ❖

president, shot him. Surgeons probed the wound but could find nothing. A recent discovery called the X ray was on display at the exposition, but it was not used. On September 14, McKinley died, and Vice President Theodore Roosevelt became president. A new century had begun.

CONCLUSION: A DECADE'S DRAMATIC CHANGES

As the funeral train carried McKinley's body back to Ohio, Mark Hanna, McKinley's old friend and ally, sat slumped in his parlor car. "I told William McKinley it was a mistake to nominate that wild man at Philadelphia," he mourned. "I asked him if he realized what would happen if he should die. Now look, that damned cowboy is president of the United States!"

Hanna's world had changed, and so had the nation's—not so much because "that damned cowboy" was suddenly president, but because events of the 1890s had had powerful effects. In the course of that decade, political patterns shifted, the presidency acquired fresh power, and massive unrest prompted so-

cial change. The war with Spain brought a new empire and worldwide responsibilities. Economic hardship posed questions of the most difficult sort about industrialization, urbanization, and the quality of American life. Worried, people embraced new ideas and causes. Reform movements begun in the 1890s flowered in the Progressive Era after 1900.

Technology continued to alter the way Americans lived. In 1896, Henry Ford produced a two-cylinder, four-horsepower car, the first of the famous line that bore his name. In 1899, the first automobile salesroom opened in New York, and some innovative thinkers were already imagining a network of service stations to keep the new cars running. At Kitty Hawk, North Carolina, Wilbur and Orville Wright, two bicycle manufacturers, neared the birth of powered flight.

The realignments that reached their peak in the 1890s seem distant, yet they are not. Important decisions in those years shaped nearly everything that came after them. In character and influence, the 1890s were as much a part of the twentieth century as of the nineteenth and continue to have repercussions into the twenty-first century.

RECOMMENDED READING

The best study of the 1890s depression is Charles Hoffman, *The Depression of the Nineties: An Economic History* (1970). H. Wayne Morgan, *From Hayes to McKinley: National Party Politics, 1877–1896* (1969), Michael E. McGerr, *The Decline of Popular Politics: The American North, 1865–1928* (1986), Mark Lawrence Kornbluh, *Why America Stopped Voting: The Decline of Participatory Democracy and the Emergence of Modern American Politics* (2000), and Richard J. Jensen, *The Winning of the Midwest* (1971) are good on politics. David P. Thelen, *The New Citizenship: Origins of Progressivism in Wisconsin, 1885–1900* (1972), Carl Smith, *Urban Disorder and the Shape of Belief: The Great Chicago Fire, the Haymarket Bomb, and the Model Town of Pullman* (1995), and Douglas W. Steeples and David O. Whitten, *Democracy in Desperation: The Depression of 1893* (1998), stress the im-

pact of the depression on ideas and attitudes. C. Vann Woodward examines the South in *Origins of the New South, 1877–1913* (1951). Also, Michael Perman, *Struggle for Mastery: Disfranchisement in the South, 1888–1908* (2001).

On Populism, see John D. Hicks, *The Populist Revolt* (1931), Lawrence Goodwyn, *Democratic Promise: The Populist Moment in America* (1976), Steven Hahn, *The Roots of Southern Populism* (1983), and Elizabeth Sanders, *Roots of Reform: Farmers, Workers, and the American State, 1877–1917* (1999). Steven W. Usselman, *Regulating Railroad Innovation: Business, Technology, and Politics in America, 1840–1920* (2002), looks at regulatory reform.

For a list of additional titles related to this chapter's topics, please see http://www.ablongman.com/divine.

Suggested Web Sites

World's Columbian Exposition: Idea, Experience, Aftermath

http://xroads.virginia.edu/~MA96/WCE/title.html

This site has a virtual tour of the fair, along with contemporary reactions and modern analysis.

Pullman Links on the Web—Historic Pullman Foundation

http://www.pullmanil.org/links.htm

This page offers several links to sites with Pullman related information, including a section of sites on the Pullman strike and labor history.

Election of 1896

http://jefferson.village.virginia.edu/seminar/unit8/home.htm

This University of Virginia site contains biographical information, images, cartoons, and related links about the pivotal 1896 election.

The Era of William McKinley

http://www.history.ohio-state.edu/projects/mckinley/default.htm

This site contains numerous images from various stages of William McKinley's career along with a brief biographical essay. This Ohio State University site also has a section with an excellent collection of cartoons from the era.

Return of the Conquerors *by Edward Moran celebrates the triumphant return of America's Great White Fleet. The fleet of 16 white-hulled battleships and supporting craft set off in December 1907 on a 14-month, round-the-world cruise as a dramatic show of America's naval strength.* ❖

Toward Empire

Roosevelt and the Rough Riders

Many Americans regretted the start of the war with Spain that began in April 1898, but many others welcomed it. Many highly respected people believed that nations must fight every now and then to prove their power and test the national spirit.

Theodore Roosevelt, 39 years old in 1898, was one of them. Nations needed to fight in order to survive, he thought. For months, Roosevelt argued strenuously for war with Spain for three reasons: first, on grounds of freeing Cuba and expelling Spain from the hemisphere; second, because of "the benefit done to our people by giving them something to think of which isn't material gain"; and third, because the army and navy needed the practice.

In April 1898, Roosevelt was serving in the important post of assistant secretary of the navy. When war broke out, he quickly resigned to join the army, rejecting the advice of the secretary of the navy, who warned he would only "ride a horse and brush mosquitoes from his neck in the Florida sands." The secretary was wrong—dead wrong—and later had the grace to admit it. "Roosevelt was right," he said. "His going into the Army led straight to the Presidency."

In 1898, officers supplied their own uniforms, and Roosevelt, the son of well-to-do parents, wanted his to be stylish. He wired Brooks Brothers, the expensive New York clothier, for a "regular Lieutenant-Colonel's uniform without yellow on the collar and with leggings," to be ready in a week. Joining a friend, he chose to enlist his own regiment, and after a few telephone calls to friends, and telegrams to the governors of Arizona, New Mexico, and Oklahoma asking for "good shots and good riders," he had more than enough men. The First United States Volunteer Cavalry, an intriguing mixture of Ivy League athletes and western frontiersmen, was born.

Known as the Rough Riders, it included men from the Harvard, Yale, and Princeton clubs of New York City, the Somerset Club of Boston, and New York's exclusive Knickerbocker Club. Former college athletes—football players, tennis players, and track stars—enlisted. Woodbury Kane, a wealthy yachtsman, signed up and promptly volunteered for kitchen duty.

Other volunteers came from the West—natural soldiers, Roosevelt called them, "tall and sinewy, with resolute, weather-beaten faces, and eyes that looked a man straight in the face without flinching." Among the cowboys, hunters, and prospectors, there were Bucky O'Neill, a legendary Arizona sheriff and Indian fighter; a half dozen other sheriffs and Texas Rangers; a large number of Indians; a famous broncobuster; and an ex-marshal of Dodge City, Kansas.

Eager for war, the men trained hard, played harder, and rarely passed up a chance for an intellectual discussion—if Roosevelt's memoir of the war is to be believed. Once, he overheard Bucky O'Neill and a Princeton graduate "discussing Aryan word-roots together, and then sliding off into a review of the novels of Balzac, and a discussion as to how far Balzac could be said to be the founder of the modern realistic school of fiction." Roosevelt himself spent his spare time reading *Superiorité des Anglo-Saxons*, a French work that strove to prove the superiority of English-speaking

OUTLINE
❖❖❖

America Looks Outward

War with Spain

Acquisition of Empire

Conclusion: Outcome of the War with Spain

FEATURE ESSAY
❖❖❖

Americans by the Numbers: The 1890 Census

Colonel Theodore Roosevelt poses in his custom-designed uniform. With surgeon Leonard Wood, Roosevelt organized the First U.S. Volunteer Cavalry—the Rough Riders—for service in the Spanish-American War. ❖

peoples. In such a camp, discipline was lax, and enlisted men got on easily with the officers.

The troops howled with joy when orders came to join the invasion army for Cuba. They won their first victories in Florida, fighting off other regiments to capture a train to take them to the wharf and then seizing the only available troopship to Cuba. The Rough Riders set sail on June 14, 1898, and Lieutenant Colonel Roosevelt, who had performed a war dance for the troops the night before, caught their mood: "We knew not whither we were bound, nor what we were to do; but we believed that the nearing future held for us many chances of death and hardship, of honor and renown. If we failed, we would share the fate of all who fail; but we were sure that we would win, that we should score the first great triumph in a mighty world-movement."

THAT "WORLD-MOVEMENT," ROOSEVELT WAS SURE, would establish the United States as a world power, whose commerce and influence would extend around the globe, particularly in Latin America and Asia. As he hoped, the nation in the 1890s underwent dramatic expansion, building on the foreign policy approaches of administrations from Lincoln to William McKinley. Policymakers fostered business interests abroad, strengthened the navy, and extended American influence into Latin America and the Pacific. Differences over Cuba resulted in a war with Spain that brought new colonies and colonial subjects, establishing for the first time an American overseas empire.

AMERICA LOOKS OUTWARD

The overseas expansion of the 1890s differed in several important respects from earlier expansionist moves of the United States. From its beginning, the American republic had been expanding. After the first landings in Jamestown and Plymouth, settlers pushed westward: into the trans-Appalachian region, the Louisiana Territory, Florida, Texas, California, Arizona, and New Mexico. Most of these lands were contiguous with existing territories of the United States, and most were intended for settlement, usually agricultural.

The expansion of the 1890s was different. It sought to gain island possessions, the bulk of them already thickly populated. The new territories were intended less for settlement than for use as naval bases, trading outposts, or commercial centers on major trade routes. More often than not, they were viewed as colonies, not as states-in-the-making.

Historian Samuel F. Bemis described the overseas expansion of the 1890s as "the great aberration," a time

when the country adopted expansionist policies that did not fit with prior experience. Other historians, pointing to expansionist tendencies in thought and foreign policy that surfaced during the last half of the nineteenth century, have found a developing pattern that led naturally to the overseas adventures of the 1890s. In the view of Walter LaFeber, "the United States did not set out on an expansionist path in the late 1890s in a sudden, spur-of-the-moment fashion. The overseas empire that Americans controlled in 1900 was not a break in their history, but a natural culmination."

Catching the Spirit of Empire

Most people in most times in history tend to look at domestic concerns, and Americans in the years following the Civil War were no exception. Among other things, they focused on Reconstruction, the movement westward, and simply making a living. They took seriously the well-remembered advice of George Washington's

❖ A Look at the Past ❖

Trade Card

Trade cards—postcard-sized advertisements—provided manufacturers with attractive, richly colored attention-grabbers. As firms entered national and even international markets, advertising became increasingly important as a way to promote brand identification and loyalty. The Singer Sewing Machine Company commissioned a set of trade cards in the 1890s, including the one shown here, that showed its products being used around the world. This card, made in 1892, reveals U.S. interest in the Philippines before the Spanish-American War broke out. Why would Singer depict sewing machines used in foreign lands as a way to attract U.S. consumers? How would you characterize the depiction of Filipinos on this card? How do you suppose Americans viewed Filipinos and other Asians?

farewell address to "steer clear" of foreign entanglements. Throughout the nineteenth century, Americans enjoyed "free security" without fully appreciating it. Sheltered by two oceans and the British navy, they could enunciate bold policies such as the Monroe Doctrine, which instructed European nations to stay out of the affairs of the Western Hemisphere, while remaining virtually impregnable to foreign attack.

In those circumstances a sense of **isolationism** spread, fostering a desire to stay out of foreign entanglements. Some people even urged abolition of the foreign service, considering it an unnecessary expenditure, a dangerous profession that might lead to involvement in the struggles of the world's great powers. A New York newspaper called it a "relic of medieval, monarchical trumpery," and if not that, it certainly became at times a dumping ground of the spoils system. Presidents named leaders who, though successful in their own fields, had no training in languages or diplomatic relations.

In the 1870s and after, however, Americans began to take an increasing interest in events abroad. There was a growing sense of internationalism, which stemmed in part from the telegraphs, telephones, and undersea cables that kept people better informed about political and economic developments in distant lands. Many Americans continued to be interested in expansion of the country's borders; relatively few were interested in **imperialism**. Expansion meant the kind of growth that had brought California and Oregon into the American system. Imperialism meant the imposition of control over other peoples through annexation, military conquest, or economic domination.

Reasons for Expansion

Several developments in these years combined to shift attention outward across the seas. The end of the frontier, announced officially in the census report of 1890, sparked fears about diminishing opportunities at home. (See the Feature Essay, "Americans by the Numbers: The 1890 Census," pp. 604–605.) Further growth, it seemed to some, must take place abroad, as John A. Kasson, an able and experienced diplomat, said in the *North American Review:* "We are rapidly utilizing the whole of our continental territory. We must turn our eyes abroad, or they will soon look inward upon discontent."

Factories and farms multiplied, producing more goods than the domestic market could consume. Both farmers and industrialists looked for new overseas markets, and the growing volume of exports—including more and more manufactured goods—changed the nature of American trade relations with the world. American exports of merchandise amounted to $393 million in 1870, $858 million in 1890, and $1.4 billion in 1900. In 1898, the United States exported more than it imported, beginning a trend that lasted through the 1960s.

Political leaders such as James G. Blaine began to argue for the vital importance of foreign markets to continued economic growth. Blaine, secretary of state under Garfield and again under Harrison, aggressively sought wider markets in Latin America, Asia, and

AMERICANS BY THE NUMBERS

The 1890 Census

Censuses measure many things, including their own purposes. In the nation's first census, in 1790, census takers had set out mainly to measure the population, as a way to apportion representatives in Congress. By 1890, one hundred years later, it did that and more, growing into an enormous compilation of numbers covering nearly every aspect of national life. It had become, as a contemporary expert put it, "a leading instrument in the sci-entific investigation of the social and economic conditions of the nation."

"Scientific" investigation in those years meant the generous use of statis-tics, a relatively new discipline, and statistics in turn involved the collec-tion and interpretation of massive amounts of data. As recently as 1880, census takers had counted that data by hand, using essentially the same meth-ods people had used in 1790. But it was a slow process at best, futile at worst, and matters looked little different as 1890 dawned. When the new superintendent of the census took charge that year, he found, as he later said, "one clerk and a mes-senger, and a desk with some white paper on it."

Fortunately, he found something else as well, a new invention, the brainchild of a young graduate of Columbia University named Herman Hollerith, who had worked with the census in 1880 and had seen its problems firsthand. Experimenting largely on his own, Hollerith devised an ingenious system in which clerks translated data into punched holes in cards, then fed the cards through a machine that used electric current to read the location of the holes. It was a revolu-tion in method—the machine tabula-tion of data.

Using the Hollerith system, an ex-perienced clerk could tabulate as many as ten thousand cards in a single day and, equally important, calculate all sorts of informative correlations. For the first time, experts could calculate quickly the number of girls between the ages of ten and fifteen working in textile mills in eastern Massachusetts, or the death rate among African Americans raising cotton on tenant farms in Mississippi, or almost any-thing else they wanted to know. A forerunner of the modern computer industry, Hollerith's system later be-came part of the International Business Machines Corporation (IBM) and helped begin the information rev-olution that so influenced the United States into the twenty-first century.

The results were startling. In 1790, 650 census takers had counted nearly 4 million people and printed the results in a booklet of 56 pages. In 1890, 46,804 census takers counted 63 million people and printed the results in 32 large volumes, with 22,000 pages of statistics tracking nearly every as-pect of American life.

The new ability to count allowed census takers to ask more questions about more things, which enabled them in turn to respond to the grow-ing desire of government and business to have detailed information about manufacturing, wages, crops, personal debt, mortality, and a host of other matters.

Some of the new questions would not be asked today. Reflecting the era's racial views, the 1890 census called for specific definitions of race, dividing African Americans into black, mu-

Observing a train conductor punch tickets gave Herman Hollerith the idea for developing a system of punched cards to record census data and an electrical tabulator to read the information. ❖

Using the tabulating machine invented by Herman Hollerith, a worker operates a presslike device to bring an array of pins into contact with a punch card. As a pin passed through a hole in the punch card, it came into contact with a small cup of mercury to complete a circuit that registered on one of the dials at the top of the electro-mechanical tabulator. To the worker's right is the card sorter. The press/pin/cup device also opened one of the sorter's chutes into which the operator would deposit the punch card. ❖

latto, quadroon, and octoroon, depending on each persons' ancestry. Because some people were worried about the growing number of immigrants in the country, it also wanted to know about place of birth and citizenship, the ability to speak the English language, and differences in birthrates between native- and foreign-born women.

The news, for some, was disturbing. Hollerith's machines turned up the fact that 5,750,000 immigrants had arrived in the United States in the ten years between 1880 and 1890, more than twice as many as in any former decade. Fully a third of the population had parents who were born in another country, a figure quickly pounced upon by those wanting laws that would cut down on immigration.

Out in Madison, Wisconsin, a young historian at the University of Wisconsin studied the new data and noted another important trend as well. From 1790 to 1880, the country had always had "a frontier of settlement," as the superintendent of the census called it, areas of land still awaiting population and development. As of 1890 it did not. Thanks to the rapid spread of population, the "frontier

line" had ceased to exist, and no longer would the frontier and the westward movement "have a place in the census reports."

From that official observation, Frederick Jackson Turner, the young historian, drew a rich and powerful interpretation of the nation's history. In an essay entitled "The Significance of the Frontier in American History," published in 1893, he argued that the frontier had made American society what it was. Settling and surviving on the western edge of settlement had sparked innovation, adaptation, and invention; spurred the growth of democratic institutions; and set in place particularly "American" ways of life and thought.

The end of the frontier, Turner wrote, "marks the closing of a great historical movement. Up to our own day American history has been in large degree the history of the colonization of the Great West," but "the frontier has gone, and with its going has closed the first period of American history."

Although "the Turner thesis," as it was quickly known, would later arouse controversy, in the 1890s it became instantly popular, persuading Theodore Roosevelt and others that

with the closing of the frontier, a new era had begun in the nation's life. That new era, the 1890 data seemed to make clear, had little to do with frontiers and farms, and everything to do with the growing, bustling world of cities and factories. In 1890, for the first time, more than half the labor force worked in some form of manufacturing, mining, trade, or transportation. People were flocking to the cities to work in the factories and enjoy new opportunities. New York City that year had 1.5 million inhabitants, Philadelphia and Chicago (which had doubled in population during the prior decade) more than a million.

If some people found cause for worry in all the figures, others found reason for hope. With the beginnings of the progressive movement in the late 1890s, reformers drew on the census statistics to study and understand the way people lived, to improve their health, enrich their lives, increase their safety at work, and protect the young and the weak. The census, in short, had become more than ever an instrument with which to monitor the state of society, and in 1902, reflecting that fact, the Census Office at last became a permanent bureau of the government.

Africa, using tariff reciprocity agreements and other measures. To some extent, he and others were also caught up in a worldwide scramble for empire. In the last third of the century, Great Britain, France, and Germany divided up Africa and looked covetously at Asia. The idea of imperialistic expansion was in the air, and the great powers measured their greatness by the colonies they acquired. Inevitably, some Americans—certain business interests and foreign policy strategists, for example—caught the spirit and wanted to enter the international hunt for territory.

Intellectual currents that supported expansion drew on Charles Darwin's theories of evolution. Adherents pointed, for example, to *The Origin of Species,* which mentioned in its subtitle *The Preservation of Favoured Races in the Struggle for Life.* Applied to human and social development, biological concepts seemed to call for the triumph of the fit and the elimination of the unfit. "In this world," said Theodore Roosevelt, who thought of himself as one of the fit, "the nation that has trained itself to a career of unwarlike and isolated ease is bound, in the end, to go down before other nations which have not lost the manly and adventurous qualities."

The "biogenetic law" formulated by German biologist Ernst Haeckel suggested that the development of the race paralleled the development of the individual. Primitive peoples thus were in the arrested stages of childhood or adolescence; they needed supervision and protection. In a similar vein, John Fiske, a popular writer and lecturer, argued for Anglo-Saxon racial superiority, a result of the process of natural selection. The English and Americans, Fiske said, would occupy every land on the globe that was not already "civilized," bringing the advances of commerce and democratic institutions.

Such views were widespread among the lettered and unlettered alike. In Cuba, one of the Rough Riders ushered a visiting Russian prince around the trenches, informing him with ill-considered enthusiasm: "You see, Prince, the great result of this war is that it has united the two branches of Anglo-Saxon people; and now that they are together they can whip the world, Prince! they can whip the world!" Eminent scholars such as John W. Burgess, a professor of political science at Columbia University, argued in similar though more dignified fashion that people of English origin were destined to impose their political institutions on the world.

The career of Josiah Strong, a Congregational minister and fervent expansionist, suggested the strength of the developing ideas. A champion of overseas missionary work, Strong traveled extensively through the West for the Home Missionary Society, and in 1885, drawing on his experiences, he published

a book titled *Our Country: Its Possible Future and Its Present Crisis.* An immediate best-seller, the book called on foreign missions to civilize the world under the Anglo-Saxon races. Strong became a national celebrity.

Our Country argued for expanding American trade and dominion. Trade was important, it said, because the desire for material things was one of the hallmarks of civilized people. So was the Christian religion, and by exporting both trade and religion, Americans could civilize and Christianize "inferior" races around the world. As Anglo-Saxons, they were members of a God-favored race destined to lead the world. Anglo-Saxons already owned one-third of the earth, Strong said, and in a famous passage he concluded that they would take more. In "the final competition of races," they would win and "move down upon Mexico, down upon Central and South America, out upon the islands of the sea, over upon Africa and beyond."

Taken together, these developments in social, political, and economic thought prepared Americans for a larger role in the world. The change was gradual, and there was never a day when people awoke with a sudden realization of their interests overseas. But change there was, and by the 1890s, Americans were ready to reach out into the world in a more determined and deliberate fashion than ever before. For almost the first time, they felt the need for a foreign "policy."

Foreign Policy Approaches, 1867–1900

Rarely consistent, American foreign policy in the last half of the nineteenth century took different approaches to different areas of the world. In relation to Europe, seat of the dominant world powers, policymakers promoted trade and tried to avoid diplomatic entanglements. In North and South America, they based policy on the Monroe Doctrine, a recurrent dream of annexing Canada or Mexico, a hope for extensive trade, and Pan-American unity against the nations of the Old World. In the Pacific, they coveted Hawaii and other outposts on the sea-lanes to China.

Secretary of State William Henry Seward, who served from 1861 to 1869, aggressively pushed an expansive foreign policy. "Give me . . . fifty, forty, thirty more years of life," he told a Boston audience in 1867, "and I will give you possession of the American continent and control of the world." Seward, it turned out, had only five more years of life, but he developed a vision of an American empire stretching south into Latin America and west to the shores of Asia. His vision included Canada and Mexico; islands in the Caribbean as strategic bases to protect a canal across the isthmus; and Hawaii and other islands as stepping-stones to Asia, which Seward and many others considered a virtually bottomless outlet for farm and manufactured goods.

Seward tried unsuccessfully to negotiate a commercial treaty with Hawaii in 1867, and the same year he annexed the Midway Islands, a small atoll group twelve hundred miles northwest of Hawaii. In 1867, he concluded a treaty with Russia for the purchase of Alaska (which was promptly labeled "Seward's Folly") partly to sandwich western Canada between American territory and lead to its annexation. As the American empire spread, Seward thought, Mexico City would become its capital.

Secretary of State Hamilton Fish, an urbane New Yorker, followed Seward in 1869, serving under President Ulysses S. Grant. An avid expansionist, Grant wanted to extend American influence in the Caribbean and Pacific, though the more conservative Fish often restrained him. They moved first to repair relations with Great Britain. The first business was settlement of the *Alabama* claims—demands that Britain pay the United States for damages to Union ships caused by Confederate vessels which, like the *Alabama,* had been built and outfitted in British shipyards. Negotiating patiently, Fish signed the Treaty of Washington in 1871, providing for arbitration of the *Alabama* issue and other nettlesome controversies. The treaty, one of the landmarks in the peaceful settlement of international disputes, marked a significant step in cementing Anglo-American relations.

Grant and Fish looked most eagerly to Latin America. In 1870, Grant became the first president to proclaim the nontransfer principle—"hereafter no territory on this continent shall be regarded as subject to transfer to a European power." Fish also promoted the independence of Cuba, restive under Spanish rule, while holding off the annexation desired by the more eager Grant. Influenced by speculators, Grant tried to annex Santo Domingo in 1869 but was thwarted by powerful Republicans in the Senate who disliked foreign involvement and feared a subsequent attempt to annex Haiti.

James G. Blaine served briefly as secretary of state under President James Garfield and laid extensive plans to establish closer commercial relations with Latin America. Blaine's successor, Frederick T. Frelinghuysen, changed Blaine's approach but not his strategy. Like Blaine, Frelinghuysen wanted to find Caribbean markets for American goods; he negotiated separate reciprocity treaties with Mexico, Cuba and Puerto Rico, the British West Indies, Santo Domingo, and Colombia. Using these treaties, Frelinghuysen hoped not only to obtain markets for American goods but to bind these countries to American interests.

When Blaine returned to the State Department in 1889 under President Benjamin Harrison, he moved again to expand markets in Latin America. Drawing on earlier ideas, he envisaged a hemispheric system of peaceful intercourse, arbitration of disputes, and expanded trade. He also wanted to annex Hawaii. "I think there are only three places that are of value and not already taken, that are not continental," he wrote in a letter to President Harrison in 1891. "One is Hawaii and the others are Cuba and Puerto Rico." The last two might take a generation to acquire, but "Hawaii may come up for decision at any unexpected hour and I hope we shall be prepared to decide it in the affirmative."

Harrison and Blaine toyed with naval acquisitions in the Caribbean and elsewhere, but in general they focused on Pan-Americanism and tariff reciprocity. Blaine presided over the first Inter-American Conference in Washington on October 2, 1889, where delegates from nineteen American nations negotiated several agreements to promote trade and created the International Bureau of the American Republics, later renamed the Pan-American Union, for the exchange of general information, including political, scientific, and cultural knowledge. The conference, a major step in hemispheric relations, led to later meetings promoting trade and other agreements.

Reciprocity, Harrison and Blaine hoped, would divert Latin American trade from Europe to the United States. Working hard to sell the idea in Congress, Blaine lobbied for a reciprocity provision in the McKinley Tariff Act of 1890, and once that was enacted, he negotiated reciprocity treaties with most Latin American nations. The treaties failed to foster the hoped-for trade because of the depression of the 1890s; nevertheless, they resulted in greater American exports of flour, grain, meat, iron, and machinery. Exports to Cuba jumped by one-third between 1891 and 1893, then dropped precipitously when the 1894 Wilson-Gorman Tariff Act ended reciprocity.

Grover Cleveland, Harrison's successor, also pursued an aggressive policy toward Latin America. In 1895, he brought the United States precariously close to war with Great Britain over a boundary dispute between Venezuela and British Guiana. Cleveland sympathized with Venezuela, and he and Secretary of State Richard Olney urged Britain to arbitrate the dispute. When Britain failed to act, Olney drafted a stiff diplomatic note affirming the Monroe Doctrine and denying European nations the right to meddle in Western Hemisphere affairs.

Four months passed before Lord Salisbury, the British foreign secretary, replied. Rejecting Olney's arguments, he sent two letters, the first bluntly repudiating the Monroe Doctrine as international law.

The second letter, carefully reasoned and sometimes sarcastic, rejected Olney's arguments for the Venezuelan boundary. Enraged, Cleveland defended the Monroe Doctrine, and he asked Congress for authority to appoint a commission to decide the boundary and enforce its decision. "I am fully alive to the responsibility incurred and keenly realize all the consequences that may follow," he told Congress, plainly implying war.

Preoccupied with larger diplomatic problems in Africa and Europe, Britain changed its position. In November 1896, the two countries signed a treaty of arbitration, under which Great Britain and Venezuela divided the disputed territory. Though Cleveland's approach was clumsy—throughout the crisis, for example, he rarely consulted Venezuela—the Venezuelan incident demonstrated a growing determination to exert American power in the Western Hemisphere. Cleveland and Olney had persuaded Great Britain to recognize the United States' dominance, and they had increased American influence in Latin America. The Monroe Doctrine assumed new importance. In averting war, an era of Anglo-American friendship was begun.

The Lure of Hawaii and Samoa

The islands of Hawaii offered a tempting way station to Asian markets. In the early 1800s, they were already called the "Crossroads of the Pacific," and trading ships of many nations stopped there. In 1820, the first American missionaries arrived to convert the islanders to Christianity. Like missionaries elsewhere, they advertised Hawaii's economic and other benefits and attracted new settlers. Their children later came to dominate Hawaiian political and economic life and played an important role in annexation.

After the Civil War, the United States tightened its connections with the islands. The reciprocity treaty of 1875 allowed Hawaiian sugar to enter the United States free of duty and bound the Hawaiian monarchy to make no territorial or economic concessions to other powers. The treaty increased Hawaiian economic dependence on the United States; its political clauses effectively made Hawaii an American protectorate. In 1887, a new treaty reaffirmed these arrangements and granted the United States exclusive use of Pearl Harbor, a magnificent harbor that had early caught the eye of naval strategists.

Following the 1875 treaty, white Hawaiians became more and more influential in the islands' political life. The McKinley Tariff Act of 1890 ended the special status given Hawaiian sugar and at the same time awarded American producers a bounty of two cents a pound. Hawaiian sugar production dropped dramatically, unemployment rose, and property values fell. The following year, the weak King Kalakaua died, bringing to power a strong-willed nationalist, Queen Liliuokalani. Resentful of white minority rule, she decreed a new constitution that gave greater power to native Hawaiians.

The first step toward American annexation of Hawaii came in 1893 when Queen Liliuokalani was removed from the throne. Hawaii was annexed to the United States as a possession in 1898 and became a U.S. territory in 1900. This photograph from ca. 1898 shows the former queen with guests and members of her household at Washington Place, her residence from 1896 until her death in 1917. ❖

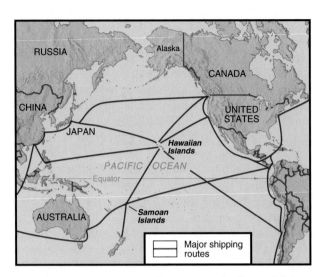

HAWAIIAN ISLANDS *The Hawaiian Islands provided the United States with both a convenient stopping point on the way to Asian markets and a strategic naval station in the Pacific.* ❖

Unhappy, the American residents revolted in early 1893 and called on the United States for help. John L. Stevens, the American minister in Honolulu, sent 150 marines ashore from the cruiser *Boston,* and within three days, the bloodless revolution was over. Queen Liliuokalani surrendered "to the superior force of the United States," and the victorious rebels set up a provisional government. Stevens urged annexation, telling Washington that the "Hawaiian pear is now fully ripe, and this is the golden hour for the United States to pluck it." On February 14, 1893, Harrison's secretary of state, John W. Foster, and delegates of the new government signed a treaty annexing Hawaii to the United States.

But only two weeks remained in Harrison's term, and the Senate refused to ratify the agreement. Five days after taking office, Cleveland withdrew the treaty; he then sent a representative to investigate the cause of the rebellion. The investigation revealed that the Americans' role in it had been improper, and Cleveland decided to restore the queen to her throne. He made the demand, but the provisional government in Hawaii politely refused and instead established the Republic of Hawaii, which the embarrassed Cleveland, unable to do otherwise, recognized.

The debate over Hawaiian annexation, continuing through the 1890s, foreshadowed the later debate over the treaty to end the Spanish-American War. People in favor of annexation pointed to Hawaii's strategic location, argued that Japan or other powers might seize the islands if the United States did not, and suggested that Americans had a responsibility to civilize and Christianize the native Hawaiians. Opponents warned

that annexation might lead to a colonial army and colonial problems, the inclusion of a "mongrel" population in the United States, and rule over an area not destined for statehood.

Annexation came swiftly in July 1898 in the midst of excitement over victories in the Spanish-American War. The year before, President William McKinley had sent a treaty of annexation to the Senate, but opposition quickly arose, and the treaty stalled. Japan protested against it, pointing out that Japanese made up a quarter of the Hawaiian population. Japan dispatched a cruiser to Honolulu; the Navy Department sent the battleship *Oregon* and ordered naval forces to take Hawaii if the Japanese made threatening moves.

In 1898, annexationists redoubled arguments about Hawaii's commercial and military importance. McKinley and congressional leaders switched strategies to seek a joint resolution, rather than a treaty, for annexation. A joint resolution required only a majority of both houses, while a treaty needed a two-thirds vote in the Senate. Bolstered by the new strategy, the annexation measure moved quickly through Congress, and McKinley signed it on July 7, 1898. His signature, giving the United States a naval and commercial base in the mid-Pacific, realized a goal held by policymakers since the 1860s.

While annexation of Hawaii represented a step toward China, the Samoan Islands, three thousand miles to the south, offered a strategic location astride the sea-lanes of the South Pacific. Americans showed early interest in Samoa, and in 1872, a naval officer negotiated a treaty granting the United States the use of Pago Pago, a splendid harbor on one of its islands. The Senate rejected the treaty but six years later approved a similar agreement providing for a naval station there. The agreement bound the United States to use its good offices to adjust any disputes between the Samoan chiefs and foreign governments. Great Britain and Germany also secured treaty rights in Samoa, and thereafter the three nations jockeyed for position.

The situation grew tense in 1889, when warships from all three countries gathered in a Samoan harbor. But a sudden typhoon damaged the fleets, and tensions eased. A month later, delegates from Britain, Germany, and the United States met in Berlin to negotiate the problem. Britain and Germany wanted to divide up the islands; Secretary of State Blaine held out for some degree of authority by the indigenous population, with American control over Pago Pago.

The agreement, an uneasy one, ended in 1899 when the United States and Germany divided Samoa and compensated Britain with lands elsewhere in the Pacific. Germany claimed the two larger islands in the chain; the United States kept the harbor at Pago Pago.

The New Navy

Large navies were vital in the scramble for colonies, and in the 1870s the United States had almost no naval power. One of the most powerful fleets in the world during the Civil War, the American navy had fallen into rapid decline. By 1880, there were fewer than two thousand vessels, only forty-eight of which could fire a gun. Ships rotted, and many officers left the service. "It was easy then," said George Dewey, later a hero of the war with Spain, "for an officer to drift along in his grade, losing interest and remaining in the navy only because he was too old to change his occupation."

Conditions changed during the 1880s. A group of rising young officers, steeped in a new naval philosophy, argued for an expanded navy equipped with fast, aggressive fleets capable of fighting battles across the seas. This group had its greatest influence in a special Naval Advisory Board, formed by the secretary of the navy in 1881. Big-navy proponents pointed to the growing fleets of Great Britain, France, and Germany, arguing that the United States needed greater fleet

This 1881 cartoon depicted "our top heavy navy," a decrepit vessel sinking with idle officers. ❖

strength to protect its economic and other interests in the Caribbean and Pacific.

In 1883, Congress authorized construction of four steel ships, marking the beginning of the new navy. Experts also worked to improve naval management and the quality of fleet personnel, and between 1885 and 1889, Congress budgeted funds for thirty additional ships. The initial building program focused on lightly armored fast cruisers for raiding enemy merchant ships and protecting American shores, but after 1890, the program shifted to the construction of a seagoing offensive battleship navy capable of challenging the strongest fleets of Europe.

Alfred Thayer Mahan and Benjamin F. Tracy were two of the main forces behind the new navy. Austere and scholarly, Mahan was the era's most influential naval strategist. After graduating from the Naval Academy in 1859, he devoted a lifetime to studying the influence of sea power in history; for more than two decades, he headed the Newport Naval War College, where officers imbibed the latest in strategic thinking. A clear, logical writer, Mahan summarized his beliefs in several major books, including *The Influence of Sea Power upon History, 1660–1783* (1890), and *The Interest of America in Sea Power* (1897).

Mahan's reasoning was simple and, to that generation, persuasive. Industrialism, he argued, produced vast surpluses of agricultural and manufactured goods, for which markets must be found. Markets involved distant ports; reaching them required a large merchant marine and a powerful navy to protect it. Navies, in turn, needed coaling stations and repair yards. Coaling stations meant colonies, and colonies became strategic bases, the foundation of a nation's wealth and power. The bases might serve as markets themselves, but they were more important as stepping-stones to other objectives, such as the markets of Latin America and Asia.

Mahan called attention to the worldwide race for power, a race, he warned, the United States could not afford to lose. "All around us now is strife; 'the struggle of life,' 'the race of life' are phrases so familiar that we do not feel their significance till we stop to think about them. Everywhere nation is arrayed against nation; our own no less than others." To compete in the struggle, Mahan argued, the United States must expand. It needed strategic bases, a powerful oceangoing navy, a canal across the isthmus to link the East Coast with the Pacific, and Hawaii as a way station on the route to Asia.

Mahan influenced a generation of policymakers in the United States and Europe; one of them, Benjamin F. Tracy, became Harrison's secretary of the navy in 1889. Tracy organized the Bureau of Construction and Repair to design and build new ships, established the

Naval Reserve in 1891, and ordered construction of the first American submarine in 1893. He also adopted the first heavy rapid-fire guns, smokeless powder, torpedoes, and heavy armor. Above all, Tracy joined with big-navy advocates in Congress to push for a far-ranging battleship fleet capable of attacking distant enemies. He wanted two fleets of battleships, eight ships in the Pacific and twelve in the Atlantic. He got four first-class battleships.

In 1889, when Tracy entered office, the United States ranked twelfth among world navies; in 1893, when he left, it ranked seventh and was climbing rapidly. "The sea," he predicted in 1891, "will be the future seat of empires. And we shall rule it as certainly as the sun doth rise." By the end of the decade, the navy had seventeen steel battleships, six armored cruisers, and many smaller craft. It ranked third in the world.

WAR WITH SPAIN

The war with Spain in 1898 built a mood of national confidence, altered older, more insular patterns of thought, and reshaped the way Americans saw themselves and the world. Its outcome pleased some people but troubled others, who raised questions about war itself, colonies, and subject peoples. The war left a lingering strain of isolationism and antiwar feeling that affected later policy. It also left an American empire, small by European standards, but quite new to the American experience by virtue of its overseas location. When the war ended, American possessions stretched into the Caribbean and deep into the Pacific. American influence went further still, and the United States was recognized as a "world power."

The Spanish-American War established the United States as a dominant force for the twentieth century. It brought America colonies and millions of colonial subjects; it brought the responsibilities of governing an empire and protecting it. For better or worse, it involved the country in other nations' arguments and affairs. The war strengthened the office of the presidency, swept the nation together in a tide of emotion, and confirmed the long-standing belief in the superiority of the New World over the Old. When it was over, Americans looked outward as never before, touched, they were sure, with a special destiny.

They seemed a chosen people, as Mr. Dooley, a character created by humorist Finley Peter Dunne, pointed out to his friend Hennessy over the Archey Road bar. "We're a gr-reat people," said Hennessy, in his rolling Irish brogue. "We ar-re that," replied Mr. Dooley. "We ar-re that. An th' best iv it is we know we ar-re."

A War for Principle

By the 1890s, Cuba and the nearby island of Puerto Rico comprised nearly all that remained of Spain's once vast empire in the New World. Several times, Cuban insurgents had rebelled against Spanish rule, including a decade-long rebellion from 1868 to 1878 (the Ten Years' War) that failed to settle the conflict. The depression of 1893 damaged the Cuban economy,

This print titled "Bohío de Reconcentrados" ("A Reconcentrado Shack") depicts Cubans suffering brutal conditions in one of General Weyler's "reconcentration" camps. Such images appearing in American newspapers and magazines strengthened U.S. sympathy for the Cubans. ❖

and the Wilson-Gorman Tariff of 1894 prostrated it. Duties on sugar, Cuba's lifeblood, were raised 40 percent. With the island's sugar market in ruins, discontent with Spanish rule heightened, and in late February 1895, revolt again broke out.

Recognizing the importance of the nearby United States, Cuban insurgents established a junta in New York City to raise money, buy weapons, and wage a propaganda war to sway American public opinion. Conditions in Cuba were grim. The insurgents pursued a hit-and-run scorched-earth policy to force the Spanish to leave. Spain committed more than 200,000 soldiers; the Spanish commander, who had won with similar tactics in 1878, tried to pin the insurgents in the eastern part of the island where they could be cornered and destroyed.

When this strategy failed, Spain in January 1896 sent a new commander, General Valeriano Weyler y Nicolau. Relentless and brutal, Weyler gave the rebels ten days to lay down their arms. He then put into effect a "reconcentration" policy designed to move the native population into camps and destroy the rebellion's popular base. Herded into fortified areas, Cubans died by the thousands, victims of unsanitary conditions, overcrowding, and disease.

There was a wave of sympathy for the insurgents, stimulated by the newspapers, but so-called **yellow journalism**, sensationalist reporting practiced mainly by a handful of newspapers in New York City that were eager to increase sales, did not cause the war. The conflict stemmed from larger disputes in policies and perceptions between Spain and the United States. Grover Cleveland, under whose administration the rebellion began, preferred Spanish rule to the kind of turmoil that might invite foreign intervention. Opposed to the annexation of Cuba, he issued a proclamation of neutrality and tried to restrain public opinion. In 1896, Congress passed a resolution favoring recognition of Cuban belligerence, but Cleveland ignored it. Instead, he offered to mediate the struggle, an offer Spain declined.

Taking office in March 1897, President McKinley also urged neutrality but leaned slightly toward the insurgents. He immediately sent a trusted aide on a fact-finding mission to Cuba; the aide reported in mid-1897 that Weyler's policy had wrapped Cuba "in the stillness of death and the silence of desolation." The report in hand, McKinley offered to mediate the struggle, but, concerned over the suffering, he protested against Spain's "uncivilized and inhuman" conduct. The United States, he made clear, did not contest Spain's right to fight the rebellion but insisted it be done within humane limits.

Late in 1897, a change in government in Madrid brought a temporary lull in the crisis. The new govern-ment recalled Weyler and agreed to offer the Cubans some form of autonomy. It also declared an amnesty for political prisoners and released Americans from Cuban jails. The new initiatives pleased McKinley, though he again warned Spain that it must find a humane end to the rebellion. Then, in January 1898, Spanish army officers led riots in Havana against the new autonomy policy, shaking the president's confidence in Madrid's control over conditions in Cuba.

McKinley ordered the battleship *Maine* to Havana to demonstrate strength and protect American citizens if necessary. On February 9, 1898, the *New York Journal,* a leader of the yellow press, published a letter stolen from Enrique Dupuy de Lôme, the Spanish ambassador in Washington. In the letter, which was private correspondence to a friend, de Lôme called McKinley "weak," "a would-be politician," and "a bidder for the admiration of the crowd." Many Americans were angered by the insult; McKinley himself was more worried about other sections of the letter that revealed Spanish insincerity in the negotiations. De Lôme immediately resigned and went home, but the damage was done.

A few days later, at 9:40 in the evening of February 15, an explosion tore through the hull of the *Maine,* riding at anchor in Havana harbor. The ship, a trim symbol of the new steel navy, sank quickly; 266 lives were lost. McKinley cautioned patience and promised an immediate investigation. Crowds gathered quietly on Capitol Hill and outside the White House, mourning the lost men. Soon there was a new slogan: "Remember the *Maine* and to Hell with Spain!"

The most recent study of the *Maine* incident blames the sinking on an accidental internal explosion, caused perhaps by spontaneous combustion in poorly ventilated coal bunkers. In 1898, Americans blamed it on Spain. Spaniards were hanged in effigy in many communities. Roosevelt, William Jennings Bryan, and others urged war, but McKinley delayed, hopeful that Spain might yet agree to an armistice and perhaps Cuban independence. "I have been through one war; I have seen the dead piled up; and I do not want to see another," he told a White House visitor.

In early March 1898, wanting to be ready for war if it came, McKinley asked Congress for $50 million in emergency defense appropriations, a request Congress promptly approved. The unanimous vote stunned Spain; allowing the president a latitude that was highly unusual for the era, it appropriated the money "for the National defense and for each and every purpose connected therewith to be expended at the discretion of the President." In late March, the report of the investigating board blamed the sinking of the *Maine* on an external (and thus presumably Spanish) explosion. Pressures for war increased.

Lithograph commemorating the sinking of the Maine *in Havana harbor on February 15, 1898, killing 266 men. Coverage of the incident in the "yellow" press encouraged readers to believe that Spanish bombs or torpedoes had sunk the ship.* ❖

On March 27, McKinley cabled Spain his final terms. He asked Spain to declare an armistice, end the reconcentration policy, and—implicitly—move toward Cuban independence. When the Spanish answer came, it conceded some things, but not, in McKinley's judgment, the important ones. Spain offered a suspension of hostilities (but not an armistice) and left the Spanish commander in Cuba to set the length and terms of the suspension. It also revoked the reconcentration policy. But the Spanish response made no mention of a true armistice, McKinley's offer to mediate, or Cuba's independence.

Reluctantly McKinley prepared his war message. It was long and temperate—at seven thousand words even deliberately boring; it suggested the possibility of further negotiations. Congress heard it on April 11, 1898. On April 19, Congress passed a joint resolution declaring Cuba independent and authorizing the president to use the army and navy to expel the Spanish from it. The **Teller Amendment,** offered by Colorado senator Henry M. Teller, pledged that the United States had no intention of annexing the island.

On April 21, Spain severed diplomatic relations. The following day, McKinley proclaimed a blockade of Cuba and called for 125,000 volunteers. On Monday, April 25, Congress passed a declaration of war. Late that afternoon, McKinley signed it.

Some historians have suggested that in leading the country toward war, McKinley was weak and indecisive, a victim of war hysteria in the Congress and the country; others have called him a wily manipulator for war and imperial gains. In truth, he was neither. Throughout the Spanish crisis, McKinley pursued a moderate middle course that sought to end the suffering in Cuba, promote Cuba's independence, and allow Spain time to adjust to the loss of the remnant of empire. He also wanted peace, as did Spain, but in the end, the conflicting national interests of the two countries brought them to war.

"A Splendid Little War"

Ten weeks after the declaration of war, the fighting was over. For Americans, they were ten glorious, dizzying weeks, with victories to fill every headline and slogans to suit every taste. No war can be a happy occasion for those who fight it, but the Spanish-American War came closer than most. Declared in April, it ended in August. Relatively few Americans died, and the quick victory seemed to verify burgeoning American power, though Sherwood Anderson, the author, suggested

A solemn crowd observes the funeral procession of the victims of the USS Maine *as it passes along M Street in Georgetown on the way to Arlington National Cemetery.* ❖

that fighting a weakened Spain was "like robbing an old gypsy woman in a vacant lot at night after a fair." John Hay, soon to be McKinley's secretary of state, called it "a splendid little war."

At the outset, the United States was militarily unprepared. Unlike the navy, the army had not been rebuilt or modernized, and it had shrunk drastically since the day thirty-three years before when Grant's great Civil War army marched sixty abreast, 200,000 strong, down Washington's Pennsylvania Avenue. In 1898, the regular army consisted of only 28,000 officers and men, most of them more experienced in quelling Indian uprisings than fighting large-scale battles. The Indian wars did produce effective small-scale forces, well trained and tightly disciplined, but the army was unquestionably too small for war against Spain.

When McKinley called for 125,000 volunteers, as many as 1 million young Americans responded. Ohio alone had 100,000 volunteers. Keeping the regular army units intact, War Department officials enlisted the volunteers in National Guard units that were then integrated into the national army. Men clamored to join. William Jennings Bryan, a pacifist by temperament, took command of a regiment of Nebraska volunteers; Roosevelt chafed to get to the front; and young Cordell Hull, who became secretary of state in the 1930s, was "wildly eager to leave at once." The secretary of war feared "there is going to be more trouble to satisfy those who are not going than to find those who are willing to go."

In an army inundated with men, problems of equipment and supply quickly appeared. The regulars

had the new .30-caliber Krag-Jorgensen rifles, but National Guard units carried Civil War Springfield rifles that used old black-powder cartridges. The cartridges gave off a puff of smoke when fired, neatly marking the troops' position. Spanish troops were better equipped; they had modern Mausers with smokeless powder, which they used to devastating effect. Food was also a problem, as was sickness. The War Department fell behind in supplies and received many complaints about the canned beef it offered the men. Tropical disease felled many soldiers. Scores took ill after landing in Cuba and the Philippines, and it was not uncommon for half a regiment to be unable to answer the bugle call.

Americans then believed that "a foreign war should be fought by the hometown military unit acting as an extension of their community." Soldiers identified with their hometowns, dressed in the local fashion, and thought of themselves as members of a town unit in a national army. The poet Carl Sandburg, 20 years old in 1898, rushed to join the army and called his unit a "living part" of his hometown of Galesburg, Illinois. And the citizens of Galesburg, for their part, took a special interest in Sandburg's unit, in a fashion repeated in countless towns across the country.

Not surprisingly, then, National Guard units mirrored the social patterns of their communities. Since everyone knew each other, there was an easygoing familiarity, tempered by the deference that went with hometown wealth, occupation, education, and length of residence. Enlisted men resented officers who grabbed too much authority, and they expected officers and men to call each other by their first names. Sandburg knew most of the privates in his unit, had worked for his corporal, and had gone to school with the first lieutenant. "Officers and men of the Guard mingle on a plane of beautiful equality," said a visitor to one volunteer camp. "Privates invade the tents of their officers at will, and yell at them half the length of the street."

Each community thought of the hometown unit as its own unit, an extension of itself. In later wars, the government censored news and dominated press relations; there was little censorship in the war with Spain, and the freshest news arrived in the latest letter home. Small-town newspapers printed news of the men and townswomen knit special red or white bellybands of stitched flannel, thought to ward off tropical fevers. Towns sent food, clothing, and occasionally even local doctors to the front. At the close of the war, the Clyde (Ohio) Ladies Society collected funds to provide each member of the town's company a medal struck on behalf of the town.

"Smoked Yankees"

When the invasion force sailed for Cuba, nearly one-fourth of it was African American. In 1898, the regular army included four regiments of African American soldiers, the Twenty-fourth and Twenty-fifth Infantry and the Ninth and Tenth Cavalry. Black regiments had served with distinction in campaigns against the Indians in the West. Most African American troops in fact were posted in the West; no eastern community would accept them. A troop of the Ninth Cavalry was stationed in Virginia in 1891, but whites protested and the troop was ordered back to the West.

When the war broke out, the War Department called for five black volunteer regiments. The army needed men, and military authorities were sure that black men had a natural immunity to the climate and diseases of the tropics. But most state governors refused to accept black volunteers. Only Alabama, Ohio, and Massachusetts mustered in black units in response to McKinley's first call for volunteers. Company L of the Sixth Massachusetts Regiment took part in the invasion of Puerto Rico in July 1898, the only one of the black volunteer units to see action in the Caribbean. African American leaders, among them P. B. S. Pinchback, former acting governor of Louisiana, and George White of North Carolina, the lone African American member of Congress, protested the discrimination. The McKinley administration intervened, and in the end, the volunteer army included more than ten thousand black troops.

Orders quickly went out to the four black regular army regiments in the West to move to camps in the South to prepare for the invasion of Cuba. Crowds and cheers followed the troop trains across the Plains, but as they crossed into Kentucky and Tennessee, the cheering stopped. Welcoming crowds were kept away from the trains, and the troops were hustled onward. Station restaurants refused to serve them; all waiting rooms were segregated. "It mattered not if we were soldiers of the United States, and going to fight for the honor of our country," Sergeant Frank W. Pullen of the Twenty-fourth Infantry wrote; "we were 'niggers' as they called us and treated us with contempt."

Many soldiers were not prepared to put up with the treatment. Those stationed near Chickamauga Park, Tennessee, shot "at some whites who insulted them" and forcibly desegregated the railroad cars on the line into Chattanooga. Troops training near Macon, Georgia, refused to ride in the segregated "trailers" attached to the trolleys, and fights broke out. Discovering a Macon park with a sign saying "Dogs and niggers not allowed," they invaded it and removed

Charge of the 24th and 25th Colored Infantry and Rescue of the Rough Riders at San Juan Hill, July 2, 1898, *colored lithograph by Kurz and Allison, 1899 (right). The twenty-fourth and twenty-fifth Colored Infantry regiments served with exceptional gallantry in the Spanish-American War. Charles Young (above), an 1889 graduate of West Point, was the only African American officer in the army during the Spanish-American War except for a few chaplains.* ❖

the sign. They also chopped down a tree in the park that had been used for lynchings.

More than four thousand black troops training near Tampa and Lakeland, Florida, found segregated saloons, cafes, and drugstores. "Here the Negro is not allowed to purchase over the same counter in some stores as the white man purchases over," Chaplain George W. Prioleau charged. "Why sir, the Negro of this country is a freeman and yet a slave. Talk about fighting and freeing poor Cuba and of Spain's brutality; of Cuba's murdered thousands, and starving reconcentradoes. Is America any better than Spain?"

Near Lakeland, units of the Tenth Cavalry pistol-whipped a drugstore owner who refused to serve a black soldier at the soda fountain. Just before the army's departure for Cuba, the tensions in Tampa erupted in a night of rioting. Drunken white soldiers from an Ohio regiment shot at a black child and black soldiers retaliated. When the night ended, three white and twenty-seven black soldiers were wounded.

When the invasion force sailed a few days later, segregation continued on some of the troopships. Blacks were assigned to the lowest decks, or whites and blacks were placed on different sides of the ship. But the confusion of war often ended the problem, if only temporarily. Blacks took command as white officers died, and Spanish troops soon came to fear the "smoked Yankees," as they called them. Black soldiers played a major role in the Cuban campaign and probably staved off defeat for the Rough Riders at San Juan Hill. In Cuba, they won twenty-six Certificates of Merit and five Congressional Medals of Honor.

The Course of the War

Mahan's Naval War College had begun studying strategy for a war with Spain in 1895. By 1898, it had a detailed plan for operations in the Caribbean and Pacific. Naval strategy was simple: Destroy the Spanish fleet, damage Spain's merchant marine, and harry the colonies or the coast of Spain. Planners were excited; two steam-powered armored fleets had yet to meet in battle anywhere in the world. The army's task was more difficult. It had to defend the United States, invade Cuba and probably Puerto Rico, and undertake possible action in far-flung places such as the Philippines or Spain.

Even before war was declared, the secretary of war arranged joint planning between the army and navy. Military intelligence was plentiful, and planners knew the numbers and locations of the Spanish troops. Earlier they had rejected a proposal to send an officer in disguise to map Cuban harbors; such things, they said, were simply not done in peacetime. Still, the War Department's new Military Information Division, a

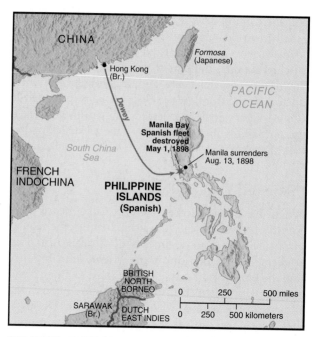

SPANISH-AMERICAN WAR: PACIFIC THEATER
Commodore Dewey, promoted to admiral immediately after the naval victory at Manila Bay, was the first hero of the war. ❖

sign of the increasing professionalization of the army, had detailed diagrams of Spanish fortifications in Havana and other points. On the afternoon of April 20, 1898, McKinley summoned the strategists to the White House; to the dismay of those who wanted a more aggressive policy, they decided on the limited strategy of blockading Cuba, sending arms to the insurgents, and annoying the Spanish with small thrusts by the army.

Victories soon changed the strategy. In case of war, long-standing naval plans had called for a holding action against the Spanish base in the Philippines. On May 1, 1898, with the war barely a week old, Commodore George Dewey, commander of the Asiatic Squadron located at Hong Kong, crushed the Spanish fleet in Manila Bay. Suddenly, Manila and the Philippines lay within American grasp. At home, Dewey portraits, songs, and poems blossomed everywhere, and his calm order to the flagship's captain—"You may fire when ready, Gridley"—hung on every tongue. Dewey had two modern cruisers, a gunboat, and a Civil War paddle steamer. He sank eight Spanish warships. Dewey had no troops to attack the Spanish army in Manila, but the War Department, stunned by the speed and size of the victory, quickly raised an expeditionary force. On August 13, 1898, the troops accepted the surrender of Manila, and with it, the Philippines.

McKinley and his aides were worried about Admiral Pascual Cervera's main Spanish fleet, thought to be headed across the Atlantic for an attack on

Florida. On May 13, the navy found Cervera's ships near Martinique in the Caribbean but then lost them again. A few days later, Cervera slipped secretly into the harbor of Santiago de Cuba, a city on the island's southern coast. But a spy in the Havana telegraph office alerted the Americans, and on May 28, a superior American force under Admiral William T. Sampson bottled Cervera up.

In early June, a small force of Marines seized Guantánamo Bay, the great harbor on the south of the island. They established depots for the navy to refuel and pinned down Spanish troops in the area. On June 14, an invasion force of about seventeen thousand men set sail from Tampa. Seven days later, they landed at Daiquiri on Cuba's southeastern coast. All was confusion, but the Spanish offered no resistance. Helped by Cuban insurgents, the Americans immediately pushed west toward Santiago, which they hoped to surround and capture. At first, the advance through the lush tropical countryside was peaceful.

The first battle broke out at Las Guasimas, a crossroads on the Santiago road. After a sharp fight,

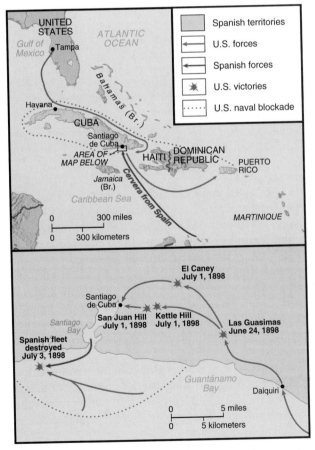

SPANISH-AMERICAN WAR: CARIBBEAN THEATER *President McKinley set up a "war room" in the White House, following the action on giant war maps with red and white marking pins.* ❖

the Spanish fell back. On July 1, the Rough Riders, troops from the four black regiments, and the other regulars reached the strong fortifications at El Caney and San Juan Hill. Black soldiers of the Twenty-fifth Infantry charged the El Caney blockhouses, surprising the Spanish defenders with Comanche yells. For the better part of a day, the defenders fought stubbornly and held back the army's elite corps. In the confusion of battle, Roosevelt rallied an assortment of infantry and cavalry to take Kettle Hill, adjacent to San Juan Hill.

They charged directly into the Spanish guns, Roosevelt at their head, mounted on a horse, a blue polka-dot handkerchief floating from the brim of his sombrero. "I waved my hat and we went up the hill with a rush," he recalled in his autobiography. Actually, it was not quite so easy. Losses were heavy; eighty-nine Rough Riders were killed or wounded in the attack. Dense foliage concealed the enemy and smokeless powder gave no clue to their position. At nightfall, the surviving Spanish defenders withdrew, and the Americans prepared for the counterattack. "We have won so far at a heavy cost," Roosevelt wrote home, "but the Spaniards fight very hard and charging these entrenchments against modern rifles is terrible. We are within measurable distance of a terrible military disaster."

American troops now occupied the ridges overlooking Santiago. They were weakened by sickness, a fact unknown to the Spanish, who decided the city was lost. The Spanish command in Havana ordered Cervera to run for the open sea, although he knew the attempt to escape was hopeless. On the morning of July 3, Cervera's squadron steamed down the bay and out through the harbor's narrow channel, but the waiting American fleet closed in, and in a few hours every Spanish vessel was destroyed. Two weeks later, Santiago surrendered.

Soon thereafter, army troops, meeting little resistance, occupied Puerto Rico. Cervera had commanded Spain's only battle fleet, and when it sank, Spain was helpless against attacks on the colonies or even its own shores. The war was over. Lasting 113 days, it took relatively few lives, most of them the result of accident, yellow fever, malaria, and typhoid in Cuba. Of the 5500 Americans who died in the war, only 379 were killed in battle. The navy lost one man in the battle at Santiago Bay, and only one to heatstroke in the stunning victory in Manila Bay.

ACQUISITION OF EMPIRE

Late in the afternoon of August 12, 1898, representatives of Spain and the United States met in McKinley's White House office to sign the preliminary instrument of peace. Secretary of State William R. Day beckoned a

✦ A Look at the Past ✦

Cartoon "School Begins"

Uncle Sam teaches a diverse group of students about civilization in this *Puck* cartoon. In the first row, receiving special attention, are recent U.S. acquisitions: Cuba, Puerto Rico, Hawaii, and the Philippines. Carefully examine all the individuals in the cartoon. Who stands outside the classroom and why? How do the students in the first row compare to others in the classroom? Read the message on the chalkboard and consider its meaning. According to this cartoon, how do Americans regard other races and ethnicities? How would Americans define civilization?

presidential aide over to a large globe, remarking, "Let's see what we get by this."

What the United States got was an expansion of its territory and an even larger expansion of its responsibilities. According to the preliminary agreement, Spain granted independence to Cuba, ceded Puerto Rico and the Pacific island of Guam to the United States, and allowed Americans to occupy Manila until the two countries reached final agreement on the Philippines. To McKinley, the Philippines were the problem. Puerto Rico was close to the mainland, and it appealed even to many of the opponents of expansion. Guam was small and unknown; it escaped attention. The Philippines, on the other hand, were huge, sprawling, and thousands of miles from America.

McKinley weighed a number of alternatives for the Philippines, but he liked none of them. He believed he could not give the islands back to Spain; public opinion would not allow it. He might turn them over to another nation, but then they would fall, as he later

said, "a golden apple of discord, among the rival powers." Germany, Japan, Great Britain, and Russia had all expressed interest in acquiring them. Germany even sent a large fleet to Manila and laid plans to take the Philippines if the United States let them go.

Rejecting those alternatives, McKinley considered independence for the islands but was soon talked out of it. People who had been there, reflecting the era's racism, told him the Filipinos were not ready for independence. He thought of establishing an American protectorate but discarded the idea, convinced it would bring American responsibilities without full American control. Sifting the alternatives, McKinley decided there was only one practical policy: Annex the Philippines, with an eye to future independence after a period of tutelage.

At first hesitant, American opinion was swinging to the same conclusion. Religious and missionary organizations appealed to McKinley to hold on to the Philippines in order to "Christianize" them. Some merchants and industrialists saw them as the key to the China market and the wealth of Asia. Many Americans simply regarded them as the legitimate fruits of war. In October 1898, representatives of the United States and Spain met in Paris to discuss a peace treaty. Spain agreed to recognize Cuba's independence, assume the Cuban debt, and cede Puerto Rico and Guam to the United States.

Acting on instructions from McKinley, the American representatives demanded the cession of the Philippines. "Grave as are the responsibilities and unforeseen as are the difficulties which are before us, the President can see but one plain path of duty—the acceptance of the archipelago," the instructions said. In return, the United States offered a payment of $20 million. Spain resisted but had little choice, and on December 10, 1898, the American and Spanish representatives signed the **Treaty of Paris.**

The Treaty of Paris Debate

Submitted to the Senate for ratification, the treaty set off a storm of debate throughout the country.

Industrialist Andrew Carnegie, reformer Jane Addams, labor leader Samuel Gompers, prominent Republicans such as Thomas B. Reed and John Sherman, Mark Twain, William Dean Howells, and a host of others argued forcefully against annexing the Philippines. Annexation of the Philippines, the anti-imperialists protested over and over again, violated the very principles of independence and self-determination on which the United States was founded.

Some labor leaders feared the importation of cheap labor from new Pacific colonies. Gompers warned about the "half-breeds and semi-barbaric people" who might undercut wages and the union movement. Other anti-imperialists argued against assimilation of different races, "Spanish-Americans," as one said, "with all the mixture of Indian and negro blood, and Malays and other unspeakable Asiatics, by the tens of millions!" Such racial views were also common among those favoring expansion, and the anti-imperialists usually focused on different arguments. If the United States established a tyranny abroad, they were sure, there would soon be tyranny at home. "This nation," declared William Jennings

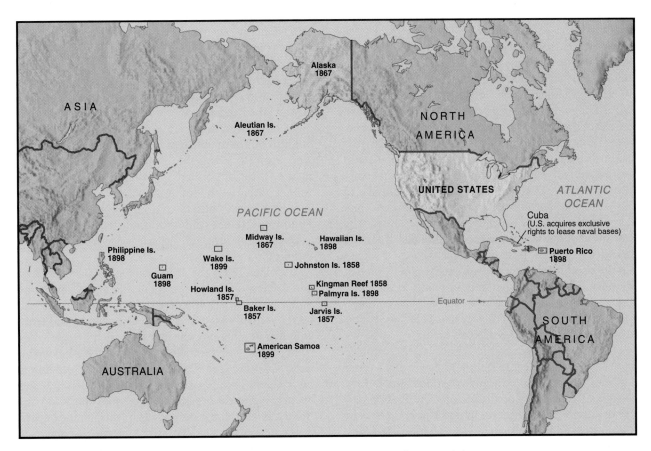

AMERICAN EMPIRE, 1900   *With the Treaty of Paris, the United States gained an expanded colonial empire stretching from the Caribbean to the far Pacific. It embraced Puerto Rico, Alaska, Hawaii, part of Samoa, Guam, the Philippines, and a chain of Pacific islands. The dates on the map refer to the date of U.S. acquisition.* ❖

Bryan, "cannot endure half republic and half colony—half free and half vassal."

Charles Francis Adams, Jr., warned that the possession of colonies meant big armies, government, and debts ("an income tax looms up in the largest possible proportions," he said). Bryan scoffed at the argument that colonies were good for trade, pointing out, "It is not necessary to own people to trade with them." E. L. Godkin, the editor of *The Nation;* George F. Hoar, a leading Republican senator; and many others thought there was no way to reconcile the country's republican ideals with the practice of keeping people under heel abroad. As one of them put it, "Dewey took Manila with the loss of one man—and all our institutions."

William James, the psychologist, said America was about to "puke up its heritage." Unless the Philippines were freed, Americans would rob Filipinos of "the one sacred thing in the world, the spontaneous budding of a national life." To Booker T. Washington, the country had more important things to think about at home, including its treatment of Indians and blacks. Carnegie was so upset that he offered to buy Filipino independence with a personal check for $20 million. He was sure that keeping the Philippines would divert attention from industrial development to foreign adventure, would glorify physical force, and would lead to a war against the Filipinos themselves, in which American soldiers who had signed up "to fight the oppressor" would end up "shooting down the oppressed."

In November 1898, opponents of expansion formed the **Anti-Imperialist League** to fight against the peace treaty. Local leagues sprang up in Boston, New York, Philadelphia, and many other cities; the parent league claimed thirty thousand members and more than half a million "contributors." Membership centered in New England; the cause was less popular in the West and South. It enlisted more Democrats than Republicans, though never a majority of either. The anti-imperialists were weakened by the fact that they lacked a coherent program. Some favored keeping naval bases in the conquered areas. Some wanted Hawaii and Puerto Rico but not the Philippines. Others wanted nothing at all to do with any colonies. Most simply wished that Dewey had sailed away after beating the Spanish at Manila Bay.

The treaty debate in the Senate lasted a month. Pressing hard for ratification, McKinley earlier toured the South to rally support and consulted closely with senators. Though opposed to taking the Philippines, Bryan supported ratification in order to end the war; his support influenced some Democratic votes. Still, on the final weekend before the vote, the treaty was two votes short. That Saturday night, news reached Washington that fighting had broken out between American troops and Filipino insurgents who de-

manded immediate independence. The news increased pressure to ratify the treaty, which the Senate did on February 6, 1899, with two votes to spare. An amendment promising independence as soon as the Filipinos established a stable government lost by one vote. The United States had a colonial empire.

Guerrilla Warfare in the Philippines

Historians rarely write of the **Philippine-American War,** but it was an important event in American history. The war with Spain was over a few months after it began, but war with the Filipinos lasted more than three years. Four times as many American soldiers fought in the Philippines as in Cuba. For the first time, Americans fought men of a different color in an Asian guerrilla war. The Philippine-American War of 1898–1902 took a heavy toll: 4300 American lives and untold thousands of Filipino lives (estimates range from 50,000 to 200,000).

Emilio Aguinaldo, the Filipino leader, was 29 years old in 1898. An early organizer of the anti-Spanish resistance, he had gone into exile in Hong Kong, from where he welcomed the outbreak of the Spanish-American War. Certain the United States would grant independence, he worked for an American victory. Filipino insurgents helped guide Dewey into Manila Bay, and Dewey himself sent a ship to Hong Kong to bring back Aguinaldo to lead a native uprising against the Spanish. On June 12, 1898, the insurgents proclaimed their independence.

Cooperating with the Americans, they drove the Spanish out of many areas of the islands. In the liberated regions, Aguinaldo established local governments with appointed provincial governors. He waited impatiently for American recognition, but McKinley and others had concluded that the Filipinos were not ready. Soon, warfare broke out between the Filipinos and Americans over the question of Filipino independence.

By late 1899, the American army had defeated and dispersed the organized Filipino army, but claims of victory proved premature. Aguinaldo and his advisers shifted to guerrilla tactics, striking suddenly and then melting into the jungle or friendly native villages. In many areas, the Americans ruled the day, the guerrillas the night. There were terrible atrocities on both sides. The Americans found themselves using brutal, Weyler-like tactics. After any attack on an American patrol, the Americans burned all the houses in the nearest district. They tortured people and executed prisoners. They established protected "zones" and herded Filipinos into them. Seizing or destroying all food outside the zones, they starved many guerrillas into submission.

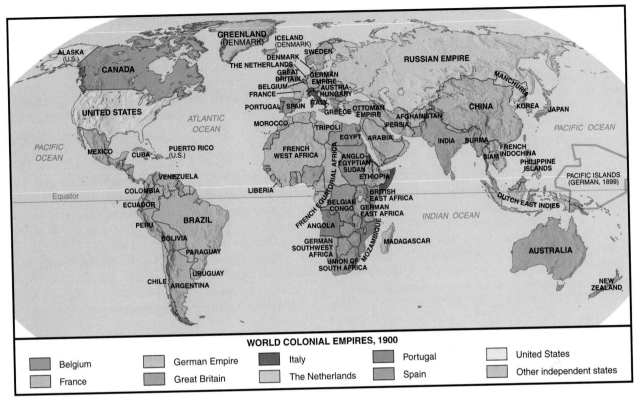

WORLD COLONIAL EMPIRES, 1900

Belgium	German Empire	Italy	Portugal	United States
France	Great Britain	The Netherlands	Spain	Other independent states

WORLD COLONIAL EMPIRES, 1900   *Events of the nineteenth century increased European hegemony over the world. By 1900, most independent African nations had disappeared and the major European nations had divided the continent among themselves. In the East, the European powers and Japan took advantage of China's internal weakness to gain both trading ports and economic concessions.* ❖

Emilio Aguinaldo (seated, in vest) and his advisors in the Philippines, 1896. Aguinaldo's forces helped the Americans drive Spain out of the Philippines, expecting that the United States would recognize Filipino independence. When the United States failed to do so, Aguinaldo led his forces in warfare against the Americans. ❖

Bryan tried to turn the election of 1900 into a debate over imperialism, but the attempt failed. For one thing, he himself refused to give up the silver issue, which cost him some support among anti-imperialists in the Northeast who were for gold. McKinley, moreover, was able to take advantage of the surging economy, and he could defend expansion as an accomplished fact. "It is no longer a question of expansion with us," he told one audience. "If there is any question at all it is a question of contraction; and who is going to contract?" Riding a wave of patriotism and prosperity, McKinley won the election handily—by an even larger margin than he had in 1896.

In 1900, McKinley sent a special Philippine Commission to the islands under William Howard Taft, a prominent Ohio judge. Directed to establish a civil government, the commission organized municipal administrations and, in stages, created a government for the Philippines. In March 1901, five American soldiers tricked their way into Aguinaldo's camp deep in the mountains and took him prisoner. Back in Manila, he signed a proclamation urging his people to end the fighting. Some guerrillas held out for another year, but to no avail. On July 4, 1901, authority was transferred from the army to Taft, who was named civilian governor of the islands, and his civilian commission. McKinley reaffirmed his purpose to grant the Filipinos self-government as soon as they were deemed ready for it.

Given broad powers, the Taft Commission introduced many changes. New schools provided education and vocational training for Filipinos of all social classes. The Americans built roads and bridges, reformed the judiciary, restructured the tax system, and introduced sanitation and vaccination programs. They established local governments built on Filipino traditions and hierarchies. Taft encouraged Filipino participation in government. During the following decades, other measures broadened Filipino rights. Independence finally came on July 4, 1946, nearly fifty years after Aguinaldo proclaimed it.

Governing the Empire

Ruling the colonies raised new and perplexing questions. How could—and how should—the distant dependencies be governed? Did their inhabitants have the rights of American citizens? Some people contended that acquisition did not automatically incorporate the new possessions into the United States and endow them with constitutional privileges. Others argued that "the Constitution followed the flag," meaning that acquisition made the possessions part of the nation and thus entitled them to all constitutional guarantees. A third group suggested that only "fundamental" constitutional guarantees—citizenship, the

right to vote, and the right to trial by jury—not "formal" privileges—the right to use American currency, the right to be taxed, and the right to run for the presidency—were applicable to the new empire.

In a series of cases between 1901 and 1904 (*De Lima* v. *Bidwell, Dooley* v. *U.S., and Downes* v. *Bidwell*), the Supreme Court asserted the principle that the Constitution did not automatically and immediately apply to the people of an annexed territory and did not confer upon them all the privileges of U.S. citizenship. Instead, Congress could specifically extend such constitutional provisions as it saw fit. "Ye-es," the secretary of war said of the Court's ambiguous rulings, "as near as I can make out the Constitution follows the flag—but doesn't quite catch up with it."

Four dependencies—Hawaii, Alaska, Guam, and Puerto Rico—were organized quickly. In 1900, Congress granted territorial status to Hawaii, gave American citizenship to all citizens of the Hawaiian republic, authorized an elective legislature, and provided for a governor appointed from Washington. A similar measure made Alaska a territory in 1912. Guam and American Samoa were simply placed under the control of naval officers.

Unlike the Filipinos, Puerto Ricans readily accepted the war's outcome, and McKinley early withdrew troops from the island. The **Foraker Act** of 1900 established civil government in Puerto Rico. It organized the island as a territory, made its residents citizens of Puerto Rico (U.S. citizenship was extended to them in 1917), and empowered the president to appoint a governor general and a council to serve as the upper house of the legislature. A lower house of delegates was to be elected.

Cuba proved a trickier matter. McKinley asserted the authority of the United States over conquered territory and promised to govern the island until the Cubans had established a firm and stable government of their own. "I want you to go down there to get the people ready for a republican form of government," he instructed General Leonard Wood, commander of the army in Cuba until 1902. "I leave the details of procedure to you. Give them a good school system, try to straighten out their ports, and put them on their feet as best you can. We want to do all we can for them and to get out of the island as soon as we safely can."

Wood moved quickly to implement the instructions. Early in 1900, he completed a census of the Cuban population, conducted municipal elections, and arranged the election of delegates to a constitutional convention. The convention adopted a constitution modeled on the U.S. Constitution and, at Wood's prodding, included provisions for future relations with the United States. Known as the **Platt Amendment** to the new Cuban Constitution, the provisions stipulated that Cuba should make no treaties with other powers that might impair its independence, acquire no debts it could not pay, and lease naval bases such as Guantánamo Bay to the United States. Most important, the amendment empowered the United States to intervene in Cuba to maintain orderly government.

Between 1898 and 1902, the American military government worked hard for the economic and political revival of the island, though it often demonstrated a paternalistic attitude toward the Cubans themselves. It repaired the damage of the civil war, built roads and schools, and established order in rural areas. A public health campaign headed by Dr. Walter Reed, an army surgeon, wiped out yellow fever. Most troops withdrew at the end of 1899, but a small American occupation force remained until May 1902. When it sailed for home, the Cubans at last had a form of independence, but they were still under the clear domination of their neighbor to the north.

The Open Door

Poised in the Philippines, the United States had become an Asian power on the doorstep of China. Weakened by years of warfare, China in 1898 and 1899 was unable to resist foreign influence. Japan, England, France, Germany, and Russia eyed it covetously, dividing parts of the country into "spheres of influence." They forced China to grant "concessions" that allowed them exclusive rights to develop particular areas and threatened American hopes for extensive trade with the country.

McKinley first outlined a new China policy in September 1898 when he said that Americans sought more trade, "but we seek no advantages in the Orient which are not common to all. Asking only the open door for ourselves, we are ready to accord the open door to others." In September 1899, Secretary of State John Hay addressed identical diplomatic notes to England, Germany, and Russia, and later to France, Japan, and Italy, asking them to join the United States in establishing the **Open Door policy.** This policy urged three agreements: Nations possessing a sphere of influence would respect the rights and privileges of other nations in that sphere; the Chinese government would continue to collect tariff duties in all spheres; and nations would not discriminate against other nations in levying port dues and railroad rates within their respective spheres of influence.

Under the Open Door policy, the United States would retain many commercial advantages it might lose if China was partitioned into spheres of influence. McKinley and Hay also attempted to preserve for the Chinese some semblance of national authority. Great Britain most nearly accepted the principle of the Open Door. Russia declined to approve it, and the other powers, sending evasive replies, stated they would agree only if all the other nations did. Hay turned the situation to American advantage by boldly announcing in March 1900 that all the powers had accepted the Open Door policy.

The policy's first test came just three months later with the outbreak of the Boxer Rebellion in Peking (now Beijing). In June 1900, a secret, intensely nationalistic Chinese society called the Boxers tried to oust all foreigners from their country. Overrunning Peking, they drove foreigners into their legations and penned them up for nearly two months. In the end, the United States joined Britain, Germany, and other powers in sending troops to lift the siege.

In this 1899 cartoon, "Putting His Foot Down" from Puck, *the nations of Europe are getting ready to cut up China to expand their spheres of influence, but Uncle Sam stands firm on American commitments to preserve China's sovereignty.* ❖

Fearing that the rebellion gave some nations, especially Germany and Russia, an excuse to expand their spheres of influence, Hay took quick action to emphasize American policy. In July, he sent off another round of Open Door notes affirming U.S. commitment to equal commercial opportunity and respect for China's independence. While the first Open Door notes had implied recognition of China's continued independence, the second notes explicitly stated the need to preserve it. Together, the two notes comprised the Open Door policy, which became a central element in American policy in the Far East.

To some degree, the policy tried to help China, but it also led to further American meddling in the affairs of another country. Moreover, by committing itself to a policy that Americans were not prepared to defend militarily, the McKinley administration left the opportunity for later controversy with Japan and other expansion-minded powers in the Pacific.

CHRONOLOGY

1867	United States purchases Alaska from Russia ❖ Midway Islands are annexed
1871	Treaty of Washington between United States and Great Britain sets precedent for peaceful settlement of international disputes
1875	Reciprocity treaty with Hawaii binds Hawaii economically and politically to United States
1878	United States acquires naval base in Samoa
1883	Congress approves funds for construction of first modern steel ships; beginning of modern navy
1887	New treaty with Hawaii gives United States exclusive use of Pearl Harbor
1889	First Inter-American Conference meets in Washington, D.C.
1893	American settlers in Hawaii overthrow Queen Liliuokalani; provisional government established
1895	Cuban insurgents rebel against Spanish rule
1898	Battleship *Maine* explodes in Havana harbor (February) ❖ Congress declares war against Spain (April) ❖ Commodore Dewey defeats Spanish fleet at Manila Bay (May) ❖ United States annexes Hawaii (July) ❖ Americans defeat Spanish at El Caney, San Juan Hill (actually Kettle Hill), and Santiago (July) ❖ Spain sues for peace (August) ❖ Treaty of Paris ends Spanish-American War (December)
1899	Congress ratifies Treaty of Paris ❖ United States sends Open Door notes to Britain, Germany, Russia, France, Japan, and Italy ❖ Philippine-American War erupts
1900	Foraker Act establishes civil government in Puerto Rico
1901	Platt Amendment authorizes American intervention in Cuba
1902	Philippine-American War ends with American victory

CONCLUSION: OUTCOME OF THE WAR WITH SPAIN

The war with Spain over, Roosevelt and the Rough Riders sailed for home in mid-August 1898. They sauntered through the streets of New York, the heroes of the city. A few weeks later, Roosevelt bade them farewell. They presented him with a reproduction of Frederick Remington's famed bronze *The Bronco-Buster,* and, close to tears, he told them, "I am proud of this regiment beyond measure." Roosevelt later wrote an account of the war in which he played so central a role that Mr. Dooley suggested, "If I was him, I'd call th' book 'Alone in Cubia.'" By then, Roosevelt was already governor of New York and on his way to the White House.

Other soldiers were also glad to be home, although they were sometimes resentful of the reception they found. "The war is over now," said Winslow Hobson, a black trooper from the Ninth Ohio, "and Roosevelt . . . and others (white of course) have all there is to be gotten out of it." Bravery in Cuba and the Philippines won some recognition for black soldiers, but the war itself set back the cause of civil rights. It spurred talk about "inferior" races, at home and abroad, and united whites in the North and South. "The Negro might as well know it now as later," a black editor said, "the closer the North and South get together by this war, the harder he will have to fight to maintain a footing." A fresh outburst of segregation and lynching occurred during the decade after the war.

McKinley and the Republican party soared to new heights of popularity. Firmly established, the Republican majority dominated politics until 1932. Scandals arose about the canned beef and the conduct of the War Department, but there was none of the sharp sense of deception and betrayal that was to mark the years after World War I. In a little more than a century, the United States had grown from thirteen states stretched along a thin Atlantic coastline into a world power that reached from the Caribbean to the Pacific. As Seward and others had hoped, the nation now dominated its own hemisphere, dealt with European powers on more equal terms, and was a major power in Asia.

RECOMMENDED READING

The best general account of the development of American foreign policy during the last part of the nineteenth century is Walter LaFeber, *The New Empire: An Interpretation of American Expansion, 1860–1898* (1963). William Appleman Williams, *The Tragedy of American Diplomacy* (1959), examines the economic motives for expansion. See also Paul Wolman, *Most Favored Nation: The Republican Revisionists and U.S. Tariff Policy, 1897–1912* (1992) and Laura Wexler, *Tender Violence: Domestic Visions in an Age of U.S. Imperialism* (2000). Lewis L. Gould persuasively reassesses McKinley's diplomacy and wartime leadership in *The Presidency of William McKinley* (1980).

Also helpful are Michael H. Hunt, *Ideology and Foreign Policy* (1987), Tom E. Terrill, *The Tariff, Politics, and American Foreign Policy, 1874–1901* (1973), and Matthew Frye Jacobson, *Barbarian Virtues: The United States Encounters Foreign Peoples at Home and Abroad, 1876–1917* (2000).

Graham A. Cosmas presents a detailed account of military organization and strategy in *An Army for Empire: The United States Army in the Spanish-American War* (1971); Willard B. Gatewood, Jr., offers a fascinating glimpse of the thoughts of some black soldiers in the war in *"Smoked Yankees" and the Struggle for Empire: Letters from Negro Soldiers, 1898–1902* (1971). Ivan Musicant, *Empire by Default: The Spanish-American War and the Dawn of the American Century* (1998), Kristin L. Hoganson, *Fighting for American Manhood: How Gender Politics Provoked the Spanish-American and Philippine-American Wars* (1998), and John L. Offner, *An Unwanted War: The Diplomacy of the United States and Spain over Cuba, 1895–1898* (1992), trace the background to the war with Spain. Brian McAllister Linn, *The Philippine War, 1899–1902* (2000), examines the often forgotten war against the Filipinos. Gerald F. Linderman relates the war to the home front in *The Mirror of War: American Society and the Spanish-American War* (1974).

For a list of additional titles related to this chapter's topics, please see http://www.ablongman.com/divine.

SUGGESTED WEB SITES

William McKinley and the Spanish-American War

http://www.history.ohio-state.edu/projects/mckinley/SpanAmWar.htm
Part of Ohio State University's site about William McKinley, this part highlights the Spanish-American War with an essay and photos.

The Spanish-American War in Motion Pictures

http://memory.loc.gov/ammem/sawhtml/sawhome.html
This Library of Congress Web presentation features sixty-eight films of the Spanish American War, the first war to be documented in motion pictures.

The World of 1898: The Spanish-American War

http://www.loc.gov/rr/hispanic/1898/
This Library of Congress site offers resources and documents about the Spanish-American War and the people who participated in or commented about it.

Sentenaryo/Centennial: The Philippine Revolution and Philippine-American War

http://www.boondocksnet.com/centennial/index.html
Jim Zwick organizes primary documents, images, and essays focusing on the Philippines and American involvement.

Anti-Imperialism in the United States, 1898–1935

http://www.boondocksnet.com/ail98-35.html
Jim Zwick edits this extensive site, collating a large number of primary documents about anti-imperialism in America.

The Age of Imperialism

http://www.smplanet.com/imperialism/toc.html
Focusing on the period around the turn of the century, this site puts much information about American imperialism in one place.

Images from the Philippine-United States War

http://historicaltextarchive.com/USA/twenty/filipino.html
The Philippine-American War is one of the least discussed military engagements in American history. This site includes several images from the war.

Theodore Roosevelt Association

http://www.theodoreroosevelt.org/
This site contains much biographical and research information about this famous American.

Hester Street (1905), a New York street scene by George Benjamin Luks. Luks was one of a group of artists associated with the Ashcan School, so named because of the artists' preference for painting the realities of modern urban life, including its streets and slums, backyards and bars. ❖

The Progressive Era

Muckrakers Call for Reform

In 1902, Samuel S. McClure, the shrewd owner of *McClure's Magazine*, sensed something astir in the country that his reporters were not covering. Like *Life*, *Munsey's*, the *Ladies' Home Journal*, and *Cosmopolitan*, *McClure's* was reaching more and more people—more than a quarter million readers a month. Americans were snapping up the new popular magazines filled with eye-catching illustrations and up-to-date fiction. Advances in photoengraving during the 1890s dramatically reduced the cost of illustrations; at the same time, income from advertisements rose sharply. By the turn of the century, some magazines earned as much as $60,000 an issue from advertising alone, and publishers could price them as low as 10 cents a copy.

McClure was always chasing new ideas and readers, and in 1902, certain that something was happening in the public mood, he told one of his editors, 36-year-old Lincoln Steffens, a former Wall Street reporter, to find out what it was. "Get out of here, travel, go—somewhere," he said to Steffens. "Buy a railroad ticket, get on a train, and there, where it lands you, there you will learn to edit a magazine."

McClure's, it turned out, had an unpaid bill from the Lackawanna Railroad, and Steffens traveled west. In St. Louis, he came across a young district attorney named Joseph W. Folk who had found a trail of corruption linking politics and some of the city's respected business leaders. Eager for help, Folk did not mind naming names to the visiting editor from New York. "It is good business men that are corrupting our bad politicians," he stressed again and again. "It is the leading citizens that are battening on our city." Steffens's story, "Tweed Days in St. Louis," appeared in the October 1902 issue of *McClure's*.

The November *McClure's* carried the first installment of Ida Tarbell's scathing "History of the Standard Oil Company," and in January 1903, Steffens was back with "The Shame of Minneapolis," another tale of corrupt partnership between business and politics. McClure had what he wanted, and in the January issue he printed an editorial, "Concerning Three Articles in This Number of *McClure's*, and a Coincidence That May Set Us Thinking." Steffens on Minneapolis, Tarbell on Standard Oil, and an article on abuses in labor unions—all, McClure said, on different topics but actually on the same theme: corruption in American life. "Capitalists, workingmen, politicians, citizens—all breaking the law, or letting it be broken."

Readers were enthralled, and articles and books by other **muckrakers**—Theodore Roosevelt coined the unflattering term in 1906 to describe the practice of exposing the corruption of public and prominent figures—spread swiftly. *Collier's* had articles on questionable stock market practices, patent medicines, and the beef trust. Novelist Upton Sinclair tackled the meatpackers in *The Jungle* (1906). In 1904, Steffens collected his McClure's articles in *The Shame of the Cities*, with an introduction expressing confidence that reform was possible, "that our shamelessness is superficial, that beneath it lies a pride which, being real, may save us yet."

Muckraking flourished from 1903 to 1909, and while it did, good writers and bad investigated almost every corner of American life: government, labor unions,

OUTLINE

The Changing Face of Industrialism

Society's Masses

Conflict in the Workplace

A New Urban Culture

Conclusion: A Ferment of Discovery and Reform

FEATURE ESSAY

Margaret Sanger and the Birth Control Movement

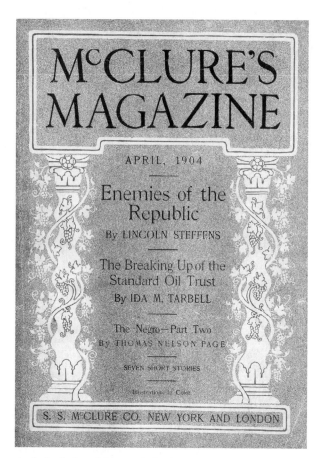

At the beginning of the twentieth century magazines enjoyed increasing popularity. McClure's Magazine *pioneered investigative journalism. The cover of the April 1904 edition draws readers not with lively illustrations, but with the best in muckraking, and reveals American interest in corruption. One of the leading muckrakers was Ida Tarbell, whose two-year series on Standard Oil exposed the corrupt practices and deals that had helped create the company.* ❖

big business, Wall Street, health care, the food industry, child labor, women's rights, prostitution, ghetto living, and life insurance. "Time was," Mr. Dooley, the fictional character of humorist Finley Peter Dunne, said to Mr. Hennessy, when magazines

was very ca'ming to the mind. Angabel an' Alfonso dashin' f'r a marriage license. Prom'nent lady authoresses makin' pomes at the moon. . . . Th' idee ye got fr'm these here publications was that life was wan glad sweet song. . . .

But now whin I pick me fav-rite magazine off th' flure, what do I find? Ivrything has gone wrong. . . . All th' pomes by th' lady authoresses that used to begin: "Oh, moon, how fair!" now begin: "Oh, Ogden Armour, how awful!" . . . Graft ivrywhere. "Graft in th' Insurance Companies," "Graft in Congress," "Graft Be an Old Grafter," "Graft in Its Relations to th' Higher Life.". . .

An' so it goes, Hinnissy . . . till I don't thrust anny man anny more. . . . I used to be nervous about burglars, but now I'm afraid iv a night call fr'm th' prisidint iv th' First National Bank.

AS MCCLURE HAD HOPED, Steffens *had* found something astir in the country, something so important and pervasive that it altered the course of American history in the twentieth century. The muckrakers were a journalistic voice of this larger movement in American society. Called **progressivism,** it lasted from the mid-1890s through World War I. Like muckraking itself, progressivism reflected worry about the state of society, the effects of industrialization and urbanization, social disorder, political corruption, and a host of other issues. With concerns so large, progressivism often had a sense of crisis and urgency, although it was rooted in a spirit of hopefulness and confidence in human progress. For varying reasons, thousands of people became concerned about their society, and, separately and together, they set out to cure some of the ills they saw around them. The efforts of the so-called progressives changed the nation and gave the era its name.

THE CHANGING FACE OF INDUSTRIALISM

"Life in the States," an English visitor said in 1900, "is one perpetual whirl of telephones, telegrams, phonographs, electric bells, motors, lifts, and automatic instruments." If not quite as automated as the visitor described, conditions in America were better than just a few years before. Farms and factories were once again prosperous; in 1901, for the first time in years, the economy reached full capacity. Farm prices rose almost 50 percent between 1900 and 1910. Unemployment dropped. "In the United States of today," a Boston newspaper said in 1904, "everyone is middle class. The resort to force, the wild talk of the nineties are over. Everyone is busily, happily getting ahead."

Everyone, of course, was not middle class, nor was everyone getting ahead. "Wild talk" persisted. Many of the problems that had angered people in the 1890s continued into the new century, and millions of Americans still suffered from poverty and disease. Racism sat even more heavily on African Americans in both South and North, and there was increasing hostility against immigrants from southern and eastern Europe and from Mexico and Asia. Yet to some degree the Boston newspaper was right: Economic conditions were better for many people, and as a result, prosperity became one of the keys to understanding the era and the nature of progressive reform.

The start of the new century was another key as well, for it influenced people to take a fresh look at themselves and their times. Excited about beginning the twentieth century, people believed technology and enterprise would shape a better life. Savoring the word *new,* they talked of the new poetry, new cinema, new history, new democracy, new woman, new art, new immigration, new morality, and new city. Magazines picked up the word; there were the *New Republic* and the *New Statesman.* Presidents Theodore Roosevelt and Woodrow Wilson called their political programs the New Nationalism and the New Freedom.

The word *mass* also cropped up frequently. Victors in the recent war with Spain, Americans took pride in teeming cities, burgeoning corporations, and other marks of the mass society. They enjoyed the fruits of mass production, read mass circulation newspapers and magazines, and took mass transit from the growing spiral of suburbs into the central cities.

Behind mass production lay significant changes in the nation's industrial system. Businesses grew at a rapid rate. They were large in the three decades after the Civil War, but in the years between 1895 and 1915, industries became mammoth, employing thousands of workers and equipped with assembly lines to turn out huge quantities of the company's product. Inevitably, changes in management attitudes, business organization, and worker roles influenced the entire society. Inevitably, too, the growth of giant businesses gave rise to a widespread fear of "trusts" and a desire among many progressive reformers to break them up or regulate them.

The Innovative Model T

In the movement toward large-scale business and mass production, the automobile industry was one of those that led the way. In 1895, there were only four cars on the nation's roads; in 1917, there were nearly five million, and the automobile had already helped work a small revolution in industrial methods and social mores.

Mass production of automobiles began in the first years of the century. Using an assembly-line system that foreshadowed later techniques, Ransom E. Olds turned out five thousand Olds runabouts in 1904. But Olds's days of leadership were numbered. In 1903, Henry Ford and a small group of associates formed the Ford Motor Company, the firm that transformed the business.

Ford was 40 years old. He had tried farming and hated it. During the 1890s, he worked as an engineer

Henry Ford built his first car in 1896, then produced a number of improved models, each designated by a letter of the alphabet. The Model T debuted in 1908. The "Tin Lizzie" was Ford's "motorcar for the multitudes," affordably priced so that every family could own one. The automobile wrought vast changes in American life and in the American landscape as it spawned the development of paved roads, traffic lights, and numerous auto-related businesses. ❖

for Detroit's Edison Company but spent his spare time designing internal combustion engines and automobiles. At first, like many others in the industry, he concentrated on building luxury and racing cars. Racing his own cars, Ford became the "speed demon" of Detroit; in 1904, he set the world's land speed record—more than 90 miles per hour—in the 999, a large red racer that shot flames from the motor.

In 1903, Ford sold the first Ford car. The price was high, and in 1905, Ford raised prices still higher. Sales plummeted. In 1907, he lowered the price; sales and revenues rose. Ford learned an important lesson of the modern economy: A smaller unit profit on a large number of sales meant enormous revenues. Early in 1908, he introduced the Model T, a four-cylinder, 20-horsepower "Tin Lizzie," costing $850, and available only in black. Eleven thousand were sold the first year.

"I am going to democratize the automobile," Ford proclaimed. "When I'm through everybody will be able to afford one, and about everyone will have one." The key was mass production, and after many experiments, Ford copied the techniques of meat-packers who moved animal carcasses along overhead trolleys from station to station. Adapting the process to automobile assembly, Ford in 1913 set up moving assembly lines in his plant in Highland Park, Michigan, that dramatically reduced the time and cost of producing cars. Emphasizing continuous movement, he strove for a nonstop flow from raw material to finished product. In 1914, he sold 248,000 Model T cars.

That year, Ford workers assembled a car in 93 minutes, one-tenth the time it had taken just eight months before. By 1925, the Ford plant turned out 9109 Model T's, a new car for every ten seconds of the workday.

While Ford was putting more and more cars on the road, the 1916 Federal Aid Roads Act, a little noticed measure, set the framework for road building in the twentieth century. Removing control from county governments, it required every state desiring federal funds to establish a highway department to plan routes, oversee construction, and maintain roads. In states that had such departments, the federal government paid half the cost of building the roads. Providing for a planned highway system, the act produced a national network of two-lane all-weather intercity roads.

The Burgeoning Trusts

As businesses like Ford's grew, capital and organization became increasingly important, and the result was the formation of a growing number of trusts. Standard Oil started the trend in 1882, but the greatest momentum came two decades later. Between 1898 and 1903, a series of mergers and consolidations swept the economy. Many smaller firms disappeared, swallowed up in giant corporations. By 1904, large-scale combinations of one form or another controlled nearly two-fifths of the capital in manufacturing in the country.

The result was not monopoly but oligopoly—control of a commodity or service by a small number of large, powerful companies. Six great financial groups dominated the railroad industry; a handful of holding companies controlled utilities and steel. Rockefeller's Standard Oil owned about 85 percent of the oil business. Large companies such as Standard Oil and American Tobacco had weathered the depression of the 1890s, and after 1898, financiers and industrialists followed their example and formed the Amalgamated Copper Company, Consolidated Tobacco, U.S. Rubber, and a host of others.

By 1909, just 1 percent of the industrial firms were producing nearly half of all manufactured goods. Giant businesses reached abroad for raw materials and

BUSINESS CONSOLIDATIONS (MERGERS), 1895–1905

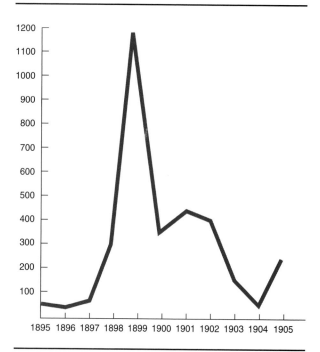

new markets. United Fruit, an empire of plantations and steamships in the Caribbean, exploited opportunities created by victory in the war with Spain. U.S. Steel worked with overseas companies to fix the price of steel rails, an unattainable dream just a few years before. For decades, competition had sent rail prices up and down; now they stayed at $28 a ton, and through the famous "Gary dinners" in which Elbert H. Gary of U.S. Steel brought steel executives from "competing" firms together to set prices, market conditions were fixed for wide areas of the industry.

Though the trend has been overstated, finance capitalists such as J. P. Morgan tended to replace the industrial capitalists of an earlier era. Able to finance the mergers and reorganizations, investment bankers played a greater and greater role in the economy. A multibillion-dollar financial house, J. P. Morgan and Company operated a network of control that ran from New York City to every industrial and financial center in the nation. Like other investment firms, it held directorships in many corporations, creating "interlocking directorates" that allowed it to control many businesses. In 1913, two banking groups—Morgan's and Rockefeller's—held 341 directorships in 112 corporations with an aggregate capital of more than $22 billion.

Massive business growth set off a decade-long debate over what government should do about the trusts. Some critics who believed that the giant companies

As early as 1886, cartoonist Thomas Nast attacked trusts. Here the people's welfare is sinking as the Statue of Liberty is defaced. ❖

were responsible for stifling individual opportunity and raising prices wanted to break them up into small competitive units. Others argued that large-scale business was a mark of the times, and that it produced more goods and better lives.

The debate over the trusts was one of the issues that shaped the Progressive Era, but it was never a simple contest between high-minded reformers and greedy business titans. Some progressives favored big business; others wanted it broken up. Business leaders themselves were divided in their viewpoints, and some welcomed reform-led assaults on giant competitors. As a rule, both progressives and business leaders drew on similar visions of the country: complex, expansive, hopeful, managerially minded, and oriented toward results and efficiency. They both believed in private property and the importance of economic progress. In fact, in working for reform, the progressives often drew on the managerial methods of a business world they sought to regulate.

Managing the Machines

Mass production changed the direction of American industry. Size, system, organization, and marketing became increasingly important. Management focused on speed and product, not on workers. Assembly-line technology changed tasks and, to some extent, values. The goal was no longer to make a unique product that would be better than the one before. "The way to make automobiles," Ford said as early as 1903, "is to make one automobile like another automobile, to make them all alike, to make them come through the factory just alike."

In a development that rivaled assembly lines in importance, businesses established industrial research laboratories where scientists and engineers developed new products. General Electric founded the first one in 1900, housed in a barn. It soon attracted experts who designed improvements in light bulbs, invented the cathode-ray tube, worked on early radio, and even tinkered with atomic theory. Du Pont opened its labs in 1911, Eastman Kodak in 1912, and Standard Oil in 1919. As the source of new ideas and technology, the labs altered life in the twentieth century.

Through all this, business became large-scale, mechanized, and managed. While many shops still employed fewer than a dozen workers, the proportion of such shops shrank. By 1920, close to one-half of all industrial workers toiled in factories employing more than 250 people. More than one-third worked in factories that were part of multiplant companies.

Industries that processed materials—iron and steel, paper, cement, and chemicals—were increasingly automated and operated continuously. In the glass industry, machines ended the domination of highly skilled and well-paid craftspeople. In 1908, Irving W. Colburn invented a machine to manufacture plate glass; the Libbey-Owens-Ford Company bought the patent; and Ford soon had a glassmaking machine from which emerged every day for two years a $3\frac{1}{2}$-mile ribbon of automobile window glass. Eventually, the plant produced almost 2000 miles of glass.

Workers tending such ribbons could not fall behind. Foremen still managed the laborers on the factory floor, but more and more, the rules came down from a central office where trained professional managers supervised production flow. Systematic record keeping, cost accounting, and inventory and production controls became widespread. Workers lost control of the work pace. "If you need to turn out a little more," a manager at Swift and Company said, "you speed up the conveyor a little and the men speed up to keep pace." It worked. For that and other reasons, in the automobile industry, output per worker-hour multiplied an extraordinary four times between 1909 and 1919.

Folkways of the workplace—workers passing job-related knowledge to each other, performing their tasks with little supervision, setting their own pace, and in effect running the shop—began to give way to "scientific" labor management. More than anyone else, Frederick Winslow Taylor, an inventive mechanical engineer, strove to extract maximum efficiency from each worker. "In the past," he believed, "the man has been first; in the future the system must be first."

In his book *The Principles of Scientific Management* (1911), Taylor proposed two major reforms. First, management must take responsibility for job-related knowledge and classify it into "rules, laws, and formulae." Second, management should control the workplace "through *enforced* standardization of methods, *enforced* adoption of the best implements and working conditions, and *enforced* cooperation." Although few factories wholly adopted Taylor's principles, he had great influence, and the doctrines of scientific management spread through American industry.

Workers caught up in the changing industrial system experienced the benefits of efficiency and productivity; in some industries, they earned more. But they suffered important losses as well. Performing repetitive tasks, they seemed part of the machinery, moving to the pace and needs of their mechanical pacesetters. Bored, they might easily lose pride of workmanship, though many workers, it is clear, did not. Efficiency engineers experimented with tools and methods, a process many workers found unsettling. Yet the goal was to establish routine—to work out, as someone said of a garment worker, "one single precise motion each second, 3600 in one hour, and all exactly the same." Praising that worker, the manager said, "She is a sure machine."

Jobs became not only monotonous but dangerous. As machines and assembly lines sped up, boredom or miscalculation could bring disaster. Meat cutters sliced fingers and hands. Illinois steel mills, a magazine said, were "Making Steel and Killing Men"; one mill had forty-six deaths in 1906 alone. Injuries were part of many jobs. "The machines go like mad all day," a garment worker said, "because the faster you work the more money you get. Sometimes in my haste I get my finger caught and the needle goes right through it . . . I bind the finger up with a piece of cotton and go on working."

In March 1911, a fire at the Triangle Shirtwaist Company in New York focused nationwide attention on unsafe working conditions. When the fire started, five hundred men and women, mostly Italians and Jews from eastern Europe, were just finishing their workday. Firefighters arrived within minutes, but they were already too late. Terrified seamstresses raced to the exits to try to escape the flames, but most exit doors were closed, locked by the company to prevent theft and shut out union organizers. Many died in the stampede down the narrow stairways or the single fire escape. Still others, trapped on the building's top stories far above the reach of the fire department's ladders, jumped to their deaths on the street below. One hundred forty-six people died.

A few days later, eighty thousand people marched silently in the rain in a funeral procession up Fifth Avenue. A quarter million people watched. At a mass meeting held to protest factory working conditions, Rose Schneiderman, a dynamic 29-year-old organizer for the Women's Trade Union League, told New York City's civic and religious leaders that they had not done enough, they had not cared. "We have tried you good people of the public and we have found you wanting. . . . Every week I must learn of the untimely death of one of my sister workers. Every

Fire nets were of no avail to the workers at the Triangle Shirtwaist Company who jumped from the upper stories to escape the flames. Speaking to a mass meeting after the fire, labor organizer Rose Schneiderman inveighed against a system that treated human beings as expendable commodities. ◆

year thousands of us are maimed. The life of men and women is so cheap and property is so sacred."

The outcry impelled New York's governor to appoint a State Factory Investigating Commission that recommended laws to shorten the workweek and improve safety in factories and stores.

SOCIETY'S MASSES

Spreading consumer goods through society, mass production not only improved people's lives but sometimes cost lives, too. Tending the machines, as Rose Schneiderman pointed out, took hard, painful labor, often under dangerous conditions. As businesses expanded, they required more and more people, and the labor force increased tremendously to keep up with the demand for workers in the factories, mines, and forests. Women, African Americans, Asian Americans, and Mexican Americans played larger and larger roles. Immigration soared. Between 1901 and 1910, nearly 8.8 million immigrants entered the United States; between 1911 and 1920, another 5.7 million came.

For many of these people, life was harsh, spent in crowded slums and long hours on the job. Fortunately, the massive unemployment of the 1890s was over, and in many skilled trades, such as cigar making, there was plenty of work to go around. Though the economic recovery helped nearly everyone, the less skilled continued to be the less fortunate. Migrant workers, lumberjacks, ore shovelers, and others struggled to find jobs that paid decently.

Under such circumstances, many people fought to make a living, and many, too, fought to improve their lot. Their efforts, along with the efforts of the reform-minded people who came to their aid, became another important hallmark of the Progressive Era.

Better Times on the Farm

While people continued to flee the farms—by 1920, fewer than one-third of all Americans lived on farms, and fewer than one-half lived in rural areas—farmers themselves prospered, the beneficiaries of greater production and expanding urban markets. Rural free delivery, begun in 1893, helped diminish the farmers' sense of isolation and changed farm life. The delivery of mail to the farm door opened that door to a wider world; it exposed farmers to urban thinking, national advertising, and political events. In 1911, more than one billion newspapers and magazines were delivered over RFD routes.

Parcel post (1913) permitted the sending of packages through the U.S. mail. Mail-order houses flourished; rural merchants suffered. Packages went both ways—President Woodrow Wilson's first parcel-post

delivery held 8 pounds of New Jersey apples—and within a year, 300 million packages were being mailed annually. While telephones and electricity did not reach most rural areas for decades, better roads, mail-order catalogs, and other innovations knit farmers into the larger society. Early in the new century, Mary E. Lease—who in her Populist days had urged Kansas farmers to raise less corn and more hell—moved to Brooklyn.

Farmers still had problems. Land prices rose with crop prices, and farm tenancy increased, especially in the South. Tenancy grew from one-quarter of all farms in 1880 to more than one-third in 1910. In South Carolina, Georgia, Alabama, and Mississippi, nearly two-thirds of the farms were run by tenant farmers. Many southern tenant farmers were African Americans, and they suffered from farm-bred diseases. In one of the reforms of the Progressive Era, in 1909, the Rockefeller Sanitary Commission, acting on recent scientific discoveries, began a sanitation campaign that eventually wiped out the hookworm disease, and in

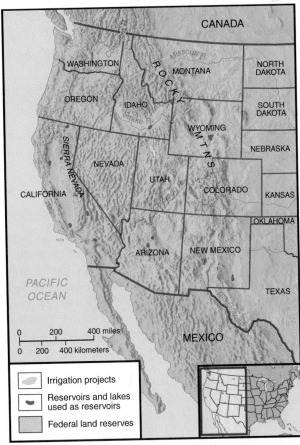

IRRIGATION AND CONSERVATION IN THE WEST TO 1917 *To make the arid lands of the western states productive, the state and federal governments regulated the water supply through irrigation projects and the creation of water reservoirs. The federal government also created land reserves.* ◆

1912, the U.S. Public Health Service began work on rural malaria.

In the arid West, irrigation transformed the land as the federal government and private landholders joined to import water from mountain watersheds. The dry lands bloomed, and so did a rural class structure that sharply separated owners from workers. Under the Newlands Act of 1902, the secretary of the interior formed the U.S. Reclamation Service, which gathered a staff of thousands of engineers and technicians, "the largest bureaucracy ever assembled in irrigation history."

Dams and canals channeled water into places such as California's Imperial Valley, and as the water streamed in, cotton, cantaloupes, oranges, tomatoes, lettuce, and a host of other crops streamed out to national markets. By 1920, Idaho, Montana, Utah, Wyoming, Colorado, and Oregon had extensive irrigation systems, all drawing on scarce water supplies; California, the foremost importer of water, had 4.2 million acres under irrigation, many of them picked by migrant workers from Mexico, China, and Japan. The work was backbreaking—and poorly paid. A worker from India called picking asparagus a "ghastly" job, paid at the rate of ten cents a box:

> They gave us miles and miles of asparagus rows. As soon as I had knelt down with my knife and cut out one head and put it in the box, there would be another one sprouting before me. Then I would have to stoop again, and it was continuous picking and stooping that made it a terrible form of exercise. It is walk and bend, bend and walk, from half past four [in the morning] or thereabouts, until seven in the evening.

Women and Children at Work

Women worked in larger and larger numbers. In 1900, more than five million worked—one-fifth of all adult women—and among those aged 14 to 24, the employment rate was almost one-third. Of those employed, single women outnumbered married women by seven to one, yet more than one-third of married women worked. Most women held service jobs. Only a small number held higher-paying jobs as professionals or managers.

In the 1890s, women made up more than one-quarter of medical school graduates. Using a variety of techniques, men gradually squeezed them out, and by the 1920s, only about 5 percent of the graduates were women. Few women taught in colleges and universities, and those who did were expected to resign if they married. In 1906, Harriet Brooks, a promising physicist at Barnard College in New York, became engaged and refused to resign; the dean told her icily that Barnard expected a married woman to "dignify her home-making into a profession, and not assume that she can carry on two full professions at a time."

More women than men graduated from high school, and with professions like medicine and science largely closed to them, they often turned to the new "business schools" that offered training in stenography, typing, and bookkeeping. In 1920, more than one-quarter of all employed women held clerical jobs. Many others taught school.

In 1907 and 1908, investigators studied 22,000 women workers in Pittsburgh; 60 percent of them earned less than $7 a week, a minimum for "decent living." Fewer than 1 percent held skilled jobs; most tended machines, wrapped and labeled, or did handwork that required no particular skill. In New York, many women toiled six days a week as garment workers from eight in the morning to six in the evening, with an extra hour off on Saturdays. They earned $7 to $12 a week, nothing at all during slack season. They had to buy their own needles and thread and pay for electricity and chairs to sit on.

Black women had always worked, and in far larger numbers than their white counterparts. The reason was usually economic; an African American man or woman alone could rarely earn enough to support a family. Unlike many white women, black women tended to remain in the labor force after marriage or the start of a family. They also had less opportunity for job advancement, and in 1920, between one-third and one-half of all African American women who were working were restricted to personal and domestic service jobs.

Critics charged that women's employment endangered the home, threatened their reproductive functions, and even, as one man said, stripped them of "that modest demeanor that lends a charm to their kind." Adding to these fears, the birthrate continued to drop between 1900 and 1920, and the divorce rate soared, in part because working-class men took advantage of the newer moral freedom and deserted their families in growing numbers. By 1916, there was one divorce for every nine marriages as compared to one for twenty-one in 1880.

David Graham Phillips, a novelist troubled by the woman's problem, depicted a husband's oppression of his wife in *The Hungry Heart*, published in 1909. "He kissed her, patted her cheek, went back to his work." When the wife grew restless, the husband knew why: "A few more years'll wash away the smatter she got at college, and this restlessness of hers will yield to nature, and she'll be content and happy in her womanhood. . . . As grandfather often said, it's a dreadful mistake, educating women beyond their sphere." Such views, mild as they were, got Phillips assassinated by a

LAD FELL TO DEATH IN BIG COAL CHUTE

Dennis McKee Dead and Arthur Allbecker Had Leg Burned In the Lee Mines.

Falling into a chute at the Chauncey colliery of the George S. Lee Coal Company at Avondale, this afternoon, Dennis McKee, aged 14, of West Nanticoke, was smothered to death and Arthur Allbecker, aged 15, had both of his legs burned and injured. Dr. Biel, of Plymouth, was summoned and dressed the burns of the injured boy.

He was removed to his home at Avondale.

Both boys were employed as breaker boys, and going too close to the chutes fell in. Fellow workmen rushed to their assistance and soon had them out of the chutes. When taken out McKee was found to be dead. His remains were removed to his home at West Nanticoke. Allbecker will recover.

Breaker boys, who picked out pieces of slate from the coal as it rushed past, often became bent-backed and suffered respiratory diseases such as bronchitis and tuberculosis after years of working fourteen hours a day in the coal mines. Accidents—and deaths— were common in the mines. ❖

lunatic who claimed the novelist was "trying to destroy the whole ideal of womanhood."

Many children also worked. In 1900, about three million children—nearly 20 percent of those between the ages of 5 and 15—held full-time or almost full-time jobs. Twenty-five thousand boys under 16 worked in mining; twenty thousand children under 12, mainly girls, worked in southern cotton mills. Gradually, as public indignation grew, the use of child labor shrank.

Determined to do something about the situation, the Women's Trade Union League lobbied the federal Bureau of Labor to investigate the conditions under which women and children worked. Begun in 1907, the investigation took four years and produced nineteen volumes of data, some of it shocking, all of it factual. In 1911, spurred by the data, the Children's Bureau was formed within the U.S. Bureau of Labor, with Grace Abbott, a social worker, at its head. It immediately began its own investigations, showing among other things the need for greater protection of maternal and infant health. In 1921, Congress passed the Sheppard-Towner Maternity and Infancy Protection Act, which helped fund maternity and pediatric clinics. Providing a precedent for the Social Security Act of 1935, it demonstrated the increasing effectiveness of women reformers in the Progressive Era.

Numerous middle-class women became involved in the fight for reform, while many others, reflecting the ongoing changes in the family, took increasing pride in homemaking and motherhood. Mother's Day, the national holiday, was formally established in 1913. Women who preferred smaller numbers of children turned increasingly to birth control, which became a more acceptable practice. Margaret Sanger, a nurse and outspoken social reformer, led a campaign to give physicians broad discretion in prescribing contraceptives. When Sanger became involved in the birth control movement, the federal Comstock Law banned the interstate transport of contraceptive devices and information (see the Feature Essay, "Margaret Sanger and the Birth Control Movement," pp. 636–637).

The Niagara Movement and the NAACP

At the turn of the century eight of every ten African Americans still lived in rural areas, mainly in the South. Most were poor sharecroppers. Jim Crow laws segregated many schools, railroad cars, hotels, and hospitals. Poll taxes and other devices disfranchised blacks and many poor whites. Violence was common; from 1900 to 1914, white mobs murdered more than a thousand black people.

Two murders occurred near Vicksburg, Mississippi, in 1904, and they revealed a great deal about the kind of violence African Americans faced. Looking for the killer of a white planter, a mob captured a black man and woman, their guilt or innocence unknown. They were tied to trees, and their fingers and ears were cut off as

MARGARET SANGER AND THE BIRTH CONTROL MOVEMENT

At the start of the twentieth century, birth control was an issue fraught with social and religious controversy. Devout Christians—Protestants and Catholics—opposed it as a violation of God's law; the overseers of society's moral behavior feared it might foster promiscuity. Theodore Roosevelt—whose young wife Alice Lee died after giving birth to their first child—said it meant "race death: a sin for which there is no atonement." The Comstock Act of 1873 banned from the U.S. mails all information on birth control, and by 1914 twenty-two states had enacted laws that hindered the dissemination of such information. That year, Margaret Sanger formally launched her campaign for birth control.

Born in 1883, Sanger grew up in Corning, New York. Her father, an Irish-born stonecutter, encouraged his children to think for themselves. "Leave the world better because you, my child, have dwelt in it," he told Margaret. One of eleven children, Margaret from an early age linked poverty to large families. "Our childhood," she said, "was one of longing for things that were always denied."

Longing for excitement and romance, Sanger settled in New York City, married, and had three children. Restless, and finding her marriage confining, she discovered Greenwich Village, a favorite haunt of the period's intense young radicals. There Sanger met Socialist leader Eugene V. Debs; young reporter and revolutionary John Reed, later to be honored by the Bolsheviks and buried in the Kremlin; William D. "Big Bill" Haywood of the radical Industrial Workers of the World (IWW); and feminist and socialist agitator Emma Goldman.

The Village was filled with people determined to improve the world. Stimulated by the exciting talk, Sanger joined the Socialist party and worked to organize women for socialism in New York City. In 1912, she marched in the IWW picket lines in the great strike at the textile mills in Paterson, New Jersey. Pursuing a nursing career, Sanger worked on the Lower East Side of New York where people were crowded into tenement houses. Struck by the ignorance of tenement women about their own bodies, she wrote in 1912 a series of newspaper articles about venereal disease and personal hygiene, titled "What Every Girl Should Know"; the post office banned it from the mails.

All around her, she saw poor working women burdened with unwanted pregnancies and, on occasion, dying from self-induced abortions. When one woman asked her doctor for contraceptive advice, he suggested only that she make her husband sleep on the roof. Sanger spent hours walking the streets and thinking about birth and children and poverty. She resolved, she later said, "to seek out the root of the evil, to do something to change the destinies of mothers whose miseries were as vast as the sky."

The answer was birth control—a term she and several friends coined in 1914. Sanger spent a year absorbing medical opinion and learning about contraceptives, and then she began publishing the journal *Woman Rebel*, which urged "women to look the whole world in the face with a go-to-hell look in the eyes; to have an ideal; to speak and act in defiance of convention." Aimed at the working class, the journal touched on birth control, but its chief focus was on social revolution, particularly on raising the social con-

Margaret Higgins Sanger with her son Stuart in 1904. In 1921, Sanger organized the American Birth Control League, which later became the Planned Parenthood Federation of America. ❖

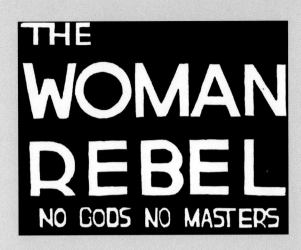

Masthead of Margaret Sanger's radical newspaper. The first issue, published in 1914, included an article titled "The Prevention of Conception," in which Sanger said she would defy the law prohibiting the distribution of information about birth control. ❖

sciousness of working women. It ran for only seven issues before it was banned by the post office. Sanger, indicted under the Comstock Act, fled to Europe.

There, after reflection, she decided that birth control was a medical matter, not a social or revolutionary one. It belonged in the hands of physicians and their patients, with physicians free to prescribe contraception and other measures when appropriate. Women should "decide for themselves whether they shall become mothers, under what conditions, and when." Working through the National Birth Control League and other groups, Sanger broadened the movement's base beyond the socialists and feminists who had originally backed it. Settlement house workers had been cool to birth control at first, but soon they too lent support.

Sanger returned to the United States, and the government, preoccupied with other issues, dropped the indictment against her. In October 1916, again defying the law, she opened the nation's first birth control clinic in the teeming Brownsville section of Brooklyn, New York. Police soon raided the clinic, and Sanger was sentenced to thirty days in jail. The New York State Court of Appeals upheld the sentence, but in a victory for Sanger, it ruled that physicians should have greater discretion in prescribing birth control.

Late in 1916, Sanger formed the New York Birth Control League to push for laws to give physicians even broader discretion. The league's argument that birth control would be an

effective means of promoting social welfare was a persuasive idea that convinced a wide variety of groups. Some reformers thought that smaller families would raise the standard of living of the poor. Other people thought that birth control might limit the number of "undesirables" in the population. Eugenicists who wanted to improve the human species through genetic control saw it as a way to reduce the proportion of the unwanted and unfit in the society. Gradually, Sanger herself came to reflect such arguments. "More children from the fit, less from the unfit—that is the chief issue," she said in 1919.

In 1921, Sanger organized the nationwide American Birth Control

League; it held clinics and conferences to educate the public. Although the Catholic Church remained opposed, the movement spread among Protestants, Jews, and those who did not attend church. In 1940, Eleanor Roosevelt, the popular First Lady, came out in support of family planning, and by the 1940s every state with the exception of Massachusetts and Connecticut had legalized the distribution of birth control information.

When Margaret Sanger died in 1966, the birth control pill had the approval of the Federal Drug Administration, and its use was widespread. The cause she had championed—once thought so shocking and radical—was won in American society.

Volunteers selling copies of the Birth Control League's *Birth Control Review.* ❖

souvenirs. "The most excruciating form of punishment consisted in the use of a large corkscrew in the hands of some of the mob. This instrument was bored into the flesh of the man and the woman, in the arms, legs and body, and then pulled out, the spirals tearing out big pieces of raw, quivering flesh every time it was withdrawn." Finally, both people were thrown on a fire and burned to death, "a relief," a witness said, "to the maimed and suffering victims."

Many African Americans labored on the cotton farms and in the railroad camps, sawmills, and mines of the South under conditions of peonage. Peons traded their lives and labor for food and shelter. Often illiterate, they were forced to sign contracts allowing the planter "to use such force as he or his agents may deem necessary to require me to remain on his farm and perform good and satisfactory services." Armed guards patrolled the camps and whipped those trying to escape. "In the woods," a peon said, "they can do anything they please, and no one can see them but God."

Few blacks belonged to labor unions, and blacks almost always earned less than whites in the same job.

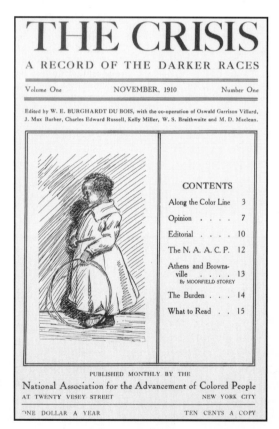

Cover of the first issue of The Crisis. *Founded in 1910 by the NAACP and edited by W. E. B. Du Bois, the monthly periodical served as the voice of the organization in its crusade for civil rights.* ❖

In Atlanta, white electricians earned $5.00 a day, blacks $3.50. Black songs such as "I've Got a White Man Workin' for Me" (1901) voiced more hope than reality. The illiteracy rate among African Americans dropped from 45 percent in 1900 to 30 percent in 1910, but nowhere were they given equal school facilities, teachers' salaries, or educational materials. In 1910, scarcely eight thousand African American youths were attending high schools in all the states of the Southeast. South Carolina spent $13.98 annually for the education of each white child, $1.13 for each black child.

African American leaders grew increasingly impatient with this kind of treatment, and in 1905 a group of them, led by sociologist W. E. B. Du Bois, met near Niagara Falls, New York (they met on the Canadian side of the Falls, since no hotel on the American side would take them). There they pledged action in the matters of voting, equal access to economic opportunity, integration, and equality before the law. Rejecting Booker T. Washington's gradualist approach, the **Niagara Movement** claimed for African Americans "every single right that belongs to a freeborn American, political, civil and social; and until we get these rights we will never cease to protest."

The Niagara Movement focused on equal rights and the education of African American youth, of whom it said, "They have a right to know, to think, to aspire." Keeping alive a program of militant action, it spawned later civil rights movements. Du Bois was its inspiration. In *The Souls of Black Folk* (1903) and other works, he called eloquently for justice and equality. "By every civilized and peaceful method," he said, "we must strive for the right which the world accords to man."

Peace was sometimes hard to come by. Race riots broke out in Atlanta, Georgia, in 1906 and in Springfield, Illinois, in 1908, the latter the home of Abraham Lincoln. Unlike the riots of the 1960s, white mobs invaded black neighborhoods, burning, looting, and killing. They lynched two blacks—one 84 years old—in Springfield.

Outrage was voiced by William E. Walling, a wealthy southerner and settlement house worker; Mary Ovington, a white anthropology student; and Oswald Garrison Villard, grandson of the famous abolitionist William Lloyd Garrison. Along with other reformers, white and black (among them Jane Addams and John Dewey), they issued a call for the conference that organized the **National Association for the Advancement of Colored People (NAACP),** which swiftly became the most important civil rights organization in the country. Created in 1909, within five years the NAACP grew to fifty branches and more than six thousand members. Walling headed it, and Du Bois, the only African American among the top officers, directed publicity and edited *The Crisis*, the voice of the organization.

Joined by the National Urban League, which was created in 1911, the NAACP pressured employers, labor unions, and the government on behalf of African Americans. It had some victories. In *Guinn* v. *United States* (1915), the Supreme Court overturned a "grandfather clause" that kept African Americans from voting in Oklahoma, and in *Buchanan* v. *Worley* (1917), it struck down a law in Louisville, Kentucky, that required residential segregation. In 1918, in the midst of World War I, the NAACP and the National Urban League persuaded the federal government to form a special Bureau of Negro Economics within the Labor Department to look after the interests of African American wage earners.

Despite these gains, African Americans continued to experience disfranchisement, poor job opportunities, and segregation. As Booker T. Washington said in 1913, "I have never seen the colored people so discouraged and so bitter as they are at the present time."

"I Hear the Whistle": Immigrants in the Labor Force

While women and African Americans worked in growing numbers, much of the huge increase in the labor force in these years came from outside the country, particularly from Europe and Mexico. Between 1901 and 1920, the extraordinarily high total of 14.5 million immigrants entered the country, more than in any previous twenty-year period. Continuing the trend begun in the 1880s, many came from southern and eastern Europe. Still called the "new" immigrants, they met hostility from "older" immigrants of northern European stock who questioned their values, religion (often Catholic or Jewish), traditions, and appearance.

Labor agents—called *padroni* among the Italians, Greeks, and Syrians—recruited immigrant workers, found them jobs, and deducted a fee from their wages. Headquartered in Salt Lake City, Leonidas G. Skliris, the "czar of the Greeks," provided workers for the Utah Copper Company and the Western Pacific Railroad. In Chicago at the turn of the century, padroni employed more than one-fifth of all Italians; in New York City, they controlled two-thirds of the entire labor force.

Immigrant patterns often departed from traditional stereotypes. Immigrants, for example, moved both to and from their homelands. Fifty percent or more of the members of some groups returned home, although the proportion varied. Jews and Czechs often brought their families to resettle in America; Serbs and Poles tended to come singly, intent on earning enough money to make a fresh start at home. Some migrants—Italian men, in particular—virtually com-

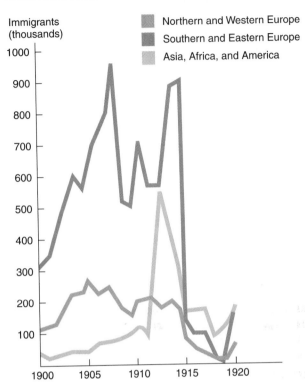

IMMIGRATION TO THE UNITED STATES, 1900–1920 (BY AREA OF ORIGIN)

Immigrants (thousands)

- Northern and Western Europe
- Southern and Eastern Europe
- Asia, Africa, and America

Note: For purposes of classification, "Northern and Western Europe" includes Great Britain, Ireland, Scandinavia, the Netherlands, Belgium, Luxembourg, Switzerland, France, and Germany. "Southern and Eastern Europe" includes Poland, Austria-Hungary, Russia and the Baltic States, Romania, Bulgaria, European Turkey, Italy, Spain, Portugal, and Greece. "Asia, Africa, and America" includes Asian Turkey, China, Japan, India, Canada, the Caribbean, Latin America, and all of Africa.

Source: U.S. Bureau of the Census, *Historical Statistics of the United States, Colonial Times to 1970*, Bicentennial Edition, Washington, D.C., 1975.

muted, returning home every slack season. These temporary migrants became known as **birds of passage.** The outbreak of World War I interrupted the practice and trapped thousands of Italians and others who had planned to return to Europe.

Older residents lumped the newcomers together, ignoring geographic, religious, and other differences. Preserving important regional distinctions, Italians tended to settle as Calabreses, Venetians, Abruzzis, and Sicilians. Old-stock Americans viewed them all simply as Italians. Henry Ford and other employers tried to erase the differences through English classes and deliberate "Americanization" programs. The Ford Motor Company ran a school where immigrant employees were first taught to say, "I am a good American." At the graduation ceremony, the pupils acted out a gigantic pantomime in which, clad in their old-country dress, they filed into a large "melting pot." When they emerged, they were wearing identical American-made clothes, and each was waving a little American flag.

In similar fashion, the International Harvester Corporation taught Polish laborers to speak English, but it had other lessons in view as well. According to Lesson One, drilled into the Polish "pupils":

> I hear the whistle. I must hurry.
> I hear the five minute whistle.
> It is time to go into the shop.
> I take my check from the gate board and hang it on the department board.
> I change my clothes and get ready to work.
> The starting whistle blows.
> I eat my lunch.
> It is forbidden to eat until then.
> The whistle blows at five minutes of starting time.
> I get ready to go to work.
> I work until the whistle blows to quit.
> I leave my place nice and clean.
> I put all my clothes in the locker.
> I must go home.

Labor groups soon learned to counter these techniques. The **Women's Trade Union League (WTUL)** urged workers to ignore business-sponsored English lessons because they did not "tell the girl worker the things she really wants to know. They do not suggest that $5 a week is not a living wage. They tell her to be respectful to her employer." Designing its own educational program, the WTUL in 1912 published "New World Lessons for Old World Peoples," which provided quite a different kind of English lesson:

> A Union girl takes me into the Union.
> The Union girls are glad to see me.
> They call me sister.
> I will work hard for our Union.
> I will come to all the Union meetings.

In another significant development at the beginning of the twentieth century, Mexicans for the first time immigrated in large numbers, especially after a revolution in Mexico in 1910 forced many to flee across the northern border into Texas, New Mexico, Arizona, and California. Their exact numbers were unknown. American officials did not count border crossings until 1907, and even then, many migrants avoided the official immigration stations. Almost all came from the Mexican lower class, eager to escape peonage and violence in their native land. Labor agents called *coyotes*—usually in the employ of large corporations or working for ranchers—recruited Mexican workers.

Between 1900 and 1910, the Mexican population of Texas and New Mexico nearly doubled; in Arizona, it more than doubled; in California, it quadrupled. In all four states, it doubled again between 1910 and

MEXICAN IMMIGRATION TO THE UNITED STATES, 1900–1920

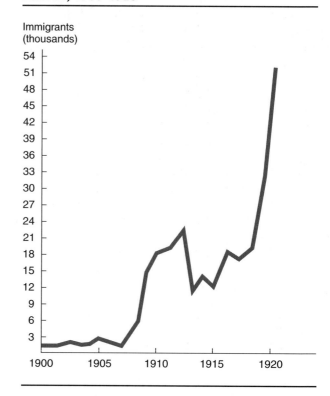

1920. After the turn of the century, almost 10 percent of the total population of Mexico moved to the American Southwest.

In time, these Mexican Americans and their children transformed the Southwest. They built most of the early highways in Texas, New Mexico, and Arizona; dug the irrigation ditches that watered crops throughout the area; laid railroad track; and picked the cotton and vegetables that clothed and fed millions of Americans. Many lived in shacks and shanties along the railroad tracks, isolated in a separate Spanish-speaking world. Like other immigrant groups, they also formed enclaves in the cities; these *barrios* became cultural islands of family life, foods, church, and festivals.

Fewer people immigrated from China in these years, deterred in part by anti-Chinese laws and hostility. Like many other immigrants, most Chinese who came did not intend to remain. Wanting to make money and return home, they mined, farmed, and worked as common laborers. In their willingness to work hard for low wages, their desire to preserve clan and family associations from China, and their maintenance of strong ties with their home villages, Chinese Americans resembled other immigrant groups, but they differed in two important respects. As late as 1920, men outnumbered women by ten to one in the Chinese American population, and with a

Japanese immigrants with a Methodist deaconess in the administration buiding of the immigration station at Angel Island, near San Francisco. Quota systems and exclusionary laws severely limited Asian immigration, while other laws placed restrictions on the immigrants, curtailing their right to own or even rent agricultural land. Some Asian immigrants, after months of detention at Angel Island, were refused permission to enter the United States and were forced to return to their homelands. ❖

male median age of 42, their communities were generally dominated by the elderly.

The Chinese American population differed in another respect as well. Unlike other immigrant groups, whose numbers tended to grow, the number of Chinese Americans shrank in these years—from about 125,000 in the early 1880s to just over 60,000 in 1920. After 1910, the U.S. government set up a special immigration facility at Angel Island in San Francisco Bay, but unlike European immigrants who landed at Ellis Island in New York and were quickly sent on, Chinese immigrants were kept for weeks and months, examined and reexamined, before being allowed to cross the narrow band of water to San Francisco. Angel Island remained open until 1940, and a poem carved into the wall of Building 317 showed the feelings of some of those who waited:

There are tens of thousands of poems composed on
  these walls,
They are all cries of complaint and sadness.
The day I am rid of this prison and attain success,
I must remember that this prison once existed.
In my daily needs I must be frugal.
Needless extravagance leads youth to ruin.
All my compatriots please be mindful.
Once you have some small gains, return home early.

By One from Xiangshan

Many Japanese also arrived at Angel Island, and though at first fewer in numbers than the Chinese, they developed communities along the Pacific Coast, where they settled mainly on farms. The number of Japanese Americans grew. In 1907, the heaviest year of immigration from Japan, nearly 31,000 Japanese entered the United States; by 1920, there were 111,000 Japanese in the country, nearly three-quarters of them in California.

As the newcomers arrived from Asia, Europe, and Mexico, nativist sentiment, which had criticized earlier waves of immigrants, intensified. Old-stock Americans sneered at their dress and language. Racial theories emphasized the superiority of northern Europeans, and the new "science" of eugenics suggested the need to control the population growth of "inferior" peoples. Hostility toward Catholics and Jews was common but touched other groups as well.

In 1902, Congress enacted a law prohibiting immigration from China. Statutes requiring literacy tests designed to curtail immigration from southern and eastern Europe were vetoed by William Howard Taft in 1913 and by Woodrow Wilson in 1915 and 1917. In 1917, such a measure passed despite Wilson's veto. Other measures tried to limit immigration from Mexico and Japan.

CONFLICT IN THE WORKPLACE

Assembly lines, speedups, long hours, and low pay produced a dramatic increase in American industrial output (and profits) after 1900; they also gave rise to numerous strikes and other kinds of labor unrest. Sometimes strikes took place through the action of unions; sometimes workers just decided they had had enough and walked off the job. Whatever the cause, strikes were frequent. In one industry, in one city—the meatpacking industry in Chicago—there were 251 strikes in 1903 alone.

Strikes and absenteeism increased after 1910; labor productivity dropped 10 percent between 1915 and 1918, the first such decline in memory. In many industries, labor turnover became a serious problem; workers changed jobs in droves. Union membership grew. In 1900, only about a million workers—less than 4 percent of the workforce—belonged to unions. By 1920, five million workers belonged, increasing the unionized portion of the workforce to about 13 percent.

As tensions grew between capital and labor, some people in the middle class became fearful that, unless something was done to improve the workers' situation, there might be violence or even revolution. This fear motivated some of the labor-oriented reforms of the Progressive Era. While some reform supporters genuinely wanted to improve labor's lot, others embraced reform because they were afraid of something else.

Organizing Labor

Samuel Gompers's American Federation of Labor increased from 250,000 members in 1897 to 1.7 million in 1904. By far the largest union organization, it remained devoted to the interests of skilled craftspeople. While it aimed partly at better wages and working conditions, it also sought to limit entry into the crafts and protect worker prerogatives. Within limits, the AFL found acceptance among giant business corporations eager for conservative policies and labor stability.

Of the 8 million female workers in 1910, only 125,000 belonged to unions. Gompers continued to resist organizing them, saying they were too emotional and, as union organizers, "had a way of making serious mistakes." Margaret Dreier Robins, an organizer of proven skill, scoffed at that. "These men died twenty years ago and are just walking around dead!" she protested.

Robins helped found the Women's Trade Union League in 1903. The WTUL led the effort to organize women into trade unions, to lobby for legislation protecting female workers, and to educate the public on the problems and needs of working women. It took in all working women who would join, regardless of skill (although not, at first, African American women), and it won crucial financial support from well-to-do women such as Anne Morgan, daughter of the feared financier J. P. Morgan. Robins's close friend Jane Addams belonged, as did Mary McDowell, the "Angel of the Stockyards," who worked with slaughterhouse workers in Chicago; Julia Lathrop, who tried to improve the lot of wage-

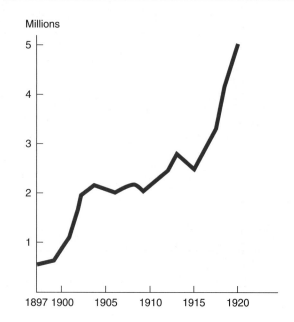

LABOR UNION MEMBERSHIP, 1897–1920

Source: U.S. Bureau of the Census, *Statistical Abstract of the United States: 1982–83* (103rd edition), Washington, D.C., 1982.

earning children; and Dr. Alice Hamilton, a pioneer in American research on the causes of industrial disease.

The WTUL never had many members—a few thousand at most—but its influence extended far beyond its membership. In 1909, it supported the "Uprising of the 20,000," a strike of shirtwaist workers in New York City. When female employees of the Triangle Shirtwaist Company tried to form a union, the company fired them, and they walked out; 20,000 men and women in 500 other shops followed. Strike meetings were conducted in three languages—English, Yiddish, and Italian—and before being forced to go back to work, the strikers won a shorter workweek and a few other gains. Sadly, the Triangle women lost out on another important demand—for unlocked shop doors and safe fire escapes. Their loss proved lethal in the famous Triangle Shirtwaist Company fire of 1911.

The WTUL also backed a strike in 1910 against Hart, Schaffner and Marx, Chicago's largest manufacturer of men's clothing. One day, Annie Shapiro, the 18-year-old daughter of Russian immigrants, was told her wages were being cut from $7 a week to $6.20. That was a large cut, and along with sixteen other young women, Shapiro refused to accept it and walked out. "We had to be recognized as people," she said later. Soon other women walked out, and the revolt spread.

Holding signs and banners that proudly display their union allegiance, including a sign with the slogan "An injury to one is an injury to all," women of the Industrial Workers of the World participate in a strike at the Oliver Iron and Steel Company in Pittsburgh, Pennsylvania, in 1913. The Clayton Act, passed by Congress in 1914, legalized picketing and other union activity. ❖

Managers quickly promised to restore the cuts, but as one woman said, "just then there was big noise outside and we all rushed to the windows and there we saw the police beating the strikers on our account, and when we saw that we went out."

In a matter of days, some forty thousand garment workers were on strike, about half of them women. Manufacturers hurried to negotiate, and the result was the important Hart, Schaffner agreement, which created an arbitration committee composed of management and labor to handle grievances and settle disputes. The first successful experiment in collective bargaining, the Hart, Schaffner agreement became the model for the kind of agreements that govern industrial relations today.

Another union, the **Industrial Workers of the World (IWW)**, attracted by far the greatest attention (and the most fears) in these years. Unlike the WTUL, it welcomed everyone regardless of gender or race. Unlike the AFL, it tried to organize the unskilled and foreign-born laborers who worked in the mass production industries. Founded in Chicago in 1905, it aimed to unite the American working class into a mammoth union to promote labor's interests. Its motto—"An injury to one is an injury to all"—stressed labor solidarity, as had the earlier Knights of Labor. But unlike the Knights, the IWW, or Wobblies as they were often known, urged social revolution.

"It is our purpose to overthrow the capitalist system by forcible means if necessary," William D. "Big Bill" Haywood, one of its founders, said; and he went on in his speeches to say he knew of nothing a worker could do that "will bring as much anguish to the boss as a little sabotage in the right place." Joe Hill, the IWW's legendary folk poet, reminded labor of its potential strength:

If the workers took a notion
    They could stop all speeding trains;
Every ship upon the ocean
    They can tie with mighty chains.

Every wheel in the creation
    Every mine and every mill;
Fleets and armies of the nation,
    Will at their command stand still.

IWW leaders included Mary Harris ("Mother") Jones, a famous veteran of battles in the Illinois coalfields; Elizabeth Gurley Flynn, a fiery young radical who joined as a teenager; and Big Bill Haywood himself, the strapping one-eyed founder of the Western Federation of Miners.

The IWW led a number of major strikes. Strikes in Lawrence, Massachusetts (1912) and Paterson, New Jersey (1912) attracted national attention: in Lawrence when the strikers sent their children, ill-clad and hungry, out of the city to stay with sympathetic families; in Paterson when they rented New York's Madison Square Garden for a massive labor pageant. IWW leaders welcomed the revolutionary tumult sweeping Russia and other countries. In the United States, they thought, a series of local strikes would bring about capitalist repression, then a general strike, and eventually a workers' commonwealth.

The IWW fell short of these objectives, but during its lifetime—from 1905 to the mid-1920s—it made major gains among immigrant workers in the Northeast, migrant farm laborers on the Plains, and loggers and miners in the South and Far West. In factories like Ford's, it recruited workers resentful of the speedups on the assembly lines. Although IWW membership probably amounted to no more than 100,000 at any one time, workers came and left so often that its total membership may have reached as high as 1 million.

Working with Workers

Concerned about labor unrest, some business leaders used violence and police action to keep workers in line, but others turned to the new fields of applied psychology and personnel management. A school of industrial psychology emerged. As had Taylor, industrial psychologists studied workers' routines, and, further, they showed that output was also affected by job satisfaction. While most businesses pushed ahead with efficiency campaigns, a few did establish industrial relations departments, hire public relations firms to improve their corporate image, and link productivity to job safety and worker happiness.

Ivy L. Lee, a pioneer in the field of corporate public relations, advised clients such as the Pennsylvania Railroad and Standard Oil on how to improve relations with labor and the public. Calling himself a "physician to corporate bodies," Lee urged complete openness on the company's part. To please employees, companies printed newsletters and organized softball teams; they awarded prizes and celebrated retirements. Ford created a "sociology department" staffed by 150 experts who showed workers how to budget their incomes and care for their health. They even taught them how to shop for meat.

On January 5, 1914, Ford took another significant step. He announced the five-dollar day, "the greatest revolution," he said, "in the matter of rewards for workers ever known to the industrial world." With a stroke, he doubled the wage rate for common labor, reduced the working day from nine hours to eight, and established a personnel department to place workers in appropriate jobs. The next day, ten thousand applicants stood outside the gates.

As a result, Ford had the pick of the labor force. Turnover declined; absenteeism, previously as much as one-tenth of all Ford workers every day, fell to 0.3 percent. Output increased; the IWW at Ford collapsed. The plan increased wages, but it also gave the company greater control over a more stable labor force. Workers had to meet a behavior code in order to qualify for the five-dollar day. At first scornful of the "utopian" plan, business leaders across the country soon copied it, and on January 2, 1919, Ford announced the six-dollar day.

Amoskeag

In size, system, and worker relations, the record of the Amoskeag Company textile mills was revealing. Located beside the Merrimack River in Manchester, New Hampshire, the mills—an enormous complex of factories, warehouses, canals, and machinery—had been built in the 1830s. By the turn of the century, they were producing nearly 50 miles of cloth an hour, more cloth each day than any other mills in the entire world.

The face of the mills, an almost solid wall of red brick, stretched nearly a mile. Archways and bridges pierced the facade. Amoskeag resembled a walled medieval city within which workers found "a total institution, a closed and almost self-contained world." At first the mills employed young women for labor, but by 1900, more and more immigrant males staffed the machines. French Canadians, Irish, Poles, and Greeks—seventeen thousand in all—worked there, and their experiences revealed a great deal about factory work and life at the turn of the century.

The company hired and fired at will, and it demanded relentless output from the spindles and spinning frames. Yet it also viewed employees as its "children" and looked for total loyalty in return, an expectation often realized. Workers identified with Amoskeag and, decades later, still called themselves Amoskeag men and women. "We were all like a family," one said.

Most Amoskeag workers preferred the industrial world of the mills to the farms they had left behind. They did not feel displaced; they knew the pains of industrial life; and they adapted in ways that fit their own needs and traditions. Families played a large role. They neither disintegrated nor lost their relationships. French Canadians and others often came in family units. One or two family members left the farm for the mills, maintained close ties with those back home, and then sent for others, creating a form of "chain migration."

Once in Manchester, families often toiled in the same workrooms. Looking after each other, they asked for transfers and promotions for relatives; they taught their children technical skills and how to get along with bosses and fellow workers. Although low paid, Amoskeag employees took pride in their work, and for many of them, a well-turned-out product provided dignity and self-esteem.

As part of its paternal interest in employee welfare, in 1910 the company inaugurated a welfare and efficiency program, which aimed to increase productivity, accustom immigrants to industrial work, instill

The playground at Amoskeag, provided for the children of the company's workers. The Amoskeag Textile Club, part of the employer-sponsored employee welfare program, had reading rooms, card tables, billiard and pool tables, a golf course, and a baseball field for the use of the workers. All was demolished when the mill closed in 1935. Many firms between 1910 and 1917 established employee programs similar to those introduced at Amoskeag. ❖

company loyalty, and curb labor unrest. Playgrounds and visiting nurses, home-buying plans, a cooking school, and dental service were part of the plan. The Amoskeag Textile Club held employee dinners and picnics, organized shooting clubs and a baseball team, sponsored Christmas parties for the children, and put out the *Amoskeag Bulletin,* a monthly magazine of employee news.

From 1885 to 1919, no strike touched the mills. Thereafter, however, labor unrest increased. Overproduction and foreign competition took their toll, and Amoskeag closed in 1935.

A New Urban Culture

For many Americans, the quality of life improved significantly between 1900 and 1920. Jobs were relatively plentiful, and, in a development of great importance, more and more people were entering the professions as doctors, lawyers, teachers, and engineers. With comfortable incomes, a growing middle class could take advantage of new lifestyles, inventions, and forms of entertainment. Mass production could not have worked without mass consumption, and Americans in these years increasingly became a nation of consumers.

Production and Consumption

In 1900, business firms spent about $95 million on advertising; twenty years later, they spent more than $500 million. Ads and billboards touted cigarettes, cars, perfumes, and cosmetics. Advertising agencies boomed. Using new sampling techniques, they developed modern concepts of market testing and research. Sampling customer preferences affected business indirectly as well, making it more responsive to public opinion on social and political issues.

Mass production swept the clothing industry and dressed more Americans better than any people ever before. Using lessons learned in making uniforms during the Civil War, manufacturers for the first time developed standard clothing and shoe sizes that fit most bodies. Clothing prices dropped; the availability of inexpensive "off-the-rack" clothes lessened distinctions between rich and poor. By 1900, nine of every ten men and boys wore the new "ready-to-wear" clothes.

In 1900, people employed in manufacturing earned on average $418 a year. Two decades later, they earned $1342 a year, though inflation took much of the increase. While the middle class expanded, the rich also grew richer. In 1920, the new income tax showed the first accurate tabulation of income, and it

✦ A Look at the Past ✦

Sears Catalog

Rural Americans gained access to the same array of consumer goods that urban dwellers had when mail-order companies, such as Sears, Roebuck and Company, offered goods through the mail. Rural Free Delivery, begun in 1893, made shopping by mail easier than visiting the local general store. Sears targeted rural consumers and designed the catalog to appeal to those consumers. Notice the cover decoration depicting goods spilling out in front of the farmstead. Why do you think the cover includes information about the firm's incorporation and capital? Why are there references from banks? Does the cover suggest that rural Americans were completely comfortable about mail order or that they needed reassurance? Why might some consumers have been nervous about mail order?

confirmed what many had suspected all along. Five percent of the population received almost one-fourth of all income.

Living and Dying in an Urban Nation

In 1920, the median age of the population was only 25. (It is now 35.) Immigration accounted for part of the population's youthfulness, since most immigrants were young. Thanks to medical advances and better living conditions, the death rate dropped in the early years of the century; the average life span increased. Between 1900 and 1920, life expectancy rose from 49 to 56 years for white women and from 47 to 54 years for white men. It rose from 33 to 45 years for blacks and other racial minorities.

Despite the increase in life expectancy, infant mortality remained high; nearly 10 percent of white babies and 20 percent of minority babies died in the first year of life. In comparison to today, fewer babies on average survived to adolescence, and fewer people survived beyond middle age. In 1900, the death rate among people between 45 and 65 was more than twice the modern rate. As a result, there were relatively fewer older people—in 1900, only 4 percent of the population was older than 65 compared to nearly 13 percent today. Fewer children than today knew their grandparents. Still, improvements in health care helped people live longer, and as a result, the incidence of cancer and heart disease increased.

Cities grew, and by any earlier standards, they grew on a colossal scale. Downtowns became a central hive of skyscrapers, department stores, warehouses, and hotels. Strips of factories radiated from the center. As street railways spread, cities took on a systematic pattern of socioeconomic segregation, usually in rings. The innermost ring filled with immigrants, circled by a belt of working-class housing. The remaining rings marked areas of rising affluence outward toward wealthy suburbs, which themselves formed around shopping strips and grid patterns of streets that restricted social interaction.

The giants were New York, Chicago, and Philadelphia, industrial cities that turned out every kind of product from textiles to structural steel. Smaller cities such as Rochester, New York, or Cleveland, Ohio, specialized in manufacturing a specific line of goods or processing regional products for the national market. Railroads instead of highways tied things together; in 1916, the rail network, the largest in the world, reached its peak—254,000 miles of track that carried more than three-fourths of all intercity freight tonnage.

Step by step, cities adopted their twentieth-century forms. Between 1909 and 1915, Los Angeles, a city of 300,000 people, passed a series of ordinances that gave rise to modern urban zoning. For the first time, the ordinances divided a city into three districts of specified use: a residential area, an industrial area, and an area open to residence and a limited list of industries. Other cities followed. Combining several features, the New York zoning law of 1916 became the model for the nation; within a decade, 591 cities copied it.

Zoning ordered city development, keeping skyscrapers out of factory districts, factories out of the suburbs. It also had powerful social repercussions. In the South, zoning became a tool to extend racial segregation; in northern cities, it acted against ethnic minorities. Jews in New York, Italians in Boston, Poles in Detroit, African Americans in Chicago—zoning laws held them all at arm's length. Like other migrants, African Americans often preferred to settle together, but zoning also helped put them there. By 1920, ten districts in Chicago were more than three-quarters black. In Los Angeles, Cleveland, Detroit, and Washington, DC, most blacks lived in only two or three wards.

Popular Pastimes

Thanks to changing work rules and mechanization, many Americans enjoyed more leisure time. The average workweek for manufacturing laborers fell from 60 hours in 1890 to 51 in 1920. By the early 1900s, white-collar workers might spend only 8 to 10 hours a day at work and a half day on weekends. Greater leisure time gave more people more opportunity for play and people flocked to places of entertainment. Baseball entrenched itself as the national pastime. Automobiles and streetcars carried growing numbers of fans to ballparks; attendance at major league games doubled between 1903 and 1920. Football also drew fans, although critics attacked the sport's violence and the use of "tramp athletes," nonstudents whom colleges paid to play. In 1905, the worst year, 18 players were killed and 150 seriously injured.

Alarmed, President Theodore Roosevelt—who had once said, "I am the father of three boys [and] if I thought any one of them would weigh a possible broken bone against the glory of being chosen to play on Harvard's football team I would disinherit him"—called a White House conference to clean up college sports. The conference founded the Intercollegiate Athletic Association, which in 1910 became the National Collegiate Athletic Association (NCAA).

Movie theaters opened everywhere. By 1910, there were 10,000 of them, drawing a weekly audience of 10 million people. Admission was usually 5 cents, and movies stressing laughter and pathos appealed to a mass market. In 1915, D. W. Griffith, a talented and creative director—as well as a racist—produced the first movie spectacular: *Birth of a Nation*. Griffith adopted new film techniques, including close-ups, fade-outs, and artistic camera angles, and he staged dramatic battle scenes. (For further discussion of the film, see the Chapter 16 Feature Essay, "Changing Views of Reconstruction," pp. 476–477.)

The "movies" quickly became one of the most popular forms of mass entertainment, and by the 1920s nearly a hundred million Americans were going to the movies each week. Movie theaters sprang up across America, offering patrons a short and inexpensive escape from daily life, such as the popular silent film serial Perils of Pauline (1914). Viewers flocked to see twenty suspenseful installments in which the heroine evades various attempts on her life, including the abduction shown in this poster for the sixth episode. ❖

Phonographs brought ready-made entertainment into the home. By 1901, phonograph and record companies included the Victor Talking Machine Company, the Edison Speaking Machine Company, and Columbia Records. Ornate mahogany Victrolas became standard fixtures in middle-class parlors. Early records were usually of vaudeville skits; orchestral recordings began in 1906. In 1919, 2.25 million phonographs were produced; two years later, more than 100 million records were sold.

As record sales grew, families sang less and listened more. Music became a business. In 1909, Congress enacted a copyright law that provided a two-cent royalty on each piece of music on phonograph records or piano rolls. The royalty, small as it was, offered welcome income to composers and publishers, and in 1914, composer Victor Herbert and others formed the American Society of Composers, Authors, and Publishers (ASCAP) to protect musical rights and royalties.

The faster rhythms of syncopated ragtime became the rage, especially after 1911, when Irving Berlin, a Russian immigrant, wrote "Alexander's Ragtime Band." Ragtime set off a nationwide dance craze. Secretaries danced on their lunch hour, the first nightclubs opened, and restaurants and hotels introduced dance floors. Waltzes and polkas gave way to a host of new dances, many with animal names: the fox-trot, bunny hop, turkey trot, snake, and kangaroo dip. Partners were not permitted to dance too close; bouncers tapped them on the shoulder if they got closer than 9 inches. The aging John D. Rockefeller hired a private instructor to teach him the tango; Yale University, however, banned that dance at its 1914 junior prom.

Vaudeville, increasingly popular after 1900, reached maturity around 1915. Drawing on the immigrant experience, it voiced the variety of city life and included skits, songs, comics, acrobats, and magicians. Dances and jokes showed an earthiness new to mass audiences. By 1914, stage runways extended into the crowd; women performers had bared their legs and were beginning to show glimpses of the midriff. Fanny Brice; Ann Pennington, the "shimmy" queen; and Eva Tanguay, who sang "It's All Been Done Before But Not the Way I Do It," starred in Florenz Ziegfeld's Follies, the peak of vaudeville.

In songs like "St. Louis Blues" (1914), W. C. Handy took the black southern folk music of the blues to northern cities. Gertrude "Ma" Rainey, the daughter of minstrels, sang in black vaudeville for nearly thirty-five years. Performing in Chattanooga, Tennessee, about 1910, she came across a 12-year-old orphan, Bessie Smith, who became the "Empress of the Blues." Smith's voice was huge and sweeping. Recording for the Race division of Columbia Records, she made more than eighty records that together sold nearly ten million copies.

Another musical innovation came north from New Orleans. Charles (Buddy) Bolden, a cornetist; Ferdinand "Jelly Roll" Morton, a pianist; and a youngster named Louis Armstrong played an improvisational music that had no formal name. Reaching Chicago, it became "jas," then "jass," and finally "jazz." Jazz jumped, and jazz musicians relied on feeling and mood. A restaurant owner once asked Jelly Roll Morton to play a waltz. "Waltz?" Morton exclaimed. "Man, these people want to dance! And you talking about waltz. This is the Roll you're talking to."

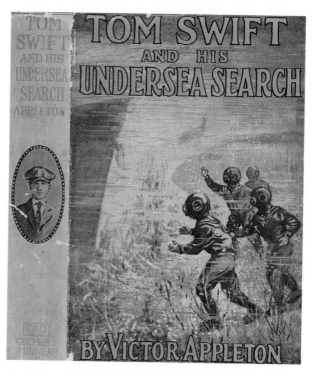

The front jacket cover for Tom Swift and His Undersea Search by Victor Appleton, one of the pseudonyms used by Edward Stratemeyer. The Stratemeyer Literary Syndicate turned out more than forty volumes about the boy inventor. Stratemeyer and his daughter, Harriet Stratemeyer Adams, also wrote the Nancy Drew mysteries, under the name Carolyn Keene. ❖

Popular fiction reflected changing interests. Kate Douglas Wiggins's *Rebecca of Sunnybrook Farm* (1903) and Lucy M. Montgomery's *Anne of Green Gables* (1908) showed the continuing popularity of rural themes. Westerns also sold well, but readers turned more and more to detective thrillers with hard-bitten city detectives and science fiction featuring the latest dream in technology. The Tom Swift series, begun in 1910, looked ahead to spaceships, ray guns, and gravity nullifiers.

Edward L. Stratemeyer, the mind behind Tom Swift, brought the techniques of mass production to book writing. In 1906, he formed the Stratemeyer Literary Syndicate, which employed a stable of writers to turn out hundreds of Tom Swift, Rover Boys, and Bobbsey Twins stories for young readers. Burt Standish, another prolific author, took the pen name Gilbert Patten and created the character of Frank Merriwell, wholesome college athlete. As Patten said, "I took the three qualities I most wanted him to represent—frank and merry in nature, well in body and mind—and made the name Frank Merriwell." The Merriwell books sold twenty-five million copies.

Experimentation in the Arts

"There is a state of unrest all over the world in art as in all other things," the director of New York's Metropolitan Museum said in 1908. "It is the same in literature, as in music, in painting, and in sculpture."

Isadora Duncan and Ruth St. Denis transformed the dance. Departing from traditional ballet steps, both women stressed improvisation, emotion, and the human form. "Listen to the music with your soul," Duncan told her students. "Unless your dancing springs from an inner emotion and expresses an idea, it will be meaningless." Draped in flowing robes, she revealed more of her legs than some thought tasteful, and she proclaimed that the "noblest art is the nude." After a triumphant performance with the New York Symphony in 1908, her ideas and techniques swept the country. Duncan died tragically in 1927, her neck broken when her long red scarf caught in the wheel of a racing car.

The lofts and apartments of New York's Greenwich Village attracted artists, writers, and poets interested in experimentation and change. To these artists, the city was the focus of national life and the sign of a new culture. Robert Henri and the realist painters—known to their critics as the **Ashcan School**—relished the city's excitement. They wanted, a friend said, "to paint truth and to paint it with strength and fearlessness and individuality."

To the realists, a painting carried into the future the look of life as it happened. Their paintings depicted street scenes, colorful crowds, and slum children swimming in the river. In paintings such as the *Cliff Dwellers,* George W. Bellows captured the color and excitement of the tenements; John Sloan, one of Henri's most talented students, painted the vitality of ordinary people and familiar scenes.

In 1913, a show at the New York Armory presented sixteen hundred modernist paintings, prints, and sculptures. The work of Picasso, Cézanne, Matisse, Brancusi, Van Gogh, and Gauguin dazed and dazzled American observers. Critics attacked the show as worthless and depraved; a Chicago official wanted it banned from the city because the "idea that people can gaze at this sort of thing without [it] hurting them is all bosh."

George Bellows, Cliff Dwellers *(1913). Bellows's work served as a commentary on contemporary urban life.* ❖

The postimpressionists changed the direction of twentieth-century art and influenced adventuresome American painters. John Marin, Max Weber, Georgia O'Keeffe, Arthur Dove, and other modernists experimented in ways foreign to Henri's realists. Defiantly avant-garde, they shook off convention and experimented with new forms. Using bold colors and abstract patterns, they worked to capture the energy of urban life. "I see great forces at work, great movements," Marin said, "the large buildings and the small buildings, the warring of the great and the small. . . . I can hear the sound of their strife, and there is a great music being played."

There was an extraordinary outburst of poetry. In 1912, Harriet Monroe started the magazine *Poetry* in Chicago, the hotbed of the new poetry; Ezra Pound and Vachel Lindsay, both daring experimenters with ideas and verse, published in the first issue. T. S. Eliot published the classic "Love Song of J. Alfred Prufrock" in *Poetry* in 1915. Attacked bitterly by conservative critics, the poem established Eliot's leadership among a group of poets, many of them living and writing in London, who rejected traditional meter and rhyme as artificial constraints. Eliot, Pound, and Amy Lowell, among others, believed the poet's task was to capture fleeting images in verse.

Others experimenting with new techniques in poetry included Robert Frost (*North of Boston*, 1915), Edgar Lee Masters (*Spoon River Anthology*, 1915), and Carl Sandburg (*Chicago Poems*, 1916). Sandburg's poem "Chicago" celebrated the vitality of the city:

> Come and show me another city with lifted head
>   singing so proud to be
>   alive and coarse and strong and cunning.
> . . . .
> Fierce as a dog with tongue lapping for action,
>   cunning as a savage
>   pitted against the wilderness,
>   Bareheaded,
>   Shoveling,
>   Wrecking,
>   Planning,
>   Building, breaking, rebuilding,
> . . . .
> Bragging and laughing that under his wrist is the
>   pulse, and under his
>   ribs the heart of the people,
>   Laughing!
> Laughing the stormy, husky, brawling laughter of
>   Youth, half-naked,
>   sweating, proud to be Hog Butcher, Tool
>   Maker, Stacker of Wheat,
>   Player with Railroads and Freight Handler to
>   the Nation.

CHRONOLOGY

1898	Mergers and consolidations begin to sweep the business world, leading to fear of trusts
1903	Ford Motor Company formed ◆ W. E. B. Du Bois calls for justice and equality for African Americans in *The Souls of Black Folk* ◆ Women's Trade Union League (WTUL) formed to organize women workers
1905	Industrial Workers of the World (IWW) established ◆ African American leaders inaugurate the Niagara Movement, advocating integration and equal opportunity for African Americans
1909	Shirtwaist workers in New York City strike in the Uprising of the 20,000 ◆ Campaign by Rockefeller Sanitary Commission wipes out hookworm disease
1910	NAACP founded ◆ Strike at Hart, Schaffner and Marx leads to pioneering collective bargaining agreement ◆ National Collegiate Athletic Association (NCAA) formed
1911	Fire at the Triangle Shirtwaist Company kills 146 people ◆ Irving Berlin popularizes rhythm of ragtime with Alexander's Ragtime Band ◆ Frederick Winslow Taylor publishes *The Principles of Scientific Management*
1912	Harriet Monroe begins publishing magazine *Poetry* ◆ IWW leads strikes in Massachusetts and New Jersey
1913	Ford introduces the moving assembly line in Highland Park, Michigan, plant ◆ Mother's Day becomes national holiday
1915	D. W. Griffith produces the first movie spectacular, *Birth of a Nation* ◆ T. S. Eliot publishes "The Love Song of J. Alfred Prufrock"
1916	Margaret Sanger forms New York Birth Control League ◆ Federal Aid Roads Act creates national road network ◆ New York zoning law sets the pattern for zoning laws across the nation
1917	Congress passes law requiring literacy test for all immigrants
1921	Congress passes the Sheppard-Towner Act to help protect maternal and infant health

CONCLUSION: A FERMENT OF DISCOVERY AND REFORM

Manners and morals change slowly, and many Americans overlooked the importance of the first two decades of the twentieth century. Yet sweeping change was under way; anyone who doubted it could visit a gallery, see a film, listen to music, or read one of the new literary magazines. Garrets and galleries were filled with a breathtaking sense of change. "There was life in all these new things," Marsden Hartley, a modernist painter, recalled. "There was excitement, there was healthy revolt, investigation, discovery, and an utterly new world out of it all."

The ferment of progressivism in city, state, and nation reshaped the country. In a burst of reform, people built playgrounds, restructured taxes, regulated business, won the vote for women, shortened working hours, altered political systems, opened kindergartens, and improved factory safety. They tried to fulfill the national promise of dignity and liberty.

Marsden Hartley, it turned out, had voiced a mood that went well beyond painters and poets. Across society, people in many walks of life were experiencing a similar sense of excitement and discovery. Racism, repression, and labor conflict were present, to be sure, but there was also talk of hope, progress, and change. In politics, science, journalism, education, and a host of other fields, people believed for a time that they could make a difference, and in trying to do so, they became part of the progressive generation.

RECOMMENDED READING

There are several important analyses of the Progressive Era, including Robert H. Wiebe, *The Search for Order, 1877–1920* (1967); Richard Hofstadter, *The Age of Reform* (1955); Samuel P. Hays, *The Response to Industrialism* (1957); and Gabriel Kolko, *The Triumph of Conservatism* (1963). C. Vann Woodward, *Origins of the New South 1877–1913* (1951), is a superb account of developments in the South, along with William A. Link, *The Paradox of Southern Progressivism, 1880–1930* (1992).

George William Shea, *Spoiled Silk: The Red Mayor and the Great Paterson Textile Strike* (2001), and Elliot J. Gorn, *Mother Jones: The Most Dangerous Woman in America* (2001), look at radical labor movements; David I. Macleod, *The Age of the Child: Children in America, 1890–1920* (1998), at children; Nancy C. Unger, *Fighting Bob LaFollette: The Righteous Reformer* (2000), and Patricia A. Schechter, *Ida B.*

Wells-Barnett and American Reform, 1880–1930 (2001), at specific reformers. Gary Scott Smith, *The Search for Social Salvation: Social Christianity and America, 1880–1925* (2000), and Thomas Winter, *Making Men, Making Class: The YMCA and Workingmen, 1877–1920* (2002), examine the role of religion.

James T. Kloppenberg, *Uncertain Victory: Social Democracy and Progressivism in European and American Thought, 1870–1920* (1986), examines progressivism at home and abroad. C. Vann Woodward, *The Strange Career of Jim Crow* (1955), traces the civil rights setbacks of the Progressive Era.

For a list of additional titles related to this chapter's topics, please see http://www.ablongman.com/divine.

SUGGESTED WEB SITES

NAACP Online

http://www.naacp.org/

The National Association for the Advancement of Colored People official Web site explains its mission and includes a primary document explaining the start of the NAACP.

The Evolution of the Conservation Movement, 1850–1920

http://memory.loc.gov/ammem/amrvhtml/conshome.html

This American Memory site brings together scores of primary sources and photographs about "the historical formation and cultural foundations of the movement to conserve and protect America's natural heritage."

The Triangle Shirtwaist Factory Fire, March 25, 1911

http://www.ilr.cornell.edu/trianglefire/

The Kheel Center for Labor-Management Documentation and Archives at Cornell University put together this excellent site composed of oral histories, cartoons, images, and essays.

Labor-Management Conflict in American History

http://www.history.ohio-state.edu/projects/laborconflict/

This site at Ohio State University includes primary accounts of some of the major events in the history of labor-management conflict in the late nineteenth and early twentieth centuries.

Inside an American Factory: The Westinghouse Works, 1904

http://lcweb2.loc.gov/ammem/papr/west/westhome.html

Part of the American Memory Project at the Library of Congress, this site provides a glimpse inside a turn-of-the-century factory.

African American Women Writers of the Nineteenth Century

http://digital.nypl.org/schomburg/writers_aa19/

The New York Public Library's Schomburg Center for Research in Black Culture maintains this site that contains a large number of digital texts by African American women of the nineteenth century.

Touring Turn-of-the-Century America: Photographs from the Detroit Publishing Company, 1880–1920

http://memory.loc.gov/ammem/detroit/dethome.html

This Library of Congress collection has thousands of photographs from turn-of-the-century America.

Bill Haywood Trial (1907)

http://www.law.umkc.edu/faculty/projects/ftrials/haywood/haywood.htm

This site contains images, chronology, court, and official documents maintained by Dr. Doug Linder at University of Missouri–Kansas City Law School.

Margaret Sanger Papers Project

http://www.nyu.edu/projects/sanger/

This site at New York University contains information about Margaret Sanger and digital versions of several of her works.

Scott Joplin, 1868–1817

http://www.lsjunction.com/people/joplin.htm

This site offers information on Joplin and ragtime music.

National Arts and Crafts Archives

http://arts-crafts.com/index.html

This site serves as a guide to materials on the Arts and Crafts movement, which lasted roughly from 1890 to 1929.

A collage celebrating the career of TR (Theodore Roosevelt)—Rough Rider, assistant secretary of the Navy, builder of the Panama Canal, organizer of the Bull Moose party, and carrier of a "big stick." ❖

From Roosevelt to Wilson in the Age of Progressivism

$\mathcal{T}$he Republicans Split

On a sunny spring morning in 1909, Theodore Roosevelt, wearing the greatcoat of a colonel of the Rough Riders, left New York for a safari in Africa. An ex-president at the age of 50, he had turned over the White House to his chosen successor, William Howard Taft, and was now off for "the joy of wandering through lonely lands, the joy of hunting the mighty and terrible lords" of Africa, "where death broods in the dark and silent depths."

Some of Roosevelt's enemies hoped he would not return. "I trust some lion will do its duty," Wall Street magnate J. P. Morgan said. Always prepared, Roosevelt took nine extra pairs of eyeglasses, and, just in case, several expert hunters accompanied him. When the nearsighted Roosevelt took aim, three others aimed at the same moment. "Mr. Roosevelt had a fairly good idea of the general direction," the safari leader said, "but we couldn't take chances with the life of a former president." Though he had built a reputation as an ardent conservationist, Roosevelt shot nine lions, five elephants, thirteen rhinoceroses, seven hippopotamuses, and assorted other game—acquiring nearly three hundred trophies in all.

It was all good fun, and afterward Roosevelt set off on a tour of Europe. He attended the funeral of the king of England with the crowned heads of Europe, dined with the king and queen of Italy—an experience he likened to "a Jewish wedding on the East Side of New York"—and happily spent five hours reviewing troops of the German empire. Less happily, he followed events back home where, in the judgment of many friends, Taft was not working out as president. Gifford Pinchot, Roosevelt's close companion in the conservation movement, came to Italy to complain personally about Taft, and at almost every stop there were letters waiting for him from other disappointed Republicans.

For his part, Taft was puzzled by it all. Honest and warmhearted, he had intended to continue Roosevelt's policies, even writing Roosevelt that he would "see to it that your judgment in selecting me as your successor and bringing about that succession shall be vindicated." But events turned out differently. The conservative and progressive wings of the Republican party split, and Taft often sided with the conservatives. Among progressive Republicans, Taft's troubles stirred talk of a Roosevelt "back from Elba" movement, akin to Napoleon's return from exile.

Thousands gathered to greet Roosevelt on his return from Europe. He sailed into New York harbor on June 18, 1910, to the sound of naval guns and loud cheers. In characteristic fashion, he had helped make the arrangements: "If there is to be a great crowd, do arrange it so that the whole crowd has a chance to see me and that there is as little disappointment as possible." Greeting Pinchot, one of Taft's leading opponents, with a hearty "Hello, Gifford," Roosevelt slipped away to his home in Oyster Bay, New York, where other friends awaited him.

OUTLINE

The Spirit of Progressivism

Reform in the Cities and States

The Republican Roosevelt

Roosevelt Progressivism at Its Height

The Ordeal of William Howard Taft

Woodrow Wilson's New Freedom

Conclusion: The Fruits of Progressivism

FEATURE ESSAY

Madam C.J. Walker: African American Business Pioneer

LAW AND SOCIETY

Muller v. *Oregon:* Expanding the Definition of Acceptable Evidence

Teddy Roosevelt, with his hunting party in Africa, poses with one of the more than three hundred animals he and his group took down. As president, Roosevelt had supported measures protecting wildlife in the United States, including designating Pelican Island, Florida, as the nation's first wildlife refuge. ❖

He carried with him a touching letter from Taft, received just before he left Europe. "I have had a hard time—I do not know that I have had harder luck than other Presidents, but I do know that thus far I have succeeded far less than have others. I have been conscientiously trying to carry out your policies but my method of doing so has not worked smoothly." Taft invited Teddy to spend a night or two at the White House, but Roosevelt declined, saying that ex-presidents should not visit Washington. Relations between the two friends cooled. "It is hard, very hard," Taft said in 1911, "to see a devoted friendship going to pieces like a rope of sand."

A YEAR LATER, THERE WAS NO longer thought of friendship, only a desperate fight between Taft and Roosevelt for the Republican presidential nomination. Taft won the nomination, but, angry and ambitious, Roosevelt bolted and helped form a new party, the Progressive (or "Bull Moose") party, to un-seat Taft and capture the White House. With Taft, Roosevelt, Woodrow Wilson (the Democratic party's candidate), and Socialist party candidate Eugene V. Debs all in the race, the election of 1912 became one of the most exciting in American history.

It was also one of the most important. People were worried about the social and economic effects of urban-industrial growth. The election of 1912 provided a forum for those worries, and, to a degree unusual in American politics, it pitted deeply opposed candidates against one another and outlined differing views of the nation's future. In the spirited battle between Roosevelt and Wilson, it also brought to the forefront some of the currents of progressive reform.

Those currents built on a number of important developments, including the rise of a new professional class, reform movements designed to cure problems in the cities and states, and the activist, achievement-oriented administrations of Roosevelt and Wilson. Together they produced the age of progressivism.

THE SPIRIT OF PROGRESSIVISM

In one way or another, progressivism touched all aspects of society. Politically, it fostered a reform movement that sought cures for the problems of city, state, and nation. Intellectually, it drew on the expertise of the new social sciences and reflected a shift from older absolutes such as religion to newer schools of thought that emphasized relativism and the role of the environment in human development. Culturally, it inspired fresh modes of expression in dance, film, painting, literature, and architecture. Touching individuals in different ways, progressivism became a set of attitudes as well as a definable movement.

Though broad and diverse, progressivism as a whole had a half dozen characteristics that gave it definition. First, the progressives acted out of concern about the effects of industrialization and the conditions of industrial life. While their viewpoints varied, they did not, as a rule, set out to harm big business, but instead sought to humanize and regulate it.

In pursuing these objectives, the progressives displayed a second characteristic: a fundamental optimism about human nature, the possibilities of progress, and the capacity of people to recognize problems and take action to solve them. Progressives believed they could "investigate, educate, and legislate"—learn about a problem, inform people about it, and, with the help of an informed public, find and enforce a solution.

Third, more than many earlier reformers, the progressives were willing to intervene in people's lives, confident that it was their right to do so. They knew best, some of them thought, and as a result, there was an element of coercion in a number of their ideas. Fourth, while progressives preferred if possible to use voluntary means to achieve reform, they tended to turn more and more to the authority of the state and government at all levels in order to put into effect the reforms they wanted.

As a fifth characteristic, many progressives drew on a combination of evangelical Protestantism (which gave them the desire—and, they thought, the duty—to purge the world of sins such as prostitution and drunkenness) and the natural and social sciences (whose theories made them confident that they could understand and control the environment in which people lived). Progressives tended to view the environment as a key to reform, thinking—in the way some economists, sociologists, and other social scientists were suggesting—that if they could change the environment, they could change the individual.

Finally, progressivism was distinctive because it touched virtually the whole nation. Not everyone, of course, was a progressive, and there were many who opposed or ignored the ideas of the movement. There were also those who were untouched by progressive reforms and those whom the movement overlooked. But in one way or another, a remarkable number of people were caught up in it, giving progressivism a national reach and a mass base.

That was one of the features, in fact, that set it off from populism, which had grown mostly in the rural South and West. Progressivism drew support from across society. "The thing that constantly amazed me," said William Allen White, a leading progressive journalist, "was how many people were with us." Progressivism appealed to the expanding middle class, prosperous farmers, and skilled laborers; it also attracted significant support in the business community.

The progressives believed in progress and disliked waste. No single issue or concern united them all. Some progressives wanted to clean up city governments, others to clean up city streets. Some wanted to purify politics or control corporate abuses, others to eradicate poverty or prostitution. Some demanded social justice in the form of women's rights, child labor laws, temperance, and factory safety. They were Democrats, Republicans, Socialists, and independents.

Progressives believed in a better world and in the ability of people to achieve it. They paid to people, as a friend said of social reformer Florence Kelley, "the high compliment of believing that, once they knew the truth, they would act upon it." Progress depended on knowledge. The progressives stressed individual morality and collective action, the scientific method, and the value of expert opinion. Like contemporary business leaders, they valued system, planning, management, and predictability. They wanted not only reform but efficiency. In the introduction to *The Shame of the Cities*, Steffens said that the cure for American ills lay in "good conduct in the individual, simple honesty, courage, and efficiency."

Historians once viewed progressivism as the triumph of one group in society over another. In this view, farmers took on the hated and powerful railroads; upstart reformers challenged the city bosses; business interests fought for favorable legislation; youthful professionals carved out their place in society. Now, historians stress the way progressivism brought people together rather than drove them apart. Disparate groups united in an effort to improve the well-being of many groups in society.

The Rise of the Professions

Progressivism fed on an organizational impulse that encouraged people to join forces, share information, and solve problems. Between 1890 and 1920, a host of national societies and associations took shape—nearly four hundred of them in just three decades. Groups such as the National Child Labor Committee, which lobbied for legislation to regulate the employment and working conditions of children, were formed to attack specific issues. Other groups reflected one of the most significant developments in American society at the turn of the century—the rise of the professions.

Growing rapidly in these years, the professions—law, medicine, religion, business, teaching, and social work—were the source of much of the leadership of the progressive movement. The professions attracted young, educated men and women, who in turn were part of a larger trend: a dramatic increase in the number of individuals working in administrative and professional jobs. In businesses, these people were managers, architects, technicians, and accountants. In city governments, they were experts in everything from education to sanitation. They organized and ran the urban-industrial society.

These professionals formed part of a new middle class whose members did not derive their status from birth or inherited wealth, as had many members of the older middle class. Instead, they moved ahead through education and personal accomplishment and worked to become doctors, lawyers, ministers, and teachers. Proud of their skills, they were ambitious and self-confident, and they thought of themselves as experts who could use their knowledge for the benefit of society. (See the Feature Essay, "Madam C.J. Walker: African American Business Pioneer," pp. 680–681.)

As a way of asserting their status, they formed professional societies to look after their interests and govern entry into their professions. Just a few years before, for example, a doctor had become a doctor simply by stocking up on patent medicines and hanging out a sign. Now doctors began to insist they were part of a medical profession, and they wanted to set educational requirements and minimum standards for practice. In 1901, they reorganized the American Medical Association (AMA) and made it into a modern national professional society. The AMA had 8400 members that year. A decade later, it had more than 70,000, and by 1920, nearly two-thirds of all doctors belonged.

Other groups and professions showed the same pattern. Lawyers formed bar associations, created examining boards, and lobbied for regulations restricting entry into the profession. Teachers organized the National Education Association (1905) and pressed for teacher certification and compulsory education laws. Social workers formed the National Federation of Settlements (1911); business leaders created the National Association of Manufacturers (1895) and the U.S. Chamber of Commerce (1912); and farmers joined the National Farm Bureau Federation to spread information about farming and to try to improve their lot.

Working both as individuals and groups, members of the professions had a major impact on the era, as the career of one of them, Dr. Alice Hamilton, illustrated. Hamilton early decided to devote her life to helping the less fortunate. Choosing medicine, she went to the University of Michigan Medical School, one of a shrinking number of medical schools that admitted women, and then settled in Chicago, where she met Jane Addams and took a room in Hull House. Soon thereafter, she traced a local typhoid epidemic to flies carrying germs from open privies. The study won national acclaim, but Hamilton had already turned her attention to the work-related illnesses she found everywhere around Hull House.

Combining field study with meticulous laboratory techniques, she pioneered research into the causes of lead poisoning and other industrial disease. In 1908, the governor of Illinois appointed her to a commission on occupational diseases; two years later, she headed a statewide survey of industrial poisons. Thanks to her work, in 1911, Illinois passed the first state law providing compensation for industrial disease caused by poisonous fumes and dust. By the end of the 1930s, all the major industrial states had such laws.

One of the new professionals, Hamilton had used her education and skill to broaden knowledge of her subject, change industrial practices, and improve the lives of countless workers. "For me," she said later in a comment characteristic of the progressives, "the satisfaction is that things are better now, and I had some part in it."

The Social-Justice Movement

As Alice Hamilton's career exemplified, progressivism began in the cities during the 1890s. It first took form around settlement workers and others interested in freeing individuals from the crushing impact of cities and factories.

Ministers, intellectuals, social workers, and lawyers joined in a **social-justice movement** that focused national attention on the need for tenement house laws, more stringent child labor legislation, and better working conditions for women. They brought pressure on municipal agencies for more and better parks, playgrounds, day nurseries, schools, and community services. Blending private and public action, settlement leaders turned increasingly to government aid. "Private beneficence," Jane Addams said, "is totally inadequate to deal with the vast numbers of the city's disinherited."

Social-justice reformers were more interested in social cures than individual charity. Unlike earlier reformers, they saw problems as endless and interrelated; individuals became part of a city's larger patterns. With that insight, social-service casework shifted from a focus on an individual's well-being to a scientific analysis of neighborhoods, occupations, and classes.

In the spring of 1900, the Charity Organization Society of New York held a tenement house exhibition that graphically presented the new kind of sociological data. Put together by Lawrence Veiller, a young social worker, the exhibition included more than a thousand photographs, detailed maps of slum districts, statistical tables and charts, and graphic cardboard depictions of tenement blocks. Never before had so much information been pulled together in one place. Veiller correlated data on poverty and disease with housing

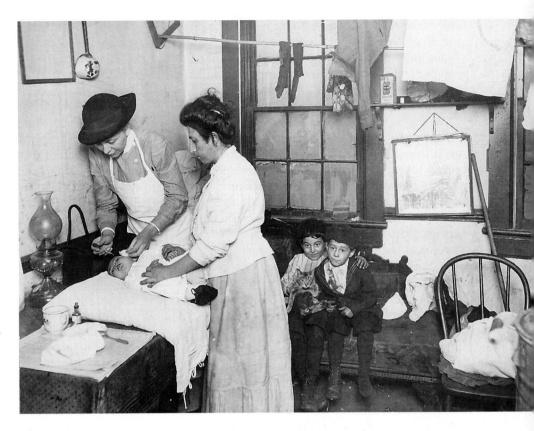

An Infant Welfare Society nurse treats the baby of an immigrant family in Chicago. A host of medical discoveries and improvements in the quality of medical education fostered an interest in public health work among the social-justice reformers. ❖

conditions, and he pointed out that new slums were springing up in more areas of the city. Stirred by the public outcry, Governor Theodore Roosevelt appointed the New York State Tenement House Commission to do something about the problem.

With Veiller's success as a model, study after study analyzed the condition of the poor. Books and pamphlets such as *The Standard of Living Among Working Men's Families in New York City* (1909) contained pages of data on family budgets, women's wages and working conditions, child labor, and other matters. Between 1910 and 1913, the U.S. Commissioner of Labor issued a massive nineteen-volume report on *Conditions of Women and Children Wage-Earners in the United States.*

Social-justice reformers, banding together to work for change, formed the National Conference of Charities and Corrections, which in 1915 became the National Conference of Social Work. Controlled by social workers, the conference reflected the growing professionalization of reform. Through it, social workers discovered each other's efforts, shared methodology, and tried to establish themselves as a separate field within the social sciences. Once content with informal training sessions in a settlement house living room, they now founded complete professional schools at Chicago, Harvard, and other universities. After 1909, they had their own professional magazine, the *Survey,*

and instead of piecemeal reforms, they aimed at a comprehensive program of minimum wages, maximum hours, workers' compensation, and widows' pensions.

The Purity Crusade

Working in city neighborhoods, social-justice reformers were often struck by the degree to which alcohol affected the lives of the people they were trying to help. Workers drank away their wages; some men spent more time at the saloon than at home. Drunkenness caused violence, and it angered employers who did not want intoxicated workers on the job. In countless ways, alcohol wasted human resources, the reformers believed, and along with business leaders, ministers, and others, they launched a crusade to remove the evils of drink from American life.

At the head of the crusade was the Women's Christian Temperance Union (WCTU), which had continued to grow since it was founded in the 1870s. By 1911, the WCTU had nearly a quarter of a million members; it was the largest organization of women in American history to that time. In 1893, it was joined by the Anti-Saloon League, and together the groups pressed to abolish alcohol and the places where it was consumed. By 1916, they had succeeded in nineteen states, but as drinking continued elsewhere, they pushed for a nationwide law. In the midst of the moral fervor of World War I, they succeeded, and the Eighteenth Amendment to the Constitution, prohibiting the manufacture, sale, and transportation of intoxicating liquors, took effect in January 1920.

The amendment encountered troubles later in the 1920s as the social atmosphere changed, but at the time it passed, progressives thought Prohibition was a major step toward eliminating social instability and moral wrong. In a similar fashion, some progressive reformers also worked to get rid of prostitution, convinced that poverty and ignorance drove women to the trade. By 1915, nearly every state had banned brothels, and in 1910, Congress passed the Mann Act, which prohibited the interstate transportation of women for immoral purposes. Like the campaign against liquor, the campaign against prostitution reflected the era's desire to purify and elevate, often through the instrument of government action.

Woman Suffrage, Women's Rights

Women played a large role in the social-justice movement. Feminists were particularly active, especially in the political sphere, between 1890 and 1914—feminists were more active then, in fact, than at any other time until the 1960s. Some working-class women pushed for higher wages and better working conditions. College-educated women—five thousand a year graduated after 1900—took up careers in the professions, from which some of them supported reform. From 1890 to 1910, the work of a number of national women's organizations, including the National Council of Jewish Women, the National Congress of Mothers, and the Women's Trade Union League, furthered the aims of the progressive movement.

Excluded from most of these organizations, African American women formed their own groups. The National Association of Colored Women was founded in 1895, fourteen years before the better known male-oriented National Association for the Advancement of Colored People (NAACP). Aimed at social welfare, the women's organization was the first African American social-service agency in the country. At the local level, African American women's clubs established kindergartens, day nurseries, playgrounds, and retirement homes.

From 200,000 members in 1900, the General Federation of Women's Clubs grew to more than 1 million by 1912. The clubs met, as they had before, for coffee and literary conversation, but they also began to look closely at conditions around them. In 1904, Mrs. Sarah P. Decker, the federation's new president, told the national convention, "Ladies, you have chosen me your leader. Well, I have an important piece of news to give you. Dante is dead. He has been dead for several centuries, and I think it is time that we dropped the study of his *Inferno* and turned our attention to our own."

Forming an Industrial Section and a Committee on Legislation for Women and Children, the federation supported reforms to safeguard child and women workers, improve schools, ensure pure food, and beautify the community. Reluctant at first, the federation finally lent support in 1914 to woman suffrage, a cause that dated back to the first women's rights convention in Seneca Falls, New York, in 1848. Divided over tactics since the Civil War, the suffrage movement suffered from disunity, male opposition, indecision over whether to seek action at the state or at the national level, resistance from the Catholic Church, and opposition from liquor interests, who linked the cause to Prohibition.

Women in the social-justice movement needed to influence elected officials—most of them men, whom they could not reach through the vote. Because politics was an avenue for reform, growing numbers of women activists became involved in the suffrage movement. After years of disagreement, the two major suffrage organizations, the National Woman Suffrage Association and the American Woman Suffrage Association, merged in 1890 to form the National American Woman Suffrage Association. The merger opened a new phase of the suffrage movement, characterized by unity and a tightly controlled national organization.

In 1900, Carrie Chapman Catt, a superb organizer, became president of the National American Woman Suffrage Association, which by 1920 had nearly two million members. Catt and Anna Howard Shaw, who became the association's head in 1904, believed in organization and peaceful lobbying to win the vote. Alice Paul and Lucy Burns, founders of the Congressional Union, were more militant; they interrupted public meetings, focused on Congress rather than the states, and in 1917 picketed the White House.

Significantly, Catt, Paul, and others made a major change in the argument for woman suffrage. When the campaign began in the nineteenth century, suffragists had claimed the vote as a natural right, owed to women as much as men. Now, they stressed a pragmatic argument: Since women were more sensitive to moral issues than men, they would use their votes to help create a better society. They would support temperance, clean government, laws to protect workers, and other reforms. This argument attracted many progressives who believed the women's vote would purify politics. In 1918, the House passed a constitutional amendment stating simply that the right to vote shall not be denied "on account of sex." The Senate and enough states followed, and, after three generations of suffragist efforts, the Nineteenth Amendment took effect in 1920.

The social-justice movement had the most success in passing state laws limiting the working hours of women. By 1913, thirty-nine states set maximum working hours for women or banned the employment of women at night. Illinois had a ten-hour law; California and Washington had eight-hour laws. Wisconsin, Oregon, and Kansas allowed expert commissions to set different hours depending on the degree of strain in various occupations. As early as 1900, thanks to groups such as the National Child Labor Committee, twenty-eight states had laws regulating child labor. But the courts often ruled against such laws, and families—needing extra income—sometimes ignored them. Parents sent children off to jobs with orders to lie about their ages.

In 1916, President Woodrow Wilson backed a law to limit child labor, the Keating-Owen Act, but in *Hammer* v. *Dagenhart* (1918), the Supreme Court overturned it as an improper regulation of local labor conditions. In 1919, Congress tried again in the Second Child Labor Act, but in *Bailey* v. *Drexel Furniture Company* (1922) the legislation was again struck down. Not until the 1930s did Congress

WOMAN SUFFRAGE BEFORE 1920

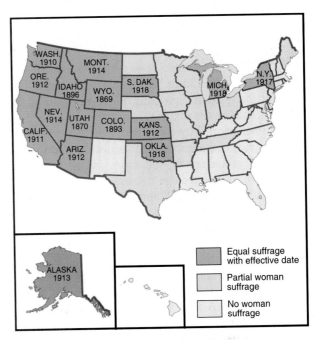

Equal suffrage with effective date

Partial woman suffrage

No woman suffrage

State-by-state gains in woman suffrage were limited to the Far West and were agonizingly slow in the early years of the twentieth century.

Woman suffrage was a key element in the social-justice movement. Without the right to vote, women working actively for reform had little real power to influence elected officials to support their endeavors. ❖

succeed in passing a court-supported national child labor law.

A Ferment of Ideas: Challenging the Status Quo

A dramatic shift in ideas became one of the most important forces behind progressive reform. Most of the ideas focused on the role of the environment in shaping human behavior. Progressive reformers accepted society's growing complexity, called for factual treatment of piecemeal problems, allowed room for new theories, and, above all, rejected age-encrusted divine or natural "laws" in favor of thoughts and actions that worked.

A new doctrine called **pragmatism** emerged in this ferment of ideas. It came from William James, a brilliant Harvard psychologist who became the key figure in American thought from the 1890s to World War I. A warm, tolerant person, James was impatient with theories that regarded truth as abstract. Truth, he believed, should work for the individual, and it worked best not in abstraction, but in action. "True ideas are those we can assimilate, validate, corroborate, and verify. False ideas are those we cannot."

People, James thought, not only were shaped by their environment; they shaped it. In *Pragmatism* (1907), he praised "tough-minded" individuals who could live effectively in a world with no easy answers. The tough-minded accepted change; they knew how to pick manageable problems, gather facts, discard ideas that did not work, and act on those that did. Ideas that worked became truth. "What is the 'cash value' of a thought, idea, or belief?" James asked. Does it work? Does it make a difference to the individual who experiences it? "The ultimate test for us of what a truth means," said James, "is the conduct it dictates."

The most influential educator of the Progressive Era, John Dewey, applied pragmatism to educational reform. A friend and disciple of William James, he argued that thought evolves in relation to the environment and that education is directly related to experience. In 1896, Dewey founded a separate School of Pedagogy at the University of Chicago, with a laboratory in which educational theory based on the newer philosophical and psychological studies could be tested and practiced.

Dewey introduced an educational revolution that stressed children's needs and capabilities. He described his beliefs and methods in a number of books, notably *School and Society* (1899) and *Democracy and Education* (1916). New ideas in education, he said, are "as much a product of the changed social situation, and as much an effort to meet the needs of the society that is forming, as are changes in modes of industry and commerce." He opposed memorization, rote learning, and dogmatic, authoritarian teaching methods; he emphasized personal growth, free inquiry, and creativity.

Rejecting the older view of the law as universal and unchanging, lawyers and legal theorists instead viewed it as a reflection of the environment—an instrument for social change. Law reflected the environment that shaped it. A movement grew among judges for "sociological jurisprudence" that related the law to social reform instead of only to legal precedent, a shift most evident in the famed **Brandeis brief,** presented in the case of *Muller v. Oregon* that came before the Supreme Court in 1908. (see *Muller v. Oregon,*" pp. 684–687).

In Denver, Colorado, after Judge Ben Lindsey sentenced a boy to reform school for stealing coal, the boy's mother rushed forward and, grief-stricken, beat her head against the wall. Lindsey investigated the case and found that the father was a smelting worker dying of lead poisoning; the family needed coal for heat. From such experiences, Lindsey concluded that children were not born with a genetic tendency to crime; they were made good or bad by the environment in which they grew. Lindsey "sentenced" youthful offenders to education and good care. He worked for playgrounds, slum clearance, public baths, and technical schools. Known as the "Kids' Judge," he attracted visitors from as far away as Japan, who wanted to study and copy his methods.

Socialism, a reformist political philosophy, grew dramatically before World War I. Socialist political parties, composed of followers of Karl Marx, first appeared in New York, Chicago, Milwaukee, and other cities after the Civil War. They urged workers to join a worldwide revolution to overthrow capitalism. Such public appeals, however, drew little support. Leaders of a new Socialist Labor party, founded in 1877, tried in secret to gain control of important labor unions. That strategy also failed.

Daniel De Leon, a brilliant tactician, took over leadership of the Socialist Labor party during the 1890s, but he too lacked mass support. Arguing for a more moderate form of socialism, Eugene V. Debs, president of the American Railway Union, in 1896 formed a rival organization, the Social Democratic party. Gentle and reflective, not at all the popular image of the wild-eyed radical, Debs was thrust into prominence by the Pullman strike. In 1901, persuading opponents of De Leon to join him, he formed the important Socialist party of America. Neither Debs nor the party ever developed a cohesive platform, nor was Debs an effective organizer. But he was eloquent, passionate, and visionary. An excellent speaker, he captivated audiences, attacking the injustices of capitalism and urging a workers' republic.

The Socialist party of America enlisted some intellectuals, factory workers, disillusioned Populists,

Some of Eugene Debs's supporters surround the "Red Special," the train Debs used in his 1908 presidential campaign. To attract voters to his socialist message, Debs traveled over 9000 miles in less than four weeks. A Detroit newspaper, trying to discredit the socialist candidate, criticized Debs's use of a "magnificent parlor car." ❖

tenant farmers, miners, and lumberjacks. By 1911, there were Socialist mayors in thirty-two cities, including Berkeley, California; Butte, Montana; and Flint, Michigan. Although its doctrines were aimed at an urban proletariat, the Socialist party drew support in rural Texas, Missouri, Arkansas, Idaho, and Washington. In Oklahoma, it attracted as much as one-third of the vote. Most Socialists who won promised progressive reform rather than threatening to overthrow capitalists.

Although torn by factions, the Socialist party doubled in membership between 1904 and 1908, then tripled in the four years after that. Running for president, Debs garnered 100,000 votes in 1900; 400,000 in 1904; and 900,000 in 1912, the party's peak year.

REFORM IN THE CITIES AND STATES

Progressive reformers realized government could be a crucial agent in accomplishing their goals. They wanted to curb the influence of "special interests" and,

through such measures of political reform as the direct primary and the direct election of senators, make government follow the public will. Once it did, they welcomed government action at whatever level was appropriate.

As a result of this thinking, the use of federal power increased, as did the power and prestige of the presidency. Progressives not only lobbied for government-sponsored reform but also worked actively in their home neighborhoods, cities, and states; much of the significant change occurred in local settings, outside the national limelight. Most important, the progressives believed in the ability of experts to solve problems. At every level—local, state, and federal—thousands of commissions and agencies took form. Staffed by trained experts, they oversaw a multitude of matters ranging from railroad rates to public health.

Interest Groups and the Decline of Popular Politics

Placing government in the hands of experts was one way to get it out of the hands of politicians and political parties. The direct primary, which allowed voters rather than parties to choose candidates for office, was another way. These initiatives and others like them were part of a fundamental change in the way Americans viewed their political system.

As one sign of the change, fewer and fewer people were going to the polls. Voter turnout dropped dramatically after 1900, when the intense partisanship of the decades after the Civil War gave way to media-oriented political campaigns based largely on the personalities of the candidates. From 1876 to 1900, the average turnout in presidential elections was 77 percent. From 1900 to 1916, it was 65 percent, and in the 1920s, it dropped to 52 percent, close to the average today. Turnout was lowest among young people, immigrants, the poor, and, ironically, the newly enfranchised women.

It was particularly low in the South where conservative whites used restrictive election laws to keep blacks and others from the polls. Turnout in the South fell sharply, from an average of 64 percent in the presidential elections of the 1880s to just 20 percent in 1920 and 1924. Although the decline in the North was less sharp, the reasons for it were more complex. By the 1920s, as many as one-quarter of all eligible northern voters never cast a ballot.

There were numerous causes for the falloff, but among the most important was the fact that people had found another way to achieve some of the objectives they had once assigned to political parties. They had found the "interest group," a means of action that assumed importance in this era and became a major feature of politics ever after. Professional societies,

VOTER PARTICIPATION IN PRESIDENTIAL ELECTIONS, 1876–1920

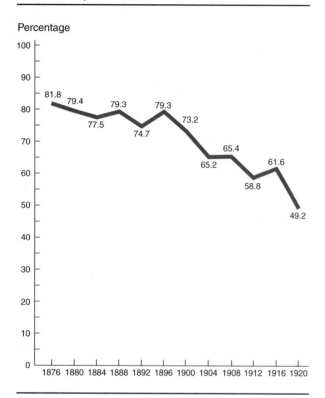

trade associations, labor organizations, farm lobbies, and scores of other interest groups worked outside the party system to pressure government for things their members wanted. Social workers, women's clubs, reform groups, and others learned to apply pressure in similar ways, and the result was much significant legislation of the Progressive Era.

Reform in the Cities

During the early years of the twentieth century, urban reform movements, many of them born in the depression of the 1890s, spread across the nation. In 1894, the National Municipal League was organized, and it became the forum for debate over civic reform, changes in the tax laws, and municipal ownership of public utilities. Within a few years, nearly every city had a variety of clubs and organizations directed at improving the quality of city life.

"For two generations," Frederic C. Howe said in 1905, "we have wrought out the most admirable laws and then left the government to run itself. This has been our greatest fault." In the 1880s, reformers such as Howe would call an evening conference, pass resolutions, and then go home; after 1900, they formed associations, adopted long-range policies, and hired a staff to achieve them. In the mid-1890s, only Chicago

had an urban reform league with a full-time paid executive; within a decade, there were such leagues in every major city.

In city after city, reformers reordered municipal government. Tightening controls on corporate activities, they broadened the scope of utility regulation and restricted city franchises. They updated tax assessments, often skewed in favor of corporations, and tried to clean up the electoral machinery. Devoted to efficiency, they developed a trained civil service to oversee planning and operations. The generation of the 1880s also had believed in civil service, but the goal then was mostly negative: to get spoilsmen out and "good" people in. Now the goal was efficiency and, above all, results.

In constructing their model governments, urban reformers often turned to recent advances in business management and organization. They stressed continuity and expertise, a system in which professional experts staffed a government overseen by elected officials. At the top, the elected leader surveyed the breadth of city, state, or national affairs and defined directions. Below, a corps of experts—trained in the various disciplines of the new society—funneled the definition into specific scientifically based policies.

Reformers created a growing number of regulatory commissions and municipal departments. They hired engineers to oversee utility and water systems, physicians and nurses to improve municipal health, and city planners to oversee park and highway development. They created specialized "academies" to train police and firefighters. Imitated by the state and federal governments, the proliferation of experts and commissions widened the gap between voters and decision makers but dramatically improved the efficiency of government.

As cities exploded in size, they freed themselves from the tight controls of state legislatures and began to experiment with their own governments. Struggling to recover from a devastating hurricane in 1900, Galveston, Texas, pioneered the commission form of government: a form of municipal government in which commissions of appointed experts, rather than elected officials, ran the city. Wanting nonpartisan expertise, Staunton, Virginia, was the first to hire a city manager. Other cities followed, and by 1910 more than one hundred cities were using either the commission or manager type of government.

In the race for reform, a number of city mayors won national reputations—among them Seth Low in New York City and Hazen S. Pingree in Detroit—working to modernize taxes, clean up politics, lower utility rates, and control the awarding of valuable city franchises. In Toledo, Ohio, Mayor Samuel M. ("Golden Rule") Jones, a wealthy manufacturer, took

Aftermath of the devastating 1900 hurricane in Galveston, Texas, in which thousands of people were killed or left homeless and a large part of the city was reduced to rubble. In the recovery effort the city created a new commission form of municipal government. ❖

billy clubs away from the police; established free kindergartens, playgrounds, and night schools; and improved wages for city workers.

In Cleveland, Ohio, Tom L. Johnson demonstrated an innovative approach to city government. A millionaire who had made his fortune manipulating city franchises, Johnson one day read Henry George's *Progress and Poverty* and turned to reform. Elected mayor of Cleveland, he served from 1901 to 1909 and collected a group of aggressive and talented young advisers. Frederic C. Howe, Newton D. Baker, and Edward Bemis—all of whom later won national reputations—shaped Johnson's ideas on taxes, prison reform, utility regulation, and other issues facing the city.

Johnson combined shrewdness and showmanship. Believing in an informed citizenry, he held outdoor meetings in huge tents. He used colorful charts to give Cleveland residents a course in utilities and taxation. He cut down on corruption, cut off special privilege, updated taxes, and gave Cleveland a reputation as the country's best governed city.

Finding it difficult to regulate powerful city utilities and keep their costs down, Johnson and mayors in other cities turned more and more to public ownership of gas, electricity, water, and transportation. The idea of "gas and water socialism"—in which cities owned their own gas, electricity, water, and other utilities—spread swiftly. In 1896, fewer than half of

American cities owned their own waterworks; by 1915, almost two-thirds did.

Action in the States

Reformers soon discovered, however, that many problems lay beyond a city's boundaries, and they turned for action to the state governments. From the 1890s to 1920, reformers worked to stiffen state laws regulating the labor of women and children, to create and strengthen commissions to regulate railroads and utilities, to impose corporate and inheritance taxes, to improve mental and penal institutions, and to allocate more funds for state universities, which were viewed as the training ground for the experts and educated citizenry needed for the new society.

Maryland passed the first workers' compensation law in 1902; soon most industrial states had such legislation. After 1900, many states adopted factory inspection laws, and by 1916, almost two-thirds of the states mandated insurance for the victims of factory accidents. By 1914, twenty-five states had enacted employers' liability laws.

New York was one of the states that led the way in adopting significant reforms. Around 1905, a series of dramatic investigations in the state revealed a systematic and corrupt alliance between politicians and business leaders in the gas, electricity, and insurance industries—all of which directly touched the general public. An angry public responded immediately, supporting greater state regulation and management by independent expert commissions. In 1905 and 1906, the state established regulatory boards to oversee utilities and insurance; it also outlawed corporate contributions to political campaigns and restricted business lobbying in the state legislature.

To regulate business, virtually every state created regulatory commissions empowered to examine corporate books and hold public hearings. Building on earlier experience, state commissions after 1900 were given new power to initiate actions, rather than await complaints, and in some cases to set maximum prices and rates. Dictating company practices, they pioneered regulatory methods later adopted in federal legislation of 1906 and 1910. Some business leaders supported the federal laws in order to get rid of "the intolerable supervision" of dozens of separate state commissions.

Historians have long praised the regulation movement, but the commissions did not always act wisely or even in the public interest. Elective commissions often produced commissioners who had little knowledge of corporate affairs. In addition, to win election, some promised specific rates or reforms, obligations that might bias the commission's investigative functions. Appointive commissions sometimes fared better, but they too had to oversee extraordinarily complex businesses such as the railroads. Shaping everything from wages to train schedules, the regulatory commissions affected railroad profits and growth negatively and, in the end, damaged the railroad industry.

To the progressives, commissions offered a way to end the corrupt alliance between business and politics. There was another way, too, and that was to "democratize" government by reducing the power of politicians and increasing the influence of the electorate. To do that, progressives backed three measures to make officeholders responsive to popular will: the initiative, which allowed voters to propose new laws; the referendum, which allowed them to accept or reject a law at the ballot box; and the recall, which gave them a way to remove an elected official from office.

The most famous of the reform leaders in the states was Wisconsin's Robert M. "Fighting Bob" La Follette. He was unanimously nominated for governor in 1900 and won the election with the largest plurality of votes ever received by a candidate for that office. He is shown here on his special campaign train during a stop at La Valle, Wisconsin, in October 1900. ✦

Oregon adopted the initiative and referendum in 1902; by 1912, twelve states had them. That year Congress added the Seventeenth Amendment to the Constitution to provide for the direct election of U.S. senators. By 1916, all but three states had direct primaries, which allowed the people, rather than nominating conventions, to choose candidates for office.

As attention shifted from the cities to the states, reform governors throughout the country earned greater visibility. Joseph Folk, Steffens's hero in St. Louis, became the governor of Missouri in 1904. Hiram Johnson won fame in California for his shrewd and forceful campaign against the Southern Pacific Railroad. In the East, the cause of reform was upheld by Charles Evans Hughes in New York and Woodrow Wilson, the former president of Princeton University, in New Jersey.

Robert M. La Follette became the most famous reform governor. A graduate of the University of Wisconsin, La Follette served three terms in Congress during the late 1880s. A staunch Republican, he supported the tariff and other Republican doctrines, but the Democratic landslide of 1890 turned him out of office. Moving to state politics, he became interested in reform, spurred in part, as so many were, by the depression of the 1890s. In 1901, he became governor of Wisconsin. Then 45 years old, La Follette was talented, aggressive, and a superb stump speaker.

In the following six years, he put together the "Wisconsin Idea," one of the most important reform programs in the history of state government. He established an industrial commission, the first in the country, to regulate factory safety and sanitation. He improved education, workers' compensation, public utility controls, and resource conservation. He lowered railroad rates and raised railroad taxes. Under La Follette's prodding, Wisconsin became the first state to adopt a direct primary for all political nominations. It also became the first to adopt a state income tax.

Like other progressives, La Follette drew on expert advice and relied on academic figures such as Richard Ely and Edward Ross at the University of Wisconsin. La Follette supporters established the first Legislative Reference Bureau in the university's library; the bureau stocked the governor and his allies with facts and figures to support the measures they wanted. Theodore Roosevelt called La Follette's Wisconsin "the laboratory of democracy," and the Wisconsin Idea soon spread to many other states, including New York, California, Michigan, Iowa, and Texas.

After 1905, the progressives looked more and more to Washington. For one thing, Teddy Roosevelt was there, with his zest for publicity and his alluring grin. But progressives also had a growing sense that many concerns—corporations and conservation, factory safety and child labor—crossed state lines. Federal action seemed desirable; specific reforms fit into a larger plan perhaps best seen from the nation's center. Within a few years, La Follette and Hiram Johnson became senators, and while reform went on back home, the focus of progressivism shifted to Washington.

THE REPUBLICAN ROOSEVELT

When President William McKinley died of gunshot wounds in September 1901, Vice President Theodore Roosevelt succeeded him in the White House. The new president initially vowed to carry on McKinley's policies. He continued some, developed others of his own, and in the end brought to them all the particular exuberance of his own personality.

At age 42, Roosevelt was then the youngest president in American history. In contrast to the dignified McKinley, he was open, aggressive, and high-spirited. At his desk by 8:30 every morning, he worked through the day, usually with visitors for breakfast, lunch, and dinner. Politicians, labor leaders, industrialists, poets, artists, and writers paraded through the White House.

In personal conversation Roosevelt was persuasive and charming. He read widely, and he held opinions on every issue—literature, art, marriage, divorce, conservation, business, football, and even spelling. An advocate of simplified spelling, he once instructed government printers to use "thru" for "through" and "dropt" for "dropped." Public opposition forced him to withdraw the order, and shortly afterward, as he was watching a naval review in Long Island Sound, a launch marked "Pres Bot" steamed by. Roosevelt laughed with delight.

If McKinley cut down on presidential isolation, Roosevelt virtually ended it. The presidency, he thought, was the "bully pulpit," a forum of ideas and leadership for the nation. The president was "a steward of the people bound actively and affirmatively to do all he could for the people." Self-confident, Roosevelt enlisted talented associates, including Elihu Root, secretary of war and later secretary of state; William Howard Taft, secretary of war; Gifford Pinchot, the nation's chief forester and leading conservationist; and Oliver Wendell Holmes, Jr., whom he named to the Supreme Court.

In 1901, Roosevelt invited Booker T. Washington, the prominent African American educator, to dinner at the White House. Many southerners protested—"a crime equal to treason," a newspaper said—and they protested again when Roosevelt appointed several African Americans to important federal offices in South Carolina and Mississippi. At first, Roosevelt considered building a biracial "black-and-tan" southern Republican party, thinking it would foster racial progress and his own renomination in 1904. He denounced lynching and ordered the Justice Department to act against peonage.

But Roosevelt soon retreated. In some areas of the South, he supported "lily-white" Republican organizations, and his policies often reflected his own belief in African American inferiority. He said nothing when a race riot broke out in Atlanta in 1906, although twelve persons died. He joined others in blaming African American soldiers stationed near Brownsville, Texas, after a night of violence there in August 1906. Acting quickly and on little evidence, he discharged "without honor" three companies of African American troops. Six of the soldiers who were discharged held the Congressional Medal of Honor.

Busting the Trusts

"There is a widespread conviction in the minds of the American people that the great corporations known as trusts are in certain of their features and tendencies hurtful to the general welfare," Roosevelt reported to Congress in 1901. Like most people, however, the president wavered on the trusts. Large-scale production and industrial growth, he believed, were natural and beneficial; they needed only to be controlled. Still he distrusted the trusts' impact on local enterprise and individual opportunity. Distinguishing between "good" and "bad" trusts, he pledged to protect the former while controlling the latter.

At first, Roosevelt hoped the combination of investigative journalism and public opinion would be enough to uncover and correct business evils, and in public he both praised and attacked the trusts. Mr. Dooley poked fun at his wavering: "'Th' trusts,' says he, 'are heejous monsthers built up be th' enlightened intherprise iv th' men that have done so much to advance progress in our beloved country,' he says. 'On wan hand I wud stamp thim undher fut; on th' other hand not so fast.'"

In 1903, Roosevelt asked Congress to create a Department of Commerce and Labor, with a Bureau of Corporations empowered to investigate corporations engaged in interstate commerce. Congress balked; Roosevelt called in reporters and, in an off-the-record interview, charged that John D. Rockefeller had organized the opposition to the measure. The press spread the word, and in the outcry that followed, the proposal passed easily in a matter of weeks.

Roosevelt was delighted. With the new Bureau of Corporations publicizing its findings, he thought, the glare of publicity would eliminate most corporate abuses.

Roosevelt also undertook direct legal action. On February 18, 1902, he instructed the Justice Department to bring suit against the Northern Securities Company for violation of the Sherman Antitrust Act. It was a shrewd move. A mammoth holding company, Northern Securities controlled the massive rail networks of the Northern Pacific, Great Northern, and Chicago, Burlington & Quincy railroads. Some of the most prominent names in business were behind the giant company—J. P. Morgan and Company; the Rockefeller interests; Kuhn, Loeb and Company; and railroad operators James J. Hill and Edward H. Harriman.

Shocked by Roosevelt's action, Morgan charged that the president had not acted like a "gentleman," and Hill talked glumly of having "to fight for our lives against the political adventurers who have never done anything but pose and draw a salary." Morgan rushed to Washington to complain and to ask whether there were plans to "attack my other interests," notably U.S. Steel. "No," Roosevelt replied, "unless we find out they have done something that we regard as wrong."

In 1904, the Supreme Court, in a 5 to 4 decision, upheld the suit against Northern Securities and ordered the company dissolved. Roosevelt was jubilant, and he followed up the victory with several other antitrust suits. In 1902, he had moved against the beef trust, an action applauded by western farmers and urban consumers alike. After a lull, he initiated suits in 1906 and 1907 against the American Tobacco Company, the Du Pont Corporation, the New Haven Railroad, and Standard Oil.

But Roosevelt's policies were not always clear, nor his actions always consistent. He invited Morgan to the White House to confer with him and allowed the president of National City Bank to preview a draft of the president's third annual message to Congress. Roosevelt also asked for (and received) business support in his bid for reelection in 1904. Large donations came in from industrial leaders, and Morgan himself later testified that he gave $150,000 to Roosevelt's campaign. In 1907, acting in part to avert a threatened financial panic, the president permitted Morgan's U.S. Steel to absorb the Tennessee Coal and Iron Company, an important competitor.

Roosevelt, in truth, was not a trustbuster, although he was frequently called that. William Howard Taft, his successor in the White House, initiated forty-three antitrust indictments in four years—nearly twice as many as the twenty-five Roosevelt initiated in the seven years of his presidency. Instead, Roosevelt used antitrust threats to keep businesses within bounds.

A cartoon illustrating Theodore Roosevelt's promise to break up only those "bad trusts" that were hurtful to the general welfare. Despite his reputation as a "trust buster," Roosevelt dissolved relatively few trusts. ❖

Regulation, he believed, was a better way to control large-scale enterprise.

"Square Deal" in the Coalfields

A few months after announcing the Northern Securities suit, Roosevelt intervened in a major labor dispute involving the anthracite coal miners of northeastern Pennsylvania. Led by John Mitchell, a moderate labor leader, the United Mine Workers demanded wage increases, an eight-hour workday, and company recognition of the union. The coal companies refused, and in May 1902, 140,000 miners walked off the job. The mines closed.

As the months passed and the strike continued, coal prices rose. With winter coming on, schools, hospitals, and factories ran short of coal. Public opinion turned against the companies. Morgan and other industrial leaders privately urged them to settle, but George F. Baer, head of one of the largest companies, refused: "The rights and interests of the laboring man," Baer said, "will be protected and cared for—not by the labor agitators, but by the Christian men to whom God in his infinite wisdom has given the control of the property interests of this country."

Roosevelt was furious. Complaining of the companies' arrogance, he invited both sides in the dispute to an October 1902 conference at the White House. There, Mitchell took a moderate tone and offered to submit the issues to arbitration, but the companies again refused to budge. Roosevelt ordered the army to prepare to seize the mines and then leaked word of his intent to Wall Street leaders.

Alarmed, Morgan and others again urged settlement of the dispute, and at last the companies retreated. They agreed to accept the recommendations of an independent commission the president would appoint. In late October, the strikers returned to work, and in March 1903, the commission awarded them a 10 percent wage increase and a cut in working hours. It recommended, however, against union recognition. The coal companies, in turn, were encouraged to raise prices to offset the wage increase.

More and more, Roosevelt saw the federal government as an honest and impartial "broker" between powerful elements in society. Rather than leaning toward labor, he pursued a middle way to curb corporate and labor abuses, abolish privilege, and enlarge individual opportunity. Conservative by temperament, he sometimes backed reforms in part to head off more radical measures.

During the 1904 campaign, Roosevelt called his actions in the coal miners' strike a "square deal" for both labor and capital, a term that stuck to his administration. Roosevelt was not the first president to take a stand for labor, but he was the first to bring opposing sides in a labor dispute to the White House to settle it. He was the first to threaten to seize a major industry, and he was the first to appoint an arbitration commission whose decision both sides agreed to accept.

ROOSEVELT PROGRESSIVISM AT ITS HEIGHT

In the election of 1904, the popular Roosevelt soundly drubbed his Democratic opponent, Alton B. Parker of New York, and the Socialist party candidate, Eugene V. Debs of Indiana. Roosevelt attracted a large campaign chest and won votes everywhere. In a landslide victory, he received 57 percent of the vote to Parker's 38 percent, and on election night, he savored the public's confidence. Overjoyed, he pledged that "under no

THE ELECTION OF 1904

Candidate	Party	Popular Vote	Electoral Vote
T. Roosevelt	Republican	7,626,593	336
Parker	Democrat	5,082,898	140
Debs	Socialist	402,489	0
Swallow	Prohibition	258,596	0

circumstances will I be a candidate for or accept another nomination," a statement he later regretted.

Regulating the Railroads

Following his election, Roosevelt in late 1904 laid out a reform program that included railroad regulation, employers' liability for federal employees, greater federal control over corporations, and laws regulating child labor, factory inspection, and slum clearance in the District of Columbia. He turned first to railroad regulation. In 1903, he had worked with Congress to pass the Elkins Act to prohibit railroad rebates and increase the powers of the Interstate Commerce Commission (ICC). The Elkins Act, a moderate law, was framed with the consent of railroad leaders. In 1904 and 1905, the president wanted much more, and he urged Congress to empower the ICC to set reasonable and nondiscriminatory rates and prevent inequitable practices.

Widespread demand for railroad regulation strengthened Roosevelt's hand. In the Midwest and Far West, the issue was a popular one, and reform governors La Follette in Wisconsin and Albert B. Cummins in Iowa urged federal action. Roosevelt maneuvered cannily. As the legislative battle opened, he released figures showing that Standard Oil had reaped $750,000 a year from railroad rebates. He also skillfully traded congressional support for a strong railroad measure in return for his promise to postpone a reduction of the tariff, a stratagem that came back to plague President Taft.

Triumph came with passage of the **Hepburn Act** of 1906. A significant achievement, the act strengthened the rate-making power of the Interstate Commerce Commission. It increased membership on the ICC from five to seven, empowered it to fix reasonable maximum railroad rates, and broadened its jurisdiction to include oil pipeline, express, and sleeping car companies. ICC orders were binding, pending any court appeals, thus placing the burden of proof of injustice on the companies. Delighted, Roosevelt viewed the Hepburn Act as a major step in his plan for continuous expert federal control over industry.

Cleaning Up Food and Drugs

Soon Roosevelt was dealing with two other important bills, these aimed at regulating the food and drug industries. Muckraking articles had touched frequently on filthy conditions in meatpacking houses, but Upton Sinclair's *The Jungle* (1906) set off a storm of indignation. Ironically, Sinclair had set out to write a novel about the packinghouse workers, the "wage slaves of the Beef Trust," hoping to do for wage slavery what Harriet Beecher Stowe had done for chattel slavery. But readers largely ignored his story of the workers

Europe. Demand for reform grew. Alarmed, the meat-packers themselves supported a reform law, which they hoped would be just strong enough to still the clamor. The Meat Inspection Act of 1906, stronger than the packers wanted, set rules for sanitary meatpacking and government inspection of meat products.

A second measure, the Pure Food and Drug Act, passed more easily. Samuel Hopkins Adams, a muckraker, exposed the dangers of patent medicines in several sensational articles in *Collier's*. Patent medi-

A poster for the movie version of Upton Sinclair's **The Jungle** promises a "wonderful story of the beef packing industry." The conditions that Sinclair described in the book brought to public attention the scandals of the meatpacking industry knowingly selling diseased meat and the filthy, disease-ridden, dangerous conditions in which the workers toiled for their subsistence wages. ❖

and seized instead on the graphic descriptions of the things that went into their meat:

> There would be meat stored in great piles in rooms; and the water from leaky roofs would drip over it, and thousands of rats would race about on it. It was too dark in these storage places to see well, but a man could run his hand over these piles of meat and sweep off handfuls of the dried dung of rats. These rats were nuisances, and the packers would put poisoned bread out for them; they would die, and then rats, bread, and meat would go into the hoppers together.

Sinclair was disappointed at the reaction. "I aimed at the public's heart," he later said, "and by accident I hit it in the stomach." He had, indeed. After reading *The Jungle*, Roosevelt ordered an investigation. The result, he said, was "hideous," and he threatened to publish the entire "sickening report" if Congress did not act. Meat sales plummeted in the United States and

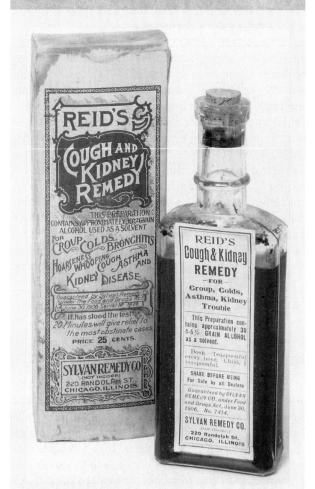

A Look at the Past

Patent Medicine

Patent medicines such as this cough and kidney remedy had long been popular. Note the many ailments it claimed to relieve, the ingredients, and the statement of compliance with the Pure Food and Drug Act. Based on this information, do you think Reid's Cough & Kidney Remedy was effective? If not, why do you suppose people continued to buy it? What questions does this medicine raise about health, medical care, and the effectiveness of government regulations in the early 1900s?

cines, Adams pointed out, contained mostly alcohol, drugs, and "undiluted fraud." Dr. Harvey W. Wiley, the chief chemist in the Department of Agriculture, led a "poison squad" of young assistants who experimented with the medicines. With evidence in hand, Wiley pushed for regulation; Roosevelt and the recently reorganized American Medical Association joined the fight, and the act passed on June 30, 1906. Requiring manufacturers to list certain ingredients on the label, it represented a pioneering effort to ban the manufacture and sale of adulterated, misbranded, or unsanitary food or drugs.

Conserving the Land

An expert on birds, Roosevelt loved nature and the wilderness, and some of his most enduring accomplishments came in the field of **conservation.** Working closely with Gifford Pinchot, chief of the Forest Service, he established the first comprehensive national conservation policy. To Roosevelt, conservation meant the wise use of natural resources, not locking them away, so those who thought the wilderness should be preserved rather than developed generally opposed his policies.

Using experts in the federal government, Roosevelt undertook a major reclamation program, created the federal Reclamation Service, and strengthened the forest preserve program in the Department of Agriculture. Broadening the concept of conservation,

he placed power sites, coal lands, and oil reserves as well as national forest in the public domain.

When Roosevelt took office in 1901, there were 45 million acres in government preserves. In 1908, there were almost 195 million. That year, he called a National Conservation Congress attended by forty-four governors and hundreds of experts. Roosevelt formed the National Commission on the Conservation of Natural Resources to look after waters, forests, lands, and minerals. With Pinchot as head, it drew up an inventory of the nation's natural resources.

As 1908 approached, Roosevelt became increasingly strident in his demand for sweeping reforms. He attacked "malefactors of great wealth," urged greater federal regulatory powers, criticized the conservatism of the federal courts, and called for laws protecting factory workers. Many business leaders blamed him for a severe financial panic in the autumn of 1907, and conservatives in Congress stiffened their opposition. Divisions between Republican conservatives and progressives grew.

Immensely popular, Roosevelt prepared in 1908 to turn over the White House to William Howard Taft, his close friend and colleague. "The Roosevelt policies will not go out with the Roosevelt administration," a party leader said. "If Taft weakens, he will annihilate himself." As expected, Taft soundly defeated the Democratic standard-bearer William Jennings Bryan, who was making his third try for the presidency. The Republicans retained control of Congress. Taft

NATIONAL PARKS AND FORESTS   *During the presidency of Theodore Roosevelt, who considered conservation his most important domestic achievement, millions of acres of land were set aside for national parks and forests.* ❖

prepared to move into the White House, ready and willing to carry on the Roosevelt legacy.

THE ORDEAL OF WILLIAM HOWARD TAFT

The Republican national convention that nominated Taft had not satisfied either Roosevelt or Taft. True, Taft won the presidential nomination as planned, but conservative Republicans beat back the attempts of progressive Republicans to influence the convention. They named a conservative, James S. Sherman, for vice president and built a platform that reflected conservative views on labor, the courts, and other issues. Taft wanted a pledge to lower the tariff but got only a promise of revision, which might lower—or raise—it. La Follette, Cummins, Jonathan P. Dolliver of Iowa, Albert J. Beveridge of Indiana, and other progressive Republicans were openly disappointed.

Taking office in 1909, Taft felt "just a bit like a fish out of water." The son of a distinguished Ohio family and a graduate of Yale Law School, he became an Ohio judge, solicitor general of the United States, and a judge of the federal circuit court. In 1900, McKinley asked him to head the Philippine Commission, charged with the difficult and challenging task of forming a civil government in the Philippines. Later Taft was named the first governor general of the Philippines. In 1904, Roosevelt appointed him secretary of war. In all these positions, Taft made his mark as a skillful administrator. He worked quietly behind the scenes, avoided controversy, and shared none of Roosevelt's zest for politics. A good-natured man, Taft had personal charm and infectious humor. He fled from fights rather than seeking them out, and he disliked political maneuvering, preferring instead quiet solitude. "I don't like politics," he said. "I don't like the limelight."

THE ELECTION OF 1908

Candidate	Party	Popular Vote	Electoral Vote
Taft	Republican	7,676,258	321
Bryan	Democrat	6,406,801	162
Debs	Socialist	420,380	0
Chafin	Prohibition	252,821	0

Weighing close to 300 pounds, Taft enjoyed conversation, golf and bridge, good food, and plenty of rest. Compared to the hardworking Roosevelt and Wilson, he was lazy. He was also honest, kindly, and amiable, and in his own way he knew how to get things done. Reflective, he preferred the life of a judge, but his wife, Helen H. Taft, who enjoyed politics, prodded him toward the White House. When a Supreme Court appointment opened in 1906, Taft reluctantly turned it down. "Ma wants him to wait and be president," his youngest son said.

Taft's years as president were not happy. Mrs. Taft's health soon collapsed, and as it turned out, Taft presided over a Republican party torn with tensions that Roosevelt had either brushed aside or concealed. The tariff, business regulation, and other issues split conservatives and progressives, and Taft often wavered or sided with the conservatives. Taft revered the past and distrusted change; although an ardent supporter of Roosevelt, he never had Roosevelt's faith in the ability of government to impose reform and alter individual behavior. He named five corporation attorneys to his cabinet, leaned more to business than to labor, and spoke of a desire to "clean out the unions."

At that time and later, Taft's reputation suffered by comparison to the flair of Roosevelt and the moral majesty of Woodrow Wilson. He deserved better. Taft

A 1910 Puck cartoon shows Taft snarled in the intricacies of office as his disappointed mentor looks on. ❖

was an honest and sincere president, who—sometimes firm, sometimes befuddled—faced a series of important and troublesome problems during his term of office.

Party Insurgency

Taft started his term with an attempt to curb the powerful Republican speaker of the House, Joseph "Uncle Joe" Cannon of Illinois. Using the powers of his position, Cannon had been setting House procedures, appointing committees, and virtually dictating legislation. Straightforward and crusty, he often opposed reform. In March 1909, thirty Republican congressmen joined Taft's effort to curb Cannon's power, and the president sensed success. But Cannon retaliated and, threatening to block all tariff bills, forced a compromise. Taft stopped the anti-Cannon campaign in return for Cannon's pledge to help with tariff cuts.

Republicans were divided over the tariff, and there was a growing party insurgency against high rates. The House quickly passed a bill providing for lower rates, but in the Senate, protectionists raised them. Senate leader Nelson W. Aldrich of Rhode Island introduced a revised bill that added more than eight hundred amendments to the rates approved in the House. It placed no duties on curling stones, false teeth, canary-bird seed, and hog bristles, which brought a chuckle from Mr. Dooley. "Th' new Tariff Bill," he said, "put these familyar commodyties within th' reach iv all."

Angry, La Follette and other Republicans attacked the bill as the child of special interests. In speeches on the Senate floor they called themselves "progressives," invoked Roosevelt's name, and urged Taft to defeat the high-tariff proposal. Caught between protectionists and progressives, Taft wavered, then tried to compromise. In the end, he backed Aldrich. The Payne-Aldrich Act, passed in November 1909, called for higher rates than the original House bill, though it lowered them from the Dingley Tariff of 1897. An unpopular law, Payne-Aldrich helped discredit Taft and revealed the tensions in the Republican party.

Republican progressives and conservatives drifted apart. Thin-skinned, Taft resented the persistent pinpricks of the progressives who criticized him for virtually everything he did. He tried to find middle ground but leaned more and more toward the conservatives. During a nationwide speaking tour in the autumn of 1909, he praised Aldrich, scolded the low-tariff insurgents, and called the Payne-Aldrich Act "the best bill that the Republican party ever passed." Traveling through the Midwest, he pointedly ignored La Follette, Cummins, and other progressive Republicans.

By early 1910, progressive Republicans in Congress no longer looked to Taft for leadership. As before, they challenged Cannon's power, and Taft wa-vered. In an outcome embarrassing to the president, the progressives won, managing to curtail Cannon's authority to dictate committee assignments and schedule debate. In progressive circles there was growing talk of a Roosevelt return to the White House.

The Ballinger-Pinchot Affair

The conservation issue dealt another blow to relations between Roosevelt and President Taft. In 1909, Richard A. Ballinger, Taft's secretary of the interior, offered for sale a million acres of public land that Pinchot, who had stayed on as Taft's chief forester, had withdrawn from sale. Pinchot, fearing that Ballinger would hurt conservation programs, protested and, seizing on a report that Ballinger had helped sell valuable Alaskan coal lands to a syndicate that included J. P. Morgan, asked Taft to intervene. After investigating, Taft supported Ballinger on every count, although he asked Pinchot to remain in office.

Pinchot refused to drop the matter. Behind the scenes, he provided material for two anti-Ballinger magazine articles, and he wrote a critical public letter that Senator Dolliver of Iowa read to the Senate. Taft had had enough. He fired the insubordinate Pinchot, an action which, though appropriate, again lost support for Taft. Newspapers followed the controversy for months, and muckrakers assailed the administration's "surrender" to Morgan and other "despoilers of the national heritage."

The Ballinger-Pinchot controversy obscured Taft's important contributions to conservation. He won from Congress the power to remove lands from sale, and he used it to conserve more land than Roosevelt did. Still, the controversy tarred Taft, and it upset his old friend Roosevelt. Pinchot hurried to Italy where Roosevelt was on tour; he talked again with Roosevelt within days of the ex-president's arrival home in June 1910.

Taft Alienates the Progressives

Interested in railroad regulation, Taft backed a bill in 1910 to empower the ICC to fix maximum railroad rates. Progressive Republicans favored that plan but attacked Taft's suggestion of a special Commerce Court to hear appeals from ICC decisions because most judges were traditionally conservative in outlook and usually rejected attempts to regulate railroad rates. They also thought the railroads had been consulted too closely in drawing up the bill. Democratic and Republican progressives tried to amend the bill to strengthen it; Taft made support of it a test of party loyalty.

The Mann-Elkins Act of 1910 gave something to everyone. It gave the ICC power to set rates, stiffened long- and short-haul regulations, and placed telephone and telegraph companies under ICC jurisdiction. These provisions delighted progressives. The act also created a Commerce Court, pleasing conservatives. In a trade-off, conservative Republican Senate leaders pledged their support for a statehood bill for Arizona and New Mexico, which were both predicted to be Democratic. In return, enough Democratic senators promised to vote for the Commerce Court provision to pass the bill. While pleased with the act, Taft and the Republican party lost further ground. In votes on key provisions of the Mann-Elkins Act, Taft raised the issue of party regularity, and progressive Republicans defied him.

Taft attempted to defeat the progressive Republicans in the 1910 elections. He helped form antiprogressive organizations, and he campaigned against progressive Republican candidates for the Senate. In California, he opposed Hiram Johnson, the progressive Republican champion; in Wisconsin, the home of La Follette, he sent Vice President James S. Sherman to take control of the state convention. Progressive Republicans retaliated by organizing a nationwide network of anti-Taft Progressive Republican Clubs.

The 1910 election results were a major setback for Taft and the Republicans—especially conservative Republicans. A key issue in the election, the high cost of living, gave an edge to the progressive wings in both major parties, lending support to their attack on the tariff and the trusts. In party primaries, progressive Republicans overwhelmed most Taft candidates, and in the general election, they tended to fare better than the conservatives, which increased progressive influence in the Republican party.

For Republicans of all persuasions, however, it was a difficult election. The Democrats swept the urban-industrial states from New York to Illinois. New York, New Jersey, Indiana, and even Taft's Ohio elected Democratic governors. For the first time since 1894, Republicans lost control of both the House and the Senate. In all, they lost fifty-eight seats in the House and ten in the Senate. Disappointed, Taft called it "not only a landslide, but a tidal wave and holocaust all rolled into one general cataclysm."

Despite the defeat, Taft pushed through several important measures before his term ended. With the help of the new Democratic House, he backed laws to regulate safety in mines and on railroads, create a Children's Bureau in the federal government, establish

According to this 1913 cartoon, the new income tax legislation distributed the tax burden more evenly, so that contributions from the wealthy eased some of the burden on the working class. ❖

employers' liability for all work done on government contracts, and mandate an eight-hour workday for government workers.

In 1909, Congress initiated a constitutional amendment authorizing an income tax, which, along with woman suffrage, was one of the most significant legislative measures of the twentieth century. The Sixteenth Amendment took effect early in 1913. A few months later, an important progressive goal was realized when the direct election of senators was ratified as the Seventeenth Amendment to the Constitution.

An ardent supporter of competition, Taft relentlessly pressed a campaign against trusts. The Sherman Antitrust Act, he said in 1911, "is a good law that ought to be enforced, and I propose to enforce it." That year, the Supreme Court in cases against Standard Oil and American Tobacco established the "rule of reason," which allowed the Court to determine whether a business presented "reasonable" restraint on trade. Taft thought the decisions gave the Court too much discretion, and he pushed ahead with the antitrust effort.

In October 1911, he sued U.S. Steel for its acquisition of the Tennessee Coal and Iron Company in 1907. Roosevelt had approved the acquisition (see p. 668), and the suit seemed designed to impugn his action. Enraged, he attacked Taft, and Taft, for once, fought back. He accused Roosevelt of undermining the conservative tradition in the country and began working to undercut the influence of the progressive Republicans. Increasingly now, Roosevelt listened to anti-Taft Republicans who urged him to run for president in 1912. In February 1912, he announced, "My hat is in the ring."

Differing Philosophies in the Election of 1912

Delighted Democrats looked on as Taft and Roosevelt fought for the Republican nomination. As the incumbent president, Taft controlled the party machinery, and when the Republican convention met in June 1912, he took the nomination. In early July, the Democrats met in Baltimore and, confident of victory for the first time in two decades, struggled through forty-six ballots before finally nominating Woodrow Wilson, the reform-minded governor of New Jersey.

A month later, some of the anti-Taft and progressive Republicans—now calling themselves the **Progressive party**—whooped it up in Chicago. Roosevelt was there to give a stirring "Confession of Faith" and listen to the delegates sing:

> Thou wilt not cower in the dust,
> Roosevelt, O Roosevelt!
> Thy gleaming sword shall never rust,
> Roosevelt, O Roosevelt!

Naming Roosevelt for president at its convention, the Progressive party—soon known as the Bull Moose party—set the stage for the first important three-cornered presidential contest since 1860.

Taft was out of the running before the campaign even began. "I think I might as well give up so far as being a candidate is concerned," he said in July. "There are so many people in the country who don't like me." Taft stayed at home and made no speeches before the election. Roosevelt campaigned strenuously, even completing one speech after being shot in the chest by an anti-third-term fanatic. "I have a message to deliver," he said, "and will deliver it as long as there is life in my body."

Roosevelt's message involved a program he called the **New Nationalism.** An important phase in the shaping of twentieth-century American political thought, it demanded a national approach to the country's affairs and a strong president to deal with them. The New Nationalism called for efficiency in government and society. It exalted the executive and the expert; urged social-justice reforms to protect

"I'm feeling like a bull moose!" declared Teddy Roosevelt while campaigning in 1912 as a Progressive and inadvertently renaming the new political party. The patch depicts a strong, independent animal, much like TR himself. In 1904 Roosevelt had won reelection by promising to give Americans a "square deal." ❖

workers, women, and children; and accepted "good" trusts. The New Nationalism encouraged large concentrations of labor and capital, serving the nation's interests under a forceful federal executive.

For the first time in the history of a major political party, the Progressive campaign enlisted women in its organization. Jane Addams, the well-known settlement worker, seconded Roosevelt's nomination at Chicago, and she and other women played a leading role in his campaign. Some labor leaders, who saw potential for union growth, and some business leaders, who saw relief from destructive competition and labor strife, supported the new party.

Wilson, in contrast, set forth a program called the **New Freedom** that emphasized business competition and small government. A states' rights Democrat, he wanted to rein in federal authority, using it only to sweep away special privilege, release individual energies, and restore competition. Drawing on the thinking of Louis D. Brandeis, the brilliant shaper of reform-minded law, he echoed the Progressive party's social-justice objectives, while continuing to attack Roosevelt's planned state. For Wilson, the vital issue was not a planned economy but a free one. "The history of liberty is the history of the limitation of governmental power," he said in October 1912. "If America is not to have free enterprise, then she can have freedom of no sort whatever."

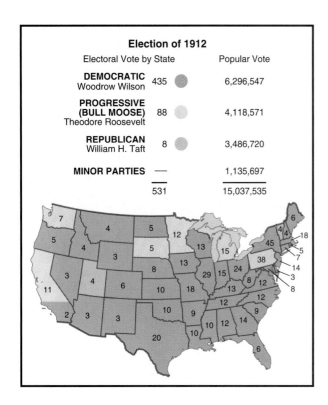

Election of 1912

	Electoral Vote by State		Popular Vote
DEMOCRATIC Woodrow Wilson	435		6,296,547
PROGRESSIVE (BULL MOOSE) Theodore Roosevelt	88		4,118,571
REPUBLICAN William H. Taft	8		3,486,720
MINOR PARTIES	—		1,135,697
	531		15,037,535

In the New Nationalism and New Freedom, the election of 1912 offered competing philosophies of government. Both Roosevelt and Wilson saw the central problem of the American nation as economic growth and its effect on individuals and society. Both focused on the government's relation to business, both believed in bureaucratic reform, and both wanted to use government to protect the ordinary citizen. But Roosevelt welcomed federal power, national planning, and business growth; Wilson distrusted them all.

On election day, Wilson won 6.3 million votes to 4.1 million for Roosevelt (who had recovered quickly from his wound) and 900,000 for Eugene V. Debs, the Socialist party candidate. Taft, the incumbent president, finished third with 3.5 million votes; he carried only Vermont and Utah for 8 electoral votes. The Democrats also won outright control of both houses.

WOODROW WILSON'S NEW FREEDOM

If under Roosevelt social reform took on the excitement of a circus, "under Wilson it acquired the dedication of a sunrise service." Born in Virginia in 1856 and raised in the South, Wilson was the son of a Presbyterian minister. As a young man, he wanted a career in public service, and he trained himself carefully in history and oratory. A moralist, he reached judgments easily. Once reached, almost nothing shook

them. Opponents called him stubborn and smug. "He gives me the creeps," a Maryland ward boss said. "The time I met him, he said something to me, and I didn't know whether God or him was talking."

After graduating from Princeton University and the University of Virginia Law School, Wilson found that practicing law bored him. Shifting to history, from 1890 to 1902 he served as professor of jurisprudence and political economy at Princeton. In 1902, he became president of the university. Eight years later, he was governor of New Jersey, where he led a campaign to reform election procedures, abolish corrupt practices, and strengthen railroad regulation.

Wilson's rise was rapid, and he knew relatively little about national issues and personalities. But he learned fast, and in some ways the lack of experience served him well. He had few political debts to repay, and he brought fresh perspectives to older issues. Ideas intrigued Wilson; details bored him. Although he was outgoing at times, he could also be cold and aloof, and aides soon learned that he preferred loyalty and flattery to candid criticism.

Prone to self-righteousness, Wilson often turned differences of opinion into bitter personal quarrels. Like Roosevelt, he believed in strong presidential leadership. A scholar of the party system, he cooperated closely with Democrats in Congress, and his legislative record placed him among the most effective presidents in terms of passing bills that he supported. Forbidding in individual conversation, Wilson could move crowds with graceful oratory. Unlike Taft, and to a greater degree than Roosevelt, he could inspire.

His inaugural address was eloquent. "The Nation," he said, "has been deeply stirred, stirred by a solemn passion, stirred by the knowledge of wrong, of ideals lost, of government too often debauched and made an instrument of evil. The feelings with which we face this new age of right and opportunity sweep across our heartstrings like some air out of God's own presence."

The New Freedom in Action

On the day of his inauguration, Wilson called Congress into special session to lower the tariff. When the session opened on April 8, 1913, Wilson himself was there, the first president since John Adams in 1801 to appear personally before Congress. In forceful language, he urged Congress to reduce tariff rates.

As the bill moved through Congress, Wilson showed exceptional skill. He worked closely with congressional leaders, and when lobbyists threatened the bill in the Senate, he appealed for popular support. The result was a triumph for Wilson and the Democratic party. The **Underwood Tariff Act** passed in 1913. The first tariff cut in nineteen years, it lowered rates about 15 percent and removed duties from sugar, wool, and several other consumer goods.

To make up for lost revenue, the act also levied a modest graduated income tax, authorized under the just ratified Sixteenth Amendment. Marking a significant shift in the American tax structure, it imposed a 1 percent tax on individuals and corporations earning more than $4000 annually and an additional 1 percent tax on incomes more than $20,000. Above all, the act reflected a new unity within the Democratic party, which had worked together to pass a difficult tariff law.

Wilson himself emerged as an able leader. "At a single stage," a foreign editor said, "[he went] from the man of promise to the man of achievement." Encouraged by his success, Wilson decided to keep Congress in session through the hot Washington summer. Now he focused on banking reform, and the result in December 1913 was the **Federal Reserve Act,** the most important domestic law of his administration.

Meant to provide the United States with a sound yet flexible currency, the act established the country's first efficient banking system since Andrew Jackson killed the second Bank of the United States in 1832. It created twelve regional banks, each to serve the banks of its district. The regional banks answered to a Federal Reserve Board, appointed by the president, which governed the nationwide system.

A compromise law, the act blended public and private control of the banking system. Private bankers owned the federal reserve banks but answered to the presidentially appointed Federal Reserve Board. The reserve banks were authorized to issue currency, and through the discount rate—the interest rate at which they loaned money to member banks—they could raise or lower the amount of money in circulation. Monetary affairs no longer depended solely on the price of gold. Within a year, nearly half the nation's banking resources were in the Federal Reserve System.

The **Clayton Antitrust Act** (1914) completed Wilson's initial legislative program. Like previous antitrust measures, it reflected confusion over how to discipline a growing economy without putting a brake on output. In part it was a response to the revelations of the Pujo Committee of the House, publicized by Brandeis in a disquieting series of articles, "Other People's Money." In its investigation of Wall Street, the committee discovered a pyramid of money and power capped by the Morgan-Rockefeller empire that, through "interlocking directorates," controlled companies worth $22 billion, more than one-tenth of the national wealth.

The Clayton Act outlawed such directorates and prohibited unfair trade practices. It forbade pricing policies that created monopoly, and it made corporate officers personally responsible for antitrust violations. Delighting Samuel Gompers and the labor movement, the act declared that unions were not conspiracies in restraint of trade, outlawed the use of injunctions in labor disputes unless necessary to protect property, and approved lawful strikes and picketing. To Gompers's dismay, the courts continued to rule against union activity.

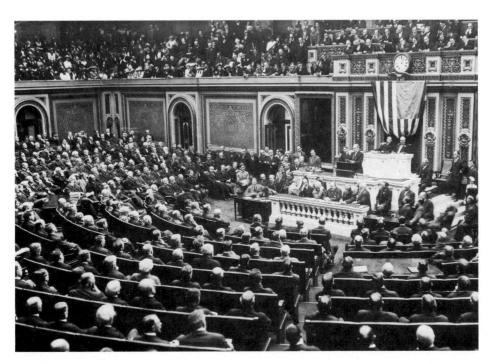

By appearing personally before Congress, President Wilson broke the precedent established by Thomas Jefferson of submitting messages to Congress in writing. Appealing for popular support in his plea for tariff reform, Wilson denounced the tariff lobbyists for seeking "to overcome the interests of the public for their private profit." ❖

A related law established a powerful Federal Trade Commission to oversee business methods. Composed of five members, the commission could demand special and annual reports, investigate complaints, and order corporate compliance, subject to court review. At first, Wilson opposed the commission concept, which was an approach more suitable to Roosevelt's New Nationalism, but he changed his mind and, along with Brandeis, called it the cornerstone of his antitrust plan. To reassure business leaders, he appointed a number of conservatives to the new commission and to the Federal Reserve Board.

In November 1914, Wilson proudly announced the completion of his New Freedom program. Tariff, banking, and antitrust laws promised a brighter future, he said, and it was now "a time of healing because a time of just dealing." Many progressives were aghast. That Wilson could think society's ills were so easily cured, the *New Republic* said, "casts suspicion either upon his own sincerity or upon his grasp of the realities of modern social and industrial life."

Wilson Moves Toward the New Nationalism

Distracted by the start of war in Europe, Wilson gave less attention to domestic issues for more than a year. When he returned to concern with reform, he adopted more and more of Roosevelt's New Nationalism and blended it with the New Freedom to set it off from his earlier policies.

One of Wilson's problems was the Congress. To his dismay, the Republicans gained substantially in the 1914 elections. Reducing the Democratic majority in the House, they swept key industrial and farm states. At the same time, a recession struck the economy, which had been hurt by the outbreak of the European war in August 1914. Some business leaders blamed the tariff and other New Freedom laws. On the defensive, Wilson soothed business sentiment and invited bankers and industrialists to the White House. He allowed companies fearful of antitrust actions to seek advice from the Justice Department.

Preoccupied with such problems, Wilson blocked significant action in Congress through most of 1915. He refused to support a bill providing minimum wages for women workers, sidetracked a child labor bill on the ground that it was unconstitutional, and opposed a bill to establish long-term credits for farmers. He also refused to endorse women's suffrage, arguing that the right to vote was a state matter, not a federal one.

Wilson's record on race disappointed African Americans and many progressives. He had appealed to African American voters during the 1912 election, and a number of African American leaders campaigned for him. Soon after the inauguration, Oswald Garrison Villard, a leader of the NAACP, proposed a National Race Commission to study the problem of race relations. Initially sympathetic, Wilson rejected the idea because he feared he might lose southern Democratic votes in Congress. A Virginian himself, he appointed many Southerners to high office, and for the first time since the Civil War, southern views on race dominated the nation's capital.

At one of Wilson's first cabinet meetings, the postmaster general proposed the segregation of all African Americans in the federal service. No one dissented, including Wilson. Several government bureaus promptly began to segregate workers in offices, shops, rest rooms, and restaurants. Employees who objected were fired. African American leaders protested, and they were joined by progressive leaders and clergymen. Surprised at the protest, Wilson backed quietly away from the policy, although he continued to insist that segregation benefited African Americans.

As the year 1916 began, Wilson made a dramatic switch in focus and again pushed for substantial reforms. The result was a virtual river of reform laws, which was significant because it began the second, more national-minded phase of the New Freedom. With scarcely a glance over his shoulder, Wilson embraced important portions of Roosevelt's New Nationalism campaign.

In part, he was motivated by the approaching presidential election. A minority president, Wilson owed his victory in 1912 to the split in the Republican party, now almost healed. Roosevelt was moving back into Republican ranks, and there were issues connected with the war in Europe that he might use against Wilson. Moreover, many progressives were voicing disappointment with Wilson's limited reforms and his failure to support more advanced reform legislation on matters such as farm credits, child labor, and woman suffrage.

Moving quickly to patch up the problem, Wilson named Brandeis to the Supreme Court in January 1916. Popular among progressives, Brandeis was also the first person of Jewish faith to serve on the Court. When conservatives in the Senate tried to defeat the nomination, Wilson stood firm and won, earning further praise from progressives, Jews, and others. In May, he reversed his stand on farm loans and accepted a rural credits bill to establish farm-loan banks backed by federal funds. The Federal Farm Loan Act of 1916 created a Federal Farm Loan Board to give farmers credit similar to the Federal Reserve's benefits for trade and industry.

Wilson was already popular within the labor movement. Going beyond Roosevelt's policies, which had sought a balance between business and labor, he

Miners in Ludlow, Colorado, went on strike in September 1913 for better working conditions and union recognition. Expecting eviction from company housing, they built a tent colony near the company town. The company, John D. Rockefeller's Colorado Fuel and Iron Company, hired guards to break the strike. On April 20, 1914, state troops and guards sprayed the tents with gunfire, then soaked the tents with kerosene and set the colony afire. Twenty-one of the colonists died, including eleven children. ❖

defended union recognition and collective bargaining. In 1913, he appointed William B. Wilson, a respected leader of the United Mine Workers, as the first head of the Labor Department, and he strengthened the department's Division of Conciliation. In 1914, in Ludlow, Colorado, state militia and mine guards fired machine guns into a tent colony of coal strikers, killing twenty-one men, women, and children. Outraged, Wilson stepped in and used federal troops to end the violence while negotiations to end the strike went on.

In August 1916, a threatened railroad strike again revealed Wilson's sympathies with labor. Like Roosevelt, he invited the two sides to the White House, where he urged the railroad companies to grant an eight-hour day and labor leaders to abandon the de-

mand for overtime pay. Labor leaders accepted the proposal; railroad leaders did not. "I pray God to forgive you, I never can," Wilson said as he left the room. Soon he signed the Adamson Act (1916) that imposed the eight-hour day on interstate railways and established a federal commission to study the railroad problem. Ending the threat of a strike, the act marked a milestone in the expansion of the federal government's authority to regulate industry.

With Wilson leading the way, the flow of reform legislation continued until the election. The Federal Workmen's Compensation Act established workers' compensation for government employees. The Keating-Owen Act, the first federal child labor law, prohibited the shipment in interstate commerce of

MADAM C.J. WALKER

African American Business Pioneer

At the 1912 convention of the National Negro Business League, a group devoted to promoting African American businesses, a 45-year-old woman, Madam C.J. Walker, tried to catch the eye of Booker T. Washington, the League's founder and head. But Washington ignored her until finally, her patience gone, she sprang to her feet and said, "Surely you are not going to shut the door in my face. I feel that I am in a business that is a credit to the womanhood of our race."

"I . . . came from the cotton fields of the South," she went on. "I was promoted from there to the wash-tub; then I was promoted to the cook kitchen, and from there *I promoted myself* into the business of manufacturing hair goods and preparations . . .

I have built my own factory on my own ground."

Had Washington listened, Madam Walker had a remarkable story to tell. She was born Sarah Breedlove in 1867 on a plantation in Delta, Louisiana, the first in her sharecropper family born free. Orphaned at age 7, she married at 14 to escape a cruel brother-in-law and find a home. Her husband died when she was 20, leaving her with a young daughter and a back already aching from years of picking cotton and doing laundry. Looking for a better life, she moved to St. Louis and then to Denver, working as a cook and laundress. In Denver, she married Charles J. Walker and began calling herself "Madam," a title that lent prestige to a new business she had just begun.

For years, Walker had had trouble with her hair. It came out in bunches, partly because of the painful "wrap and twist" method that was popular for styling African American hair. After trying various remedies, she developed her own formula that she said came to her in a dream. "I tried it on my friends," she said. "It helped them. I made up my mind to begin to sell it." Filling jars of the mixture in the attic of her home, she sold it door-to-door.

Madam Walker began promoting her system of hair care in 1905. The Walker system called for women first to wash their hair with Madam Walker's Vegetable Shampoo, then apply her Wonderful Hair Grower, add a light oil called Glossine, and finally press and relax the hair with a wide-toothed "hot comb."

As her business grew, Walker opened schools to teach her system, hired thousands of African American women as sales agents, and in 1910 moved her factory to Indianapolis for its central location. Knowing that white stores would not stock her products, she relied on churches and women's clubs, two key institutions of the black community. Sales soon extended throughout the United States, Central America, and the Caribbean; Josephine Baker, the famous dancer, used Walker's products in Paris.

Dressed in white shirts and long black skirts, Walker agents became a familiar sight in African American neighborhoods everywhere. There were twenty thousand agents by 1916, most of them former maids, laundresses, and farm workers. "I have made it possible for many colored women to abandon the wash-tub for more pleasant and profitable occupation," she said.

Photographs of Madam C.J. Walker before and after using her hair care formula. Madam Walker was the first black woman millionaire and a pioneer in the development and manufacture of beauty products for African American women. ✦

BEFORE USING

Madam Walker before and after her wonderful discovery.

As her income grew, Walker gave generously to various causes, including the YMCA, Mary McLeod Bethune's Educational and Industrial Institute for Negro Girls (now Bethune-Cookman College), the Tuskegee Institute, and the NAACP. "Lady Bountiful," she was called, and she encouraged her agents to contribute to charity, too. "I love to use a part of what I make in trying to help others," she said.

When the country entered World War I, Walker helped sell war bonds and joined the many black leaders who encouraged African Americans to aid in the war effort, hoping that contributions to victory abroad would improve race relations at home. But she grew impatient as lynchings and other racial incidents continued. Angered by a race riot in East St. Louis, Illinois, in 1917, she supported the Negro Silent Protest Parade, in which ten thousand black New Yorkers marched in silence down Fifth Avenue while another twenty thousand African Americans looked on.

Walker went to Washington to ask President Woodrow Wilson to support legislation making lynching a federal crime, but Wilson was too "busy" to see her. Refusing to give up, Walker donated $5000 to the NAACP's antilynching campaign and defended the rights of returning war veterans.

In 1918, Walker built Villa Lewaro, a mansion overlooking the Hudson River above New York City, near the estate of John D. Rockefeller. Walker called her home a symbol, to show "young Negroes what a lone woman accomplished and to inspire them to do big things." Madam Walker died at the villa in 1919, aged 51. At her death, *The Crisis,* the journal of the NAACP, said she had "revolutionized the personal habits and appearance of millions of human beings."

According to the *Guinness Book of World Records,* Madam Walker was the first self-made woman millionaire. What she did, said Ida B. Wells-Barnett, the militant black leader, "made me take pride anew in Negro womanhood." Mary McLeod Bethune, the black educator, said, "She has gone, but her work still lives and shall live as an inspiration to not only her race but to the world." Walker be-

Madam C.J. Walker Hair Culturists Union of America convention in Philadelphia, 1917, one of the first national meetings of U.S. businesswomen. ❖

queathed her company to her daughter—asking that a woman always serve at the head—but it began to fail during the Great Depression. Housed in the Walker Building, a National Historic Landmark, the Madam Walker Theatre Center today serves as a cultural center for the performing arts in downtown Indianapolis.

Even at the height of Madam Walker's business, "hot combs" and hair straighteners were controversial. Some black leaders (Booker T. Washington among them) denounced them as attempts to imitate whites, but many African American women straightened their hair anyway. Walker herself argued that she had no interest in straightening hair, only in boosting confidence and personal hygiene.

Walker's business dwindled, but the debate over hair continued, carrying important economic as well as social dimensions. In recent years, African Americans spent three times more per person than other consumer groups on hair-care products, cosmetics, toiletries, and other grooming aids.

Famous African American singers, actresses, and television personalities, including Oprah Winfrey,

relax their hair. Others object. Alice Walker, an African American and one of the nation's foremost authors, calls hair straightening a form of oppression, a "ceiling on the brain" that keeps people from fulfillment. Hip-hop music reinforces the message, taking hair, as one music magazine has said, "back to its African roots. From dreads, cornrows, and braids to twists, coils to 'fros, hip hop is keeping it real . . . natural. For many, hair is more than just a style—it's a statement."

Madam Walker would have agreed. Hair care, she believed, involved more than hair; it meant pride, better health, and new opportunities for black women everywhere. When she returned to the Negro Business League convention in 1913, she talked about economic independence for African American women. "The girls and women of our race," she said, "must not be afraid to take hold of business endeavor . . . wring success out of a number of business opportunities that lie at their very doors. . . . I want to say to every Negro woman present, don't sit down and wait for the opportunities to come. . . . Get up and make them!"

CHRONOLOGY

1894	National Municipal League formed to work for reform in cities
1900	Galveston, Texas, is first city to try commission form of government
1901	Theodore Roosevelt becomes president ❖ Robert M. La Follette elected reform governor of Wisconsin ❖ Doctors reorganize the American Medical Association ❖ Socialist party of America organized
1902	Roosevelt sues Northern Securities Company for violation of Antitrust Act ❖ Coal miners in northeastern Pennsylvania strike ❖ Maryland is first state to pass workers' compensation law ❖ Oregon adopts the initiative and referendum
1904	Roosevelt elected president
1906	Hepburn Act strengthens Interstate Commerce Commission (ICC) ❖ Upton Sinclair attacks meatpacking industry in *The Jungle* ❖ Congress passes Meat Inspection Act and Pure Food and Drug Act
1908	Taft elected president ❖ Supreme Court upholds Oregon law limiting working hours for women in *Muller* v. *Oregon*
1909	Payne-Aldrich Tariff Act divides Republican party
1910	Mann-Elkins Act passed to regulate railroads ❖ Taft fires Gifford Pinchot, head of U.S. Forest Service ❖ Democrats sweep midterm elections
1912	Progressive party formed; nominates Roosevelt for president ❖ Woodrow Wilson elected president
1913	Underwood Tariff Act lowers rates ❖ Federal Reserve Act reforms U.S. banking system ❖ Sixteenth Amendment authorizes Congress to collect taxes on incomes
1914	Clayton Act strengthens antitrust legislation
1916	Wilson wins reelection
1918	Supreme Court strikes down federal law limiting child labor in *Hammer* v. *Dagenhart*
1920	Nineteenth Amendment gives women the right to vote

products manufactured by children under the age of 14. It too expanded the authority of the federal government, though it was soon struck down by the Supreme Court. The Warehouse Act authorized licensed warehouses to issue negotiable receipts for farm products deposited with them.

In September, Wilson signed the Tariff Commission Act creating an expert commission to recommend tariff rates. The same month, the Revenue Act of 1916 boosted income taxes and furthered tax reform. Four thousand members of the National American Woman Suffrage Association cheered when Wilson finally came out in support of woman suffrage. Two weeks later he endorsed the eight-hour day for all the nation's workers.

The 1916 presidential election was close, but Wilson won it on the issues of peace and progressivism. By the end of 1916, he and the Democratic party had enacted most of the important parts of Roosevelt's Progressive party platform of 1912. To do it, Wilson abandoned portions of the New Freedom and accepted much of the New Nationalism, including greater federal power and commissions governing trade and tariffs. In mixing the two programs, he blended some of the competing doctrines of the Progressive Era, established the primacy of the federal government, and foreshadowed the pragmatic outlook of Franklin D. Roosevelt's New Deal of the 1930s.

CONCLUSION: THE FRUITS OF PROGRESSIVISM

The election of 1916 showed how deeply progressivism had reached into American society. "We have in four years," Wilson said that fall, "come very near to carrying out the platform of the Progressive party as well as our own; for we are also progressives."

In retrospect, however, 1916 also marked the beginning of progressivism's decline. At most, the years of progressive reform lasted from the 1890s to 1921, and in large measure they were compressed into a single decade between 1906 and American entry into World War I in 1917. Many problems the progressives addressed but did not solve; and some important ones, such as race, they did not even tackle. Yet their regulatory commissions, direct primaries, city improvements, and child labor laws marked an era of important and measured reform.

The institution of the presidency expanded. From the White House radiated executive departments that guided a host of activities. Independent commissions, operating within flexible laws, supplemented executive authority.

These developments owed a great deal to both Roosevelt and Wilson. To manage a complex society, TR developed a simple formula: expert advice; growth-minded policies; a balancing of business, labor, and other interests; the use of publicity to gather support; and stern but often permissive oversight of the economy. TR strengthened the executive office, and he called on the newer group of professional, educated, public-minded citizens to help him. "I believe in a strong executive," he said; "I believe in power."

At first, Wilson had different ideas, wanting to dismantle much of Roosevelt's governing apparatus. But driven by outside forces and changes in his own thinking, Wilson soon moved in directions similar to those Roosevelt had championed. Starting out to disperse power, he eventually consolidated it.

Through such movements, government at all levels accepted responsibility for the welfare of various elements in the social order. A reform-minded and bureaucratic society took shape, in which men and women, labor and capital, political parties and social classes competed for shares in the expansive framework of twentieth-century life. But there were limits to

reform. As both TR and Wilson found, the new government agencies, understaffed and underfinanced, depended on the responsiveness of those they sought to regulate.

Soon there was a far darker cloud on the horizon. The spirit of progressivism rested on a belief in human potential, peace, and progress. After Napoleon's defeat in 1815, a century of peace began in western Europe, and as the decades passed, war seemed a dying institution. "It looks as though this were going to be the age of treaties rather than the age of wars," an American said in 1912, "the century of reason rather than the century of force." It was not to be. Two years later, the most devastating of wars broke out in Europe, and in 1917, Americans were fighting on the battlefields of France.

RECOMMENDED READING

George Mowry, *The Era of Theodore Roosevelt* (1958), and Arthur S. Link, *Woodrow Wilson and the Progressive Era* (1954), trace the social and economic conditions of the period. See also John M. Blum's perceptive and brief *The Republican Roosevelt* (1954) and Kathleen Dalton, *Theodore Roosevelt: A Strenuous Life* (2002). The definitive biography of Wilson is Arthur S. Link, *Wilson*, 5 vols. (1947–1965).

Samuel P. Hays offers an influential interpretation of progressivism in *Conservation and the Gospel of Efficiency* (1959) as does Nancy Cohen, *The Reconstruction of*

American Liberalism, 1865–1914 (2002), for the broader period. Albro Martin, *Enterprise Denied: Origins of the Decline of American Railroads, 1897–1917* (1971), argues persuasively that reformers damaged as well as regulated. Samuel Haber, *The Quest for Authority and Honor in the American Professions, 1750–1900* (1991), examines the changing nature of the professions.

For a list of additional titles related to this chapter's topics, please see http://www.ablongman.com/divine.

SUGGESTED WEB SITES

Theodore Roosevelt Association

http://www.theodoreroosevelt.org/
This site contains much biographical and research information about Theodore Roosevelt.

History of the Suffrage Movement

http://www.rochester.edu/SBA
This site includes a chronology, important texts relating to woman suffrage, and biographical information about Susan B. Anthony and Elizabeth Cady Stanton.

Woodrow Wilson

http://www.ipl.org/ref/POTUS/wwilson.html
This page contains basic factual data about Wilson's election and presidency, speeches, and on-line biographies.

Women and Social Movements in the United States, 1775–2000

http://womhist.binghamton.edu
This site offers essays and primary documents on women in social movements.

Muller v. Oregon

Expanding the Definition of Acceptable Evidence

People in the Progressive Era asked new questions about their society and often refused to be bound by "traditional" rules. This was true in most aspects of human life, and certainly in the law, where lawyers and jurists looked for new ways to make the law more responsive to human needs. One especially important case tried during this era was *Muller v. Oregon,* a case that set a precedent for protective labor laws and that expanded the definition of legal evidence.

On September 4, 1905, which happened to be Labor Day, the manager of the Grand Laundry in Portland, Oregon, the city's finest hand laundry, ordered the women who worked there to stay past the normal time, in violation of a 1903 Oregon law that barred women in factories and laundries from working more than ten hours a day. Emma Gotcher, one of the women, complained, and Curt Muller, the laundry's owner, was arrested, found guilty, and fined $10. When the Oregon Supreme Court upheld the law, Muller, with backing from business groups interested in overturning it, appealed to the U.S. Supreme Court.

Alarmed, several women in Oregon flashed word of the appeal to Florence Kelley, head of the National Consumers' League, an organization in New York City dedicated to bettering the lot of women and children. Kelley immediately saw the danger. If the Supreme Court struck down the Oregon law, similar laws in nineteen other states would be in jeopardy, along with other reform legislation as well.

Kelley needed a topflight attorney to defend the law, so she and Josephine Goldmark, the League's research director, went first to Joseph H. Choate, one of the country's most famous lawyers. But Choate was puzzled why the two women were even there. What did

he, busy as he was, have to do with some Oregon law regulating the number of hours a woman could work?

"A law *prohibiting* more than ten hours a day in laundry work," he boomed. "Big, strong, laundry women. Why shouldn't they work longer?"

Getting out of Choate's office as fast as she could, Kelley turned to Goldmark: "That's over, thank God. Tomorrow we'll go to Boston."

In Boston was Louis D. Brandeis, Goldmark's brother-in-law and an attorney renowned for his work for reform. Brandeis had not always been very interested in reform. Once a prosperous corporate lawyer, he, like so many others, had changed his outlook during the depression of the 1890s. Human misfortune sharpened his social conscience, and soon Brandeis became known as the "people's attorney," a fighter against corporate abuses and political corruption.

To Brandeis, the law was a living, evolving thing, not just law books and legal precedents but part of the present—changing, growing, responsive to current needs. He liked a poem of James Russell Lowell's:

> New times demand new issues and new men,
>   The world advances, and in time outgrows the
>   laws
> That in our fathers' time were best;
>   And, doubtless, after us some purer scheme
> Will be shaped out by wiser men than we,—
>   Made wiser by the steady growth of truth.

Evolving, the law should reflect not abstract philosophy but actual facts, carefully gathered and "scientifically" interpreted. In this, Brandeis mirrored the outlook of his progressive generation: Define the problem, collect the facts bearing on it, and devise a solution.

At first glance, however, the facts in the Muller case posed some major difficulties. For one thing,

Brandeis had barely a month to get ready before the case came before the Court.

Even more troublesome, the Court in the case of *Lochner* v. *New York* (1905) had just struck down a New York state law setting maximum hours for bakery workers, calling it a wrongful attempt "to regulate the hours of labor between the master and his employees." In trying to justify the law, the Court held, the state of New York had not shown enough of a link between the law and the health of the bakers. The *Lochner* decision heartened conservatives who were tired of progressive reforms; *Muller,* they thought, with all its similarities to the New York case, must surely be decided in the same way.

But there was an opening in *Lochner,* and both Kelley and Brandeis saw it at once. They had to do for *Muller* what the state of New York had failed to do for the bakers. They had to link the Oregon law squarely to the safety and welfare of the women it covered.

The way to do that, they thought, was to offer the Court detailed evidence showing the effects of long hours of labor on women. Enlisting ten women from various reform groups in New York City, Kelley and Goldmark haunted the city's libraries. "In these days of abundant tools of research," Goldmark recalled decades later, "the paucity of our means seems almost laughable." Using pencils and loose-leaf notebooks, the researchers combed reports from American and European factory inspectors, medical commissions, labor unions, economists, and social workers. A young medical student gathered statistics on the hygiene of occupations. As the evidence piled up, it was taken to Boston, where Brandeis organized it in the legal brief he would present to the Court.

That brief, the "Brandeis brief," was soon famous worldwide. In a dramatic departure from prior custom, it included only two pages of traditional legal precedents. Fifteen pages were devoted to showing that other states and countries believed long hours of labor affected women's health. The brief closed with nearly a hundred pages on "The World's Experience upon which the Legislation Limiting the Hours of Labor for Women is Based."

"Long hours of labor are dangerous for women primarily because of their special physical organization," the brief argued, citing as proof eleven authorities, including a British parliamentary committee, reports of the Nebraska and Massachusetts bureaus of labor statistics, and medical handbooks. "The evil effect of overwork before as well as after marriage upon childbirth is marked and disastrous." Nine authorities supported that conclusion, and six more agreed that "accidents to working women occur most frequently at the close of the day, or after a long period of uninterrupted work."

In the opinion of twenty-three sources, "When the health of women has been injured by long hours, . . . the deterioration is handed down to succeeding generations. . . . The overwork of future mothers thus directly attacks the welfare of the nation." Long hours also kept women from their housework, the brief argued, and with little time for leisure or home life, they sought relief in alcohol "and other excesses." "I have noticed that the hard, slavish overwork is driving those girls into the saloons," a male mill worker was quoted as saying.

Brandeis's "authorities" would not satisfy standards today, but they were the best he had, and he cited more than ninety of them on the link between the number of hours worked and a person's physical and moral well-being. It all seemed very

Laundry owner Curt Muller, standing in the laundry doorway with his arms folded, challenged an Oregon law limiting the length of the workday for women. ❖

Lawyer Louis D. Brandeis used sociological data to defend the Oregon law limiting women's working hours when he argued the case before the U.S. Supreme Court. ❖

"scientific," though Brandeis wanted to title his brief "What Any Fool Knows."

On January 15, 1908, five days after the brief was finished and rushed to Washington, the Supreme Court heard the arguments in the case. Muller's attorney took a traditional tack, arguing from legal precedent—including *Lochner*—that the Oregon law infringed on a woman's right to hire out her labor. The law, he suggested, did not protect women but instead discriminated against them. "We may regret that all women may not be sheltered in happy homes, free from the exacting demands upon them in pursuit of a living, but their right to pursue any honorable vocation . . . is just as sacred . . . as the same right enjoyed by men."

Brandeis, as usual, was eloquent and imposing in rebuttal. Building from the evidence in his brief, he argued it was "common knowledge" that women differed from men, a line of reasoning that makes interesting reading today:

In structure and function women are differentiated from men. Besides these anatomical and physiological differences, physicians are agreed that women are fundamentally weaker than men in all that makes for endurance: in muscular strength, in nervous energy, in the powers of persistent attention and application. Overwork, therefore, which strains endurance to the utmost, is more disastrous to the health of women than of men, and entails upon them more lasting injury.

Women, more than men, Brandeis argued, felt the strain of modern industry, and when the health of a nation's women was injured, it imperiled the future of the nation and "the race."

In its decision a few weeks later, the Court agreed unanimously with Brandeis, even taking the unusual step of mentioning him by name. It was "obvious," the Court said in upholding the Oregon law, that "woman's physical structure and the performance of maternal functions place her at a disadvantage in the struggle for subsistence."

This is especially true when the burdens of motherhood are upon her . . . and as healthy mothers are essential to vigorous offspring, the physical well-being of woman becomes an object of public interest and care in order to preserve the strength and vigor of the race.

Still again, history discloses the fact that woman has always been dependent upon man. He established his control at the outset by superior physical strength, and this control in various forms, with diminishing intensity, has continued to the present. . . . Doubtless there are individual exceptions, and there are many respects in which she has an advantage over him; but looking at it from the view point of the effort to maintain an independent position in life, she is not upon an equality.

Set off by such matters from men, the Court concluded, "[woman] is properly placed in a class by herself, and legislation designed for her protection may be sustained, even when like legislation is not necessary for men and could not be sustained."

The decision in hand, Brandeis, Kelley, and other reformers celebrated. Kelley, who had done so much to shape the case, called it "epoch-making," and Goldmark spoke of the "incalculable benefit it bestows on working women." "There have been," a leading journal said, "military victories acclaimed with the ringing of bells and with bonfires that have had no more significance for the future of the land than this sober decision. It is, in brief, that American women can be protected by law against commercial greed. . . . Although nominally a Constitutional question, it is really a vast social question that the Court has answered."

In the decade after *Muller*, Brandeis, Kelley, and their allies won other important court decisions using similar methods. Their briefs, filled with the kind of so-called scientific data Brandeis had used, grew longer and longer, in some cases reaching a thousand pages or more. Florence Kelley continued to fight for special protection for women, rejecting the arguments of "topsy-turvy" feminists, as she called them, until her death in 1932 at the age of 72. In 1916, Brandeis himself was appointed to the Supreme Court, and sociological jurisprudence of the kind he pioneered continued to play a large role in legal thinking. Among other instances, it strongly influenced the Supreme Court's 1954 ruling in *Brown v. Board of Education* to end segregation in the nations' public schools.

Back in Portland, Oregon, the story of *Muller* v. *Oregon* took another twist. The Supreme Court having ruled against him, Curt Muller fired the women who worked in the laundry and hired men instead.

But *Muller* soon became a landmark in the history of American law and the Supreme Court, one of the most famous and influential cases ever argued. The Brandeis brief, based on sociological and other data rather than on legal precedent, influenced lawyers, courts, and legislatures across the country. "Far and wide this little volume spread its message of humanity and hope," Goldmark wrote. "Gone was the deadening weight of legal precedent. A movement to extend and strengthen women's hour legislation spread over the country."

Goldmark in a sense was right, but there were those who raised questions about just what *Muller* in fact had accomplished. That famous Brandeis brief, after all, had classified women as different, dependent, and subordinate, a judgment with which the Supreme Court had clearly agreed. Reformers such as Kelley and Goldmark tended to accept parts of this, believing, as Goldmark once said, that "women as women should have certain safeguards secured by law, that women need special legislation."

But other people did not accept it, including a number who were devoted to improving women's rights. Had not Brandeis, they asked, invited a Supreme Court composed entirely of men to agree that women were the "weaker" sex, dependent on men like themselves for protection and safekeeping? Had *Lochner* and *Muller* been decided in different ways simply because one involved men and the other women? Why did Brandeis's arguments and the Court's decision touch so little on the welfare of women themselves and instead focus on women as mothers and homemakers? Wasn't there a tendency in that to view women as property rather than as people on a par with men? Were women, or any group in society for that matter, benefited or harmed from securing special consideration under the law?

Questions of this sort about *Muller* have mounted through the years. While some people have continued to praise the decision as a breakthrough for women and reform, others have called it "crudely patronizing" and "romantic paternalism," arguing that measures like the Oregon law made women "the virtual victims of a form of protection that in practice perpetuated their dependency." Critics have also noted that legislatures and employers, in some cases using *Muller* itself, have "protected" women right out of their jobs. Ruth Bader Ginsburg, the second woman to sit on the Supreme Court, recently noted, "From a contemporary perspective, *Muller* v. *Oregon* has been described as a 'roadblock to full equality for women.'"

Questions for Discussion

- What were the main points of Brandeis's argument? Muller's attorney's argument? How do these arguments reflect the time period of the case? How do you think they would be received today? Do you agree or disagree with Brandeis's argument?

- How did the Brandeis brief change the definition of acceptable evidence? Can we still see effects of this change in modern court cases?

Florence Kelley served as general secretary of the National Consumers' League from 1899 until her death in 1932. The evidence Kelley and her researcher Josephine Goldmark amassed for the "Brandeis brief" helped establish the principle of the constitutional validity of protective legislation for industry. ❖

Sheet music cover for "Let's Keep the Glow in Old Glory," an unofficial but nonetheless popular bit of propaganda during the World War I era. ✦

The Nation at War

The Sinking of the Lusitania

On the morning of May 1, 1915, the German government took out the following important advertisement in the *New York World* as a warning to Americans and other voyagers setting sail for England:

> NOTICE—
>
> Travellers intending to embark on the Atlantic voyage are reminded that a state of war exists between Germany and her allies and Great Britain and her allies; that the zone of war includes the waters adjacent to the British Isles; that, in accordance with formal notice given by the Imperial German Government, vessels flying the flag of Great Britain, or of any of her allies, are liable to destruction in those waters and that travelers sailing in the war zone on ships of Great Britain or her allies do so at their own risk.

At 12:30 that afternoon, the British steamship *Lusitania* set sail from New York to Liverpool. Secretly, it carried a load of ammunition as well as passengers.

The steamer was two hours late in leaving, but it held several speed records and could easily make up the time. The passenger list of 1257 was the largest since the outbreak of war in Europe in 1914. Alfred G. Vanderbilt, the millionaire sportsman, was aboard; so were Charles Frohman, a famous New York theatrical producer, and Elbert Hubbard, a popular writer who jested that a submarine attack might help sell his new book. While some passengers chose the *Lusitania* for speed, others liked the modern staterooms, more comfortable than the older ships of the competing American Line.

Six days later, the *Lusitania*, back on schedule, reached the coast of Ireland. German U-boats were known to patrol the dangerous waters. When the war began, Great Britain imposed a naval blockade of Germany. In return, Germany in February 1915 declared the area around the British Isles a war zone; all enemy vessels, armed or unarmed, were at risk. Germany had only a handful of U-boats, but the submarines were a new and frightening weapon. On behalf of the United States, President Woodrow Wilson protested the German action, and on February 10, he warned Germany of its "strict accountability" for any American losses resulting from U-boat attacks.

Off Ireland, the passengers lounged on the deck of the *Lusitania*. As if it were peacetime, the ship sailed straight ahead, with no zigzag maneuvers to throw off pursuit. But the submarine U-20 was there, and its commander, seeing a large ship, fired a single torpedo. Seconds after it hit, a boiler exploded and blew a hole in the *Lusitania*'s side. The ship listed immediately, hindering the launching of lifeboats, and in eighteen minutes it sank. Nearly 1200 people died, including 128 Americans. As the ship's bow lifted and went under, the U-20 commander for the first time read the name: *Lusitania.*

The sinking, the worst since the *Titanic* went down with 1500 people in 1912, horrified Americans. Theodore Roosevelt called it "an act of piracy" and demanded war. Most Americans, however, wanted to stay out of war; like Wilson, they hoped negotiations could solve the problem. "There is such a thing," Wilson said a few days after the sinking, "as a man being too proud to fight. There is such a thing as a nation being so right that it does not need to convince others by force."

OUTLINE

A New World Power

Foreign Policy Under Wilson

Toward War

Over There

Over Here

The Treaty of Versailles

Conclusion: Postwar Disillusionment

FEATURE ESSAY

Measuring the Mind

THE LUSITANIA, SUNK BY GERMAN TORPEDO, WITH HEAVY LOSS OF LIFE.

With the sinking of the Lusitania, *the American people learned firsthand of the horrors of total war. President Wilson's decision to protest the incident through diplomacy kept the United States out of the war— but only temporarily.* ❖

In a series of diplomatic notes, Wilson demanded a change in German policy. The first *Lusitania* note (May 13, 1915) called on Germany to abandon unrestricted submarine warfare, disavow the sinking, and compensate for lost American lives. Germany sent an evasive reply, and Wilson drafted a second *Lusitania* note (June 9) insisting on specific pledges. Fearful the demand would lead to war, Secretary of State William Jennings Bryan resigned rather than sign the note. Wilson sent it anyway and followed with a third note (July 21)—almost an ultimatum—warning Germany that the United States would view similar sinkings as "deliberately unfriendly."

Unbeknownst to Wilson, Germany had already ordered U-boat commanders not to sink passenger liners without warning. In August 1915, a U-boat mistakenly torpedoed the British liner *Arabic*, killing two Americans. Wilson protested, and Germany, eager to keep the United States out of the war, backed down. The *Arabic* pledge (September 1) promised that U-boats would stop and warn liners, unless they tried to resist or escape. Germany also apologized for American deaths on the *Arabic*, and for the rest of 1915, U-boats hunted freighters, not passenger liners.

ALTHOUGH WILSON'S DIPLOMACY had achieved his immediate goal, the *Lusitania* and *Arabic* crises contained the elements that led to war. Trade and travel tied the world together, and Americans no longer hid behind safe ocean barriers. New weapons, such as the submarine, strained old rules of international law. But while Americans sifted the conflicting claims of Great Britain and Germany, they hoped for peace. A generation of progressives, inspired with confidence in human progress, did not easily accept war.

Wilson also hated war, but he found himself caught up in a worldwide crisis that demanded the best in American will and diplomacy. In the end, diplomacy failed, and in April 1917, the United States entered a war that changed the nation's history. Building on several major trends in American foreign policy since the 1890s, the years around World War I firmly established the United States as a world power, confirmed the country's dominance in Latin America, and ended with a war with Germany and her allies that had far-reaching results, including establishing the United States as one of the world's foremost economic powers.

A NEW WORLD POWER

As they had in the late nineteenth century, Americans after 1900 continued to pay relatively little attention to foreign affairs. Newspapers and magazines ran stories every day about events abroad, but people paid closer attention to what was going on at home. Walter Lippmann, one of the twentieth century's most outstanding political commentators, once said, "I cannot remember taking any interest whatever in foreign affairs until after the outbreak of the First World War."

For Americans at the time, foreign policy was something to be left to the president in office, an attitude the presidents themselves favored. Foreign affairs became an arena in which they could exert a free hand largely unchallenged by Congress or the courts, and Roosevelt, Taft, and Wilson all took advantage of the opportunity to do so.

The foreign policy they pursued from 1901 to 1920 was aggressive and nationalistic. During these years, the United States intervened in Europe, the Far East, and Latin America. It dominated the Caribbean.

In 1898, the United States left the peace table possessing the Philippines, Puerto Rico, and Guam. Holding distant possessions required a colonial policy; it also required a change in foreign policy, reflecting an outward approach. From the Caribbean to the Pacific, policymakers paid attention to issues and countries they had earlier ignored. Like other nations in these years, the United States built a large navy, protected its colonial empire, and became increasingly involved in international affairs.

The nation also became more and more involved in economic ventures abroad. Turning out goods from textiles to steel, mass production industries sold products overseas, and financiers invested in Asia, Africa, Latin America, and Europe. During the years between the Spanish-American War and World War I, investments abroad rose from $445 million to $2.5 billion. While investments and trade never wholly dictated American foreign policy, they fostered greater involvement in foreign lands.

"I Took the Canal Zone"

Convinced the United States should take a more active international role, Theodore Roosevelt spent his presidency preparing the nation for world power. Working with Secretary of War Elihu Root, he modernized the army, using lessons learned from the war with Spain. Roosevelt and Root established the Army War College, imposed stiff tests for the promotion of officers, and in 1903 created a general staff to oversee military planning and mobilization. Determined to end dependence on the British fleet, Roosevelt doubled the strength of the navy during his term in office.

Stretching his authority to the limits, Roosevelt took steps to consolidate the country's new position in the Caribbean and Central America. European powers, which had long resisted American initiatives there, now accepted American supremacy. Preoccupied with problems in Europe and Africa, Great Britain agreed to U.S. plans for an Isthmian canal in Central America and withdrew much of its military force from the area.

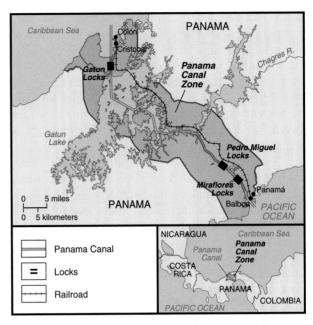

THE PANAMA CANAL ZONE *Construction of the canal began in 1904, and despite landslides, steamy weather, and yellow fever, work was completed in 1914.* ❖

Roosevelt wanted a canal to link the Atlantic and Pacific oceans across the isthmus connecting North and South America. When the war with Spain started in 1898, the battleship *Oregon* took seventy-one days to sail from San Francisco around Cape Horn to its battle station in the Atlantic; years later, naval experts still shuddered at the memory. Secretary of State John Hay negotiated with Britain the Hay-Pauncefote Treaty of 1901 that permitted the United States to construct and control an Isthmian canal, providing it would be free and open to ships of all nations.

Delighted, Roosevelt began selecting the route. One route, fifty miles long, wandered through the rough, swampy terrain of the Panama region of Colombia. A French company had recently tried and failed to dig a canal there. To the northwest, another route ran through mountainous Nicaragua. Although two hundred miles in length, it followed natural waterways, a factor that would make construction easier.

An Isthmian Canal Commission investigated both routes in 1899 and recommended the shorter route through Panama. Roosevelt backed the idea, and he authorized Hay to negotiate an agreement with the Colombian chargé d'affaires, Thomas Herrán. The Hay-Herrán Convention (1903) gave the United States a 99-year lease, with option for renewal, on a canal zone 6 miles in width. In exchange, the United States agreed to pay Colombia a onetime fee of $10 million and an annual rental of $250,000.

To Roosevelt's dismay, the Colombian Senate rejected the treaty, in part because it infringed on Colombian sovereignty. The Colombians also wanted more money. Calling them "jack rabbits" and "contemptible little creatures," Roosevelt considered seizing Panama, then hinted he would welcome a Panamanian revolt from Colombia. In November 1903, the Panamanians took the hint, and Roosevelt moved quickly to support them. Sending the cruiser *Nashville* to prevent Colombian troops from putting down the revolt, he promptly recognized the new Republic of Panama.

Two weeks later, the **Hay-Bunau-Varilla Treaty** with Panama granted the United States control of a canal zone 10 miles wide across the Isthmus of Panama. In return, the United States guaranteed the independence of Panama and agreed to pay the same fees offered Colombia. Using giant steam shovels and thousands of laborers from Jamaica, engineers cut their way across the isthmus. On August 15, 1914, the first ocean steamer sailed through the completed canal, which had cost $375 million to build.

Roosevelt's actions angered many Latin Americans. Trying to soothe feelings, Wilson agreed in 1914 to pay Colombia $25 million in cash, give it preferential treatment in using the canal, and express "sincere regret" over American actions. Roosevelt was furious, and his friends in the Senate blocked the agreement. Colombian-American relations remained strained until 1921, when the two countries signed a treaty that included Wilson's first two provisions but omitted the apology.

For his part, Roosevelt took great pride in the canal, calling it "by far the most important action in foreign affairs." Defending his methods, he said in 1911, "If I had followed traditional conservative methods, I would have submitted a dignified state paper of 200 pages to Congress and the debate on it would have been going on yet; but I took the Canal Zone and let Congress debate; and while the debate goes on the Canal does also."

The Roosevelt Corollary

With interests in Puerto Rico, Cuba, and the canal, the United States developed a Caribbean policy to ensure its dominance in the region. It established protectorates over some countries and subsidized others to keep them dependent. When necessary, the United States purchased islands to keep them out of the hands of other powers, as in the case of the Danish West Indies (now the Virgin Islands), bought in 1917 to prevent the Germans from acquiring them.

From 1903 to 1920, the United States intervened often in Latin America to protect the canal, promote regional stability, and exclude foreign influence. One problem worrying American policymakers was the scale of Latin American debts to European powers. Many countries in the Western Hemisphere owed money to European governments and banks, and often these nations were poor, prone to revolution, and unable to pay. The situation invited European intervention. In 1902, Venezuela defaulted on debts; England, Germany, and Italy sent Venezuela an ultimatum and blockaded its ports. American pressure

A cartoon from Judge titled "The World's Constable." The Roosevelt Corollary claimed the right of the United States to exercise "an international police power," enforced by what many referred to as a "big stick" diplomacy. ❖

forced a settlement of the issue, but the general problem remained.

Roosevelt was concerned about it, and in 1904, when the Dominican Republic defaulted on its debts, he was ready with a major announcement. Known as the **Roosevelt Corollary** of the Monroe Doctrine, the policy warned Latin American nations to keep their affairs in order or face American intervention.

Applying the new policy immediately, Roosevelt in 1905 took charge of the Dominican Republic's revenue system. American officials collected customs and saw to the payment of debt. Within two years, Roosevelt also established protectorates in Cuba and Panama. In 1912, the U.S. Senate added the Lodge Corollary, which warned foreign corporations not to purchase harbors and other sites of military significance in Latin America. Continued by Taft, Wilson, and other presidents, the Roosevelt Corollary guided American policy in Latin America until the 1930s, when Franklin D. Roosevelt's Good Neighbor policy replaced it.

Ventures in the Far East

The Open Door policy toward China and possession of the Philippine Islands shaped American actions in the Far East. Congress refused to arm the Philippines, and the islands were vulnerable to the growing power of Japan. Roosevelt wanted to balance Russian and Japanese power, and he was not unhappy at first when war broke out between them in 1904. As Japan won victory after victory, however, Roosevelt grew worried. Acting on a request from Japan, he offered to mediate the conflict, and both Russia and Japan accepted: Russia because it was losing, and Japan because it was financially drained.

In August 1905, Roosevelt convened a peace conference at Portsmouth, New Hampshire. The conference ended the war, but Japan emerged as the dominant force in the Far East. Adjusting policy, Roosevelt sent Secretary of War Taft to Tokyo to negotiate the Taft-Katsura Agreement (1905), which recognized Japan's dominance over Korea in return for its promise not to invade the Philippines. Giving Japan a free hand in Korea violated the Open Door policy, but Roosevelt argued that he had little choice.

Relations between Japan and the United States were again strained in 1906 when the San Francisco school board ordered the segregation of Japanese, Chinese, and Korean children into a separate Oriental school. A year later, the California legislature considered a bill limiting the immigration of Japanese laborers into the state. As resentment mounted in Japan, Roosevelt intervened to persuade the school board to rescind its order, while at the same time he obtained from Japan the "Gentlemen's Agreement" (1907) promising to stop the flow of Japanese agricultural laborers into the United States.

In case Japan viewed his policy as a sign of weakness, Roosevelt sent sixteen battleships of the new American fleet around the world, including a stop in Tokyo in October 1908. Critics at home predicted dire consequences, and European naval experts felt certain Japan would attack the fleet. Instead, the Japanese welcomed it, even posting ads to sell the sailors Mitsukoshi washing powder to "rid yourselves of the seven blemishes on the way home." For the moment, Japanese-American relations improved, and in 1908 the two nations, in an exchange of diplomatic notes, reached the comprehensive Root-Takahira Agreement in which they promised to maintain the status quo in the Pacific, uphold the Open Door, and support Chinese independence.

In later years, tensions again grew in the Far East. Anger mounted in Japan in 1913 when the California legislature prohibited Japanese residents from owning property in the state. At the start of World War I, Japan seized some German colonies, and in 1915 it issued the Twenty-One Demands insisting on authority over China. Coveting an Asian empire, Japan eyed American possessions in the Pacific.

Taft and Dollar Diplomacy

In foreign as well as domestic affairs, President Taft tried to continue Roosevelt's policies. For secretary of state he chose Philander C. Knox, Roosevelt's attorney general, and together they pursued a policy of **"dollar diplomacy"** to promote American financial and business interests abroad. The policy had profit-seeking motives, but it also aimed to substitute economic ties for military alliances with the idea of increasing American influence and bringing lasting peace.

Intent, like Roosevelt, on supremacy in the Caribbean, Taft worked to replace European loans with American ones, thereby reducing the danger of outside meddling. In 1909, he asked American bankers to assume the Honduran debt in order to fend off English bondholders. A year later, he persuaded them to take over the assets of the National Bank of Haiti, and in 1911 he helped Nicaragua secure a large loan in return for American control of Nicaragua's National Bank. When Nicaraguans revolted against the agreement, Taft sent marines to put them down. A marine detachment was stationed in the country intermittently until the 1930s.

In the Far East, Knox worked closely with Willard Straight, an agent of American bankers, who argued that dollar diplomacy was the financial arm of the Open Door. Straight had close ties to Edward H.

Harriman, the railroad magnate, who wanted to build railroads in Manchuria in northern China. Roosevelt had tacitly promised Japan he would keep American investors out of the area, and Knox's plan reversed the policy. Trying to organize an international syndicate to loan China money to purchase the Manchurian railroads, Knox approached England, Japan, and Russia. In January 1910, all three turned him down.

The outcome was a blow to American policy and prestige in Asia. Russia and Japan found reasons to cooperate with each other and staked out spheres of influence in violation of the Open Door. Japan resented Taft's initiatives in Manchuria, and China's distrust of the United States deepened. Instead of cultivating friendship, as Roosevelt had envisioned, Taft had started an intense rivalry with Japan for commercial advantage in China.

FOREIGN POLICY UNDER WILSON

When he took office in 1913, Woodrow Wilson knew little about foreign policy. As a Princeton professor, he had studied Congress and the presidency, but his books made only passing reference to foreign issues, and during the 1912 campaign he mentioned foreign policy only when it affected domestic concerns. "It would be the irony of fate if my administration had to deal chiefly with foreign affairs," he said to a friend before becoming president. And so it was. During his two terms, Wilson faced crisis after crisis in foreign affairs, including the outbreak of World War I.

A supremely self-confident man, Wilson conducted his own diplomacy. He composed important diplomatic notes on his own typewriter, sent personal emissaries abroad, and carried on major negotiations without the knowledge of his secretaries of state. Failing to find the right persons for key diplomatic posts, he filled the positions with party regulars such as James W. Gerard, his ambassador to Germany, for whom he had contempt. On Gerard's dispatches, Wilson penciled notes: "Ordinarily our Ambassador ought to be backed up as [a matter] of course, but— this ass? It is hard to take it seriously." Or, the next day: "Who can fathom this? I wish they would hand this idiot his passports!"

The idealistic Wilson believed in a principled, ethical world in which militarism, colonialism, and war were brought under control. He stressed moral purposes over material interests and said during one crisis, "The force of America is the force of moral principle." Rejecting the policy of dollar diplomacy, Wilson initially chose a course of **moral diplomacy,** designed to bring right to the world, preserve peace, and extend to other peoples the blessings of democracy.

Conducting Moral Diplomacy

William Jennings Bryan, whom Wilson appointed as secretary of state, was also an amateur in foreign relations. Trusting in the common people, Bryan was skeptical of experts in the State Department. To key posts abroad he appointed "deserving Democrats," believing they could do the job as well as career diplomats. Bryan was a fervent pacifist, and like Wilson, he believed in the American duty to "help" less favored nations.

In 1913 and 1914, he embarked on an idealistic campaign to negotiate treaties of arbitration throughout the world. Known as "cooling-off" treaties, they provided for submitting all international disputes to permanent commissions of investigation. Neither party could declare war or increase armaments until the investigation ended, usually within one year. The idea drew on the era's confidence in commissions and the sense that human reason, given time for emotions to fade, could settle problems without war. Bryan negotiated cooling-off treaties with thirty nations, including Great Britain, France, and Italy. Germany refused to sign one. Based on a generous idea, the treaties were naive, and they did not work.

Wilson and Bryan promised a dramatic new approach in Latin America, concerned not with the "pursuit of material interest" but with "human rights" and "national integrity." Signaling the change, in 1913 they negotiated the treaty with Colombia apologizing for Roosevelt's Panamanian policy. Yet in the end, Wilson, distracted by other problems and impatient with the results of his idealistic approach, continued the Roosevelt-Taft policies. He defended the Monroe Doctrine, gave unspoken support to the Roosevelt Corollary, and intervened in Latin America more than had either Roosevelt or Taft.

In 1914, Wilson negotiated a treaty with Nicaragua to grant the United States exclusive rights to build a canal and lease sites for naval bases. This treaty made Nicaragua an American satellite. In 1915, he sent marines into Haiti to quell a revolution; they stayed until 1934. In 1916, he occupied the Dominican Republic, establishing a protectorate that lasted until 1924. By 1917, American troops "protected" Nicaragua, Haiti, the Dominican Republic, and Cuba—four nations that were U.S. dependencies in all but name.

Troubles Across the Border

Wilson's moral diplomacy encountered one of its greatest challenges across the border in Mexico. Porfirio Díaz, president of Mexico for thirty-seven years, was overthrown in 1911. Díaz had encouraged

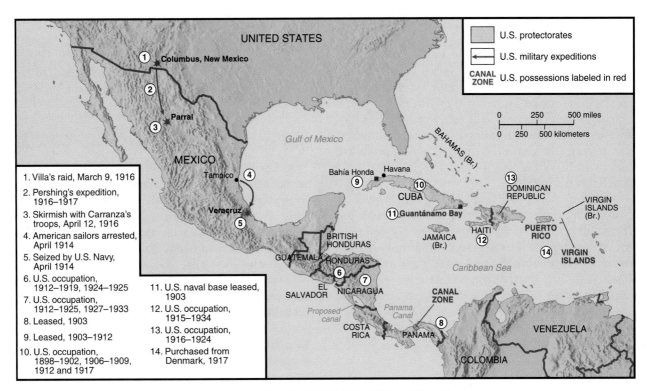

1. Villa's raid, March 9, 1916
2. Pershing's expedition, 1916–1917
3. Skirmish with Carranza's troops, April 12, 1916
4. American sailors arrested, April 1914
5. Seized by U.S. Navy, April 1914
6. U.S. occupation, 1912–1919, 1924–1925
7. U.S. occupation, 1912–1925, 1927–1933
8. Leased, 1903
9. Leased, 1903–1912
10. U.S. occupation, 1898–1902, 1906–1909, 1912 and 1917
11. U.S. naval base leased, 1903
12. U.S. occupation, 1915–1934
13. U.S. occupation, 1916–1924
14. Purchased from Denmark, 1917

ACTIVITIES OF THE UNITED STATES IN THE CARIBBEAN, 1898–1930   *During the first three decades of the twentieth century, the United States policed the Caribbean, claiming the right to take action when it judged Latin American countries were doing a bad job of running their affairs.* ❖

foreign investments in Mexican mines, railroads, oil, and land; by 1913, Americans had invested more than $1 billion. But most Mexicans remained poor and uneducated, and Díaz's overthrow led to a decade of violence that tested Wilson's policies and brought the United States close to war with Mexico.

A liberal reformer, Francisco I. Madero, followed Díaz as president in 1911. But Madero could not keep order in the troubled country, and opponents of his reforms undermined him. With support from wealthy landowners, the army, and the Catholic Church, General Victoriano Huerta ousted Madero in 1913, threw him in jail, and arranged his murder. Most European nations immediately recognized Huerta, but Wilson, calling him a "butcher," refused to do so. Instead, he announced a new policy toward revolutionary regimes in Latin America. To win American recognition, they must not only exercise power but reflect "a just government based upon law, not upon arbitrary or irregular force."

On that basis, Wilson withheld recognition from Huerta and maneuvered to oust him. Early in 1914, he stationed naval units off Mexico's ports to cut off arms shipments to the Huerta regime. The action produced trouble. On April 9, 1914, several American sailors, who had gone ashore in Tampico to purchase supplies,

were arrested. They were promptly released, but the American admiral demanded an apology and a 21-gun salute to the American flag. Huerta agreed—if the Americans also saluted the Mexican flag.

Wilson asked Congress for authority to use military force if needed; then, just as Congress acted, he learned that a German ship was landing arms at Veracruz on Mexico's eastern coast. With Wilson's approval, American warships shelled the harbor, and marines went ashore. Against heavy resistance, they took the city. Outraged, Mexicans of all factions denounced the invasion, and for a time the two countries hovered on the edge of war.

Retreating hastily, Wilson explained that he desired only to help Mexico. Argentina, Brazil, and Chile came to his aid with an offer to mediate the dispute, and tensions eased. In July 1914, weakened by an armed rebellion, Huerta resigned. Wilson recognized the new government, headed by Venustiano Carranza, an associate of Madero. Early in 1916, Francisco ("Pancho") Villa, one of Carranza's generals, revolted. Hoping to goad the United States into an action that would help him seize power, he raided border towns, injuring American civilians. In January, he removed seventeen Americans from a train in Mexico and murdered them. Two months later he invaded Columbus,

New Mexico, killing sixteen Americans and burning the town.

Stationing militia along the border, Wilson ordered General John J. Pershing on a punitive expedition to seize Villa in Mexico. Pershing led six thousand troops deep into Mexican territory. At first, Carranza agreed to the drive, but as the Americans pushed farther and farther into his country, he changed his mind. As the wily Villa eluded Pershing, Carranza protested bitterly, and Wilson, worried about events in Europe, ordered Pershing home.

Wilson's policy had laudable goals; he wanted to help the Mexicans achieve political and agrarian reform. But his motives and methods were condescending. Wilson tried to impose gradual progressive reform on a society sharply divided along class and other lines. With little forethought, he interfered in the affairs of another country, and in doing so he revealed the themes—moralism, combined with pragmatic self-interest and a desire for peace—that also shaped his policies in Europe.

TOWARD WAR

In May 1914, Colonel Edward M. House, Wilson's close friend and adviser, sailed to Europe on a fact-finding mission. Tensions there were rising. "The situation is extraordinary," he reported to Wilson. "It is jingoism [extreme nationalism] run stark mad.... There is too much hatred, too many jealousies."

Large armies dominated the European continent. A web of alliances entangled nations, maximizing the risk that a local conflict could produce a wider war. In Germany, the ambitious Kaiser Wilhelm II coveted a world empire to match those of Britain and France. Germany had military treaties with Turkey and Austria-Hungary, a sprawling central European country of many nationalities. Linked in another alliance, England, France, and Russia agreed to aid each other in case of attack.

On June 28, 1914, a Bosnian assassin linked to Serbia murdered Archduke Franz Ferdinand, heir to the Austro-Hungarian throne. Within weeks, Germany, Turkey, and Austria-Hungary (the Central Powers) were at war with England, France, and Russia (the Allied Powers). Americans were shocked at the events. "I had a feeling that the end of things had come," one of Wilson's cabinet members said. "I stopped in my tracks, dazed and horror-stricken." Wilson immediately proclaimed neutrality and asked Americans to remain "impartial in thought as well as in action."

The war, he said, was one "with which we have nothing to do, whose causes cannot touch us." In private, Wilson was stunned. A man who loved peace, he had long admired the British parliamentary system, and he respected the leaders of the British Liberal party, who supported social programs akin to his own. "Everything I love most in the world," he said, "is at stake."

The Neutrality Policy

In general, Americans accepted neutrality. They saw no need to enter the conflict, especially after the Allies in September 1914 halted the first German drive toward Paris. America resisted involvement in other countries' problems, with the notable exception of Latin America, and had a tradition of freedom from foreign entanglements.

Many of the nation's large number of progressives saw additional reasons to resist. War, they thought, violated the very spirit of progressive reform. Why demand safer factories in which people could work and then kill them by the millions in war? To many progressives, moreover, England represented international finance, an institution they detested. Germany, on the other hand, had pioneered some of their favorite social reforms.

Furthermore, progressives and others tended to put the blame for war on the greed of "munition manufacturers, stockbrokers, and bond dealers" eager for wartime profits. "Do you want to know the cause of the war?" Henry Ford, who was no progressive, asked. "It is capitalism, greed, the dirty hunger for dollars." Above all, progressives were sure that war would end reform. It consumed money and attention; it inflamed emotions.

As a result, Jane Addams, Florence Kelley, Frederic C. Howe, Lillian Wald, and other progressives fought to keep the United States out of war. In late 1915, they formed the American Union Against Militarism, to throw, they said, "a monkey wrench into the machinery" of war. Throughout 1915 and 1916, *La Follette's Magazine,* the voice of the progressive leader, railed against the Morgans, Rockefellers, Du Ponts, and "the thirty-eight corporations most benefited by war orders." In 1915, Addams and Wald helped organize the League to Limit Armament, and shortly thereafter, Addams and Carrie Chapman Catt formed the Woman's Peace Party to organize women against the war.

The war's outbreak also tugged at the emotions of millions of immigrant Americans. Those who came from the British Isles tended to support the Allies; those from Ireland tended to support Germany, hoping Britain's wartime troubles might free their homeland from British domination. The large population of German Americans often sympathized with the

A Look at the Past

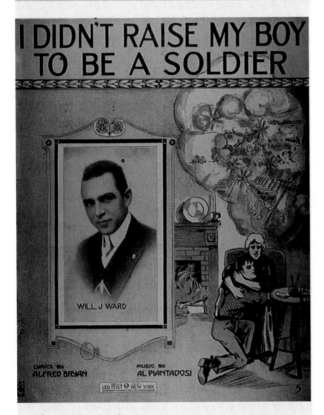

I DIDN'T RAISE MY BOY TO BE A SOLDIER

WILL J WARD

LYRICS BY
ALFRED BRYAN

MUSIC BY
AL PIANTADOSI

LEO FEIST ♦ NEW YORK

Sheet Music Cover

In 1915, the song "I Didn't Raise My Boy to Be a Soldier," written by Alfred Bryan and Al Piantadosi and performed by many different singers, was very popular in the United States. This cover of the song's sheet music includes a photograph of one of the performers and an illustration of a mother embracing her son with scenes of battle in their thoughts. What emotions do you think this image stirred in its audience? What do the song title and cover art suggest about the role women played in the peace movement during World War I? Do the sentiments expressed by this cover help explain why it took years before the United States entered the war? Had attitudes changed by 1918, when songs such as "Let's Keep the Glow in Old Glory" (see the sheet music cover on p. 688) were published?

United States in its early years. Germany, on the other hand, seemed arrogant and militaristic. When the war began, it invaded Belgium to strike at France and violated a treaty which the German chancellor called "just a scrap of paper." Many Americans resented the violation, and they liked it even less when German troops executed Belgian civilians who resisted.

Both sides sought to sway American opinion, and fierce propaganda campaigns flourished. The German Literary Defense Committee distributed more than a million pamphlets during the first year of the war. German propaganda tended to stress strength and will; Allied propaganda called on historical ties and took advantage of German atrocities, both real and alleged. In the end, the propaganda probably made little difference. Ties of heritage and the course of the war, not propaganda, decided the American position. At the outset, no matter which side they cheered for, Americans of all persuasions preferred simply to remain at peace.

Freedom of the Seas

The demands of trade tested American neutrality and confronted Wilson with difficult choices. Under international law, neutral countries were permitted to trade in nonmilitary goods with all belligerent countries. But Great Britain controlled the seas, and it intended to cut off shipments of war materials to the Central Powers.

As soon as war broke out, Britain blockaded German ports and limited the goods Americans could sell to Germany. American ships had to carry cargoes to neutral ports from which, after examination, they could be carried to Germany. As time passed, Britain stepped up the economic sanctions by forbidding the shipment to Germany of all foodstuffs and most raw materials, seizing and censoring mail, and "blacklisting" American firms that dealt directly with the Central Powers. British ships often stopped American ships and confiscated cargoes.

Again and again, Wilson protested against such infringements on neutral rights. Sometimes Britain complied, sometimes not, and Wilson often grew angry. But needing American support and supplies, Britain pursued a careful strategy to disrupt German-American trade without disrupting Anglo-American relations. After forbidding cotton shipments to Germany in 1915, it agreed to buy enough cotton to make up for the losses. When necessary, it also promised to reimburse American businesses after the war's end.

Other than the German U-boats, there were no constraints on trade with the Allies, and a flood of Allied war orders fueled the American economy.

Central Powers. But many people thought that, in a nation of immigrants, a policy of neutrality would be wise from a domestic point of view as well as from the viewpoint of foreign policy.

At the deepest level, a majority in the country, bound by common language and institutions, sympathized with the Allies and blamed Germany for the war. Like Wilson, many Americans admired English literature, customs, and law; they remembered Lafayette and the times when France had helped the

England and France bought huge amounts of arms, grain, cotton, and clothing. To finance the purchases, the Allies turned to American bankers for loans. By 1917, loans to Allied governments exceeded $2 billion; loans to Germany came to only $27 million.

In a development that influenced Wilson's policy, the war produced the greatest economic boom in the nation's history. Loans and trade drew the United States ever closer to the Allied cause. And even though Wilson often protested English maritime policy, the protests involved American goods and money, whereas Germany's submarine policy threatened American lives.

The U-Boat Threat

A relatively new weapon, the *Unterseeboot*, or submarine, strained the guidelines of international law. Traditional law required a submarine to surface, warn the target to stop, send a boarding party to check papers and cargo, then allow time for passengers and crew to board lifeboats before sinking the vessel. Flimsy and slow, submarines could ill afford to surface while the prey radioed for help. If they did surface, they might be rammed or blown up by deck guns.

When Germany announced the submarine campaign in February 1915, Wilson protested sharply, calling the sinking of merchant ships without checking cargo "a wanton act." The Germans promised not to sink American ships—an agreement that lasted until 1917—and thereafter the issue became the right of Americans to sail on the ships of belligerent nations. In March, an American citizen aboard the British liner *Falaba* perished when the ship was torpedoed off the Irish coast. Bryan urged Wilson to forbid Americans to travel in the war zones, but the president, determined to stand by the principles of international law, refused.

Wilson reacted more harshly in May and August of 1915 when U-boats sank the *Lusitania* and the *Arabic*. He demanded that the Germans protect passenger vessels and pay for American losses. At odds with Wilson's understanding of neutrality, Bryan resigned as secretary of state and was replaced by Robert Lansing, a lawyer and counselor in the State Department. Lansing brought a very different spirit to the job. He favored the Allies and believed that democracy was threatened in a world dominated by Germany. He urged strong stands against German violations of American neutrality.

In February 1916, Germany declared unrestricted submarine warfare against all armed ships. Lansing protested and told Germany it would be held strictly accountable for American losses. A month later, a U-boat torpedoed the unarmed French channel steamer *Sussex* without warning, injuring several Americans. Arguing that the sinking violated the *Arabic* pledge, Lansing urged Wilson to break relations with Germany. Wilson rejected the advice, but on April 18 he sent an ultimatum to Germany, stating that unless the Germans immediately called off attacks on cargo and passenger ships, the United States would sever relations.

The Kaiser, convinced he did not yet have enough submarines to risk war, yielded. In the *Sussex* pledge of May 4, 1916, he agreed to Wilson's demands and promised to shoot on sight only ships of the enemy's navy. But he attached the condition that the United States compel the Allies to end their blockade and comply with international law. Wilson accepted the pledge but turned down the condition.

A new and terrifying weapon of the war was the German U-boat, which attacked silently and without warning. ❖

The *Sussex* pledge marked the beginning of a short period of friendly relations between Germany and the United States. The agreement applied not only to passenger liners but to all merchant ships, belligerent or not. There was one problem: Wilson had taken such a strong position that if Germany renewed submarine warfare on merchant shipping, war was likely. Most Americans, however, viewed the agreement as a diplomatic stroke for peace by Wilson, and the issues of peace and preparedness dominated the presidential election of 1916.

"He Kept Us Out of War"

The "preparedness" issue pitted antiwar groups against those who wanted to prepare for war. The American Rights Committee, the National Security League, and other groups urged stepped-up military measures in case of war. In the summer of 1915, they persuaded the War Department to hold a training camp in Plattsburg, New York, in which regular army officers trained 1200 civilian volunteers in modern warfare. The following summer, 16,000 volunteers participated in such training camps.

Bellicose as always, Teddy Roosevelt led the preparedness campaign. He called Wilson "yellow" for not pressing Germany harder and scoffed at the popular song "I Didn't Raise My Boy to Be a Soldier," which he compared to singing "I Didn't Raise My Girl to Be a Mother." Defending the military's state of readiness, Wilson refused to be stampeded just because "some amongst us are nervous and excited." In fact, when government revenue dropped in 1915, he cut military appropriations.

Wilson's position was attacked from both sides as preparedness advocates charged cowardice, while pacifists denounced any attempt at military readiness. The difficulty of his situation, plus the growing U-boat crisis, soon changed Wilson's mind. In mid-1915, he asked the War Department to increase military planning, and he quietly notified congressional leaders of a switch in policy. Later that year, Wilson approved large increases in the army and navy, a move that upset many peace-minded progressives. In January 1916, he toured the country to promote preparedness, and in June, with an American flag draped over his shoulder, he marched in a giant preparedness parade in Washington.

For their standard-bearer in the presidential election of 1916, the Republicans nominated Charles Evans Hughes, a moderate justice of the Supreme Court. Hughes seemed to have all the qualifications for victory. A former reform governor of New York, he could lure back the Roosevelt progressives while at the same time appealing to the Republican conserva-

Roosevelt's campaign for war preparedness became a personal attack on Wilson, whom TR called a coward and a weakling. According to this cartoon titled "White House or Bust," Roosevelt had the election of 1916 in mind as well as military preparedness. ❖

tives. To woo the Roosevelt wing, Hughes called for a tougher line against Germany, thus allowing the Democrats to label him the "war" candidate. Even so, Roosevelt and others considered Hughes a "bearded iceberg," a dull campaigner who wavered on important issues.

The Democrats renominated Wilson in a convention marked by spontaneous demonstrations for peace. Determined to outdo Republican patriotism, Wilson himself had ordered the convention's theme to be "Americanism." The delegates were to sing "America" and "The Star-Spangled Banner" and to cheer any mention of America and the flag. They did it all dutifully but then broke into spontaneous applause at the mention of Wilson's careful diplomatic moves. As the keynote speaker reviewed them, the delegates shouted, "What did we do? What did we do?" The speaker shouted back, "We didn't go to war! We didn't go to war!"

Picking up the theme, perhaps with reservations, Wilson said in October, "I am not expecting this country to get into war." The campaign slogan "He kept us out of war" was repeated again and again, and just before the election, the Democrats took full-page ads in leading newspapers:

You Are Working—Not Fighting!
   Alive and Happy—Not Cannon Fodder!
   Wilson and Peace with Honor?
      or
   Hughes with Roosevelt and War?

On election night, Hughes had swept most of the East, and Wilson retired at 10 P.M. thinking he had lost. During the night, the results came in from California, New Mexico, and North Dakota; all supported Wilson—California by a mere 3773 votes. Wilson won with 9.1 million votes against 8.5 million for Hughes. Holding the Democratic South, he carried key states in the Midwest and West and took large portions of the labor and progressive vote. Women—who were then allowed to vote in presidential elections in twelve states—also voted heavily for Wilson.

The Final Months of Peace

Just before election day, Great Britain further limited neutral trade, and there were reports from Germany of a renewal of unrestricted submarine warfare. Fresh from his victory, Wilson redoubled his efforts for peace. Aware that time was running out, he hoped to start negotiations to end the bloodshed and create a peaceful postwar world.

In December 1916, he sent messages to both sides asking them to state their war aims. Should they do so, he pledged the "whole force" of the United States to end the war. The Allies refused, although they promised privately to negotiate if the German terms were reasonable. The Germans replied evasively and in January 1917 revealed their real objectives. Close to forcing Russia out of the war, Germany sensed victory and wanted territory in eastern Europe, Africa, Belgium, and France.

On January 22, in an eloquent speech before the Senate, Wilson called for a "peace without victory." Outlining his own ambitious aims, he urged respect for all nations, freedom of the seas, arms limitations, and a League of Nations to keep the peace. "Only a peace between equals can last, only a peace the very principle of which is equality and a common participation in a common benefit." The speech made a great impression on many Europeans, but it was too late. The Germans had decided a few weeks before to unleash the submarines and gamble on a quick end to the war. Even as Wilson spoke, U-boats were in the Atlantic west of Ireland, preparing to attack.

On January 31, the German ambassador in Washington informed Lansing that beginning February 1, U-boats would sink on sight all ships—passenger or merchant, neutral or belligerent, armed or unarmed—in the waters around England and

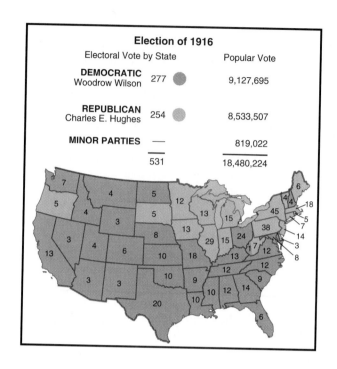

Election of 1916

	Electoral Vote by State		Popular Vote
DEMOCRATIC Woodrow Wilson	277		9,127,695
REPUBLICAN Charles E. Hughes	254		8,533,507
MINOR PARTIES	—		819,022
	531		18,480,224

France. Staking everything on a last effort, the Germans calculated that if they could sink 600,000 tons of shipping a month, they could defeat England in six months. As he had pledged in 1916, Wilson broke off relations with Germany, although he still hoped for peace.

On February 25, the British government privately gave Wilson a telegram intercepted from Arthur Zimmermann, the German foreign minister, to the German ambassador in Mexico. A day later, Wilson asked Congress for authority to arm merchant ships to deter U-boats attacks. When La Follette and a handful of others threatened to filibuster, Wilson divulged the contents of the Zimmermann telegram. It proposed an alliance with Mexico in case of war with the United States, offering financial support and recovery of Mexico's "lost territory" in New Mexico, Texas, and Arizona.

Spurred by a wave of public indignation toward the Germans, the House passed Wilson's measure, but La Follette and others still blocked action in the Senate. On March 9, 1917, Wilson ordered merchant ships armed on his own authority. Three days later, he announced the arming, and on March 13, the navy instructed all vessels to fire on submarines. Between March 12 and March 21, U-boats sank five American ships, and Wilson decided to wait no longer.

He called Congress into special session and at 8:30 in the evening on April 2, 1917, asked for a declaration of war. "It is a fearful thing to lead this great peaceful people into war, into the most terrible and disastrous of all wars, civilization itself seeming to be in the balance.

But the right is more precious than peace, and we shall fight for the things which we have always carried nearest our hearts,—for democracy, . . . for the rights and liberties of small nations, for a universal dominion of right by such a concert of free peoples as shall bring peace and safety to all nations and make the world itself at last free."

Congressmen broke into applause and crowded the aisles to congratulate Wilson. "My message today was a message of death for our young men," he said afterward. "How strange it seems to applaud that."

Pacifists in Congress continued to hold out, and for four days they managed to postpone action. Finally, on April 6, the declaration of war passed, with fifty members of the House and six senators voting against it. Even then, the country was divided over entry into the war.

OVER THERE

With a burst of patriotism, the United States entered a war its new allies were in danger of losing. That same month, the Germans sank 881,000 tons of Allied shipping, the highest amount for any one month during the war. There were mutinies in the French army; a costly British drive in Flanders stalled. In November, the Bolsheviks seized power in Russia, and, led by V. I. Lenin, they soon signed a separate peace treaty with Germany, freeing German troops to fight in the West. German and Austrian forces routed the Italian army on the southern flank, and the Allies braced for a spring 1918 offensive.

Mobilization

The United States was not prepared for war. Some Americans hoped the declaration of war itself might daunt the Germans; there were those who thought that naval escorts of Allied shipping would be enough. Others hoped money and arms supplied to the Allies would be sufficient to produce victory without sending troops. "Good Lord!" an influential senator exclaimed just after war was declared. "You're not going to send soldiers over there, are you?"

Bypassing older generals, Wilson named John J. ("Black Jack") Pershing, leader of the Mexican campaign, to head the American Expeditionary Force (AEF). Pershing inherited an army unready for war. In April 1917, it had 200,000 officers and men, equipped with 300,000 old rifles, 1500 machine guns, 55 out-of-date airplanes, and 2 field radio sets. Its most recent battle experience had been chasing Pancho Villa around northern Mexico. It had not caught him.

The armed forces had just two war plans: War Plan Orange, for a defensive war against Japan in the Pacific, and War Plan Black, to counter a possible German attack in the Caribbean. Wilson had ordered military commanders not to plan because to do so violated neutrality. "When the Acting Chief of Staff went to look at the secret files where the plans to meet the situation that confronted us should have been found," Pershing later said, "the pigeonhole was empty."

Although some in Congress preferred a voluntary army of the kind that had fought in the Spanish-American War, Wilson turned to conscription, which he believed was both efficient and democratic. In May

U.S. LOSSES TO THE GERMAN SUBMARINE CAMPAIGN, 1916–1918

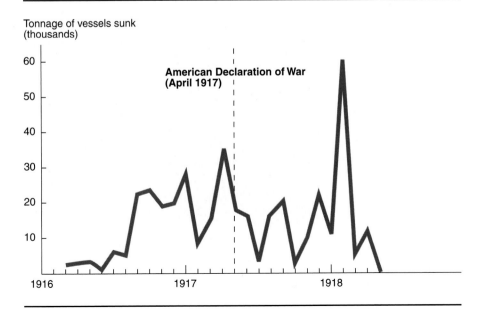

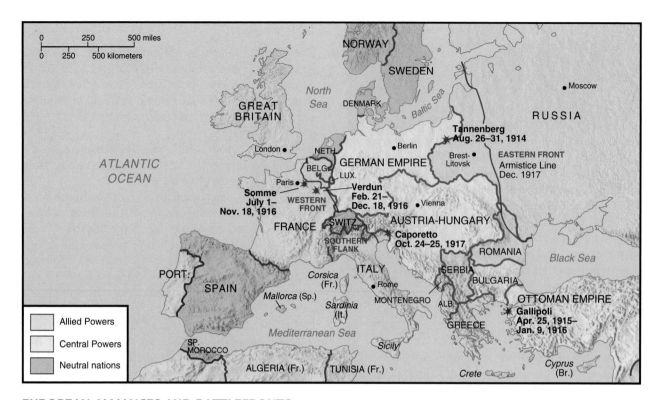

EUROPEAN ALLIANCES AND BATTLEFRONTS, 1914–1917   *Allied forces suffered early defeats on the eastern front (Tannenberg) and in the Dardanelles (Gallipoli). In 1917, the Allies were routed on the southern flank (Caporetto); the western front then became the critical theater of the war.* ❖

1917, Congress passed the **Selective Service Act,** providing for the registration of all men between the ages of 21 and 30 (later changed to 18 and 45). Early in June, 9.5 million men registered for the draft. By the end of the war, the act had registered 24.2 million men, about 2.8 million of whom were inducted into the army. Defending the draft, Wilson said it was not really a draft at all, but a "selection from a nation which has volunteered in mass." Newly devised intelligence tests became part of the selection process. (See the Feature Essay, "Measuring the Mind," pp. 704–705.)

The draft included black men as well as white, and four African American regiments were among the first sent into action. Despite their contributions, however, no black soldiers were allowed to march in the victory celebrations that eventually took place in Paris. Nor were they included in a French mural of the different races in the war, even though black servicemen from English and French colonies were represented.

War in the Trenches

World War I may have been the most terrible war of all time, more terrible even than World War II and its vast devastation. After the early offensives, the European

In The Victorious Retreat Back to the Rhine *(1918), American illustrator and painter Frank Schoonover captures the intensity of aerial bombardment supporting the gathering momentum of Allied ground forces to drive back the Germans in the final stages of the war.* ❖

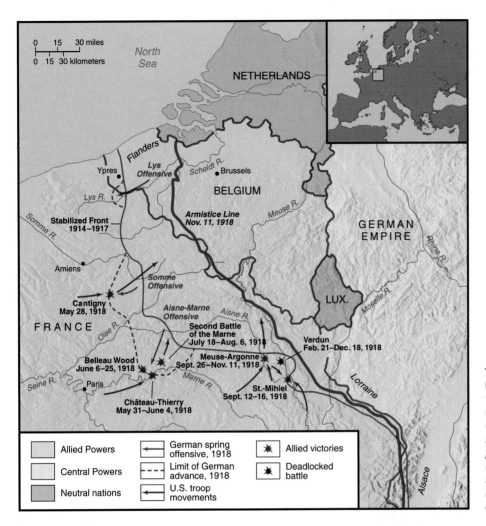

THE WESTERN FRONT: U.S. PARTICIPATION, 1918 *The turning point of the war came in July, when the German advance was halted at the Marne. The "Yanks," now a fighting force, were thrown into the breach. They played a dramatic role in stemming the tide and mounting the counteroffensives that ended the war.* ❖

armies dug themselves into trenches only hundreds of yards apart in places. Artillery, poison gas, hand grenades, and a new weapon—rapid-fire machine guns—kept them pinned down.

Even in moments of respite, the mud, rats, cold, fear, and disease took a heavy toll. Deafening bombardments shook the earth, and there was a high incidence of shell shock. From time to time, troops went "over the top" of the trenches in an effort to break through the enemy's lines, but the costs were enormous. The German offensive at Verdun in 1916 killed 600,000 men; the British lost 20,000 on the first day of an offensive on the Somme.

The first American soldiers reached France in June 1917. By March of the following year, 300,000 Americans were there, and by war's end, 2 million men had crossed the Atlantic. No troop ships were sunk, a credit to the British and American navies. In the summer of 1917, Admiral William S. Sims, a brilliant American strategist, pushed through a convoy plan that used Allied destroyers to escort merchant vessels across the ocean. At first resisted by English captains

who liked to sail alone, the plan soon cut shipping losses in half.

As expected, on March 21, 1918, the Germans launched a massive assault in western Europe. Troops from the Russian front added to the force, and by May they had driven Allied forces back to the Marne River, just 50 miles from Paris. There, the Americans saw their first action. The American forces blocked the Germans at the town of Château-Thierry and four weeks later forced them out of Belleau Wood, a crucial stronghold. On July 15, the Germans threw everything into a last drive for Paris, but they were halted at the Marne, and in three days of battle they were finished. "On the 18th," the German chancellor said, "even the most optimistic among us knew that all was lost. The history of the world was played out in three days."

With the German drive stalled, the Allies counterattacked along the entire front. On September 12, 1918, a half million Americans and a smaller contingent of French drove the Germans from the St. Mihiel salient, 12 miles south of Verdun. Two weeks later, 896,000 American soldiers attacked between the

Feature Essay

MEASURING THE MIND

From 1870 to 1920, scientists and physicians explored new ideas about the mind. In Europe, the Viennese psychiatrist Sigmund Freud studied the unconscious, which, he thought, shaped human behavior. Russia's Ivan Pavlov tested the conditioned reflex in mental activity (Pavlov's dogs), and in the United States William James, the psychologist and philosopher, examined emotions and linked psychology to everyday problems.

As one way of understanding the mind, psychologists studied the mental processes of a great many minds, a task to which the relatively new science of statistics lent a hand. Testing large samples of subjects, they developed the concept of the "normal" and "average," helpful boundaries used to determine an individual's place in the population. In 1890, the psychologist James McKeen Cattell tested one hundred first-year students at the University of Pennsylvania for vision and hearing, sensitivity to pain, reaction time, and memory. He called these examinations by a new name—mental tests—and the idea spread. In 1895, the American Psychological Association (APA) set up a special committee to promote the nationwide collection of mental statistics.

Work was under way on both sides of the ocean, and in 1905 Alfred Binet and Theodore Simon, two French psychologists, devised a metric intelligence scale. Seizing on the idea that intelligence increases with age until maturity, they tested children to find an average level of performance for different ages. Once they had determined the average, they could compare any child's test performance to it and thus distinguish between the child's "mental age" and chronological age. In 1912, William Stein, a German psychologist, introduced the "intelligence quotient," found by dividing a person's mental age by the chronological age. In 1916, Lewis M. Terman of Stanford University improved Binet's test, and the term *IQ* became part of the American vocabulary.

Employers and educators, however, remained skeptical of measuring intelligence. Thus, when the United States entered World War I, psychologists at once saw the opportunity to overcome the doubts and prove their theories. Huge numbers of men needed to be recruited, classified, and assigned to units quickly. Why not use the new mental tests? APA leaders formed twelve committees, including one on the Psychological Examination of Recruits, to explore the military uses of psychology.

Preferring to issue promotions on the basis of seniority, the army resisted the "mental meddlers," but the APA persuaded the War Department to use the tests. In early 1918, psychological examiners were posted at all training camps to administer the Alpha Test to literates and the Beta Test (with instructions given in pantomime) to illiterates and recruits who did not understand English. At the start of each Alpha Test, the examiners put the men at ease by explaining that the army was "not looking for crazy people. The aim is to help find out what we are best fit-

Administered to soldiers in groups, the IQ test was used in World War I to classify recruits and determine which of them were "officer material." The results of the tests raised questions not only about the mental abilities and backgrounds of the men but also about possible biases in the tests themselves. ◆

TEST 8

Notice the sample sentence:

People hear with the   eyes   _ears_   nose   mouth

The correct word is _ears_, because it makes the truest sentence.

In each of the sentences below you have four choices for the last word. Only one of them is correct. In each sentence draw a line under the one of these four words which makes the truest sentence. If you can not be sure, guess. The two samples are already marked as they should be.

SAMPLES
{ People hear with the   eyes   _ears_   nose   mouth
{ France is in   _Europe_   Asia   Africa   Australia

1. America was discovered by   Drake   Hudson   Columbus   Balboa 1
2. Pinochle is played with   rackets   cards   pins   dice 2
3. The most prominent industry of Detroit is   automobiles   brewing   flour   packing 3
4. The Wyandotte is a kind of   horse   fowl   cattle   granite 4
5. The U. S. School for Army Officers is at   Annapolis   West Point   New Haven   Ithaca .. 5
6. Food products are made by   Smith & Wesson   Swift & Co.   W. L. Douglas   B. T. Babbitt 6
7. Bud Fisher is famous as an   actor   author   baseball player   comic artist 7
8. The Guernsey is a kind of   horse   goat   sheep   cow 8
9. Marguerite Clark is known as a   suffragist   singer   movie actress   writer 9
10. "Hasn't scratched yet" is used in advertising a   duster   flour   brush   cleanser 10
11. Salsify is a kind of   snake   fish   lizard   vegetable 11
12. Coral is obtained from   mines   elephants   oysters   reefs 12
13. Rosa Bonheur is famous as a   poet   painter   composer   sculptor 13
14. The tuna is a kind of   fish   bird   reptile   insect 14
15. Emeralds are usually   red   blue   green   yellow 15
16. Maize is a kind of   corn   hay   oats   rice 16
17. Nabisco is a   patent medicine   disinfectant   food product   tooth paste 17
18. Velvet Joe appears in advertisements of   tooth powder   dry goods   tobacco   soap 18
19. Cypress is a kind of   machine   food   tree   fabric 19
20. Bombay is a city in   China   Egypt   India   Japan 20
21. The dictaphone is a kind of   typewriter   multigraph   phonograph   adding machine .. 21
22. The pancreas is in the   abdomen   head   shoulder   neck 22
23. Cheviot is the name of a   fabric   drink   dance   food 23
24. Larceny is a term used in   medicine   theology   law   pedagogy 24
25. The Battle of Gettysburg was fought in   1863   1813   1778   1812 25
26. The bassoon is used in   music   stenography   book-binding   lithography 26
27. Turpentine comes from   petroleum   ore   hides   trees 27
28. The number of a Zulu's legs is   two   four   six   eight 28
29. The scimitar is a kind of   musket   cannon   pistol   sword 29
30. The Knight engine is used in the   Packard   Lozier   Stearns   Pierce Arrow 30
31. The author of "The Raven" is   Stevenson   Kipling   Hawthorne   Poe 31
32. Spare is a term used in   bowling   football   tennis   hockey 32
33. A six-sided figure is called a   scholium   parallelogram   hexagon   trapezium 33
34. Isaac Pitman was most famous in   physics   shorthand   railroading   electricity 34
35. The ampere is used in measuring   wind power   electricity   water power   rainfall .. 35
36. The Overland car is made in   Buffalo   Detroit   Flint   Toledo 36
37. Mauve is the name of a   drink   color   fabric   food 37
38. The stanchion is used in   fishing   hunting   farming   motoring 38
39. Mica is a   vegetable   mineral   gas   liquid 39
40. Scrooge appears in   Vanity Fair   The Christmas Carol   Romola   Henry IV 40

Questions from one portion of the U.S. Army Intelligence Alpha Test. ❖

ted to do." On the Beta Test, which was made up largely of pictures, the examiners were reminded that Beta men "sometimes sulk and refuse to work."

On the basis of the tests, the examiners classified recruits as "superior," "average," or "inferior." From the "superior" category, they selected men for officer training, a helpful winnowing process in an army that expanded quickly from 9000 officers to 200,000. They then distributed the remaining "superior," "average," and "inferior" men among each military unit. In all, the examiners tested 1.7 million men—by far the largest testing program in human history to that time. To some degree, the tests served their purpose, but they also seemed to raise questions about the education and mental ability of many American men.

For one thing, there was the extent of illiteracy—nearly one-quarter of the draft-age men in 1918 could neither read nor write. (One-third, in-cidentally, were physically unfit for service.) There was also the limited schooling of the recruits, most of whom had left school between the fifth and seventh grades. More alarming, according to the test results, 47 percent of the white draftees and 89 percent of the black draftees had a "mental age" of 12 years or under, which classified them as "feebleminded." Did that mean half or more of the American population was feebleminded?

The tests also turned up racial and national distinctions—or so some of the examiners concluded. Men of "native" backgrounds and "old" immigrant stock (from northern Europe and the British Isles) tended to score well and fall in the "superior" category; "new" immigrants (from central and southern Europe) tended to score less well and rank as "inferior." Among Russian, Polish, and Italian draftees, more than half were classified as "inferior."

Such results came as no surprise to those who had long doubted the intelligence of the "new" immigrants, nor did the fact that 80 percent of the African American men taking the Alpha Test scored in the "inferior" range.

Some observers, however, wondered what the tests really measured. The APA examiners claimed they measured "native intelligence," but questions about Edgar Allan Poe's poem "The Raven" or the paintings of Rosa Bonheur, a French artist of the mid-nineteenth century, required answers that native intelligence alone could not supply. When blacks and whites scored comparably on the early Beta Test, the examiners decided that something must be wrong with the test, so they changed the questions until the scores showed the expected racial differences. Most of those taking the Beta Test had never taken a written test before; many had probably never held a pencil.

Still skeptical, the army discontinued the tests the moment the war ended, but what the army rejected, the nation adopted. Businesses, government, and above all, educational institutions found more and more uses for intelligence testing. In 1926, the College Entrance Examination Board (CEEB) administered the first Scholastic Aptitude Test (SAT), designed to test "intelligence" and predict performance in college. In 1935, it established scoring ranges from 200 to 800, with the average score set at 500. During World War II, SAT tests were widely used. In 1947, the CEEB became part of a new Educational Testing Service that spurred an educational revolution by making "intelligence" instead of social or economic standing the main criterion of college admissions.

Before long, intelligence testing—the measuring of minds—touched every aspect of American life. Shaping lives and careers, it pushed some people forward and held others back, in the military, industry, the civil service, and higher education. "Intelligence tests . . . ," an expert said in 1971, "have more and more become society's instrument for the selection of human resources."

German prisoners and American wounded returning from the front lines of the Meuse-Argonne. More Americans died in that campaign than in the rest of the war. The painting is by Harvey Dunn, one of eight official artists with the American Expeditionary Force. ❖

Meuse River and the Argonne Forest. Focusing their efforts on a main railroad supply line for the German army in the West, American troops broke through in early November, cut the line, and drove the Germans back along the whole front.

The German high command knew that the war was lost. On October 6, 1918, Germany appealed to Wilson for an armistice, and by the end of the month, Turkey, Bulgaria, and Austria-Hungary were out of the war. At 4 A.M. on November 11, Germany signed the armistice. The AEF lost 48,909 dead and 230,000 wounded; losses to disease brought the total of dead to more than 112,000.

The American contribution, although small in comparison to the enormous costs to European nations, was vital. Fresh, enthusiastic American troops raised Allied morale; they helped turn the tide at a crucial point in the war.

OVER HERE

Victory at the front depended on economic and emotional mobilization at home. Consolidating federal authority, Wilson moved quickly in 1917 and 1918 to organize war production and distribution. An idealist who knew how to sway public opinion, he also recognized the need to enlist American emotions. To him, the war for people's minds, the "conquest of their convictions," was as vital as events on the battlefield.

The Conquest of Convictions

A week after war was declared, Wilson formed the **Committee on Public Information (CPI)** and asked George Creel, an outspoken progressive journalist, to head it. Creel hired progressives such as Ida Tarbell and Ray Stannard Baker and recruited thousands of people in the arts, advertising, and film industries to publicize the war. He worked out a system of voluntary censorship with the press, plastered walls with colorful posters, and issued more than 75 million pamphlets.

Creel also enlisted 75,000 "four-minute men" to give quick speeches at public gatherings and places of entertainment on "Why We Are Fighting" and "The Meaning of America." At first, they were instructed to stress facts and stay away from emotions, particularly hatred, but by the beginning of 1918, the instructions shifted; the Germans were to be depicted as bloodthirsty Huns bent on world conquest. Exploiting a new medium, the CPI promoted films such as *The Prussian Cur* and *The Kaiser, the Beast of Berlin*. Creel secretly subsidized several prowar groups and formed the CPI's Division of Industrial Relations to rally labor to the war.

Helped along by the propaganda campaign, anti-German sentiment spread rapidly. Many schools stopped offering instruction in the German language—California's state education board called it a language "of autocracy, brutality, and hatred." Sauerkraut became "liberty cabbage"; saloonkeepers removed pretzels from the bar. Orchestral works by Bach, Beethoven, and Brahms vanished from some symphonic programs, and the New York Philharmonic agreed not to perform the music of living German composers. Government agents harassed Karl Muck, the German conductor of the Boston Symphony, imprisoned him for more than a year, and then, after the war ended, deported him. German Americans and antiwar figures were badgered, beaten, and in some cases killed.

Vigilantism, sparked often by superpatriotism of a ruthless sort, flourished. Frequently, it focused on radical antiwar figures such as Frank Little, an official of the Industrial Workers of the World (IWW) in Butte, Montana, who was taken from his boarding-house in August 1917, tied to the rear of an automobile, and dragged through the streets until his kneecaps were scraped off. Little was then hanged from a railroad trestle. In April 1918, a Missouri mob seized Robert Prager, a young man whose sole crime was being born in Germany. They bound him with an American flag, paraded him through town, and then lynched him. A jury acquitted the mob's members—who wore red, white, and blue ribbons to court—as one juror shouted, "Well, I guess nobody can say we aren't loyal now."

Rather than curbing the repression, Wilson encouraged it. "Woe be to the man or group of men that seeks to stand in our way," he told peace advocates soon after the war began. At his request, Congress passed the **Espionage Act** of 1917, which imposed sentences of up to twenty years in prison for persons found guilty of aiding the enemy, obstructing recruitment of soldiers, or encouraging disloyalty. It allowed the postmaster general to remove from the mails materials that incited treason or insurrection. The Trading-with-the-Enemy Act of 1917 authorized the government to censor the foreign language press.

In 1918, Congress passed the **Sedition Act,** imposing harsh penalties on anyone using "disloyal, profane, scurrilous, or abusive language" about the government, flag, or armed forces uniforms. In all, more than fifteen hundred persons were arrested under the new laws. People indicted or imprisoned included a Californian who laughed at rookies drilling at an army camp, a woman who greeted a Red Cross solicitor in a "hostile" way, and an editor who printed this sentence: "We must make the world safe for democracy even if we have to 'bean' the Goddess of Liberty to do it."

The sedition laws clearly went beyond any clear or present danger. There were, to be sure, German spies in the country, Germans who wanted to encourage strikes in American arms factories. Moreover, the U.S. government and other national leaders were painfully aware of how divided Americans had been about entering the war. They set out to promote unity—by force, if necessary—in order to convince Germany that the nation was united behind the war.

But none of these matters warranted a nationwide program of repression. Conservatives took advantage of wartime feelings to try to stamp out American socialists, who in fact were vulnerable because, unlike their European counterparts, they continued to oppose the war even after their country had entered it. Using the sedition laws, conservatives harried the Socialist party and another favorite target, the Industrial Workers of the World. In 1921, ill and facing imprisonment, "Big Bill" Haywood, one of the IWW's best known members, fled to the Soviet Union, where he died a few years later.

Wilson's postmaster general banned from the mails more than a dozen socialist publications, including the *Appeal to Reason,* which went to more than half a million people weekly. In 1918, Eugene V. Debs, the Socialist party leader, delivered a speech denouncing capitalism and the war. He was convicted for violation of the Espionage Act and spent the war in a penitentiary in Atlanta. Nominated as the

Anti-German sentiment spread in America during World War I, escalating dramatically after the United States entered the war in April 1917. A wave of verbal and physical attacks on German Americans was accompanied by a campaign to repress German culture. In this photograph from 1917, a group of children stand in front of an anti-German sign posted in the Edison Park community of Chicago, Illinois. As the sign suggests, some Americans questioned the loyalty of their German American neighbors. ❖

Eugene V. Debs, serving time in an Atlanta penitentiary for speaking out against the war, is shown here after receiving word of his nomination for the presidency. Debs campaigned in 1920 from behind bars. ✤

Socialist party candidate in the presidential election of 1920, Debs—prisoner 9653—won nearly a million votes, but the Socialist movement never fully recovered from the repression of the war.

In fostering hostility toward anything that smacked of dissent, the war also gave rise to the great "Red Scare" that began in 1919. Pleased at first with the Russian revolution, Americans in general turned quickly against it, especially after Lenin and the Bolsheviks seized control late in 1917. The Americans feared Lenin's anticapitalist program, and they denounced his decision in early 1918 to make peace with Germany because it freed German troops to fight in France.

Once again, Wilson himself played a prominent role in the development of anti-Bolshevik sentiment. In the summer of 1918, he sent fifteen thousand American troops into the Soviet Union, where they joined other Allied soldiers. Ostensibly, the troops were there to protect Allied supplies from the Germans and to rescue a large number of Czechs who wanted to return home to fight Germany. But the underlying rea-

son for their presence was that Wilson and others hoped to bring down the fledgling Bolshevik government, fearful it would spread revolution around the world.

Besides sending troops, Wilson joined in an economic blockade of Russia, sent weapons to anti-Bolshevik insurgents, and refused to recognize Lenin's government. He also blocked Russian participation in the peace conference that ended the war. American troops remained in Russia until April 1920, and on the whole, American willingness to interfere soured Russian-American relations for decades to come.

A Bureaucratic War

Quick, effective action was needed to win the war. To meet the need, Wilson and Congress set up an array of new federal agencies, nearly five thousand in all. Staffed largely by businessmen, the agencies drew on funds and powers of a hitherto unknown scope. At night, the secretary of the treasury sat in bed, a yellow pad on his knees, adding up the money needed to finance the war. "The noughts attached to the many millions were so boisterous and prolific," he later said, "that, at times, they would run clear over the edge of the paper."

By the time the war was over, the "noughts" had boisterously added up to $32 billion in direct war expense—in an era when the entire federal budget rarely exceeded $1 billion. To raise the money, the administration sold about $23 billion in "Liberty Bonds," and, using the new Sixteenth Amendment, boosted taxes on corporations and personal incomes. The taxes brought in another $10 billion to help pay for the war.

At first, Wilson tried to organize the wartime economy along decentralized lines, almost in the fashion of his early New Freedom thinking. But that proved unworkable, and he moved instead to a series of highly centralized planning boards, each with broad authority over a specific area of the economy. There were boards to control virtually every aspect of transportation, agriculture, and manufacturing. Though only a few of them were as effective as Wilson had hoped, they did coordinate the war effort to some degree.

The **War Industries Board (WIB),** one of the most powerful of the new agencies, oversaw the production of all American factories. Headed by millionaire Bernard M. Baruch, a Wall Street broker and speculator, it determined priorities, allocated raw materials, and fixed prices. It told manufacturers what they could and could not make. The WIB set the output of steel and regulated the number of stops on elevators. Working closely with business, Baruch for a time acted as the dictator of the American economy.

Herbert Hoover, the hero of a campaign to feed starving Belgians, headed a new **Food Administration,** and he set out with customary energy to supply food to the armies overseas. Appealing to the "spirit of self-sacrifice," Hoover convinced people to save food by observing "meatless" and "wheatless" days. He fixed prices to boost production, bought and distributed wheat, and encouraged people to plant "victory gardens" behind homes, churches, and schools. He sent a half million campaigners door to door to get housewives to sign cards pledging their cooperation. One householder—Wilson—set an example by grazing sheep on the White House lawn.

At another new agency, the Fuel Administration, Harry A. Garfield, the president of Williams College, introduced daylight saving time, rationed coal and oil, and imposed gasless days when motorists could not drive. To save coal, he shut down nonessential factories one day a week, and in January 1918, he closed all factories east of the Mississippi for four days to divert coal to munitions ships stranded in New York harbor. A fourth agency, the Railroad Administration, dictated rail traffic

The U.S. Food Administration urged immigrants and newcomers to America to make sacrifices in the cause of freedom. ❖

over nearly 400,000 miles of track—standardizing rates, limiting passenger travel, and speeding arms shipments. The War Shipping Board coordinated shipping, the Emergency Fleet Corporation supervised shipbuilding, and the War Trade Board oversaw foreign trade.

As never before, the government intervened in American life. When strikes threatened the telephone and telegraph companies, the government simply seized and ran them. Businessmen, paid a nominal dollar a year, flocked to Washington to run the new agencies, and the partnership between government and business grew closer. As government expanded, business expanded as well, responding to wartime contracts. Industries such as steel, aluminum, and cigarettes boomed, and corporate profits increased threefold between 1914 and 1919.

Labor in the War

The war also brought organized labor into the partnership with government, although the results were more limited than in the business-government alliance. Samuel Gompers, president of the AFL, served on Wilson's Council of National Defense, an advisory group formed to unify business, labor, and government. Gompers hoped to trade labor peace for labor advances, and he formed a War Committee on Labor to enlist workers' support for the war. With the blessing of the Wilson administration, membership in the AFL and other unions grew from about 2.7 million in 1916 to more than 4 million in 1919.

Hoping to encourage production and avoid strikes, Wilson adopted many of the objectives of the social-justice reformers. He supported an eight-hour day in war-related industries and improved wages and working conditions. In May 1918, he named Felix Frankfurter, a brilliant young law professor, to head a new War Labor Board (WLB). The agency standardized wages and hours, and at Wilson's direction, it protected the right of labor to organize and bargain collectively. Although it did not forbid strikes, it used various tactics to discourage them. It enforced decisions in well-publicized cases; when the Smith and Wesson arms factory in Massachusetts and the Western Union telegraph company disobeyed the WLB's union rules, the agency took them over.

The WLB also ordered that women be paid equal wages for equal work in war industries. In 1914, the flow of European immigrants suddenly stopped because of the war, and in 1917, the draft began to take large numbers of American men. The result was a labor shortage, filled by women, African Americans, and Mexican Americans. One million women worked in war industries. Some of them took jobs previously held by men, but for the most part, they moved from

Housewives did not leave home for the factory en masse in 1917 as they later did during World War II, but many women already employed outside the home found new, well-paying opportunities in jobs previously held by men. ❖

one set of "women's jobs" into another. From the beginning of the war to the end, the number of women in the workforce held steady at about eight million, and unlike the experience in World War II, large numbers of housewives did not leave the home for machine shops and arms plants.

Still, there were some new opportunities and in some cases higher pay. In food, airplane, and electrical plants, women made up one-fifth or more of the workforce. As their wages increased, so did their expectations; some became more militant, and conflict grew between them and male coworkers. To set standards for female employment, a Women's Bureau was established in the Department of Labor, but the government's influence varied. In the federally run railroad industry, women often made wages equal to those of men; in the federally run telephone industry, they did not.

Looking for more people to fill wartime jobs, corporations found another major source among southern blacks. Beginning in 1916, northern labor agents traveled across the South, promising jobs, high wages, and free transportation. Soon the word spread, and the movement northward became a flood. Between 1916 and 1918, more than 450,000 African Americans left the Old South for the booming industrial cities of St. Louis, Chicago, Detroit, and Cleveland. In the decade before 1920, Detroit's black population grew by more than 600 percent, Cleveland's by more than 300 percent, and Chicago's by 150 percent.

Most of the newcomers were young, unmarried, and skilled or semiskilled. The men found jobs in factories, railroad yards, steel mills, packinghouses, and coal mines; black women worked in textile factories, department stores, and restaurants. In their new homes, African Americans found greater racial freedom but also different living conditions. If the South was often hostile, the North could be impersonal and lonely. Accustomed to the pace of the farm—ruled by the seasons and the sun—those blacks who were able to enter the industrial sector now worked for hourly wages in mass production industries, where time clocks and line supervisors dictated the daily routine.

Racial tensions increased, resulting in part from growing competition for housing and jobs. In mid-1917, a race war in East St. Louis, Illinois, killed nine whites and about forty blacks. In July 1919, the month President Wilson returned from the peace conference in Paris, a race riot in Washington, D.C., killed six people. Riots in Chicago that month killed thirty-eight—fifteen whites and twenty-three blacks—and there were later outbreaks in New York City and Omaha. Lynch mobs killed forty-eight blacks in 1917, sixty-three in 1918, and seventy-eight in 1919. Ten of the victims in 1919 were war veterans, several still in uniform.

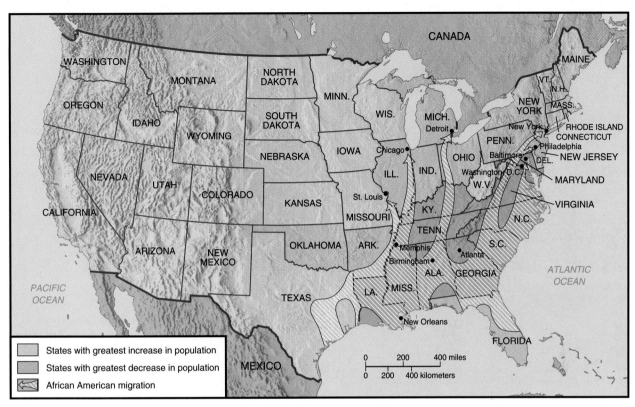

AFRICAN AMERICAN MIGRATION NORTHWARD, 1910–1920   *The massive migration of African Americans from the South to the North during World War I changed the dynamics of race relations in the United States.* ❖

Blacks were more and more inclined to fight back. Two hundred thousand blacks served in France—forty-two thousand as combat troops. Returning home, they expected better treatment. "I'm glad I went," a black veteran said. "I done my part and I'm going to fight right here till Uncle Sam does his." Roscoe Jameson, Claude McKay, and other black poets wrote biting poetry, some of it—such as Fenton Johnson's "The New Day"—drawn from the war experience:

> For we have been with thee in No Man's Land,
> Through lake of fire and down to Hell itself;
> And now we ask of thee our liberty,
> Our freedom in the land of Stars and Stripes.

"Lift Ev'ry Voice and Sing," composed in 1900, became known as the "Negro National Anthem." Parents bought black dolls for their children, and W. E. B. Du Bois spoke of a "New Negro," proud and more militant: "We return. We return from fighting. We return fighting."

Eager for cheap labor, farmers and ranchers in the Southwest persuaded the federal government to relax immigration restrictions, and between 1917 and 1920, more than 100,000 Mexicans migrated into Texas, Arizona, New Mexico, and California. The Mexican American population grew from 385,000 in 1910 to 740,000 in 1920. Tens of thousands of Mexican Americans moved to Chicago, St. Louis, Omaha, and other northern cities to take wartime jobs. Often scorned and insecure, they created urban barrios similar to the Chinatowns and Little Italys around them.

Like most wars, World War I affected patterns at home as much as abroad. Business profits grew, factories expanded, and industries turned out huge amounts of war goods. Government authority swelled, and people came to expect different things of their government. Labor made some gains, as did women and blacks. Society assimilated some of the shifts, but social and economic tensions grew, and when the war ended, they spilled over in the strikes and violence of the Red Scare that followed.

The United States emerged from the war the strongest economic power in the world. In 1914, it was a debtor nation, and American citizens owed foreign investors about $3 billion. Five years later, the United States had become a creditor nation. Foreign governments owed more than $10 billion, and foreign

The 369th infantry regiment returning from the war on the Stockholm *in February 1919. They were awarded the Croix de Guerre for bravery in the Meuse-Argonne.* ❖

citizens owed American investors nearly $3 billion. The war marked a shift in economic power rarely equaled in history.

THE TREATY OF VERSAILLES

Long before the fighting ended, Wilson began to formulate plans for the peace. Like many others, he was disconcerted when the new Bolshevik government in Russia began revealing the terms of secret agreements among Britain, France, and czarist Russia to divide up Germany's colonies. To try to place the war on a higher plane, he appeared before Congress on January 8, 1918, and outlined terms for a far-reaching, nonpunitive settlement. Wilson's **Fourteen Points** were generous and farsighted, but they failed to satisfy wartime emotions that sought vindication.

England and France distrusted Wilsonian idealism as the basis for peace. They wanted Germany disarmed and crippled; they wanted its colonies; and they were skeptical of the principle of self-determination. As the end of the war neared, the Allies, who had in fact made secret commitments with one another, balked at making the Fourteen Points the basis of peace. When Wilson threatened to negotiate a separate treaty with Germany, however, they accepted.

Wilson had won an important victory, but difficulties lay ahead. As Georges Clemenceau, the 78-year-old French premier, said, "God gave us the Ten Commandments, and we broke them. Wilson gives us the Fourteen Points. We shall see."

A Peace at Paris

Unfortunately, Wilson made a grave error just before the peace conference began. He appealed to voters to elect a Democratic Congress in the November 1918 elections, saying that any other result would be "interpreted on the other side of the water as a repudiation of my leadership." Many Republicans were furious, especially those who had supported the Fourteen Points; Wilson's problems deepened when the Democrats went on to lose both the House and Senate.

Wilson's opponents immediately announced that voters had rejected his policies, as he had suggested they could. In fact, the Democratic losses stemmed largely from domestic problems, such as the price of wheat and cotton. But they hurt Wilson, who had alienated some important Republican party leaders. Soon, he would be negotiating with European leaders buoyed by rousing victories at their own polls.

Two weeks after the elections, Wilson announced he would attend the peace conference. This was a

WOODROW WILSON'S FOURTEEN POINTS, 1918: SUCCESS AND FAILURE IN IMPLEMENTATION

1. Open covenants of peace openly arrived at	Not fulfilled
2. Absolute freedom of navigation on the seas in peace and war	Not fulfilled
3. Removal of all economic barriers to the equality of trade among nations	Not fulfilled
4. Reduction of armaments to the level needed only for domestic safety	Not fulfilled
5. Impartial adjustments of colonial claims	Not fulfilled
6. Evacuation of all Russian territory; Russia to be welcomed into the society of free nations	Not fulfilled
7. Evacuation and restoration of Belgium	**Fulfilled**
8. Evacuation and restoration of all French lands; return of Alsace-Lorraine to France	**Fulfilled**
9. Readjustment of Italy's frontiers along lines of Italian nationality	Compromised
10. Self-determination for the former subjects of the Austro-Hungarian Empire	Compromised
11. Evacuation of Rumania, Serbia, and Montenegro; free access to the sea for Serbia	Compromised
12. Self-determination for the former subjects of the Ottoman Empire; secure sovereignty for Turkish portion	Compromised
13. Establishment of an independent Poland, with free and secure access to the sea	**Fulfilled**
14. Establishment of a League of Nations affording mutual guarantees of independence and territorial integrity	Not fulfilled

Sources: Data from G. M. Gathorne-Hardy, *The Fourteen Points and the Treaty of Versailles* (Oxford Pamphlets on World Affairs, no. 6, 1939), pp. 8–34; Thomas G. Paterson et al., *American Foreign Policy: A History Since 1900*, 2nd ed., vol. 2, pp. 282–293.

dramatic break from tradition, and his personal involvement drew attacks from Republicans. They renewed criticism when he named the rest of the delegation: Secretary of State Lansing; Colonel House; General Tasker H. Bliss, a military expert; and Henry White, a career diplomat. Wilson named no member of the Senate, and the only Republican in the group was White.

In selecting the delegation, Wilson passed over Henry Cabot Lodge, the powerful Republican senator from Massachusetts who opposed the Fourteen Points and would soon head the Senate Foreign Relations Committee. He also decided not to appoint Elihu Root or ex-President Taft, both of them enthusiastic internationalists. Never good at accepting criticism or delegating authority, Wilson wanted a delegation he could control—an advantage at the peace table but not in any battle over the treaty at home.

Upon his arrival, Wilson received a tumultuous welcome in England, France, and Italy. Never before had such crowds acclaimed a democratic political figure. In Paris, two million people lined the Champs-Elysées, threw flowers at him, and shouted, "Wilson le Juste [the just]" as his carriage drove by. Overwhelmed, Wilson was sure that the people of Europe shared his goals and would force their leaders to accept his peace. He was wrong. Like their leaders,

many people on the Allied side hated Germany and wanted victory unmistakably reflected in the peace.

Opening in January 1919, the Peace Conference at Paris continued until May. Although twenty-seven nations were represented, the "Big Four" dominated it: Wilson; Clemenceau of France, tired and stubborn, determined to end the German threat forever; David Lloyd George, the crafty British prime minister who had pledged to squeeze Germany "until the pips squeak"; and the Italian prime minister, Vittorio Orlando. A clever negotiator, Wilson traded various "small" concessions for his major goals—national self-determination, a reduction in tensions, and a League of Nations to enforce the peace.

Wilson had to surrender some important principles. Departing from the Fourteen Points by violating the principle of self-determination, the treaty created two new independent nations—Poland and Czechoslovakia—with large German-speaking populations. It divided up the German colonies in Asia and Africa. Instead of a peace without victory, it made Germany accept responsibility for the war and demanded enormous reparations—which eventually totaled $33 billion. It made no mention of disarmament, free trade, or freedom of the seas. Instead of an open covenant openly arrived at, the treaty was drafted behind closed doors.

Sir William Orpen, The Signing of Peace in the Hall of Mirrors, Versailles, 28th of May 1919.
Although the United States played a major role in drafting the treaty, the Senate never ratified the document. Instead, the United States made a separate peace with Germany in 1921. ❖

But Wilson deflected some of the most extreme Allied demands, and he won his coveted Point 14, a League of Nations, designed "to achieve international peace and security." The League included a general assembly; a smaller council composed of the United States, Great Britain, France, Italy, Japan, and four nations to be elected by the assembly; and a court of international justice. League members pledged to submit to arbitration every dispute threatening peace and to enjoin military and economic sanctions against nations resorting to war. Article X, for Wilson the heart of the League, obliged members to look out for one another's independence and territorial integrity.

The draft treaty in hand, Wilson returned home in February 1919 to discuss it with Congress and the people. Most Americans, the polls showed, favored the League; thirty-three governors endorsed it. But over dinner with the Senate and House Foreign Relations Committees, Wilson learned of the strength of congressional opposition to it. On March 3, Senator Lodge produced a "round robin" signed by thirty-seven senators declaring they would not vote for the treaty without amendment. Should the numbers hold, Lodge had enough votes to defeat it.

Returning to Paris, Wilson attacked his critics, while he worked privately for changes to improve the chances of Senate approval. In return for major con-

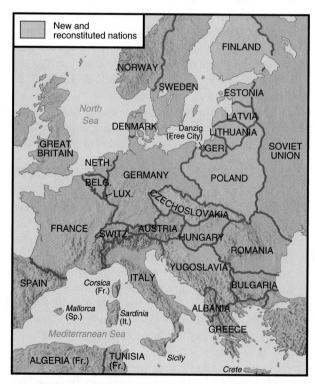

EUROPE AFTER THE TREATY OF VERSAILLES, 1919 *The treaty changed the map of Europe, creating a number of new and reconstituted nations. (Note the boundary changes from the prewar map on p. 702.)* ❖

cessions, the Allies amended the League draft treaty, agreeing that domestic affairs remained outside League jurisdiction (exempting the Monroe Doctrine) and allowing nations to withdraw after two years' notice. On June 28, 1919, they signed the treaty in the Hall of Mirrors at Versailles, and Wilson started home for his most difficult fight.

Rejection in the Senate

There were ninety-six senators in 1919, forty-nine of them Republicans. Fourteen Republicans, led by William E. Borah of Idaho, were the "irreconcilables" who opposed the League on any grounds. "If the Savior of man," Borah said, "would revisit the earth and declare for a League of Nations, I would be opposed to it." Frank B. Kellogg of Minnesota led a group of twelve "mild reservationists" who accepted the treaty but wanted to insert several reservations that would not greatly weaken it. Finally, there were the Lodge-led "strong reservationists," twenty-three of them in all, who wanted major changes that the Allies would have to approve.

With only four Democratic senators opposed to the treaty, the Democrats and Republicans willing to compromise had enough votes to ratify it, once a few reservations were inserted. Bidding for time to allow public opposition to grow, Lodge scheduled lengthy hearings and spent two weeks reading the 268-page treaty aloud. Democratic leaders urged Wilson to appeal to the Republican "mild reservationists," but he refused: "Anyone who opposes me in that I'll crush!"

Fed up with Lodge's tactics, Wilson set out in early September to take the case directly to the people. Crossing the Midwest, his speeches aroused little emotion, but on the Pacific Coast he won ovations, which heartened him. On his way back to Washington, he stopped in Pueblo, Colorado, where he delivered one of the most eloquent speeches of his career. People wept as he talked of Americans who died in battle and the hope that they would never fight again in foreign lands. That night Wilson felt ill. He returned to Washington, and on October 2, Mrs. Wilson found him lying unconscious on the floor of the White House, the victim of a stroke that paralyzed his left side.

After the stroke, Wilson could not work more than an hour or two at a time. No one was allowed to see him except family members, his secretary, and his physician. For more than seven months, he did not meet with the cabinet. Secretary of State Lansing convened cabinet meetings, but when Wilson learned of them, he ordered Lansing to stop and then cruelly forced Lansing to resign. Focusing his remaining energy on the fight over the treaty, Wilson lost touch with other issues, and critics charged that his wife, Edith Bolling Wilson, ran the government.

Humanity is the accuser, the U.S. Senate is the assassin, and the Treaty of Versailles is the victim in this commentary on the Senate's rejection of the treaty. Isolationists, who wanted to keep the United States out of European affairs, opposed the treaty because it included the Covenant for the League of Nations. ❖

On November 6, 1919, while Wilson convalesced, Lodge finally reported the treaty out of committee, along with "Fourteen Reservations," one for each of Wilson's points. The most important reservation stipulated that implementation of Article X, Wilson's key article, required the action of Congress before any American intervention abroad.

The next day, the president's floor leader in the Senate told him that the Democrats could not pass the treaty without reservations. "Is it possible?" Wilson asked sadly. "It might be wise to compromise," the senator said. "Let Lodge compromise!" Wilson replied. When Mrs. Wilson urged her husband to accept the Lodge reservations, he said, "Better a thousand times to go down fighting than to dip your colors to dishonorable compromise."

On November 19, the treaty—with the Lodge reservations—failed, 39 to 55. Following Wilson's instructions, the Democrats voted against it. A motion to approve without the reservations lost 38 to 53, with only one Republican voting in favor. The defeat brought pleas for compromise, but neither Wilson nor Lodge would back down. When the treaty with reservations again came up for vote on March 19, 1920, Wilson ordered the Democrats to hold firm against it. Although twenty-one of them defied him, enough obeyed his orders to defeat it, 49 to 35, seven votes short of the necessary two-thirds majority.

THE ELECTION OF 1920

Candidate	Party	Popular Vote	Electoral Vote
Harding	Republican	16,133,314	404
Cox	Democrat	9,140,884	127
Debs	Socialist	913,664	0

To Wilson, walking now with the help of a cane, one chance remained: the presidential election of 1920. For a time, he thought of running for a third term himself, but his party shunted him aside. The Democrats nominated Governor James M. Cox of Ohio, along with the young and popular Franklin D. Roosevelt, assistant secretary of the navy, for vice president. Wilson called for "a great and solemn referendum" on the treaty. The Democratic platform endorsed the treaty but agreed to accept reservations that clarified the American role in the League.

On the Republican side, Senator Warren G. Harding of Ohio, who had nominated Taft in 1912, won the presidential nomination. Harding waffled on the treaty, but that issue made little difference. Voters wanted a change. Harding won in a landslide, taking 61 percent of the vote and beating Cox by seven million votes. Without a peace treaty, the United States remained technically at war, and it was not until July 1921, almost three years after the last shot was fired, that Congress passed a joint resolution ending the war.

CONCLUSION: POSTWAR DISILLUSIONMENT

After 1919, there was disillusionment. World War I was feared before it started, popular while it lasted, and hated when it ended. To a whole generation that followed, it appeared futile, killing without cause, sacrificing without benefit. Books, plays, and movies—Hemingway's *A Farewell to Arms* (1929), John Dos Passos's *Three Soldiers* (1921), Laurence Stallings and Maxwell Anderson's *What Price Glory?* (1924), among others—showed it as waste, horror, and death.

The war and its aftermath damaged the humanitarian, progressive spirit of the early years of the century. It killed "something precious and perhaps irretrievable in the hearts of thinking men and women." Progressivism survived well into the 1920s and the New Deal, but it no longer had the old conviction and broad popular support. Bruising fights over the war and the League drained people's energy and enthusiasm.

Confined to bed, Woodrow Wilson died in Washington in 1924, three years after Harding, the

CHRONOLOGY

1901	Hay-Pauncefote Treaty with Great Britain empowers United States to build Isthmian canal
1904	Theodore Roosevelt introduces corollary to Monroe Doctrine
1904–1905	Russo-Japanese War
1905	Taft-Katsura Agreement recognizes Japanese power in Korea
1908	Root-Takahira Agreement vows to maintain status quo in the Pacific ❖ Roosevelt sends the fleet around the world
1911	Revolution begins in Mexico
1913–1914	Bryan negotiates "cooling-off" treaties to end war
1914	World War I begins ❖ U.S. Marines take Veracruz ❖ Panama Canal completed
1915	Japan issues Twenty-one Demands to China (January) ❖ Germany declares water around British Isles a war zone (February) ❖ *Lusitania* torpedoed (May) ❖ Bryan resigns; Robert Lansing becomes secretary of state (June) ❖ *Arabic* pledge restricts submarine warfare (September)
1916	Germany issues *Sussex* pledge (March) ❖ General John J. Pershing leads unsuccessful punitive expedition into Mexico to seize Pancho Villa (April) ❖ Wilson wins reelection
1917	Wilson calls for "peace without victory" (January) ❖ Germany resumes unrestricted U-boat warfare (February) ❖ United States enters World War I (April) ❖ Congress passes Selective Service Act (May) ❖ First American troops reach France (June) ❖ War Industries Board established (July)
1918	Wilson outlines Fourteen Points for peace (January) ❖ Germany asks for peace (October) ❖ Armistice ends the war (November)
1919	Peace negotiations begin in Paris (January) ❖ Treaty of Versailles defeated in Senate
1920	Warren G. Harding elected president

new president, promised "not heroics but healing; not nostrums but normalcy; not revolution but restoration." Nonetheless, the "war to end all wars" and the spirit of Woodrow Wilson left an indelible imprint on the country.

RECOMMENDED READING

American foreign policy between 1901 and 1921 has been the subject of considerable study. Richard W. Leopold, *The Growth of American Foreign Policy* (1962), is balanced and informed. Robert E. Osgood, *Ideals and Self-Interest in America's Foreign Relations* (1953), and William Appleman Williams, *Roots of the Modern American Empire* (1969), explore the forces underlying American foreign policy.

For American policy toward Latin America, see Dana G. Munro's detailed account, *Intervention and Dollar Diplomacy in the Caribbean, 1900–1920* (1964); Mary A. Renda, *Taking Haiti: Military Occupation and the Culture of U.S. Imperialism, 1915–1940* (2001); and Emily S. Rosenberg, *Financial Missionaries to the World: The Politics and Culture of Dollar Diplomacy, 1900–1930* (1999). Arthur S. Link examines Wilson's foreign policy in his exceptional five-volume biography, *Wilson* (1947–1965), and in *Woodrow Wilson: Revolution, War, and Peace* (1979).

Studies of events at home during the war include David M. Kennedy, *Over Here* (1980); Robert D. Cuff, *The War Industries Board* (1973); and Maurine W. Greenwald, *Women, War, and Work* (1980). Susan Zeiger, *In Uncle Sam's Service: Women Workers with the American Expeditionary Force, 1917–1919* (1999), and Kathleen Kennedy, *Disloyal Mothers and Scurrilous Citizens: Women and Subversion During World War I* (1999), look at the role of women; Jennifer D. Keene, *Doughboys, the Great War, and the Remaking of America* (2001), at the war's effects on the soldiers; and Mark Robert Schneider, *"We Return Fighting": The Civil Rights Movement in the Jazz Age* (2001), Mark Ellis, *Race, War, and Surveillance: African Americans and the United States Government during World War I* (2001), and Theodore Kornweibel, Jr., *"Investigate Everything": Federal Efforts to Compel Black Loyalty During World War I* (2002), at its impact on African Americans.

Arthur Walworth, *America's Moment, 1918: American Diplomacy at the End of World War I* (1977), examines Wilson's attempt to create a peaceful world order.

For a list of additional titles related to this chapter's topics, please see http://www.ablongman.com/divine.

SUGGESTED WEB SITES

Woodrow Wilson

http://www.ipl.org/ref/POTUS/wwilson.html
This page contains basic factual data about Wilson's election and presidency, speeches, and on-line biographies.

World War I Document Archive

http://www.lib.byu.edu/~rdh/wwi/
This archive contains sources about World War I in general, not just America's involvement.

World War One: Trenches on the Web

http://www.worldwar1.com/index.htm
This site provides a mass of data concerning the prosecution of the world's first global war.

The Great Migration in Chicago

http://lcweb.loc.gov/exhibits/african/afam011.html
This site looks at the black experience in the Great Migration at one prominent destination.

The American Experience: Influenza

http://www.pbs.org/wgbh/pages/amex/influenza
This PBS site reveals the impact of the great flu epidemic of 1918.

Howard Thain's painting, The Great White Way—Times Square, *captures the bright lights and excitement of New York's entertainment center in the "Roaring Twenties."* ❖

Transition to Modern America

*W*heels for the Millions

The moving assembly line that Henry Ford perfected in 1913 for manufacture of the Model T marked only the first step toward full mass production and the beginning of America's worldwide industrial supremacy. A year later, Ford began buying large plots of land along the Rouge River southeast of Detroit, Michigan. He already had a vision of a vast industrial tract where machines, moving through a sequence of carefully arranged manufacturing operations, would transform raw materials into finished cars, trucks, and tractors. The key would be control over the flow of goods at each step along the way—from lake steamers and railroad cars bringing in the coal and iron ore, to overhead conveyor belts and huge turning tables carrying the moving parts past the stationary workers on the assembly line. "Everything must move," Ford commanded, and by the mid-1920s at River Rouge, as the plant became known, it did.

Ford began fulfilling his industrial dream in 1919 when he built a blast furnace and foundry to make engine blocks for both the Model T and his tractors. By 1924, more than forty thousand workers were turning out nearly all the metal parts used in making Ford vehicles. One tractor factory was so efficient that it took just over twenty-eight hours to convert raw ore into a new farm implement.

Visitors from all over the world came to marvel at River Rouge. Some were disturbed by the jumble of machines (by 1926, there were forty-three thousand in operation) and the apparent congestion on the plant floor, but industrial experts recognized that the arrangement led to incredible productivity because "the work moves and the men stand still." A trained engineer summed it up best when he wrote that a visitor to the plant "sees each unit as a carefully designed gear which meshes with other gears and operates in synchronism with them, the whole forming one huge, perfectly-timed, smoothly-operating industrial machine of almost unbelievable efficiency."

In May 1927, after producing more than fifteen million Model Ts, Ford closed the assembly line at Highland Park. For the next six months, his engineers worked on designing a more compact and efficient assembly line at River Rouge for the Model A, which went into production in November. By then, River Rouge had more than justified Ford's vision. "Ford had brought together everything at a single site and on a scale no one else had ever attempted," concluded historian Geoffrey Perrett. "The Rouge plant became to a generation of engineers far more than a factory. It was a monument."

Mass production, born in Highland Park in 1913 and perfected at River Rouge in the 1920s, became the hallmark of American industry. Other carmakers copied Ford's methods, and soon his emphasis on the flow of parts moving past stationary workers became the standard in nearly every American factory. The moving assembly line—with its emphasis on uniformity, speed, precision, and coordination—took

OUTLINE
❖❖❖

The Second Industrial Revolution

City Life in the Jazz Age

The Rural Counterattack

Politics of the 1920s

Conclusion: The Old and the New

FEATURE ESSAY
❖❖❖

Marcus Garvey: Racial Redemption and Black Nationalism

LAW AND SOCIETY
❖❖❖

The Scopes "Monkey" Trial: Contesting Cultural Differences

On the assembly line at Ford's River Rouge plant, workers performed repetitive tasks on the car chassis that rushed by at a rate of 6 feet per minute. ❖

away the last vestiges of craftsmanship and turned workers into near robots. It led to amazing efficiency that produced both high profits for manufacturers and low prices for buyers. By the mid-1920s, the cost of the Model T had dropped from $950 to $290.

MOST IMPORTANT, MASS PRODUCTION CONTRIBUTED to a consumer goods revolution. American factories turned out a flood of automobiles, electrical appliances, and other items that made life easier and more pleasant for most Americans. The result was the creation of a distinctively modern America, one marked by the material abundance that has characterized American society ever since.

But the abundance came at a price. The 1920s have been portrayed as a decade of escape and frivolity, and for many Americans they were just that. But those years also were an era of transition: a time when the old America of individualistic rural values gave way to a new America of conformist urban values. The transition was often wrenching, and many Americans clung desperately to the old ways. Modernity finally won, but not without a struggle.

THE SECOND INDUSTRIAL REVOLUTION

The first Industrial Revolution in the late nineteenth century had catapulted the United States into the forefront among the world's richest and most highly developed nations. With the advent of the new consumer goods industries, the American people by the 1920s enjoyed the highest standard of living of any nation on earth. After a brief postwar depression, 1922 saw the beginning of a great boom that peaked in 1927 and lasted until 1929. In this brief period, American industrial output nearly doubled, and the gross national product rose by 40 percent. Most of this explosive growth took place in industries producing consumer goods—automobiles, appliances, furniture, and clothing. Equally important, the national per capita income increased by 30 percent to $681 in 1929. American workers became the highest paid in history. Combined with the expansion of installment credit programs that allowed customers to buy now and pay later, this income growth allowed a purchasing spree like nothing the nation had ever experienced.

The key to the new affluence lay in technology. The moving assembly line pioneered by Ford became a standard feature in nearly all American plants. Electric motors replaced steam engines as the basic source of energy in factories; by 1929, 70 percent of all industrial power came from electricity. Efficiency experts broke down the industrial process into minute parts, using time and motion studies, and then showed managers and workers

how to maximize the output of their labor. Production per worker-hour increased an amazing 75 percent over the decade; in 1929, a workforce no larger than that of 1919 was producing almost twice as many goods.

The Automobile Industry

The nature of the consumer goods revolution can best be seen in the automobile industry, which became the nation's largest in the 1920s. Rapid growth was its hallmark. In 1920, there were ten million cars in the nation; by the end of the decade, twenty-six million were on the road. Production jumped from fewer than two million units a year to more than five million by 1929.

The automobile boom, at its peak from 1922 to 1927, depended on the apparently insatiable appetite of the American people for cars. But as the decade continued, the market became saturated as more and more of those who could afford the new luxury had become car owners. Marketing became as crucial as production. Automobile makers began to rely heavily on advertising and annual model changes, seeking to make customers dissatisfied with their old vehicles and eager to order new ones. Despite these efforts, sales slumped in 1927 when Ford stopped making the Model T, picked up again the next year with the new Model A, but began to slide again in 1929. The new industry revealed a basic weakness in the consumer goods economy; once people had bought an item with a long life, they would be out of the market for a few years.

In the affluent 1920s, few noticed the emerging economic instability. Instead, contemporary observers focused on the stimulating effect the automobile had on the rest of the economy. The mass production of cars required huge quantities of steel; entire new rolling mills had to be built to supply sheet steel for car bodies. Rubber factories boomed with the demand for tires, and paint and glass suppliers had more business than ever before. The auto changed the pattern of city life, leading to a suburban explosion. Real estate developers, no longer dependent on streetcars and railway lines, could now build houses in ever wider concentric circles around the central cities.

The automobile had a profound effect on all aspects of American life in the 1920s. Filling stations appeared on the main streets, replacing the smithies and stables of the past. In Kansas City, Jess D. Nichols built the first shopping center, Country Club Plaza, and thus set an example quickly followed by other suburban developers.

Even in smaller communities, the car ruled. In Muncie, Indiana, site of a famous sociological survey in the 1920s, one elder replied when asked what was taking place, "I can tell you what's happening in just four letters: A-U-T-O!" A nation that had always revered symbols of movement, from the *Mayflower* to the covered wagon, now had a new icon to worship.

Patterns of Economic Growth

Automobiles were the most conspicuous of the consumer products that flourished in the 1920s, but certainly not the only ones. The electrical industry grew almost as quickly. Central power stations, where massive steam generators converted coal into electricity, brought current into the homes of city and town dwellers. Two-thirds of all American families enjoyed electricity by the end of the decade, and they spent vast sums on washing machines, vacuum cleaners, refrigerators, and ranges. The new appliances eased the burdens of housework and ushered in an age of leisure.

Radio broadcasting and motion picture production also boomed in the 1920s. The early success of KDKA in Pittsburgh stimulated the growth of more than eight hundred independent radio stations, and by 1929, NBC had formed the first successful radio network. Five nights a week, *Amos 'n Andy,* a comic serial featuring two "blackface" vaudevillians, held the attention of millions of Americans. The film industry thrived in Hollywood, reaching its maturity in the mid-1920s when in every large city there were huge theaters seating as many as four thousand people. With the advent of the "talkies" by 1929, average weekly movie attendance climbed to nearly 100 million.

Other industries prospered as well. Production of light metals such as aluminum and magnesium

✦ A Look at the Past ✦

THE GOLD MEDAL GLENWOOD

Perfect Baking
Here's the secret—at the tip of your fingers

SUCCESS is never a matter of lucky guessing when you have a Gold Medal Glenwood to depend on. Perfect control of every baking temperature is right at your finger tips on the dial of the Glenwood Robertshaw oven heat control.

Suppose you are baking sponge cake. The Glenwood cooking chart shows you that 320 degrees is exactly the right temperature to assure the slow, even heat which sponge cake requires. Set the indicator, and come back an hour later. Look through the glass oven door and

you'll see your cake raised and browned as perfectly as though you had been there watching it every minute.

With its three roomy ovens the Gold Medal combines all the conveniences and all the capacity of two separate ranges—one for gas and one for coal. Yet it will take up surprisingly little space in your kitchen.

Everything a good cook wants to know about a new range is shown and described in our Booklet "G," recently published. We'll be glad to mail you one if you will send us your name and address.

WEIR STOVE COMPANY, TAUNTON, MASS.
Western Branch: American Furniture Mart Building
666 Lake Shore Drive, Chicago

Glenwood Ranges
make cooking easy
COAL, WOOD, OIL AND GAS RANGES · HEATING STOVES AND FURNACES

Glenwood Stove Ad

This Glenwood stove, fueled by wood, coal, or gas, reveals the unevenness of technological change. While some women were able to cook with convenient, clean natural gas, others still used dirty coal or carried armloads of wood. The Glenwood also demonstrated that consumers wanted to purchase fashionable, up-to-date, and labor-saving products even if they depended on wood rather than the modern fuel, gas. Why do you suppose standardization had become a goal for consumers as well as for producers?

grew into a major business. Chemical engineering came of age with the invention of synthetics, ranging from rayon for clothing to cellophane for packaging. Americans found a whole new spectrum of products to buy—cigarette lighters, wristwatches, heat-resistant glass cooking dishes, and rayon stockings, to name just a few.

The corporation continued to be the dominant economic unit in the 1920s. Growing corporations now had hundreds of thousands of stockholders; and one individual or family rarely held more than 5 percent of the stock. The enormous profits generated by the corporations enabled their managers to finance growth and expansion internally, thus freeing companies from their earlier dependence on investment bankers like J. P. Morgan. Voicing a belief in social responsibility and enlightened capitalism, the new professional class operated independently, free from outside restraint. In the final analysis, the corporate managers were accountable only to other managers.

Another wave of mergers accompanied the growth of corporations during the 1920s. From 1920 to 1928, some eight thousand mergers took place as more and more small firms proved unable to compete effectively with the new giants. By the end of the decade, the two hundred largest nonfinancial corporations owned almost half of the country's corporate wealth. The automobile industry set the example for other areas. The greatest abuses took place in public utilities; promoters such as Samuel Insull built vast paper empires by gaining control of power companies and then draining them of their assets.

The most distinctive feature of the new consumer-oriented economy was the emphasis on marketing. Advertising earnings rose from $1.3 billion in 1915 to $3.4 billion in 1926. Skillful practitioners such as Edward Bernays and Bruce Barton sought to control public taste and consumer spending by identifying the good life with the possession of the latest product of American industry, whether it be a car, a refrigerator, or a brand of cigarettes. Chain stores advanced rapidly at the expense of small retail shops. A&P dominated the retail food industry, growing from 400 stores in 1912 to 15,500 by 1932. Woolworth's "five-and-tens" spread almost as rapidly, while such drugstore chains as Rexall and Liggetts—both owned by one huge holding company—opened outlets in nearly every town and city in the land.

Uniformity and standardization, the characteristics of mass production, now prevailed. The farmer in Kansas bought the same kind of car, the same groceries, and the same pills as the factory worker in Pennsylvania. Sectional differences in dress, food, and furniture began to disappear. Even the regional accents that distinguished Americans in different parts of the country were threatened with extinction by the advent of radio and films, which promoted a standard national dialect devoid of any local flavor.

Economic Weaknesses

The New Era, as business leaders labeled the decade, was not as prosperous as it first appeared. The revolution in consumer goods disguised the decline of many traditional industries in the 1920s. Railroads, overcapitalized and poorly managed, suffered from internal woes and from competition with the growing trucking industry. The coal industry was also troubled, with petroleum and natural gas beginning to replace coal as a

fuel. The use of cotton textiles declined with the development of rayon and other synthetic fibers. The New England mills moved south in search of cheap labor, leaving behind thousands of unemployed workers and virtual ghost towns in the nation's oldest industrial center.

Hardest hit of all was agriculture. American farmers had expanded production to meet the demands of World War I, when they fed their own nation and most of Europe as well. A sharp cutback of exports in 1919 caused a rapid decline in prices. By 1921, farm exports had fallen by more than $2 billion. Throughout the 1920s, the farmers' share of the national income dropped, until by 1929, the per capita farm income was only $273, compared to the national average of $681.

Urban workers were better off than farmers in the 1920s, but they did not share fully in the decade's affluence. The industrial labor force remained remarkably steady during this period of economic growth; technical innovations meant the same number of workers could produce far more than before. Most new jobs appeared in the lower-paying service industry. During the decade, factory wage rates rose only a modest 11 percent; in 1929, nearly half of all American families had an income of less than $1500. At the same time, however, conditions of life improved. Prices remained stable, even dropping somewhat in the early 1920s, so workers enjoyed a gain in real wages.

Organized labor proved unable to advance the interests of workers in the 1920s. Conservative leadership in the AFL neglected the task of organizing the vast number of unskilled laborers in the mass production industries. Aggressive management weakened the appeal of unions by portraying them as radical organizations after a series of strikes in 1919. Many businesses used injunctions and "yellow-dog contracts"—which forbade employees to join unions—to establish open shops and deny workers the benefits of collective bargaining. Other employers wooed their workers away from unions, using techniques of welfare capitalism—spending money to improve plant conditions and winning employee loyalty with pensions, paid vacations, and company cafeterias. The net result was a decline in union membership from a postwar high of five million to less than three million by 1929.

Black workers remained on the bottom, both economically and socially. Nearly half a million African Americans had migrated northward from the rural South during World War I. Some found jobs in northern industries, but many more worked in menial service areas, collecting garbage, washing dishes, and sweeping floors. Yet even these jobs offered them a better life than they found on the depressed southern farms, where millions of African Americans still lived in poverty, and so the migration continued. The black

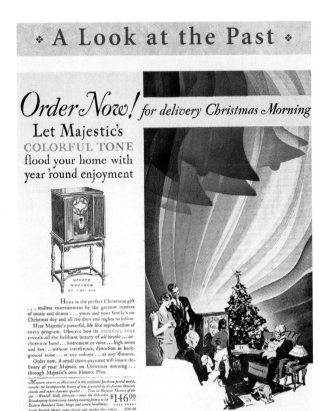

Radio

Radios became enormously popular during the 1920s and 1930s, giving people access to news and entertainment in their homes. While some radios fit on table tops, other models were large, fine pieces of furniture suitable for covering with doilies and treasured photographs. What do expensive, fancy models suggest about the place of radio in the home? Why would radios attain a privileged position in the home?

ghettos in northern cities grew rapidly in the 1920s; Chicago's African American population doubled during the decade, while New York's rose from 152,467 to 327,706, with most African Americans living in Harlem.

Middle- and upper-class Americans were the groups who thrived in the 1920s. The rewards of this second Industrial Revolution went to the managers—the engineers, bankers, and executives—who directed the new industrial economy. Corporate profits nearly doubled in ten years, and income from dividends rose 65 percent, nearly six times the rate of increase in workers' wages. Bank accounts, reflecting the accumulated savings of the upper-middle and wealthy classes, rose from $41.1 billion to $57.9 billion. These were the people who bought the fine new houses in the suburbs

and who could afford more than one car. Their conspicuous consumption helped fuel the prosperity of the 1920s, but their disposable income eventually became greater than their material wants. The result was speculation, as those with idle money began to invest heavily in the stock market to reap the gains from industrial growth.

The economic trends of the decade had both positive and negative implications for the future. On the one hand, there was the solid growth of new consumer-based industries. Automobiles and appliances were not passing fancies; their production and use became a part of the modern American way of life, creating a high standard of living that roused the envy of the rest of the world. The future pattern of American culture—cars and suburbs, shopping centers and skyscrapers—was determined by the end of the 1920s.

But at the same time, there were ominous signs of danger. The unequal distribution of wealth, the growth of consumer debt, the saturation of the market for cars and appliances, and the rampant speculation all contributed to economic instability. The boom of the 1920s would end in a great crash; yet the achievements of the decade would survive even that dire experience to shape the future of American life.

CITY LIFE IN THE JAZZ AGE

The city replaced the countryside as the focal point of American life in the 1920s. The 1920 census revealed that for the first time, slightly more than half of the population lived in cities (defined broadly to include all places of more than 2500 people). During the decade, the metropolitan areas grew rapidly as both whites and blacks from rural areas came seeking jobs in the new consumer industries. Between 1920 and 1930, cities with populations of 250,000 or more had added some eight million people to their ranks. New York City grew by nearly 25 percent, while Detroit more than doubled its population during the decade.

The skyscraper soon became the most visible feature of the city. Faced with inflated land prices, builders turned upward—developing a distinctively American architectural style in the process. New York led the way with the ornate Woolworth Building in 1913. The sleek 102-story Empire State Building, completed in 1931, was for years the tallest building in the world. Other cities erected their own jagged skylines. By 1929, there were 377 buildings more than 20 stories tall across the nation. Most significantly, the skyscraper came to symbolize the new mass culture. "The New York skyscrapers are the most striking manifestation of the triumph of numbers," wrote one French observer. "One cannot understand or like them without first having tasted and enjoyed the

Chicago Tribune editor Col. Robert R. McCormick sponsored in 1922 an international competition for "the most beautiful office building in the world." Architects Raymond M. Hood and John Mead Howells won the competition—and the $50,000 first prize—basing their design for the Tribune Tower on the style of the cathedrals of medieval Europe. Entries for the competition influenced skyscraper architecture throughout the 1920s. ❖

thrill of counting or adding up enormous totals and of living in a gigantic, compact and brilliant world."

In the metropolis, life was different. The old community ties of home, church, and school were absent, but there were important gains to replace them—new ideas, new creativity, new perspectives. Some city dwellers became lost and lonely without the old institutions; others thrived in the urban environment.

Women and the Family

The urban culture of the 1920s witnessed important changes in the American family. This vital institution began to break down under the impact of economic and social change. A new freedom for women and children seemed to be emerging in its wake.

Although World War I accelerated the process by which women left the home for work, the postwar decade witnessed a return to the slower pace of the prewar years. During the 1920s there was no permanent gain in the number of working women. Two million more women were employed in 1930 than in 1920, but this represented an increase of only 1 percent. Most women workers, moreover, had low-paying jobs, ranging from stenographers to maids. The number of women doctors actually decreased, and even though women earned nearly one-third of all graduate degrees, only 4 percent of full professors were female. For the most part, the professions were reserved for men, with women relegated to such fields as teaching and nursing.

Women had won the right to vote in 1920, but the Nineteenth Amendment proved to have less impact than its proponents had hoped. Adoption of the amendment robbed women of a unifying cause, and the exercise of the franchise itself did little to change prevailing sex roles. Men remained the principal breadwinners in the family; women cooked, cleaned, and reared the children. "The creation and fulfillment of a successful home," a *Ladies Home Journal* writer advised women, "is a bit of craftsmanship that compares favorably with building a beautiful cathedral."

The feminist movement, however, still showed signs of vitality in the 1920s. Social feminists pushing for humanitarian reform won enactment of the Sheppard-Towner Act of 1921, which provided for federal aid to establish state programs for maternal and infant health care. Although the failure to enact the child labor amendment in 1925 marked the beginning of a decline in humanitarian reform, for the rest of the decade, women's groups continued to work for good-government measures, for the inclusion of women on juries, and for consumer legislation.

One group of activists, led by Alice Paul's National Woman's Party (NWP), lobbied for full equality for women under the law. In 1923, the NWP succeeded in having an Equal Rights Amendment introduced in Congress. The amendment stated simply, "Men and women shall have equal rights throughout the United States and every place subject to its jurisdiction." Most other women's organizations, notably the League of Women Voters, opposed the amendment because it threatened gender-specific legislation such as the Sheppard-Towner Act that women had fought so hard to enact. The drive for the ERA in the 1920s failed.

Growing assertiveness had a profound impact on feminism in the 1920s. Instead of crusading for social progress, young women concentrated on individual self-expression by rebelling against Victorian restraints. In the larger cities, some quickly adopted what critic H. L. Mencken called the flapper image, portrayed most strikingly by artist John Held, Jr. Cutting their hair short, raising their skirts above the knee, and binding their breasts, "flappers" set out to compete on equal terms with men on the golf course and in the speakeasy. Young women delighted in shocking their elders—they rouged their cheeks and danced the Charleston. Women smoked cigarettes and drank alcohol in public more freely than before. The flappers assaulted the traditional double standard in sex, demanding that equality with men should include sexual fulfillment before and during marriage. New and more liberal laws led to a sharp rise in the divorce rate; by 1928, there were 166 divorces for every 1000 marriages, compared to only 81 in 1900.

The sense of woman's emancipation was heightened by a continuing drop in the birthrate and by the abundance of consumer goods. With fewer children to care for and with washing machines and vacuum cleaners to ease their household labor, it seemed that women of the 1920s would have more leisure time. Yet appearances were deceptive. Advertisers eagerly sought out women as buyers of laborsaving consumer products, but wives exercised purchasing power only as delegated by their husbands. In addition, many women were not in the position to put the new devices to use—one-fourth of the homes in Cleveland lacked running water in the 1920s, and three-quarters of the nation's families did not have washing machines. The typical childless woman spent between forty-three and fifty hours a week on household duties; for mothers, the average workweek was fifty-six hours, far longer than that of their husbands. And despite the talk of the "new woman," the flappers fell victim to the sex-role conditioning of their parents. Boys continued to play with guns and grew up to head their families; girls played with dolls and looked forward to careers as wives and mothers. "In the 1920s, as in the 1790s," concluded historian June Sochen, "marriage was the only approved state for women."

The family, however, did change. It became smaller as easier access to effective birth control methods enabled couples to limit the number of their offspring. More and more married women took jobs outside the home, bringing in an income and gaining a measure of independence (although their rate of pay was always lower than that for men). Young people, who had once joined the labor force when they entered their teens, now discovered adolescence as a stage of life. A high school education was no longer uncommon, and college attendance increased.

Prolonged adolescence led to new strains on the family in the form of youthful revolt. Freed of the traditional burden of earning a living at an early age, youths in the 1920s went on a great spree. Heavy drinking, casual sexual encounters, and a constant search for excitement became the hallmarks of the upper-class youth immortalized by F. Scott Fitzgerald. "I have been kissed by dozens of men," one of his characters commented. "I suppose I'll kiss dozens more." The theme of rebellion against parental authority, which runs through all aspects of the 1920s, was at the heart of the youth movement.

Alice Paul broadcasts plans for the dedication of the National Woman Party new national headquarters in Washington, D.C. An ardent campaigner for woman suffrage and equality, Alice Paul rallied support for the cause of women's rights with marches, parades, picketing, and hunger strikes. After passage of the Nineteenth Amendment, Paul and the NWP continued to fight for women's equality; their efforts included drafting an Equal Rights Amendment and proposing it to Congress in 1923. ❖

The Roaring Twenties

Excitement ran high in the cities as both crime waves and highly publicized sports events flourished. Prohibition ushered in such distinctive features of the decade as speakeasies, bootleggers, and bathtub gin. Crime rose sharply as middle- and upper-class Americans willingly broke the law to gain access to alcoholic beverages. City streets became the scene of violent shoot-outs between rival bootleggers; by 1929, Chicago had witnessed more than five hundred gangland murders. Underworld czars controlled illicit empires; Al Capone's produced revenue of $60 million a year.

Sports became a national mania in the 1920s as people found more leisure time. Golf boomed, with some two million men and women playing on nearly five thousand courses across the country. Spectator sports attracted even more attention. Boxing drew huge crowds to see fighters such as Jack Dempsey and Gene Tunney. Baseball attendance soared. More than twenty million fans attended games in 1927, the year Babe Ruth became a national idol by hitting sixty home runs. On college campuses, football became more popular than ever. Universities vied with each other in building massive stadiums, seating upward of seventy thousand people.

In what Frederick Lewis Allen called "the ballyhoo years," the popular yearning for excitement led people to seek vicarious thrills in all kinds of ways—applauding Charles Lindbergh's solo flight across the Atlantic, cheering Gertrude Ederle's swim across the English Channel, and flocking to such bizarre events as six-day bicycle races, dance marathons, and flagpole sittings. It was a time of pure pleasure seeking, when people sought to escape from the increasingly drab world of the assembly line by worshiping heroic individuals.

Sex became another popular topic in the 1920s as Victorian standards began to crumble. Sophisticated city dwellers seemed to be intent on exploring a new freedom in sexual expression. Plays and novels focused on adultery, and the new urban tabloids—led by the *New York Daily News*—delighted in telling their readers about love nests and kept women. The popular songs of the decade, such as "Hot Lips" and "Burning Kisses," were less romantic and more explicit than

Sheik with Sheba *is the title of this John Held, Jr., drawing, which appeared on a 1925 cover of* Judge *magazine. Held's drawings define the image of the "flapper" era—the young woman with rolled-down stockings and rouged knees and the young man with cigarette and pocket flask at the wheel of his car.* ❖

Several new dances were introduced on the dance floors of ballrooms and clubs in the 1920s jazz era. The wild rhythms of the new music encouraged energetic new steps. One of the most popular new dances was the Charleston—a dance associated with the rebellious image of the "flapper." Here, two daring flappers dance the Charleston on the roof of Chicago's Hotel Sherman in 1926. ❖

those of years before. Hollywood exploited the obsession with sex by producing movies with such provocative titles as *Up in Mabel's Room, A Shocking Night,* and *Women and Lovers.* Theda Bara and Clara Bow, the "vamp" and the "It" girl, set the model for feminine seductiveness while Rudolph Valentino became the heartthrob of millions of American women. Young people embraced the new permissiveness joyfully, with the automobile giving couples an easy way to escape parental supervision.

There is considerable debate, however, over the extent of the sexual revolution in the 1920s. Later studies by Dr. Alfred C. Kinsey showed that premarital intercourse was twice as common among women born after 1900 than for those born before the turn of the century. But a contemporary survey of more than two thousand middle-class women by Katherine B. Davis found that only 7 percent of those who were married had had sexual relations before marriage and that only

14 percent of the single women had engaged in intercourse. Actual changes in sexual behavior are beyond the historian's reach, hidden in the privacy of the bedroom, but the old Victorian prudishness was a clear casualty of the 1920s. Sex was no longer a taboo subject, at least in urban areas; men and women now could discuss it openly, and many of them did.

The Flowering of the Arts

The greatest cultural advance of the 1920s was visible in the outpouring of literature. The city gave rise to a new class of intellectuals—writers who commented on the new industrial society. Many had been uprooted by World War I. They were bewildered by the rapidly changing social patterns of the 1920s and appalled by the materialism of American culture. Some fled to Europe to live as expatriates, congregating in Paris cafés to bemoan the loss of American innocence and purity. Others stayed at home, observing and condemning the excesses of a business civilization. All shared a sense of disillusionment and wrote pessimistically of the flawed promise of American life. Yet, ironically, their body of writing revealed a profound creativity that suggested America was coming of age intellectually.

The exiles included the poets T. S. Eliot and Ezra Pound and the novelist Ernest Hemingway. Pound discarded rhyme and meter in a search for clear, cold images that conveyed reality. Like many of the writers of the 1920s, he reacted against World War I, expressing a deep regret for the tragic waste of a whole generation in defense of a "botched civilization."

Eliot, who was born in Missouri but became a British subject, displayed even more profound despair. In *The Waste Land,* which appeared in 1922, he evoked images of fragmentation and sterility that had a powerful impact on the other disillusioned writers of the decade. He reached the depths in *The Hollow Men* (1925), a biting description of the emptiness of modern man.

Ernest Hemingway sought redemption from the modern plight in the romantic individualism of his heroes. Preoccupied with violence, he wrote of men alienated from society who found a sense of identity in their own courage and quest for personal honor. His own experiences, ranging from driving an ambulance in the war to stalking lions in Africa, made him a legendary figure; his greatest impact on other writers, however, came from his sparse, direct, and clean prose style.

The writers who stayed home were equally disdainful of contemporary American life. F. Scott Fitzgerald chronicled American youth in *This Side of Paradise* (1920) and *The Great Gatsby* (1925), writing

T. S. Eliot, whose long poem The Waste Land *owed much to Ezra Pound's critical eye, set the standard by which modern American poetry was judged in the mid-twentieth century. The painting is by English artist Wyndham Lewis.* ❖

in bittersweet prose about "the beautiful and the damned." Amid the glitter of life among the wealthy on Long Island's North Shore came the haunting realization of emptiness and lack of human concern.

Sinclair Lewis became the most popular of the critical novelists. *Main Street,* published in 1920, satirized the values of small-town America as dull, complacent, and narrow-minded; *Babbitt,* which appeared two years later, poked fun at the commercialism of the 1920s, portraying George Babbitt as the stereotype of the lazy, smug middle-class businessman who hailed the decade as a New Era.

Most savage of all was H. L. Mencken, the Baltimore newspaperman and literary critic who founded *American Mercury* magazine in 1923. Declaring war on "Homo boobiens," Mencken mocked everything he found distasteful in America, from the Rotary Club to the Ku Klux Klan. "From Boy Scouts, and from Home Cooking, from Odd Fellows' funerals, from Socialists, from Christians—Good Lord, deliver us," he pleaded. It was not difficult to discover Mencken's dislikes (including Jews, as his published

diary makes clear); the hard part was finding out what he affirmed, other than wit and a clever turn of phrase. A born cynic, he served as a zealous guardian of public rationality in an era of excessive boosterism.

The cultural explosion of the 1920s was surprisingly broad. It included novelists such as Sherwood Anderson and John Dos Passos, who described the way the new machine age undermined such traditional American values as craftsmanship and a sense of community, and playwrights such as Eugene O'Neill, Maxwell Anderson, and Elmer Rice, who added greatly to the stature of American theater. Women writers were particularly effective in dealing with regional themes. Edith Wharton continued to write penetratingly about eastern aristocrats in books such as *The House of Mirth* (1905) and *The Age of Innocence* (1921); Willa Cather and Ellen Glasgow focused on the plight of women in the Midwest and the South, respectively, in their short stories and novels. These writers portrayed their heroines in the traditional roles of wives and mothers; playwright Zona Gale, on the other hand (who won the Pulitzer Prize for drama in 1920 for *Miss Lulu Bett*), used her title character to depict the dilemmas facing an unmarried woman in American society.

Art and especially music made significant advances as well. Edward Hopper and Charles Burchfield

Edward Hopper, Sunday, 1926. *Concentrating on the commonplace in urban life and using light to isolate his subjects, Hopper conveys a sense of the detachment, mystery, and loneliness of life in the modern city.* ❖

captured the ugliness of city life and the loneliness of its inhabitants in their realistic paintings. Aaron Copland and George Gershwin added a new vitality to American music. But African Americans migrating northward brought the most significant contribution: the spread of jazz—first to St. Louis, Kansas City, and Chicago, and finally to New York. The form of jazz known as the blues, so expressive of the suffering of African Americans, became an authentic national folk music, and performers such as Louis Armstrong enjoyed popularity around the world.

The cultural growth of the 1920s was the work of blacks as well as whites. W. E. B. Du Bois, the editor of the newspaper *Crisis,* became the intellectual voice of the black community developing in New York City's Harlem. In 1917, James Weldon Johnson, who had been a professor of literature at Fisk University, published *Fifty Years and Other Poems,* in which the title poem commented on the half century of suffering that had followed the Emancipation Proclamation, and called for the promise of that period to be redeemed:

> Think you that John Brown's spirit stops?
> That Lovejoy was but idly slain?
> Or do you think those precious drops
> From Lincoln's heart were shed in vain?

As other African American writers gathered around them, Du Bois and Johnson became the leaders of the **Harlem Renaissance.** The NAACP moved its headquarters to Harlem, and in 1923, the Urban League began publishing *Opportunity,* a magazine devoted to scholarly studies of racial issues, including black nationalism and emigration to Africa. (See the Feature Essay, "Marcus Garvey: Racial Redemption and Black Nationalism," pp. 730–731.)

African American literature blossomed rapidly. In 1922, critics hailed the appearance of Claude McKay's book of verses, *White Shadows.* In stark images, McKay expressed both his resentment against racial injustice and his pride in blackness. Countee Cullen and Langston Hughes won critical acclaim for the beauty of their poems and the eloquence in their portrayals of the black tragedy.

Art and music also flourished during Harlem's golden age. Plays and concerts at the 135th Street YMCA; floor shows at Happy Rhone's nightclub (attended by many white celebrities); rent parties where jazz musicians played to raise money to help writers, artists, and neighbors pay their bills—all were part of the ferment that made Harlem "the Negro Capital of the World" in the 1920s. "Almost everything seemed possible above 125th Street in the early twenties for these Americans who were determined to thrive separately to better proclaim the ideals of integration," commented historian David Lewis. "You could be black and proud, politically assertive and economically independent, creative and disciplined—or so it seemed."

Although its most famous writers were identified with New York's Harlem, the new African American

Archibald Motley, The Jazz Singers. *Motley, one of the artists of the Harlem Renaissance, combined the traditions of his native New Orleans with the energy and rhythms of 1920s Harlem.* ❖

MARCUS GARVEY

Racial Redemption and Black Nationalism

In a world of wolves one should go armed," wrote Marcus Garvey in 1919, "and one of the most powerful defensive weapons within the reach of Negroes is the practice of race first in all parts of the world." This stress on black solidarity reflected Garvey's belief that racial oppression and exploitation lay at the heart of most of the world's societies. Negro equality, he insisted, would come not through integration or civil rights legislation, but only by transforming black heritage from a mark of inferiority into the basis of a program of pride and liberation. "The world has made being black a crime," he declared, "and instead of making it a crime I hope to make it a virtue."

Nowhere did these ideas find a more enthusiastic reception than in the United States. World War I brought American blacks to northern cities in unprecedented numbers, but the postwar economic slump aggravated already existing racial tensions. Urban slums, job discrimination, disfranchisement, and segregation gave powerful reinforcement to black disillusionment with white America, and to Garvey's message of black nationalism and racial redemption.

Garvey's upbringing in Jamaica, under the color-based caste system of the British-ruled West Indies, convinced him that only black solidarity could lead his race out of subjugation. Dreaming of an independent black Africa, he embraced black nationalism and economic self-help, and in 1914 he molded these ideas into a vision of the Negro race re-

deemed through his new organization, the United Negro Improvement Association (UNIA). In 1916, Garvey toured the United States, and American blacks responded so strongly to his message that he moved UNIA headquarters to Harlem. With a new weekly, the *Negro World*, Garvey advanced his crusade for racial redemption and separatism. The paper extolled the beauty of black skin color and African features, and his editorials demanded economic self-reliance and collective black action. "Up, you mighty race," he exhorted. "You can accomplish what you will."

Garvey put his principles into practice in 1919 when he launched the Black Star Line (BSL), a steamship corporation that he believed would demonstrate black competence in business, enhance racial pride, and strengthen the bonds among blacks worldwide. A company brochure offered every black investor the promise of easy dividends and an opportunity to climb the ladder of success for only $5 per share. In November 1919, the BSL launched its first of three ships and stock sales soared. Spirits were equally high at UNIA's first international convention, held in New York in 1920, which brought together several thousand delegates from all forty-eight states and more than twenty countries. After leading the opening day parade, which stretched for several miles through the streets of Harlem, Garvey delivered the keynote address before a crowd of twenty-five-thousand:

We are the descendants of a suffering people. We are the descendents

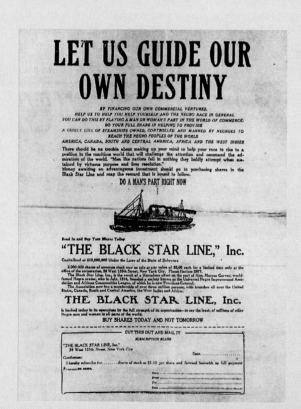

Marcus Garvey sought investors for his Black Star Line with ads such as this in his weekly newspaper, *The Negro World*. He hoped to use ships of the line to transport blacks from America to Africa and there to realize his dream of an independent black Africa. ◆

of a people determined to suffer no longer. We shall now organize the 400,000,000 Negroes of the world into a vast organization to plant the banner of freedom on the great continent of Africa . . . If Europe is for Europeans, then Africa shall be for the black peoples of the world.

Others echoed his sentiments. UNIA delegates meeting in Harlem approved the Declaration of Rights of the Negro Peoples of the World, which declared that the black man had "an inherent right . . . to possess himself of Africa." The convention also urged the teaching of black history in schools, demanded an end to lynching and segregation, and elected Garvey as the provisional president of Africa.

Garvey's vision began to unravel with his Liberian Rehabilitation project. The black African republic welcomed his offer of financial and technical assistance through the UNIA, and in late 1920 he began to raise money for a reconstruction loan. In subsequent months, however, he diverted much of the proceeds to keep the ailing BSL afloat. With large capital outlays, poor management, and high operating costs, Garvey's dream of a maritime empire verged on financial collapse. The "establishment" black press accused Garvey of adventurism, opportunism, and diversion from the real path of progress. His views on the Klu Klux Klan made him even more controversial. While deploring Klan terror and violence, Garvey voiced appreciation of Klan candor on race relations:

I regard the Klan, the Anglo-Saxon Clubs, and White American societies as better friends of the race than all other groups of hypocritical whites put together. I like honesty and fair play. You may call me a Klansman if you will, but potentially every white man is a Klansman, as far as the Negro in competition with whites socially, economically, and politically is concerned . . .

So stark a statement of racial separatism and suspicion of whites appalled other black leaders. W. E. B. Du Bois described him as "the most dangerous enemy of the Negro race," and a black newspaper promised to "drive Garvey and Garveyism in all its sinister viciousness from the American soil." Yet Marcus Garvey and his message endured; by 1921, the UNIA had more than eight hundred official and unofficial branches.

Garvey's battle with black leaders was but one of his challenges. In May 1923, he and three associates went on trial for mail fraud in the sale of BSL stock. The evidence suggested that while BSL's leaders made poor business decisions, neither Garvey nor his executives drew large salaries or lived lavishly at company expense. The BSL may have been ill-advised and badly managed, but it does not appear to have been fraudulent. The jury, however, found Garvey guilty (despite acquitting his codefendants), and the judge sentenced him to the maximum five-year-term.

On February 8, 1925, Garvey entered the federal penitentiary at Atlanta. Ironically, once he was behind bars, he gained the support of many of his erstwhile detractors who protested the severity of white justice. Under mounting pressure, President Coolidge commuted Garvey's sentence in 1927. Immediate deportation followed, as required by U.S. immigration law. On December 10, 1927, Garvey returned to Jamaica, where one of the largest crowds in the island's history greeted him with a hero's welcome.

Garvey tried in vain to revitalize the UNIA in Jamaica, but with the onset of the Great Depression, American blacks concentrated more on survival than on racial nationalism. Garvey slipped into obscurity and died in 1940 at the age of fifty-two. Despite this end, however, his movement had inspired many blacks who were disgusted by the hypocrisy of American democracy and frustrated by the failure of gradualism to improve their lot. His appeals offered them an alternative to the legalistic approach of the more conservative black establishment, and an emphasis on pride in their heritage that influenced many black Americans in succeeding generations.

Marcus Garvey's advocacy of black nationalism and independent black entrepreneurship were, in part, discredited by his trial and conviction for mail fraud. ❖

W. E. B. Du Bois (left), editor of The Crisis, *was one of the intellectual and political leaders of the Harlem Renaissance, which fostered the rise of literary figures such as Zora Neale Hurston (center) and Langston Hughes (right). Hurston wrote four novels and two books of black folklore that "helped to remind the Renaissance . . . of the richness in racial heritage." Hughes wrote sensitively and eloquently of the world of common black people.* ❖

cultural awareness spread to other cities in the form of poetry circles and theater groups. The number of African Americans graduating from college rose from 391 in 1920 to 1903 by 1929. Although blacks were still an oppressed minority in the America of the 1920s, they had taken major strides toward achieving cultural and intellectual fulfillment.

In retrospect, there is a striking paradox about the literary flowering of the 1920s. Nearly all the writers, black as well as white, cried out against the conformity and materialism of the contemporary scene. They were critical of mass production and reliance on the machine; they wrote wistfully of the disappearance of the artisan and of a more relaxed way of life. Few took any interest in politics or in social reform. They retreated instead into individualism, seeking an escape into their art from the prevailing business civilization. Whether they went abroad or stayed home, the writers of the 1920s turned inward to avoid being swept up in the consumer goods revolution. Yet despite their withdrawal, and perhaps because of it, they produced an astonishingly rich and varied body of work. American writing had a greater intensity and depth than in the past; American writers, despite their alienation, had placed their country in the forefront of world literature.

THE RURAL COUNTERATTACK

The shift of population from the countryside to the city led to heightened social tensions in the 1920s. Intent on preserving traditional social values, rural Americans saw in the city all that was evil in contem-

porary life. Saloons, whorehouses, little Italys and little Polands, communist cells, free love, and atheism—all were identified with the city. Accordingly, the countryside struck back at the newly dominant urban areas, aiming to restore the primacy of the Anglo-Saxon and predominantly Protestant culture they revered. This counterattack won considerable support in the cities from those so recently uprooted from their rural backgrounds.

Other factors contributed to the intensity of the counterattack. The war had unleashed a nationalistic spirit that craved unity and conformity. In a nation where one-third of the people were foreign born, the attack on immigrants and the call for 100 percent Americanism took on a frightening zeal. When the war was over, groups such as the American Legion tried to root out "un-American" behavior and insisted on cultural as well as political conformity. The prewar progressive reform spirit added to the social tension. Stripped of much of its former idealism, progressivism focused on such social problems as drinking and illiteracy to justify repressive measures such as Prohibition and immigration restriction. The result was tragic. Amid the emergence of a new urban culture, the movements aimed at preserving the values of an earlier America succeeded only in complicating life in an already difficult period of cultural transition.

The Fear of Radicalism

The first and most intense outbreak of national alarm, the **Red Scare,** came in 1919. The heightened nationalism of World War I, aimed at achieving unity at the expense of ethnic diversity, found a new target in bolshevism. The Russian Revolution and the triumph of Marxism frightened many Americans. A growing turn to communism among American radicals (especially the foreign born) accelerated these fears. Although the numbers involved were tiny—at most there were sixty thousand communists in the United States in 1919—they were highly visible. Located in the cities, their influence appeared to be magnified with the outbreak of widespread labor unrest.

A general strike in Seattle, a police strike in Boston, and a violent strike in the iron and steel industry thoroughly alarmed the American people in the spring and summer of 1919. A series of bombings led to panic. First the mayor of strikebound Seattle received a small brown package containing a homemade bomb; then an alert New York postal employee detected sixteen bombs addressed to a variety of famous citizens (including John D. Rockefeller); and finally, on June 2, a bomb shattered the front of Attorney General A. Mitchell Palmer's home. Although the man who delivered it was blown to pieces, authorities quickly identified him as an Italian anarchist from Philadelphia.

In the ensuing public outcry, Attorney General Palmer led the attack on the alien threat. A Quaker and progressive, Palmer abandoned his earlier liberalism to launch a massive roundup of foreign-born radicals. In a series of raids that began on November 7, federal agents seized suspected anarchists and communists and held them for deportation with no regard for due process of law. In December, 249 aliens—including such well-known radical leaders as Emma Goldman and Alexander Berkman—were sent to Russia aboard the *Buford*, dubbed the "Soviet Ark" by the press. Nearly all were innocent of the charges against them. A month later, Palmer rounded up nearly four thousand suspected communists in a single evening. Federal agents broke into homes, meeting halls, and union offices without search warrants. Many native-born Americans were caught in the dragnet and spent several days in jail before being released; aliens rounded up were deported without hearings or trials.

For a time, it seemed that the Red Scare reflected the prevailing views of the American people. Instead of condemning their government's action, citizens voiced their approval and even urged more drastic steps. One patriot said his solution to the alien problem was simple: "S.O.S.—ship or shoot." General Leonard Wood, the former army chief of staff, favored placing Bolsheviks on "ships of stone with sails of lead," while evangelist Billy Sunday preferred to take "these ornery, wild-eyed Socialists" and "stand them up before a firing squad and save space on our ships." Inflamed by public statements like these, a group of legionnaires in Centralia, Washington, dragged a radical from the town jail, castrated him, and hanged him from a railway bridge. The coroner's report blandly stated that the victim "jumped off with a rope around his neck and then shot himself full of holes."

The very extremism of the Red Scare led to its rapid demise. In early 1920, courageous government officials from the Department of Labor insisted on due process and full hearings before anyone else was deported.

The explosion in Wall Street on September 16, 1920, left thirty-three dead and nearly two hundred wounded. Attorney General Palmer saw the blast as the work of a communist conspiracy, but relatively few Americans subscribed to his view. ❖

Ben Shahn's work The Passion of Sacco and Vanzetti *(1931–1932) depicts the members of the committee who investigated the trial and confirmed its fairness. (*The Passion of Sacco and Vanzetti *[1931–1932] by Ben Shahn, from Sacco and Vanzetti series of 23 paintings. Tempera, 84-1/2 x 48 inches. From the collection of Whitney Museum of American Art. Gift of Edith and Milton Lowenthal. © Estate of Ben Shahn/Licensed by VAGA, New York, NY.)* ❖

Prominent public leaders began to speak out against the acts of terror. Charles Evans Hughes, the defeated GOP candidate in 1916, offered to defend six socialists expelled from the New York legislature; Ohio Senator Warren G. Harding, the embodiment of middle-class values, expressed his opinion that "too much has been said about bolshevism in America." Finally, Palmer himself, with evident presidential ambition, went too far. In April 1920, he warned of a vast revolution to occur on May 1; the entire New York City police force, some eleven thousand strong, was placed on duty to prepare for imminent disaster. When no bombings or violence took place on May Day, the public began to react against

Palmer's hysteria. Despite a violent explosion on Wall Street in September that killed thirty-three people, the Red Scare died out by the end of 1920. Palmer passed into obscurity, the tiny Communist party became torn with factionalism, and the American people tried hard to forget their loss of balance.

Yet the Red Scare exerted a continuing influence on American society in the 1920s. The foreign born lived in the uneasy realization that they were viewed with hostility and suspicion. Two Italian aliens in Massachusetts, Nicola Sacco and Bartolomeo Vanzetti, were arrested in May 1920 for a payroll robbery and murder. They faced a prosecutor and jury who condemned them more for their ideas than for any evidence of criminal conduct and a judge who referred to them as "those anarchist bastards." Despite a worldwide effort that became the chief liberal cause of the 1920s, the courts rejected all appeals. Sacco, a shoemaker, and Vanzetti, a fish peddler, died in the electric chair on August 23, 1927. Their fate symbolized the bigotry and intolerance that lasted through the 1920s and made that decade one of the least attractive in American history.

Prohibition

In December 1917, Congress adopted the Eighteenth Amendment, prohibiting the manufacture and sale of alcoholic beverages. A little over a year later, Nebraska was the necessary thirty-sixth state to ratify, and **prohibition** became the law of the land.

Beginning January 16, 1920, the Volstead Act, which implemented prohibition, banned most commercial production and distribution of beverages containing more than one-half of 1 percent of alcohol by volume. (Exceptions were made for medicinal and religious uses of wine and spirits. Production for one's own private use was also allowed.) Prohibition was the result of both a rural effort of the Anti-Saloon League, backed by Methodist and Baptist clergymen, and the urban progressive concern over the social disease of drunkenness, especially among industrial workers. The moral issue had already led to the enactment of prohibition laws in twenty-six states by 1920; the real tragedy would occur in the effort to extend this "noble experiment" to the growing cities, where it was deeply resented by ethnic groups such as the Germans and the Irish and was almost totally disregarded by the well-to-do and the sophisticated.

Prohibition did in fact lead to a decline in drinking. Americans consumed much less alcohol in the 1920s than in the prewar years. Rural areas became totally dry, and in the cities, the consumption of alcoholic beverages dropped sharply among the lower classes, who could not afford the high prices for bootleg liquor. Among the middle class and the wealthy, however, drinking became fashionable. Bootleggers supplied whiskey, which quickly replaced lighter spirits such as wine and beer. The alcohol was either smuggled from abroad (a $40 million a year business by 1924) or illicitly manufactured in America. Exotic products such as Jackass Brandy, Soda Pop Moon, and Yack Yack Bourbon were common—and all could be fatal. Despite the risk of illness or death from extraordinarily high alcohol content or poorly controlled distillation, Americans consumed some 150 million quarts of liquor a year in the 1920s. Bootleggers took in nearly $2 billion annually, about 2 percent of the gross national product.

Urban resistance to prohibition finally led to its repeal in 1933. But in the intervening years, it damaged American society by breeding a profound disrespect for the law. The flamboyant excesses of bootleggers were only the more obvious evils spawned by prohibition. In city after city, police openly tolerated the traffic in liquor, and judges and prosecutors agreed to let bootleggers pay merely token fines, creating almost a system of licenses. Prohibition satisfied the countryside's desire for vindication, yet rural and urban America alike suffered from this overzealous attempt to legislate morals.

The Ku Klux Klan

The most ominous expression of protest against the new urban culture was the rebirth of the Ku Klux Klan. On Thanksgiving night in 1915, on Stone Mountain in Georgia, Colonel William J. Simmons and thirty-four followers founded the modern Klan. Only "native born, white, gentile Americans" were permitted to join "the Invisible Empire, Knights of the Ku Klux Klan." Membership grew slowly during World War I, but after 1920, fueled by postwar fears and shrewd promotional techniques, the Klan mushroomed. In villages, towns, and small cities across the nation, Anglo-Saxon Protestant men flocked into the newly formed chapters, seeking to relieve their anxiety over a changing society by embracing the Klan's unusual rituals and by demonstrating their hatred against blacks, aliens, Jews, and Catholics.

The Klan of the 1920s, unlike the night riders of the post–Civil War era, was not just antiblack; the threat to American culture, as Klansmen perceived it, came from aliens—Italians and Russians, Jews and Catholics. They attributed much of the tension and conflict in society to the prewar flood of immigrants,

A 1925 Ku Klux Klan demonstration in Cincinnati, Ohio, attended by nearly thirty thousand robed members and marked by the induction of eight thousand young boys in the Junior Order. Only native-born, white Americans "who believe in the tenets of the Christian religion" were admitted into the Klan. The original Klan, formed during the Reconstruction era to terrorize former slaves, disbanded in 1869. The Klan that formed in 1915 declined after the mid-1920s but did not officially disband until 1944. Two years later, a third Klan emerged, focusing on the civil rights movement and communism. ❖

foreigners who spoke different languages, worshiped in strange churches, and lived in distant, threatening cities. The Klansmen struck back by coming together and enforcing their own values. They punished blacks who did not know their place, women who practiced the new morality, and aliens who refused to conform. Beating, flogging, burning with acid—even murder—were condoned. They also tried more peaceful methods of coercion, formulating codes of behavior and seeking communitywide support.

The Klan entered politics, at first hesitantly, then with growing confidence. The KKK gained control of the legislatures in Texas, Oklahoma, Oregon, and Indiana; in 1924, it blocked a resolution of censure at the Democratic national convention. With an estimated five million members by the mid-1920s, the Klan seemed to be fully established.

Its appeal lay in the sanctuary it offered to insecure and anxious people. Protestant to the core, the members found in the local Klavern a reassurance missing in their churches. The poor and ignorant became enchanted with the titles, ranging from Imperial Wizard to Grand Dragon, and gloried in the ritual that centered around the letter K. Thus each Klan had its own Klalendar, held its weekly Klonklave in the local Klavern, and followed the rules set forth in the Kloran. Members found a sense of identity in the group activities, whether they were peaceful picnics, ominous parades in white robes, or fiery cross burnings at night.

Although it was a men's organization, the Klan did not neglect the family. There was a Women's Order, a Junior Order for boys, and a Tri-K Klub for girls. Members had to be born in America, but foreign-born Protestants were allowed to join a special Krusaders affiliate. Only blacks, Catholics, Jews, and prostitutes were beyond redemption to these lonely and anxious men who came together to chant:

> United we stick
> Divided we're stuck.
> The better we stick
> The better we Klux!

The Klan fell even more quickly than it rose. Its more violent activities—which included kidnapping, lynching, setting fire to synagogues and Catholic churches, and, in one case, murdering a priest—began to offend the nation's conscience. Misuse of funds and sexual scandals among Klan leaders, notably in Indiana, repelled many of the rank and file; effective counterattacks by traditional politicians ousted the KKK from control in Texas and Oklahoma. Membership declined sharply after 1925; by the end of the decade, the Klan had virtually disappeared. But its spirit lived on, testimony to the recurring demons of nativism and hatred that have surfaced periodically throughout the American experience.

Immigration Restriction

The nativism that permeated the Klan found its most successful outlet in the immigration legislation of the 1920s. The sharp increase in immigration in the late nineteenth century had led to a broad-based movement, spearheaded by organized labor and by New England aristocrats such as Henry Cabot Lodge, to restrict the flow of people from Europe. In 1917, over Wilson's veto, Congress enacted a literacy test that reduced the number of immigrants allowed into the country. The war caused a much more drastic decline—from an average of 1 million a year between 1900 and 1914 to only 110,000 in 1918.

After the armistice, however, rumors began to spread of an impending flood of people seeking to escape war-ravaged Europe. Kenneth Roberts, a popular historical novelist, warned that all Europe was on the move, with only the limits of available steamship space likely to stem the flow. Worried congressmen spoke of a "barbarian horde" and a "foreign tide" that would inundate the United States with "dangerous and deadly enemies of the country." Even though the actual number of immigrants, 810,000 in 1920 (fewer than the prewar yearly average), did not match these projections, Congress in 1921 passed an emergency immigration act. The new quota system restricted immigration from Europe to 3 percent of the number of nationals from each country living in the United States in 1910.

The 1921 act failed to satisfy the nativists. The quotas still permitted more than 500,000 Europeans to come to the United States in 1923, nearly half of them from southern and eastern Europe. The declining percentage of Nordic immigrants alarmed writers such as Madison Grant, who warned the American people the Anglo-Saxon stock that had founded the nation was about to be overwhelmed by lesser breeds with inferior genes. "These immigrants adopt the language of the native American, they wear his clothes and are beginning to take his women, but they seldom adopt his religion or understand his ideals," Grant wrote.

Psychologists, relying on primitive IQ tests used by the army in World War I, confirmed this judgment. (See the Feature Essay in Chapter 24, "Measuring the Mind," pp. 704–705.) One senator claimed that all the nation's ills were due to an "intermingled and mongrelized people" as he demanded that racial purity replace the older reliance on the melting pot. In 1924, Congress adopted the **National Origins Quota Act,** which limited immigration from Europe to 150,000 a year; allocated most of the available slots to immigrants from Great Britain, Ireland, Germany, and Scandinavia; and banned all Asian immigrants. The measure passed Congress with overwhelming rural support.

The new restrictive legislation marked the most enduring achievement of the rural counterattack. Unlike the Red Scare, Prohibition, and the Klan, the quota system would survive until the 1960s, enforcing a racist bias that excluded Asians and limited the immigration of Italians, Greeks, and Poles to a few thousand a year while permitting a steady stream of Irish, English, and Scandinavian immigrants. The large corporations, no longer dependent on armies of unskilled immigrant workers, did not object to the 1924 law; the machine had replaced the immigrant on the assembly line. Yet even here the victory was not complete. A growing tide of Mexican laborers, exempt from the quota act, flowed northward across the Rio Grande to fill the continuing need for unskilled workers on the farms and in the service trades. The Mexican immigrants, as many as 100,000 a year, marked the strengthening of an element in the national ethnic mosaic that would grow in size and influence until it became a major force in modern American society.

The Fundamentalist Challenge

The most significant—and, as it turned out, longest-lasting—challenge to the new urban culture was rooted in the traditional religious beliefs of millions of Americans who felt alienated from city life, from science, and from much of what modernization entailed. Sometimes this challenge was direct, as when Christian fundamentalists campaigned against the teaching of evolution in the public schools. Their success in Tennessee touched off a court battle, the **Scopes trial,** that drew the attention of the entire country to the small town of Dayton in the summer of 1925. (See the Law and Society essay, "The Scopes 'Monkey' Trial," pp. 743–748.)

Other aspects of the fundamentalist challenge were more subtle but no less important in countering the modernizing trend. As middle- and upper-class Americans drifted into a genteel Christianity that stressed good works and respectability, the Baptist and Methodist churches continued to hold on to the old faith. In addition, aggressive fundamentalist sects such as the Churches of Christ, the Pentecostals, and Jehovah's Witnesses grew rapidly. While church membership increased from 41.9 million in 1916 to 54.5 million in 1926, the number of churches actually declined during the decade. More and more rural dwellers drove their cars into town instead of going to the local crossroads chapel.

Many of those who came to the city in the 1920s brought their religious beliefs with them and found new outlets for their traditional ideas. Thus evangelist Aimee Semple McPherson enjoyed amazing success in Los Angeles with her Church of the Four-Square Gospel, building the Angelus Temple to seat more than 5000 worshipers. And in Fort Worth, the Reverend J. Frank Norris erected a 6000-seat sanctuary for the First Baptist Church, bathing it in spotlights so it could be seen for thirty miles across the North Texas prairie.

Far from dying out, as divinity professor Thomas G. Oden noted, biblical fundamentalism retained "remarkable grassroots strength among the organization men and the industrialized mass society of the 20th century." The rural counterattack, while challenged by the city, did enable some older American values to survive in the midst of the new mass production culture.

POLITICS OF THE 1920s

The tensions between the city and the countryside also shaped the course of politics in the 1920s. On the surface, it was a Republican decade. The GOP ("Grand Old Party") controlled the White House from 1921 to 1933 and had majorities in both houses of Congress from 1919 to 1931. The Republicans used their return to power after World War I to halt further reform legislation and to establish a friendly relationship between government and business. Important shifts were taking place, however, in the American electorate. The Democrats, although divided into competing urban and rural wings, were laying the groundwork for the future by winning over millions of new voters, especially among the ethnic groups in the cities. The rising tide of urban voters indicated a fundamental shift away from the Republicans toward a new Democratic majority.

Harding, Coolidge, and Hoover

The Republicans regained the White House in 1920 with the election of Warren G. Harding of Ohio. A dark-horse contender, Harding won the GOP nomination when the convention deadlocked and he became the compromise choice. Handsome and dignified, Harding reflected both the virtues and blemishes of small-town America. Originally a newspaper publisher in Marion, he had made many friends and few enemies throughout his career as a legislator, lieutenant governor, and finally, after 1914, U.S. senator. Conventional in outlook, Harding was a genial man who lacked the capacity to govern and who, as president, broadly delegated power.

He made some good cabinet choices, notably Charles Evans Hughes as secretary of state and

Herbert C. Hoover as secretary of commerce, but two corrupt officials—Attorney General Harry Daugherty and Secretary of the Interior Albert Fall—sabotaged his administration. Daugherty became involved in a series of questionable deals that led ultimately to his forced resignation; Fall was the chief figure in the **Teapot Dome scandal.** Two oil promoters gave Fall nearly $400,000 in loans and bribes; in return, he helped them secure leases on naval oil reserves in Elk Hills, California, and Teapot Dome, Wyoming. The scandal came to light after Harding's death from a heart attack in 1923. Fall eventually served a year in jail, and the reputation of the Harding administration never recovered.

Vice President Calvin Coolidge assumed the presidency upon Harding's death, and his honesty and integrity quickly reassured the nation. Coolidge, born in Vermont of old Yankee stock, had first gained national attention in 1919 as governor of Massachusetts when he had dealt firmly with a Boston police strike by declaring, "There is no right to strike against the public safety by anybody, anywhere, any time." A reserved, reticent man, Coolidge became famous for his epigrams, which contemporaries mistook for wisdom. "The business of America is business," he proclaimed. "The man who builds a factory builds a temple; the man who works there worships there." Consistent with this philosophy, he believed his duty was simply to preside benignly, not govern the nation. "Four-fifths of all our troubles in this life would disappear," he said, "if we would just sit down and be still." Calvin Coolidge, one observer noted, "aspired to become the least President the country ever had; he attained his desire." Satisfied with the prosperity of the mid-1920s, the people responded favorably. Coolidge was elected to a full term by a wide margin in 1924.

When Coolidge announced in 1927 that he did not "choose to run," Herbert Hoover became the Republican choice to succeed him. By far the ablest GOP leader of the decade, Hoover epitomized the American myth of the self-made man. Orphaned as a boy, he had worked his way through Stanford University and had gained both wealth and fame as a mining engineer. During World War I, he had displayed admirable administrative skills in directing Wilson's food program at home and relief activities abroad. Sober, intelligent, and immensely hardworking, Hoover embodied the nation's faith in individualism and free enterprise.

As secretary of commerce under Harding and Coolidge, he had sought cooperation between government and business. He used his office to assist American manufacturers and exporters in expanding their overseas trade, and he strongly supported a trade association movement to encourage cooperation rather than cutthroat competition among smaller American companies. He did not view business and government as antagonists. Instead, he saw them as partners, working together to achieve efficiency and affluence for all Americans. His optimistic view of the future led him to declare in his speech accepting the Republican presidential nomination in 1928 that "we in America today are nearer to the final triumph over poverty than ever before in the history of any land."

Republican Policies

During the 1920 campaign, Warren Harding urged a return to "not heroism, but healing, not nostrums, but normalcy." Misreading his speechwriter's "normality," he coined a new word that became the theme for the Republican administrations of the 1920s. Aware that the public was tired of zealous reform-minded presidents such as Teddy Roosevelt and Woodrow Wilson, Harding and his successors sought a return to traditional Republican policies. In some areas they were successful, but in others the Republican leaders were forced to adjust to the new realities of a mass production society. The result was a mixture of traditional and innovative measures that was neither wholly reactionary nor entirely progressive.

The most obvious attempt to go back to the Republicanism of William McKinley came in tariff and tax policy. Fearful of a flood of postwar European imports, Congress passed an emergency tariff act in 1921 and followed it a year later with the protectionist Fordney-McCumber Tariff Act. The net effect was to raise the basic rates substantially over the moderate Underwood Tariff schedules of the Wilson period.

Secretary of the Treasury Andrew Mellon, a wealthy Pittsburgh banker and industrialist, worked hard to achieve a similar return to normalcy in taxation. Condemning the high wartime tax rates on businesses and wealthy individuals, Mellon pressed for repealing an excess profits tax on corporations and slashing personal rates on the very rich. Using the new budget system adopted by Congress in 1921, he reduced government spending from its World War I peak of $18 billion to just over $3 billion by 1925, thereby creating a slight surplus. Congress responded in 1926 by cutting the highest income tax bracket to a modest 20 percent.

The revenue acts of the 1920s greatly reduced the burden of taxation; by the end of the decade, the government was collecting one-third less than it had in 1921, and the number of people paying income taxes dropped from more than 6.5 million to 4 million. Yet

In this 1925 political cartoon, Clifford Berryman depicts Calvin Coolidge and Andrew Mellon in a car racing downhill to tax reductions. The wealthy benefited most from Mellon's tax reduction policies, paying as much as one third less in 1926 than they had paid in 1921. ❖

the greatest relief went to the wealthy. The public was shocked to learn in the 1930s that J. P. Morgan, Jr., and his nineteen partners had paid no income tax at all during the depths of the Great Depression.

The growing crisis in American farming during the decade forced the Republican administrations to seek new solutions. The end of the European war led to a sharp decline in farm prices and a return to the problem of overproduction. Southern and western lawmakers formed a farm bloc in Congress to press for special legislation for American agriculture. The farm bloc supported the higher tariffs, which included protection for constituents' crops, and helped secure passage of legislation to create federal supervision over stockyards, packinghouses, and grain trading.

This special-interest legislation failed to get at the root of overproduction, however. Farmers then supported more controversial measures designed to raise domestic crop prices by having the government sell the surplus overseas at low world prices. Coolidge vetoed the legislation on grounds that it involved unwarranted government interference in the economy.

Yet the government's role in the economy increased rather than lessened in the 1920s. Republicans widened the scope of federal activity and nearly doubled the ranks of government employees. Herbert

Hoover led the way in the Commerce Department, establishing new bureaus to help make American industry more efficient in housing, transportation, and mining. Under his leadership, the government encouraged corporations to develop welfare programs that undercut trade unions, and he tried to minimize labor disturbances by devising new federal machinery to mediate disputes. Instead of going back to the laissez-faire tradition of the nineteenth century, the Republican administrations of the 1920s were pioneering a close relationship between government and private business.

The Divided Democrats

While the Republicans ruled in the 1920s, the Democrats seemed bent on self-destruction. The Wilson coalition fell apart in 1920 as pent-up dissatisfaction stemming from the war enabled Harding to win by a landslide. The pace of the second Industrial Revolution and the growing urbanization split the party in two. One faction was centered in the rural South and West. Traditional Democrats who had supported Wilson stood for prohibition, fundamentalism, the Klan, and other facets of the rural counterattack against the city. In contrast, a new breed of Democrat was emerging in the metropolitan areas of the North and Midwest. Immigrants and their descendants began to become active in the Democratic party. Catholic or Jewish in religion and strongly opposed to prohibition, they had little in common with their rural counterparts.

The split within the party surfaced dramatically at the national convention in New York in 1924. Held in Madison Square Garden, a hall built in the 1890s and too small and cramped for the more than one thousand delegates, the convention soon degenerated into what one observer described as a "snarling, cursing, tenuous, suicidal, homicidal roughhouse." City slickers mocked the "rubes and hicks" from the "sticks"; populist orators struck back by denouncing the city as "wanting in national ideals, devoid of conscience . . . rooted in corruption, directed by greed and dominated by selfishness." An urban resolution to condemn the Ku Klux Klan led to a spirited response from the rural faction and its defeat by a single vote. Then for nine days, in the midst of a stifling heat wave, the delegates divided between Alfred E. Smith, the governor of New York, and William G. McAdoo of California,

THE ELECTION OF 1924

Candidate	Party	Popular Vote	Electoral Vote
Coolidge	Republican	15,717,553	382
Davis	Democrat	8,386,169	136
La Follette	Progressive	4,814,050	13

Wilson's secretary of the treasury. When it became clear that neither the city nor the rural candidate could win a majority, both men withdrew; on the 103rd ballot, the weary Democrats finally chose John W. Davis, a former West Virginia congressman and New York corporation lawyer, as their compromise nominee.

In the ensuing election, the conservative Davis had difficulty setting his views apart from those of Republican president Calvin Coolidge. For the discontented, Senator Robert La Follette of Wisconsin offered an alternative by running on an independent Progressive party ticket. Coolidge won easily, receiving 15 million votes to 8 million for Davis and nearly 5 million for La Follette. Davis had made the poorest showing of any Democratic candidate in the twentieth century.

Yet the Democrats were in far better shape than this setback indicated. Beginning in 1922, the party had made heavy inroads into the GOP majority in Congress. The Democrats took seventy-eight seats away from the Republicans in that election, many of them in the cities of the East and Midwest. In New York alone, they gained thirteen new congressmen, all but one in districts with heavy immigrant populations. Even in 1924, the Republican vote in large cities declined as many urban voters chose La Follette in the absence of an attractive Democratic candidate. In 1926, the Democrats came within one vote of controlling the Senate and picked up nine more seats in the House in metropolitan areas. The large cities were swinging clearly into the Democratic column; all the party needed was a charismatic leader who could fuse the older rural elements with the new urban voters.

The Election of 1928

The selection of Al Smith as the Democratic candidate in 1928 indicated the growing power of the city. Born on the Lower East Side of Manhattan of mixed Irish-German ancestry, Smith was the prototype of the urban Democrat. He was Catholic; he was associated with a big-city machine; he was a "wet" who wanted to end prohibition. Starting out in the Fulton Fish Market as a boy, he had joined Tammany Hall and gradually climbed the political ladder, rising from sub-

poena server to state legislator to governor, a post he held with distinction for nearly a decade. Rejected by rural Democrats in 1924, he still had to prove he could unite the South and West behind his leadership. His lack of education, poor grammar, and distinctive New York accent all hurt him, as did his eastern provincialism. When reporters asked him about his appeal in the states west of the Mississippi, he replied, "What states are west of the Mississippi?"

The choice facing the American voter in 1928 seemed unusually clear-cut. Herbert Hoover was a Protestant, a dry, and an old-stock American, who stood for efficiency and individualism; Smith was a Catholic, a wet, and a descendant of immigrants, who was closely associated with big-city politics. Just as Smith appealed to new voters in the cities, so Hoover won the support of many old-line Democrats who feared the city, Tammany Hall, and the pope.

Yet beneath the surface, as Allan J. Lichtman points out, there were "striking similarities between Smith and Hoover." Both were self-made men who embodied the American belief in freedom of opportunity and upward mobility. Neither advocated any significant degree of economic change nor any redistribution of national wealth or power. Though religion proved to be the most important issue in the minds of the voters, hurting Smith far more than prohibition or his identification with the city, the Democratic candidate's failure to spotlight the growing cracks in prosperity or to offer alternative economic policies ensured his defeat.

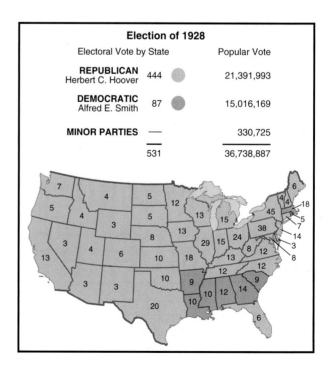

Election of 1928

	Electoral Vote by State	Popular Vote
REPUBLICAN Herbert C. Hoover	444	21,391,993
DEMOCRATIC Alfred E. Smith	87	15,016,169
MINOR PARTIES	—	330,725
	531	36,738,887

CHRONOLOGY

1919	U.S. agents arrest 1700 in Red Scare raids ❖ Congress passes Volstead Act over Wilson's veto (October)
1920	Budget Bureau set up to oversee federal spending ❖ Nineteenth Amendment passed, granting women the right to vote ❖ Transcontinental airmail service inaugurated (September) ❖ WWJ-Detroit broadcasts first commercial radio program (November)
1921	Congress enacts quotas for European immigrants
1923	Newspapers expose Ku Klux Klan graft, torture, and murder ❖ Henry Luce begins publishing *Time* magazine (March)
1924	Senate probes Teapot Dome scandal ❖ Veterans' World War I bonus bill passed
1925	John Scopes convicted of teaching theory of evolution in violation of Tennessee law (July)
1926	First Martha Graham modern dance recital (April)
1927	Charles Lindbergh completes first nonstop transatlantic flight from New York to Paris (May) ❖ Coolidge vetoes farm price-control bill ❖ Sacco and Vanzetti executed (August) ❖ The movie *The Jazz Singer* features singing-talking soundtrack

The 1928 election was a dubious victory for the Republicans. Hoover won easily, defeating Smith by more than six million votes and carrying such traditionally Democratic states as Oklahoma, Texas, and Florida. But Smith succeeded for the first time in winning a majority of votes for the Democrats in the nation's twelve largest cities. A new Democratic electorate was emerging, consisting of Catholics and Jews, Irish and Italians, Poles and Greeks. Now the task was to unite the traditional Democrats of the South and West with the urban voters of the Northeast and Midwest.

CONCLUSION: THE OLD AND THE NEW

The election-night celebrations at Hoover campaign headquarters were muted by prohibition and by the president-elect's natural reserve. Had Hoover known what lay just ahead for the country, and for his presidency, no doubt the party would have been even more somber.

During the 1920s, America struggled to enter the modern era. The economics of mass production and the politics of urbanization drove the country forward, but the persistent appeal of individualism and rural-based values held it back. Americans achieved greater prosperity than ever before, but the prosperity was unevenly distributed. Further, as the outbursts of nativism, ethnic and racial bigotry, and intolerance revealed, prosperity hardly guaranteed generosity or unity. Nor, for that matter, did it guarantee continued prosperity, even for those who benefited initially. As much as America changed during the 1920s, in one crucial respect the country remained as before. The American economy, for all its remarkable productive capacity, was astonishingly fragile. This was the message Hoover was soon to learn.

RECOMMENDED READING

William Leuchtenburg provides the best overview of the 1920s in *The Perils of Prosperity, 1914–1932* (1958). He stresses the theme of rural-urban conflict and claims that the achievements of the decade were more significant than its failures. Ellis Hawley, *The Great War and the Search for a Modern Order* (1979), and Donald McCoy, *Coming of Age* (1973), are also valuable as surveys of the period. Frederick Lewis Allen, *Only Yesterday: An Informal History of the 1920s* (1931), is a classic, and still delightfully readable. The changing political alignments of the 1920s are covered in David Burner, *The Politics of Provincialism* (1968). The essays in John Braeman, Robert H. Bremner, and David Brody, eds., *Change and Continuity in Twentieth-Century America: The 1920s* (1968), provide various perspectives on important facets of the period.

Economic developments of the 1920s are the subject of George Soule, *Prosperity Decade* (1947). Helen Lynd and Robert Lynd, *Middletown* (1929), examine the social and cultural trends of the decade. David J. Goldberg, *Discontented America* (1999), finds unhappiness beneath the apparent prosperity.

Edward J. Larson, *Summer for the Gods* (1998), is the most recent and accessible account of the Scopes trial. Lawrence Levine, *Defender of the Faith* (1965), covers the last ten years of William Jennings Bryan's life. The lives of other public figures of the 1920s are traced in David Levering Lewis, *W. E. B. Du Bois*, vol. 2 (2000); Terry Teachout, *The Skeptic* (2002), on H. L. Mencken; Elisabeth Israels Perry, *Belle Moskowitz* (2000); and Robert A. Slayton, *Empire Statesman* (2001), and Christopher M. Finan, *Alfred E. Smith* (2002), both on the leading Democrat of the 1920s.

For a list of additional titles related to this chapter's topics, please see http://www.ablongman.com/divine.

SUGGESTED WEB SITES

Automotive History at the Michigan Electronic Library

http://mel.org/business/autos-history.html

This page has several links to sites about automotive history in America.

Harlem 1900–1940: An African American Community

http://www.si.umich.edu/CHICO/Harlem/

The New York Public Library's Schomburg Center for Research in Black Culture hosts this site that includes a database, a timeline, and an exhibit.

William P. Gottlieb Photographs from the Golden Age of Jazz

http://memory.loc.gov/ammem/wghtml/wghome.html

The Music Division of the Library of Congress has numerous images, audio, and scanned articles from the 1940s.

The Scopes Trial

http://www.law.umkc.edu/faculty/projects/ftrials/scopes/scopes.htm

This site provides a detailed discussion of the trial, biographies of the major figures, images, and excerpts from the trial transcript.

American Temperance and Prohibition

http://prohibition.history.ohio-state.edu/

This site looks at the temperance movement over time and contains many informative links.

National Arts and Crafts Archives

http://arts-crafts.com/archive/archive.shtml

This site serves as a guide to materials on the Arts and Crafts movement, which lasted roughly from 1890 to 1929.

The Jazz Age: Flapper Culture and Sytle

http://www.geocities.com/flapper_culture

This site contains many links to information about the popular culture of the 1920s with special reference to the flapper.

The Calvin Coolidge Experience

http://www.geocities.com/CapitolHill/4921/

This site is an unusual look at one of America's less colorful presidents.

The Scopes "Monkey" Trial

Contesting Cultural Differences

During the postwar 1920s, a "new" America emerged. Largely urban, secular, and focused on the future, the "modern" culture challenged the traditional values and familiar way of life of many Americans, especially those living in rural areas. Intense cultural conflict characterized the decade. Those who saw in modern culture numerous threats to the moral fabric of the nation increasingly turned to their faith for stability and comfort. The popularity of Protestant fundamentalism, which held to a literal interpretation of the Bible, increased dramatically during this period, particularly in the South. According to fundamentalists, one of the key modernist attacks on traditional religious beliefs came from the realm of science.

Advancements in science in the late nineteenth and early twentieth centuries fueled modernization, and Americans increasingly placed their faith in the authority of science and progress. There was growing acceptance of Charles Darwin's theory of evolution, which demonstrated that plants and animals—including humans—evolved from lower life forms by a process of natural selection. By the 1920s, discussion of evolution theory had entered public school classrooms. Though many Americans could reconcile a belief in evolution with their religious beliefs, fundamentalists thought the theory of evolution contradicted the Biblical story of creation and was therefore blasphemous—particularly the notion that humans evolved from a lower primate form. Fundamentalists led a charge against evolution, particularly against its teaching in the schools, and several southern states turned to legislation to keep the scientific theory of out of the classroom.

Such a law was introduced in Tennessee by John W. Butler, a state representative. The statute passed both houses of the Tennessee legislature by a large majority and was signed into law by the governor in March 1925. The Butler Act, as it became known, made it unlawful for a teacher in state-supported schools "to teach any theory that denies the story of Divine Creation of man as taught in the Bible, and to teach instead that man has descended from a lower order of animals." Violating the law was designated a misdemeanor punishable by a fine of $100 to $500 for each offense.

In response to the Butler Act, the American Civil Liberties Union (ACLU) advertised for teachers in Tennessee willing to challenge the new law in court. Civic boosters in Dayton, eager to draw attention to their small town in eastern Tennessee, persuaded John Scopes, a science teacher and assistant football coach in Dayton, to accept the ACLU offer. Scopes was a logical choice. He opposed the antievolution law on philosophical grounds, and he had little to lose personally, being twenty-four and single and with no particular desire to remain in Dayton. Furthermore, he was a likable young man, popular around town and with otherwise conventional views, and so wouldn't muddy the legal waters by provoking the judge or jury unnecessarily. Scopes admitted that anyone teaching from the state's approved biology textbook, Hunter's *Civic Biology*, which included sections on evolution of animals and humans, would be breaking the new law. Scopes had used the text as a substitute biology teacher. He agreed to be arrested to test the law in court.

From the start, *Tennessee* v. *John Thomas Scopes* was about far more than Scopes. Supporters and opponents of the antievolution law converged on Dayton from around the country. The law's supporters brought in the renowned orator William Jennings Bryan, a three-time Democratic nominee for president, former secretary of state, and fervent Christian fundamentalist, to assist the prosecution, led by chief prosecutor A. Thomas Stewart, attorney general of Tennessee. Since the early 1920s Bryan had led the

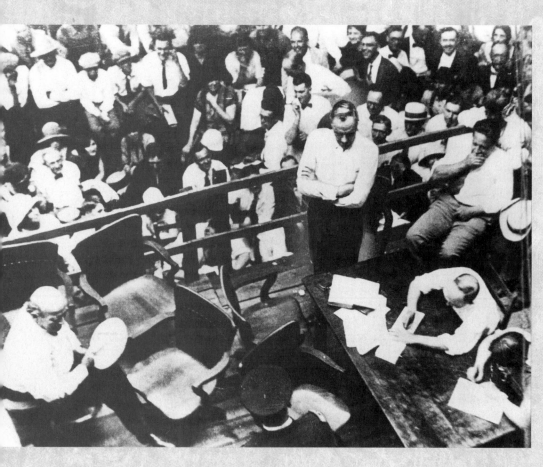

Crowds of spectators and reporters throng the courtroom during the Scopes trial as defense attorney Clarence Darrow stands with his arms folded. William Jennings Bryan, seated, is holding a fan. The soaring temperature and overcrowding eventually drove the proceedings outdoors. ❖

charge against the theories of Charles Darwin and the teaching of evolution in the schools; his syndicated newspaper column, "Weekly Bible Talks," frequently hammered Darwinism and what Bryan considered excessive faith in science.

The ACLU summoned counsel for the defense and Clarence Darrow, one of the most celebrated trial lawyers in America in the 1920s, volunteered his services as the chief defense attorney. He delighted in defending unpopular causes, including labor activists (he had defended Socialist leader Eugene V. Debs in the Pullman strike of 1894), political radicals, and murder suspects. He was also an outspoken agnostic, doubting the existence of God, and a vocal critic of Christian fundamentalists, including Bryan.

A small army of reporters descended upon Dayton, including journalist H. L. Mencken, widely known for his biting wit and disdain for middle America, who was writing for the *Baltimore Sun* and the *American Mercury*. From all over America and from various foreign countries the journalists came, eager to convey to their readers every detail of "the Monkey trial," as the trial was dubbed. The new technology of radio supplemented the newspaper coverage, especially after Judge John Raulston agreed to allow microphones in the courtroom.

For Dayton, the trial was a windfall. Business had been slow since a local steel mill shut down prior to World War I, and the owners of the town's restaurants and hotels hoped to capitalize on their community's moment of fame. "It is not a fight for evolution or against evolution, but a fight against obscurity," remarked a politician from Chattanooga, whose own city had tried to land the antievolution trial. The substantial media coverage, and the drama of the trial itself, ensured Dayton considerable attention. Spectators and entrepreneurs selling books and souvenirs flocked to the Rhea County Courthouse. The trial had taken over the town—and attracted the nation.

The proceedings opened on Friday, July 10, with a prayer. Darrow might have objected but decided to save his fire for the main battle. (In fact he did object to court prayers once the jury was chosen. His objection was overruled.) After some initial business of the court, selection of the jury began. Of the nineteen potential jurors examined, twelve were selected. Darrow queried the potential jurors about their religious beliefs, their knowledge of evolution, and their ability to render a fair verdict. "Are you a member of any church?" he asked Jim Riley. Riley replied that he had been a member of the Baptist church for a long time. Darrow continued his questioning:

Q: Do you know anything about evolution?
A: No, not particularly.
Q: Heard about it?
A: Yes, I have heard about it.
Q: Know what it is?
A: I don't know much about it.

Darrow asked whether Riley had read anything Bryan had written about evolution.

A: No, sir; I can't read.

"Well, you are fortunate," Darrow responded, in the first of many jabs at Bryan. Riley became one of the jurors.

Darrow and the defense argued principally that the antievolution law violated several clauses of the Tennessee constitution as well as guarantee of freedom of speech and provision for separation of church and state in the First Amendment of the U.S. Constitution. Contending that the law also violated the Fourteenth Amendment's declaration that no state was permitted to pass a law that abridged citizens' privileges, Darrow argued, "If today you can take a thing like evolution and make it a crime to teach it in the public school, tomorrow you can make it a crime to teach it in the private schools, and the next year you can make it a crime to teach it to the hustings or in the church."

To the prosecution, the case was fairly simple. They held that the state had the constitutional right to set the curriculum in state-funded schools. The question to be decided was whether Scopes had violated the Butler Act by covering the theory of evolution in his classroom. Prosecution witnesses, including a school official and several of Scope's students, testified that he had.

Darrow and the defense team wanted to introduce scientific evidence supporting the theory of evolution by summoning a number of scientists from various fields as expert witnesses. The prosecution protested opening the case to this wider issue. "I say, bar the door and not allow science to enter," declared Stewart, the chief prosecutor. After hearing arguments from both sides and initial testimony from the defense's first witness, the court sided with Stewart and Tennessee. "The evidence of experts would shed no light on the issues," Judge Raulston ruled.

It was Bryan's speech for the prosecution that brought real excitement to the courtroom and the nationwide attention to Dayton that the city's supporters had hoped for. The Great Commoner, as Bryan was known, commenced softly, conveying an impression of calm reason. But as he warmed to his subject, his voice rose and his words became more intense. He denied that he or most of the citizens of Tennessee advocated teaching the Bible in schools. And even if they did advocate it, the Tennessee constitution prevented them. The question at hand was different, Bryan said.

The question is, can a minority in this state come in and compel a teacher to teach that the Bible is not true, and make the parents of these children pay the expenses of the teacher to tell their children what these people believe is false and dangerous? Has it come to a time when the minority can take charge of a state like Tennessee and compel the majority to pay their teachers while they take religion out of the heart of the children of the parents who pay the teachers?

Bryan was a master at working an audience, and the jurors and spectators in the courtroom—and larger group listening in the yard outside the court—hung on his every word. They laughed as he lampooned the Darwinians; they nodded agreement as he affirmed the teachings of the Bible. They thundered their approval of his wry observation: "The Christian believes that man came from above, but the evolutionist believes he must have come from below." Following a loud "Amen!" from the audience, Darrow, who had been sitting silently through Bryan's long speech interjected: "I hope the reporters got the amens in the record. I want somewhere, at some point, to find some court where a picture of this will be painted." Such information in the official record would ensure higher courts a more complete picture of the atmosphere in the courtroom.

Denied the opportunity to call on expert witnesses to provide support for the theory of evolution, Darrow found another opportunity after the defense made an unusual request to place Bryan on the witness stand. There was some question as to whether Bryan could or should testify, as he had no firsthand knowledge of what Scopes had or hadn't done, and was no expert on the constitutions of Tennessee or the United States. But the defense asked permission to question Bryan as an expert witness on the Bible. Bryan indicated willingness and Judge Raulston—who seemed to relish the publicity the case was generating—let the two celebrities go at each other. What resulted was one of the most dramatic courtroom scenes in American history.

Darrow asked Bryan whether he had given "considerable study to the Bible." Bryan responded, "I have studied the Bible for about fifty years, or some time more than that. . . . "

Given that opening, Darrow went on to ask questions designed to undermine a strictly literal interpretation of the Bible.

Darrow: Do you claim that everything in the Bible should be literally interpreted?
Bryan: I believe everything in the Bible should be accepted as it is given there. Some of the Bible is given illustratively. For instance: "Ye are the salt of the earth." I would not insist that man was actually salt, or that he had flesh of salt, but it is used in the sense of salt as saving God's people.

Darrow pressed on. Did Bryan believe that a whale swallowed Jonah?

Bryan:	When I read that a big fish swallowed Jonah—it does not say whale—
Darrow:	Doesn't it? Are you sure?
Bryan:	That is my recollection of it. A big fish, and I believe it, and I believe in a God who can make a whale and can make a man and make both do what He pleases.

Darrow continued his line of questioning, asking Bryan to interpret other passages of the Bible. Had Joshua really made the sun stand still?

Bryan:	I believe what the Bible says.

Did that mean that the sun actually stood still, or that the earth stopped spinning? For that matter, did Mr. Bryan believe that the earth circled the sun, or vice versa? Bryan assured Darrow and the court that he knew that the earth orbited the sun. But he allowed that the author of the Joshua passage might not have. "I believe that the Bible is inspired, an inspired author. Whether one who wrote as he was directed to write understood the things he was writing about, I don't know." Darrow interrupted, but Bryan went on: "I believe it was inspired by the Almighty, and He may have used language that could be understood at that time—instead of using language that could not be understood until Darrow was born."

Listeners, siding with Bryan but squirming under Darrow's questioning, broke into loud applause here. When the applause recurred, Darrow said sarcastically, "Great applause from the bleachers."

Bryan:	From those whom you call "yokels."
Darrow:	I have never called them yokels.

The exchange grew nastier.

Bryan:	Those are the people whom you insult.
Darrow:	You insult every man of science and learning in the world because he does not believe in your fool religion.
Judge Raulston:	I will not stand for that.
Darrow:	For what he is doing?
Judge Raulston:	I am talking to both of you.

Such dignity as the trial initially possessed had disappeared by now. After the exchange continued for some time, Darrow asked Bryan if he had ever wondered where Cain's wife came from. "No, sir," Bryan replied. "I leave the agnostics to hunt for her." Darrow asked Bryan if the six days of creation were twenty-four-hour days. Bryan allowed that they might have been longer.

People examine the Anti-Evolution League's book stall during the Scopes trial. As noted in one of the banners, the display included books by Bryan. ❖

Finally Tom Stewart broke into Darrow's questioning. "What is the purpose of this examination?" the chief prosecutor demanded.

"The purpose is to cast ridicule on everybody who believes in the Bible," Bryan asserted.

Darrow answered differently. "We have the purpose of preventing bigots and ignoramuses from controlling the education of the United States."

Darrow was allowed to continue his questioning about creation. Might it have lasted more than a modern week? Bryan granted that it could have. How much more? "It might have continued for millions of years."

Darrow's examination of Bryan lasted two hours. Before the end it was obvious that it had little to do with the case at hand—but everything to do with the larger issue joined by Darrow and Bryan. As a reporter for the *Nashville Banner* explained, "In reality, it was a debate between Darrow and Bryan on Biblical history, on agnosticism and belief in revealed religion."

Not surprisingly, judgments regarding the outcome of the debate depended on the source of those judgments. The *New York Times* thought Darrow scored a clear victory. "Mr. Bryan's complete lack of interest in many of the things closely connected with such religious questions as he had been supporting for many years was strikingly shown again and again by Mr. Darrow," the *Times* explained. The Memphis *Commercial Appeal* thought Bryan had held his own: "Darrow succeeded in showing that Bryan knows little about the science of the world. Bryan succeeded in bearing witness bravely to the faith which he believes transcends all the learning of men."

The reaction to the trial's verdict was similar. Scopes, to no one's surprise, was convicted of violating the law and Judge Raulston fined him $100. Even Darrow, intending to appeal the verdict to a higher court, recommended that the jury find Scopes guilty. Antievolutionists in Tennessee and elsewhere took the conviction as vindication of their beliefs. But to many Americans with more secular views, the conviction was simply further evidence of the wrongheadedness of Bryan and the Tennessee legislature. When Bryan died suddenly just five days after the trial ended, a southern journalist approached Darrow for comment. "People down here believe that Bryan died of a broken heart because of your questioning," the journalist said. Darrow, referring to Bryan's notoriously large appetite, reportedly responded, "Broken heart nothing. He died of a busted belly." H. L. Mencken remarked, "God aimed at Darrow, missed, and hit Bryan instead."

The Scopes trial settled nothing. The defense appealed the conviction to the Tennessee Supreme Court, where it was set aside on a technicality (the jury rather than the judge should have set Scopes's fine).

But the antievolution law was left intact, and stood for another forty years, until the Tennessee legislature overturned it in 1967. In the immediate aftermath of the Scopes trial, both sides claimed moral victory, and the rift that gave rise to the case simply grew wider. Fundamentalism was discredited in large parts of urban America, but it sank roots in the rural regions of the country, becoming stronger than ever, if sometimes less visible. Several states submitted antievolution bills in the latter half of the 1920s, but most, with the exceptions of Georgia and Mississippi, did not succeed in passing laws restricting teaching of Darwin's theory. Concern over diminishing sales in the South and West, however, drove textbook publishers to revise coverage of evolution in many textbooks—de-emphasizing the topic or eliminating it entirely. With or without legislation opposing its teaching, evolution did disappear from many classrooms.

In 1960, the liberal *New Republic* declared, "The Monkey Trial is now a historical curiosity"—a judgment that proved premature when evolution reemerged as a controversial issue. The constitutional question of whether the First Amendment permitted states to ban teaching of a theory that contradicted religious beliefs had not been resolved by the Scopes case. In the 1968 case *Epperson* v. *Arkansas*, however, the U.S. Supreme Court ruled that such bans were unconstitutional. During the 1970s and 1980s various Sunbelt school districts took a different approach, passing "equal time" laws requiring that "creationism"—essentially the Biblical version of life's origins, though typically without the explicit references to Genesis—be given equal time in the classroom with evolution. Arkansas and Louisiana passed such laws, but in 1987 the U.S. Supreme Court ruled in *Edwards* v. *Aguillard* that these laws were also unconstitutional. Still the issue refused to die. In 1999, the Kansas school board mandated that the theory of evolution should be de-emphasized in the state's classrooms. The Kansas board eventually changed its mind, but not before the debate there drew national attention and demonstrated that the Scopes trial was far more than a curiosity from the past.

Questions for Discussion

- Why did different observers interpret the outcome of the Scopes trial so differently?

- Why does the issue of evolution in the public schools continue to resurface decades after laws banning its teaching were found unconstitutional?

Maynard Dixon, Okie Camp, 1935. With the encouragement of the second of his three wives, the depression-era documentary photographer Dorothea Lange, Dixon turned his art to social criticism, making his paintings commentaries on victims of the Great Depression. ❖

Franklin D. Roosevelt and the New Deal

The Struggle Against Despair

Oscar Heline never forgot the terrible waste of the Great Depression. "Grain was being burned," he told interviewer Studs Terkel. "It was cheaper than coal." Heline lived in Iowa, in the heart of the farm belt. "A county just east of here, they burned corn in their courthouse all winter. . . . You couldn't hardly buy groceries for corn." Farmers, desperate for higher prices, resorted to destruction. As Heline recalled, "People were determined to withhold produce from the market—livestock, cream, butter, eggs, what not. If they would dump the produce, they would force the market to a higher level. The farmers would man the highways, and cream cans were emptied in ditches and eggs dumped out. They burned the trestle bridge, so the trains wouldn't be able to haul grain."

Film critic Pauline Kael recounted a different memory of the 1930s. Kael was a college student in California during the Great Depression, and was struck by the number of students who were missing fathers. "They had wandered off in disgrace because they couldn't support their families. Other fathers had killed themselves, so the family could have the insurance. Families had totally broken down." Kael and many of her classmates struggled to stay in school. "There were kids who didn't have a place to sleep, huddling under bridges on the campus. I had a scholarship, but there were times when I didn't have any food. The meals were often three candy bars."

Howard Worthington resorted to trickery after losing his job in Chicago. One Easter Sunday during the depression, when his son was four years old, Worthington couldn't afford enough eggs for a proper egg hunt. So he devised a plan. "I hid a couple in the piano and all around. Tommy got his little Easter basket, and as he would find the eggs, I'd steal 'em out of the basket and re-hide them. . . . He hunted Easter eggs for three hours and he never knew the difference."

NO AMERICAN WHO LIVED THROUGH the Great Depression ever forgot the experience. As the stories of Heline, Kael, and Worthington show, the individual memories were of hard times, but also of determination, adaptation, and survival.

The depression decade had an equally profound effect on American institutions. To cope with the problems of poverty and dislocation, Americans looked to government as never before, and in doing so transformed American politics and public life. The agent of the transformation—the man America turned to in its moment of trial—was Franklin D. Roosevelt. His answer to the country's demands for action was an ambitious program of relief and reform called the **New Deal.**

OUTLINE

The Great Depression

Fighting the Depression

Roosevelt and Reform

Impact of the New Deal

End of the New Deal

Conclusion: The New Deal and American Life

FEATURE ESSAY

Eleanor Roosevelt and the Quest for Social Justice

During the Great Depression, market prices for produce were so low that farmers could scarcely afford to harvest their crops. Many resorted to destroying produce in an attempt to limit supplies and force prices higher, such as these striking dairy farmers in Illinois dumping cans of milk into the street. ❖

THE GREAT DEPRESSION

The depression of the 1930s came as a shock to Americans who had grown used to the prosperity of the 1920s. The consumer revolution of that earlier decade had fostered a general confidence that the American way of life would continue to improve. But following the collapse of the stock market in late 1929, factories closed, machines fell silent, and millions of Americans walked the streets looking for jobs that didn't exist.

The Great Crash

The consumer goods revolution contained the seeds of its own demise. The productive capacity of the automobile and appliance industries grew faster than the effective demand. Each year after 1924, the rate of increase in the sale of cars and refrigerators and ranges slowed, a natural consequence as more and more people already owned these durable goods. Production began to falter, and in 1927, the nation underwent a mild recession. The sale of durable goods declined, and construction of houses and buildings fell slightly. If corporate leaders had heeded these warning signs, they might have responded by raising wages or lowering prices, both effective ways to stimulate purchasing

power and sustain the consumer goods revolution. Or if government officials had recognized the danger signals and forced a halt in installment buying and slowed bank loans, the nation might have experienced a sharp but brief depression.

Neither government nor business leaders were so farsighted. The Federal Reserve Board lowered the discount rate, charging banks less for loans in an attempt to stimulate the economy. Much of this additional credit, however, went not into solid investment in factories and machinery but instead into the stock market, touching off a new wave of speculation that obscured the growing economic slowdown and ensured a far greater crash to come.

Individuals with excess cash began to invest heavily in the stock market, betting the already impressive rise in security prices would bring them even greater windfall profits. The market had advanced in spurts during the decade; the value of all stocks listed on the New York Stock Exchange rose from $27 billion in 1925 to $67 billion in early 1929. The strongest surge began in the spring of 1928, when investors ignored the declining production figures in the belief they could make a killing in the market. People bet their savings on speculative stocks. Corporations used their large cash reserves to supply money to brokers who in

U.S. UNEMPLOYMENT, 1929–1942

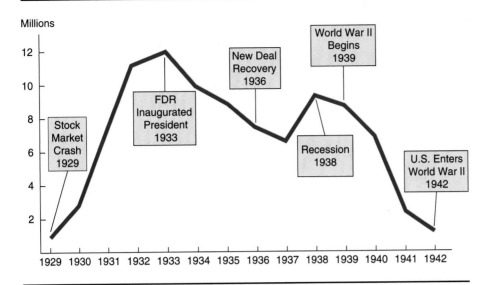

turn loaned it to investors on margin; in 1929, for example, the Standard Oil Company of New Jersey loaned out $69 million a day in this fashion.

Investors could now play the market on credit, buying stock listed at $100 a share with $10 down and $90 on margin, the broker's loan for the balance. If the stock advanced to $150, the investor could sell and reap a gain of 500 percent on the $10 investment. And in the bull market climate of the 1920s, everyone was sure the market would go up.

By 1929, it seemed the whole nation was engaged in speculation. In city after city, brokers opened branch offices, each complete with a stock ticker and a huge board covered with the latest Wall Street quotations. People crowded into the customers' rooms in the offices, filling the seats and greeting the latest advances of their favorite stocks with shouts of approval. So great was the public's interest in the stock market that newspapers carried the stock averages on their front pages.

In reality, though, more people were spectators than speculators; fewer than three million Americans owned stocks in 1929, and only about a half million were active buyers and sellers. But the bull market became a national obsession, assuring everyone that the economy was healthy and preventing any serious analysis of its underlying flaws. When the market soared to more than $80 billion in total value by midsummer, the *Wall Street Journal* discounted any possibility of a decline, proclaiming, "The outlook for the fall months seems brighter than at any time."

And then things changed, almost overnight. On October 24—later known as Black Thursday—the rise in stock prices faltered, and when it did investors nervously began to sell. Such leading stocks as RCA and Westinghouse plunged, losing nearly half their value in a single day. Speculators panicked as their creditors demanded new collateral, and the panic caused prices to plummet still further. Within weeks the gains of the previous two years had vanished.

The great crash of the stock market soon spilled over into the larger economy. Banks and other financial institutions suffered heavy losses in the market and were forced to curtail lending for consumer purchases. As consumers came up short, factories cut back production, laying off some workers and reducing hours for others. The layoffs and cutbacks lowered purchasing power even further, so fewer people bought cars and appliances. More factory layoffs resulted, and some plants closed entirely, leading to the availability of even less money for the purchase of consumer goods.

This downward economic spiral continued for four years. By 1932, unemployment had swelled to 25 percent of the workforce. Steel production was down to 12 percent of capacity, and the vast assembly lines in Detroit produced only a trickle of cars each day. The gross national product fell to 67 percent of the 1929 level. The bright promise of mass production had ended in a nightmare.

The basic explanation for the Great Depression lies in the fact that U.S. factories produced more goods than the American people could consume. The problem was not that the market for such products was fully saturated. In 1929, there were still millions of Americans who did not own cars or radios or refrigerators, but many of them could not afford the new products. There were other contributing causes—unstable economic conditions in Europe, the agricultural decline since 1919, corporate mismanagement, and excessive speculation—but it all came down to the fact that people did not have enough money to buy the consumer products coming off the assembly lines. Installment sales helped bridge the gap, but by 1929 the burden of debt was just too great.

The new economic system had failed to distribute wealth more broadly. Too much money had gone into profits, dividends, and industrial expansion, and not enough had gone into the hands of the workers, who were also consumers. Factory productivity had increased 43 percent during the decade, but the wages of industrial workers had gone up only 11 percent. If the billions that went into stock market speculation had been used instead to increase wages—which would then have increased consumer purchasing power—production and consumption could have been brought into balance. Yet it is too much to expect that the prophets of the new era could have foreseen this flaw and corrected it. They were pioneering a new industrial system, and only out of the bitter experience of the Great Depression would they discover the full dynamics of the consumer goods economy.

Effect of the Depression

It is difficult to measure the human cost of the Great Depression. The material hardships were bad enough. Men and women lived in lean-tos made of scrap wood and metal, and families went without meat and fresh vegetables for months, existing on a diet of soup and beans. The psychological burden was even greater: Americans suffered through year after year of grinding poverty with no letup in sight. The unemployed stood in line for hours waiting for relief checks; veterans sold apples or pencils on street corners, their manhood—once prized so highly by the nation—now in question. People left the city for the countryside but found no salvation on the farm. Crops rotted in the fields because prices were too low to make harvesting worthwhile; sheriffs fended off angry crowds as banks foreclosed long-overdue mortgages on once prosperous farms.

The Great Depression devastated millions who lost their jobs and often then the means to provide food and shelter for themselves and their families. Overwhelmed local and private charities could not keep up with the demands for assistance, and many looked to the federal government for direct relief from their suffering. Breadlines stretched as far as the eye could see as impoverished workers lined up in the hope of obtaining some meager rations for their hungry families. ❖

Reginald Marsh, The Park Bench *(1933). Marsh's city scenes portray the gritty, dirty side of urban life. The monochromatic tone and compact composition of* The Park Bench *create a powerful scene of human desolation.* ❖

Few escaped the suffering. African Americans who had left the poverty of the rural South for factory jobs in the North were among the first to be laid off. Mexican immigrants, who had flowed in to replace European immigrants, met with competition from angry citizens now willing to do stoop labor in the fields and work as track layers on the railroads. Immigration officials used technicalities to halt the flow across the Rio Grande and even to reverse it; nearly a half million Mexicans were deported in the 1930s, including families with children born in the United States.

The poor—black, brown, and white—survived because they knew better than most Americans how to exist in poverty. They stayed in bed in cold weather, both to keep warm and to avoid unnecessary burning up of calories; they patched their shoes with pieces of rubber from discarded tires, heated only the kitchens of their homes, and ate scraps of food that others would reject.

The middle class, which had always lived with high expectations, was hit hard. Professionals and white-collar workers refused to ask for charity even while their families went without food; one New York dentist and his wife turned on the gas and left a note saying, "We want to get out of the way before we are forced to accept relief money." People who fell behind in their mortgage payments lost their homes and then faced eviction when they could not pay the rent. Health care declined. Middle-class people stopped going to doctors and dentists regularly, unable to make the required cash payment in advance for services rendered.

Even the well-to-do were affected, giving up many of their former luxuries and weighed down with guilt as they watched former friends and business associates join the ranks of the impoverished. "My father lost everything in the depression" became an all-too-familiar refrain among young people who dropped out of college.

Many Americans sought escape in movement. Men, boys, and some women rode the rails in search of jobs, hopping freights to move south in the winter or west in the summer. On the Missouri Pacific alone, the number of vagrants increased from just over 13,000 in 1929 to nearly 200,000 in 1931. One town in the Southwest hired special police to keep vagrants from leaving the boxcars. Those who became tramps had to keep on the move, but they did find a sense of community in the hobo jungles that sprang up along the major railroad routes. Here the unfortunate could find a place to eat and sleep, and people with whom to share their misery. Louis Banks, a black veteran, told interviewer Studs Terkel what these informal camps were like:

> Black and white, it didn't make any difference who you were, 'cause everybody was poor. All friendly, sleep in a jungle. We used to take a big pot and cook food, cabbage, meat and beans all together. We all set together, we made a tent. Twenty-five or thirty would be out on the side of the rail, white and colored: They didn't have no mothers or sisters, they didn't have no home, they were dirty, they had overalls on, they didn't have no food, they didn't have anything.

FIGHTING THE DEPRESSION

The Great Depression presented an enormous challenge for American political leadership. The inability of the Republicans to overcome the economic catastrophe provided the Democrats with the chance to regain power. Although they failed to achieve full recovery before the outbreak of World War II, the Democrats did succeed in alleviating some of the suffering and establishing political dominance.

Hoover and Voluntarism

Herbert Hoover was the Great Depression's most prominent victim. When the economic downturn began in late 1929, he tried to rally the nation with bold forecasts of better days ahead. His repeated assertion that prosperity was just around the corner bred cynicism and mistrust. Expressing complete faith in the American economic system, Hoover blamed the depression on foreign causes, especially unstable European banks. The president rejected proposals for bold government action and relied instead on voluntary cooperation within business to halt the slide. He called the leaders of industry to the White House and secured their agreement to maintain prices and wages at high levels. Yet within a few months, employers were reducing wages and cutting prices in a desperate effort to survive.

Hoover also believed in voluntary efforts to relieve the human suffering brought about by the depression. He called on private charities and local governments to help feed and clothe those in need. But when these sources were exhausted, he rejected all requests for direct federal relief, asserting that such handouts would undermine the character of proud American citizens.

As the depression deepened, Hoover reluctantly began to move beyond voluntarism to undertake more sweeping government measures. A new Federal Farm Board loaned money to aid cooperatives and bought up surplus crops in the open market in a vain effort to raise farm prices. At Hoover's request, Congress cut taxes in an attempt to restore public confidence and adopted a few federal public works projects, such as Boulder (Hoover) Dam, to provide jobs for idle men.

To help imperiled banks and insurance companies, Hoover proposed the Reconstruction Finance Corporation (RFC), which Congress established in early 1932. The RFC loaned government money to financial institutions to save them from bankruptcy. Hoover's critics, however, pointed out that while he favored aid to business, he still opposed measures such as direct relief and massive public works that would help the millions of unemployed.

BANK FAILURES, 1929–1933

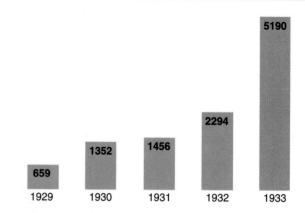

Source: Data compiled from C. D. Bremer, *American Bank Failures* (New York: Columbia University Press, 1935), p. 42.

By 1932, Hoover's efforts to overcome the Depression had clearly failed. The Democrats had gained control of the House of Representatives in the 1930 elections and were pressing the president to take bolder action, but Hoover stubbornly resisted. His public image suffered its sharpest blow in the summer of 1932 when he ordered General Douglas MacArthur to clear out the **bonus army.** This ragged group of some twenty-two thousand World War I veterans had come to Washington in the summer of 1932 to lobby Congress to pay immediately a bonus for military service that was due them in 1945. After the Senate rejected the bonus bill, some of the veterans stayed in Washington, living in ramshackle huts in Anacostia Flats along the Potomac. Mounted troops drove the bonus army out of the capital, blinding the veterans with tear gas and burning their shacks.

Meanwhile, the nation's banking structure approached collapse. Bank failures rose steadily in 1931 and 1932 as customers responded to rumors of bankruptcy by rushing in to withdraw their deposits. The banking crisis completed the nation's disenchantment with Hoover; people were ready for a new leader in the White House.

The Emergence of Roosevelt

The man who came forward to meet this national need was Franklin D. Roosevelt. Born into the old Dutch colonial aristocracy of New York, FDR was a distant cousin of the Republican Teddy. He grew up with all the advantages of wealth: private tutors, his own sailboat and pony, frequent trips to Europe, and education at Groton and Harvard. His strong-willed mother smoothed all the obstacles in the path of her only child and gave him a priceless sense of inner security. After graduation from Harvard, he briefly attended law school but left to plunge into politics. He served in the New York legislature and then went to Washington as assistant secretary of the navy under Wilson, a post he filled capably during World War I. Defeated as the Democratic vice presidential candidate in 1920, Roosevelt had just begun a banking career when he suffered an attack of polio in the summer of 1921. Refusing to give in, he fought back bravely, and though he never again walked unaided, he reentered politics in the mid-1920s and was elected governor of New York in 1928.

Roosevelt's dominant trait was his ability to persuade and convince other people. He possessed a marvelous voice, deep and rich; a winning smile; and a buoyant confidence he could easily transmit to others. Some believed he was too vain and superficial as a young man, but his bout with polio gave him both an understanding of human suffering and a broad political appeal as a man who had faced heavy odds and overcome them. He understood the give-and-take of politics, knew how to use flattery to win over doubters, and was especially effective in exploiting the media, whether in bantering with newspaper reporters or reaching out to the American people on the radio. Although his mind was quick and agile, he had little patience with philosophical nuances; he dealt with the appearance of issues, not their deeper substance, and he displayed a flexibility toward political principles that often dismayed even his warmest admirers.

PRESIDENTIAL VOTING IN CHICAGO BY ETHNIC GROUPS, 1924–1932 (PERCENTAGE DEMOCRATIC)

	1924	1928	1932
Czechoslovakians	40	73	83
Poles	35	71	80
Lithuanians	48	77	84
Yugoslavs	20	54	67
Italians	31	63	64
Germans	14	58	69
Jews	19	60	77

Source: John M. Allswang, *A House for All Peoples: Ethnic Politics in Chicago, 1890–1936* (Lexington: University of Kentucky Press, 1971).

Roosevelt took advantage of the opportunity offered by the Great Depression. With the Republicans discredited, he cultivated the two wings of the divided Democrats, appealing to both the traditionalists from the South and West and the new urban elements in the North. After winning the party's nomination in 1932, he broke with tradition by flying to Chicago and accepting in person, telling the cheering delegates, "I pledge you—I pledge myself to a new deal for the American people."

In the fall, he defeated Herbert Hoover in a near landslide for the Democrats. Roosevelt tallied 472 electoral votes as he swept the South and West and carried nearly all the large industrial states as well. Farmers and workers, Protestants and Catholics, immigrants and native born rallied behind the new leader who promised to restore prosperity. Roosevelt not only met the challenge of the depression but also solidified the shift to the Democratic party and created an enduring coalition that would dominate American politics for a half century.

The Hundred Days

When Franklin Roosevelt took the oath of office on March 4, 1933, the nation's economy was on the brink of collapse. Unemployment stood at nearly thirteen million, one-fourth of the labor force; banks were closed in thirty-eight states. On inauguration morning, the governors of New York and Illinois closed the banks in the nation's two largest cities, thus bringing the country's financial transactions to a halt. Speaking from the steps of the Capitol, FDR declared boldly, "First of all, let me assert my firm belief that the only thing we have to fear is fear itself—nameless, unreasoning, unjustified terror." Then he announced he

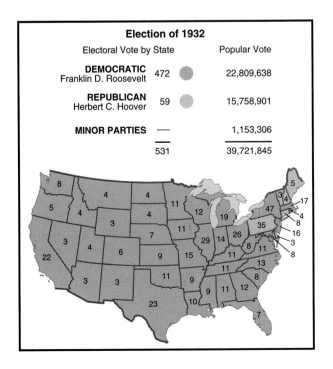

Election of 1932

	Electoral Vote by State		Popular Vote
DEMOCRATIC Franklin D. Roosevelt	472		22,809,638
REPUBLICAN Herbert C. Hoover	59		15,758,901
MINOR PARTIES	—		1,153,306
	531		39,721,845

⬧ A Look at the Past ⬧

Jefferson Monument

During the 1930s, history became popular in the United States. Feature films such as *Young Man Lincoln* and *Gone with the Wind* drew large audiences. New monuments and museums opened, including Colonial Williamsburg in Virginia. At a time when people feared that economic hardship might contribute to rising fascism, apparent in Europe, Americans turned to their past for reassurance that they would not lose their ideals. The Jefferson Monument, commissioned in 1933 and completed in 1944, honored the president some people called the "Father of American democracy." Costing millions of dollars and stirring considerable public interest, the monument physically expressed American interest in the past. Why was the federal government willing to spend on a monument? How many New Deal programs also celebrated the past or American values?

would call Congress into special session and request "broad executive power to wage a war against the emergency, as great as the power that would be given to me if we were in fact invaded by a foreign foe."

Within the next ten days, Roosevelt won his first great New Deal victory by saving the nation's banks. On March 5, he issued a decree closing the banks and called Congress back into session. His aides drafted new banking legislation and presented it to Congress on March 9; a few hours later, both houses passed it, and FDR signed the new legislation that evening. The measure provided for government supervision and aid to the banks. Strong ones would be reopened with federal support, weak ones closed, and those in difficulty bolstered by government loans.

On March 12, FDR addressed the nation by radio in the first of his fireside chats. In conversational tones, he told the public what he had done. Some banks would begin to reopen the next day, with the government standing behind them. Other banks, once they became solvent, would open later, and the American people could safely put their money back into these institutions. The next day, March 13, the nation's largest and strongest banks opened their doors; at the end of the day, customers had deposited more cash than they withdrew. The crisis was over; gradually, other banks opened, and the runs and failures ceased.

"Capitalism was saved in eight days," boasted one of Roosevelt's advisers. Most surprising was the conservative nature of FDR's action. Instead of nationaliz-

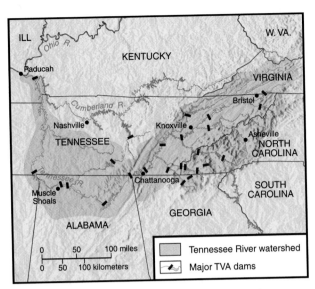

THE TENNESSEE VALLEY AUTHORITY *The Tennessee Valley Authority (TVA) served a seven-state region in the Southeast. Developing such a vast project required federal funding and management, both of which were provided through a federally owned corporation.* ❖

ing the banks, he had simply thrown the government's resources behind them and preserved private ownership. Though some other New Deal measures would be more radical, Roosevelt set a tone in the banking crisis. He was out to reform and restore the American economic system, not change it drastically. He drew on the progressive tradition and his experience with World War I mobilization to fashion a moderate program of government action.

For the next three months, until it adjourned in June, Congress responded to a series of presidential initiatives. During these "Hundred Days," Roosevelt sent fifteen major requests to Congress and received back fifteen pieces of legislation. A few created agencies that have become a part of American life. The **Tennessee Valley Authority (TVA)** was one of the most ambitious of Roosevelt's New Deal measures. This innovative effort at regional planning resulted in the building of a series of dams in seven states to control floods, ease navigation, and produce electricity. Although critics lamented the cost of the project and its impact on the environment and certain local communities, it went far toward bringing one of the most underdeveloped parts of the country into the modern era.

Other New Deal agencies were temporary in nature, designed to meet the specific economic problems of the depression. None were completely successful; the depression would continue for another six years, immune even to Roosevelt's magic. But psychologically, the nation turned the corner in the spring of 1933. Under FDR, the government seemed to be responding

to the economic crisis, enabling people for the first time since 1929 to look to the future with hope.

Roosevelt and Recovery

Two major New Deal programs launched during the Hundred Days were aimed at industrial and agricultural recovery. The first was the **National Recovery Administration (NRA)**, FDR's attempt to achieve economic advance through planning and cooperation among government, business, and labor. In the midst of the depression, business owners were intent on stabilizing production and raising prices for their goods. Labor leaders were equally determined to spread work through maximum hours and to put a floor under workers' income with minimum wages.

The NRA hoped to achieve both goals by permitting companies in each major industry to cooperate in writing codes of fair competition that would set realistic limits on production, allocate percentages to individual producers, and set firm guidelines for prices. Section 7a of the enabling act mandated protection for

The National Recovery Administration blue eagle signaled a firm's participation in the National Recovery Act. Roosevelt's innovative program met with considerable resistance, and signs modeled on this original example attempted to make participation patriotic and respectable. The eagle, a traditional symbol for a strong United States, is clutching symbols of industrial might. ❖

labor in all the codes by establishing maximum hours, minimum wages, and the guarantee of collective bargaining by unions. No company could be compelled to join, but the New Deal sought complete participation by appealing to patriotism. Each firm that took part could display a blue eagle and stamp the symbol on its products. With energetic Hugh Johnson in charge, the NRA quickly enrolled the nation's leading companies and unions. By the summer of 1933, more than five hundred industries had adopted codes that covered 2.5 million workers.

The NRA quickly bogged down in a huge bureaucratic morass. The codes proved to be too detailed to enforce easily. Written by the largest companies, the rules favored big business at the expense of smaller competitors. Labor quickly became disenchanted with Section 7a. The minimum wages were often near starvation level, while business avoided the requirement for collective bargaining by creating company unions that did not represent the real needs of workers. After a brief upsurge in the spring of 1933, industrial production began to sag as disillusionment with the NRA grew. By 1934, more and more business owners were complaining about the new agency, calling it the "National Run Around." When the Supreme Court finally invalidated the NRA in 1935 on constitutional grounds, few mourned its demise. The idea of trying to overcome the depression by relying on voluntary cooperation between competing businesses and labor leaders had collapsed in the face of individual self-interest and greed.

The New Deal's attempt at farm recovery fared a little better. Henry A. Wallace, FDR's secretary of agri-culture, came up with an answer to the farmers' old dilemma of overproduction. The government would act as a clearinghouse for producers of major crops, arranging for them to set production limits for wheat, cotton, corn, and other leading crops. The **Agricultural Adjustment Administration (AAA)** created by Congress in May 1933, would allocate acreage among individual farmers, encouraging them to take land out of production by paying them subsidies (raised by a tax on food processors). Unfortunately, Wallace preferred not to wait until the 1934 planting season to implement this program, and so farmers were paid in 1933 to plow under crops they had already planted and to kill livestock they were raising. Faced with the problem of hunger in the midst of plenty, the New Deal seemed to respond by destroying the plenty.

The AAA program worked better in 1934 and 1935 as land removed from production led to smaller harvests and rising farm prices. Farm income rose for the first time since World War I, increasing from $2 billion in 1933 to $5 billion by 1935. Severe weather, especially Dust Bowl conditions on the Great Plains, contributed to the crop-limitation program, but most of the gain in farm income came from the subsidy payments themselves rather than from higher market prices.

On the whole, large farmers benefited most from the program. Possessing the capital to buy machinery and fertilizer, they were able to farm more efficiently than before on fewer acres of land. Small farmers, tenants, and sharecroppers did not fare as well, receiving

Drought and soil erosion brought on by overfarming turned the agricultural land of the Great Plains into a giant dust bowl during the 1930s. Especially hard hit were western Kansas and Oklahoma, eastern Colorado, and the Texas Panhandle. Giant dust storms, such as the one approaching this Oklahoma ranch, forced many farmers from their land. ❖

very little of the government payments and often being driven off the land as owners took the acreage previously cultivated by tenants and sharecroppers out of production. Some three million people left the land in the 1930s, crowding into the cities where they swelled the relief rolls. In the long run, the New Deal reforms improved the efficiency of American agriculture, but at a real human cost.

The Supreme Court eventually found the AAA unconstitutional in 1936, but Congress reenacted it in modified form that year and again in 1938. The system of allotments, now financed directly by the government, became a standard feature of the farm economy. Other New Deal efforts to assist the rural poor, notably the Farm Security Administration (FSA), sought to loan money to tenants and sharecroppers so they could ac-

quire land of their own, but the sums appropriated by Congress were too modest. The FSA was able to extend loans to fewer than 2 percent of the nation's tenant farmers. "Obviously," the FSA director informed Roosevelt, "this . . . program can be regarded as only an experimental approach to the farm tenancy problem." The result of the New Deal for American farming was to hasten its transformation into a business in which only the efficient and well capitalized would thrive.

Roosevelt and Relief

The New Deal was far more successful in meeting the most immediate problem of the 1930s—relief for the millions of unemployed and destitute citizens. Roosevelt never shared Hoover's distaste for direct

❖ A Look at the Past ❖

FSA Photos

"Migrant Mother" (left) is one of the best-known photographs commissioned by the Farm Security Administration (FSA) during the 1930s. The FSA used photographs to document rural problems and to build support for its resettlement program. Roy Stryker, the project's director, wanted the photographs to convince the public that rural Americans faced difficulties but with help were capable of overcoming those troubles. Dorothea Lange, who took these photographs, experimented with compositions in an effort to capture artistically pleasing images that provoked the reactions Stryker wanted. Compare Lange's famous image to the one she never intended to publish. Why would the photograph on the right fail to meet Stryker's demands? What emotions does the photograph on the left evoke? How does the image on the left meet Stryker's requirements?

Federal work relief programs helped millions maintain their self-respect. Workers in the CCC (top, left) received $30 a month for planting trees and building parks and trails. As indicated on the map, the PWA hired workers to build schools, dig irrigation ditches, construct sewage treatment plants, and erect bridges across the country. Artists and writers found work in the WPA (top, right). ❖

federal support; on May 12, 1933, in response to FDR's March request, Congress authorized the RFC to distribute $500 million to the states to help individuals and families in need.

Roosevelt brought in Harry Hopkins to direct the relief program. A former social worker who seemed to live on black coffee and cigarettes, Hopkins set up a desk in the hallway of the RFC building and proceeded to spend more than $5 million in less than two hours. By the end of 1933, Hopkins had cut through red tape to distribute money to nearly one-sixth of the American people. The relief payments were modest in size, but they enabled millions to avoid starvation and stay out of humiliating breadlines.

Another, more imaginative early effort was the **Civilian Conservation Corps (CCC),** which was Roosevelt's own idea. The CCC enrolled young males from city families on relief and sent them to work on the nation's public lands, cutting trails, planting trees, building bridges, and paving roads. Ultimately, more than two million young people served in the CCC, contributing both to their families' incomes and to the nation's welfare.

Hopkins realized the need to do more than just keep people alive, and he soon became an advocate of work relief. Hopkins argued that the government should put the jobless to work, not just to encourage self-respect, but also to enable them to earn enough to purchase consumer goods and thus stimulate the entire economy. A Public Works Administration (PWA) headed by Secretary of the Interior Harold Ickes had been authorized in 1933, but Ickes, intent on the quality of the projects rather than human needs, failed to put many people to work. In the fall of 1933, Roosevelt created the Civil Works Administration (CWA) and charged Hopkins with getting people off the unemployment lines and relief rolls and back to work. Hopkins had more than four million men and women at work by January 1934, building roads, schools, playgrounds, and athletic fields. Many of the workers were unskilled, and some of the projects were shoddy, but the CWA at least enabled people to work and earn enough money to survive the winter. Roosevelt, appalled at the huge expenditures involved, shut down the CWA in 1934 and forced Hopkins to return to federal relief payments as the only source of aid to the jobless.

The final commitment to the idea of work relief came in 1935 when Roosevelt established the **Works Progress Administration (WPA)** to spend nearly $5 billion authorized by Congress for emergency relief. The WPA, under Hopkins, put the unemployed on the federal payroll so they could earn enough to meet their basic needs and help stimulate the stagnant economy. Conservatives complained that the WPA amounted to nothing more than hiring the jobless to do make-work

tasks with no real value. But Hopkins cared less about what was accomplished than about helping those who had been unemployed for years to get off the dole and gain self-respect by working again.

In addition to funding the usual construction and conservation projects, the WPA tried to preserve the skills of American artists, actors, and writers. The Federal Theatre Project produced plays, circuses, and puppet shows that enabled entertainers to practice their crafts and to perform before people who often had never seen a professional production before. Similar projects for writers and artists led to a series of valuable state guidebooks and to murals that adorned public buildings across the land. A separate National Youth Administration (NYA) found part-time jobs for young people still in school and developed projects—ranging from automobile repairing in New York City to erecting tuberculosis isolation units in Arizona—for 2.5 million young adults.

The WPA helped ease the burden for the unemployed, but it failed to overcome the depression. Rather than spending too much, as his critics charged, Roosevelt's greatest failure was not spending enough. The WPA never employed at any one time more than three million of the ten million jobless. The wages, although larger than relief payments, were still pitifully low, averaging only $52 a month. Thus the WPA failed to prime the American economy by increasing consumer purchasing power. Factories remained closed and machinery idle because the American people still did not have the money, either from relief or the WPA, to buy cars, radios, appliances, and the other consumer goods that had been the basis for the prosperity of the 1920s. By responding to basic human needs, Roosevelt had made the depression bearable. The New Deal's failure, however, to go beyond relief to achieve prosperity led to a growing frustration and the appearance of more radical alternatives that challenged the conservative nature of the New Deal and forced FDR to shift to the left.

ROOSEVELT AND REFORM

In 1935, the focus of the New Deal shifted from relief and recovery to reform. During his first two years in office, FDR had concentrated on fighting the Great Depression by shoring up the sagging American economy. Only a few new agencies, notably TVA, sought to make permanent changes in national life. Roosevelt was developing a "broker-state" concept of government, responding to pressures from organized elements such as corporations, labor unions, and farm groups while ignoring the needs and wants of the dispossessed who had no clear political voice. The early New Deal tried to assist bankers and industrialists, large farmers, and members of the labor unions, but it did little to help unskilled workers and sharecroppers.

The continuing depression and high unemployment began to build pressure for more sweeping changes. Roosevelt faced the choice of either providing more radical programs, ones designed to end historical inequities in American life, or deferring to others who put forth solutions to the nation's ills. Bolstered by an impressive Democratic victory in the 1934 congressional elections, Roosevelt responded by embracing a reform program that marked the climax of the New Deal.

Challenges to FDR

The signs of discontent were visible everywhere by 1935. In the upper Midwest, progressives and agrarian radicals, led by Minnesota governor Floyd Olson, were calling for government action to raise farm and labor income. "I am a radical in the sense that I want a definite change in the system," Olson declared. "I am not satisfied with patching." Upton Sinclair, the muckraking novelist, nearly won the governorship of California in 1934 running on the slogan "End poverty in California," while in the East a violent strike in the textile industry shut down plants in twenty states. The most serious challenge to Roosevelt's leadership, however, came from three demagogues who captured national attention in the mid-1930s.

The first was Father Charles Coughlin, a Roman Catholic priest from Detroit, who had originally supported FDR. Speaking to a rapt nationwide radio audience in his rich, melodious voice, Coughlin appealed to the discontented with a strange mixture of crank monetary schemes and anti-Semitism. He broke with the New Deal in late 1934, denouncing it as the "Pagan Deal," and founded his own National Union for Social Justice. Increasingly vitriolic, he called for monetary inflation and the nationalization of the banking system in his weekly radio sermons to an audience of more than thirty million.

A more benign but equally threatening figure appeared in California. Francis Townsend, a 67-year-old physician, came forward in 1934 with a scheme to assist the elderly, who were suffering greatly during the depression. The Townsend Plan proposed giving everyone over the age of 60 a monthly pension of $200 with the proviso that it must be spent within thirty days. Although designed less as an old-age pension plan than as a way to stimulate the economy, the proposal understandably had its greatest appeal among the elderly. They embraced it as a holy cause, joining Townsend Clubs across the country. Despite the criticism from economists that the plan would transfer more than half the national income to less than 10

percent of the population, more than ten million people signed petitions endorsing the Townsend Plan, and few politicians dared oppose it.

The third new voice of protest was that of Huey Long, the flamboyant senator from Louisiana. Like Coughlin, an original supporter of the New Deal, Long turned against FDR and by 1935 had become a major political threat to the president. A shrewd, ruthless, yet witty man, Long had a remarkable ability to mock those in power. The Kingfish (a nickname he borrowed from *Amos 'n Andy*) announced a nationwide "Share the Wealth" movement in 1934. He spoke grandly of taking from the rich to make "every man a king," guaranteeing each American a home worth $5000 and an annual income of $2500. To finance the plan, Long advocated seizing all fortunes of more than $5 million and levying a tax of 100 percent on incomes greater than $1 million. By 1935, Long claimed to have founded twenty-seven thousand Share the Wealth clubs and had a mailing list of more than seven million people, including workers, farmers, college professors, and even bank presidents. Threatening to run as a third-party candidate in 1936, Long generated fear among Democratic leaders that he might attract three to four million votes, possibly enough to swing the election to the Republicans. Although an assassin killed Huey Long in Louisiana in late 1935, his popularity showed the need for the New Deal to do more to help those still in distress.

Social Security

When the new Congress met in January 1935, Roosevelt was ready to support a series of reform measures designed to take the edge off national dissent. The recent elections had increased Democratic congressional strength significantly, with the Republicans losing thirteen seats in the House and retaining less than one-third of the Senate. Many of the Democrats were to the left of Roosevelt, favoring increased spending and more sweeping federal programs. "Boys—this is our hour," exulted Harry Hopkins. "We've got to get everything we want ... now or never." Congress quickly appropriated $4.8 billion for the WPA and was prepared to enact virtually any proposal that Roosevelt offered.

The most significant reform enacted in 1935 was the **Social Security Act.** The Townsend movement had reminded Americans that the United States, alone among modern industrial nations, had never developed a welfare system to aid the aged, the disabled, and the unemployed. A cabinet committee began studying the problem in 1934, and President Roosevelt sent its recommendations to Congress the following January.

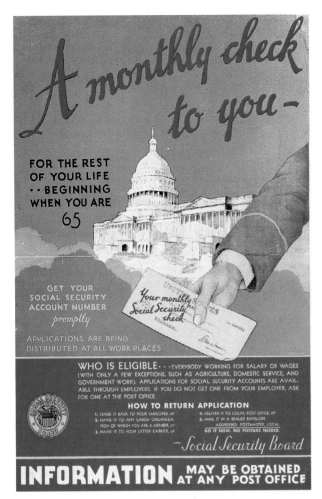

Despite the administration's boosterism, many believed that Social Security could not fulfill its promises. ❖

The proposed legislation had three major parts. First, it provided for old-age pensions financed equally by a tax on employers and workers, without government contributions. In addition, it gave states federal matching funds to provide modest pensions for the destitute elderly. Second, it set up a system of unemployment compensation on a federal-state basis, with employers paying a payroll tax and with each state setting benefit levels and administering the program locally. Finally, it provided for direct federal grants to the states, on a matching basis, for welfare payments to the blind, handicapped, needy elderly, and dependent children.

Although there was criticism from conservatives who mourned the passing of traditional American reliance on self-help and individualism, the chief objections came from those who argued that the administration's measure did not go far enough. Democratic leaders, however, defeated efforts to incorporate Townsend's proposal for $200 monthly pensions and increases in unemployment benefits.

Congress then passed the Social Security Act by overwhelming margins.

Critics began to point out its shortcomings, as they have ever since. The old-age pensions were paltry. Designed to begin in 1942, they ranged from $10 to $85 a month. Not everyone was covered; many of those who most needed protection in their old age, such as farmers and domestic servants, were not included. And all participants, regardless of income or economic status, paid in at the same rate, with no supplement from the general revenue. The trust fund also took out of circulation money that was desperately needed to stimulate the economy in the 1930s.

Other portions of the act were equally open to question. The cumbersome unemployment system offered no aid to those currently out of work, only to people who would lose their jobs in the future, and the benefits (depending on the state) ranged from barely adequate to substandard. The outright grants to the handicapped and dependent children were minute in terms of the need; in New York City, for example, a blind person received only $5 a week in 1937.

The conservative nature of the legislation reflected Roosevelt's own fiscal orthodoxy, but even more it was a product of his political realism. Despite the severity of the depression, he realized that establishing a system of federal welfare went against deeply rooted American convictions. He insisted on a tax on participants to give those involved in the pension plan a vested interest in Social Security. He wanted them to feel they had earned their pensions and that in the future no one would dare take them away. "With those taxes in there," he explained privately, "no damned politician can ever scrap my social security program." Above all, FDR had succeeded in establishing the principle of government responsibility for the aged, the handicapped, and the unemployed. Whatever the defects of the legislation, Social Security stood as a landmark of the New Deal, creating a system to provide for the welfare of individuals in a complex industrial society.

Labor Legislation

The other major reform achievement in 1935 was passage of the National Labor Relations Act, or the **Wagner Act,** as it became known. Senator Robert Wagner of New York introduced legislation in 1934 to outlaw company unions and other unfair labor practices in order to ensure collective bargaining for unions. FDR, who had little knowledge of labor-management relations and apparently little interest in them, opposed the bill. In 1935, however, Wagner began to gather broad support for his measure, which passed the Senate in May with only twelve opposing votes, and the president, seeing passage as likely, gave it his approval. The bill moved quickly through the House, and Roosevelt signed it into law in July.

The Wagner Act created a National Labor Relations Board to preside over labor-management relations and enable unions to engage in collective bargaining with federal support. The act outlawed a variety of union-busting tactics and in its key provision decreed that whenever the majority of a company's workers voted for a union to represent them, management would be compelled to negotiate with the union on all matters of wages, hours, and working conditions. With this unprecedented government sanction, labor unions could now recruit the large number of unorganized workers throughout the country. The Wagner Act, the most far-reaching of all New Deal measures, led to the revitalization of the American labor movement and a permanent change in labor-management relations.

Three years later, Congress passed a second law that had a lasting impact on American workers—the Fair Labor Standards Act. A long-sought goal of the New Deal, this measure aimed to establish both minimum wages and maximum hours of work per week. Since labor unions usually were able to negotiate adequate levels of pay and work for their members, the act was aimed at unorganized workers and met with only grudging support from unions. Southern conservatives opposed it strongly, both on ideological grounds (it meant still greater government involvement in private enterprise) and because it threatened the low southern wages that had attracted northern industry since Reconstruction.

Roosevelt finally succeeded in winning passage of the Fair Labor Standards Act in 1938, but only at the cost of exempting many key industries from its coverage. The act provided for a minimum wage of 40 cents an hour by 1940 and a standard workweek of forty hours, with time and a half for overtime. Despite its loopholes, the legislation did lead to pay raises for the twelve million workers earning less than 40 cents an hour. More important, like Social Security it set up a system—however inadequate—that Congress could build on in the future to reach more generous and humane levels.

Other New Deal reform measures met with a mixed reception in Congress. Proposals to break up the huge public utility holding companies created by promoters in the 1920s and to levy a "soak the rich" tax on the wealthy stirred up bitter debate, and these bills were passed only in greatly weakened form. Roosevelt was more successful in passing a banking act that made important reforms in the Federal Reserve System. He also gained congressional approval of the Rural Electrification Administration (REA), which helped bring electricity to the 90 percent of American farms that still did not have it in the 1930s.

All in all, Roosevelt's record in reform was similar to that in relief and recovery—modest success but no sweeping victory. A cautious and pragmatic leader, FDR moved far enough to the left to overcome the challenges of Coughlin, Townsend, and Long without venturing too far from the mainstream. His reforms improved the quality of life in America significantly, but he made no effort to correct all the nation's social and economic wrongs.

IMPACT OF THE NEW DEAL

The New Deal had a broad influence on the quality of life in the United States in the 1930s. Government programs reached into areas hitherto untouched. Many of them brought about long-overdue improvements, but others failed to make any significant dent in historic inequities. The most important advances came with the dramatic growth of labor unions; the conditions for working women and minorities in nonunionized industries showed no comparable advance.

Rise of Organized Labor

Trade unions were weak at the onset of the Great Depression, with a membership of fewer than three million workers. Most were in the American Federation of Labor (AFL), composed of craft unions that served the needs of skilled workers. The nation's basic industries, such as steel and automobiles, were unorganized; the great mass of unskilled workers thus fared poorly in terms of wages and working conditions. Section 7a of the NRA had led to some growth in AFL ranks, but the union's conservative leaders, eager to cooperate with business, failed to take full advantage of the opportunity to organize the mass production industries.

John L. Lewis, head of the United Mine Workers, took the lead in forming the Committee on Industrial Organization (CIO) in 1935. The son of a Welsh coal miner, Lewis was a dynamic and ruthless man. He had led the mine workers since 1919 and was determined to spread the benefits of unions throughout industry. Lewis first battled with the leadership of the AFL, and then—after being expelled—he renamed his group the Congress of Industrial Organizations and announced in 1936 that he would use the Wagner Act to extend collective bargaining to the nation's auto and steel industries.

Within five years, Lewis had scored a remarkable series of victories. Some came easily. The big steel companies, led by U.S. Steel, surrendered without a fight in 1937; management realized that federal support put the unions in a strong position. There was greater resistance in the automobile industry. When General Motors, the first target, resisted, the newly cre-

In some cases, striking union members met with brute force. Philip Evergood's 1937 painting The American Tragedy *recounts the violence of the Republic Steel strike.* ❖

ated United Automobile Workers (UAW) developed an effective strike technique. In late December 1936, GM workers in Flint, Michigan, simply sat down in the factory, refusing to leave until the company recognized their union, and threatening to destroy the valuable tools and machines if they were removed forcibly. When the Michigan governor refused to call out the national guard to break the strike, General Motors conceded defeat and signed a contract with the UAW. Chrysler quickly followed suit, but Henry Ford refused to give in and fought the UAW, hiring strikebreakers and beating up organizers. In 1941, however, Ford finally recognized the UAW. Smaller steel companies, led by Republic Steel, engaged in even more violent resistance; in one incident in 1937, police shot ten strikers. The companies eventually reached a settlement with the steelworkers' union in 1941.

By the end of the 1930s, the CIO had some five million members, slightly more than the AFL. The successes were remarkable—in addition to the automaking and steel unions, organizers for the CIO and the AFL had been successful in the textile, rubber, electrical, and metal industries. For the first time, unskilled as well as skilled were unionized. Women and African Americans benefited from the creation of the CIO, not because the union followed enlightened policies, but simply because they made up a substantial proportion of the unskilled workforce that the CIO organized.

Yet despite these impressive gains, only 28 percent of all Americans (excluding farmworkers) belonged to unions by 1940. Millions in the restaurant, retail, and service trades remained unorganized, working long hours for very low wages. Employer resistance and traditional hostility to unions blocked further progress, as did the aloof attitude of President Roosevelt, who commented to labor and management, "A plague on both your houses" during the steel strike. The Wagner Act had helped open the way, but labor leaders such as Lewis, Philip Murray of the Steel Workers Organizing Committee, and Walter Reuther of the United Automobile Workers deserved most of the credit for union achievements.

The New Deal Record on Help to Minorities

The Roosevelt administration's attempts to aid the downtrodden were least effective with African Americans and other racial minorities. The Great Depression had hit blacks with special force. Sharecroppers and tenant farmers had seen the price of cotton drop from 18 to 6 cents a pound, far below the level to sustain a family on the land. In the cities, the saying "Last hired, First fired" proved all too true; by 1933, more than 50 percent of urban blacks were unemployed. Hard times sharpened racial prejudice. "No jobs for niggers until every white man has a job" became a rallying cry for many whites in Atlanta.

The New Deal helped African Americans survive the depression, but it never tried to confront squarely the racial injustice built into the federal relief programs. Although the programs served blacks as well as whites, in the South the weekly payments blacks received were much smaller. In the early days, NRA codes permitted lower wage scales for blacks, while the AAA led to the eviction of thousands of Negro tenants and sharecroppers. African American leaders referred to the NRA as standing for "Negro Robbed Again" and

dismissed the AAA as "a continuation of the same old raw deal." Nor did later reform measures help very much. Neither the minimum wage nor Social Security covered those working as farmers or domestic servants, categories that comprised 65 percent of all African American workers. Thus an NAACP official commented that Social Security "looks like a sieve with the holes just large enough for the majority of Negroes to fall through."

Despite this bleak record, African Americans rallied behind Roosevelt's leadership, abandoning their historic ties to the Republican party. In 1936, more than 75 percent of those African Americans who voted supported FDR. In part, this switch came in response to Roosevelt's appointment of a number of prominent African Americans to high-ranking government positions, such as William H. Hastie in the Interior Department and Mary McLeod Bethune (founder and president of Bethune-Cookman College) in the National Youth Administration. Eleanor Roosevelt spoke out eloquently throughout the decade against racial discrimination, most notably in 1939 when the Daughters of the American Revolution refused to let African American contralto Marian Anderson sing in Constitution Hall. The first lady and Interior Secretary Harold Ickes arranged for the singer to perform at the Lincoln Memorial, where 75,000 people gathered to hear her on Easter Sunday.

Perhaps the most influential factor in the African Americans' political switch was the color-blind policy of Harry Hopkins. He had more than one million blacks working for the WPA by 1939, many of them in teaching and artistic positions as well as in construction jobs. Overall, the New Deal provided assistance to 40 percent of the nation's blacks during the depression. Uneven as his record was, Roosevelt had still done more to aid this oppressed minority than any previous president since Lincoln. One African American newspaper commented that while "relief and WPA are not ideal, they are better than the Hoover bread lines and they'll have to do until the real thing comes along."

The New Deal did far less for Mexican Americans. Engaged primarily in agricultural labor, these people found their wages in California fields dropping from 35 to 14 cents an hour by 1933. The pool of unemployed migrant labor expanded rapidly with Dust Bowl conditions in the Great Plains and the subsequent flight of "Okies" and "Arkies" to the cotton fields of Arizona and the truck farms of California. The Roosevelt administration cut off any further influx from Mexico by barring entry of any immigrant "likely to become a public charge"; local authorities rounded up migrants and shipped them back to Mexico to reduce the welfare rolls.

With the statue of Abraham Lincoln as a backdrop, African American contralto Marian Anderson sang on the steps of the Lincoln Memorial in a concert given April 9, 1939. ❖

Roosevelt appointed John Collier as commissioner of Indian affairs to bring the New Deal to Native Americans. Under the Indian Reorganization Act of 1934, more than 7 million acres of land were restored to Native American control. Still, many Indians continued to distrust the government and its New Deal programs. Collier is shown here with a group of Flathead Indian chiefs standing behind Secretary of the Interior Harold L. Ickes on October 28, 1935, as Ickes signs the first constitution providing for Indian self-rule. Previously, the Bureau of Indian Affairs had directed the government of the Indians. ❖

The New Deal relief program did aid many thousands of Mexican Americans in the Southwest in the 1930s, although migrant workers had difficulty meeting state requirements. The WPA hired Mexican Americans for a variety of construction and cultural programs, but after 1937 such employment was denied to aliens. Overall, the pattern was one of great economic hardship and relatively little federal assistance for Mexican Americans.

Native Americans, after decades of neglect, fared slightly better under the New Deal. Roosevelt appointed John Collier, a social worker who championed Indian rights, to serve as commissioner of Indian affairs. In 1934, Congress passed the Indian Reorganization Act, a reform measure designed to stress tribal unity and autonomy instead of attempting (as previous policy had done) to transform Indians into self-sufficient farmers by granting them small plots of land. Collier employed more Native Americans in the Indian Bureau, supported educational programs on the reservations, and encouraged tribes to produce native handiwork such as blankets and jewelry. Despite modest gains however, the nation's one-third million Indians remained the most impoverished citizens in America.

Women at Work

The decade witnessed no significant gain in the status of American women. In the midst of the Great Depression, there was little concern expressed for protecting or extending their rights. The popular idea that women worked for "pin money" while men were the breadwinners for their families led employers to discriminate in favor of men when cutting the workforce. Working women "are holding jobs that rightfully belong to the God-intended providers of the household," declared a Chicago civic group. More than three-fourths of the nation's school boards refused to hire married women, and more than half of them fired women teachers who married. Federal regulations prohibited more than one member of a family from working in the civil service, and almost always it was the wife who had to defer to her husband. A Gallup poll revealed that 82 percent of the people disapproved of working wives, with 75 percent of the women polled agreeing.

Many of the working women in the 1930s were either single or the sole supporters of an entire family. Yet their wages remained lower than those for men, and their unemployment rate ran higher than 20 percent throughout the decade. Women over age 40 found it particularly hard to find or retain jobs during the depression. The New Deal offered little encouragement. NRA codes sanctioned lower wages for women, permitting laundries, for example, to pay them as little as 14 cents an hour. The minimum wage did help those women employed in industry, but too many worked as maids and waitresses—jobs not covered by the law—for the new law to have much overall effect on women's income. Despite these hardships, the number of married women and women between the ages of 25 and 40 in the labor force increased during the 1930s. Relatively few women worked in heavy industry, where unemployment was greatest; most were employed in the clerical and service sectors, areas of traditional female employment, in which jobs were more plentiful.

The one area of advance in the 1930s came in government. Eleanor Roosevelt set an example that encouraged millions of American women. Not content to

Women working at a Campbell's soup factory in the 1930s inspect and cut out the bad parts of tomatoes. The number of married women in the paid labor force increased during the 1930s, but their opportunities were limited, their hours long, and their wages low. ❖

be mistress of the White House, she traveled around the country, eager to uncover wrongs, bring them to the president's attention, and, if possible, rectify them. (See the Feature Essay, "Eleanor Roosevelt and the Quest for Social Justice," pp. 770–771) Frances Perkins, the secretary of labor, became the first woman cabinet member, and FDR appointed women as ambassadors and federal judges for the first time.

Women also were elected to office in larger numbers in the 1930s. Hattie W. Caraway of Arkansas succeeded her husband in the Senate, winning a full term in 1934. That same year, voters elected six women to the House of Representatives. Public service, however, was one of the few professions open to women. The nation's leading medical and law schools discouraged women from applying, and the percentage of female faculty members in colleges and universities continued to decline in the 1930s. In sum, a decade that was grim for most Americans was especially hard on American women.

END OF THE NEW DEAL

The New Deal reached its high point in 1936, when Roosevelt was overwhelmingly reelected and the Democratic party strengthened its hold on Congress. This political triumph was deceptive. In the next two

years, Roosevelt met with a series of defeats in Congress. Yet despite the setbacks, he remained a popular political leader who had restored American self-confidence as he strove to meet the challenges of the Great Depression.

The Election of 1936

Franklin Roosevelt enjoyed his finest political hour in 1936. A man who loved the give-and-take of politics, FDR faced challenges from both the left and the right as he sought reelection. Father Coughlin and Gerald L. K. Smith, who inherited Huey Long's following after the senator's assassination in 1935, organized a Union party, with North Dakota Progressive Congressman William Lemke heading the ticket. At the other extreme, a group of wealthy industrialists formed the Liberty League to fight what they saw as the New Deal's assault on property rights. The Liberty League attracted prominent Democrats, including Al Smith, but in 1936 it endorsed the Republican presidential candidate, Governor Alfred M. Landon of Kansas. A moderate, colorless figure, Landon disappointed his backers by refusing to campaign for repeal of the popular New Deal reforms.

Roosevelt ignored Lemke and the Union party, focusing attention instead on the assault from the right. Democratic spokesmen condemned the Liberty League as a "millionaire's union" and reminded the American people of how much Roosevelt had done for them in fighting unemployment and providing relief. In his speeches, FDR condemned the "economic royalists" who were "unanimous in their hatred for me." "I welcome their hatred," he declared, and promised that in his second term, these forces would meet "their master."

This frank appeal to class sympathies proved enormously successful. Roosevelt won easily, receiving five million more votes than he had in 1932 and outscoring Landon in the electoral college by 523 to 8. The Democrats did almost as well in Congress, piling up margins of 331 to 89 in the House and 76 to 16 in the Senate (with 4 not aligned with either major party).

Equally important, the election marked the stunning success of a new political coalition that would

THE ELECTION OF 1936

Candidate	Party	Popular Vote	Electoral Vote
Roosevelt	Democratic	27,752,869	523
Landon	Republican	16,674,665	8

dominate American politics for the next three decades. FDR, building on the inroads into the Republican majority that Al Smith had begun in 1928, carried urban areas by impressive margins, winning 3.6 million more votes than his opponents in the nation's twelve largest cities. He held on to the traditional Democratic votes in the South and West and added to them by appealing strongly to the diverse religious and ethnic groups in the northern cities—Catholics and Jews, Italians and Poles, Irish and Slavs. The strong support of labor, together with three-quarters of the black vote, indicated that the nation's new alignment followed economic as well as cultural lines. The poor and the oppressed, who in the depression years included many middle-class Americans, became attached to the Democratic party, leaving the GOP in a minority position, limited to the well-to-do and to rural and small-town Americans of native stock.

The Supreme Court Fight

FDR proved to be far more adept at winning electoral victories than in achieving his goals in Congress. In 1937, he attempted to use his recent success to overcome the one obstacle remaining in his path—the Supreme Court. During his first term, the Court had ruled several New Deal programs unconstitutional, most notably the NRA and the AAA. Only three of the nine justices were sympathetic to the need for emergency measures in the midst of the depression. Two others were unpredictable, sometimes approving New Deal measures and sometimes opposing them. Four justices were bent on using the Constitution to block Roosevelt's proposals. All were elderly men, and one, Willis Van Devanter, had planned to retire in 1932 but remained on the Court because he believed Roosevelt to be "unfitted and unsafe for the Presidency."

When Congress convened in 1937, the president offered a startling proposal to overcome the Court's threat to the New Deal. Instead of seeking a constitutional

Courtesy, D. R. Fitzpatrick. *St. Louis Post-Dispatch*, June 28, 1935

FDR's battle with the Supreme Court provoked both sympathy and contempt among political cartoonists of the day. In the cartoon on the right, the NRA blue eagle lies dead, nailed to the wall by the Supreme Court. The cartoon on the left, titled "Do We Want a Ventriloquist Act in the Supreme Court?" satirizes FDR's "court-packing" scheme. ❖

ELEANOR ROOSEVELT AND THE QUEST FOR SOCIAL JUSTICE

*I*n August 1933, Eleanor Roosevelt journeyed to Scotts Run, a poor mining community in West Virginia, to observe life in one of the nation's poorest and most desolate areas. The first lady toured the dilapidated homes and listened to the problems of the unemployed miners, some of whom had not worked in eight years. She also met with their wives and children, and visited with local African Americans. It was an experience few would forget; "Some of the Negroes," wrote a local newspaper editor to Eleanor's husband, President Franklin Delano Roosevelt, "think she is God." Millions of Americans held her in similar esteem. At the height of the Great Depression, ER's willingness to listen to, and act

on behalf of, those whose voices often went unheard made her one of the nation's leading symbols of hope and compassion.

Eleanor Roosevelt entered public life as a reformer long before she became first lady. Growing up shy and insecure in a prominent New York family (she was the niece of Theodore Roosevelt), she sought personal fulfillment through voluntary social work. Like many reformers of her day, she found her sense of social justice upset by the existence of poverty and inequality. Avoiding politics, which she then considered a "sinister affair," she limited her activities to nonpartisan reform and relief organizations, such as settlement houses and the Consumer's League. She curtailed her

social work after her 1905 marriage to Franklin Roosevelt, placing her responsibilities as wife and mother first, as she believed a woman should. FDR, as a New York state senator and later as assistant secretary of the Navy, carried the political torch for the family. However, her role changed in 1921 when Franklin was stricken with polio. Eleanor was determined to return him to political life as soon as possible, which she believed was the best antidote to his pain and depression. While working tirelessly to speed his recovery, she also struck out on her own to keep the Roosevelt name alive in New York politics, making speeches, writing magazine articles, and chairing the Women's Platform Committee at the Democratic National Convention in 1924. In the newly formed League of Women Voters and other activist organizations, she brought her reformer's impulse to politics by advocating measures such as a maximum hours law for working women. Through these efforts, she also formed the nucleus of a "woman's network" that she would employ extensively during the New Deal years.

Focusing on those whose needs were greatest, Eleanor became the administration's champion for the dispossessed. While her husband appealed to the "Forgotten Man," she concerned herself with the "Forgotten Woman." She worked with Harry Hopkins to achieve equity for women on relief and to create more jobs for women under the auspices of the CWA and the WPA. With Frances Perkins, she helped establish camps for unemployed girls patterned after the CCC, and worked with the Women's Trade Union League to guarantee

During the Great Depression, Eleanor Roosevelt traveled thousands of miles each year to learn about conditions throughout the country. She is shown here in Des Moines, Iowa, in 1936, inspecting a WPA project to convert a city dump into a waterfront park. ❖

women equal pay for equal work on federal projects. She saw to it that whenever possible, women administrators were hired to supervise projects for women, and in her syndicated newspaper column, "My Day," she often dealt with the problems faced by women during the Great Depression. Her 1933 book, *It's Up To The Women,* urged American women to join her in a crusade for decency and fairness. "For more than a century," wrote one reviewer, "the Great White Father in the White House has been instructing his people in right conduct . . . But now the Great White Mother emerges as a personality in her own right and starts an independent course of instruction on her own account."

Eleanor worked hard for African Americans, whose position at the bottom of American society deeply offended her sense of fairness and decency; in the late 1930s, three quarters of adult blacks in America had not finished high school, and almost 90 percent lived below the federal poverty standard. The first lady spoke out eloquently in favor of equal opportunity for blacks and sought their inclusion in New Deal programs. She worked with Hopkins to employ more African Americans in federal projects, and lobbied within the administration for the appointment of black men and women to administer programs designed specifically for them. Publicly, she endeavored to set an example by addressing black audiences throughout the country, presiding over a more egalitarian White House, and resigning her membership in the Daughters of the American Revolution over the Marian Anderson incident (see p. 766).

Her struggle against racial discrimination sometimes put Mrs. Roosevelt in conflict with her husband's efforts to keep the Democratic Party intact. His fear of alienating southern supporters caused him to temporize on bills to ban lynching and abolish the poll tax; his wife's support of these measures, however, put the Roosevelt name behind them without the same damaging political consequences. In her efforts to advance the cause of civil rights, Eleanor arranged for White House meetings between FDR and African American leaders, supported interracial projects, and spoke out forcefully against racial discrimination. To ER, such change did not help just one element of society, but brought benefits to the entire country. "To deny any part of a population the opportunities for more enjoyment in life, for higher aspirations," she declared, "is a menace to the nation as a whole."

Like other first ladies, Eleanor Roosevelt had to strike a balance between capitalizing on her unique access to the president and intruding illegitimately into the affairs of the nation's elected officials. Her position was complicated, as well, by her own ambivalence on certain issues. Although she advocated greater rights for women, for example, she did not believe in full equality between men and women. She thought that women required protective legislation on account of their special roles as wives and mothers.

Although Mrs. Roosevelt was instrumental in the few gains made by women and African Americans in the 1930s, her advocacy could not overcome the sexual and racial stereotypes that continued to limit their role in the workplace and society. Thus despite her efforts, the plight of these groups during the depression was only slightly relieved. However, this is not to minimize her achievements. As the self-appointed conscience of the Roosevelt Administration, she exposed the areas where the New Deal had not been realized. Her courage and vitality in the pursuit of human rights and equality made her the embodiment of reform and social justice in the New Deal. Eleanor Roosevelt's goal was a simple one, concluded one biographer, "a life of dignity and decency for all."

Eleanor Roosevelt visited many sites in her efforts to bring the New Deal to the forgotten and the dispossessed. She is shown here visiting an African American nursery school run by the WPA in Des Moines, Iowa. ❖

amendment either to limit the Court's power or to clarify the constitutional issues, FDR chose an oblique attack. Declaring the Court was falling behind schedule because of the age of its members, he asked Congress to appoint a new justice for each member of the Court over the age of 70, up to a maximum of six.

Although this **"court-packing" scheme,** as critics quickly dubbed it, was perfectly legal, it outraged not only conservatives but liberals as well, who realized it could set a dangerous precedent for the future. Republicans wisely kept silent, letting prominent Democrats such as Senator Burton Wheeler of Montana lead the fight against Roosevelt's plan. Despite all-out pressure from the White House, resistance in the Senate blocked early action on the proposal.

The Court defended itself well. Chief Justice Charles Evans Hughes testified tellingly to the Senate Judiciary Committee, pointing out that in fact the Court was up to date and not behind schedule as Roosevelt charged. The Court then surprised observers with a series of rulings approving such controversial New Deal measures as the Wagner Act and Social Security. In the midst of the struggle, Justice Van Devanter resigned, enabling FDR to make his first appointment to the Court since taking office in 1933. Believing he had proved his point, the president allowed his court-packing plan to die in the Senate.

During the next few years, four more vacancies occurred, and Roosevelt was able to appoint such distinguished jurists as Hugo Black, William O. Douglas, and Felix Frankfurter to the Supreme Court. Yet the price was high. The Court fight had badly weakened the president's relations with Congress, opening deep rifts with members of his own party. Many senators and representatives who had voted reluctantly for Roosevelt's measures during the depths of the Great

MAJOR NEW DEAL LEGISLATION AND AGENCIES

Year Created	Act or Agency	Provisions
1933	Agricultural Adjustment Administration (AAA)	Attempted to regulate agricultural production through farm subsidies; reworked after the Supreme Court ruled its key regulatory provisions unconstitutional in 1936; coordinated agricultural production during World War II, after which it was disbanded.
	Banking Act of 1933 (Glass-Steagall Act)	Prohibited commercial banks from selling stock or financing corporations; created FDIC.
	Civilian Conservation Corps (CCC)	Young men between the ages of 18 and 25 volunteered to be placed in camps to work on regional environmental projects, mainly west of the Mississippi; they received $30 a month, of which $25 was sent home; disbanded during World War II.
	Civil Works Administration (CWA)	Emergency work relief program put more than four million people to work during the extremely cold winter of 1933–1934, after which it was disbanded.
	Federal Deposit Insurance Corporation (FDIC)	A federal guarantee of savings bank deposits initially of up to $2500, raised to $5000 in 1934, and frequently thereafter; continues today with a limit of $100,000.
	Federal Emergency Relief Administration (FERA)	Combined cash relief to needy families with work relief; superseded in early 1935 by the extensive work relief projects of the WPA and unemployment insurance established by Social Security.
	National Recovery Administration (NRA)	Attempted to combat the Great Depression through national economic planning by establishing and administering a system of industrial codes to control production, prices, labor relations, and trade practices among leading business interests; ruled unconstitutional by the Supreme Court in 1935.
	Public Works Administration (PWA)	Financed more than 34,000 federal and nonfederal construction projects at a cost of more than $6 billion; initiated the first federal public housing program, made the federal government the nation's leading producer of power, and advanced conservation of the nation's natural resources; discontinued in 1939 due to its effectiveness at reducing unemployment and promoting private investment.
	Tennessee Valley Authority (TVA)	An attempt at regional planning. Included provisions for environment and recreational design; architectural, educational, and health projects; and controversial public power projects; continues today to meet the Tennessee Valley's energy and flood-control needs.

Depression now felt free to oppose any further New Deal reforms.

The New Deal in Decline

The legislative record during Roosevelt's second term was meager. Aside from the minimum wage and a maximum-hour law passed in 1938, Congress did not extend the New Deal into any new areas. Attempts to institute national health insurance met with stubborn resistance, as did efforts by civil rights advocates to pass antilynching legislation. Disturbed by the growing congressional resistance, Roosevelt set out in the spring of 1938 to defeat a number of conservative Democratic congressmen and senators, primarily in the South. His targets gleefully charged the president with interference in local politics; only one of the men he sought to defeat lost in the primaries. The failure of this attempted purge further undermined Roosevelt's strained relations with Congress.

The worst blow came in the economic sector. The slow but steady improvement in the economy suddenly gave way to a sharp recession in the late summer of 1937. In the following ten months, industrial production fell by one-third, and nearly four million workers lost their jobs. Critics of the New Deal quickly labeled the downturn "the Roosevelt recession," and business executives claimed that it reflected a lack of confidence in FDR's leadership.

The criticism was overblown but not without basis. In an effort to reduce expanding budget deficits, Roosevelt had cut back sharply on WPA and other government programs after the election. Federal contributions to consumer purchasing power fell from $4.1 billion in 1936 to less than $1 billion in 1937. For several months, Roosevelt refused to heed calls from

Year Created	Act or Agency	Provisions
1934	Federal Communications Commission (FCC)	Regulatory agency with wide discretionary powers established to oversee wired and wireless communication; reflected growing importance of radio in everyday lives of Americans during the Great Depression; continues to regulate television as well as radio.
	Federal Housing Administration (FHA)	Expanded private home ownership among moderate-income families through federal guarantees of private mortgages, the reduction of down payments from 30 to 10 percent, and the extension of repayment from 20 to 30 years; continues to function today.
	Securities and Exchange Commission (SEC)	Continues today to regulate trading practices in stocks and bonds according to federal laws.
1935	National Labor Relations Board (NLRB); established by Wagner Act	Greatly enhanced power of American labor by overseeing collective bargaining; continues to arbitrate labor-management disputes today.
	National Youth Administration (NYA)	Established by the WPA to reduce competition for jobs by supporting education and training of youth; paid grants to more than 2 million high school and college students in return for work performed in their schools; also trained another 2.6 million out-of-school youths as skilled labor to prepare them for later employment in the private sector; disbanded during World War II.
	Rural Electrification Administration (REA)	Transformed American rural life by making electricity available at low rates to American farm families in areas that private power companies refused to service; closed the cultural gap between rural and urban everyday life by making modern amenities, such as radio, available in rural areas.
	Social Security Act	Guaranteed retirement payments for enrolled workers beginning at age 65; set up federal-state system of unemployment insurance and care for dependent mothers and children, the handicapped, and public health; continues today.
	Works Progress Administration (WPA)	Massive work relief program funded projects ranging from construction to acting; disbanded by FDR during World War II.
1937	Farm Security Administration (FSA)	Granted loans to small farmers and tenants for rehabilitation and purchase of small-sized farms; Congress slashed its appropriations during World War II when many poor farmers entered the armed forces or migrated to urban areas.
1938	Fair Labor Standards Act	Established a minimum wage of 40 cents an hour and a maximum workweek of 40 hours for businesses engaged in interstate commerce.

economists to restore heavy government spending. Finally, in April 1938, Roosevelt asked Congress for a $3.75 billion relief appropriation, and the economy began to revive. But FDR's premature attempt to balance the budget had meant two more years of hard times and had marred his reputation as the energetic foe of the depression.

The political result of the attempted purge and the recession was a strong Republican upsurge in the elections of 1938. The GOP won an impressive 81 seats in the House and 8 more in the Senate, as well as 13 governorships. The party many thought dead suddenly had new life. The Democrats still held a sizable majority in Congress, but their margin in the House was particularly deceptive. There were 262 Democratic representatives to 169 Republicans, but 93 southern Democrats held the balance of power. More and more often after 1938, anti–New Deal Southerners voted with Republican conservatives to block social and economic reform measures. Thus not only was the New Deal over by the end of 1938, but a new bipartisan conservative coalition that would prevail for a quarter century had formed in Congress.

CONCLUSION: THE NEW DEAL AND AMERICAN LIFE

The New Deal lasted a brief five years, and most of its measures came in two legislative bursts in the spring of 1933 and the summer of 1935. Yet its impact on American life was enduring. Nearly every aspect of economic, social, and political development in the decades that followed bore the imprint of Roosevelt's leadership.

The least impressive achievement of the New Deal came in the economic realm. Whatever credit Roosevelt is given for relieving human suffering in the depths of the Great Depression must be balanced against his failure to achieve recovery in the 1930s. The moderate nature of his programs, especially the unwieldy NRA, led to slow and halting industrial recovery. Although much of the improvement that was made came as a result of government spending, FDR never embraced the concept of planned deficits, striving instead for a balanced budget. As a result, the nation had barely reached the 1929 level of production a decade later, and there were still nearly ten million men and women unemployed.

Equally important, Roosevelt refused to make any sweeping changes in the American economic system. Aside from the TVA, there were no broad experiments in regional planning and no attempt to alter free enterprise beyond imposing some limited forms of government regulation. The New Deal did nothing to alter the basic distribution of wealth and power in the nation. The outcome was the preservation of the traditional capitalist system with a thin overlay of federal control.

More significant change occurred in American society. With the adoption of Social Security, the government acknowledged for the first time its responsibility to provide for the welfare of those unable to care for themselves in an industrial society. The Wagner Act helped stimulate the growth of labor unions to balance corporate power, and the minimum wage law provided a much needed floor for many workers.

Yet the New Deal tended to help only the more vocal and organized groups, such as union members and commercial farmers. Those without effective voices or political clout—African Americans, Mexican Americans, women, sharecroppers, restaurant and laundry workers—received little help from the New Deal. For all the appealing rhetoric about the "forgotten man," Roosevelt did little more than Hoover in responding to the long-term needs of the dispossessed.

The most lasting impact of the Roosevelt leadership came in politics. Taking advantage of the emerging power of ethnic voters and capitalizing on the frustration growing out of the depression, FDR proved to be a genius at forging a new coalition. Overcoming the friction between rural and urban Democrats that had prolonged Republican supremacy in the 1920s, he attracted new groups to the Democratic party, principally African Americans and organized labor. His political success led to a major realignment that lasted long after he left the scene.

CHRONOLOGY

1932	Franklin D. Roosevelt elected president
1933	Emergency Banking Relief Act passed in one day (March) ❖ Twenty-first Amendment repeals prohibition (December)
1934	Securities and Exchange Commission authorized (June)
1935	Works Progress Administration (WPA) hires unemployed (April) ❖ Wagner Act grants workers collective bargaining (July) ❖ Congress passes Social Security Act (August)
1936	FDR wins second term as president
1937	United Automobile Workers sit-down strike forces General Motors contract (February) ❖ FDR loses court-packing battle (July) ❖ "Roosevelt recession" begins (August)
1938	Congress sets minimum wage at 40 cents an hour (June)

His political achievement also reveals the true nature of Roosevelt's success. He was a brilliant politician who recognized the essence of leadership in a democracy—appealing directly to the people and giving them a sense of purpose. He succeeded in infusing them with the same indomitable courage and jaunty optimism that had marked his own battle with polio. Thus, despite his limitations as a reformer, Roosevelt proved to be the leader the American people needed in the 1930s—a president who provided the psychological lift that helped them endure and survive the Great Depression.

RECOMMENDED READING

The best overall account of political developments in the 1930s is William Leuchtenburg, *Franklin D. Roosevelt and the New Deal* (1963). Leuchtenburg offers a balanced treatment but concludes by defending Roosevelt's record. For a more critical view, see James MacGregor Burns, *Roosevelt: The Lion and the Fox* (1956), which portrays FDR as an overly cautious political leader; and Robert A. McElvaine, *The Great Depression: America, 1929–1941* (1984), which laments the New Deal's failure to make more sweeping changes in American life. Gene Smiley, *Rethinking the Great Depression* (2002), succinctly challenges conventional wisdom on the subject.

David M. Kennedy provides a comprehensive portrait of American life during both the Great Depression and World War II in *Freedom from Fear* (1999). More succinct is Gerald D. Nash, *The Crucial Era: The Great Depression and World War II, 1929–1945* (1992). For a sympathetic examination of the New Deal through 1936, see Arthur M. Schlesinger, Jr., *The Age of Roosevelt,* 3 vols. (1957–1960); Paul Conkin offers a brief but provocative critique of Roosevelt's policies in *The New Deal* (1967). George McJimsy, *The Presidency of Franklin Delano Roosevelt* (2000), is the most recent and best-balanced account.

John Kenneth Galbraith, *The Great Crash, 1929* (1961), has long been the standard treatment of that stomach-churning event, but Maury Klein, *Rainbow's End* (2001), may displace it. Alan Brinkley, *Voices of Protest* (1982), assesses the challenges to Roosevelt from the left and the right. Lizabeth Cohen, *Making a New Deal: Industrial Workers in Chicago, 1919–1939* (1990), examines the effects of the Great Depression and the New Deal on the working class. Blanche Wiesen Cook's continuing biography, *Eleanor Roosevelt,* 2 vols. to date (1992–), shows the transformation of the first lady into an advocate of the poor and dispossessed. Franklin Roosevelt's troubles with the Supreme Court are traced in William Leuchtenburg, *The Supreme Court Reborn* (1995); and Barry Cushman, *Rethinking the New Deal Court* (1998). The waning of the New Deal is the theme of Alan Brinkley, *The End of Reform* (1995).

For a list of additional titles related to this chapter's topics, please see http://www.ablongman.com/divine.

SUGGESTED WEB SITES

Voices from the Dust Bowl: The Charles L. Todd and Robert Sonkin Migrant Worker Collection, 1940–1941

http://memory.loc.gov/ammem/afctshtml/tshome.html
Farm Security Administration (FSA) studies of migrant work camps in central California in 1940 and 1941 are the bulk of this site. The collection includes audio recordings, photographs, manuscript materials, and publications.

New Deal Network

http://newdeal.feri.org/
This database includes photographs, political cartoons, and texts—including speeches, letters, and other historic documents—from the New Deal period.

Franklin Delano Roosevelt

http://www.ipl.org/ref/POTUS/fdroosevelt.html
This site provides information about FDR, the only president to serve more than two terms.

A New Deal for the Arts

http://www.archives.gov/exhibit_hall/new_deal_for_the_arts/index.html
Artwork, documents, and photographs recount the federal government's efforts to fund artists in the 1930s in the National Archives site.

America from the Great Depression to World War II: Photographs from the FSA and OWI, ca. 1935–1945

http://memory.loc.gov/ammem/fsowhome.html
These images in the Farm Security Administration–Office of War Information Collection show Americans from all over the nation experiencing everything from despair to triumph in the 1930s and 1940s.

The Landing at Saipan *by William Draper, who painted combat scenes he witnessed while serving in the U.S. Navy. The global conflict of World War II involved every major power in the world as it was fought on land, at sea, and in the air.* ❖

America and the World, 1921–1945

A Pact Without Power

On August 27, 1928, U.S. Secretary of State Frank B. Kellogg, French Foreign Minister Aristide Briand, and representatives of twelve other nations met in Paris to sign a treaty outlawing war. Several hundred spectators crowded into the ornate clock room of the Quai d'Orsay to watch the historic ceremony. Six huge klieg lights illuminated the scene so photographers could record the moment for a world eager for peace. Briand opened the ceremony with a speech in which he declared, "Peace is proclaimed," and then Kellogg signed the document with a foot-long gold pen given to him by the citizens of Le Havre as a token of Franco-American friendship. In the United States, a senator called the **Kellogg-Briand Pact** "the most telling action ever taken in human history to abolish war."

In reality, the Pact of Paris was the result of a determined American effort to avoid involvement in the European alliance system. In June 1927, Briand had sent a message to the American people inviting the United States to join with France in signing a treaty to outlaw war between the two nations. The invitation struck a sympathetic response, especially among pacifists who had advocated the outlawing of war throughout the 1920s, but the State Department feared correctly that Briand's true intention was to establish a close tie between France and the United States. The French had already created a network of alliances with the smaller countries of eastern Europe; an antiwar treaty with the United States would at least ensure American sympathy, if not involvement, in case of another European war. Kellogg delayed several months and then outmaneuvered Briand by proposing the pledge against war not be confined just to France and the United States, but instead be extended to all nations. An unhappy Briand, who had wanted a bilateral treaty with the United States, had no choice but to agree, and so the diplomatic charade finally culminated in the elaborate signing ceremony in Paris.

Eventually the signers of the Kellogg-Briand Pact included nearly every nation in the world, but the effect was negligible. All promised to renounce war as an instrument of national policy, except of course, as the British made clear in a reservation, in matters of self-defense. Enforcement of the treaty relied solely on the moral force of world opinion. The Pact of Paris was, as one senator shrewdly commented, only "an international kiss."

UNFORTUNATELY, THE KELLOGG-BRIAND PACT was symbolic of American foreign policy in the years immediately following World War I. Instead of asserting the role of world leadership its resources and power commanded, the United States retreated from involvement with other nations. America went its own way, extending trade and economic dominance but refusing to take the lead in maintaining world order. This retreat from responsibility seemed unimportant in the 1920s when exhaustion from World War I ensured relative peace and tranquility. But in the 1930s,

OUTLINE
❖❖❖

Retreat, Reversal, and Rivalry

Isolationism

The Road to War

Turning the Tide Against the Axis

The Home Front

Victory

Conclusion: The Transforming Power of War

FEATURE ESSAY
❖❖❖

The Face of the Holocaust

777

Secretary of State Frank Kellogg signs the Kellogg-Briand Treaty renouncing war. A grand document, the treaty included no method to enforce its provisions. The agreement was formally broken when Japan invaded Manchuria in 1931. ❖

when threats to world order arose in Europe and Asia, the American people retreated even deeper, searching for an isolationist policy that would spare them the agony of another great war.

There was no place to hide in the modern world. The Nazi onslaught in Europe and the Japanese expansion in Asia finally convinced America to reverse its isolationist stance and become involved in World War II in late 1941, at a time when the chances for an Allied victory seemed most remote. With incredible swiftness, the nation mobilized its military and industrial strength. American armies were soon fighting on three continents,

the U.S. Navy controlled the world's oceans, and the nation's factories were sending a vast stream of war supplies to more than twenty Allied countries.

When the Allied victory came in 1945, the United States was by far the most powerful nation in the world. But instead of the enduring peace that might have permitted a return to a less active foreign policy, the onset of the Cold War with the Soviet Union brought on a new era of tension and rivalry. This time the United States could not retreat from responsibility. World War II was a coming of age for American foreign policy.

RETREAT, REVERSAL, AND RIVALRY

"The day of the armistice America stood on the hilltops of glory, proud in her strength, invincible in her ideals, acclaimed and loved by a world free of an ancient fear at last," wrote journalist George Creel in 1920. "Today we writhe in a pit of our own digging; despising ourselves and despised by the betrayed peoples of earth." The bitter disillusionment Creel described ran through every aspect of American foreign policy in the 1920s. In contrast to diplomatic actions under Wilsonian idealism, American diplomats in the 1920s made loans, negotiated treaties and agreements, and pledged the nation's good faith, but they were careful not to make any binding commitments on behalf of world order. The result was neither isolation nor involvement but rather a cautious

middle course that managed to alienate friends and encourage foes.

Retreat in Europe

The United States emerged from World War I as the richest nation on earth, displacing England from its prewar position of economic primacy. The Allied governments owed the United States a staggering $10 billion in war debts, money they had borrowed during and immediately after the conflict. Each year of the 1920s saw the nation increase its economic lead as the balance of trade tipped heavily in America's favor. The war-ravaged countries of Europe borrowed enormous amounts from American bankers to rebuild their economies; Germany alone absorbed more than $3 billion in

American investments during the decade. By 1929, American exports totaled more than $7 billion a year, three times the prewar level, and American overseas investment had risen to $17.2 billion.

The European nations could no longer compete on equal terms. The high American tariff, first imposed in 1922, was raised again with enactment of the Hawley-Smoot Tariff in 1930. The high tariff frustrated attempts by England, France, and a defeated Germany to earn the dollars necessary to meet their American financial obligations. The Allied partners in World War I asked Washington to cancel the $10 billion in war debts, particularly after they were forced to scale down their demands for German reparations payments. American leaders from Wilson to Hoover refused the request, claiming the ungrateful Allies were trying to repudiate their obligations.

Only a continuing flow of private American capital to Germany allowed the payment of reparations to the Allies and the partial repayment of the Allies' war debts in the 1920s. The financial crash of 1929 halted the flow of American dollars across the Atlantic and led to subsequent default on the debt payments, with accompanying bitterness on both sides of the ocean.

Political relations fared little better. The United States never joined the League of Nations, nor did it take part in the attempts by England and France to negotiate European security treaties. American observers attended League sessions and occasionally took part in economic and cultural missions in Geneva. But the Republican administrations of the 1920s refused to compromise American freedom of action by embracing collective security, the principle on which the League was founded. And FDR, always realistic, made no effort to renew Wilson's futile quest. Thus the United States remained aloof from the European balance of power and refused to stand behind the increasingly shaky Versailles settlement.

The U.S. government ignored the Soviet Union throughout the 1920s. American businesses, however, exported large quantities of heavy machinery to Russia as part of its rapid industrialization. When that trade began to slump after 1930, business leaders hoped to revive it by calling on Washington to extend diplomatic recognition to the Bolshevik regime that had come to power in the Russian Revolution of 1917. In 1933, Franklin Roosevelt finally ended the long estrangement by signing an agreement opening up diplomatic relations between the two countries. The Soviets soon went back on promises to stop all subversive activity in the United States and to settle prerevolutionary debts, but even if they rarely understood one another, at least the two nations had opened a channel of communication.

Cooperation in Latin America

U.S. policy was both more active and more enlightened in the Western Hemisphere than in Europe. The State Department sought new ways in the 1920s to pursue traditional goals of political dominance and economic advantage in Latin America. The outcome of World War I lessened any fears of European threats to the area and thus enabled the United States to dismantle the interventions in the Caribbean carried out by Roosevelt, Taft, and Wilson. At the same time, both Republican and Democratic administrations worked hard to extend American trade and investment in the nations to the south.

Under Harding, Coolidge, and Hoover, American marines were withdrawn from Haiti and the Dominican Republic, and in 1924 the last detachment left Nicaragua, ending a twelve-year occupation. Renewed unrest there the next year, however, led to a second intervention in Nicaragua, which did not end until the early 1930s.

Showing a new sensitivity, the State Department released the Clark Memorandum in 1930, a policy statement repudiating the controversial Roosevelt Corollary to the Monroe Doctrine. Under the Monroe Doctrine, the United States had no right to intervene in neighboring states, declared Undersecretary of State J. Reuben Clark, although he asserted a traditional claim to protect American lives and property under international law.

When FDR took office in 1933, relations with Latin America were far better than they had been under Wilson, but American trade in the hemisphere had fallen drastically as the depression worsened. Roosevelt moved quickly to solidify the improved relations and gain economic benefits. With his usual flair for the dramatic, he proclaimed a **Good Neighbor policy** and then proceeded to win goodwill by renouncing the imperialism of the past.

In 1933, Secretary of State Cordell Hull signed a conditional pledge of nonintervention at the Pan-American Conference in Montevideo, Uruguay. A year later, the United States renounced the right to intervene in Cuban affairs it had asserted under the Platt Amendment and loosened its grip on Panama. By 1936, American troops were no longer occupying any Latin American nation. FDR personally cemented the new policy by traveling to Buenos Aires to sign an agreement that forbade intervention "directly or indirectly, and for whatever reason" in the internal affairs of a Central or South American state.

The United States had not changed its basic goal of political and economic dominance in the hemisphere; rather, the new policy of benevolence reflected Roosevelt's belief that cooperation and friendship were more effective tactics than threats and armed intervention. Mexico tried his patience in 1938 by nationalizing its oil resources; with admirable restraint, the president finally negotiated a settlement in 1941 on terms favorable to Mexico. Yet this economic loss was more than offset by the new trade opportunities opened up by the Good Neighbor policy. American commerce with Latin America increased fourfold in the 1930s, and investment rose substantially from its Great Depression low. Most important, FDR succeeded in forging a new policy of regional collective security. As the ominous events leading to World War II unfolded in Europe and Asia, the nations of the Western Hemisphere looked to the United States for protection against external danger.

Rivalry in Asia

In the years following World War I, the United States and Japan were on a collision course in the Pacific. The Japanese, lacking the raw materials to sustain their developing industrial economy, were determined to expand onto the Asian mainland. They had taken Korea by 1905 and during World War I had extended their control over the mines, harbors, and railroads of Manchuria, the industrial region of northeast China. The American Open Door policy remained the primary obstacle to complete Japanese dominion over China. The United States thus faced the clear-cut choice of either abandoning China or forcefully opposing Japan's expansion. American efforts to avoid making this painful decision postponed the eventual showdown but not the growing rivalry.

The first attempt at a solution came in 1921 when the United States convened the Washington Disarmament Conference, which included delegates from the United States, Japan, Great Britain, and six other nations. The major objective was a political settlement of the tense Asian situation, but the most pressing issue was a dangerous naval race between Japan and the United States. Both nations were engaged in extensive shipbuilding programs begun during the war. Great Britain was forced to compete in order to preserve its traditional control of the sea; even so, projected construction indicated that both the United States and Japan would overtake the British navy by the end of the decade. Japan, spending nearly one-third of its total budget on naval construction, was eager for an agreement; in the United States, growing congressional concern over appropriations suggested the need for slowing the naval buildup.

In his welcoming address at the Washington Conference, Secretary of State Charles Evans Hughes outlined a specific plan for naval disarmament, calling for the scrapping of sixty-six battleships—thirty

American, nineteen British, and seventeen Japanese. Three months later, delegates signed a Five Power Treaty embodying the main elements of Hughes's proposal: limitation of capital ships (battleships and aircraft carriers) in a ratio of 5:5:3 for the United States, Britain, and Japan, respectively, and 1.67:1.67 for France and Italy. England reluctantly accepted equality with the United States, while Japan agreed to the lower ratio only in return for an American pledge not to fortify Pacific bases such as the Philippines and Guam. The treaty cooled off the naval race even though it did not include cruisers, destroyers, or submarines.

The Washington Conference produced two other major agreements: the Nine Power Treaty and the Four Power Treaty. The first simply pledged all the countries involved to uphold the Open Door policy, while the other compact replaced the old Anglo-Japanese alliance with a new Pacific security pact signed by the United States, Great Britain, Japan, and France. Neither document contained any enforcement provision beyond a promise to consult in case of a violation. In essence, the Washington treaties formed a parchment peace, a pious set of pledges that attempted to freeze the status quo in the Pacific.

This compromise lasted less than a decade. In September 1931, Japanese forces violated the Nine Power Treaty and the Kellogg-Briand Pact by overrunning Manchuria in a brutal act of aggression. The United States, paralyzed by the depression, responded feebly. Secretary of State Henry L. Stimson sent an observer to Geneva to assure cooperation with the League of Nations, which was content to investigate the "incident." In January 1932, Stimson fell back on moral force, issuing notes vowing the United States would not recognize the legality of the Japanese seizure of Manchuria. Despite concurrence by the League on nonrecognition, the Japanese ignored the American moral sanction and incorporated the former Chinese province, now renamed Manchukuo, into their rapidly expanding empire.

Aside from the Good Neighbor approach in the Western Hemisphere, American foreign policy faithfully reflected the prevailing disillusionment with world power that gripped the country after World War I. The United States avoided taking any constructive steps toward preserving world order, preferring instead the empty symbolism of the Washington treaties and the Kellogg-Briand Pact.

ISOLATIONISM

The retreat from an active world policy in the 1920s turned into a headlong flight back to isolationism in the 1930s. Two factors were responsible. First, the depression made foreign policy seem remote and unimportant to most Americans. As unemployment increased and the economic crisis intensified after 1929, many people grew apathetic about events abroad. Second, the danger of war abroad, when it did finally penetrate the American consciousness, served only to strengthen the desire to escape involvement.

Three powerful and discontented nations were on the march in the 1930s—Germany, Italy, and Japan. In Germany, Adolf Hitler came to power in 1933 as the head of a National Socialist, or Nazi, movement. A shrewd and charismatic leader, Hitler capitalized on both domestic discontent and bitterness over World War I. Blaming the Jews for all of Germany's ills and asserting the supremacy of the "Aryan" race of blond, blue-eyed Germans, he quickly imposed a totalitarian dictatorship in which the Nazi party ruled and the *Führer* was supreme. At first, his foreign policy seemed harmless, but as he consolidated his power, the ultimate threat to world peace became clearer. Hitler took Germany out of the League of Nations, reoccupied the Rhineland, and formally denounced the Treaty of Versailles. His boasts of uniting all Germans into a Greater Third Reich that would last a thousand years filled his European opponents with terror, blocking any effective challenge to his regime.

In Italy, another dictator, Benito Mussolini, had come to power in 1922. Emboldened by Hitler's success, he embarked on an aggressive foreign policy in 1935. His invasion of the independent African nation of Ethiopia led its emperor, Haile Selassie, to call on the League of Nations for support. With England and France far more concerned about Hitler, the League's halfhearted measures utterly failed to halt Mussolini's conquest. "Fifty-two nations had combined to resist aggression," commented historian A. J. P. Taylor; "all they accomplished was that Haile Selassie lost all his country instead of only half." Collective security had failed its most important test.

Japan formed the third element in the threat to world peace. Militarists began to dominate the government in Tokyo by the mid-1930s, using tactics of fear and even assassination against their liberal opponents. By 1936, Japan had left the League of Nations and had repudiated the Washington treaties. A year later, its armies began an invasion of China that marked the beginning of the Pacific phase of World War II.

The resurgence of militarism in Germany, Italy, and Japan undermined the Versailles settlement and threatened to destroy the existing balance of power. England and France in Europe proved as powerless as China in Asia to stop the tide of aggression. In 1937, the three totalitarian nations signed an anti-Comintern pact completing a Berlin-Rome-Tokyo axis. The alliance of the **Axis Powers** ostensibly was

Millions of Germans idolized Adolf Hitler, portrayed in this captured German painting as a white knight. After the painting came into American hands, a GI slashed Hitler's face to indicate his displeasure with the mystique of the Führer. ❖

aimed at the Soviet Union, but in fact it threatened the entire world. Only a determined American response could unite the other nations against the Axis threat. Unfortunately, the United States deliberately abstained from assuming this role of leadership until it was nearly too late.

The Lure of Pacifism and Neutrality

The growing danger of war abroad led to a rising American desire for peace and noninvolvement. Memories of World War I contributed heavily. Erich Maria Remarque's novel *All Quiet on the Western Front*, as well as the movie based on it, reminded people of the brutality of war. Historians began to treat the Great War as a mistake, criticizing Wilson for failing to preserve American neutrality and claiming the clever British had duped the United States into entering the war. Walter Millis advanced this thesis in *America's Road to War, 1914–1917*, published in 1935. It was hailed as a vivid description of the process by which "a peace-loving democracy, muddled but excited, misinformed and whipped to a frenzy, embarked upon its greatest foreign war."

American youth made clear their determination not to repeat the mistakes of their elders. Pacifism swept across college campuses. A Brown University poll indicated 72 percent of the students opposed military service in wartime. At Princeton, undergraduates formed the Veterans of Future Wars, a parody on veterans' groups, to demand a bonus of $1000 apiece before they marched off to a foreign war. In April 1934, students and professors alike walked out of class to attend massive antiwar rallies, which became an annual rite of spring in the 1930s. Demonstrators carried signs reading "Abolish the R.O.T.C." and "Build Schools—Not Battleships," and pacifist orators urged students to sign a pledge not to support their country "in any war it might conduct."

The pacifist movement found a scapegoat in the munitions industry. The publication of several books exposing the unsavory business tactics of large arms dealers such as Krupp in Germany and Vickers in Britain led to a demand to curb these "merchants of death." Senator Gerald Nye of North Dakota headed a special Senate committee that spent two years investigating American munitions dealers. The committee revealed the enormous profits firms such as Du Pont reaped from World War I, but Nye went further, charging that bankers and munitions makers were responsible for American intervention in 1917. No proof was forthcoming, but the public—prepared to believe the worst of businessmen during the Great Depression—accepted the "merchants of death" thesis.

The Nye Committee's revelations culminated in neutrality legislation. In 1935, Senator Nye and another Senate colleague introduced measures to ban arms sales and loans to belligerents and to prevent Americans from traveling on belligerent ships. By outlawing the activities that led to World War I, they hoped, the United States could avoid involvement in the new conflict. This "never again" philosophy proved irresistible. In August 1935, Congress passed the first of three **neutrality acts.** The 1935 law banned the sale of arms to nations at war and warned American citizens not to sail on belligerent ships. In 1936, a second act added a ban on loans, and in 1937, a third neutrality act made these prohibitions permanent and required, on a two-year trial basis, that all trade other than munitions be conducted on a cash-and-carry basis.

President Roosevelt played a passive role in the adoption of the neutrality legislation. At first opposed to the arms embargo, he finally approved it for six months in 1935 in a compromise designed to save important New Deal legislation in Congress. Yet he also appeared to share the isolationist assumption that a European war would have no impact on vital national interests. He termed the first neutrality act "entirely satisfactory" when he signed it. Others in the administration criticized the mandatory nature of the new law,

The pacifism that swept college campuses in the 1930s touched students at the University of Chicago. The university undergraduates shown here hold placards bearing antiwar slogans as they wait to join a parade as part of a nationwide demonstration against war. ❖

pointing out that it prevented the United States from distinguishing between aggressors and their victims. Privately, Roosevelt expressed some of the same reservations, but publicly he bowed to the prevailing isolationism. He signed the subsequent neutrality acts without protest, and during the 1936 election, he delivered an impassioned denunciation of war. "I hate war," he told an audience in Chautauqua, New York. "I have passed unnumbered hours, I shall pass unnumbered hours, thinking and planning how war may be kept from this nation."

Yet FDR did take a few steps to try to limit the nation's retreat into isolationism. His failure to invoke the neutrality act after the Japanese invasion of China in 1937 enabled the hard-pressed Chinese to continue buying arms from the United States. In January 1938, he used his influence to block a proposal by Indiana Congressman Louis Ludlow to require a nationwide referendum before Congress could declare war. FDR's strongest public statement came earlier, in Chicago in October 1937, when he denounced "the epidemic of world lawlessness" and called for an international effort to "quarantine" the disease. When reporters asked him if his call for "positive efforts to preserve peace" signaled a repeal of the neutrality acts, however, Roosevelt quickly reaffirmed this isolationist legislation. Whatever his private yearning for cooperation against aggressors, the president had no intention of challenging the prevailing public mood of the 1930s.

War in Europe

The neutrality legislation played directly into the hands of Adolf Hitler. Bent on the conquest of Europe, he could now proceed without worrying about American interference. In March 1938, he seized Austria in a bloodless coup. Six months later, he was demanding the Sudetenland, a province of Czechoslovakia with a large German population. When the British and French leaders agreed to meet with Hitler at Munich, FDR voiced his approval. Roosevelt carefully kept the United States aloof from the decision to surrender the Sudetenland in the hopes of appeasing Hitler's demand for land. At the same time, the president gave his tacit approval of the policy of appeasement by telling the British prime minister

Hitler sent his armies into Poland with tremendous force and firepower, devastating the country. Here German troops observe as the German Luftwaffe bombs Warsaw in September 1939, destroying the city and forcing its inhabitants to surrender. ❖

that he shared his "hope and belief that there exists to-day the greatest opportunity in years for the establishment of a new order based on justice and on law."

Six months after the meeting at Munich, Hitler violated his promises by seizing nearly all of Czechoslovakia. In the United States, Roosevelt permitted the State Department to press for neutrality revision. The administration proposal to repeal the arms embargo and place *all* trade with belligerents, including munitions, on a cash-and-carry basis soon met stubborn resistance from isolationists. They argued that cash-and-carry would favor England and France, who controlled the sea. The House rejected the measure by a narrow margin, and the Senate's Foreign Relations Committee voted 12 to 11 to postpone any action on neutrality revision.

In July 1939, Roosevelt finally abandoned his aloof position and met with Senate leaders to plead for reconsideration. Warnings of the imminence of war in Europe by both the president and the secretary of state failed to impress the isolationists. Senator William Borah, who had led the fight against the League of Nations in 1919, responded that he believed the chances for war in Europe were remote. After canvassing the senators present, Vice President John Nance Garner bluntly told FDR that the neutrality revision was dead. "You haven't got the votes," Garner commented, "and that's all there is to it."

On September 1, 1939, Hitler began World War II by invading Poland. England and France responded two days later by declaring war, although there was no way they could prevent the German conquest of Poland. Russia had played a key role, refusing Western overtures for a common front against Germany and finally signing a nonaggression treaty with Hitler in late August. The Nazi-Soviet Pact enabled Germany to avoid a two-front war; the Russians were rewarded with a generous slice of eastern Poland.

President Roosevelt reacted to the outbreak of war by proclaiming American neutrality, but the successful aggression by Nazi Germany brought into question the isolationist assumption that American well-being did not depend on the European balance of power. Strategic as well as ideological considerations began to undermine the earlier belief that the United States could safely pursue a policy of neutrality and noninvolvement. The long retreat from responsibility was about to end as Americans came to realize that their own democracy and security were at stake in the European war.

THE ROAD TO WAR

For two years, the United States tried to remain at peace while war raged in Europe and Asia. In contrast to the climate of the country while Wilson attempted

to be impartial during most of World War I, however, the American people displayed an overwhelming sympathy for the Allies and total distaste for Germany and Japan. Roosevelt made no secret of his preference for an Allied victory, but a fear of isolationist criticism compelled him to move slowly, and often deviously, in adopting a policy of aid for England and France.

From Neutrality to Undeclared War

Two weeks after the outbreak of war in Europe, Roosevelt called Congress into special session to revise the neutrality legislation. He wanted to repeal the arms embargo in order to supply weapons to England and France, but he refused to state this aim openly. Instead he asked Congress to replace the arms embargo with cash-and-carry regulations. Belligerents would be able to purchase war supplies in the United States, but they would have to pay cash and transport the goods in their own ships. Public opinion strongly supported the president, and Congress passed the revised neutrality policy by heavy margins in early November 1939.

A series of dramatic German victories had a profound impact on American opinion. Quiet during the winter of 1939–1940, the Germans struck with lightning speed and devastating effect in the spring. In April, they seized Denmark and Norway, and on May 10, 1940, they unleashed the *blitzkrieg* (lightning war) on the western front. Using tanks, armored columns, and dive-bombers in close coordination, the German army cut deep into the Allied lines, dividing the British and French forces. Within three weeks, the British were driven off the Continent. In another three weeks, France fell to Hitler's victorious armies.

Americans were stunned. Hitler had taken only six weeks to achieve what Germany had failed to do in four years of fighting in World War I. Suddenly they realized they did have a stake in the outcome; if England fell, Hitler might well gain control of the British navy. The Atlantic would no longer be a barrier; instead, it would be a highway for German penetration of the New World.

Roosevelt responded by invoking a policy of all-out aid to the Allies, short of war. In a speech at Charlottesville, Virginia, in June (just after Italy entered the war by invading France), he denounced Germany and Italy as representing "the gods of force and hate" and vowed, "The whole of our sympathies lies with those nations that are giving their life blood in combat against these forces." It was too late to help France, but in early September, FDR announced the transfer of fifty old destroyers to England in exchange for rights to build air and naval bases on eight British possessions in the Western Hemisphere. Giving warships to a belligerent nation was clearly a breach of neutrality, but Roosevelt stressed the importance of guarding the Atlantic approaches, calling the destroyers-for-bases deal "the most important action in the reinforcement of our national defense that has been taken since the Louisiana Purchase."

Isolationists cried out against this departure from neutrality. A bold headline in the *St. Louis Post-Dispatch* read, "Dictator Roosevelt Commits Act of War." A group of Roosevelt's opponents in the Midwest formed the America First Committee to protest the drift toward war. Such diverse individuals as aviator-hero Charles Lindbergh, conservative Senator Robert A. Taft of Ohio, socialist leader Norman Thomas, and liberal educator Robert M. Hutchins condemned FDR for involving the United States in a foreign conflict. Voicing belief in a "Fortress America," they denied that Hitler threatened American security and claimed that the nation had the strength to defend itself regardless of what happened in Europe.

To support the administration's policies, opponents of the isolationists organized the Committee to Defend America by Aiding the Allies. Eastern Anglophiles, moderate New Dealers, and liberal Republicans made up the bulk of the membership, with Kansas newspaper editor William Allen White serving as chairman. The White Committee, as it became known, advocated unlimited assistance to England short of war, although some of its members privately favored entry into the conflict. Above all, the interventionists challenged the isolationist premise that events in Europe did not affect American security. "The future of western civilization is being decided upon the battlefield of Europe," White declared.

In the ensuing debate, the American people gradually came to agree with the interventionists. The battle of Britain helped. "Every time Hitler bombed London, we got a couple of votes," noted one interventionist. Frightened by the events in Europe, Congress approved large sums for preparedness, increasing the defense budget from $2 billion to $10 billion during 1940. Roosevelt courageously asked for a peacetime draft, the first in American history, to build up the army; in September, Congress agreed.

The sense of crisis affected domestic politics. Roosevelt ran for an unprecedented third term in 1940 because of the European war; the Republicans nominated Wendell Willkie, a former Democratic businessman who shared FDR's commitment to aid for England. Both candidates made appeals to peace sentiment during the campaign, but Roosevelt's decisive victory made it clear that the nation supported his increasing departure from neutrality.

After the election, FDR took his boldest step. Responding to British Prime Minister Winston

THE ELECTION OF 1940

Candidate	Party	Popular Vote	Electoral Vote
Roosevelt	Democratic	27,263,448	449
Willkie	Republican	22,336,260	82

Churchill's warning that England was running out of money, the president asked Congress to approve a new program to lend and lease goods and weapons to countries fighting against aggressors. Roosevelt's call for America to become "the great arsenal of democracy" seemed straightforward enough, but he acted somewhat deviously by naming the program **Lend-Lease** and by comparing it to loaning a neighbor a garden hose to put out a fire.

Isolationists angrily denounced Lend-Lease as both unnecessary and untruthful. "Lending war equipment is a good deal like lending chewing gum," commented Senator Taft. "You don't want it back." In March 1941, however, Congress voted by substantial margins to authorize the president to "sell, transfer title to, exchange, lease, lend, or otherwise dispose of" war supplies to "any country the President deems vital to the defense of the United States." The accompanying $7 billion appropriation ended the "cash" part of cash-and-carry and ensured Britain full access to American war supplies.

The "carry" problem still remained. German submarines were sinking more than 500,000 tons of shipping a month. England desperately needed the help of the American navy in escorting convoys across the U-boat–infested waters of the North Atlantic. Roosevelt, fearful of isolationist reaction, responded with naval patrols in the western half of the ocean. Hitler placed his submarine commanders under strict restraints to avoid drawing America into the European war. Nevertheless, incidents were bound to occur. In September 1941, after a U-boat narrowly missed torpedoing an American destroyer tracking it, Roosevelt denounced the German submarines as the "rattlesnakes of the Atlantic" and issued orders for the navy to convey British ships halfway across the ocean.

Undeclared naval war quickly followed. On October 17, 1941, a German submarine damaged the U.S. destroyer *Kearney;* ten days later, another U-boat sank the *Reuben James,* killing more than one hundred American sailors. FDR issued orders for the destroyers to shoot U-boats on sight. He also asked Congress to repeal the "carry" section of the neutrality laws and permit American ships to deliver supplies to England. In mid-November, Congress approved these moves by slim margins. Now American merchant ships as well as destroyers would become targets for German attacks.

Kneeling at the Capitol Plaza in Washington, members of the "Mothers' Crusade" conduct a pray-in to protest the passage of the Lend-Lease Act. ❖

By December, it seemed only a matter of weeks—or months at most—until repeated sinkings would lead to a formal declaration of war against Germany.

In leading the nation to the brink of war in Europe, Roosevelt opened himself to criticism from both sides in the domestic debate. Interventionists believed he had been too cautious in dealing with the danger to the nation from Nazi Germany. Isolationists were equally critical of the president, claiming he had misled the American people by professing peace while plotting for war. Roosevelt was certainly less than candid, relying on executive discretion to engage in highly provocative acts in the North Atlantic. He agreed with the interventionists that in the long run a German victory in Europe would threaten American security. But he also was aware that a poll taken in September 1941 showed nearly 80 percent of the American people wanted to stay out of World War II. Realizing that leading a divided nation into war would be disastrous, FDR played for time, inching the country toward war while waiting for the Axis nations to make the ultimate move. Japan finally obliged at Pearl Harbor.

Showdown in the Pacific

Japan had taken advantage of the war in Europe to expand farther in Asia. Although successful after 1937 in conquering the populous coastal areas of China, the Japanese had been unable to defeat Chiang Kai-shek, whose forces retreated into the vast interior of the country. The German defeat of France and the Netherlands in 1940, however, left their colonial possessions in the East Indies and Indochina vulnerable and defenseless. Japan now set out to incorporate these territories—rich in oil, tin, and rubber—into a Greater East Asia Co-Prosperity Sphere.

The Roosevelt administration countered with economic pressure. Japan depended heavily on the United States for petroleum and scrap metal. In July 1940, President Roosevelt signed an order setting up a licensing and quota system for the export of these crucial materials to Japan and banned the sale of aviation gasoline altogether. With Britain fighting for survival and France and the Netherlands occupied by Germany, the United States was now employing economic sanctions to defend Southeast Asia against Japanese expansion.

Tokyo appeared to be unimpressed. In early September, Japanese troops occupied strategic bases in the northern part of French Indochina. Later in the month, Japan signed the Tripartite Pact with Germany and Italy, a defensive treaty that confronted the United States with a possible two-ocean war. The new Axis alignment confirmed American suspicions that Japan was part of a worldwide totalitarian threat. Roosevelt and his advisers, however, saw Germany as the primary danger; thus they pursued a policy of all-out aid to England while hoping that economic measures alone would deter Japan.

The embargo on aviation gasoline, extended to include scrap iron and steel in late September 1940, was a burden Japan could bear, but a possible ban on all oil shipments was a different matter. Japan lacked petroleum reserves of its own and was entirely dependent on imports from the United States and the Dutch East Indies. In an attempt to ease the economic pressure through negotiation, Japan sent a new envoy to Washington in the spring of 1941. But the talks quickly broke down. Tokyo wanted nothing less than a free hand in China and an end to American sanctions, while the United States insisted on an eventual Japanese evacuation of all China.

In July 1941, Japan invaded southern Indochina, beginning the chain of events that led to war. Washington knew of this aggression before it occurred. Naval intelligence experts had broken the Japanese diplomatic code and were intercepting and reading all messages between Tokyo and the Japanese embassy in Washington. President Roosevelt responded on July 25, 1941, with an order freezing all Japanese assets in the United States. This step, initially intended only as a temporary warning to Japan, soon became a permanent embargo due to positive public reaction and State Department zeal. Trade with Japan, including the vital oil shipments, came to a complete halt. When the Dutch government in exile took similar action, Japan faced a dilemma: In order to have oil shipments resumed, Tokyo would have to end its aggression; the alternative would be to seize the needed petroleum supplies in the Dutch East Indies, an action that would mean war.

After one final diplomatic effort failed, General Hideki Tojo, an army militant, became the new premier of Japan. To mask its war preparations, Tokyo sent yet another envoy to Washington with new peace proposals. Code breaking enabled American diplomats to learn that the Japanese terms were unacceptable even before they were formally presented. Army and navy leaders urged President Roosevelt to seek at least a temporary settlement with Japan to give them time to prepare American defenses in the Pacific. Secretary of State Cordell Hull, however, refused to allow any concession; on November 26, he sent a stiff ten-point reply to Tokyo that included a demand for Japanese withdrawal from China.

The Japanese response came two weeks later. On the evening of December 6, 1941, the first thirteen parts of the reply to Hull's note arrived in Washington, with the fourteenth part to follow the next morning. Naval intelligence actually decoded the message faster than the Japanese embassy clerks. A messenger delivered the text to President Roosevelt late that night; after glancing at it, he commented, "This means war." The next day, December 7, the fourteenth part arrived, revealing that Japan totally rejected the American position.

Officials in Washington immediately sent warning messages to American bases in the Pacific, but they failed to arrive in time. At 7:55 in the morning, just before 1 P.M. in Washington, squadrons of Japanese carrier-based planes caught the American fleet at Pearl Harbor totally by surprise. In little more than an hour, they crippled the American Pacific fleet and its major base, sinking eight battleships and killing more than twenty-four hundred American sailors.

In Washington, the Japanese envoys had requested a meeting with Secretary Hull at 1 P.M. Just before the meeting, news arrived of the attack on **Pearl Harbor.** An irate Cordell Hull read the note the Japanese handed him and then, unable to restrain himself any longer, burst out, "In all my fifty years of public service, I have never seen a document that was more crowded with infamous falsehoods and distortions—on a scale so huge that I never imagined until today that any government was capable of uttering them."

Speaking before Congress the next day, President Roosevelt termed December 7 "a date which will live in infamy" and asked for a declaration of war on Japan. With only one dissenting vote, both branches passed the measure. On December 11, Germany and Italy declared war against the United States; the nation was now fully involved in World War II.

The whole country united behind Roosevelt's leadership to seek revenge for Pearl Harbor and to defeat the Axis threat to American security. After the war, however, critics charged that FDR had entered the conflict by a back door, claiming the president had deliberately exposed the Pacific fleet to attack. Subsequent investigations uncovered negligence in both Hawaii and Washington but no evidence to support the conspiracy charge. Commanders in Hawaii, like most military experts, believed the Japanese would not launch an attack on a base four thousand miles from Japan. FDR, like too many Americans, had badly underestimated the daring and skill of the Japanese; he and the nation alike paid a heavy price for this cultural and racial prejudice. But there was no plot. Roosevelt could not have known that Hitler, so restrained in the Atlantic, would reverse his policy and foolishly declare war against the United States after Pearl Harbor. Perhaps the most frightening aspect of the whole episode is that it took the shock of the Japanese sneak attack to make the American people

American ships were destroyed in the surprise attack on Pearl Harbor, December 7, 1941. Caught completely off guard, U.S. forces still managed to shoot down twenty-nine enemy planes. ❖

aware of the extent of the Axis threat to their well-being and lead them to end the long American retreat from responsibility.

TURNING THE TIDE AGAINST THE AXIS

In the first few months after the United States entered the war, the outlook for victory was bleak. In Europe, Hitler's armies controlled virtually the entire continent, from Norway in the north to Greece in the south. Despite the nonaggression pact, German armies had penetrated deep into Russia after an initial invasion in June 1941. Although they had failed to capture either Moscow or Leningrad, the Nazi forces had conquered the Ukraine and by the spring of 1942 were threatening to sweep across the Volga River and seize vital oil fields in the Caucasus. In North Africa, General Erwin Rommel's Afrika Korps had pushed the British back into Egypt and threatened the Suez Canal (see the map on p. 799).

The situation was no better in Asia. The Pearl Harbor attack had enabled the Japanese to move unopposed across Southeast Asia. Within three months, they had conquered Malaya and the Dutch East Indies, with its valuable oil fields, and were pressing the British back both in Burma and New Guinea. American forces under General Douglas MacArthur had tried vainly to block the Japanese conquest of the Philippines. MacArthur finally escaped by torpedo boat to Australia; the American garrison at Corregidor surrendered after a long siege, the survivors then enduring the cruel death march across the Bataan peninsula. With the American navy still recovering from the devastation at Pearl Harbor, Japan controlled the western half of the Pacific (see the map on p. 792).

Over the next two years, the United States and its allies would finally halt the German and Japanese offensives in Europe and Asia. But then they faced the difficult process of driving back the enemy, freeing the vast conquered areas, and finally defeating the Axis powers on their home territory. It would be a difficult and costly struggle that would require great sacrifice and heavy losses; World War II would test American will and resourcefulness to the utmost.

Wartime Partnerships

The greatest single advantage that the United States and its partners possessed was their willingness to form a genuine coalition to bring about the defeat of the Axis powers. Although there were many strains within the wartime alliance, it did permit a high de-

✦ A Look at the Past ✦

Service Stars

Households with members enlisted in the armed forces earned the privilege to display service stars in their windows. Each star represented one family member, whether male or female, involved in the armed services. A blue star indicated that someone from the household was in the service; a yellow star flag denoted that a household member had died in service. Why would the federal government issue service stars? How would displaying service stars aid the war effort? How might families with no family members eligible for serving in the military have felt about having no service stars?

gree of coordination. In striking contrast was the behavior of Germany and Japan, each fighting a separate war without any attempt at cooperation.

The United States and Britain achieved a complete wartime partnership. Prewar military talks led to the formation of a Combined Chiefs of Staff, headquartered in Washington, which directed Anglo-American military operations. The close cooperation between President Roosevelt and Prime Minister Churchill ensured a common strategy. The leaders decided at the outset that a German victory posed the greater danger and thus gave priority to the European theater in the conduct of the war. In a series of meetings in December 1941, Roosevelt and Churchill signed a Declaration of the United Nations, eventually sub-

scribed to by twenty-six countries, that pledged them to fight together until the Axis powers were defeated.

Relations with the other members of the United Nations coalition in World War II were not quite so harmonious. The decision to defeat Germany first displeased the Chinese, who had been at war with Japan since 1937. Roosevelt tried to appease Chiang Kai-shek with a trickle of supplies, flown in at great risk by American airmen over the Himalayas from India. France posed a more delicate problem. FDR virtually ignored the Free French government in exile under General Charles de Gaulle. Roosevelt preferred to deal with the Vichy regime, despite its collaboration with Germany, because it still controlled the French fleet and retained France's overseas territories.

At their meeting at Casablanca, Morocco, in January 1943, President Roosevelt and British Prime Minister Winston Churchill announced that the unconditional surrender of the Axis powers would be the only acceptable basis for ending the war. ❖

The greatest strain of all within the wartime coalition was with the Soviet Union. Although Roosevelt had ended the long period of nonrecognition in 1933, close ties had failed to develop. The Russian refusal to pay prerevolutionary debts, together with continued Soviet support of domestic communist activity in the United States in the 1930s, intensified American distaste for Stalin's regime. The great Russian purge trials and the temporary Nazi-Soviet alliance from 1939 to 1941, along with deep-seated cultural and ideological differences, made wartime cooperation difficult.

Ever the pragmatist, Roosevelt tried hard to break down the old hostility and establish a more cordial relationship with Russia during the war. Even before Pearl Harbor, he extended Lend-Lease aid to Russia, and after American entry into the war, this economic assistance grew rapidly, limited only by the difficulty of delivering the supplies. Eager to keep Russia in the war, the president promised a visiting Russian diplomat in May 1942 that the United States would create a second front in Europe by the end of that year—a pledge he could not fulfill. In January 1943, Roosevelt and Churchill met in Casablanca, Morocco, where they declared a policy of unconditional surrender, vowing

that the Allies would fight until the Axis nations were completely defeated.

Despite these promises, the Soviet Union bore the brunt of battle against Hitler in the early years of the war, fighting alone against more than two hundred German divisions. The United States and England, grateful for the respite to build up their forces, could do little more than offer promises of future help and send Lend-Lease supplies. The result was a rift that never fully healed—one that did not prevent the defeat of Germany but did ensure future tensions and uncertainties between the Soviet Union and the Western nations.

Halting the German Blitz

From the outset, the United States favored an invasion across the English Channel. Army planners, led by Chief of Staff George C. Marshall and his protégé, Dwight D. Eisenhower, were convinced such a frontal assault would be the quickest way to win the war. Roosevelt concurred, in part because it fulfilled his second-front commitment to the Soviets.

The initial plan, drawn up by Eisenhower, called for a full-scale invasion of Europe in the spring of

1943, with provision for a temporary beachhead in France in the fall of 1942 if necessary to keep Russia in the war. Marshall surprised everyone by placing Eisenhower, until then a relatively junior general, in charge of implementing the plan.

But the British, remembering the heavy casualties of trench warfare in World War I, and hoping to protect the route to India, their most important colony, preferred a perimeter approach. Air and naval attacks around the edge of the continent, especially in the Mediterranean, would be a prelude to a final invasion of Germany. British strategists assented to the basic plan but strongly urged a preliminary invasion of North Africa in the fall of 1942. Roosevelt, too, wanted American troops engaged in combat against Germany before the end of 1942 to offset growing pressure at home to concentrate on the Pacific; hence, after he overruled objections from his military advisers, American and British troops landed on the Atlantic and Mediterranean coasts of Morocco and Algeria in November 1942.

The British launched an attack against Rommel at El Alamein in Egypt and soon forced the Afrika Korps to retreat across Libya to Tunisia. Eisenhower, delayed by poor roads and bad weather, was slow in bringing up his forces, and in their first encounter with Rommel at the Kasserine Pass in the desert south of Tunis, inexperienced American troops suffered a humiliating defeat. General George Patton quickly rallied the demoralized soldiers, and by May 1943, Germany had been driven from Africa, leaving behind nearly 300,000 troops.

During these same months, the Soviet Union's Red Army had broken the back of German military power in the battle of Stalingrad. Turned back at the critical bend in the Volga, Hitler had poured in division after division in what was ultimately a losing cause; never again would Germany be able to take the offensive in Europe.

At Churchill's insistence, FDR agreed to follow up the North African victory with the invasion first of Sicily and then Italy in the summer of 1943. Italy dropped out of the war when Mussolini fled to Germany, but the Italian campaign proved to be a strategic dead end. Germany sent in enough divisions to establish a strong defensive line in the mountains south of Rome; American and British troops were forced to fight their way slowly up the peninsula, suffering heavy casualties.

More important, these Mediterranean operations delayed the second front, postponing it eventually to the spring of 1944. Meanwhile, the Soviets began to push the Germans out of Russia and looked forward to the liberation of Poland, Hungary, and Romania, where they could establish "friendly" communist regimes. Having borne the brunt of the fighting against Nazi Germany, Russia was ready to claim its reward—the postwar domination of eastern Europe.

Checking Japan in the Pacific

Both the decision to defeat Germany first and the vast expanses of the Pacific dictated the nature of the war against Japan. The United States conducted amphibious island-hopping campaigns rather than attempting to reconquer the Dutch East Indies, Southeast Asia, and China. There would be two separate American operations. One, led by Douglas MacArthur based in Australia, would move from New Guinea back to the Philippines, while the other, commanded by Admiral Chester Nimitz from Hawaii, was directed at key Japanese islands in the Central Pacific. The original plan called for the two offensives to come together for the final invasion of the Japanese home islands.

Success in the Pacific depended above all else on control of the sea. The devastation at Pearl Harbor gave Japan the initial edge, but fortunately, the United States had not lost any of its four aircraft carriers. In the battle of the Coral Sea in May 1942, American naval forces blocked a Japanese thrust to outflank Australia. The turning point came one month later at Midway. A powerful Japanese task force threatened to seize this remote American outpost more than a thousand miles west of Pearl Harbor; Japan's real objective was the destruction of what remained of the American Pacific fleet. Superior American airpower enabled Nimitz's forces to engage the enemy at long range. Japanese fighters shot down thirty-five of forty-one attacking torpedo bombers, but a second wave of dive-bombers scored hits on three Japanese carriers. The battle of Midway ended with the loss of four Japanese aircraft carriers compared to just one American carrier. It was the first defeat the modern Japanese navy had ever suffered, and it left the United States in control of the Central Pacific.

Encouraged by the victory, American forces launched their first Pacific offensive in the Solomon Islands, east of New Guinea, in August 1942. Both sides suffered heavy losses, but six months later the last Japanese were driven from the key island of Guadalcanal. At the same time, MacArthur began the long, slow, and bloody job of driving the Japanese back along the north coast of New Guinea.

By early 1943, the defensive phase of the war with Japan was over. The enemy surge had been halted in both the central and the southwestern Pacific, and the United States was preparing to penetrate the Gilbert, Marshall, and Caroline Islands and recapture the Philippines. Just as Russia had broken German power

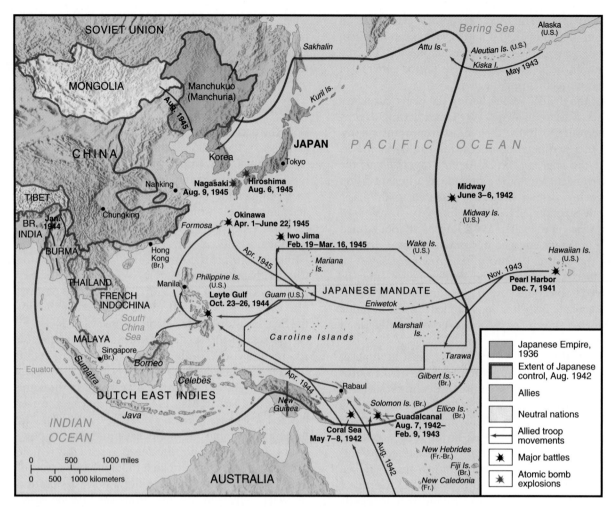

WORLD WAR II IN THE PACIFIC *The tide of battle turned in the Pacific the same year as in Europe. The balance of sea power shifted back to the United States from Japan after the naval victories of 1942.* ❖

in Europe, so the United States, fighting alone except for Australia and New Zealand, had halted the Japanese. And, like the USSR with its plans for eastern Europe, America expected to reap the rewards of victory by dominating the Pacific in the future.

THE HOME FRONT

World War II had a greater impact than the Great Depression on American life. While American soldiers and sailors fought abroad, the nation underwent sweeping social and economic changes at home. American industry worked to capacity to meet the need for war materials. Increased production in both industry and agriculture benefited workers and farmers alike. The expansion of war-related industries encouraged many people to move to where new jobs had sprung up. Women moved out of the home into the paid workforce; rural

dwellers relocated to urban areas, and northerners and easterners sought new opportunities and new homes in the South and West. Another beneficiary of the return to prosperity brought on by the war was FDR, who had seen the nation through the dark days of the depression. The nation's economic recovery helped him win reelection to the presidency for a fourth term in 1944.

The Arsenal of Democracy

American industry made the nation's single most important contribution to victory. Even though more than fifteen million Americans served in the armed forces, it was the nearly sixty million who worked on farms and factories who achieved the miracle of production that ensured the defeat of Germany and Japan. The manufacturing plants that had run at half capacity through the 1930s now hummed with activity. In Detroit, automobile assembly lines were converted to produce tanks and airplanes; Henry Ford built the giant Willow Run factory, covering 67 acres, where forty-two thousand workers turned out a B-24 bomber every hour. Henry J. Kaiser, a California industrialist who constructed huge West Coast shipyards to meet the demand for cargo vessels and landing craft, operated on an equally large scale. His plant in Richmond, California, reduced the time to build a merchant ship from 105 to 14 days. In part, America won the battle of the Atlantic by building ships faster than German U-boats could sink them.

This vast industrial expansion, however, created many problems. In 1942, President Roosevelt appointed Donald Nelson, a Sears, Roebuck executive, to head a War Production Board (WPB). A jovial, easygoing man, Nelson soon was outmaneuvered by the army and the navy, which preferred to negotiate directly with large corporations. The WPB allowed business to claim rapid depreciation, and thus huge tax credits, for new plants and awarded lucrative cost-plus contracts for urgently needed goods. Shortages of critical materials such as steel, aluminum, and copper led to an allocation system based on military priorities. Rubber, cut off by the Japanese conquest of Southeast Asia, was particularly scarce; the administration finally began gasoline rationing in 1943 to curb pleasure driving and prolong tire life. The government itself built fifty-one synthetic-rubber plants, which by 1944 were producing nearly one million tons a year for the tires of American airplanes

and military vehicles. All in all, the nation's factories turned out twice as many goods as did German and Japanese industry combined.

Roosevelt revealed the same tendency toward compromise in directing the economic mobilization as he did in shaping the New Deal. When the Office of Price Administration—which tried to curb inflation by controlling prices and rationing scarce goods such as sugar, canned food, and shoes—clashed with the WPB, FDR appointed James Byrnes to head an Office of Economic Stabilization. Byrnes, a former South Carolina senator and Supreme Court justice, used political judgment to settle disputes between agencies and keep all groups happy. The president was also forced to compromise with Congress, which pared down the administration's requests for large tax increases. Half the cost of the war was financed by borrowing; the other half came from revenues. A $7 billion revenue increase in 1942 included so many first-time taxpayers that in the following year the Treasury Department instituted a new practice—withholding income taxes from workers' wages.

A result of the wartime economic explosion was a growing affluence. Despite the federal incentives to business, heavy excess-profit taxes and a 94 percent tax rate for the very rich kept the wealthy from benefiting unduly. The huge increase in federal spending, from $9 billion in 1940 to $98 billion in 1944, spread through American society. A government agreement with labor unions in 1943 held wage rates to a 15 percent increase,

To keep up with the demand for war matériel, shipyards and factories operated around the clock, such as this North American aviation factory in Kansas City, where workers are shown assembling B-25 bombers. ❖

❖ **A Look at the Past** ❖

Ration Stamps

Ration stamps became necessary during World War II when gasoline, tires, selected foodstuffs, and other products became scarce. Stamps with patriotic or military symbolism suggest that rationing was an honorable sacrifice, not a hardship. How effective was the tactic of using such symbols? If Americans accepted rationing as their duty, what does that suggest about attitudes toward the war effort and government?

A Nation on the Move

The war led to a vast migration of the American population. Young men left their homes for training camps and then for service overseas. Defense workers and their families, some nine million people in all, moved to work in the new booming shipyards, munitions factories, and aircraft plants. Norfolk, Virginia; San Diego, California; Mobile, Alabama; and other centers of defense production grew by more than 50 percent in just a year or two. Rural areas lost population while coastal regions, especially along the Pacific and the Gulf of Mexico, drew millions of people. The location of army camps in the South and West created boom conditions in the future Sunbelt, as did the concentration of aircraft factories and shipyards in this region. California had the greatest gains, adding nearly two million to its population in less than five years.

This movement of people caused severe social problems. Housing was in short supply. Migrating workers crowded into house trailers and boarding-houses, bringing unexpected windfalls to landlords. In one boomtown, a reporter described an old Victorian house that had five bedrooms on the second floor. "Three of them," he wrote, "held two cots apiece, the two others held three cots." But the owner revealed that "the third floor is where we pick up the velvet. . . . We rent to workers in different shifts . . . three shifts a day . . . seven bucks a week apiece."

Family life suffered under these crowded living conditions. An increase in the number of marriages, as young people searched for something to hang on to in the midst of wartime turmoil, was offset by a rising divorce rate. The baby boom that would peak in the 1950s began during the war and brought its own set of problems. Only a few publicly funded day-care centers were available, and working mothers worried about their "latchkey children." Schools in the boom areas were unable to cope with the influx of new students; a teacher shortage, intensified by the lure of higher wages in war industries, compounded the education crisis.

Despite these problems, women found the war a time of economic opportunity. The demand for workers led to a dramatic rise in women's employment, from fourteen million working women in 1940 to nineteen million by 1945. Most of the new women workers were married and many were middle-aged, thus broadening the composition of the female workforce, which in the past had been composed primarily of young single women. Women entered industries once viewed as exclusively male; by the end of the war, they worked alongside men tending blast furnaces in steel mills and welding hulls in shipyards. Few challenged the traditional view of gender roles, yet the wartime experience helped temporarily undermine the concept that woman's only proper place was in the

but the long hours of overtime resulted in doubling and sometimes tripling the weekly paychecks of factory workers. Farmers shared in the new prosperity as their incomes quadrupled between 1940 and 1945. For the first time in the twentieth century, the lowest fifth of wage earners increased their share of the national income in relation to the more affluent; their income rose by 68 percent between 1941 and 1945, compared to a 20 percent increase for the well-to-do. Most important, this rising income ensured postwar prosperity. Workers and farmers saved their money, channeling much of it into government war bonds, waiting for the day when they could buy the cars and home appliances they had done without during the long years of depression and war.

As men left for military service in World War II and U.S. industry expanded to keep up with the defense needs, millions of women joined the paid labor force. By 1944, the peak year for female wartime employment, women made up 36 percent of the American workforce. Women took jobs that before had been done by men, such as riveting, welding, and operating heavy equipment. The women shown here are assembling jeeps to be used by U.S. army personnel. ✤

home. Women enjoyed the hefty weekly paychecks, which rose by 50 percent from 1941 to 1943, and they took pride in their contributions to the war effort. "To hell with the life I have had," commented a former fashion designer. "This war is too damn serious, and it is too damn important to win it."

African Americans shared in the wartime migration, but racial prejudice limited their social and economic gains. Nearly one million served in the armed forces, but relatively few saw combat. The army placed black soldiers in segregated units, usually led by white officers, and used them for service and construction tasks. The navy was even worse, relegating them to menial jobs until late in the war. African Americans were denied the chance to become petty officers, Secretary of the Navy Frank Knox explained, because experience had shown that "men of the colored race . . . cannot maintain discipline among men of the white race."

African American civilians fared a little better. In 1941, black labor leader A. Philip Randolph threatened a massive march on Washington to force President Roosevelt to end racial discrimination in defense industries and government employment and to integrate the armed forces. FDR compromised, persuading Randolph to call off the march and drop his integration demand in return for an executive order creating a Fair Employment Practices Committee (FEPC) to ban racial discrimination in war industries. As a result, African American employment by the federal government rose from 60,000 in 1941 to 200,000 by the end of the war. The FEPC proved less successful in the private sector. Weak in funding and staff, the FEPC was able to act on only one-third of the eight thousand

complaints it received. The nationwide shortage of labor was more influential than the FEPC in accounting for the rise in black employment during wartime. African Americans moved from the rural South to northern and western cities, finding jobs in the automobile, aircraft, and shipbuilding industries.

The movement of an estimated 700,000 people helped transform black-white relations from a regional issue into a national concern that could no longer be ignored. The limited housing and recreational facilities for both black and white war workers created tensions that led to urban race riots. On a hot Sunday evening in June 1943, blacks and whites began exchanging insults and then blows near Belle Isle recreation park in Detroit. The next day, a full-scale riot broke out in which twenty-three blacks and nine whites died. The fighting raged for twenty-four hours until national guard troops were brought in to restore order. Later that summer, only personal intervention by New York Mayor Fiorello LaGuardia quelled a Harlem riot that took the lives of six blacks.

These outbursts of racial violence fueled the resentments that would grow into the postwar civil rights movement. For most African Americans, despite economic gains, World War II was a reminder of the inequality of American life. "Just carve on my tombstone," remarked one black soldier in the Pacific, "'Here lies a black man killed fighting a yellow man for the protection of a white man.'"

One-third of a million Mexican Americans served in the armed forces and shared some of the same experiences as African Americans. Although they were not as completely segregated, many served in the 88th

The migration of African Americans from the South to northern cities was recorded in a series of sixty tempera panels by African American artist Jacob Lawrence. The paintings are done in sharp primary colors and a forceful but simple design. They form a continuous narrative of visual history and African American experience. ❖

Division, made up largely of Mexican American officers and troops, which earned the nickname "Blue Devils" in the Italian campaign. At home, Spanish-speaking people left the rural areas of Texas, New Mexico, and California for jobs in the cities, especially in aircraft plants and petroleum refineries. Despite low wages and union resistance, they improved their economic position substantially. But they still faced discrimination based both on skin color and language, most notably in the Los Angeles "zoot suit" riots in 1943 when white sailors attacked Mexican American youths dressed in their distinctive outfits—long jackets worn with pants tightly pegged at the ankles. The racial prejudice heightened feelings of ethnic identity and led returning Mexican American veterans to form organizations such as the American G.I. Forum to press for equal rights in the future.

A tragic counterpoint to the voluntary movement of American workers in search of jobs was the forced relocation of 120,000 Japanese Americans from the West Coast. Responding to racial fears in California after Pearl Harbor, President Roosevelt approved an army order in February 1942 to move all Japanese Americans on the West Coast to concentration camps in the interior. More than two-thirds of those detained were *Nisei*, native-born Americans whose only crime was their Japanese ancestry. Forced to sell their farms and businesses at distress prices, the Japanese Americans lost not only their liberty but also most of their worldly goods. Herded into ten hastily built detention centers in seven western and southern states, they lived as prisoners in tar-papered barracks behind barbed wire, guarded by armed troops.

Appeals to the Supreme Court proved fruitless; in 1944, six justices upheld relocation on grounds of national security in wartime. Beginning in 1943, individual Nisei could win release by pledging their loyalty and finding a job away from the West Coast. Some thirty-five thousand left the camps during the next

JAPANESE AMERICAN INTERNMENT CAMPS
Following the attack on Pearl Harbor, President Roosevelt established the War Relocation Authority and charged the agency with the task of evacuating Japanese Americans from the West Coast and transporting them to internment camps. ❖

Family in Jerome Camp, *by Japanese American painter Henry Sugimoto, depicts a family in their quarters at an internment camp in a southern Arkansas swampland. Like many Japanese Americans living on the West Coast, the Sugimotos were first ordered from their homes to large assembly centers such as the former fairgrounds at Fresno, California. There whole families were assigned to individual horse stalls while they awaited relocation to one of the internment camps located in isolated areas of California, Arizona, Idaho, Utah, Colorado, Wyoming, and Arkansas. Conditions in the camps were equally dismal. Whole families lived in a single room furnished with little more than a few cots, some blankets, and a single light bulb.* ❖

two years, including more than thirteen thousand who joined the armed forces. The all-Nisei 442nd Combat Team served gallantly in the European theater, losing more than five hundred men in battle and winning more than a thousand citations for bravery. One World War II veteran remembers that when his unit was in trouble, the commander would issue a familiar appeal: "Call in the Japs."

For other Nisei, the experience was bitter. More than five thousand renounced their American citizenship and chose to live in Japan at the war's end. The government did not close down the last detention center until March 1946. Japanese Americans never experienced the torture and mass death of the German concentration camps, but their treatment was a disgrace to a nation fighting for freedom and democracy. Finally, in 1988, Congress voted an indemnity of $1.2 billion for the estimated sixty thousand surviving Japanese Americans detained during World War II. Susumi Emori, who had been moved with his wife and four children from his farm in Stockton, California, to a camp in Arkansas, felt vindicated. "It was terrible," he said, with tears in his eyes, "but it was a time of war. Anything can happen. I didn't blame the United States for that."

Win-the-War Politics

Franklin Roosevelt used World War II to strengthen his leadership and maintain Democratic political dominance. As war brought about prosperity and removed the economic discontent that had sustained the New Deal, FDR announced that "Dr. New Deal" had given way to "Dr. Win-the-War." Congress, already controlled by a conservative coalition of southern Democrats and northern Republicans, had almost slipped into GOP hands in 1942. With a very low voter turnout, due in part to the large numbers of men in service and uprooted workers who failed to meet residency requirements for voting, the Republicans won forty-four new seats in the House and nine in the Senate and elected governors in New York and California as well.

In 1944, Roosevelt responded to the Democratic slippage by dropping Henry Wallace, his liberal and visionary vice president, for Harry Truman, a moderate and down-to-earth Missouri senator who was acceptable to all factions of the Democratic party. Equally important, FDR received increased political support from organized labor, which had grown in membership during the war from ten to fifteen million. The newly organized Political Action Committee (PAC) of the CIO, headed by Sidney Hillman, conducted massive door-to-door drives to register millions of workers and their families.

The Republicans nominated Thomas E. Dewey, who had been elected governor of New York after gaining fame as a prosecutor of organized crime. Dewey, moderate in his views, played down opposition to the New Deal and instead tried to make Roosevelt's age and health the primary issues, along with the charge that the Democrats were soft on communism.

THE ELECTION OF 1944

Candidate	Party	Popular Vote	Electoral Vote
Roosevelt	Democrat	25,611,936	432
Dewey	Republican	22,013,372	99

Despite his abrasive campaign style, Dewey did not advocate a return to isolationism. The Republican party was trying hard to shake the obstructionist image it had gained during the League of Nations fight in 1919; it went on record in 1943 as favoring American postwar cooperation for world peace. Indeed, Dewey pioneered a bipartisan approach to foreign policy. He accepted wartime planning for the future United Nations and kept the issue of an international organization out of the campaign.

Reacting to the issues of his age and health, especially after a long bout with influenza in the spring, FDR disregarded the advice of his doctors and took a five-hour drive in an open car through the rain-soaked streets of New York City just before the election. His vitality impressed the voters, and in November 1944 he swept back into office for a fourth term. The campaign, however, had taken its toll. The president, suffering from high blood pressure and congestive heart failure, had only a few months left to lead the nation.

VICTORY

World War II ended with surprising swiftness. By 1943, the Axis tide had been turned in Europe and Asia, and it did not take long for Russia, the United States, and England to mount the offensives that drove Germany and Japan back across the vast areas they had conquered and set the stage for their final defeat.

The long-awaited second front finally came on June 6, 1944. For two years, the United States and England concentrated on building up an invasion force of nearly three million troops and a vast armada of ships and landing craft to carry them across the English Channel. Hoping to catch Hitler by surprise, Eisenhower chose the Normandy peninsula, where the absence of good harbors had led to lighter German fortifications. Allied aircraft bombed northern France for six weeks preceding the assault in order to block the movement of German reinforcements once the invasion began.

D-Day was originally set for June 5, but bad weather forced a delay. Relying on a forecasted break in the storm, Eisenhower gambled on going ahead on June 6. During the night, three divisions parachuted down behind the German defenses; at dawn, the British and American troops fought their way ashore at five points along a sixty-mile stretch of beach, encountering stiff German resistance at several points. By the end of the day, however, Eisenhower had won his beachhead; a week later, more than one-third of a million men were slowly pushing back the German forces through the hedgerows of Normandy. The breakthrough came on July 25 when General Omar Bradley decimated the enemy with a massive artillery and aerial bombardment at Saint-Lô, opening a gap for General George Patton's Third Army. American tanks raced across the French countryside, trapping thousands of Germans and liberating Paris by August 25. Allied troops reached the Rhine River by September, but a shortage of supplies, especially gasoline, forced a three-month halt.

Hitler took advantage of this breathing spell to deliver a daring counterattack. In mid-December, the remaining German armored divisions burst through a weak point in the Allied lines in the Ardennes Forest, planning a breakout to the coast that would have cut off nearly one-third of Eisenhower's forces. A combination of tactical surprise and bad weather, which prevented Allied air support, led to a huge bulge in the American lines. But an airborne division dug in at the key crossroads of Bastogne, in Belgium, and held off a much larger German force. Allied reinforcements and clearing weather then combined to end the attack. By committing nearly all his reserves to the Battle of the Bulge, Hitler had delayed Eisenhower's advance into Germany, but he also had fatally weakened German resistance in the west.

The end came quickly. A massive Russian offensive began in mid-January and swept across the Oder River toward Berlin. General Bradley's troops, finding a bridge left virtually intact by the retreating Germans, crossed the Rhine on March 7. Eisenhower overruled the British, who favored one concentrated drive on Berlin. Instead the Allied forces advanced on a broad front, capturing the industrial Ruhr basin and breaking the Nazi death grip on prisoner populations. (See the Feature Essay, "The Face of the Holocaust," pp. 800–801.) The Americans and British met the Russians at the Elbe in late April. With the Red Army already in the suburbs of Berlin, Adolf Hitler committed suicide on April 30. A week later, on May 7, 1945, Eisenhower accepted the unconditional surrender of all German forces. Just eleven months and a day after the landings in Normandy, the Allied forces had brought the war in Europe to a successful conclusion.

War Aims and Wartime Diplomacy

The American contribution to Hitler's defeat was relatively minor compared to the damage inflicted by the Soviet Union. At the height of the German invasion of

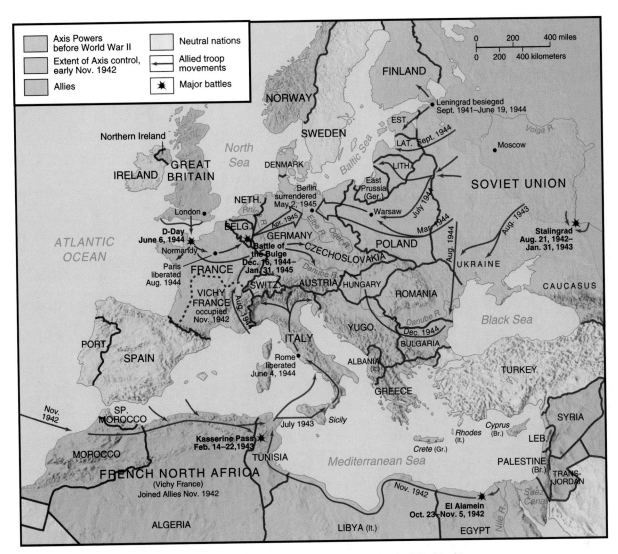

WORLD WAR II IN EUROPE AND NORTH AFRICA *The tide of battle shifted in this theater during the winter of 1942–1943. The massive German assault on the eastern front was turned back by the Russians at Stalingrad, and the Allied forces recaptured North Africa.* ❖

Russia, more than 300 Soviet divisions had been locked in battle with 250 German ones, a striking contrast to the 58 divisions the United States and Britain used in the Normandy invasion. As his armies overran Poland and the Balkan countries, Joseph Stalin was determined to retain control over this region, which had been the historic pathway for Western invasion into Russia. Delay in opening the second front and an innate distrust of the West convinced the Soviets that they should maximize their territorial gains by imposing communist regimes on eastern Europe.

American postwar goals were quite different. Now believing the failure to join the League of Nations in 1919 had led to the coming of World War II, the American people and their leaders vowed to put their faith in a new attempt at collective security. At Moscow in 1943, Secretary of State Cordell Hull had won

Russian agreement to participate in a future world organization at the war's end. The first wartime Big Three conference brought together Roosevelt, Churchill, and Stalin at Teheran, Iran, in late 1943. Stalin reaffirmed this commitment and also indicated to President Roosevelt that Russia would enter the war against Japan once Germany was defeated.

By the time the Big Three met again in February 1945 at the **Yalta Conference,** the military situation favored the Russians. While British and American forces were still recovering from the Battle of the Bulge, the Red Army was advancing to within fifty miles of Berlin. Stalin drove a series of hard bargains. He refused to give up his plans for communist domination of Poland and the Balkans, although he did agree to Roosevelt's request for a Declaration of Liberated Europe, which called for free elections without providing for any

Feature Essay

THE FACE OF THE HOLOCAUST

The liberation of the Nazi death camps near the end of World War II was not a priority objective; nor was it a planned operation. Convinced that military victory was the surest way to end Nazi oppression, Allied strategists organized their campaigns without specific reference to the camps; they staged no daring commando raids to rescue the survivors of Nazi genocide. It was by chance that Allied forces first stumbled upon the camps, and the GIs who threw open the gates to that living hell were totally unprepared for what they found.

Not until November 1944 did the U.S. Army discover its first camp, Natzwiller-Struthof, which had been abandoned by the Germans months

before. Viewing Natzwiller from a distance, Milton Bracker of the *New York Times* noted its deceptive similarity to an American Civilian Conservation Corps camp: "The sturdy green barracks buildings looked exactly like those that housed forestry trainees in the U.S. during the early New Deal."

As he toured the grounds, however, he faced a starker reality and slowly came to think the unthinkable. In the crematorium, he reported, "I cranked the elevator tray a few times and slid the furnace tray a few times, and even at that moment, I did not believe what I was doing was real."

"There were no prisoners," he wrote, "no screams, no burly guards, no taint of death in the air as on a battlefield." Bracker had to stretch his imagination to its limits to comprehend the camp's silent testimony to the Nazi attempt to exterminate the Jews of Europe. U.S. military personnel who toured Natzwiller shared this sense of the surreal. In their report to headquarters, they carefully qualified every observation. They described "what appeared to be a disinfection unit," a room "allegedly used as a lethal gas chamber," "a cellar room with a special type elevator," and "an incinerator room with equipment

Two survivors at the Mittlebau Dora camp at Nordhausen, Germany, lie among hundreds of dead on the barrack floors. Photos of the death camps made the almost unimaginable atrocities of the *Führer's* regime real to Americans at home. ❖

obviously intended for the burning of human bodies." They saw before them the evidence of German atrocities, but the truth was so horrible, they could not quite bring themselves to draw the obvious conclusions.

Inside the Vicious Heart, Robert Abzug's study of the liberation of the concentration camps, refers to this phenomenon as "double vision." Faced with a revelation so terrible, witnesses could not fully comprehend the evidence of the systematic murder of more than six million men, women, and children. But as the Allied armies advanced into Germany, the shocking evidence mounted. On April 4, 1945, the Fourth Armored Division of the Third Army unexpectedly discovered Ohrdruf, a relatively small concentration camp. Ohrdruf's liberation had a tremendous impact on American forces. It was the first camp discovered intact, with its grisly array of the dead and dying. Inside the compound, corpses were piled in heaps in the barracks. An infantryman recalled, "I guess the most vivid recollection of the whole camp is the pyre that was located on the edge of the camp. It was a big pit, where they stacked bodies— stacked bodies and wood and burned them."

On April 12, generals Eisenhower, Bradley, and Patton toured Ohrdruf. The generals, professional soldiers familiar with the devastation of battle, had never seen its like. Years later, Bradley recalled, "The smell of death overwhelmed us even before we passed through the stockade. More than 3200 naked, emaciated bodies had been flung into shallow graves. Others lay in the street where they had fallen."

Eisenhower ordered every available armed forces unit in the area to visit Ohrdruf. "We are told that the American soldier does not know what

800

he is fighting for," said Eisenhower. "Now at least he will know what he is fighting against." He urged government officials and journalists to visit the camps and tell the world. In an official message Eisenhower summed it up:

> We are constantly finding German camps in which they have placed political prisoners where unspeakable conditions exist. From my own personal observation, I can state unequivocally that all written statements up to now do not paint the full horrors.

On April 11, the Timberwolf Division of the Third Army uncovered Nordhausen. They found three thousand dead and only seven hundred survivors. The scene sickened battle-hardened veterans:

> The odors, well there is no way to describe the odors. . . . Many of the boys I am talking about now— these were tough soldiers, there were combat men who had been all

the way through the invasion— were ill and vomiting, throwing up, just at the sight of this.

For some, the liberation of Nordhausen changed the meaning of the war.

> I must also say that my fellow GIs, most thought that any stories they had read in the paper . . . were either not true or at least exaggerated. And it did not sink in, what this was all about, until we got into Nordhausen.

If the experience at Nordhausen gave many GIs a new sense of mission in battle, it also forced them to distance themselves from the realities of the camps. Only by closing off their emotions could they go about the grim task of sorting out the living from the dead and tending to the survivors. Margaret Bourke-White, whose *Life* magazine photographs brought the horrors of the death camps to millions on the home front, recalled working "with a veil over my mind."

People often ask me how it is possible to photograph such atrocities. In photographing the murder camps, the protective veil was so tightly drawn that I hardly knew what I had taken until I saw prints of my own photographs.

By the end of 1945, most of the liberators had come home and returned to civilian life. Once home, their experiences produced no common moral responses. No particular pattern emerged in their occupational, political, and religious behavior, beyond a fear of the rise of postwar totalitarianism shared by most Americans. Few spoke publicly about their role in the liberation of the camps; most found that after a short period of grim fascination, their friends and families preferred to forget. Some had nightmares, but most were not tormented by memories. For the liberators, the ordeal was over. For the survivors of the Holocaust, liberation was but the first step in the tortuous process of rebuilding broken bodies and shattered lives.

Victims at the Bergen-Belsen concentration camp were buried in a mass grave. The camp was liberated by the Allies April 14, 1945, less than a month before Germany's surrender. ❖

The nation's grief at FDR's death is mirrored in the face of this serviceman as the president's funeral cortege passes. ❖

method of enforcement or supervision. More important for the United States, Stalin promised to enter the Pacific war three months after Germany surrendered. In return, Roosevelt offered extensive concessions in Asia, including Russian control over Manchuria. While neither a sellout nor a betrayal, as some critics have charged, Yalta was a significant diplomatic victory for the Soviets—one that reflected Russia's major contribution to a victory in Europe.

For the president, the long journey to Yalta proved to be too much. His health continued to fail after his return to Washington. In early April, FDR left the capital for Warm Springs, Georgia, where he had always been able to relax. He was sitting for his portrait at midday on April 12, 1945, when he suddenly complained of a "terrific headache," then slumped forward and died.

The nation mourned a man who had gallantly met the challenge of depression and global war. Unfortunately, FDR had taken no steps to prepare his successor for the difficult problems that lay ahead. The defeat of Nazi Germany dissolved the one strong bond between the United States and the Soviet Union. With very different histories, cultures, and ideologies, the two nations were bound to drift apart. It was now up to the inexperienced Harry Truman to manage the growing rivalry that was destined to develop into the future Cold War.

Triumph and Tragedy in the Pacific

The total defeat of Germany in May 1945 turned all eyes toward Japan. Although the combined chiefs of staff had originally estimated it would take eighteen

months after Germany's surrender to conquer Japan, American forces moved with surprising speed. Admiral Nimitz swept through the Gilbert, Caroline, and Marshall Islands in 1944, securing bases for further advances and building airfields for American B-29s to begin a deadly bombardment of the Japanese home islands. General MacArthur cleared New Guinea of the last Japanese defender in early 1944 and began planning his long-heralded return to the Philippines. American troops landed on the island of Leyte on October 20, 1944, and Manila fell in early February 1945. The Japanese navy, in a Pacific version of the Battle of the Bulge, launched a daring three-pronged attack on the American invasion fleet in Leyte Gulf. The U.S. Navy rallied to blunt all three Japanese thrusts, sinking four carriers and ending any further Japanese naval threat.

The defeat of Japan was now only a matter of time. The United States had three possible ways to proceed. The military favored a full-scale invasion, beginning on the southernmost island of Kyushu in November 1945 and culminating with an assault on Honshu (the main island of Japan) and a climactic battle for Tokyo in 1946; casualties were expected to run into the hundreds of thousands. Diplomats suggested a negotiated peace, urging the United States to modify the unconditional surrender formula to permit Japan to retain the institution of the emperor.

The third possibility involved the highly secret **Manhattan Project.** Since 1939, the United States had spent $2 billion to develop an atomic bomb based on the fission of radioactive uranium and plutonium. Scientists, many of them refugees from Europe, worked to perfect this deadly new weapon at the

The atomic bomb dropped on Nagasaki, a provincial capital and naval base in southern Japan, on August 9, 1945, virtually obliterated the city and killed about 40,000 people. Only buildings made with reinforced concrete remained standing after the blast. ❖

University of Chicago; Oak Ridge, Tennessee; Hanford, Washington; and a remote laboratory in Los Alamos, New Mexico. In the New Mexico desert on July 16, 1945, they successfully tested the first atomic bomb, creating a fireball brighter than several suns and a telltale mushroom cloud that rose some 40,000 feet above an enormous crater in the desert floor.

Truman had been unaware of the existence of the Manhattan Project before he became president on April 12. Now he simply followed the recommendation of a committee headed by Secretary of War Henry L. Stimson to drop the bomb on a Japanese city. The committee discussed but rejected the possibility of inviting the Japanese to observe a demonstration shot at a remote Pacific site and even ruled out the idea of giving advance notice of the bomb's destructive power. Neither Truman nor Stimson had any qualms about the decision to drop the bomb without warning. They viewed it as a legitimate wartime measure, one designed to save the lives of hundreds of thousands of Americans—and Japanese—that would be lost in a full-scale invasion.

Weather conditions on the morning of August 6 dictated the choice of Hiroshima as the bomb's target. The explosion incinerated 4 square miles of the city, instantly killing more than sixty thousand. Two days later, Russia entered the war against Japan, and the next day, August 9, the United States dropped a second bomb on Nagasaki. There were no more atomic bombs available, but no more were needed. The emperor personally broke a deadlock in the Japanese cabinet and persuaded his ministers to surrender unconditionally on August 14, 1945. Three weeks later, Japan signed a formal capitulation agreement on the decks of the battleship *Missouri* in Tokyo Bay to bring World War II to its official close.

Many years later, scholars charged that Truman had more in mind than defeating Japan when he decided to use the atomic bomb. Citing air force and naval officers who claimed Japan could be defeated by a blockade or by conventional air attacks, these revisionists suggested the real reason for dropping the bomb was to impress the Soviet Union with the fact that the United States had exclusive possession of the ultimate weapon. The available evidence indicates that while Truman and his associates were aware of the possible effect on the Soviet Union, their primary motive was to end World War II as quickly and effortlessly as possible. The saving of American lives, along with a desire for revenge for Pearl Harbor, were uppermost in the decision to bomb Hiroshima and Nagasaki. Yet in using the atomic bomb to defeat Japan, the United States virtually guaranteed a postwar arms race with the Soviet Union.

CHRONOLOGY

1922	Washington Naval Conference limits tonnage
1926	World Court rejects qualified U.S. entry
1928	Kellogg-Briand Pact outlaws war (August) ❖ Clark Memorandum repudiates Roosevelt Corollary (December)
1931	Japan occupies China's Manchurian province
1933	FDR extends diplomatic recognition to USSR
1936	Hitler's troops reoccupy Rhineland
1937	FDR signs permanent Neutrality Act (May) ❖ FDR urges quarantine of aggressor nations (October) ❖ Japanese planes sink USS *Panay* in China (December)
1938	Ludlow war referendum buried in Congress (January) ❖ Munich Conference appeases Hitler (September)
1939	Germany invades Poland; World War II begins
1941	Germany invades USSR ❖ Japan attacks Pearl Harbor; United States enters World War II
1942	U.S. defeats Japanese at battle of Midway (June) ❖ Allies land in North Africa (November)
1943	Soviets smash Nazis at Stalingrad
1944	Allies land on Normandy beachheads
1945	Big Three meet at Yalta (February) ❖ FDR dies; Harry Truman becomes president (April) ❖ Germany surrenders unconditionally (May) ❖ United States drops atomic bombs on Hiroshima and Nagasaki; Japan surrenders (August)

CONCLUSION: THE TRANSFORMING POWER OF WAR

The second great war of the twentieth century had a lasting impact on American life. For the first time, the nation's military potential had been reached. In 1945, the United States was unquestionably the strongest country on the earth, with eleven million men and women in uniform; a vast array of shipyards, aircraft plants, and munitions factories in full production; and a monopoly over the atomic bomb. For better or worse, the nation was now launched on a global career. In the future, the United States would be involved in all parts of the world, from western Europe to remote jungles in Asia, from the nearby Caribbean to the distant Persian Gulf. And despite its enormous strength in 1945, the nation's new world role would encompass failure and frustration as well as power and dominion.

The legacy of war was equally strong at home. Four years of fighting brought about industrial recovery and unparalleled prosperity. The old pattern of unregulated free enterprise was as much a victim of the war as of the New Deal; big government and huge deficits had now become the norm as economic control passed from New York and Wall Street to Washington and Pennsylvania Avenue. The war led to far-reaching changes in American society that would become apparent only decades later. Such distinctive patterns of recent American life as the baby boom and the growth of the Sunbelt can be traced back to wartime origins. World War II was a watershed in twentieth-century America, ushering in a new age of global concerns and domestic upheaval.

RECOMMENDED READING

The best general account of American attitudes toward the world in the 1920s can be found in Warren I. Cohen, *Empire Without Tears* (1987). Robert Dallek provides a thorough account of FDR's diplomacy in *Franklin D. Roosevelt and American Foreign Policy, 1932–1945* (1979). For a more critical view, see Robert A. Divine, *Roosevelt and World War II* (1969). David M. Kennedy, *Freedom from Fear* (1999), sets Roosevelt's foreign and wartime policies against the background of domestic politics.

Two good books on the continuing controversy over Pearl Harbor are Roberta Wohlstetter, *Pearl Harbor: Warning and Decision* (1962), and Gordon W. Prange, *At Dawn We Slept* (1981). Both authors deny the charge that Roosevelt deliberately exposed the naval base to attack.

In his brief overview of wartime diplomacy, *American Diplomacy During the Second World War,* 2nd ed. (1985), Gaddis Smith stresses the tensions within the victorious coalition. So does Mark Stoler in *Allies and Adversaries* (2000). Kenneth S. Davis, *FDR: The War President* (2000);

Thomas Fleming, *The New Dealers' War* (2001); and Michael Beschloss, *The Conquerors* (2002), portray American leadership during the war. Williamson Murray and Allan R. Millett, *A War to Be Won* (2000), and Carlo D'Este, *Eisenhower: A Soldier's Life* (2002), focus on the fighting. Robert S. Norris, *Racing for the Bomb* (2002), and Gregg Herken, *Brotherhood of the Bomb* (2002), describe the Manhattan Project and what it led to.

The best accounts of the home front are Kennedy, *Freedom from Fear*; Richard Polenberg, *War and Society* (1972); John M. Blum, *V Was for Victory* (1976); and Doris Kearns Goodwin, *No Ordinary Time* (1995). Daniel Kryder, *Divided Arsenal* (2000); Ronald Takaki, *Double Victory* (2000); and Greg Robinson, *By Order of the President* (2001), trace the war's effects on racial and ethnic minorities in the United States.

For a list of additional titles related to this chapter's topics, please see http://www.ablongman.com/divine.

SUGGESTED WEB SITES

A People at War

http://www.archives.gov/exhibit_hall/a_people_at_war.html

This National Archives exhibit takes a close look at the contributions millions of Americans made to the war effort.

Powers of Persuasion—Poster Art of World War II

http://www.archives.gov/exhibit_hall/powers_of_persuasion_home.html

These powerful posters at the National Archives were part of the battle for the hearts and minds of the American people.

America from the Great Depression to World War II: Photographs from the FSA and OWI, ca. 1935–1945

http://memory.loc.gov/ammem/fsowhome.html

These images in the Farm Security Administration–Office of War Information Collection show Americans from all over the nation experiencing everything from despair to triumph in the 1930s and 1940s.

A-Bomb WWW Museum

http://www.csi.ad.jp/ABOMB/

This site offers information about the impact of the first atomic bomb as well as the background and context of weapons of total destruction.

The United States Holocaust Memorial Museum

http://www.ushmm.org/

This is the official Web site of the Holocaust Museum in Washington, D.C.

Tuskegee Airmen

http://www.wpafb.af.mil/museum/history/prewwii/ta.htm

The Air Force Museum at Wright-Patterson Air Force Base maintains this site about the African American pilots of World War II.

Abraham Lincoln Brigade Archives

http://www.alba-valb.org

This Brandeis University site has posters and photographs from the Spanish civil war and the unit of American volunteers who fought in it.

World War II Resources: Primary Source Materials on the Web

http://www.ibiblio.org/pha/index.html

This site has a large number of searchable primary texts from all aspects of World War II.

Chapter 28

The explosion of a U.S. test bomb over an uninhabited island in the Pacific on November 1, 1952, demonstrated to the world the fearsome power of the hydrogen bomb. This early H-bomb was capable of destroying a city the size of Washington, D.C. Over the next decade both the United States and the Soviet Union developed far more powerful bombs. ❖

The Onset of
the Cold War

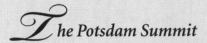 The Potsdam Summit

I am getting ready to go see Stalin and Churchill," President Truman wrote to his mother in July 1945, "and it is a chore." On board the cruiser *Augusta*, the new president continued to complain about the upcoming **Potsdam Conference** in his diary. "How I hate this trip!" he confided. "But I have to make it win, lose, or draw and we must win. I am giving nothing away except to save starving people and even then I hope we can only help them to help themselves."

Halfway around the world, Joseph Stalin left Moscow a day late because of a slight heart attack. The Russian leader hated to fly, so he traveled by rail. Moreover, he ordered the heavily guarded train to detour around Poland for fear of an ambush, further delaying his arrival. When he made his entrance into Potsdam, a suburb of Berlin miraculously spared the total destruction that his forces had created in the German capital, he was ready to claim the spoils of war.

These two men, one the veteran revolutionary who had been in power for two decades, the other an untested leader in office for barely three months, symbolized the enormous differences that now separated the wartime allies. Stalin was above all a realist. Brutal in securing total control at home, he was more flexible in his foreign policy, bent on exploiting Russia's victory in World War II rather than aiming at world domination. Cunning and caution were the hallmarks of his diplomatic style. Small in stature, ungainly in build, he radiated a catlike quality as he waited behind his unassuming facade, ready to dazzle an opponent with his "brilliant, terrifying tactical mastery." Truman, in contrast, personified traditional Wilsonian idealism. Lacking Roosevelt's guile, the new president placed his faith in international cooperation. Like many Americans, he believed implicitly in his country's innate goodness. Self-assured to the point of cockiness, he came to Potsdam clothed in the armor of self-righteousness.

Truman and Stalin met for the first time on July 17, 1945. "I told Stalin that I am no diplomat," the president recorded in his diary, "but usually said yes and no to questions after hearing all the argument." The Russian dictator's reaction to Truman remains a mystery, but Truman believed the first encounter went well. "I can deal with Stalin," he wrote. "He is honest—but smart as hell."

Together with Winston Churchill and his replacement, Clement Attlee, whose Labour party had just triumphed in British elections, Truman and Stalin clashed for the next ten days over such difficult issues as reparations, the Polish border, and the fate of eastern Europe. Truman presented the ideas and proposals formulated by his advisers; he saw his task as essentially procedural, and when he presided, he moved the agenda along in brisk fashion. After he had "banged through" three items one day, he commented, "I am not going to stay around this terrible place all summer, just to listen to speeches. I'll go home to the Senate for that." In an indirect, roundabout way, he informed Stalin of the existence of the atomic bomb, tested successfully in the New

OUTLINE

The Cold War Begins

Containment

The Cold War Expands

The Cold War at Home

Eisenhower Wages the
Cold War

Conclusion: The Continuing
Cold War

FEATURE ESSAY

The "Lost Sheep" of the
Korean War

Churchill, Truman, and Stalin during the Potsdam Conference in July 1945. The conference revealed the growing divergence among the wartime allies that soon led to the onset of the Cold War. ❖

Mexico desert just before the conference began. Truman offered no details, and the impassive Stalin asked for none, commenting only that he hoped the United States would make "good use of it against the Japanese."

Reparations proved to be the crucial issue at Potsdam. The Russians wanted to rebuild their war-ravaged economy with German industry; the United States feared it would be saddled with the entire cost of caring for the defeated Germans. A compromise was finally reached. Each side would take reparations primarily from its own occupation zone, a solution that foreshadowed the future division of Germany. "Because they could not agree on how to govern Europe," wrote historian Daniel Yergin, "Truman and Stalin began to divide it." The other issues were referred to the newly created Council of Foreign Ministers, which would meet in the fall in London.

THE POTSDAM CONFERENCE THUS ENDED on an apparent note of harmony; beneath the surface, however, the bitter antagonism of the Cold War was festering. A dozen years later, Truman reminisced to an old associate about Potsdam. "What a show that was!" Describing himself as "an innocent idealist" surrounded by wolves, he claimed that all the agreements reached there were "broken as soon as the unconscionable Russian Dictator returned to Moscow!" He added ruefully, "And I liked the little son of a bitch."

Potsdam marked the end of the wartime alliance. America and Russia, each distrustful of the other, began to engage in a long and bitter confrontation. For the next decade, the two superpowers would vie for control of postwar Europe, and later clash over the spread of communism to Asia. By the time Truman's and Stalin's successors met for the next summit conference, at Geneva in 1955, the Cold War was at its height.

THE COLD WAR BEGINS

The conflict between the United States and the Soviet Union began gradually. For two years, the nations tried to adjust their differences over the division of Europe, postwar economic aid, and the atomic bomb through discussion and negotiation. The Council of Foreign Ministers provided the forum. Beginning in London during the fall of 1945 and meeting with their Russian counterparts in Paris, New York, and Moscow,

American diplomats searched for a way to live in peace with a suspicious Soviet Union.

The Division of Europe

The fundamental disagreement was over who would control postwar Europe. In the east, the Red Army had swept over Poland and the Balkans, laying the basis for Soviet domination there. American and British forces had liberated western Europe from Scandinavia to

Italy. The Russians, mindful of past invasions from the west across the plains of Poland, were intent on imposing communist governments loyal to Moscow in the Soviet sphere. The United States, on the other hand, upheld the principle of national self-determination, insisting the people in each country should freely choose their postwar rulers. The Soviets saw the demand for free elections as subversive, since they knew that popularly chosen regimes would be unfriendly to Russia. Suspecting American duplicity, Stalin brought down an **Iron Curtain** (Churchill's phrase) from the Baltic to the Adriatic as he created a series of satellite governments.

Germany was the key. The temporary zones of occupation gradually hardened into permanent lines of division. Ignoring the Potsdam Conference agreement that the country be treated as an economic unit, the United States and Great Britain were by 1946 refusing to permit the Russians to take reparations from the industrial western zones. The initial harsh occupation policy gave way to more humane treatment of the German people and a slow but steady economic recovery. The United States and England merged their zones and championed the idea of the unification of all Germany. Russia, fearing a resurgence of German military power, responded by intensifying the communization of its zone, which included the jointly occupied city of Berlin. By 1947, England, France, and the United States were laying plans to transfer their authority to an independent West Germany.

The Soviet Union consolidated its grip on eastern Europe in 1946 and 1947. One by one, communist regimes replaced coalition governments in Poland, Hungary, Romania, and Bulgaria. Moving cautiously to avoid provoking the West, Stalin used communism as a means to dominate half of Europe, both to protect the security of the Soviet state and to advance its international power. The climax came in March 1948 when a coup in Czechoslovakia overthrew a democratic government and gave the Soviets a strategic foothold in central Europe.

The division of Europe was an inevitable after-effect of World War II. Both sides were intent on imposing their values in the areas liberated by their troops. The Russians were no more likely to withdraw from eastern Europe than the United States and Britain were from Germany, France, and Italy. A frank recognition of competing spheres of influence might have avoided

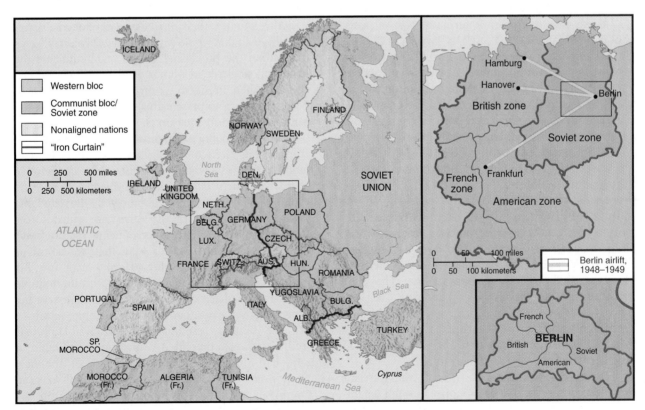

EUROPE AFTER WORLD WAR II   *The heavy red line splitting Germany shows in graphic form the division of Europe between the Western and Soviet spheres of influence. "From Stettin in the Baltic to Trieste in the Adriatic," said Winston Churchill in a speech at Fulton, Missouri, in 1956, "an iron curtain has descended across the Continent."* ❖

further escalation of tension. But the Western nations, remembering Hitler's aggression in the 1930s, began to see Stalin as an equally dangerous threat to their well-being. Instead of accepting him as a cautious leader bent on protecting Russian security, they perceived him as an aggressive dictator leading a communist drive for world domination.

Withholding Economic Aid

World War II had inflicted enormous damage on Russia. The brutal fighting had taken between fifteen and twenty million Russian lives, destroyed more than thirty thousand factories, and torn up forty thousand miles of railroad track. The industrialization that Stalin had achieved at such great sacrifice in the 1930s had been badly set back; even agricultural production had fallen by half during the war. Outside aid and assistance were vital for the reconstruction of the Soviet Union.

American leaders knew of Russia's plight and hoped to use it to good advantage. Wartime ambassador Averell Harriman wrote in 1944 that economic aid was "one of the most effective weapons at our disposal" in dealing with Russia. President Truman was convinced that economically "we held all the cards and the Russians had to come to us."

There were two possible forms of postwar assistance: loans and Lend-Lease. In January 1945, the Soviets requested a $6 billion loan to finance postwar reconstruction. Despite initial American encouragement, President Roosevelt deferred action on this request; as relations with Russia cooled, the chances for action dimmed. "Our experience," commented Harriman in April 1945, had "incontrovertibly proved it was not possible to bank goodwill in Moscow." By the war's end, the loan request, though never formally turned down, was dead.

Lend-Lease proved no more successful. In the spring of 1945, Congress instructed the administration not to use Lend-Lease for postwar reconstruction. President Truman went further, however, by signing an order on May 11, 1945, terminating all shipments to Russia, including those already at sea. The State Department saw the action as applying "leverage against the Soviet Union"; Stalin termed it "brutal." Heeding Russian protests, Truman resumed Lend-Lease shipments, but only until the war was over in August. After that, all Lend-Lease ended.

Deprived of American assistance, the Russians were forced to rebuild their economy through reparations. American and British resistance prevented them from taking reparations in western Germany, but the Soviets systematically removed factories and plants from other areas they controlled, including their zone of Germany, eastern Europe, and Manchuria. Slowly, the Russian economy recovered from the war, but the bitterness over the American refusal to extend aid convinced Stalin of Western hostility and thus deepened the growing antagonism between the Soviet Union and the United States.

The Atomic Dilemma

Overshadowing all else was the atomic bomb. Used by the United States with deadly success at Hiroshima and Nagasaki, the new weapon raised problems that would have been difficult for even friendly nations to resolve. Given the uneasy state of Soviet-American relations, the effect was disastrous.

The wartime policy followed by Roosevelt and Churchill ensured a postwar nuclear arms race. Instead of informing their major ally of the developing atomic bomb, they kept it a closely guarded secret. Stalin learned of the Manhattan Project through espionage and responded by starting a Soviet atomic program in 1943. By the time Truman informed Stalin of the weapon's existence at Potsdam, the Russians, aided by a steady stream of information from spies in the United States, were well on the way to making their own bomb.

After the war, the United States developed a disarmament plan that would turn control of fissionable material, then the processing plants, and ultimately the American stockpile of bombs over to an international agency. When President Truman appointed financier Bernard Baruch to present this proposal to the United Nations, Baruch insisted on changing it in several important ways, adding sanctions against violators and exempting the international agency from the UN veto. Ignoring scientists who pleaded for a more cooperative position, Baruch followed instead the advice of Army Chief of Staff Dwight D. Eisenhower, who cited the rapid demobilization of the American armed forces (from nearly twelve million personnel in 1945 to fewer than two million in 1947) to argue that "we cannot at this time limit our capability to produce or use this weapon." In effect, the **Baruch Plan,** with its multiple stages and emphasis on inspection, would preserve the American atomic monopoly for the indefinite future.

The Soviets responded predictably. Diplomat Andrei Gromyko presented a simple plan calling for a total ban on the production and use of the new weapon as well as the destruction of all existing bombs. The Russian proposal was founded on the same perception of national self-interest as the Baruch Plan. Although Russia had also demobilized rapidly, it still had nearly three million men under arms in 1947 and wanted to use its conventional strength to the utmost by outlawing the atomic bomb.

No agreement was possible. Neither the United States nor the Soviet Union could abandon its position without surrendering a vital national interest. Wanting to preserve its monopoly, America stressed inspection and control; hoping to neutralize the U.S. advantage, Russia advocated immediate disarmament. The nuclear dilemma, inherent in the Soviet-American rivalry, blocked any national settlement. Instead, the two superpowers agreed to disagree. Trusting neither each other nor any form of international cooperation, each concentrated on taking maximum advantage of its wartime gains. Thus the Russians exploited the territory they had conquered in Europe while the United States retained its economic and strategic advantages over the Soviet Union. The result was the Cold War.

CONTAINMENT

A major departure in American foreign policy occurred in January 1947, when General George C. Marshall, the wartime army chief of staff, became secretary of state. Calm, mature, and orderly of mind, Marshall had the capability—honed in World War II—to think in broad strategic terms. An extraordinarily good judge of ability, he relied on gifted subordinates to handle the day-to-day implementation of his policies. In the months after taking office, he came to rely on two men in particular: Dean Acheson and George Kennan.

Acheson, an experienced Washington lawyer and bureaucrat, was appointed undersecretary of state and given free rein by Marshall to conduct American diplomacy. In appearance, he seemed more British than American, with his impeccable Ivy League clothes and bushy mustache. A man of keen intelligence, he had a carefully cultivated reputation for arrogance and a low tolerance for mediocrity. As an ardent Anglophile, he wanted to see the United States take over a faltering Britain's role as the supreme arbiter of world affairs. Recalling the lesson of Munich, he opposed appeasement and advocated a policy of negotiating only from strength.

George Kennan, Marshall's other mainstay, headed the newly created Policy Planning Staff. A career foreign service officer, Kennan had become a Soviet expert, mastering Russian history and culture as well as speaking the language fluently. He served in Moscow after U.S. recognition in 1933 and again during World War II, developing there a profound distrust for the Soviet regime. In a crucial telegram in 1946, he warned that the Kremlin believed "that there can be no

compromise with rival power" and advocated a policy of containment, arguing that only strong and sustained resistance could halt the outward flow of Russian power. As self-assured as Acheson, Kennan believed that neither Congress nor public opinion should interfere with the conduct of foreign policy by the experts.

In the spring of 1947, a sense of crisis impelled Marshall, Acheson, and Kennan to set out on a new course in American diplomacy. Dubbed **containment,** after an article by Kennan in *Foreign Affairs,* the new policy both consolidated the evolving postwar anti-communism and established guidelines that would shape America's role in the world for more than two decades. What Kennan proposed was "a long-term, patient but firm, and vigilant containment of Russian expansive tendencies." Such a policy of halting Soviet aggression would not lead to any immediate victory, Kennan warned. In the long run, however, he believed that the United States could force the Soviet Union to adopt more reasonable policies and live in peace with the West.

The Truman Doctrine

The initial step toward containment came in response to an urgent British request. Since March 1946, England had been supporting the Greek government in a bitter civil war against communist guerrillas. On February 21, 1947, the British informed the United States that they could no longer afford to aid Greece or Turkey, the latter under heavy pressure from the Soviets for access to the Mediterranean. Believing the Russians responsible for the strife in Greece (in fact, they were not), Marshall, Acheson, and Kennan quickly decided the United States would have to assume Britain's role in the eastern Mediterranean.

Worried about congressional support, especially since the Republicans had gained control of Congress in 1946, Marshall called a meeting with the legislative leadership in late February. He outlined the problem; then Acheson took over to warn that "a highly possible Soviet breakthrough might open three continents to Soviet penetration." Comparing the situation in Greece to one rotten apple spoiling an entire barrel, Acheson warned that "the corruption of Greece would infect Iran and all to the east. It would also carry infection to Africa through Asia Minor and Egypt, and to Europe through Italy and France." Claiming that the Soviets were "playing one of the greatest gambles in history," Acheson concluded that "we and we alone were in a position to break up the play."

The bipartisan group of congressional leaders was deeply impressed. Finally, Republican Senator Arthur

M. Vandenberg spoke up, saying he would support the president, but adding that to ensure public backing, Truman would have to "scare hell" out of the American people.

The president followed the senator's advice. On March 12, 1947, he asked Congress for $400 million for military and economic assistance to Greece and Turkey. In stating what would become known as the **Truman Doctrine,** he made clear that more was involved than just these two countries—the stakes in fact were far higher. "It must be the policy of the United States," Truman told the Congress, "to support free peoples who are resisting attempted subjugation by armed minorities or by outside pressure." After a brief debate, both the House and the Senate approved the program by margins of better than three to one.

The Truman Doctrine marked an informal declaration of cold war against the Soviet Union. Truman used the crisis in Greece to secure congressional approval and build a national consensus for the policy of containment. In less than two years, the civil war in Greece ended, but the American commitment to oppose communist expansion, whether by internal subversion or external aggression, placed the United States on a collision course with the Soviet Union around the globe.

The Marshall Plan

Despite American interest in controlling Soviet expansion into Greece, western Europe was far more vital to U.S. interests than was the eastern Mediterranean. Yet by 1947, many Americans believed that western Europe was open to Soviet penetration. The problem was economic in nature. Despite $9 billion in piecemeal American loans, England, France, Italy, and the other European countries had great difficulty in recovering from World War II. Food was scarce, with millions existing on less than fifteen hundred calories a day; industrial machinery was broken down and obsolete; and workers were demoralized by years of depression and war. The cruel winter of 1947, the worst in fifty years, compounded the problem. Resentment and discontent led to growing communist voting strength, especially in Italy and France. If the United States could not reverse the process, it seemed as though all Europe might drift into the communist orbit.

In the weeks following proclamation of the Truman Doctrine, American officials dealt with this problem. Secretary of State Marshall, returning from a frustrating Council of Foreign Ministers meeting in Moscow, warned that "the patient is sinking while the doctors deliberate." Acheson believed that it was time to extend American "economic power" in Europe, both "to call an effective halt to the Soviet Union's expansionism" and "to create a basis for political stability and economic well-being." The experts drew up a plan for the massive infusion of American capital to finance the economic recovery of Europe. Speaking at a Harvard commencement on June 5, 1947, Marshall presented the broad outline. He offered extensive economic aid to all the nations of Europe if they could reach agreement on ways to achieve "the revival of a working economy in the world so as to permit the emergence of political and social conditions in which free institutions can exist."

George Marshall, seated at left, talks with the president of Harvard at the university's commencement ceremonies on June 5, 1947, where Marshall delivered a speech announcing the outlines of his plan for economic aid to assist European recovery after World War II. In 1953, Marshall was awarded the Nobel Peace Prize for his efforts. ❖

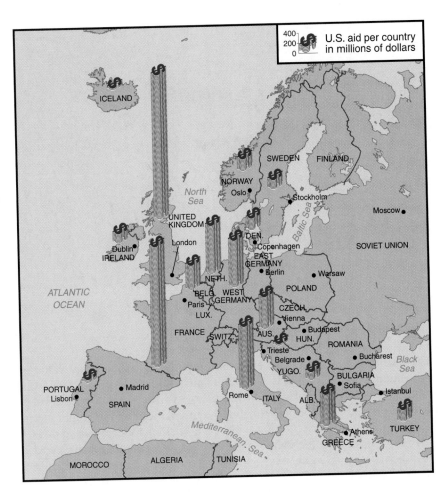

400
200
0

U.S. aid per country
in millions of dollars

MARSHALL PLAN AID TO EUROPE, 1948–1952 *The Marshall Plan, also known as the European Recovery Program, provided aid totaling $13 billion to European countries following World War II. Most went to former allies Great Britain and France but former enemies Italy and West Germany also received substantial aid. To receive the grants, countries pledged to control inflation and lower tariffs.* ❖

The fate of the **Marshall Plan** depended on the reaction of the Soviet Union and the U.S. Congress. Marshall had taken, in the words of one American diplomat, "a hell of a gamble" by including Russia in his offer of aid. At a meeting of the European nations in Paris in July 1947, the Soviet foreign minister ended the suspense by abruptly withdrawing. Neither the Soviet Union nor its satellites would take part, apparently because Moscow saw the Marshall Plan as an American attempt to weaken Soviet control over eastern Europe. The other European countries then made a formal request for $17 billion in assistance over the next four years.

Congress responded cautiously to the proposal, appointing a special joint committee to investigate. The administration lobbied vigorously, pointing out that the Marshall Plan would help the United States by stimulating trade with Europe as well as checking Soviet expansion. It was the latter argument, however, that proved decisive. When the Czech coup touched off a war scare in March 1948, Congress quickly approved the Marshall Plan by heavy majorities. Over the next four years, the huge American investment paid rich dividends, generating a broad industrial revival in western Europe that became self-sustaining by the 1950s. The threat of communist domination faded, and a prosperous Europe proved to be a bonanza for American farmers, miners, and manufacturers.

The Western Military Alliance

The third and final phase of containment came in 1949 with the establishment of the **North Atlantic Treaty Organization (NATO).** NATO grew out of European fears of Russian military aggression. Recalling Hitler's tactics in the 1930s, the people of western Europe wanted assurance that the United States would protect them from attack as they began to achieve economic recovery. American diplomats were sympathetic. "People could not go ahead and make investments for the future," commented Averell Harriman, "without some sense of security."

England, France, and the Low Countries (Belgium, the Netherlands, and Luxembourg) began the process in March 1948 when they signed the Brussels Treaty, providing for collective self-defense. In January 1949, President Truman called for a broader defense pact including the United States; ten European nations, from

The Soviet view of the Cold War, as depicted in this Soviet cartoon, shows the United States stretching out long arms to take hold of Korea, Iran, Turkey, Taiwan, and Vietnam. ❖

Norway in the north to Italy in the south, joined the United States and Canada in signing the North Atlantic Treaty in Washington on April 4, 1949. This historic departure from the traditional policy of isolation—the United States had not signed such a treaty since the French alliance in the eighteenth century—caused extensive debate, but the Senate ratified it in July by a vote of 82 to 13.

There were two main features of NATO. First, the United States committed itself to the defense of Europe in the key clause, which stated that "an armed attack against one or more shall be considered an attack against them all." In effect, the United States was extending its atomic shield over Europe. The second feature was designed to reassure worried Europeans that the United States would honor this commitment. In late 1950, President Truman appointed General Dwight D. Eisenhower to the post of NATO supreme commander and authorized the stationing of four American divisions in Europe to serve as the nucleus of the NATO army. It was believed the threat of American troop involvement in any Russian assault would deter the Soviet Union from making such an attack.

The Western military alliance escalated the developing Cold War. Whatever its advantage in building a sense of security among worried Europeans, it represented an overreaction to the Soviet danger. Americans and Europeans alike were attempting to apply the lesson of Munich to the Cold War. But Stalin was not Hitler, and the Soviets were not the Nazis. There was no evidence of any Russian plan to invade western Europe, and in the face of the American atomic bomb, none was likely. NATO only intensified Russian fears of the West and thus increased the level of international tension.

The Berlin Blockade

The main Russian response to containment came in 1948 at the West's most vulnerable point. American, British, French, and Soviet troops each occupied a sector of Berlin, but the city was located more than a hundred miles within the Russian zone of Germany (see the map of postwar Europe on p. 809). Stalin decided to test his opponents' resolve by cutting off all rail and highway traffic to Berlin on June 20, 1948.

The timing was very awkward for Harry Truman. He had his hands full resisting efforts to force him off the Democratic ticket, and he faced a difficult reelection effort against a strong Republican candidate, Governor Thomas E. Dewey of New York. Immersed in election-year politics, Truman was caught unprepared by the Berlin blockade. The alternatives were not very appealing. The United States could withdraw its forces and lose not just a city, but the confidence of all Europe; it could try to send in reinforcements and fight for Berlin; or it could sit tight and attempt to find a diplomatic solution. Truman made the basic decision in characteristic fashion, telling the military that there would be no thought of pulling out. "We were going to stay, period," an aide reported Truman as saying.

In the next few weeks, the president and his advisers developed ways to implement the decision. Rejecting proposals for provoking a showdown by sending an armored column down the main highway, the administration adopted a two-phase policy. The first part was a massive airlift of food, fuel, and supplies for the ten thousand troops and the two million civilians in Berlin. A fleet of fifty-two C-54s and eighty C-47s began making two daily round-trip flights to Berlin, carrying 2500 tons every twenty-four hours. Then, to guard against

Soviet interruption of the **Berlin airlift,** Truman transferred sixty American B-29s, planes capable of delivering atomic bombs, to bases in England. The president was bluffing; the B-29s were not equipped with atomic bombs, but at the time, the threat was effective.

For a few weeks, the world teetered on the edge of war. Stalin did not attempt to disrupt the flights to Berlin, but he rejected all American diplomatic initiatives. Although at any time the Russians could have halted it by jamming radar or shooting down the defenseless cargo planes, the airlift gradually increased to more than 4000 tons a day. Governor Dewey patrioti-

The Berlin airlift of 1948–1949 broke the Soviet blockade. Called Operation Vittles, it provided food and fuel for West Berliners. Here, children atop a pile of rubble wave to an American cargo plane flying overhead. In addition to necessities, airlift pilots dropped candy in tiny handkerchief parachutes. ❖

cally supported the president's policy, thus removing foreign policy from the presidential campaign. Yet for Truman, the tension was fierce. In early September, he asked his advisers to brief him "on bases, bombs, Moscow, Leningrad, etc." "I have a terrible feeling afterward that we are very close to war," he confided in his diary. "I hope not."

Slowly, the tension eased. The Russians did not shoot down any planes, and the daily airlift climbed to nearly 7000 tons. Truman, a decided underdog, won a surprising second term in November over a complacent Dewey, in part because the Berlin crisis had rallied the nation behind his leadership. In early 1949, the Soviets gave in, ending the blockade in return for another meeting of the Council of Foreign Ministers on Germany—a conclave that proved as unproductive as all the earlier ones.

The Berlin crisis marked the end of the initial phase of the Cold War. The airlift had given the United States a striking political victory, showing the world the triumph of American ingenuity over Russian stubbornness. Yet it could not disguise the fact that the Cold War had cut Europe in two. Behind the Iron Curtain, the Russians had consolidated control over the areas won by their troops in the war, while the United States had used the Marshall Plan to revitalize western Europe. But a divided continent was a far cry from the wartime hopes for a peaceful world. And the

rivalry that began in Europe would soon spread into a worldwide contest between the superpowers.

THE COLD WAR EXPANDS

The rivalry between the United States and the Soviet Union grew in the late 1940s and early 1950s. Both sides began to rebuild their military forces with new methods and new weapons. Equally significant, the diplomatic competition spread from Europe to Asia as each of the superpowers sought to enhance its influence in the Far East. By the time Truman left office in early 1953, the Cold War had taken on global proportions.

The Military Dimension

After World War II, American leaders were intent on reforming the nation's military system in light of their wartime experience. Two goals were uppermost. First, nearly everyone agreed in the aftermath of Pearl Harbor that the U.S. armed services should be unified into an integrated military system. The developing Cold War reinforced this decision. Without unification, declared George Marshall in 1945, "there can be little hope that we will be able to maintain through the years a military posture that will secure for us a lasting peace." Equally important, planners realized, was the need for new institutions to coordinate military and diplomatic strategy so the nation could cope effectively with threats to its security.

In 1947, Congress passed the **National Security Act.** It established a Department of Defense, headed by a civilian secretary of cabinet rank presiding over three separate services—the army, the navy, and the new air force. In addition, the act created the Central Intelligence Agency (CIA) to coordinate the intelligence-gathering activities of various government agencies. Finally, the act provided for a National Security Council (NSC)—composed of the service secretaries, the secretary of defense, and the secretary of state—to advise the president on all matters regarding the nation's security.

Despite the appearance of equality among the services, the air force quickly emerged as the dominant power in the atomic age, based on its capability both to deter an enemy from attacking and to wage war if deterrence failed. President Truman, intent on cutting back defense expenditures, favored the air force in his 1949 military budget, allotting this branch more than one-half the total sum. After the Czech coup and the resulting war scare, Congress granted an additional $3 billion to the military. The appropriation included funds for a new B-36 to replace the B-29 as the nation's primary strategic bomber.

American military planners received even greater support in the fall of 1949 when the Soviet Union exploded its first atomic bomb. President Truman appointed a high-level committee to explore mounting an all-out effort to build a hydrogen bomb to maintain American nuclear supremacy.

Some scientists had technical objections to the H-bomb, which was still far from being perfected, while others opposed the new weapon on moral grounds, claiming that its enormous destructive power (intended to be one thousand times greater than the atomic bomb) made it unthinkable. George Kennan suggested a new effort at international arms control with the Soviets, but Dean Acheson—who succeeded Marshall as secretary of state in early 1949—believed it was imperative that the United States develop the hydrogen bomb before the Soviet Union. When Acheson presented the committee's favorable report to the president in January 1950, Truman took only seven minutes to decide to go ahead with the awesome new weapon.

At the same time, Acheson ordered the Policy Planning Staff (headed by Paul Nitze after Kennan resigned in protest) to draw up a new statement of national defense policy. **NSC-68,** as the document eventually became known, was based on the premise that the Soviet Union sought "to impose its absolute authority over the rest of the world" and thus "mortally challenged" the United States. Rejecting such options as appeasement or a return to isolation, Nitze advocated a massive expansion of American military power so the United States could halt and overcome the Soviet threat. Contending the nation could afford to spend "upward of 50 percent of its gross national product" for security, NSC-68 proposed increasing defense spending from $13 to $45 billion annually. Approved in principle by the National Security Council in April 1950, NSC-68 stood as a symbol of the Truman administration's determination to win the Cold War regardless of cost.

The Cold War in Asia

The Soviet-American conflict developed more slowly in Asia. At Yalta, the two superpowers had agreed to a Far Eastern balance of power, with the Russians dominating Northeast Asia and the Americans in control of the Pacific, including both Japan and its former island empire.

The United States moved quickly to consolidate its sphere of influence. General Douglas MacArthur, in charge of Japanese occupation, denied the Soviet Union any role in the reconstruction of Japan. Instead, he supervised the transition of the Japanese government into a constitutional democracy, shaped along Western lines, in which communists were barred from all government posts. The Japanese willingly renounced war in their new constitution, relying instead on American forces to protect their security. American policy was equally nationalistic in the Pacific. A trusteeship arrangement with the United Nations merely disguised the fact that the United States held full control over the Marshall, Mariana, and Caroline Islands. American scientists conducted atomic bomb tests at Bikini atoll in 1946, and by 1949, MacArthur was declaring that the entire Pacific "had become an Anglo-Saxon lake and our line of defense runs through the chain of islands fringing the coast of Asia."

As defined at Yalta, China lay between the Soviet and American spheres. When World War II ended, the country was torn between Chiang Kai-shek's Nationalists in the South and Mao Tse-tung's Communists in the North. Chiang had many advantages, including American political and economic backing and official Soviet recognition. But corruption was widespread among the Nationalist leaders, and a raging inflation that soon reached 100 percent a year devastated the Chinese middle classes and thus eroded Chiang's base of power. Mao used tight discipline and patriotic appeals to strengthen his hold on the peasantry and extend his influence. When the Soviets abruptly vacated Manchuria in 1946, after stripping it of virtually all the industrial machinery Japan had installed, Mao inherited control of this rich northern province. Ignoring American advice, Chiang rushed north to occupy Manchurian cities, overextending his supply lines and exposing his forces to Communist counterattack.

American policy sought to prevent a Chinese civil war. Before he became secretary of state, George Marshall undertook the difficult task of forming a coalition government between Chiang and Mao. For a few months in early 1946, Marshall appeared to have succeeded, but Chiang's attempts to gain control of Manchuria doomed the agreement. In reality, there was no basis for compromise. Chiang insisted he "was going to liquidate Communists," while Mao was trying to play the United States against Russia in his bid for power. By 1947, as China plunged into full-scale civil war, the Truman administration had given up any meaningful effort to influence the outcome. Political mediation had failed, military intervention was out of the question so soon after World War II, and a policy of continued American economic aid served only to appease domestic supporters of Chiang Kai-shek; 80 percent of the military supplies ended up in Communist hands.

The Chinese conflict climaxed at the end of the decade. Mao's forces drove the Nationalists out of Manchuria in late 1948 and advanced across the Yangtze by mid-1949. Acheson released a lengthy report justifying American policy in China on the grounds that the civil war there "was beyond the control of the government of the United States." An American military adviser concurred, telling Congress that the Nationalist defeat was due to "the world's worst leadership" and "a complete loss of will to fight." Republican senators, however, disagreed, blaming American diplomats for sabotaging the Nationalists and terming Acheson's report "a 1054-page whitewash of a wishful, do-nothing policy." While the domestic debate raged over responsibility for the loss of China, Chiang's forces fled the mainland for sanctuary on Formosa (Taiwan) in December 1949. Two months later, Mao and Stalin signed a Sino-Soviet treaty of mutual assistance that clearly placed China in the Russian orbit.

The American response to the Communist triumph in China was twofold. First, the State Department refused to recognize the legitimacy of the new regime in Peking, maintaining instead formal diplomatic relations with the Nationalists on Formosa. Citing the Sino-Soviet alliance, Assistant Secretary of State Dean Rusk called the Peking regime "a colonial Russian government" and declared, "It is not the Government of China. It does not pass the first test. It is not Chinese." Then, to compensate for the loss of China, the United States focused on Japan as its main ally in Asia. The State Department encouraged the buildup of Japanese industry, and the Pentagon expanded American bases on the Japanese home islands and Okinawa. A Japanese-American security pact led to the end of American occupation by 1952. The Cold War had now split Asia in two.

The Korean War

The showdown between the United States and the Soviet Union in Asia came in Korea. Traditionally the cockpit of international rivalry in Northeast Asia, Korea had been divided at the 38th parallel in 1945. The Russians occupied the industrial North, installing a communist government under the leadership of Kim Il-Sung. In the agrarian South, Syngman Rhee, a conservative nationalist, emerged as the American-sponsored ruler. Neither regime heeded a UN call for elections to unify the country. The two superpowers pulled out most of their occupation forces by 1949. The Russians, however, helped train a well-equipped army in the North, while the United States—fearful

Chairman Mao Tse-tung inspects his People's Liberation Army troops at the Hsiyuan airfield near Peking in March 1949. By the end of the year, Mao's Communist forces had defeated the Nationalists under Chiang Kai-shek and forced them off the mainland to the island of Taiwan. ❖

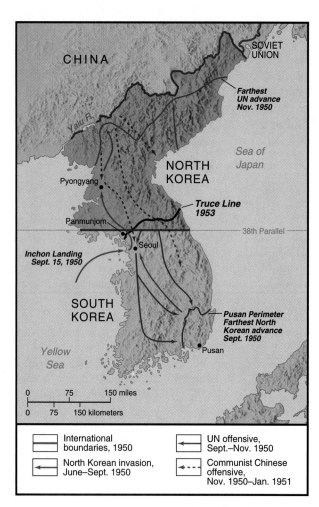

THE KOREAN WAR, 1950–1953 *After a year of rapid movement up and down the Korean peninsula, the fighting stalled just north of the 38th parallel. The resulting truce line has divided North and South Korea since the July 1953 armistice.* ❖

Rhee would seek unification through armed conquest—gave much more limited military assistance to South Korea.

On June 25, 1950, the North Korean army suddenly crossed the 38th parallel in great strength. Stalin had approved this act of aggression in advance. In January 1950, the Soviet leader had told Mao Tse-tung that he was ready to overthrow the Yalta settlement in the Far East ("and to hell with it," he exclaimed to Mao). In April, when Kim Il-Sung came to Moscow to gain approval for the assault on South Korea, Stalin gave it willingly, apparently in the belief that the United States was ready to abandon Syngman Rhee. But the ever cautious Stalin warned Kim not to count on Soviet assistance, saying, "If you should get kicked in the teeth, I shall not lift a finger. You have to ask Mao for all the help." Despite expressing some reservations, in May, Mao also approved the planned North Korean aggression.

Both Stalin and Mao had badly miscalculated the American response. President Truman saw the invasion as a clear-cut case of Soviet aggression reminiscent of the 1930s. "Communism was acting in Korea just as Hitler, Mussolini, and the Japanese had acted ten, fifteen, and twenty years earlier," he commented in his memoirs. Following Acheson's advice, the president convened the UN Security Council and, taking advantage of a temporary Soviet boycott, secured a resolution condemning North Korea as an aggressor and calling on the member nations to engage in a collective security action. Within a few days, American troops from Japan were in combat in South Korea. The conflict, which would last for more than three years, was technically a police action fought under UN auspices; in reality, the United States was at war with a Soviet satellite in Asia.

In the beginning, the fighting went badly as the North Koreans continued to drive down the peninsula. But by August, American forces had halted the communist advance near Pusan. In September, General MacArthur changed the whole complexion of the war by carrying out a brilliant amphibious assault at Inchon, on the waist of Korea, cutting off and destroying most of the North Korean army in the South. Encouraged by this victory, Truman began to shift from his original goal of restoring the 38th parallel to a new one: the unification of Korea by military force.

The administration ignored Beijing's repeated warnings not to invade North Korea. "I should think it would be sheer madness for the Chinese to intervene," commented Acheson. Despite CIA reports of a massive Chinese force assembling in Manchuria, President Truman and his advisers continued to believe that the Soviet Union, not ready for all-out war, would hold China in check. General MacArthur was equally certain that China would not attack his troops in Korea. "We are no longer fearful of their intervention," he told Truman in October, adding that if they crossed the Yalu into Korea, "there would be the greatest slaughter."

Rarely has an American president received worse advice. China was not a Soviet puppet. When UN forces crossed the 38th parallel and moved confidently toward the Yalu, the Chinese launched a devastating counterattack in late November which caught MacArthur by surprise and drove his armies out of North Korea by the end of the year. MacArthur finally stabilized the fighting near the 38th parallel, but when Truman decided to give up his attempt to unify Korea, the general protested to Congress, calling for a renewed offensive and proclaiming, "There is no substitute for victory."

Truman courageously relieved the popular hero of the Pacific of his command on April 11, 1951. At first, MacArthur seemed likely to force the president to back

Douglas MacArthur, supreme commander of UN forces in Korea, launched the invasion at Inchon in September 1950 and within a few days recaptured Seoul, the South Korean capital. ❖

down. Huge crowds came forward to welcome him home and hear him call for victory over the communists in Asia. At a special congressional hearing, the administration struck back effectively by warning that MacArthur's strategy would expose all Europe to Soviet attack. General Omar Bradley, Truman's chief military adviser, succinctly pointed out that a "showdown" with communism in Asia would be "the wrong war, at the wrong place, at the wrong time, and with the wrong enemy."

Congress and the American people came to accept MacArthur's recall. The Korean War settled into a stalemate near the 38th parallel as truce talks with the communists bogged down. The president had achieved his primary goal, defense of South Korea and the principle of collective security. Yet by taking the gamble to unify Korea by force, he had confused the American people and humiliated the United States in the eyes of the world. (See the Feature Essay, "The 'Lost Sheep' of the Korean War," pp. 820–821.)

In the last analysis, the most significant result of the Korean conflict was the massive American rearmament it brought about. The war led to the implemen-

tation of NSC-68—the army expanded to 3.5 million troops, the defense budget increased to $50 billion a year by 1952, and the United States acquired distant military bases from Saudi Arabia to Morocco. America was now committed to waging a global contest against the Soviet Union with arms as well as words.

THE COLD WAR AT HOME

The Cold War cast a long shadow over American life in the late 1940s and early 1950s. Truman tried to carry on the New Deal reform tradition he had inherited from FDR, but the American people were more concerned about events abroad. The Republican party used both growing dissatisfaction with postwar economic adjustment and fears of communist penetration of the United States to revive its sagging fortunes and regain control of the White House in 1952 for the first time in twenty years.

Truman's Troubles

Matching his foreign policy successes with equal achievements at home was not easy for Harry S Truman. As a loyal supporter of Franklin D. Roosevelt's New Deal programs during his Senate career, Truman had earned a reputation for being a hardworking, reliable, and intensely partisan legislator. But he was relatively unknown to the general public, and his background as a Missouri county official associated with Kansas City machine politics did little to inspire confidence in his ability to lead the nation. Surprisingly well-read—especially in history and biography—Truman possessed sound judgment, the ability to reach decisions quickly, and a fierce and uncompromising sense of right and wrong.

Two weaknesses marred his performance in the White House. One was a fondness for old friends, which resulted in the appointment of many Missouri and Senate cronies to high office. Men such as Attorney General Tom Clark, Secretary of the Treasury Charles Snyder, and White House military aide Harry Vaughn brought little credit to the Truman administration, while the loss of such effective public servants as Secretary of the Interior Harold Ickes and Labor Secretary Frances Perkins hurt it. The president's other serious limitation was his lack of political vision. Failing to pursue a coherent legislative program of his own, he tried to perpetuate FDR's New Deal and, as a result, engaged in a running battle with Congress.

The postwar mood was not conducive to an extension of New Deal reforms. Americans were weary of shortages and sacrifices; they wanted the chance to buy the consumer goods denied them under wartime

THE "LOST SHEEP" OF THE KOREAN WAR

*I*t was unthinkable.

Twenty-three young American prisoners of war, who should have been overjoyed because they were free and returning home after nearly three years in captivity, instead joined the enemy. Laughing and chanting anti-U.S. slogans, they rolled into Panmunjom on September 24, 1953, aboard three Russian-made trucks. They traveled down the same dusty road taken earlier by more than thirty-five hundred fellow POWs who had been returned by the Chinese and North Koreans during Operation Big Switch, the prisoner exchange at the end of the Korean War. But these twenty-three were not interested in returning home. Instead, they sang the communist anthem, "The Internationale," and pledged to stay with their captors and fight for world peace.

One of the men, speaking in a rich southern accent, yelled at an American news reporter: "Go home, you imperialist Yankee." Another called to a Chinese soldier, "See you in Peiping," as they headed for temporary quarters in the neutral zone that separated United Nations forces from the Chinese and North Koreans. Accompanying the men as they climbed from the trucks was a mascot, a dog wearing a small banner proclaiming his name as "Non-repat," short for "nonrepatriate." For the next ninety days, the men would be in the custody of neutral troops from India while they mulled over their decision to defect.

The American defectors were an unexpected by-product of the prisoner repatriation debate that had held up armistice talks at Panmunjom for more than a year. The communists,

aware that many of their captured soldiers would refuse to come back, first demanded that all prisoners of war be returned. The United States had insisted that no POWs be forced to return home against their will. After months of hard negotiations, the communists reluctantly agreed to voluntary repatriation. The United States anticipated the propaganda victory that could be reaped from the spectacle of thousands of Chinese and North Korean POWs spurning communism. U.S. policymakers initially gave little thought to the possibility that Americans might also refuse repatriation and create their own spectacle.

Officially, the army called the twenty-three American defectors "voluntary nonrepatriates," but soon they were dubbed "turncoats" by the media. In sheer numbers they were few, especially in comparison to the more than twenty thousand Chinese and North Korean prisoners who refused to return home. The U.S. government feared the defectors would be used to discredit the American way of life, particularly in the eyes of the Third World countries.

Such fears were not groundless. The communists already had made far-fetched charges that American bombers had dropped insects and disease cultures on North Korea. Some captive U.S. airmen had made "confessions" of germ warfare. Other POWs had attacked their government in letters sent to newspapers back home or in stories printed in camp papers and magazines. The defectors appeared to be just one more salvo in the Cold War's propaganda barrage.

Even in this Cold War context, the scene at Panmunjom was a shock.

Never before had American soldiers captured on foreign soil opted to stay with the enemy after hostilities were over. Why would God-fearing American boys, most in their early twenties and hailing from small towns from New York to California, turn their backs on their nation and their families and join the enemy?

Some said the men were pitiful products of communist torture and brainwashing. Others, particularly the army, saw the men strictly as opportunistic collaborators who earlier had betrayed their fellow POWs in exchange for favors from their captors. General Mark Clark, commander of U.S. and UN troops in Korea, dismissed the defectors as "rats." However, Secretary of State John Foster Dulles dubbed the men "lost sheep," and President Eisenhower urged sympathy since no one knew what they had undergone. Mothers of the defectors saw their sons as misguided and confused, pointing to their lack of worldliness and their youth. More than half were teenagers when they were captured, and most had traveled little outside their hometowns before they joined the army.

During the ninety-day period they spent in the neutral zone, the defectors held the attention of an American public anxious to change their minds. Fund drives were launched nationwide to send their mothers to Korea, but the United States ruled out the plan as unworkable. Radio commentator Paul Harvey urged the young men's parents to go to their nearest radio station and record pleas for their sons to come home. Evangelist Billy Graham prayed for the defectors and asked

The Korean War POWs, including 21 Americans, 1 Brit, and 325 South Koreans who rejected their home countries and chose instead to espouse communism, await the arrival of trucks to take them from Panmunjom to the town of Kaesong in North Korea. ❖

Eisenhower to send him to Korea to talk with them. The Cleveland Indians offered the men jobs if they would return. One Hollywood resident telegraphed Eisenhower with a suggestion that a team of actors, including Jimmy Stewart, Clark Gable, Henry Fonda, and William Holden, be dispatched to Korea to try to change the defectors' minds.

Instead, the army selected a team of twelve young college-educated officers and gave them special training on how to lure back the defectors. The twelve pored over background material about the defectors. They memorized their photos so they could greet them by name in face-to-face meetings allowed by the repatriation agreement signed with the communists. But this team never had a chance. The defectors declined to meet with them and refused to accept individually addressed, custom-written letters. In a last-ditch effort, the army blared a loudspeaker broadcast into the defectors' compound, urging them to return before it was too late. The defectors drowned out the words with songs and chants and said they would never go home.

Two of the men did change their minds and returned home before the deadline. Corporal Edward Dickenson said he had decided "Communism is not my belief" and that he missed his mother's home cooking back in Cracker's Neck, Virginia. Corporal Claude Batchelor of Kermit, Texas, was moved to return in part by love letters from his Japanese fiancée, which actually were ghostwritten by news people. In a move that generated considerable controversy, the army later court-martialed the two men for collaborating with the enemy and sentenced them to long prison terms. Both were paroled by the end of the 1950s.

On January 28, 1954, the twenty-one Americans, along with a single British soldier and 325 South Korean soldiers who also defected, boarded Russian trucks and drove north out of the neutral zone. Before going, they gave a press conference and told reporters they were staying with the communists because they wanted to be "peace fighters." The Americans soon ended up in China, where they worked in factories, attended school, or taught English.

The defectors eventually drifted back to the United States, sometimes accompanied by Chinese wives and children. By the mid-1960s, all but two had left China. The returnees expressed disillusionment with communism and China and said they missed their families and the United States. Some viewed their sojourn in China as a lark. "I would never get a chance like that to go to a big country and I thought to learn Chinese would be very nice," said one.

After an initial flurry of publicity that accompanied each man's arrival, the "lost sheep" quickly drifted into obscurity and became a forgotten postscript of the Korean War.

conditions. But in the rush to convert industry from producing planes and tanks to cars and appliances, problems soon emerged. Prices and wages rose quickly as Congress voted to end wartime controls. With prices going up 25 percent in two years, workers demanded higher wages to offset the loss of overtime pay. A wave of labor unrest swept over the country in the spring of 1946, culminating in two critical strikes: a walkout by coal miners that threatened to close down much of American industry and a paralyzing strike by railroad workers.

President Truman was caught in the middle. Sensitive to union demands, he permitted businesses to negotiate large pay increases for their workers and then pass on the cost to consumers in the form of higher prices. He criticized Congress for weakening wartime price controls, but he failed to offer anything else to curb inflation. Homemakers blamed him for the rising price of food, while organized labor condemned Truman as the country's "No. 1 Strikebreaker" when he asked Congress for power to draft striking railway workers into the army.

In the face of this rising discontent, Truman's efforts to extend the New Deal met with little success. Congress ignored his September 1945 call for measures to ensure economic security and enacted only the Employment Act of 1946. This legislation created the Council of Economic Advisers to assist the president and asserted the principle that the government was responsible for the state of the economy, but it failed to address Truman's original goal of mandatory federal planning to achieve full employment.

The Republicans took advantage of increasing public dissatisfaction with postwar economic woes to attack the Democrats. "To err is Truman," the GOP proclaimed and then adopted a very effective two-word slogan for the 1946 congressional elections: "Had enough?" The American people, weary of inflation and labor unrest, responded by electing Republican majorities in both the House and Senate for the first time since 1930.

Truman Vindicated

The president's relations with Congress became even stormier after the 1946 elections. Truman successfully vetoed two GOP measures to give large tax cuts to the wealthy, but Congress overrode his veto of the **Taft-Hartley Act** in 1947. Designed to correct the imbalance in labor-management relations created by the Wagner Act, the Taft-Hartley Act outlawed specific labor union activities—including the closed shop and secondary boycotts—and it permitted the president to invoke an eighty-day cooling-off period to delay strikes that might endanger national health or safety. Despite Truman's claim that it was a "slave-labor" bill, unions were able to survive its provisions.

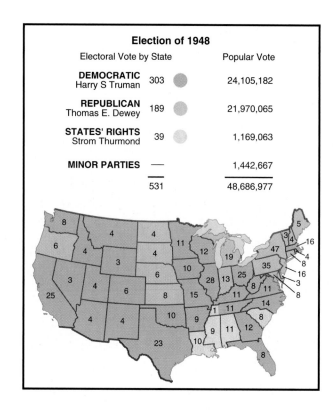

President Truman's political fortunes reached their lowest ebb in early 1948. Former vice president Henry A. Wallace, claiming to represent the New Deal, announced his third-party (Progressive) candidacy in the presidential contest that year. Worried Democratic party leaders sought to persuade Truman to step aside and allow General Dwight D. Eisenhower to become the Democratic candidate. When Eisenhower turned down bids from both parties, the Democrats reluctantly nominated Truman. His prospects for victory in the fall, however, looked very dim—especially after disgruntled Southerners bolted the Democratic party in protest over a progressive civil rights platform. The **Dixiecrats,** as they became known, nominated Strom Thurmond, the governor of South Carolina, on a States' Rights party ticket.

The defection of the Dixiecrats in the South and Wallace's liberal followers in the North led political experts to predict an almost certain Republican victory. Governor Thomas E. Dewey of New York, the GOP candidate, was so sure of winning that he waged a cautious and bland campaign designed to give him a free hand once he was in the White House. With nothing to lose, Truman barnstormed around the country denouncing the "do-nothing" Republican Eightieth Congress. The president's "give-'em hell" tactics reminded voters of how much they owed the Democrats for helping them survive the Great Depression. To the amazement of the pollsters, Truman won a narrow but decisive victory in November. The old Roosevelt coalition—farmers, organized labor, urban ethnic groups, and blacks—had held together, enabling Truman to remain in the White House and the Democrats to regain control of Congress.

There was one more reason for Truman's win in 1948. During this election, held at the height of the Berlin crisis, the GOP failed to challenge Truman's conduct of the Cold War. Locked in a tense rivalry with the Soviet Union, the American people saw no reason to reject a president who had countered aggression overseas with the Truman Doctrine and the Marshall Plan. The Republicans, committed to support the bipartisan policy of containment, had allowed the Democrats to preempt the foreign policy issue. Until they found a way to challenge Truman's Cold War policies, GOP leaders had little chance to regain the White House.

The Loyalty Issue

Despite Truman's surprising victory in 1948, there was one area on which the Democrats were vulnerable. The fear of communism abroad that had led to the bipartisan containment policy could be used against them at home by politicians who were more willing to exploit the public's deep-seated anxiety.

Fear of radicalism had been a recurrent feature of American life since the early days of the republic. Federalists had tried to suppress dissent with the Alien and Sedition Acts in the 1790s; the Know-Nothings had campaigned against foreigners and Catholics in the 1850s; and the Red Scare after World War I had been directed against both aliens and radicals. The Cold War heightened the traditional belief that subversion from abroad endangered the republic. Bold rhetoric from members of the Truman administration, portraying the men in the Kremlin as inspired revolutionaries bent on world conquest, frightened the American people. They viewed the Soviet Union as a successor to Nazi Germany—a totalitarian police state that threatened the basic liberties of a free people.

A series of revelations of communist espionage activities reinforced these fears, sparking a second Red Scare. Canadian officials uncovered a Soviet spy ring in 1946, and the **House Un-American Activities Committee (HUAC)** held hearings indicating that communist agents had flourished in the Agriculture and Treasury Departments in the 1930s.

Although Truman tried to dismiss the loyalty issue as a "red herring," he felt compelled to take protective measures, thus lending substance to the charges of subversion. In March 1947, he had initiated a loyalty program, ordering security checks of government employees in order to root out communists. Originally intended to remove subversives for whom "reasonable grounds exist for belief that the person involved is disloyal," within four years the Loyalty Review Board was

A jubilant Harry Truman, on the morning after his 1948 election win, displays the headline blazoned on the front page of the Chicago Daily Tribune—a newspaper that believed the pollsters. ❖

dismissing workers as security risks if there was "reasonable doubt" of their loyalty. Thousands of government workers lost their jobs, charged with guilt by association with radicals or with membership in left-wing organizations. Often those who were charged had no chance to face their accusers.

The most famous disclosure came in August 1948, when Whittaker Chambers, a repentant communist, accused Alger Hiss of having been a Soviet spy in the 1930s. When Hiss, who had been a prominent State Department official, denied the charges, Chambers led investigators to a hollowed-out pumpkin on his Maryland farm. Inside the pumpkin were microfilms of confidential government documents. Chambers claimed that Hiss had passed the State Department materials to him in the late 1930s. Although the statute of limitations prevented a charge of treason against Hiss, he was convicted of perjury in January 1950 and sentenced to a five-year prison term.

In 1948, the Justice Department further heightened fears of subversion. It charged eleven officials of the Communist party with advocating the violent overthrow of the government. After a long trial, the jury found them guilty, and the party officials received prison sentences and heavy fines; in 1951, the Supreme Court upheld the convictions as constitutional.

Such repressive measures failed, however, to reassure the nation. Events abroad intensified the sense of danger. The communist triumph in China in the fall of 1949 came as a shock; soon there were charges that "fellow travelers" in the State Department were responsible for "the loss of China." In September 1949,

Alger Hiss, accused of being a Communist spy by Whittaker Chambers, takes an oath during his August 1948 hearings before the House Un-American Activities Committee. Chambers, a former editor of Time *magazine, holds the headline announcing Hiss's conviction on charges of perjury. Hiss's conviction convinced many Americans that internal subversion threatened the nation's survival.* ❖

when the Truman administration announced that the Russians had detonated their first atomic bomb, the end of America's nuclear monopoly was blamed on Soviet espionage. In early 1950, Klaus Fuchs—a British scientist who had worked on the wartime Manhattan Project—admitted giving the Russians vital information about the A-bomb.

A few months later, the government charged American communists Ethel and Julius Rosenberg with conspiracy to transmit atomic secrets to the Soviet Union. In 1951, a jury found the Rosenbergs guilty of treason, and Judge Irving Kaufman sentenced them to die for what he termed their "loathsome of-

fense." Despite their insistent claims of innocence and worldwide appeals on their behalf, the Rosenbergs were electrocuted on June 19, 1953. Thus by the early 1950s, nearly all the ingredients were at hand for a new outburst of hysteria—fear of Russia, evidence of espionage, and a belief in a vast unseen conspiracy. The only element missing was a leader to release the new outburst of intolerance.

McCarthyism in Action

On February 12, 1950, Senator Joseph R. McCarthy of Wisconsin delivered a routine Lincoln's Birthday

Ethel and Julius Rosenberg, charged with spying for the Soviet Union, were found guilty of treason in 1951 and sentenced to death. Sympathetic protesters appealed to the president for clemency. Here, Sophie Rosenberg, Julius's mother, carries a sign that reads "If we die it will be murder of innocent people," the statement of her son and daughter-in-law. ❖

speech in Wheeling, West Virginia. This little known Republican suddenly attracted national attention when he declared, "I have here in my hand a list of 205—a list of names that were made known to the secretary of state as being members of the communist party and who nevertheless are still working and shaping policy in the State Department." The charge that there were communists in the State Department—repeated on different occasions with the number changed to 57, then 81—was never substantiated. But McCarthy's Wheeling speech triggered a four-and-a-half-year crusade to hunt down alleged communists in government. The stridency and sensationalism of the senator's accusations soon won the name **McCarthyism.**

McCarthy's basic technique was the multiple untruth. He leveled a bevy of charges of treasonable activities in government. While officials were refuting his initial accusations, he brought forth a steady stream of new ones, so the corrections never caught up with the latest blast. He failed to unearth a single confirmed communist in government, but he kept the Truman administration in turmoil. Drawing on an army of informers, primarily disgruntled federal workers with grievances against their colleagues and superiors, McCarthy charged government agencies with harboring and protecting communist agents and accused the State Department of deliberately losing the Cold War. His briefcase bulged with documents, but he did very little actual research, relying instead on reports (often outdated) from earlier congressional investigations. He exploited the press with great skill, combining current accusations with promises of future disclosures to guarantee headlines.

The secret of McCarthy's power was the fear he engendered among his Senate colleagues. In 1950, Maryland Senator Millard Tydings, who headed a committee critical of McCarthy's activities, failed to win reelection when McCarthy opposed him; after that, other senators ran scared. McCarthy delighted in making sweeping, startling charges of communist sympathies against prominent public figures. A favorite target was patrician Secretary of State Dean Acheson, whom McCarthy ridiculed as the "Red Dean," with his "cane, spats and tea-sipping little finger"; he even went after General George Marshall, claiming that the wartime army chief of staff was an agent of the communist conspiracy. Nor were follow Republicans immune. One GOP senator was described as "a living miracle in that he is without question the only man who has lived so long with neither brains nor guts."

The attacks on the wealthy, famous, and privileged won McCarthy a devoted national following, though at the height of his influence in early 1954, he gained the approval of only 50 percent of the respondents in a

Senator Joseph McCarthy maintained a steady stream of unsubstantiated charges, always ready to make new accusations of communist infiltration before the preceding ones could be proven untrue. McCarthy's ruthless, vicious attacks cost hundreds of people their jobs and careers. ❖

Gallup poll. McCarthy drew a disproportionate backing from working-class Catholics and ethnic groups, especially the Irish, Poles, and Italians, who normally voted Democratic. He offered a simple solution to the complicated Cold War: Defeat the enemy at home rather than continue to engage in costly foreign aid programs and entangling alliances abroad. Above all, McCarthy appealed to conservative Republicans in the Midwest who shared his right-wing views and felt cheated by Truman's upset victory in 1948. Even GOP leaders who viewed McCarthy's tactics with distaste, such as Robert A. Taft of Ohio, quietly encouraged him to attack the vulnerable Democrats.

The Republicans in Power

In 1952, the GOP capitalized on a growing sense of national frustration to capture the presidency. The stalemate in Korea and the second Red Scare created a

Eisenhower's landslide victories in the presidential elections of 1952 and 1956 seemed to prove his slogan that Americans did, indeed, "like Ike," as expressed on this campaign pennant. ❖

desire for political change; revelations of scandals by several individuals close to Truman intensified the feeling that someone needed to clean up "the mess in Washington." In Dwight D. Eisenhower, the Republican party found the perfect candidate to explore what one senator called K_1C_2—Korea, communism, and corruption.

Immensely popular because of his amiable manner, winning smile, and heroic stature, Eisenhower alone appeared to have the ability to unite a divided nation. In the 1952 campaign, Ike displayed hidden gifts as a politician in running against Adlai Stevenson, the eloquent Illinois governor whose appeal was limited to diehard Democrats and liberal intellectuals. Eisenhower allowed his young running mate, Senator Richard M. Nixon of California, to hammer away at the Democrats on the communist and corruption issues, but he himself delivered the most telling blow of all on the Korean War. Speaking in Detroit in late October, just after the fighting had intensified again in Korea, Ike promised if elected he would go personally to the battlefield in an attempt "to bring the Korean War to an early and honorable end."

"That does it—Ike is in," several reporters exclaimed after they heard this pledge. The hero of World War II had clinched his election by committing himself to end an unpopular war. Ten days later, he won the presidency handily, carrying thirty-nine states, including four in the formerly solid Democratic South. The Republican party, however, did not fare as well in Congress; it gained just a slight edge in the House and controlled the Senate by only one seat.

Once elected, Eisenhower moved quickly to fulfill his campaign pledge. He spent three days in early December touring the battlefront in Korea, quickly ruling out the new offensive the military favored. "Small attacks on small hills," he later wrote, "would not end the war." Instead he turned to diplomacy, relying on subtle hints to China on the possible use of nuclear weapons to break the stalemated peace talks. These tactics, together with the death of Joseph Stalin in early March, finally led to the signing of an armistice on July 27, 1953, which ended the fighting but left Korea divided—as it had been before the war—near the 38th parallel.

The new president was less effective in dealing with the problem raised by Senator McCarthy's continuing witch-hunt. Instead of toning down his anticommunist crusade after the Republican victory in 1952, McCarthy used his new position as chairman of the Senate Committee on Government Operations as a base for ferreting out communists on the federal payroll. He made a series of charges against the foreign affairs agencies and demanded that certain books be purged from American information libraries overseas. Eisenhower's advisers urged the president to use his own great prestige to stop McCarthy. But Ike refused such a confrontation, saying, "I will not get into a pissing contest with a skunk." Eisenhower preferred to play for time, hoping the American people would eventually come to their senses.

THE ELECTION OF 1952

Candidate	Party	Popular Vote	Electoral Vote
Eisenhower	Republican	33,936,137	442
Stevenson	Democratic	27,314,649	89

Senator Joseph McCarthy appeared on television on April 6, 1954, in a filmed reply to CBS newscaster Edward R. Murrow's anti-McCarthy broadcast of the television show See It Now *(March 9). Murrow's attack and McCarthy's response—in which he accused Murrow of being engaged in propaganda for Communist causes—helped turned public opinion against McCarthy.* ❖

The Wisconsin senator finally overreached himself. In early 1954, he uncovered an army dentist suspected of disloyalty and proceeded to attack the upper echelons of the U.S. Army, telling one much decorated general that he was "not fit to wear the uniform." The controversy culminated in the televised Army-McCarthy hearings. For six weeks, the senator revealed his crude, bullying behavior to the American people. Viewers were repelled by his frequent outbursts that began with the insistent cry, "Point of order, Mr. Chairman, point of order," and by his attempt to slur the reputation of a young lawyer associated with army counsel Joseph Welch. This last maneuver led Welch to condemn McCarthy for his "reckless cruelty" and ask rhetorically, as millions watched on television, "Have you no sense of decency, sir?"

Courageous Republicans, led by Senators Ralph Flanders of Vermont and Margaret Chase Smith of Maine, joined with Democrats to bring about the Senate's censure of McCarthy in December 1954, by a vote of 67 to 22. Once rebuked, McCarthy fell quickly from prominence. He died three years later virtually unnoticed and unmourned.

Yet his influence was profound. Not only did he paralyze national life with what a Senate subcommittee described as "the most nefarious campaign of half-truth and untruth in the history of the Republic," but he also helped impose a political and cultural conformity that froze dissent for the rest of the 1950s. Long after McCarthy's passing, the nation tolerated loyalty oaths for teachers, the banning of left-wing books in public libraries, and the blacklist-

ing of entertainers in radio, television, and films. Freedom of expression was inhibited, and the opportunity to try out new ideas and approaches was lost as the United States settled into a sterile Cold War consensus.

While Dwight Eisenhower could claim that his policy of giving McCarthy enough rope to hang himself had worked, it is possible that a bolder and more forthright presidential attack on the senator might have spared the nation some of the excesses of the second Red Scare.

EISENHOWER WAGES THE COLD WAR

Dwight D. Eisenhower came into the presidency in 1952 unusually well prepared to lead the nation at the height of the Cold War. His long years of military service had exposed him to a wide variety of international issues, both in Asia and in Europe, and to an even broader array of world leaders, such as Winston Churchill and Charles de Gaulle. He was not only an experienced military strategist but a gifted politician and diplomat as well. He was blessed with a sharp, pragmatic mind and organizational genius that enabled him to plan and carry out large enterprises, grasping the precise relationship between the parts and the whole. Above all, he had a serene confidence in his own ability. At the end of his first day in the White House, he confided in his diary: "Plenty of worries and difficult problems. But such has been my portion for a long time—the result is that this just seems like a continuation of all I've been doing since July 1941."

Eisenhower chose John Foster Dulles as his secretary of state. The myth soon developed that Ike had given Dulles free rein to conduct American diplomacy. Appearances were deceptive. Eisenhower preferred to work behind the scenes. He let Dulles make the public speeches and appearances before congressional commit-tees, where the secretary's hard-line views placated GOP extremists. But Dulles carefully consulted with the president before every appearance, meeting frequently with Eisenhower at the White House and telephoning him several times a day. Ike respected his secre-

President Eisenhower and Secretary of State John Foster Dulles consult before the final session of a summit meeting of the United States, the Soviet Union, Great Britain, and France in Geneva, Switzerland, in 1955. ❖

tary of state's broad knowledge of foreign policy and skill in conducting American diplomacy, but he made all the major decisions himself. "There's only one man I know who has seen *more* of the world and talked with more people and *knows* more than he does," Ike said of Dulles, "and that's me."

From the outset, Eisenhower was determined to bring the Cold War under control. Ideally, he wanted to end it, but as a realist, he would settle for a relaxation of tensions with the Soviet Union. In part, he was moti-vated by a deeply held concern about the budget. Defense spending had increased from $13 billion to $50 billion under Truman; Ike was convinced the nation was in danger of going bankrupt unless military spend-ing was reduced. As president, he inaugurated a "new look" for American defense, cutting back on the army and navy and relying even more heavily than Truman had on the air force and its nuclear striking power. As a result, the defense budget dropped below $40 billion an-nually. In 1954, Dulles announced reliance on **massive retaliation**—in fact a continuance of Truman's policy of deterrence. Rather than becoming involved in limited wars such as Korea, the United States would consider the possibility of using nuclear weapons to halt any

Cartoonist Herblock, a sharp critic of Dulles's hard line, depicts him in a Superman suit pushing Uncle Sam to the brink of nuclear war. ❖

communist aggression that threatened vital U.S. interests anywhere in the world.

While he permitted Dulles to make his veiled nuclear threats, Eisenhower's fondest dream was to end the arms race. Sobered by the development of the hydrogen bomb, successfully tested by the United States in November 1952 and by the Soviet Union in August 1953, the president began a new effort at disarmament with the Russians. Yet before this initiative could take effect, Ike had to weather a series of crises around the world that tested his skill and patience to the utmost.

Entanglement in Indochina

The first crisis facing the new president came in Indochina. Since 1950, the United States had been giving France military and economic aid in a war in Indochina against communist guerrillas led by Ho Chi Minh. The Chinese increased their support to Ho's forces, known as the Vietminh, after the Korean War ended; by the spring of 1954, the French were on the brink of defeat. The Vietminh had surrounded nearly ten thousand French troops at **Dien Bien Phu** deep in the interior of northern Indochina; in desperation, France turned to the United States for help. Admiral Arthur Radford, chairman of the Joint Chiefs of Staff, proposed an American air strike to lift the siege. Although the other Joint Chiefs had strong objections to involving American forces in another Asian war so

soon after Korea, hawkish Republican senators were clamoring for action.

Eisenhower decided against Radford's bold proposal, but he killed it in his typically indirect fashion. Fearful that an air attack would lead inevitably to the use of ground troops, Ike insisted that both Congress and American allies in Europe approve the strike in advance. Congressional leaders, recalling the recent Korean debacle, were reluctant to agree; the British were appalled and ruled out any joint action. The president used these objections to reject intervention in Indochina in 1954. Years later, he stated his reasons more candidly. "The jungles of Indochina would have swallowed up division after division of United States troops," he explained. Equally important, he believed that U.S. involvement in France's war would have compromised the American "tradition of anti-colonialism."

Dien Bien Phu fell to the Vietminh in May 1954. At an international conference held in Geneva a few weeks later, Indochina was divided at the 17th parallel. Ho gained control of North Vietnam, while the French continued to rule in the South, with provision for a general election within two years to unify the country. The election was never held, largely because Eisenhower feared it would result in an overwhelming mandate for Ho. Instead, the United States gradually took over from the French in South Vietnam, sponsoring a new government in Saigon headed by Ngo Dinh Diem, a Vietnamese nationalist from a northern Catholic family. While Eisenhower can be given credit

A French soldier stands guard over a truckload of Vietnamese nationalists captured in the fighting in Indochina. French efforts to quash the rebellion in Vietnam ended on May 7, 1954, when the Vietminh took the French stronghold at Dien Bien Phu. ❖

for refusing to engage American forces on behalf of French colonialism in Indochina, his determination to resist communist expansion had committed the United States to a long and eventually futile struggle to prevent Ho Chi Minh from achieving his long-sought goal of a unified, independent Vietnam.

Containing China

The communist government in Peking posed a serious challenge for the Eisenhower administration. Senate Republicans, led by William Knowland of California, blamed the Democrats for the "loss" of China. They viewed Mao as a puppet of the Soviet Union and insisted the United States recognize the Nationalists on Formosa as the only legitimate government of China. While State Department experts realized there were underlying tensions between China and Russia, Mao's intervention in the Korean War had convinced most Americans that the Chinese communists were an integral part of a larger communist effort at world domination. Thus Truman and Acheson had abandoned any hope of trying to exploit differences between Mao and Stalin by wooing China away from the Soviet Union.

Eisenhower and Dulles chose to accentuate the potential conflict between Russia and China. By taking a strong line against China, the United States could make the Chinese realize that Russia was unable to protect their interests; at the same time, such a hawkish policy would please congressional conservatives such as Knowland. Ultimately, Eisenhower and Dulles hoped that a policy of firmness would not only contain communist Chinese expansion in Asia but also drive a wedge between Moscow and Peking.

A crisis in the Formosa Straits provided the first test of the new policy. In the fall of 1954, communist China threatened to seize coastal islands, notably Quemoy and Matsu, occupied by the Nationalists. Fearful that seizure of these offshore islands would be the first step toward an invasion of Formosa, Eisenhower permitted Dulles to sign a security treaty with Chiang Kai-shek committing the United States to defend Formosa. When the communists began shelling the offshore islands, Eisenhower persuaded Congress to pass a resolution authorizing him to use force to defend Formosa and "closely related localities."

Despite repeated requests, however, the president refused to say whether he would use force to repel a Chinese attack on Quemoy or Matsu. Instead he and Dulles hinted at the use of nuclear weapons, carefully stating that their action would depend on whether they considered an attack on the offshore islands part of a larger offensive aimed at Formosa. The Chinese leaders, unsure whether Eisenhower was bluffing, decided not to test American resolve. The shelling ended

in 1955, and when the communists resumed it again in 1958, another firm but equally ambiguous American response forced them to desist. The apparent refusal of the Soviet Union to come to China's aid in these crises with the United States contributed to a growing rift between the two communist nations by the end of the 1950s. Unfortunately, the Eisenhower administration failed to take full advantage of the opportunity that it had helped to create.

Turmoil in the Middle East

The gravest crisis for Eisenhower came in the Middle East when Egyptian leader Gamal Nasser seized the Suez Canal in July 1956. England and France were ready to use force immediately; their citizens owned the canal company, and their economies were dependent on the canal for the flow of oil from the Persian Gulf. President Eisenhower, however, was staunchly opposed to intervention, preferring to seek a diplomatic solution with Nasser, who kept the canal running smoothly. For three months, Dulles did everything possible to restrain the European allies, but finally they decided to take a desperate gamble—they invaded Egypt and seized the canal, relying on the United States to prevent any Russian interference.

Eisenhower was furious when England and France launched their attack in early November. Campaigning for reelection against Adlai Stevenson on the slogan of keeping the peace, Ike had to abandon domestic politics to deal with the threat of war. "The White House crackled with barracks-room language," reported one observer; the president told an aide that the Western allies had made "a complete *mess* and *botch* of things." Unhesitatingly, he instructed Dulles to sponsor a UN resolution calling for British and French withdrawal from Egypt. Yet when the Russians supported the American proposal and went further, threatening rocket attacks on British and French cities and even offering to send "volunteers" to fight in Egypt, Eisenhower made it clear he would not tolerate Soviet interference. He put the Strategic Air Command on alert and said of the Russians, "If those fellows start something, we may have to hit 'em—and, if necessary, with everything in the bucket."

Just after noon on election day, November 6, 1956, British Prime Minister Anthony Eden called the president to inform him that England and France were ending their invasion. Eisenhower breathed a sigh of relief. American voters rallied behind Ike, electing him to a second term by a near landslide. As a result of the **Suez crisis,** the United States replaced England and France as the main Western influence in the Middle East. With Russia strongly backing Egypt and Syria, the Cold War had found yet another battleground.

Two years later, Eisenhower found it necessary to intervene in the strategic Middle Eastern country of Lebanon. Political power in this neutral nation was divided between Christian and Muslim elements. When the outgoing Christian president, Camille Chamoun, broke with tradition by seeking a second term, Muslim groups (aided by Egypt and Syria) threatened to launch a rebellion. At first, Eisenhower turned down Chamoun's request for American intervention to avert a civil war, but after an unexpected nationalist coup overthrew the pro-Western government of Iraq, Ike decided to act in order to uphold the U.S. commitment to political stability in the Middle East.

American marines from the Sixth Fleet moved swiftly ashore on July 15, 1958, securing the Beirut airport and preparing the way for a force of some fourteen thousand troops airlifted from bases in Germany. The military wanted to occupy the entire country, but Eisenhower insisted on limiting American forces to the area of Beirut. The mission of the troops, he argued, was "not primarily to fight," but simply to show the flag. Lebanese political leaders quickly agreed on a successor to Chamoun, and American soldiers left the country before the end of October. The restrained use of force achieved Eisenhower's primary goal of quieting the explosive Middle East. It also served, as Secretary of State Dulles pointed out, "to reassure many small nations that they could call on us in a time of crisis."

Covert Actions

Amid these dangerous crises, the Eisenhower administration worked behind the scenes in the 1950s to expand the nation's global influence. In 1953, the CIA was instrumental in overthrowing a popularly elected government in Iran and placing the shah in full control of that country. American oil companies were rewarded with lucrative concessions, and Eisenhower believed he had gained a valuable ally on the Russian border. But these short-run gains created a deep-seated animosity among Iranians that would haunt the United States in the future.

Closer to home, in Latin America, Eisenhower once again relied on covert action. In 1954, the CIA masterminded the overthrow of a leftist regime in Guatemala. The immediate advantage was in denying the Soviets a possible foothold in the Western Hemisphere, but Latin Americans resented the thinly disguised interference of the United States in their internal affairs. More important, when Fidel Castro came to power in Cuba in 1959, the Eisenhower administration—after a brief effort at conciliation—adopted a hard line that helped drive Cuba into the Soviet orbit and led to new attempts at covert action.

Eisenhower's record as a cold warrior was thus mixed. His successful ending of the Korean War and his peacekeeping efforts in Indochina and Formosa and in the Suez crisis are all to his credit. Yet his reliance on coups and subversion directed by the CIA in Iran and Guatemala reveal Ike's corrupting belief that the ends justified the means. And despite the 1952 campaign call for the liberation of eastern Europe, Eisenhower accepted Soviet domination of this region, refusing to act on behalf of East German protesters in 1953 or Hungarian freedom fighters in 1956.

Nevertheless, Eisenhower did display an admirable ability to stay calm and unruffled in moments of great tension, reassuring the nation and the world. And above all, he could boast, as he did in 1962, of his ability to keep the peace. "In those eight years," he reminded the nation, "we lost no inch of ground to tyranny. One war was ended and incipient wars were blocked."

Waging Peace

Eisenhower hoped to ease Cold War tensions by ending the nuclear arms race. The advent of the hydrogen bomb intensified his concern over nuclear warfare; by 1955, both the United States and the Soviet Union had added this dread new weapon to their arsenals. With new long-range ballistic missiles being perfected, it was only a matter of time before Russia and the United States would be capable of destroying each other completely. Peace, as Winston Churchill noted, now depended on a balance of terror.

Throughout the 1950s, Eisenhower sought a way out of the nuclear dilemma. In April 1953, shortly after Stalin's death, he gave a speech in which he called on the Russians to join him in a new effort at disarmament, pointing out that "every warship launched, every rocket fired signifies, in the final sense, a theft from those who hunger and are not fed, those who are cold and are not clothed." When the Soviets ignored this appeal, the president tried again in December 1953. Addressing the UN General Assembly, he outlined an "atoms for peace" plan whereby the United States and the Soviet Union would donate fissionable material to a new UN agency to be used for peaceful purposes. Despite Ike's appeal "to serve the needs rather than the fears of mankind," the Russians again rebuffed him. Undaunted, Eisenhower tried once more. At a summit conference in Geneva, Switzerland, in 1955, Ike proposed to Nikita Khrushchev, just emerging as Stalin's successor after a two-year struggle for power, a way to break the disarmament deadlock. "Open skies," as reporters dubbed the plan, would overcome the traditional Russian objection to on-site inspection by having both superpowers open their territory to mutual aerial surveillance. Unfortunately,

✦ A Look at the Past ✦

Fallout Shelter

Fallout shelters caught the interest and attention of both private citizens and entire communities during the early years of the Cold War. Directions for constructing and stocking the shelters appeared in official government documents as well as magazines such as *Popular Mechanics*. Whether specially constructed, elaborate shelters, or merely a protected corner of the basement as shown here, fallout shelters revealed how seriously Americans viewed the threat of nuclear war. The shelters also indicated that people believed it possible to survive a nuclear war. Contrast those attitudes to ours. Do we consider nuclear war to be a real threat or survivable if it did occur? Examine the design and furnishings of this shelter. Was this designed only to meet standards for survival? Could this be used for other purposes? What do the supplies shown here suggest about how long people expected to remain in the shelter in the event of a nuclear attack?

untarily suspended further weapons tests pending the outcome of a conference held at Geneva to work out a test ban treaty. Although the Geneva Conference failed to make progress, neither the United States nor the Soviet Union resumed testing for the remainder of Ike's term in office.

The suspension of testing halted the pollution of the world's atmosphere, but it did not lead to the improvement in Soviet-American relations that Eisenhower sought. Instead, the Soviet feat in launching *Sputnik,* the first artificial satellite to orbit the earth, intensified the Cold War. Fearful that the Russians were several years ahead of the United States in the development of intercontinental ballistic missiles (ICBMs), Democrats criticized Eisenhower for not spending enough on defense and warned that a dangerous missile

CHRONOLOGY

1945	Truman meets Stalin at Potsdam Conference (July) ✦ World War II ends with Japanese surrender (August)
1946	Winston Churchill gives "Iron Curtain" speech
1947	Truman Doctrine announced to Congress (March) ✦ George Marshall outlines Marshall Plan (June) ✦ Truman orders loyalty program for government employees (March)
1948	Soviets begin blockade of Berlin (June) ✦ Truman scores upset victory in presidential election
1949	NATO treaty signed in Washington (April) ✦ Soviet Union tests its first atomic bomb (August)
1950	Truman authorizes building of hydrogen bomb (January) ✦ Senator Joseph McCarthy claims communists in government (February) ✦ North Korea invades South Korea (June)
1951	Truman recalls MacArthur from Korea
1952	Dwight D. Eisenhower elected president
1953	Julius and Ethel Rosenberg executed for atomic-secrets spying (June) ✦ Korean War truce signed at Panmunjom (July)
1954	Fall of Dien Bien Phu to Vietminh ends French control of Indochina
1956	England and France touch off Suez crisis
1957	Russia launches *Sputnik* satellite
1959	Fidel Castro takes power in Cuba
1960	American U-2 spy plane shot down over Russia

Khrushchev dismissed open skies as "a very transparent espionage device," and the conference ended without any significant breakthrough in the Cold War.

After his reelection in 1956, the president renewed his efforts toward nuclear arms control. Concern over atmospheric fallout from nuclear testing had led presidential candidate Adlai Stevenson to propose a mutual ban on such experiments. At first, Eisenhower rejected the test ban idea, arguing that it could be effective only as part of a comprehensive disarmament agreement, but the Russians supported it. Finally, in 1958, the president changed his mind after American and Soviet scientists developed a system to detect nuclear testing in the atmosphere without on-site inspection. In October 1958, Eisenhower and Khrushchev each vol-

Conclusion: The Continuing Cold War 833

gap would open up by the early 1960s—a time when the Russians might have such a commanding lead in ICBMs that they could launch a first strike and destroy America. Despite the president's belief that the American missile program was in good shape, he allowed increased defense spending to speed up the building of American ICBMs and the new Polaris submarine–launched intermediate range missile (IRBM).

Nikita Khrushchev took full advantage of the furor over *Sputnik* to put the United States on the defensive. "We will bury you," he boasted, telling Americans, "Your grandchildren will live under communism." The most serious threat of all came in November 1958, when the Russian leader declared that within six months he would sign a separate peace treaty with East Germany, calling for an end to American, British, and French occupation rights in Berlin.

Eisenhower met the second Berlin crisis as firmly as Truman had the first. He refused to abandon the city but also tried to avoid a military showdown. Prudent diplomacy forced Khrushchev to extend his deadline indefinitely. After a trip to the United States, culminating in a personal meeting with Eisenhower at Camp David, the Russian leader agreed to attend a summit conference in Paris in May 1960.

This much heralded meeting never took place. On May 1, two weeks before the leaders were to convene in Paris, the Soviets shot down an American U-2 plane piloted by Francis Gary Powers. The United States had been overflying Russia since 1956 in the high-altitude spy planes, gaining vital information about the Soviet missile program which showed there was little basis for the public's fear that the Russians had opened up a dangerous missile gap. After initially denying any knowledge, Eisenhower took full responsibility for Powers's overflight, and Khrushchev responded with a scathing personal denunciation and a refusal to meet with the American president.

CONCLUSION: THE CONTINUING COLD WAR

The breakup of the Paris summit marked the end of Eisenhower's attempts to moderate the Cold War. The disillusioned leader told an aide that "he saw nothing

Russians view the wreckage of the U-2 reconnaissance plane piloted by Francis Powers that was shot down over Soviet territory on May 1, 1960. Although Eisenhower originally disavowed any knowledge of Powers's mission, Khrushchev produced photographs of Soviet military and industrial sites, which he said had been taken by the U-2 pilot. Powers was held in a Soviet prison for two years before he was released in exchange for a Russian spy. ❖

worthwhile left for him to do now until the end of his presidency." But Eisenhower did make a final effort for peace by delivering a somber warning about the danger of massive military spending in his farewell address to the American people. "In the councils of government, we must guard against the acquisition of unwarranted influence, whether sought or unsought, by the military-industrial complex," he declared. "The potential for the disastrous rise of misplaced power exists and will persist."

Rarely has an American president been more prophetic. In the next few years, the level of defense spending would skyrocket as the Cold War escalated. The **military-industrial complex** reached its acme of power in the 1960s when the United States realized the full implications of Truman's doctrine of containment. Eisenhower had succeeded in keeping the peace for eight years, but he had failed to halt the momentum of the Cold War he had inherited from Harry Truman. Ike's efforts to ease tension with the Soviet Union were dashed by his own distrust of communism and by Khrushchev's belligerent rhetoric and behavior. Still, he had begun to relax tensions, a process that would survive the troubled 1960s and, after several false starts, would finally begin to erode the Cold War by the end of the 1980s.

RECOMMENDED READING

The Cold War spawned a vast array of books, some enduring in nature and many that are already outdated. The best general guide to American diplomacy since World War II is Walter LaFeber, *America, Russia and the Cold War, 1945–2000,* 9th ed. (2002). On the much debated question of the origins of the Cold War, the most balanced account is Daniel Yergin, *Shattered Peace* (1977); for a dissenting view, see Thomas G. Paterson, *On Every Front* (1979). John Lewis Gaddis, *We Now Know* (1997), integrates new disclosures from Soviet and Chinese archives to provide the best rounded account of the Cold War through the early 1960s.

The classic account of containment is still the lucid recollection of its chief architect, George Kennan, *Memoirs, 1925–1950* (1967). John Lewis Gaddis uses Kennan's ideas as a point of departure for his account of the changing nature of American Cold War policy in *Strategies of Containment* (1982). Melvyn P. Leffler offers a full account of the development of containment in *A Preponderance of Power* (1992); Arnold A. Offner is more critical of Truman's policies in *Another Such Victory* (2002). For developments in the Far East, consult the perceptive book by Akira Iriye,

The Cold War in Asia (1974). On the Korean conflict, see Burton Kaufman, *The Korean War,* 2nd ed. (1997), and Bruce Cumings, *The Origins of the Korean War,* 2 vols. (1981 and 1991).

The best book on the Truman period is Alonzo L. Hamby, *Man of the People* (1995), which provides a balanced portrait of a controversial leader. Richard M. Fried offers a perceptive overview of the postwar anticommunist crusade in *Nightmare in Red: The McCarthy Era in Perspective* (1990); the best biography of McCarthy is David Oshinsky, *A Conspiracy So Immense* (1983).

Stephen A. Ambrose evaluates Dwight D. Eisenhower positively in the second volume of his biography, *Eisenhower: The President* (1985). For an equally favorable analysis, see Robert A. Divine, *Eisenhower and the Cold War* (1981). Richard H. Immerman provides a balanced portrait of Eisenhower's secretary of state in *John Foster Dulles* (1999).

For a list of additional titles related to this chapter's topics, please see http://www.ablongman.com/divine.

SUGGESTED WEB SITES

Harry S Truman

http://www.ipl.org/ref/POTUS/hstruman.html
This page contains basic factual data about his election and presidency, speeches, and on-line biographies.

Harry S Truman Library and Museum

http://www.trumanlibrary.org
This presidential library site has numerous photos and various important primary documents relating to Truman.

Cold War

http://cnn.com/SPECIALS/cold.war/
This is the companion site to the CNN Perspectives series on the Cold War. It contains information including interactive timelines and a quiz.

Korean War Project

http://www.koreanwar.org
This site has information about the Korean War and is a guide to resources on the struggle.

NATO at 50

http:www.cnn.com/SPECIALS/1999/nato/
This site from CNN has an excellent timeline and images telling the history of the North Atlantic Treaty Organization.

Senator Joe McCarthy—A Multimedia Celebration

http://webcorp.com/mccarthy/
This webcorp site includes audio and visual clips of McCarthy's speeches.

The houses of Levittown spread over 1200 acres of former potato fields on Long Island, New York. ❖

Affluence and Anxiety

Levittown: The Flight to the Suburbs

On May 7, 1947, William Levitt announced plans to build two thousand rental houses in a former potato field on Long Island, thirty miles from Midtown Manhattan. Using mass production techniques he had learned while erecting navy housing during the war, Levitt quickly built four thousand homes and rented them to young veterans eager to leave crowded city apartments or their parents' homes to begin raising families. A change in government financing regulations led him to begin offering his houses for sale in 1948 for a small amount down and a low monthly payment. Young couples, many of them the original renters, quickly bought the first four thousand; by the time **Levittown**—as he called the new community—was completed in 1951, it contained more than seventeen thousand homes. So many babies were born in Levittown that it soon became known as "Fertility Valley" and "the Rabbit Hutch."

Levitt eventually built two more Levittowns, one in Pennsylvania and one in New Jersey; each contained the same curving streets, neighborhood parks and playgrounds, and community swimming pools characteristic of the first development. The secret of Levittown's appeal was the basic house, a 720-square-foot Cape Cod design built on a concrete slab. It had a kitchen, two bedrooms and bath, a living room complete with a fireplace and 16-foot picture window, and an expansion attic with room for two more bedrooms. Levitt built only one interior, but there were four different facades to break the monotony. The original house sold for $6990 in 1948; even the improved model, a ranch-style house, sold for less than $10,000 in 1951.

Levitt's houses were ideal for young people just starting out in life. They were cheap, comfortable, and efficient, and each home came with a refrigerator, cooking range, and washing machine. Despite the conformity of the houses, the three Levittowns were surprisingly diverse communities; residents had a wide variety of religious, ethnic, and occupational backgrounds. African Americans, however, were rigidly excluded. In time, as the more successful families moved on to larger homes in more expensive neighborhoods, the Levittowns became enclaves for lower-middle-class families.

LEVITTOWN SYMBOLIZED THE MOST SIGNIFICANT social trend of the postwar era in the United States—the flight to the suburbs. The residential areas surrounding cities such as New York and Chicago nearly doubled in the 1950s. While central cities remained relatively stagnant during the decade, suburbs grew by 46 percent; by 1960, some sixty million people, one-third of the nation, lived in suburban rings around the cities. This massive shift in population from the central city was accompanied by a **baby boom** that started during World War II. Young married couples began to have three, four, or even five children (compared with only one or two children in

OUTLINE

The Postwar Boom

The Good Life?

Farewell to Reform

The Struggle over Civil Rights

Conclusion: Restoring National Confidence

FEATURE ESSAY

Rise of a New Idiom in Modern Painting: Abstract Expressionism

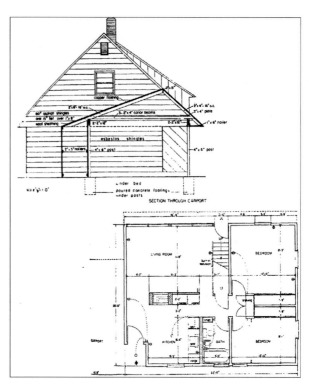

A photograph, floor plan, and elevation for a Levittown house. The Levittown builders applied the principles of mass production used in auto manufacturing to house construction. One important difference was the fact that the product stood stationary while workers came to the site to perform their specialized tasks. Construction was broken down into twenty-seven separate tasks, and a house could be assembled in fifteen minutes. ❖

American families during the 1930s). These larger families led to a 19 percent growth in the nation's population between 1950 and 1960, the highest growth rate since 1910.

The economy boomed as residential construction soared. By 1960, one-fourth of all existing homes were less than ten years old, and factories were turning out large quantities of appliances and television sets for the new households. A multitude of new consumer products—ranging from frozen foods to filter cigarettes, from high-fidelity phonographs to cars equipped with automatic transmissions and tubeless tires—appeared in stores and showrooms. In the suburbs, the corner grocery gave way to the supermarket carrying a vast array of items that enabled homemakers to provide their families with a more varied diet.

A new affluence replaced the poverty and hunger of the Great Depression for most Americans, but many had haunting memories of the 1930s. The obsession with material goods took on an almost desperate quality, as if a profusion of houses, cars, and home appliances could guarantee that the nightmare of depression would never return. Critics were quick to disparage the quality of life in suburban society. They

condemned the conformity, charging the newly affluent with forsaking traditional American individualism to live in identical houses, drive look-alike cars, and accumulate the same material possessions. Folksinger Malvina Reynolds caught the essence of postwar suburbia in a 1963 song:

> Little boxes on the hillside,
> Little boxes made of ticky tacky
> Little boxes on the hillside,
> Little boxes all the same.
> There's a green one and a pink one
> And a blue one and a yellow one
> And they're all made out of ticky tacky
> And they all look just the same.*

Events abroad added to the feeling of anxiety in the postwar years. Nuclear war became a frighteningly real possibility. The rivalry with the Soviet Union had led to the second Red Scare, with charges of treason and disloyalty being leveled at loyal Americans. Many

*"Little Boxes," words and music by Malvina Reynolds. Copyright © 1962 Schroder Music Co. [ASCAP]. Used by permission. All rights reserved.

Americans joined Senator Joseph McCarthy in searching for the communist enemy at home rather than abroad. Loyalty oaths and book burning revealed how insecure Americans had become in the era of the Cold War. The 1950s also witnessed a growing demand by African Americans for equal opportunity in an age of abundance. The civil rights movement, along with strident criticism of the consumer culture, revealed that beneath the bland surface of suburban affluence forces for change were at work.

THE POSTWAR BOOM

For fifteen years following World War II, the nation witnessed a period of unparalleled economic growth. A pent-up demand for consumer goods fueled a steady industrial expansion. Heavy government spending during the Cold War added an extra stimulus to the economy, offsetting brief recessions in 1949 and 1953 and moderating a steeper one in 1957–1958. By the end of the 1950s, the American people had achieved an affluence that finally erased the lingering fears of the Great Depression.

Postwar Prosperity

The economy began its upward surge as the result of two long-term factors. First, American consumers—after being held in check by depression and then by wartime scarcities—finally had a chance to indulge their suppressed appetites for material goods. At the

war's end, personal savings in the United States stood at more than $37 billion, providing a powerful stimulus to consumption. Initially, American factories could not turn out enough automobiles and appliances to satisfy the horde of buyers. By 1950, however, production lines had finally caught up with the demand. In that year, Americans bought more than six million cars, and the gross national product (GNP) reached $318 billion (50 percent higher than in 1940).

The Cold War provided the additional stimulus the economy needed when postwar expansion slowed. The Marshall Plan and other foreign aid programs financed a heavy export trade. The Korean War helped overturn a brief recession and ensured continued prosperity as the government spent massive amounts on guns, planes, and munitions. In 1952, the nation spent $44 billion, two-thirds of the federal budget, on national defense. Although Eisenhower managed to bring about some modest reductions, defense spending continued at a level of $40 billion throughout the decade.

The nation achieved an affluence in the 1950s that made the persisting fear of another Great Depression seem irrational. The baby boom and the spectacular growth of suburbia served as great stimulants to the consumer goods industries. Manufacturers turned out an ever increasing number of refrigerators, washing machines, and dishwashers to equip the kitchens of Levittown and its many imitators across the country. The automobile industry thrived with suburban expansion as two-car families became more and more common. In 1955, in an era when oil was abundant and gasoline sold for less than 30 cents a gallon, Detroit sold a record eight million cars. The electronics industry boomed. Consumers were eager to acquire the latest marvel of home entertainment—the television set.

Commercial enterprises snapped up office machines and the first generation of computers; industry installed electronic sensors and processors as it underwent extensive automation; and the military displayed an insatiable appetite for electronic devices for its planes and ships. As a result, American industry averaged more than $10 billion a year in capital investment, and the number of persons employed rose above the long-sought goal of sixty million nationwide.

Yet the economic abundance of the 1950s was not without its problems. While some sections of the nation (notably the emerging Sunbelt areas of the South

BIRTHRATE, 1940–1970

Source: Compiled from U.S. Bureau of the Census, *Historical Statistics of the United States, Colonial Times to 1970,* Bicentennial Edition, Washington, D.C., 1975.

and West) benefited enormously from the growth of the aircraft and electronics industries, older manufacturing regions, such as New England, did not fare as well. The steel industry increased its capacity during the decade, but it began to fall behind the rate of national growth. Agriculture continued to experience bumper crops and low prices, so rural regions, like the vast areas of the Plains states, failed to share in the general affluence. Unemployment persisted despite the boom, rising to more than 7 percent in a sharp recession that hit the country in the fall of 1957 and lasted through the summer of 1958. The rate of economic growth slowed in the second half of the decade, causing concern about the continuing vitality of the American economy.

None of these flaws, however, could disguise the fact that the nation was prospering to an extent no one dreamed possible in the 1930s. The GNP grew to $440 billion by 1960, more than double the 1940 level. More important, workers now labored fewer than forty hours a week; they rarely worked on Saturdays,

and nearly all enjoyed a two-week paid vacation each year. By the mid-1950s, the average American family had twice as much real income to spend as its counterpart had possessed in the boom years of the 1920s. From 1945 to 1960, per capita disposable income rose by $500—to $1845—for every man, woman, and child in the country. The American people, in one generation, had moved from poverty and depression to the highest standard of living the world had ever known.

Life in the Suburbs

Sociologists had difficulty describing the nature of suburban society in the 1950s. Some saw it as classless, while others noted the absence of both the very rich and the very poor and consequently labeled it "middle class." Rather than forming a homogeneous social group, though, the suburbs contained a surprising variety of people, whether classified as "upper lower," "lower middle," and "upper middle" or simply as blue collar, white collar, and professional. Doctors and lawyers often lived in the same developments as salesclerks and master plumbers. The traditional distinctions of ancestry, education, and size of residence no longer differentiated people as easily as they had in the past.

Yet suburbs could vary widely, from working-class communities clustered near factories built in the countryside to old, elitist areas such as Scarsdale, New York, and Shaker Heights, Ohio. Most were almost exclusively white and Christian, but suburbs such as Great Neck on Long Island and Richmond Heights outside Miami enabled Jews and blacks to take part in the flight from the inner city.

Life in all the suburban communities depended on the automobile. Highways and expressways allowed fathers to commute to jobs in the cities, often an hour or more away. Children might ride buses to and from school, but mothers had to drive them to piano lessons and Little League ballgames. Two cars became a necessity for almost every suburban family, thus helping spur the boom in automobile production. In 1948, only 59 percent of American families owned a car; just a few years later, nearly every suburban family had at least one vehicle, and many had several.

In the new drive-in culture, people shopped at the stores that grew up first in "miracle miles" along the highways and later at the shopping centers that spread across the countryside in the 1950s. There were only eight shopping centers in the entire country in 1946; hundreds appeared over the next fifteen years, including Poplar Plaza in Memphis, with one large department store, thirty retail shops, and parking for more than five hundred cars. In 1956, the first enclosed air-conditioned mall, the Southdale Shopping Center, opened outside Minneapolis.

❖ A Look at the Past ❖

Western-Themed Toys

Following World War II, westerns enjoyed enormous popularity. TV and movie westerns provided inspiration to both children and manufacturers. Plastic cowboys and Indians, miniature frontier towns, ranches and forts invited children to reenact western dramas. Western-themed toys, with heroes adults approved, enabled children to extend screen fantasies into their lives. Westerns permitted adults to escape their worries and experience a world where good and evil were clearly defined and good always triumphed. Why do you think westerns and their associated goods appealed so strongly to Americans during the postwar period?

Despite the increased mobility provided by the car, the home became the focus for activities and aspirations. The postwar shortage of housing that often forced young couples to live with their parents or in-laws created an intense demand for new homes in the suburbs. When questioned, prospective buyers expressed a desire for "more space," for "comfort and roominess," and for "privacy and freedom of action" in their new residences. Men and women who moved to the suburbs prized the new kitchens with their built-in dishwashers, electric ovens, and gleaming counters; the extra bedrooms that ensured privacy from and for the children; the large garages that could be converted into recreation rooms; and the small, neat lawns that gave them an area for outdoor activities as well as a new way to compete with their neighbors. "Togetherness" became the code word of the 1950s. Families did things together, whether gathering around the TV sets that dominated living rooms, attending community activities, or taking vacations in the huge station wagons of the era.

But there were some less attractive consequences of the new suburban lifestyle. The extended family, in which several generations had lived in close proximity, was a casualty of the boom in small detached homes. As historian Kenneth Jackson noted, suburban life "ordained that most children would grow up in intimate contact only with their parents and siblings." For many families, grandparents, aunts and uncles, cousins, and more distant relatives would become remote figures, seen only on special occasions.

The nuclear family, typical of the suburb, did little to encourage the development of feminism. The end of the war saw many women who had entered the workforce return to the home, where the role of wife and mother continued to be viewed as the ideal for women in the 1950s. Trends toward getting married earlier and having larger families reinforced the pattern of women devoting all their efforts to housework and child raising rather than acquiring professional skills and pursuing careers outside the home. Adlai Stevenson, extolling "the humble role of housewife," told Smith College graduates that there was much they could do "in the living room with a baby in your lap or in the kitchen with a can opener in your hand." Dr. Benjamin Spock's 1946 best-seller, *Baby and Child Care*, became a fixture in millions of homes, while the traditional women's magazines such as *McCall's* and *Good Housekeeping* thrived by featuring articles on natural childbirth and inspirational pieces such as "Homemaking Is My Vocation."

Nonetheless, the number of working wives doubled between 1940 and 1960. By the end of the 1950s, 40 percent of American women, and nearly one-third of all married women, had jobs outside the home. The heavy expenses involved in rearing and educating children led wives and mothers to seek ways to augment the family income, inadvertently preparing the way for a new demand for equality in the 1960s.

THE GOOD LIFE?

Consumerism became the dominant social theme of the 1950s. Yet even with an abundance of creature comforts and added hours of leisure time, the quality of life left many Americans anxious and dissatisfied.

Areas of Greatest Growth

Organized religion flourished in the climate of the 1950s. Ministers, priests, and rabbis all commented on the rise in church and synagogue attendance in the new communities. Will Herberg claimed that religious affiliation had become the primary identifying feature of modern American life, dividing the nation into three separate segments—Protestant, Catholic, and Jewish.

Some observers condemned the bland, secular nature of suburban churches, which seemed to be an integral part of the consumer society. "On weekdays one shops for food," wrote one critic, "on Saturdays one shops for recreation, and on Sundays one shops for the Holy Ghost." But the popularity of religious writer Norman Vincent Peale, with his positive gospel that urged people to "start thinking faith, enthusiasm and joy," suggested that the new churches filled a genuine if shallow human need. At the same time, the emergence of neo-orthodoxy in Protestant seminaries (notably through the ideas of Reinhold Niebuhr) and the rapid spread of radical forms of fundamentalism (such as the Assemblies of God) indicated that millions of Americans still were searching for a more personal religious faith.

Schools provided an immediate problem for the growing new suburban communities. The increase in the number of school-age children, from twenty to thirty million in the first eight grades, overwhelmed the resources of many local districts, leading to demands for federal aid. Congress granted limited help for areas affected by defense plants and military bases, but Eisenhower's reluctance to unbalance the budget—along with traditional adherence to state control over public education—blocked further federal assistance prior to 1957, when the government reacted to *Sputnik*.

Equally important, a controversy arose over the nature of education in the 1950s. Critics of "progressive" education called for sweeping educational reforms and a new stress on traditional academic subjects. Suburban communities often had bitter fights; affluent parents demanded kindergarten enrichment programs and grade school foreign language

One of the most popular television programs of the 1950s was I Love Lucy, *a situation comedy featuring the real-life husband-and-wife team of Lucille Ball and Desi Arnaz portraying the fictional couple Lucy and Ricky Ricardo. Millions of families settled down in front of their television sets on Monday nights to watch the zany antics of the red-haired comedienne, her Cuban husband, and their landlord-neighbors Ethel and Fred Mertz, played by Vivian Vance and William Frawley.* ❖

instruction while working-class people resisted such costly innovations. The one thing all seemed to agree on was the desirability of a college education. The number of young people attending colleges increased from 1.5 million in 1940 to 3.6 million in 1960.

The largest advances were made in the exciting new medium of television. From a shaky start just after the war, TV boomed in the 1950s, pushing radio aside and undermining many of the nation's magazines. By 1957, three networks controlled the airwaves, reaching forty million sets over nearly five hundred stations. Advertisers soon took charge of the new medium, using techniques first pioneered in radio—including pretaped commercials, quiz shows, and soap operas.

At first, the insatiable demand for programs encouraged a burst of creativity. Playwrights such as Reginald Rose, Rod Serling, and Paddy Chayefsky wrote a series of notable dramas for *Playhouse 90, Studio One,* and the *Goodyear Television Playhouse.* Broadcast live from cramped studios, these productions thrived on tight dramatic structures, movable scenery, and frequent close-ups of the actors.

Advertisers, however, quickly became disillusioned with the live anthology programs, which usually dealt with controversial subjects or focused on ordinary people and events. In contrast, sponsors wanted shows that stressed excitement, glamour, and

instant success. Aware that audiences were fascinated by contestants with unusual expertise (a shoemaker answering tough questions on operas, a grandmother stumping experts on baseball), producers began giving away huge cash prizes on *The $64,000 Question* and *Twenty-one.* In 1959, the nation was shocked when Charles Van Doren, a Columbia University professor, confessed he had been given the answers in advance to win $129,000 on *Twenty-one.* The three networks quickly dropped all the big-prize quiz programs, replacing them with comedy, action, and adventure shows such as *The Untouchables* and *Bonanza.* Despite its early promise of artistic innovation, television had become a technologically sophisticated but safe conveyor of the consumer culture.

Critics of the Consumer Society

One striking feature of the 1950s was the abundance of self-criticism. A number of widely read books explored the flaws in the new suburbia. John Keats's *The Crack in the Picture Window* described the endless rows of tract houses "vomited up" by developers as "identical boxes spreading like gangrene." Their occupants—whom he dubbed the Drones, the Amiables, and the Fecunds—lost any sense of individuality in their obsession with material goods.

Richard Gordon, Katherine Gordon, and Max Gunther were more concerned about the psychological toll of suburban life in their 1960 book *The Split-Level Trap.* They labeled the new lifestyle "Disturbia" and bemoaned the "haggard" men, the "tense and anxious" women, and the "gimme" kids it produced. The most sweeping indictment came in William H. Whyte's *The Organization Man* (1956), based on a study of the Chicago suburb of Park Forest. Whyte perceived a change from the old Protestant ethic, with its emphasis on hard work and personal responsibility, to a new social ethic centered on "the team" with the ultimate goal of "belongingness." The result was a stifling conformity and the loss of personal identity.

The most influential social critic of the 1950s was Harvard sociologist David Riesman. His book *The Lonely Crowd* appeared in 1950 and set the tone for intellectual commentary about suburbia for the rest of the decade. Riesman described the shift from the "inner-directed" Americans of the past who had relied on such traditional values as self-denial and frugality to the "other-directed" Americans of the consumer society who constantly adapted their behavior to conform to social pressures. The consequences—a decline in individualism and a tendency for people to become acutely sensitive to the expectations of others—produced a bland and tolerant society of consumers lacking creativity and a sense of adventure.

C. Wright Mills was a far more caustic commentator on American society in the 1950s. Anticipating government statistics that revealed white-collar workers (salesclerks, office workers, bank tellers) now outnumbered blue-collar workers (miners, factory workers, millhands), Mills described the new middle class in ominous terms in his books *White Collar* (1951) and *Power Elite* (1956). The corporation was the villain for Mills, depriving office workers of their own identities and imposing an impersonal discipline through manipulation and propaganda. The industrial assembly line had given way to an even more dehumanizing workplace, the modern office. "At rows of blank-looking counters sat rows of blank-looking girls with blank, white folders in their blank hands, all blankly folding blank papers."

This disenchantment with the consumer culture reached its most eloquent expression with the **beats,** literary groups that rebelled against the materialistic society of the 1950s. Jack Kerouac's novel *On the Road,* published in 1957, set the tone for the new movement. The name came from the quest for beatitude, a state of inner grace sought in Zen Buddhism. Flouting the respectability of suburbia, the "beatniks"—as middle America termed them—were easily identified by their long hair and bizarre clothing; they also had a penchant for sexual promiscuity and drug experimentation. They were conspicuous dropouts from a society they found senseless. Poet Lawrence Ferlinghetti, who held forth in the City Lights Bookshop in San Francisco (a favorite resort of the beats), summed it up this way: "I was a wind-up toy someone had dropped wound up into a world already running down."

The social protest inherent in the books and poems of the beats found its artistic counterpart in the rise of abstract expressionism. Abstract expressionists worked in styles that emphasized individuality and freedom from the constraints of representational, realistic art. Painters Jackson Pollock and Mark Rothko, among others, challenged mainstream America's

Novelist Jack Kerouac and his fellow "beat" writers bemoaned the moral bankruptcy of popular culture. They sought not to improve conditions but to find release from the moral and social confines constricting their lives and the literary conventions circumscribing their writing. In order to avoid feeding single sheets of paper into his typewriter, Kerouc wrote his novel On the Road *on a series of twelve foot long rolls of paper taped together to form this 120 foot long scroll.* ❖

RISE OF A NEW IDIOM IN MODERN PAINTING

Abstract Expressionism

The literary critique of the consumer society in the 1950s was matched by an artistic rebellion against traditional values. Just as the beats protested the stifling confor-

Number 10 (1950) by Mark Rothko. (Mark Rothko, *Number 10, 1950.* Oil on canvas, 7ft. 6-3/8 x 57-1/8 inches. The Museum of Modern Art. Gift of Philip Johnson. Photograph © 2001 The Museum of Modern Art, New York/Art Resource, NY. © 2005 Kate Rothko Prizel & Christopher Rothko/Artists Rights Society [ARS], New York.) ✦

mity of Cold War America, so did the painters intent on finding new ways to express their sense of individual identity.

In the 1950s, New York replaced Paris as the Western world's capital of avant-garde art. The artists at the center of this phenomenon were the abstract expressionists—notably Jackson Pollock, Mark Rothko, Robert Motherwell, Willem de Kooning, Barnett Newman, Adolph Gottlieb, and Franz Kline. These artists did not share a common style or motif of painting. Rather they shared a mutual conception of what constituted art: a portrayal of individual feelings and psychological traumas through improvised visual expressions.

The abstract expressionists abandoned representational art—the use of figures—and geometric design for a freer use of color and line. They strove to express transcendental themes by capturing a moment in their own lives rather than depicting a figure or a premeditated idea. Their

work, wrote art critic Harold Rosenberg, "was not a picture but an event."

The careers of Jackson Pollock and Mark Rothko exemplify the common and contrasting themes that characterized the abstract expressionists. Jackson Pollock was born in Cody, Wyoming, in 1912. Mark Rothko was born nine years earlier in Dvinsk, Russia, emigrated to the United States as a boy, and was reared in Portland, Oregon. By the early 1930s, both painters had settled in New York City, the crucible of avant-garde American painting during the Great Depression.

The New Deal's Federal Art Project under the Works Progress Administration (WPA) contributed to the development of a self-conscious artistic community in New York. The Art Project also provided Pollock and Rothko their first opportunities to paint full time. Like many artists of their generation, they adopted leftist political concerns. Their early 1930s works in social realism—a style of monumental narrative painting that emphasized social themes and collective action—reflected these beliefs.

In the late 1920s and 1930s, several important museums opened in New York. Among them, the Museum of Modern Art, opened in 1929, displayed works by such masters as Pablo Picasso. These collections gave New York artists the opportunity to study firsthand the leaders of the dominant movements in twentieth-century European art. Pollock, for instance, studied Wassily Kandinsky's expres-

Pollock began each painting without a preconceived plan, spontaneously dripping pigment across a canvas on the floor until the composition began to suggest its own development. His *Convergence* (1952), a typically complex work of varied colors, is shown at right. (Jackson Pollock, *Convergence*, 1952, oil on canvas, overall; 93-1/2 x 155 inches, Albright-Knox Art Gallery, Buffalo, New York, Gift of Seymour H. Knox, Jr., 1956. © 2005 The Pollock-Krasner Foundation/ Artists Rights Society [ARS], New York.) ❖

sionist works while working as a custodian at the Museum of Non-Objective Art (today's Solomon R. Guggenheim Museum). Also, prominent European artists—such as André Breton, Mark Chagall, André Masson, Piet Mondrian, and Yves Tanguy, to name a few—fled to New York to escape fascist regimes. The arrival of the Europeans provided "American painters," noted critic Clement Greenberg, "the sense, wholly new in this country, of being in the center of art in their time."

The presence of these artists had a major impact on Pollock and Rothko. With the onset of World War II, they abandoned their leftist politics and what they now considered the provincialism of social realism. Inspired by cubism's radical abstraction of figures and surrealism's juxtaposition of ordinary objects and symbols in psychologically provocative ways, Pollock and Rothko each began to experiment. Both became intrigued, for instance, with the surrealists' use of automatism—a form of free association in painting—to probe the unconscious.

The Great Depression and World War II compelled American artists to explore ways to confront the national consciousness forged by these two momentous events. This search for a new idiom evolved into abstract expression-

ism. Like other artists in their circle, Pollock and Rothko in the early 1940s focused on archetypal myths—present in the unconscious of the individual and basic to human experience—as a source for examining universal psychological themes. Such fundamental concepts would transcend the cultural and social differences that separated individuals in complex modern societies.

The absence of any new generation of European talent after World War II augmented the growing self-assurance of American artists. In the late 1940s, Rothko and Pollock led the transition into the new genre of abstract expressionism.

Pollock physically involved himself in the painting process by using the floor of his studio as an easel. This allowed him to traverse the canvas while he cathartically dripped paint. Although Rothko worked more conventionally, his visions were as radical as Pollock's. Rothko painted introspective floating color masses that captured the somber mood of his more conventional 1930s paintings. Their shared commitment "to work from within" rather than "go to a subject matter outside from themselves," as Pollock put it, conceptually linked their very different visions.

Avant-garde painters, like many other artists and intellectuals in the 1950s, abhorred the dominance of

middle-class cultural values and social conformity that stifled individualism and led to alienation. And although the avant-garde painters avoided political interpretations of their work, there was an intellectual agreement between their aesthetic concerns—which emphasized freedom—and the emerging Cold War ethos condemning totalitarianism. According to art historian Serge Guilbaut, the abstract expressionist school became the "protégé of the new liberalism" that sought to defend freedom from the "authoritarianism of the left and the right."

Whatever their social message, these artists tapped feelings that produced moving paintings but sometimes had tragic impact on their lives. After 1953, Pollock's work declined as he turned to alcohol. Following much personal anguish, he died in a possibly suicidal 1956 automobile accident. Mark Rothko battled serious bouts of depression throughout his career; he took his own life in 1970.

Pollock, Rothko, and the other abstract expressionists collectively left an enduring legacy. Their paintings stand both as a striking aesthetic commentary on culture in the Cold War and as a testimony to the emergence of the United States as the center of avant-garde art and New York City as its capital.

notions about the form and function of art. For Pollock, the act of creating a painting was as important as the painting itself. Rothko pioneered a style known as color field painting; his works in this style are monumental pieces in which enormous areas of color lacking any distinct structure or central focus are used to create a mood. (See the Feature Essay, "Rise of a New Idiom in Modern Painting: Abstract Expressionism," pp. 844–845.)

Despite the disapproval they evoked from mainstream Americans, the beat generation had some compassion for their detractors. "We love everything," Kerouac proclaimed, "Billy Graham, the Big Ten, Rock and Roll, Zen, apple pie, Eisenhower—we dig it all." Yet as highly visible nonconformists in an era of stifling conformity, the beats demonstrated a style of social protest that would flower into the counterculture of the 1960s.

The Reaction to Sputnik

The profound insecurity that underlay American life throughout the 1950s burst into view in October 1957, when the Soviets sent the 184-pound satellite *Sputnik* into orbit. People around the world applauded the scientific feat, but in the United States the reaction was one of dismay at being bested by a communist rival. The declining rate of economic growth; the recession of 1957–1958; the growing concern that American schools, with their frills and frivolities and their emphasis on social adjustment, were lagging behind their

Russian counterparts—all contributed to a conviction that the nation had somehow lost its previously unquestioned primacy in the eyes of the world.

The national sense of humiliation only deepened in December, when TV cameras showed the rocket bearing the first American satellite exploding only a few feet after liftoff. Finally, on January 31, 1958, the United States launched its first orbiting satellite. Although the *Explorer*, only 6 inches wide and weighing just over 30 pounds, was tiny compared to *Sputnik*, it carried a much more sophisticated set of scientific instruments to probe the mysteries of space.

In the late 1950s, the president and Congress moved to restore national confidence. Eisenhower appointed James R. Killian, president of the Massachusetts Institute of Technology (MIT), as his special assistant for science and technology and to oversee a crash program in missile development. The House and Senate followed by creating the National Aeronautics and Space Administration (NASA) in 1958. Congress appropriated vast sums to allow the agency to compete with the Russians in the space race. Soon a new group of heroes, the astronauts, began the training that led to suborbital flights and eventually to John Glenn's five-hour flight around the globe in 1962.

Congress also sought to match the Soviet educational advances by passing the **National Defense Education Act (NDEA)**. This legislation authorized federal financing of scientific and foreign language

Sputnik I on its support stand before launching. The first news of Sputnik *was not carried in Soviet newspapers until two days after the launch.* ❖

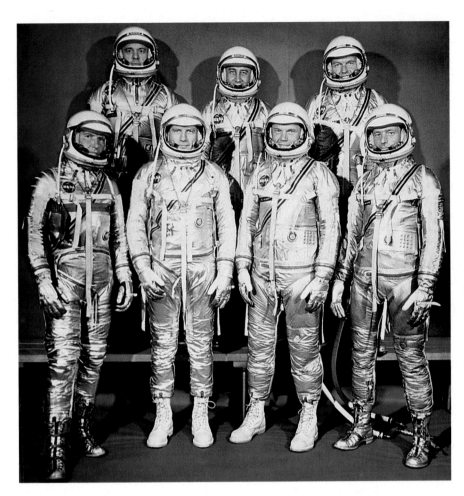

Heroes for the new age of space
exploration included the astronauts of
the United States first manned space
program, Project Mercury. The
program's mission was to put a man in
space and to investigate the capabilities
of humans in space. The first Project
Mercury astronauts were (front row,
left to right) Walter M. Schirra, Jr.,
Donald "Deke" K. Slayton, John H.
Glenn, and M. Scott Carpenter, and
(back row, left to right) Alan B.
Shepard, Jr., Virgil I. "Gus" Grissom,
and L. Gordon Cooper, Jr. In 1961,
Shepard became the first American to
fly in space with his fifteen-minute flight
aboard the capsule Freedom 7. ◈

programs in the nation's schools and colleges. Soon
American students were hard at work mastering the
"new physics" and the "new math."

The belief persisted, however, that the faults lay
deeper, that in the midst of affluence and abundance
Americans had lost their competitive edge.
Economists pointed to the higher rate of Soviet economic growth, and social critics bemoaned a supermarket culture that stressed consumption over
production, comfort over hard work. It would take
time for the American people to recover their traditional optimism and sense of national purpose after
the shock of *Sputnik*.

FAREWELL TO REFORM

It is not surprising that the spirit of reform underlying
the New Deal failed to flourish in the postwar years.
Growing affluence took away the sense of grievance
and the cry for change that was so strong in the 1930s.
Eager to enjoy the new prosperity after years of want
and sacrifice, the American people turned away from
federal regulation and welfare programs.

Truman and the Fair Deal

Harry Truman tried to capitalize on his upset victory
in 1948 to offer a broad program of reform to the nation on January 5, 1949. Venturing beyond earlier proposals by FDR to increase the minimum wage and
broaden Social Security coverage, he called for a **Fair
Deal,** a reform package that comprised a new program
of national medical insurance, federal aid to education, enactment of a Fair Employment Practices
Commission (FEPC) to prevent economic discrimination against blacks, and an overhaul of the farm subsidy program.

The Fair Deal was never enacted. Except for raising the minimum wage to 75 cents an hour and broadening Social Security to cover ten million more
Americans, Congress refused to pass any of Truman's
health, education, or civil rights measures. The nation's doctors waged an effective campaign against the
president's health insurance plan, and southern senators blocked any action on the FEPC. Aid to education,
repeal of Taft-Hartley, and the new farm program all
failed to win congressional approval. In part, Truman
was to blame for trying to secure too much too soon; if

he had selected one or two measures and given them priority, he might have been more successful. More important, however, was the fact that despite the Democratic victory in 1948, Congress remained under the control of a bipartisan conservative coalition of northern Republicans and southern Democrats, the same alignment that had halted Roosevelt's reforms after 1938.

Although his legislative failure became certain in 1950, when war once again subordinated domestic issues to foreign policy, President Truman deserves credit for maintaining and consolidating the New Deal. His spirited leadership prevented any Republican effort to repeal the gains of the 1930s. Moreover, even though he failed to get any new measures enacted, he broadened the reform agenda and laid the groundwork for future advances in health care, aid to education, and civil rights.

Eisenhower's Modern Republicanism

The American people found that moderation was the keynote of the Eisenhower presidency. His major goal from the outset was to restore calm and tranquility to a badly divided nation. Unlike FDR and Truman, Eisenhower had no commitment to social change or economic reform. Ike was a fiscal conservative who was intent on balancing the budget. Yet unlike some Republicans of the extreme right wing, he had no plans to dismantle the social programs of the New Deal. He sought instead to keep military spending in check, to encourage as much private initiative as possible, and to reduce federal activities to the bare minimum. Defining his position as **Modern Republicanism,** he claimed that he was "conservative when it comes to money and liberal when it comes to human beings."

On domestic issues, Eisenhower preferred to delegate authority and to play a passive role. He concentrated his own efforts on the Cold War abroad. The men he chose to run the nation reflected his preference for successful corporation executives. Thus George Humphrey, an Ohio industrialist, carried out a policy of fiscal stringency as secretary of the treasury, while Charles E. Wilson (the former head of General Motors) sought to keep the Pentagon budget under control as secretary of defense. Neither man was wholly successful, and both were guilty of tactless public statements. Humphrey warned that unless Congress showed budgetary restraint, "we're gonna have a depression which will curl your hair," and Wilson gained notoriety by proclaiming that "what was good for our country was good for General Motors, and vice versa."

Eisenhower was equally reluctant to play an active role in dealing with Congress. A fervent believer in the separation of powers, Ike did not want to engage in intensive lobbying. He left congressional relations to aides such as Sherman Adams, a former New Hampshire governor who served as White House chief of staff. Adams's skill at resolving problems at lower levels insulated Eisenhower from many of the nation's pressing domestic concerns.

Republican losses in the midterm election of 1954 weakened Eisenhower's relations with Congress. The Democrats regained control of both houses and kept it throughout the 1950s. The president had to rely on two Texas Democrats, Senate Majority Leader Lyndon B. Johnson and Speaker of the House Sam Rayburn, for legislative action; at best, it was an awkward and uneasy relationship.

The result was a very modest legislative record. Eisenhower did continue the basic social measures of the New Deal. In 1954, he signed bills extending Social Security benefits to more than seven million Americans, raising the minimum wage to $1 an hour, and adding four million workers to those eligible for unemployment benefits. He consolidated the administration of welfare programs by creating the Department of Health, Education, and Welfare in 1953. Oveta Culp Hobby, the first woman to hold a cabinet post in a Republican administration, headed the new department. But Ike steadfastly opposed Democratic plans for compulsory health insurance—which he condemned as the "socialization of medicine"—and comprehensive federal aid to education, preferring to leave everything except school construction in the hands of local and state authorities. This lack of presidential support and the continuing grip of the conservative coalition in Congress blocked any further reform in the 1950s.

The one significant legislative achievement of the Eisenhower years came with the passage of the **Highway Act of 1956.** After a twelve-year delay, Congress appropriated funds for a 41,000-mile interstate highway system consisting of multilane divided expressways that would connect the nation's major cities. Justified on grounds of national defense, the 1956 act pleased a variety of highway users: the trucking industry, automobile clubs, organized labor (eager for construction jobs), farmers (needing to speed their crops to market), and state highway officials (anxious for the 90 percent funding contributed by the federal government). Eisenhower's insistence that general revenue funds not be used to provide the federal share—estimated at $25 billion—of the total cost led to the creation of a highway trust fund raised by taxes on fuel, tires, and new cars and trucks. Built over the next twenty years, the interstate highway system had a profound influence on American life. It stimulated the economy and shortened travel time dramatically, while at the same time intensifying the nation's depen-

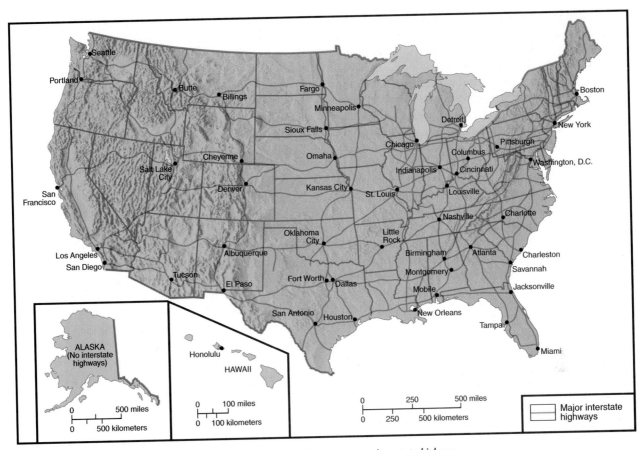

THE INTERSTATE HIGHWAY SYSTEM   *The 1956 plan to create an interstate highway system drastically changed America's landscape and culture. Today, the system covers about forty-five thousand miles, only a few thousand more miles than called for in the original plan.* ❖

dence on the automobile and distorting metropolitan growth patterns into long strips paralleling the new expressways.

Overall, the Eisenhower years marked an era of political moderation. The American people, enjoying the abundance of the 1950s, seemed quite content with legislative inaction. The president was sensitive to the nation's economic health; when recessions developed in 1953 and again in 1957 after his landslide reelection victory, he quickly abandoned his goal of a balanced budget in favor of a policy advocating government spending to restore prosperity. These steps, along with modest increases in New Deal welfare programs, led to a steady growth in the federal budget from $29.5 billion in 1950 to $76.5 in 1960.

THE ELECTION OF 1956

Candidate	Party	Popular Vote	Electoral Vote
Eisenhower	Republican	35,585,245	457
Stevenson	Democratic	26,030,172	73

Eisenhower was able to balance the budget in only three of his eight years in office, and the $12 billion deficit in 1959 was larger than any ever before recorded in peacetime. In this manner, Eisenhower was able to maintain the New Deal legacy of federal responsibility for social welfare and the state of the economy while at the same time successfully resisting demands for more extensive government involvement in American life.

THE STRUGGLE OVER CIVIL RIGHTS

Despite President Eisenhower's reluctance to champion the cause of reform, powerful pressures for change forced long-overdue action in one area of American life—the denial of basic rights to the nation's black minority. In the midst of the Cold War, the contradiction between the denunciation of the Soviet Union for its human rights violations and the second-class status of African Americans began to arouse the national conscience. Fighting for freedom against communist tyranny abroad, Americans had to face the reality of the continued denial of freedom to a submerged minority at home.

African Americans had benefited economically from World War II, but they were still a seriously disadvantaged group. Those who had left the South for better opportunities in northern and western cities were concentrated in blighted and segregated neighborhoods, working at low-paying jobs, suffering economic and social discrimination, and failing to share fully in the postwar prosperity. The rising expectations of African Americans in the postwar years led them to challenge the older patterns of racial segregation and inequality.

In the South, conditions were much worse. State laws forced blacks to live almost totally segregated from white society. Not only did African Americans attend separate (and almost always inferior) schools, but they also were rigidly segregated in all public facilities. They were forced to use separate waiting rooms in train stations, separate seats on all forms of transportation, separate drinking fountains, and even separate telephone booths. "Segregation was enforced at all places of public entertainment, including libraries, auditoriums, and circuses," Chief Justice Earl Warren noted. "There was segregation in the hospitals, prisons, mental institutions, and nursing homes. Even ambulance service was segregated."

Civil Rights as a Political Issue

Truman was the first president to attempt to alter the historic pattern of racial discrimination in the United States. In 1946, he appointed a presidential commission on civil rights. A year later, in a sweeping report titled "To Secure These Rights," the commission recommended the reinstatement of the wartime Fair Employment Practices Committee (FEPC), the establishment of a permanent civil rights commission, and the denial of federal aid to any state that condoned segregation in schools and public facilities. The president's ten-point legislative program proposed in 1948 included some of these measures, notably the establishment of a permanent FEPC and a civil rights commission. But southern resistance had blocked any action by Congress, and the inclusion of a strong civil rights plank in the 1948 Democratic platform had led to the walkout of some southern delegations and a separate States' Rights (Dixiecrat) ticket in several states of the South that fall.

African American voters in the North overwhelmingly backed Truman over Dewey in the 1948 election. The African American vote in key cities—Los Angeles, Cleveland, and Chicago—ensured the Democratic victory in California, Ohio, and Illinois. Truman responded by including civil rights legislation in his Fair

Deal program in 1949. Once again, however, determined southern opposition blocked congressional action on both a permanent FEPC and an anti-lynching measure.

Even though President Truman was unable to secure any significant legislation, he did succeed in adding civil rights to the liberal agenda. From this time forward, it would be an integral part of the Democratic reform program. Also, Truman used his executive power to assist African Americans. He strengthened the civil rights division of the Justice Department, which aided black groups in their efforts to challenge school segregation and restrictive housing covenants in the courts. Most important, in 1948 Truman issued an order calling for the desegregation of the armed forces. The navy and the air force quickly complied, but the army resisted until the personnel needs of the Korean War finally overcame the military's objections. By the end of the 1950s, the armed forces had become far more integrated than American society at large.

Desegregating the Schools

The nation's schools soon became the primary target of civil rights advocates. The NAACP concentrated first on universities, successfully waging an intensive legal battle to win admission for qualified African Americans to graduate and professional schools. Led by Thurgood Marshall, NAACP lawyers then took on the broader issue of segregation in the country's public schools. Challenging the 1896 Supreme Court decision that upheld the constitutionality of separate but equal public facilities (see "*Plessy* v. *Ferguson*: The Shaping of Jim Crow," pp. 567–571), Marshall argued that even substantially equal but separate schools did profound psychological damage to African American children and thus violated the Fourteenth Amendment.

The Supreme Court was unanimous in its 1954 decision in the case of **Brown v. Board of Education of Topeka.** Chief Justice Earl Warren, recently appointed by President Eisenhower, wrote the landmark opinion flatly declaring that "separate educational facilities are inherently unequal." To divide grade school children "solely because of their race," Warren argued, "generates a feeling of inferiority as to their status in the community that may affect their hearts and minds in a way unlikely ever to be undone." Despite this sweeping language, Warren realized it would be difficult to change historic patterns of segregation quickly. Accordingly, in 1955 the Court ruled that desegregation of the schools should proceed "with all deliberate speed" and left the details to the lower federal courts.

"All deliberate speed" proved to be agonizingly slow. Officials in the border states quickly complied

Demonstrators bearing signs in support of the Supreme Court's 1954 Brown v. Board of Education *ruling to desegregate the nation's schools. The ruling also sparked protests, many of them violent and destructive, from opponents of integration.* ❖

with the Court's ruling, but states deeper in the South responded with a policy of massive resistance. Local white citizens' councils organized to fight for retention of racial separation; 101 representatives and senators signed a Southern Manifesto in 1956 that denounced the *Brown* decision as "a clear abuse of judicial power." School boards, encouraged by this show of defiance, found a variety of ways to evade the Court's ruling. The most successful was the passage of pupil placement laws. These laws enabled local officials to assign individual students to schools on the basis of scholastic aptitude, ability to adjust, and "morals, conduct, health and personal standards." These stalling tactics led to long disputes in the federal courts; by the end of the decade, fewer than 1 percent of the black children in the Deep South attended school with whites.

A conspicuous lack of presidential support further weakened the desegregation effort. Dwight Eisenhower believed that people's attitudes could not be altered by "cold lawmaking"—only "by appealing to reason, by

prayer, and by constantly working at it through our own efforts" could change be enacted. Quietly and unobtrusively, he worked to achieve desegregation in federal facilities, particularly in veterans' hospitals, navy yards, and the District of Columbia school system. Yet he refrained from endorsing the *Brown* decision, which he told an aide he believed had "*set back* progress in the South *at least fifteen years.*"

Southern leaders mistook Ike's silence for tacit support of segregation. In 1957, Governor Orval Faubus of Arkansas called out the national guard to prevent the integration of Little Rock's Central High School on grounds of a threat to public order. After 270 armed troops turned back 9 young African American students, a federal judge ordered the guardsmen removed; but when the black students entered the school, a mob of 500 jeering whites surrounded the building. Eisenhower, who had told Faubus that "the Federal Constitution will be upheld by me by every legal means at my command," sent in 1000 paratroopers to ensure the rights of the Little Rock Nine to attend Central High. The students finished the school year under armed guard. Then Little Rock authorities closed Central High School for the next two years; when it reopened, there were only three African Americans in attendance.

Angry whites taunt Elizabeth Eckford, one of nine African American students who enrolled at Little Rock's Central High School in 1957. The Arkansas National Guard, acting on orders from the state's governor Orval Faubus, refused the students entry into the school. The students were finally able to enter the school under the escort of paratroopers from the 101st Airborne Division. ❖

Despite the snail's pace of school desegregation, the *Brown* decision led to other advances. In 1957, the Eisenhower administration proposed the first general civil rights legislation since Reconstruction. Senate Majority Leader Lyndon B. Johnson overcame strong southern resistance to avoid a filibuster, but at the expense of weakening the measure considerably. The final act, however, did create a permanent Commission for Civil Rights, one of Truman's original goals. It also provided for federal efforts aimed at "securing and protecting the right to vote." A second civil rights act in 1960 slightly strengthened the voting rights section.

Like the desegregation effort, the attempt to ensure African American voting rights in the South was still largely symbolic. Southern registrars used a variety of devices, ranging from intimidation to unfair tests, to deny African Americans suffrage. Yet the actions of Congress and the Supreme Court marked a vital turning point in national policy toward racial justice.

The Beginnings of Black Activism

The most dynamic force for change came from African Americans themselves. The shift from legal struggles in the courts to protest in the streets began with an incident in Montgomery, Alabama. On December 1, 1955, Rosa Parks—a black seamstress who had been active in the local NAACP chapter—violated a city ordinance by refusing to give up her seat to a white person on a local bus. Her action, often viewed as spontaneous, grew out of a long tradition of black protest against the rigid segregation of the races in the South. Rosa Parks herself had been ejected from a bus a decade earlier for refusing to obey the driver's command, "Niggers move back." In 1953, black church leaders in Baton Rouge, Louisiana, had mounted a weeklong boycott of that city's bus system and succeeded in modifying the traditional segregated seating rules.

In Montgomery, Rosa Parks's arrest sparked a massive protest movement. Black women played a particularly important role in the protest, printing and handing out 50,000 leaflets to rally the African American community behind Parks. The movement also led to the emergence of Martin Luther King, Jr., as an eloquent new spokesman for African Americans.

King agreed to lead the subsequent bus boycott. The son of a famous Atlanta preacher, he had recently taken his first church in Montgomery after years of studying theology while earning a Ph.D. at Boston University. Now he would be able to combine his wide learning with his charismatic appeal in behalf of a practical goal—fair treatment for the African Americans who made up the bulk of the riders on the city's buses.

The **Montgomery bus boycott** started out with a modest goal. Instead of challenging the legality of seg-

Rosa Parks's refusal to surrender her seat to a white man on a Montgomery, Alabama, bus led to a citywide bus boycott that brought Rev. Martin Luther King, Jr., to prominence as a leader of the civil rights movement. Parks remained active in the movement as well; she is shown here being fingerprinted in February 1956 after her arrest for violating an antiboycott law. ❖

regated seating, King simply asked that seats be taken on a first-come, first-served basis, with African Americans being seated from the back and the whites from the front of each bus. As the protest continued, however, and as they endured both legal harassment and sporadic acts of violence, the protesters began to be more assertive. An effective system of car pools enabled them to avoid using the city buses. Soon they were insisting on a complete end to segregated seating as they sang their new song of protest:

Ain't gonna ride them buses no more
Ain't gonna ride no more
Why in the hell don't the white folk know
That I ain't gonna ride no more.

The boycott ended in victory a year later when the Supreme Court ruled the Alabama segregated seating law unconstitutional. The protest movement had triumphed, not only in denting the wall of southern segregation, but in featuring the leadership of Martin Luther King, Jr. He had emerged as the charismatic leader of a new civil rights movement—a man who won acclaim not only at home but around the world. A year after the successful bus boycott, King founded the **Southern Christian Leadership Conference (SCLC)** to direct the crusade against segregation. He visited Third World leaders in Africa and Asia and paid homage to India's Mahatma Gandhi, who had influenced his reliance on civil disobedience. He led a triumphant

Prayer Pilgrimage to Washington in 1957 on the third anniversary of the *Brown* decision, stirring the crowd of thirty thousand with his ringing demand for the right to vote. His cry "Give us the ballot" boomed in salvos that civil rights historian Taylor Branch likened to "cannon bursts in a diplomatic salute." His remarkable voice became familiar to the entire nation. Unlike many African American preachers, he never shouted, yet he captured his audience by presenting his ideas with both passion and a compelling cadence. "Though still a boy to many of his older listeners," Branch noted, "he had the commanding air of a burning sage."

Even more important, he had a strategy and message that fitted perfectly with the plight of his followers. Drawing on sources as diverse as Gandhi and Henry David Thoreau, King came out of the bus boycott with the concept of passive resistance. "If cursed," he had told protesters in Montgomery, "do not curse back. If struck, do not strike back, but evidence love and goodwill at all times." The essence of his strategy was to use the apparent weakness of southern blacks—their lack of power—and turn it into a conquering weapon. His message to southern whites was clear and unmistakable: "We will match your capacity to inflict suffering with our capacity to endure suffering. We will meet your physical force with soul force. We will not hate you, but we will not obey your evil laws. We will soon wear you down by pure capacity to suffer."

In February 1960, black students from North Carolina A&T College staged a sit-in at a "whites only" Woolworth's lunch counter in Greensboro, North Carolina. Their act of nonviolent protest spurred similar demonstrations in public spaces across the South in an effort to draw national attention to racial injustice, to demand desegregation of public facilities, and to prompt the federal government to take a more active role to end segregation. At right, civil rights activists from Tougaloo College in Mississippi bear the verbal and physical abuse of white hecklers at a sit-in demonstration at a Woolworth's lunch counter on May 28, 1963. ❖

CHRONOLOGY

1946	Republicans win control of both houses of Congress in November elections
1947	William Levitt announces first Levittown
1948	Truman orders end to segregation in armed forces
1949	Minimum wage raised from 40 to 75 cents an hour
1950	Gwendolyn Brooks becomes first African American woman to be awarded Pulitzer Prize
1951	Remington Rand unveils UNIVAC, the first electronic digital computer to be marketed commercially
1952	Edward R. Murrow inaugurates television news show *See It Now*
1953	McDonald's chooses golden arches design for its hamburger shops
1954	Supreme Court orders schools desegregated in *Brown* v. *Board of Education of Topeka*
1955	Dr. Jonas Salk reports success of antipolio vaccine (April) ◆ African Americans begin boycott of Montgomery, Alabama, bus company (December)
1956	Eisenhower signs legislation creating the interstate highway system
1957	Congress passes first Civil Rights Act since Reconstruction
1958	Charles Van Doren confesses to cheating on television quiz show *Twenty-one*
1960	African American college students stage sit-in in Greensboro, North Carolina

His ultimate goal was to unite the broken community through bonds of Christian love. He hoped to use nonviolence to appeal to middle-class white America, "to the conscience of the great decent majority who through blindness, fear, pride or irrationality have allowed their consciences to sleep." The result, King prophesied, would be to enable future historians to say of the effort, "There lived a great people—a black people—who injected new meaning and dignity into the veins of civilization."

King was not alone in championing the cause of civil rights. JoAnn Robinson helped pave the way in Montgomery with the Woman's Political Caucus, and leaders as diverse as Bayard Rustin and Ella Baker were advancing the cause at the grassroots level.

In February 1960, another spontaneous event sparked a further advance for passive resistance. Four African American students from North Carolina Agricultural and Technical College sat down at a dime-store lunch counter in Greensboro, North Carolina, and refused to move after being denied service. Other students, both whites and blacks, joined in similar "sit-ins" across the South, as well as "kneel-ins" at churches and "wade-ins" at swimming pools. By the end of the year, some fifty thousand young people had succeeded in desegregating public facilities in more than a hundred southern cities. Several thousand of the demonstrators were arrested and put in jail, but the movement gained strength, leading to the formation of the **Student Nonviolent Coordinating Committee (SNCC)** in April 1960. From this time on, the SCLC and SNCC, with their tactic of direct, though peaceful, confrontation, would replace the NAACP and its reliance on court action in the forefront of the civil rights movement. The change would eventually lead to dramatic success for the movement, but it also ushered in a period of heightened tension and social turmoil in the 1960s.

CONCLUSION: RESTORING NATIONAL CONFIDENCE

In 1959, disturbed by the criticism of American society sparked by *Sputnik*, President Eisenhower appointed a Commission on National Goals "to develop a broad outline of national objectives for the next decade and longer." Ten prominent citizens from all walks of life, led by Henry W. Wriston of Brown University, issued a report that called for increased military spending abroad, greater economic growth at home, broader educational opportunities, and more government support for both scientific research and the advancement of the arts. The consensus seemed to be that rather than a change of direction, all the United States needed was a renewed commitment to the pursuit of excellence.

The 1950s ended with the national mood less troubled than when the decade began amid the turmoil of the second Red Scare and the Korean War, yet hardly as tranquil or confident as Eisenhower had hoped it would be. The American people felt reassured about the state of the economy, no longer fearing a return to the grim years of the Great Depression. At the same time, however, they were aware that abundance alone did not guarantee the quality of everyday life and realized that there was still a huge gap between American ideals and the reality of race relations, in the North as well as the South.

RECOMMENDED READING

Two excellent books survey the social, cultural, and political trends in the United States during the postwar period. In *One Nation Divisible* (1980), Richard Polenberg analyzes class, ethnic, and racial changes; James T. Patterson offers a perceptive overview of American life from the end of World War II through the mid-1970s in *Grand Expectations* (1996).

Richard Pells provides a sweeping survey of the American intellectual community's response to the Cold War in *The Liberal Mind in a Conservative Age* (1985). The broadest account of American life during the decade is David Halberstam, *The Fifties* (1993). Other important books on social and cultural trends include Elaine Tyler May, *Homeward Bound: American Families in the Cold War Era* (1988); Kenneth A. Jackson, *Crabgrass Frontier* (1986); Lisabeth Cohen, *A Consumer's Republic* (2003); and Serge Guilbaut, *How New York Stole the Idea of Modern Art* (1983).

Charles Alexander provides a balanced view of the Eisenhower years in *Holding the Line* (1975), portraying the Republican president as an able chief executive who was well suited to the times. Fred Greenstein, *The Hidden Hand Presidency* (1982), explores Eisenhower's fondness for indirect leadership. For the impact of *Sputnik* and the space program, see Walter A. MacDougall, *The Heavens and the Earth* (1985) and Robert A. Divine, *The Sputnik Challenge* (1993).

Taylor Branch gives a comprehensive account of the genesis of the civil rights movement in *Parting the Waters: America in the King Years, 1954–1963* (1988). Three fine biographies—David L. Lewis's *King* (1970), Stephen B. Oates's *Let the Trumpet Sound* (1982), and David Garrow's *Bearing the Cross* (1986)—present perceptive portraits of Martin Luther King, Jr., the movement's most influential leader. On civil rights, see also Adam Fairclough, *To Redeem the Soul of America* (1987), Joanne Grant, *Ella Baker* (1999); and James T. Patterson, *Brown v. Board of Education* (2001).

For a list of additional titles related to this chapter's topics, please see http://www.ablongman.com/divine.

SUGGESTED WEB SITES

Fifties Website Home Page

http://www.fiftiesweb.com/

This entertaining site tells about and samples music and television from the 1950s. It also includes a related links page.

1950s America

http://www.english.upenn.edu/~afilreis/50/home.html

This site by Professor Al Filreis of the University of Pennsylvania contains a large array of 1950s literature and images in an alphabetical index.

Levittown: Documents of an Ideal American Suburb

http://www.uic.edu/~pbhales/Levittown/

The postwar boom in housing made suburban living the cultural norm in America and shaped a generation. The story of the classic suburb, Levittown, is told on this site in pictures and text.

Beyond the Playing Field: Jackie Robinson, Civil Rights Advocate

http://www.archives.gov/digital_classroom/lessons/jackie_robinson/jackie_robinson.html

This National Archives and Records Administration teaching materials site contains images, essays, and documents about Robinson and Civil Rights.

Negro Leagues Baseball On-line Archive

http://www.negroleaguebaseball.com/

Essays about desegregation, baseball, and Jim Crow as well as images of teams and players comprise much of this site.

Dwight David Eisenhower

http://www.ipl.org/ref/POTUS/ddeisenhower.html

This site contains basic factual data about Eisenhower's election and presidency, including speeches and other materials.

The Dwight D. Eisenhower Library and Museum

http://www.eisenhower.utexas.edu/

This site contains mainly photos of the presidents.

Robert Rauschenberg memorialized some of the events of the 1960s in this screen print (Signs, 1970). Robert Rauschenberg, Signs, 1970. © Robert Rauschenberg/Licensed by VAGA, New York, NY. *(Robert Rauschenberg, Signs, 1970. © Robert Rauschenberg/Licensed by VAGA, New York, NY.)* ❖

The Turbulent Sixties

Kennedy versus Nixon: The First Televised Presidential Candidate Debate

On Monday evening, September 26, 1960, John F. Kennedy and Richard M. Nixon faced each other in the nation's first televised debate between two presidential candidates. Kennedy, the relatively unknown Democratic challenger, had proposed the debates; Nixon, confident of his mastery of television, had accepted even though, as Eisenhower's vice president and the early front-runner in the election, he had more to lose and less to gain.

Richard Nixon arrived an hour early at the CBS studio in Chicago, looking tired and ill at ease. He was still recovering from a knee injury that had slowed his campaign and left him pale and weak as he pursued a hectic catch-up schedule. Makeup experts offered to hide Nixon's heavy beard and soften his prominent jowls, but the GOP candidate declined, preferring to let an aide apply a light coat of Max Factor's "Lazy Shave," a pancake cosmetic. John Kennedy, tanned from open-air campaigning in California and rested by a day spent nearly free of distracting activity, wore very light makeup. He also changed from a gray to a dark blue suit better adapted to the intense television lighting.

At 8:30 P.M. central time, moderator Howard K. Smith welcomed a viewing audience estimated at seventy-seven million. Kennedy led off, echoing Abraham Lincoln by saying that the nation faced the question of "whether the world will exist half-slave and half-free." Although the ground rules limited the first debate to domestic issues, Kennedy argued that foreign and domestic policy were inseparable. He accused the Republicans of letting the country drift at home and abroad. "I think it's time America started moving again," he concluded. Nixon, caught off guard, seemed to agree with Kennedy's assessment of the nation's problems, but he contended that he had better solutions. "Our disagreement," the vice president pointed out, "is not about the goals for America but only about the means to reach those goals."

For the rest of the hour, the two candidates answered questions from a panel of journalists. Radiating confidence and self-assurance, Kennedy used a flow of statistics and details to create the image of a man deeply knowledgeable about all aspects of government. Nixon fought back with a defense of the Eisenhower record, but he seemed nervous and unsure of himself. The reaction shots of each candidate listening to the other's remarks showed Kennedy calm and serene, Nixon tense and uncomfortable.

Polls taken during the following few weeks revealed a sharp swing to Kennedy. Many Democrats and independents who had thought him too young or too inexperienced were impressed by his performance. Nixon suffered more from his unattractive image than from what he said; those who heard the debate on radio thought the Republican candidate more than held his own. In the three additional debates held during the campaign, Nixon improved his performance notably, wearing makeup to soften his appearance and taking the offensive from Kennedy on the issues. But the damage had been done. A postelection poll revealed that of four million voters who were influenced by the debates, three million voted for Kennedy.

OUTLINE
❖❖❖

Kennedy Intensifies the Cold War

The New Frontier at Home

"Let Us Continue"

Johnson Escalates the Vietnam War

Years of Turmoil

The Return of Richard Nixon

Conclusion: The End of an Era

FEATURE ESSAY
❖❖❖

Unintended Consequences: The Second Great Migration

Both candidates did well in the televised Kennedy-Nixon debates, but Nixon lost the advantage of greater name recognition while Kennedy won supporters with his healthier appearance and more confident manner. ❖

The televised debates were only one of many factors influencing the outcome of the 1960 election. In essence, Kennedy won because he took full advantage of all his opportunities. Lightly regarded by Democratic leaders, he won the nomination by appealing to the rank and file in the primaries, but then he astutely chose Lyndon Johnson of Texas as his running mate to blunt Nixon's southern strategy.

DURING THE FALL CAMPAIGN, Kennedy exploited the national mood of frustration that had followed *Sputnik*. At home, he promised to stimulate the lagging economy and carry forward long-overdue reforms in education, health care, and civil rights under the banner of the **New Frontier.** Abroad, he pledged a renewed commitment to the Cold War, vowing he would lead the nation to victory over the Soviet Union. He met the issue of his Catholicism head on, telling a group of Protestant ministers in Houston that as president he would always place country above religion. In the shrewdest move of all, he won over African American voters by helping to secure the release of Martin Luther King, Jr., from a Georgia jail where the civil rights leader was being held on a trumped-up charge.

The Democratic victory in 1960 was paper-thin. Kennedy's edge in the popular vote was only two-tenths of 1 percent, and his wide margin in the electoral college (303 to 219) was tainted by voting irregularities in several states—notably Illinois and Texas—which went Democratic by very slender majorities. Yet even though he had no mandate, Kennedy's triumph did mark a sharp political shift. In contrast to the aging Eisenhower, Kennedy symbolized youth, energy, and ambition. His mastery of the new medium of

television reflected his sensitivity to the changes taking place in American life in the 1960s. He came to office promising reform at home and advances abroad. Over the next eight years, he and Lyndon Johnson achieved many of their goals. Yet the nation also became engulfed in angry protests, violent demonstrations, and sweeping social change in one of the stormiest decades in American history.

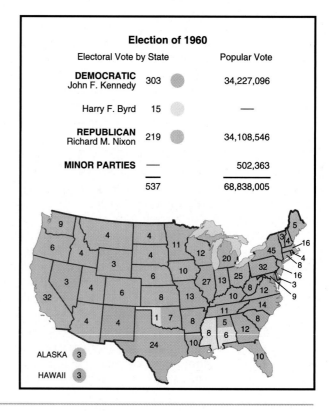

Election of 1960

	Electoral Vote by State	Popular Vote
DEMOCRATIC John F. Kennedy	303	34,227,096
Harry F. Byrd	15	—
REPUBLICAN Richard M. Nixon	219	34,108,546
MINOR PARTIES	—	502,363
	537	68,838,005

ALASKA 3

HAWAII 3

KENNEDY INTENSIFIES THE COLD WAR

John F. Kennedy was determined to succeed where he believed Eisenhower had failed. Critical of his predecessor for holding down defense spending and apparently allowing the Soviet Union to open up a dangerous lead in ICBMs, Kennedy sought to warn the nation of its peril and lead it to victory in the Cold War.

In his inaugural address, the young president sounded the alarm. Ignoring the domestic issues aired during the campaign, he dealt exclusively with the world. "Let every nation know, whether it wishes us well or ill, that we shall pay any price, bear any burden, meet any hardship, support any friend, oppose any foe," Kennedy declared, "to assure the survival and success of liberty. We will do all this and more."

From the day he took office, John F. Kennedy gave foreign policy top priority. In part, the decision reflected the perilous world situation, the immediate dangers ranging from the unresolved Berlin crisis, through a developing civil war in Vietnam, to the emergence of Fidel Castro as a Soviet ally in Cuba. But it also corresponded to Kennedy's personal priorities. As a congressman and senator, he had been an intense cold warrior. Bored by committee work and legislative details, he had focused on foreign policy in the Senate, gaining a seat on the Foreign Relations Committee and publishing a book of speeches, *The Strategy of Peace,* in early 1960.

His appointments reflected his determination to win the Cold War. His choice of Dean Rusk, an experienced but unassertive diplomat, to head the State Department indicated that Kennedy planned to be his own secretary of state. He surrounded himself with young pragmatic advisers who prided themselves on toughness: McGeorge Bundy, dean of Harvard College, became national security adviser; Walt W. Rostow, an MIT economist, was Bundy's deputy; and Robert McNamara, the youthful president of the Ford Motor Company, took over as secretary of defense.

These New Frontiersmen, later dubbed "the best and the brightest" by journalist David Halberstam, all shared a hard-line view of the Soviet Union and the belief that American security depended on superior force and the willingness to use it. Walt Rostow summed up their view of the contest with Russia best when he wrote, "The cold war comes down to this test of whether we and the democratic world are fundamentally tougher and more purposeful in the defense of our vital interests than they are in the pursuit of their global ambitions."

Flexible Response

The first goal of the Kennedy administration was to build up the nation's armed forces. During the 1960 campaign, Kennedy had warned that the Soviets were opening a missile gap. In fact, due largely to Eisenhower's foresight, the United States had a significant lead in nuclear striking power by early 1961, with a fleet of more than 600 B-52 bombers, 2 Polaris submarines, and 16 Atlas ICBMs capable of delivering more than 2000 warheads against Russian targets. Nevertheless, the new administration, intent on putting the Soviets on the defensive, authorized the construction of an awesome nuclear arsenal that included 1000 Minuteman solid-fuel ICBMs (five times the number Eisenhower had believed necessary) and 32 Polaris submarines carrying 656 missiles. The United States thus opened a missile gap in reverse, creating the possibility of a successful American first strike.

At the same time, the Kennedy administration augmented conventional military strength. Secretary of Defense McNamara developed plans to add five combat-ready army divisions, three tactical air wings, and a ten-division strategic reserve. These vast increases led to a $6 billion jump in the defense budget in 1961 alone. The president took a personal interest in counterinsurgency. He expanded the Special Forces unit at Fort Bragg, North Carolina, and insisted, over army objections, that it adopt a distinctive green beret as a symbol of its elite status.

The purpose of this buildup was to create an alternative to Eisenhower's policy of massive retaliation. Instead of responding to communist moves with nuclear threats, the United States could now call on a wide spectrum of force—ranging from ICBMs to Green Berets. Thus, as Robert McNamara explained, the new strategy of **flexible response** meant the United States could "choose among several operational plans. We shall be committed only to a system that gives us the ability to use our forces in a controlled and deliberate way." The danger was that such a powerful arsenal might tempt the new administration to test its strength against the Soviet Union.

Crisis over Berlin

The first confrontation came in Germany. Since 1958, Soviet Premier Khrushchev had been threatening to sign a peace treaty that would put access to the isolated western zones of Berlin under the control of East Germany. The steady flight of skilled workers to the West through the Berlin escape route weakened the East German regime dangerously, and the Soviets believed they had to resolve this issue quickly.

The wall built by the Soviet Union split Berlin. Here West Berliners watch East Berliners construct roadblock reinforcements at a section of the wall in order to prevent trucks from escaping. The wall later became much higher than shown here. ❖

Aware of superior American nuclear striking power, Khrushchev settled for a stalemate. On August 13, the Soviets sealed off their zone of the city. They began the construction of the **Berlin Wall** to stop the flow of brains and talent to the West. For a brief time, Russian and American tanks maneuvered within sight of each other at Checkpoint Charlie (where the American and Soviet zones met), but by fall, the tension gradually eased. The Soviets signed a separate peace treaty that did not affect U.S. occupation rights; Berlin—like Germany and, indeed, all of Europe—remained divided between the East and the West. Neither side could claim a victory, but Kennedy believed that at least he had proved to the world America's willingness to honor its commitments.

Containment in Southeast Asia

Two weeks before Kennedy's inauguration, Khrushchev gave a speech in Moscow in which he declared Soviet support for "wars of national liberation." The Russian leader's words were actually aimed more at China than the United States; the two powerful communist nations were now rivals for influence in the Third World. But the new American president, ignoring the growing Sino-Soviet split, concluded the United States and Russia were locked in a struggle for the hearts and minds of the uncommitted in Asia, Africa, and Latin America.

Calling for a new policy of nation building, Kennedy advocated financial and technical assistance designed to help Third World nations achieve economic modernization and stable pro-Western governments. Measures ranging from the formation of the idealistic Peace Corps to the ambitious Alliance for Progress—a massive economic aid program for Latin America—were part of this effort. Unfortunately, Kennedy relied even more on counterinsurgency and the Green Berets to beat back the communist challenge in the Third World.

Southeast Asia offered the gravest test. The American decision to back Ngo Dinh Diem (see p. 829) had prevented the holding of elections throughout Vietnam in 1956, as called for in the Geneva accords. Instead, Diem sought to establish a separate government in the South with large-scale American economic and military assistance. By the time Kennedy entered the White House, however, the com-

At a summit meeting in Vienna in June 1961, Kennedy and Khrushchev focused on Berlin as the key issue. The Russian leader called the current situation "intolerable" and announced the Soviet Union would proceed with an East German peace treaty. Kennedy was equally adamant, defending the American presence in Berlin and refusing to give up occupation rights that he considered crucial to the defense of western Europe. In their last session, the failure to reach agreement took on an ominous tone. "I want peace," Khrushchev declared, "but, if you want war, that is your problem." "It is you, not I," the young president replied, "who wants to force a change." When the Soviet leader said he would sign a German peace treaty by December, Kennedy added, "It will be a cold winter."

The climax came sooner than either man expected. On July 25, Kennedy delivered an impassioned televised address to the American people in which he called the defense of Berlin "essential" to "the entire Free World." Announcing a series of arms increases, including $3 billion more in defense spending, the president took the unprecedented step of calling more than 150,000 reservists and national guardsmen to active duty.

munist government in North Vietnam, led by Ho Chi Minh, was directing the efforts of Vietcong rebels in the South. As the guerrilla war intensified in the fall of 1961, the president sent two trusted advisers, Walt Rostow and General Maxwell Taylor, to South Vietnam. They returned favoring the dispatch of eight thousand American combat troops. "As an area for the operation of U.S. troops," reported General Taylor, "SVN [South Vietnam] is not an excessively difficult or unpleasant place to operate. . . . The risks of backing into a major Asian war by way of SVN are present but are not impressive."

The president decided against sending in combat troops in 1961, but he authorized substantial increases in economic aid to Diem and in the size of the military mission in Saigon. The number of American advisers in Vietnam grew from fewer than one thousand in 1961 to more than sixteen thousand by late 1963. The flow of supplies and the creation of "strategic hamlets," fortified villages designed to protect the peasantry from the Vietcong, slowed the communist momentum. American helicopters gave government forces mobility against the Vietcong, but by 1963, the situation had again become critical. Diem had failed to win the support of his own people; Buddhist monks set themselves aflame in public protests against him; and even Diem's own generals plotted his overthrow.

President Kennedy was in a quandary. He realized that the fate of South Vietnam would be determined not by America but by the Vietnamese. "In the final analysis," he said in September 1963, "it is their war. They are the ones who have to win it or lose it." But at the same time, Kennedy was not prepared to accept the possible loss of all Southeast Asia. Saying it would be "a great mistake" to withdraw from South Vietnam, he told reporters, "Strongly on our mind is what happened in the case of China at the end of World War II, where China was lost. We don't want that." Although aides later claimed he planned to pull out after the 1964 election, Kennedy raised the stakes by tacitly approving a coup that led to Diem's overthrow and death on November 1, 1963. The resulting power vacuum in Saigon made further American involvement in Vietnam almost certain.

Containing Castro: The Bay of Pigs Fiasco

Kennedy's determination to check global communist expansion reached a peak of intensity in Cuba. In the 1960 campaign, pointing to the growing ties between the Soviet Union and Fidel Castro's regime, he had accused the Republicans of permitting a "communist satellite" to arise on "our very doorstep." Kennedy had

Flames engulf Buddhist monk, the Reverend Quang Duc, who set himself afire at an intersection in Saigon, Vietnam, to protest persecution of Buddhists by Vietnam president Ngo Dinh Diem and his government. Other monks placed themselves in front of the wheels of nearby fire trucks to prevent them from reaching Duc. ❖

even issued a statement backing "anti-Castro forces in exile," calling them "fighters for freedom" who held out hope for "overthrowing Castro."

In reality, the Eisenhower administration had been training a group of Cuban exiles in Guatemala since March 1960 as part of a CIA plan to topple the Castro regime. Many of the new president's advisers had doubts about the proposed invasion. Some saw little chance for success because the operation depended heavily on a broad uprising of the Cuban people. Others—notably Senator William Fulbright of Arkansas, chairman of the Foreign Relations Committee—viewed it as an immoral act that would discredit the United States. "The Castro regime is a thorn in the flesh," Fulbright argued, "but it is not a dagger in the heart." The president, however, committed by his own campaign rhetoric and assured of success by the military, decided to proceed.

On April 17, 1961, fourteen hundred Cuban exiles moved ashore at the Bay of Pigs on the southern coast of Cuba. Even though the United States had masterminded the entire operation, Kennedy insisted on covert action, even canceling at the last minute a planned American air strike on the beachhead. With air superiority, Castro's well-trained forces had no difficulty in quashing the invasion. They killed nearly five hundred exiles and forced the rest to surrender within forty-eight hours.

Aghast at the swiftness of the defeat, President Kennedy took personal responsibility for the **Bay of Pigs.** In his address to the American people, however, he showed no remorse for arranging the violation of a neighboring country's sovereignty, only regret at the outcome. Above all, he expressed renewed defiance, warning the Soviets that "our restraint is not inexhaustible." He went on to assert that the United States would resist "communist penetration" in the Western Hemisphere, terming it part of the "primary obligations . . . to the security of our nation." For the remainder of his presidency, Kennedy continued to harass the Castro regime, imposing an economic blockade on Cuba, supporting a continuing series of raids by exile groups operating out of Florida, and failing to stop the CIA from experimenting with bizarre plots to assassinate Fidel Castro.

Containing Castro: The Cuban Missile Crisis

The climax of Kennedy's crusade came in October 1962 with the **Cuban missile crisis.** Throughout the summer and early fall, the Soviets engaged in a massive arms buildup in Cuba, ostensibly to protect Castro from an American invasion. In the United States, Republican candidates in the 1962 congressional elections called for a firm American response; Kennedy contented himself with a stern warning against the introduction of any offensive weapons, believing their presence would directly threaten American security. Khrushchev publicly denied any such intent, but secretly he took a daring gamble, building sites for twenty-four medium-range (1000-mile) and eighteen intermediate-range (2000-mile) missiles in Cuba. Later he claimed his purpose was purely defensive, but most likely he was responding to the pressures from his own military to close the enormous strategic gap in nuclear striking power that Kennedy had opened.

On October 14, 1962, an American U-2 plane finally discovered the missile sites that were nearing completion. As soon as he learned of the Russian action, Kennedy decided to seek a showdown with Khrushchev. Insisting on absolute secrecy, he convened a special group of advisers to consider the way to respond.

An initial preference for an immediate air strike gradually gave way to discussion of either a full-scale invasion or a naval blockade. The president and his advisers ruled out diplomacy, rejecting a proposal to offer the withdrawal of obsolete American Jupiter missiles from Turkey in return for a similar Russian pullout in Cuba. Kennedy finally agreed to a two-step procedure. He would proclaim a quarantine of Cuba to prevent the arrival of new missiles and threaten a nuclear confrontation to force the removal of those already there. If the Russians did not cooperate, then the United States would invade Cuba and dismantle the missiles by force.

On the evening of October 22, the president informed the nation of the existence of the Soviet missiles and his plans to remove them. He spared no words in blaming Khrushchev for "this clandestine, reckless, and provocative threat to world peace," and he made it clear that any missile attack from Cuba would lead to "a full retaliatory response upon the Soviet Union."

For the next six days, the world hovered on the brink of nuclear catastrophe. Khrushchev replied defiantly, accusing Kennedy of pushing mankind "to the abyss of a world nuclear-missile war." In the Atlantic, some sixteen Soviet ships continued on course toward Cuba, while the American navy was deployed to intercept them five hundred miles from the island. In Florida, nearly a quarter million men were being concentrated in the largest invasion force ever assembled in the continental United States.

The first break came at midweek when the Soviet ships suddenly halted to avert a confrontation at sea. "We're eyeball to eyeball," commented Secretary of State Dean Rusk, "and I think the other fellow just blinked." On Friday, Khrushchev sent Kennedy a long, rambling letter offering a face-saving way out: Russia would remove the missiles in return for an American promise never to invade Cuba. The president was ready to accept when a second Russian message raised the stakes by insisting that American Jupiter missiles be withdrawn from Turkey. Heeding the advice of his brother, attorney general Robert Kennedy, the president refused to bargain; Khrushchev had endangered world peace by putting the missiles in Cuba secretly, and he must take them out immediately. Nevertheless, while the military went ahead with plans for the invasion of Cuba, the president, heeding his brother's advice, decided to make one last appeal for peace. Ignoring the second Russian message, he sent a cable to Khrushchev accepting his original offer.

On Saturday night, October 27, Robert Kennedy met with Soviet ambassador Anatoly Dobrynin to make clear it was the last chance to avert nuclear confrontation. "We had to have a commitment by tomorrow that those bases would be removed," Robert Kennedy recalled telling him. "He should understand that if they did not remove those bases, we would remove them." Then the president's brother calmly remarked that if Khrushchev did not back down, "there would be not only dead Americans but dead Russians as well."

In reality, John F. Kennedy was not quite so ready to risk nuclear war. He instructed his brother to assure

MEDIUM RANGE BALLISTIC MISSILE BASE IN CUBA

Aerial photographs taken by a U-2 reconnaissance plane flying over Cuba revealed the presence of Russian missile sites under construction on the island. Recently released information about the type and number of Soviet nuclear warheads in Cuba reveals just how imminent was the threat of nuclear war had not the Soviets capitulated to U.S. demands for removal of the missiles. ❖

Dobrynin that the Jupiter missiles would soon be removed from Turkey. The president preferred that the missile swap be done privately, but twenty-five years later, Secretary of State Dean Rusk revealed that JFK had instructed him to arrange a deal through the United Nations involving "the removal of both the Jupiters and the missiles in Cuba." In recently released transcripts of his meetings with his advisers, the president reaffirmed his intention of making a missile trade with Khrushchev publicly as a last resort to avoid nuclear war. "We can't very well invade Cuba with all its toil," he commented, "when we could have gotten them out by making a deal on the same missiles in Turkey."

President Kennedy never had to make this final concession. At nine the next morning, Khrushchev agreed to remove the missiles in return only for Kennedy's promise not to invade Cuba. The crisis was over.

The world, however, had come perilously close to a nuclear conflict. We now know the Soviets had nuclear warheads in Cuba, not only for twenty of the medium-range missiles, but also for short-range tactical launchers designed to be used against an American invading force. If Kennedy had approved the military's recommendations for an invasion of Cuba, the consequences might have been disastrous.

The peaceful resolution of the Cuban missile crisis became a personal and political triumph for John F. Kennedy. His party successfully overcame the Republican challenge in the November elections, and his own popularity reached new heights. The American people, on the defensive since *Sputnik,* suddenly felt that they had proved their superiority over the Russians. Arthur Schlesinger, Jr., Kennedy's confidant and later his biographer, claimed that the Cuban crisis showed the "whole world . . . the ripening of an American leadership unsurpassed in the responsible management of power. . . . It was this combination of toughness and restraint, of will, nerve and wisdom, so brilliantly controlled, so matchlessly calibrated, that dazzled the world."

The Cuban missile crisis had more substantial results as well. Shaken by their close call, Kennedy and Khrushchev agreed to install a "hot line" to speed direct communication between Washington and Moscow in an emergency. Long-stalled negotiations over the reduction of nuclear testing suddenly resumed, leading to the limited test ban treaty of 1963, which outlawed tests in the atmosphere while still permitting them underground. Above all, Kennedy displayed a new maturity as a result of the crisis. In a speech at American University in June 1963, he shifted from the rhetoric of confrontation to that of conciliation. Speaking of the Russians, he said, "Our most basic common link is the fact that we all inhabit this planet. We all breathe the same air. We all cherish our children's future. And we are all mortal."

Despite these hopeful words, the missile crisis also had an unfortunate consequence. Those who believed that the Russians understood only the language of force were confirmed in their penchant for a hard line. Hawks who had backed Kennedy's military buildup believed events had justified a policy of nuclear superiority. The Russian leaders drew similar conclusions. Aware the United States had a four-to-one advantage in nuclear striking power during the Cuban crisis, one Soviet official told his American counterpart, "Never will we be caught like this again." After 1962, the Soviets embarked on a crash program to build up their navy and to overtake the American lead in nuclear missiles. Within five years, they had the nucleus of a modern fleet and had surpassed the United States in ICBMs. Kennedy's fleeting moment of triumph thus ensured the escalation of the arms race. His legacy was a bittersweet one of short-term success and long-term anxiety.

THE NEW FRONTIER AT HOME

Kennedy hoped to change the course of history at home as well as abroad. His election marked the arrival of a new generation of leadership. For the first time, people born in the twentieth century who had entered political life after World War II were in charge of national affairs. Kennedy's inaugural call to get the nation moving again was particularly attractive to young people, who had shunned political involvement during the Eisenhower years.

The new administration reflected Kennedy's aura of youth and energy. Major cabinet appointments went to activists—notably Connecticut governor Abraham Ribicoff as secretary of Health, Education, and Welfare; labor lawyer Arthur J. Goldberg as secretary of Labor; and Arizona congressman Stuart Udall as secretary of the Interior. The most controversial choice was Robert F. Kennedy, the president's brother, as attorney general. Critics scoffed at his lack of legal experience, leading JFK to note jokingly he wanted to give Bobby "a little experience before he goes out to practice law." In fact, the president prized his brother's loyalty and shrewd political advice.

Equally important were the members of the White House staff who handled domestic affairs. Like their counterparts in foreign policy, these New Frontiersmen—Kenneth O'Donnell, Theodore Sorensen, Richard Goodwin, and Walter Heller—prided themselves on being tough-minded and pragmatic. In contrast to Eisenhower, Kennedy relied heavily on academics and intellectuals to help him infuse the nation with energy and a new sense of direction.

Kennedy's greatest asset was his own personality. A cool, attractive, and intelligent man, he possessed a sense of style that endeared him to the American public. Encouraged by his wife, Jacqueline, the president invited artists and musicians as well as corporate executives to White House functions, and he sprinkled his speeches with references to Emerson and Shakespeare. He seemed to be a new Lancelot, bent on calling forth the best in national life; admirers likened his inner circle to King Arthur's court at Camelot. Reporters loved him, both for his fact-filled and candid press conferences and for his witty comments. After an embarrass-

Jacqueline Kennedy turned the White House into a center for culture and ceremony, frequented by poets, composers, singers, and musicians. Here, poet Robert Frost (right) and novelist Pearl Buck (left) exchange greetings after a dinner honoring winners of the Nobel Prize. ❖

ing foreign policy failure, when his standing in the polls actually went up, he remarked, "It's just like Eisenhower. The worse I do, the more popular I get."

The Congressional Obstacle

Neither Kennedy's wit nor his charm proved strong enough to break the logjam in Congress. Since the late 1940s, a series of reform bills ranging from health care to federal aid to education had been stalled on Capitol Hill. Despite JFK's victory, the election of 1960 clouded the outlook for his New Frontier program. The Democrats had lost twenty seats in the House and two in the Senate; even though they retained majorities in both branches, a conservative coalition of northern Republicans and southern Democrats opposed all efforts at reform.

The situation was especially critical in the House, where 101 southern representatives held the balance of power between 160 northern Democrats and 174 Republicans. Aided by Speaker Sam Rayburn, Kennedy was able to enlarge the Rules Committee and overcome a traditional conservative roadblock, but the narrowness of the vote, 217 to 212, revealed how difficult it would be to enact reform measures. The president gave up the fight for health care in the Senate and settled instead for a modest increase in the minimum wage and the passage of manpower training and area-redevelopment legislation.

Kennedy had no more success in enacting his program in 1962 and 1963. The conservative coalition stood firmly against education and health-care proposals. Shifting ground, the president did win approval for a trade expansion act in 1962 designed to lower tariff barriers, but no significant reform legislation was passed. Although the composition of Congress was his main obstacle, Kennedy's greater interest in foreign policy and his distaste for legislative infighting contributed to the outcome. JFK did not enjoy "blarneying with pompous congressmen and simply would not take the time to do it," one observer noted. As a result, the New Frontier languished in Congress.

Economic Advance

Kennedy gave a higher priority to the sluggish American economy. During the last years of Eisenhower's administration, the rate of economic growth had slowed to just over 2 percent annually, while unemployment rose to new heights with each recession. JFK was determined to stimulate the economy to achieve a much higher rate of long-term growth. In part, he wanted to redeem his campaign pledge to get the nation moving again; he also believed the United States had to surpass the Soviet Union in economic vitality.

Kennedy received conflicting advice from the experts. Those who claimed the problem was essentially a technological one urged manpower training and area-redevelopment programs to modernize American industry. Others called for federal spending to rebuild the nation's public facilities—from parks and playgrounds to decaying bridges and urban courthouses. Kennedy sided with the first group, largely because Congress was opposed to massive spending on public works.

The actual stimulation of the economy, however, came not from social programs but from greatly increased appropriations for defense and space. A $6 billion increase in the arms budget in 1961 gave the economy a great lift, and Kennedy's decision to send an astronaut to the moon eventually cost $25 billion. By 1962, more than half the federal budget was devoted to space and defense; aircraft and computer companies in the South and West benefited, but unemployment remained uncomfortably high in the older industrial areas of the Northeast and Midwest.

The administration's desire to keep the inflation rate low led to a serious confrontation with the business community. Kennedy relied on informal wage and price guidelines to hold down the cost of living. But in April 1962, just after the president had persuaded the steelworkers' union to accept a new contract with no wage increases and only a few additional benefits, U.S. Steel head Roger Blough informed Kennedy that his company was raising steel prices by $6 a ton. Outraged, the president publicly called the increase "a wholly unjustifiable and irresponsible defiance of the public interest" and accused Blough of displaying "contempt for the interests of 185 million Americans." Privately, Kennedy was even blunter. He confided to aides, "My father always told me that all businessmen were sons-of-bitches, but I never believed it till now."

Roger Blough soon gave way. The president's tongue-lashing, along with a cutoff in Pentagon steel orders and the threat of an antitrust suit, forced him to reconsider. When several smaller steel companies refused to raise their prices in hopes of expanding their share of the market, U.S. Steel rolled back its prices. The business community deeply resented the president's action, and when the stock market, which had been rising steadily since 1960, suddenly fell sharply in late May 1962, analysts were quick to label the decline "the Kennedy market."

Troubled by his strained relations with business and by the continued lag in economic growth, the president decided to adopt a more unorthodox approach in 1963. Walter Heller, chairman of the Council of Economic Advisers, had been arguing since 1961 for a major cut in taxes in the belief it would stimulate consumer spending and give the economy the jolt it needed. The idea of a tax cut and resulting deficits during a period of prosperity went against economic orthodoxy, but Kennedy finally gave his approval. In January 1963, the president proposed a tax reduction of $13.5 billion, asserting that "the unrealistically heavy drag of federal income taxes on private purchasing power" was the "largest single barrier to full employment." When finally enacted by Congress in 1964, the massive tax cut led to sustained economic advance for the rest of the decade.

Kennedy's economic policy was far more successful than his legislative efforts. Although the rate of economic growth doubled to 4.5 percent by the end of 1963 and unemployment was reduced substantially, the cost of living rose only 1.3 percent a year. Personal income went up 13 percent in the early 1960s, but the greatest gains came in corporate profits—up 67 percent in the period. Yet critics pointed to the Kennedy administration's failure to close the glaring loopholes in the tax laws that benefited the rich and its lack of effort to help those at the bottom by forcing redistribution of national wealth. Despite the overall economic growth, the public sector continued to be neglected. "I am not sure what the advantage is," complained economist John Kenneth Galbraith, "in having a few more dollars to spend if the air is too dirty to breathe, the water too polluted to drink, the commuters are losing out in the struggle to get in and out of the cities, the streets are filthy, and the schools so bad that the young, perhaps wisely, stay away."

Moving Slowly on Civil Rights

Kennedy faced a genuine dilemma over the issue of civil rights. Despite his own lack of a strong record while in the Senate, he had portrayed himself during the 1960 campaign as a crusader for African American rights. He had promised to launch an attack on segregation in the Deep South, but his fear of alienating the large bloc of southern Democrats forced him to downplay civil rights legislation.

The president's solution was to defer congressional action in favor of executive leadership in this area. He directed his brother, Attorney General Robert Kennedy, to continue and expand the Eisenhower administration's efforts to achieve voting rights for southern blacks. To register previously disfranchised citizens, the Justice Department worked with the civil rights movement—notably the Student Nonviolent Coordinating Committee (SNCC)—in the Deep South. In two years, the Kennedy administration increased the number of voting rights suits fivefold. Yet the attorney general could not force the FBI to provide

protection for the civil rights volunteers who risked their lives by encouraging African Americans to register. "SNCC's only contact with federal authority," noted one observer, "consisted of the FBI agents who stood by taking notes while local policemen beat up SNCC members."

Other efforts had equally mixed results. Vice President Lyndon Johnson headed a presidential Commission on Equal Employment Opportunities that worked with defense industries and other government contractors to increase the number of jobs for African Americans. But a limited budget and a reliance on voluntary cooperation prevented any dramatic gains; African American employment improved only in direct proportion to economic growth in the early 1960s.

Kennedy did succeed in appointing a number of African Americans to high government positions: Robert Weaver became chief of the federal housing agency, and Thurgood Marshall, who pleaded the *Brown* v. *Topeka* school desegregation case before the Supreme Court, was named to the U.S. Circuit Court. On the other hand, among his judicial appointments, Kennedy included one Mississippi jurist who referred to African Americans in court as "niggers" and once compared them to "a bunch of chimpanzees."

The civil rights movement refused to accept Kennedy's indirect approach. In May 1961, the Congress of Racial Equality (CORE) sponsored a **freedom ride** in which a biracial group attempted to test a 1960 Supreme Court decision outlawing segregation in all bus and train stations used in interstate commerce. When they arrived in Birmingham, Alabama, the freedom riders were attacked by a mob of angry whites. The attorney general quickly dispatched several hundred federal marshals to protect the freedom riders, but the president, deeply involved in the Berlin crisis, was more upset at the distraction the protesters created. Kennedy directed one of his aides to get in touch with the leaders of CORE. "Tell them to call it off," he demanded. "Stop them."

In September, after the attorney general finally convinced the Interstate Commerce Commission to issue an order banning segregation in interstate terminals and buses, the freedom rides ended. The Kennedy administration then sought to prevent further confrontations by involving civil rights activists in its voting drive.

A pattern of belated reaction to southern racism marked the basic approach of the Kennedys. When James Meredith courageously sought admission to the all-white University of Mississippi in 1962, the president and the attorney general worked closely with Mississippi governor Ross Barnett to avoid violence. A transcript of Robert Kennedy's conversation with

Governor Barnett on September 25 indicates that the attorney general focused on the legal rather than the moral issues involved:

RFK: I think the problem is that the federal courts have acted and when there is a conflict between your state and the federal courts under arrangements made some years ago—

Barnett: The institution is supported by the tax-payers of this state and controlled by the Trustees.

RFK: Governor, you are a part of the United States.

Barnett: . . . I am going to treat you with every courtesy, but I won't agree to let that boy get to Ole Miss. I will never agree to that. I would rather spend my whole life in a penitentiary than do that.

RFK: I have a responsibility to enforce the laws of the United States.

Barnett: I appreciate that. You have a responsibility. Why don't you let the NAACP run their own affairs and quit cooperating with that crowd?

Despite Barnett's later promise of cooperation, the night before Meredith enrolled at the University of Mississippi, a mob attacked the federal marshals and national guard troops sent to protect him. The violence left 2 dead and 375 injured, including 166 marshals and 12 guardsmen, but Meredith attended the university and eventually graduated.

In 1963, Kennedy sent the deputy attorney general to face down Governor George C. Wallace, an avowed segregationist who had promised "to stand in the schoolhouse door" to prevent the integration of the University of Alabama. After a brief confrontation, Wallace yielded to federal authority, and two African American students peacefully desegregated the state university.

"I Have a Dream"

Martin Luther King, Jr., finally forced Kennedy to abandon his cautious tactics and come out openly in behalf of racial justice. In the spring of 1963, King began a massive protest in Birmingham, one of the South's most segregated cities. Public marches and demonstrations aimed at integrating public facilities and opening up jobs for African Americans quickly led to police harassment and many arrests, including that of King himself. Police Commissioner Eugene "Bull" Connor was determined to crush the civil rights movement; King was equally determined to prevail. Writing from his cell in Birmingham, he vowed an active campaign to bring the issue of racial injustice to national attention.

The attempts of African Americans to end discrimination and secure their civil rights met with violent resistance in Birmingham, Alabama, where police used snarling dogs, fire hoses, clubs, and electric cattle prods to turn back the unarmed demonstrators. ✦

Bull Connor played directly into King's hands. On May 3, as six thousand children marched in place of the jailed protesters, authorities broke up a demonstration with clubs, snarling police dogs, and high-pressure water hoses strong enough to take the bark off a tree. With a horrified nation watching scene after scene of this brutality on television, the Kennedy administration quickly intervened to arrange a settlement with the Birmingham civic leaders that ended the violence and granted the protesters most of their demands.

More important, Kennedy finally ended his long hesitation and sounded the call for action. "We are confronted primarily with a moral issue," he told the nation on June 11. "It is as old as the Scriptures and is as clear as the American Constitution." Eight days later, the administration sponsored civil rights legislation providing equal access to all public accommodations as well as an extension of voting rights for African Americans.

Despite pleas from the government for an end to demonstrations and protests, civil rights leaders kept pressure on the administration. They scheduled a massive **March on Washington** for August 1963. On August 28, more than 200,000 marchers gathered for a daylong rally in front of the Lincoln Memorial where they listened to hymns, speeches, and prayers for racial justice. The climax of the event was Martin Luther King, Jr.'s eloquent description of his dream for America. It concluded:

Reverend Martin Luther King, Jr., addresses the crowd at the March on Washington in August 1963. The largest single demonstration of the early 1960s, the march reflected the spirit and determination of many devoted to the cause of equality for African Americans. In his speech, King recounted the difficulties of blacks' struggle for freedom, then stirred the crowd with the description of his dream for America: "I have a dream that one day this nation will rise up and live out the true meaning of its creed—we hold these truths to be self-evident, that all men are created equal." ❖

When we let freedom ring, when we let it ring from every village and every hamlet, from every state and every city, we will be able to speed up that day when all God's children, black men and white men, Jews and Gentiles, Protestants and Catholics, will be able to join hands and sing, in the words of that old Negro spiritual, "Free at last! Free at last! Thank God almighty, we are free at last!"

By the time of Kennedy's death in November 1963, his civil rights legislation was well on its way to passage in Congress. Yet even this achievement did not fully satisfy his critics. For two years, they had waited for him to deliver on his campaign promise to wipe out housing discrimination "with a stroke of the pen." The executive order on housing finally issued in November 1962, proved disappointing; it ignored all past discrimination and applied only to houses and apartments financed by

the federal government. For many, Kennedy had raised hopes for racial equality that he never fulfilled.

But unlike Eisenhower, he had provided presidential leadership for the civil rights movement. His emphasis on executive action gradually paid off, especially in extending voting rights. By early 1964, 40 percent of southern blacks had the franchise, compared to only 28 percent in 1960. Moreover, Kennedy's sense of caution and restraint, painful and frustrating as it was to African American activists, had proved well founded. Avoiding an early, and possibly fatal, defeat in Congress, he had waited until a national consensus emerged and then had carefully channeled it behind effective legislation. Behaving very much the way Franklin Roosevelt did in guiding the nation into World War II, Kennedy chose to be a fox rather than a lion on civil rights.

The Supreme Court and Reform

The most active impulse for social change in the early 1960s came from a surprising source: the usually staid and conservative Supreme Court. Under the leadership of Earl Warren, a pragmatic jurist more noted for his political astuteness than his legal scholarship, the Court ventured into new areas. A group of liberal judges—especially William O. Douglas, Hugo Black, and William J. Brennan, Jr.—argued for social reform, while advocates of judicial restraint (such as John Marshall Harlan and Felix Frankfurter) fought stubbornly against the new activism.

The resignation of Felix Frankfurter in 1962 enabled President Kennedy to appoint Secretary of Labor Arthur Goldberg, a committed liberal, to the Supreme Court. With a clear majority now favoring judicial intervention, the Warren Court issued a series of landmark decisions designed to extend to state and local jurisdictions the traditional rights afforded the accused in federal courts. Thus in *Gideon* v. *Wainwright* (1963), *Escobedo* v. *Illinois* (1964), and *Miranda* v. *Arizona* (1966), the majority decreed that defendants had to be provided lawyers, had to be informed of their constitutional rights, and could not be interrogated or induced to confess to a crime without defense counsel being present. In effect, the Court extended to the poor and the ignorant those constitutional guarantees that had always been available to the rich and to the legally informed—notably hardened criminals.

The most far-reaching Warren Court decisions came in the area of legislative reapportionment. In 1962, the Court ruled in *Baker* v. *Carr* that Tennessee had to redistribute its legislative seats to give citizens in Memphis equal representation. Subsequent decisions reinforced the ban on rural overrepresentation as the Court proclaimed that places in all legislative bodies, including the House of Representatives, had to be allocated on the basis of "people, not land or trees or pastures." The principle of "one man, one vote" greatly increased the political power of cities at the expense of rural areas; it also involved the Court directly in the reapportionment process, frequently forcing judges to draw up new legislative and congressional districts.

The activism of the Supreme Court stirred up a storm of criticism. The rulings that extended protection to criminals and those accused of subversive activity led some Americans to charge that the Court was encouraging crime and weakening national security. The John Birch Society, an extreme anticommunist group, demanded the impeachment of Chief Justice Warren. The 1962 *Engel* v. *Vitale* decision banning school prayer incensed many conservative Americans, who saw the Court as undermining moral values. Legal scholars worried more about the weakening of the Court's prestige as it became more directly involved in the political process. On balance, however, the Warren Court helped achieve greater social justice by protecting the rights of the underprivileged and by permitting dissent and free expression to flourish.

"LET US CONTINUE"

The New Frontier came to a sudden and violent end on November 22, 1963, when Lee Harvey Oswald assassinated John F. Kennedy as the president rode in a motorcade in downtown Dallas. The shock of losing the young president, who had become a symbol of hope and promise for a whole generation, stunned the entire world. The American people were bewildered by the rapid sequence of events: the brutal killing of their young president; the televised slaying of Oswald by Jack Ruby in the basement of the Dallas police station; the composure and dignity of Kennedy's widow, Jacqueline, at the ensuing state funeral; and the hurried Warren Commission report, which identified Oswald as the lone assassin. Afterward, critics would charge that Oswald had been part of a vast conspiracy, but at the time, the prevailing national reaction was a numbing sense of loss.

Vice President Lyndon B. Johnson moved quickly to fill the vacuum left by Kennedy's death. Sworn in on board Air Force One as he returned to Washington, Johnson soon met with a stream of world leaders to reassure them of American political stability. Five days after the tragedy in Dallas, Johnson spoke eloquently to a special joint session of Congress. Recalling JFK's inaugural summons, "Let us begin," the new president declared, "Today in the moment of new resolve, I would say to all my fellow Americans, 'Let us continue.'" Asking Congress to enact Kennedy's tax and civil rights bills as a tribute to the fallen leader, LBJ concluded, "Let us here highly resolve that John Fitzgerald Kennedy did not live or die in vain."

President Kennedy smiles at the crowd as his motorcade moves through downtown Dallas, Texas, on November 22, 1963. Minutes later the president was assassinated. ❖

Johnson in Action

Lyndon Johnson suffered from the inevitable comparison with his young and stylish predecessor. LBJ was acutely aware of his own lack of polish; he sought to surround himself with Kennedy advisers and insiders, hoping their sophistication would rub off on him. Johnson's assets were very real—he possessed an intimate knowledge of Congress, an incredible energy and determination to succeed, and a fierce ego. When a young marine officer tried to direct him to the proper helicopter, saying, "This one is yours," Johnson replied, "Son, they are all my helicopters."

LBJ's height and intensity gave him a powerful presence; he dominated any room he entered, and he delighted in using his physical power of persuasion. One Texas politician explained why he had given in to Johnson: "Lyndon got me by the lapels and put his face on top of mine and he talked and talked and talked. I figured it was either getting drowned or joining."

Yet LBJ found it impossible to project his intelligence and vitality to large audiences. Unlike Kennedy, he wilted before the camera, turning his televised speeches into stilted and awkward performances. Trying to belie his reputation as a riverboat gambler, he came across like a foxy grandpa, clever, calculating, and not to be trusted. He lacked Kennedy's wit and charm, and reporters delighted in describing the way he berated his aides or shocked the nation by baring his belly to show the scar from a recent operation.

Whatever his shortcomings in style, however, Johnson possessed far greater ability than Kennedy in dealing with Congress. He entered the White House with more than thirty years of experience in Washington as a legislative aide, congressman, and senator. His encyclopedic knowledge of the legislative process and his shrewd manipulation of individual senators had enabled him to become the most influential Senate majority leader in history. Famed for "the Johnson treatment," a legendary ability to use personal persuasion to reach his goals, Johnson in fact relied more on his close ties with the Senate's power brokers—or "whales," as he called them—than on his exploitation of the "minnows."

Above all, Johnson sought consensus. Indifferent to ideology, he had moved easily from New Deal liberalism to oil-and-gas conservatism as his career advanced. He had carefully cultivated Richard Russell of Georgia, leader of the Dixie bloc, but he also had taken Hubert Humphrey, a Minnesota liberal, under his wing. He had performed a balancing act on civil rights, working with the Eisenhower administration

President Johnson applies the "Johnson treatment" to Senator Theodore Francis Green of Rhode Island. A shrewd politician and master of the legislative process, Johnson always knew which votes he could count on, those he couldn't, and where and how to apply pressure to swing votes his way. ❖

on behalf of the 1957 Voting Rights Act, yet carefully weakening it to avoid alienating southern Democrats. When Kennedy dashed Johnson's own intense presidential ambitions in 1960, LBJ had gracefully agreed to be his running mate and had endured the humiliation of the vice presidency loyally and silently. Suddenly thrust into power, Johnson used his gifts wisely. Citing his favorite scriptural passage from Isaiah, "Come now, and let us reason together, saith the Lord," he concentrated on securing passage of Kennedy's tax and civil rights bills in 1964.

The tax cut came first. Aware of the power wielded by Senate Finance Committee Chairman Harry Byrd, a Virginia conservative, Johnson astutely lowered Kennedy's projected $101.5 billion budget for 1965 to $97.9 billion. Although Byrd voted against the tax cut, he let the measure out of his committee, telling Johnson, "I'll be working for you behind the scenes." In February, Congress reduced personal income taxes by more than $10 billion, touching off a sustained economic boom. Consumer spending increased by an impressive $43 billion during the next eighteen months, and new jobs opened up at the rate of one million a year.

Johnson was even more influential in passing the Kennedy civil rights measure. Staying in the background, he encouraged liberal amendments that strengthened the bill in the House. With Hubert Humphrey leading the floor fight in the Senate, Johnson refused all efforts at compromise, counting on growing public pressure to force northern Republicans to abandon their traditional alliance with southern Democrats. Everett M. Dirksen of Illinois, the GOP leader in the Senate, met repeatedly with Johnson at the White House. When LBJ refused to yield, Dirksen finally announced, "The time has come for equality of opportunity in sharing in government, in education, and in employment," and led a Republican vote to end a 57-day filibuster.

The 1964 Civil Rights Act, signed on July 2, made illegal the segregation of African Americans in public facilities, established an Equal Employment Opportunity Commission to lessen racial discrimination in employment, and protected the voting rights of African Americans. An amendment sponsored by segregationists in an effort to weaken the bill added gender to the prohibition of discrimination in Title VII of the act; in the future, women's groups would use the clause to secure government support for greater equality in employment and education.

The Election of 1964

Passage of two key Kennedy measures within six months did not satisfy Johnson who wanted now to win the presidency in his own right. Eager to surpass Kennedy's narrow victory in 1960, he hoped to win by a great landslide.

Searching for a cause of his own, LBJ found one in the issue of poverty. Beginning in the late 1950s, economists had warned that the prevailing affluence disguised a persistent and deep-seated problem of poverty. In 1962, Michael Harrington's book *The Other America* attracted national attention. Writing with passion and eloquence, Harrington claimed that nearly one-fifth of the nation, some thirty-five million Americans, lived in poverty.

Three groups predominated among the poor—African Americans, the aged, and households headed by women. The problem, Harrington contended, was that the poor were invisible, living in slums or depressed areas such as Appalachia. They were cut off from the educational facilities, medical care, and employment opportunities afforded more affluent Americans. Moreover, poverty was a vicious cycle. The children of the poor were trapped in the same culture of poverty as their parents, living without hope or knowledge of how to enter the mainstream of American life.

Johnson quickly took over proposals that Kennedy had been developing and made them his own. In his January 1964 State of the Union address, LBJ announced, "This administration, today, here and now, declares unconditional war on poverty in America." During the next eight months, Johnson fashioned a comprehensive poverty program under the direction of R. Sargent Shriver, Kennedy's brother-in-law. The president added $500 million to existing programs to come up with a $1 billion effort that Congress passed in August 1964.

The new Office of Economic Opportunity (OEO) set up a wide variety of programs, ranging from Head Start for preschoolers to the Job Corps for high school dropouts in need of vocational training. The emphasis was on self-help, with the government providing money and know-how so the poor could reap the benefits of neighborhood day care centers, consumer education classes, legal aid services, and adult remedial reading programs. The level of funding was never high enough to meet the OEO's ambitious goals, and a controversial attempt to include representatives of the poor in the Community Action Program led to bitter political feuding with city and state officials. Nonetheless, the **war on poverty,** along with the economic growth provided by the tax cut, helped reduce the ranks of the poor by nearly ten million between 1964 and 1967.

The new program established Johnson's reputation as a reformer in an election year, but he still faced two challenges to his authority. The first was Robert F. Kennedy, the late president's brother, who continued as attorney general but who wanted to become vice

THE ELECTION OF 1964

Candidate	Party	Popular Vote	Electoral Vote
Johnson	Democratic	43,126,584	486
Goldwater	Republican	27,177,838	52

president and Johnson's eventual successor in the White House. Desperate to prove his ability to succeed without Kennedy help, LBJ commented, "I don't need that little runt to win" and chose Hubert Humphrey as his running mate.

The second challenge was the Republican candidate, Senator Barry Goldwater, an outspoken conservative from Arizona. An attractive and articulate man, Goldwater advocated a rejection of the welfare state and a return to unregulated free enterprise. To Johnson's delight, Goldwater chose to place ideology ahead of political expediency. The senator spoke out boldly against the Tennessee Valley Authority, denounced Social Security, and advocated a hawkish foreign policy. "In Your Heart, You Know He's Right," read the Republican slogan, leading the Democrats to reply, "Yes, Far Right," and in reference to a careless Goldwater comment about using nuclear weapons, Johnson backers punned, "In Your Heart, You Know He Might."

Johnson stuck carefully to the middle of the road, embracing the liberal reform program—which he now called the **Great Society**—while stressing his concern for balanced budgets and fiscal orthodoxy. The more Goldwater sagged in the polls, the harder Johnson campaigned, determined to achieve his treasured landslide. On election day, LBJ received 61.1 percent of the popular vote and an overwhelming majority in the electoral college; Goldwater carried only Arizona and five states of the Deep South. Equally important, the Democrats achieved huge gains in Congress, controlling the House by a margin of 295 to 140 and the Senate by 68 to 32. Kennedy's legacy and Goldwater's candor had enabled Johnson to break the conservative grip on Congress for the first time in a quarter century.

The Triumph of Reform

LBJ moved quickly to secure his legislative goals. Despite solid majorities in both Houses, including seventy first-term Democrats who had ridden into office on his coattails, Johnson knew he would have to enact the Great Society as swiftly as possible. "You've got to give it all you can, that first year," he told an aide. "Doesn't matter what kind of majority you come in with. You've got just one year when they treat you right, and before they start worrying about themselves."

Johnson gave two traditional Democratic reforms—health care and education—top priority. Aware of strong opposition to a comprehensive medical program, LBJ settled for **Medicare,** which mandated health insurance under the Social Security program for Americans over age 65, and a supplementary Medicaid program for the indigent. To symbolize the end of a long struggle, Johnson flew to Independence, Missouri, so Truman could witness the ceremonial signing of the Medicare law, which had its origins in Truman's 1949 health insurance proposal.

LBJ overcame the religious hurdle on education by supporting a child-benefit approach, allocating federal money to advance the education of students in parochial as well as public schools. The Elementary and Secondary Education Act of 1965 provided more than $1 billion in federal aid, the largest share going to school districts with the highest percentage of impoverished pupils.

Civil rights proved to be the most difficult test of Johnson's leadership. Martin Luther King, Jr., concerned that three million southern blacks were still denied the right to vote, in early 1965 chose Selma, Alabama, as the site for a test case. The white authorities in Selma, led by Sheriff James Clark, used cattle prods and bullwhips to break up the demonstrations. More than two thousand African Americans were jailed. Johnson intervened in March, after TV cameras showed Sheriff Clark's deputies brutally halting a march from Selma to Montgomery. The president ordered the Alabama National Guard to federal duty to protect the demonstrators, had the Justice Department draw up a new voting rights bill, and personally addressed the Congress on civil rights. "I speak tonight for the dignity of man and the destiny of democracy," he began. Calling the denial of the right to vote "deadly wrong," LBJ issued a compelling call to action. "Their cause must be our cause, too. Because it is not just Negroes, but really it is all of us who must overcome the crippling legacy of bigotry and injustice."

Five months later, Congress passed the **Voting Rights Act of 1965.** Once again Johnson had worked with Senate Republican leader Dirksen to break a southern filibuster and assure passage of a measure. The act banned literacy tests in states and counties in which less than half the population had voted in 1964 and provided for federal registrars in these areas to assure African Americans the franchise.

The results were dramatic. In less than a year, 166,000 African Americans were added to the voting rolls in Alabama; African American registration went up 400 percent in Mississippi. By the end of the decade, the

AFRICAN AMERICAN VOTER REGISTRATION BEFORE AND AFTER PASSAGE OF THE VOTING RIGHTS ACT OF 1965

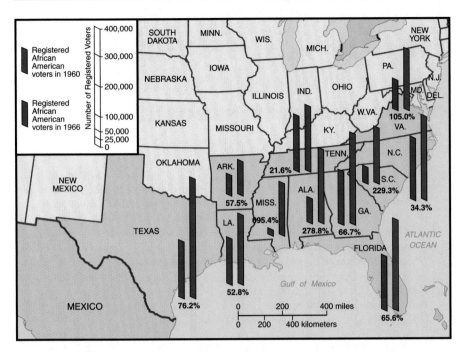

The percentages shown on the map indicate the increase in African American voter registration between 1960 and 1966.

percentage of eligible African American voters who had registered had risen from 40 to 65 percent. For the first time since Reconstruction, African Americans had become active participants in southern politics.

Before the 89th Congress ended its first session in the fall of 1965, it had passed eighty-nine bills. These included measures to create two new cabinet departments (Transportation and Housing and Urban Affairs); acts to provide for highway safety and to ensure clean air and water; large appropriations for higher education, public housing, and the continuing war on poverty; and sweeping immigration reform legislation. (See the Feature Essay, "Unintended Consequences: The Second Great Migration," pp. 874–875.) In nine months, Johnson had enacted the entire Democratic reform agenda.

The man responsible for this great leap forward, however, had failed to win the public adulation he so deeply desired. His legislative skills had made the most of the opportunities offered by the 1964 Democratic landslide, but the people did not respond to Johnson's leadership with the warmth and praise they had showered on Kennedy. Reporters continued to portray him as a crude wheeler-dealer; as a maniac who drove around Texas back roads at 90 miles an hour, one hand on the wheel and the other holding a can of beer; or as

a bully who picked up his dog by the ears. No one was more aware of this lack of affection than LBJ himself. His public support, he told an aide, is "like a Western river, broad but not deep."

Johnson's realization of the fleeting nature of his popularity was all too accurate. The dilemmas of the Cold War began to divert his attention from domestic concerns and eventually, in the case of Vietnam, would overwhelm him. Yet his legislative achievements were still remarkable. In one brief outburst of reform, he had accomplished more than any president since FDR.

Difficulties abroad would dim the luster of the Johnson presidency, but they could not diminish the lasting impact of the Great Society on American life. Federal aid to education, the enactment of Medicare and Medicaid, and, above all, the civil rights acts of 1964 and 1965 changed the nation irrevocably. The aged and the poor now were guaranteed access to medical care; communities saw an infusion of federal funds to improve local education; and African Americans could now begin to attend integrated schools, enjoy public facilities, and gain political power by exercising the right to vote. But even at this moment of triumph for liberal reform, new currents of dissent and rebellion were brewing.

UNINTENDED CONSEQUENCES

The Second Great Migration

This is not a revolutionary bill," President Lyndon Johnson declared when he signed the Immigration Act of 1965 into law. Rarely has a president been so wrong. The changes Congress made in American immigration policy led a second great migration, larger and even more diverse than the first, which took place in the thirty years before World War I. By the end of the century, the second great wave of immigration had profoundly altered the ethnic composition of the United States.

The political leaders responsible for changing immigration policy in the 1960s had very different intentions. Focused on removing long-standing inequities in the law, they sought to replace the national origins system, adopted in the 1920s, which favored people from western Europe, with a new set of criteria designed to bring in newcomers with economic skills the United States needed and to reunite broken families. Above all, the architects of change wanted to end the unfair race-based quotas for people of Asian extraction and the evident discrimination against applicants from eastern and southern Europe. Attorney General Robert Kennedy called the national origins quotas "a standing affront to many Americans and to many countries." At the height of the Cold War, realism seemed to join with idealism in the effort to end a discriminatory immigration policy that smacked of racism.

The legislative process, however, often works in mysterious ways. The bill passed by Congress did end the national origins system, as its framers desired, but reversed the new priorities, giving highest preference to family reunification, and less emphasis to job skills and asylum for refugees. As enacted and later amended, the 1965 Immigration Act set an annual limit of 170,000 for immigrants from Europe, Asia, and Africa, and 120,000 for those from Western Hemisphere countries, with a ceiling of 20,000 for any one country. The total, 290,000, would be only slightly larger than the number admitted under the old system.

By the end of the 1970s, it was clear that the family preferences, which made up nearly 70 percent of the allotted visas, were allowing recent immigrants to bring in large numbers of relatives, instead of reuniting immigrants who had been in the United States for years with their families. The figure, "The Second Great Migration: A Theoretical Example," shows how one postgraduate student with a non-immigrant visa, by adroit use of the available family preferences, could easily gain the admission of eighteen relatives in just a decade. Moreover, once resident aliens became citizens, they could bring in "immediate relatives"—spouses, children under 21, and parents—without regard to visa limits.

Two significant developments flowed directly from the Great Society's immigration policy. First, annual immigration increased steadily from an average of 250,000 in the 1950s to at least 1 million by the end of the century. In 1990, in an effort to place "immediate relatives" under an effective limit, Congress approved an overall ceiling of just less than 700,000 immigrants a year, except for refugees. But other legislation allowing undocu-mented workers to gain legal status, as well as an estimated 300,000 illegal immigrants a year, swelled the actual total to more than one million. In effect, the 1965 legislation had led to a quadrupling of newcomers entering the United States every year.

The other unintended consequence of the 1965 Immigration Act was a rapid shift in the source of the new immigrants. Europe, the traditional place of origin for immigrants, fell from providing 70 percent of newcomers in the 1950s to just 16 percent by the mid-1990s. Latin American immigrants rose from 25 to 49 percent of the total, while Asia supplied 32 percent by the end of the century, up from just 6 percent in the 1950s. This change in the countries of origin was as striking as the similar shift from western to eastern Europe in the first great migration. Where once Germany, Great Britain, and Ireland had furnished the majority of newcomers, by 1989 it was Mexico, the Philippines, and Vietnam that led the list, with no European country among the top ten (see table at right).

The result was a growing diversity that promised to make the United States a truly multiethnic society in the twenty-first century. By the 1990s, the number of foreign-born Americans had more than doubled to 10 percent of the population. Hispanic Americans were the most rapidly growing segment, replacing African Americans as the nation's largest minority in 2001. Asian Americans, although much smaller in number, grew at a fast pace and had greater success economically than any other ethnic group.

THE SECOND GREAT MIGRATION: A THEORETICAL EXAMPLE

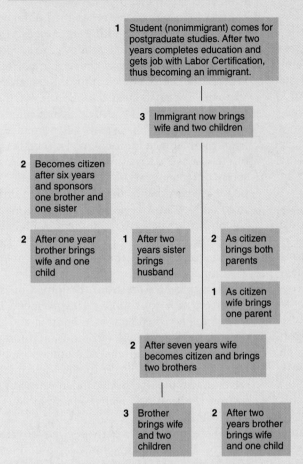

1 Student (nonimmigrant) comes for postgraduate studies. After two years completes education and gets job with Labor Certification, thus becoming an immigrant.

3 Immigrant now brings wife and two children

2 Becomes citizen after six years and sponsors one brother and one sister

2 After one year brother brings wife and one child

1 After two years sister brings husband

2 As citizen brings both parents

1 As citizen wife brings one parent

2 After seven years wife becomes citizen and brings two brothers

3 Brother brings wife and two children

2 After two years brother brings wife and one child

Note: Total is nineteen after original student arrived for postgraduate education ten years earlier. Adapted from David M. Reimer, *Still the Golden Door,* 2d ed. (New York: Columbia University Press, 1992), p. 95.

By the end of the century it was clear that the Immigration Act of 1965 had led to a major shift in the racial and ethnic composition of the United States. The effort to erase past discriminatory and race-based quotas resulted in an unexpected flow of people from Asia and Latin America that ensured the end of traditional European dominance. By 2050, according to Census Bureau projections, the country will be almost evenly divided between non-Hispanic whites and minorities. Social harmony in the twenty-first century will depend on whether the melting pot continues to melt, blending ethnic groups into mainstream America, or whether these groups, as their numbers grew, will shape the society into one that political leaders of the 1960s such as Lyndon Johnson and Robert Kennedy could never have foreseen.

REGION OF BIRTH OF FOREIGN BORN, 2000

Region	Number
Latin America	16,086,974
Asia	8,226,254
Europe	4,915,557
Africa	881,300
North America	829,442
Australia, New Zealand, and Pacific Islands	168,046

Source: Associated Press, June 9, 2002.

JOHNSON ESCALATES THE VIETNAM WAR

Lyndon Johnson stressed continuity in foreign policy just as he had in enacting Kennedy's domestic reforms. He not only inherited the policy of containment from his fallen predecessor, but he shared the same Cold War assumptions and convictions. And, feeling less confident about dealing with international issues, he tended to rely heavily on Kennedy's advisers—notably Secretary of State Rusk, Secretary of Defense McNamara, and McGeorge Bundy (the national security adviser until he was replaced in 1966 by the even more hawkish Walt Rostow).

Johnson had broad exposure to national security affairs. He had served on the Naval Affairs Committee in the House before and during World War II, and as Senate majority leader he had been briefed and consulted regularly on the crises of the 1950s. A confirmed cold warrior, he had also seen in the 1940s the devastating political impact on the Democratic party of the communist triumph in China. "I am not going to lose Vietnam," he told the American ambassador to Saigon just after taking office in 1963. "I am not going to be the president who saw Southeast Asia go the way China went."

Aware of the problem Castro had caused John Kennedy, LBJ moved firmly to contain communism in the Western Hemisphere. When a military junta overthrew a leftist regime in Brazil, Johnson offered covert aid and open encouragement. He was equally forceful in compelling Panama to restrain rioting aimed at the continued American presence in the Canal Zone.

In 1965, to block the possible emergence of a Castro-type government, LBJ sent twenty thousand American troops to the Dominican Republic. Johnson's flimsy justifications—ranging from the need to protect American tourists to a dubious list of suspected communists among the rebel leaders—served only to alienate liberal critics in the United States, particularly Senate Foreign Relations Committee Chairman J. William Fulbright, a former Johnson favorite. The intervention ended in 1966 with the election of a conservative government. Senator Fulbright, however, continued his criticism of Johnson's foreign policy by publishing *The Arrogance of Power,* a biting analysis of the fallacies of containment. Fulbright's defection symbolized a growing gap between the president and liberal intellectuals; the more LBJ struggled to uphold the Cold War policies he had inherited from Kennedy, the more he found himself under attack from Congress, the media, and the universities.

The Vietnam Dilemma

It was Vietnam rather than Latin America that became Lyndon Johnson's obsession and led ultimately to his political downfall. Inheriting an American commitment that dated back to Eisenhower to support an independent South Vietnam, the new president believed he had little choice but to continue Kennedy's policy in Vietnam. The crisis created by Diem's overthrow only three weeks before Kennedy's assassination led to a vacuum of power in Saigon that prevented Johnson from conducting a thorough review and reassessment of the strategic alternatives in Southeast Asia. In 1964, seven different governments ruled South Vietnam; power changed hands three times within one month. According to an American officer, the atmosphere in Saigon "fairly smelled of discontent," with "workers on strike, students demonstrating, [and] the local press pursuing a persistent campaign of criticism of the new government."

Resisting pressure from the Joint Chiefs of Staff for direct American military involvement, LBJ continued Kennedy's policy of economic and technical assistance. He sent in seven thousand more military advisers and an additional $50 million in aid. While he insisted it was still up to the Vietnamese themselves to win the war, he expanded American support for covert operations, including amphibious raids on the North.

These undercover activities led directly to the Gulf of Tonkin affair. On August 2, 1964, North Vietnamese torpedo boats attacked the *Maddox,* an American destroyer engaged in electronic intelligence gathering in the Gulf of Tonkin. The attack was prompted by the belief the American ship had been involved in a South Vietnamese raid nearby. The *Maddox* escaped unscathed, but to show American resolve, the navy sent in another destroyer, the *C. Turner Joy.* On the evening of August 4, the two destroyers, responding to sonar and radar contacts, opened fire on North Vietnamese gunboats in the area. Johnson ordered retaliatory air strikes on North Vietnamese naval bases. Later investigation indicated that the North Vietnamese gunboats had not launched a second attack on the American ships.

The next day, the president asked Congress to pass a resolution authorizing him to take "all necessary measures to repel any armed attack against the forces of the United States and to prevent further aggression." He did not in fact need this authority; he had already ordered the retaliatory air strike without it. Later, critics charged that LBJ wanted a blank check from Congress to carry out the future escalation of the Vietnam War, but such a motive is unlikely. He had already rejected immediate military intervention. In

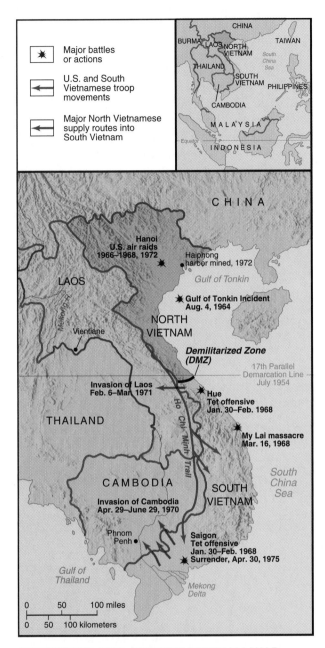

Major battles
or actions

U.S. and South
Vietnamese troop
movements

Major North Vietnamese
supply routes into
South Vietnam

CHINA
BURMA LAOS NORTH
VIETNAM
THAILAND
South
China
Sea
SOUTH
VIETNAM
PHILIPPINES
CAMBODIA
MALAYSIA
Equator
INDONESIA
TAIWAN

CHINA

Hanoi
U.S. air raids
1966–1968, 1972
Haiphong
harbor mined, 1972
Gulf of Tonkin

LAOS

Gulf of Tonkin Incident
Aug. 4, 1964

NORTH
VIETNAM

Vientiane

Demilitarized Zone
(DMZ)
17th Parallel
Demarcation Line
July 1954

Invasion of Laos
Feb. 6–Mar. 1971
Hue
Tet offensive
Jan. 30–Feb. 1968

THAILAND
My Lai massacre
Mar. 16, 1968

South
China
Sea

CAMBODIA
SOUTH
VIETNAM

Invasion of Cambodia
Apr. 29–June 29, 1970

Phnom
Penh
Saigon
Tet offensive
Jan. 30–Feb. 1968
Surrender, Apr. 30, 1975

Gulf of
Thailand

Mekong
Delta

0   50   100 miles
0   50   100 kilometers

SOUTHEAST ASIA AND THE VIETNAM WAR
*American combat forces in South Vietnam rose from sixteen
thousand in 1963 to a half million in 1968, but a successful
conclusion to the conflict was no closer.* ❖

the Gulf of Tonkin incident, Johnson could both impress the North Vietnamese and outmaneuver a political rival at home.

Congress responded with alacrity. The House acted unanimously, while only two senators voted against the Gulf of Tonkin Resolution. Johnson appeared to have won a spectacular victory. His standing in the Gallup poll shot up from 42 to 72 percent, and he had effectively blocked Goldwater from exploiting Vietnam as a campaign issue.

In the long run, however, this easy victory proved costly. Having used force once against North Vietnam, LBJ was more likely to do so in the future. And although he apparently had no intention of widening the conflict in August 1964, the congressional resolution was phrased broadly enough to enable him to use whatever level of force he wanted—including unlimited military intervention. Above all, when he did wage war in Vietnam, he left himself open to the charge of deliberately misleading Congress. Presidential credibility proved ultimately to be Johnson's Achilles' heel; his political downfall began with the Gulf of Tonkin Resolution.

Escalation

Full-scale American involvement in Vietnam began in 1965 in a series of steps designed primarily to prevent a North Vietnamese victory. With the political situation in Saigon growing more hopeless every day, the president's advisers urged the bombing of the North. American air attacks would serve several purposes: They would block North Vietnamese infiltration routes, make Hanoi pay a heavy price for its role, and lift the sagging morale of the South Vietnamese. But most important, as McGeorge Bundy reported after a visit to Pleiku (site of a Vietcong attack on an American base that took nine lives), "Without new U.S. action defeat appears inevitable—probably not in a matter of weeks or perhaps even months, but within the next year or so." In February 1965, Johnson cited the Pleiku attack in ordering a long-planned aerial bombardment of selected North Vietnamese targets.

The air strikes, aimed at impeding the communist supply line and damaging Hanoi's economy, proved ineffective. In April, Johnson authorized the use of American combat troops in South Vietnam, restricting them to defensive operations intended to protect American air bases. The Joint Chiefs then pressed the president for both unlimited bombing of the North and the aggressive use of American ground forces in the South. In mid-July, Secretary of Defense McNamara recommended sending a hundred thousand combat troops to Vietnam, more than doubling the American forces there. He believed this escalation

part, he wanted the **Gulf of Tonkin Resolution** to demonstrate to North Vietnam the American determination to defend South Vietnam at any cost. "The challenge we face in Southeast Asia today," he told Congress, "is the same challenge that we have faced with courage and that we have met with strength in Greece and Turkey, in Berlin and Korea." He also wanted to preempt the Vietnam issue from his Republican opponent, Barry Goldwater, who had been advocating a tougher policy. By taking a firm stand on would lead to a "favorable outcome," but he also told the president that an additional hundred thousand soldiers might be needed in 1966 and that American battle deaths could rise as high as five hundred a month (by early 1968, they hit a peak of more than five hundred a week).

At the same time, other advisers, most notably Undersecretary of State George Ball, spoke out against military escalation in favor of a political settlement. Warning that the United States was likely to suffer France's fate in Vietnam of "national humiliation," Ball told the president that he had "serious doubt that an army of westerners can successfully fight Orientals in an Asian jungle."

Lyndon Johnson was genuinely torn, asking his advisers at one point, "Are we starting something that in two to three years we simply can't finish?" But he finally decided he had no choice but to persevere in Vietnam. Although he insisted on paring down McNamara's troop request, LBJ settled on a steady military escalation designed to compel Hanoi to accept a diplomatic solution. In late July, the president permitted a gradual increase in the bombing of North Vietnam and allowed American ground commanders to conduct offensive operations in the South. Most ominously, he approved the immediate dispatch of fifty thousand troops to Vietnam and the future commitment of fifty thousand more.

These July decisions formed "an open-ended commitment to employ American military forces as the situation demanded," wrote historian George Herring, and they were "the closest thing to a formal decision for war in Vietnam." Convinced that withdrawal would destroy American credibility before the world and that an invasion of the North would lead to World War III, Johnson opted for large-scale but limited military intervention. Moreover, LBJ feared the domestic consequences of either extreme. A pullout could cause a massive political backlash at home, as conservatives condemned him for betraying South Vietnam to communism. All-out war, however, would mean the end of his social programs. Once Congress focused on the conflict, he explained to biographer Doris Kearns, "that bitch of a war" would destroy "the woman I really loved—the Great Society." So he settled for a limited war, committing a half million American troops to battle in Southeast Asia, all the while pretending it was a minor engagement and refusing to ask the American people for the support and sacrifice required for victory.

Lyndon Johnson was not solely responsible for the Vietnam War. He inherited both a policy that assumed Vietnam was a vital national interest and a deteriorating situation in Saigon that demanded a more active American role. Truman, Eisenhower, and Kennedy had

taken the United States deep into the Vietnam maze; it was Johnson's fate to have to find a way out. But LBJ bears full responsibility for the way he tried to resolve his dilemma. The failure to confront the people with the stark choices the nation faced in Vietnam, the insistence on secrecy and deceit, the refusal to acknowledge that he had committed the United States to a dangerous military involvement—these were Johnson's sins in Vietnam. His lack of self-confidence in foreign policy and fear of domestic reaction led directly to his undoing.

Stalemate

For the next three years, Americans waged an intensive war in Vietnam and succeeded only in preventing a

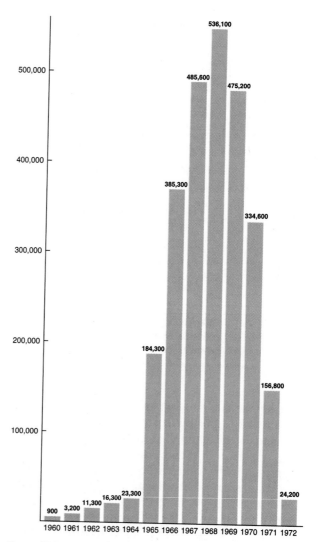

U.S. TROOP LEVELS IN VIETNAM

(as of Dec. 31 of each year)

Year	Troops
1960	900
1961	3,200
1962	11,300
1963	16,300
1964	23,300
1965	184,300
1966	385,300
1967	485,600
1968	536,100
1969	475,200
1970	334,600
1971	156,800
1972	24,200

Source: U.S. Department of Defense.

U.S. troops wade through marshland during an operation on South Vietnam's Mekong Delta. Although the United States conducted thousands of air strikes over North Vietnam and committed a half million troops to the South, it failed to win the advantage. North Vietnamese regulars and Vietcong guerrillas were better able to use the jungle terrain to advantage than their American adversaries. ❖

communist victory. American bombing of the North proved ineffective. The rural, undeveloped nature of the North Vietnamese economy meant there were few industrial targets; a political refusal to bomb the main port of Haiphong allowed Soviet and Chinese arms to flow freely into the country. Nor were the efforts to destroy supply lines any more successful. American planes pounded the Ho Chi Minh Trail that ran down through Laos and Cambodia, but the North Vietnamese used the jungle canopy effectively to hide their shipments and their massive efforts to repair damaged roads and bridges. In fact, the American air attacks, with their inadvertent civilian casualties, gave North Vietnam a powerful propaganda weapon, which it used to sway world opinion against the United States.

The war in the South went no better. Despite the steady increase in American ground forces, from 184,000 in late 1965 to more than 500,000 by early 1968, the Vietcong still controlled much of the countryside. The search-and-destroy tactics employed by the American commander, General William Westmoreland, proved ill-suited to the situation. The

A North Vietnamese truck driver sleeps in a hammock during the day, resting before resuming his nighttime duties on the Ho Chi Minh Trail. The trail, the main supply route for the Vietcong, was a principal target for American bombers. ❖

Vietcong, aided by North Vietnamese regulars, were waging a war of insurgency, avoiding fixed positions and striking from ambush. In a vain effort to destroy the enemy, Westmoreland used superior American firepower wantonly, devastating the countryside, causing many civilian casualties, and driving the peasantry into the arms of the guerrillas. Inevitably, these tactics led to the slaughter of innocent civilians, most notably at the hamlet of My Lai. In March 1968, an American company led by Lieutenant William Calley, Jr., killed more than two hundred unarmed villagers.

The main premise of Westmoreland's strategy was to wage a war of attrition that would finally reach a "crossover point" when communist losses each month would be greater than the number of new troops they could recruit. He hoped to lure the Vietcong and the North Vietnamese regulars into pitched battles in which American firepower would inflict heavy casualties. But soon it was the communists who were deciding where and when the fighting would take place, provoking American attacks in remote areas of South Vietnam that favored the defenders and made Westmoreland pay heavily in American lives for the communist losses. By the end of 1967, the nearly half million American troops Johnson had sent to Vietnam had failed to defeat the enemy. At best, LBJ had only achieved a bloody stalemate that gradually turned the American people against a war they had once eagerly embraced.

YEARS OF TURMOIL

The Vietnam War became the focal point for a growing movement of youthful protest that made the 1960s the most turbulent decade of the twentieth century. Disenchantment with conventional middle-class values, a rapid increase in college enrollments as a result of the post–World War II baby boom, a reaction against the crass materialism of the affluent society—with its endless suburbs and shopping malls—all led American youth to embrace an alternative lifestyle based on the belief that people are "sensitive, searching, poetic, and capable of love." They were ready to create a counterculture.

The agitation of the 1960s was at its height between 1965 and 1968, the years that marked the escalation of the Vietnam War. Disturbances on college campuses reflected growing discontent in other parts of society, from the urban ghettos to the lettuce fields of the Southwest. All who felt disadvantaged and dissatisfied—students, African Americans, Hispanics, Native Americans, women, hippies—took to the streets to give vent to their feelings.

The Student Revolt

The first sign of student rebellion came in the fall of 1964 at the prestigious University of California at Berkeley. A small group of radical students resisted university efforts to deny them a place to solicit volunteers and funds for off-campus causes. Forming the Free Speech movement, they struck back by occupying administration buildings and blocking the arrest of a nonstudent protester. For the next two months, the campus was in turmoil.

In the end, the protesters won the rights of free speech and association that they championed. Their hero was Mario Savio, a student who had eloquently summed up the cause by likening the university to a great machine and telling others, "You've got to put your bodies upon the gears, and upon the wheels, upon the levers, upon all the apparatus, and you've got to make it stop."

The Free Speech movement at Berkeley offered many insights into the causes of campus unrest. It was fueled in part by student suspicion of an older, depression-born generation that viewed affluence as the answer to all problems. Unable to exert much influence on the power structure that directed the consumer society, the students turned on the university. They viewed higher education as the faithful servant of a corporate culture: The university trained hordes of technicians, harbored research laboratories that perfected dreadful weapons, and used IBM punch cards to regiment students. The feeling of powerlessness that underlay the Berkeley riots was best revealed by a protester carrying a sign that read, "I am a UC student. Please don't bend, fold, spindle or mutilate me."

Student protest found its full expression in the explosive growth of the **Students for a Democratic Society (SDS)**. Founded in Port Huron, Michigan, in 1962, the radical organization wanted to rid American society of poverty, racism, and violence. Although the SDS embraced many traditional liberal reforms, such as expanded public housing and comprehensive health insurance, its founders advocated a new approach called participatory democracy. In contrast to both liberalism and old-style socialism, the SDS sought salvation through the individual rather than the group. Personal control of one's life and destiny, not the creation of new bureaucracies, was the hallmark of the New Left.

In the next few years, the SDS grew phenomenally. Spurred on by the Vietnam War and massive campus unrest, the SDS could count more than a hundred thousand followers and was responsible for disruptions at nearly a thousand colleges in 1968. Yet its very emphasis on the individual and its fear of bureaucracy left it leaderless and subject to division and disunity. By 1970, a split between factions, some of which were given to violence, led to its complete demise.

The meteoric career of the SDS symbolized the turbulence of the 1960s. For a brief time, it seemed as though the nation's youth had gone berserk, indulging in a wave of experimentation with drugs, sex, and rock music. Older Americans believed that all the nation's traditional values, from the Puritan work ethic to the family, were under attack. Not all American youth joined in the cultural insurgency; the rebellion was generally limited to children of the upper middle class. But like the flappers of the 1920s, the protesters set the tone for an entire era and left a lasting impression on American society.

Protesting the Vietnam War

The most dramatic aspect of the youthful rebellion came in opposing the Vietnam War. The first student "teach-ins" began at the University of Michigan in March 1965; soon they spread to campuses across the nation. More than twenty thousand protesters, under SDS auspices, gathered in Washington in April to listen to entertainers Joan Baez and Judy Collins sing anti-war songs. "End the War in Vietnam Now, Stop the Killing" read the signs.

One of the great ironies of the Vietnam War was the system of student draft deferments, which enabled most of those enrolled in college to avoid military service. As a result, the children of the well-to-do, who were more likely to attend college, were able to escape the draft. One survey revealed that men from disadvantaged families, including a disproportionately large number of African and Hispanic Americans, were twice as likely to be drafted and engage in combat in Vietnam as those from more privileged backgrounds. Consequently, a sense of guilt led many college activists who were safe from Vietnam because of their student status to take the lead in denouncing an unjust war.

As the fighting in Southeast Asia intensified in 1966 and 1967, the protests grew larger and the slogans more extreme. "Hey, Hey, LBJ, how many kids did you kill today?" chanted students as they proclaimed, "Hell, no, we won't go!" At the Pentagon in October 1967, more than a hundred thousand demonstrators—mainly male students but housewives, teachers, and young professionals as well—confronted a cordon of

Antiwar protesters came face-to-face with military police in the October 1967 March on the Pentagon. Leaders of the march announced that the demonstration marked the end of peaceful protest against the war and the beginning of a new stage of "active resistance." Borrowing techniques from the civil rights movement, some of the demonstrators staged a sit-down in the Pentagon parking lot. ❖

❖ A Look at the Past ❖

Army Fatigue Jacket

Gray flannel suits with conservative ties and dresses with tightly fitted bodices represented the standard uniform during the years of 1950s conformity. By the late 1960s, American youth had cast aside those conservative clothes and instead wore tie-dyed shirts, jeans, and clothes made from Indian print fabrics. Many young people, especially anti-war protesters, also wore military surplus clothing such as this army fatigue jacket. Why do you think civilians protesting the Vietnam War would adopt military attire? Can you think of other examples of clothing used for political or social protest?

hundred colleges, from Cheyney State in Pennsylvania to Northwestern in Illinois.

The students failed to stop the war, but they did succeed in gaining a voice in their education. University administrations allowed undergraduates to sit on faculty curriculum-planning committees and gave up their once rigid control of dormitory and social life. But the students' greatest impact lay outside politics and the campus. They spawned a cultural uprising that transformed the manners and morals of America.

The Cultural Revolution

In contrast to the elitist political revolt of the SDS, the cultural rebellion by youth in the 1960s was pervasive. Led by college students, young people challenged the prevailing adult values in clothing, hairstyles, sexual conduct, work habits, and music. Blue jeans and love beads took the place of business suits and wristwatches; long hair and unkempt beards for men, bare feet and bralessness for women became a new uniform of protest. Families gave way to communes for the "flower children" of the 1960s.

Music became the touchstone of the new departure. Folksingers such as Joan Baez and Bob Dylan, popular for their songs of social protest in the mid-1960s, gave way first to rock groups such as the Beatles, whose lyrics were often suggestive of drug use, and then to "acid rock" as symbolized by the Grateful Dead. The climactic event of the decade came at the Woodstock concert at Bethel in upstate New York when 400,000 young people indulged in a three-day festival of rock music, drug experimentation, and public sexual activity.

Former Harvard psychology professor Timothy Leary encouraged youth to join him in trying out the drug scene. Millions accepted his invitation to "tune in, turn on, drop out" literally, as they experimented with marijuana and with LSD, a new and dangerous chemical hallucinogen. The ultimate expression of insurgency was the Yippie movement, led by Jerry Rubin and Abbie Hoffman. Shrewd buffoons who mocked the consumer culture, they delighted in capitalizing on the mood of social protest to win attention. Once, when testifying before a congressional committee investigating internal subversion, Rubin dressed as a Revolutionary War soldier; Hoffman appeared in the gallery of the New York Stock Exchange in 1967, raining money down on the cheering brokers below.

"Black Power"

The civil rights movement, which had spawned the mood of protest in the 1960s, fell on hard times later

military policemen guarding the heart of the nation's war machine.

The climax came in the spring of 1968. Driven by both opposition to the war and concern for social justice, the SDS and African American radicals at Columbia University joined forces in April. They seized five buildings, effectively paralyzing one of the country's leading colleges. After eight days of tension, the New York City police regained control. The brutal repression quickened the pace of protest elsewhere. Students held sit-ins and marches at more than one

WOODSTOCK MUSIC & ART FAIR
presents
AN AQUARIAN EXPOSITION
in
WHITE LAKE, N.Y.*

3 DAYS of PEACE & MUSIC

WITH

Joan Baez	Keef Hartley	The Band
Arlo Guthrie	Canned Heat	Jeff Beck Group
Tim Hardin	Creedence Clearwater	Blood, Sweat and Tears
Richie Havens	Grateful Dead	Joe Cocker
Incredible String Band	Janis Joplin	Crosby, Stills and Nash
Ravi Shankar	Jefferson Airplane	Jimi Hendrix
Sly And The Family Stone	Mountain	Iron Butterfly
Bert Sommer	Quill	Ten Years After
Sweetwater	Santana	Johnny Winter
	The Who	

FRI.   **SAT.**   **SUN.**
AUG. 15   **AUG. 16**   **AUG. 17**

All programs subject to change without notice
*White Lake, Town of Bethel, Sullivan County, N.Y.

Woodstock Brochure

The dove and guitar on this brochure for the 1969 Woodstock Music Festival graphically present Woodstock's purpose: peaceful, joyful coexistence. More than 400,000 revelers ignored bad weather and poor conditions to listen to folk and rock music. The Age of Aquarius, when peace and harmony would triumph, had seemingly arrived. How do you explain the contradiction between the call for peace and harmony and the growing violence of the 1960s?

in the decade. The legislative triumphs of 1964 and 1965 were relatively easy victories over southern bigotry; now the movement faced the far more complex problem of achieving economic equality in the cities of the North, where more than half of the nation's African Americans lived in poverty. The civil rights movement had raised the expectations of urban African Americans for improvement; frustration mounted as they failed to experience any significant economic gain.

The first sign of trouble came in the summer of 1964, when African American teenagers in Harlem and Rochester, New York, rioted. The next summer, a massive outburst of rage and destruction swept over the Watts area of Los Angeles as the inhabitants burned buildings and looted stores. Riots in the summer of 1966 were less destructive, but in 1967 the worst ones yet took place in Newark and in Detroit, where forty-three were killed and thousands were injured. The mobs attacked the shops and stores, expressing a burning grievance against a consumer society from which they were excluded by their poverty.

The civil rights coalition fell apart, a victim of both its legislative success and economic failure. Black militants took over the leadership of the Student Nonviolent Coordinating Committee (SNCC); they disdained white help and even reversed Martin Luther King's insistence on nonviolence. The SNCC's new leader, Stokely Carmichael, told blacks they should seize power in those parts of the South where they outnumbered whites. "I am not going to beg the white man for anything I deserve," he said, "I'm going to take it." Soon his calls for "black power" became a rallying cry for more militant blacks who advocated the need for African Americans to form "our own institutions, credit unions, co-ops, political parties" and even write "our own history."

Others went further than calls for ethnic separation. H. Rap Brown, who replaced Carmichael as the leader of the SNCC in 1967, told an African American crowd in Cambridge, Maryland, to "get your guns" and "burn this town down"; Huey Newton, one of the founders of the militant Black Panther party, proclaimed, "We make the statement, quoting from Chairman Mao, that Political Power comes through the Barrel of a Gun."

King suffered the most from this extremism. His denunciation of the Vietnam War cost him the support of the Johnson administration and alienated him from the more conservative civil rights groups such as the NAACP and the Urban League. He finally seized on poverty as the proper enemy for attack, but before he could lead his Poor People's March on Washington in 1968, he was assassinated in Memphis in early April.

Both blacks and whites realized the nation had lost its most eloquent voice for racial harmony. His tragic death elevated King to the status of a martyr, but it also led to one last outbreak of urban violence. African Americans exploded in angry riots in 125 cities across the nation; the worst rioting took place in

Washington, D.C., where buildings were set on fire within a few blocks of the White House. "It was as if the city were being abandoned to an invading army," wrote a British journalist. "Clouds of smoke hung over the Potomac, evoking memories of the London blitz."

Yet there was a positive side to the emotions engendered by black nationalism. Leaders urged African Americans to take pride in their ethnic heritage, to embrace their blackness as a positive value. African Americans began to wear Afro hairstyles and dress in dashikis, stressing their African roots. Students began to demand new black studies programs in the colleges; the word *Negro*—identified with white supremacy of the past—virtually disappeared from usage overnight, replaced by the favored *Afro-American* or *black*. Singer James Brown best expressed the sense of racial identity: "Say It Loud—I'm Black and I'm Proud."

Ethnic Nationalism

Other groups quickly emulated the African American phenomenon. Native Americans decried the callous use of their identity as football mascots; in response, universities such as Stanford changed their symbols. Puerto Ricans demanded their history be included in school and college texts. Polish, Italian, and Czech

In March 1966, César Chávez, shown here talking with workers, led striking grape pickers on a 250-mile march from Delano, California, to the state capital at Sacramento to dramatize the plight of the migrant farmworkers. With the slogan "God is beside you on the picket line," the march took on the character of a religious pilgrimage. ❖

groups insisted on respect for their nationalities. Congress acknowledged these demands with passage of the Ethnic Heritage Studies Act of 1972. Instead of trying to melt all groups down into a standard American type, Congress now gave what one sponsor of the measure called "official recognition to ethnicity as a positive constructive force in our society today."

Mexican Americans were in the forefront of the ethnic groups that became active in the 1970s. The primary impulse came from the efforts of César Chávez to organize the poorly paid grape pickers and lettuce workers in California into the National Farm Workers Association (NFWA). Chávez appealed to ethnic nationalism in mobilizing Mexican American field hands to strike against grape growers in the San Joaquin Valley in 1965. A national boycott of grapes by Mexican Americans and their sympathizers among the young people of the counterculture led to a series of hard-fought victories over the growers. The five-year struggle resulted in a union victory in 1970, but at an enormous cost—95 percent of the farmworkers involved had lost their homes and their cars. Nevertheless, Chávez succeeded in raising the hourly wage of farmworkers in California to $3.53 by 1977 (it had been $1.20 in 1965).

Chávez's efforts helped spark an outburst of ethnic consciousness among Mexican Americans that swept through the urban barrios of the Southwest. Mexican American leaders campaigned for bilingual programs and improved educational opportunities. Young activists began to call themselves Chicanos, which had previously been a derogatory term, and to take pride in their cultural heritage; in 1968, they succeeded in establishing the first Mexican American studies program at California State College at Los Angeles. Campus leaders called for reform, urging high school students to insist on improvements. Heeding such appeals, nearly ten thousand students at East Los Angeles high schools walked out of class in March 1968. These walkouts sparked similar movements in San Antonio, Texas, and Phoenix, Arizona, and led to the introduction of bilingual programs in grade schools and the hiring of more Chicano teachers at all levels.

Women's Liberation

Active as they were in the civil rights and antiwar movements, women soon learned that the male leaders of these causes were little different from corporate executives—they expected women to fix the food and type the communiqués while the men made the decisions. Understandably, women soon realized that they could only achieve respect and equality by mounting their own protest.

Betty Friedan poses with a copy of her groundbreaking book, The Feminine Mystique. *In the work, Friedan castigated advertisers, educators, and others for promoting what she labeled the feminine mystique—the idea that women could find fulfillment only in their roles as wives and mothers. Friedan helped spark the modern feminist movement, which had its roots in the nineteenth-century women's rights movement and built on the efforts of earlier activists such as Susan B. Anthony, Lucretia Mott, and Elizabeth Cady Stanton.* ❖

In some ways, the position of women in American society was worse in the 1960s than it had been in the 1920s. After forty years, a lower percentage of women were enrolled in the nation's colleges and professional schools. Women were still relegated to stereotyped occupations such as nursing and teaching; there were few female lawyers and even fewer women doctors. And gender roles, as portrayed on television commercials, continued to call for the husband to be the breadwinner and the wife to be the homemaker.

Betty Friedan was one of the first to seize on the sense of grievance and discrimination that developed among white middle-class women in the 1960s. The beginning of the effort to raise women's consciousness was her 1963 book, *The Feminine Mystique.* Calling the American home "a comfortable concentration camp," she attacked the prevailing view that women were completely contented with their housekeeping and child-rearing tasks, claiming that housewives had no self-esteem and no sense of identity. "I'm a server of food and putter on of pants and a bedmaker," a mother of four told Friedan, "somebody who can be called on when you want something. But who am I?"

The 1964 Civil Rights Act helped women attack economic inequality head-on by making it illegal to discriminate in employment on the basis of gender. Women filed suit for equal wages, demanded that companies provide day care for their infants and preschool children, and entered politics to lobby against laws that—in the guise of protection of a weaker gender—were unfair to women. As the women's liberation movement grew, its advocates began to attack laws banning abortion and waged a campaign to toughen the enforcement of rape laws.

The women's movement met with many of the same obstacles as other protest groups in the 1960s. The moderate leadership of the **National Organization for Women (NOW),** founded by Betty Friedan in 1966, soon was challenged by those with more extreme views. Ti-Grace Atkinson and Susan Brownmiller attacked revered institutions—the family and the home—and denounced sexual intercourse with men, calling it a method of male domination. Many women were repelled by the harsh rhetoric of the extremists and expressed satisfaction with their lives. But despite these disagreements, most women supported the effort to achieve equal status with men, and in 1972, Congress responded by voting to send the Equal Rights Amendment to the state legislatures for ratification.

THE RETURN OF RICHARD NIXON

The turmoil of the 1960s reached a crescendo in 1968 as the American people responded to the two dominant events of the decade—the war in Vietnam and the cultural insurgency at home. In an election marked by a series of bizarre events, including riots and an assassination, Richard Nixon staged a remarkable comeback to win the post denied him in 1960.

Vietnam Undermines Lyndon Johnson

A controversial Vietcong offensive in early 1968 proved to be the decisive event in breaking the stalemate in Vietnam and driving Lyndon Johnson from office. Using deceptive tactics, the North Vietnamese began a prolonged siege of an American marine base at Khe Sanh, deep in the northern interior. Fearing another Dien Bien Phu, Westmoreland rushed in reinforcements, sending more than 40 percent of all American infantry and armor battalions into the two northernmost provinces of South Vietnam.

The Vietcong then used the traditional lull in the fighting at Tet, the lunar New Year, to launch a surprise attack in the heavily populated cities. Beginning on January 30, 1968, the Vietcong struck at thirty-six of the forty-four provincial capitals. The most daring raid came at the American embassy compound in Saigon. Although the guerrillas were unable to penetrate the embassy proper, for six hours television cameras caught the dramatic battle that ensued in the courtyard before military police finally overcame the attackers.

Although caught off guard, American and South Vietnamese forces succeeded in repulsing the **Tet offensive** quickly everywhere except in Hue, the old imperial capital, which was retaken only after three weeks of heavy fighting that left this beautiful city, in the words of one observer, "a shattered, stinking hulk, its streets choked with rubble and rotting bodies."

Tet proved to be the turning point of the Vietnam War. Although the communists failed to win control of the cities and suffered heavy losses, they still held on to most of the rural areas and had scored an impressive political victory. For months, President Johnson had been telling the American people the war was almost over and victory was in sight; suddenly it appeared to be nearly lost. CBS-TV newscaster Walter Cronkite took a quick trip to Saigon to find out what had happened. Horrified at what he saw, he exclaimed to his guides, "What the hell is going on? I thought we were winning the war." He returned home to tell the American people, "It seems now more certain than ever that the bloody experience of Vietnam is to end in a stalemate."

President Johnson reluctantly came to the same conclusion after the Joint Chiefs of Staff requested an additional 205,000 troops to achieve victory in Vietnam following the Tet offensive. He began to listen to his new secretary of defense, Clark Clifford, who had replaced Robert McNamara in January 1968. In mid-March, after receiving advice from the "wise men," a group of experienced cold warriors that included such illustrious figures as Dean Acheson and Omar Bradley, the president decided to limit the bombing of North Vietnam in an effort to open up peace negotiations with Hanoi. In a speech to the nation on Sunday evening, March 31, 1968, Johnson outlined his plans for a new effort at ending the war peacefully and then concluded by saying, as proof of his sincerity, "I shall not seek, and I will not accept, the nomination of my party for another term as your president."

In the fourteen years since the siege of Dien Bien Phu, American policy had gone full cycle in Vietnam. Even though Eisenhower had decided against using force to rescue the French, his commitment to the Diem regime in Saigon had led eventually to American military involvement on a massive scale. Three years of inconclusive fighting and a steadily mounting loss of American lives had disillusioned the American people and finally cost Lyndon Johnson the presidency. And the full price the nation would have to pay for its folly in Southeast Asia was still unknown—the Vietnam experience would continue to cast a shadow over American life for years to come.

The Democrats Divide

Lyndon Johnson's withdrawal from the presidential race after the Tet offensive set the tone for the 1968 election. LBJ's decision had come in response to political as well as military realities. By 1966, the antiwar movement had spread from the college campuses to Capitol Hill. Chairman J. William Fulbright gave the protests a new respectability when his Senate Foreign Relations Committee held probing hearings on the war, broadcast on television to the entire country. Johnson began to feel like a prisoner in the White House, since in his infrequent public appearances he was hounded by larger and larger groups of antiwar demonstrators, whose taunts and jeers wounded him.

The essentially leaderless protest against the war had taken on a new quality on January 3, 1968, when Senator Eugene McCarthy, a Democrat from Minnesota, announced he would challenge LBJ for the party's presidential nomination. Intellectual, cool, aloof, and almost arrogant, McCarthy raised the banner of idealism, telling audiences, "Whatever is morally necessary must be made politically possible." College students flocked to his campaign, shaving their beards and cutting their hair to be "clean for Gene." In the New Hampshire primary in early March, the nation's earliest political test, McCarthy shocked the political experts by coming within a few thousand votes of defeating President Johnson.

McCarthy's strong showing in New Hampshire led Robert Kennedy, who had been weighing the risks in challenging Johnson, to enter the presidential race. Elected senator from New York in 1964, Bobby Kennedy had become an effective voice for the disadvantaged, as well as an increasingly severe critic of the Vietnam War. Unlike McCarthy, whose appeal was largely limited to upper-middle-class whites and college students, Kennedy attracted strong support among blue-collar workers, African Americans,

President Johnson, alone in the Cabinet room, rests his head on his hand as he listens to a tape from his son-in-law Marine Captain Charles Robb recounting his combat experiences in Vietnam. Johnson stunned the nation with his announcement on March 31, 1968, that he would not seek reelection. Poor results in the March primaries and public opinion polls indicated that support for LBJ was eroding. ❖

Chicanos, and other minorities who formed the nucleus of the continuing New Deal coalition.

Lyndon Johnson's dramatic withdrawal caused an uproar in the Democratic party. With Johnson's tacit backing and strong support from party regulars and organized labor, Vice President Hubert H. Humphrey immediately declared his candidacy. Humphrey, a classic Cold War liberal who had worked equally hard for social reform at home and American expansion abroad, was totally unacceptable to the antiwar movement. Accordingly, he decided to avoid the primaries and work for the nomination within the framework of the party.

Kennedy and McCarthy, the two antiwar candidates, were thus left to compete in the spring primaries, requiring agonizing choices among those who desired change. Kennedy won everywhere except in Oregon, but his narrow victory in California ended in tragedy when a Palestinian immigrant, Sirhan Sirhan, assassinated him in a Los Angeles hotel.

With his strongest opponent struck down, Hubert Humphrey had little difficulty at the Chicago convention. Backed by that city's political boss, Mayor Richard Daley, the vice president relied on party leaders to defeat an antiwar resolution and win the nomination on the first ballot by a margin of more than two to one.

Humphrey's triumph was marred by violence outside the heavily guarded convention hall. Radical groups had urged their members to come to Chicago to agitate; the turnout was relatively small but included many who were ready to provoke the authorities in their despair over the convention's outcome. Epithets and cries of "pigs" brought on a savage response from Daley's police. "The cops had one thing on their mind," commented journalist Jimmy

While party factions quarreled inside the convention hall at the 1968 Democratic National Convention in Chicago, in the streets outside police clashed violently with antiwar demonstrators, who had been denied permits to march. Here, a Chicago policeman clubs a protester in Grant Park, the site of the only legal rally during the convention. ❖

Breslin. "Club and then gas, club and then gas, club and then gas."

The bitter fumes of tear gas hung in the streets for days afterward; the battered heads and bodies of demonstrators and innocent bystanders alike flooded the city's hospital emergency rooms. What an official investigation later termed a "police riot" marred Humphrey's nomination and made a sad mockery out of his call for "the politics of joy." The Democratic party itself had become the next victim of the Vietnam War.

The Republican Resurgence

The primary beneficiary of the Democratic debacle was Richard Nixon. Written off as politically dead after his unsuccessful race for governor of California in 1962, Nixon had slowly rebuilt his place within the party by working loyally for Barry Goldwater in 1964 and for GOP congressional candidates two years later. Positioning himself squarely in the middle, he quickly became the front-runner for the Republican nomina-

tion. At the GOP convention in Miami Beach, Nixon won an easy first-ballot nomination and chose Maryland governor Spiro Agnew as his running mate. Agnew, little known on the national scene, had won the support of conservatives by taking a strong stand against African American rioters.

In the fall campaign, Nixon opened up a wide lead by avoiding controversy and reaping the benefit of discontent with the Vietnam War. He played the peace issue shrewdly, appearing to advocate an end to the conflict without ever taking a definite stand. The United States should "end the war and win the peace," he declared, hinting he had a secret formula for peace but never revealing what it was. Above all, he chose the role of reconciler for a nation torn by emotion, a leader who promised to bring a divided country together again.

Humphrey, in contrast, found himself hounded by antiwar demonstrators who heckled him constantly. He walked a tightwire, desperate for the continued support of President Johnson but handicapped by LBJ's stubborn refusal to end all bombing of North Vietnam. Only when he broke with Johnson in late September by announcing that if elected he would "stop the bombing of North Vietnam as an acceptable risk for peace" did his campaign begin to gain momentum.

Unfortunately for Humphrey, a third-party candidate cut deeply into the normal Democratic majority.

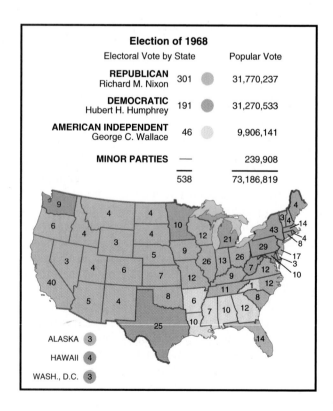

Election of 1968

	Electoral Vote by State		Popular Vote
REPUBLICAN Richard M. Nixon	301		31,770,237
DEMOCRATIC Hubert H. Humphrey	191		31,270,533
AMERICAN INDEPENDENT George C. Wallace	46		9,906,141
MINOR PARTIES	—		239,908
	538		73,186,819

CHRONOLOGY

1961	JFK establishes Peace Corps (March) ❖ U.S.-backed Bay of Pigs invasion crushed by Cubans (April)
1962	Astronaut John H. Glenn, Jr., becomes first American to orbit the earth (February) ❖ President Kennedy forces U.S. Steel to roll back price hike (April) ❖ Cuban missile crisis takes world to brink of nuclear war (October)
1963	United States, Great Britain, and USSR sign Limited Nuclear Test Ban treaty (August) ❖ JFK assassinated; Lyndon B. Johnson sworn in as president (November)
1964	President Johnson declares war on poverty (January) ❖ Congress overwhelmingly passes Gulf of Tonkin Resolution (August) ❖ Johnson wins presidency in landslide (November)
1965	LBJ commits fifty thousand American troops to combat in Vietnam (July) ❖ Congress enacts Medicare and Medicaid (July)
1966	National Organization for Women (NOW) formed
1967	Israel wins Six Day War in Middle East (June) ❖ Riots in Detroit kill forty-three, injure two thousand, leave five thousand homeless (July)
1968	Vietcong launch the offensive (January) ❖ Johnson announces he will not seek reelection (March) ❖ Martin Luther King, Jr., assassinated in Memphis (April) ❖ Robert Kennedy assassinated in Los Angeles (June)

George C. Wallace had first gained national attention as the racist governor of Alabama whose motto was "Segregation now . . . segregation tomorrow . . . segregation forever." In 1964, he had shown surprising strength in Democratic primaries in northern states. By attacking both black leaders and their liberal white allies, Wallace appealed to the sense of powerlessness among the urban working classes. "Liberals, intellectuals, and longhairs have run the country for too long," Wallace told his followers. "When I get to Washington," he promised, "I'll throw all these phonies and their briefcases into the Potomac."

Running on the ticket of the American Independent Party, Wallace was a close third in the September polls, gaining support from more than 20 percent of the electorate. But as the election neared, his following declined. Humphrey continued to gain, especially after Johnson agreed in late October to end all bombing of North Vietnam. By the first week in November, the outcome was too close for the experts to call.

Nixon won the election with the smallest share of the popular vote of any winning candidate since 1916. But he swept a broad band of states from Virginia and the Carolinas through the Midwest to the Pacific for a clear-cut victory in the electoral college. Humphrey held on to the urban Northeast; Wallace took just five states in the Deep South, but his heavy inroads into blue-collar districts in the North shattered the New Deal coalition.

CONCLUSION: THE END OF AN ERA

The election of 1968 was a repudiation of the politics of protest and the cultural insurgency of the mid-1960s. The combined popular vote for Nixon and Wallace, 56.5 percent of the electorate, signified there was a silent majority that was fed up with violence and confrontation. A growing concern over psychedelic drugs, rock music, long hair, and sexual permissiveness had offset the usual Democratic advantage on economic issues and led to the election of a Republican president.

Richard Nixon's victory marked the end of an era with the passing of two concepts that had guided American life since the 1930s. First, the liberal reform impulse, which reached its zenith with the Great Society legislation in 1965, had clearly run its course. Civil rights, Medicare, and federal aid to education would continue in place, but Nixon's election signaled a strong reaction against the growth of federal power. At the same time, the Vietnam fiasco spelled the end of activist foreign policy that had begun with American entry into World War II. Containment, so successful in protecting western Europe against the Soviet threat, had proved a disastrous failure when applied on a global scale. The last three decades of the twentieth century would witness a struggle to replace outmoded liberal internationalism with new policies at home and abroad.

RECOMMENDED READING

The best general account of the 1960s is Jim F. Heath, *Decade of Disillusionment* (1975), which stresses the continuity in policy between the Kennedy and Johnson administrations. Arthur M. Schlesinger, Jr., *A Thousand Days* (1965) is the classic history of the Kennedy administration; for a more balanced view, see Richard Reeves, *President Kennedy* (1993). The best study of Kennedy's foreign policy is Michael R. Beschloss, *The Crisis Years: Kennedy and*

Khrushchev, 1960–1963 (1991); for the Cuban missile crisis, consult Graham Allison and Philip Zelikow, *Essence of Decision,* 2nd ed. (1999).

Victor S. Navasky offers a critical view of Robert Kennedy as attorney general in *Kennedy Justice* (1971). The best overview of civil rights developments in the 1960s is Hugh Davis Graham, *The Civil Rights Era, 1960–1972* (1990).

Robert Dallek offers a balanced view of Johnson's presidential years in *Flawed Giant* (1998). The best one-volume biography of Lyndon Johnson is Irwin Unger and Debi Unger, *LBJ* (1999); John A. Andrew III provides a concise account of LBJ's domestic program in *Lyndon Johnson and the Great Society* (1998). For the impact of the l965 immigration legislation, see Hugh Davis Graham, *Collision Course* (2002). For LBJ's foreign policy, see H. W. Brands, *The Wages of Globalism* (1995). The best introduction to the Vietnam War is the balanced survey by George Herring,

America's Longest War, 4th ed. (2002). For contrasting views of Johnson's responsibility for the Vietnam conflict, see Fredrik Logevall, *Choosing War* (1999), highly critical, and Lloyd Gardner, *Pay Any Price* (1995), more understanding.

The most comprehensive account of the student protests is Terry Anderson, *The Movement and the Sixties* (1995), but see also Todd Gitlin, *The Sixties* (1987), more sympathetic to the youthful protesters; W. J. Rorabaugh, *Berkeley at War* (1989); and Rhodri Jeffrey-Jones, *Peace Now!* (1999).

Garry Wills provides the most revealing portrait of Richard Nixon's character and prepresidential career in *Nixon Agonistes* (1970). The best account of the 1968 election is Lewis L. Gould, *1968: The Election That Changed America* (1993).

For a list of additional titles related to this chapter's topics, please see http://www.ablongman.com/divine.

SUGGESTED WEB SITES

The Avalon Project: The Cuban Missile Crisis

http://www.yale.edu/lawweb/avalon/diplomacy/forrel/cuba/cubamenu.htm
Part of the foreign relations series of the Avalon Project at Yale Law School, this site includes a collection of on-line documents pertaining to the Cuban Missile Crisis and its aftermath.

John Fitzgerald Kennedy

http://www.ipl.org/ref/POTUS/jfkennedy.html
This site contains basic factual data about Kennedy's election and presidency, speeches, and on-line biographies.

The Kennedy Assassination

http://mcadams.posc.mu.edu/home.htm
This well-organized site has images, essays, and photos on the assassination.

Lyndon B. Johnson

http://www.ipl.org/ref/POTUS/lbjohnson.html
This page contains basic factual data about his election and presidency, speeches, and on-line biographies.

Lyndon B. Johnson Library and Museum

http://www.lbjlib.utexas.edu/
This presidential library contains images and on-line exhibits.

National Aeronautics and Space Administration

http://www.hq.nasa.gov/office/pao/History/histsub.htm
NASA's Office of Policy and Plans History Office maintains this site about NASA and its history.

Investigating the Vietnam War

http://www.spartacus.schoolnet.co.uk/vietintro.htm
This site from Spartacus Educational Publishing, U.K., has an excellent list of annotated links to the best Vietnam-related sites.

Vietnam War Bibliography

http://hubcap.clemson.edu/~eemoise/bibliography.html
Edwin Moise of Clemson University maintains this extensive bibliography of print works about Vietnam and the Vietnam War.

Vietnam On-line

http://www.pbs.org/wgbh/pages/amex/vietnam/index.html
From PBS and the American Experience, this site contains a detailed, interactive timeline of the war, interpretive essays, and autobiographical reflections.

My Lai Courts-Martial (1970)

http://www.law.umkc.edu/faculty/projects/ftrials/mylai/mylai.htm
This site contains images, chronology, court and official documents maintained by Dr. Doug Linder at University of Missouri–Kansas City Law School.

JFK Assassination Web Page

http://ourworld.compuserve.com/homepages/MGriffith_2/jfk.htm
This is a personal but thorough page that is a guide to the best Internet resources for the assassination.

Martin Luther King, Jr. Papers Project

http://www.stanford.edu/group/King/
This site at Stanford University has links and selected digital documents by and concerning Martin Luther King, Jr.

National Civil Rights Museum

http://www.mecca.org/~crights/nc2.html
This site allows a virtual tour of the museum with its interpretive exhibits.

The Digger Archives

http://www.diggers.org/

This site provides information about The San Francisco Diggers, which became one of the legendary groups in the Haight-Ashbury from 1966 to 1968.

Free Speech Movement: Student Protest–U.C. Berkeley, 1964–65

http://www.lib.berkeley.edu/BANC/FSM/

The Bancroft Library at U.C. Berkeley houses this exhibit with oral histories, a chronology, and documents.

Voices of the Civil Rights Era

http://www.webcorp.com/civilrights/index.htm

Webcorp provides audio clips from prominent figures of the Civil Rights era including Martin Luther King, Jr., and Malcolm X.

Martin Luther King, Jr.

http://www.seattletimes.com/mlk/

This site from the *Seattle Times* has several articles about King and the civil rights movement.

The Sixties Project

http://lists.village.virginia.edu/sixties/

This University of Virginia site has extensive exhibits, documents, and personal narratives from the 1960s.

Civil Rights Oral History Bibliography

http://www-dept.usm.edu/~mcrohb/

This University of Southern Mississippi site includes complete transcripts of the selected oral resources.

1969 Woodstock Festival and Concert

http://www.woodstock69.com/index.htm

This site provides pictures and lists of songs from the famous rock festival.

United States v. Cecil Price et al. (The "Mississippi Burning" Trial), 1967

http://www.law.umkc.edu/faculty/projects/ftrials/price&bowers/price&bowers.htm

This site contains images, chronology, and court and official documents maintained by Dr. Doug Linder at University of Missouri–Kansas City Law School.

The Arab oil embargo of 1973 threatened Americans' love affair with the automobile. As gas prices rose and supplies dwindled, service stations cut their hours of operation and restricted the amount of gasoline customers could buy. Long lines of cars circled around gas stations as motorists waited to buy fuel for their cars. ❖

A Crisis in Confidence, 1969–1980

The Watergate Break-in

On the evening of June 17, 1972, five men broke into the headquarters of the Democratic National Committee in the Watergate complex. They wore surgical gloves and carried cans of Mace, lock-picking tools, camera equipment, and telephone bugging devices. Busy filming documents and checking on electronic bugs planted two weeks before, the burglars were caught by police after an alert security guard discovered they had carelessly left doors taped open.

The leader of the group, James McCord, a former CIA employee, was working for CREEP (the Committee to Re-Elect the President), and police quickly found the telephone number of White House aide E. Howard Hunt in his address book. Despite this obvious tie to the Nixon administration, presidential press secretary Ron Ziegler denied any White House involvement in the Watergate break-in, dismissing it as "a third-rate burglary attempt."

In fact, this criminal act was a direct outgrowth of the paranoia that characterized the Nixon presidency. Aware that he had won office by a very narrow margin in 1968, Nixon was determined to do everything possible to ensure his reelection in 1972. Concerned about leaks from the White House, he authorized wiretaps on the telephones of both reporters and key aides. In 1971, Nixon's paranoia intensified after Daniel Ellsberg, a former Defense Department official, leaked the **Pentagon Papers,** a compilation of secret documents on the Vietnam War, to the *New York Times.* The president ordered the Justice Department to ask the Supreme Court to halt the publication of papers the White House claimed "prejudiced the defense interests of the United States." But Nixon was too late. By the time the Court heard the case, Ellsberg had leaked the Pentagon Papers to the *Washington Post,* which, along with some twenty other newspapers, began publishing various portions of the papers. On June 30, the Supreme Court ruled 6 to 3 to dismiss the government's case, upholding the constitutional right to freedom of the press.

After this setback, Nixon took drastic measures to plug any further leaks of secret documents. His aides created a self-styled "plumbers" unit within the White House directed by G. Gordon Liddy, a former FBI agent, and E. Howard Hunt, a veteran of the CIA. Charged with preserving secrecy and discrediting those who spoke to the press, Hunt and Liddy set out to embarrass Daniel Ellsberg, going so far as to break into his psychiatrist's office in search of damning information.

Convinced that people throughout society were working for his defeat in 1972, Nixon ordered aides John Dean and Charles Colson to prepare an "enemies list." They eventually compiled a roster of several hundred prominent citizens, ranging from movie stars such as Jane Fonda and Paul Newman to journalists and educators such as columnist James Reston and Kingman Brewster, president of Yale University, as well as twelve African American congressmen. The plan was to direct the IRS and other government agencies to target these "enemies" for audits and investigations,

OUTLINE

Nixon in Power

The Crisis of Democracy

Energy and the Economy

Private Lives—Public Issues

Politics after Watergate

From Détente to Renewed Cold War

Conclusion: A Failed Presidency

FEATURE ESSAY

Three Mile Island and Chernobyl: The Promise and Peril of Nuclear Power

LAW AND SOCIETY

Roe v. *Wade:* The Struggle over Women's Reproductive Rights

893

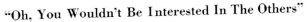

Alarmed by publication of the Pentagon Papers, Nixon and his administration sought various ways to prevent sensitive information about government activities and individuals from reaching the press and the public. (From Herblock's State of the Union [Simon & Schuster, 1972].) ❖

or, as John Dean put it, to use "the available federal machinery to screw our political enemies." Operating under a siege mentality, the Nixon White House was prepared to do anything necessary to defeat its opponents, who were thought to include the media, the intellectual community, and virtually all minority groups.

The president's greatest concern was guaranteeing his reelection. He appointed Attorney General John Mitchell to head CREEP and gave him access to extensive funds and the use of men like Liddy and Hunt. Specialists in political "dirty tricks" harassed Democratic contenders, while Liddy developed an elaborate plan to disrupt the Democratic convention in Miami and to spy on party activities. The bungled Watergate break-in, directed by Liddy and Hunt, was thus the culmination of abuses of power that grew directly out of Nixon's personal insecurity.

The president probably did not have any advance knowledge of the break-in, but he committed a criminal act by authorizing a far-reaching cover-up. On June 23, he ordered his aides to instruct the FBI to defer to the CIA in regard to the Watergate burglary, invoking nonexistent national security concerns to block an investigation that might expose White House in-

volvement. Determined to contain the damage, Nixon told John Mitchell, "I want you to stonewall it, let them plead the Fifth Amendment, cover-up, or anything else." Putting John Dean in charge, Nixon successfully covered up the Watergate affair while winning reelection in 1972, only to have the whole matter later unravel and drive him from office.

THE WATERGATE BREAK-IN was but the first of a series of shocks in the 1970s that shook the confidence of the American people. At home, a dramatic increase in the price of oil following the October War between Israel and its Arab neighbors had a devastating impact on the American economy. Not only did the price of gasoline at the pump triple, but traditional manufacturing companies, hit hard by foreign competition, began to decline sharply. A second wave of inflation, touched off by the Iranian revolution in 1978, drove interest rates to double-digit levels and eroded consumer purchasing power, ending the decades of post–World War II prosperity that Americans had taken for granted.

Events abroad proved equally threatening. Despite Nixon's efforts at détente, the Cold War intensified by the late 1970s with new Soviet thrusts into Africa and

Central Asia, culminating in the invasion of Afghanistan in 1979. The fall of the Shah and rise of a fundamentalist Muslim regime in Iran transformed a former friend into a dangerous enemy. And even closer to home, the Sandinista revolution in Nicaragua caused some to fear that communism would sweep across Central America.

By the end of the decade, the American people were beginning to question the validity of traditional national values and institutions as they tried to cope with these difficult challenges at home and abroad. Fear for the future threatened to replace the nation's historic optimism.

NIXON IN POWER

Before Watergate cast its long shadow over his presidency, Nixon dealt ably with a wide range of issues at home and abroad. While his domestic policies had only limited success, he proved both skillful and effective in the international arena, achieving a significant, though temporary, reduction in Cold War tensions.

The man who took office as the thirty-sixth president of the United States on January 20, 1969, seemed to be a new Nixon. Gone were the fiery rhetoric and the penchant for making enemies. In their place, observers found an air of moderation and restraint. He appeared to have his emotions under firm control, but beneath the surface he remained bitter, hurt, and sensitive to criticism.

An innately shy man, Nixon hoped to enjoy the power of the presidency in splendid solitude. Described by Barry Goldwater as "the most complete loner I've ever known," Nixon assembled a powerful White House staff whose main task was to isolate him from Congress, the press, and even his own cabinet. Loyal subordinates such as H. R. Haldeman and John Ehrlichman took charge of domestic issues, often making decisions without consulting Nixon. Foreign policy was Nixon's great passion, and here he relied heavily on Henry Kissinger, his national security adviser, to formulate policy, leaving Secretary of State William Rogers to keep the State Department bureaucrats busy with minor details.

The Nixon White House soon could be likened to a fortress under siege. Distrusting everyone, from the media to members of his own party, the president sought to rule the nation without help from either Congress or his cabinet. In his quest for privacy, the president cut himself off from the nation and thus sowed the seeds of his downfall.

Reshaping the Great Society

Nixon began his first term on a hopeful note, promising the nation peace and respite from the chaos of the 1960s. Rejecting the divisions that had split Americans apart, he promised in his inaugural address to "bring us together." "We cannot learn from one another until we stop shouting at one another—until we speak quietly enough so that our words can be heard as well as our voices."

Nixon's moderation promised a return to the politics of accommodation that had characterized the Eisenhower era. Faced with a Democratic Congress, Nixon, like Ike, appeared ready to accept the main outlines of the welfare state. Instead of any massive overthrow of the Great Society, he focused on making the federal bureaucracy function more efficiently.

Nixon was successful in shifting responsibility for social problems from Washington to state and local authorities. He developed the concept of revenue sharing, by which federal funds would be dispersed to state, county, and city agencies to meet local needs. In 1972, Congress finally approved a measure to share $30.1 billion with local governments over a five-year period. An accompanying ceiling of $2.5 billion a year on federal welfare payments, however, meant that much of the revenue-sharing payments had to be allocated by cities and states to programs previously paid for by the federal government.

In the area of civil rights, Nixon made a shrewd political move. Action by Congress and the outgoing Johnson administration had ensured that massive desegregation of southern schools, delayed for more than a decade by legal action, would finally begin just as Nixon took office. Nixon and his attorney general, John Mitchell, decided to shift the responsibility for this process to the courts. In the summer of 1969, the Justice Department asked a federal judge to delay the integration of thirty-three school districts in Mississippi. The Supreme Court quickly ruled against the Justice Department, declaring that "the obligation of every school district is to terminate dual school systems at once." Thus, in the minds of southern white voters, it was the hated Supreme Court, not Richard Nixon, who had forced them to integrate their schools.

Nixon used similar tactics in his attempt to reshape the Supreme Court along more conservative lines. His appointment of Warren Burger, an experienced federal judge with moderate views, to replace the retiring Earl Warren as chief justice, met with little objection. But liberal Democrats succeeded in blocking the nomination first of Clement Haynesworth of South Carolina and then of G. Harrold Carswell of Florida. Nixon denounced his opponents for insulting "millions of Americans who live in the South" by turning down his two southern nominees. Once again, the president had used the Supreme Court to enhance his political appeal to Southerners.

Nixon finally filled the Court position with Harry Blackmun, a respected moderate from Minnesota, who easily won confirmation. Subsequently, the president appointed Lewis Powell, a distinguished Virginia lawyer, and William Rehnquist, a rigidly conservative Justice Department attorney from Arizona, to the Supreme Court. Surprisingly, the Burger Court, despite its more conservative makeup, did not engage in any massive overturn of the Warren Court's decisions. It continued to uphold the legality of desegregation, ruling in 1971 that busing was a necessary and proper way to achieve integrated schools.

The moderation of the Supreme Court and the legislative record of the Nixon administration indicated that the nation was not yet ready to abandon the reforms adopted in the 1960s. The pace of change slowed down, but the commitment to social justice was still clear.

Nixonomics

The economy posed a more severe test for Richard Nixon. He inherited growing inflation stemming from the Vietnam War. Although Lyndon Johnson finally secured a tax increase from Congress in 1968 which produced a balanced budget in 1969, the heavy expense of the fighting in Vietnam since 1965 had led to massive deficit spending. As a result, in 1968 the cost of living rose 5 percent. Strongly opposed to the idea of federal controls, Nixon at first opted for a reduction in government spending while encouraging the Federal Reserve Board to raise interest rates, thereby slowing the rate of business expansion.

The result was disastrous. Inflation continued, reaching nearly 6 percent by the end of 1970, the highest rate since the Korean War. At the same time, the economy underwent its first major recession since 1958. Unemployment rose to 6 percent by the end of 1970, and business failures jumped alarmingly. The collapse of the Penn Central Railroad was the most spectacular bankruptcy in the nation's history to date. Democrats quickly coined a new word, *Nixonomics,* to describe the disaster.

Conditions seemed to worsen in 1971. Inflation continued unabated, and the nation's balance of trade became negative as imports exceeded exports by a substantial margin, leading to a weakening of the dollar abroad.

In mid-August, Nixon acted boldly to halt the economic decline. Abandoning his earlier resistance to controls, he announced a ninety-day freeze on

"Damndest seesaw I've ever seen"

Economic problems tested President Nixon soon after he took office in 1969. The cost of living rose as the government attempted to pay for the Vietnam War and Great Society programs with massive deficit spending. At the same time, declines in manufacturing and industrialization contributed to rising unemployment. ❖

To cope with the economic problems of increasing inflation and increasing unemployment, in August 1971 Nixon instituted a ninety-day freeze on both wages and prices. But neither Nixon nor his Treasury Secretary John Connally had announced what would constitute Phase Two of the program when the freeze ended in November. ❖

wages and prices to be followed by federally imposed guidelines in both areas. The new secretary of the treasury, Democrat John Connally, carried out a devaluation of the dollar, which, along with a 10 percent surtax on all imports, led to a greatly improved balance of trade. The sudden Nixon economic reversal quickly ended the recession, with industrial production increasing more than over 5 percent in the first quarter of 1972.

Building a Republican Majority

"The Great Nixon Turnaround," as historian Lloyd Gardner termed it, came too late to help the Republicans in the 1970 congressional elections. From the time he took office in 1969, the president was obsessed with the fact that he had received only 43 percent of the popular vote in 1968. The Republicans were still a minority party, and to be reelected in 1972, Nixon would need to win over southern whites and blue-collar workers who had voted for Wallace in 1968.

Attorney General John Mitchell, who had been Nixon's campaign manager in 1968, had devised a southern strategy to help achieve a Republican majority by 1972. The administration's well-publicized objection to school desegregation in the South and the attempt to put Haynesworth and Carswell on the Court were part of this design. Kevin Phillips, one of Mitchell's aides, urged the Nixon administration to direct its appeal to "middle Americans"—southern whites, Catholic ethnic groups, blue-collar workers, and, above all, the new suburbanites of the South and West, the emerging Sunbelt.

Nixon unleashed Vice President Spiro Agnew in an attempt to exploit the social issue in the 1970 election. Blaming all of society's problems—from drug abuse and sexual permissiveness to crime in the streets—on Democratic liberals and their allies in the media, Agnew delivered a series of scathing speeches. He denounced intellectuals as "an effete corps of impudent snobs," branded television commentators as "a tiny and closed fraternity of privileged men," and damned the press in general as "nattering nabobs of negativism."

The Democrats struck back by changing their tactics. Warned by Richard Scammon and Ben Wattenberg in *The Real Majority* (1970) that most voters were not young, black, or poor, Democratic candidates were careful to stress economic issues, blaming the Republicans for both inflation and recession. On social issues, they joined in the chorus against crime, pornography, and drugs.

The outcome was a standoff. Agnew's attacks helped the GOP limit the usual off-year losses in the House to nine seats, while the Republicans gained two

votes in the Senate. But the Democrats did well in state elections and proved once again that economic issues were crucial in American politics. Nixon and the Republicans still did not command a national majority.

In Search of Détente

Richard Nixon gave foreign policy top priority, and he proved surprisingly adept at it. In Kissinger, he had a White House specialist who had devoted his life to the study of diplomacy. A refugee from Nazi Germany, Kissinger had become a professor of government at Harvard, the author of several influential books, and an acknowledged authority on international affairs. Nixon and Kissinger approached foreign policy from a similar realistic perspective. Instead of viewing the Cold War as an ideological struggle for survival with communism, they saw it as a traditional great-power rivalry, one to be managed and controlled rather than to be won.

Kissinger and Nixon had a grand design. Realizing that recent events, especially the Vietnam War and the rapid Soviet arms buildup of the 1960s, had eroded America's position of primacy in the world, they planned a strategic retreat. Russia had great military strength, but its economy was weak and it had a dangerous rival in China. Kissinger planned to use American trade—notably grain and high technology—to induce Soviet cooperation, while at the same time improving U.S. relations with China.

Nixon and Kissinger shrewdly played the China card as their first step toward achieving **détente**—that is, a relaxation of tension—with the Soviet Union. In February 1972, accompanied by a planeload of reporters and television camera crews, Nixon made a triumphal tour of China, meeting with the communist leaders and ending more than two decades of Sino-American hostility. Nixon agreed to establish an American liaison mission in Beijing as a first step toward diplomatic recognition.

The Soviets, who viewed China as a dangerous adversary along a 2000-mile frontier in Asia, responded by agreeing to reach an arms control pact with the United States. The **Strategic Arms Limitation Talks (SALT)** had been under way since 1969. During a visit to Moscow in May 1972, President Nixon signed two vital documents with Soviet leader Leonid Brezhnev. The first limited the two superpowers to two hundred antiballistic missiles (ABMs) apiece; the second froze the number of offensive ballistic missiles for a five-year period. SALT I recognized the existing Soviet lead in missiles, but the American deployment of multiple independently targeted reentry vehicles (MIRVs) ensured a continuing strategic advantage for the United States.

Kissinger's search for détente began with a calculated decision to improve relations with China. In a highly publicized state visit, Nixon and Chinese leaders were photographed sharing banquets and touring the Great Wall of China. ❖

The SALT I agreements were most important as a symbolic first step toward control of the nuclear arms race. They signified that the United States and Russia were trying to achieve a settlement of their differences by peaceful means.

Ending the Vietnam War

Vietnam remained the one foreign policy challenge that Nixon could not overcome. He had a three-part plan to end the conflict—gradual withdrawal of American troops and training of South Vietnamese forces to take over the combat role, renewed bombing, and a hard line in negotiations with Hanoi. The number of American soldiers in Vietnam fell from 543,000 in early 1969 to less than 30,000 by 1972; domestic opposition to the war declined sharply with the accompanying drop in casualties and reductions in the draft call.

Renewed bombing proved the most controversial part of the plan. As early as the spring of 1969, Nixon secretly ordered raids on communist supply lines in neutral Cambodia. Then in April 1970, he ordered both air and ground strikes into Cambodia, causing a massive outburst of antiwar protests at home. Students demonstrated against the invasion of Cambodia on campuses across the nation. Tragedy struck at Kent State University in Ohio in early May. After rioters had firebombed an ROTC building, the governor sent in national guard troops who were taunted and harassed by irate students. The guards-

men then opened fire, killing four students and wounding eleven more. The victims were innocent bystanders; two were young women caught in the fusillade on their way between classes. A week later, two African American student demonstrators were killed at Jackson State College in Mississippi; soon riots and protests raged on more than four hundred campuses across the country.

Nixon had little sympathy for the demonstrators, calling the students "bums" who were intent on "blowing up the campuses." The "silent majority" to whom he appealed seemed to agree; one poll showed that most Americans blamed the students, not the national guard, for the deaths at Kent State. An "Honor America Day" program, held in Washington, D.C., on July 4, attracted 250,000 people who heard Billy Graham and Bob Hope endorse the president's policies. Nixon's Cambodian invasion did little to shorten the Vietnam War, but the public reaction reinforced the president's resolve not to surrender.

The third tactic, negotiation with Hanoi, finally proved successful. Beginning in the summer of 1969, Kissinger held a series of secret meetings with North Vietnam's foreign minister, Le Duc Tho. In the summer and fall of 1972, the two sides were near agreement, but South Vietnamese objections blocked a settlement before the 1972 election. When the North Vietnamese tried to make last-minute changes, Nixon ordered a series of savage B-52 raids on Hanoi that finally led to the signing of a truce on January 27, 1973.

The renewed bombing of North Vietnam and invasion of Cambodia ordered by Nixon in hopes of ending the conflict precipitated student protests at many campuses. At Kent State University in Ohio, demonstrators and bystanders were shot by national guardsmen. ❖

In return for the release of all American prisoners of war, the United States agreed to remove its troops from South Vietnam within sixty days. The political clauses allowed the North Vietnamese to keep their troops in the South, thus virtually guaranteeing future control of all Vietnam by the communists.

The agreement was, in fact, a disguised surrender, but finally the American combat role in the Vietnam War was over. After eight years of fighting, the United States had emerged from the quagmire in Southeast Asia. Yet, known only to a few insiders around the president, the nation was already deeply enmeshed in another dilemma—what Gerald R. Ford termed "the long national nightmare" of Watergate.

THE CRISIS OF DEMOCRACY

The June 1, 1972, break-in at the Democratic National Committee offices came back to haunt Richard Nixon in 1973 and 1974. His determination to stonewall the press on any White House involvement in the burglary—including instructions to his aides to lie under oath—proved successful in the short run, but eventually the cover-up led to his downfall.

The Election of 1972

The irony of the Watergate break-in was that by the time it occurred, Nixon's election was assured. Aided by Republican dirty tricks, the Democrats self-destructed.

First, Edmund Muskie, the front-runner, replying in the New Hampshire primary to a letter accusing him of prejudice against French Canadians, lost his composure. Then a lone assassin, Arthur Bremer, shot and seriously wounded George Wallace. Paralyzed, Wallace was forced

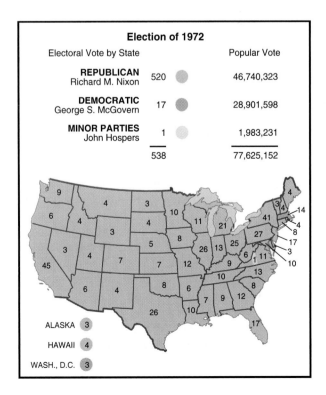

Election of 1972

	Electoral Vote by State		Popular Vote
REPUBLICAN Richard M. Nixon	520	●	46,740,323
DEMOCRATIC George S. McGovern	17	●	28,901,598
MINOR PARTIES John Hospers	1	●	1,983,231
	538		77,625,152

ALASKA 3
HAWAII 4
WASH., D.C. 3

to drop out of the race, leaving Nixon with a complete monopoly over the political right.

Senator George McGovern of South Dakota finally emerged as the Democratic nominee. He ran on a platform that advocated a negotiated settlement in Vietnam, the right to abortion, and tolerance of diverse lifestyles. The South Dakota senator hoped to unite the New Left with traditional Democratic voters, but his strong stand against the Vietnam War and in favor of income redistribution at home was perceived as "anti-establishment" by middle-class America and greatly strengthened Nixon's appeal.

Instead of focusing on his own record in office, Richard Nixon shrewdly let McGovern's perceived extremism and New Left support become the main issue in the campaign. Staying carefully aloof from partisanship, Nixon let others campaign for him, relying heavily on the recent improvement in the economy and his foreign policy triumphs with China and Russia to sway the nation's voters.

The result was a stunning victory. Nixon won a popular landslide with 60.8 percent of the vote—second only to Lyndon Johnson's record in 1964—and an even more decisive sweep of the electoral college, taking every state but Massachusetts. The very low turnout and Democratic control of both Houses of Congress suggests the election was primarily a repudiation of George McGovern, rather than an endorsement of Richard Nixon. The voting patterns did suggest, however, the beginning of a major political realignment, as only blacks, Jews, and low-income voters continued to vote overwhelmingly Democratic, while the GOP made significant gains in the Sunbelt states of the South and West.

The Watergate Scandal

Despite the best efforts of John Dean, the Watergate cover-up began to unravel in early 1973. Hunt and Liddy were convicted and went to prison without implicating anyone else in the Nixon administration; James McCord became the first to break the silence. Sentenced to a long jail term by Judge John Sirica, McCord asked for leniency, informing Sirica he had received money from the White House and had been promised a future pardon in return for his silence. By April 1973, Nixon was forced to fire John Dean, who refused to become the scapegoat for the cover-up, and to allow Haldeman and Ehrlichman, who were deeply implicated, to resign. The Senate then appointed a special committee to investigate the **Watergate scandal.** In a week of dramatic testimony, John Dean revealed the president's personal involvement in the cover-up. Still, it was basically a matter of whose word was to be believed, that of the president or that of a discredited aide, and Nixon hoped to weather the storm.

In an April 29, 1974, television address, Nixon announced that he would release Watergate tape transcripts, shown stacked in the background, to the House Judiciary Committee's impeachment probe. The transcripts were edited versions of taped conversations in the Oval Office. The transcripts and, later, the release of the actual tapes, eventually forced Nixon to resign the presidency. ❖

The existence of tapes of conversations in the Oval Office, recorded regularly since 1970, finally brought Nixon down. At first, the president tried to invoke executive privilege to withhold the tapes. When Archibald Cox, appointed as Watergate special prosecutor, demanded the release of the tapes, Nixon fired him. But the new Watergate prosecutor, Leon Jaworski, continued to press for the tapes. Nixon tried to release only a few of the less damaging ones, but the Supreme Court ruled unanimously in June 1974 that the tapes had to be turned over to Judge Sirica.

By that time, the House Judiciary Committee, acting on evidence compiled by the staff of the Senate committee, had voted three articles of impeachment, charging Nixon with obstruction of justice, abuse of power, and contempt of Congress. Faced with the release of tapes that directly implicated him in the cover-up, the president finally chose to resign on August 9, 1974.

Nixon's resignation proved to be the culmination of the Watergate scandal. The entire episode revealed both the weaknesses and strengths of the American political system. Most regrettable was the abuse of presidential authority—a reflection both of the growing power of the modern presidency and of the fatal flaws in Richard Nixon's character. Unlike previous executive branch scandals such as the Whiskey Ring and Teapot Dome, Watergate involved a lust for power rather than for money. Realizing he had reached the White House almost by accident, Nixon did everything possible to retain his hold on his office. He used the plumbers to maintain executive secrecy, and he directed the Internal Revenue Service and the Justice Department to punish his enemies and reward his friends.

But Watergate also demonstrated the vitality of a democratic society. The press showed how investigative reporting could unlock even the most closely guarded executive secrets. Judge Sirica proved that an independent judiciary was still the best bulwark for individual freedom. And Congress rose to the occasion, both by carrying out a successful investigation of executive misconduct and by following a scrupulous and nonpartisan impeachment process that left Nixon with no chance to escape his fate.

The nation survived the shock of Watergate with its institutions intact. Attorney General John Mitchell and twenty-five presidential aides were sentenced to jail terms. Congress, in decline since Lyndon Johnson's exercise of executive dominance, was rejuvenated, with its members now intent on extending congressional authority into all areas of American life.

ENERGY AND THE ECONOMY

In the midst of Watergate, the outbreak of war in the Middle East threatened a vital national interest—the supply and price of the fuel on which the American way of life was based. In the course of the 1970s, the resulting energy crisis helped touch off an inflationary impulse that had a profound impact on the national economy.

The October War

On October 6, 1973, Egypt and Syria launched a surprise attack on Israel. The fighting caught American leaders completely off guard. After recovering from the initial shock, President Nixon and Henry Kissinger, who had become secretary of state in September, expected Israel to repel the Arab invaders and display the same military dominance it had used to win the Six Day War in 1967. In that conflict, Israel had devastated its Arab neighbors, taking possession of the Golan Heights from Syria, the Sinai peninsula from Egypt, and Jerusalem and the West Bank from Jordan. Instead of increasing Israeli security, however, the conquests had only added to Middle East tensions. They unified the Arab countries, who now called for the return of their lands, and increased Egyptian and Syrian dependence on the Soviet Union for arms and political support.

Henry Kissinger used the October War, which began on the Jewish holy day of Yom Kippur, as an opportunity to shift American policy from its traditional pro-Israeli position to a more neutral stance—as the honest broker between Israel and its Arab neighbors. At

first, Nixon and Kissinger had to approve a massive resupply in mid-October to help Israel stem the Egyptian and Syrian offensives. But when the Israelis quickly routed their opponents, the United States intervened diplomatically to prevent a victory for Israel that would preclude American mediation. The fighting finally ended in late October; Israel had repulsed the Arab attack but had been stopped short of complete victory.

Kissinger's apparent diplomatic triumph, however, was offset by an unforeseen consequence of the Yom Kippur War. On October 17, the Arab members of the **Organization of Petroleum Exporting Countries (OPEC)** announced a 5 percent cut in oil production, with additional cuts of 5 percent each month until Israel gave up the lands it had taken in 1967. President Nixon announced a $2.2 billion aid package for Israel on October 19, and the next day Saudi Arabia cut off oil shipments to the United States and to the Netherlands, the European nation that had most strongly supported American policy in the Middle East.

❖ A Look at the Past ❖

Locking Gas Cap

The energy crisis of the 1970s brought rationing and long lines at gasoline stations. As gas became increasingly difficult to obtain and rose in expense, consumers took many measures to deal with their fuel problems. Some bought fuel-efficient Japanese cars. The market for protective devices such as this locking gas cap grew as reports circulated about thieves siphoning gasoline out of cars. Before long, locking gas caps became standard on most cars. What do the reports and the caps suggest about the depth of consumer fears? Do you think the widespread use of locking caps reflected an enduring change in public confidence and willingness to trust fellow Americans?

The Arab oil embargo had a disastrous impact on the American economy. First, it produced a worldwide shortage of oil. Arab producers cut production by 25 percent from the September 1973 level, leading to a 10 percent curtailment in the world supply. For the United States, which imported one-third of its daily consumption, this meant a loss of nearly 2 million barrels a day. Long lines formed at automobile service stations as motorists who feared running out of gas kept filling their tanks.

A dramatic increase in oil prices proved to be a far more significant result of the embargo. After the Arab embargo began, OPEC, led by the shah of Iran, raised crude oil prices fourfold. In the United States, gasoline prices at the pumps nearly doubled in a few weeks' time while the cost of home heating fuel rose even more sharply.

President Nixon responded with a series of temporary measures, including pleas to turn down thermostats in homes and offices, close service stations on weekends to curb pleasure driving, and reduce automobile speed limits to 50 miles an hour. When the Arab oil embargo ended in March, after Kissinger negotiated an Israeli pullback in the Sinai, the American public relaxed. Gasoline once again became plentiful, thermostats were raised, and people resumed their love affair with the automobile.

The energy crisis, however, did not end with the lifting of the embargo. The Arab action marked the beginning of a new era in American history. The United States, with only 6 percent of the world's population, had been responsible for nearly 40 percent of the earth's energy consumption. In 1970, domestic oil production began to decline; the embargo served only to highlight the fact that the nation was now dependent on other countries, notably those in the Persian Gulf, for its economic well-being. A nation that based its way of life on abundance and expansion suddenly was faced with the reality of limited resources and economic stagnation.

The Oil Shocks

Cheap energy had been the underlying force behind the amazing growth of the American economy after World War II. The world price of oil had actually declined in the 1950s and 1960s as huge new fields in the Middle East and North Africa began to produce. The GNP had more than doubled between 1950 and 1973; the American people had come to base their way of life on gasoline prices that averaged about 35 cents a gallon. The huge gas-guzzling cars, the flight to the suburbs, the long drives to work each day, the detached houses heated by fuel oil and natural gas and cooled by central air-conditioning represented a dependence on inexpensive energy that everyone took for granted.

The first great oil shock of the 1970s came with the October War and the resulting Arab oil embargo. Few had noticed a gradual increase in OPEC prices in the early 1970s; global demand for oil, intensified by the explosive economic development of western Europe and Japan as well as the United States, had now caught up with oil production. In the ensuing shortfall, the OPEC nations quickly raised prices, first from $3 to more than $5 a barrel, then to $11.65.

THE OIL SHOCKS: PRICE INCREASES OF CRUDE OIL AND GASOLINE, 1973–1985

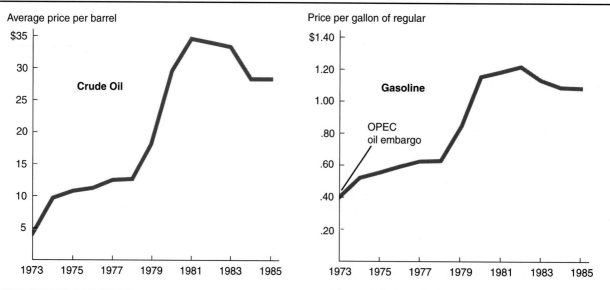

The effect on the American economy was devastating. Gasoline prices jumped from 35 to 65 cents a gallon; the cost of manufacturing went up proportionately, while utility rates rose sharply as a result of the higher cost of fuel oil and natural gas. Suddenly, Americans faced drastic and unexpected increases in such everyday expenses as driving to work and heating their homes.

The result was a sharp decline in consumer spending and the worst recession since World War II. The GNP dropped by 6 percent in 1974, and unemployment rose to more than 9 percent, the highest level since the Great Depression of the 1930s. Detroit was hit the hardest. Buyers shied away from big cars with their low gas mileage, but many were skeptical of the first generation of American-made small cars. Sales declined by 20 percent, and by the fall of 1974, Detroit's Big Three automakers had laid off more than 225,000 workers.

President Gerald R. Ford, who followed Richard Nixon into the White House (see p. 912), responded belatedly to the economic crisis by proposing a tax cut to stimulate consumer spending. Congress passed a $22.8 billion reduction in taxes in early 1975, which led to a gradual recovery by 1976. The resulting budget deficits, however, helped keep inflation above 5 percent and prevented a return to full economic health.

Jimmy Carter of Georgia, who succeeded Ford (see p. 913), had little more success in achieving a rapid rate of economic growth. Continued federal deficits and relatively high interest rates kept the economy sluggish throughout 1977 and 1978. Then in 1979, the outbreak of the Iranian Revolution and the overthrow of the shah touched off another oil shock. Although the cutoff of Iranian oil led to a shortfall of only 3 percent of the world's oil supply, the members of the OPEC cartel took advantage of the situation to double prices over the next eighteen months. A barrel of crude oil now cost more than $30. Gasoline prices climbed to more than $1 a gallon at American service stations, leading to an even greater wave of inflation than in 1973.

The American people panicked. When lines began to form at gas stations in California and Florida in early May 1979, drivers started filling their tanks every day or two. The long lines frustrated American drivers; incidents of violence began to mount, and the public took out its fury on the Carter administration. In June, the president's staff warned him of the danger in the "worsening short-term energy crisis." "Nothing else has so frustrated, confused, angered the American people," Carter was told, "or so targeted their distress at you personally."

By the fall of 1979, world supply had caught up with demand, and the oil scare ended. But the price of gasoline remained at more than $1 a gallon, and the inflation rate began to reach double-digit levels again. The twin oil shocks of the 1970s had left the economy battered and had undermined the average American's faith in the future.

The Search for an Energy Policy

The oil shocks of 1973 and 1979 were but two symptoms of a much deeper energy crisis. Put simply, the United States was running out of the fossil fuels on which it had relied for its economic growth in the past. Domestic oil production peaked in 1970 and declined every year thereafter; there were more ample reserves of natural gas, but both fuels were nonrenewable sources of energy that eventually would be exhausted. American political leaders had to devise a national policy to meet not only the temporary shortfalls of the 1970s but also the long-term energy problem inherent in past reliance on fossil fuels.

The success of the environmental movement in the late 1960s and early 1970s compounded the problem. Efforts to protect the environment and curtail pollution of the nation's air and water had led to significant legislative restrictions on American industry. Congress created the **Environmental Protection Agency** in 1970 to monitor industry and passed a

Environmentalist activists protesting at a 1979 "no nukes" demonstration in Washington, D.C., advocate solar power as a safe, environmentally friendly energy alternative. ◈

Clean Air Act that encouraged public utilities to shift from using coal, which polluted the atmosphere, to clean-burning fuel oil and natural gas to generate electricity. The observance of Earth Day in April 1970, complete with a massive parade up New York City's Fifth Avenue, and outrage over an oil spill in the Santa Barbara channel, reflected the national consensus behind the environmental movement.

The energy crunch pitted the environmentalists and advocates of economic growth in direct confrontation with each other. Those who put ecology first lost out. By the end of the decade, groups such as the Sierra Club and Friends of the Earth had failed in their efforts to halt the gradual relaxation of environmental regulations that prohibited strip mining of coal and offshore drilling for oil.

The nation's leaders had a difficult time devising a coherent and workable long-term national energy policy. Gerald Ford favored expanding production to overcome the shortage. The Republicans advocated removing price controls on oil and natural gas to bring in new supplies of the fuels. Greater production of coal and expanded nuclear power plants were key parts of the Republican approach to the energy problem. The tragic accident at Three Mile Island in Pennsylvania in 1979, however, led to a moratorium on the building of new nuclear power plants. (See the Feature Essay, "Three Mile Island and Chernobyl: The Promise and Peril of Nuclear Power," pp. 906–907.)

The Democrats, in contrast, stressed price controls and conservation. Intent on shielding American consumers from the full brunt of the world price increase, Democratic leaders in Congress wanted to continue an elaborate system of price controls instituted by Nixon in 1973. They preferred standby plans for gas rationing to reliance on the marketplace to allocate scarce supplies.

The nation failed to adopt either the Republican or the Democratic energy plans; instead, Congress tried to muddle through with elements of both approaches. Thus, on the production front, it approved construction of the Alaskan pipeline, which brought an additional 1.5 million barrels of oil a day to American consumers. On the conservation side, Congress continued the price controls on domestic oil for another forty months in late 1975 and mandated annual increases in automobile gasoline mileage that forced Detroit to produce more fuel-efficient cars. Since nearly 10 percent of the world's oil production was burned up every day on American highways, this one congressional act eventually resulted in substantial gasoline savings.

The overall outcome, however, was a patchwork that fell far short of a coherent national strategy for solving the energy problem. Oil imports actually increased by 50 percent between 1973 and 1979, rising from 6 million to 9 million barrels a day, an amount nearly half of the nation's daily petroleum usage.

The Great Inflation

The gravest consequence of the oil shocks was inflation. The startling increase in price levels in the 1970s stemmed from many causes. The Vietnam War created budget deficits that grew from $63 billion for the entire decade of the 1960s to a total of $420 billion in the 1970s. A worldwide shortage of food, resulting from both rapid population increases and poor harvests around the globe in the mid-1970s, triggered a 20 percent rise in American food prices in 1973 alone. But above all else, the primary source of the great inflation of the 1970s was the sixfold increase in petroleum prices.

The impact on consumers was staggering. The price of an automobile jumped 72 percent between 1973 and 1978. During the decade, the price of a hamburger doubled, milk went from 28 to 59 cents a quart, and the cost of a loaf of bread—the proverbial staff of life—rose from 24 to 89 cents. Corresponding wage increases failed to keep pace with inflation; in 1980, the real income of the average American family fell by 5.5 percent.

Curbing inflation proved to be beyond the power of the federal government. President Ford's early efforts to roll back prices by rhetoric were a casualty of the 1974 recession. President Carter proved equally powerless. Finally, in October 1979, the Federal Reserve Board, led by Carter appointee Paul Volcker, began a sustained effort to halt inflation by mandating increased bank reserves to curtail the supply of money in circulation. The new tight-money policy served only to heighten inflation in the short run by driving interest rates up to record levels. By the spring of 1980, the prime interest rate reached 20 percent.

The Shifting American Economy

Inflation and the oil shocks helped bring about significant changes in American business and industry in the 1970s. The most obvious result was the slowing of the rate of economic growth, with the GNP advancing only 3.2 percent for the decade, compared to 3.7 percent in the 1960s. More important, American industry began to lose its position of primacy in world markets. In 1959, U.S. firms had been the leaders in eleven of thirteen major industrial sectors, ranging from manufacturing to banking. By 1976, American companies led in only seven areas, and in all but one category—aerospace—U.S. corporations had declined in relation to Japanese and western European competitors.

The most serious losses came in the heavy industries in which the United States had once led the world. New steel producers in western Europe, Japan, and the Third World, using more advanced technology and aided by government subsidies, were producing steel far more efficiently than their American counterparts. As a result, by the end of the 1970s, American firms were closing down their obsolete mills in the East and Midwest, idling thousands of workers.

Foreign competition did even more damage in the automobile industry. The oil shocks led to a consumer demand for small, efficient cars. German and Japanese automakers seized the opportunity to expand their once low volume of sales in the United States. By 1977, imported cars had captured 18.3 percent of the American market, with Japan leading the way. In response, Detroit spent $70 billion retooling to produce a new fleet of smaller, lighter front-wheel-drive cars; but American manufacturers barely survived the foreign invasion. Only government-backed loans helped the Chrysler Corporation stave off bankruptcy.

The decline in manufacturing led to significant shifts in the labor movement. The industrial unions such as the United Automobile Workers (UAW) lost members steadily in the 1960s and 1970s. At the same time, public employee unions enjoyed rapid growth and acceptance. The Great Society legislation, the baby boom with the resulting need for many more teachers, and the growth of social agencies on the state and local level opened up new jobs for social workers, teachers, and government employees. By the end of the 1980s, members of public employee unions made up over 20 percent of the AFL-CIO ranks, while the separate National Education Association (NEA) became the nation's largest single union, with 2 million members—600,000 more than the Teamsters. The rise of public employee unions also opened the way for greater participation by African Americans and women than in the older trade and industrial unions.

Just as public employee unions prospered from the shifts in the American economy in the 1970s, so did many American corporations. The multinationals that had emerged in the boom years of the 1960s continued to thrive. IBM sold computers all over the globe. The growth of conglomerates—huge corporations that combined many dissimilar industrial concerns—accelerated as companies such as Gulf & Western and the Transamerica Corporation diversified by buying up Hollywood studios, insurance companies, and recreational equipment manufacturers. The growth of high-technology industries proved to be the most profitable new trend of the 1970s. Computer companies and electronics firms grew at a rapid rate, especially after the development of the silicon chip, a small, wafer-thin microprocessor capable of performing complex calculations almost instantly.

The result was a geographic shift of American industry from the East and Midwest to the Sunbelt.

Increasing imports of foreign cars, many of them smaller and more fuel-efficient than American-made autos, alarmed U.S. automobile manufacturers who scrambled to produce lighter and more economical cars. Here dockworkers unload imports at Baltimore's Dundalk Marine Terminal, the nation's largest entry port for foreign automobiles. ❖

Electronics manufacturers flourished in California, Texas, and North Carolina, where they grew up around major universities. The absence of well-entrenched labor unions, the availability of skilled labor, and the warm and attractive climate of the southern and western states lured many new concerns to the Sunbelt. At the same time, the decline of the steel and auto industries was leading to massive unemployment and economic stagnation in the northern industrial heartland.

The overall pattern was one of an economy in transition. The oil shocks had caused serious problems of inflation, slower economic growth, and rising unemployment rates. But American business still displayed the enterprise and the ability to develop new technologies that gave promise of renewed economic vitality.

PRIVATE LIVES—PUBLIC ISSUES

Sweeping changes in the private lives of the American people began in the 1970s and continued for the rest of the century. The traditional American family, with

THREE MILE ISLAND AND CHERNOBYL

The Promise and Peril of Nuclear Power

In March 1979, it appeared to the world that its worst nightmares about nuclear power might come true when a near meltdown occurred at the Three Mile Island nuclear power plant outside of Harrisburg, Pennsylvania. Only a few years later, an accident of even greater proportions, the explosion of a reactor at the Chernobyl plant in the Soviet Ukraine on April 26, 1986, stirred fears once again. These incidents were frightful reminders of what could happen and they cast serious doubt on the future viability of nuclear power.

In the 1960s, the United States and other industrialized nations had turned to nuclear power to fulfill the need for clean, inexpensive, and renewable energy. By 1979, there were seventy-two nuclear power plants operating in the United States, and they generated 12.5 percent of the nation's electricity. Another ninety-two plants were under construction, and thirty more were in the planning stage. The Soviet Union had also embarked on a nuclear program. By 1984, Russia had built forty-three plants that supplied 10 percent of that country's electrical needs. Advocates insisted that nuclear power plants posed no serious danger to public health, and in both countries the industry expected to play an ever larger part in meeting the growing demand for electricity.

The accident at Three Mile Island (TMI) caught the American people by surprise and touched off a strong reaction against reliance on nuclear power. Early reports on the meltdown were sketchy. It was not clear what exactly had gone wrong on Wednesday, March 28, 1979, except that one unit of the TMI facility had released some radioactivity into the environment. State officials and company representatives assured the anxious public that radiation levels outside were not—repeat, not—dangerous. Inside TMI, the water system used to cool the reactor core had broken down, and company employees, scientists, and industry experts fought to get the cooling water moving again. And even though the chain reaction inside the reactor had stopped, the radioactive materials within continued to release tremendous quantities of heat.

By Friday, March 30, the crisis had become intense. Radiation readings outside the plant had risen but were not yet considered dangerous. Pennsylvania Governor Richard Thornburgh advised that those most susceptible to radiation, namely preg-

Cooling towers at Three Mile Island, Pennsylvania. The partial meltdown at the plant in March 1979 released some radioactive particles into the environment, endangering nearby residents and frightening Americans about reliance on nuclear power. ❖

nant women and preschool-age children living within a 5-mile radius of TMI, ought to leave. Taking no chances, more than forty thousand people streamed out of the area that afternoon and evening.

The greatest danger came from a hydrogen bubble that had formed above the reactor core. Authorities feared that if the bubble continued to expand, it could lead to a catastrophic meltdown. By Monday, April 2, however, the bubble began to shrink dramatically, ending the threat to public safety. Studies made twenty years later showed no significant increase in cancer deaths among those living within five miles of TMI.

Soviet citizens living near the Chernobyl nuclear power station were not as lucky. The Chernobyl plant housed four reactors. On April 26, 1986, while conducting a safety test in Unit IV, plant personnel violated regulations, removing all of the control rods from the reactor core. The core temperature shot up, triggering an uncontrolled nuclear reaction and steam build-up. At 1:23 A.M., the reactor exploded, destroying the concrete shield above it and causing approximately thirty fires in the immediate vicinity.

Over the course of the next ten days, Soviet officials worked to cool off the damaged core. In the meantime, the reactor spewed a radioactive cloud of dust into the air—a plume that eventually spread over the Ukraine, Scandinavia, and much of Central and Eastern Europe.

Soviet authorities, unlike their American counterparts, refused to warn the people living near Chernobyl of the danger they faced from escaping radioactive particles. Mikhail Byckau, a Belarusian scientist, later reported that he and other experts were sworn to secrecy about the risks facing the public. Watching rain he knew contained Iodine-131 falling in Minsk, he commented that "it was painful to see how the children were playing in the radioactive sand."

Estimating the human cost of the Chernobyl disaster is difficult even today. The Kremlin reported that 237 persons were hospitalized for significant radiation exposure and thirty-one died in the immediate aftermath of the accident. In 1990, however, a Moscow newspaper claimed that at least 250 people had died during the accident or the subsequent rescue and cleanup operations. A more important—and controversial—question is the number of individuals who will ultimately die of cancer or various defects as a consequence of Chernobyl. Despite some alarming estimates, so far the most serious consequence has been a reported 1800 cases of thyroid cancer, mainly among children and adolescents, but only a handful of deaths from radiation exposure. A United Nations report in 2000 found no increase in leukemia and concluded that, aside from the thyroid cancer cases, "there is no evidence of a major public health impact attributable to radiation exposure fourteen years after the accident."

Today, the three remaining nuclear reactors at Chernobyl and the one at Three Mile Island continue to produce electricity. The TMI plant is due to be decommissioned in 2014, while plans to close the Chernobyl facility have been postponed for lack of alternative power sources for the Ukraine. An intensive international effort is underway, however, to build a huge containment dome over Chernobyl-4 to replace a temporary cap built after the 1986 explosion. This 20,000-ton steel shell, estimated to cost $768 million, will keep the radioactive sludge contained for at least one hundred years.

The two crises affected the American and Soviet nuclear power industries in strikingly similar ways. In both countries, the governments stepped up their regulation of nuclear facilities rather than totally abandoning their programs. By the end of the 1980s, nuclear power plants still generated more than 17 percent of America's electricity and 11 percent of the Soviet Union's.

Nuclear power, however, has lost much of its luster. In the United States, every nuclear reactor ordered since 1974 has either been canceled or postponed indefinitely. The Soviet Union likewise scrapped some of its plans to build new stations. And in both countries, TMI and Chernobyl left a legacy of fear that has eroded popular support for nuclear power.

Nuclear power has not, in all likelihood, been permanently discredited. Consumption of electricity in the United States has risen by more than one-third since the 1973 Arab oil embargo. Except in certain regions where hydroelectric power and wind and solar energy are readily available, Americans will have to choose between fossil fuels and nuclear power. Growing environmental concern over acid rain and global warming tend to weigh against the burning of coal, oil, and natural gas. It is thus possible that the nuclear alternative may regain some of the credibility it lost as a consequence of TMI and Chernobyl.

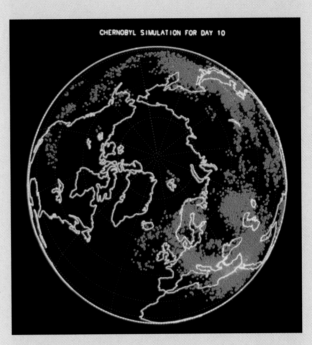

Within a few days of the Chernobyl accident, the U.S. agency ARAC produced simulations of the estimated dispersion of radioactive particles to assist emergency response. This image shows the northern hemisphere on day ten. ✦

the husband as wage earner and the wife as home-maker, gave way to much more diverse living arrangements. The number of working women, including wives and mothers, increased sharply; the wage gap between the sexes narrowed, but women still lagged noticeably behind men in earnings. Then, in the years following 1970 came the emergence of an active gay rights movement as more and more homosexuals began to disclose their sexual identities and demand an end to discrimination.

The Changing American Family

Family life underwent a number of significant shifts after 1970. The most notable was a decline in the number of families with two parents and one or more children under 18. By 1990, in only 21 percent of the two-parent families was the mother solely engaged in child rearing. A few fathers stayed at home with the children, but in the great majority of these families, both parents worked outside the home.

The traditional nuclear family of the 1950s no longer prevailed in America by the end of the twentieth century. The number of married couple households with children dropped from 30 percent in the 1970s to 23.5 percent by 2000. The number of unmarried couples doubled in the 1990s, while adults living alone surpassed the number of married couples with children for the first time in American history. "Being married is great," commented demographer William H. Frey, "but being married with kids is tougher in today's society with spouses in different jobs and expensive day care and schools."

The divorce rate, which doubled between the mid-1960s and the late 1970s, leveled off for the rest of the century. Nevertheless, half of all first marriages still ended in divorce. After a sharp fall in the 1970s, the birthrate climbed again as the baby boom generation began to mature. There was a marked increase in the number of births to women over age 30, as well as a very high proportion of children born to single mothers, who composed 7 percent of all households by 2000, a 25 percent increase since 1990. Conservatives, alarmed by the decline of the nuclear family, called for change. "We need to discourage people from living together outside of marriage," observed Bridget Maher of the Family Research Council, "and encourage them to have children within marriage."

For better or worse, the American family structure changed significantly in the last three decades of the twentieth century, with a large number of people either never marrying or postponing marriage until late in the childbearing period. The traditional family unit, with the working father and the mother rearing the children at home, rapidly declined. Most mothers work outside the home, and many are the sole support for their children. The proportion of children living with only one parent doubled in twenty years. Women without partners headed more than one-third of all impoverished families, and children made up 40 percent of the nation's poor. Although politicians, especially Republicans, refer to family values during campaigns, the fact remains that the American family underwent great stress due to social changes in the last third of the twentieth century, and children have suffered disproportionately.

Gains and Setbacks for Women

American women experienced significant changes in their way of life and their place in society in the last quarter of the twentieth century. The prevailing theme

TYPES OF HOUSEHOLDS IN THE UNITED STATES, 2000

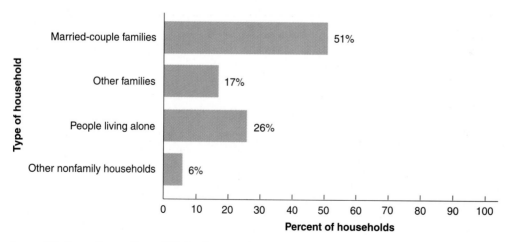

Source: U.S. Census Bureau, Census 2000 Supplementary Survey.

concerned the increasing percentage of working women. There was a rapid movement of women into the labor force in the 1970s; six million more married women held jobs by the end of the decade as two incomes became increasingly necessary to keep up with inflation. The trend continued through the 1980s. Fully 61 percent of the nearly nineteen million new jobs created during the decade were filled by women; many of these new jobs, however, were entry-level or low-paying service positions.

Women scored some impressive breakthroughs. They began to enter corporation boardrooms, became presidents of major universities, and were admitted to West Point and Annapolis. Women entered blue-collar, professional, and small-business fields traditionally dominated by men. Reagan's appointment of Sandra Day O'Connor to the Supreme Court in 1981 marked a historic first; Clinton doubled the number of women on the Court with his selection of Ruth Bader Ginsburg.

Yet at the same time, women encountered a great deal of resistance. Most women continued to work in female-dominated fields—as nurses, secretaries, teachers, and waitresses. Those who entered such "male" areas as management and administration soon encountered the so-called "glass ceiling," which kept them from advancing beyond mid-level executive status. In 1990, only 4.3 percent of corporate officers were women. Most in business worked at the middle and lower rungs of management with staff jobs in personnel and public relations, not key operational positions in sales and marketing that would lead to the boardroom; women held fewer than 3 percent of the top jobs in Fortune 500 companies. The economic boom of the 1990s, however, led to a steady increase in the number of women executives; in 1998, there was an increase of 514,000.

Even with these gains, however, by 2002 women's wages still averaged only 77.5 percent of men's earnings. A college education helped close the gap, but a woman with a degree made only $600 a year more on the average than a man with a high school diploma. Younger women did best; those between 16 and 24 earned almost 90 cents for every dollar paid to a male in the same age group. Older women, who often had no other source of support, fared poorly; those over the age of 50 earned only 64 percent as much as men their age. Feminists had once hoped to close the gender gap by the year 2000, but experts predicted women would not reach pay equity with men until 2018.

The most encouraging development for women came in business ownership. Often blocked by the glass ceiling and seeking flexible schedules, more and more women went into business for themselves. The number of female business owners increased 40 percent between 1987 and 1992, twice the national rate of business growth. A women's trade group estimated that in 1996 women owned almost eight million businesses, employing more than eighteen million workers—one out of four American workers. A speaker at the first National Women's Economic Summit

Many women sought economic opportunity and equity through business ownership, even of businesses in traditionally male-based occupations. Anna Glavda of Queens, New York, for example, owned her own construction company and employed other female workers. ❖

VOTING ON THE EQUAL RIGHTS AMENDMENT

By the end of 1974, thirty-four states had ratified the ERA; Indiana finally approved the amendment in 1977, but the remaining fifteen states held out, leaving ratification three states short of the required three-fourths majority.

in 1996 exaggerated only slightly in crediting her group with restoring prosperity, claiming that "the American economy has been revitalized in good measure because of the participation of and contributions of women business owners."

Beyond economic opportunity, the women's movement had two goals. The first was ratification of the **Equal Rights Amendment (ERA).** Approved by Congress in 1972, the ERA stated simply, "Equality of rights under the law shall not be denied or abridged by the United States or any state on account of sex." Within a year, twenty-two states had approved the amendment, but the efforts gradually faltered just three states short of ratification. The opposition came in part from working-class women who feared, as one union leader explained, that those employed as "maids, laundry workers, hospital cleaners, or dishwashers" would lose the protection of state laws that regulated wages and hours of work for women. Right-wing activist Phyllis Schlafly led an organized effort to defeat the ERA, claiming the amendment would lead to unisex toilets, homosexual marriages, and the drafting of women. The National Organization of Women (NOW) fought back, persuading Congress to extend the time for ratification by three years and waging intense campaigns for approval in Florida and Illinois. But the deadline for ratification finally passed on June 30, 1982, with the ERA forces still three states short. NOW leader Eleanor Smeal vowed a continuing struggle: "The crusade is not over. We know that we are the wave of the future."

The women's movement focused even more of its energies in protecting a major victory it had won in *Roe v. Wade* in 1973. (See the Law and Society essay, "*Roe v. Wade:* The Struggle Over Women's Reproductive Rights," pp. 920–924.) "Right-to-life" groups, consisting mainly of orthodox Catholics, fundamentalist Protestants, and conservatives, fought back. In 1978, with strong support from President Carter, Congress passed the Hyde amendment, which denied the use of federal funds to pay for abortions for poor women. Nevertheless, prochoice groups organized privately funded family planning agencies and abortion clinics to give more women a chance to exercise their constitutional right to abortion.

As Presidents Reagan and Bush appointed more conservative judges to the Court, however, prochoice groups began to fear the future overturn of *Roe v. Wade.* The Court avoided a direct challenge, contenting itself with lesser actions that upheld the rights of states to regulate abortion clinics, impose a 24-hour waiting period, and require the approval of one parent or a judge before a minor could have an abortion. Abortion became an issue in presidential contests, with the Republicans upholding a prolife position and the Democrats taking a prochoice stand. Bill Clinton's election and appointment of Ruth Bader Ginsburg to the Court appeared to end the danger to *Roe v. Wade,* but in 2000 the Court margin in rejecting a Nebraska law forbidding certain late-term abortions fell to a bare majority, 5–4. And even the exercise of the right to abortion proved difficult and sometimes dangerous in view of the often violent protests of prolife groups outside abortion clinics. For many women, abortion was a hard-won right they still had to struggle to protect.

The Gay Liberation Movement

On the evening of July 29, 1969, a squad of New York policemen raided the Stonewall Inn, a Greenwich Village bar frequented by "drag queens" and lesbians. As the patrons were being herded into vans, a crowd of gay onlookers began to jeer and taunt the police. A riot quickly broke out. "Beer cans and bottles were heaved at the windows and a rain of coins descended on the cops," reported the *Village Voice.* "Almost by signal the crowd erupted into cobblestone and bottle heaving." The next night, more than four hundred police officers battled two thousand gay demonstrators through the streets of Greenwich Village. The two-day Stonewall Riots marked the beginning of the modern **gay liberation movement.** Refusing to play the role of victims any longer, gays and lesbians decided to affirm their sexual orientation and demand an end to discrimination against homosexuals.

Within a few days, two new organizations were formed in New York, the Gay Liberation Front and the Gay Activist Alliance, with branches and offshoots quickly appearing in cities across the country. The basic theme of gay liberation was to urge all homosexuals to "come out of the closet" and affirm with pride their sexual identity; instead of shame, they would find freedom and self-respect in the very act of coming out. "Come out for freedom! Come out now!" proclaimed the Gay Liberation Front's newspaper. "Come out of the closet before the door is nailed shut!"

In the course of the 1970s, hundreds of thousands of gays and lesbians responded to this call. They formed more than a thousand local clubs and organizations and won a series of notable victories. In 1974, the American Psychiatric Association stopped classifying homosexuality as a mental disorder, and by the end of the decade, half the states had repealed their sodomy statutes. Gays fought hard in cities and states for laws forbidding discrimination against homosexuals in housing and employment, and in 1980, they finally succeeded in getting a gay rights plank in the Democratic National Platform.

In the 1980s, the onset of the AIDS epidemic (see pp. 944–946) forced the gay liberation movement on the defensive. Stung by the accusation that AIDS was a "gay disease," male homosexuals faced new public condemnation at a time when they were trying desperately to care for the growing number of victims of the disease within their ranks. The gay organizations formed in the 1970s to win new rights now were channeling their energies into caring for the ill, promoting safe sex practices, and fighting for more public funding to help conquer AIDS. In 1986, ACT UP (AIDS Coalition to Unleash Power) began a series of violent demonstrations in an effort to shock the nation into doing more about AIDS. ACT UP members disrupted public meetings, chained themselves to a New York Stock Exchange balcony, and spray-painted outlines of corpses on the streets of San Francisco to call attention to those who had died of AIDS.

The movement also continued to stimulate gay consciousness in the 1980s. In 1987, an estimated 600,000 gays and lesbians took part in a march on Washington on behalf of gay rights. Every year afterward, gay groups held a National Coming Out Day in October to encourage homosexuals to proclaim proudly their sexual identity. In a more controversial move, some gay leaders encouraged "outing"—releasing the names of prominent homosexuals, primarily politicians and movie stars, in an effort to make the nation aware of how many Americans were gay or lesbian. Gay leaders claimed there were more than twenty million gays and lesbians in the nation, basing this estimate on a Kinsey report which had stated in the late 1940s that one in ten American males had engaged in homosexual behavior. A sociological survey released in the spring of 1993 contradicted those numbers, finding only 1.1 percent of American males exclusively homosexual. Whatever the actual number, it was clear by the 1990s that gays and lesbians formed a significant minority that had succeeded in forcing the nation, however grudgingly, to respect its rights.

There was one battle, however, in which victory eluded the gay liberation movement. In the 1992 election, gays and lesbians strongly backed Democratic candidate Bill Clinton, who promised, if elected, to end the ban on homosexuals in the military. In his first days in office, however, President Clinton stirred up great resistance in the Pentagon and Congress when he

Backtracking on his campaign promise to end the ban on homosexuals in the military, President Clinton disappointed many by agreeing to the compromise "don't ask, don't tell" policy that permitted gays to serve in the military as long as they did not reveal their sexual orientation. ❖

"*This one's for not asking, and this one's for not telling.*"

tried to issue an executive order forbidding such discrimination. The Joint Chiefs of Staff and many Democrats, led by Georgia Senator Sam Nunn, warned that acceptance of gays and lesbians would destroy morale and seriously weaken the armed forces. Clinton finally settled for the Pentagon's compromise "Don't ask, don't tell" policy that would permit homosexuals to continue serving in the military as they had in the past as long as they did not reveal their sexual preference and refrained from homosexual conduct. However disappointed gays and lesbians were in Clinton's retreat, their leaders understood that the real problem was the resistance of mainstream America to full acceptance of homosexuality.

Public attitudes toward gays and lesbians seemed to be changing in the 1990s, but the growing tolerance had definite limits. In a 1996 poll, 85 percent of those questioned believed that gays should be treated equally in the workplace, up from 76 percent in 1992. Violence against gays, however, continued, most notably in the 1998 fatal beating of Matthew Shepard, a 21-year-old gay college student, in Wyoming. The brutal attack spurred calls for hate-crime legislation and the judge in the case, banning a so-called gay-panic defense, sentenced Shepard's assailant to two consecutive terms of life imprisonment.

The issue of same-sex marriage came to a head at the end of the century. In 1996, President Clinton signed the Defense of Marriage Act, which decreed that states did not have to recognize same-sex marriages performed elsewhere. But in 2000, following a state supreme court ruling, the Vermont legislature legalized "civil unions" between individuals of the same sex, enabling gays and lesbians to receive all the legal benefits available to married couples. Whether sanctioned by law or not, the number of gay and lesbian households steadily increased; the 2000 census revealed that there were nearly 600,000 homes in America headed by same sex couples. While nearly one-quarter were in California and New York, there was at least one gay or lesbian couple living in 99 percent of the nation's counties.

POLITICS AFTER WATERGATE

The energy crisis and the economic dislocations of the mid-1970s could not have come at a worse time. Watergate had a paralyzing impact on the American political system. An awareness that the Cold War had led to an imperial presidency created a growing demand to weaken the power of the president and strengthen congressional authority. The result was increasing tension between the White House and Capitol Hill, preventing the strong, effective leadership needed to meet the unprecedented problems of the 1970s.

The Ford Administration

Gerald R. Ford had the distinction of being the first president who had not been elected to national office. Richard Nixon had appointed him to the vice presidency to succeed Spiro Agnew, who had been forced to resign in order to avoid prosecution for accepting bribes while he was governor of Maryland. Ford, an amiable and unpretentious Michigan congressman who had risen to the post of House minority leader, seemed ready to restore public confidence in the presidency when he replaced Nixon in August 1974.

Ford's honeymoon lasted only a month. On September 8, 1974, he shocked the nation by announcing he had granted Richard Nixon a full and unconditional pardon for all federal crimes he may have committed. Some critics charged darkly that Nixon and Ford had made a secret bargain; others pointed out how unfair it was for Nixon's aides to serve their prison terms while the chief criminal went free. Ford apparently acted in an effort to end the bitterness over Watergate, but his attempt backfired, eroding public confidence in his leadership and linking him indelibly with the scandal.

Ford soon found himself fighting an equally difficult battle on behalf of the beleaguered CIA. The Watergate scandal and the Vietnam fiasco had eroded public confidence in the government and lent credibility to a startling series of disclosures about past covert actions. The president allowed the CIA to confirm some of the charges, and then he made things worse by blurting out to the press the juiciest item of all: The CIA had been involved in plots to assassinate foreign leaders.

Senate and House select committees appointed to investigate the CIA now focused on the assassination issue, eventually charging that the agency had been involved in no less than eight separate attempts to kill Fidel Castro. The chairman of the Senate committee, Frank Church of Idaho, worried that the revelations would damage the reputations of Democratic Presidents Kennedy and Johnson; he tried to put all the blame on the CIA, likening it to "a rogue elephant on the rampage."

In late 1975, President Ford finally moved to limit the damage to the CIA. He appointed George Bush, then a respected former Republican congressman, as the agency's new director and gave him the authority both to reform the CIA and to strengthen its role in shaping national security policy. Most notably, Ford issued an executive order outlawing assassination as an instrument of American foreign policy. To prevent future abuses, Congress created permanent House and Senate intelligence committees to exercise general oversight for covert CIA operations.

Ford proved less successful in his dealings with Congress on other issues. Although he prided himself on his good relations with members of both houses, he opposed Democratic measures such as federal aid to education and control over strip mining. In a little more than a year, he vetoed thirty-nine separate bills. In fact, Ford, who as a congressman had opposed virtually every Great Society measure, proved far more conservative than Nixon in the White House.

The 1976 Campaign

Ford's lackluster record and the legacy of Watergate made the Democratic nomination a prize worth fighting for in 1976. A large field of candidates entered the contest, but a virtual unknown, former Georgia governor James Earl Carter, quickly became the front-runner. Aware of the voters' disgust with politicians of both parties, Jimmy Carter ran as an outsider, portraying himself as a Southerner who had no experience in Washington and one who could thus give the nation fresh and untainted leadership.

Appearing refreshingly candid, Carter claimed to be an honest man, ready to deal fairly with the American people. On television, the basic Carter commercial showed him at his Georgia peanut farm, dressed in blue jeans, looking directly into the camera and saying, "I'll never tell a lie."

Carter swept through the primaries and won the Democratic nomination easily, naming Senator Walter Mondale of Minnesota as his running mate. The polls gave Carter a 33-point lead when the campaign began, but he quickly lost ground as he began to hedge on the issues. President Ford counterattacked, saying of his Democratic opponent that "he wavers, he wanders, he wiggles, and he waffles." But Ford, whose reputation as a bumbler developed from both his uninspired leadership and his occasional physical stumbles on golf courses and airport ramps, reinforced his own image of ineptitude. In a televised debate, responding to a question about Iron Curtain countries, he declared, "There is no Soviet domination of eastern Europe."

Carter won an extremely narrow victory in 1976. Despite Watergate and Ford's weak record, the Democratic candidate took only 49.98 percent of the popular vote. Ford swept nearly the entire West, but Carter carried the South and key northern industrial states such as New York and Ohio. Far more than most recent elections, the outcome turned on class and racial factors. "The affluent, the well-educated, the suburbanites largely went for Ford," commented one

THE ELECTION OF 1976

Candidate	Party	Popular Vote	Electoral Vote
Jimmy Carter	Democratic	40,830,763	297
Gerald Ford	Republican	39,147,793	240

observer, "the socially and economically disadvantaged for Carter." The black vote clinched the victory for the Democrats. Carter received more than 90 percent of the votes of African Americans, and their ballots provided the margin of victory in Ohio, Pennsylvania, and seven southern states.

Disenchantment with Carter

The new president, described by an associate as "superficially self-effacing but intensely shrewd," was an ambitious and intelligent politician. He had a rare gift for sensing what people wanted and appearing to give it to them. Liberals thought he clearly stood with them; conservatives were equally convinced he was on their side. He was especially adept at utilizing symbols. He emerged from airplanes carrying his own garment bag; after his inauguration, he walked up Pennsylvania Avenue hand in hand with his wife Rosalynn and daughter Amy. "Look," he seemed to be saying, "I am just an ordinary citizen who happens to be in the White House."

The substance, however, failed to match the style. He had no discernible political philosophy, no clear sense of direction. He sought the White House convinced that he was brighter and better than his competitors, but once there, he had no cause or mission to fulfill. He called himself a populist, but that label meant little more than an appeal to the common man, a somewhat ironic appeal, given Carter's personal wealth. "The idea of a millionaire populist has always amused me," commented his attorney general, fellow Georgian Griffin Bell.

The makeup of his administration reflected the conflicting tendencies that would eventually prove destructive. In the White House, he surrounded himself with close associates from Georgia, fellow outsiders such as presidential adviser Hamilton Jordan and press secretary Jody Powell. Yet he picked established Democrats for key cabinet positions: Cyrus Vance, a New York lawyer, as secretary of state; and Joseph Califano, a former aide to Lyndon Johnson, to head Health, Education, and Welfare. In the lower ranks, however, he selected liberal activists, followers of George McGovern, Edward (Ted) Kennedy, and Ralph Nader, people who were intent on regulating business

Despite his intelligence, integrity, and hard work, Jimmy Carter suffered a crisis in leadership. The electorate perceived him as ineffectual at solving problems and indecisive at setting priorities. ✦

and preserving the environment. The result was bound to be tension and conflict, as the White House staff and the federal bureaucracy worked at cross-purposes, one group seeking change while the other attempted to protect the president.

Lacking both a clear set of priorities and a coherent political philosophy, the Carter administration had little chance to succeed. The president strove hard for a balanced budget but was forced to accept mounting deficits. Federal agencies fought to save the environment and help consumers but served only to anger industry.

In the crucial area of social services, Joseph Califano failed repeatedly in his efforts to carry out long-overdue reforms. His attempts to overhaul the nation's welfare program, which had become a $30 billion annual operation serving some thirty million Americans, won little support from the White House. Carter's unwillingness to take the political risks involved in revamping the overburdened Social Security system by reducing benefits and raising the retirement age blocked Califano's efforts. And the HEW secretary

finally gave up his attempt to draw up a workable national health insurance plan.

Informed by his pollsters in 1979 that he was losing the nation's confidence, Carter sought desperately to redeem himself. After a series of meetings at Camp David with a wide variety of advisers, he gave a speech in which he seemed to blame his failure on the American people, accusing them of creating "a crisis of confidence . . . that strikes at the very heart and soul and spirit of our national will." Then, a week after what his critics termed the "national malaise" speech, he requested the resignation of Califano and the secretary of the treasury. But neither the attempt to pin responsibility on the American people nor the firing of cabinet members could hide the fact that Carter, despite his good intentions and hard work, had failed to provide the bold leadership the nation needed.

FROM DÉTENTE TO RENEWED COLD WAR

America's political position in the world declined sharply in the 1970s. In part, the fault was internal. The Vietnam War left the American people convinced that the nation should never again intervene abroad, and Watergate discredited strong presidential leadership, shifting power over foreign policy to Congress. The new national consensus was symbolized by the War Powers Act, passed in 1973, which required the president to consult with Congress before sending American troops into action overseas. At the same time, external events and developments, notably the control over oil exercised by OPEC and the threats posed by revolutionary nationalism in the Middle East and Latin America, further weakened American foreign policy. No longer able to dominate the international scene, the United States began to play the role of spectator, and at times even of victim.

Retreat in Asia

It was Gerald Ford's fate to reap where Nixon had sown. In 1974, Congress cut in half the administration's request for $1.4 billion in military aid to South Vietnam. A year later, when a North Vietnamese offensive proved surprisingly successful, Ford was unable to get Congress to grant any additional aid. Bereft of American assistance and weakened by internal corruption, the South Vietnamese government was unable to stop the advance on Saigon in April 1975. American forces concentrated on evacuating 150,000 loyal South Vietnamese, but many more were left behind when the last helicopter left the roof of the embassy in Saigon. After a quarter century of futile effort, the United

A North Vietnamese tank crashes through the gates of the Presidential Palace in Saigon during the fall of the city to communist forces in May 1975. ❖

States finally had to admit defeat in the nation's longest and most humiliating foreign war.

Less than a month later, Ford had a chance to remind the world of American power. The Khmer Rouge government of Cambodia seized an American freighter, the *Mayaguez*, and imprisoned its crew. When the communists ignored the initial American protest, Ford authorized an armed attack on Cambodia by two thousand marines from bases in Thailand. By the time the American forces landed on a small offshore island, Cambodia had freed the crewmen. The nation took pride in the president's resort to force, but forty Americans paid for his decision with their lives.

Accommodation in Latin America

President Carter was more successful than Ford in adjusting to the growing nationalism in the world, particularly in Central America, where the United States had imposed order for most of the twentieth century by backing reactionary regimes.

The first test came in Panama. Resentment over American ownership of the Panama Canal had led Lyndon Johnson to enter into negotiations aimed at the eventual return of the waterway to Panama. Carter completed the long diplomatic process in 1977 by signing two treaties. One restored sovereignty in the 500-square-mile Canal Zone to Panama, while the other provided for gradual Panamanian responsibility

for operating the canal, with appropriate safeguards for its use and defense by the United States. In negotiating the treaties, Carter was trying both to right an ancient wrong and to create stability in a highly volatile region.

The real struggle over the treaties took place in the Senate. Conservative Republicans expressed outrage over what they termed a "giveaway" of the Panama Canal. "It's ours. We stole it fair and square," claimed California Senator S. I. Hayakawa. Intensive personal lobbying by President Carter, as well as bipartisan support from influential Republicans such as Gerald Ford and Henry Kissinger, finally led to Senate ratification with just one vote to spare, thus paving the way for the return of the canal to Panama by the year 2000.

Carter was less successful, however, in dealing with a growing problem of left-wing uprisings in Central America. In mid-1979, dictator Anastasio Somoza capitulated to the Sandinista forces in Nicaragua. Despite American attempts to moderate the Sandinista revolution, the new regime moved steadily to the left, developing close ties with Castro's Cuba. In neighboring El Salvador, a growing leftist insurgency against a repressive regime put the United States in an awkward position. Unable to find a workable alternative between the extremes of reactionary dictatorship and radical revolution in Central America, Carter tried to use American economic aid to encourage the military junta in El Salvador to carry out democratic reforms. But after the guerrillas launched a major offensive in January 1981, he authorized large-scale military assistance to the government for its war against the insurgents, setting a precedent for the future.

The Quest for Peace in the Middle East

The inconclusive results of the 1973 October War gave Henry Kissinger the opportunity to play the role of peacemaker in the troubled Middle East. Shuttling back and forth between Cairo and Jerusalem, and then to Damascus, the secretary of state finally succeeded in arranging a pullback of Israeli forces in both the Sinai and the Golan Heights. Although he failed to achieve his goal of an Arab-Israeli settlement, Kissinger had succeeded in demonstrating that the United States could play the role of neutral mediator between the Israelis and Arabs. And equally important, he had detached Egypt from dependence on the Soviet Union, thereby weakening Russian influence in the Middle East.

In November 1977, Egyptian president Anwar Sadat stunned the world by traveling to Jerusalem in an effort to reach agreement directly with Israel. The next year, President Carter invited both Sadat and Israeli prime minister Menachem Begin to negotiate under his guidance at Camp David. For thirteen days,

A highlight of Carter's presidency was his role in helping negotiate the Camp David accords between Israeli Prime Minister Menachem Begin (right) and Egyptian President Anwar Sadat (left). The agreements set the stage for a peace treaty between Israel and Egypt. ❖

Carter met with Sadat and Begin, finally emerging with the ambiguous **Camp David accords.** A framework for negotiations rather than an actual peace settlement, the Camp David agreements dealt gingerly with the problem of Palestinian autonomy in the West Bank and Gaza Strip areas.

In 1979, Israel and Egypt signed a peace treaty that provided for the gradual return of the entire Sinai to Egypt but left the fate of the Palestine Arabs vague and unsettled. By excluding both the Palestine Liberation Organization (PLO) and the Soviet Union from the negotiations, the United States alienated Egypt from the other Arab nations and drove the more radical states closer to the Soviet Union.

Any sense of progress in the Middle East as a result of Camp David was quickly offset in 1979 with the outbreak of the Iranian Revolution. Under Nixon and Kissinger, the United States had come to depend heavily on the shah and his powerful army for defense of the vital Persian Gulf. Carter continued the close relationship with the shah, despite growing signs of domestic discontent with his leadership. By 1978, Iran was in chaos as the exiled Ayatollah Ruholla Khomeini led a fundamentalist Muslim revolt against the shah.

Unaware of the deep resentment most Iranians felt toward the shah—a resentment based both on dislike of sweeping modernization programs and police-state rule—the Carter administration misjudged the nature of the Iranian Revolution. At first, the United States encouraged the shah to remain in Iran, but when he decided to leave the country in January 1979, Carter tried to work with a moderate regime rather than encourage an army coup. With Khomeini's return from exile, Muslim militants quickly came to power in Tehran. In October 1979, Carter permitted the exiled shah to enter the United States for medical treatment. Irate mobs in Iran denounced the United States, and on November 4, militants seized the U.S. embassy in Teheran and took fifty-three Americans prisoner.

The prolonged **Iranian hostage crisis** revealed the extent to which American power had declined in the 1970s. Carter relied first on diplomacy and economic reprisals in a vain attempt to free the hostages. The United States concentrated its naval forces in the Indian Ocean as a warning to the Iranians. In his State of the Union message in January 1980, the president enunciated a new Carter doctrine, telling the world the United States would fight to protect the vital oil supplies of the Persian Gulf. "Twin threats to the flow of oil—from regional instability and now potentially from the Soviet Union—require that we firmly defend our vital interest when threatened."

Carter was unable to back up his brave words with meaningful action. In April 1980, the president

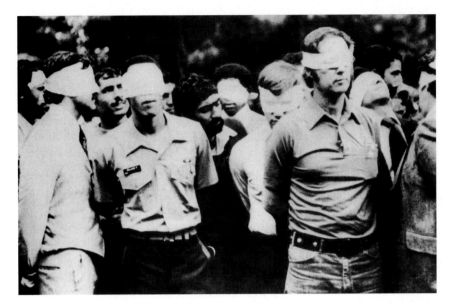

Blindfolded American hostages stand among their Iranian captors after Iranian militants captured the American embassy in Tehran on November 4, 1979. The Iranians' capture of fifty-three Americans as hostages and their violent attacks on the embassy shocked U.S. citizens. The hostage crisis dragged on for the rest of Carter's administration; the hostages were not released until January 1981. ❖

authorized a desperate rescue mission that ended in failure when several helicopters broke down in the Iranian desert and an accident cost the lives of eight crewmen. The mission was aborted. Secretary of State Cyrus Vance—who had opposed the rescue attempt—resigned in protest. The hostage crisis dragged on through the summer and fall of 1980, a symbol of American weakness that proved to be a powerful political handicap to Carter in the upcoming presidential election.

The Cold War Resumes

The policy of détente was already in trouble when Carter took office in 1977. Congressional refusal to relax trade restrictions on the Soviet Union had doomed Kissinger's attempts to win political concessions from the Soviets through economic incentives. The Kremlin's repression of the growing dissident movement and its harsh policy restricting the emigration of Soviet Jews had caused many Americans to doubt the wisdom of seeking accommodation with the Soviet Union.

President Carter's emphasis on human rights appeared to the Russians to be a direct repudiation of détente. In his inaugural address, Carter reaffirmed his concern over the mistreatment of human beings anywhere in the world, declaring that "our commitment to human rights must be absolute." It was easier said than done. Carter did withhold aid from authoritarian governments in Chile and Argentina, but equally repressive regimes in South Korea and the Philippines continued to receive generous American support. The Soviets, however, found even an inconsistent human

rights policy to be threatening, particularly after Carter received Soviet exiles in the White House.

Secretary of State Vance concentrated on continuing the main pillar of détente, the Strategic Arms Limitation Talks (SALT). In 1974, President Ford had met with Brezhnev in Vladivostok and reached tentative agreement on the outline of SALT II. The chief provision was for a ceiling of 2400 nuclear launchers by each side, a level that would not require either Russia or the United States to give up any existing delivery vehicles. In March 1977, Vance went to Moscow to propose a drastic reduction in this level; the Soviets, already angry over human rights, rejected the American proposal as an attempt to overcome the Russian lead in land-based ICBMs.

Zbigniew Brzezinski, Carter's national security adviser, worked from the outset to reverse the policy of détente. Commenting that he was "the first Pole in three hundred years in a position to really stick it to the Russians," he favored confrontation with the Kremlin. Although Carter signed a SALT II treaty with Russia in 1979, lowering the ceiling on nuclear delivery systems to 2250, growing opposition in the Senate played directly into Brzezinski's hands. He prevailed on the president to advocate adoption of a new MX missile to replace the existing Minuteman ICBMs, which some experts thought were now vulnerable to a Soviet first strike. This new weapons system, together with the planned Trident submarine, ensured that regardless of SALT, the nuclear arms race would be speeded up in the 1980s.

Brzezinski also was successful in persuading the president to use China to outmaneuver the Soviets. On January 1, 1979, the United States and China exchanged

CHRONOLOGY

1969	Two American astronauts land on the moon
1970	U.S. forces invade Cambodia (April) ❖ Ohio National Guardsmen kill four students at Kent State University (May)
1971	States ratify Twenty-sixth Amendment to the Constitution, giving 18-year-olds the right to vote (July) ❖ President Nixon freezes wages and prices for ninety days (August)
1972	President Nixon visits China (February) ❖ U.S. and USSR sign SALT I accords in Moscow (May) ❖ White House "plumbers" unit breaks into Democratic headquarters in Watergate complex (June) ❖ Richard Nixon wins reelection in landslide victory over George McGovern (November)
1973	United States and North Vietnam sign truce (January) ❖ Arab oil embargo creates energy crisis in the United States (October)
1974	Supreme Court orders Nixon to surrender White House tapes (June) ❖ Richard M. Nixon resigns presidency (August)
1975	Last evacuation helicopter leaves roof of U.S. embassy in Saigon, South Vietnam (April)
1976	Nation celebrates bicentennial with fireworks, patriotic music, and parade of sailing ships (July) ❖ Jimmy Carter defeats Gerald Ford in presidential election (November)
1977	President Carter signs Panama Canal treaties restoring sovereignty to Panama (September) ❖ Sales of imported cars, mainly from Japan, surpass two million a year for first time
1978	President Carter signs law raising mandatory retirement age from 65 to 70 (April) ❖ Over nine hundred followers of Rev. Jim Jones die in a mass suicide in Guyana (November)
1979	Iranian militants take fifty-three Americans hostage in U.S. embassy in Teheran (November) ❖ Soviet invasion of Afghanistan leads to U.S. withdrawal from 1980 Moscow Olympics (December) ❖ Congress approves loan of $1.5 billion to rescue the ailing Chrysler Corporation (December)
1980	Prime lending rate hits all-time peak of 21.5 percent

ambassadors, thereby completing the reconciliation that Nixon had begun in 1971. The new relationship between Beijing and Washington presented the Soviet Union with the problem of a link between its two most powerful enemies.

The Cold War, in abeyance for nearly a decade, resumed with full fury in December 1979 when the Soviet Union invaded Afghanistan. Although this move was designed to ensure a regime friendly to the Soviet Union, it appeared to many like the beginning of a Soviet thrust toward the Indian Ocean and the Persian Gulf. Carter responded to this aggression with a series of symbolic acts: The United States banned the sale of high technology to Russia, embargoed the export of grain, resumed draft registration, and even boycotted the 1980 Moscow Olympics. These American moves did not halt the invasion of Afghanistan; instead, they put the United States and Russia back on a collision course.

The results doomed détente. Aware that he could not get a two-thirds vote in the Senate, Carter withdrew the SALT II treaty. The hopeful phrases of détente gave way to belligerent rhetoric as groups such as the Committee on the Present Danger called for an all-out effort against the Soviet Union. Jimmy Carter, who had come into office hoping to advance human rights and control the nuclear arms race, now found himself a victim of the renewed Cold War.

CONCLUSION: A FAILED PRESIDENCY

National frustration over the hostages in Iran and the Soviet invasion of Afghanistan destroyed public confidence in the Carter administration. The irony lay in the relationship between events and presidential leadership. The failures of Lyndon Johnson and Richard Nixon, most notably the defeat in Vietnam and the Watergate scandal, had helped the relatively unknown Jimmy Carter reach the White House as the outsider who would avoid the mistakes of his predecessors. But events beyond Carter's control proved equally damaging to his presidency. The inability to wield American power in the world effectively, as well as the failure to overcome the ravages of inflation, destroyed Carter's dream of achieving prosperity at home and peace abroad.

President Carter, despite his incredibly long hours and determined efforts, lost the most crucial of all presidential assets—the support of the American people. His substantial achievements—environmental reform, the Camp David agreements, the Panama Canal treaties—were soon forgotten as the nation only remembered double-digit inflation and the humiliating hostage crisis. By mid-1980, the president's overall approval rating had fallen to 23 percent in the Gallup poll. American voters, disappointed by the performances of Johnson, Nixon, Ford, and Carter in the White House, yearned for new political leadership to meet the mounting challenges facing the nation.

RECOMMENDED READING

The most comprehensive account of Nixon's political career and presidency is the three-volume biography by Stephen E. Ambrose, *Nixon* (1987–1992). Melvin Small offers a balanced assessment of Nixon's White House years in *The Presidency of Richard Nixon* (1999); for a more detailed view, see Richard Reeves, *President Nixon* (2001). Stanley Kutler provides a thorough account of the scandal that drove Nixon from office in *The Wars of Watergate* (1990).

H. W. Brands offers a good survey of American foreign policy from the mid-1970s through the mid-1990s in *Since Vietnam* (1995). For foreign policy under Nixon, see William P. Bundy, *A Tangled Web* (1998), and Jeffrey Kimball, *Nixon's Vietnam War* (1998). Raymond L. Garthoff, *Détente and Confrontation* (1985) covers relations with the Soviet Union in the 1970s. The best biography of Henry Kissinger is Walter Isaacson, *Kissinger* (1989). James Bamford, *Body of Secrets* (2001), deals with the highly secretive National Security Agency.

In *The Prize* (1991), Daniel Yergin puts the energy crisis of the 1970s in historical perspective. Richard Barnet gives a thorough description of the impact of the energy crisis and foreign competition on the American economy in the 1970s in *The Lean Years* (1980). For economic policy under Carter, see W. Carl Biven, *Jimmy Carter's Economy* (2002).

Two books survey popular culture in the 1970s: David Frum, *How We Got Here: The 70's* (2000) and Bruce J. Schulman, *The Seventies* (2001).

For the Ford and Carter administrations, see John R. Greene, *The Presidency of Gerald R. Ford* (1995), and Burton I. Kaufman, *The Presidency of Jimmy Carter* (1993). Gaddis Smith surveys Carter's foreign policy in *Morality, Reason, and Power* (1985). For the crisis with Iran, see Barry Rubin, *Paved with Good Intentions* (1980).

For a list of additional titles related to this chapter's topics, please see http://www.ablongman.com/divine.

SUGGESTED WEB SITES

May 4, 1970: Twenty-five Years of Remembrance

http://www.library.kent.edu/exhibits/4may95/index.html

This site commemorates the twenty-fifth anniversary of the shootings at Kent State University with a detailed chronology and other information.

Documents from the Women's Liberation Movement

http://scriptorium.lib.duke.edu/wlm/

Primary documents on-line from the Special Collections Library at Duke University provide firsthand information about the women's liberation movement.

Constitutional Issues: Watergate and the Constitution

http://www.nara.gov/education/teaching/watergate/watergat.html

From the National Archives' teaching materials, this site has a good chronology of Watergate and a 1974 memorandum from the Watergate Special Prosecution Force weighing the pros and cons of seeking an indictment against former President Richard Nixon.

CNN 1970s Interactive Timeline

http://cnn.com/SPECIALS/1999/century/episodes/08/

CNN has a series of interactive timelines with several interesting sites. This one covers the years from 1970 to 1979.

Watergate 25

http://www.washingtonpost.com/wp-srv/national/longterm/watergate/front.htm

This site features a chronology, images, searchable articles, and a good deal of background information about the burglary and its consequences.

Richard Milhous Nixon

http://www.ipl.org/ref/POTUS/rmnixon.html

This site contains basic factual data about Nixon's election and presidency, speeches, and on-line biographies.

Gerald Rudolph Ford

http://www.ipl.org/ref/POTUS/grford.html

This site contains basic factual data about Ford's election and presidency, speeches, and on-line biographies.

James Earl Carter, Jr.

http://www.ipl.org/ref/POTUS/jecarter.html

This site contains basic factual data about Carter's election and presidency, speeches, and on-line biographies.

Giant Leap

http://cnn.com/TECH/specials/apollo/

This CNN site commemorates the thirtieth anniversary of the 1969 moonwalk and tells the story of NASA and the ongoing space program.

The American Experience: Meltdown at Three Mile Island

http://www.pbs.org/wgbh/amex/three/

Companion to the PBS documentary, this site includes a chronology and description of the 1979 nuclear accident.

U.S. Environmental Protection Agency

http://www.epa.gov/history

This history of the EPA includes a timeline, topical information, publications, and a document collection.

Law and Society

Roe v. Wade

The Struggle over Women's Reproductive Rights

In colonial America, abortion had been a legal and acceptable way to terminate a pregnancy. Throughout the nineteenth century, states began restricting or outlawing the procedure, and by 1900 every state except Kentucky had enacted some form of anti-abortion law. Despite laws criminalizing abortion, the number of illegal abortions each year—whether performed privately by physicians or by unlicensed practitioners—numbered anywhere from 200,000 to 1.2 million. And each year about two hundred of the women who obtained illegal abortions died as a result of the procedure.

Abortion rights advocates mobilized in the 1960s, helped by the growing women's rights movement, the declining health risk involved in the procedure, and the wave of fetal deformities and birth defects that swept the nation in the early 1960s, largely attributable to an outbreak of German measles. Their argument centered on the belief that a woman had the right to control her own body. Just as vocal as abortion rights advocates were those who opposed abortion, believing that human life began at conception and that a fetus's right to life outweighed a woman's right to end a pregnancy. In 1973, in the case of *Roe* v. *Wade,* the U.S. Supreme Court handed down a momentous decision on the abortion debate—a decision that continues to generate controversy, to rally support, and to provoke opposition thirty years later.

On January 22, 1998, Norma McCorvey joined thousands of Americans who braved the freezing weather of Washington, D.C, to protest the Supreme Court decision in the case of *Jane Roe et. al.* v. *Henry Wade.* Exactly twenty-five years earlier the court had sided with Jane Roe, the pseudonym for an anonymous

Texas woman seeking an abortion, and overturned a state law that made abortion illegal in all cases except when the life of the mother was at risk. The ruling had voided forty-six state laws that denied or restricted a woman's access to the controversial procedure. Now Norma McCorvey and other abortion opponents were observing the anniversary of the decision by taking to the streets to demonstrate their opposition. In many ways, McCorvey's presence was unsurprising; she was a "born-again" Christian, an active abortion opponent, and the founder of an anti-abortion ministry. In 1997, she had publicly denounced abortion in America as "a terrible, terrible holocaust." Yet, one thing made Norma different from the other protestors: twenty-five years earlier, she had been Jane Roe.

The intensity of the debate over abortion reached unprecedented heights in the 1970s, and state legislatures began to pay attention to the cries for reform of laws governing abortion. Between 1967 and 1970, twelve states liberalized their laws, usually to permit abortion in cases of rape, incest, or fetal deformity, or to protect the life and health of the pregnant woman. Most states, however, retained their restrictive laws, and by 1973 only four states guaranteed their residents virtually unhindered access to an abortion. Texas, the home of Norma McCorvey, was not one of them.

McCorvey was largely unaware of these legal struggles. A poor Texas woman from a broken home, she had dropped out of school in tenth grade and at the age of sixteen married an abusive spouse. The marriage quickly collapsed, and Norma spent the next five years working odd jobs and traveling across Texas. Her first child, born while she was sixteen, was eventually adopted by her mother, and her second, the product of a short affair with a co-worker a few years later, was given up for adoption. In late 1969,

Norma McCorvey, the Jane Roe of *Roe* v. *Wade,* with one of her lawyers, Gloria Allred. ❖

Norma again became pregnant. Twenty-two years old, depressed, poor, and lacking access to good medical care, she sought a solution—any solution—other than carrying the unwanted child to term. Her attempt to induce an abortion by drinking castor oil and eating a few pounds of peanuts only made her sick. Texas's abortion law, which had stood virtually unchanged since 1857, proscribed a punishment of up to five years in prison to anyone convicted of performing an abortion for reasons other than saving the mother's life. Adoption, it seemed, was her only option.

Surprisingly, her path toward adoption led McCorvey into the struggle for abortion rights. An adoption lawyer referred her to Sarah Weddington and Linda Coffee, two young lawyers who were preparing to challenge Texas's abortion law, but needed a pregnant woman willing to serve as the name plaintiff. In December 1969, the three women met for dinner in Dallas. McCorvey agreed to join the

lawsuit without much prodding, but had one request: the use of a pseudonym to hide her identity. Three months later, Weddington and Coffee filed a class action lawsuit on behalf of all Texas women against Henry Wade, the District Attorney of Dallas County, demanding that he stop enforcing the state's abortion laws; McCorvey, the name plaintiff, was identified only as Jane Roe.

At first, the case attracted little notice. When Dallas's Fifth Circuit three-judge Federal Court heard oral arguments on May 22, 1970, there were no reporters, no television cameras, and no Norma McCorvey. Coffee and Weddington asked the court to overturn the Texas law on two grounds. First, they claimed, it was written too vaguely to be applied fairly. More significantly, they argued that the Texas law violated a woman's right to privacy. They cited recent Supreme Court decisions articulating a zone of personal privacy; this zone, the justices had admitted, was not explicitly written into the Constitution but could be inferred from a number of amendments. In 1965, the Supreme Court had made their most specific statement on this concept, writing in *Griswold* v. *Connecticut* of a "zone of privacy created by several fundamental constitutional guarantees." In *Griswold,* the justices struck down a one-hundred-year-old Connecticut law forbidding the sale of birth control devices; now, Weddington and Coffee argued that this personal privacy zone included reproductive rights as well.

Texas's lawyers rejected the claims. Jay Floyd of the Attorney General's Office contended that Jane Roe, whoever she was, had no standing to sue since the law only punished doctors who performed abortions, not the women who received them. Besides, Floyd claimed, Roe had to be so far along in her pregnancy by now that either she had already given birth or would do so fairly soon; thus, regardless of the court's decision, the whole case was moot. Assistant District Attorney John Tolle took a different approach, arguing that the state had the right to protect life in all forms, and hence the fetus was entitled to the full protection of the state. "I personally think and I think the state's position," he concluded, "is that the right of the child to life is superior to that woman's right to privacy."

It took almost a month for the judges to announce their decision. The Texas laws, they ruled, were unconstitutional, "because they deprive single women and married couples of their right [to privacy], secured by the Ninth Amendment." They also found the statute too vague to be allowed to continue under the Fourteenth Amendment. The law would have to be eliminated. However, they refused to issue an injunction ordering the district attorney's office to stop enforcing it immediately; such an action, they announced, would be too intrusive considering that the state had not yet been given the opportunity to revise its laws. Quickly, the Texas attorney general announced his intention to appeal the case and to continue prosecuting doctors who violated the statute. Weddington and Coffee also appealed, citing the court's refusal to issue an injunction. The first battle for abortion rights had been fought, but nothing had been resolved.

For Weddington and Coffee, the decision would mean an eventual appeal to the Supreme Court; for Norma McCorvey it meant only crushing disappointment. McCorvey had never seen herself as a crusader for women's rights, and despite being the name plaintiff she had played virtually no role in the case. She had joined the lawsuit only in the hope of obtaining an abortion, and for six months had drifted across Texas, clinging to the lawsuit as her last chance. Now, she discovered, she had won her case, but without an immediate injunction she would have to deliver the baby after all. The lawsuit, she realized for the first time, was "not really for me. It was about me, and maybe all the women who've come before me, but it was really for all the women who were coming after me." A few months later she had her third baby, which she gave up for adoption.

In March 1971, the United States Supreme Court agreed to hear the case. Supreme Court involvement prior to a case being argued before an appeals court was an unusual step, but since a constitutional right was at issue, the justices agreed to intervene immediately. Undoubtedly, the growing intensity of the abortion debate also influenced the court; by the time the *Roe* appeal was filed, eleven state courts had abortion cases pending, twenty cases were before three-judge federal panels, and four others were on the Supreme Court docket for consideration. Local and state disputes also kept the topic at the center of public attention. In 1969, a woman's rights organization in New York, furious at a federal court's refusal to hear the testimony from people who had suffered through illegal abortions, took public depositions at a church in Greenwich Village. The following year, Washington residents debated Proposition 20, a proposal to repeal their abortion laws. Anti-abortion advocates adorned billboards throughout the state with pictures of a four-month-old fetus in a human hand, above the slogan, "Kill Referendum 20, Not Me."

In the end, the Supreme Court would hear *Roe v. Wade* not once but twice. At oral arguments on December 13, 1971, both sides reiterated their positions to the nation's highest court. The justices quickly

Abortion rights advocates supported the Supreme Court decision in *Roe* v. *Wade*. Demonstrators, like these picketers in Cincinnati, Ohio, affirmed that the decision gave women the right to choose. ❖

dismissed the state's claim that Roe did not have standing to sue, since the case was a class-action suit on behalf of all Texas women. "I suppose," declared Justice Potter Stewart, "we could almost take judicial notice of the fact that there are, at any given time, unmarried, pregnant females in the state of Texas." The verdict seemed clear in postargument discussions, as five of the justices favored striking down the Texas law, while only two sided with the state. Due to recent retirements, however, the court was operating with only seven members, two short of its full complement. This fact, combined with general unhappiness with the majority opinion written by Justice Harry Blackmun, led the Court to the unusual decision of putting the case over for reargument the following year.

On October 10, 1972, the two sides rehashed their arguments for a final time. Again, McCorvey remained in Texas while Weddington stressed her constitutional right to privacy. "We are not here to advocate abortion," she told the court. "We do not ask this Court to rule that abortion is good or desirable in any particular situation. We are here to advocate that the decision as to whether or not a particular woman will continue to carry or will terminate a pregnancy is a decision that should be made by that individual." A number of groups filed briefs in support of *Roe*, including the American Medical Association, the National Organization for Women, the American Bar Association, and the American Association of University Women, while Texas's case received supporting briefs from the attorney generals of Connecticut, Kentucky, Arizona, and Nebraska.

The justices announced their verdict on January 22, 1973, striking down the Texas law by a 7 to 2 vote. Justice Blackmun's eighty-page majority opinion echoed Weddington and Coffee's argument about an implied zone of privacy. "The right of privacy," he wrote, "whether it be founded in the Fourteenth Amendment's concept of personal liberty and restrictions upon state action, as we feel it is, or, as the District Court determined, in the Ninth Amendment's reservation of rights to the people, is broad enough to encompass a woman's decision whether or not to terminate her pregnancy." The fetus, the majority also agreed, had never been given legal recognition as a person, and as such could not expect to receive equal protections.

Once again the verdict was not an unqualified victory for Coffee and Weddington. Blackmun's decision forbade states from restricting abortion in the first trimester of pregnancy and allowed them to regulate it only in the interests of preserving maternal health in the second. However, he recognized a legitimate state interest in protecting "potential life," which he defined as occurring when the fetus had "the capacity for meaningful life outside of the mother's womb." Accordingly, he permitted states to regulate abortion under almost all circumstances during the last trimester. Only Justices Byron White and William Rehnquist sided with Texas. In a scathing dissent, White attacked his brethren for making a decision that should have been left to the individual states, calling the verdict "an improvident and extravagant exercise of the power of judicial review." The Court, he concluded, "apparently values the convenience of the pregnant mother more than the continued existence and development of the life or potential life which she carries."

The ruling set off both celebration and protest. In Texas, Norma McCorvey read about the decision in the newspaper and immediately broke into tears. When Weddington finally reached her a few days later, Norma was thrilled. "It makes me feel like I'm on top of Mt. Everest," she told her lawyer. The sentiment was hardly unanimous. John Cardinal Krol, president of the National Catholic Conference, predicted that the Court was ushering in "the greatest slaughter of innocent life in the history of mankind." Personal letters to the justices, most of them negative, were so overwhelming that the guards had to construct a separate sorting area in the basement of the Supreme Court building (Justice Hugo Black received more than a thousand derogatory letters, despite the fact that he had died eighteen months earlier).

The struggle, however, was far from over. Shocked by the decision, anti-abortion forces redoubled their efforts. Although a few chose violence, most opponents of the *Roe* decision turned to lobbying and legislation to undo the verdict. Congressmen introduced hundreds of constitutional amendments limiting abortion, but none was approved. In 1976, Congress did prohibit the use of Medicaid funds for abortions, except when the life of the mother was at risk, and twelve years later, the Department of Health and Human Services banned government-employed doctors from counseling women about abortions. Even the Supreme Court showed a willingness to chip away at its earlier decision. In *Bellotti v. Baird* (1979), the Court allowed states to require unmarried minors to get parental consent for abortions, as long as the state offered an alternative procedure such as allowing her to obtain a judge's permission instead. The Court, in *Planned Parenthood of Southeastern Pennsylvania* v. *Casey* (1992), later upheld a Pennsylvania law that placed various restrictions on abortion rights, including a mandatory twenty-four

Anti-abortion activists, like these demonstrators in Washington, D.C., equated abortion with murder in their protests against *Roe* v. *Wade*. ❖

hour waiting period and a requirement that doctors present alternative options before performing the surgery. Still, while the Court modified the *Roe* decision, it never renounced the basic principle of guaranteeing American women the right to choose an abortion early in a pregnancy.

Throughout the intense debate, no figure remained more central to the struggle than Norma McCorvey. For two decades, many who supported abortion rights admired her as a courageous individual who led American women in their fight to recapture control of their own bodies. Yet, more than twenty years later, McCorvey, who revealed her identity in 1984, stunned her supporters by renouncing her past position and embracing the anti-abortion movement. She then became an inspirational symbol to those on the other side of the debate, who applauded her wisdom and courage in renouncing the errors of her past. By 1997, she had joined the controversial anti-

abortion group Operation Rescue and the following year opened her own ministry, "Roe No More." Yet, despite her role as a symbol of this intense struggle, McCorvey remained just a typical American struggling to come to grips with a difficult and complex topic. "Deep inside," she recalled twenty years after Jane Roe had become famous, "I'm still nobody but Norma McCorvey."

Questions for Discussion

- What is the constitutional basis for the assertion of a woman's right to privacy?

- Why was Justice Blackmon's opinion so controversial? Why did he limit the right to abortion to the first two trimesters of a pregnancy?

- To what extent have subsequent court decisions limited a woman's right to abortion? How likely do you think it is that the Court will overturn *Roe v. Wade* in the future?

Chapter 32

Aerial view of Los Angeles in 1983. The relaxation of federal regulations adopted in the 1970s to reduce air pollution, increasing population and automobile traffic, as well as the city's valley location, all contributed to the smog visible in this photograph. ❖

The Republican Resurgence, 1980–1992

*R*eagan and the Rise of Conservatism

In October 1964, the Republican National Committee sponsored a televised address by Hollywood actor Ronald Reagan on behalf of Barry Goldwater's presidential candidacy. Reagan's speech had originally been aired on a Los Angeles station; the resulting outpouring of praise and campaign contributions led to its national rebroadcast.

In contrast to Goldwater's strident rhetoric, Reagan used relaxed, confident, and persuasive terms to put forth the case for a return to individual freedom. Instead of the usual choice between increased government activity and less government involvement, often couched in terms of the left and the right, Reagan presented the options of either going up or down—"up to the maximum of human freedom consistent with law and order, or down to the ant heap of totalitarianism." Then, borrowing a phrase from FDR, he told his audience: "You and I have a rendezvous with destiny. We can preserve for our children this the last best hope of man on earth, or we can sentence them to take the first step into a thousand years of darkness."

Although the speech did not rescue Goldwater's unpopular candidacy, it marked the beginning of Ronald Reagan's remarkable political career. A popular Hollywood actor whose movie career had begun to fade in the 1950s, Reagan had become an effective television performer as host of "The General Electric Theater." His political views, once liberal, moved steadily to the right as he became a spokesperson for a major American corporation. In 1965, a group of wealthy friends persuaded him, largely on the basis of the success of "the speech," to run for the California governorship.

Reagan proved to be an attractive candidate. His friendly, relaxed manner and his mastery of television enabled him to present his strongly conservative message without appearing to be a rigid ideologue of the right. He won handily by appealing effectively to rising middle-class suburban resentment over high taxes, expanding welfare programs, and bureaucratic regulation.

In two terms as governor, Reagan displayed natural ability as a political leader. Instead of insisting on implementing all of his conservative beliefs, he proved surprisingly flexible. Faced with a Democratic legislature, he yielded on raising taxes and increasing state spending while managing to trim the welfare rolls. Symbolic victories were his specialty; in one example he managed to confront campus radicals and fire Clark Kerr, chancellor of the University of California, while at the same time generously funding higher education.

By the time Reagan left the governor's office in 1974, many signs pointed to a growing conservative mood across the nation. In a popular rebellion against escalating property taxes in 1978, California's voters passed Proposition 13, which called for a 57 percent cut in taxes and resulted in a gradual reduction in social services. Religious leaders were especially outraged over the 1962 Supreme Court ruling in *Engel* v. *Vitale* outlawing school prayer on the grounds that it was "no part of the business of government to compose official prayers." In the South, where daily prayers were the customary

OUTLINE
❖❖❖

Reagan in Power

Reaganomics

Reagan and the World

Social Dilemmas

Passing the Torch to Bush

Conclusion: Republican
Economic Woes

FEATURE ESSAY
❖❖❖

The Christian Right

LAW AND SOCIETY
❖❖❖

Bakke v. *Regents of the
University of California:* The
Question of Affirmative Action

way of beginning the school day, the reaction was intense. One Alabama congressman denounced the Supreme Court justices, proclaiming, "They put the Negroes in the schools and now they're driving God out."

Concern over school prayer, along with rising abortion and divorce rates, impelled religious groups to engage in political activity to defend what they viewed as traditional family values. Jerry Falwell, a successful Virginia radio and television evangelist, founded the **Moral Majority,** a fundamentalist group dedicated to preserving the "American way of life." (See the Feature Essay, "The Christian Right," pp. 934–935.)

The population shift of the 1970s, especially the rapid growth of the Sunbelt region in the South and West (see p. 963), added momentum to the conservative upsurge. Those moving to the Sunbelt tended to be white, middle- and upper-class suburbanites—mainly skilled workers, young professionals, and business executives who were attracted both by economic opportunity and by a political climate stressing low taxes, less government regulation, and more reliance on the marketplace. The political impact of population shifts from East to West and North to South during the 1970s was reflected in the congressional gains (seventeen seats) by Sunbelt and Far West states after the 1980 census.

Conservatives also succeeded, for the first time since World War II, in making their cause intellectually respectable. Scholars and academics on the right flourished in new "think tanks"; writer William Buckley and economist Milton Friedman proved to be effective advocates of conservative causes in print and on television. **Neoconservatism,** led by Norman Podhoretz's magazine *Commentary*, became fashionable among many intellectuals who were former liberal stalwarts. They denounced liberals for being too soft on the communist threat abroad and too willing to compromise high standards at home in the face of demands for equality from African Americans, women, and the disadvantaged. Neoconservatives called for a reaffirmation of capitalism and a new emphasis on what was right about America rather than an obsessive concern with social ills.

BY THE END OF THE 1970s, Ronald Reagan was recognized as the nation's most effective leader of the conservative resurgence. His personal charm softened the hard edges of his right-wing call to arms, and his conviction that America could regain its traditional self-confidence by reaffirming basic ideals had a broad appeal to a nation shaken by inflation at home and humiliation abroad. In 1976, Reagan had barely lost to Gerald Ford at the Republican convention; four years later, he overcame an early upset by George Bush in Iowa to win the GOP presidential nomination handily.

In his acceptance speech at the Republican convention in Detroit, he set forth the themes that endeared him to conservatives: less government, balanced budget, family values, and peace through increased military spending. Unlike Barry Goldwater, who frightened people with his rigid ideology, Reagan offered reassurance and hope for the future. He spoke of restoring to the federal government "the capacity to do the people's work without dominating their lives." As historian Robert Dallek pointed out, Reagan "assured

Republican presidential candidate Ronald Reagan greets supporters in Cincinnati during his 1980 campaign. Reagan won the election, carrying all but six states. ❖

his listeners that he was no radical idealist courting defeat, but a sensible, thoroughly likable American with a surefire formula for success that would please everyone." In Ronald Reagan, the Republicans had found the perfect candidate to exploit both the American people's frustration with the failures in domestic and foreign policy of the 1970s and the growing conservative mood of the nation.

In the White House, Reagan would have a lasting impact on American life. At home, his success in reducing taxes and cutting spending on social programs reversed the trend toward greater reliance on the federal government that had prevailed since the New Deal. Yet

his economic policies, along with a sharp increase in defense spending, created unprecedented budget deficits that would plague his successors through the mid-1990s. Abroad, Reagan was successful in rebuilding American military power and compelling the Soviet Union to choose diplomacy rather than confrontation, culminating in the dramatic end of the Cold War during the presidency of George Bush. Yet even this unexpected victory led not to a new era of peace in the world, but rather to dangerous crises in the Middle East and the Balkans. For better or worse, President Reagan left an enduring legacy.

REAGAN IN POWER

The liberal Democratic political coalition, originally created by Franklin D. Roosevelt in the Great Depression, finally split apart by the end of the 1970s. The Watergate scandal gave the Democrats a brief reprieve, but by the end of the decade, the Republicans were using the conservative upsurge to make inroads among such traditionally Democratic groups of voters as Jews, Southerners, and blue-collar workers. Yet the continuing appeal of the New Deal legacy prevented a total political realignment.

The Reagan Victory

In 1980, Jimmy Carter, who had used the Watergate trauma to win the presidency, found himself in trouble. Inflation, touched off by the second oil shock of the 1970s, reached double-digit figures. The Federal Reserve Board's effort to tighten the money supply had led to a recession, with unemployment climbing to 7.8 percent by July 1980. What Ronald Reagan dubbed the "misery index," the combined rate of inflation and unemployment, hit 28 percent early in 1980 and stayed above 20 percent throughout the year.

Foreign policy proved almost as damaging to Carter. The Soviet invasion of Afghanistan eroded hopes for continued détente; the hostage crisis in Iran highlighted the nation's sense of helplessness. In the short run, Carter used that crisis to beat back the challenge to his renomination by fellow Democrat Edward Kennedy; the president stayed in the White House during the spring primaries, reminding the voters of his devotion to duty. The Democrats rallied behind Carter, although the delegates to the party's convention displayed a notable lack of enthusiasm in renominating him.

Ronald Reagan and his running mate, George Bush, hammered away at the state of the economy and the world. Reagan scored heavily among traditionally

Democratic blue-collar groups by blaming Carter for inflation, which robbed workers of any gain in real wages. Reagan also accused Carter of allowing the Soviets to outstrip the United States militarily and promised a massive buildup of American forces if he was elected. Although Republican strategists feared Carter might spring an "October surprise"—a negotiated release of the American hostages at the height of the campaign—the Iranian situation actually helped Reagan by accentuating U.S. weakness in the world. Carter's position was further hurt by the independent candidacy of liberal Republican John Anderson of Illinois, who appealed to voters disenchanted with Carter but not yet ready to embrace Reagan.

The president struck back by claiming that Reagan was too reckless to conduct American foreign policy in the nuclear age. Charging that the election would decide "whether we have peace or war," Carter tried to portray his Republican challenger as a warmonger. The attack backfired. In a televised debate arranged late in the campaign, Reagan assured the American people of his devotion to peace, leaving Carter with the onus of trying to land a low blow. At the end of the confrontation, Reagan scored impressively when he summed up the country's dire economic condition by suggesting that voters ask themselves simply, "Are you better off now than you were four years ago? Is it easier for you to go and buy things in the stores than it was four years ago?"

On election day, the American people answered with a resounding "no." Reagan carried forty-four states and gained 51 percent of the popular vote. Carter won only six states and 41 percent of the popular vote, while John Anderson received the remaining 8 percent but failed to carry a single state. Reagan clearly benefited from the growing political power of the Sunbelt; he carried every state west of the Mississippi except Minnesota, the home state of Carter's running mate, Walter Mondale. In the South, Reagan lost only Georgia, Carter's home state. Even more impressive

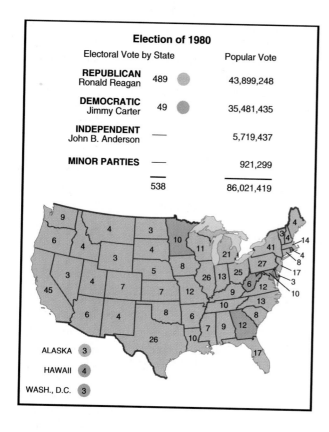

Election of 1980

Electoral Vote by State		Popular Vote
REPUBLICAN Ronald Reagan	489	43,899,248
DEMOCRATIC Jimmy Carter	49	35,481,435
INDEPENDENT John B. Anderson	—	5,719,437
MINOR PARTIES	—	921,299
	538	86,021,419

ALASKA 3
HAWAII 4
WASH., D.C. 3

Journalist Theodore White disagreed, viewing the outcome as a repudiation of the Democratic coalition that had dominated American politics since the days of Franklin D. Roosevelt and the New Deal. White had a strong case. In the eight presidential elections from 1952 to 1980, Republican candidates received 52.3 percent of the popular vote, compared to 47.7 percent for the Democrats. Reagan's victory in 1980 thus marked the culmination of a Republican presidential realignment that ended a half-century of Democratic dominance.

Cutting Spending and Taxes

When Ronald Reagan took office in January 1981, the ravages of inflation had devastated the economy. Interest rates hovered near 20 percent, while the value of the dollar, compared to 1960, had dropped to just 36 cents. The new president blamed what he termed "the worst economic mess since the Great Depression" on high federal spending and excessive taxation. "Government is not the solution to our problems," Reagan announced in his inaugural address, "government is the problem."

The president embraced the concept of **supply-side economics** as the proper remedy for the nation's economic ills. Supply-side economists believed that the private sector, freed of the ever increasing burden of government spending, would shift its resources from tax shelters to productive investment, leading to an economic boom that would provide enough new income to offset the lost revenue. Although many other economists worried that the 30 percent cut in income taxes that Reagan favored would lead to staggering deficits, the president was confident that his program would both stimulate the economy and reduce the role of government.

The president made spending the first target. Quickly deciding not to attack such popular middle-class entitlement programs as Social Security and Medicare, and sparing critical social services for the "truly deserving needy," the so-called safety net, Republicans concentrated on slashing $41.4 billion from the budget by cutting heavily into other social services such as food stamps and by reducing public service jobs, student loans, and support for urban mass transit. Reagan used his charm and powers of persuasion to woo conservative Democrats from the West and South. Appearing before a joint session of Congress only weeks after an attempt on his life, Reagan won a commanding 253 to 176 margin of victory for his budget in the House, and an even more lopsided vote of 78 to 20 in the Senate in May. A jubilant Reagan told a Los Angeles audience that he had achieved "the greatest reduction in government spending that has ever been attempted."

were Reagan's inroads into the old New Deal coalition. He received 50.5 percent of the blue-collar vote and 46 percent of the Jewish vote, the best showing by a Republican since 1928. Only one group remained loyal to Carter: African American voters gave him 85 percent of their ballots.

Republican gains in Congress were even more surprising. For the first time since 1954, the GOP gained control of the Senate, 53 to 46, and the party picked up 33 seats in the House to narrow the Democratic margin from 114 to 50. Liberals were the chief losers in Congress. Prominent Democratic senators such as George McGovern and Frank Church met with defeat, victims of a vendetta waged by the Moral Majority.

The meaning of the election was less clear than its outcome. Nearly all observers agreed that the voters had rendered an adverse judgment on the Carter administration. But most experts did not assess the outcome to be a major realignment in American politics equivalent to the Democratic victory of FDR in 1932. Voters in 1980 expressed distaste for current economic conditions, not a strongly held ideological preference. The fact that the Democrats still held a sizable majority in the House was seen as proof of their party's continuing strength. Political scientist Walter Dean Burnham termed the result "a conservative revitalization," but one that stopped short of making the GOP the dominant party.

President Reagan jubilantly acknowledges the crowd just moments before being shot by John Hinckley, Jr., on March 30, 1981. After the assassination attempt, Secret Service personnel and police rushed to rescue the president and the others wounded in the gunfire. ❖

The president proved equally successful in reducing taxes. Adopting a proposal originally put forth by Senator William Roth of Delaware and Congressman Jack Kemp of New York, he advocated a cut of 10 percent in personal income taxes for three consecutive years. When the Democrats countered with a two-year plan that would reduce taxes by only 15 percent, Reagan compromised with a proposal to cut taxes by 5 percent the first year but insisted on the full 10 percent reduction for the second and third years. In July, both houses passed the tax cut by impressive margins. In se-

curing reductions in spending and lowering taxes, Reagan had demonstrated beyond any doubt his ability to wield presidential power effectively. As *Time* magazine commented, no president since FDR had "done so much of such magnitude so quickly to change the economic direction of the country."

Limiting the Role of Government

Reagan met with only mixed success in his other efforts to restrict government activity and reduce federal regulation of the economy. Cutting back on the scope of federal agencies and limiting their impact on American business was a central tenet of the president's political philosophy. To achieve his goal of **deregulation** he appointed men and women who shared his belief in relying on the marketplace rather than the bureaucracy to direct the nation's economy. To the outrage of environmentalists, Secretary of the Interior James Watt opened up federal land to coal and timber production, halted the growth of national parkland, and made more than a billion acres of land available for offshore oil drilling. Though Watt was eventually forced to resign, the Reagan administration continued its policy of reducing government intervention in business long after Watt's departure.

Transportation Secretary Drew Lewis proved to be the most effective cabinet member in the administration's first two years. He helped relieve the troubled American automobile industry of many of the regulations adopted in the 1970s to reduce air pollution and increase passenger safety. At the same time, he played a key role in the behind-the-scenes negotiations that led Japan to agree in the spring of 1981 to restrict its automobile exports to the United States for the next three years. This unilateral Japanese action enabled the Reagan administration to help Detroit's carmakers without openly violating its free market position by endorsing protectionist measures.

Lewis gained notoriety in opposing a strike by the air traffic controllers' union (PATCO) in the summer of 1981. The president, denouncing PATCO for threatening to interrupt "the protective services which are government's reason for being," fired the striking workers, decertified the union, and ordered Lewis to hire and train thousands of new air traffic controllers at a cost of $1.3 billion. For the Reagan administration, the price was worth paying to prove that no group of government employees had the right to defy the public interest.

The Reagan administration was less successful in trying to cut back on the entitlement programs that it viewed as the primary cause of the growing budget deficits. Social Security was the greatest offender. A 500 percent increase in Social Security benefits in the 1970s threatened to bankrupt the system's trust fund by the end of the century. Reagan, overconfident from his budget victory, met a sharp rebuff when he tried to make substantial cuts in future benefits. The president then appointed a bipartisan commission to recommend ways to protect the system's endangered trust fund. In March 1983, Congress approved a series of changes that guaranteed the solvency of Social Security by gradually raising the retirement age, delaying cost-of-living increases for six months, and taxing pensions paid to the well-to-do elderly.

The Professional Air Traffic Controllers' Organization (PATCO) was one of the few unions to support Reagan in the 1980 campaign. But when PATCO struck in August 1981, Reagan unhesitatingly fired the striking air traffic controllers and refused to rehire them when the strike collapsed. ❖

The administration's record in dealing with women's concerns and civil rights proved clumsy and divisive. Although feminist groups were disappointed by the administration's strong rhetorical attacks on legalized abortion, the appointment of Sandra Day O'Connor to the Supreme Court pleased them. By this one shrewd move, Reagan was able both to fulfill a campaign pledge and to make a symbolic gesture to women. His appointments to the lower federal courts were a better indication of his administration's relatively low regard for women. Of the first seventy-two Reagan nominees to the federal judiciary, only three were women; just one of the sixty-nine men was African American.

The administration's civil rights record proved especially revealing. Aware of how few African Americans had supported the GOP in 1980, Reagan made no effort to reward this group with government jobs or favors. Instead, the Justice Department actively opposed busing to achieve school integration and affirmative action measures that resulted in minority hiring quotas.

Chief Justice Warren Burger swears in Sandra Day O'Connor, the first woman to serve on the U.S. Supreme Court, in September 1981. ✧

REAGANOMICS

The sweeping reductions in domestic spending and income taxes that Reagan achieved in 1981 gave rise to conflicting economic expectations. Supply-side economists believed that the tax relief granted investors would lead to rapid business growth, which would raise more than enough new revenue to offset the lower rates. The administration's critics, on the other hand, were sure that heavy defense spending coupled with tax reductions would create massive deficits and result in economic stagnation. Neither group proved to be right.

Recession and Recovery

The supply-side theory became the first economic casualty of the 1980s. The naive belief that a combination of cuts in social spending and sharply reduced taxes could unleash an economic boom that would avoid huge deficits was the victim of both Reagan's insistence on huge increases in defense spending (projected at more than $1 trillion over five years) and the Federal Reserve Board's tight-money policy. It was the latter that touched off a recession that began in the fall of 1981 and grew steadily worse throughout 1982, with unemployment reaching a postwar high of 10.4 percent in October.

Still, Reagan refused to give up his income tax cuts. With the first 10 percent reduction due to come in July 1982, he claimed that his policies had not yet been given a chance. But he did prove flexible in other ways, slightly moderating the defense buildup, accepting fewer cuts in social programs than he proposed, and finally agreeing to a $98 billion increase in miscel-

laneous federal taxes. He refused, however, to cancel the final 10 percent cut in income taxes due in mid-1983. Instead, he declared that all signs pointed to "a strong recovery," adding, "Our economic game plan is working."

Whether by design or good luck, the president's optimism proved justified. In the second quarter of 1983, the economy came to life. The final 10 percent tax cut in July stimulated consumer spending. The long-depressed automobile industry, helped by Japan's voluntary quotas on car exports, began to boom, with annual sales reaching $13.6 million in 1984. The American people went on a great buying spree with consumer installment debt increasing as much in the first six months of 1983 as in all of 1982.

Best of all, inflation remained under control as the economy expanded. The cost of living dropped to 3.8 percent in 1983, the lowest rate since 1972. At the same time, interest rates, which had been hovering around 16.5 percent in 1982, fell to 10.5 percent and remained below 11 percent, enabling consumers to buy goods and corporations to expand their inventories much more easily. A combination of long-term Federal Reserve policy, the impact of the recession, and a worldwide decline in energy and food prices enabled the Reagan administration to take credit for solving the problem that had proved fatal for Carter and the Democrats.

The Growing Deficit

A new problem emerged in the mid-1980s to cloud Reagan's claims of economic recovery—the growing federal budget deficit. As the economy weakened and unemployment increased, tax revenues fell below projections while government spending on unemployment insurance and other social programs climbed. The deficit reached $207.8 billion in 1983, nearly triple the pre-Reagan high of $70.5 billion in 1976.

Some economists were predicting that at current spending and tax rates, the deficit would rise to more than $300 billion a year by the end of the decade. The result, many feared, would be soaring interest rates as the government competed with the private sector for the limited amount of investment capital in the nation. In fact, a slumping world economy led to a massive infusion of foreign investment, which kept the prime rate from rising above 11 percent.

When the deficit continued to climb during the economic recovery of the mid-1980s, Congress finally came forward with what appeared to be a drastic solution. Republican senators Phil Gramm of Texas and Warren Rudman of New Hampshire joined with Democrat Ernest Hollings of South Carolina to set a series of budgetary ceilings designed to eliminate the

THE CHRISTIAN RIGHT

*I*n early 1979, Rev. Jerry Falwell was flying to Lynchburg, Virginia, when he suddenly felt God calling him to enlist "the good people of America" in a crusade to battle permissiveness and moral decay. Falwell, who had built a small church in Lynchburg into a huge religious enterprise with eighteen thousand members, sixty associate pastors, and a television and radio audience of a million and a half, plus fifteen hundred students at Liberty Baptist College, launched his new enterprise on Capitol Hill in April 1979. Announcing that it was time to "fight the pornography, obscenity, vulgarity, profanity that, under the guise of sex education and 'values clarification,'" pervaded public school education, Falwell founded an overtly political organization to purify American society. He invited Roman Catholics, Jews, Protestants, Mormons, and even non-religious conservatives to join his "Moral Majority."

Falwell's Moral Majority highlighted the emergence in the 1970s of what journalists called the Christian Right. Throughout American history, many church members have been swept up in religious "awakenings." Leaders of the revivals have called Americans back to personal piety and a concern for their society and its changing values. At those times, Christians have been urged to work actively to change their communities.

The Supreme Court's 1962 and 1963 decisions to ban school-sponsored prayer and Bible reading sparked increased political activity among conservative Christians. Many joined organizations working at the local level to gain greater control over public education and the content of textbooks and science lectures. Church leaders often encouraged their congregations to become more active in local politics; they endorsed candidates and causes and passed out literature at church services. Conservative Christians also supported candidates who promised measures that would reverse the perceived decline in traditional family values as evidenced by feminism, abortion, and overt homosexuality.

Concern for the changing values of Americana resulted in a new series of revivals. The open-air "camp meetings" of past awakenings developed into gatherings that packed thousands into large arenas for events broadcast by television to extended audiences. A number of Christian preachers used television to broaden their ministries. Several, like Falwell, produced their own weekly or daily television broadcasts. The new television evangelists—dubbed *televangelists*—combined commentary on social, economic, and foreign policy issues with their more traditional sermons and advice on living the Christian life. The televangelists produced publications and solicited contributions for their ministries. Their mailing lists formed the first "membership roles" of the new Christian Right. Jimmy Carter was one of their earliest national beneficiaries and suffered the consequences.

Carter was a devoted Baptist who taught Sunday school, readily professed his Christianity, and emphasized family values in his speeches. He received the endorsement of some of the televangelists for his campaign to become president of the United States, and the national press began to pay closer attention to his personal religious beliefs. But support from the budding Christian Right was not necessarily an asset; such Christians hold themselves, their preachers, and other Christians to very high standards of moral behavior and ideological purity. When Carter discussed his Christian commitment in an interview in *Playboy* magazine, it cost him some votes in a close election; *Playboy* was the cultural antithesis of the family values advocated by the Christian Right. Other voters feared that Carter was crossing the traditional barrier placed between religion and politics in America.

As president, Carter's actions continually reminded conservatives that he was, after all, a Democrat and a liberal one. Carter was unwilling to reform welfare, to work for the return of prayer in public schools, or to ban abortion. The developing Christian Right wanted more than just Christians in office; they wanted to see their program enacted. They found a new darling—Ronald Reagan.

Reagan was not a practicing Christian, he was divorced, and his children were not the model products of a "family values" home. But he was a bona fide conservative. He knew the right words to answer questions about his faith; and he peppered his speeches with the program of the Christian Right. With his words, Reagan brought the growing power of the Christian Right solidly into the Republican party. Their numbers and the enthusiasm of their individual political workers were sufficient to swing close elections; and candidates at all levels sought their endorsement. The Moral Majority, and conservative Christians in general, were energized by the recognition they received while working hard for Ronald Reagan. However, President Reagan paid them for their support with little more than

Ronald Reagan appears with Rev. Jerry Falwell at a Moral Majority rally in Dallas, Texas, in 1980. Falwell's Moral Majority and other similar evangelical groups endorsed conservative positions on a variety of issues, including abortion and school prayer. In his two presidential election campaigns, Reagan vigorously sought the support of Falwell's followers. ❖

the words in his speeches. So the Christian Right began to carefully consider the choice of a successor.

Pat Robertson stepped forward. He was the son of a congressman and a Phi Beta Kappa graduate of Washington and Lee University, Yale Law School, and the New York Theological Seminary. He had first joined the Baptist Church but later became a charismatic Christian and one of the most prominent preachers and healers on television with his *700 Club*. Like Falwell, Robertson formed a coalition of religious conservatives from many faiths, with the intent of teaching the members how to be effective in politics. That organization provided the grassroots workers for his effort to win the Republican nomination for president in 1988.

Unfortunately, Robertson became the innocent victim of the televangelist scandals—the "fallen angels"—that filled newspapers and television throughout 1987 and 1988. Oral Roberts demanded that his supporters send him $8 million or God would "call him home." Jim and Tammy

Bakker, of the *PTL Club,* were accused of sexual, drug, and financial misconduct; Jim Bakker was sentenced to prison. Jimmy Swaggart, famous for his exhortations calling Christians to morally upright lives, was caught with a prostitute. The scandals cut into the income of every religious broadcast, including the ministries of Falwell and Robertson. The Moral Majority folded. Pat Robertson received good seats for his supporters and some attention at the Republican convention; George Bush got the nomination.

By the end of the twentieth century, the Christian Right had grown into a powerful political force but its national program remained unrealized. Conservative Christians had become experts at mobilizing support for national elections and local causes and candidates, but they did not form a mature political entity willing to negotiate, compromise, or trade one goal in order to achieve another. Many religious activists quickly became disillusioned with politics when their candidates could not fulfill all their promises once elected. Likewise, can-

didates who campaigned on the programs of the Christian Right often lost the support of the general electorate because they were seen as too extreme. Clearly, the ideological purity demanded by the Christian Right was at odds with the pragmatism needed to achieve their goals through the actions of government.

U.S. BUDGET DEFICITS, 1980–1997

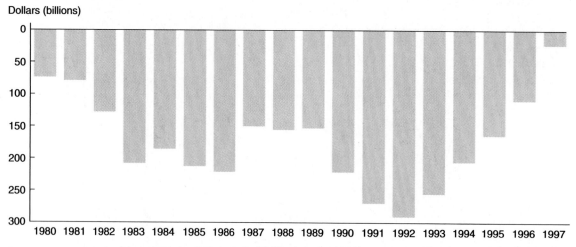

Source: *Economic Report of the President, 1997*, p. 389; *Newsweek,* January 19, 1998, p. 28.

deficit entirely by 1991 through mandatory, across-the-board spending cuts. After the Supreme Court ruled the compulsory features were unconstitutional, the revised Gramm-Rudman-Hollings Balanced Budget Act did succeed in halting the deficit spiral. As altered by Congress in 1986 and 1987, **Gramm-Rudman,** as it became known, stretched out the goal of ending the deficit until 1993. The president and Congress were able to lower the deficit from a peak of $221 billion in 1986 to a more manageable $155 billion by 1988. Even more important, the deficit as a percentage of the GNP fell from more than 5 percent to close to 3 percent, a level common in many industrial nations.

In essence, Gramm-Rudman was a political compromise. The price Reagan had to pay for Democratic help in resolving his budgetary crisis was to stop the increase in defense spending; the Pentagon budget, which went from less than $200 billion to just under $300 billion in three years, was frozen for the rest of the decade. But at the same time, by agreeing to sizable budget deficits for the next few years, the Democrats who controlled Congress had to give up any hope of expanding existing social programs or enacting new ones, such as a comprehensive national health plan.

Another alarming deficit—in the balance of overseas trade—also became an important issue in the mid-1980s. American exports had been falling steadily since the 1970s as a result of the decline in traditional manufacturing industries—iron and steel, electronics, and automobiles. The Japanese had been the biggest gainers as they dominated the American market in consumer goods.

In the 1980s, the American people had begun living beyond their means. Just as the government in-

curred large deficits rather than raising taxes to pay for the huge defense buildup, so consumers had cut back on personal saving in order to buy imported cars, television sets, and VCRs, encouraging further foreign investment. By 1988, foreigners held $400 billion in U.S. Treasury securities (almost 20 percent of the national debt), had invested another $300 billion in American industry, and owned 21 percent of the nation's banking assets. At the end of the decade, the American people were sending $60 billion a year overseas just to pay the interest on the public and private obligations. Reaganomics had succeeded in continuing America's traditional high standard of living, but at a very high price—massive borrowing that mortgaged the nation's future.

The Rich Grow Richer

There were both gains and losses in the Reagan years. Inflation fell from double-digit levels by 1982 and averaged about 4 percent for the rest of the decade. A sharp drop in the world price of oil in late 1985 helped lower the trade deficit and brought inflation down to less than 2 percent, although cheap oil had a devastating impact on oil-producing states such as Texas, Louisiana, and Oklahoma.

After the end of the 1982 recession, employment grew steadily; by 1990, there were nearly nineteen million more Americans working than in 1980. There were losers as well, however. Blue-collar jobs declined as American industry, notably steel and autos, streamlined operations by closing obsolete plants, switching to automated production, and farming out manufacturing to foreign producers with far lower labor costs.

Companies that specialized in labor-intensive consumer products, such as Eastman Kodak and General Electric, virtually stopped all manufacturing in the United States, concentrating instead on marketing and distributing goods made abroad to their specifications.

At the same time, however, the service sector expanded rapidly, especially the financial, transportation, and health care industries. Accountants, lawyers, and technicians flourished, with women especially benefiting from the change from blue- to white-collar jobs. Union membership no longer guaranteed a high-wage job; education and technical training were the keys to success in the postindustrial economy. By 1990, nearly one in three workers was an executive, technician, or professional; only one in five worked in factories. Labor unions were especially hard hit; union membership dropped from 23 percent of the workforce in 1980 to 15.5 percent by 1992.

The most striking change in the decade was the growing inequality of wealth in America. In the five income categories used by the Census Bureau, the poorest 20 percent of Americans fared badly, dropping 6 percent in pretax income in the 1980s. The three middle groups gained about 5 percent, largely as a result of the increased employment of women as middle-class families increasingly needed two wage earners to maintain their standard of living. The top fifth did far better, increasing their incomes by 20 percent over the decade. The top 1 percent, the truly rich, did best of all, doubling their after-tax income in ten years. By 1989, the top fifth made as much money as the other 80 percent combined, while the top 1 percent alone earned as much as the middle fifth of the population.

The income disparity was the product of both economic restructuring and Republican tax policy. The decline in manufacturing meant that many assembly-line workers, who averaged more than $20 an hour in the 1970s, lost their jobs and were working for little more than the minimum wage in the service sector. At the same time, income tax cuts and adjustments

SHARE OF AGGREGATE HOUSEHOLD INCOME BY QUINTILES, 1975–1995 (IN PERCENT)

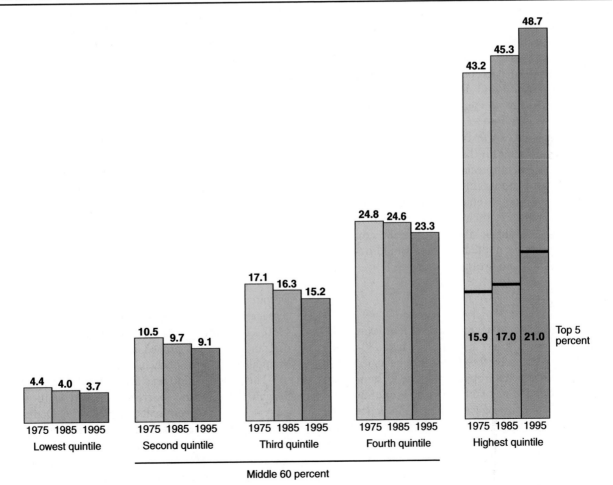

reduced the top tax rate from 70 percent to 31 percent. A parallel increase in Social Security payroll taxes meant that by the end of the decade, the tax burden for a middle-class family was 37.3 cents of every dollar earned, compared to 35 cents for the wealthy.

The economic inequities of the 1980s were most clearly reflected in the transfer of actual wealth—housing, property, stocks, savings, and retirement accounts. Between 1983 and 1989, family wealth increased from $13.6 trillion to $16.1 trillion; 55 percent of the gain in net assets went to the top 0.5 percent of the population. The poor and the lower middle class actually lost $256 billion in wealth during this boom period. As a result, wealth became even more concentrated than income in the 1980s. By the end of the decade, the top fifth of the population owned 80 percent of the nation's entire household wealth.

The economic changes of the 1980s hit the middle class particularly hard. Median family income, which had doubled between 1947 and 1973, remained stagnant for the next twenty years, only reaching the 1973 level by the mid-1990s. Middle class fathers responded by working longer hours and their wives left the home for the workplace in increasing numbers in order to maintain a decent standard of living for their families.

By the 1990s, middle class Americans came to believe that their children would not fare as well as they had. This feeling of diminished expectations came for several reasons. In part, people began to realize that the rapid expansion and prosperity of the 1950s and 1960s was a happy accident unlikely to occur again. The inflation in real estate values by the 1980s added greatly to the net worth of an older generation but made it very difficult for their children to benefit from the same kind of appreciation. Above all, the baby boom generation took affluence for granted and expected to continue to enjoy all the blessings of an abundant society. Yet their parents feared that while their children would be able to live a life envied by most of the world's population, they would not share fully in the American dream.

Reagan Affirmed

"Are you better off now than you were four years ago?" Reagan had asked voters at the end of his 1980 debate with Jimmy Carter. By the mid-1980s, he appeared to have delivered on his implicit promise to stem inflation and revive the stagnant American economy.

Despite the growing gap between the rich and the poor, Reagan could boast of impressive economic gains after weathering the 1982 recession. The recovery led to 16 million new jobs as the unemployment rate dropped back under 6 percent. Inflation remained low and even median family income, although still be-

low the post–World War II peak reached in the early 1970s, moved steadily upward.

The economic boom that began in 1983 came at just the right time for the Republican party. By early 1984, with personal income rising at an annual rate of 10.3 percent from January to June and unemployment shrinking rapidly, Democratic prospects dimmed for the presidential election. After a long, bruising primary battle, Walter Mondale, former Minnesota senator and Carter's vice president, won the Democratic nomination. In a bold break with tradition, he chose a woman as a running mate, Congresswoman Geraldine Ferraro of New York.

When the Republicans renominated Reagan and Bush, the campaign quickly came down to one issue: leadership. The GOP claimed that Reagan had overcome the problems that overwhelmed Carter, notably inflation at home and disrespect abroad. Asserting that he wanted to "make America great again," the president told voters they should reelect him: "You ain't seen nothin' yet."

Mondale and Ferraro, in contrast, accused Reagan of helping the rich at the expense of the poor, saddling future generations with huge deficits, and risking war in the Middle East and Central America. In a surprise move, the Democratic candidate announced he intended to raise taxes to curb the deficit and then accused Reagan of harboring a "secret plan" to increase taxes himself.

These tactics failed to gain support; the outcome was a far greater Reagan victory than in 1980. With a solid base in the South and West, the president cut deeply into the normally Democratic states of the Northeast and the swing states of the Midwest to take the electoral votes of all but Minnesota and the District of Columbia. Exit surveys revealed that economic issues were uppermost in the minds of voters; in the midst of a strong economic recovery, Reagan won a majority among all voters earning more than $12,500 a year. More than two-thirds of the white male voters in the nation stood behind Reagan, who won even a majority of the blue-collar and women's votes. Despite Ferraro's presence on the ballot, a higher percentage of women voted for Reagan in 1984 than in 1980. Of all the traditional Democratic groups, only African Americans proved loyal to the party, giving Mondale 90 percent of their votes.

The 1984 election was far more of a triumph for Reagan than for his party. In Congress, the GOP gained only fourteen seats, leaving the Democrats firmly in control of the House; in the Senate, the Republicans lost two places, narrowing their majority to 54 to 46. Despite minor gains at the state level, the GOP failed to achieve the party realignment it sought. Republicans were encouraged by a strong showing

THE ELECTION OF 1984

Candidate	Party	Popular Vote	Electoral Vote
Reagan	Republican	54,451,521	525
Mondale	Democratic	37,565,334	13

among the young, with Reagan taking 56 percent of the vote of the baby boomers (those aged 25 to 34) and 60 percent of the postboomers (those aged 18 to 24). The nation seemed to be dividing politically along economic lines, with the wealthy and affluent who fared best from Reagan's economic policies supporting the president while a growing underclass of African Americans, Hispanics, and the working poor were voting solidly Democratic. Middle-class Americans who held the balance revealed their mixed feelings by backing a Republican for president and Democratic candidates for the House and Senate.

REAGAN AND THE WORLD

Ronald Reagan was even more determined to reverse the course of American policy abroad than at home. He believed that under Carter, American prestige and standing in the world had dropped to an all-time low. Intent on restoring traditional American pride and self-respect, Reagan's mission was to strengthen America's defenses and recapture world supremacy from the Soviet Union.

In reality, the new president was simply continuing the hard line that Carter had begun to take after the invasion of Afghanistan. The Democrats had begun a massive military buildup in 1979 that included plans for cruise missiles in Europe, a rapid deployment force in the Middle East, and a 5 percent increase in the defense budget.

Under Reagan, the Pentagon flourished. Secretary of Defense Caspar Weinberger, once known as a budget cutter, presented a plan that would more than double defense spending. The emphasis was on new weapons, ranging from the B-1 bomber and the controversial MX nuclear missile to the expansion of the navy from 456 to 600 ships. Despite growing opposition in Congress, by 1985 the defense budget grew to more than $300 billion at the very time the administration was cutting back on domestic spending.

The president scored his first foreign policy victory on the day he took office, thanks again to efforts begun under Carter. On January 20, 1981, Iran released the fifty-three Americans held hostage and thus enabled Reagan to begin his presidency on a positive note.

After some initial difficulty, Reagan proved more successful than Jimmy Carter in bringing harmony and order to the conduct of American foreign policy. His first secretary of state was Alexander Haig, a former general, NATO commander, Kissinger aide, and White House chief of staff under Nixon. Haig, outspoken and assertive, tried to establish his primacy over the policymaking process, only to alienate the entire White House staff. Finally, in mid-1982, Reagan replaced Haig as secretary of state with George Shultz, a professional economist with extensive government experience, whose low-key and relaxed style brought an air of calm reassurance to the conduct of American

Defense spending during the Reagan administration focused on new weapons such as this B-2 bomber unveiled at U. S. Air Force Plant 42 in 1988. The B-2, also called the stealth bomber, was designed with a low profile to be undetectable in flight. ❖

foreign policy. Shultz, moreover, proved more than able to hold his own in bureaucratic infighting with the White House staff, Defense Secretary Weinberger, and the administration's most outspoken hard-liner, UN Ambassador Jeane Kirkpatrick.

Despite the steady increase in defense spending and the formation of a smoothly functioning foreign policy team, Reagan soon found his diplomatic goals were more difficult to achieve than the budgetary and tax measures he had pushed through Congress so speedily. Yet in the long run, he could claim credit for a goal that had eluded his predecessors in the White House—the end of the Cold War.

Challenging the "Evil Empire"

The belief that the Soviet Union was a deadly enemy that threatened the well-being and security of the United States was the central tenet of Reagan's approach to foreign policy. He saw the Russians as bent on world revolution, ready "to commit any crime, to lie, to cheat" to advance their cause. Citing what he called a "record of tyranny," Reagan denounced the Russians before the UN in 1982, claiming, "Soviet-sponsored guerrillas and terrorists are at work in Central and South America, in Africa, the Middle East, in the Caribbean and in Europe, violating human rights and unnerving the world with violence."

Given this view of Russia as "the focus of evil in the modern world," it is not surprising that the new president continued the hard line that Carter had

adopted after the invasion of Afghanistan. Abandoning détente, Reagan proceeded to implement a 1979 decision to place 572 Pershing II and cruise missiles in western Europe within range of Moscow and other Russian population centers to match Soviet deployment of medium-range missiles aimed at NATO countries. Despite strong protests from the Soviet Union, as well as growing uneasiness in Europe and an increasingly vocal nuclear freeze movement at home, the United States began putting the weapons in bases in Great Britain and Germany in November 1983. The Soviets, claiming the move gave them only ten minutes of warning time in case of an American attack, responded by breaking off disarmament negotiations in Geneva.

The nuclear arms race had now reached a more dangerous level than ever before. The United States stepped up research and development of the **Strategic Defense Initiative (SDI),** an antimissile system based on the use of lasers and particle beams to destroy incoming missiles in outer space. SDI was quickly dubbed "star wars" by the media. Critics doubted that SDI could be perfected, but they warned that even if it were, the result would be to escalate the arms race by forcing the Russians to build more offensive missiles in order to overcome the American defense system. The Reagan administration, however, defended SDI as a legitimate attempt to free the United States from the deadly trap of deterrence, with its reliance on the threat of nuclear retaliation to keep the peace. Meanwhile, the Soviet Union kept deploying larger and more accurate land-based

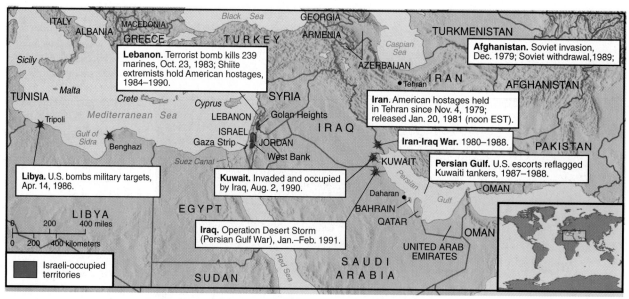

TROUBLE SPOTS IN THE MIDDLE EAST *Armed conflict and territorial attacks in this region intensified in the 1980s and early 1990s.* ❖

ICBMs. Although both sides continued to observe the unratified SALT II agreements, the fact remained that between them the two superpowers had nearly fifty thousand warheads in their nuclear arsenals.

Turmoil in the Middle East

Reagan tried to continue Carter's basic policy in the turbulent Middle East. In April 1982, the Israelis honored a Camp David pledge by making their final withdrawal from the Sinai. Reagan hoped to achieve the other Camp David objective of providing a homeland for the Palestinian Arabs on the West Bank, but Israel instead continued to extend Jewish settlements into the disputed area. The threat of the Palestine Liberation Organization (PLO), based in southern Lebanon and frequently raiding across the border into Israel, seemed to be the major obstacle to further progress.

On June 6, 1982, with tacit American encouragement, Israel invaded southern Lebanon in order to secure its northern border and destroy the PLO. The Reagan administration made no effort to halt the offensive but did join with France and Italy in sending a multinational force to permit the PLO to evacuate to Tunisia. Unfortunately, the United States soon became enmeshed in the Lebanese civil war, which had been raging since 1975. American marines, sent to Lebanon as part of the multinational force to restore order, were caught up in the renewed hostilities between Muslim and Christian militia. The Muslims perceived the marines as aiding the Christian-dominated government of Lebanon instead of acting as neutral peacekeepers, and they began firing on the vulnerable American troops.

In the face of growing congressional demands for the withdrawal of the marines, Reagan declared they were there to protect Lebanon from the designs of Soviet-backed Syria. But finally, after terrorists drove a truck loaded with explosives into the American barracks, killing 239 marines, the president had no choice but to pull out. The last American unit left Beirut in late February 1984. Despite his good intentions, Reagan had experienced a humiliation similar to Carter's in Iran—one that left Lebanon in shambles and the Arab-Israeli situation worse than ever.

Confrontation in Central America

Reagan faced a difficult situation in Central America. In an area marked by great extremes of wealth, with a small landowning elite and a mass of peasants mired in dire poverty, the United States sought moderate middle-class regimes to support. Washington usually ended up backing repressive right-wing dictatorships rather than the more leftist groups who raised the radical issues of land reform and redistribution of wealth. Yet it was often oppression by U.S.-supported regimes that drove those seeking political change to embrace revolutionary tactics.

This is precisely what happened in Nicaragua, where the leftist Sandinista coalition finally succeeded in overthrowing the repressive Somoza regime in 1979. In an effort to strengthen the many middle-class elements in the original Sandinista government and to avoid forcing Nicaragua into the Cuban and Soviet orbit, Carter extended American economic aid.

The Reagan administration quickly reversed this policy. Alexander Haig cut off all aid to Nicaragua in the spring of 1981, accusing the Sandinistas of driving out the moderates, welcoming Cuban advisers and Soviet military assistance, and serving as a supply base for leftist guerrillas in nearby El Salvador. The criticism became a self-fulfilling prophecy as Nicaragua became even more dependent on Cuba and the Soviet Union.

The United States and Nicaragua were soon on a collision course. In April 1983, declaring that "the national security of all the Americas is at stake in Central America," President Reagan asked Congress for the money and authority to oust the Sandinistas. When Congress, fearful of repeating the Vietnam fiasco, refused, Reagan opted for covert action. The CIA began supplying the Contras, exiles fighting against the Sandinistas from bases in Honduras and Costa Rica. The U.S.-backed rebels tried to disrupt the Nicaraguan economy, raiding villages, blowing up oil tanks, and even mining harbors. Then, in 1984, Congress passed the Boland Amendment prohibiting any U.S. agency from spending money in Central America. The withdrawal of U.S. financial backing left the Contras in a precarious position.

Reagan's only clear-cut triumph in the hemisphere came in the Caribbean. In October 1983, a military coup led to the death of the leftist prime minister of Grenada, who was subsequently replaced by an even more radical regime. The Reagan administration, already upset by Grenada's close ties to Cuba and the construction of a large airfield on this small Caribbean island, decided to intervene to prevent the communists from acquiring a strategic military base.

Nearly two thousand U.S. marines invaded Grenada on October 25, 1983. After brief but spirited resistance from eight hundred Cuban workers and troops on the island, the American forces claimed a victory that cost eighteen lives. The administration proudly displayed pictures of captured Soviet arms to justify the resort to force; American medical students, shown on television kissing the ground as they returned

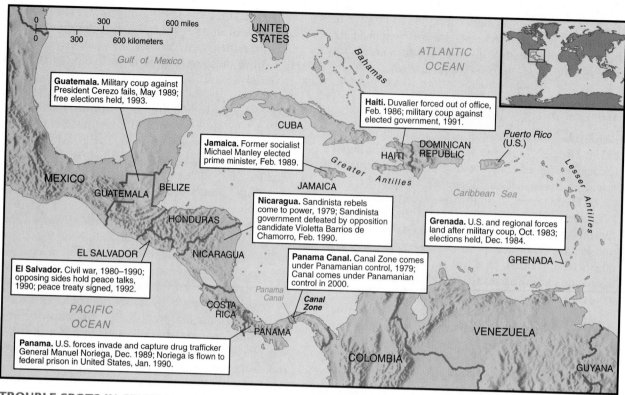

TROUBLE SPOTS IN CENTRAL AMERICA AND THE CARIBBEAN   *U.S. involvement in Central American trouble spots intensified in the 1980s and early 1990s.* ❖

to the United States, enabled the administration to label the operation a "rescue mission."

Aside from Grenada, however, the Reagan administration had little to show for its massive military buildup. In the Middle East, its well-intentioned use of marines had ended in disaster; its determined opposition to left-wing groups in Central America had at best achieved a stalemate. Relations with the Soviet Union had fallen into one of the deepest chills of the entire Cold War with the nuclear arms race more intense than ever.

Trading Arms for Hostages

The Reagan administration's policies in the Middle East and Central America reached a tragic convergence in the **Iran-Contra affair.** In mid-1985, Robert McFarlane, a retired marine officer who had become national security adviser a year earlier, began a new initiative designed to restore American influence in the troubled Middle East. Concerned over the fate of six Americans held hostage in Lebanon by groups thought to be loyal to Iran's Ayatollah Khomeini, McFarlane proposed trading American antitank missiles to Iran in return for the hostages' release. Although he realized the president was primarily concerned with the fate of the hostages, McFarlane's main

goal in proposing the exchange was to establish good relations with moderate elements in Iran, anticipating the aged Khomeini's death. The Iranians, desperate for weapons in the war they had been waging against Iraq since 1980, seemed willing to comply.

McFarlane soon found himself in over his head. He relied heavily on a young marine lieutenant colonel assigned to the National Security Council (NSC), Oliver North, and North in turn sought the assistance of CIA director William Casey. A veteran of the Office of Strategic Services in World War II, Casey saw the Iran initiative as an opportunity to use the NSC to mount the kind of covert operation denied the CIA under the post-1975 congressional oversight policy. By early 1986, when John Poindexter, a naval officer with little political experience, replaced a burned-out McFarlane as national security adviser, Casey was able to persuade the president, over the strenuous objections of both Secretary of State Shultz and Secretary of Defense Weinberger, to go ahead with shipments of TOW antitank missiles and HAWK anti-aircraft missiles to Iran.

The arms deal with Iran was bad policy, but what came next was criminal. Ever since the Boland Amendment in late 1984 had cut off congressional funding, the Reagan administration had been searching for ways to supply the Contras in Nicaragua. Oliver

North was put in charge of soliciting donations from wealthy right-wing Americans. In early 1986, North had what he later described as a "neat idea" (apparently shared by Casey as well)—he could use the enormous profits from the sale of weapons to Iran (charging as much as $10,000 for a TOW that cost the United States only $3,500) to finance the Contras. North's ploy was clearly not only illegal but unconstitutional, since it meant usurping the congressional power of the purse.

Unlike the policy of trading arms for hostages, the diversion of the profits to the Contras was a closely held secret. Apparently, only North, Casey, and Poindexter were aware of the illegal activity until November 1986, when the press finally learned of the Iranian arms sales. North then hurriedly destroyed most of the incriminating documents, but he overlooked one key memo that revealed the Contra diversion.

The political fallout was very heavy. The administration, having learned from the Watergate cover-up, tried to control the damage by breaking the bad news itself. Every effort was made to protect President Reagan; Attorney General Edwin Meese blamed Poindexter and North, who both were dropped from the NSC. Despite these efforts to spare the president's reputation, a CBS–*New York Times* poll taken in

Despite Oliver North's questionable conduct, the public elevated him to near hero status during the televised Iran-Contra hearings. The bemedaled marine testified that he believed his deeds were justified as a defense of democracy. ❖

December 1986 revealed that Reagan's popularity had dropped from 67 percent to 46 percent in just a month, the steepest decline ever recorded.

The vital question of whether Ronald Reagan had approved of the Contra diversion was never answered satisfactorily. Public opinion polls indicated that most Americans suspected the president was at least aware of the Contra diversion. In the absence of firm evidence, however, they were willing to give Reagan the benefit of the doubt. A protracted congressional hearing in the summer of 1987 did little to clear up the confusion. Oliver North used his televised appearances to win public sympathy if not approval. Poindexter insisted under oath that he had never informed the president he and North had used the profits from arms sales to Iran to fund the Contras in defiance of Congress. The only other man who knew what had actually happened was William Casey; his death from a brain tumor in mid-1987 left the mystery unsolved.

While Reagan escaped the Iran-Contra affair without being held fully responsible for it, his presidency was in serious trouble. In Congress, the Democrats, who gained control of the Senate as well as the House in the 1986 elections, began to override his vetoes, reject his nominees, and bring a total halt to even humanitarian aid to the Contras, whose cause now became hopeless. Ronald Reagan was still in the White House, but his reliance on others to conduct the affairs of state had robbed him of his power to lead the nation.

Reagan the Peacemaker

By the end of 1987, the president had made a remarkable recovery. Stepping into the foreign affairs arena, Reagan, with strong pressure from his wife, Nancy, shed his image as a hawk and set out to reverse the course of Soviet-American relations.

A momentous change in leadership in the Soviet Union proved fortunate. The illness and death of Leonid Brezhnev in 1982, followed in rapid succession by the deaths of his aged successors, Yuri Andropov and Konstantin Chernenko, led finally to the selection of Mikhail Gorbachev, a younger and more dynamic Soviet leader. Gorbachev was intent on improving relations with the United States as part of his new policy of *perestroika* (restructuring the Soviet economy) and *glasnost* (political openness). Soviet economic performance had been deteriorating steadily and the war in Afghanistan had become a major liability. Gorbachev needed a breathing spell in the arms race and a reduction in Cold War tensions in order to carry out his sweeping changes at home.

The first meeting between Reagan and Gorbachev, at Geneva in 1985, went well, but it did not lead to any

Reagan and Gorbachev in Red Square. During the summits between the two leaders, the American public grew to admire the Soviet premier for his policies of perestroika *(restructuring) and* glasnost *(openness).* ❖

A fourth Reagan-Gorbachev summit in Moscow in mid-1988 did not achieve any further progress toward the goal of reducing the nuclear arsenals, but the pictures of Reagan and Gorbachev strolling amiably about Red Square in front of Lenin's tomb, saluting tourists, and taking turns kissing babies, gave rise to the hope that an end to the Cold War was finally in sight.

When Reagan returned home, his popularity soared to 70 percent, higher than it had been before the Iran-Contra affair. He had not only succeeded in making a major breakthrough in the nuclear arms race, but he could also claim that his policies had led to a moderation in Soviet behavior. During the president's last year in office, the Soviets cooperated with the United States in pressuring Iran and Iraq to end their long war. Most impressive of all, Gorbachev moved to end the war in Afghanistan. The first Soviet units pulled out in April 1988, with the final evacuation due to be completed early the next year. By the time Reagan left office in January 1989, he had scored a series of foreign policy triumphs that offset the Iran-Contra fiasco and thus helped redeem his presidency.

SOCIAL DILEMMAS

Two complex social issues arose in the 1980s that stood in sharp contrast to the prevailing sense of well-being. A massive viral epidemic and a new drug crisis threatened the social fabric of the United States, yet President Reagan failed to respond promptly or effectively to either one; his successors in the White House, George Bush and Bill Clinton, would find the problems equally frustrating.

The AIDS Epidemic

The outbreak of **AIDS** (acquired immune deficiency syndrome) in the early 1980s took most Americans by surprise. Even health experts had difficulty grasping the nature and extent of the new public health threat. Doctors first noticed a few cases of a rare form of pneumonia and an unusual type of skin cancer in male patients in New York City and San Francisco in 1981. The Centers for Disease Control noted the phenomenon in a June 1981 bulletin, but it was several years before researchers finally identified it as a hitherto unknown human immunodeficiency virus (HIV). HIV apparently originated in Central Africa and spread to the United States, where it found its first victims primarily among gay men.

Initially, AIDS was perceived as a threat only to gay men. With a growing sense of urgency as the death toll mounted, gay men began to practice safer sex, using condoms and confining themselves to trusted

significant agreements. A hurried summit at Reykjavik, Iceland, in October 1986, just before the Iran-Contra affair had become public, nearly led to a historic breakthrough. The two men reached general agreement on the long-disputed issue of Intermediate Nuclear Forces (INF) in Europe. Only Soviet insistence that Reagan cancel SDI blocked agreement on an ambitious proposal to abolish all nuclear weapons within a decade.

The apparent failure at Reykjavik, however, did not halt the new momentum toward peace; both leaders needed a foreign policy triumph too much not to continue the dialogue. Throughout 1987, experts worked out the details of an **Intermediate Nuclear Forces agreement** that promised to become the most significant disarmament achievement since SALT I in 1972. Meeting in Washington in December 1987, Reagan and Gorbachev agreed to remove and destroy all intermediate-range missiles and to permit on-site inspection to verify the process.

Understanding AIDS

A Message From The Surgeon General

This brochure has been sent to you by the Government of the United States. In preparing it, we have consulted with the top health experts in the country.

I feel it is important that you have the best information now available for fighting the AIDS virus, a health problem that the President has called "Public Enemy Number One."

Stopping AIDS is up to you, your family and your loved ones.

Some of the issues involved in this brochure may not be things you are used to discussing openly. I can easily understand that. But now you must discuss them. We all must know about AIDS. Read this brochure and talk about it with those you love. Get involved. Many schools, churches, synagogues, and community groups offer AIDS education activities.

I encourage you to practice responsible behavior based on understanding and strong personal values. This is what you can do to stop AIDS.

C. Everett Koop, M.D., Sc.D.
Surgeon General

Este folleto sobre el SIDA se publica en Español.
Para solicitar una copia, llame al 1-800-344-SIDA.

U.S. Department of Health
& Human Services
Public Health Service
Centers for Disease Control
P.O. Box 6003
Rockville, MD 20850

Official Business

HHS Publication No. (CDC) HHS-88-8404. Reproduction of the contents of this brochure is encouraged.

AIDS Brochure

In response to the rapid spread of AIDS in the 1980s and the growing public concern about the new and deadly disease, Surgeon General C. Everett Koop wrote an eight-page brochure titled *Understanding AIDS* that was mailed out by the Public Health Service in 1988 to all 107 million U.S. households. It was the largest public health mailing ever done. Shown here is the first page of the booklet with a message from the surgeon general. Note the availability of a Spanish version of the publication. Why do you think the government sponsored a mass mailing on AIDS? According to this brochure, what is one chief weapon in stopping the AIDS epidemic? Why do you suppose that many people found the mailing controversial? Do you think it would still be considered controversial if it were mailed today?

partners. It soon became clear, however, that AIDS could not be so easily contained. It began to appear among intravenous (IV) drug users who shared the same needles and eventually among hemophiliacs and others receiving frequent blood transfusions. The threat of a contaminated national blood supply terrified middle-class America, as did the possibility of the spread of AIDS to heterosexuals.

Scientists tried to reassure the public by explaining that the virus could be spread only by the exchange of bodily fluids, primarily blood and semen, and not by casual contact. The death of former movie star Rock Hudson from AIDS in the summer of 1985, however, intensified the sense of national panic. Controversy soon developed over proposals for mandatory blood tests for suspected HIV carriers and for the quarantine of AIDS victims. The integrity of hospital blood supplies caused the most realistic concern; in 1985, a new test finally gave reassurance that transfusions could be performed safely.

The Reagan administration proved slow and halting in its approach to the AIDS epidemic. The lack of sympathy for gays and a need to reduce the deficit worked against any large increase in health spending; what little money was devoted to AIDS went almost entirely for research rather than for educational measures to slow its spread. The only real leadership came from Surgeon General C. Everett Koop, who surprised his conservative backers in 1986 by coming out boldly with proposals for sex education, the use of condoms to ensure "safer sex," and confidential blood testing to help contain the disease.

While the administration dallied, the grim toll mounted. Because the average time between the initial HIV infection and the first symptoms of AIDS was five years and the delay could be as long as fourteen years, efforts at prevention had little immediate impact. In November 1983, there were 2803 known cases and 1416 deaths; by the time Rock Hudson died in mid-1985, more than 12,000 cases and more than 6000 deaths had been reported.

Growing public concern finally led to action. In 1987, Ronald Reagan appointed a special presidential commission headed by Admiral James Watkins, a former chief of naval operations, to study the AIDS epidemic. The Watkins report in 1988 criticized the administration's AIDS efforts as "inconsistent" and recommended a new effort that included antidiscrimination legislation and explicit prevention education. Koop responded by sending out a pamphlet titled "Understanding AIDS" to 107 million households, while in the fall, Congress voted to spend $1.3 billion to fight AIDS, with much of the money going for confidential testing and counseling and home care for victims.

Despite the new efforts, the epidemic continued to grow. In 1987, there were 50,000 cases; by mid-1989, the count had reached 100,000. The U.S. Centers for Disease Control in Atlanta reported more than 200,000 cases at the end of 1991; the total had increased to more than 500,000 by mid-1996. By then, 345,000 AIDS victims had died, making it the leading cause of death for Americans aged 25 to 44.

The number of those infected with HIV appeared to be stabilizing by the mid-1990s at between 650,000 and 900,000. Yet what was once known as the "gay disease" had spread far beyond that one group in society by the end of the century. Minorities and the young were at greatest risk. African American youths made up two-thirds of the new HIV cases among people under 25. "The disease is disappearing from the mainstream" claimed a Washington, D.C., clinic director, "and becoming a disease of kids who are disenfranchised anyway."

The most encouraging development was a fall-off in the death rate from AIDS that began in the mid-1990s. Health officials attributed the decline to heavier spending on treatment and prevention and, above all, to powerful new drug combinations. By 2001, however, the drop in new cases and deaths from AIDS began to level off. "The latest data," commented one expert in August 2001, "suggest that the era of dramatic declines is now over." There was a particularly alarming increase in the number of new cases among young gay men who apparently believed that the new treatment had made the disease manageable. But unfortunately the so-called AIDS cocktail was very expensive, running as high as $15,000 a year, and did not work for everyone. And even more disturbing was the growing realization that AIDS was threatening to decimate the population of Third World countries, especially in sub-Sahara Africa.

In the mid-1980s, cocaine suddenly was perceived as a danger to American society. The deaths of several celebrities from cocaine overdoses alarmed the public. More ominous was the emergence of "crack," a cheap cocaine derivative that could be smoked in a pipe to give a very intense high. Dealers sold this new form of cocaine for as little as $10 a dose, opening up a vast new market among the poor in the urban ghettos. By 1986, an estimated 5.8 million people were using cocaine at least once a month, and more than 600,000 were confirmed addicts.

Despite its relatively low cost, crack led to an explosion of urban crime. The intense high lasted only a few minutes, leading users to keep smoking more, desensitizing their nervous systems and forcing them to use ever larger amounts to achieve the by now indispensable euphoria. Needing as much as $1000 worth of crack each day to sustain their habits, users turned to crime to gain the necessary funds. By 1987, more than 70 percent of all those arrested for burglary in Manhattan tested positive for cocaine.

The Reagan administration tried several approaches to the problem posed by cocaine. In 1982, First Lady Nancy Reagan chose drug education as her special project. Using the slogan "Just say no," she

The War on Drugs

The 1980s witnessed the rapid spread of cocaine use in America, leading to a growing sense of social crisis by the end of the decade. Cocaine had long been viewed as a relatively harmless recreational drug used by only a few people—rock musicians, Hollywood producers, and the very wealthy. By the end of the 1970s, the snorting of the pure white powder, distilled from the leaves of coca plants grown in the foothills of the Andes, had spread throughout the upper middle class. Bankers, lawyers, and doctors began to use it occasionally to achieve a moment of ecstasy, striving for what has been called "the illusion of instant happiness." The costs, however, were very high—$100 for a few snorts and the danger of dying from an overdose or literally blowing one's mind. "Chronic cocaine use," warned one expert, "is the same as putting one's car in neutral with the brakes on and pressing the accelerator to the floor for hours—eventually, the engine will burn out." Nevertheless, the number of users reached more than four million by 1982.

Investigators from the Federal Bureau of Alcohol, Tobacco, and Firearms examine twenty tons of cocaine seized in a 1989 drug bust in Los Angeles. Though the war on drugs initiated in the 1980s led to an increase in the number of drug raids and arrests and raised the public's awareness of the nation's illegal drug problem, government efforts have made little progress in stopping the drug trade. ✦

urged schools, churches, and civic groups to inform young people about the dangers of cocaine. Her program helped educate the middle class but had little impact on crack smokers in the ghetto.

In the mid-1980s, the administration began to place greater emphasis on interdiction, using agents of the Drug Enforcement Agency (the DEA—a body created by Nixon in 1973), the Customs Bureau, and the Coast Guard to try to seal off the nation's borders. An international cartel of drug dealers, led by a group of Colombians, overcame this effort by saturating the nation with cocaine, losing only a fraction to the hard-pressed DEA. In reality, the Reagan administration was unwilling to devote the personnel and resources that truly effective interdiction would require; with one eye on the deficit, Washington was content with a few highly publicized skirmishes in what it termed the war on drugs.

The very nature of the cocaine industry frustrated a third, and potentially most promising, countermeasure—wiping out the coca fields and processing plants in South America. The administration relied on diplomatic efforts in cooperation with the governments of Colombia, Bolivia, and Peru to curb the trade in cocaine, but with little success. South American farmers could make five times as much money growing coca leaves as food crops; it was estimated that Bolivia received $600 million a year in hard currency from the drug trade, compared to profits of only $400 million from tin and other legal exports.

The efforts of the Bush administration proved no more successful than the Reagan program. An ambitious "Andean Strategy," funded at more than $2 billion, pledged American support for antidrug programs in Columbia, Bolivia, and Peru. Yet by 1992, coca leaf production had reached a record level of 336,300 tons, nearly three times as high as in 1984. As one critic, Ted Galen Carpenter, explained, "The United States is asking Latin American governments to do the impossible: Wage war on a drug trade that now represents a vital part of their economies and around which have arisen powerful political constituencies."

The Clinton administration proved equally unsuccessful in its two-part approach to the drug problem. One aspect of the new Democratic strategy was to focus primarily on trying to curtail drug use in the United States. But a reduced budget and the inherent difficulty in attacking the causes of drug addiction blocked any progress. By 1996, the number of Americans engaging in illicit drug use, primarily marijuana, had dropped to twelve million, but the number of heroin and cocaine users remained stable at about three million.

The Clinton administration's other approach to the drug war was to focus its overseas efforts primarily on eradicating the source of cocaine in Colombia, Bolivia, and Peru. A presidential directive issued in November 1993 targeted foreign drug cartels as a "national security threat." Although the new policy led to the arrest of eight major cartel chieftains in Colombia, the flow of drugs into the United States continued unabated, with Mexico becoming the new pipeline, funneling an estimated 210 tons of cocaine to the United States in 1995. By the turn of the century, it was clear that there was no end in sight to the war on drugs.

PASSING THE TORCH TO BUSH

Reagan's triumphal reelection in 1984 raised Republican hopes that they had achieved a major political realignment in 1980. The economic boom that had begun after the 1982 recession, along with the promise of the end of the Cold War, reinforced this trend and enabled George Bush to replace Ronald Reagan in the White House.

The Changing Palace Guard

Ronald Reagan had always been unusually dependent on aides and assistants. He saw his own role as one above the heat of bureaucratic battle—providing the nation with a set of goals and a vision for the future. As the great communicator, he would build the public consensus and let others manage the more mundane task of turning his dreams into reality.

His initial success depended heavily on the very effective White House team of James Baker, Edwin Meese, and Michael Deaver. Baker, a Texan with extensive Washington experience, became the chief of staff, managing the White House and directing legislative strategy.

Ronald Reagan's laid-back style was misleading. Although it is true he preferred to be presented with solutions rather than problems, it was Reagan's personal commitment to cutting taxes, reducing domestic spending, and rebuilding America's defenses that gave shape and coherence to his administration's policies. In the Oval Office, he thrived on the interplay among Baker, Meese, and Deaver, letting them present various alternatives and then instinctively suggesting compromises. Neither brilliant nor well-read, Reagan had a quick mind and a remarkable feel for the public's emotions that enabled him to perform effectively as a detached but charismatic chief executive.

An abrupt change in the White House staff in 1985 nearly proved disastrous for Reagan. Tired of the constant infighting, Baker agreed to Secretary of the Treasury Donald Regan's suggestion that the two men swap jobs. A self-made Wall Street operator, Regan possessed a confident, abrasive manner and a determination to assert his authority as White House chief of staff. When Meese became attorney general and Deaver left the government later in 1985, Regan extended his own control and thus ended the give-and-take in the Oval Office that had allowed Reagan to shape the final policy choices during his first term.

At first, Regan and Baker were able to score a major victory. Intent on lowering taxes still more on the wealthy while capitalizing on growing congressional demands for a simpler and fairer revenue system, the two men pressed for a major overhaul of the income tax. Making the necessary compromises with leaders in Congress, they shaped the 1986 Tax Reform Act, which cut the top rate from 50 to 28 percent while sharply reducing unproductive tax shelters. The new rates exempted six million people at the lower end from paying taxes while an alternative minimum tax prevented the rich from escaping their fair share. Although designed to bring in the same total revenue, the new act led to short-term increases in business taxes that kept the federal deficit from growing any larger.

The administration had only partial success in another area—appointing conservative federal judges who would simply follow the law and leave policy issues to Congress and state legislatures. In 1986, after a brief skirmish with the Senate, Reagan succeeded in replacing outgoing Chief Justice Warren Burger with the Supreme Court's strongest conservative, William Rehnquist. Equally conservative appeals court judge Antonin Scalia joined the Supreme Court at the same time. But in 1987, when the president nominated Robert Bork, an outspoken opponent of judicial activism, to fill the next vacancy, Democrats drew the line. Opposition from labor and civil rights groups finally led the Senate to reject Bork's nomination by a vote of 58 to 42. It was a bittersweet victory, however, as Reagan responded by appointing the moderately conservative, but far more diplomatic, Anthony Kennedy to the Court.

George Bush, Reagan's successor in the White House, made two appointments to the Supreme Court. His first choice, David H. Souter of New Hampshire, reflected the president's desire to avoid the kind of controversy stirred by the Bork nomination. Souter, dubbed "the stealth nominee" because of his unknown views on controversial issues, won Senate approval easily in 1991, but then, to the dismay of conservatives, sided consistently with the liberal minority on the Court. Bush's second choice, Clarence Thomas, proved far more controversial. Picked in 1991 to replace Thurgood Marshall, Thomas was an African American conservative who opposed affirmative action. Despite his race, civil rights groups opposed his nomination on ideological grounds. The Senate

Judiciary Committee hearings became explosive when University of Oklahoma law school professor Anita Hill accused Thomas of sexual harassment when she had been employed by him in a government agency a decade earlier. Thomas denied the charges and defended himself by accusing the Judiciary Committee of conducting "a high tech lynching of an uppity black who in any way deigns to think for himself." The Senate finally confirmed Thomas by a vote of just 52 to 48, the narrowest margin ever for a Supreme Court appointment. The American people, however, had fewer reservations about Thomas, as polls showed 58 percent believing him and only 24 percent finding Hill's charges credible. On the Court, Thomas regularly voted in tandem with Justice Antonin Scalia, leader of the conservative bloc, and thus, despite Souter's defection, his appointment ensured that the Court would continue to champion free market principles over increased governmental regulation.

The Election of 1988

The Democrats approached the 1988 election with growing optimism. They had regained control of the Senate in 1986, Reagan no longer would be on the Republican ticket, and Iran-Contra and the vast increase in the national debt since 1980 all appeared to place the GOP on the defensive. Michael Dukakis, the successful governor of Massachusetts, emerged from the grueling primary contests as the clear-cut winner. With the selection of moderate Texas senator Lloyd Bentsen as his vice presidential running mate, Dukakis left the convention at Atlanta confident of victory, with polls showing him ahead by 17 points.

The Republican nominee, Vice President George Bush, proved to be a much stronger candidate than anyone had expected. Despite the controversial choice of Indiana senator Dan Quayle as his running mate, Bush quickly regained the lead. The Republicans waged a ruthless attack on Dukakis, portraying him as soft on crime and defense. Above all, the GOP candidate repeatedly promised not to raise taxes, reiterating his favorite line: "Read my lips—no new taxes."

Dukakis fought back, but failed to close the narrow gap separating the two candidates in the polls. In the last weeks, the vice president, with the South se-

THE ELECTION OF 1988

Candidate	Party	Popular Vote	Electoral Vote
Bush	Republican	48,886,097	426
Dukakis	Democratic	41,809,074	112

cure, concentrated on holding his slim leads in crucial states such as California and Ohio.

The outcome confirmed the pollsters' projections. Bush won overwhelmingly in the South, carried most of the West, and defeated Dukakis in such key industrial states as Michigan and Pennsylvania. His victory reflected the continuing GOP dominance of the electoral college, as well as the natural advantage of an incumbent at a time when the economy was healthy and the world at relative peace. Yet Dukakis could take some comfort in blocking a Republican landslide. Although the voters elected a Republican president, they also increased the Democratic margins in both the House and Senate. Bush would be the first new president since John F. Kennedy to enter the White House while his party lost ground in Congress.

The election of 1988 indicated that, at least on the presidential level, a significant change had taken place in American politics in 1980. Bush consolidated the GOP's grip on the electoral college, winning in the Sunbelt states of the South and West. He held much of Reagan's inroads into the working-class vote, scoring 49 percent compared to Reagan's 55 percent among blue-collar voters. At the same time, racial polarization in politics continued, with Dukakis getting 88 percent of the African American vote and 69 percent of the Hispanic ballots. The Democrats, despite their success in Congress, faced the challenge of trying to regain the support of white middle-class voters for their presidential candidates.

Bush's Domestic Agenda

Many people expected the Bush administration to reflect the reputation of the new president—bland and cautious, lacking in vision but safely predictable. At home, he lived up to his reputation, sponsoring few initiatives in education, health care, and environmental protection while continuing the Reagan theme of limiting federal interference in the everyday lives of American citizens. He vetoed family leave legislation, refused to sponsor meaningful health care reform, and watered down civil rights proposals in Congress. The one exception was the **Americans with Disabilities Act (ADA)**, passed by Congress in 1991, which prohibited discrimination against the disabled in hiring, transportation, and public accommodations. Beginning in July 1992, ADA called for all public buildings, restaurants, and stores to be made accessible to those with physical handicaps and required that businesses with twenty-five or more workers hire new employees without regard to disability.

Most of Bush's time was taken up with two pressing domestic problems. First, the nation's savings and loan industry, based on U.S. government–insured deposits, was in grave trouble as a result of lax regulation and unwise, even possibly fraudulent, loan policies. After record losses of $13.4 billion in 1988, more than 250 savings and loans had been forced to close. The continuing budget deficit provided an even greater challenge. Despite Gramm-Rudman, the nation continued to spend beyond its means, with deficits still running over $150 billion a year.

The president and Congress finally reached agreement on both issues. In August 1989, Congress passed an administration bill to close or merge more than seven hundred ailing savings and loans at a cost of $157 billion over a ten-year period. The proposal included a restructuring of the federal regulatory system and bond provisions to keep the thrift

Advocates for the disabled and a sign language interpreter look on as President Bush signs the Americans with Disabilities Act of 1990. ❖

❖ A Look at the Past ❖

EMPOWER YOURSELF
LEAN ON THE LORD

WWW.TELLITRIGHT.COM

Christian Right Bumper Sticker

Religion and politics became partners in the 1970s and found a champion in Ronald Reagan, who became president in 1980. The New Right Coalition had political goals as well as social and cultural goals—what could be called a crusading moralism. Opposing what they called degenerate lifestyles, they defended traditional family values. The New Right became adept at using the media and at increasing awareness of their moral crusade. Religion became part of popular culture with the rise of televangelism and a wide variety of personal products. Why do you think someone would proclaim his or her conversion by wearing a belt buckle or pasting a sticker onto a car bumper? What do such items suggest about the place of religion in American life?

bailout from adding to the deficit. A new federal agency, the Resolution Trust Corporation, closed more than five hundred savings and loans, primarily in the Sunbelt states. It took over the properties on which developers had secured loans many times their actual value and gradually sold them off at discount prices. By the time the Resolution Trust Corporation expired in 1992, the initial cost to the government was more than $150 billion, and the eventual bill for the savings and loan cleanup, including interest, was estimated at between $500 and $700 billion.

Action on the budget proved even more difficult. Facing a Gramm-Rudman goal of $110 billion for the 1991 budget, Bush finally persuaded Congress to accept a deficit of $105 billion in late 1989; accounting gimmicks and a surplus in the Social Security account disguised the true figure of nearly $200 billion. In the fall of 1990, Bush finally agreed to break his "no new taxes" pledge and support a budget that included new taxes on the wealthy along with substantial spending cuts, mainly for the military. The resulting agreement projected a savings of $500 billion over five years, half from reduced spending and half from new revenue generated mainly by increasing the top tax rate from 28 percent to 31 percent and raising the gasoline tax by 5.1 cents a gallon.

Unfortunately for the president, the budget deal coincided with the beginning of a slow but painful re-

cession that ended the Republican prosperity of the 1980s. Not only did Bush face recriminations from voters for breaking his "Read my lips" pledge, but the economic decline led to greatly reduced government revenues. As a result, the deficit continued to soar, rising from $150 billion in fiscal year 1989 to just under $300 billion in 1992. Despite the 1990 budget agreement, the national debt increased by more than $1 trillion during Bush's presidency.

The End of the Cold War

Abroad, the Bush administration faced an unprecedented year of change that appeared to mark the end of the post–World War II era. In country after country, communism gave way to freedom as the Cold War faded away more quickly than anyone had expected.

The first attempt at internal liberation proved tragically abortive. In May 1989, students in China began a monthlong demonstration for freedom in Beijing's Tiananmen Square that attracted worldwide attention. Watching American television coverage of Gorbachev's visit to China in mid-May, Americans were fascinated to see the Chinese students call for democracy with a hunger strike and a handcrafted replica of the Statue of Liberty. But on the evening of June 4, the Chinese leaders sent tanks and troops to

Fed up with the corruption that accompanied the economic benefits of Chinese leader Deng Xiaoping's reforms, Chinese students demonstrated for democracy in the spring of 1989. Their nonviolent protest in Beijing's Tiananmen Square at first evoked a surprisingly passive government response. Here, student leader Wang Dan, standing before a large crowd in Tiananmen Square on May 27, calls for a citywide march. In early June, military action was called for to break the students' resistance. Tanks, armored personnel carriers, and trucks cleared the square after firing on the unarmed students. ❖

Tiananmen Square to crush the student demonstration. By the next day, full-scale repression swept over China; several hundred protesters were killed, and thousands were injured. Chinese leaders imposed martial law to quell the dissent and shatter American hopes for a democratic China.

President Bush responded cautiously. He wanted to preserve American influence with the Chinese government. Hence, despite official statements denouncing the crackdown, Bush permitted National Security Adviser Brent Scowcroft to undertake a secret mission to Beijing to maintain a working relationship with the Chinese leaders.

A far more promising trend toward freedom began in Europe in mid-1989. In June, Lech Walesa and his

Solidarity movement came to power in free elections in Poland. Soon the winds of change were sweeping over the former Iron Curtain countries. A new regime in Hungary opened its borders to the West in September, allowing thousands of East German tourists in Hungary to flee to freedom. One by one, the repressive governments of East Germany, Czechoslovakia, Bulgaria, and Romania fell. The most heartening scene of all took place in East Germany in early November when the new communist leaders suddenly announced the opening of the Berlin Wall. Workers quickly demolished a 12-foot-high section of this despised physical symbol of the Cold War, joyously singing a German version of "For He's a Jolly Good Fellow."

Most people realized it was Mikhail Gorbachev who was responsible for the liberation of eastern Europe. In late 1988, he signaled the spread of his reforms to the Soviet satellites by announcing that the Brezhnev doctrine, which called for Soviet control of eastern Europe, was now replaced with "the Sinatra doctrine," which meant that the people of this region could now do things "their way." It was Gorbachev's refusal to use armed force to keep repressive regimes in power that permitted the long-delayed liberation of the captive peoples of central and eastern Europe.

Yet by the end of 1991, both Gorbachev and the Soviet Union had become victims of the demise of communism. On August 19, 1991, eight right-wing plotters placed Gorbachev under arrest. Boris Yeltsin, the newly elected president of the Russian Republic, broke up the coup by mounting a tank in Moscow and demanding Gorbachev's release. The Red Army rallied to Yeltsin's side. The coup failed and Gorbachev was released, only to resign in December 1991 after the fifteen republics dissolved the Soviet Union. Russia, by far the largest and most powerful of the former Soviet republics, took the lead in joining with ten others to form a loose alignment called the Commonwealth of Independent States (CIS). Yeltsin then disbanded the Communist party and continued the reforms begun by Gorbachev to establish democracy and a free market system in Russia.

The Bush administration, although criticized for its cautious approach, welcomed the demise of communism and offered economic assistance to Russia and the other members of the new CIS. The most important steps came in the critical area of nuclear weapons. In 1991, Bush and Gorbachev signed START I, agreeing to reduce nuclear warheads to less than ten thousand apiece; in late 1992, Bush and Yeltsin agreed on the terms of START II, which would eliminate land missiles with multiple warheads and reduce the number of nuclear weapons on each side to just over three thousand, a level not seen since the mid-1960s.

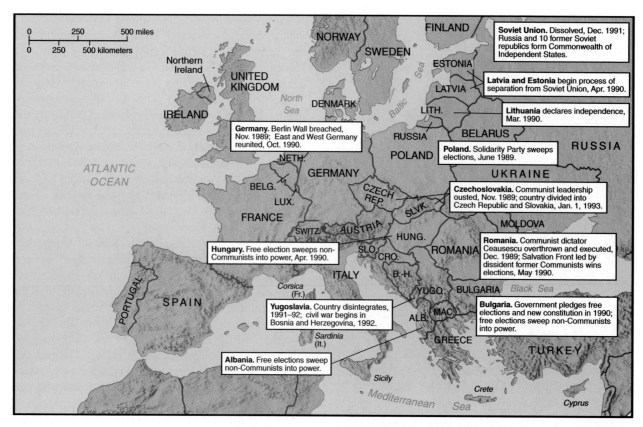

THE END OF THE COLD WAR   *Free elections in Poland in June 1989 triggered the domino effect in the fall of communism in eastern Europe and the former Soviet Union. Changes in policy came quickly, but the restructuring of social and economic institutions continues to take time.* ❖

Waging Peace

The end of the Cold War, however, did not bring about a world free of violence. In December 1989, twenty-seven thousand American troops invaded Panama and quickly installed a new government friendly to the United States in the largest American military operation since the Vietnam War. Despite the death of twenty-three Americans and several hundred Panamanians, this action won approval from the people of both countries when it resulted in the capture of drug-trafficking General Manuel Noriega. By taking such bold and decisive action in Panama, Bush was able to shake his reputation for caution. But critics noted that the president, in the best tradition of the Cold War, had waged war without consulting Congress. Eight months later, Bush suddenly faced a much graver challenge. On August 2, 1990, Saddam Hussein, the dictatorial ruler of Iraq, stunned the world by invading defenseless Kuwait and threatening Saudi Arabia and the oil-rich Persian Gulf region. The president responded firmly, despite an earlier balance-of-power policy of supporting Iraq against Iran. He accused Saddam of naked aggression and carefully built up a UN coalition to uphold what he termed "a new world order." Equally important, he

quickly persuaded Saudi Arabia to accept a huge American troop buildup, dubbed Desert Shield. With the United States importing nearly half of the oil the American people used every day, there was a compelling strategic need to prevent the bulk of the world's oil reserves from falling under the sway of Saddam Hussein. Whatever the appeal of the president's call for a "new world order," control of the Persian Gulf was clearly a vital national interest.

Debate raged, however, on the best way to meet the Iraqi threat. Many Democrats in Congress supported Bush's efforts to place international economic sanctions on Iraq but opposed the use of force. Bush had clearly opted for a different solution by November, massing far more troops in the Persian Gulf area than were needed to defend Saudi Arabia—Operation Desert Shield was giving way to **Desert Storm.** After securing UN support, Bush narrowly persuaded Congress (with just five votes to spare in the Senate) to approve the use of force to liberate Kuwait.

On January 17, 1991, the president unleashed a devastating aerial assault on Iraq. After knocking out the Iraqi air defense network in a few hours, F-117A stealth fighters and Tomahawk cruise missiles hit key targets in Baghdad. The air attack, virtually unchal-

lenged by the Iraqis, wiped out command and control centers and enabled the coalition bombers to demoralize the beleaguered enemy troops. After five weeks, Bush gave his approval for the long-awaited ground assault. Led by General H. Norman Schwarzkopf, the allied armored units swept across the desert in a great flanking operation while a combined force of U.S. marines and Saudi troops drove directly into Kuwait City. In just one hundred hours, the American-led offensive liberated Kuwait and sent Saddam Hussein's vaunted Republican Guard fleeing back into Iraq.

In a controversial decision, President Bush, acting on the advice of General Colin Powell, chairman of the Joint Chiefs, halted the advance and agreed to an armistice with Iraq. Critics claimed that with just a few more days of fighting, perhaps even just a few more hours, American forces could have encircled the Republican Guard and ended Saddam's cruel regime. But the president, fearful of disrupting the allied coalition and of having American troops mired down in a guerrilla war, stopped when he had achieved his announced goal of liberating Kuwait. Moreover, he hoped that a chastened Saddam would help balance the threat of Iran in the volatile Persian Gulf region.

Desert Storm brought mixed blessings. It was a great personal victory for George Bush, who saw his approval rating climb to an unprecedented level—nearly 90 percent, higher than even Eisenhower and Kennedy at the height of the Cold War. American military leaders believed they had finally atoned for Vietnam, a sentiment widely shared by an euphoric public. The United States had deployed more than

Anti-aircraft fire lights up the sky over Baghdad, Iraq, during the Persian Gulf War. A month of strikes on Iraqi targets was followed by a ground offensive that lasted only one hundred hours before Iraqi troops began to surrender and President Bush ordered a cease-fire. Critics of Bush's decision argued that stopping the advance allowed an unvanquished Saddam Hussein to remain in power in Iraq. ❖

CHRONOLOGY

1980	Ronald Reagan wins presidency in landslide
1981	American hostages in Iran released after 444 days in captivity (January) ❖ Sandra Day O'Connor becomes first woman U.S. Supreme Court justice (September)
1982	Equal Rights Amendment fails state ratification (June) ❖ Unemployment reaches post-war record high of 10.4 percent (October)
1983	Soviets shoot down Korean airliner (September) ❖ U.S. invades Grenada (October)
1984	Russia boycotts summer Olympics in Los Angeles (July) ❖ Ronald Reagan reelected president (November)
1985	Mikhail Gorbachev becomes leader of the Soviet Union (March)
1986	Space shuttle *Challenger* explodes, killing seven astronauts (January) ❖ Iran-Contra affair made public (November)
1987	Reagan and Gorbachev sign INF treaty at Washington summit
1988	George Bush defeats Michael Dukakis decisively in presidential election
1989	*Exxon Valdez* oil spill pollutes over 500 square miles of Alaskan waters (March) ❖ San Francisco rocked by massive earthquake (October) ❖ Berlin Wall crumbles (November)
1990	Saddam Hussein invades Kuwait (August) ❖ Bush breaks "no new taxes" campaign pledge, supports $500 billion budget deal (November)
1991	Operation Desert Storm frees Kuwait and crushes Iraq (January–February) ❖ Soviet Union dissolved, replaced by Commonwealth of Independent States (December)

500,000 troops, as many as were in Vietnam in 1968, and had lost just 146 lives in inflicting a stinging defeat on a dangerous bully. Best of all, the price of oil, which had climbed to nearly $40 a barrel in October, fell back to less than $20, allowing Americans to fill the gas tanks of their cars for just over $1 a gallon.

At the same time, however, Saddam Hussein continued to rule in Baghdad, persecuting Kurds in northern Iraq and Shi'ite Muslims in the south. He survived several attempts on his life and tightened his grip on Iraq, frustrating U.S. efforts to uncover and destroy his suspected chemical, biological, and nuclear weapons facilities. In retrospect, Bush's failure to oust Saddam in 1991 meant that American troops would have to invade Iraq again in 2003 in an effort to complete this task.

CONCLUSION: REPUBLICAN ECONOMIC WOES

In the long run, the Persian Gulf War may have damaged George Bush more than it helped him politically. It was his concentration on the Gulf crisis that led the president to enter into the budget deal with congressional Democrats in the fall of 1990—a deal that alienated conservative Republicans and left Bush open to the charge of violating his 1988 campaign pledge not to raise taxes. When the deficit continued to increase despite the budget deal, Bush became very vulnerable at the ballot box.

Even more dangerous for the president was the way in which the Gulf War interrupted the slow recovery from the lingering recession and revived fears about America's economic vitality in the post–Cold War era. For twelve years, the Republicans had relied on a robust economy to enact their programs and consolidate their power—now the Democrats finally had a chance to accuse the GOP of endangering the nation's economic health.

RECOMMENDED READING

A British observer, Godfey Hodgson, gives a perceptive and balanced analysis of the conservative movement that led to Reagan's election in *The World Turned Right Side Up* (1996). The most detailed account of the Reagan presidency is the second volume of journalist Lou Cannon's biography, *President Reagan* (1991). Bob Schieffer and Gary Paul Gates offer a critical overview of the Reagan administration in *The Acting President* (1989), which focuses on Reagan's detached style of leadership.

Michael Schaller, *Reckoning with Reagan* (1992), and Haynes Johnson, *Sleepwalking Through History* (1991), offer critical accounts of the Reagan administration. For a more positive view by a Reagan aide, see Martin Anderson, *Revolution* (1988). Thomas Ferguson and Joel Rogers analyze the political realignment of the 1980s in *Right Turn* (1985).

For Reagan's foreign policy, the most complete account is by his secretary of state, George Shultz, *Turmoil and Triumph* (1992). Frances Fitzgerald provides a critical analysis of the Strategic Defense Initiative in *Way Out There in the Blue* (2000). The two best accounts of how the Cold War ended are Don Oberdorfer, *The Turn* (1991), and Raymond L. Garthoff, *The Great Transition* (1994). Jay Winik, *On the Brink* (1996), gives the Reagan administration full credit for winning the Cold War.

John Robert Greene provides a balanced view of the Bush administration in *The Presidency of George Bush* (2000); the best biography of the president is Herbert Parmet, *George Bush* (1997). For foreign policy, see George Bush and Brent Scowcroft, *A World Transformed* (1998). Bob Woodward traces the decisions leading to the Gulf War in *The Commanders* (1991); the best overview of the military operations is Michael R. Gordon and Bernard F. Trainor, *The Generals' War* (1995).

For a list of additional titles related to this chapter's topics, please see http://www.ablongman.com/divine.

SUGGESTED WEB SITES

The 80s Server

http://www.80s.com/

This site has a variety of sources of information about the 1980s, including an extensive reference database open to 80s server members.

The Gulf War

http://www.pbs.org/pages/frontline/gulf/index.html

This Frontline and PBS site combines personal accounts with a chronology and general information about the war.

Ronald Wilson Reagan

http://www.ipl.org/ref/POTUS/rwreagan.html

This site contains basic factual data about Reagan's election and presidency, speeches, and on-line biographies.

George Herbert Walker Bush

http://www.ipl.org/ref/POTUS/ghwbush.html

This site contains basic factual data about Bush's election and presidency, speeches, and on-line biographies.

In Their Own Words: NIH Online AIDS History Project

http://aidshistory.nih.gov

National Institutes of Health site documenting the early years of HIV/AIDS. Resources include oral histories of AIDS researchers, a timeline of key events in AIDS history from 1981–1988, document and image archives, and a links page.

Bakke v. Regents of the University of California

The Question of Affirmative Action

In June 1974, an attorney for NASA engineer and Vietnam veteran Allan Bakke filed a complaint against the University of California. Bakke could not have realized he was beginning a legal battle that would last four years and end in the U.S. Supreme Court. His case would capture the attention of the nation and raise concerns about the direction of civil rights in America. In his lawsuit, Bakke claimed to be a victim of racial discrimination. His case attracted so much attention because Allan Bakke was white.

The civil rights victories of the early 1960s had benefited minorities in many ways, but economic progress was not one of them. Most minority Americans continued to live in poverty. In 1965, President Lyndon Johnson heralded the "next and the more profound stage of the battle for civil rights," as he called for efforts to improve the economic status of minorities. "We seek not just freedom but opportunity," LBJ declared. Polls showed that most Americans approved of financial aid and job-training programs that assisted minorities in competing equally for educational opportunities and employment. However, Americans did not approve of programs that set quotas guaranteeing minorities a certain percentage of jobs. As the economy began to stagnate in the early 1970s and competition for work and school admissions became more fierce, many white Americans came to believe that "affirmative action" programs gave opportunities to unqualified minorities at the expense of more deserving whites. The Bakke case would make this concern the subject of a national debate to be decided in the courts.

The School of Medicine at the University of California at Davis had voluntarily created a special admissions program in 1969. The university reserved sixteen of the hundred entering class seats for students accepted under an alternative admissions program known as the Task Force. A separate admissions committee composed of faculty and minority students reviewed the applications of students who claimed to have come from "educationally and economically disadvantaged backgrounds." Bakke learned about the Task Force program after the university rejected his application for the 1973 school year. He discovered that several students admitted through the Task Force had lower grade-point averages and Medical College Aptitude Test scores than he did. Bakke also learned that no white student had ever been accepted through the alternative admissions program. When the university rejected his application for the 1974 school year, Bakke, claiming he had been denied the opportunity to compete for sixteen of the hundred seats solely because he was white, initiated his lawsuit accusing the university of racial discrimination.

Bakke v. Regents of the University of California was first heard on September 27, 1974, in the Superior Court in Yolo County, California. Judge F. Leslie Manker presided over a nearly empty courtroom; no one at the time realized Bakke's case would become nationally famous. Bakke's attorney, Reynold Colvin, contended the Task Force program was in fact a racial quota system. Bakke had been prevented from competing for one of the sixteen seats solely because of his race, a violation of the Equal Protection Clause of the Fourteenth Amendment, which guarantees that "no state shall deny to any person within its jurisdiction the equal protection under the laws." Colvin argued that if "the Constitution prohibits exclusion of blacks and other minorities on racial grounds it cannot permit the exclusion of whites on racial grounds. For it must be the exclusion on racial grounds that offends the Constitution and not the particular skin color of

Supporters of affirmative action demonstrate outside the Supreme Court to protest the decision in the *Bakke* case. The Court ruled against the use of racial quota systems to achieve racial balance. However, the Court did uphold the principle of affirmative action by ruling that race could be one of several factors in making hiring or admissions decisions. ❖

the person excluded." Colvin asked the judge to issue an order directing the university to admit Bakke immediately.

The university not only argued against Bakke's admission, it asked the judge to declare the special admissions program to be lawful. University officials and attorneys argued that the Task Force program, far from violating the Equal Protection Clause, ensured that minorities would have an equal opportunity to attend medical school—without the Task Force program, the student body would be overwhelmingly white. The attorneys maintained that the university had a "compelling interest" in promoting diversity in the student body and the medical profession. Minority physicians would bring new viewpoints to the medical community. They would serve as role models to minority children. They would be more likely to return to disadvantaged neighborhoods, which typically suffered from a dearth of physicians. The admission of minorities through the Task Force thus benefited not only the students but society as a whole.

The decision Judge Manker issued on November 22, 1974, pleased no one. He found that since no whites had been admitted under the Task Force, it was in fact a racial quota system. No matter how beneficial its operation was to society, the program was racially discriminatory and therefore illegal:

> This Court cannot conclude that there is any compelling or even legitimate public purpose to be served in granting preference to minority students in admission to the medical school when to do so denies white persons an equal opportunity for admittance. Accordingly, the Court holds in this case that the special admissions program at the Davis Medical School as the same in operation at the time of plaintiff's rejection as an applicant to the school and as the school intends to continue it is violative of the Equal Protection Clause of the Fourteenth Amendment of the United States Constitution.

Much to Bakke's dismay, however, the judge did not order the university to admit him. Judge Manker declared that Bakke had not proved he would have been admitted if the Task Force did not exist. Other students with higher scores than Bakke had been denied admission, and one of those students, not Allan Bakke, might have been accepted.

Dissatisfied with Judge Manker's ruling, both sides appealed. The California Supreme Court accepted the case on the grounds that it was "of great and pressing statewide importance." The case began attracting national attention. Civil rights groups, which had been confident the university would win in the trial court, now worried about the impact of an adverse decision on affirmative action programs.

The court announced its decision on September 16, 1976. By a 6 to 1 vote, the court ruled the admissions program was illegal because it violated the equal protection clause—race could never be the determining factor in the admissions process. The university could fulfill its "compelling interest" of providing opportunities for minorities through nondiscriminatory methods such as remedial schooling programs or expanded admissions. In addition, the court ordered Bakke's admission to the medical school because the university could not prove he would have been rejected if the Task Force program had not existed.

The lone dissenter argued that the students admitted under the Task Force were fully qualified to be medical students, and that the university could use nonacademic factors, including race, in determining which qualified students to accept. He contended that the Constitution permitted racial classifications that had a positive effect, such as the compelling interests that the university claimed, arguing that "as a practical matter" race had to be considered "if the effects of past discrimination and exclusion are to be overcome."

Although the California Supreme Court found in his favor, Bakke still could not enter medical school. The university obtained a stay of the ruling from the court while debating whether to appeal to the U.S. Supreme Court, which, with four of the nine justices being Nixon appointees, now had a strongly conservative cast. Fearful of an adverse decision, concerned civil rights groups counseled the university not to appeal; they preferred to wait for a case more favorable to their position. Nonetheless, in November 1976, the university regents voted to appeal the case to the U.S. Supreme Court; three months later, a majority of justices voted to hear the appeal.

Bakke's case now captured the attention of the nation. Demonstrators opposing Bakke held rallies and parades in California and Washington, D.C. Articles about the case appeared in newspapers and magazines. Fifty-eight individuals and organizations filed briefs containing their opinions. Eager to hear the case, people began lining up outside the Court on October 11, the evening before oral arguments were to be heard. An overflow audience watched attorneys for the two sides present their arguments on October 12, 1977, but those in attendance, along with the rest of the nation, had to wait another eight months before the Court rendered its verdict.

Court insiders later revealed that the justices "really agonized" over the Bakke case. Drafts of the decision were recalled from the printer three times for revisions. Finally, on June 28, 1978, Justice Lewis Powell, author of the majority opinion, addressed the courtroom. After acknowledging the difficulties of the Bakke case, Powell announced that six different opinions had been written and that the Court's judgment was divided. Four justices, Stevens, Burger, Rehnquist, and Stewart, upheld the judgment of the California Supreme Court. Avoiding the constitutional issues, they declared the Task Force in violation of Title VI of the Civil Rights Act of 1964. Largely ignored in the earlier trials, Title VI bans racial discrimination "under any program or activity receiving Federal assistance." These four justices agreed that Bakke should be admitted to the medical school. Justices Brennan, Marshall, White, and Blackmun maintained that Title VI prohibited "only those uses of racial criteria that would violate the Fourteenth Amendment if employed by a State or its agencies; it does not bar the preferential treatment of racial minorities as a means of remedying past societal discrimination." Speaking for the four justices who upheld the university's Task Force approach under the Fourteenth Amendment, Harry Blackmun asserted, "In order to get beyond racism, we must first take account of race."

Justice Powell held the deciding vote. He agreed that the Fourteenth Amendment and not Title VI

Allan Bakke finally won admission to the medical school at University of California at Davis. Here, he walks to his car after his first day of class on September 26, 1978. ✧

should be used in judging the case. Powell argued that the Task Force, which used race as the sole determining factor for admissions, violated the equal protection clause. He declared the Task Force invalid. However, pointing to Harvard University's admissions procedure, Powell ruled that programs that used race as one of many factors in selecting students would not be invalid. Powell had adroitly left the door open for affirmative action programs. Finally, Powell affirmed the California Supreme Court's judgment that Bakke should be admitted to the medical school.

The mixed public reaction reflected the split nature of the Court's ruling. Many viewed the decision as a blow to civil rights. A UC Davis employee complained, "There goes all the progress, everything that's happened in the past ten years," and a science major worried that "this decision seems like a step backwards to before the Sixties." Civil rights activist Jesse Jackson claimed that universities might use the ruling as an excuse to scale back their affirmative action programs. Other observers were more optimistic. Civil rights leader Vernon Jordan claimed that the decision gave "a green light to go forward with acceptable affirmative action programs," and Stanford law professor John Kaplan argued that "the Bakke people have lost. There are five votes on the Supreme Court saying that while you can't have quotas, you can manipulate admissions standards to get a desired level of minorities."

In the short run, at least, Jordan and Kaplan appeared to be right. For the next twenty years, colleges and universities regularly relied on the Bakke decision to use race as one way to admit black and other minority students in a quest for diverse student bodies. In 1996, however, the 5th U.S. Circuit Court of Appeals in New Orleans ruled against this form of affirmative action in the case of Cheryl Hopwood and three other white students who claimed they had higher qualifications than minority candidates admitted to the University of Texas Law School. The Circuit Court ruled that neither race nor ethnicity could be used as factors in granting admission, even for "the wholesome practice of correcting perceived racial imbalance in the student body." In July 1996, the Supreme Court refused to hear the case on appeal. Thus *Hopwood,* as the case came to be known, applied only to institutions in Texas, Louisiana, and Mississippi.

Hopwood, along with a ruling by the University of California Board of Regents in 1996, ended the practice of admitting black and Hispanic students with lower academic qualifications than white students, the policy that had prevailed since *Bakke* in the nation's two most populous states. This denial of affirmative action had immediate consequences; the number of African Americans and Hispanics admitted to major state universities in Texas and California fell sharply in the fall of 1997. Graduate enrollment was hit hardest. Only four black applicants were admitted to the University of Texas Law School for the fall of 1997, and all four declined to attend. The University of Texas admitted just twenty-four blacks to its medical schools in 1997, a decline of 41 percent; at the University of California medical school at San Diego, none of the two hundred African Americans who had applied was accepted.

In 2003, in two cases involving the University of Michigan, the Supreme Court reaffirmed Lewis Powell's opinion in the *Bakke* case and overturned the *Hopwood* decision. Justice Sandra Day O'Connor played the key role. She joined five of her colleagues in ruling against an undergraduate admission procedure at Michigan that arbitrarily gave 20 points (on a scale of 150) to African American and Hispanic candidates. But in the case of the Michigan law school, which used race and ethnicity as one of several factors in determining admission, she wrote the majority opinion in a 5 to 4 decision in favor of affirmative action. In her opinion, she accepted the contention of the University of Michigan

that racial diversity was vital to the educational process, benefiting all students. Her ruling drew a distinction between mechanical formulas for fostering diversity, such as the 20-point undergraduate bonus at Michigan, and what Chief Justice Rehnquist called "narrowly tailored" procedures designed to consider all aspects of an applicant's qualifications. "A university's admissions program," O'Connor asserted, "must remain flexible enough to ensure that each applicant is evaluated as an individual and not in a way that makes an applicant's race or ethnicity the defining feature."

The resolution of the Michigan cases ended the confusion stemming from the divided nature of the Court's ruling in *Bakke.* O'Connor had put the Court clearly in favor of affirmative action procedures designed to achieve diversity in higher education without making race the sole determinant for admission. The attempts to qualify and limit the *Bakke* case, such as the *Hopwood* decision, died with O'Connor's ruling; she had reestablished Powell's opinion as the law of the land.

In the twenty-five years since the Court's original ruling, Allan Bakke had fulfilled his desire to become a physician. He entered the UC Davis medical school in the fall of 1978 and graduated three years later. Trained as an anesthesiologist, he began practicing at a community hospital in Minnesota. In the long run, however, Bakke's brief moment of fame, like that of so many others in the annals of the Supreme Court–Dred Scott, Homer Plessy, Ernesto Miranda–matters less than the constitutional principles to which he appealed. The American people will remember Bakke not as the aspiring medical student who fought to become a doctor, but as a symbol of the ongoing debate over the wisdom and justice of affirmative action.

Questions for Discussion

- Why do most Americans oppose the use of racial quotas?

- On what grounds did advocates of affirmative action justify their support for making race a factor in university admission policy?

- Why did Justice O'Connor approve the University of Michigan Law School admission policy while objecting to the same university's undergraduate procedures?

An aerial view of a real estate development on the edge of Lake Tahoe. The region, which includes portions of California and Nevada, has experienced a huge growth in population and development continues to move into the surrounding wilderness. ❖

America in Flux

The Buck Starts Here

The two men who met in Little Rock, Arkansas, on December 2, 1992, could not have been more different. Bill Clinton, the president-elect, was gregarious and charming; his guest, Federal Reserve Chairman Alan Greenspan, was shy, gloomy, and reserved. Clinton was noted for his ability to use words eloquently; Greenspan for his uncanny ability to use them to confuse rather than enlighten his listeners.

Alan Greenspan was also a genius at statistical analysis. He had founded a private consulting firm in New York City that compiled and analyzed economic data to advise major corporations on how to adapt to the vagaries of the marketplace. A lifelong Republican with libertarian instincts such as a strong belief in free markets and the power of the individual, Greenspan had served as chairman of the Council of Economic Advisers in the Ford administration and Ronald Reagan had appointed him chairman of the Federal Reserve Board in 1987. Reappointed to a second four-year term in 1991 by George Bush, Greenspan oversaw the nation's fiscal policy from a modest Washington office dominated by a wall plaque proclaiming, "The Buck Starts Here."

Despite their personal and political differences, Clinton and Greenspan shared a common goal: to rein in the alarming growth of the federal deficit while stimulating the expansion of the stagnant economy. George Bush's $500 billion deal with Congress in 1990 to cut spending and raise taxes had failed to reduce the deficit because of declining government revenues in the recession of 1990 to 1991. Already over $200 billion a year, the shortfall was expected to reach $400 billion by the end of Clinton's first term. As a result, the interest on the ever-expanding national debt, running $300 billion annually, would continue to grow, threatening to surpass defense spending as the government's largest single expense. Even though Clinton had focused on economic revitalization during the campaign, promising a middle-class tax cut and job creation, he realized he would have to give deficit reduction, the issue advocated by third-party candidate Ross Perot, his highest priority. Greenspan reinforced this perception by delivering a lengthy economic lecture stressing the importance of lower long-term bond rates to the president-elect.

The benefits of deficit reduction and lower bond rates, Greenspan argued, could be enormous. A drop in the cost of borrowing money, both for businesses that were expanding and for home mortgages, could lead to rapid economic growth. And renewed economic growth would create jobs and thus help lower the 6 percent unemployment rate that was hurting American workers.

Greenspan's argument hit home with Clinton. As an experienced politician, Clinton made no binding commitment, but after the meeting he commented, "We can do business." To the dismay of his liberal advisers, Clinton followed Greenspan's advice and made deficit reduction the centerpiece of his economic policy. He did so, however, with some reservations, commenting to aides that the success of his administration "hinges on the Federal Reserve and a bunch of f—— bond traders."

On February 17, 1993, the president gave his first State of the Union address. Striking a bipartisan note, President Clinton outlined a bold plan to reduce the deficit

OUTLINE

The Changing American Population

Democratic Revival

Clinton and the World

The End of the Century

The New Millennium

Conclusion: The American Century?

FEATURE ESSAY

The Dot.com Boom and Bust

Newly elected President Clinton meets with Federal Reserve Board Chair Alan Greenspan in the Oval Office in 1993. ❖

by more than $500 billion over four years, half by cutting spending and half by raising taxes, mainly on the wealthy. It was time, the president declared, "to say there can be no more something for nothing and admit we are all in this together."

The applause for Clinton's economic plan reverberated far beyond the halls of Congress. Polls showed his approval rating rising from 51 to 63 percent as the public endorsed his decision to give the deficit highest priority. More important, in less than two weeks interest rates on 30-year bonds dropped below 7 percent for the first time ever. Greenspan was proved right and Clinton had won his biggest gamble.

Over the next seven years, the Clinton-Greenspan partnership paid off handsomely. The economy boomed with the creation of 20 million new jobs, the stock market soared to new highs year after year, and unemployment fell to an all-time low of 4 percent. Moreover, rising government revenues wiped out the deficit and even produced a $100 billion surplus in 2000. The future promised to be even brighter, with the Congressional Budget Office predicting a $2.2 trillion windfall in the first decade of the twenty-first century.

THE BOOM OF THE 1990s owed its success to more than just wise fiscal policy. An enormous increase in productivity, made possible by new technology, especially computers, enabled workers to turn out more goods without increasing costs, which kept inflation in check. Continued declines in defense spending with the end of the Cold War helped, as did the in-

creases in American exports as a result of new trade policies and agreements. American consumers were the real heroes, buying vast numbers of cars, computers, and household goods in pursuit of the good life. Best of all, even though the wealthy continued to reap the greatest rewards, prosperity reached every level, with those at the bottom making real, if modest, advances.

American life at the turn of the century consisted of more than just material abundance. The population shift to the Sunbelt that began in the 1970s continued through the end of the century, though at a somewhat slower pace. The equally important flow of immigrants from Latin America and Asia, made possible by the Immigration Act of 1965, remained strong, helping to transform the United States into a more ethnically diverse country.

The most surprising development came overseas as the end of the Cold War led not to a peaceful world but rather spawned a series of crises in Africa, the Balkans, and the Middle East that led to frequent American military involvement. Yet even these traditional foreign policy challenges proved minor compared to the threat of international terrorism engendered by America's world supremacy. Attacks on the World Trade Center in 1993 and American embassies in East Africa in 1998 were but the forerunners of the tragic events of September 11, 2001. The hijacking and suicide mission that used American airliners to destroy the twin towers of the World Trade Center and damage the Pentagon shocked the nation and made September 11 a day of infamy equal to December 7, 1941, the day of the Japanese attack on Pearl Harbor.

Bill Clinton, whose second term was marred by his affair with a White House intern, left office in early 2001, replaced by George W. Bush, son of the former President Bush. In his last year in office, Clinton appointed Alan Greenspan to a fourth term as Fed chairman, but a downturn in the economy in early 2001 soon wiped out the projected budget surplus and tarnished Greenspan's reputation for economic wizardry.

The new president, however, faced an even greater challenge than a declining economy as he waged war against the campaign of terrorism conducted by al Qaeda and Osama bin Laden. It was ironic that Clinton, despite his economic success, had never faced the kind of challenge that gives rise to claims of presidential greatness in his eight years in office. Yet President Bush was presented with such an opportunity in only his first year in the White House.

THE CHANGING AMERICAN POPULATION

From the *Mayflower* to the covered wagon, movement has always characterized the American people. The last three decades of the twentieth century witnessed two significant shifts in the American population: movement internally to the Sunbelt region of the South and West and a remarkable influx of immigrants from developing nations. These changes led to increased urbanization, greater ethnic diversity, and growing social unrest.

A People on the Move

The most striking finding in the 1980 census was that for the first time in American history, more than half the people lived in the South and West; the **Sunbelt** had boomed. The Sunbelt, best defined as a broad band running across the country below the 37th parallel from the Carolinas to Southern California, had begun to flourish with the buildup of military bases and defense plants during World War II. Rapid population growth continued with the stimulus of heavy Cold War defense spending and accelerated in the 1970s when both new high-technology firms and more established industries were attracted by lower labor costs and the favorable climate of the Sunbelt states. Florida,

Texas, and California led the way, each gaining more than two million new residents in the 1970s.

The flow continued at a slightly lower rate over the next two decades. The Northeast and the Middle West continued losing people to the South and West, and in 1994 Texas surpassed New York as the nation's second most populous state. The 2000 census revealed that while all regions had gained population in the 1990s, the South and West had expanded by nearly 20 percent, compared to around 6 percent for the Northeast and Middle West. Phoenix was typical of the phenomenal growth of Sunbelt cities, adding a million residents in the 1990s to grow at a 45 percent rate. "Phoenix is flat and it's easy," explained a geographer who saw no end in sight. "You stick a shovel in the ground and pour a slab and you have a house."

The increasing urbanization of America had both positive and negative aspects. People living in the large metropolitan areas were both more affluent and better educated than their rural counterparts. Family income among people living in the bigger cities and their suburbs ran $9000 a year more and three-fourths of the urban population had graduated from high school, compared to two-thirds of other Americans. A metropolitan American was twice as likely to be a college graduate than a rural resident. Yet these advantages were offset by rising urban crime rates, longer commuting time in heavy traffic, and

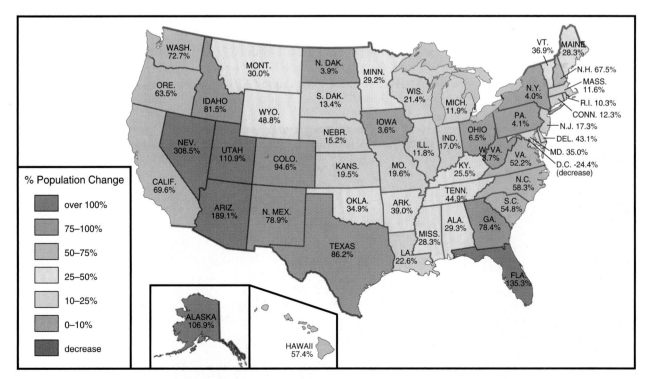

POPULATION SHIFTS, 1970–2000   *Although all fifty states experienced some population growth between 1970 and 2000, states in the West and the South saw the largest percentage increases.* ❖

higher living costs. Nevertheless, the big cities and their suburbs continued to thrive, accounting for 80 percent of all Americans by 2000.

Another striking population trend was the nationwide rise in the number of the elderly. At the beginning of the century, only 4.1 percent of the population was aged 65 or older; by 1997, those over 65 made up 13 percent of the population, with the nearly four million over 85 the fastest growing group of all. Census Bureau projections suggest that by the year 2030, one out of every five Americans will be over age 65.

Six of every ten older Americans were women, and they tended to have a higher rate of chronic disease and to be worse off economically than men the same age. Many of the oldest old, those over 85, lived in nursing homes and accounted for one-third of all Medicaid payments. Yet only 9.9 percent of the elderly lived below the poverty line and three-fourths owned their own homes. The annual cost-of-living increases in Social Security payments spared them the worst ravages of inflation. Most impressive of all was their political power: Two-thirds of those over 65 voted regularly, compared to just under half of the entire population. With more than 30 million members, the AARP (formerly known as the American Association of Retired People) proved very effective in Washington in representing the interests of the elderly, particularly in regard to Medicare.

The Revival of Immigration

The flow of immigrants into the United States reached record proportions in the 1990s as a result of the new policies adopted in 1965. (See the Feature Essay in Chapter 30, "Unintended Consequences: The Second Great Migration," pp. 874–875.) The number of new arrivals peaked at more than 2 million in 2001, but then fell back to 1.2 million in 2002 as a result of tighter immigration controls following the September 11 terrorist attacks. By 2002, there was a record high of 32.2 million foreign-born residents of the United States, 11.5 percent of the total population.

The new wave of immigrants came mainly from Latin America and Asia. By 2002, just over half the foreign-born population of the United States came from Latin America, slightly more than one-quarter from Asia, and only 15 percent from Europe. The new immigrants tended to settle in urban areas in six states—California, Texas, New York, Florida, Illinois, and New Jersey. In California, the influx of immigrants from Asia and Mexico created growing pressure on public services, especially during the recession of the early 1990s.

The arrival of more than 30 million immigrants in three decades was bound to lead to controversy over whether immigrants were a benefit or a liability to American society. A study by the National Academy of Sciences in 1997 reported that while government services used by immigrants—schools, welfare, health clinics—cost more initially than was collected from them in taxes, in the long run, immigrants and their families more than paid their way. In 1992, one scholar estimated that immigrants who had entered the country since 1970 had contributed $27 million more in taxes than the cost of social services they had used. In regard to employment, immigrants tended to help consumers and employers by working for relatively low wages in restaurants, the textile industry, and farming, but they hurt low-skilled U.S. workers, notably high school dropouts and many African Americans, by keeping wages low.

Mexican-born Audelia Ordaz (center) was one of 1700 naturalized immigrants sworn in as U.S. citizens at a ceremony in San Francisco in 1996. The mass swearing-in was part of Citizenship USA, an initiative of the U.S. Immigration and Naturalization Service to reduce the backlog of applications for citizenship and speed up the process of naturalization. ❖

Economist George J. Borjas, a refugee from Cuba, claimed that immigrants from developing countries lacked the education and job skills needed to achieve the level of prosperity attained by newcomers in the past; instead of entering the mainstream of American life, they were likely to remain a permanent underclass.

Public attitudes began to shift toward the end of the century. Legislation adopted in 1996 dropped restrictions on legal immigrants in favor of provisions aimed at illegal aliens—more money to guard the nation's borders and a ban on social services for illegal immigrants. A 1997 poll showed that the number of people who believed immigrants were bad for the nation had dropped from 60 percent in 1993 to 42 percent, with 43 percent affirming the benefits of immigration for the country. The booming economy, with resulting low unemployment, made newcomers willing to do the hard jobs shunned by the native-born appear to be a blessing rather than a threat. But the fear of terrorism engendered by the September 11 attacks revived concern that those hostile to the American way of life could exploit lax immigration procedures to enter the country and carry out destructive acts.

The Surging Hispanics

People of Hispanic origin became the nation's largest ethnic group in 2002, surpassing African Americans for the first time. The rapidly growing Hispanic population had climbed to nearly 39 million, a rise of more than 60 percent, accounting for 13 percent of the nation's population. "It doesn't surprise me," commented the leader of the League of Latin American Citizens. "Anybody that travels around . . . can see Latinos everywhere, working everywhere, trying to reach the American dream."

The Census Bureau identified four major Hispanic categories: Mexican Americans, Puerto Ricans, Cuban Americans, and other Hispanics, including many from Central America. Even though most of the Hispanic population was concentrated in cities like New York, Los Angeles, San Antonio, and Miami, the 2000 census showed a surprising geographical spread. Hispanics made up 20 percent of the population in individual counties in states such as Georgia, Iowa, and Minnesota. "The Latinization of the country is not just happening in New York, Miami, or L.A.," observed a Puerto Rican leader. "Its greatest impact is in the heartland in places like Reading, Pa.; Lorain, Ohio; and Lowell, Mass."

The Hispanic groups had several features in common. All were relatively youthful, with a median age of 22 and a high fertility rate. They tended to be relatively poor, with one-fourth falling below the poverty line,

and to be employed in low-paying positions as manual laborers, domestic servants, and migrant workers. Although the position of Hispanics had improved considerably in the boom years of the 1980s and 1990s, they still lagged behind mainstream America. The poverty rate among Hispanics was twice the national average, and family median income in 1998 was $28,330, only two-thirds of the level for other Americans.

Lack of education was a key factor in preventing economic progress for Hispanics. The American Council on Education released a report in 1991 that found Hispanics "are grossly under-represented at every rung of the educational ladder." Fewer Hispanics graduated from high school than other minorities and their school dropout rate was the nation's highest at more than 50 percent. Hispanic leaders warned that these figures boded ill not just for their own group, but for society as a whole. "You either educate us," claimed a San Antonio activist, "or you pay for building more jails or for more welfare."

The entry of several million illegal immigrants from Mexico, once derisively called "wetbacks" and now known as **undocumented aliens,** created a substantial social problem for the nation and especially for the Southwest. Critics charged that the flagrant violation of the nation's border with Mexico had led to an "invisible subculture outside the boundaries of law and legitimate institutions." They argued that the aliens took jobs away from U.S. citizens, kept wages artificially low, and received extensive welfare and medical benefits that strained budgets in states such as Texas and California.

Defenders of the undocumented aliens contended that the nation gained from the abundant supply of workers who were willing to work in fields and factories at backbreaking jobs shunned by most Americans. Moreover, defenders stated, illegal entrants usually paid sales and withholding taxes but rarely used government services for fear of being deported. Whichever view was correct, an exploited class of illegal aliens was living on the edge of poverty. The *Wall Street Journal* summed it up best by observing, "The people who benefit the most from this situation are certainly the employers, who have access to an underground market of cheap, productive labor, unencumbered by minimum wage laws, union restrictions, or pension requirements."

Concern over economic competition from an estimated four million Mexican "illegals" led Congress to pass legislation in 1986 that penalized employers who hired undocumented workers. Congress permitted those aliens who could show that they were living in the United States before 1982 to become legal residents; nearly three million accepted this offer of amnesty to become legal residents. The reform effort, however, failed to stem the continued flow of undocumented workers northward from Mexico in the 1990s —perhaps as many as 500,000 a year. While experts debated the exact number, the Immigration and Naturalization Service estimated in 1997 that 5 million foreigners, mainly from Mexico and Central America, were living illegally in the United States—two million in California alone.

Despite stepped-up border enforcement efforts after the September 11 attacks, illegal immigrants continued to move northward from Mexico and Central America in the early years of the twenty-first century. The trip was not without hazards. Mexican experts estimated that more than 2000 migrants lost their lives attempting to enter the United States illegally between 1997 and 2003. Nineteen Mexican and Central American workers died from suffocation in south Texas in May 2003—nearly one hundred illegal aliens had been jammed into a truck trailer without access to water or fresh air. Yet the movement continued. As one rural Mexican official commented, "There are great problems in the countryside. And that famous American dream keeps calling."

Advance and Retreat for African Americans

African Americans formed the second largest of the nation's ethnic minorities. In 2002, there were just over 38 million blacks in the United States, 12.8 percent of the population. Although the heaviest concentration of African Americans was in northern cities, notably New York and Chicago, there was a significant movement back to the South. This shift, which began in the 1970s and accelerated in the 1990s, meant that by 2000 nearly 54 percent of those identifying themselves as black for the census lived in the sixteen states of the Sunbelt. Family ties and a search for ancestral roots helps explain this movement, but it also reflects the same economic incentives that drew so many Americans to this region in the last three decades of the twentieth century.

Middle-class African Americans had made some gains during the 1970s and 1980s. By 1976, one-third of all black workers held white-collar jobs—double the rate of 1960. Education proved the key to African American advances. Black graduates of the nation's colleges and universities had relatively easy entry into higher paying jobs in banks, corporations, and government agencies. Black college enrollment increased by 43 percent between 1970 and 2000, giving more African Americans the opportunity for a middle-class lifestyle.

Yet despite these gains, there were setbacks as well for African Americans. In the *Bakke* decision (see pp. 956–959), the Supreme Court ruled against racial quotas for blacks at a University of California medical school, although the ruling did permit universities to consider race as "simply one element" in efforts to select diverse student bodies. In subsequent decisions, the Court upheld an affirmative action program designed by Kaiser Aluminum to help advance minority workers and ordered American Telephone and Telegraph to hire more African Americans and women to make up for past discrimination.

Affirmative action yielded only mixed results for blacks. For those able to gain university admission, such programs proved helpful, but even blacks who graduated from college did not do as well economically as their white counterparts. The Census Bureau reported in 1991 that African American college graduates received only 77 percent as much as white graduates employed in executive and administrative positions. For black males with a high school degree, the gap was even larger. "It seems whether with a high school education or a bachelor's degree," commented a Census Bureau demographer, "the earnings differential is still there for black and white men."

For blacks without education, the situation was much worse. Even in the boom years of the 1980s, unemployment rates for African Americans remained over 10 percent, and among black teenagers, the level was a staggering 40 percent. In the recession of 1990–1991, black workers lost 59,579 jobs. Blue-collar African American workers were especially hard hit, losing one-third of the 180,210 blue-collar jobs lost during the recession. Nor did blacks share equally in the economic recovery of the 1990s. More than two million black families were living below the poverty line in 1998; the poverty rate for blacks was nearly double that for white Americans.

Rodney King became a symbol of black frustration in the United States. In March 1991, a bystander videotaped four Los Angeles policemen brutally beating King, an African American, who had been stopped for a traffic violation. The pictures of the rain of blows on King shocked the nation. Nearly a year later, when an all-white jury acquitted the four officers of charges of police brutality, rioting erupted in South Central Los Angeles that for a time threatened the entire city when the police failed to respond promptly. In the aftermath of the riot, which took fifty-three lives (compared to thirty-four deaths in the 1965 riot in the nearby Watts area) and did more than $1 billion in damage, government and state agencies promised new efforts to help the ghetto dwellers. Urban blacks, however, saw little hope for improvement. A poll taken in

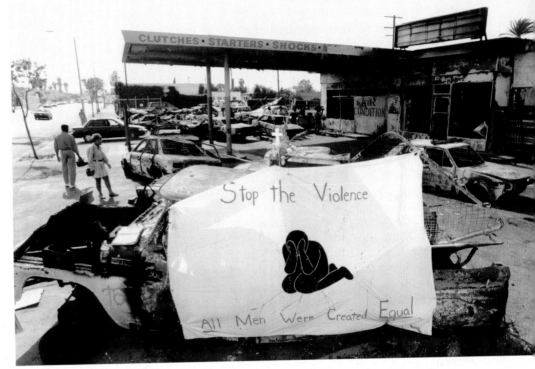

The acquittal of four Los Angeles police officers on charges of police brutality in the 1991 Rodney King case touched off the worst incident of urban violence in the twentieth century. More than fifty people died in the rioting in Los Angeles, and property damage exceeded $1 billion. Here, a poster against violence stands out against the ruins of a service station. ❖

the early 1990s revealed that 51 percent of African Americans believed life had "gotten worse" during the past ten years. For black youths in Los Angeles, surrounded by gang warfare and drive-by shootings, their aspiration was simply to stay alive.

Americans from Asia and the Middle East

Asian Americans were the fasting-growing minority group at the end of the century. In 2000, there were more than 12 million Americans of Asian or Pacific Island descent. Although they represented only 4 percent of the total population, they were increasing at seven times the national rate, and future projections indicated that by 2050 one in ten Americans would be of Asian ancestry.

The Chinese formed the largest single group of Asian Americans, followed by Filipinos, Japanese, Indians, Koreans, and Vietnamese. Immigration was the primary reason for the rapid growth of all these groups except the Japanese; in the 1980s, Asia provided 46 percent of all immigrants to the United States.

Compared to other minorities, Asian Americans are relatively well educated and affluent. Three out of four Asian youths graduate from high school, compared to less than one out of two for blacks and Hispanics. Asian Americans also have the highest per-

centage of college graduates and recipients of doctoral degrees of any minority group; in fact, they are better represented in colleges and universities than the white majority. Many Asians have entered professional fields, and as a result, the median income for Asian American families is more than $4000 higher than the 1998 national level.

Not all Asian Americans have fared well, however. Refugees from Southeast Asia have experienced both economic hardship and persecution. The median family income for Vietnamese Americans in the mid-1980s was $8000 below that for whites. Nearly half the Laotian refugees living in Minnesota were unemployed because they had great difficulty learning to read and write English. Vietnamese fishermen who settled on the Gulf Coast experienced repeated attacks on their livelihood in Texas and Louisiana; the Ku Klux Klan in the early 1980s burned three fishing boats belonging to Vietnamese immigrants and fire-bombed one house in Seadrift, Texas. In the Los Angeles riots in 1992, Korean stores and shops became a main target for looting and firebombing.

But the overall experience of Asian Americans has been a positive one. They came to America seeking economic opportunity, or as many put it, "to climb the mountain of gold." "People are looking for a better life," a Chinese spokeswoman explained. "It's as simple as that, and we will continue to come here, especially if the situations over there [in Asia] stay tight, or get worse."

The number of Americans from the Middle East grew almost as fast as the number of those from Asia in the 1990s. The 2000 census counted 1.5 million Americans of Middle Eastern ancestry, up from 200,000 thirty years earlier. Most came from Arab countries, as well as Israel and Iran. Concentrated in California, New York, and Michigan, Middle Eastern Americans were well-educated, with nearly half having college degrees.

Melting Pot or Multiethnic Diversity?

"Cultural diversity probably accelerated more in the 1980s than any other decade," noted demographer Carl Haub. The influx of people from all around the world, not just from Europe, had profound implications for American culture. Traditionally, the favorite American self-image was the melting pot, the title of Israel Zangwill's play written in 1908, at the height of European immigration into the nation. "America is God's crucible, the great Melting-Pot where all the races of Europe are melting and reforming," one of his characters proclaimed. "Germans and Frenchmen, Irishmen and Englishmen, Jews and Russians—into the Crucible with you all! God is making the American!"

The melting pot image carried with it the concept of stripping newcomers of their culture and national traits and casting them into an Anglo-Saxon mold. Dubious for European immigration in view of the way each ethnic group retained its separate identity, this analogy has seemed increasingly irrelevant to the Third World migration to America in recent times. Instead of recasting immigrants into an American type, immigration could better be seen as broadening the diversity that always has characterized the United States. Now, instead of the usual division between blacks and whites, America is composed of Asians as well as Europeans, Hispanics as well as African Americans. Sociologist Amitai Etzioni suggested replacing the melting pot image with a "mosaic" portraying a nation in which ethnic groups retain their own identities "while recognizing that they are integral parts of a more encompassing whole."

The new awareness of ethnic diversity manifested itself in many ways. In public education, blacks led a crusade against Eurocentric curriculum and demanded a new emphasis on the influence of African culture; on college campuses, the call for multicultural courses and separate departments for African American, Asian American, and Hispanic studies created controversy. Citing the forecasts of a declining Anglo dominance and the rise of minority groups in the next century, ethnic leaders advocated cultural pluralism. Raul Yzaguirre, president of the National Council of La Raza, an Hispanic advocacy group, argued that America has never had a real melting pot in which all races contributed to the mix. "What we've had is a pressure cooker, where everybody has had to come in and become Anglophiles." Yzaguirre claimed that the "new demographics ask America to live up to its own conception of itself as a pluralistic society."

Many Americans found themselves perplexed and uncertain of their cultural identity by the end of the twentieth century. A Census Bureau survey, asking people to state their ancestry, revealed that fully one-fourth of Americans listed Germany first, with Ireland and England a distant second and third. Some Hispanics found the census racial classifications—black, Asian–Pacific Islander, white, or American Indian—meaningless. "I don't really consider myself Caucasian," objected Jose Arroyo of San Jose, California. "My roots go down into the Indians of Mexico." People of Arab descent felt equally confused. Maha El-Sheikh, a Californian of mixed Egyptian and Jordanian parentage, resented the fact that "on tests and things like that, I either have to put that I'm 'Caucasian' or I'm 'Asian'—which I'm not. . . . I say I am Arabic—or I leave it blank."

In the 1990s, people of mixed racial parentage demanded that the census for 2000 include a box labeled "multiracial" rather than just the meaningless "other." A group called Project RACE (Reclassify All Children Equally) argued that the four million children of more than a million interracial marriages deserved their own census category. The professional golf champion Tiger Woods—whose ancestry is part black, part Thai, part Chinese, part Native American, and part Caucasian—agreed, saying that as a child he called himself "Cablinasian." Civil rights groups, however, objected, fearing cuts in government benefits to minorities based on the census figures. The Census Bureau compromised in 2000 by adding four new dual race categories—American Indian-white, American Indian-black, Asian-white, and black-white. In addition, individuals of mixed ancestry could mark several racial categories, not just one as in the past.

The results were startling. Nearly seven million Americans claimed to be multiracial, with most choosing either black-white or Asian-white. Levonne Gaddy, president of the Association of Multiethnic Americans, was ecstatic. "This is the beginning of our having to redefine this social myth that we call race," she declared. A more neutral Census Bureau official observed, "The nation is much more diverse in the year 2000 than it was in 1990." "That diversity," he added, "is much more complex than we've ever measured before."

Project RACE argues that forms requiring racial data should include a category labeled "multiracial" so that people of mixed race can acknowledge their entire heritage. Among the best-known of persons fitting the "multiracial" classification is professional golf star Eldrick "Tiger" Woods, whose father Earl is African American and mother Kultida is a native of Thailand. ❖

Horace Kallen, one of the early critics of Zangwill's melting pot analogy, offered the most appealing image of the nation's diverse heritage. He likened the United States to a symphony orchestra, in which each nationality and ethnic group contributed its "own specific timbre and tonality" to create "a multiplicity in a unity, an orchestration of mankind." As Americans wrestle with the continuing dilemma embodied in the national motto, *E pluribus unum*, the image of a great symphony in which all groups blend harmoniously offers a way to balance the pride individuals find in ethnic identity with the need for national unity.

DEMOCRATIC REVIVAL

The Democrats, victims of the runaway inflation of the 1970s, became the beneficiaries of a lingering recession of the early 1990s. Moving away from its traditional liberal reliance on big government, the party regained strength by choosing moderate candidates and tailoring its programs to appeal to the hard-pressed middle class. These new tactics enabled the Democrats to regain the White House in 1992 and retain it in 1996, despite a Republican sweep of Congress in 1994. The key figure in this political shift was Bill Clinton, who overcame some early setbacks to reap the rewards of a sustained economic boom.

The Election of 1992

The persistence of the recession that had begun two years earlier became a major political issue in 1992. Although mild by postwar standards, the economic downturn that began in July 1990 proved unusually stubborn, especially in states such as California that relied heavily on the defense industry, which was hurt by the end of the Cold War. The recovery, which started just after the end of the Persian Gulf War in the spring of 1991, proved slow and uneven. Unemployment remained high for eighteen months and the gross domestic product rose only an anemic 2.9 percent in the same period.

The political impact was devastating for the Bush administration. Three million Americans joined the ranks of the unemployed, and unlike earlier recessions, many were white-collar employees rather than factory workers. Although the economy began to advance more briskly in 1992, unemployment persisted as businesses still hesitated to hire new workers. As a result, the average American worker was ready to look beyond the Republican party for relief.

As Bush's popularity plummeted, two men sought to capitalize on the dismal state of the U.S. economy. First, Arkansas governor Bill Clinton defeated a field of five other challengers for the Democratic nomination by becoming the champion of economic renewal. Forgoing traditional liberal appeals to interest groups, Clinton stressed the need for investment in the nation's future—rebuilding roads and bridges, training workers for high-tech jobs, and solving the growing national health care crisis.

Despite his victories in the Democratic primaries, however, Clinton faced a new rival in H. Ross Perot. An eccentric Texas billionaire, Perot singled out the deficit as the nation's gravest problem and agreed to run as an independent candidate in response to a grassroots movement (which he financed) to place his name on the November ballot.

When Clinton and his running mate, Senator Albert Gore, Jr., of Tennessee, succeeded in unifying the Democratic party and gaining agreement on a moderate platform promising economic change, Perot stunned his supporters by suddenly dropping out of the race in July. Clinton immediately became the front-runner, rising from 30 percent to more than 50 percent in the polls, leaving Bush far behind. With unemployment continuing unabated, the American people turned their backs on George Bush and the Reagan revolution.

A relentless Democratic attack on the administration's lackluster economic performance overcame all the president's efforts to remind the nation of Reagan prosperity and Bush triumphs abroad. Even GOP assaults on Clinton's character, notably his evasion of the draft during the Vietnam War, failed to halt the Democratic momentum. The message that Clinton's political advisers tacked up at the Democratic candidate's headquarters in Little Rock—"The economy, stupid"—provided the key to victory in November. Clinton wound up with 43 percent of the popular vote but with a commanding lead in the electoral college, 370 to 168 for Bush. Perot, who had reentered the race, won 19 percent of the popular vote but failed to carry a single state.

For political scientists, 1992 was a clear case of a negative referendum. Voters had decisively rejected the Reagan-Bush programs. Troubled by both the frightening deficit and the sluggish economy, they had chosen Clinton's program of economic renewal over Perot's call for short-term sacrifice to achieve long-term prosperity. Clinton maintained the Democratic grip on ethnic minorities, winning 83 percent support from African Americans and 62 percent from Hispanics; gained back both the elderly and the blue-collar Reagan Democrats; and cut deeply into the cru-

cial middle class by doing better than Bush among those earning between $30,000 and $75,000 a year.

Most important, Clinton had broken the GOP's grip on the South and West—only Texas and the interior western states had remained Republican strongholds. When the boom of the 1980s collapsed, the Sunbelt states proved to be as receptive as the rest of the nation to the call for change. Yet while there was no doubt about the rejection of Bush, there remained a question of precisely what change the electorate wanted most—responsible budgetary policies to reduce the deficit or federal spending programs to achieve jobs and economic growth.

Economic Recovery

In the White House, Bill Clinton proved to be the most adept politician since Franklin Roosevelt. Born William Jefferson Clinton in Hope, Arkansas, in 1946, he weathered a difficult childhood with an alcoholic stepfather by developing skills at dealing with people and using personal charm to achieve his goals. Intelligent and ambitious, he completed his undergraduate work at Georgetown University, studied law at Yale, and spent two years as a Rhodes scholar at Oxford University in England. Entering politics after teaching law briefly at the University of Arkansas, he won election first as Arkansas attorney general and then as governor. Defeated after his first term in 1980, Clinton won the nickname "Comeback Kid" by regaining the governor's office in 1982, using it to earn a reputation as one of the nation's most successful young political leaders during the following ten years.

Bill Clinton's political gifts centered on the easy way in which he was able to reconcile what biographer Martin Walker called "the ambivalence between the bubba and the brains, between the redneck and [the] Rhodes scholar." His legendary charm appealed both to sophisticated intellectuals and to the MTV audience. Empathy, charm, and understanding, combined with a genuine desire to serve, made him a formidable political leader with broad appeal across the electorate.

Unfortunately, serious flaws marred his political gifts. His eagerness to please undercut his devotion to principle. He wanted so much to prevail that he often ignored the cost of winning. Despite his apparently sincere devotion to causes such as civil rights and equality for women, even those who voted for Clinton had doubts about his personal integrity. One writer summed up his contradictory nature by describing him as "a man who loves the fruits of compromise but treasures the idea of his own unbending goodness."

What often saved Clinton from his own worst faults was his loyal wife, Hillary Rodham Clinton. An accomplished attorney, she rescued his candidacy in

Election of 1992

	Electoral Vote by State	Popular Vote
DEMOCRATIC Bill Clinton	370	44,908,232
REPUBLICAN George Bush	168	39,102,282
INDEPENDENT H. Ross Perot	—	19,725,433
MINOR PARTIES	—	773,161
	538	104,509,108

ALASKA 3

HAWAII 4

WASH., D.C. 3

1992 by defending him against charges of adultery. But more important, from the outset she was his political partner, sharing in the strategic planning that won him the presidency. They made a formidable political team, her idealism offsetting his pragmatism. Her ability to master detail and impose organization helped translate his vague ideas and lofty concepts into realistic proposals.

In his first months in office, Bill Clinton's political skills appeared to evaporate as he had difficulty in making the transition from governor of a small state to president of the nation, a position under intense media scrutiny. His inept handling of the "gays in the military" issue (see p. 911), made worse by his own draft evasion during the Vietnam War and several botched cabinet appointments, robbed him of the usual honeymoon period new presidents enjoy. He reacted with bitter indignation to media criticism, refusing to hold a White House press conference during his first two months in office.

In appointing his cabinet, Clinton did try to live up to his pledges of ethnic and gender diversity. Hazel O'Leary, a black woman, served as secretary of energy, while Janet Reno, a political unknown, became attorney general. The cabinet included two Hispanics, Henry Cisneros and Federico Peña, and two African Americans, Mike Espy and Ronald Brown.

Diversity ended there, however. Fourteen of the eighteen cabinet members were lawyers, and most were wealthy; there were more attorneys and more millionaires in Clinton's cabinet than in Bush's. Secretary of Labor Robert Reich, a Harvard professor, was one of the few advocates for working-class Americans. Beyond the cabinet, two-thirds of the Clinton administration appointees were white men; minorities made up just 14 percent of the Clinton team, barely higher than the 13 percent under Bush.

Clinton's most important appointments came in the economic realm. Senator Lloyd Bentsen, a fiscal conservative, became secretary of the treasury, with Robert Rubin, a Wall Street bond trader, serving as special assistant for economic policy; former Congressman Leon Panetta, a longtime deficit hawk, took on the key job of White House budget director. By choosing such a conservative team to guide economic policy, Clinton was risking the fate of his administration on the single issue of deficit reduction.

These advisers helped the president shape the economic program calling for tax increases and spending cuts to achieve a balanced budget that he presented to Congress and the nation on February 17, 1993. Despite the warm reception for his State of the Union address, Clinton still had to wage a long and determined fight to complete his economic program. It took all-out arm-twisting from the White House to get Congress to approve the final budget terms—$241 billion in new taxes and $255 billion in spending cuts, for a total reduction of $496 billion over four years. In late August, the House approved the budget by just two votes, and in the Senate, Vice President Gore cast his vote to break a 50 to 50 deadlock.

Despite the narrow margin, it was a major achievement. Clinton stood firm on deficit reduction, compromising on details but insisting on a program that promised to cut the deficit in half within four years. Moreover, he succeeded in winning approval for some of his education and job-training programs while increasing income tax rates on the wealthy from 33 to 39.6 percent. At the same time, he secured passage of the earned income tax credit for the working poor, providing as much as $3500 a year to keep a low-income family above the poverty line. And best of all, lower interest rates created by action of the Federal Reserve Board and the growing confidence of financial markets led to a steadily expanding economy that made Clinton's deficit reduction goals realistic (see the opening vignette for more on Federal Reserve Chairman Alan Greenspan's role in the economic policy). Unlike George Bush in 1990, who sealed his political doom by reneging on his promise not to raise taxes, a healthier economy enabled Clinton both to raise taxes and to win respect by standing on principle. He did, however, risk the same fate as Bush since Republicans were quick to call the budget deal "the biggest tax increase in the history of the world."

President versus Congress

Deficit reduction marked only the beginning of Bill Clinton's struggles with Congress. For the next four years, he engaged in a series of confrontations, winning some and losing some with first Democratic and then Republican majorities in the two houses.

His most important triumph came when Congress approved the **North American Free Trade Agreement (NAFTA)** in the fall of 1993. NAFTA, initiated and nearly completed by Bush, was a free trade plan that united the United States, Mexico, and Canada into a common market without tariff barriers. Although Clinton had muted his support for NAFTA during the 1992 campaign, once elected, he saw it as the first step in creating similar free trade associations with Asia and Europe that would enable the United States to dominate global markets. Calling NAFTA "a defining moment" for the nation, he proclaimed, "This country is now the most productive country in the world." Asserting that "we can win" in the global economic struggle, he continued, "We have to decide whether we are going to reach out and win or try to withdraw."

Critics of NAFTA did not share Clinton's optimism. Representing both ends of the political spectrum, leaders as diverse as Pat Buchanan on the right and Ralph Nader on the left warned that free trade would undermine small American companies and send millions of American jobs to exploited and underpaid workers in Third World countries. The issue of free trade divided the Democratic party, with many liberals and labor union members strongly opposed. Ross Perot, the defeated 1992 third-party candidate, became the best known critic, especially with his vivid claim about the loud "sucking sound" that would signal the flushing of American jobs down the drain.

The toughest fight came in the House, but 102 Democrats finally joined with 132 Republicans to approve NAFTA by a 34-vote margin, giving Clinton a solid victory there. The Senate added its consent by a vote of 61 to 38. Thus Clinton triumphed over key elements within his own party to achieve a significant goal.

At the height of the debate over NAFTA, President Clinton allowed his wife to make public his administration's massive plan for health reform in an unprecedented appearance before the House Ways and Means Committee. "I am here as a mother, as a wife, a daughter, a sister, a woman, as an American citizen concerned about the health of her family and the health of her nation," Hillary Clinton told the startled representatives as she presented the 1364-page health care reform plan.

When he first took office, Bill Clinton had signaled the importance of the health care issue by appointing a task force, headed by his wife, to find a comprehensive solution to the nation's health care problem. Clinton had two primary objectives. The first was an all-embracing health care system that would include the thirty-seven million Americans who lacked health insurance. At the same time, the president was committed to reducing the skyrocketing cost of health care. Medicare was one of the prime culprits—the cost of medical services to the elderly had risen to more than one-fifth of all federal revenues by 1991. The trick would be to devise a system that would reduce costs while extending medical insurance to everyone in the nation, without raising taxes or adding to the deficit. The only possible solution involved rationing health care by having someone in authority place limits on the medical services each American could receive—a strategy that was political dynamite.

The plan that Hillary Clinton presented to the House Ways and Means Committee in October 1993 had two key features. First, it required large companies to offer a generous health care package to all workers, with employers paying 80 percent of the estimated $4200 annual cost per family. The second feature dealt with small businesses, which were required to form large health alliances so that they could purchase equally generous benefit packages from insurance companies. The task force believed that these mandatory health alliances would have enough clout to bargain for competitive rates, thereby sharply reducing health costs.

The initial public reception was favorable. According to a CNN poll, 61 percent of the American people said they were ready to pay higher taxes for a truly comprehensive health care system. When Congress began studying the details, however, attitudes started to change. The complex bill was referred to ten separate committees, inviting legislative chaos. And then opponents, primarily Republicans and representatives of small business, counterattacked. Spending nearly $60 million to fight the Clinton program, its critics claimed that it would deprive Americans of the right to choose their own doctors. A coalition of small insurers struck the most telling blow

Anti-NAFTA demonstrators broadcast their views at a rally in Austin, Texas, in 1993. Opponents of the North American Free Trade Agreement feared that passage of the act would mean loss of jobs for U.S. workers. ❖

with a series of "Harry and Louise" ads, which featured dialogue between a middle-class husband and wife who wanted to reduce their health bills but worried about "a new army of government bureaucrats." The tactic of embracing the concept of reform but questioning the specifics of the Clinton plan proved highly effective.

By January 1994, the administration's health care plan was in deep trouble. The longer congressional committees debated the plan, the lower support for it fell in the polls. By midsummer, only 39 percent of the American people expressed confidence in the administration's health proposal. When Democrats were unable to round up sixty votes to break a Republican filibuster on procedural issues in late August 1994, the Senate dropped the issue, effectively killing the Clinton health plan.

In retrospect, it seems evident that the incompatible goals of reducing costs while striving for universal coverage had doomed the plan from the outset. Shrewder political maneuvering by the Clintons might have enabled them to salvage a scaled-down health reform. Instead, by insisting on a sweeping overhaul of the American health system rather than accepting incremental changes, Bill Clinton would have to pay a heavy political price.

Contract with America

Clinton's failure to deliver on his health care promise helped fuel a dramatic Republican resurgence. A young maverick congressman from Georgia, Newton Leroy "Newt" Gingrich, had been leading a Republican attack against the House Democratic leadership, scoring a big victory in 1989 when he forced Speaker Jim Wright of Texas to resign over corruption charges. Using a well-funded political action committee, GOPAC, Gingrich supported other young, conservative Republicans who opposed the Democratic leadership. Sensing that the nation was ready for change, Gingrich believed that 1994 was the right year for an all-out effort to capture control of both houses of Congress.

In an attempt to transform 435 separate races into one national contest, Gingrich asked all GOP candidates to sign a ten-point **Contract with America.** The contract consisted of familiar conservative goals, including a balanced budget amendment to the Constitution, term limits for members of Congress, a line-item veto for the president, and a middle-class tax cut. For the first time in recent political history, a party sought to win Congress on ideological issues rather than relying on individual personalities.

A series of embarrassing disclosures involving Bill Clinton's character made this tactic particularly effec-

tive in 1994. During the 1992 campaign, the *New York Times* had raised questions about a bankrupt Arkansas land development called Whitewater in which the Clintons had lost a modest investment. In late 1993, the Resolution Trust Corporation, charged with cleaning up the savings and loan debacle of the 1980s, began exploring Hillary Clinton's relationship with Madison Guaranty, a failed financial institution that had loaned the Clintons money for their Whitewater investment. Republicans were quick to charge that, in effect, American taxpayers were left holding the bill for a corrupt Arkansas bank that had close ties to the Clintons. Although there was no evidence of illegal acts, at the president's request, Attorney General Janet Reno appointed a special prosecutor to investigate the Whitewater affair.

Additional scandals cropped up over activities that had taken place after Clinton was elected president. Travelgate was the name given to the firing, apparently at the urging of Hillary Clinton, of several career White House employees who arranged travel for the press covering the president. Then in early 1994, Paula Jones, a former Arkansas state employee, filed a sexual harassment suit against Clinton, charging that in 1991 then-Governor Clinton had made sexual advances to her.

While there was no clear-cut evidence to substantiate any of the charges against the president or his wife, Republicans used these episodes to revive earlier questions about Bill Clinton's character. More important, they were able to make more substantial attacks on the president, pointing to his failure to enact health care reform and, above all, reminding voters that in 1993 Clinton had enacted "the biggest tax increase" of all time.

The outcome of the November 1994 vote stunned political observers. The Republicans gained 9 seats in the Senate and an astonishing 53 in the House to take control of both houses. Newt Gingrich, who had worked so hard to ensure the change in leadership in the Congress, became speaker of the House. The GOP also captured 32 governorships, including those of New York, California, and Texas, where George W. Bush, the son of the man whom Clinton beat in 1992, won handily.

There were two ways to view the remarkable about-face. Claiming that voters endorsed their Contract with America, the GOP hailed the outcome as a mandate to dismantle the welfare state and government in general in favor of free market economics. Clinton and some of his advisers, however, noted that the 1994 election was hardly representative of the country as a whole. The turnout was low—less than 40 percent, compared to 56 percent when Clinton won the presidency just two years before. Nationally, barely more than half of those voting supported Republicans, so that in effect just 20 percent of the electorate had determined the outcome.

The most striking statistic lay in the gender breakdown. Women voted for Democratic candidates by a margin of 53 to 47, while men went Republican by a much bigger differential, 57 to 43. In effect, an outpouring of "angry white males" who believed that Clinton was unfit to be president determined the outcome. The lesson for Clinton was clear. He could not convert his diehard opponents, but if he could win back the women and minorities who had voted for him in 1992 but stayed home in 1994, he had a chance to be the "Comeback Kid" once again.

The Clinton Rebound

After Clinton's surprising victory in 1992, the slogan in his Little Rock war room—"The economy, stupid"— became the easiest way to explain the outcome. Four years later, the same pithy commentary proved even more apt. The candidate who had accused his opponent of ignoring the economic suffering accompanying the recession of 1990–1991 now became the beneficiary of the recovery that had actually begun before the 1992 election.

The scope of the prosperity that spread throughout America in the 1990s was astonishing. Leaner American corporations, benefiting from downsizing— the ruthless firing of employees to achieve greater efficiency—now found they could compete on favorable terms with Japanese and German rivals. Productivity shot up, keeping labor costs down, while technological advances, especially in microprocessors, made American products the envy of the world. By 1996, Clinton could boast that nine million new jobs had been created since he took office and that the United States now led all other nations in the export of manufactured goods.

Clinton not only could claim credit for this remarkable resurgence, but he had the political skill to assuage the heavy human costs involved. He criticized corporations for dismissing so many employees in their quest for competitive advantages in the global marketplace, and he expressed concern over the growing inequality of wealth that benefited the educated and penalized the unskilled. In persuading Congress to pass the Family and Medical Leave Act in 1993 and increasing the minimum wage in 1996, the president was able to present himself as a caring leader concerned about the welfare of all Americans, not just the rich and powerful.

The Republicans, fresh from their sweeping victory in Congress, ironically became the vehicle for Clinton's political rehabilitation. Mistaking a negative referendum against Clinton for a ringing endorsement of his Contract with America, Newt Gingrich played directly into the president's hands. In 1995, despite majorities in both houses, the GOP enacted only four minor parts of the contract. Although the House of Representatives passed all but one item, the more cautious Senate refused to go along with such measures as term limits for members of Congress, a $500 per child tax cut, and a constitutional amendment requiring a balanced budget.

The president found Gingrich and his followers a perfect foil. When they demanded a balanced budget by early in the next century, Clinton agreed in principle, but then refused to accept GOP plans to slash programs such as Medicare and Medicaid. Portraying himself as the defender of the downtrodden, Clinton claimed that the Republican cuts in education, college loans, and health care would hurt children, ambitious young people, and the elderly.

The GOP leadership in Congress then made a gross miscalculation by threatening to close down the government to force Clinton to give way. The president, glad to have the chance to redeem his reputation for softness, stood firm, aware that Gingrich's negative ratings were higher than his own. Twice the Republicans shut down all but the most vital of federal services. The public outcry, directed almost entirely against Gingrich and the GOP, finally forced the Republicans to relent. They accepted a compromise in early 1996 that optimistically promised a balanced budget in seven years. Clinton was thus able to begin the campaign year by taking credit for balancing the budget while making the Republicans appear to be the enemies of Medicare and Social Security.

Once he had regained the initiative, Clinton pressed his advantage. Relying on the advice of political consultant Dick Morris, the president pursued a policy of "triangulation," in which he distanced himself from both conservative Republicans and liberal Democrats to take the political high ground—the center. He signed a welfare reform bill, slightly more acceptable than the two he had vetoed before, to fulfill his earlier promise "to end welfare as we know it." The new legislation turned the welfare program over to the states, funded by scaled-down federal grants, and required recipients to find work within two years or lose their benefits.

While Republican hopefuls fought each other in a series of grueling and expensive party primaries, Clinton—again on Morris's advice—began raising huge sums to conduct a massive television campaign. Throughout the spring and summer, the airwaves were filled with 30-second commercials picturing the Republicans as trying to weaken Medicare and deny social services to those in need while Clinton fought to preserve the heritage of the New Deal and the Great Society. By the time the GOP nominated Bob Dole, the

Consumers were the losers in the battle over the balanced budget waged by President Clinton and the Republican Congress when the failure to provide monies for operating expenses forced the shutdown of government services and facilities, such as the Smithsonian Institution. ❖

respected but dour Senate majority leader from Kansas, the contest was all but over. Having used up nearly all his federal matching funds in the primaries, Dole was unable to counter Clinton's television blitz. By the traditional Labor Day starting date for the presidential campaign, Clinton had established a double-digit lead in the polls.

The ensuing fall campaign turned out to be anticlimactic. Everything Dole tried proved ineffective. His proposal of a 15 percent across-the-board tax cut found little acceptance and many questions about how Dole expected to balance the budget while reducing federal revenue. The GOP candidate began raising questions about Clinton's integrity, but an electorate that had grown bored with the unsubstantiated Whitewater charges and had proved indifferent to character issues failed to respond.

On election day, the president won his expected victory. A low turnout (10 million fewer voters than in 1992) and the third-party candidacy of Ross Perot (only a nuisance factor in 1996) prevented Clinton from winning a clear majority of the popular vote. But he carried 31 states with 379 electoral votes, for a decisive victory over Dole, who won just 19 states with 159 electoral votes. Clinton's strategy of winning back the vote of women and minorities with his stress on education, health care, and providing opportunities for the young paid off handsomely. If the angry white male was the symbol of the GOP congressional victory in 1994, then "soccer moms"—suburban middle-class women concerned about social issues—proved the key

to Clinton's comeback in 1996. The gender gap was evident—men split evenly between Dole and Clinton, but 54 percent of female voters backed the president and only 38 percent voted for his GOP challenger. And, in contrast to 1994, women outnumbered men at the polls by a margin of 52 to 48.

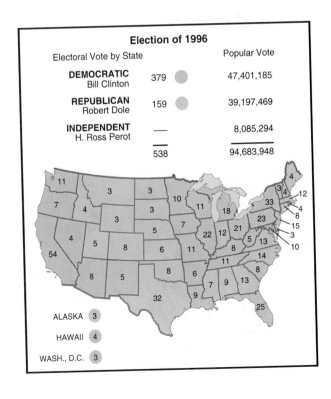

Election of 1996

	Electoral Vote by State		Popular Vote
DEMOCRATIC Bill Clinton	379		47,401,185
REPUBLICAN Robert Dole	159		39,197,469
INDEPENDENT H. Ross Perot	—		8,085,294
	538		94,683,948

ALASKA 3
HAWAII 4
WASH., D.C. 3

In winning a second term, Clinton was both skillful and lucky. He benefited from the powerful economic growth that surpassed even his own expectations. With the deficit falling faster than either Clinton or Greenspan had estimated, the economy had proved to be his greatest ally. But Clinton was also fortunate in the men who opposed him. Gingrich and Dole were experienced and able congressional leaders, but neither possessed the charisma or the public sensitivity that enabled Clinton to connect with the voter. Worse still, they made tactical mistakes that played directly into the president's hands.

Yet it took both political skill and daring to weather the rejection Clinton experienced in 1994 and to adapt to the changing mood of the American people. Dick Morris proved to be a shrewd adviser, but it was Clinton himself who took the gamble that he could turn the Republican shutdown of government into a political victory. And even though the president probably had little to do with the underlying causes of the economic boom, his willingness to adopt Greenspan's fiscal strategy and stake everything on deficit reduction gave him a reasonable claim to some of the credit. Most important, Clinton won in large measure because, unlike his opponents in 1992 and 1996, he seemed to embody, in the words of a British observer, "all the characteristics of his generation, distilled to an intensity that matched his ambition."

CLINTON AND THE WORLD

American foreign policy underwent notable changes in the 1990s. Unlike his predecessor, Bill Clinton gave top priority to domestic issues rather than international affairs. And where Bush had viewed the world largely in geopolitical terms, stressing American strategic interests, Clinton gave economics top consideration, seeking markets abroad to stimulate the dormant American economy. Yet there was one similarity—under Clinton, as under Bush, American foreign policy continued to drift, lacking direction in the confusing post–Cold War world.

In choosing his foreign policy team, Clinton wisely went with experienced professionals to whom he could delegate foreign policy while he carried out his domestic agenda. Secretary of State Warren M. Christopher, who had served under Jimmy Carter, pursued a cautious, lawyerly approach to world problems, while National Security Adviser Anthony Lake carefully kept a low profile. These veteran diplomats, and their second-term replacements, Madeleine Albright and Sandy Berger, worked skillfully on the international issues confronting the nation, but they were hampered by the lack of any overarching principle to guide them.

Global Tensions in the Post–Cold War Era

Clinton's greatest challenge was in dealing with America's old Cold War rivals, Russia and China. Inheriting the chaos left by the breakup of the Soviet Union, the president concentrated on two issues. First, as Bush had done, he supported Russian President Boris Yeltsin to the hilt. In 1993, Clinton persuaded Congress to provide a $2.5 billion aid package to help Yeltsin carry out his free market reforms of the devastated Russian economy. The Clinton administration

The lack of any clear principle or philosophy guiding Clinton's foreign policy hampered the effort to define the proper role for and responsibilities of the United States, the only remaining superpower, in the post–Cold War era. ❖

strongly supported Yeltsin and his successor, Vladimir V. Putin, despite Russia's continuing brutal war with Chechnya. Although the expansion of NATO to include Poland, Hungary, and the Czech Republic, and plans for a missile defense system created some tension, the Clinton administration succeeded in maintaining good relations with Russia.

Clinton was even more successful on the second issue—preventing the proliferation of nuclear weapons among the former republics of the Soviet Union. With patient diplomacy, Christopher and his aides won agreements from Belarus and Kazakhstan to scrap their deadly ICBMs. Ukraine proved more difficult, but in 1994, Clinton persuaded the president of Ukraine to surrender his country's entire nuclear stockpile. Clinton's effort on behalf of nuclear nonproliferation in the former Soviet Union was perhaps his most important, if least heralded, achievement.

The president's policy toward China was more questionable. Clinton ignored China's dismal human rights record and continued Bush's policy of extending most favored nation status to Beijing annually. The growing importance of trade with China, whose economic output in 1993 exceeded Britain's, led Clinton to overlook the memory of the Tiananmen Square massacre and the continued persecution of dissidents in China. As trade with China began to rival that with Japan, the president announced a policy of "constructive engagement." It was better, he and his spokespeople declared, to keep talking, and trading, with China than to harden Chinese resentment against the West by harping on moral issues. In 2000, Clinton won a notable victory for free trade when the House voted to give China permanent most favored nation status.

The Chinese, however, proved to be less than cooperative. China ignored U.S. protests over its exports of missiles to Iran and nuclear technology to Pakistan and continued to stifle dissent at home. The administration did send aircraft carriers to signify its support for Taiwan when China conducted provocative missile tests near the island on the eve of an election. Anthony Lake helped defuse the crisis, but only after one Chinese official talked casually about raining nuclear missiles on Los Angeles. Constructive engagement clearly had its limitations.

In other parts of the world, the Middle East proved as perplexing for Clinton as it had for his predecessors. The administration continued the efforts to broker a peace between Israel and the Palestinian Arabs. Despite a promising beginning at a meeting between Palestinian Liberation Organization Chairman Yasir Arafat and Israeli Prime Minister Yitzhak Rabin in Washington in 1993, Clinton was unable to overcome the ethnic and religious tensions that blocked the path to peace in the Middle East. Clinton's final attempt, a meeting between Arafat and Israeli Prime Minister Ehud Barak at Camp David in July 2000, proved futile.

In Iraq, Clinton met the continued defiance of Saddam Hussein by twice ordering American cruise missile attacks on Iraqi military targets. U.S. relations with Iran failed to improve, even with the election of a more moderate prime minister in 1997. Saudi Arabia remained a staunch ally, despite strains from a terrorist attack that killed nineteen American air force personnel in 1996. More worrisome was the increasingly heavy U.S. reliance on Persian Gulf oil as a result of Americans' love affair with gas-guzzling vans, pickup trucks, and sport utility vehicles. A sharp increase in the price of oil in early 2000 brought howls of protest from angry motorists and highlighted the risk of continuing American dependence on foreign oil.

Intervening in Somalia and Haiti

The most difficult foreign policy decisions for the Clinton administration came over the question of whether to use American troops to intervene abroad. The absence of the Cold War threat, with its implicit need to counter communist rivals, made it much more difficult for the president and his advisers to decide when the national interest required sending American men and women into harm's way. Between 1993 and 1999, Clinton opted for foreign intervention in four areas—Somalia, Haiti, Bosnia, and Kosovo—with decidedly mixed results.

Clinton inherited the Somalian venture. In December 1992, George Bush had sent 25,000 American troops to that starving country on a humanitarian mission. Under Clinton, however, the original aim of using troops to protect the flow of food supplies and relief workers fighting the ravages of famine gradually shifted to supporting a UN effort at nation building. Tragedy struck in October 1993 when eighteen American soldiers died in a botched attempt to capture a local warlord in Mogadishu. When television cameras recorded the naked corpse of a U.S. helicopter pilot being dragged through the streets of Somalia's capital, an angry Congress demanded a quick end to the intervention. Secretary of Defense Les Aspin resigned his office, after accepting responsibility for refusing to provide the U.S. commander with the tanks and aerial gunships he had requested. American forces left Somalia by the end of March 1994 in what was unquestionably the low point of Clinton's foreign policy.

The lack of clear criteria governing intervention that had brought on the disaster in Somalia almost led to another fiasco in Haiti. Seeking to halt the flow into Florida of thousands of Haitians fleeing both poverty and tyranny, Clinton worked to compel the military rulers of Haiti to abdicate in favor of the man they had overthrown in 1991, Jean-Bertrand Aristide.

After nearly a year of trade sanctions and increasing diplomatic pressure, the president prepared to use force to remove the military regime. At the last minute, a three-member peace mission led by former President Jimmy Carter worked out a compromise that allowed U.S. troops to land unopposed in late September 1994. Aristide returned to Haiti to take power in mid-October, but he could do little either to restore democracy or achieve economic progress in view of his country's bankrupt treasury, devastated economy, and deep political divisions. By the time Aristide turned over the presidency to his elected successor in 1996, Haiti remained mired in hopeless poverty. The reality of Haiti's plight had frustrated Clinton's effort to use American power righteously.

Halting Civil War in Bosnia

Bosnia provided an even more stern test for the president's foreign policy. The breakup of Yugoslavia in 1991 led the Muslim president of Bosnia to ask the European community to recognize the independence of Bosnia-Herzegovina. Bosnia's ethnic and religious makeup—44 percent Muslim, 31 percent Serb, and 17 percent Croat—quickly led to civil war by the spring of 1992. The Bosnian Serbs used the guns and heavy weaponry of the former Yugoslavian army to seize more than 70 percent of Bosnian territory. The Muslim and Croatian forces were unable to mount effective resistance as the Serbs began a policy of "ethnic cleansing," driving Muslims and Croats from their ancestral homes and farms and beginning a lethal bombardment of the capital, Sarajevo.

Although Clinton had criticized Bush's failure to stop the fighting in Bosnia during the campaign, the new president at first followed an equally cautious policy. He backed a plan to divide Bosnia into ten ethnic provinces. When the Serbs rejected the proposal in the spring of 1993, the president fell back on using American air power to patrol no-fly zones over Bosnia designed to protect UN peacekeeping efforts. Meanwhile, Serb artillery continued to pour a withering fire on the civilian population of Sarajevo, and journalists reported a series of brutal atrocities in which Serb troops slaughtered thousands of Muslim men and raped thousands of Muslim women.

After two years of passively watching Bosnian suffering, Clinton acted in 1995, unleashing American air power. In the summer of 1995, American planes under NATO auspices began a series of air strikes on the Serb forces, shelling Sarajevo from the surrounding mountains.

The air campaign, which lasted for two weeks, along with a major counteroffensive by better equipped Croatian and Muslim forces, finally led to a

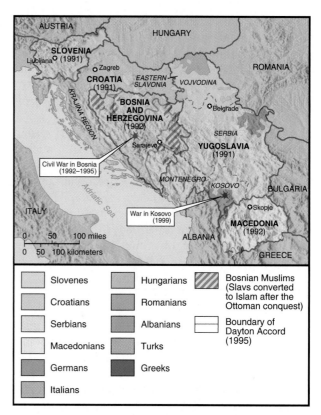

THE BREAKUP OF YUGOSLAVIA/CIVIL WAR IN BOSNIA   *With the end of the communist regime in Yugoslavia in the early 1990s, the country broke apart into ethnically distinct regions. In Bosnia, Muslims, Croatians, and Serbians fought a bloody civil war rife with atrocities on all sides over the issue of ethnic cleansing.* ❖

cease-fire in mid-October 1995. The three warring factions sent delegations to Dayton, Ohio, to discuss a settlement. After three weeks of talks, U.S. mediator Richard Holbrooke secured their agreement to create a weak central government for all Bosnia at Sarajevo and to divide the rest of the country into two parts—a Muslim-Croatian federation with 51 percent of the territory and a Serbian enclave with 49 percent. The Dayton plan called for free elections, the return of refugees to their former homes, and a NATO force to oversee the peace process.

Clinton took a calculated risk in sponsoring the Dayton settlement. The division of Bosnia into two competing halves meant only a temporary halt to the fighting rather than an end to the struggle for control of the country. But in stopping the fighting at least temporarily, and especially in lifting the siege of Sarajevo, Clinton could take credit for a major humanitarian achievement. He displayed uncharacteristic political courage in agreeing to commit 20,000 American troops to the International Force (IFOR) that would undertake the dangerous task of supervising the implementation of the Dayton accords. The fact that there was no clear-cut American national interest at stake, beyond the desire to save human life, made it an even more impressive achievement.

The American troops, originally scheduled to leave by late 1996, stayed on in reduced numbers when the original departure date was postponed indefinitely. Few refugees were able to return to their original farms and villages, and suspected war criminals remained at large in the Serbian enclave. British, French, and U.S. members of IFOR faced tense confrontations with angry Serb mobs. Yet, the net result was an uneasy truce without fighting and without peacekeeping casualties. Clinton had not only been brave; he had been lucky as well.

Saving Kosovo

President Clinton faced an even more serious challenge in another Balkan trouble spot—Kosovo. Serbian leader Slobodan Milosevic had ended the province's autonomy within Yugoslavia and imposed Serbian rule in 1989, even though 90 percent of the population was ethnic Albanian. When these people, who called themselves Kosovars, resisted by waging guerrilla war against the Serbian police, Milosevic responded with a campaign of repression and ethnic cleansing that outraged world opinion. After diplomatic efforts failed in 1998 and early 1999, the United States and NATO began an aerial assault on Serbia on March 24, 1999, in an effort to end the persecution of the Kosovars.

At first it appeared that Clinton and his outspoken secretary of state, Madeleine Albright, had miscalculated. The initial air attacks, largely directed at empty barracks and remote military bases, failed to persuade Milosevic to seek peace. Instead, he stepped up the ethnic cleansing in Kosovo, forcing hundreds of thousands of Kosovars to leave their homes and flee to neighboring Albania and Macedonia. NATO pilots, restricted to flying above 15,000 feet to avoid antiaircraft fire, were unable to hit the elusive Serbian forces in Kosovo. When Clinton ordered more intense bombing of Serbia, some of the strikes led to heavy civilian casualties; the most embarrassing incident was the accidental bombing of the Chinese embassy in Belgrade in early May 1999.

Clinton, despite his reputation as an opportunist, stayed the course in Kosovo. He took the high ground, explaining to the American people his devotion to a humanitarian cause. "It is perhaps the first conflict ever fought where no one wanted any land, or money, or geopolitical advantage," he declared. "We just wanted to stop and reverse ethnic cleansing."

His perseverance paid off. Unable to strike effectively at the Serbian army in Kosovo, NATO planes concentrated on the infrastructure of Serbia, targeting bridges, oil refineries, and, most important of all, power stations. By the end of May, Serbia had lost 60 percent of its electrical capacity and the domestic pressure on Milosevic began to mount. With Russian diplomats acting as go-betweens, Milosevic finally agreed to end his attempts to purge Kosovo of its Albanian inhabitants. An agreement signed on June 10, 1999, called for the withdrawal of all Serb forces and placed Kosovo under UN supervision, with NATO troops acting as peacekeepers.

The conflict over Kosovo revealed both the strengths and weaknesses of the United States in the

With NATO peacekeepers looking on, ethnic Albanian refugees return to their homes in southern Kosovo in June 1999. Nearly one million Kosovars had been uprooted during Serbian leader Slobodan Milosevic's campaign of repression and ethnic cleansing. ❖

turbulent post–Cold War world. American military power, while great, was limited by a strong desire to avoid risking American lives. Clinton could boast of an amazing result—NATO had waged a 12-week air campaign without the loss of a single pilot. Yet the United States had been unable to prevent Milosevic from uprooting and terrorizing nearly one million Kosovars. When the fighting ended, the Kosovars returned to their devastated homeland and soon NATO troops had the thankless task of preventing the Albanians from seeking revenge against the Serbian minority in Kosovo.

The Clinton record abroad highlights the dilemma facing the United States in the post–Cold War world. Lacking the central focus of rivalry with another super power, the United States must decide when and where to bring its great power to bear without exhausting itself in endless adventures overseas. Clinton failed in Somalia, achieved only limited success in Haiti, but he could claim credit for ending a bloody civil war in Bosnia and for rescuing the Kosovars from Milosevic's ethnic cleansing. Like his predecessor, however, Clinton was unable to define a clear international mission for post–Cold War America. As a result, instead of setting the global agenda, the United States remained the prisoner of events abroad.

THE END OF THE CENTURY

It was the best of times; it was the worst of times. The 1990s witnessed an unparalleled burst of economic growth that clearly established the United States as the world's richest nation. Yet in the same decade, violence in the form of angry protests from both the extreme right and the extreme left, as well as a series of senseless school shootings, shocked the nation. Waco, Oklahoma City, Seattle, Littleton—these sites of violence and devastation revealed deep flaws in American society. Even the man who claimed credit for the prosperity, Bill Clinton, nearly lost the presidency over a sexual affair with a White House intern.

From Deficit to Surplus

In early 2000, the boom of the 1990s officially became the longest sustained period of economic growth in American history. Since March 1991, the economy had expanded by an incredible 64 percent, creating 20 million new jobs. Unemployment dropped below 5 percent in 1997 and stayed there for the rest of the decade. Best of all, inflation remained low, averaging just over 2 percent a year and thus enabling family income not only to recover from the 1990–1991 recession, but even to surpass the previous all-time high of the early 1970s.

Economists had difficulty explaining this happy situation. The primary factor appeared to be continued increases in productivity, which allowed the economy to expand without creating inflationary pressures. Businesses invested heavily not just in new plants and machinery, but in new technology—especially computers and sophisticated software—that enabled workers to increase their output steadily. The growth in exports that Clinton fought for acted as a stimulus, yet foreign trade accounted for only about 10 percent of the output. The real driving force was American consumers with their purchases of cars, computers, household goods, and the myriad items that made up the largest national market in the world. Any doubt about the domestic roots of the boom were dispelled with the Asian crash of 1997–1998, which, despite sparking a brief downturn in the stock market, failed to halt the American economic advance.

Federal Reserve Chairman Alan Greenspan helped sustain the boom by keeping inflation in check. He lowered interest rates in late 1997 to stimulate the economy during the Asian turmoil. Then he began to raise them in 1999 and 2000 to the highest level of the decade to slow down the economy and prevent surging world oil prices from leading to a repetition of the great inflation of the 1970s.

The greatest benefit of the remarkable economic boom was the transformation of the federal budget. Deficits disappeared, replaced with surpluses, at first modest, but then substantial. In 1997, the deficit had been $5 billion; by 2000, the surplus was more than $100 billion.

The two political parties could not agree on how to spend the unexpected bonanza. Republicans called for across-the-board tax reductions, while Democrats wanted to shore up the faltering Social Security and Medicare programs. Clinton's veto of congressional tax cuts led to a deadlock that actually seemed to accomplish what most Americans preferred—paying off the national debt that had grown so large from past deficits.

The optimistic forecasts all depended on sustaining economic expansion. A recession, the normal pattern in the business cycle of the past, would make the debate over whether to reduce taxes or shore up social programs irrelevant. Those who won control of the White House and Congress in 2000, therefore, would face the challenge not only of spending the surplus wisely, but also of ensuring its continued existence.

Violence in the 1990s

Amid the unprecedented prosperity, a series of violent episodes disturbed the nation in the last decade of the century. Across the political spectrum, those who feared the loss of personal freedom resorted to force to express their discontent.

On the right, a militia movement accelerated after a shoot-out at Ruby Ridge, Idaho, in August 1992. Trying to arrest Christian survivalist Randy Weaver for illegal arms sales, federal agents shot and killed Weaver's wife and son during an eleven-day siege. Ruby Ridge became the rallying cry for right-wing activists who expressed their hatred for blacks, homosexuals, abortionists, and above all, the federal government, which they saw as a threat to individual freedom.

A second tragic incident—the siege and destruction of the Branch Davidian compound in Waco, Texas, in 1993—intensified the militia impulse. What began in January as an attempt to arrest charismatic leader David Koresh on gun-dealing charges finally ended in April with the death of seventy-five Branch Davidians. As a stunned nation tried to understand what had happened at Waco, many dissidents had a ready explanation. An evil government, part of an international conspiracy to create a new world order at the expense of traditional American liberties, was responsible. Across the nation, citizens began joining the nearly 150 militia units that sprang up in thirty-three states.

On April 19, 1995, the second anniversary of the Waco tragedy, Timothy McVeigh, who shared the viewpoint of the movement but was not a member of any militia unit, set off a powerful bomb in a rented truck in the street next to the federal building in Oklahoma City, killing 169 men, women, and children. Caught by chance less than a hundred miles away, McVeigh would eventually be sentenced to die for his crime. Yet he showed no remorse, reflecting the views expressed by the bomber in a novel McVeigh sold at gun shows around the country: "There is no way we can destroy the System without hurting many thousands of innocent people—no way."

The hatred of corporate America was as strong on the far left as on the far right. Its most dramatic expression came from the Unabomber—an unknown enemy of the global economy who sent sixteen bombs through the mail to corporation executives and university professors between 1978 and 1995, killing three people and injuring twenty-three others. In 1995, the *Washington Post* published his "manifesto," a 35,000 word polemic in which he blamed modern technology for all of humanity's ills.

Nearly a year later, in April 1996, federal agents arrested Theodore J. Kaczynski at a remote cabin in Montana. His brother, David, recognized Theodore as the author of the Unabomber manifesto and informed the FBI. Theodore Kaczynski had earned a doctorate in mathematics at Harvard and held a tenure-track teaching position at the University of California in Berkeley, but in 1969 he resigned in order to live in seclusion without modern conveniences. After refusing to agree to an insanity defense, Kaczynski pled guilty to thirteen federal charges and was sentenced to prison for life without the possibility of parole. While few condoned his violent acts, some sympathized with Kaczynski's resentment over the degree to which technology encroached on individual privacy and curtailed personal freedom.

The clearest expression of unhappiness with the global economy of the 1990s came at the **World Trade Organization (WTO)** meeting in Seattle in late 1999. More than forty thousand protesters gathered to denounce the secret and autocratic way that the WTO

An aerial view of the destroyed Alfred P. Murrah Federal Building in Oklahoma City suggests the extent of the physical damage caused by the bomb blast on April 19, 1995, but cannot come close to expressing the human tragedy of the loss of 169 lives and the hundreds of injuries suffered. ❖

encouraged the exploitation of both low-paid workers and natural resources in developing countries. At first, orderly marches led by organized labor and environmental groups drew large crowds and sent an important message of dissent. But then more violent demonstrators began smashing windows, spray-painting graffiti on Nike and Gap stores, and trashing Starbucks coffee bars. The police used tear gas, nightsticks, and rubber bullets to clear the streets and arrest more than 500 demonstrators. Despite the violence, the protesters succeeded not only in interrupting the WTO meeting, which adjourned without reaching any new trade agreements, but also in gaining worldwide attention for their grievances.

Subsequent protest efforts were less successful, but the protesters, united behind their slogan, "Human Need, Not Corporate Greed," made a statement that reflected a growing concern over economic globalization. Many Americans began to wonder whether the stunning advances in technology and world trade were compromising the traditional values and personal freedom they had always prized.

Even more perplexing were the series of senseless school shootings that occurred in the late 1990s. They began in Pearl, Mississippi, on October 1, 1997, when a 16-year-old boy stabbed his mother to death and then fatally shot two girls and wounded seven other high school students. Similar outbursts at West Paducah, Kentucky; Jonesboro, Arkansas; and Springfield, Oregon, in the 1997–1998 school year saw angry teenagers kill nine of their classmates and three adults, as well as wounding a score of others. The culmination came at Columbine High School in Littleton, Colorado, in April 1999. Eric Harris and Dylan Klebold used automatic weapons to slaughter twelve fellow students and a teacher in the worst incident of school violence in American history.

The youthful killers had much in common. They all were white, above average in intelligence, attended nonurban schools, came from middle-class families, and were deeply alienated. All appeared to hold grudges against classmates they believed had ostracized them. Luke Woodham of Pearl explained that he acted "because people like me are mistreated every day."

Explanations for their violent behavior ranged from easy access to guns to the violence of pop culture. Parents were criticized for leading such busy lives that they neglected their emotionally fragile children. In all five cases, it was clear afterward that those who committed the crimes gave ample warning that something was very wrong.

Critics called for tighter gun controls, greater parental supervision of teenagers, and restrictions on the extreme lyrics of popular music and the violent nature of video games. "When you look at the overall pattern," commented one expert, "it's a pretty serious wake-up call." If nothing else, the school shootings revealed that beneath the veneer of prosperity there were deep flaws in both family structure and popular culture at the end of the century.

Shadow on the White House

"CLINTON ACCUSED OF URGING AIDE TO LIE," read the headline in the *Washington Post* on the morning of January 21, 1998. For the first time, the American people learned that Kenneth Starr, the special prosecutor appointed in 1994 to probe the Whitewater affair, was now investigating reports that President Clinton had conducted a clandestine affair with a White House intern, Monica Lewinsky. In early 1998 Lewinsky, subpoenaed in the Paula Jones sexual harassment case against Clinton (see p. 973), filed an affidavit in which she denied ever having a sexual relationship with the president. But Starr had information from another source that contradicted this claim. For the next year, the Lewinsky scandal dominated national attention as Bill Clinton fought hard to save his presidency.

Clinton's relationship with the twenty-two-year-old intern began in November 1995 and continued into early 1997, before the president terminated the relationship in April. The affair came to light in January 1998 when Linda Tripp, a co-worker of Lewinsky at the Pentagon, handed tapes of telephone conversations to the special prosecutor on which the intern described her sexual encounters with the president. When Starr's office leaked this development to the media, reporters besieged Clinton. On January 26, 1998, the president flatly denied the charges, saying, "I did not have sexual relations with that woman, Miss Lewinsky."

For the next six months, the president stoutly maintained his innocence, aided greatly by Hillary Clinton who stood by her husband and charged that Starr's investigation was part of a "vast right-wing conspiracy" designed to drive him from the White House. Impressed with her devotion, many Americans withheld judgment. Indeed, with the economy booming, Clinton's approval rate in the polls went from the low 60s to more than 70 percent.

Matters finally culminated in August when Starr offered Lewinsky immunity from prosecution for any prior acts she committed that might be considered criminal (such as filing a false affidavit in the Jones case) in return for her truthful testimony. She gave a detailed account of her sexual encounters with the president and provided crucial physical evidence implicating Clinton.

Realizing that he could no longer deny the affair, the president sought to limit the damage. On August

17 he appeared before Starr's grand jury and admitted to having "inappropriate intimate contact" with Lewinsky. That evening Clinton spoke briefly to the nation. Claiming that he had given the grand jury "legally accurate" answers, the president for the first time admitted to a relationship with Lewinsky that was "not appropriate" and "wrong." He said he regretted misleading the people and especially his wife, but he refused to apologize for his behavior or his false denials.

Clinton's fate hung in the balance. For the first time, some Democrats began to speak out, most notably Senator Joseph Lieberman of Connecticut, who denounced the president's behavior as "disgraceful" and "immoral." But just when Clinton was most vulnerable, the special prosecutor rescued him. In early September, Starr sent a 452-page report to Congress outlining eleven possible impeachment charges against Clinton. The key one was perjury, and Starr provided painstakingly graphic detail on all of the sexual encounters between Clinton and Lewinsky to prove that the president had lied when he denied engaging in sexual relations with the intern.

Many Americans responded by condemning Starr rather than the president. Shocked by the sordid details, they blamed the prosecutor for exposing families to distasteful sexual practices on the evening news. When Hillary Clinton continued to support her husband, a majority of the public seemed to conclude that however bad the president's conduct, it was a private matter, one to be settled between a husband and a wife, not in the public arena.

Republican leaders ignored public sentiment and pressed ahead with impeachment proceedings. In December, the House (where the 1998 midterm elections had narrowed the GOP advantage to six) voted on four articles of impeachment, rejecting two, but approving two others—perjury and obstruction of justice—by small margins in nearly straight party-line votes.

The final showdown in the Senate was anticlimatic. With a two-thirds vote required to find the president guilty and remove him from office, there was no chance of conviction in the highly charged partisan mood that prevailed. On February 12, 1999, the GOP was unable to muster even a majority on the perjury charge, with 45 in favor and 55 opposed. After a second, closer vote, 50 to 50, on obstruction of justice, the presiding officer, Chief Justice William Rehnquist, declared, "Acquitted of the charges."

Clinton had survived the Monica Lewinsky affair because once again he proved to be a far more skillful politician than his Republican opponents. With his wife's unflagging public support, he was able to persuade the American people that his political opponents were waging a vendetta against him. Starr and the GOP played right into his hands, displaying a vindictive quality that appeared to confirm Hillary Clinton's claims of a "vast right-wing conspiracy" against her husband.

Yet Bill Clinton emerged from the ordeal with his presidency badly damaged. His final two years in office would be devoted to a concerted effort to restore his damaged reputation. Desperate for a legacy to mark his White House years, Clinton failed to realize that he

Members of the House Judiciary Committee listen to Clinton's testimony during the hearings on the president's impeachment in December 1998. The Committee sent four articles of impeachment to the full House, and the House adopted two—one count of perjury and one of obstruction of justice. The Senate could not muster the two-thirds majority required for conviction, and so Clinton was acquitted of both articles. ❖

had already created an enduring one—he would always be remembered as the president who dishonored his office by his affair with a young intern.

THE NEW MILLENNIUM

The eve of the twenty-first century was for many a time of anxiety as well as celebration. Since the mid-1990s, experts had warned of what became known as the Year 2000, or Y2K, problem—the likely failure of computers because they had been programmed with only the last two digits for each year of the twentieth century. Concern that the entire technology-based modern way of life would crash as computers confused 2000 with 1900 led to a massive effort to reprogram financial and public service systems. Consumers responded by stockpiling canned goods, generators, and survival gear. The billions spent in preparing for Y2K helped sustain the boom of the 1990s, but proved unnecessary as the United States made the transition to the new millennium without interruptions in basic services.

Yet the new age did bring unforeseen challenges. A close and controversial election resulted in Republican control of the White House and Congress. In 2001, the boom collapsed with the crash of the technology laden Nasdaq stock market (see the Feature Essay, "The Dot.com Boom and Bust," pp. 988–989.) A brief recession and a sluggish recovery led to a steadily-rising unemployment rate despite extensive tax cuts that helped unbalance the federal budget. Then on September 11, 2001, terrorist attacks on the World Trade Center and the Pentagon ushered in a new age of fear and reprisal. Efforts to protect the homeland clashed with traditional civil liberties, while abroad the war on terrorism led to the invasion of Afghanistan and Iraq, yet failed to eliminate completely the terrorist threat to the United States. The world of the twenty-first century thus proved to be not only different but dangerous.

The Disputed Election of 2000

Two dominant trends shaped the presidential contest in 2000. The first, which favored the Democrats, was the economic boom that had erased the budget deficit and brought prosperity to nearly all Americans in the 1990s. At the same time, however, many voters felt a sense of disappointment and even betrayal over Clinton's personal failings. The conflict between material abundance and moral values resulted in the closest election in more than a century.

The two candidates, Governor George W. Bush of Texas and Vice President Al Gore of Tennessee, had little in common beyond being the sons of successful

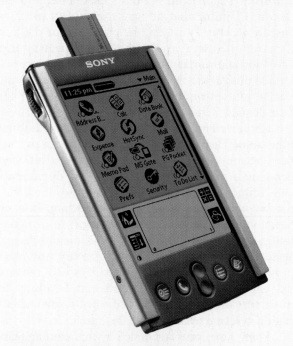

❖ A Look at the Past ❖

Handheld Computer

During the 1980s, personal computers became available and affordable. Desktop computers soon became standard office equipment and in high demand at both home and at school. Computers revolutionized office work and almost every other kind of work. By the 1990s, desktop computers no longer met consumer processing requirements and powerful, portable laptops entered the market. A decade later, the even more portable and affordable handheld computers, such as the personal digital assistant (PDA) device shown here, allowed users to do work or send email from almost anywhere. The speed at which new computer technology becomes dated suggests that even devices we use today may be historical artifacts tomorrow. Why do you think the trend has been for computers to get smaller? Why would someone need a portable computer rather than a desktop version? What does such a portable computer suggest about business and work practices? What other products suggest similar work patterns?

political fathers. Gore had spent eighteen years in Washington as a congressman, senator, and vice president. Somewhat stiff and aloof in manner, he had mastered the intricacies of all the major policy issues and had the experience and knowledge to lead the nation. Bush, in contrast, had pursued a business career before winning the governorship of Texas in 1994. Personable and outgoing, Bush had the temperament for leadership but lacked not only experience but a full grasp of national issues. Journalists were quick to seize on the weaknesses of both men, accusing Gore of frequent and misleading exaggeration and Bush of mangling words and speaking only in generalities.

The conventional political wisdom pointed to an easy win for Al Gore in the November election, but two factors reduced his chances. In the past, the candidate of a party in power during prosperous times had a clear advantage. A perceived need to separate himself from Clinton's scandals, however, led Gore to run as his own man and fail to capitalize on the president's glowing economic record. The decision of consumer advocate Ralph Nader to run for president on the Green Party ticket further complicated Gore's campaign and forced him to move to the left, enabling Bush to appeal more effectively to moderate independents.

In the fall campaign, the candidates presented American voters with a clear choice. Under the banner of "compassionate conservatism," Bush called for limiting the role of government and relying instead on the free market. The centerpiece of his campaign was a proposed across-the-board tax cut that would be of greatest benefit to the wealthy, who paid the most income tax. He also favored partial privatization of Social Security and placed greater weight on the private sector in his prescription drug plan and other reform proposals. Gore, in contrast to Clinton's efforts to move the Democratic Party to the center in 1992 and 1996, became the advocate of government action, calling for an expanded federal role in education and health care. Delivering a fervent populist attack on big business, especially oil and drug companies, Gore repeatedly charged that Bush's tax cut would not benefit the average American but only help "the wealthiest 1 percent."

The race for the White House, to the delight of the media, proved to be close and exciting. Bush led in the polls until Gore moved ahead after the Democratic convention in August. His vice presidential choice of Connecticut Senator Joe Lieberman, a moderate and a Jew, proved popular, while Bush's running mate, former defense secretary Dick Cheney, failed to excite the electorate. But the vice president's surprisingly uneven performance in three televised debates, along with GOP and media attacks on his truthfulness, allowed Bush to regain a narrow lead in the polls in October until Gore began to draw even in the final week of the campaign.

The early returns on election night proved that the polls were right in stressing the closeness of the presidential race. Gore seemed the likely winner when the networks mistakenly predicted a Democratic victory in Florida. When the TV analysts put Florida back in the undecided column, Bush began to forge ahead,

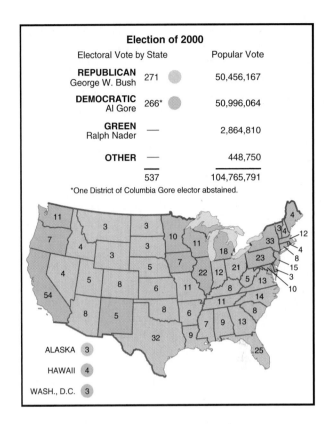

sweeping the rest of the south, including the Clinton-Gore home states of Arkansas and Tennessee. After midnight, when the networks again mistakenly called Florida, this time for Bush, the vice president telephoned the governor to concede, only to recant an hour later when it became clear that the Bush margin in Florida was paper thin.

For the next five weeks, all eyes were on Florida. Gore had 200,000 more popular votes nationwide than Bush and 267 electoral votes to Bush's 246. Yet with Florida's 25 electoral votes, Bush could win the presidency. Both sides sent teams of lawyers to Florida. Bush's team, working with Florida's Republican secretary of state, sought to certify the results that showed the GOP candidate with a lead of 930 votes out of nearly 6 million cast. Citing many voting problems disclosed by the media, Gore asked for a recount in three heavily Democratic counties in south Florida. All three used antiquated punch card machines that resulted in some ballots not being clearly marked for any presidential candidate when the chads, the bits of paper removed when a card is punched, were not completely detached from the cards. For weeks the results in Florida, and hence of the entire election, appeared to depend on how one divined the intent of a voter based on hanging, dimpled, or bulging chads.

The decision finally came in the courts. Democrats appealed the initial attempt to certify Bush as the victor to the Florida Supreme Court. The Florida court twice ordered recounts, the second time for all counties in the state, but Bush's lawyers appealed to the United States Supreme Court. On December 12, five weeks after the election, the Court overruled the state court's call for a recount in a 5 to 4 decision that reflected a long-standing ideological divide among the nine justices. The next day, Gore gracefully conceded, and Bush finally became president-elect.

Although the rule of law prevailed, neither the winner nor the loser could take much pride in their party's behavior. The Republicans displayed an unseemly haste to have Bush declared the victor in Florida despite obvious voting irregularities. And the Democrats, while championing the principle of counting every vote, damaged their case from the outset by asking for recounts in just the three counties they believed would help their cause. The courts proved equally susceptible to partisan rather than legal considerations, issuing rulings that mirrored their political makeup.

When the electoral college finally voted on December 18, there were 271 votes cast for Bush and 266 for Gore (one District of Columbia Gore elector abstained). Nearly complete election totals showed that Gore had received at least 500,000 more popular votes than Bush. The governor had carried more states, 30 to 20, but the vice president had won in the large states with major metropolitan areas such as California, New York, and Illinois. Later studies of the Florida ballots by the media revealed that the limited recount requested by Gore would only have confirmed Bush's narrow victory. Ironically, only an examination of the entire state's disputed ballots might have resulted in Gore winning the election.

Bush's narrow victory revealed deep divisions in American life at the end of the twentieth century. The rural west and south went for Bush, along with a few key Midwest and border states, while Gore won the urban states along both coasts. There was an equally strong divide along economic lines, with the poor voting for Gore, the rich for Bush, and the middle class dividing evenly between the two candidates. Gore continued to benefit from the gender gap, winning 54 percent of the women's vote, and he won an even larger share of the black vote, 90 percent, than Clinton in 1996. Bush did succeed in narrowing the Democratic margin among Hispanic voters, taking 35 percent, compared to only 28 percent for Dole four years earlier. The two candidates split the suburban vote evenly and Bush succeeded in recapturing the lead among Catholic voters.

Exit polls confirmed the underlying split in the electorate. More than 60 percent of voters surveyed said issues were more important than personality. Yet Bush was the overwhelming choice of those who placed primary emphasis on character and values. It was clear that Bush, who ended every campaign speech with a promise to restore dignity and honor to the White House, had used Clinton's foibles to counter Democratic claims of achieving prosperity. By the narrowest of margins, the American people appeared to have placed values ahead of material well-being in the election of 2000.

George W. Bush never looked back. He took the oath of office on January 20, 2001, and began governing without regard to his controversial election. He appointed a strong cabinet filled with conservative Republicans and he succeeded in persuading a closely divided Congress to pass a huge tax cut and adopt his education program. The new president weathered some difficult times on the domestic front, notably when the Democrats regained control of the Senate in mid-2001 and the economy turned down to end the longest boom in American history.

Bush's Domestic Agenda

Bush's first few months in office provided a demanding test of the inexperienced president's leadership qualities. As governor of Texas, he had been able to achieve bipartisan goals by working easily with rural, conservative Democrats who held the balance of power in the legislature. In Washington, however, he faced urban, liberal Democrats who resisted his efforts at conciliation out of a determination to stand up for their constituencies, mainly organized labor, environmental activists, and civil rights groups. With only a narrow Republican majority in the House and just a one-vote margin in the Senate, the president faced a difficult task. The result was a mixed record—some sweeping victories but also several stinging setbacks.

Before battling with Congress, Bush had to organize his administration. Like most modern presidents, he relied heavily on past associates in staffing the White House. Colin Powell, the former chairman of the Joint Chiefs of Staff, became secretary of state, where he belied his military background by becoming an advocate for cooperation with other nations, urging diplomacy over the use of force. In contrast, Donald Rumsfeld, the new secretary of defense (a post he had held in the Ford administration) was intent on streamlining the armed forces in order to enable the United States to fulfill its post–Cold War position of world preeminence. Along with Vice President Cheney, Rumsfeld was on a collision course with Powell, leaving the delicate task of reconciling the ensuing conflict to National Security Adviser Condoleezza Rice.

Bush's most controversial choice was former senator John Ashcroft of Missouri for attorney general. A staunch conservative and favorite of the Christian right, Ashcroft stirred fears among Democrats of using the Justice Department to restrict traditional religious and civic freedoms. His former Senate colleagues finally confirmed him by a narrow margin. Bush's remaining cabinet appointees were more routine. Norman Minetta, the secretary of transportation, who had served as secretary of commerce under Clinton, was the lone Democrat among the conservative Republicans who made up Bush's cabinet.

The first order of business was the tax cut, which required intense lobbying from the White House. The president had to win over several conservative southern Democrats without losing a handful of Republican moderates who favored debt reduction over tax relief. Through adroit maneuvering, Bush finally succeeded in persuading Congress to pass legislation in early June that cut taxes by a staggering $1.35 trillion over a ten-year period. Many of the cuts would only take effect in future years, but Congress offered an immediate stimulus to the economy by authorizing rebate payments to taxpayers: $600 for couples and $300 for individuals earning more than $6000 a year. While critics saw this measure as a betrayal of the long effort to balance the budget, Bush contended that future budget surpluses would more than make up for the loss of tax revenue.

The slowing American economy, which soon turned the projected budget surplus into annual deficits, failed to halt the Bush administration's tax cut momentum. In 2003, arguing that a further reduction in taxes would stimulate the stalled economy, Bush prevailed upon Congress to adopt another $350 billion in cuts. Like the 2001 cuts, the new reductions were temporary in order to preserve the possibility of a balanced budget by 2010. Opponents charged that if a future Congress made these tax cuts permanent, as seemed likely, the total cost would rise to nearly $1 trillion. While Clinton had favored a policy of eliminating the deficit, Bush made tax reduction the centerpiece of his economic policy.

Although it took six months longer, the president also succeeded in getting Congress to enact his education reform program in December 2001. Borrowing the label "No Child Left Behind" from liberal Democrats, the administration pushed hard for a new policy requiring states to give annual performance tests to all elementary school students. Democrats countered with demands for increased federal funding of public education to assist states and local school boards in raising their standards. Bush shrewdly cultivated the support of Senator Ted Kennedy, a leading liberal Democrat, to forge a bipartisan consensus. The final measure increased federal aid to education by $4 billion, to a total of $22 billion annually, and man-

dated state tests in reading and math for all students in grades three through eight, and at least once during grades ten to twelve.

The new administration's successes in cutting taxes and educational reform were balanced by setbacks in the Senate and in the economy. On May 24, 2001, Senator James M. Jeffords, a Republican moderate from Vermont, surprised the GOP by announcing that he was leaving the party. By becoming an independent and aligning himself with the Democrats, Jeffords reduced the number of Republicans to 49 in the Senate, thus giving the Democrats control of the upper chamber. The new majority leader, Senator Tom Daschle of South Dakota, quickly asserted his authority to block a number of administration initiatives, including a proposal to drill for oil in environmentally sensitive areas of the Arctic National Wildlife Refuge in Alaska. The Democratic leadership prevented a Senate vote on several key Bush judicial appointees and served notice they would insist on a moderate nominee for the next Supreme Court vacancy.

In the spring of 2001 the American economy experienced its first recession in ten years. A glut of unsold goods forced manufacturers to curtail production and lay off workers. Unemployment rose to 6 percent by 2002, despite the efforts of the Federal Reserve to stem the decline by cutting interest rates eleven times in 2001. The tax rebates authorized by Congress helped stimulate recovery in the summer, but then the September 11 attacks led to a further decline. In 2002, the economy once again began to recover, only to be stalled late in the year by concern over the threat of war with Iraq.

One of the most troubling aspects of the economic downturn was the collapse of several major corporations and the subsequent revelation of shocking financial practices. WorldCom, Inc., a major telecommunications company, became the largest corporation in American history to declare bankruptcy, while a New York grand jury charged executives of Tyco International, a large electronics company, with stealing more than $600 million from shareholders through stock fraud, false expense reports, and unauthorized bonuses. These scandals, however, paled before the misdeeds of Enron, a Houston energy company that failed in late 2001 as the result of astonishingly corrupt business practices including fraudulent accounting and private partnerships designed to inflate profits and hide losses. When investors began to sell their overvalued Enron stock, shares that were once worth nearly $100 fell to less than $1. Enron declared bankruptcy and the remaining shareholders lost over $50 billion, while rank-and-file employees lost not only their jobs but much of their retirement savings, invested largely in now worthless Enron stock.

THE DOT.COM BOOM AND BUST

On March 30, 1999, a company named Priceline.com went public, offering 30 million shares of its stock for sale. The opening price was $16 per share, but by the end of the day, investors had bid the price up 425 percent, to close at $68 per share. The market value of Priceline.com was now almost $10 billion—more than the combined value of United, Continental, and Northwest Airlines. A few weeks after it went public, Priceline.com stock hit a peak of $150 a share.

Priceline.com owned no fleet of planes, nor did it employ thousands of pilots and mechanics. Instead, possessing only some software, a few powerful computers, and a brand name, it planned to revolutionize the way people bought airline tickets and hotel reservations by allowing customers to name their own prices. After a customer named a desired price for a plane ticket, for example, Priceline would then submit the price request to participating airlines. If an airline accepted the offer, it would be able to select the flight time based on available seats. Believing that consumers would jump at the chance to name their own price for airline tickets, even if they had to be flexible about their travel plans, Priceline.com expected to make millions of dollars and reward its investors with handsome dividends. Indeed, in its first year of operation, Priceline.com sold $35 million worth of tickets—for which it had paid $36.5 million. This million-dollar-plus trading loss, however, was dwarfed by the company's expenditures for advertising and marketing; those costs put the company's total losses at more than $100 million in 1998. Investors were out of luck. By 2000, the price per

share of Priceline.com stock had plummeted to under $2.

In just five years, from 1995 to 2000, hundreds of dot.coms, as companies like Priceline.com became known, came into being, with a total market value of $1 trillion. In the rising stock market of the mid-1990s, the reports of huge gains by technology companies involved in the rapid growth of the Internet set off a dot.com revolution. The phenomenon began when Netscape.com, an Internet browser and the first company to use "dot.com" in its name, went public in 1995 and made its owners wealthy overnight. On the first day of trading, share prices climbed from $28 to $58.50, giving the company a value of $2.2 billion. Netscape developer Marc Andersson's shares were suddenly worth $70 million. Other high-tech companies quickly followed Netscape.com's example.

In the United States, venture capital firms—companies that invest shareholders' money in risky but potentially very profitable ventures—began to funnel millions of dollars into new high-tech companies in return for a share of future profits. Foreign investors also poured billions into the American market; from 1995 to 2000, $1.2 trillion more investment capital flowed into the United States than out of the country. A new cable TV channel, CNBC, kept viewers constantly updated on the rising price of their stocks. Some investors who caught the dot.com fever quit their jobs to become day traders, sitting before a computer all day long, buying and selling stocks, hoping to get rich quick.

Many investors were so eager to participate in what commentators were now calling the "New Economy"

that they often bought stock without a clear understanding of its true worth. In the market frenzy, amateur and professional investors alike bought shares of companies that had never made a profit and had little prospect of doing so. Pets.com, for example, which planned to dominate the pet supply business through the Internet, attracted many investors when it emerged in 1999. Managers of the company, however, failed to take into account the high cost of delivering 40-pound bags of dog food and lost more on the cost of delivery than they made on sales. Pets.com quickly failed, losing $100 million in investor money, including $2 million spent on advertising aired during the Super Bowl.

The centerpiece of the dot.com revolution was Nasdaq (National Association of Securities Dealers Automated Quotation System). Founded in 1971, Nasdaq was a "virtual" market that existed only in cyberspace. Securities dealers across the country, linked by computers, created a market for stocks of companies too small to be traded on the floor of the New York Stock Exchange. Nasdaq grew slowly in the 1970s and 1980s, but made rapid strides in the 1990s, becoming the main vehicle through which the new dot.coms launched the sale of their stock to the public. Nasdaq's lax policies, however, made it possible for companies with little more than a business plan and a few millions in capital to hoodwink unwary investors.

On March 10, 2000, Nasdaq's Composite Index, which measures the market value of stocks, reached an all-time high of 5048.62. A month later, it had dropped below 4000. By October 2002 it had fallen to 1114, a decline of

The online pet supply company Pets.com was one of many companies that went under in the dot.com bust, taking jobs and investor capital with it. ❖

nearly 75 percent. Nasdaq's collapse took much of the dot.com world with it; some companies declared bankruptcy, others were taken over by stronger competitors, many just quietly dropped out of sight. The burst of the dot.com bubble helped bring on the recession that began in March 2001 and proved to be unusually long lasting.

The dot.com craze, however, was not a total loss. Although the Internet had largely failed as a profitable form of retail commerce, it continued to expand as an efficient way of distributing information and communicating through email. And there were dot.coms that succeeded. Companies such as the on-line auction site eBay, which provided a unique Internet service by bringing together buyers and sellers in an auction format without incurring any inventory or delivery costs, prospered, as did successful portals such as Yahoo! or e-merchants such as Amazon.com, which built up a brand name by selling books, relatively cheap to deliver, at a healthy discount.

Despite these successes, many sought a villain to blame for the dot.com debacle. How could a nation of supposedly well-informed investors place their faith—and their fortunes—in such ill-defined ventures? Some investors saw stockbrokers and financial analysts as the culprits for urging their clients to buy shares in companies no one really understood and that often proved worthless. Some dishonest and unethical brokers and financial advisers, who purposely misled their clients about the value of dot.com stocks, do bear a portion of the blame. Other investors found fault with the media for contributing to the speculative mania and failing to warn the public of the risks involved. Some investors accepted that they themselves were responsible for both boom and bust. Driven by greed, too many people had tried to get rich too quickly. When the dot.com bubble burst, so did their dreams of great wealth evaporate.

Most of the company's executives escaped criminal charges, with the exception of Andrew Fastow, who was indicted for fraud in the fall of 2002.

The public disclosures of the corrupt practices of these major corporations further weakened public confidence in American business and served to slow recovery from the recession of 2001. President Bush contended that the tax cut he had pushed through Congress would provide the necessary stimulus for full recovery. The stock market began to rally in the spring of 2003 after three straight years of losses, and consumer spending helped drive the economy's growth rate to over 7 percent in the third quarter of the year. But unemployment continued to rise, going over 6 percent by mid-2003 as companies kept trimming their payrolls to cut costs and become profitable again. The political outlook for George W. Bush, very much aware of the way a sluggish economy had made his father a one-term president, depended on how quickly the recovering economy could produce new jobs and thus restore the confidence of voters in the party in power.

Terrorism: Attack and Counterattack

On the morning of September 11, 2001, nineteen Islamic militant terrorists hijacked four U.S. airliners and turned them to attack targets in New York City and Washington, D.C. The hijackers took over two planes flying out of Boston's Logan Airport en route to California, and flew them into the World Trade Center (WTC) in New York. One plane slammed into the north tower just before 9 A.M. and the second hit the south tower only 20 minutes later. Within two hours, both towers had collapsed, taking the lives of nearly 3000 victims trapped in the buildings or crushed by the debris and more than 300 firefighters and other rescue workers who attempted to save them.

In Washington, an American Airlines flight that left Dulles Airport bound for Los Angeles met a similar fate. Taken over by five terrorists, the Boeing 757 plowed into the Pentagon, destroying one wing of the building and killing 189 military personnel and civilian workers. The terrorists had seized a fourth plane, United Airlines flight 93, scheduled to fly from Newark, New Jersey, to San Francisco. Over Pennsylvania, as the hijackers attempted to turn the plane toward the nation's capital, the passengers fought to regain control of the plane. They failed to do so, but did succeed in preventing the plane from hitting another target in Washington—perhaps the White House or the Capitol building. Flight 93 crashed in southern Pennsylvania, killing all forty-four passengers and crew as well as the hijackers.

President Bush was in Florida talking to second grade students when he was informed of the attacks. His security detail, fearing a terrorist attempt to kill

❖ A Look at the Past ❖

Patriotic Symbols

Throughout U.S. history, Americans have used to patriotic symbols to express feelings of national unity and pride. Images of Uncle Sam, the Liberty Bell, and the Statue of Liberty are a few such emblems, but the most popular and enduring insignia have been the American flag and its red, white, and blue colors. In the aftermath of the terrorist attacks of September 11, 2001, many Americans decorated their homes, clothing, and cars with flags and other patriotic symbols. Storekeepers could not keep flags on the shelves and there were even reports of flag being stolen from businesses and homes. This September 2002 photograph shows a van in New York City decorated with flags and references to September 11 to commemorate the first anniversary of the attacks. Why do you think people responded to the tragic events of September 11 with such public displays of patriotic symbols? From your study of U.S. history, can you recall other times in which Americans responded to events with similar public displays? Do you notice any differences in the ways in which Americans express patriotism today as compared with the past? How do the ways we use patriotic symbols reflect contemporary culture?

the president, immediately put him on Air Force One. Flying first to an air force base in Louisiana, and then to another in Nebraska, Bush finally rejected the advice of the secret service and insisted on returning to Washington. Back in the White House, he began to display qualities of leadership and determination that few suspected he possessed.

"None of us will forget this day," he told the American people in a televised speech on the evening of September 11. "Yet we go forward to defend freedom and all that is good and just in the world." In a key sentence, the president had strengthened the vague wording in the original speechwriter's draft to insist that the United States would not only pursue the terrorists responsible for the assault, but any person or nation that assisted them. In declaring a **war on terrorism,** Bush vowed, "We will make no distinction between those who planned these acts and those who harbor them."

Three days later, the president reinforced his determination to punish anyone aiding in terrorist attacks on the nation. Flying to New York City to visit the scene of the attack, what quickly became known as Ground Zero, he was overwhelmed by the devastation at the site of the fallen towers. When someone in the crowd of rescue workers shouted, "I can't hear you," the president shouted back into a bullhorn, "I can hear you. The rest of the world hears you. And the people who knocked these buildings down will hear all of us soon!"

Bush then returned to Washington to prepare a speech to a joint session of Congress on September 20— a speech that 80 million Americans watched on television. In it the president promised to pursue those responsible for September 11: "Our grief has turned to anger and anger to resolution. Whether we bring our enemies to justice or bring justice to our enemies, justice will be done." And the counterattack, he cautioned, would take time. "Americans should not expect one battle but a lengthy campaign, unlike any other we have ever seen." The outcome, however, would never be in doubt.

"I will not yield; I will not rest," Bush declared to thunderous applause, "I will not relent in waging this struggle for freedom and security for the American people."

It would take far more than words to avenge the acts of September 11 and end the terrorist threat to the United States. It soon became evident that Osama bin Laden, a wealthy Saudi, and his terrorist organization, al-Qaeda ("the Base" in Arabic), had planned and carried out the attacks. Bin Laden had originally been part of the international Muslim resistance to the Soviet invasion of Afghanistan that had received support and weapons from the CIA in the 1980s. He turned against the United States at the time of the Gulf War, outraged by the presence of large numbers of American troops in his native Saudi Arabia. Earlier, in the late 1980s, he had formed al-Qaeda as a determined group of Islamic fundamentalists intent on restoring orthodox religion in the Arab world and cleansing it of foreign influence, especially American. The CIA had evidence linking bin Laden and al-Qaeda to the bombing of two American embassies in East Africa in 1998 and the attack on the American destroyer *USS Cole* in Yemen in 2000. And bin Laden soon released video tapes gloating over the September 11 attacks.

The United States had been trying to neutralize al-Qaeda for at least a decade without any success. Ordered out of Saudi Arabia in 1991, bid Laden had sought refuge, first in the Sudan, and later in Afghanistan after the Taliban, another extremist Muslim group, had taken over that country. In Afghanistan, bin Laden set up camps to train hundreds of would-be terrorists, mainly from Arab countries but including recruits from the Philippines, Indonesia, and Central Asia. After the embassy bombings, President Clinton ordered cruise missile attacks on several of these camps in the hope of

As rescue efforts continued in the rubble of the World Trade Center, President Bush toured the site on September 14, 2001. In CNN's televised coverage of the visit, Bush is shown here addressing rescue workers through a bullhorn. Firefighter Bob Beckwith stands beside him. ✢

killing bin Laden. The al-Qaeda leader survived, though, leaving one of the targets only a few hours before the strike.

Bush's determination to go after those harboring terrorists made Afghanistan the prime target for the American counterattack. The president ordered the Pentagon and the CIA, which already had agents on the scene, to launch an invasion of Afghanistan to destroy the Taliban, wipe out al-Qaeda, and capture or kill Osama bin Laden.

In early October, the CIA and Army Special Forces began the operation, relying on the Northern Alliance, an Afghan political coalition still resisting the Taliban. Using a variety of methods, ranging from substantial bribes of local warlords to frequent air strikes, American forces quickly routed the Taliban and by December had installed a U.S.-friendly regime in Kabul. Most of Afghanistan, however, remained in chaos, and despite extensive efforts and several near misses, bin Laden had avoided capture, apparently taking refuge in the rugged mountain areas along the Pakistan border.

The quick victory in Afghanistan marked only the beginning of the war on terrorism waged by the Bush administration. With help from a broad international coalition including a cooperative government in Pakistan, the CIA and FBI were able to capture a number of high-ranking al-Qaeda officials. Other Muslim countries, notably Egypt and Jordan, also proved invaluable in interrogating suspected terrorists and helping foil their plans for new attacks against the United States. The CIA gained a rich harvest of intelligence data in Afghanistan and received additional useful information from several hundred terrorists imprisoned at the American naval base in Guantanamo, Cuba.

There were setbacks as well as victories in the conflict. The futile search for bin Laden, despite reports of his death, frustrated American leaders. And in the spring of 2003, al-Qaeda proved it still was very dangerous by using suicide bombers to set off deadly blasts in Casablanca, Morocco, and Riyadh, Saudi Arabia, killing more than fifty people, including eight Americans.

While waging the war abroad, the Bush administration also focused on the problem of securing the United States from any further terrorist assaults. The president favored the creation of a new Department of Homeland Security, combining Customs, the Coast Guard, the Immigration and Naturalization Service (INS), and other government bureaus into one central agency to protect the nation. In November 2002, Congress approved the new Department of Homeland Security, to be headed by Tom Ridge, former governor of Pennsylvania.

The difficulty in protecting the nation from terrorist attack was highlighted by the anthrax scare in the fall of 2001. Several employees of a Florida newspaper publishing company became ill in October with the anthrax bacteria, one dying after inhaling the spores in an envelope that came through the mail. Later in the month, a secretary at NBC News in New York City was exposed to the deadly white powder while opening a letter addressed to anchorman Tom Brokaw. In November, similar envelopes arrived in Washington addressed to members of Congress. After the deaths of two postal workers forced authorities to close the central mail processing facility in the nation's capital, letters filled with anthrax were found addressed to Senators Tom Daschle and Patrick Leahy. There were no further anthrax incidents, but the episode showed how vulnerable the nation was to biological attack. Officials traced the infected envelopes to a rural New Jersey post office, but were unable to discover the person responsible for this act of terror.

The homeland security department faced a particularly hard task in policing the nation's borders and alerting the public to potential threats. With more than 1 million immigrants and 42 million more visitors entering the United States each year, neither the INS—later replaced by the Bureau of Citizenship and Immigration Services (BCIS)—nor the customs service could guarantee that they had prevented any terrorist from slipping into the country. Ridge's office stepped up patrols of such likely targets as nuclear power plants and public water supply systems. Using a color-coded chart, from time to time homeland security raised the nation's alert status from yellow (elevated risk) to orange (high risk), just one level below red (highest risk). By the spring of 2003, the public tended to ignore these danger signals as nearly two years had passed without a further terrorist attack on American soil.

A primary focus of homeland security was on ensuring the safety of airline travel in the wake of the September 11 hijackings. In November 2001, President Bush signed legislation replacing private companies with government employees at all airport screening stations. The airlines were required to replace cockpit doors with secure barriers and to permit armed air marshals to ride among the passengers. The understandable public fear of flying after September 11 nevertheless had a devastating effect on the airline industry, forcing the cancellation of many flights and the laying off of thousands of pilots and other workers. Despite a $15 billion government bailout approved in late September 2001, the airlines continued to experience heavy losses. Several, including United Airlines, filed for bankruptcy. Although air travel began to revive slowly in 2002, the industry, along with other forms of tourism, continued to be a drag on an already sluggish economy.

The war on terrorism raised an even more fundamental question than economic stagnation. Attorney General John Ashcroft, using new powers granted by

In March 2002, Homeland Security Director Tom Ridge implemented a color-coded advisory system to identify security risk levels. The system of colored warnings garnered some ridicule but continued to be used. ❖

Congress, conducted a broad crackdown on possible terrorists, detaining many Muslim Americans on flimsy evidence and insisting that concern for national security outweighed traditional civil liberties. Opponents quickly challenged Ashcroft, arguing that the terrorists would win their greatest victory if the United States violated its own historic principles of individual freedom in the name of fighting terrorism. It was a debate that troubled many Americans who had difficulty reconciling the need for security with respect for civil liberties.

The real winner in the war against terrorism, at least in the short run, was George W. Bush. His resolute stand against terrorism and his determination to avenge September 11 attacks struck a responsive chord among the American people. His approval rating, a respectable 53 percent before September 11, shot up to over 90 percent in the weeks following the attack, and then settled into the 65 to 75 percent range, extraordinarily high for a first-term president. The way the American people had rallied around his leadership helped offset growing doubts about his tax cuts and the stalled economy. The attacks on the twin towers and the Pentagon had transformed his presidency and improved his chance of winning a second term in the White House.

The New American Empire?

The terrorist attacks on the United States were the catalyst for a major change in direction for American foreign policy. Not only did the Bush administration wage an intensive effort to avenge the September 11 attacks and prevent further assaults; it initiated a new global policy of American preeminence. For the first time since the end of the Cold War, the United States had a clear, if controversial, blueprint for international affairs.

The new administration rejected traditional forms of international cooperation. President Bush withdrew U.S. participation in the Kyoto Protocol to control global warming and announced plans to terminate the 1972 Antiballistic Missile (ABM) treaty with Russia. And he was outspoken in refusing to expose American servicemen to the jurisdiction of the International Criminal Court for possible crimes committed in worldwide peacekeeping efforts.

The new direction of American foreign policy became clear on January 29, 2002, when Bush delivered his second State of the Union address to Congress and the nation. Not only did he repeat his vow to punish all nations sponsoring terrorism, but he became specific. In a memorable phrase, he accused Iraq, Iran, and North Korea of forming "an axis of evil." Nine months later, in September 2002, the Bush administration released a fully-developed statement of its new world policy, "National Security Strategy (NSS) of the United States." The goal of American policy, Bush's NSS declared, was to "extend the peace by encouraging free and open societies on every continent."

There were two main components of the new strategy, which critics quickly called **unilateralism.** The first was to accept fully the role the nation had been playing since the end of the Cold War—global police. The United States would not shrink from its responsibility to defend freedom anywhere in the world—with allies if possible, by itself if necessary. To implement this policy, NSS asserted that the Bush administration would maintain "military strength beyond challenge." "Our forces," the NSS declared, "will be strong enough to dissuade potential adversaries from pursuing a military buildup in hopes of surpassing, or equaling, the power of the United States."

In playing the role of world police, Bush and his advisers asserted the right to the preemptive use of force. Learning from September 11, the NSS continued, "We cannot let our enemies strike first." Although promising to seek the support of the international community before using force, the NSS stated, "we will not hesitate to act alone, if necessary, to exercise our right of self-defense." In other words, the Bush administration, aware that the United States was far stronger militarily and economically than any other nation, accepted its new role as final arbiter of all international disputes.

The new strategy reflected the triumph of Rumsfeld and Cheney over Colin Powell. Instead of the traditional reliance on diplomacy and international cooperation that Powell and the State Department favored, the United States would act on its own. The result, in the eyes of both its critics and defenders, would be a new American empire.

Iraq quickly became the test case for this new shift in American foreign policy. After his "axis of evil" speech in January, President Bush focused on what he and his Pentagon advisers called **weapons of mass destruction (WMD)** that they claimed Saddam Hussein had been secretly amassing in large quantities. The United States demanded that Iraq permit UN inspectors (forced out of the country in 1998) to search for such weapons. Iraq had promised the UN it would do so in 1991 at the end of the Gulf War. In

August 2002, more than ten years later, Bush agreed to allow Secretary of State Powell to attempt to have the UN resume its weapons inspection and force Saddam to disarm. The Pentagon, meanwhile, would perfect its own plans for a unilateral American military solution.

Slowly, but inevitably, the United States moved toward war with Iraq in late 2002 and early 2003. Congress approved a resolution in October authorizing the president to use force against Saddam Hussein's regime. A month later, the UN Security Council voted unanimously to send its team of inspectors back into Iraq, warning Saddam of "severe consequences" if he failed to comply. Despite the failure of the international inspectors to find any evidence of chemical, biological, or nuclear weapons in Iraq, the Bush administration kept pressing for a Security Council resolution authorizing the use of force to compel Saddam to disarm. When France and Russia vowed to veto any such measure, Bush and his advisers decided to ignore the world body and proceed on their own. Preemption would have its first real test.

The ensuing war with Iraq surprised both the backers and the critics of unilateralism. On March 18, two days before the planned start of hostilities, President Bush made a last-minute decision to launch a cruise missile and laser bomb air strike on a bunker in Baghdad, in the belief that Saddam was inside. The results were unknown, but the next day, twenty-four hours earlier than planned, three columns of American troops, a total of 65,000, began to execute a two-pronged invasion of Iraq from bases in Kuwait. Britain, the only major power to join the United States in the fighting, helped by besieging the city of Basra and taking control of southern Iraq. After a week of rapid advance and only light casualties, the main American thrust seemed to bog down less than

In a memorable image from the war in Iraq, Iraqi civilians and U.S. soldiers pull down a statue of Saddam Hussein in Baghdad on April 9, 2003. Eight months later, U.S. soldiers captured the former Iraqi president near Tikrit. ❖

one-hundred miles from Baghdad. Unexpected attacks by guerrilla forces forced a pause while newly arriving American troops destroyed these irregular units and increased patrols to protect the long supply line. The media, listening to armchair generals at home, claimed that the invasion was stymied, asserted that hundreds of thousands of more troops would be required, and warned that the battle for Baghdad might turn into another Stalingrad, which had endured a sixty-six-day siege in World War II.

In reality, victory was within sight. The turning point came on March 25 when the three columns of American troops resumed their advance northward. Saddam sent elite units of the Republican Guard to engage the Americans south of Baghdad only to see them decimated by air strikes and then overrun by American armor. Within a week, the army had captured the Baghdad international airport, and on April 8, just three weeks after the fighting had begun, marines marched virtually unopposed into the heart of the city. The American people watched the televised scene of joyous Iraqis toppling a statue of Saddam in Fardos Square. An Iraqi major summed up the enormity of his country's defeat: "Losing a war is one thing, but losing Baghdad is another," he explained. "It was like losing the dearest thing in life."

The war was essentially over by April 8, although sporadic resistance continued north of Baghdad until early May, when President Bush formally declared an end to the combat phase of the conflict. In less than half the time that it had taken to liberate Kuwait in 1991, and with even fewer American casualties, the United States had driven Saddam Hussein from power. But the subsequent failure to find any evidence of weapons of mass destruction led critics to question the validity of the war. In response, the president's defenders stressed the importance of deposing Saddam by pointing to his brutal prisons and to the killing fields south of Baghdad where thousands of Shi'ite rebels had been slaughtered in 1991.

The problems of restoring order and rebuilding the shattered Iraqi economy quickly overshadowed the debate over the war's legitimacy. Daily attacks on American troops in the Sunni triangle north of Baghdad began in the summer of 2003 and increased in intensity during the fall, killing an average of three American soldiers each week. By October, more troops had died from these attacks than had been killed during the combat phase in March and April. Widespread looting, sabotage of oil pipelines, and the difficulty in repairing and operating outdated power plants and oil facilities made economic recovery very slow and halting. U.S. efforts to involve occupation forces from other UN members yielded only a few troops. In the fall of 2003, a group of wealthier

CHRONOLOGY

1992	Riots devastate South Central Los Angeles after verdict in Rodney King case (May) ◆ Bill Clinton elected president (November)
1993	General Motors announces loss of $23.4 billion, the largest one-year loss in U.S. corporate history
1994	Former football star O. J. Simpson charged with killing ex-wife Nicole Brown Simpson and her friend Ronald Goldman (June) ◆ Republicans gain control of both houses of Congress (November)
1995	U.S. troops arrive in Bosnia as part of international peacekeeping force (December)
1996	FBI arrests Theodore Kaczynzki, suspected Unabomber, in Montana (April) ◆ Clinton signs major welfare reform measure (August)
1997	Federal jury gives Timothy McVeigh death sentence for Oklahoma City bombing
1998	Terrorists bomb American embassies in Kenya and Tanzania
1999	Senate acquits Clinton of impeachment charges (February) ◆ Dow Jones Industrial Average goes over 10,000 for first time (March)
2000	Y2K furor proves unfounded ◆ George W. Bush wins contested presidential election
2001	American economy goes into recession, ending the longest period of expansion in U.S. history (March) ◆ Terrorist attacks on World Trade Center and the Pentagon (September 11) ◆ Anthrax spores found in mail (October) ◆ United States military action against the Taliban regime in Afghanistan (October–December)
2002	Police arrest suspected D.C. snipers who killed 10 and wounded three residents of the metro area (October) ◆ Department of Homeland Security created (November)
2003	U.S. troops invade Iraq and overthrow Saddam Hussein's regime (March–April) ◆ Saddam Hussein captured (December)

nations led by Japan pledged $13 billion for Iraq's reconstruction; Congress, after considerable debate, finally authorized another $18.6 billion to help rebuild Iraq, along with $51 billion to support the American army of occupation.

The capture of Saddam Hussein in December 2003 helped boost President Bush's approval rating, which had begun to sag as problems persisted in postwar Iraq. The situation in Iraq, however, still remained troubling after Saddam's capture. Despite slow but steady progress in restoring public services such as electric power and the gradual recovery of the Iraq oil industry, the armed insurrection continued. Mortar attacks on Baghdad hotels, roadside bombs aimed at American armored convoys, and hand-held missile attacks on American helicopters made Iraq a very dangerous place. Equally disturbing, conflicts of interest between Shi'ite and Sunni Muslims, as well as the Kurdish demand for autonomy, threatened the American goal of creating a stable Iraqi government. George W. Bush, bolstered by a reviving economy, still faced a likely campaign attack by Democrats in 2004 on his handling of the war with Iraq.

Conclusion: The American Century?

On the eve of American entry into World War II, Henry Luce, founder of the *Time-Life* publishing empire, predicted that the 1900s would become known in history as the American century. The onset of the Cold War made Luce's prediction premature. But the demise of the Soviet Union in 1991, leaving the United States as the world's sole superpower, and the subsequent assertion of American preeminence by the George W. Bush administration suggest that the next one hundred years may well be the real American century. The United States, despite a slow recovery from the 2001 recession and hostile world opinion, remains by far the strongest nation on the globe. Its military power is unrivaled and its economy is still the engine driving the world's markets.

Yet daunting challenges face the United States in the twenty-first century. History has repeatedly shown how brief a time most nations have to enjoy their moment of world supremacy. Like the empires of Greece and Rome, or even of Great Britain in more recent times, the United States must guard against the powerful force of imperial decay. In a world suspicious of American motives, the challenge facing the United States is to convince its own citizens, as well as those of other nations, that the American mission of spreading democracy, of being a beacon of liberty to all peoples, remains a worthwhile and attainable goal.

Recommended Reading

Bob Woodward offers the fullest account of the Clinton-Greenspan effort to end the budget deficits in two books, *The Agenda* (1994), on Clinton's economic policy, and *Maestro* (2000), on Greenspan's service as chairman of the Federal Reserve Board.

The best book on recent immigration from developing countries is David Reimers, *Still the Golden Door,* 2nd ed. (1992). Peter Skerry provides a thoughtful survey of the largest single Hispanic group in *Mexican-Americans* (1993). For the role of blacks in politics since World War II, see Steven F. Lawson, *Running for Freedom* (1991).

British journalist Martin Walker gives a balanced account of Clinton's first term in *The President We Deserve* (1996). For the first lady's perspective, see Hillary Clinton, *Living History* (2003). Two books cover the Monica Lewinsky scandal and the ensuing impeachment proceedings: Michael Isikoff, *Uncovering Clinton* (2000), and Richard A. Posner, *An Affair of State* (1999).

Haynes Johnson traces the boom years of the 1990s in *The Best of Times* (2001). For the stock market bubble, see John Cassidy, *dot.com: The Greatest Story Ever Sold* (2002).

The best survey of foreign policy in the Clinton years is David Halberstam, *War in a Time of Peace* (2001). For Bosnia, see Richard Holbrooke, *To End a War* (1998); David Fromkin deals with the other Balkan crisis in *Kosovo Crossing* (1999).

In *Gathering Storm* (1996), Morris Dees and James Corcoran offer a somber assessment of the militia movement from the Ruby Ridge shootout to the Oklahoma City bombing.

The most balanced account of the disputed 2000 election is Howard Gillman, *The Votes that Counted* (2001). For contrasting opinions, see Richard A. Posner, *Breaking the Deadlock* (2001), in support of the Supreme Court decision, and Alan M. Dershowitz, *Supreme Injustice* (2001), sharply critical.

The first memoir to come out of the George W. Bush White House is David Frum, *The Right Man* (2003), favorable to the president but not entirely uncritical. On the events of September 11 and their aftermath, see Richard Bernstein, et al., *Out of the Blue* (2002), based on *New York Times* reporting; and Steven Brill, *After* (2003), on the way people came to terms with the tragedy. For the war on terrorism, see Paul Pillar, *Terrorism and U.S. Foreign Policy* (2001), and Victor Davis Hanson, *An Autumn of War* (2002), essays supportive of Bush's efforts.

Williamson Murray and Robert H. Scales, Jr., survey the fighting that led to the defeat of Saddam Hussein's regime in *The Iraq War* (2003).

For a list of additional titles related to this chapter's topics, please see http://www.ablongman.com/divine.

SUGGESTED WEB SITES

American Identities

http://xroads.virginia.edu/~YP/ethnic.html
This site suggests resources for studying America's multiple ethnic identities.

Census 2000

http://www.census.gov/main/www/cen2000.html
U.S. Census Bureau gateway to 2000 census information and data.

William Jefferson Clinton

http://www.ipl.org/ref/POTUS/wjclinton.html
This site contains basic factual data about Clinton's election and presidency, speeches, and on-line biographies.

Investigating the President: The Trial

http://www.cnn.com/ALLPOLITICS/resources/1998/lewinsky
This site from CNN provides information and documents about the scandals surrounding President Clinton and his impeachment.

A Brief History of the Internet, Version 3.1

http://www.isoc.org/internet-history/
The Internet Society puts out this site that explores the development and impact of the Internet.

The Computer Museum History Center

http://computerhistory.org
This site for the Computer Museum History Center features on-line archives and exhibits tracing five decades of computer history.

George Walker Bush

http://www.ipl.org/ref/POTUS/gwbush.html
This site contains basic factual data about Bush's election and presidency, speeches, and on-line biographies.

September 11, 2001: Attack on America

http://www.yale.edu/lawweb/avalon/sept_11/sept_11.htm
The Avalon Project at Yale Law School sponsors this collection of documents relating to the September 11 terrorist attacks.

War in Iraq

http://www.cnn.com/SPECIALS/2003/Iraq
A CNN special report on the war, including interactive maps, headlines, video, and topical information.

Appendix

The Declaration of Independence

The Articles of Confederation

The Constitution of the United States of America

Amendments to the Constitution

Presidential Elections

For additional reference material, go to
http://www.ablongman.com/divine/appendix
The on-line appendix includes the following:

The Declaration of Independence
The Articles of Confederation
The Constitution of the United States of America
Amendments to the Constitution
Presidential Elections
Vice Presidents and Cabinet Members by Administration
Supreme Court Justices
Presidents, Congresses, and Chief Justices, 1789–2001
Territorial Expansion of the United States (map)
Admission of States of the Union
U.S. Population, 1790–2000

Ten Largest Cities by Population, 1700–1900
Birthrate, 1820–2000 (chart)
Death Rate, 1900–2000 (chart)
Life Expectancy, 1900–2000 (chart)
Urban/Rural Population, 1750–1900 (chart)
Women in the Labor Force, 1890–1990
United States Physical Features (map)
United States Native Vegetation (map)
Ancient Native American Communities (map)
Native American Peoples, c. 1500 (map)
Present-Day United States (map)

THE DECLARATION OF INDEPENDENCE

In Congress, July 4, 1776

The Unanimous Declaration of the Thirteen United States of America,

When, in the course of human events, it becomes necessary for one people to dissolve the political bonds which have connected them with another, and to assume, among the powers of the earth, the separate and equal station to which the laws of nature and of nature's God entitle them, a decent respect to the opinions of mankind requires that they should declare the causes which impel them to the separation.

We hold these truths to be self-evident: That all men are created equal; that they are endowed by their Creator with certain unalienable rights; that among these are life, liberty, and the pursuit of happiness; that, to secure these rights, governments are instituted among men, deriving their just powers from the consent of the governed; that whenever any form of government becomes destructive of these ends, it is the right of the people to alter or to abolish it, and to institute new government, laying its foundation on such principles, and organizing its powers in such form, as to them shall seem most likely to effect their safety and happiness. Prudence, indeed, will dictate that governments long established should not be changed for light and transient causes; and accordingly all experience hath shown that mankind are more disposed to suffer, while evils are sufferable, than to right themselves by abolishing the forms to which they are accustomed. But when a long train of abuses and usurpations, pursuing invariably the same object, evinces a design to reduce them under absolute despotism, it is their right, it is their duty, to throw off such government, and to provide new guards for their future security. Such has been the patient sufferance of these colonies; and such is now the necessity which constrains them to alter their former systems of government. The history of the present King of Great Britain is a history of repeated injuries and usurpations, all having in direct object the establishment of an absolute tyranny over these states. To prove this, let facts be submitted to a candid world.

He has refused his assent to laws, the most wholesome and necessary for the public good.

He has forbidden his governors to pass laws of immediate and pressing importance, unless suspended in their operation till his assent should be obtained; and, when so suspended, he has utterly neglected to attend to them.

He has refused to pass other laws for the accommodation of large districts of people, unless those people would relinquish the right of representation in the legislature, a right inestimable to them, and formidable to tyrants only.

He has called together legislative bodies at places unusual, uncomfortable, and distant from the depository of their public records, for the sole purpose of fatiguing them into compliance with his measures.

He has dissolved representative houses repeatedly, for opposing, with manly firmness, his invasions on the rights of the people.

He has refused for a long time, after such dissolutions, to cause others to be elected; whereby the legislative powers, incapable of annihilation, have returned to the people at large for their exercise; the state remaining, in the mean time, exposed to all the dangers of invasions from without and convulsions within.

He has endeavored to prevent the population of these states; for that purpose obstructing the laws for naturalization of foreigners; refusing to pass others to encourage their migration hither, and raising the conditions of new appropriations of lands.

He has obstructed the administration of justice, by refusing his assent to laws for establishing judiciary powers.

He has made judges dependent on his will alone, for the tenure of their offices, and the amount and payment of their salaries.

He has erected a multitude of new offices, and sent hither swarms of officers to harass our people and eat out their substance.

He has kept among us, in times of peace, standing armies, without the consent of our legislatures.

He has affected to render the military independent of, and superior to, the civil power.

He has combined with others to subject us to a jurisdiction foreign to our constitution, and unacknowledged by our laws, giving his assent to their acts of pretended legislation:

For quartering large bodies of armed troops among us;

For protecting them, by a mock trial, from punishment for any murder which they should commit on the inhabitants of these states;

For cutting off our trade with all parts of the world;

For imposing taxes on us without our consent;

For depriving us, in many cases, of the benefits of trial by jury;

For transporting us beyond seas, to be tried for pretended offenses;

For abolishing the free system of English laws in a neighboring province, establishing therein an arbitrary government, and enlarging its boundaries, so as to render it at once an example and fit instrument for introducing the same absolute rule into these colonies;

For taking away our charters, abolishing our most valuable laws, and altering fundamentally the forms of our governments;

For suspending our own legislatures, and declaring themselves invested with power to legislate for us in all cases whatsoever.

He has abdicated government here, by declaring us out of his protection and waging war against us.

He has plundered our seas, ravaged our coasts, burned our towns, and destroyed the lives of our people.

He is at this time transporting large armies of foreign mercenaries to complete the works of death, desolation, and tyranny already begun with circumstances of cruelty and perfidy scarcely paralleled in the most barbarous ages, and totally unworthy the head of a civilized nation.

He has constrained our fellow-citizens, taken captive on the high seas, to bear arms against their country, to become the executioners of their friends and brethren, or to fall themselves by their hands.

He has excited domestic insurrection among us, and has endeavored to bring on the inhabitants of our frontiers the merciless Indian savages, whose known rule of warfare is an undistinguished destruction of all ages, sexes, and conditions.

In every stage of these oppressions we have petitioned for redress in the most humble terms; our repeated petitions have been answered only by repeated injury. A prince, whose character is thus marked by every act which may define a tyrant, is unfit to be the ruler of a free people.

Nor have we been wanting in our attentions to our British brethren. We have warned them, from time to time, of attempts by their legislature to extend an unwarrantable jurisdiction over us. We have reminded them of the circumstances of our emigration and settlement here. We have appealed to their native justice and magnanimity; and we have

conjured them, by the ties of our common kindred, to disavow these usurpations, which would inevitably interrupt our connections and correspondence. They, too, have been deaf to the voice of justice and of consanguinity. We must, therefore, acquiesce in the necessity which denounces our separation, and hold them, as we hold the rest of mankind, enemies in war, in peace friends.

We, therefore, the representatives of the United States of America, in General Congress assembled, appealing to the Supreme Judge of the world for the rectitude of our intentions, do, in the name and by the authority of the good people of these colonies, solemnly publish and declare, that these United Colonies are, and of right ought to be, FREE AND INDEPENDENT STATES; that they are absolved from all allegiance to the British crown, and that all political connection between them and the state of Great Britain is, and ought to be, totally dissolved; and that, as free and independent states, they have full power to levy war, conclude peace, contract alliances, establish commerce, and do all other acts and things which independent states may of right do. And for the support of this declaration, with a firm reliance on the protection of Divine Providence, we mutually pledge to each other our lives, our fortunes, and our sacred honor.

John Hancock

Button Gwinnett
Lyman Hall
Geo. Walton
Wm. Hooper
Joseph Hewes
John Penn
Edward Rutledge
Thos. Heyward, Junr.
Thomas Lynch, Junr.
Arthur Middleton
Samuel Chase
Wm. Paca
Thos. Stone
Charles Carroll of Carrollton
George Wythe
Richard Henry Lee
Th. Jefferson
Benj. Harrison
Thos. Nelson, Jr.

Francis Lightfoot Lee
Carter Braxton
Robt. Morris
Benjamin Rush
Benja. Franklin
John Morton
Geo. Clymer
Jas. Smith
Geo. Taylor
James Wilson
Geo. Ross
Caesar Rodney
Geo. Read
Tho. M'kean
Wm. Floyd
Phil. Livingston
Frans. Lewis
Lewis Morris
Richd. Stockton

Jno. Witherspoon
Fras. Hopkinson
John Hart
Abra. Clark
Josiah Bartlett
Wm. Whipple
Saml. Adams
John Adams
Robt. Treat Paine
Elbridge Gerry
Step. Hopkins
William Ellery
Roger Sherman
Sam'el Huntington
Wm. Williams
Oliver Wolcott
Matthew Thornton

THE ARTICLES OF CONFEDERATION

Between the States of New Hampshire, Massachusetts Bay, Rhode Island and Providence Plantations, Connecticut, New York, New Jersey, Pennsylvania, Delaware, Maryland, Virginia, North Carolina, South Carolina, Georgia

ARTICLE 1

The stile of this confederacy shall be "The United States of America."

ARTICLE 2

Each State retains its sovereignty, freedom and independence, and every power, jurisdiction, and right, which is not by this confederation expressly delegated to the United States, in Congress assembled.

ARTICLE 3

The said states hereby severally enter into a firm league of friendship with each other for their common defence, the security of their liberties and their mutual and general welfare; binding themselves to assist each other against all force offered to, or attacks made upon them, or any of them, on account of religion, sovereignty, trade, or any other pretence whatever.

ARTICLE 4

The better to secure and perpetuate mutual friendship and intercourse among the people of the different states in this union, the free inhabitants of each of these states, paupers, vagabonds, and fugitives from justice excepted, shall be entitled to all privileges and immunities of free citizens in the several states; and the people of each State shall have free ingress and regress to and from any other State, and shall enjoy therein all the privileges of trade and commerce, subject to the same duties, impositions, and restrictions, as the inhabitants thereof respectively; provided, that such restrictions shall not extend so far as to prevent the removal of property, imported into any State, to any other State of which the owner is an inhabitant; provided also, that no imposition, duties, or restriction, shall be laid by any State on the property of the United States, or either of them.

If any person guilty of, or charged with treason, felony, or other high misdemeanor in any State, shall flee from justice and be found in any of the United States, he shall, upon demand of the governor or executive power of the State from which he fled, be delivered up and removed to the State having jurisdiction of his offence.

Full faith and credit shall be given in each of these states to the records, acts, and judicial proceedings of the courts and magistrates of every other State.

ARTICLE 5

For the more convenient management of the general interests of the United States, delegates shall be annually appointed, in such manner as the legislature of each State shall direct, to meet in Congress, on the 1st Monday in November in every year, with a power reserved to each State to recall its delegates, or any of them, at any time within the year, and to send others in their stead for the remainder of the year.

No State shall be represented in Congress by less than two, nor by more than seven members; and no person shall be capable of being a delegate for more than three years in any term of six years; nor shall any person, being a delegate, be capable of holding any office under the United States, for which he, or any other for his benefit, receives any salary, fees, or emolument of any kind.

Each State shall maintain its own delegates in a meeting of the states, and while they act as members of the committee of the states.

In determining questions in the United States, in Congress assembled, each State shall have one vote.

Freedom of speech and debate in Congress shall not be impeached or questioned in any court or place out of Congress: and the members of Congress shall be protected in their persons from arrests and imprisonments, during the time of their going to and from, and attendance on Congress, except for treason, felony, or breach of the peace.

ARTICLE 6

No State, without the consent of the United States, in Congress assembled, shall send any embassy to, or receive any embassy from, or enter into any conference, agreement, alliance, or treaty with any king, prince, or state; nor shall any person, holding any office of profit or trust under the United States, or any of them, accept of any present, emolument, office or title, of any kind whatever, from any king, prince, or foreign state; nor shall the United States, in Congress assembled, or any of them, grant any title of nobility.

No two or more states shall enter into any treaty, confederation, or alliance, whatever, between them, without the consent of the United States, in Congress assembled, specifying accurately the purposes for which the same is to be entered into, and how long it shall continue.

No State shall lay any imposts or duties which may interfere with any stipulations in treaties entered into by the United States, in Congress assembled, with any king, prince, or state, in pursuance of any treaties already proposed by Congress to the courts of France and Spain.

No vessels of war shall be kept up in time of peace by any State, except such number only as shall be deemed necessary by the United States, in Congress assembled, for the defence of such State or its trade; nor shall any body of forces be kept up by any State, in time of peace, except such number only as, in the judgment of the United States, in Congress assembled, shall be deemed requisite to garrison the forts necessary for the defence of such State; but every State shall always keep up a well regulated and disciplined militia, sufficiently armed and accoutred, and shall provide, and constantly have ready for use, in public stores, a due number of field pieces and tents, and a proper quantity of arms, ammunition and camp equipage.

No State shall engage in any war without the consent of the United States, in Congress assembled, unless such State be actually invaded by enemies, or shall have received certain advice of a resolution being formed by some nation of Indians to invade such State, and the danger is so imminent as not to admit of a delay till the United States, in Congress assembled, can be consulted; nor shall any State grant commissions to any ships or vessels of war, nor letters of marque or reprisal, except it be after a declaration of war by the United States, in Congress assembled, and then only against the kingdom or state, and the subjects thereof, against which war has been so declared, and under such regulations as shall be established by the United States, in Congress assembled, unless such States be infested by pirates, in which case vessels of war may be fitted out for that occasion, and kept so long as the danger shall continue, or until the United States, in Congress assembled, shall determine otherwise.

ARTICLE 7

When land forces are raised by any State for the common defence, all officers of or under the rank of colonel, shall be appointed by the legislature of each State respectively, by whom such forces shall be raised, or in such manner as such State shall direct; and all vacancies shall be filled up by the State which first made the appointment.

ARTICLE 8

All charges of war and all other expences, that shall be incurred for the common defence or general welfare, and allowed by the United States, in Congress assembled, shall be defrayed out of a common treasury, which shall be supplied by the several states, in proportion to the value of all land within each State, granted to or surveyed for any person, as such land and the buildings and improvements thereon shall be estimated according to such mode as the United States, in Congress assembled, shall, from time to time, direct and appoint.

The taxes for paying that proportion shall be laid and levied by the authority and direction of the legislatures of the several states, within the time agreed upon by the United States, in Congress assembled.

ARTICLE 9

The United States, in Congress assembled, shall have the sole and exclusive right and power of determining on peace and war, except in the cases mentioned in the 6th article; of sending and receiving ambassadors; entering into treaties and alliances, provided that no treaty of commerce shall be made, whereby the legislative power of the respective states shall be restrained from imposing such imposts and duties on foreigners as their own people are subjected to, or from prohibiting the exportation or importation of any species of goods or commodities whatsoever; of establishing rules for

deciding, in all cases, what captures on land or water shall be legal, and in what manner prizes, taken by land or naval forces in the service of the United States, shall be divided or appropriated; of granting letters of marque and reprisal in times of peace; appointing courts for the trial of piracies and felonies committed on the high seas, and establishing courts for receiving and determining, finally, appeals in all cases of captures; provided, that no member of Congress shall be appointed a judge of any of the said courts.

The United States, in Congress assembled, shall also be the last resort on appeal in all disputes and differences now subsisting, or that hereafter may arise between two or more states concerning boundary, jurisdiction or any other cause whatever; which authority shall always be exercised in the manner following: whenever the legislative or executive authority, or lawful agent of any State, in controversy with another, shall present a petition to Congress, stating the matter in question, and praying for a hearing, notice thereof shall be given, by order of Congress, to the legislative or executive authority of the other State in controversy, and a day assigned for the appearance of the parties by their lawful agents, who shall then be directed to appoint, by joint consent, commissioners or judges to constitute a court for hearing and determining the matter in question; but, if they cannot agree, Congress shall name three persons out of each of the United States, and from the list of such persons each party shall alternately strike out one, in the petitioners beginning, until the number shall be reduced to thirteen; and from that number not less than seven, nor more than nine names, as Congress shall direct, shall, in the presence of Congress, be drawn out by lot; and the persons whose names shall be drawn, or any five of them, shall be commissioners or judges to hear and finally determine the controversy, so always as a major part of the judges who shall hear the cause shall agree in the determination; and if either party shall neglect to attend at the day appointed, without shewing reasons which Congress shall judge sufficient, or, being present, shall refuse to strike, the Congress shall proceed to nominate three persons out of each State, and the secretary of Congress shall strike in behalf of such party absent or refusing; and the judgment and sentence of the court to be appointed, in the manner before prescribed, shall be final and conclusive; and if any of the parties shall refuse to submit to the authority of such court, or to appear or defend their claim or cause, the court shall nevertheless proceed to pronounce sentence or judgment, which shall, in like manner, be final and decisive, the judgment or sentence and other proceedings being, in either case, transmitted to Congress, and lodged among the acts of Congress for the security of the parties concerned: provided, that every commissioner, before he sits in judgment, shall take an oath, to be administered by one of the judges of the supreme or superior court of the State where the cause shall be tried, "well and truly to hear and determine the matter in question, according to the best of his judgment, without favour, affection, or hope of reward": provided, also, that no State shall be deprived of territory for the benefit of the United States.

All controversies concerning the private right of soil, claimed under different grants of two or more states, whose jurisdictions, as they may respect such lands and the states which passed such grants, are adjusted, the said grants, or either of them, being at the same time claimed to have originated antecedent to such settlement of jurisdiction, shall, on the petition of either party to the Congress of the United States, be finally determined, as near as may be, in the same manner as is before prescribed for deciding disputes respecting territorial jurisdiction between different states.

The United States, in Congress assembled, shall also have the sole and exclusive right and power of regulating the alloy and value of coin struck by their own authority, or by that of the respective states; fixing the standard of weights and measures throughout the United States; regulating the trade and managing all affairs with the Indians not members of any of the states; provided that the legislative right of any State within its own limits be not infringed or violated; establishing and regulating post offices from one State to another throughout all the United States, and exacting such postage on the papers passing through the same as may be requisite to defray the expences of the said office; appointing all officers of the land forces in the service of the United States, excepting regimental officers; appointing all the officers of the naval forces, and commissioning all officers whatever in the service of the United States; making rules for the government and regulation of the said land and naval forces, and directing their operations.

The United States, in Congress assembled, shall have authority to appoint a committee to sit in the recess of Congress, to be denominated "a Committee of the States," and to consist of one delegate from each State, and to appoint such other committees and civil officers as may be necessary for managing the general affairs of the United States, under their direction; to appoint one of their number to preside; provided that no person be allowed to serve in the office of president more than one year in any term of three years; to ascertain the necessary sums of money to be raised for the service of the United States, and to appropriate and apply the same for defraying the public expences; to borrow money or emit bills on the credit of the United States, transmitting, every half year, to the respective states, an account of the sums of money so borrowed or emitted; to build and equip a navy; to agree upon the number of land forces, and to make requisitions from each State for its quota, in proportion to the number of white inhabitants in such State; which requisitions shall be binding; and, thereupon, the legislature of each State shall appoint the regimental officers, raise the men, and cloathe, arm, and equip them in a soldier-like manner, at the expence of the United States; and the officers and men so cloathed, armed, and equipped, shall march to the place appointed and within the time agreed on by the United States, in Congress assembled; but if the United States, in Congress assembled, shall, on consideration of circumstances, judge proper that any State should not raise men, or should raise a smaller number than its quota, and that any other State should raise a greater number of men than the quota thereof, such extra number shall be raised, officered, cloathed, armed, and equipped in

the same manner as the quota of such State, unless the legislature of such State shall judge that such extra number cannot be safely spared out of the same, in which case they shall raise, officer, cloathe, arm, and equip as many of such extra number as they judge can be safely spared. And the officers and men so cloathed, armed, and equipped, shall march to the place appointed and within the time agreed on by the United States, in Congress assembled.

The United States, in Congress assembled, shall never engage in a war, nor grant letters of marque and reprisal in time of peace, nor enter into any treaties or alliances, nor coin money, nor regulate the value thereof, nor ascertain the sums and expences necessary for the defence and welfare of the United States, or any of them: nor emit bills, nor borrow money on the credit of the United States, nor appropriate money, nor agree upon the number of vessels of war to be built or purchased, or the number of land or sea forces to be raised, nor appoint a commander in chief of the army or navy, unless nine states assent to the same; nor shall a question on any other point, except for adjourning from day to day, be determined, unless by the votes of a majority of the United States, in Congress assembled.

The Congress of the United States shall have power to adjourn to any time within the year, and to any place within the United States, so that no period of adjournment be for a longer duration than the space of six months, and shall publish the journal of their proceedings monthly, except such parts thereof, relating to treaties, alliances or military operations, as, in their judgment, require secrecy; and the yeas and nays of the delegates of each State on any question shall be entered on the journal, when it is desired by any delegate; and the delegates of a State, or any of them, at his, or their request, shall be furnished with a transcript of the said journal, except such parts as are above excepted, to lay before the legislatures of the several states.

ARTICLE 10

The committee of the states, or any nine of them, shall be authorized to execute, in the recess of Congress, such of the powers of Congress as the United States, in Congress assembled, by the consent of nine states, shall, from time to time, think expedient to vest them with; provided, that no power be delegated to the said committee for the exercise of which, by the articles of confederation, the voice of nine states, in the Congress of the United States assembled, is requisite.

ARTICLE 11

Canada acceding to this confederation, and joining in the measures of the United States, shall be admitted into and entitled to all the advantages of this union; but no other colony shall be admitted into the same, unless such admission be agreed to by nine states.

ARTICLE 12

All bills of credit emitted, monies borrowed and debts contracted by, or under the authority of Congress before the assembling of the United States, in pursuance of the present confederation, shall be deemed and considered as a charge against the United States, for payment and satisfaction whereof the said United States and the public faith are hereby solemnly pledged.

ARTICLE 13

Every State shall abide by the determinations of the United States, in Congress assembled, on all questions which, by this confederation, are submitted to them. And the articles of this confederation shall be inviolably observed by every State, and the union shall be perpetual; nor shall any alteration at any time hereafter be made in any of them, unless such alteration be agreed to in a Congress of the United States, and be afterwards confirmed by the legislatures of every State.

These articles shall be proposed to the legislatures of all the United States, to be considered, and if approved of by them, they are advised to authorize their delegates to ratify the same in the Congress of the United States; which being done, the same shall become conclusive.

THE CONSTITUTION OF THE UNITED STATES OF AMERICA

PREAMBLE

We the People of the United States, in Order to form a more perfect Union, establish Justice, insure domestic Tranquility, provide for the common defence, promote the general Welfare, and secure the Blessings of Liberty to ourselves and our Posterity, do ordain and establish this Constitution for the United States of America.

ARTICLE I

Section 1

All legislative Powers herein granted shall be vested in a Congress of the United States, which shall consist of a Senate and House of Representatives.

Section 2

The House of Representatives shall be composed of Members chosen every second Year by the People of the several States, and the Electors in each State shall have the Qualifications requisite for Electors of the most numerous Branch of the State Legislature.

No Person shall be a Representative who shall not have attained to the Age of twenty five Years, and been seven Years a Citizen of the United States, and who shall not, when elected, be an inhabitant of that State in which he shall be chosen.

Representatives and direct Taxes shall be apportioned among the several States which may be included within this Union, according to their respective Numbers, *which shall be determined by adding to the whole Number of free Persons, including those bound to Service for a Term of Years, and excluding Indians not taxed, three fifths of all other Persons.** The actual Enumeration shall be made within three Years after the first Meeting of the Congress of the United States, and within every subsequent Term of ten Years, in such Manner as they shall by Law direct. The Number of Representatives shall not exceed one for every thirty Thousand, but each State shall have at Least one Representative; *and until such enumeration shall be made, the State of New Hampshire shall be entitled to chuse three, Massachusetts eight, Rhode-Island and Providence Plantations one, Connecticut five, New York six, New Jersey four, Pennsylvania eight, Delaware one, Maryland six, Virginia ten, North Carolina five, South Carolina five, and Georgia three.*

When vacancies happen in the Representation from any State, the Executive Authority thereof shall issue Writs of Election to fill such Vacancies.

The House of Representatives shall chuse their Speaker and other Officers; and shall have the sole Power of Impeachment.

Section 3

The Senate of the United States shall be composed of two Senators from each State, *chosen by the Legislature thereof,* for six Years; and each Senator shall have one Vote.

Immediately after they shall be assembled in Consequence of the first Election, they shall be divided as equally as may be into three Classes. The Seats of the Senators of the first Class shall be vacated at the Expiration of the second Year, of the second Class at the Expiration of the fourth Year, and of the third Class at the Expiration of the sixth Year so that one third may be chosen every second Year; and if Vacancies happen by Resignation, or otherwise, during the Recess of the Legislature of any state, the Executive thereof may make temporary Appointments until the next Meeting of the Legislature, which shall then fill such Vacancies.

No Person shall be a Senator who shall not have attained to the Age of thirty Years, and been nine Years a Citizen of the United States, and who shall not, when elected, be an Inhabitant of that State for which he shall be chosen.

The Vice President of the United States shall be President of the Senate, but shall have no Vote, unless they be equally divided.

The Senate shall chuse their other Officers, and also a President *pro tempore,* in the Absence of the Vice President, or when he shall exercise the Office of President of the United States.

The Senate shall have the sole Power to try all Impeachments. When sitting for that Purpose, they shall be on Oath or Affirmation. When the President of the United States is tried the Chief Justice shall preside: And no Person shall be convicted without the Concurrence of two thirds of the Members present.

Judgment in Cases of Impeachment shall not extend further than to removal from Office, and disqualification to hold and enjoy any Office of honor, Trust or Profit under the United States: but the Party convicted shall nevertheless be liable and subject to Indictment, Trial, Judgment and Punishment, according to Law.

Section 4

The Times, Places and Manner of holding Elections for Senators and Representatives, shall be prescribed in each State by the Legislature thereof; but the Congress may at any time by Law make or alter such Regulations, except as to the Places of chusing Senators.

The Congress shall assemble at least once in every Year, *and such Meeting shall be on the first Monday in December, unless they shall by Law appoint a different Day.*

Section 5

Each House shall be the Judge of the Elections, Returns and Qualifications of its own Members, and a Majority of each shall constitute a Quorum to do Business; but a smaller Number may adjourn from day to day, and may be

---

*Passages no longer in effect are printed in italic type.

authorized to compel the Attendance of absent Members, in such Manner, and under such Penalties as each House may provide.

Each House may determine the Rules of its Proceedings, punish its Members for disorderly Behaviour, and, with the Concurrence of two thirds, expel a Member.

Each House shall keep a Journal of its Proceedings, and from time to time publish the same, excepting such Parts as may in their Judgment require Secrecy; and the Yeas and Nays of the Members of either House on any question shall, at the Desire of one fifth of those Present, be entered on the Journal.

Neither House, during the Session of Congress, shall, without the Consent of the other, adjourn for more than three days, nor to any other Place than that in which the two Houses shall be sitting.

Section 6

The Senators and Representatives shall receive a Compensation for their Services, to be ascertained by Law, and paid out of the Treasury of the United States. They shall in all Cases, except Treason, Felony and Breach of the Peace, be privileged from Arrest during their Attendance at the Session of their respective Houses, and in going to and returning from the same; and for any Speech or Debate in either House, they shall not be questioned in any other Place.

No Senator or Representative shall, during the Time for which he was elected, be appointed to any civil Office under the Authority of the United States, which shall have been created, or the Emoluments whereof shall have been encreased during such time, and no Person holding any Office under the United States, shall be a Member of either House during his Continuance in Office.

Section 7

All Bills for raising Revenue shall originate in the House of Representatives; but the Senate may propose or concur with Amendments as on other Bills.

Every Bill which shall have passed the House of Representatives and the Senate, shall, before it become a Law, be presented to the President of the United States; If he approve he shall sign it, but if not he shall return it, with his Objections to the House in which it shall have originated, who shall enter the Objections at large on their Journal, and proceed to reconsider it. If after such Reconsideration two thirds of that House shall agree to pass the Bill, it shall be sent, together with the Objections, to the other House, by which it shall likewise be reconsidered, and if approved by two thirds of that House, it shall become a Law. But in all such Cases the Votes of both Houses shall be determined by yeas and Nays, and the Names of the Persons voting for and against the Bill shall be entered on the Journal of each House respectively. If any Bill shall not be returned by the President within ten Days (Sundays excepted) after it shall have been presented to him, the Same shall be a Law, in like Manner as if he had signed it, unless the Congress by their Adjournment prevent its Return, in which Case it shall not be a Law.

Every Order, Resolution, or Vote to which the Concurrence of the Senate and House of Representatives may be necessary (except on a question of Adjournment) shall be presented to the President of the United States; and before the Same shall take Effect, shall be approved by him, or being disapproved by him, shall be repassed by two thirds of the Senate and House of Representatives, according to the Rules and Limitations prescribed in the Case of a Bill.

Section 8

The Congress shall have Power To lay and collect Taxes, Duties, Imposts and Excises, to pay the Debts and provide for the common Defence and general Welfare of the United States; but all Duties, Imposts and Excises shall be uniform throughout the United States;

To borrow Money on the credit of the United States;

To regulate Commerce with foreign Nations, and among the several States, and with the Indian Tribes;

To establish an uniform Rule of Naturalization, and uniform Laws on the subject of Bankruptcies throughout the United States;

To coin Money, regulate the Value thereof, and of foreign Coin, and fix the Standard of Weights and Measures;

To provide for the Punishment of counterfeiting the Securities and current Coin of the United States;

To establish Post Offices and post Roads;

To promote the Progress of Science and useful Arts, by securing for limited Times to Authors and Inventors the exclusive Right to their respective Writings and Discoveries;

To constitute Tribunals inferior to the supreme Court;

To define and punish Piracies and Felonies committed on the high Seas, and Offences against the Law of Nations;

To declare War, grant Letters of Marque and Reprisal, and make Rules concerning Captures on Land and Water;

To raise and support Armies, but no Appropriation of Money to that Use shall be for a longer Term than two Years;

To provide and maintain a Navy;

To make Rules for the Government and Regulation of the land and naval Forces;

To provide for calling forth the Militia to execute the Laws of the Union, suppress Insurrections and repel Invasions;

To provide for organizing, arming, and disciplining, the Militia, and for governing such Part of them as may be employed in the Service of the United States, reserving to the States respectively, the Appointment of the Officers, and the Authority of training the Militia according to the discipline prescribed by Congress;

To exercise exclusive Legislation in all Cases whatsoever, over such District (not exceeding ten Miles square) as may, by Cession of particular States, and the Acceptance of Congress, become the Seat of the Government of the United States, and to exercise like Authority over all Places purchased by the Consent of the Legislature of the State in which the Same shall be, for the Erection of Forts, Magazines, Arsenals, dock-Yards, and other needful Buildings;—And

To make all Laws which shall be necessary and proper for carrying into Execution the foregoing Powers, and all other Powers vested by this Constitution in the Government of the United States, or in any Department of Officer thereof.

Section 9

The Migration or Importation of such Persons as any of the States now existing shall think proper to admit, shall not be prohibited by the Congress prior to the Year one thousand eight hundred and eight, but a Tax or duty may be imposed on such Importation, not exceeding ten dollars for each Person.

The Privilege of the Writ of Habeas Corpus shall not be suspended, unless when in Cases of Rebellion or Invasion the public Safety may require it.

No Bill of Attainder or ex post facto Law shall be passed.

No Capitation, or other direct, Tax shall be laid, unless in Proportion to the Census or Enumeration herein before directed to be taken.

No Tax or Duty shall be laid on Articles exported from any State.

No Preference shall be given by any Regulation of Commerce or Revenue to the Ports of one State over those of another: nor shall Vessels bound to, or from, one State, be obliged to enter, clear, or pay Duties in another.

No Money shall be drawn from the Treasury, but in Consequence of Appropriations made by Law; and a regular Statement and Account of the Receipts and Expenditures of all public Money shall be published from time to time.

No Title of Nobility shall be granted by the United States: And no Person holding any Office of Profit or Trust under them, shall, without the Consent of the Congress, accept of any present, Emolument, Office, or Title, of any kind whatever, from any King, Prince, or foreign State.

Section 10

No State shall enter into any Treaty, Alliance, or Confederation; grant Letters of Marque and Reprisal; coin Money; emit Bills of Credit; make any Thing but gold and silver Coin a Tender in Payment of Debts; pass any Bill of Attainder, ex post facto Law, or Law impairing the obligation of Contracts, or grant any Title of Nobility.

No State shall, without the Consent of the Congress, lay any Imposts or Duties on Imports or Exports, except what may be absolutely necessary for executing its inspection Laws: and the net Produce of all Duties and Imposts, laid by any State on Imports or Exports, shall be for the Use of the Treasury of the United States; and all such Laws shall be subject to the Revision and Controul of the Congress.

No State shall, without the Consent of Congress, lay any Duty of Tonnage, keep Troops, or Ships of War in time of Peace, enter into any Agreement or Compact with another State, or with a foreign Power, or engage in War, unless actually invaded, or in such imminent Danger as will not admit of delay.

ARTICLE II

Section 1

The executive Power shall be vested in a President of the United States of America. He shall hold his Office during the Term of four Years, and, together with the Vice President, chosen for the same Term, be elected, as follows:

Each State shall appoint, in such Manner as the Legislature thereof may direct, a Number of Electors, equal to the whole Number of Senators and Representatives to which the State may be entitled in the Congress: but no Senator or Representative, or Person holding an Office of Trust or Profit under the United States, shall be appointed an Elector.

The Electors shall meet in their respective States, and vote by Ballot for two Persons, of whom one at least shall not be an Inhabitant of the same State with themselves. And they shall make a List of all the Persons voted for, and of the Number of Votes for each; which List they shall sign and certify, and transmit sealed to the Seat of the Government of the United States, directed to the President of the Senate. The President of the Senate shall, in the Presence of the Senate and House of Representatives, open all the Certificates, and the Votes shall then be counted. The Person having the greatest Number of Votes shall be the President, if such Number be a Majority of the whole number of Electors appointed; and if there be more than one who have such Majority, and have an equal Number of Votes, then the House of Representatives shall immediately chuse by Ballot one of them for President; and if no Person have a Majority, then from the five highest on the List the said House shall in like Manner chuse the President. But in chusing the President, the Votes shall be taken by States, the Representation from each State having one Vote; A quorum for this Purpose shall consist of a Member or Members from two thirds of the States, and a Majority of all the States shall be necessary to a Choice. In every Case, after the Choice of the President, the Person having the greatest Number of Votes of the Electors shall be the Vice President. But if there should remain two or more who have equal Votes, the Senate shall chuse from them by Ballot the Vice President.

The Congress may determine the time of chusing the Electors, and the Day on which they shall give their Votes; which Day shall be the same throughout the United States.

No person except a natural born Citizen, *or a Citizen of the United States, at the time of the Adoption of this Constitution,* shall be eligible to the Office of President; neither shall any Person be eligible to that Office who shall not have attained to the Age of thirty five Years, and been fourteen Years a Resident within the United States.

In Case of the Removal of the President from Office, or of his Death, Resignation, or Inability to discharge the Powers and Duties of the said Office, the Same shall devolve on the Vice President, and the Congress may by Law provide for the Case of Removal, Death, Resignation or Inability, both of the President and Vice President, declaring what Officer shall then act as President, and such Officer shall act accordingly, until the Disability be removed, or a President shall be elected.

The President shall, at stated Times, receive for his Services, a Compensation, which shall neither be increased nor diminished during the Period for which he shall have been elected, and he shall not receive within that period any other Emolument from the United States, or any of them.

Before he enter on the Execution of his Office, he shall take the following Oath or Affirmation:—"I do solemnly swear (or affirm) that I will faithfully execute the Office of President of the United States, and will to the best of my Ability, preserve, protect and defend the Constitution of the United States."

Section 2

The President shall be Commander in Chief of the Army and Navy of the United States, and of the Militia of the several States, when called into the actual Service of the United States; he may require the Opinion, in writing, of the principal Officer in each of the executive Departments, upon any Subject relating to the Duties of their respective Offices, and he shall have Power to grant Reprieves and Pardons for Offences against the United States, except in Cases of Impeachment.

He shall have Power, by and with the Advice and Consent of the Senate, to make Treaties, provided two thirds of the Senators present concur; and he shall nominate, and by and with the Advice and Consent of the Senate, shall appoint Ambassadors, other public Ministers and Consuls, Judges of the supreme Court, and all other Officers of the United States, whose Appointments are not herein otherwise provided for, and which shall be established by Law: but the Congress may by Law vest the Appointment of such inferior Officers, as they think proper in the President alone, in the Courts of Law, or in the Heads of Departments.

The President shall have Power to fill up all Vacancies that may happen during the Recess of the Senate, by granting Commissions which shall expire at the End of their next Session.

Section 3

He shall from time to time give to the Congress Information of the State of the Union, and recommend to their Consideration such Measures as he shall judge necessary and expedient; he may, on extraordinary Occasions, convene both Houses, or either of them, and in Case of disagreement between them, with Respect to the Time of Adjournment, he may adjourn them to such Time as he shall think proper; he shall receive Ambassadors and other public Ministers; he shall take Care that the Laws be faithfully executed, and shall Commission all the officers of the United States.

Section 4

The President, Vice President and all civil Officers of the United States, shall be removed from Office on Impeachment for, and Conviction of, Treason, Bribery or other high Crimes and Misdemeanors.

ARTICLE III

Section 1

The judicial Power of the United States, shall be vested in one supreme Court, and in such inferior Courts as the Congress may from time to time ordain and establish. The Judges, both of the supreme and inferior Courts, shall hold their offices during good Behaviour, and shall, at stated Times, receive for their Services, a Compensation, which shall not be diminished during their Continuance in Office.

Section 2

The judicial Power shall extend to all Cases, in Law and Equity, arising under this Constitution, the Laws of the United States, and Treaties made, or which shall be made, under their Authority;—to all Cases affecting Ambassadors, other public Ministers and Consuls;—to all Cases of admiralty and maritime Jurisdiction;—to Controversies to which the United States shall be a Party;—to Controversies between two or more States;—*between a State and Citizens of another State;*—between Citizens of different States;—between Citizens of the same State claiming Lands under Grants of different States, and between a State, or the Citizens thereof, and foreign States, Citizens or Subjects.

In all Cases affecting Ambassadors, other public Ministers and Consuls, and those in which a State shall be Party, the supreme Court shall have original Jurisdiction. In all the other Cases before mentioned, the supreme Court shall have appellate Jurisdiction, both as to Law and Fact, with such Exceptions, and under such Regulations as the Congress shall make.

The Trial of all Crimes, except in Cases of Impeachment, shall be by Jury; and such Trial shall be held in the State where the said Crimes shall have been committed, but when not committed within any State, the Trial shall be at such Place or Places as the Congress may by Law have directed.

Section 3

Treason against the United States, shall consist only in levying War against them, or in adhering to their Enemies, giving them Aid and Comfort. No person shall be convicted of Treason unless on the Testimony of two Witnesses to the same overt Act, or on Confession in open Court.

The Congress shall have Power to declare the Punishment of Treason, but no Attainder of Treason shall work Corruption of Blood, or Forfeiture except during the Life of the Person attainted.

ARTICLE IV

Section 1

Full Faith and Credit shall be given in each State to the public Acts, Records, and judicial Proceedings of every other State. And the Congress may by general Laws prescribe the Manner in which such Acts, Records and Proceedings shall be proved, and the Effect thereof.

Section 2

The Citizens of each State shall be entitled to all Privileges and Immunities of Citizens in the several States.

A Person charged in any State with Treason, Felony, or other Crime, who shall flee from Justice, and be found in another State, shall on Demand of the executive Authority of the State from which he fled, be delivered up, to be removed to the State having Jurisdiction of the Crime.

No Person held to Service or Labour in one State, under the Laws thereof, escaping into another, shall, in Consequence of any Law or Regulation therein, be discharged from such Service or Labour, but shall be delivered up on Claim of the Party to whom such Service or Labour may be due.

Section 3

New States may be admitted by the Congress into this Union; but no new State shall be formed or erected within the Jurisdiction of any other State; nor any State be formed by the Junction of two or more States, or Parts of States, without the Consent of the Legislatures of the States concerned as well as of the Congress.

The Congress shall have Power to dispose of and make all needful Rules and Regulations respecting the Territory or other Property belonging to the United States; and nothing in this Constitution shall be so construed as to Prejudice any Claims of the United States, or of any particular States.

Section 4

The United States shall guarantee to every State in this Union a Republican Form of Government, and shall protect each of them against Invasion; and on Application of the Legislature, or of the Executive (when the Legislature cannot be convened) against domestic violence.

ARTICLE V

The Congress, whenever two thirds of both Houses shall deem it necessary, shall propose Amendments to this Constitution, or, on the Application of the Legislatures of two thirds of the several States, shall call a Convention for proposing Amendments, which, in either Case, shall be valid to all Intents and Purposes, as Part of this Constitution, when ratified by the Legislatures of three fourths of the several States, or by Conventions in three fourths thereof, as the one or the other Mode of Ratification may be proposed by the Congress; Provided *that no Amendment which may be made prior to the Year One thousand eight hundred and eight shall in any Manner affect the first and fourth Clauses in the Ninth Section of the first Article*; and that no State, without its Consent, shall be deprived of its equal Suffrage in the Senate.

ARTICLE VI

All Debts contracted and Engagements entered into, before the Adoption of this Constitution, shall be as valid against the United States under this Constitution, as under the Confederation.

This Constitution, and Laws of the United States which shall be made in Pursuance thereof; and all Treaties made, or which shall be made, under the Authority of the United States, shall be the supreme Law of the Land; and the Judges in every State shall be bound thereby, any Thing in the Constitution or Laws of any State to the Contrary notwithstanding.

The Senators and Representatives before mentioned, and the Members of the several State Legislatures, and all executive and Judicial Officers, both of the United States and of the several States, shall be bound by Oath or Affirmation, to support this Constitution; but no religious Test shall ever be required as a Qualification to any Office of public Trust under the United States.

ARTICLE VII

The Ratification of the Conventions of nine States, shall be sufficient for the Establishment of this Constitution between the States so ratifying the Same.

Done in Convention by the Unanimous Consent of the States present the Seventeenth Day of September in the Year of our Lord one thousand seven hundred and Eighty seven and of the Independence of the United States of America the Twelfth* IN WITNESS whereof We have hereunto subscribed our Names,

George Washington
President and Deputy from Virginia

Delaware
George Read
Gunning Bedford, Jr.
John Dickinson
Richard Bassett
Jacob Broom

Maryland
James McHenry
Daniel of St. Thomas Jenifer
Daniel Carroll

Virginia
John Blair
James Madison, Jr.

North Carolina
William Blount
Richard Dobbs Spraight
Hugh Williamson

South Carolina
John Rutledge
Charles Cotesworth Pinckney
Charles Pinckney
Pierce Butler

Georgia
William Few
Abraham Baldwin

New Hampshire
John Langdon
Nicholas Gilman

Massachusetts
Nathaniel Gorham
Rufus King

Connecticut
William Samuel Johnson
Roger Sherman

New York
Alexander Hamilton

New Jersey
William Livingston
David Brearley
William Paterson
Jonathan Dayton

Pennsylvania
Benjamin Franklin
Thomas Mifflin
Robert Morris
George Clymer
Thomas FitzSimons
Jared Ingersoll
James Wilson
Gouverneur Morris

*The Constitution was submitted on September 17, 1787, by the Constitutional Convention, was ratified by the Convention of several states at various dates up to May 29, 1790, and became effective on March 4, 1789.

AMENDMENTS TO THE CONSTITUTION

AMENDMENT I

Congress shall make no law respecting an establishment of religion, or prohibiting the free exercise thereof; or abridging the freedom of speech, or of the press; or the right of the people peaceably to assemble, and to petition the Government for a redress of grievances.

AMENDMENT II

A well regulated Militia being necessary to the security of a free State, the right of the people to keep and bear Arms, shall not be infringed.

AMENDMENT III

No Soldier shall, in time of peace be quartered in any house, without the consent of the Owner, nor in time of war, but in a manner to be prescribed by law.

AMENDMENT IV

The right of the people to be secure in their persons, houses, papers, and effects, against unreasonable searches and seizures, shall not be violated, and no Warrants shall issue, but upon probable cause, supported by Oath or affirmation, and particularly describing the place to be searched, and the persons or things to be seized.

AMENDMENT V

No person shall be held to answer for a capital, or otherwise infamous crime, unless on a presentment or indictment of a Grand Jury, except in cases arising in the land or naval forces, or in the Militia, when in actual service in time of War or public danger; nor shall any person be subject for the same offense to be twice put in jeopardy of life or limb; nor shall be compelled in any criminal case to be a witness against himself, nor be deprived of life, liberty, or property, without due process of law; nor shall private property be taken for public use, without just compensation.

AMENDMENT VI

In all criminal prosecutions, the accused shall enjoy the right to a speedy and public trial, by an impartial jury of the State and district wherein the crime shall have been committed, which district shall have been previously ascertained by law, and to be informed of the nature and cause of the accusation; to be confronted with the witnesses against him; to have compulsory process for obtaining witnesses in his favor, and to have the Assistance of Counsel for his defence.

AMENDMENT VII

In Suits at common law, where the value in controversy shall exceed twenty dollars, the right of trial by jury shall be preserved, and no fact tried by a jury, shall be otherwise reexamined in any Court of the United States, than according to the rules of the common law.

AMENDMENT VIII

Excessive bail shall not be required, nor excessive fines imposed, nor cruel and unusual punishments inflicted.

AMENDMENT IX

The enumeration in the Constitution, of certain rights, shall not be construed to deny or disparage others retained by the people.

AMENDMENT X*

The powers not delegated to the United States by the Constitution, nor prohibited by it to the States, are reserved to the States respectively, or to the people.

AMENDMENT XI
[ADOPTED 1798]

The Judicial power of the United States shall not be construed to extend to any suit in law or equity, commenced or prosecuted against one of the United States by Citizens of another State, or by Citizens or Subjects of any Foreign State.

AMENDMENT XII
[ADOPTED 1804]

The Electors shall meet in their respective states, and vote by ballot for President and Vice President, one of whom, at least, shall not be an inhabitant of the same state with themselves; they shall name in their ballots the person voted for as President, and in distinct ballots the person voted for as Vice President, and they shall make distinct lists of all persons voted for as President, and of all persons voted for as Vice President, and of the number of votes for each, which lists they shall sign and certify, and transmit sealed to the seat of the government of the United States, directed to the President of the Senate;—The President of the Senate shall, in the presence of the Senate and House of Representatives, open all the certificates and the votes shall then be counted;—The person having the greatest number of votes for President, shall be the President, if such number be a majority of the whole number of Electors appointed; and if no person have such majority, then from the persons having the highest numbers not exceeding three on the list of those voted for as President, the House of Representatives shall choose immediately, by ballot, the President. But in choosing the President, the votes shall be taken by states, the representation from each state having one vote; a quorum for this purpose shall consist of a member or members from two-thirds of the states, and a majority of all the states shall be necessary to a choice. And if the House of Representatives shall not choose a President whenever the

---

*The first ten amendments (the Bill of Rights) were ratified and their adoption was certified on December 15, 1791.

right of choice shall devolve upon them, before *the fourth day of March* next following, then the Vice President shall act as President, as in the case of the death or other constitutional disability of the President.—The person having the greatest number of votes as Vice President, shall be the Vice President, if such number be a majority of the whole number of Electors appointed, and if no person have a majority, then from the two highest numbers on the list, the Senate shall choose the Vice President; a quorum for the purpose shall consist of two-thirds of the whole number of Senators, and a majority of the whole number shall be necessary to a choice. But no person constitutionally ineligible to the office of President shall be eligible to that of Vice President of the United States.

AMENDMENT XIII
[ADOPTED 1865]

Section 1
Neither slavery nor involuntary servitude, except as a punishment for crime whereof the party shall have been duly convicted, shall exist within the United States, or any place subject to their jurisdiction.

Section 2
Congress shall have power to enforce this article by appropriate legislation.

AMENDMENT XIV
[ADOPTED 1868]

Section 1
All persons born or naturalized in the United States, and subject to the jurisdiction thereof, are citizens of the United States and of the State wherein they reside. No State shall make or enforce any law which shall abridge the privileges or immunities of citizens of the United States; nor shall any State deprive any person of life, liberty, or property, without due process of law; nor deny to any person within its jurisdiction the equal protection of the laws.

Section 2
Representatives shall be apportioned among the several States according to their respective numbers, counting the whole number of persons in each State, excluding Indians not taxed. But when the right to vote at any election for the choice of electors for President and Vice President of the United States, Representatives in Congress, the Executive and Judicial officers of a State, or the members of the Legislature thereof, is denied to any of the male inhabitants of such State, being twenty-one years of age, and citizens of the United States, or in any way abridged, except for participation in rebellion, or other crime, the basis of representation therein shall be reduced in the proportion which the number of such male citizens shall bear to the whole number of male citizens twenty-one years of age in such State.

Section 3
No person shall be a Senator or Representative in Congress, or elector of President and Vice President, or hold any office, civil or military, under the United States, or under any State, who, having previously taken an oath, as a member of Congress, or as an officer of the United States, or as a member of any State legislature, or as an executive or judicial officer of any State, to support the Constitution of the United States, shall have engaged in insurrection or rebellion against the same, or given aid or comfort to the enemies thereof. But Congress may by a vote of two-thirds of each House, remove such disability.

Section 4
The validity of the public debt of the United States, authorized by law, including debts incurred for payment of pensions and bounties for services in suppressing insurrection or rebellion, shall not be questioned. But neither the United States nor any State shall assume or pay any debt or obligation incurred in aid of insurrection or rebellion against the United States, or any claim for the loss or emancipation of any slave; but all such debts, obligations and claims shall be held illegal and void.

Section 5
The Congress shall have power to enforce, by appropriate legislation, the provisions of this article.

AMENDMENT XV
[ADOPTED 1870]

Section 1
The right of citizens of the United States to vote shall not be denied or abridged by the United States or by any State on account of race, color, or previous condition of servitude.

Section 2
The Congress shall have power to enforce this article by appropriate legislation.

AMENDMENT XVI
[ADOPTED 1913]
The Congress shall have power to lay and collect taxes on incomes, from whatever source derived, without apportionment among the several States, and without regard to any census or enumeration.

AMENDMENT XVII
[ADOPTED 1913]
The Senate of the United States shall be composed of two Senators from each State, elected by the people thereof, for six years; and each Senator shall have one vote. The electors in each State shall have the qualifications requisite for electors of the most numerous branch of the State legislatures.

When vacancies happen in the representation of any State in the Senate, the executive authority of such State shall issue writs of election to fill such vacancies: *Provided,* That the legislature of any State may empower the executive thereof to make temporary appointments until the people fill the vacancies by election as the legislature may direct.

This amendment shall not be so construed as to affect the election or term of any Senator chosen before it becomes valid as part of the Constitution.

AMENDMENT XVIII
[ADOPTED 1919, REPEALED 1933]

Section 1

After one year from the ratification of this article the manufacture, sale, or transportation of intoxicating liquors within, the importation thereof into, or the exportation thereof from the United States and all territory subject to the jurisdiction thereof for beverage purposes is hereby prohibited.

Section 2

The Congress and the several States shall have concurrent power to enforce this article by appropriate legislation.

Section 3

This article shall be inoperative unless it shall have been ratified as an amendment to the Constitution by the legislatures of the several States, as provided in the Constitution, within seven years from the date of the submission hereof to the States by the Congress.

AMENDMENT XIX
[ADOPTED 1920]

The right of citizens of the United States to vote shall not be denied or abridged by the United States or by any State on account of sex.

Congress shall have power to enforce this article by appropriate legislation.

AMENDMENT XX
[ADOPTED 1933]

Section 1

The terms of the President and Vice President shall end at noon on the 20th day of January, and the terms of Senators and Representatives at noon on the 3d day of January, of the years in which such terms would have ended if this article had not been ratified and the terms of their successors shall then begin.

Section 2

The Congress shall assemble at least once in every year, and such meeting shall begin at noon on the 3d day of January, unless they shall by law appoint a different day.

Section 3

If, at the time fixed for the beginning of the term of the President, the President elect shall have died, the Vice President elect shall become President. If a President shall not have been chosen before the time fixed for the beginning of his term, or if the President elect shall have failed to qualify, then the Vice President elect shall act as President until a President shall have qualified; and the Congress may by law provide for the case wherein neither a President elect nor a Vice President elect shall have qualified, declaring who

shall then act as President, or the manner in which one who is to act shall be selected, and such person shall act accordingly until a President or Vice President shall have qualified.

Section 4

The Congress may by law provide for the case of the death of any of the persons from whom the House of Representatives may choose a President whenever the right of choice shall have devolved upon them, and for the case of the death of any of the persons from whom the Senate may choose a Vice President whenever the right of choice shall have devolved upon them.

Section 5

Sections 1 and 2 shall take effect on the 15th day of October following the ratification of this article.

Section 6

This article shall be inoperative unless it shall have been ratified as an amendment to the Constitution by the legislatures of three fourths of the several States within seven years from the date of its submission.

AMENDMENT XXI
[ADOPTED 1933]

Section 1

The eighteenth article of amendment to the Constitution of the United States is hereby repealed.

Section 2

The transportation or importation into any State, Territory, or possession of the United States for delivery or use therein of intoxicating liquors in violation of the laws thereof, is hereby prohibited.

Section 3

This article shall be inoperative unless it shall have been ratified as an amendment to the Constitution by conventions in the several States, as provided in the Constitution, within seven years from the date of the submission hereof to the States by the Congress.

AMENDMENT XXII
[ADOPTED 1951]

Section 1

No person shall be elected to the office of the President more than twice, and no person who has held the office of President, or acted as President, for more than two years of a term to which some other person was elected President shall be elected to the office of the President more than once. But this Article shall not apply to any person holding the office of President when this Article was proposed by the Congress, and shall not prevent any person who may be holding the office of President, or acting as President, during the term within which this Article becomes operative from holding the office of President or acting as President during the remainder of such term.

Section 2

This article shall be inoperative unless it shall have been ratified as an amendment to the Constitution by the legislatures of three-fourths of the several States within seven years from the date of its submission to the States by the Congress.

AMENDMENT XXIII
[ADOPTED 1961]

Section 1

The District constituting the seat of Government of the United States shall appoint in such manner as the Congress shall direct:

A number of electors of President and Vice President equal to the whole number of Senators and Representatives in Congress to which the District would be entitled if it were a State, but in no event more than the least populous State; they shall be in addition to those appointed by the States, but they shall be considered, for the purposes of the election of President and Vice President, to be electors appointed by a State; and they shall meet in the District and perform such duties as provided by the twelfth article of amendment.

Section 2

The Congress shall have power to enforce this article by appropriate legislation.

AMENDMENT XXIV
[ADOPTED 1964]

Section 1

The right of citizens of the United States to vote in any primary or other election for President or Vice President, for electors for President or Vice President, or for Senator or Representative in Congress, shall not be denied or abridged by the United States or any state by reason of failure to pay any poll tax or other tax.

Section 2

The Congress shall have the power to enforce this article by appropriate legislation.

AMENDMENT XXV
[ADOPTED 1967]

Section 1

In case of the removal of the President from office or his death or resignation, the Vice President shall become President.

Section 2

Whenever there is a vacancy in the office of the Vice President, the President shall nominate a Vice President who shall take the office upon confirmation by a majority vote of both houses of Congress.

Section 3

Whenever the President transmits to the President pro tempore of the Senate and the Speaker of the House of Representatives his written declaration that he is unable to discharge the powers and duties of his office, and until he transmits to them a written declaration to the contrary, such powers and duties shall be discharged by the Vice President as Acting President.

Section 4

Whenever the Vice President and a majority of either the principal officers of the executive departments or of such other body as Congress may by law provide, transmit to the President pro tempore of the Senate and the Speaker of the House of Representatives their written declaration that the President is unable to discharge the powers and duties of his office, the Vice President shall immediately assume the powers and duties of the office as Acting President.

Thereafter, when the President transmits to the President pro tempore of the Senate and the Speaker of the House of Representatives his written declaration that no inability exists, he shall resume the powers and duties of his office unless the Vice President and a majority of either the principal officers of the executive department or of such other body as Congress may by law provide, transmit within four days to the President pro tempore of the Senate and the Speaker of the House of Representatives their written declaration that the President is unable to discharge the powers and duties of his office. Thereupon Congress shall decide the issue, assembling within 48 hours for that purpose if not in session. If the Congress, within 21 days after receipt of the latter written declaration, or, if Congress is not in session, within 21 days after Congress is required to assemble, determines by two-thirds vote of both houses that the President is unable to discharge the powers and duties of his office, the Vice President shall continue to discharge the same as Acting President; otherwise, the President shall resume the powers and duties of his office.

AMENDMENT XXVI
[ADOPTED 1971]

Section 1

The right of citizens of the United States, who are 18 years of age or older, to vote shall not be denied or abridged by the United States or any state on account of age.

Section 2

The Congress shall have the power to enforce this article by appropriate legislation.

AMENDMENT XXVII
[ADOPTED 1992]

No law, varying the compensation for the services of the Senators and Representatives shall take effect, until an election of Representatives shall have intervened.

PRESIDENTIAL ELECTIONS

Year	Candidates	Parties	Popular Vote	Electoral Vote	Voter Participation
1789	**George Washington**		*	69	
	John Adams			34	
	Others			35	
1792	**George Washington**		*	132	
	John Adams			77	
	George Clinton			50	
	Others			5	
1796	**John Adams**	Federalist	*	71	
	Thomas Jefferson	Democratic-Republican		68	
	Thomas Pinckney	Federalist		59	
	Aaron Burr	Dem.-Rep.		30	
	Others			48	
1800	**Thomas Jefferson**	Dem.-Rep.	*	73	
	Aaron Burr	Dem.-Rep.		73	
	John Adams	Federalist		65	
	C. C. Pinckney	Federalist		64	
	John Jay	Federalist		1	
1804	**Thomas Jefferson**	Dem.-Rep.	*	162	
	C. C. Pinckney	Federalist		14	
1808	**James Madison**	Dem.-Rep.	*	122	
	C. C. Pinckney	Federalist		47	
	George Clinton	Dem.-Rep.		6	
1812	**James Madison**	Dem.-Rep.	*	128	
	De Witt Clinton	Federalist		89	
1816	**James Monroe**	Dem.-Rep.	*	183	
	Rufus King	Federalist		34	
1820	**James Monroe**	Dem.-Rep.	*	231	
	John Quincy Adams	Dem.-Rep.		1	
1824	**John Quincy Adams**	Dem.-Rep.	108,740 (30.5%)	84	26.9%
	Andrew Jackson	Dem.-Rep.	153,544 (43.1%)	99	
	William H. Crawford	Dem.-Rep.	46,618 (13.1%)	41	
	Henry Clay	Dem.-Rep.	47,136 (13.2%)	37	
1828	**Andrew Jackson**	Democratic	647,286 (56.0%)	178	57.6%
	John Quincy Adams	National Republican	508,064 (44.0%)	83	

*Electors selected by state legislatures.

Year	Candidates	Parties	Popular Vote	Electoral Vote	Voter Participation
1832	**Andrew Jackson**	Democratic	687,502 (55.0%)	219	55.4%
	Henry Clay	National Republican	530,189 (42.4%)	49	
	John Floyd	Independent		11	
	William Wirt	Anti-Mason	33,108 (2.6%)	7	
1836	**Martin Van Buren**	Democratic	765,483 (50.9%)	170	57.8%
	William Henry Harrison	Whig		73	
	Hugh L. White	Whig	739,795 (49.1%)	26	
	Daniel Webster	Whig		14	
	W. P. Magnum	Independent		11	
1840	**William Henry Harrison**	Whig	1,274,624 (53.1%)	234	80.2%
	Martin Van Buren	Democratic	1,127,781 (46.9%)	60	
	J. G. Birney	Liberty	7069	—	
1844	**James K. Polk**	Democratic	1,338,464 (49.6%)	170	78.9%
	Henry Clay	Whig	1,300,097 (48.1%)	105	
	J. G. Birney	Liberty	62,300 (2.3%)	—	
1848	**Zachary Taylor**	Whig	1,360,967 (47.4%)	163	72.7%
	Lewis Cass	Democratic	1,222,342 (42.5%)	127	
	Martin Van Buren	Free-Soil	291,263 (10.1%)	—	
1852	**Franklin Pierce**	Democratic	1,601,117 (50.9%)	254	69.6%
	Winfield Scott	Whig	1,385,453 (44.1%)	42	
	John P. Hale	Free-Soil	155,825 (5.0%)	—	
1856	**James Buchanan**	Democratic	1,832,955 (45.3%)	174	78.9%
	John C. Frémont	Republican	1,339,932 (33.1%)	114	
	Millard Fillmore	American	871,731 (21.6%)	8	
1860	**Abraham Lincoln**	Republican	1,865,593 (39.8%)	180	81.2%
	Stephen A. Douglas	Democratic	1,382,713 (29.5%)	12	
	John C. Breckinridge	Democratic	848,356 (18.1%)	72	
	John Bell	Union	592,906 (12.6%)	39	
1864	**Abraham Lincoln**	Republican	2,213,655 (55.0%)	212*	73.8%
	George B. McClellan	Democratic	1,805,237 (45.0%)	21	
1868	**Ulysses S. Grant**	Republican	3,012,833 (52.7%)	214	78.1%
	Horatio Seymour	Democratic	2,703,249 (47.3%)	80	
1872	**Ulysses S. Grant**	Republican	3,597,132 (55.6%)	286	71.3%
	Horace Greeley	Dem.; Liberal Republican	2,834,125 (43.9%)	66†	
1876	**Rutherford B. Hayes‡**	Republican	4,036,298 (48.0%)	185	81.8%
	Samuel J. Tilden	Democratic	4,300,590 (51.0%)	184	
1880	**James A. Garfield**	Republican	4,454,416 (48.5%)	214	79.4%
	Winfield S. Hancock	Democratic	4,444,952 (48.1%)	155	

*Eleven secessionist states did not participate.
†Greeley died before the electoral college met. His electoral votes were divided among the four minor candidates.
‡Contested result settled by special election.

Year	Candidates	Parties	Popular Vote	Electoral Vote	Voter Participation
1884	**Grover Cleveland**	Democratic	4,874,986 (48.5%)	219	77.5%
	James G. Blaine	Republican	4,851,981 (48.2%)	182	
1888	**Benjamin Harrison**	Republican	5,439,853 (47.9%)	233	79.3%
	Grover Cleveland	Democratic	5,540,309 (48.6%)	168	
1892	**Grover Cleveland**	Democratic	5,556,918 (46.1%)	277	74.7%
	Benjamin Harrison	Republican	5,176,108 (43.0%)	145	
	James B. Weaver	People's	1,041,028 (8.5%)	22	
1896	**William McKinley**	Republican	7,104,779 (51.1%)	271	79.3%
	William Jennings Bryan	Democratic People's	6,502,925 (47.7%)	176	
1900	**William McKinley**	Republican	7,207,923 (51.7%)	292	73.2%
	William Jennings Bryan	Dem.-Populist	6,358,133 (45.5%)	155	
1904	**Theodore Roosevelt**	Republican	7,623,486 (57.9%)	336	65.2%
	Alton B. Parker	Democratic	5,077,911 (37.6%)	140	
	Eugene V. Debs	Socialist	402,283 (3.0%)	—	
1908	**William H. Taft**	Republican	7,678,908 (51.6%)	321	65.4%
	William Jennings Bryan	Democratic	6,409,104 (43.1%)	162	
	Eugene V. Debs	Socialist	420,793 (2.8%)	—	
1912	**Woodrow Wilson**	Democratic	6,293,454 (41.9%)	435	58.8%
	Theodore Roosevelt	Progressive	4,119,538 (27.4%)	88	
	William H. Taft	Republican	3,484,980 (23.2%)	8	
	Eugene V. Debs	Socialist	900,672 (6.0%)	—	
1916	**Woodrow Wilson**	Democratic	9,129,606 (49.4%)	277	61.6%
	Charles E. Hughes	Republican	8,538,221 (46.2%)	254	
	A. L. Benson	Socialist	585,113 (3.2%)	—	
1920	**Warren G. Harding**	Republican	16,152,200 (60.4%)	404	49.2%
	James M. Cox	Democratic	9,147,353 (34.2%)	127	
	Eugene V. Debs	Socialist	919,799 (3.4%)	—	
1924	**Calvin Coolidge**	Republican	15,725,016 (54.0%)	382	48.9%
	John W. Davis	Democratic	8,386,503 (28.8%)	136	
	Robert M. La Follette	Progressive	4,822,856 (16.6%)	13	
1928	**Herbert Hoover**	Republican	21,391,381 (58.2%)	444	56.9%
	Alfred E. Smith	Democratic	15,016,443 (40.9%)	87	
	Norman Thomas	Socialist	267,835 (0.7%)	—	
1932	**Franklin D. Roosevelt**	Democratic	22,821,857 (57.4%)	472	56.9%
	Herbert Hoover	Republican	15,761,841 (39.7%)	59	
	Norman Thomas	Socialist	881,951 (2.2%)	—	
1936	**Franklin D. Roosevelt**	Democratic	27,751,597 (60.8%)	523	61.0%
	Alfred M. Landon	Republican	16,679,583 (36.5%)	8	
	William Lemke	Union	882,479 (1.9%)	—	
1940	**Franklin D. Roosevelt**	Democratic	27,244,160 (54.8%)	449	62.5%
	Wendell L. Willkie	Republican	22,305,198 (44.8%)	82	
1944	**Franklin D. Roosevelt**	Democratic	25,602,504 (53.5%)	432	55.9%
	Thomas E. Dewey	Republican	22,006,285 (46.0%)	99	

Year	Candidates	Parties	Popular Vote	Electoral Vote	Voter Participation
1948	**Harry S Truman**	Democratic	24,105,695 (49.5%)	304	53.0%
	Thomas E. Dewey	Republican	21,969,170 (45.1%)	189	
	J. Strom Thurmond	State-Rights Democratic	1,169,021 (2.4%)	38	
	Henry A. Wallace	Progressive	1,156,103 (2.4%)	—	
1952	**Dwight D. Eisenhower**	Republican	33,936,252 (55.1%)	442	63.3%
	Adlai E. Stevenson	Democratic	27,314,992 (44.4%)	89	
1956	**Dwight D. Eisenhower**	Republican	35,575,420 (57.6%)	457	60.6%
	Adlai E. Stevenson	Democratic	26,033,066 (42.1%)	73	
	Other	—	—	1	
1960	**John F. Kennedy**	Democratic	34,227,096 (49.9%)	303	62.8%
	Richard M. Nixon	Republican	34,108,546 (49.6%)	219	
	Other	—	—	15	
1964	**Lyndon B. Johnson**	Democratic	43,126,506 (61.1%)	486	61.7%
	Barry M. Goldwater	Republican	27,176,799 (38.5%)	52	
1968	**Richard M. Nixon**	Republican	31,770,237 (43.4%)	301	60.6%
	Hubert H. Humphrey	Democratic	31,270,533 (42.7%)	191	
	George Wallace	American Indep.	9,906,141 (13.5%)	46	
1972	**Richard M. Nixon**	Republican	47,169,911 (60.7%)	520	55.2%
	George S. McGovern	Democratic	29,170,383 (37.5%)	17	
	Other	—	—	1	
1976	**Jimmy Carter**	Democratic	40,828,587 (50.0%)	297	53.5%
	Gerald R. Ford	Republican	39,147,613 (47.9%)	241	
	Other	—	1,575,459 (2.1%)	—	
1980	**Ronald Reagan**	Republican	43,901,812 (50.7%)	489	52.6%
	Jimmy Carter	Democratic	35,483,820 (41.0%)	49	
	John B. Anderson	Independent	5,719,722 (6.6%)	—	
	Ed Clark	Libertarian	921,188 (1.1%)	—	
1984	**Ronald Reagan**	Republican	54,455,075 (59.0%)	525	53.3%
	Walter Mondale	Democratic	37,577,185 (41.0%)	13	
1988	**George H. W. Bush**	Republican	48,886,000 (53.4%)	426	57.4%
	Michael S. Dukakis	Democratic	41,809,000 (45.6%)	111	
1992	**William J. Clinton**	Democratic	43,728,375 (43%)	370	55.0%
	George H. W. Bush	Republican	38,167,416 (38%)	168	
	H. Ross Perot	Independent	19,237,247 (19%)	—	
1996	**William J. Clinton**	Democratic	45,590,703 (50%)	379	48.8%
	Robert Dole	Republican	37,816,307 (41%)	159	
	Ross Perot	Reform	7,866,284		
2000	**George W. Bush**	Republican	50,456,167 (47.88%)	271	51.2%
	Al Gore	Democratic	50,996,064 (48.39%)	266*	
	Ralph Nader	Green	2,864,810 (2.72%)	—	
	Other		834,774 (less than 1%)	—	

*One District of Columbia Gore elector abstained.

Maps

Political and Physical Map of the United States

Political Map of the World

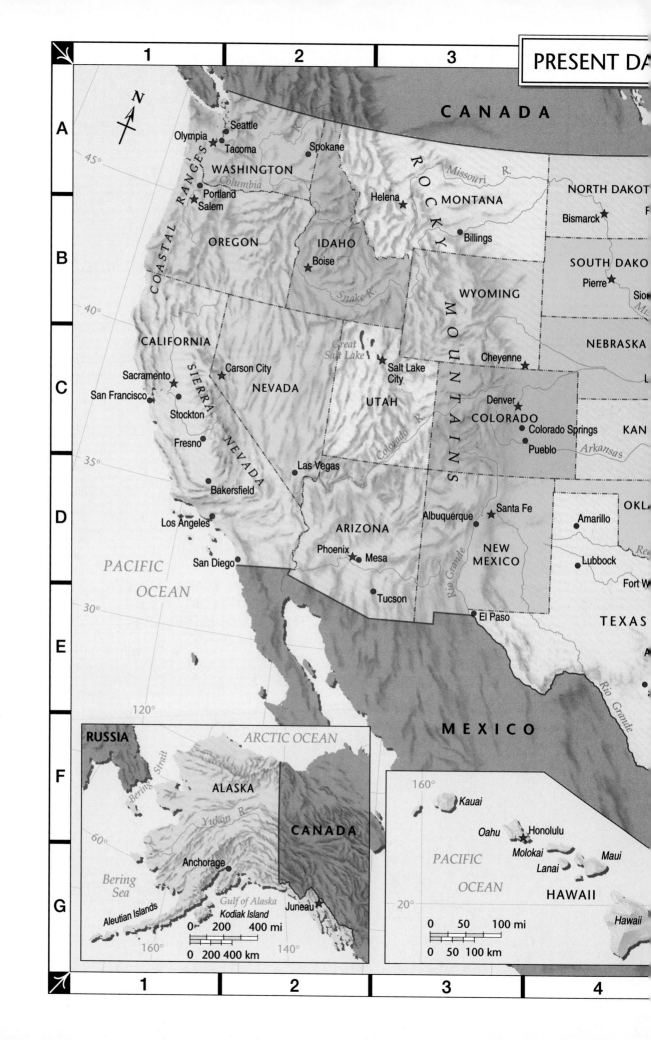

CANADA

1 2 3

A

B

C

D

E

F

G

1 2 3 4

Seattle
Olympia
Tacoma
Spokane
45°
WASHINGTON
Columbia
Portland
Salem
OREGON
IDAHO
Boise
Snake R.
40°
CALIFORNIA
Great
Salt Lake
Carson City
Sacramento
San Francisco
Stockton
Fresno
35°
Las Vegas
Bakersfield
Los Angeles
San Diego
Phoenix Mesa
Tucson
PACIFIC
OCEAN
30°
120°

ROCKY
Missouri R.
Helena
MONTANA
Billings
NORTH DAKOT
Bismarck
SOUTH DAKO
Pierre
Siou
WYOMING
Mi
M
O
U
N
T
A
I
N
S
Salt Lake
City
UTAH
Cheyenne
NEBRASKA
Denver
COLORADO
Colorado Springs
Pueblo
KAN
Arkansas
Colorado R.
Albuquerque Santa Fe
ARIZONA
NEW
MEXICO
Rio Grande
Amarillo
OKLA
Lubbock
Red
Fort W
El Paso
TEXAS
A
Rio Grande

SIERRA
NEVADA
COASTAL RANGES

MEXICO

RUSSIA
ARCTIC OCEAN
Bering Strait
ALASKA
Yukon R.
CANADA
Bering
Sea
Anchorage
60°
Aleutian Islands
Kodiak Island
Juneau
Gulf of Alaska
0   200   400 mi
0 200 400 km
160° 140°

160°
Kauai
Oahu Honolulu
Molokai
Lanai Maui
PACIFIC
OCEAN
HAWAII
Hawaii
20°
0   50   100 mi
0   50 100 km

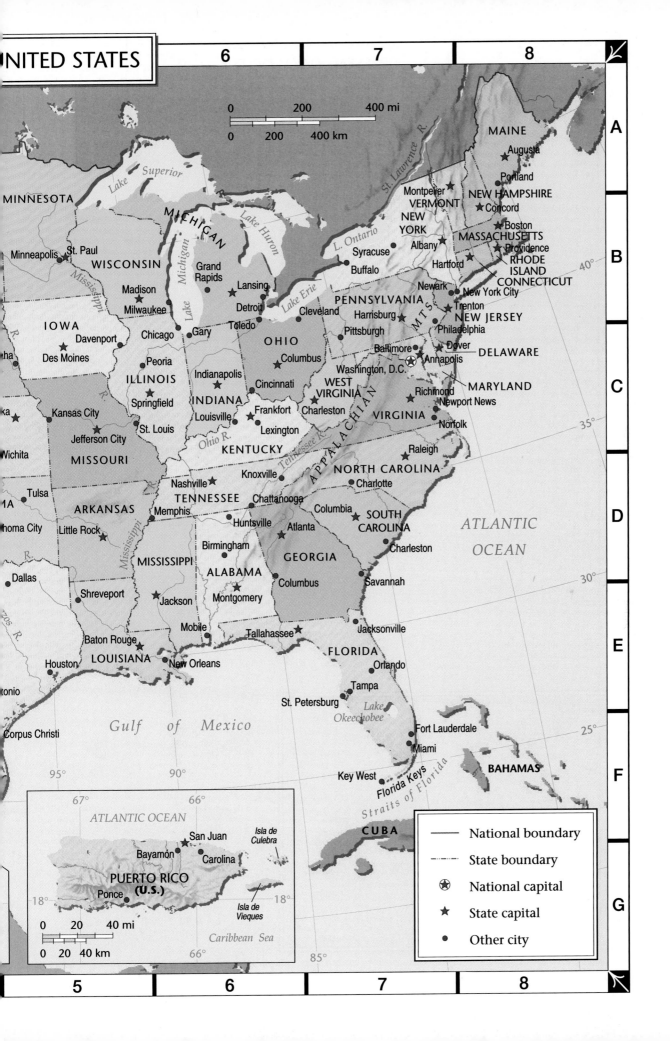

UNITED STATES

6 | **7** | **8**

0   200   400 mi
0   200   400 km

A

MAINE

★ Augusta

● Portland

Montpelier ★
VERMONT   NEW HAMPSHIRE
★ Concord

NEW
YORK   ★ Boston
MASSACHUSETTS

Syracuse ●   Albany ●   ● Providence
● Buffalo   Hartford ★   RHODE
ISLAND
CONNECTICUT

MINNESOTA

Lake Superior

MICHIGAN

St. Lawrence R.

Lake Huron

L. Ontario

B

40°

Minneapolis ● St. Paul
WISCONSIN   ● Grand
Rapids   Lansing ★
● Madison   Detroit ●
Milwaukee ●   Toledo ●
Lake Michigan

Lake Erie

Newark ●   ● New York City
PENNSYLVANIA   Trenton ★
Harrisburg ★   NEW JERSEY
Pittsburgh ●   ● Philadelphia
Baltimore ●   ● Dover   DELAWARE
Annapolis ★
Washington, D.C. ✪   MARYLAND

A P P A L A C H I A N   M T S

IOWA   ● Davenport
ha ●   Des Moines ●
Chicago ●   Gary ●
● Peoria
ILLINOIS   Indianapolis ★
INDIANA   Cincinnati ●
Springfield ●   Louisville ●   Frankfort ★
ka ★   Kansas City ●   St. Louis ●   Lexington ●
Jefferson City ★
Wichita ●   MISSOURI   KENTUCKY

Cleveland ●
OHIO
Columbus ●

WEST
VIRGINIA
Charleston ●

C

35°

Richmond ★
● Newport News
VIRGINIA   ● Norfolk

● Raleigh

Knoxville ●   NORTH CAROLINA
Nashville ★
Tulsa ●   TENNESSEE   Chattanooga ●
ARKANSAS   Memphis ●   Huntsville ●
homa City ●   Little Rock ★

● Charlotte

Columbia ★
SOUTH
CAROLINA
● Charleston

D

30°

Dallas ●
Shreveport ●   Birmingham ●   Atlanta ★
MISSISSIPPI   ALABAMA   GEORGIA
Jackson ★   Montgomery ★   Columbus ●

● Savannah

ATLANTIC
OCEAN

Ohio R.

Tennessee R.

Mississippi

tonio ●   Baton Rouge ★
Houston ●   LOUISIANA   New Orleans ●
Mobile ●   Tallahassee ★
FLORIDA

Jacksonville ●

E

25°

Corpus Christi ●

Gulf   of   Mexico

Orlando ●
Tampa ●
St. Petersburg ●   Lake
Okeechobee

Fort Lauderdale ●

Miami ●

Brazos R.

F

Key West ●   Florida Keys
Straits of Florida

BAHAMAS

ATLANTIC OCEAN

67°   66°

San Juan ★
Bayamón ●   ● Carolina
Isla de
Culebra

PUERTO RICO
(U.S.)
Ponce ●

18°   18°
Isla de
Vieques

0   20   40 mi
0   20   40 km

95°   90°   85°

CUBA

Caribbean Sea

66°

——— National boundary

–·–·– State boundary

✪ National capital

★ State capital

● Other city

G

5 | **6** | **7** | **8**

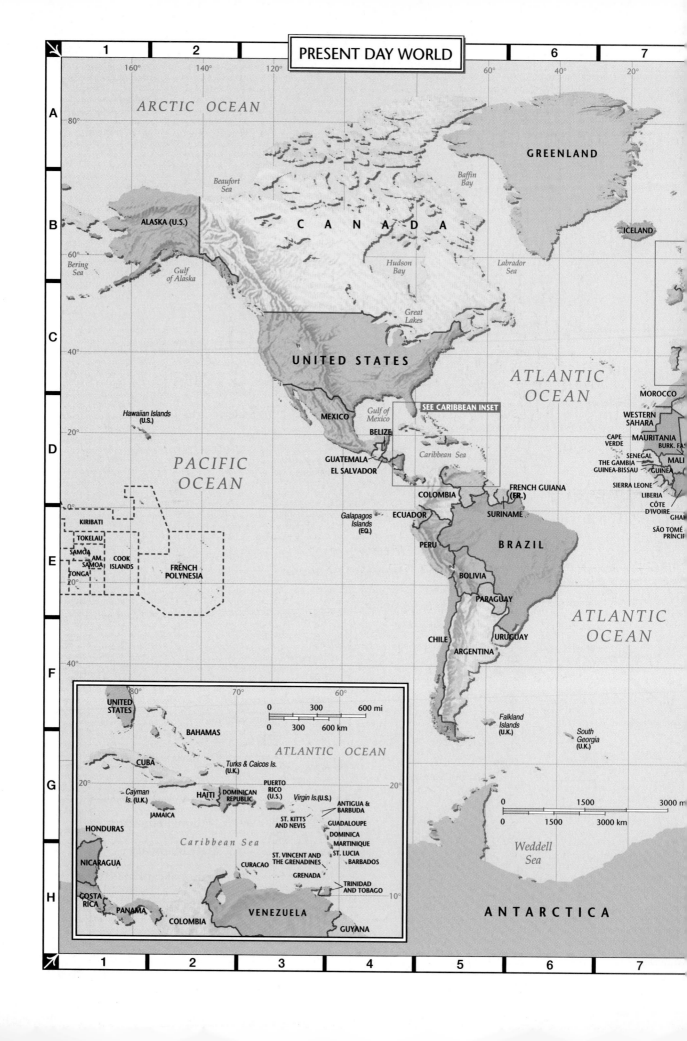

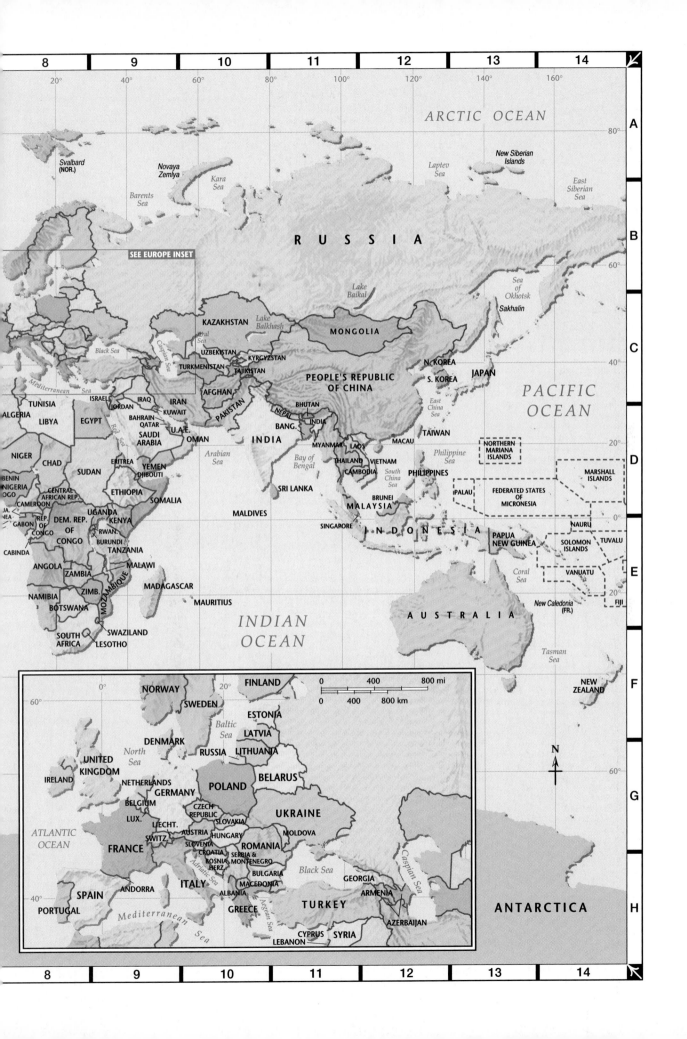

8 9 10 11 12 13 14

20° 40° 60° 80° 100° 120° 140° 160°

ARCTIC OCEAN

A 80°

Svalbard (NOR.) Novaya Zemlya Kara Sea Laptev Sea New Siberian Islands East Siberian Sea

Barents Sea B

R U S S I A 60°

SEE EUROPE INSET

Lake Baikal Sea of Okhotsk C

KAZAKHSTAN Lake Balkhash MONGOLIA Sakhalin

Aral Sea 40°

UZBEKISTAN KYRGYZSTAN N. KOREA JAPAN

Black Sea Caspian Sea TURKMENISTAN TAJIKISTAN PEOPLE'S REPUBLIC OF CHINA S. KOREA PACIFIC OCEAN

Mediterranean Sea AFGHAN.

TUNISIA ISRAEL IRAQ IRAN BHUTAN East China Sea

ALGERIA JORDAN KUWAIT PAKISTAN NEPAL INDIA TAIWAN 20°

LIBYA EGYPT BAHRAIN QATAR U.A.E. BANG. MACAU

NIGER CHAD SAUDI ARABIA OMAN INDIA MYANMAR LAOS Philippine Sea NORTHERN MARIANA ISLANDS

BENIN SUDAN ERITREA YEMEN Arabian Sea Bay of Bengal THAILAND VIETNAM MARSHALL ISLANDS

NIGERIA DJIBOUTI CAMBODIA South China Sea PHILIPPINES

TOGO CENTRAL AFRICAN REP. ETHIOPIA SOMALIA SRI LANKA BRUNEI PALAU FEDERATED STATES OF MICRONESIA 0°

JA. UGANDA MALAYSIA NAURU

NEA GABON REP. OF CONGO KENYA MALDIVES SINGAPORE I N D O N E S I A PAPUA NEW GUINEA SOLOMON ISLANDS TUVALU

CABINDA DEM. REP. OF CONGO RWAN. BURUNDI TANZANIA

ANGOLA ZAMBIA MALAWI Coral Sea VANUATU E

NAMIBIA ZIMB. MADAGASCAR MAURITIUS 20°

BOTSWANA MOZAMBIQUE INDIAN OCEAN A U S T R A L I A New Caledonia (FR.) FIJI

SOUTH AFRICA SWAZILAND LESOTHO Tasman Sea

NEW ZEALAND F

NORWAY FINLAND 0 400 800 mi

60° SWEDEN 0 400 800 km

Baltic Sea ESTONIA

DENMARK LATVIA

North Sea RUSSIA LITHUANIA N

UNITED KINGDOM 60° G

IRELAND NETHERLANDS POLAND BELARUS

GERMANY

BELGIUM CZECH REPUBLIC

LUX. LIECHT. SLOVAKIA UKRAINE

ATLANTIC OCEAN SWITZ. AUSTRIA HUNGARY MOLDOVA

FRANCE SLOVENIA ROMANIA Caspian Sea

CROATIA BOSNIA HERZ. SERBIA & MONTENEGRO

Adriatic Sea BULGARIA Black Sea GEORGIA

SPAIN ANDORRA ITALY MACEDONIA ARMENIA ANTARCTICA H

40° ALBANIA TURKEY AZERBAIJAN

PORTUGAL GREECE

Mediterranean Sea Aegean Sea CYPRUS SYRIA LEBANON

8 9 10 11 12 13 14

Glossary

Adams-Onís Treaty Signed by Secretary of State John Quincy Adams and Spanish minister Luis de Onís in 1819, this treaty allowed for U.S. annexation of Florida.

African Methodist Episcopal (AME) Church Richard Allen founded the African Methodist Episcopal Church in 1816 as the first independent black-run Protestant church in the United States. The AME Church was active in the promotion of abolition and the founding of educational institutions for free blacks.

Agricultural Adjustment Administration (AAA) Created by Congress in 1933 as part of the New Deal, this agency attempted to restrict agricultural production by paying farmers subsidies to take land out of production. The object was to raise farm prices, and it did, but the act did nothing for tenant farmers and sharecroppers. The Supreme Court declared it unconstitutional in 1936.

Agricultural Revolution The gradual shift from hunting and gathering to cultivating basic food crops that occurred worldwide from 7000 to 9000 years ago. This transition resulted in sedentary living, population growth, and establishment of permanent villages.

AIDS Acquired immune-deficiency syndrome (AIDS), a disease of the immune system transmitted through blood, especially by sexual contact or contaminated needles. AIDS reached epidemic proportions in the United States in the 1980s before it was gradually contained in the 1990s.

Alamo In 1835, Americans living in the Mexican state of Texas fomented a revolution. Mexico lost the conflict, but not before its troops defeated and killed a group of American rebels at the Alamo, a fort in San Antonio.

Albany Plan Plan of intercolonial cooperation proposed by prominent colonists including Benjamin Franklin at a conference in Albany, New York, in 1754. The plan envisioned the formation of a Grand Council of elected delegates from the colonies that would have powers to tax and provide for the common defense. It was rejected by the colonial and British governments, but was a prototype for colonial union.

Alien and Sedition Acts Collective name given to four laws passed in 1798 designed to suppress criticism of the federal government and to curb liberties of foreigners living in the United States.

American Colonization Society Founded in 1817, this abolitionist organization hoped to provide a mechanism by which slavery could gradually be eliminated. The society advocated the relocation of free blacks (followed by freed slaves) to the African colony of Monrovia, present day Liberia.

American Federation of Labor (AFL) Founded by Samuel Gompers in 1886, the AFL was a loose alliance of national craft unions that organized skilled workers by craft and worked for specific practical objectives such as higher wages, shorter hours, and better working conditions. The AFL avoided politics, and while it did not expressly forbid black and women workers from joining, it used exclusionary practices to keep them out.

American system A national economic strategy championed by Kentucky Senator Henry Clay, the American system stressed high tariffs and internal improvements.

Americans with Disabilities Act (ADA) Passed by Congress in 1991, this act banned discrimination against the disabled in employment and mandated easy access to all public and commercial buildings.

anaconda policy A key point in the Union's war strategy was encircling the South as an anaconda squeezes its prey. This plan entailed a naval blockade and the capture of the Mississippi River corridor.

Antifederalists Critics of the Constitution who expressed concern that it seemed to possess no specific provision for the protection of natural and civil rights. The antifederalists forced Congress to accept a number of amendments known as the **Bill of Rights.**

Anti-Imperialist League This organization was formed in November 1898 to fight against the **Treaty of Paris** ending the Spanish-American War. Members opposed the acquisition of overseas colonies by the United States, believing it would subvert American ideals and institutions. Membership centered in New England; the cause was less popular in the South and West.

Antinomianism Religious belief rejecting traditional moral law as unnecessary for Christians who possessed saving grace and affirming that an individual could experience divine revelation and salvation without the assistance of formally trained clergy.

Articles of Confederation Ratified in 1781, this document was the United States' first constitution, providing a framework for national government. The articles sharply limited central authority by denying the national government any taxation or coercive power.

Ashcan School This school of early twentieth-century realist painters took as their subjects the slums and streets of the nation's cities and the lives of ordinary urban dwellers. They often celebrated life in the city but also advocated political and social reform.

Axis Powers During World War II, the alliance between Italy, Germany, and Japan was known as the "Rome-Berlin-Tokyo axis," and the three members were called the Axis Powers. They fought against the Allied Powers, led by the United States, Britain, and the Soviet Union.

baby boom Post–World War II Americans idealized the family. The booming birth rate after the war led children born to this generation to be commonly referred to as "baby boomers."

backcountry In the eighteenth century, the edge of settlement extending from western Pennsylvania to Georgia. This region formed the second frontier as settlers moved westward from the Atlantic coast into the nation's interior.

Bacon's Rebellion An armed rebellion in Virginia (1675–1676) led by Nathaniel Bacon against the colony's royal governor Sir William Berkeley. Although some of his followers called for an end of special privilege in government, Bacon was chiefly interested in gaining a larger share of the lucrative Indian trade.

Bank of the United States National bank proposed by Secretary of the Treasury Alexander Hamilton and established in 1791. It served as a central depository for the U.S. government and had the authority to issue currency.

Bank war Between 1832–1836, Andrew Jackson used his presidential power to fight and ultimately destroy the second Bank of the United States.

Barbary War In response to constant attacks on trading vessels by pirates from the North African Barbary States, in 1801 President Thomas Jefferson sent a naval squadron to resolve the problem through military force. After failing to achieve most of its military objectives, the administration signed an 1805 treaty ending the war.

Baruch Plan In 1946, Bernard Baruch presented an American plan to control and eventually outlaw nuclear weapons. The plan called for United Nations control of nuclear weapons in three stages before the United States gave up its stockpile. Soviet insistence on immediate nuclear disarmament without inspection doomed the Baruch Plan and led to a nuclear arms race between the United States and the Soviet Union.

Bay of Pigs In April 1961, a group of Cuban exiles organized and supported by the U.S. Central Intelligence Agency (CIA) landed on the southern coast of Cuba in an effort to overthrow Fidel Castro. When the invasion ended in disaster, President Kennedy took full responsibility for the failure.

beats In the late 1950s, young poets and novelists such as Jack Kerouac became known as the beats or "beatniks" for their innovative writing and bizarre behavior. Calling themselves members of "the beat generation," they challenged the prevailing materialism of the consumer culture.

Berlin airlift In 1948, in response to a Soviet land blockade of Berlin, the United States carried out a massive effort to supply the two million Berlin citizens with food, fuel, and other goods by air for more than six months. The airlift forced the Soviets to end the blockade in 1949.

Berlin Wall In 1961, the Soviet Union built a high barrier to seal off their sector of Berlin in order to stop the flow of refugees out of the Soviet zone of Germany. The wall was torn down in 1989.

Bill of Rights The first ten amendments to the U.S. Constitution, adopted in 1791 to preserve the rights and liberties of individuals.

birds of passage Temporary migrants who came to the United States to work and save money and then returned home to their native countries during the slack season. World War I interrupted the practice, trapping thousands of migrant workers in the United States.

Black Codes Laws passed by southern states immediately after the Civil War in an effort to maintain the pre-war social order. The codes attempted to tie freedmen to field work and prevent them from becoming equal to white Southerners.

Bland-Allison Silver Purchase Act This act, a compromise between groups favoring the coinage of silver and those opposed to it, called for the partial coinage of silver. Those favoring silver coinage argued that it would add to the currency and help farmers and workers; those who opposed it pointed out that few other major countries accepted silver coinage. President Rutherford B. Hayes vetoed the Bland-Allison bill in 1878, but Congress overrode his veto.

bonanza farms Huge farms covering thousands of acres on the Great Plains. In relying on large size and new machinery, they represented a development in agriculture similar to that taking place in industry.

bonus army In June 1932, a group of twenty thousand World War I veterans marched on Washington, D.C., to demand immediate payment of their "adjusted compensation" bonuses voted by Congress in 1924. Congress rejected their demands, and President Hoover, fearing that their ranks were infested with criminals and radicals, had the bonus army forcibly removed from their encampment. It was a public relations disaster for Hoover.

Boston Massacre A violent confrontation between British troops and a Boston mob on March 5, 1770. Five citizens were killed when the troops fired into the crowd. The incident inflamed anti-British sentiment in Massachusetts.

Brandeis brief Filed by attorney Louis D. Brandeis in the Supreme Court case of *Muller* v. *Oregon,* this brief presented only two pages of legal precedents, but contained 115 pages of sociological evidence on the negative effects of long workdays on women's health and thus on women as mothers. The brief expanded the definition of legal evidence.

Brook Farm This transcendentalist commune, founded in Massachusetts in 1841, attracted many leading creative figures during its brief existence.

Brown* v. *Board of Education of Topeka In 1954, the Supreme Court reversed the ***Plessy* v. *Ferguson*** decision (1896) that established the "separate but equal" doctrine. The *Brown* decision found segregation in schools inherently unequal and initiated a long and difficult effort to integrate the nation's public schools.

Camp David accords In 1978, President Carter mediated a peace agreement between the leaders of Egypt and Israel at Camp David, a presidential retreat near Washington, D.C. The next year, Israel and Egypt signed a peace treaty based on the Camp David accords.

carpetbaggers This term was applied to Northerners who moved to the South after the Civil War in order to aid in the reconstruction of the South or to invest in the southern economy. It derives from the claim that these Northerners carried everything they owned in one bag.

Chinese Exclusion Act Legislation passed in 1882 that excluded Chinese immigrant workers for ten years and denied U.S. citizenship to Chinese nationals living in the United States. It was the first U.S. exclusionary law that was aimed at a specific racial group.

Civilian Conservation Corps (CCC) One of the most popular **New Deal** programs, the CCC was created by Congress to provide young men between ages 18 and 25 with government jobs in reforestation and other conservation projects. It eventually employed over 300,000.

Civil Rights Act of 1875 A federal law that forbade discrimination on public conveyances (transportation) and guaranteed African Americans "full and equal enjoyment" of such conveyances. It represented one of the last efforts on the part of the federal government to enforce civil rights.

Civil Rights Cases A group of cases in 1883 in which the Supreme Court ruled that the **Fourteenth Amendment** barred state governments from discriminating on the basis of race but did not prevent private individuals or organizations from doing so. The ruling dealt a major blow to the Republican party's earlier efforts to provide protection for African Americans.

Clayton Antitrust Act An attempt to improve the **Sherman Anti-Trust Act** of 1890, this law outlawed interlocking directorates (companies in which the same people served as directors), forbade policies that created monopolies, and made corporate officers responsible for anti-trust violations. Benefiting labor, it declared that unions were not conspiracies in restraint of trade and outlawed the use of injunctions in labor disputes unless they were necessary to protect property.

Coercive Acts Also known as the Intolerable Acts, the four pieces of legislation passed by Parliament in 1774 in response to the Boston Tea Party were meant to punish the colonies.

Columbian Exchange The exchange of plants, animals, culture, and diseases between Europe and the Americas from first contact throughout the era of exploration.

committee of correspondence Vast communication network formed in Massachusetts and other colonies to communicate grievances and provide colonists with evidence of British oppression.

Committee on Public Information (CPI) Created in 1917 by President Wilson and headed by progressive journalist George Creel, this organization rallied support for American involvement in World War I through art, advertising, and film. Creel worked out a system of voluntary censorship with the press and distributed colorful posters and pamphlets. The CPI's Division of Industrial Relations rallied labor to help the war effort.

Common Sense Revolutionary tract written by Thomas Paine in January 1776. It called for independence and the establishment of a republican government in America.

Compromise of 1850 This series of five congressional statutes temporarily calmed the sectional crisis. Among other things, the compromise made California a free state, ended the slave trade in the District of Columbia, and strengthened the Fugitive Slave Law.

Compromise of 1877 Compromise struck during the contested Presidential election of 1876, in which Democrats accepted the election of Rutherford B. Hayes (Republican) in exchange for the withdrawal of federal troops from the South and the ending of Reconstruction.

Comstock Lode Discovered in 1859 near Virginia City, Nevada, this ore deposit was the richest discovery in the history of mining. Named after T. P. Comstock, a drifter who talked his way into partnership in the claim, between 1859 and 1879 the deposit produced silver and gold worth more than $306 million.

conquistadores Sixteenth-century Spanish adventurers, often of noble birth, who subdued the Native Americans and created the Spanish empire in the New World.

conservation As President, Theodore Roosevelt made this principle one of his administration's top goals. Conservation in his view aimed at protecting the nation's natural resources, but called for the wise use of them rather than locking them away. Roosevelt's policies were opposed by those who favored preservation of the wilderness over its development.

containment First proposed by George Kennan in 1947, containment became the basic strategy of the United States throughout the Cold War. Kennan argued that firm American resistance to Soviet expansion would eventually compel Moscow to adopt more peaceful policies.

Contract with America In the 1994 congressional elections, Congressman Newt Gingrich had Republican candidates sign a document in which they pledged their support for such things as a balanced budget amendment, term limits for members of Congress, and a middle-class tax cut.

cooperationists In late 1860, southern secessionists debated two strategies: unilateral secession by each state or "cooperative" secession by the South as a whole. The cooperationists lost the debate.

Copperheads Northern Democrats suspected of being indifferent or hostile to the Union cause in the Civil War.

cotton gin Invented by Eli Whitney in 1793, this device for separating the seeds from the fibers of short-staple cotton enabled a slave to clean fifty times more cotton as by hand, which reduced production costs and gave new life to slavery in the South.

"court-packing" scheme Concerned that the conservative Supreme Court might declare all his New Deal programs unconstitutional, President Franklin Delano Roosevelt asked Congress to allow him to appoint additional justices to the Court. Both Congress and the public rejected this "court-packing" scheme and it was defeated.

Crittenden compromise Faced with the specter of secession and war, Congress tried and failed to resolve the sectional crisis in the months between Lincoln's election and inauguration. The leading proposal, introduced by Kentucky Senator John Crittenden, would have extended the **Missouri Compromise** line west to the Pacific.

Cuban missile crisis In October 1962, the United States and the Soviet Union came close to nuclear war when President Kennedy insisted that Nikita Khrushchev remove the 42 missiles he had secretly deployed in Cuba. The Soviets eventually did so, nuclear war was averted, and the crisis ended.

Cult of Domesticity Term used by historians to characterize the dominant gender role for white women in the antebellum period. The ideology of domesticity stressed the virtue of women as guardians of the home, which was considered their proper sphere.

Dartmouth College v. Woodward In this 1819 case, the Supreme Court ruled that the Constitution protected charters given to corporations by states.

Dawes Severalty Act Legislation passed by Congress in 1887 that aimed at breaking up traditional Indian life by promoting individual land ownership. It divided tribal lands into small plots that were distributed among members of each tribe. Provisions were made for Indian education and eventual citizenship. The law led to corruption, exploitation, and the weakening of Native American tribal culture.

D-Day D-Day (June 6, 1944) was the day Allied troops crossed the English Channel and opened a second front in western Europe during World War II. The "D" stands for "disembarkation": to leave a ship and go ashore.

Dien Bien Phu In 1954, Vietminh rebels besieged a French garrison at Dien Bien Phu, deep in the interior of northern Vietnam. In May, after the United States refused to intervene, Dien Bien Phu fell to the communists.

Dixiecrats In 1948, a group of southern Democrats known as the Dixiecrats bolted from their party and supported Governor Strom Thurmond of South Carolina as the presidential candidate of the States Rights party.

deregulation Ronald Reagan continued the deregulation process begun by Jimmy Carter, cutting back on the scope of federal agencies and relying instead on the free market to keep prices of consumer goods and services low and the quality high.

Desert Storm Desert Storm was the code name used by the United States and its coalition partners in waging war against Iraq in early 1991 to liberate Kuwait.

détente President Nixon and Henry Kissinger pursued a policy of détente, a French word meaning a relaxation of tension, with the Soviet Union as a way to lessen the possibility of nuclear war in the 1970s.

"dollar diplomacy" This policy, adopted by President William Howard Taft and Secretary of State Philander C. Knox, sought to promote U.S. financial and business interests abroad. It aimed to replace military alliances with economic ties, with the idea of increasing American influence and securing lasting peace. Under this policy, Taft worked in Latin America to replace European loans with American ones, assumed the debts of countries such as Honduras to fend off foreign bondholders, and helped Nicaragua secure a large loan in exchange for U.S. control of its national bank.

dry farming A farming technique developed to allow farming in the more arid parts of the West, where settlers had to deal with far less rainfall than they had east of the Mississippi. Furrows were plowed a foot or so deep and filled with a dust mulch to loosen soil and slow evaporation.

Emancipation Proclamation On January 1, 1863, President Lincoln proclaimed that the slaves of the Confederacy were free. Since the South had not yet been defeated, the proclamation did not immediately free anyone, but it made emancipation an explicit war aim of the North.

Embargo Act In response to a British attack on an American warship off the coast of Virginia, this 1807 law prohibited foreign commerce.

encomienda An exploitative labor system designed by Spanish rulers to reward **conquistadores** in the New World by granting them local villages and control over native labor.

Enlightenment Philosophical and intellectual movement that began in Europe during the eighteenth century. It stressed the application of reason to solve social and scientific problems.

enumerated goods Certain essential raw materials produced in the North American colonies, such as tobacco, sugar, and rice specified in the **Navigation Acts,** which stipulated that these goods could be shipped only to England or its colonies.

Environmental Protection Agency Congress created the Environmental Protection Agency (EPA) in 1970 as part of a broader effort to protect the environment and curb the pollution of the nation's air and water.

Equal Rights Amendment (ERA) In 1972, Congress approved the Equal Rights Amendment (ERA) to the Constitution, a measure designed to guarantee women equal treatment under the law. Despite a three-year extension in the time allowed for ratification, ERA supporters fell three states short of winning adoption.

"era of good feeling" A descriptive term for the era of President James Monroe, who served two terms from 1817-1823. During Monroe's administration, partisan conflict abated and bold federal initiatives suggested increased nationalism.

Espionage Act This law, passed after the United States entered World War I, imposed sentences of up to twenty years on anyone found guilty of aiding the enemy, obstructing recruitment of soldiers, or encouraging disloyalty. It allowed the postmaster general to remove from the mail any materials that incited treason or insurrection.

Exodusters A group of about six thousand African Americans who left their homes in Louisiana, Mississippi, and Texas in 1879, seeking freer lives in Kansas, where they worked as farmers or laborers.

Fair Deal A series of reform measures proposed by President Truman in 1949, including federal aid to education, civil rights measures, and national medical insurance. A bipartisan conservative coalition in Congress blocked this effort to move beyond the **New Deal** reforms of the 1930s.

Farewell Address In this 1796 speech, President George Washington announced his intention not to seek a third term in office. He also stressed federalist interests and warned the American people to avoid political factions and foreign entanglements that could sacrifice U.S. security.

Federal Reserve Act One of the most important laws in the history of the country, this act created a central banking system, consisting of twelve regional banks governed by the Federal Reserve Board. It was an attempt to provide the United States with a sound yet flexible currency. The Board it created still plays a vital role in the American economy today.

The Federalist A series of essays penned by Alexander Hamilton, James Madison, and John Jay that explained and defended the stronger national government created by the Constitutional Convention of 1787.

Federalists Supporters of the Constitution who advocated its ratification.

Fifteenth Amendment Ratified in 1870, this amendment prohibited the denial or abridgment of the right to vote by the federal government or state governments on the basis of race, color, or prior condition as a slave. It was intended to guarantee African Americans the right to vote in the South.

First Continental Congress A meeting of delegates from twelve colonies in Philadelphia in 1774, the Congress denied Parliament's authority to legislate for the colonies, condemned British actions toward the colonies, created the Continental Association, and endorsed a call to take up arms.

flexible response The Kennedy administration rejected the Eisenhower strategy of **massive retaliation** in favor of flexible re-sponse, which emphasized the use of conventional as well as nuclear weapons in meeting threats to American security.

Food Administration A wartime government agency that encouraged Americans to save food in order to supply the armies overseas. It fixed prices to boost production, asked people to observe "meatless" and "wheatless" days to conserve food, and promoted the planting of "victory gardens" behind homes, schools, and churches.

Foraker Act This act established Puerto Rico as an unorganized U.S. territory. Puerto Ricans were not given U.S. citizenship, but the U.S. president appointed the island's governor and governing council.

Force acts Congress attacked the Ku Klux Klan with three Enforcement or "Force" acts in 1870–1871. Designed to protect black voters in the South, these laws placed state elections under federal jurisdiction and imposed fines and imprisonment on those guilty of interfering with any citizen exercising his right to vote.

Fourteen Points In January 1918, President Wilson presented these terms for a far-reaching, nonpunitive settlement of World War I. He called, among other things, for removal of barriers to trade, open peace accords, reduction of armaments, and the establishment of a League of Nations. While generous and optimistic, the Points did not satisfy wartime hunger for revenge, and thus were largely rejected by European nations.

Fourteenth Amendment Ratified in 1868, this amendment provided citizenship to ex-slaves after the Civil War and constitutionally protected equal rights under the law for all citizens. Its provisions were used by **Radical Republicans** to enact a congressionally controlled Reconstruction policy of the former Confederate states.

Freedmen's Bureau Agency established by Congress in March 1865 to provide freedmen with shelter, food, and medical aid and to help them establish schools and find employment. The Bureau was dissolved in 1872.

freedom ride Bus trips taken by both black and white civil rights advocates in the 1960s. Sponsored by the Congress of Racial Equality (CORE), freedom rides in the South were designed to test the enforcement of federal regulations that prohibited segregation in interstate public transportation.

French Revolution A social and political revolution in France (1789–1799) that toppled the monarchy.

Free-Soil party Organized in 1848, this third party proposed to exclude slavery from federal territories and nominated former President Martin Van Buren in the presidential election of that year. Most Free Soilers eventually became Republicans.

Fugitive Slave Law Passed in 1850, this federal law made it easier for slaveowners to recapture runaway slaves; it also made it easier for kidnappers to take free blacks. The law became an object of hatred in the North.

gay liberation movement In the 1970s, homosexuals began an effort to win social and legal acceptance and to encourage gays to affirm their sexual identity. Despite some advances, the movement was slowed by the onset of the **AIDS** epidemic in the 1980s and the insistence of the military on banning openly gay individuals from the armed services.

Ghost Dances A religious movement that arose in the late nineteenth century under the prophet Wavoka, a Paiute Indian. It involved a set of dances and rites that its followers believed would cause white men to disappear and restore lands to the Native Americans. The Ghost Dance religion was outlawed by the U.S. government, and army intervention to stop it led to the **Wounded Knee Massacre.**

Gibbons v. *Ogden* In this 1824 case, the Supreme Court affirmed and expanded the power of the federal government to regulate interstate commerce.

Glorious Revolution Replacement of James II by William and Mary as English monarchs in 1688, marking the beginning of constitutional monarchy in Britain. American colonists celebrated this moment as a victory for the rule of law over despotism.

Gold Rush of 1849 Individual prospectors made the first gold strikes along the Sierra Nevada Mountains in 1849, touching off a mining boom that helped shape the development of the West and set the pattern for subsequent strikes in other regions.

Gold Standard Act Passed by Congress in 1900, this law declared gold the nation's standard of currency, meaning that all currency in circulation had to be redeemable in gold. The United States remained on the gold standard until 1933.

Good Neighbor policy President Hoover's administration initiated a new approach to Western hemispheric relations. The Good Neighbor policy declared America's intention to use cooperation and friendship in place of threats and armed intervention in its dealings with Latin America. It was extended and elaborated by the administration of Franklin Roosevelt.

Gramm-Rudman The Gramm-Rudman-Hollings Balanced Budget Act of 1985, popularly known as Gramm-Rudman, revised federal budgeting procedures. It authorized the president to impose automatic spending reductions to meet annual deficit limits.

Great Awakening Widespread evangelical religious revival movement of the mid-1700s. The movement divided congregations and weakened the authority of established churches in the colonies.

Great Society President Johnson called his version of the Democratic reform program the Great Society. In 1965, Congress passed many Great Society measures, including **Medicare,** civil rights legislation, and federal aid to education.

greenbackers Members of the National Greenback Party, founded in 1874, who wanted to keep wartime paper money (**greenbacks**) in circulation. They believed that a floating currency, not tied to either gold or silver, would provide relief to debtors and impoverished farmers by increasing the money supply.

greenbacks Paper currency issued by the Union beginning in 1862.

Gulf of Tonkin Resolution After a North Vietnamese attack on an American destroyer in the Gulf of Tonkin in 1964, President Johnson persuaded Congress to pass a resolution giving him the authority to use armed force in Vietnam.

Harlem Renaissance An African American cultural, literary, and artistic movement centered in Harlem, an area in New York City, in the 1920s. Harlem, the largest black community in the world outside of Africa, was considered the cultural capital of African Americans.

Hartford Convention An assembly of New England federalists who met in Hartford, Connecticut, in December 1814 to protest Madison's foreign policy in the War of 1812, which had undermined commercial interests in the North. They proposed amending the Constitution to prevent future presidents from declaring war without a two-thirds majority in Congress.

Hay-Bunau-Varilla Treaty This 1903 treaty granted the United States control over a canal zone ten miles wide across the Isthmus of Panama. In return, the United States guaranteed the independence of Panama and agreed to pay Colombia a onetime fee of $10 million and an annual rental of $250,000.

Haymarket Riot On May 4, 1886, a demonstration in Chicago's Haymarket Square to protest the slayings of two workers during a strike turned into a violent riot after a bomb explosion killed seven policemen. Although the bomb thrower was never found, the incident was blamed on labor "radicalism" and resulted in public condemnation of organized labor and contributed to the demise of the **Knights of Labor.**

headright System of land distribution in which settlers were granted a fifty-acre plot of land from the colonial government for each servant or dependent they transported to the New World. The system encouraged the recruitment of a large servile labor force.

Hepburn Act A law that strengthened the rate-making power of the **Interstate Commerce Commission,** again reflecting the era's desire to control the power of the railroads. It increased the ICC's membership from five to seven, empowered it to fix reasonable railroad rates, and broadened its jurisdiction. It also made ICC rulings binding pending court appeals.

Highway Act of 1956 A significant legislative achievement of Eisenhower's presidency, the Highway Act created the interstate highway system. The system, built over twenty years, provided jobs in construction, shortened travel times, and increased dependence on the automobile while weakening the railroads.

Homestead Act of 1862 Legislation granting 160 acres of land to anyone who paid a $10 fee and pledged to live on and cultivate the land for five years. Although there was a good deal of fraud, the act encouraged a large migration to the West. Between 1862 and 1900, nearly 600,000 families claimed homesteads under its provisions.

Homestead Strike In July 1892, wage-cutting at Andrew Carnegie's Homestead Steel Plant in Pittsburgh provoked a violent strike in which three company-hired detectives and ten workers died. Using ruthless force and strikebreakers, company officials effectively broke the strike and destroyed the union.

House of Burgesses An elective representative assembly in colonial Virginia. It was the first example of representative government in the English colonies.

House Un-American Activities Committee (HUAC) This congressional committee played a prominent role in attempting to uncover and punish those suspected of aiding the communist cause in the early years of the Cold War.

hustings Using tree stumps as podiums, traveling orators in America gave speeches on behalf of political parties. These visits were called "hustings" after a word for stump.

imperialism The policy of extending a nation's power through military conquest, economic domination, or annexation.

indentured servants Individuals who agreed to serve a master for a set number of years in exchange for the cost of boat transport to America. Indentured servitude was the dominant form of labor in the Chesapeake colonies before slavery.

Industrial Workers of the World (IWW). Founded in 1905, this radical union, also known as the Wobblies, aimed to unite the American working class into one union to promote labor's interests. It worked to organize unskilled and foreign-born laborers, advocated social revolution, and led several major strikes. Stressing solidarity, the IWW took as its slogan, "An injury to one is an injury to all."

Intermediate Nuclear Forces agreement Signed by President Reagan and Soviet President Gorbachev in Washington in late 1987, this agreement provided for the destruction of all intermediate-range nuclear missiles and permitted on-site inspection for the first time during the Cold War.

Interstate Commerce Commission (ICC) Created by Congress in 1887, this agency was authorized to investigate and oversee railroad activities. It also outlawed rebates and pooling agreements. An early attempt to remove certain issues from politics and turn them over to experts, the ICC became a prototype for the federal commissions that regulate many parts of the American economy today.

Iran-Contra affair The Iran-Contra affair involved officials high in the Reagan administration secretly selling arms to Iran and using the proceeds to finance the Contra rebels in Nicaragua. This illegal transaction usurped the congressional power of the purse.

Iranian hostage crisis In 1979, Iranian fundamentalists seized the American embassy in Tehran and held fifty-three American diplomats hostage for over a year. The Iranian hostage crisis weakened the Carter presidency; the hostages were finally released on January 20, 1981, the day Ronald Reagan became president.

Iron Curtain British Prime Minister Winston Churchill coined the phrase "Iron Curtain" to refer to the boundary in Europe that divided Soviet-dominated eastern and central Europe from western Europe, which was free from Soviet control.

isolationism A belief that the United States should stay out of entanglements with other nations. Isolationism was widespread after the Spanish-American War in the late 1890s and influenced later U.S. foreign policy.

itinerant preachers Traveling revivalist ministers of the **Great Awakening** movement. These charismatic preachers spread revivalism throughout America.

Jacksonian Democracy A historian's term for the political culture of white male citizens in the 1820s and 1830s. It celebrated the "self-made man" and rejected the idea that leaders should be drawn from the intellectual and economic elite. Andrew Jackson, the first "people's president," exemplified the spirit of the age.

Jay's Treaty Controversial treaty with Britain negotiated by Chief Justice John Jay in 1794 to settle American grievances and avert war. Though the British agreed to surrender forts on U.S. territory, the treaty failed to realize key diplomatic goals and provoked a storm of protest in America.

Jim Crow laws Laws enacted by states to segregate the population. They became widespread in the South after Reconstruction.

joint-stock company Business enterprise that enabled investors to pool money for commercial trading activity and funding for sustaining colonies.

Kansas-Nebraska Act This 1854 act repealed the Missouri Compromise, split the Louisiana Purchase into two territories, and allowed its settlers to accept or reject slavery by popular sovereignty. This act enflamed the slavery issue and led opponents to form the Republican party.

Kellogg-Briand Pact Also called the Pact of Paris, this 1929 agreement was the brainchild of U.S. Secretary of State Frank B. Kellogg and French premier Aristide Briand. It pledged its signatories, eventually including nearly all nations, to shun war as an instrument of policy. Derided as an "international kiss," it had little effect on the actual conduct of world affairs.

Kentucky and Virginia Resolutions Statements penned by Thomas Jefferson and James Madison to mobilize opposition to the Alien and Sedition Acts, which they argued were unconstitutional. Jefferson's statement (the Kentucky Resolution) suggested that states should have the right to declare null and void congressional acts they deemed unconstitutional. Madison produced a more temperate resolution, but most Americans rejected such an extreme defense of states' rights.

Knights of Labor Also known as the Noble and Holy Order of the Knights of Labor. Founded in 1869, this labor organization pursued broad-gauged reforms as much as practical issues like wages and hours. Unlike the **American Federation of Labor,** the Knights of Labor welcomed all laborers regardless of race, gender, or skill.

Know-Nothing party After the collapse of the Whig party in the 1850s, this anti-immigrant and anti-Catholic party rose to national prominence. Though the party enjoyed some success in local and state elections, it failed to sustain its existence and quickly disappeared.

Ku Klux Klan A secret terrorist society first organized in Tennessee in 1866. The original Klan's goals were to disfranchise Africa Americans, stop Reconstruction, and restore the pre-war social order of the South. The Ku Klux Klan re-formed after World War II to promote white supremacy in the wake of the "Second Reconstruction."

Lecompton constitution In 1857, a fraudulently-elected group of pro-slavery delegates met in Lecompton, Kansas, and drafted a state constitution. After bitter debate, Congress narrowly denied Kansas's entry into the Union under this constitution.

Leisler's Rebellion In the aftermath of England's **Glorious Revolution** in 1688, Jacob Leisler seized control of New York's government. Although Lesisler was executed as a traitor, his followers defended his memory against detractors well into the eighteenth century

Lend-Lease Arguing that aiding Britain would help America's own self-defense, President Roosevelt in 1941 asked Congress for a $7 billion Lend-Lease plan. This would allow the president to sell, lend, lease, or transfer war materials to any country whose defense he declared as vital to that of the United States.

Levittown In 1947, William Levitt used mass production techniques to build inexpensive homes in suburban New York to help relieve the postwar housing shortage. Levittown became a symbol of the movement to the suburbs in the years after World War II.

Lewis and Clark Expedition Overland expedition to the Pacific coast (1804–1806) led by Meriwether Lewis and William Clark. Commissioned by President Thomas Jefferson, the exploration of the Far West brought back a wealth of scientific data about the country and its resources.

Liberty party America's first antislavery political party, formed in 1840. When the party ran a presidential candidate in the 1844 election, it split the Republican vote and inadvertently tipped the 1844 election in favor of Democrat James Polk.

Louisiana Purchase U.S. acquisition of the Louisiana Territory from France in 1803 for $15 million. The purchase secured American control of the Mississippi River and doubled the size of the nation.

Loyalists Throughout the conflict with Great Britain, many colonists sided with the king and Parliament. Also called Tories, these people feared that American liberty might promote social anarchy.

Manhattan Project In early 1942, Franklin Roosevelt, alarmed by reports that German scientists were working on an atomic bomb, authorized a crash program to build the bomb first. The Manhattan Project, named for the Corps of Engineers district originally in charge, spent $2 billion dollars and produced the weapons that devastated Hiroshima and Nagasaki in 1945.

Manifest Destiny Coined in 1845, this term referred to a doctrine in support of territorial expansion based on the beliefs that population growth demanded territorial expansion, that God supported American expansion, and that national expansion equaled the expansion of freedom.

Marbury* v. *Madison In this 1803 landmark decision, the Supreme Court first asserted the power of judicial review by declaring an act of Congress, the Judiciary Act of 1789, unconstitutional.

March on Washington In August 1963, civil rights leaders organized a massive rally in Washington to urge passage of President Kennedy's civil rights bill. The high point came when Martin Luther King, Jr. gave his "I Have a Dream" speech to more than 200,000 marchers in front of the Lincoln Memorial.

Marshall Plan In 1947, Secretary of State George Marshall proposed a massive economic aid program to rebuild the war-torn economies of western European nations. The plan was motivated by both humanitarian concern for the conditions of those nations' economies and fear that economic dislocation would promote communism in western Europe.

massive retaliation The "new look" defense policy of the Eisenhower administration in the 1950s was to threaten "massive retaliation" with nuclear weapons in response to any act of aggression by a potential enemy.

Mayflower Compact Agreement among the Pilgrims aboard the Mayflower in 1620 to create a civil government at Plymouth Colony.

McCarthyism In 1950, Senator Joseph R. McCarthy began a sensational campaign against communists in government that led to more than four years of charges and countercharges, ending when the Senate censured him in 1954. McCarthyism became the contemporary name for the red scare of the 1950s.

McCulloch v. Maryland Ruling on this banking case in 1819, the Supreme Court propped up the idea of "implied powers" meaning the Constitution could be broadly interpreted. This pivotal ruling also asserted the supremacy of federal power over state power.

Medicare The 1965 Medicare Act provided Social Security funding for hospitalization insurance for people over age 65 and a voluntary plan to cover doctor bills paid in part by the federal government.

mercantilism An economic theory that shaped imperial policy throughout the colonial period, mercantilism was built on the assumption that the world's wealth was a fixed supply. In order to increase its wealth, a nation needed to export more goods than it imported. Favorable trade and protective economic policies, as well as new colonial possessions rich in raw materials, were important in achieving this balance.

Mexican-American War Conflict (1846–1848) between the United States and Mexico after the U.S. annexation of Texas, which Mexico still considered its own. As victor, the United States acquired vast new territories from Mexico according to the terms of the **Treaty of Guadalupe Hidalgo.**

military-industrial complex In his farewell address in January 1961, President Eisenhower used the phrase "military-industrial complex" to warn about the danger of massive defense spending and the close relationship between the armed forces and industrial corporations that supplied their weapons.

Missouri Compromise A sectional compromise in Congress in 1820 that admitted Missouri to the Union as a slave state and Maine as a free state. It also banned slavery in the remainder of the Louisiana Purchase territory above the latitude of 36°30'.

Modern Republicanism President Eisenhower characterized his views as "Modern Republicanism." Claiming he was liberal toward people but conservative about spending public money, he helped balance the federal budget and lower taxes without destroying existing social programs.

Monroe Doctrine A key foreign policy made by President James Monroe in 1823, it declared the western hemisphere off limits to new European colonization; in return, the United States promised not to meddle in European affairs.

Montgomery bus boycott In late 1955, African Americans led by Martin Luther King, Jr., boycotted the buses in Montgomery, Alabama, after seamstress Rosa Parks was arrested for refusing to move to the back of a bus. The boycott, which ended when the Supreme Court ruled in favor of the protesters, marked the beginning of a new, activist phase of the civil rights movement.

moral diplomacy Policy adopted by President Woodrow Wilson that rejected the approach of **"dollar diplomacy."** Rather than focusing mainly on economic ties with other nations, Wilson's policy was designed to bring right principles to the world, preserve peace, and extend to other peoples the blessings of democracy. Wilson, however, often ended up pursuing policies much like those followed by Roosevelt and Taft.

Moral Majority In 1979, the Reverend Jerry Falwell founded the Moral Majority to combat "amoral liberals," drug abuse, "coddling" of criminals, homosexuality, communism, and abortion. The Moral Majority represented the rise of political activism among organized religion's radical right wing.

muckrakers Unflattering term coined by Theodore Roosevelt to describe the writers who made a practice of exposing the wrongdoings of public figures. Muckraking flourished from 1903 to 1909 in magazines such as *McClure's* and *Collier's,* exposing social and political problems and sparking reform.

Mugwumps Drawing their members mainly from among the educated and upper class, these reformers crusaded for lower tariffs, limited federal government, and civil service reform to end political corruption. They were best known for their role in helping to elect Grover Cleveland to the presidency in 1884.

Muller v. Oregon This Supreme Court decision established special protections for working women, upholding an Oregon law that limited women working in factories and laundries to a ten-hour work day. Louis D. Brandeis, attorney for the state of Oregon, argued that because of the importance of women's roles as mothers, they deserved special protection from labor abuses. The **Brandeis brief,** as it was called, was based largely on sociological data rather than legal evidence, and as a result, expanded the definition of legal evidence.

National American Woman Suffrage Association Founded by Susan B. Anthony in 1890, this organization worked to secure women the right to vote. While some suffragists urged militant action, it stressed careful organization and peaceful lobbying. By 1920 it had nearly two million members.

National Association for the Advancement of Colored People (NAACP) Created in 1909, this organization quickly became one of the most important civil rights organizations in the country. The NAACP pressured employers, labor unions, and the government on behalf of African Americans.

National Defense Education Act (NDEA) The 1958 National Defense Education Act (NDEA), passed in response to *Sputnik,* provided an opportunity and stimulus for college education for many Americans. It allocated funds for upgrading studies in the sciences, foreign languages, guidance services, and teaching innovation.

National Farmers' Alliance and Industrial Union One of the largest reform movements in American history, the Farmer's Alliance sought to organize farmers in the South and West to fight for reforms that would improve their lot, including measures to overcome low crop prices, burdensome mortgages, and high railroad rates. The Alliance ultimately organized a political party, the **People's (Populist) party.**

National Grange of the Patrons of Husbandry Founded by Oliver H. Kelly in 1867, the Grange sought to relieve the drabness of farm life by providing a social, educational, and cultural outlet for its members. It also set up grain elevators, cooperative stores, warehouses, insurance companies, and farm machinery factories. Although its constitution banned political involvement, the Grange often supported railroad regulation and other measures.

National Organization for Women (NOW) Founded in 1966, the National Organization for Women (NOW) called for equal employment opportunity and equal pay for women. NOW also championed the legalization of abortion and passage of an equal rights amendment to the Constitution.

National Origins Quota Act This 1924 law established a quota system to regulate the influx of immigrants to America. The system restricted the **new immigrants** from southern and eastern Europe and Asia. It also reduced the annual total of immigrants.

National Reclamation Act (Newlands Act) Passed in 1902, this legislation set aside the majority of the proceeds from the sale of public land in sixteen Western states to fund irrigation projects in the arid states.

National Recovery Administration (NRA) A keystone of the early **New Deal,** this federal agency was created in 1933 to promote economic recovery and revive industry during the Great Depression. It permitted manufacturers to establish industry-wide codes of "fair business practices" setting prices and production levels. It also provided for minimum wages and maximum working hours for labor and guaranteed labor the right to organize and bargain collectively (Section 7a). The Supreme Court declared it unconstitutional in 1935.

National Security Act Congress passed the National Security Act in 1947 in response to perceived threats from the Soviet Union after World War II. It established the Department of Defense and created the Central Intelligence Agency (CIA) and National Security Council.

nationalists Group of leaders who favored replacing the Articles of Confederation with a stronger national government.

natural rights Fundamental rights over which the government could exercise no control. An uncompromising belief in such rights energized the popular demand for a formal bill of rights in 1791.

Navigation Acts A series of commercial restrictions passed by Parliament intended to regulate colonial commerce in such a way as to favor England's accumulation of wealth.

Neoconservatism Former liberals who advocated a strong stand against communism abroad and free market capitalism at home became known as neoconservatives. These intellectuals stressed the positive values of American society in contrast to liberals who emphasized social ills.

neutrality acts Reacting to their disillusionment with World War I and absorbed in the domestic crisis of the Great Depression, Americans backed Congress's three neutrality acts in the 1930s. The 1935 and 1936 acts forbade selling munitions or lending money to belligerents in a war. The 1937 act required that all remaining trade be conducted on a cash-and-carry basis.

New Deal In accepting the nomination of the Democratic Party in 1932, Franklin Delano Roosevelt promised a "new deal" for the American people. After his election, the label was applied to his program of legislation passed to combat the Great Depression. The New Deal included measures aimed at relief, reform, and recovery. They achieved some relief and considerable reform but little recovery.

New Freedom Woodrow Wilson's program in his campaign for the presidency in 1912, the New Freedom emphasized business competition and small government. It sought to rein in federal authority, release individual energy, and restore competition. It echoed many of the progressive social-justice objectives while pushing for a free economy rather than a planned one.

New Frontier The New Frontier was the campaign program advocated by John F. Kennedy in the 1960 election. He promised to revitalize the stagnant economy and enact reform legislation in education, health care, and civil rights.

new immigrants Starting in the 1880s, immigration into the United States began to shift from northern and western Europe, its source for most of the nation's history, to southern and eastern Europe. These "new" immigrants tended to be poor, non-Protestant, and unskilled; they tended to stay in close-knit communities and retain their language, customs, and religions. Between 1880 and 1910, approximately 8.4 million of these so-called "new" immigrants came to the United States.

New Jersey Plan Proposal of the New Jersey delegation at the Constitutional Convention that called for a strong national government with one house of Congress in which all states would have equal representation. This plan challenged the **Virginia Plan** and was the basis for a compromise in which one of the two houses of Congress, the Senate, was based on equal representation from each state regardless of size.

New Nationalism Theodore Roosevelt's program in his campaign for the presidency in 1912, the New Nationalism called for a national approach to the country's affairs and a strong president to deal with them. It also called for efficiency in government and society; it urged protection of children, women, and workers; accepted "good" trusts; and exalted the expert and the executive. Additionally, it encouraged large concentrations of capital and labor.

Niagara Movement A movement, led by W. E. B. Du Bois, that focused on equal rights and the education of African American youth. Rejecting the gradualist approach of Booker T. Washington, members kept alive a program of militant action and claimed for African Americans all the rights afforded to other Americans. It spawned later civil rights movements.

Nixonomics A word used by Democrats critical of President Richard Nixon's economic policies, in particular the inability to curb inflation at a time of high unemployment and recession.

nonimportation During their controversy with Britain over taxation, the colonists devised a strategy of political resistance in which they boycotted a wide range of British imported goods to put economic pressure on Britain. The cooperative effort promoted mutual trust among the colonists and strengthened their resistance to the British measures.

North American Free Trade Agreement (NAFTA) A free trade plan initiated in the Bush administration and enacted by a narrow vote in Congress in the early months of the Clinton administration. It established a common market without tariff barriers between the United States, Canada, and Mexico.

North Atlantic Treaty Organization (NATO) In 1949, the United States, Canada, and ten European nations formed this military mutual-defense pact. In 1955, the Soviet Union countered NATO with the formation of the Warsaw Pact, a military alliance among those nations within its own sphere of influence.

Northwest Ordinance Legislation that formulated plans for governments in America's northwestern territories, defined a procedure for the territories' admission to the Union as states, and prohibited slavery north of the Ohio River.

NSC-68 National Security Council planning paper No. 68 redefined America's national defense policy. Adopted in 1950, it committed the United States to a massive military buildup to meet the challenge posed by the Soviet Union.

nullification The supposed right of any state to declare a federal law inoperative within its boundaries. In 1832, South Carolina created a firestorm when it attempted to nullify the federal tariff.

Ocala Demands Adopted by the Farmers' Alliance at an 1890 meeting in Ocala, Florida, these demands became the organization's main platform. They called for the creation of a sub-treasury system to allow farmers to store their crops until they could get the best price, the free coinage of silver, an end to protective tariffs and national banks, a federal income tax, the direct election of senators by voters, and tighter regulation of railroads.

Old South The term refers to the slaveholding states between 1830 and 1860, when slave labor and cotton production dominated the economies of the southern states. This period is also known as the "antebellum era."

Oneida community Founded in 1848 in Oneida, New York, this Christian utopian community earned notoriety for institutionalizing a form of "free love."

Open Door policy Established in a series of notes by Secretary of State John Hay in 1900, this policy established free trade between the United States and China and attempted to enlist major European and Asian nations in recognizing the territorial integrity of China. It marked a departure from the American tradition of **isolationism** and signaled the country's growing involvement in the world.

Organization of Petroleum Exporting Countries (OPEC) A cartel of oil-exporting nations. In late 1973, OPEC took advantage of the October War and an oil embargo by its Arab members to quadruple the price of oil. This huge increase had a devastating impact on the American economy.

Ostend Manifesto Written by American officials in 1854, this secret memo—later dubbed a "manifesto"—urged the acquisition of Cuba by any means necessary. When it became public, Northerners claimed it was a plot to extend slavery and the manifesto was disavowed.

Overland Trail The route taken by thousands of travelers from the Mississippi Valley to the Pacific Coast in the last half of the nineteenth century. It was extremely difficult, often taking six months or more to complete.

Panic of 1837 A financial depression that lasted until the 1840s.

parliamentary sovereignty Principle that emphasized the power of Parliament to govern colonial affairs as the preeminent authority.

Pearl Harbor On December 7, 1941, Japanese warplanes attacked U.S. naval forces at Pearl Harbor, Hawaii, sinking several ships and killing more than 2400 American sailors. The event marked America's entrance into World War II.

Pendleton Act Passed by Congress in 1883 with the backing of President Chester A. Arthur, this act sought to lessen the involvement of politicians in the running of the government. It created a bipartisan Civil Service Commission to administer competitive exams to candidates for civil service jobs and to appoint officeholders based on merit. It also outlawed forcing political contributions from appointed officials. The measure served as the basis for later expansion of a professional civil service.

Pentagon Papers The Pentagon Papers was a secret Defense Department study of the Vietnam War. Publication of the papers in 1971 revealed how civilian and military leaders had misled the American people about the nation's role in Vietnam.

People's (or Populist) party This political party was organized in 1892 by farm, labor, and reform leaders, mainly from the Farmers' Alliance. It offered a broad-based reform platform reflecting the **Ocala Demands.** It nominated James B. Weaver of Iowa for president in 1892 and William Jennings Bryan of Nebraska in 1896. After 1896, it became identified as a one-issue party focused on free silver and gradually died away.

Philippine-American War A war fought from 1899 to 1903 to quell Filipino resistance to U.S. control of the Philippine Islands. Although often forgotten, it lasted longer than the Spanish-American War and resulted in more casualties. Filipino guerilla soldiers finally gave up when their leader, Emilio Aguinaldo, was captured.

placer mining A form of mining that required little technology or skill, placer mining techniques included using a shovel and a washing pan to separate gold from the ore in streams and riverbeds. An early phase of the mining industry, placer mining could be performed by miners working as individuals or in small groups.

Platt Amendment This amendment to the new Cuban constitution authorized U.S. intervention in Cuba to protect its interests. Cuba pledged not to make treaties with other countries that might compromise its independence, and it granted naval bases to the United States, the most notable being Guantanamo Bay.

Plessy* v. *Ferguson A Supreme Court case in 1896 that established the doctrine of "separate but equal" and upheld a Louisiana law requiring that blacks and whites occupy separate rail cars. The Court applied it to schools in *Cumming* v. *County Board of Education*

(1899). The doctrine was finally overturned in 1954, in ***Brown* v. *Board of Education of Topeka.***

popular sovereignty The concept that the settlers of a newly organized territory have the right to decide (through voting) whether or not to accept slavery. Promoted as a solution to the slavery question, popular sovereignty became a fiasco in Kansas during the 1850s.

Potsdam Conference The final wartime meeting of the leaders of the United States, Great Britain, and the Soviet Union was held at Potsdam, outside Berlin, in July, 1945. Truman, Churchill, and Stalin discussed the future of Europe but their failure to reach meaningful agreements soon led to the onset of the Cold War.

pragmatism A doctrine that emerged in the early twentieth century, built largely on the ideas of Harvard psychologist and philosopher William James. Pragmatists were impatient with theories that held truth to be abstract; they believed that truth should work for the individual. They also believed that people were not only shaped by their environment but also helped to shape it. Ideas that worked, according to pragmatists, became truth.

preemption The right of first purchase of public land. Settlers enjoyed this right even if they squatted on the land in advance of government surveyors.

progressivism Movement for social change between the late 1890s and World War I. Its origins lay in a fear of big business and corrupt government and a desire to improve the lives of countless Americans. Progressives set out to cure the social ills brought about by industrialization and urbanization, social disorder, and political corruption.

Progressive party Also known as the "Bull Moose" party, this political party was formed by Theodore Roosevelt in an attempt to advance progressive ideas and unseat President William Howard Taft in the election of 1912. After Taft won the Republican party's nomination, Roosevelt ran on the Progressive party ticket.

prohibition The ban of the manufacture, sale, and transportation of alcoholic beverages in the United States. The Eighteenth Amendment, adopted in 1919, established prohibition. It was repealed by the Twenty-first Amendment in 1933. While prohibition was in effect, it reduced national consumption of alcohol, but it was inconsistently enforced and was often evaded, especially in the cities.

Protestant Reformation Sixteenth-century religious movement to reform and challenge the spiritual authority of the Roman Catholic Church, associated with figures such as Martin Luther and John Calvin.

Pullman Strike Beginning in May 1894, this strike of employees at the Pullman Palace Car Company near Chicago was one of the largest strikes in American history. Workers struck to protest wage cuts, high rents for company housing, and layoffs; the American Railway Union, led by Eugene V. Debs, joined the strike in June. Extending into twenty-seven states and territories, it effectively paralyzed the western half of the nation. President Grover Cleveland secured an injunction to break the strike on the grounds that it obstructed the mail and sent federal troops to enforce it. The Supreme Court upheld the use of the injunction in *In re Debs* (1895).

Puritans Members of a reformed Protestant sect in Europe and America that insisted on removing all vestiges of Catholicism from popular religious practice.

Quakers Members of a radical religious group, formally known as the Society of Friends, that rejected formal theology and stressed each person's "inner light," a spiritual guide to righteousness.

Radical Reconstruction The Reconstruction Acts of 1867 divided the South into five military districts. They required the states to guarantee black male suffrage and to ratify the **Fourteenth Amendment** as a condition of their readmission to the Union.

Radical Republicans The Radical Republicans in Congress, headed by Thaddeus Stevens and Charles Sumner, insisted on black suffrage and federal protection of civil rights of African Americans. They gained control of Reconstruction in 1867 and required the ratification of the **Fourteenth Amendment** as a condition of readmission for former Confederate states.

Red Scare A wave of anticommunist, antiforeign, and antilabor hysteria that swept over America at the end of World War I. It resulted in the deportation of many alien residents and the violation of the civil liberties of many of its victims.

Redeemers A loose coalition of prewar Democrats, Confederate Army veterans, and southern Whigs who took over southern state governments in the 1870s, supposedly "redeeming" them from the corruption of Reconstruction. They shared a commitment to white supremacy and laissez-faire economics.

Renaissance A cultural awakening that began in Italy and spread throughout Europe in the fifteenth and sixteenth centuries. This powerful humanistic movement encouraged creativity and a spirit of inquiry and brought forth new forms of artistic expression and political theory.

republicanism Concept that ultimate political authority is vested in the citizens of the nation. The character of republican government was dependent on the civic virtue of its citizens to preserve the nation from corruption and moral decay.

Republicans Members of the Republican party established following the enactment of the **Kansas-Nebraska Act** in 1854. Republicans were opposed to the extension of slavery into the western territories.

Roe v. Wade In 1973, the Supreme Court ruled in *Roe* v. *Wade* that women had a constitutional right to abortion during the early stages of pregnancy. The decision provoked a vigorous right-to-life movement that opposed abortion.

Roosevelt Corollary President Theodore Roosevelt's 1904 foreign policy statement, a corollary to the **Monroe Doctrine,** which asserted that the United States would intervene in Latin American affairs if the countries themselves could not keep their affairs in order. It effectively made the United States the policeman of the western hemisphere. The Roosevelt Corollary guided U.S. policy in Latin America until it was replaced by Franklin D. Roosevelt's **Good Neighbor policy** in the 1930s.

Sanitary Commission An association chartered by the Union government during the Civil War to promote health in the northern army's camps though attention to cleanliness, nutrition, and medical care.

Scopes trial Also called the "monkey trial," the 1924 Scopes trial was a contest between modern liberalism and religious fundamentalism. John T. Scopes was on trial for teaching Darwinian evolution in defiance of a Tennessee state law. He was found guilty and fined $100.

Second Continental Congress This meeting took place in Philadelphia in May 1775, in the midst of rapidly unfolding military events. It organized the Continental Army and commissioned George Washington to lead it, then began requisitioning men and supplies for the war effort.

Second Great Awakening A series of evangelical Protestant revivals that swept over America in the early nineteenth century.

second party system A historian's term for the national two-party rivalry between Democrats and **Whigs.** The second party system began in the 1830s and ended in the 1850s with the demise of the Whig party and the rise of the Republican party.

Sedition Act A wartime law that imposed harsh penalties on anyone using "disloyal, profane, scurrilous, or abusive language" about the U.S. government, flag, or armed forces.

Selective Service Act This 1917 law provided for the registration of all American men between the ages of 21 and 30 for a military draft. By the end of World War I, 24.2 million men had registered; 2.8 million had been inducted into the army. The age limits were later changed to 18 and 45.

Seneca Falls Convention The first women's rights convention held in 1848 in Seneca Falls, New York, and co-sponsored by Elizabeth Cady Stanton and Lucretia Mott. Delegates at the convention drafted a "declaration of sentiments," patterned on the Declaration of Independence, but which declared that "all men and women are created equal."

settlement houses Located in poor districts of major cities, these were community centers that tried to soften the impact of urban life for immigrant and other families. Often run by young, educated women, they provided social services and a political voice for their neighborhoods. Chicago's Hull House, founded by Jane Addams in 1889, became the most famous of the settlement houses.

Seven Years' War Worldwide conflict (1756–1763) that pitted Britain against France for control of North America. With help from the American colonists, the British won the war and eliminated France as a power on the North American continent. Also known in America as the French and Indian War.

Shakers A religious group, formally known as the United Society of believers, that advocated strict celibacy, gender equality, and communal ownership.

sharecropping After the Civil War, the southern states adopted a sharecropping system as a compromise between former slaves, who wanted land of their own and former slave owners who needed labor. The landowners provided land, tools, and seed to a farming family, who in turn provided labor. The resulting crop was divided between them, with the farmers receiving a "share" of one-third to one-half of the crop.

Shays's Rebellion Armed insurrection of farmers in western Massachusetts led by Daniel Shays, a veteran of the Continental Army. Intended to prevent state courts from foreclosing on debtors unable to pay their taxes, the rebellion was put down by the state militia. Nationalists used the event to justify the calling of a constitutional convention to strengthen the national government.

Sherman Antitrust Act Passed by Congress in 1890, this act was the first major U.S. attempt to deal legislatively with the problem of the increasing size of business. It declared illegal "every contract, combination in the form of trust or otherwise, or conspiracy, in restraint of trade or commerce." Penalties for violations were strict, ranging from fines to imprisonment and even the dissolution of guilty trusts. The law was weakened when the Supreme Court, in *United States* v. *E. C. Knight and Co.* (1895), drew a sharp distinction between manufacturing and commerce and ruled that manufacturing was excluded from its coverage. Nonetheless, the law shaped all future antitrust legislation.

Sherman Silver Purchase Act An act that attempted to resolve the controversy over silver coinage. Under it, the U.S. Treasury would purchase 4.5 million ounces of silver each month and issue legal tender (in the form of Treasury notes) for it. The act pleased opponents of silver because it did not call for free coinage; it pleased proponents of silver because it bought up most of the nation's silver production.

social Darwinism Adapted by English social philosopher Herbert Spencer from Charles Darwin's theory of evolution, this theory held that the "laws" of evolution applied to human life, that change or reform therefore took centuries, and that the "fittest" would succeed in business and social relationships. It promoted the ideas of competition and individualism, saw as futile any intervention of government into human affairs, and was used by influential members of the economic and social elite to oppose reform.

Social Gospel Preached by a number of urban Protestant ministers, the Social Gospel focused as much on improving the conditions of life on earth as on saving souls for the hereafter. Its adherents worked for child-labor laws and measures to alleviate poverty.

Social Security Act The 1935 Social Security Act established a system of old age, unemployment, and survivors' insurance funded by wage and payroll taxes. It did not include health insurance and did not originally cover many of the most needy groups and individuals.

social-justice movement During the 1890s and after, this important movement attracted followers who sought to free people from the often devastating impact of urban life. It focused on the need for tenement house laws, more stringent child labor regulations, and better working conditions for women. Social-justice reformers also brought pressure on municipal agencies for better community services and facilities.

Southern Christian Leadership Conference (SCLC) An organization founded by Martin Luther King, Jr., to direct the crusade against segregation. Its weapon was passive resistance that stressed nonviolence and love, and its tactic direct, though peaceful, confrontation.

specie circular In 1836, President Andrew Jackson issued this executive order that required purchasers of public land to pay in "specie," gold or silver coin, rather than paper money.

spectral evidence In the Salem witch trials, the court allowed reports of dreams and visions in which the accused appeared as the devil's agent to be introduced as testimony. The accused had no defense against this kind of "evidence." When the judges later disallowed this testimony, the executions for witchcraft ended.

Sputnik In October 1957, the Soviet Union surprised the world by launching *Sputnik*, the first artificial satellite to orbit the earth. The resulting outcry in the United States, especially fears that the Soviets were ahead in both space exploration and military missiles, forced the Eisenhower administration to increase defense spending and accelerate America's space program.

Stamp Act Congress Meeting of colonial delegates in New York City in October 1765 to protest the Stamp Act, a law passed by Parliament to raise revenue in America. The delegates drafted petitions denouncing the Stamp Act and other taxes imposed on Americans without colonial consent.

Strategic Arms Limitations Talks (SALT) In 1972, the United States and the Soviet Union culminated four years of Strategic Arms Limitation Talks (SALT) by signing a treaty limiting the deployment of antiballistic missiles (ABM) and an agreement to freeze the number of offensive missiles for five years.

Strategic Defense Initiative (SDI) Popularly known as "Star Wars," President Ronald Reagan's Strategic Defense Initiative (SDI) proposed the construction of an elaborate computer-controlled, anti-missile defense system capable of destroying enemy missiles in outer space. Critics claimed that SDI could never be perfected.

Student Nonviolent Coordinating Committee (SNCC) A radical group advocating black power. The SNCC's leaders, scornful of integration and interracial cooperation, broke with Martin Luther King, Jr., to advocate greater militancy and acts of violence.

Students for a Democratic Society (SDS) Founded in 1962, the SDS was a popular college student organization that protested shortcomings in American life, notably racial injustice and the Vietnam War. It led thousands of campus protests before it split apart at the end of the 1960s.

Suez crisis Egyptian leader Gamal Abdel Nasser nationalized the Suez Canal in 1956 when the United States withdrew promised aid to build the Aswan Dam on the Nile River. Britain and France, dependent on Middle East oil that was transported through the Suez Canal, launched an armed attack to regain control. President Eisenhower protested the use of force and persuaded Britain and France to withdraw their troops.

Sunbelt This region consists of a broad band of states running across the South from Florida to Texas, extending west and north to include California and the Pacific Northwest. Beginning in the 1970s, this area has experienced rapid economic growth and major gains in population.

supply-side economics Advocates of supply-side economics claimed that tax cuts would stimulate the economy by giving individuals a greater incentive to earn more money, which would lead to greater investment and eventually larger tax revenues at a lower rate. Critics replied that supply-side economics would only burden the economy with larger government deficits.

Taft-Hartley Act This 1947 anti-union legislation outlawed the closed shop and secondary boycotts. It also authorized the president to seek injunctions to prevent strikes that posed a threat to national security.

tariff of abominations An 1828 protective tariff, or tax on imports, motivated by special interest groups. It resulted in a substantial increase in duties that angered many southern free traders.

Teapot Dome scandal A 1924 scandal in which Secretary of the Interior Albert Fall was convicted of accepting bribes in exchange for leasing government-owned oil lands in Wyoming (Teapot Dome) and California (Elks Hill) to private oil businessmen.

Teller Amendment In this amendment, sponsored by Senator Henry M. Teller of Colorado, the United States pledged that it did not intend to annex Cuba and that it would recognize Cuban independence from Spain after the Spanish-American War.

temperance movement Temperance—moderation or abstention in the use of alcoholic beverages—attracted many advocates in the early nineteenth century. Their crusade against alcohol, which grew out of the Second Great Awakening, became a powerful social and political force.

Ten Percent Plan Reconstruction plan proposed by President Abraham Lincoln as a quick way to readmit the former Confederate States. It called for full pardon of all Southerners except Confederate leaders, and readmission to the Union for any state after 10 percent of its voters in the 1860 election signed a loyalty oath and the state abolished slavery.

Tennessee Valley Authority (TVA) A New Deal effort at regional planning created by Congress in 1933, this agency built dams and power plants on the Tennessee River. Its programs for flood control, soil conservation, and reforestation helped raise the standard of living for millions in the Tennessee River valley.

Tet offensive In February 1968, the Viet Cong launched a major offensive in the cities of South Vietnam. Although caught by surprise, American and South Vietnam forces successfully quashed this attack, yet the Tet offensive was a blow to American public opinion and led President Johnson to end the escalation of the war and seek a negotiated peace.

Thirteenth Amendment Ratified in 1865, this amendment to the U.S. Constitution prohibited slavery and involuntary servitude.

Trail of Tears In the winter of 1838–1839, the Cherokee were forced to evacuate their lands in Georgia and travel under military guard to present-day Oklahoma. Due to exposure and disease, roughly one-quarter of the 16,000 forced migrants died en route.

transcendentalism An American version of the romantic and idealist thought that emerged in Europe in the early nineteenth century, this literary and philosophical movement held that individuals could rise above material reality and ordinary understanding.

Treaty of Guadalupe Hidalgo Signed in 1848, this treaty ended the Mexican-American War. Mexico relinquished its claims to Texas and ceded an additional 500,000 square miles to the United States for $15 million.

Treaty of Paris Signed by the United States and Spain in December 1898, this treaty ended the Spanish-American War. Under its terms, Spain recognized Cuba's independence and assumed the Cuban debt; it also ceded Puerto Rico and Guam to the United States. At the insistence of the U.S. representatives, Spain also ceded the Philippines. The Senate ratified the treaty on February 6, 1899.

Treaty of Tordesillas Treaty negotiated by the pope in 1494 to resolve competing land claims of Spain and Portugal in the New World. It divided the world along a north-south line in the middle of the Atlantic Ocean, granting to Spain all lands west of the line and to Portugal lands east of the line.

Truman Doctrine In 1947, President Truman asked Congress for money to aid the Greek and Turkish governments that were then threatened by communist rebels. Arguing for the appropriations, Truman asserted his doctrine that the United States was committed to support free people everywhere who were resisting subjugation by communist attack or rebellion.

trunk lines Four major railroad networks that emerged after the Civil War to connect the eastern seaports to the Great Lakes and western rivers. They reflected the growing integration of transportation across the country that helped spur large-scale industrialization.

trust A business-management device designed to centralize and make more efficient the management of diverse and far-flung business operations. It allowed stockholders to exchange their stock certificates for trust certificates, on which dividends were paid. John D. Rockefeller organized the first major trust, the Standard Oil Trust, in 1882.

Turner's thesis Put forth by historian Frederick Jackson Turner in his 1893 paper, "The Significance of the Frontier in American History," this thesis asserted that the existence of a frontier and its settlement had shaped American character; given rise to individualism, independence, and self-confidence; and fostered the American spirit of invention and adaptation. Later historians, especially a group of "new Western historians," modified the thesis by pointing out the environmental and other consequences of frontier settlement, the role of the federal government in peopling the arid West, and the clash of races and cultures that took place on the frontier.

Underground Railroad A network of safe houses organized by abolitionists (usually free blacks) to aid slaves in their attempts to escape slavery in the North or Canada.

Underwood Tariff Act An early accomplishment of the Wilson administration, this law reduced the tariff rates of the Payne-Aldrich law of 1909 by about 15 percent. It also levied a graduated income tax to make up for the lost revenue.

undocumented aliens Once derisively called "wetbacks," undocumented aliens are illegal immigrants, mainly from Mexico and Central America.

unilateralism A national policy of acting alone without consulting others.

utopianism Between the 1830s and 1850s, hopes for societal perfection—utopia—were widespread among evangelical Christians as well as secular humanists. These hopes found expression in various utopian communities and spiritual movements.

vertical integration A form of business organization in which a single firm owns and controls the entire process of production, from the procurement of raw materials to the manufacture and sale of the finished product. In the 1880s and 1890s, many important companies, including Carnegie (later U.S.) Steel and Standard Oil, were vertically integrated.

Vesey conspiracy A plot to burn Charleston, South Carolina, and thereby initiate a general slave revolt, led by a free African American, Denmark Vesey, in 1822. The conspirators were betrayed before the plan was carried out, and Vesey and thirty-four others were hanged.

Virginia Plan Offered by James Madison and the Virginia delegation at the Constitutional Convention, this proposal called for a new government with a strong executive office and two houses of Congress, each with representation proportional to a state's population. Madison's plan also recommended giving the national government veto power over bills passed by the state legislatures. Smaller states countered with the **New Jersey Plan** that gave each state equal representation in Congress.

virtual representation Notion that although colonists had not elected members to Parliament, they were nonetheless represented by it. Espoused by British leaders, this claim countered colonists' argument that they had no voice in Parliament and therefore were being taxed without proper representation.

Voting Rights Act of 1965 The 1965 Voting Rights Act effectively banned literacy tests for voting rights and provided for federal registrars to assure the franchise to minority voters. Within a few years, a majority of African Americans had become registered voters in the southern states.

Wade-Davis Bill In 1864, Congress passed the Wade-Davis bill to counter Lincoln's **Ten Percent Plan** for Reconstruction. The bill required that a majority of a former Confederate state's white male population take a loyalty oath and guarantee equality for African Americans. President Lincoln pocket-vetoed the bill.

Wagner Act The 1935 Wagner Act, formally known as the National Labor Relations Act, created the National Labor Relations Board to supervise union elections and designate winning unions as official bargaining agents. The board could also issue cease-and-desist orders to employers who dealt unfairly with their workers.

War Hawks Congressional leaders who, in 1811 and 1812, called for war against Britain to defend the national honor and force Britain to respect America's maritime rights.

War Industries Board (WIB) An example of the many boards and commissions created during World War I, this government agency oversaw the production of all American factories. It determined priorities, allocated raw materials, and fixed prices; it told manufacturers what they could and could not produce.

War of 1812 War between Britain and the United States. U.S. justifications for war included British violations of American maritime rights, impressment of seamen, provocation of the Indians, and defense of national honor.

war on poverty Lyndon Johnson declared war on poverty in his 1964 State of the Union address. A new Office of Economic Opportunity (OEO) oversaw a variety of programs to help the poor, including the Job Corps and Head Start.

war on terrorism Initiated by President George W. Bush after the attacks of September 11, 2001, the broadly defined war on terrorism aimed to weed out terrorist operatives and their supporters throughout the world.

Watergate scandal A break-in at the Democratic National Committee offices in the Watergate complex in Washington was carried out under the direction of White House employees. Disclosure of the White House involvement in the break-in and subsequent cover-up forced President Richard Nixon to resign in 1974 to avoid impeachment.

weapons of mass destruction (WMD) Biological, chemical, and nuclear weapons capable of widespread destruction.

Webster-Ashburton Treaty This 1842 agreement with Britain resolved the boundary dispute between Maine and New Brunswick, Canada, setting the northeastern U.S. border.

Whigs In mid-eighteenth century Britain, the Whigs were a political faction that dominated Parliament. Generally they were opposed to royal influence in government and wanted to increase the control and influence of Parliament. In America, a Whig party—named for the British Whigs who opposed the king in the late seventeenth century—coalesced in the 1830s around opposition to Andrew Jackson. In general, the American Whigs supported federal power and internal improvements but not territorial expansion. The Whig party collapsed in the 1850s.

Whiskey Rebellion Protests in 1794 by western Pennsylvania farmers resisting payment of a federal tax on whiskey. The uprising was forcibly suppressed when President George Washington called an army of 15,000 troops to the area, where they encountered almost no resistance.

Wilmot Proviso In 1846, shortly after outbreak of the **Mexican-American War,** Congressman David Wilmot of Pennsylvania introduced this controversial amendment stating that any lands won from Mexico would be closed to slavery.

Women's Christian Temperance Union (WCTU) Founded by Frances E. Willard, this organization campaigned to end drunkenness and the social ills that accompanied it. The largest women's organization in the country, by 1898 it had 10,000 branches and 500,000 members. The WCTU illustrated the large role women played in politics and reform long before they won the right to vote.

Women's Trade Union League (WTUL) Founded in 1903, this group worked to organize women into trade unions. It also lobbied for laws to safeguard female workers and backed several successful strikes, especially in the garment industry. It accepted all women who worked, regardless of skill, and while it never attracted many members, its leaders were influential enough to give the union considerable power.

Works Progress Administration (WPA) Congress created this **New Deal** agency in 1935 to provide work relief for the unemployed. Federal works projects included building roads, bridges, and schools; the WPA also funded projects for artists, writers, and young people. It eventually spent $11 billion on projects and provided employment for 8.5 million people.

World Trade Organization (WTO) Global international organization that deals with rules of trade between nations. It became a target for demonstrations in the late 1990s by protesters claiming that global corporations exploited workers and damaged the environment.

Wounded Knee Massacre In December 1890, troopers of the Seventh Cavalry, under orders to stop the **Ghost Dance** religion among the Sioux, took Chief Big Foot and his followers to a camp on Wounded Knee Creek in South Dakota. It is uncertain who fired the first shot, but violence ensued and approximately two hundred Native American men, women, and children were killed.

XYZ Affair A diplomatic incident in which American peace commissioners sent to France by President John Adams in 1797 were insulted with bribe demands from their French counterparts, dubbed X, Y, and Z, in American newspapers. The incident heightened war fever against France.

Yalta Conference Yalta, a city in the Russian Crimea, hosted this wartime conference of the Allies in February 1945 in which the Allies agreed to final plans for the defeat of Germany and the terms of its occupation. The Soviets agreed to allow free elections in Poland, but the elections were never held.

yellow journalism In order to sell newspapers to the public before and during the Spanish-American War, publishers William Randolph Hearst and Joseph Pulitzer engaged in blatant sensationalization of the news, which became known as "yellow journalism." Although it did not cause the war with Spain, it helped turn U.S. public opinion against Spain's actions in Cuba.

yeoman Southern small landholders who owned no slaves, and who lived primarily in the foothills of the Appalachian and Ozark mountains. These farmers were self-reliant and grew mixed crops, although they usually did not produce a substantial amount to be sold on the market.

Young America In the 1840s and early 1850s, many public figures—especially younger members of the Democratic party—used this term to describe a movement that advocated territorial expansion and industrial growth in the name of patriotism.

Credits

Unless otherwise credited, all photographs are the property of Pearson Education, Inc. Page abbreviations are as follows: **T** *top,* **C** *center,* **B** *bottom,* **L** *left,* **R** *right.*

CHAPTER 16

450 The Granger Collection, New York **452–454** The Library of Congress **455** Chicago Historical Society, (none)-00434 **457** National Archives **459** Stock Montage, Inc. **461** Collection of The New-York Historical Society. Negative number 50475 **463** © Bettmann/Corbis **464** Courtesy of the Sixth Mount Zion Baptist Church, Richmond, Virginia **465** Valentine Museum, Richmond, Virginia; **467L** Culver Pictures **467R** © Bettmann/CORBIS **468** Rutherford B. Hayes Presidential Center, Fremont, Ohio **469** Fair Street Pictures **471–473** Culver Pictures **474** © Corbis **477** © Bettmann/CORBIS **478** Yale Joel/LIFE MAGAZINE © Time Inc/Getty Images

CHAPTER 17

480 *Cowboy Camp During the Roundup* by Charles M. Russell, ca. 1885–1887. Amon Carter Museum, Forth Worth, Texas, 1961.186 **484** Neg./Transparency no. 1540-2, Department of Library Services, Courtesy of American Museum of Natural History **487** From *A Pictographic History of the Oglala Sioux* by Amos Bad Heart Bull, text by Helen Blish, University of Nebraska Press **488** Montana Historical Society, Helena **489** Courtesy, Colorado Historical Society **490L** Arizona Historical Society/Tucson, photo accession number 19831 **490R** Arizona Historical Society/Tucson, photo accession number 19830 **491** Thomas Gilcrease Institute of American History & Art **493** Denver Public Library, Western History Collection, X-21874 **494** Used by permission from the Union Pacific Museum Collection **495** Yanaguana Society Collection, Daughters of the Republic of Texas Library **497** Collection of The New-York Historical Society. Negative number 16212 **499** The Library of Congress **500** Californio Vaquero Trousers, Wool, Cotton, Silver, 1834. Autry Museum of Western Heritage, Los Angeles. Acquisition made possible by the Ramona Chapter, Native Sons of the Golden West. **502** The Library of Congress **503** From *The Black West* by William Loren Katz **504B** Haynes Foundation Collection/Montana Historical Society, Helena **504T** Joseph H. Bailey © National Geographic Society

CHAPTER 18

510 *Treasures of Art, Industry, and Manufacture Represented in the American Centennial Exhibition at Philadelphia,* 1876. Plate 35: The Corliss Engine. Publisher: Cosack & Co., Buffalo, New York, 1877. The Thomas J. Watson Library, The Metropolitan Museum of Art. Photograph © 1981 The Metropolitan Museum of Art **513** Courtesy, Colorado Historical Society **516** Culver Pictures **518** Union Pacific Railroad Museum Collection **520** The Granger Collection, NY **524L** The Library of Congress **524R** From the Collections of the Henry Ford Museum and Greenfield Village **525** The Granger Collection, New York **526** © CORBIS **527** The Library of Congress **529** The Library of Congress **530** Courtesy, Metropolitan Life Insurance Company **532** The Library of Congress **533** Carnegie Library of Pittsburgh **535** © Bettmann/Corbis

CHAPTER 19

538 Courtesy of Christopher Cardozo, Inc. **540** Chicago Historical Society **542** © The Museum of the City of New York, The Byron Collection **544** Hulton|Archive/Getty Images **545B** The Library of Congress **545T** National Archives **547** New York Public Library, Astor, Lenox and Tilden Foundations **548** The Chicago Historical Society, ICHi27477 **549** Collection of David J. and Janice L. Frent **551** The Advertising Archive **552** Collection of the New-York Historical Society, Negative Number 42976 **553** The Library of Congress **555** Courtesy of the AT&T Archives **556** Brown Brothers **558** University of Michigan Medical School records, Bentley Historical Library, University of Michigan. J. Jefferson Gibson, Photographer **559** The Library of Congress **561** © The Museum of the City of New York, The Byron Collection **563L** Brown Brothers **563R** Jane Addams Memorial Collection, Special Collections, University Library, University of Illinois at Chicago. HHA# neg 32 **567** © Bettmann/Corbis **568** The Library of Congress **570** © Elliott Erwitt/Magnum

CHAPTER 20

572 Courtesy of Janice L. and David Frent **574** The Library of Congress **575** National Museum of American History, Smithsonian Institution **578** © Bettmann/CORBIS **581** North Carolina Division of Archives & History **582** The Kansas State Historical Society, Topeka, Kansas **584** © Minnesota Historical Society/Corbis **585** The Library of Congress **586** The Granger Collection, NY **589L** Valentine Museum/Richmond History Center **589R** © Bettmann/Corbis **590** Clifton Waller Barrett Library of American Literature, Special Collections, University of Virginia Library **591** © Bettmann/CORBIS **592–593** L. Frank Baum, *The Wonderful World of Oz,* William Morrow and Company, Inc., N.Y. **595** Culver Pictures

CHAPTER 21

600 United States Naval Academy Museum **602** The Library of Congress **603** The State Historical Society of Wisconsin **604** The Granger Collection, NY **605** © Bettmann/Corbis **608** The Hawaiian Historical Society **611** Courtesy of the Cuban Heritage Collection, University of Miami Libraries, Coral Gables, Florida **613** The Granger Collection, New York **614** © Corbis **615L** Courtesy of USMA Archives, West Point, N.Y. **615R** Chicago Historical Society, ICHi-08425 **618** New York Public Library, Astor, Lenox and Tilden Foundations **621B–623** Culver Pictures

CHAPTER 22

626 *Hester Street* by George Benjamin Luks, 1905. Oil on canvas, 26 1/8 x 36 1/8 inches. Brooklyn Museum of Art, Dick S. Ramsay Fund. 40.339 **628** Culver Pictures **629** From the collections of the Henry Ford Museum & Greenfield Village **631** New York Public Library, Astor, Lenox and Tilden Foundations **632L-R** Brown Brothers **635L** The Library of Congress **635R** Courtesy George Eastman House **636** Culver Pictures **637B** Women's History Archive, Sophia Smith Collection, Smith College, Northampton, Mass. **638** © Bettmann/Corbis **641** California History Section, California State Library **643** Walter Reuther Library, Wayne State University **645** Manchester, N.H. Historic Association **646** The Granger Collection, NY **647** Photofest **648** The Granger Collection, New York **649** *Cliff Dwellers* by George Wesley Bellows (United States, 1882–1925), 1913. Los Angeles County Museum of Art, Los Angeles County Fund. Photograph © 2005 Museum Associates/LACMA

CHAPTER 23

656 Culver Pictures **659** Chicago Historical Society, ICHi-03841 **661** Culver Pictures **663** Rare Book, Manuscript, & Special Collections Library, Duke University **665** © Corbis **666** State Historical Society of Wisconsin, WHi (X3) 13031; WHi-2394 **668** The Granger Collection, New York **670L** Courtesy, The Lilly Library, Indiana University, Bloomington, Indiana **670R** Smithsonian Institution **674** The Library of Congress **675** Museum of American Political Life, University of Hartford **677** Culver Pictures **679B** Walter P. Reuther Library, Wayne State University **679T** National Archives **680–681** A'Lelia Bundles/Walker Family Collection/Washington, DC **685** Mrs. Neill Whisnant **686** The Granger Collection, NY **687** Jane Addams Memorial Collection (JAMC neg. 404) Special Collections, The University Library, University of Illinois at Chicago

CHAPTER 24

688 National Archives **690** *New York Tribune*, May 8, 1915 **697** © Bettmann/Corbis **698** Dokumentations- und Informationszentrum Munchen GmbH, Bilderdienst **699** The Library of Congress **702** *The Victorious Retreat Back to the Rhine* by Frank Earle Schoonover (1877–1972). 1918, (oil on canvas). Delaware Art Museum, Wilmington, USA / Bridgeman Art Library, Gift of the Bank of Delaware **704** National Archives **705** US Government Printing Office **706** *The Argonne* by Harvey Dunn/National Museum of American History, Smithsonian Institution **707** The Chicago Historical Society, DN-0069264 **708** Brown Brothers **709** Courtesy of the American Legion **710** © Bettmann/CORBIS **712** National Archives **714** The Imperial War Museum, London **715** The Granger Collection, NY

CHAPTER 25

718 *The Great White Way, —Times Square* by Howard Thain, 1925, oil on canvas, 30 x 36 inches, accession number 1963.150. Collection of The New-York Historical Society **720** From the collections of the Henry Ford Museum & Greenfield Village **721** Gaslight Advertising Archives **723** The Granger Collection, New York **724** Archive Photos/Getty Images **725** © Bettmann/Corbis; **726** The Granger Collection, New York **727** © Underwood & Underwood/Corbis **728B** *Sunday, 1926* by Edward Hopper. Acquired 1926, The Phillips Collection, Washington, DC **728T** Courtesy of Harvard University Portrait Collection, Gift of Mrs. Stanley B. Resor for Eliot House **729** *The Jazz Singers* by Archibald J. Motley, Jr. 1891–1981, c.1937. Oil on canvas, 32⅛" h. x 42¼" w. Permanent Collection, Western Illinois University Art Gallery/Museum, Macomb, Illinois **730** The Negro World — Schomburg Center for Research in Black Culture, New York Public Library, Astor, Lenox and Tilden Foundations **732C** Photograph by Carl Van Vechten. Reproduced by permission of Carl Van Vechten Papers, Collection of American Literature, Beinecke Rare Book and Manuscript Library, Yale University **732L** Art Resource, New York **732R** The Granger Collection, New York **733** Culver Pictures **734** *The Passion of Sacco and Vanzetti*, (1931–1932) by Ben Shahn, from the Sacci and Vanzetti series of 23 paintings. Tempera, 84-½ x 48 inches. From the collection of Whitney Museum of American Art. Gift of Edith and Milton Lowenthal. © Estate of Ben Shahn/Licensed by VAGA, New York, NY **735** © Bettmann/Corbis **739–744** The Library of Congress **745** Culver Pictures **746** © Bettmann/Corbis

CHAPTER 26

748 *Okie Camp* by Maynard Dixon,1935. The Delman Collection, San Francisco **750** AP/Wide World Photos **752** The Library of Congress **753** *The Park Bench* by Reginald March, 1933. Tempera on masonite mounted on panel, 24 x 36, Sheldon Memorial Art Gallery and Sculpture Garden, University of Nebraska-Lincoln, NAA-Nebraska Art Association Collection **756** © J.B. Grant/Leo de Wys Photo Agency/eStock Photography, LLC **757** The Franklin D. Roosevelt Library; **758** AP/Wide World Photos **759 L-R** The Library of Congress

760B The Library of Congress **760TL** The Franklin D. Roosevelt Library **760TR** The Library of Congress **763** The Library of Congress **765** Mrs. Philip Evergood/ACA Galleries **766** Hulton|Archive/ Getty Images **767** AP/Wide World Photos **768** Archive Photos/Getty Images **769L** Daniel Robert Fitzpatrick/St. Louis Post Dispatch **769R–771** The Franklin D. Roosevelt Library

CHAPTER 27

776 U.S. Navy Art Collection **778** Brown Brothers **781** U.S. Army Center of Photo History **782** AP/Wide World Photos **783** Bildarchiv Preussischer Kulturbesitz **786** UPI/Corbis-Bettmann **788** Official U.S. Navy Photograph **789L-R** Courtesy of Military Antiques, Petaluma, CA **790** © Bettmann/Corbis **793** The Library of Congress **795** AP/Wide World Photos **796** *The Migration of the Negro Panel 1* by Jacob Lawrence, 1940–41. The Phillips Collection, Washington, D.C. Jacob & Gwendolyn Lawrence Foundation **797** *Family in Camp Room* by Henry Sugimoto, 1942. Gift of Madeleine Sugimoto and Naomi Tagawa, Japanese American National Museum (92.97.88) **800** US Army Photo **801** Courtesy of the World Federation of Bergen-Belsen Associations **802** Ed Clark/LIFE MAGAZINE © Time Inc/Getty Images **803** Underwood & Underwood/Corbis-Bettmann

CHAPTER 28

806 National Archives **808–812** AP/Wide World Photos **814** The Fotomas Index **815** © Bettmann/Corbis **817** Sovfoto/Eastfoto **819** Carl Mydens, LIFE MAGAZINE © Time Inc//Getty Images **821–823** UPI/Corbis-Bettmann **824** © Bettmann/Corbis **825** Hank Walker, LIFE MAGAZINE © Time Inc/Getty Images **826** Courtesy of Janice L. and David Frent **827** © Bettmann/ CORBIS **828B** from Herblock's *Special for Today*, (Simon & Schuster, 1958). Originally appeared in *The Washington Post* **828T** Brown Brothers **829** AP/Wide World Photos **832** The National Archives **833** UPI/Corbis-Bettmann

CHAPTER 29

836–838L © Cornell Capa/Magnum **840** © Christie's Images **842** Superstock **843L** © Christie's Images **843R** Globe Photos, Inc. **844** *Number 10* by Mark Rothko,1950. Oil on Canvas, 7'6-⅜" x 57-⅛". The Museum of Modern Art. Gift of Philip Johnson. Photograph © 2001 The Museum Modern Art, New York /Art Resource, NY. © 1998 Kate Rothko Prizel & Christopher Rothko/Artists Rights Society (ARS), New York **845L** © Rudolph Burckhardt/Sygma/Corbis **845R** *Convergence* by Jackson Pollock, 1952. Oil on canvas, overall: 93 ½ x 155", Albright-Knox Art Gallery, Buffalo, New York, Gift of Seymour H. Knox, Jr., 1956. © 2005 The Pollock-Krasner Foundation/Artists Rights Society (ARS), New York **846L** Sovfoto **846R** Copyright © 1957 by The New York Times Co. Reprinted by permission **847** NASA **851B** UPI/Corbis-Bettmann **851T** Magnum Photos, Inc. **852** AP/Wide World Photos **853L** © Bettmann/ CORBIS **853R** AP/Wide World Photos

CHAPTER 30

856 *Signs* by Robert Rauschenberg, 1970. © Robert Rauschenberg/Licensed by VAGA, New York, NY **858–861** AP/Wide World Photos **863** Archive Photos/Getty Images **864** © Bettmann/ CORBIS **867** Charles Moore/Black Star/StockPhoto **868** AP/Wide World Photos **869** © Bettmann/CORBIS **870L-R** George Tames/NYT Pictures **879B** Photo by Doan Cong Tinh/American War Photo Project. © 2000 The New York Times Company; **879T** AP/Wide World Photos **881** Paul Conklin/TimePix/Getty Images **882** Courtesy of Vintage Trends.com **883** Archive Photos/Blank Archive/Getty Images **884** Getty Images **885** © Nancy Ellison/Sygma/Corbis **887** Lyndon Baines Johnson Library **888** Magnum Photos

CHAPTER 31

892 Archive Photos/Getty Images **894** from Herblock's *State of the Union*, (Simon & Schuster, 1972) **896B** © 1971, The Washington Post.

Index

Key terms and the text page on which the term is defined are highlighted in boldface type. Terms and definitions also appear in the Glossary, pp. G-1–G-13.

A

AAA. *See* Agricultural Adjustment Administration (AAA)
A&P grocery stores, 528
AARP, 964
Abbot, Grace, 635
Abilene, Kansas, 499
Ablowitz, Rebecca, 555
Abortion and abortion rights, 910, 920–924, 922 (illus.); Sanger, Margaret, and, 636; Supreme Court and, 910
"Absurd Effort to Make the World Over, The" (Sumner), 560
Abzug, Robert, 800
Acheson, Dean: McCarthy, Joseph R., and, 825; as secretary of state, 816, 817, 818, 830; as undersecretary of state, 811; Vietnam War and, 886
Acid rain, 907
ACLU. *See* American Civil Liberties Union (ACLU)
Acquired immune deficiency syndrome. *See* AIDS (acquired immune deficiency syndrome)
ACT UP (AIDS Coalition to Unleash Power), 911
ADA. *See* Americans with Disabilities Act (ADA)
Adams, Charles Francis, Jr., 573, 620
Adams, Harriet Stratemeyer, 648
Adams, Henry, 584
Adams, Samuel Hopkins, 670
Adams, Sherman, 848
Adamson Act (1916), 679
Addams, Jane, 547, 557, 563 (illus.), 564; Hull House of, 562–563; NAACP and, 638; Philippines annexation and, 619; on private beneficence, 658; Progressive party and, 675; and Women's Trade Union League, 642; World War I and, 696
Adding machine, 523
Adolescence: in late 19th century, 554, 555; prolonged, 725
Adventures of Huckleberry Finn, The (Twain), 590, 590 (illus.)
Adventures of Tom Sawyer, The (Twain), 590
Advertising, 525–528
AEF. *See* American Expeditionary Force (AEF)
Affirmative action, 570, 966; *Bakke* v. *Regents of the University of California* and, 956–959; demonstration for, 957 (illus.); Reagan and, 932
Affluence: anxiety and, 847; critics of, 842–843, 846; reform and, 847–849; suburbanization and, 836–839, 840–841; in urban

areas, 963; after World War II, 836–849. *See also* Wealth
Afghanistan: Soviet invasion of, 895, 918; terrorism and, 991–992
AFL. *See* AFL-CIO; American Federation of Labor (AFL)
AFL-CIO, membership of, 905
Africa: AIDS in, 946; after Cold War, 962; empires and, 606; imperialism in, 621 (illus.); World War I and, 700; World War II and, 788, 791
African Americans: back-to-Africa movements, 730–731; Black Codes and, 455, 456, 462; black nationalism and, 730–731, 883; Black Panthers and, 883; Black Power and, 882–884; as buffalo soldiers, 486, 488–489, 488 (illus.); in business, 680–681; churches of, 464 (illus.), 465; Colored Farmers' National Alliance and Cooperative Union, 581; in Congress, 463, 463 (illus.), 464, 615; conscription and, 702, 881; contract labor system and, 461; convict-lease system and, 474–475; on courts, 932; as cowboys, 500; in defense industries, 866; as domestics, 589 (illus.); in election of 1980, 930; employment discrimination and, 638; as Exodusters, 502, 503 (illus.); farming and, 633, 635, 638; Fifteenth Amendment and, 466–467; Fourteenth Amendment and, 456; as government appointees, 766; as governors, 615; in Great Depression, 753, 766–767, 771; hair care and, 680–681, 884; higher education and, 558–559, 732; housing discrimination and, 837, 840, 868; in Indian wars, 615; institutions of, 464–465; Jim Crow and, 473–475; Ku Klux Klan and, 467–469, 735–736; in labor force, 588; labor unions and, 532, 533, 638, 642, 765, 905; literacy and, 638; literature of, 729; lynchings of, 474, 474 (illus.); marriage and, 464–465; migration of, 539, 710, 711, 711 (illus.), 722–723, 729, 730, 796 (illus.); in military, 702, 712 (illus.), 795, 802 (illus.), 850; military honors for, 616, 667, 712 (illus.); music and, 648, 729; NAACP and, 639; National Urban League and, 639; New Deal and, 766–767; in 1950s, 839; in political office, 463, 464, 473–474; Populism and, 582; poverty and, 871; racial designations and, 604–605; radicalism of, 882; Republican party and, 462; and resistance to violence, 711; Roosevelt, Eleanor, and, 766, 770, 771; Roosevelt, Franklin D., and, 766; Roosevelt, Theodore, and, 667; second great migration and, 874; separate but equal

doctrine and, 557; sharecropping and, 461–462; Smalls, Robert, 451–452, 452 (illus.); as "smoked Yankees," 616; Social Security and, 766; social-service agencies of, 660; Southern Alliance and, 582; southern public schools and, 557; in Spanish-American War, 615–616, 615 (illus.), 616, 617, 624; status of, 966–967; Truman, Harry S., and, 850; Turner, Henry McNeal, and, 475–478, 478 (illus.); in U.S. population (1900), 550; views of Reconstruction and, 476–477; voting and, 473–474, 579, 872–873, 873 (illus.), 913; wage discrimination and, 766; Wilson, Woodrow, and, 678; women's organizations and, 660; women workers and, 530, 634; words referring to, 884; in workforce, 531; World War I and, 681, 702, 709, 710–711, 730–731; after World War II, 850; WPA and, 766. *See also* Civil rights; Civil rights movement; Desegregation; Freedmen; Segregation; Slaves and slavery; Voting and voting rights
African Methodist Episcopal (AME) Church, 465, 475
Afrika Korps, 788, 791
Age of Aquarius, 883 (illus.)
Age of Innocence, The (Wharton), 728
Agnew, Spiro, 888, 897, 912
Agricultural Adjustment Administration (AAA), 758–759, 766, 769, 772
Agricultural experiment stations, 504
Agriculture: commodity prices and, 580; contract labor system in, 461; cooperatives, 581; crop lien system, 580; land use in 1880s, 505 (illus.). *See also* Planters and plantations; Sharecropping
Agriculture Department, 671
Aguinaldo, Emilio, 620, 621 (illus.), 622
AIDS (acquired immune deficiency syndrome), 911, **944**–946, 945 (illus.)
Air brakes, 516, 525
Airline industry, after September 11, 2001, 992
Air pollution, 542, 904, 926 (illus.), 932
Alabama: African American troops in, 615; tenant farming in, 633
Alabama (ship): claims settlement with Britain, 607
Alabama National Guard, 872
Alaska: environment of, 987; oil pipeline in, 904; purchase of, 607; territorial status of, 622
Albanians, ethnic, 979, 979 (illus.)
Albright, Madeleine, 976, 979
Alcohol and alcoholism: in cities, 543; illness, death, and, 735; Native Americans and, 491;

Alcohol and alcoholism *(continued)*: products, 734–735; progressivism and, 659–660. *See also* Prohibition; Temperance movement

Alcott, Louisa May, 589

Aldrich, Nelson W., 673

"Alexander's Ragtime Band," 648

Alger, Horatio, 531, 589

Algeria, 791

Alien and Sedition Acts (1798), 823

Aliens, undocumented, 965

Allen, Frederick Lewis, 726

Alley Gang, 543

Alliances: in World War I, 696–697, 702 (illus.); in World War II, 780, 781, 788–789. *See also* specific alliances

All Quiet on the Western Front (Remarque), 781

Alpha Test, 704–705, 705 (illus.)

al Qaeda, 962–963

Alternating current, for electric lighting, 525

AMA. *See* American Medical Association (AMA)

Amador, José María, 496

Amalgamated Copper Company, 630

Amalgamated Iron and Steel Workers, 535

Amazon.com, 989

"America" (song), 699

America First Committee, 785

American Birth Control League. *See* Birth Control League

American Civil Liberties Union (ACLU), Scopes Trial and, 743–747

American Economic Association, 561

American Expeditionary Force (AEF), 701, 706

American Federation of Labor (AFL), 532–533; CIO and, 765; in Great Depression, 764–765; membership of, 642; in 1920s, 722. *See also* AFL-CIO

American G.I. Forum, 796

American Independent party, 889

American League (baseball), 553

American Line, 689

American Medical Association (AMA), 658, 671

American Mercury, 728

American Protective Association, 546

American Psychiatric Association, on homosexuality, 911

American Psychological Association (APA), 704

American Railway Association, 516

American Railway Union (ARU), 585, 662

American Rights Committee, 699

American Society of Composers, Authors and Publishers (ASCAP), 648

American Sugar Refining, 522

Americans with Disabilities Act (ADA), 949, 950 (illus.)

American Telephone and Telegraph (AT&T), 523, 966

American Tobacco Company, 630, 668, 674

American Tragedy, The (Evergood), 765 (illus.)

American Woman Suffrage Association, 660

America's Road to War, 1914-1917 (Millis), 781

Amnesty, for illegal aliens, 965–966

Amoskeag Bulletin, 645

Amoskeag Company, 644–645, 645 (illus.)

Amos 'n Andy, 721, 762

"Anaconda" system (crop lien), 580

Anacostia Flats, bonus army in, 754

Anarchists and anarchism: Haymarket Riot and, 535; in 1919, 733

Andean Strategy, antidrug program as, 947

Anderson, John, 929

Anderson, Marian, 766, 766 (illus.), 771

Anderson, Maxwell, 716, 728

Anderson, Sherwood, 613–614, 728

Andresson, Marc, 988

Andropov, Yuri, 943

Anesthetics, 551

Angel Island, 641 (illus.)

Angelus Temple, 737

Anglo-Saxons, 606

Animals: of Great Plains, 483

Anne of Green Gables (Montgomery), 648

Annexation: foreign policy and, 606; of Hawaii, 607, 608–609

Antebellum era. *See also* Civil War (U.S.); South

Anthony, Susan B., 467, 467 (illus.), 555, 885

Anthrax scare, 992

Anti-abortion advocates, 922, 923 (illus.)

Antiballistic missiles (ABMs), 897

Antiballistic Missile (ABM) treaty, termination of, 993

Anti-Catholicism, 546–547

Anti-Comintern pact, 781

Anti-Evolution League, 746 (illus.)

Anti-immigrant sentiment: census of 1890 and, 605; against Chinese, 640; in early 1900s, 628, 641; mining strikes and, 585–587. *See also* Immigrants and immigration; Know-Nothings

Anti-Imperialist League, 620

Anti-Saloon League, 659–660, 734

Anti-Semitism, 547, 762. *See also* Jews and Judaism

Antitrust movement, 522. *See also* Trusts and trust busting

Antiwar sentiment. *See* Pacifism and peace movements; Protest(s)

Apache Indians, 483, 486

Appalachian region: poverty in, 871

Appeal to Reason, 707

Appeasement, 783–784, 811

Appleton, Victor, 648

Applied Christianity (Gladden), 562

Arabic (ship), 690, 698

Arab-Israeli wars: Lebanon, Syria, and, 941; October War and, 901

Arab oil embargo (1973), 892 (illus.), 894, 902–903

Arab world: Camp David accords and, 916; Clinton and, 977; immigrants from, 968; Palestine Arabs and, 916. *See also* Arab-Israeli wars

Arafat, Yasir, 977

Arapaho Indians, 483, 485, 486, 489

Arbitration treaty, with Great Britain, 608

Architecture: skyscrapers, 540–541, 723–724, 724 (illus.)

Arctic National Wildlife Refuge, 987

Argentina, 695

Argonne Forest, battle at, 703

Aristide, Jean-Bertrand, 977, 978

Arizona, 482

Arkansas, 468; Clinton in, 970; school shooting in, 982; Unionist government in, 453

Arkansas National Guard, 851, 851 (illus.)

Arkies, 766

Arlington National Cemetery, 614

Armed forces, 705 (illus.); air force and, 816; Civil War and, 614; desegregation of, 850; IQ testing in, 704–705; in Lebanon, 940; modernization of, 691; rearmament and, 819; Spanish-American War and, 614, 616; unification of, 815–816; in Vietnam War, 878, 878 (illus.), 879, 880, 898. *See also* American Expeditionary Force (AEF); Armed forces; Military; Soldiers; specific battles and wars

Armour, Philip D., 527

Arms control: Eisenhower and, 829, 831–832; nuclear test ban and, 832

Arms race. *See* Nuclear arms race

Armstrong, Louis, 648, 729

Army-McCarthy hearings, 827

Army War College, 691

Arnaz, Desi, 842 (illus.)

Arrogance of Power, The (Fulbright), 876

Art(s): abstract expressionism and, 844–845; Ashcan School and, 626, 649; avant-garde, 845; blacklisting and, 827; critique of consumerism and, 843, 846; experimentation in, 649–650; Great Depression and, 748, 759, 760 (illus.), 761; leftism and, 844, 845; New York Armory show and, 649; in 1920s, 727–729, 732; postimpressionism and, 650; realism and, 649; social realism and, 844, 845

Arthur, Chester A., 577

Ashcan School, 626, 649

Ashcroft, John, 986–987; war on terrorism and, 992–993

Asia: financial crash in, 980; foreign policy of 1920s and 1930s in, 780; immigration from, 628, 737, 962, 964, 967–968; imperialism in, 621 (illus.); markets in, 608; scramble for empire and, 606; second great migration and, 874–875. *See also* World War II; specific countries

Asiatic Squadron, 616

Aspin, Les, 977

Assassinations: attempt against Reagan, 931 (illus.); attempt on Castro, 862; by CIA, 912; of Garfield, 577; of Kennedy, John F., 869, 869 (illus.); of Kennedy, Robert F., 887; of King, Martin Luther, Jr., 883; of McKinley, 597–598, 667

Assemblies of God, 841

Assembly line, 719–720; IWW and, 644; in meat packing industry, 523, 527

Assimilation policy, for Native Americans, 487–491

Association of Multiethnic Americans, 968

Atchison, Topeka, and Santa Fe Railroad, 517, 518

Atkinson, Ti-Grace, 885

Atlanta: rioting in, 638, 667

Atlanta Compromise, 559

Atlanta Exposition, 559

Atlas ICBMs, 859

Atomic weapons. *See* Nuclear weapons

Attlee, Clement, 807

Audiotapes, Watergate scandal and, 900

Augusta (ship), 807

Australia, World War II and, 791, 792

Austria: World War II and, 783

Austria-Hungary: immigrants from, 546; World War I and, 696

Authoritarianism, Carter's human rights policy and, 917

Automobiles and automobile industry: decline in purchases and, 903; foreign competition in, 905, 905 (illus.); fuel-efficient cars and, 904; Highway Act of 1956, 848; interstates and, 848–849, 849 (illus.); mass production of, 629–630, 631; Model T, 719–720; Reagan and, 932; suburbanization and, 840–841. *See also* Energy crisis; Oil shocks

Aviation: first flight, 598; Lindbergh and, 726; Roosevelt, Franklin D., and, 755; World War I and, 702 (illus.)

Axis of evil, 993, 994

Axis Powers, 781, 788–792, 798–799, 802–803

Ayer, N. W., and Son, 525

B

Babbitt (Lewis), 728

Babcock, Orville E., 470

Baby and Child Care (Spock), 841

Baby boom and baby boomers, **837**–838, 838 (illus.), 841; birthrate and, 908; election of 1984 and, 939

Back-to-Africa movements, 730–731

Baer, George F., 668

Baez, Joan, 881, 882

Baghdad: in Persian Gulf War, 953. *See also* Iraq

Bailey, James A., 553

Bailey v. *Drexel Furniture Company,* 661

Baker, Ella, 854

Baker, James, 947

Baker, Josephine, 680

Baker, Newton D., 665

Baker, Ray Stannard, 706

Baker v. *Carr* (1962), 868–869

Bakke, Allan, 956–959, 958 (illus.)

Bakker, Jim and Tammy, 935

Bakke v. *Regents of the University of California,* 570, 956–959, 966

Balkan region: after Cold War, 962; Soviet Union and, 799, 808

Ball, George, Vietnam War and, 878

Ball, Lucille, 842 (illus.)

Ballinger, Richard A., 673

Ballinger-Pinchot affair, 673

Ballot box, 575 (illus.)

Baltimore and Ohio (B & O) Railroad, 516, 518, 519

Bancroft, Hubert Howe, 498

Bank(s) and banking: bank holiday, 756; bond sales of 1894-1896, 587; in Great Depression, 754, 754 (illus.), 755, 756; mergers and, 630; Panic of 1893 and, 584 (illus.)

Banking Act (1933), 772

Bankruptcy: of railroads, 518, 896. *See also* Great Depression (1930s)

Banks, Louis, 753

Bannock Indians, 482, 486

Bara, Theda, 727

Barak, Ehud, 977

Barbed wire, 500, 503, 504 (illus.)

Barnard College, 558, 634

Barnett, Ross, 866–867

Barnum, P. T., 481, 553

Barry, Leonora M., 533

Baruch, Bernard M., 708, 810

Baruch Plan, 810

Baseball, 553, 553 (illus.), 726

Basketball, 553

Bataan death march, 788

Batchelor, Claude, 821

Battle(s): Native American, 485 (illus.), 486–487. *See also* Wars and warfare; specific battles and wars

"Battle of the standards," in 1886 election, 499

Battleships, 611

Baum, Frank, 592–593

Baxter Street Dudes, 543

Bay of Pigs, 861–**862**

Beats, 843, 846

Beckwith, Bob, 991 (illus.)

Beecher: Henry Ward, 562. *See also* Stowe, Harriet Beecher

Beethoven, 706

Begin, Menachem, 916, 916 (illus.)

Behavioral psychology, 551

Beirut, Lebanon, 831, 941

Belarus, 977

Belgium: Brussels Treaty and, 813; Hoover, Herbert, and, 709; World War I and, 697, 700; World War II and, 798

Belknap, William E., 470

Bell, Alexander Graham, 523

Bellamy, Edward, 561

Belleau Wood, battle at, 703

Bellotti v. *Baird,* 923

Bellows, George W., 649

Bell Telephone Company, 523

Bemis, Edward, 665

Bemis, Samuel F., 602

Ben Hur (Wallace), 589

Bentsen, Lloyd, 948, 971

Bergen-Belsen, 801 (illus.)

Berger, Sandy, 976

Berkman, Alexander, 535, 733

Berlin, Germany, 609

Berlin, Irving, 648

Berlin airlift, 814–**815,** 815 (illus.)

Berlin Blockade, 814–815, 815 (illus.)

Berlin crisis: first, 814–815; second, 833, 859–860

Berlin Wall, 860, 860 (illus.); opening of, 951

Berryman, Clifford, 739

Bessemer, Henry, 519

Bessemer process, 519, 520 (illus.)

Bessemer steel, 512

Beta Test, 704–705

Bethel, New York, 882

Bethlehem Steel, 521

Bethune, Mary McLeod, 681, 766

Bethune-Cookman College, 681

Beveridge, Albert J., 672

B-52 bomber, 859

Bible: Scopes Trial and, 743–747

Big business: railroads as, 513. *See also* Business; Corporations

Big Foot (chief), 487, 489

Big Four, after World War I, 713

Big Three conference, 799

Bikini atoll, 816

Billington, Ray Allen, 506

"Billion-dollar" Congress, 578–579, 594

Billy the Kid, 496

Binet, Alfred, 704

Bin Laden, Osama, 962, 991, 992

Biogenetic law, 606

Birds of passage, 639

Birmingham, Alabama: children's march in, 867; demonstrators in, 867 (illus.); freedom ride and, 866

Birth control, 635, 636–637; in late 19th century, 554; in 1920s, 725

Birth Control League, 637 (illus.). *See also* Planned Parenthood Federation of America

Birth Control Review, 637 (illus.)

Birth of a Nation (movie), 476, 477 (illus.), 647

Birthrate, 908; decline in, 554; 1940-1970, 838 (illus.)

Bison. *See* Buffalo

Black, Hugo, 772, 868, 923

Black Beauty (Sewell), 589

Black Codes, 455, 456, 462; apprenticeship provisions in, 464

Blackfoot Indians, 483

Black Hills, gold rush in, 498

Black Kettle (chief), 485–486

Black male suffrage, 453, 457; Fifteenth Amendment and, 467. *See also* Voting and voting rights

Blackmun, Harry, 896, 923; *Bakke* case and, 958

Black nationalism, 478

Black Panther party, 883

Black Power movement, 882–884

Black Reconstruction in America (Du Bois), 476

Blacks. *See* African Americans; Slaves and slavery

Black Star Line, 730–731, 730 (illus.)

Blaine, James G., 470, 603–606; and economic benefits of expansion, 603, 606; election of 1884 and, 577; under Garfield, 607; and Latin America, 607; and Samoa, 609

Bland-Allison Silver Purchase Act (1878), **577,** 579

Bliss, Tasker H., 713

Bliss, William Dwight Porter, 562

Blitzkrieg, 784

Blockade. *See* Berlin Blockade

Bloomer pants, 492

Blough, Roger, 865

Blue-collar jobs: African Americans in, 966; Reagan and, 936, 937

Blues (music), 729

Board of Special Inquiry (Ellis Island), 545

Bobbsey Twins series, 648

Bohemians, 585

"Bohío de Reconcentrados," 611 (illus.)

Boland Amendment, 941; Iran-Contra and, 942–943

Bolden, Charles (Buddy), 648

Bolivia, drug trade and, 947

Bolshevik Revolution, 701, 708, 733

Bolsheviks, 636

Bombs and bombings: in Oklahoma City, 980; of Vietnam, 898. *See also* Terrorism

Bonanza, 842

Bonanza farms, 504

Bonus army, 754

"Boomers" (Oklahoma homesteaders), 506

Borah, William E., 715, 784

Borders: drug trade and, 947

Borjas, George J., 965

Bork, Robert, 948

Bosnia: civil war in, 978 (illus.); intervention in, 977

Bosnia-Herzegovina, 978
Bosnian Serbs, 978
Bosses (political), 548–550
Boston: Anti-Imperialist League in, 620; foreign-born population of, 546; police strike in, 733, 738; workers' demonstration in, 584
Boston (ship), 609
Boston History Class, 557
Boston Red Sox, 553
Boulder Dam, 754
Bourke-White, Margaret, 801
Bowery, 590, 591 (illus.)
Boxer Rebellion, 623–624
Boxing, 553
Boycotts: of grapes, 884; Montgomery bus boycott, 852; of 1980 Moscow Olympics, 918
Bozeman Trail, Sioux War and, 486
Bracker, Milton, 800
Bradley, Omar: Cold War and, 819; Vietnam War and, 886; World War II and, 798, 800
Brahms, 706
Branch, Taylor, 853
Branch Davidians, siege against, 981
Brandeis, Louis D., 675, 677, 678; *Muller* v. *Oregon* and, 684–687, 686 (illus.)
Brandeis brief, 662, 685–687
Brand names, 525–528
Brazil, 695, 876
Breadlines, 752 (illus.)
Breedlove, Sarah. *See* Walker, C. J. (Madam)
Bremer, Arthur, 899
Brennan, William J., 868
Breslin, Jimmy, 887–888
Breton, André, 845
Brezhnev, Leonid, 897, 943
Brezhnev doctrine, end of, 951
Briand, Aristide, 777
Britain. *See* England (Britain)
British Guiana, 607–608
British West Indies, 607
Brokaw, Tom, 992
Bronco Buster, The (Remington), 624
Bronson House, 563
Brooklyn, New York, birth control clinic in, 637
Brooklyn Bridge, 520, 549
Brooks, Harriet, 634
Brooks Brothers, 601
Brown, H. Rap, 883
Brown, Henry Billings, 569
Brown, James, 884
Brown, Joseph E., 472
Brown, Ronald, 971
Brownmiller, Susan, 885
Brown University: pacifism and, 782
Brown v. Board of Education of Topeka, 570, 686, **850–852,** 851 (illus.), 853
Bruce, Blanche K., 463 (illus.), 464
Brussels Treaty, 813
Bryan, Alfred, 697
Bryan, Mary, 594
Bryan, William Jennings: Baum, Frank, and, 592; "Cross of Gold" speech, 594–595, 595 (illus.); election of 1896 and, 572 (illus.), 594–596, 597; election of 1900 and, 597, 622; election of 1908 and, 671–672; Philippines annexation and, 619–620, 622; Scopes Trial and, 744–747, 744 (illus.); as

secretary of state, 690, 694, 698; Spanish-American War and, 612, 614
Bryn Mawr college, 558
Brzezinski, Zbigniew, 917
B-25 bomber, 793 (illus.)
B-29 bomber, 802, 815, 816
B-36 bomber, 816
Buchanan, Pat, 972
Buchanan v. *Worley,* 639
Buck, Pearl, at White House, 864 (illus.)
Buckley, Christopher A. ("Blind Boss"), 548, 549, 550
Buckley, William, 928
Buddhists, self-immolation of monks, 861, 861 (illus.)
Budget: ceiling on federal, 933–936; Clinton and, 971; in 1920s, 738–739; surplus in, 980. *See also* Federal deficit; Spending
Buffalo, 483; Indians and, 483–484, 484 (illus.), 490–491
Buffalo, New York, 597
Buffalo nickel, 491
Buffalo Soldiers, 486, 488–489, 488 (illus.), 615, 616
Buford (ship), 733
Bulgaria, 809, 951
Bulge, battle of, 798, 799
Bull, Amos Bad Heart, 487 (illus.)
Bulldozing, 473
Bull Moose party, 656, 675, 675 (illus.)
Bundy, McGeorge, 859, 876, 877
Burchfield, Charles, 728–729
Bureau of Construction and Repair, 610
Bureau of Corporations, 667–668
Bureau of Indian Affairs, 767
Bureau of Labor, 635
Bureau of Negro Economics, 639
Burger, Warren, 895, 896, 933 (illus.), 948
Burgess, John W., 476, 606
Burma, 788
Burnham, Walter Dean, 930
Burns, Lucy, 660
Bus boycott: in Montgomery, 852
Bush, George, 948–954; ADA and, 949, 950 (illus.); China and, 951; as CIA director, 912; domestic policy of, 949–950, 969; election of 1980 and, 929; election of 1984 and, 938; election of 1988 and, 935, 948–949; election of 1992 and, 969–970, 970 (illus.); end of Cold War and, 950–951; Persian Gulf War (1990) and, 952–953; Supreme Court and, 910; Yeltsin and, 953 (illus.)
Bush, George W., 962; cabinet of, 986–987; domestic policy of, 986–990; election of 2000 and, 984–986, 985 (illus.); foreign policy of, 993–996; ratings of, 996; September 11, 2001, terrorist attacks and, 990–991, 991 (illus.); war against terrorism and, 993
Business: advertising and, 721 (illus.), 723 (illus.); consolidations (mergers) and, 630 (illus.), 722; corporation and, 721–722; covert action in Iran and, 831; female ownership of, 909, 909 (illus.); industrial psychology and, 644; interlocking directorates and, 677; marketing and, 720, 722; National Recovery Administration (NRA) and, 757–758; in 1920s, 721–722; regulation of, 665–666; standardization and, 722; trusts and trust-busting, 667–668; vertical integration of,

520; women in, 909 (illus.); World War I and, 709, 711; World War II and, 793. *See also* Corporations; Trusts and trustbusting
Business organization: holding company as, 522; trusts as, 522
Busing, Reagan and, 932
Butler, John W., 743
Butler Act (1925), 743, 745
Butte, Montana, lynching in, 707
Byckau, Mikhail, 907
Byington, Margaret, 547
Byrd, Harry F., 858 (illus.), 871
Byrnes, James, 793

C

Caballeros, 495 (illus.)
Cabinet: of Bush, George W., 986–987; of Clinton, 971
Cable, George Washington, 590
Calamity Jane (Martha Jane Canary), 498
Calculating machine, 523
Califano, Joseph, 913, 914
California, 483; anti-Asian policy in, 693; Central Valley of, 493; gold in, 483, 492; immigrants to, 964; Imperial Valley in, 634; literature about, 590; Mexican Americans in, 496; National Farm Workers Association in, 884; Native Americans in, 483; population shift to, 963; Reagan as governor of, 927–928
California State College at Los Angeles, Mexican American studies program at, 884
Californios, 496
Calley, William, Jr., 880
Call of the Wild (London), 590–591
Calzoneras, 495 (illus.)
Cambodia: bombing of, 898; Khmer Rouge in, 915; U.S. attack on, 915; Vietnam War and, 879
Campbell, Helen, 564
Campbell's Soup Company, 768 (illus.)
Camp David, Eisenhower and Krushchev at, 833
Camp David accords, 916, 916 (illus.), 941
Camp Dweller Indians, 483
Canada: foreign policy toward, 606, 607; immigrants from, 644; North Atlantic Treaty and, 814
Canadian Southern Railway, 516 (illus.)
Canary, Martha Jane. *See* Calamity Jane (Martha Jane Canary)
Cannon, Joseph "Uncle Joe," 673
Canton, Ohio, 595
Capital (financial): for railroads, 514, 518–519
Capone, Al, 726
Caporetto, battle of, 702 (illus.)
Caraway, Hattie W., 768
Caribbean region: dollar diplomacy in, 693; expansion into, 607; foreign policy toward, 606, 607; Grenada invasion and, 941–942; Roosevelt Corollary and, 692–693; trouble spots in, 942 (illus.); United Fruit in, 630; U.S. in, 1898-1930, 695 (illus.)
Carlisle Indian School, 490, 490 (illus.)
Carmichael, Stokely, 883
Carnegie, Andrew, 520, 531, 535, 619
Carnegie Steel Company, 520
Caroline Islands, 791, 802, 816
Carpenter, M. Scott, 847 (illus.)
Carpenter, Ted Galen, 947

Carpetbaggers, 462, 463, 477
Carranza, Venustiano, 695–696
Carson, Pirie, Scott (department store), 541
Carson River Valley, gold strike in, 497
Carswell, G. Harrold, 895
Cartels: of drug dealers, 947. *See also*
    Organization of Petroleum Exporting
    Countries (OPEC)
Carter, Jimmy, 903, 914 (illus.), 916 (illus.);
    Christian Right and, 934; Cold War and,
    917–918; election of 1976 and, 913; election
    of 1980 and, 929; failure of presidency, 918;
    foreign policy of, 915–917, 929; Haiti peace
    mission by, 978; Iranian hostage crisis and,
    916–917, 917 (illus.); presidency of, 913–914
Carter doctrine, 916
Casablanca, Morocco, 790, 790 (illus.)
Cascade Mountains, 482
Casey, William, 942, 943
Cash register, 523, 524 (illus.)
Caste: economic system in Southwest, 496
Castle Garden, 544
Castro, Fidel, 831, 859, 862; Bay of Pigs and,
    861–862; CIA and, 912; missile crisis and,
    862–864
Casualties: from Chernobyl, 907; in Kosovo,
    979. *See also* Wars and warfare
Catalogs, mail-order, 528, 529
Cather, Willa, 728
Catholics and Catholicism: birth control and,
    637; Coughlin, Charles, and, 762; hostility
    toward, 641; Kennedy, John F., and, 858;
    Ku Klux Klan and, 735–736; in late 19th
    century, 552; of Polish immigrants, 548;
    Republican party and, 579; settlement
    houses and, 563
Catt, Carrie Chapman, 660, 696
Cattell, James McKeen, 704
Cattle: drives, 499–500; ranching, 494,
    499–501, 502 (illus.); trails, 499–500, 501
    (illus.)
Cavalry (U.S.), buffalo soldiers in, 486,
    488–489, 488 (illus.)
CBS: Cronkite's visit to Vietnam, 886;
    Kennedy-Nixon debate and, 857
CCC. *See* Civilian Conservation Corps (CCC)
Censorship: banned books, 590; Scopes Trial
    and, 747; second Red Scare and, 839;
    Spanish-American War and, 614; World
    War I and, 706, 707
Censure: of McCarthy, Joseph, 827
Census: of 1890, 604–605; of 1920, 723; racial
    classifications in, 968
Census Bureau, 523
Centennial Exposition, 510 (illus.), 511, 512;
    telephone at, 523
Centers for Disease Control, AIDS and, 944,
    945
Central America: Carter and, 915–916; immi-
    grants from, 965, 966; Reagan and con-
    frontations in, 941–942, 942 (illus.). *See also*
    Latin America; South America; specific
    countries
Central Europe, end of Cold War and, 951
Central High School (Little Rock), 851
Central Intelligence Agency (CIA), 816; in
    Afghanistan, 992; Contras and, 941; Ford,
    Gerald, and, 912; in Guatemala, 831; in
    Iran, 831; Watergate and, 894. *See also*
    Covert action

Central Pacific Railroad, 497, 558; transconti-
    nental railroad and, 515–516
Central Park, 549
Central Valley, migration to, 493
Cervera, Pascual, 616–617
C-47 (airplane), 814
C-54 (airplane), 814
Chagall, Mark, 845
Chain gangs, 475
Chain stores, 529
Chambers, Whittaker, 823, 824 (illus.)
Chamoun, Camille, 831
Chandler, Alfred D., 513
*Charge of the 24th and 25th Colored Infantry
    and Rescue of the Rough Riders at San Juan
    Hill, July 2, 1898,* 615 (illus.)
Charity Organization Society, 658
Charleston (dance), 725, 727 (illus.)
Château-Thierry, battle at, 703
Chávez, César, 884, 884 (illus.)
Chayefsky, Paddy, 842
Checkpoint Charlie, 860
Chemical weapons, in World War I, 703
Cheney, Dick, 985, 986, 994
Chernenko, Konstantin, 943
Chernobyl, nuclear accident at, 906–907, 907
    (illus.)
Cherokee Indians, 483
Cheyenne Indians, 483, 485, 486, 489, 490
Cheyney State (Pennsylvania), student protests
    at, 882
Chiang Kai-shek, 786, 789, 816–817, 830
Chicago, 540; architecture of, 541; cattle mar-
    kets in, 499; Democratic convention of 1968
    and, 887–888, 888 (illus.); foreign-born pop-
    ulation of, 546; great fire in, 541; Haymarket
    Riot in, 535, 535 (illus.); Hull House and,
    658; innovations in, 526–527; mail-order
    business in, 528–529; in 1900, 540 (illus.);
    Pullman strike and, 585; railroads and, 513;
    "second nature" in, 526–527; Union Stock
    Yards in, 526, 526 (illus.), 527, 527 (illus.);
    World's Fair in, 564
"Chicago" (Sandburg), 650
Chicago Auditorium, 541
Chicago Bureau of Charities, 564
Chicago Commodity Exchange, 527
Chicago Daily Tribune, 724, 823 (illus.)
Chicago Poems (Sandburg), 650
Chicago River, innovations for, 526–527
Chicanos. *See* Mexicans and Mexican
    Americans
Chickamauga Park, Tennessee, 615
Chief Joseph, 487
Childbearing: birthrate and, 908
Childbirth, 551
Child labor, 529 (illus.), 530–531, 532, 564,
    588–589, 589 (illus.), 634, 635 (illus.), 642;
    Keating-Owen Act (1916) and, 679; legisla-
    tion on, 593, 724; regulation of, 661–662
Children: Black Codes and, 464; family and,
    908; of immigrants, 547; in late 19th cen-
    tury, 555–556; Victorian morality and, 551;
    in westward movement, 492; in workplace,
    529 (illus.), 530–531
Children's Bureau, 635, 674
Chile, 695; miners from, 498
Chilled-iron plow, 504
China: ambassadorial exchange with, 917–918;
    Boxer Rebellion in, 623–624; civil war in,

816–817; Clinton and, 976, 977; Cold War
    and, 830; Communist Revolution in,
    816–817, 823; dollar diplomacy in, 694;
    Formosa Straits crisis and, 830; immigrants
    from, 498, 634, 640, 641, 967; imperialism
    and, 621; Japan and, 780, 781, 783,
    786–787; Korean War and, 818; Nixon,
    Kissinger, and, 897, 898 (illus.); Open Door
    Policy and, 623 (illus.), 693; People's
    Liberation Army, 817 (illus.); Roosevelt,
    Franklin D., and, 783; Soviet Union and,
    802, 816–817, 830; spheres of influence in,
    623 (illus.); Tiananmen Square demonstra-
    tion and, 950–951, 951 (illus.); Twenty-One
    Demands and, 693; World War II and, 791.
    See also Chiang Kai-shek; Mao Tse-Tung
Chinese Americans, 481; anti-Chinese laws
    and sentiment, 640, 641; demographics of,
    640–641; higher education for, 558; segre-
    gation and, 693; in U.S. population (1900),
    550
Chinese Exclusion Act (1882), 499, **531**
Chinook Indians, 483
Chippewa Indians, 483
Chisholm Trail, 500, 501 (illus.)
Chivington, John M., 485–486
Chivington massacre. *See* Sand Creek
    Massacre
Chloroform, 551
Choate, Joseph H., 684
Christian Right, 934–935, 936 (illus.)., 950 (il-
    lus.)
Christians and Christianity: birth control and,
    636, 637; expansionism and, 606; in inter-
    national politics, 831; nonviolence and, 854;
    Scopes Trial and, 684–687. *See also*
    Missions and missionaries
Christopher, Warren M., 976, 977
Christowe, Stoyan, 544, 545
Chrysler Corporation, 765; government
    bailout of, 905
Church(es): black, 464 (illus.), 465; as immi-
    grant institutions, 548
Church, Frank, 912, 930
Churches of Christ, 737
Churchill, Winston: balance of terror and,
    831; Casablanca meeting and, 790, 790 (il-
    lus.); on Iron Curtain, 809; Lend-Lease and,
    785; Manhattan Project and, 810; at
    Potsdam, 807–808, 808 (illus.); Roosevelt,
    Franklin D., and, 789, 790; at Tehran, 799;
    at Yalta, 799, 802
Church of Jesus Christ of Latter-day Saints.
    See Mormons
Church of the Carpenter, 562
Church of the Four-Square Gospel, 737
CIA. *See* Central Intelligence Agency (CIA)
Cigar Makers' Union, 533
Cimarron (Ferber), 506
Cincinnati, Ohio, 735 (illus.)
Cincinnati College of Music, 553
Cincinnati Red Stockings, 553
CIO: African Americans and, 765; American
    Federation of Labor (AFL) and, 765; elec-
    tion of 1944 and, 797; during Great
    Depression, 764–765; women and, 765. *See
    also* AFL-CIO
Circuses, 552 (illus.), 553
CIS. *See* Commonwealth of Independent
    States (CIS)

Cisneros, Henry, 971

Cities and towns: African Americans and, 966; automobile and, 721; city managers and, 664; crime in, 543; culturally pluralistic society in, 565; 1893 depression and, 564–565; electricity and transportation in, 525; governments in, 549; growth of, 539–540, 605; immigrants in, 539, 543–548; in jazz age, 723–729, 732; in Midwest, 538 (illus.); political machines in, 548–550; population of, 963–964; in postwar South, 460; power structures in, 549; railroads and, 513; reform and, 560–565, 664–665; settlement houses in, 562–563; skyscrapers in, 540–541, 723–724, 724 (illus.); society, cultural change, and, 550–560; suburbs and, 541; tenements and, 541–543

Citizens' Committee to Test the Constitutionality of the Separate Car Law (New Orleans), 568

Citizenship: and annexed territory, 622; Fourteenth Amendment and, 456; for freedmen, 464; for Native Americans, 490

City planning, 549

Civic Biology (Hunter), 743

Civic Federation, 565

Civilian Conservation Corps (CCC), 760 (illus.), **761**, 770, 772

Civil liberties: anti-terrorism campaign and, 993. *See also* Civil rights

Civil rights: affirmative action and, 956; after Civil War, 575; Commission for Civil Rights and, 852; Eisenhower and, 851; as political issue, 850; Reagan and, 932–933; Republican party and, 575; Roosevelt, Eleanor, and, 771; after Spanish-American War, 624; Supreme Court decisions affecting black, 475, 475 (illus.); Truman and, 850. *See also* Civil rights movement; Desegregation; Lynchings; Race and racism; Segregation; Voting and voting rights

Civil Rights Act(s): of 1866, 456, 462; **of 1875,** 475, **567;** of 1957, 852; of 1960, 852; of 1964, 871, 885

Civil Rights Cases, 475 (illus.), **557,** 568

Civil rights movement, 849–854, 866–868; Birmingham and, 867; Black Power and, 882–884; *Brown* v. *Board of Education* and, 850–851; economic inequality and, 883; FBI and, 866; freedom ride and, 866; March on Washington and, 867–868, 868 (illus.); Montgomery bus boycott and, 852–853; nonviolence and, 853–854, 853 (illus.), 883; Prayer Pilgrimage to Washington and, 853; Selma-to-Montgomery march and, 872; sit-ins and, 853 (illus.), 854; University of Alabama and, 867; University of Mississippi and, 866–867; voting rights and, 866. *See also* Desegregation; King, Martin Luther, Jr.; Segregation

Civil Service Commission, 577

Civil service reform: Cleveland, Grover, and, 577; Garfield and, 577; Hayes and, 576; Pendleton Act and, 577

Civil war: in Lebanon, 940

Civil War (U.S.): African Americans during, 451; financing of, 499; Lincoln's

Reconstruction initiatives during, 453; sectional reconciliation after, 478. *See also* Reconstruction

Civil Works Administration (CWA), 761, 770, 772

Clark, J. Reuben, 779

Clark, James, 872

Clark, Mark, 820

Clark, Tom, 819

Clarke, Edward H., 558

Clark Memorandum, 779

Class. *See* specific classes

Classical economics, 561

Classical music, 552–553

Clayton Antitrust Act (1914), **677**

Clean Air Act, 904

Clemenceau, Georges, 712, 713

Clemens, Samuel Langhorne, 590. *See also* Twain, Mark

Clerical workers, women as, 530 (illus.)

Cleveland, Grover, 547, 577, 588; Cuba and, 612; 1884 election and, 577; 1888 election and, 576 (illus.), 578; 1892 election and, 583, 587; 1894 election and, 594; 1896 election and, 594–595; foreign policy of, 607–608; Hawaii and, 609; Panic of 1893 and, 587; Pullman strike and, 585, 594; silver coinage and, 594

Cleveland Indians, 821

Cliff Dwellers (Bellows), 649 (illus.)

Clifford, Clark, 886

Climate: of Great Plains, 483

Clinton, Bill, 961–962, 962 (illus.); cabinet of, 971; Congress and, 971–973; drug strategy of, 947; economy and, 961–962, 969, 970–971, 974, 980; election of 1992 and, 969–970, 970 (illus.); election of 1996 and, 975–976, 975 (illus.); foreign policy of, 976–980, 976 (illus.); homosexuals in military and, 911–912; impeachment of, 983; Lewinsky and, 982–983, 983 (illus.); Middle East and, 977; rebound of, 974–976; scandals and, 973; Supreme Court and, 910

Clinton, Hillary Rodham, 970–971; Clinton sex scandal and, 982, 983; health care and, 972

Clothing: bloomer pants, 492; of caballeros, 495 (illus.); of cowboys, 500 (illus.); producing, 523; in Victorian era, 551, 551 (illus.); of westward travelers, 492; of youth in 1960s, 882 (illus.)

CNBC, 988

Coal and coal mining: dangers in, 635 (illus.); decline of, 722; steel production and, 519; strikes and, 585–586, 668–669

Coal City, Illinois, 585

Coalitions (political). *See* Democratic party; Republican party

Coast Ranges, 482

Cocaine, 946, 946 (illus.), 947

Cody, William F. "Buffalo Bill," 490, 491

Coeur d'Alene, silver miners' strike at, 535

Coffee, Linda, 921, 923

Coin's Financial School (Harvey), 594

Coit, Stanton, 562

Colburn, Irving W., 631

Cold War, 894–895; anxiety and, 839; arts and, 844–845; in Asia, 816–819; atomic

dilemma in, 810–811; beginning of, 808–810; Berlin airlift and, 814–815, 815 (illus.); Berlin Blockade and, 814–815, 815 (illus.); Carter and, 917–918; China and, 816–817, 823, 830; civil rights movement and, 849; containment and, 811–815; covert action and, 831; détente and, 897–898; deterrence and, 816; division of Europe and, 808–810, 809 (illus.); Eisenhower and, 827–833; end of, 950–951, 952 (illus.); expansion of, 815–819; fallout shelters and, 832 (illus.); government spending and, 839; at home, 819, 822–827; Indochina and, 829–830; Korean War and, 817–819; loyalty issue and, 822–825; Marshall Plan and, 812–813; McCarthyism and, 824–825; Middle East and, 830–831; military dimension of, 815–816; military-industrial complex and, 833; missile gap and, 832–833; North Atlantic Treaty Organization (NATO) and, 813–814; NSC-68 and, 816; peace after, 952–954; Reagan and, 939–940, 943–944; *Sputnik* and, 846–847; Truman Doctrine and, 811–812; Yalta Conference and, 816, 818. *See also* Berlin Wall; Vietnam War

Cole (ship), 991

Colfax, Schuyler, 470

College Entrance Examination Board (CEEB), 705

Collier, John, 767, 767 (illus.)

Collier's magazine, 627, 670

Colombia: drug trade and, 947; Panama Canal and, 691–692, 694; reciprocity treaty with, 607

Colonies: as strategic bases, 610

Colorado, 481, 482; school shootings in, 982; woman suffrage in, 574

Colorado Fuel and Iron Company, 679

Colored Farmers' National Alliance and Cooperative Union, 581. *See also* National Farmers' Alliance and Industrial Union

Colson, Charles, 893

Columbia Records, 648

Columbia University, protest at, 882

Columbine High School, shootings at, 982

Columbus, New Mexico, 695–696

Columbus, Ohio, 586

Colvin, Reynold, 956

Comanche Indians, 483, 484, 486, 489

Commentary magazine, 928

Commerce. *See* Trade

Commerce and Labor, Department of, 667–668

Commerce Court, 674

Commission for Civil Rights, 852

Commission on Equal Employment Opportunities, 866

Commission on National Goals, 854

Committee of Industrial Organizations. *See* CIO

Committee of Industrial Organizations (CIO). *See* CIO

Committee on Public Information (CPI), **706**–708

Committee to Defend America by Aiding the Allies, 785

Common law: coverture and, 555

Commonwealth of Independent States (CIS), 951

Communication(s): revolution in, 512; telephone and, 523; transatlantic telegraph cable and, 522–523

Communists and communism: Communist party, 734; number of communists, 733. *See also* Bolshevik Revolution; Cold War; McCarthyism; Red Scare

Community Action Program, 871

Company L (Sixth Massachusetts Regiment), 615

Competition: economic, 905; between railroads, 518; Rockefeller and, 521

Compromise of 1877, 471–472

Compulsory school attendance laws, 556

Computers, 984 (illus.)

Comstock, Anthony, 552

Comstock, Henry T. P., 497

Comstock Act (1873), 552, 635, 636, 637

Comstock Lode, 497, 499

Concentration policy, for Indians, 485

"Concerning Three Articles in This Number of *McClure's*, and a Coincidence That May Set Us Thinking" (McClure), 627

Conditions of Women and Children Wage-Earners in the United States, 659

Condoms, 945

Confederacy. *See* Civil War (U.S.); Reconstruction

Congress (U.S.): African Americans in, 463, 464; Bush, George W., and, 987; CIA and, 913; Clinton and, 971–973; Contract with America and, 973–974; election of 1984 and, 938–939; ex-Confederates in, 455; Johnson, Andrew, and, 455–457, 458–460; Reconstruction and, 453, 456–458; strength of, 576; Sunbelt and western seats in, 928

Congressional Budget Office, 962

Congressional Medal of Honor, for buffalo soldiers, 489

Congressional Union, 660

Congress of Industrial Organizations (CIO). *See* CIO

Congress of Racial Equality (CORE), 866

Conkling, Roscoe, 470, 577

Connally, John, 896 (illus.), 897

Connecticut, 575

Connor, Eugene "Bull," 867

Conscription. *See* Draft (military)

Conservation, 671; Ballinger-Pinchot affair and, 673; Roosevelt, Theodore, and, 671–672

Conservatives and conservatism: intellectual support for, 928; Nixon and, 895–896; in postwar South, 463; Reagan and, 927–928. *See also* Christian Right; Moral Majority

Consolidated Tobacco, 630

Consolidation: in oil industry, 521; by railroads, 515–516, 518–519; in steel industry, 520–521

Constitution(s): in Reconstruction South, 455

Constitution (U.S.): Johnson's impeachment and, 459

Constitutional conventions, during Reconstruction, 451, 454–455, 475

Constitution Hall, 766

Consumer protection, 669

Consumers and consumerism, 633, 645–646, 750, 751–752; advertising and, 528; automobile industry and, 719–721; Clinton and, 975 (illus.); critics of, 842–843, 846; debt and, 723; in 1920s, 720–723; savings and, 936; second industrial revolution and, 720–723; shopping centers and, 721; after World War II, 819, 822, 838, 839–841

Consumer's League, The, 770

Consumption, in late 19th century, 529

Containment, 811–815

Contraception. *See* Birth control

Contract labor system, 461

Contract with America, 973–974

Contras, anti-Sandinista forces as, 941, 942–943

Convergence (Pollock), 845 (illus.)

Conversion (religious): of Hawaiians, 608

Convict-lease system, African Americans and, 474–475

Coolidge, Calvin, 739 (illus.); election of 1924 and, 738, 740; Garvey and, 731; Latin America and, 779; as president, 738–739

Cooling-off treaties, 694

Cooper, L. Gordon, Jr., 847 (illus.)

Cooper, Peter, 466

Cooperatives, agricultural, 581

Copland, Aaron, 729

Copyright law, 647

Coral Sea, battle of, 791

CORE. *See* Congress of Racial Equality (CORE)

Corliss engine, 510 (illus.), 511, 512

Cornell University, 557

Corning, New York, 636

Corporations: collapses of, 987; hatred of, 981–982

Corregidor, 788

Corruption: in Grant administration, 466, 470; of political bosses, 549; in postwar South, 463–464, 473; railroads and, 515

Cosmopolitan magazine, 627

Costa Rica, Contras in, 941

Cost of living: Nixon and, 896; Reagan and, 933

Cotton and cotton industry: decline of, 722; in postwar South, 460, 461; prices and, 584

Coughlin, "Bathhouse John," 548

Coughlin, Charles, 762, 764, 768

Council of Economic Advisers, 822, 865–866

Council of Foreign Ministers, 808, 812, 815

Council of National Defense, 709

Court(s): desegregation and, 895; freedmen and, 465; women on, 932. *See also* Supreme Court (U.S.)

Court of Indian Offenses, 487–490

Court-packing scheme, 769, 772–773

Covert action: in Guatemala, 831; in Iran, 831

Coverture, law of, 555

Cowboy Camp During Roundup (Russell), 480 (illus.)

Cowboys, 499, 500, 500 (illus.)

Cox, Archibald, 900

Cox, James M., 716

Coxey, Jacob S., 584–585, 585 (illus.)

Coxey Good Roads bill, 584–585

Coxey's Army, 584–585

CPI. *See* Committee on Public Information (CPI)

Crack cocaine, 946–947

Crack in the Picture Window, The (Keats), 842

Crane, Stephen, 590, 591

Crazy Horse (chief), 486

Creation-evolution debate, 743–747

Credit: greenbacks, gold, and, 466; in sharecropping system, 461–462. *See also* Great Depression (1930s)

Crédit Mobilier scandal, 470, 515

Creel, George, 706, 778

CREEP (Committee to Re-Elect the President), 893, 894

Crime and criminals: in cities, 543; crack cocaine and, 946; hate-crime legislation and, 912; international, 993; in 1920s, 726; Prohibition and, 735; sociological jurisprudence and, 662; Warren Court and, 869. *See also* Law(s)

Crisis, The, 639, 729

Croatians, 585; in Bosnia, 978

Crocker, Charles, 515–516

Croix de Guerre, 712 (illus.)

Croker, Richard, 548, 550

Cronkite, Walter, 886

Cronon, William, 526

Croquet, 552

"Cross of Gold" speech, 594–595, 595 (illus.)

Cross Streets of New York (Shinn), 626

Crow Indians, 483

Cruise missiles, Reagan and, 939

C. Turner Joy (ship), 876

Cuba: Bay of Pigs and, 861–862; constitution of, 622–623; economy of, 611–612; Grant and, 607; immigrants from, 965; independence of, 618–619; missile crisis and, 862–864; Platt Amendment and, 622–623; political cartoons and, 618 (illus.); as protectorate, 693; reciprocity treaty with, 607; "reconcentration" camps and, 611 (illus.), 612, 613; Roosevelt, Franklin D., and, 779; Rough Riders in, 602; social Darwinism and, 606; Spanish-American War and, 601–602, 611–617; Ten Years' War and, 611; U.S. withdrawal from, 623

Cuban missile crisis, 862–864, 863 (illus.)

Cullen, Countee, 729

Culture(s), 649; advertising, 603, 627, 629 (illus.); beats and, 843, 846; consumerism and, 633, 645–646; in early 1900s, 629; Harlem Renaissance and, 729; of immigrants in cities, 547–548; Mexican American, 640; military, 614–615; Native American, 487–491; in 1960s, 882, 882 (illus.), 883 (illus.), 884, 889; popular magazines and, 627; popular pastimes and, 647–648; shopping centers and, 840; of Spanish-speaking people, 494–495; Western-themed toys and, 840 (illus.); of work, 531, 631–632; yellow journalism and, 612. *See also* Art(s); Ethnocentrism; Literature; Society

Cumming v. *County Board of Education,* 557

Cummins, Albert B., 669, 672

Currency: Comstock Lode and, 499; greenbacks and, 466. *See also* Money

Curriculum: in late 19th century, 556; of universities, 557, 559–560

Currier and Ives, 553 (illus.)

Curtis, George William, 552

Custer, George Armstrong, 486–487, 488, 498

"Custer's Last Stand," 486, 487 (illus.)

CWA. *See* Civil Works Administration (CWA)

Czechoslovakia, 713, 951; coup in, 813, 816; Soviet Union and, 809; World War II and, 783–784

Czechs and Czech Americans: ethnic nationalism of, 884; as immigrants, 639; as voters, 755 (illus.)

Czolgosz, Leon, 597

D

Daily life. *See* Lifestyle

Dakotas. *See* North Dakota; South Dakota

Daley, Richard J., 887–888

Dallas, Kennedy assassination in, 869, 869 (illus.)

Dallek, Robert, 928

Dalrymple, Oliver, 504, 504 (illus.)

Dance: Charleston, 725; in early 1900s, 648; experimentation in, 649

Danish West Indies, 692

Dardanelles, 702 (illus.)

Darrow, Clarence, 560–561, 744–747, 744 (illus.)

Darwin, Charles, 560, 606; Scopes Trial and, 743–747. *See also* Social Darwinism

Daschle, Tom, 987, 992

Daugherty, Harry, 738

Daughters of the American Revolution, 766, 771

Davidson Mountain, 497

Davis, Jefferson, 463 (illus.)

Davis, John W., 740

Davis, Katherine B., 727

Dawes Severalty Act (1887), **490**

Day, William R., 617–618

Daybreak Boys, 543

Daylight saving time, 709

Dayton accords, 978

D-Day, 798

DEA. *See* Drug Enforcement Agency (DEA)

Deadwood, 498

Dean, John, 893, 894, 900

Death: from AIDS, 945. *See also* Casualties; Life expectancy

Deaver, Michael, 947

Debs, Eugene V., 585, 597, 636; election of 1904 and, 669; election of 1908 and, 672; election of 1912 and, 656, 676; election of 1920 and, 708; as prisoner, 707–708, 708 (illus.); Pullman strike and, 744; and Social Democratic party, 662

Debt: greenbacks and Civil War, 466

Decker, Sarah P., 660

Declaration of Liberated Europe, 799, 802

Declaration of Rights of Negro Peoples of the World, 730

Defense Department, establishment of, 816

Defense industry: pacifism and, 782; Reagan and, 933

Defense spending: during Cold War, 839, 860, 865; Reagan and, 939–940

Deficit: budget surplus and, 980; in overseas trade, 936. *See also* Federal deficit

Deficit spending, in Great Depression, 773–774

Deflation, in 1870s, 466

De Gaulle, Charles, 789

Delano, California, 884

De Leon, Daniel, 662

De Lima v. *Bidwell,* 622

Democracy and Education (Dewey), 662

Democratic-Conservatives, in South, 468, 469

Democratic National Committee, Watergate break-in and, 893–894, 899

Democratic party: after Civil War, 575; Cleveland and, 577, 594; "disappearing quorum" rule and, 578; divisions in, 739–740, 755, 886–887; 1894 election and, 587–588; energy crunch and, 904; "force bill" and, 579; Great Depression and, 754; Ku Klux Klan and, 739; New Deal and, 762; 1968 convention and, 887–888, 888 (illus.); and Populist movement, 583; in postwar South, 463, 468, 469 (illus.), 472, 473; revival of, 969; Roosevelt, Eleanor, and, 770; Roosevelt, Franklin D., and, 774; silver coinage and, 594–595; South and, 575, 587, 594, 774; Southern Alliance and, 582; split of, 588; voter coalition of, 929, 930. *See also* Election(s)

Demography: of African Americans, 966; of Hispanics, 965–966; population shift and, 963–964, 963 (illus.)

Dempsey, Jack, 726

Deng Xiaoping, 951 (illus.)

Department stores, 524 (illus.), 528

Dependent Pensions Act, 578

Deportation: Ellis Island and, 545

Depression(s): of 1870s, 502, 505; of 1893-1897, 564, 583–588, 591, 596, 611. *See also* Great Depression (1930s)

Deregulation, 932

Desdunes, Rodolphe L., 568

Desegregation: of armed services, 850; Nixon and, 895; of public transportation, 852–853; of schools, 850–851, 866–867; sit-ins and, 853 (illus.), 854. *See also* Civil rights; Civil rights movement; Segregation

Desert Land Act (1877), 494

Desert Storm, 952–953

Détente, 897–898, 898 (illus.), 917

Detroit, 629, 792–793, 795, 883

Deutsch-Amerikanischer Nationalbund, 548

Dewey, George, 610, 616, 620

Dewey, John: NAACP and, 638; School of Pedagogy and, 662

Dewey, Thomas E., 815; 1944 election and, 797–798; 1948 election and, 814, 822–823, 822 (illus.), 823 (illus.)

Díaz, Porfirio, 694–695

Dickenson, Edward, 821

Diem, Ngo Dinh, 829, 860–861, 861, 876, 886

Dien Bien Phu, 829

Diet (food): of buffalo soldiers, 488; changes in, 550–551; innovations in, 523, 527

Dingley Tariff (1897), 597, 673

Diphtheria, 551

Diplomacy: with China, 917–918; with Soviets, 917. *See also* Foreign policy

Direct current, for electric lighting, 525

Dirksen, Everett M., 871, 872

"Dirty tricks," Nixon and, 894

Disabled people, 755, 763

"Disappearing quorum" rule, 578

Disarmament, Eisenhower and, 829, 831–832

Discrimination, 868; draft and, 881; against gays, 910–911; in housing, 837, 840, 868; in postwar South, 462

Disease: AIDS and, 944–946; farm-bred, 633–634; government and, 634; jobs and, 530; medicine and, 551; Native Americans and, 483; Spanish-American War and, 614, 617; tuberculosis and, 541 (illus.); in World War I, 703, 706. *See also* Health and health care; Occupational safety and health

Disfranchisement, in South, 473

Dissent. *See* Protest(s)

District of Columbia. *See* Washington, D.C.

Diversity: in Clinton cabinet, 971; melting pot vs., 968–969

Divorce, 634; increases in, 908; women and, 555

Dixiecrats, 822, 850

Dixon, Maynard, 748

Dobrynin, Anatoly, 862–863

Dodd, Samuel T. C., 522

Dodge, Grenville M., 515–516

Dodge City, Kansas, 500

Dole, Bob, 974–975, 975 (illus.)

Dollar diplomacy, 693–694

Dolliver, Jonathan P., 672, 673

Dominican Republic, 693, 779, 876

"Don't ask, don't tell" policy, 911 (illus.), 912

Dooley v. *U.S.,* 622

Dorr, Rheta Childe, 555

Dos Passos, John, 716, 728

Dot.coms, boom and bust of, 984, 988–989

Douglas, William O., 772, 868

Douglass, Frederick, 463 (illus.)

Dove, Arthur, 650

Downes v. *Bidwell,* 622

Draft (military): African Americans and, 702; discrimination and, 881; World War I and, 701–702

Drake, Edwin L., 521

Draper, William, 776

Dred Scott v. *Sandford,* 569

Dreiser, Theodore, 591

Dress. *See* Clothing

Drug education, 946–947

Drug Enforcement Agency (DEA), 947

Drugs: IV drug users, AIDS, and, 945; Noriega and trade in, 952; use and addiction, 882; war on, 946–947, 946 (illus.)

Dry farming, 503

Du Bois, W. E. B., 476, 477, 558, 564, 732 (illus.); on Garvey, Marcus, 731; as intellectual voice of black community, 729; NAACP and, 638–639; on "New Negro," 711; Niagara Movement and, 638; Washington, Booker T., and, 559, 638

Duc, Quang, 861 (illus.)

Dukakis, Michael, 948–949

Duke, James B., 525

Dulles, John Foster: brinksmanship and, 828–829, 828 (illus.), 830; Eisenhower and, 828, 828 (illus.); Korean War and, 820; massive retaliation and, 828–829, 830; Middle East and, 830, 831

Dumbbell tenement, 541 (illus.), 542

Duncan, Isadora, 649

Dunn, Harvey, 706
Dunne, Finley Peter, 611, 627
Du Pont Corporation, 631; munitions industry and, 782; trustbusting and, 668
Du Pont family, 696
Dupuy de Lôme, Enrique, 612
Dust Bowl, 758, 758 (illus.), 766
Dutch. *See* Netherlands
Dutch East Indies, 787, 788, 791
Dylan, Bob, 882

E

Earp, Wyatt, 500
Earth Day (1970), 904
East Berlin, 860 (illus.)
Eastern Europe: end of Cold War and, 951; immigrants from, 546–547
Eastern Trunk Line Association, 518
East Germany, 831; Berlin Wall and, 860 (illus.); end of Cold War and, 951; second Berlin crisis and, 833, 859–860
East Louisiana Railway, *Plessy* v. *Ferguson* and, 568
Eastman, George, 523
Eastman Kodak, 631
East St. Louis, Illinois: race riot in, 681
eBay, 989
Eckford, Elizabeth, 851 (illus.)
Economics: classical vs. "younger," 561; Reaganomics and, 933–939
Economy: Asian crash and, 980; budget surplus and, 980; Bush, George, and, 954, 969, 970; Bush, George W., and, 987; Carter and, 929; Clinton and, 961–962, 969, 970–971, 974, 980; and dot.coms, 984, 988–989; environmentalists and, 904; greenbacks, hard money, and, 466; immigrants and, 965; manufacturing decline and, 936–937; in 1920s, 721–723; in 1970s, 904–905; Nixon and, 896–897; oil shocks and, 902–903; overseas expansion and, 603; of postwar South, 460; railroads and, 513; service sector expansion and, 937; supply-side economics and, 930; of West, 481–482. *See also* Depression(s)
Eden, Anthony, 830
Ederle, Gertrude, 726
Edison, Thomas A., 522, 523–525, 584, 647
Edison Company, 524–525, 629
Education, 452; for African Americans, 966; of Asian Americans, 967; Bush, George W., and, 987; compulsory, 589; discrimination and, 638; early elementary, 557; for freedmen, 465, 465 (illus.); higher, 842; of Hispanics, 965; IQ testing and, 704–705; Johnson, Lyndon B., and, 872; in late 19th century, 555–557; National Defense Education Act and, 846–847; professionalization of teachers and, 658; reform of, 841–842; in South, 463, 556–557; universal, 556; of women, 634, 909
Educational and Industrial Institute for Negro Girls, 681
Edwards, Laura, 464
Edwards v. *Aguillard,* 747
Egypt, 788, 830, 831; Camp David accords and, 916; October War and, 901
Ehrlichman, John, 895, 900
"Eight box" law, 574

Eighteenth Amendment, 660, 734
Eight hour day, 532
Eisenhower, Dwight D., 826 (illus.), 827–828, 828 (illus.), 829, 831; arms race and, 829, 831–832; brinksmanship and, 828–829, 830; on *Brown* decision, 851; budget concerns of, 828, 841, 848; civil rights and, 851–852; Cold War and, 827–833; Commission on National Goals, 854; Congress and, 848; covert action and, 831; Cuba and, 831, 861; defense policy of, 828–829; Dulles, John Foster, and, 828; election of 1948 and, 822; election of 1952 and, 826–827; election of 1956 and, 830, 849; Indochina and, 829–830; Iran and, 831; Johnson, Lyndon B., and, 848, 870–871; Khrushchev, Nikita, and, 831–833; Korean War and, 826; leadership style of, 848; Little Rock crisis and, 851; massive retaliation and, 828–829, 830, 859; McCarthy, Joseph R., and, 826–827; Middle East and, 830–831; military-industrial complex and, 833; missile gap and, 832–833; Modern Republicanism and, 848–849; as NATO Supreme Commander, 814; nuclear weapons and, 810, 832; second Berlin crisis and, 833; Soviet Union and, 831–833; space program and, 846; Supreme Court and, 850; Vietnam and, 829–830, 886; World War II and, 790–791, 800–801
El Caney, battle at, 617
Elderly: increase in, 964; Reagan's programs and, 932
Election(s): of 1866, 456; of 1868, 466, 466 (illus.), 467–468; of 1872, 468, 470, 470 (illus.), 555; of 1875, 468; of 1876, 451, 466, 469, 471–472, 472 (illus.), 575, 576–577; of 1878, 451, 466; of 1880, 451, 575, 577; of 1884, 575, 577; of 1886, 451; of 1888, 575, 577, 578; of 1890, 579, 587, 666; of 1892, 575, 583, 587; of 1894, 587–588; of 1896, 499, 572 (illus.), 591, 594–596; of 1900, 597; of 1904, 669; of 1908, 671–672; of 1910, 674; of 1912, 656, 674–675; of 1914, 678; of 1916, 699–700; of 1920, 708, 716, 737, 755; of 1922, 740; of 1924, 738, 739–740; of 1928, 740–741, 740 (illus.); of 1930, 754; of 1932, 755, 755 (illus.); of 1934, 762; of 1936, 768–769; of 1938, 774; of 1940, 785; of 1942, 797; of 1944, 797–798; of 1946, 822; of 1948, 814, 822 (illus.), 850; of 1952, 819, 826–827; of 1956, 830, 849; of 1960, 857–858, 858 (illus.), 865; of 1962, 863; of 1964, 871–872, 927; of 1968, 885–889, 888 (illus.); of 1970, 897; of 1972, 897, 899–900, 899 (illus.); of 1976, 913; of 1980, 929–930, 930 (illus.); of 1984, 938–939, 939 (illus.); of 1988, 948–949, 948 (illus.); of 1990, 622; of 1992, 969–970; of 1994, 973–974; of 1996, 975–976, 975 (illus.); of 2000, 984–986, 985 (illus.); direct election of senators, 666, 674; electoral college and, 575, 578; electorate and, 574; primary system and, 666; in South, 473; voter participation and, 574, 576, 595
Elective curriculum, 557
Electoral college: election of 2000 and, 985, 986
Electoral commission (1877), 471
Electricity, 524–525, 541, 553–554

Electronics industry, 905
Elementary and Secondary Education Act (1965), 872
Elevated railway, 520, 540 (illus.)
Elevators: electric, 541
Eliot, Charles W., 557
Eliot, T. S., 650, 727, 728 (illus.)
Elkins Act (1903), 669
Elliott, Robert Brown, 464
Ellis Island, 543, 544–545, 544 (illus.), 545 (illus.), 641; Detention Card from, 545 (illus.)
Ellsberg, Daniel, 893
El Salvador, 941; leftists in, 915–916
El-Sheikh, Maha, 968
Ely, Richard T., 561, 666
Emancipation, 454
Embargo: on Soviet Union, 918
Embassies: bombings of, 991
Emergency Fleet Corporation, 709
Emigration: of blacks to Africa, 478. *See also* Immigrants and immigration
Emori, Susumi, 797
Empires: American, 602–611, 993–996
Empire State Building, 723
Employment: of African Americans, 966; of immigrants, 964–965; under Reagan, 936–937; of women, 554–555
Employment Act (1946), 822
"Enemies list," of Nixon, 893–894
Energy: coal, 722; electricity, 720, 721; natural gas, 722; petroleum, 722. *See also* Energy crisis; Nuclear power
Energy crisis, 901; energy policy and, 903–904; gas rationing and, 901 (illus.); U.S. energy consumption and, 902
Engel v. *Vitale,* 869, 927
England (Britain): *Alabama* claims and, 607; battle of Britain in, 785; Brussels Treaty and, 813; China and, 623; Cold War and, 811; Five Power Treaty and, 780; Four Power Treaty and, 780; immigrants from, 585–586, 737; League of Nations and, 714; Normandy invasion and, 798–799; Paris Peace Conference and, 712–715, 713–715; and Philippines, 618; rapprochement with, 607, 608; Samoa and, 609; scramble for empire and, 606; steel production in, 519; Suez Canal and, 830; and U.S. Far East policy, 694; and Venezuela, 692; Venezuela-Guiana dispute and, 607–608; Versailles Treaty and, 712; World War II and, 789
English Channel: swimming of, 726; World War II and, 798
English-only laws, 579
Enron scandal, 987–990
Entertainment: in late 19th century, 552–554; in 1920s, 721. *See also* Movies
Entitlement programs, Reagan and, 930, 932
Entrepreneurs: industrial development and, 512; in oil industry, 521
Environment: activists and, 903 (illus.); Bush, George W., and, 987; nuclear power and, 907; of Plains, 483, 503; Tennessee Valley Authority and, 757; Watt and, 932; western, 492. *See also* Conservation
Environmental Protection Agency (EPA), **903**–904
E pluribus unum, as national motto, 969
Epperson v. *Arkansas,* 747

Equality: for gays, 912
Equal Protection Clause, *Bakke* case and, 957
Equal rights: Fifteenth Amendment and, 466–467; Fourteenth Amendment and, 456
Equal Rights Amendment (ERA), 910, 910 (illus.); in 1920s, 724, 725; ratification and, 885
ERA. *See* Equal Rights Amendment (ERA)
Era of Reconstruction (Stampp), 476
Erie Railroad, 516, 518, 519, 584
Erie Street Baptist Church, 521
Escobedo v. *Illinois* (1964), 868
Espionage: Soviet, 823–824; U.S., 833, 833 (illus.)
Espionage Act (1917), **707**
Espy, Mike, 971
Ether, 551
Ethiopia, Mussolini and, 781
Ethnic cleansing, 979
Ethnic Heritage Studies Act (1972), 884
Ethnicity: Asian, 967–968; of Bosnia, 978; Hispanic, 964, 965–966; melting pot vs. diversity and, 968–969; Middle Eastern, 968; of U.S. population (1900), 550. *See also* Race and racism
Ethnic nationalism, 884
Ethnocentrism: and anti-imperialism, 619; during Great Depression, 753; Hawaii annexation and, 609; immigration restriction and, 736, 874; IQ testing and, 704–705; Philippines annexation and, 618; *Superiorité des Anglo-Saxons* and, 601–602
Eugenics, 637, 641
Europe and Europeans: immigration and, 543, 546–547
Evangelicalism: in late 19th century, 552
Evergood, Philip, 765
"Evil Empire," Soviet Union as, 940
Evolution: creation and, 743–747; expansionism and, 606
Executive power: Johnson, Andrew, and, 458–459; Lincoln and, 453
Exodusters, 502, 503 (illus.)
Expansion and expansionism, 602–611; Alaska and, 607; foreign policy and (1867-1900), 606–608; frontier closing and, 603, 605; under Grant, 607; and Hawaii, 609; navy and, 610–611; and Philippines, 618; reasons for, 602, 603–606, 618; and Samoa, 609; Spanish-American War and, 602, 611, 617–619; spirit of empire and, 602–603. *See also* Annexation; Cold War; Communication(s); Foreign policy; Imperialism; Soviet Union; Transportation; Westward movement
"Experiment in Misery, An" (Crane), 590
Explorer (spacecraft), 846
Exports: to Cuba, 607; overseas expansion and, 603

F

Factories: women in, 530
Fair Deal, 847–848, 850
Fair Employment Practices Committee (FEPC), 795, 847, 850
Fair Labor Standards Act (1938), 763–764, 773
Falaba (ship), 698
Fall, Albert, 738
Fallout shelters, 832 (illus.)
Falwell, Jerry, 928, 934, 935 (illus.)

Families and family life: at Amoskeag Company, 644–645; baby boom and, 837–838; birth control and, 635; changing, 905–908; divorce and, 634; of freedmen, 464, 465; immigrant, 547; in late 19th century, 554; in 1960s, 882; on Overland Trail, 492–493; same sex couples in, 912; sharecropper, 461 (illus.); suburbanization and, 841; types of households and (2000), 908 (illus.); unmarried couples and, 908; women and, 634, 885; during World War II, 794
Family and Medical Leave Act (1993), 974
Family in Jerome Camp, 797 (illus.)
Family task system, 460
Farewell to Arms, A (Hemingway), 716
Farmers' Alliance, 505
Farmers' Alliance and Industrial Union. *See* National Farmers' Alliance and Industrial Union
Farmers and Mechanics Bank, 584
Farms and farming: African Americans and, 633, 635, 638; Agricultural Adjustment Administration (AAA) and, 758; bonanza farms and, 504; drought of 1894 and, 584; dry farming and, 503; Dust Bowl and, 758, 758 (illus.); in early 1900s, 628; in 1870-1900, 580–581, 591; Grange and, 505; in Great Depression, 766; greenbacks and, 466; in Imperial Valley, 634; Indian assimilation policy and, 490; international trade and, 603; irrigation and, 634; large vs. small farmers and, 758–759; minimum wage laws and, 766; by Native Americans, 483; New Deal and, 758–759; in 1920s, 722, 752; overproduction and, 739, 758; populists and, 579–580; during Progressive Era, 633–634; railroads and, 580; Redeemer regimes and, 473; Rural Free Delivery and, 646; rural vs. urban attitudes toward, 732–737, 739; sharecropping and, 635, 758–759; Social Security and, 766; technology for, 503–504; tenancy and, 633, 758–759; in West, 502–506; Wilson and, 678; after World War I, 739; after World War II, 840; World War II and, 794. *See also* Rural areas
Farm Security Administration (FSA), 759, 773
Fastow, Andrew, 990
Fathers. *See also* Families and family life
Faubus, Orval, 851
FBI (Federal Bureau of Investigation), 866, 894
FCC. *See* Federal Communications Commission (FCC)
FDIC. *See* Federal Deposit Insurance Corporation (FDIC)
Federal Aid Roads Act (1916), 630
Federal Art Project, 844
Federal building (Oklahoma city), bombing of, 981, 981 (illus.)
Federal Bureau of Investigation (FBI). *See* FBI (Federal Bureau of Investigation)
Federal Communications Commission (FCC), 773
Federal deficit, 903, 933–936, 936 (illus.), 949–950, 961, 971, 976; budget surplus and, 980; Clinton and, 961–962, 971, 976
Federal Deposit Insurance Corporation (FDIC), 772

Federal Drug Administration, 637
Federal Farm Board, 754
Federal Farm Loan Act (1916), 678
Federal Farm Loan Board, 678
Federal government. *See* Government (U.S.)
Federal Housing Administration (FHA), 773
Federal Reserve: Clinton and, 971; Greenspan and, 961
Federal Reserve Act (1913), **677**
Federal Reserve system, 677, 678, 750, 764, 896, 933
Federal Steel, 520
Federal Theater Project, 761
Federal Trade Commission, 678
Federal Workmen's Compensation Act, 679
Feminine Mystique, The (Friedan), 885, 885 (illus.)
Feminists and feminism: Fifteenth Amendment and, 467; Reagan and, 932; suburbanization, 841
Feminization of professions, 530
Femme coverte. See Coverture
FEPC. *See* Fair Employment Practices Committee (FEPC)
Ferber, Edna, 506
Ferdinand, Franz, assassination of, 696
Ferguson, John H., 568
Ferraro, Geraldine, 938
Fertility: decline in rates of, 554; Hispanic, 965
Fessenden, William Pitt, 455–456
Fetterman massacre, 486
FHA. *See* Federal Housing Administration (FHA)
Field, Cyrus W., 522
Field, Marshall, 528
Field, Stephen J., 497
Fifteenth Amendment, 457 (illus.), **466–467,** 468, 473, 579
Fifty Years and Other Poems (Johnson), 729
Filibuster, Compromise of 1877 and, 471, 472
Filipinos: on trade cards, 603 (illus.). *See also* Philippines
Films. *See* Movies
Finances: under Nixon, 895
Fink, Albert, 518
First Amendment: Scopes Trial and, 745, 747
First Reconstruction Act (1867), 457
First U.S. Volunteer Cavalry. *See* Rough Riders
First Vote, The (Ward), 450 (illus.)
First World War. *See* World War I
Fiscal policy. *See* Economy; Federal Reserve system
Fish, Hamilton, 607
Fiske, John, 606
Fisk University, 559
Fitzgerald, F. Scott, 725, 727–728
Fitzgerald, John F., 587
"Five and Ten Cent Store," 528
Five-dollar day, 644
Five Points district (New York), 562
Five Power Treaty, 780
Flanders, Ralph, 827
Flappers, 724–725, 726 (illus.), 727 (illus.)
Flathead Indians, 767 (illus.)
Flexible response, 859
Flint, Michigan, strike in, 765
Florida, 469; election of 2000 and, 985–986; population shift to, 963; rioting in, 616; segregation in, 616
Flower children, 882

Floyd, Jay, 921
Flynn, Elizabeth Gurley, 643
Folk, Joseph W., 627, 666
Folklore: Native Americans in, 491
Foner, Eric, 477, 478
Food: Spanish-American War and, 614
Food Administration, 709, 709 (illus.)
Football, 553
Foote, Edward Bliss, 555
Foraker Act of 1900, **622**
Force acts (1870-1871), **468**
Ford, Gerald R., 899, 903, 912–913; election of
    1976 and, 913; energy policy and, 904; for-
    eign policy of, 914–915; SALT II and, 917
Ford, Henry, 527, 598, 629–630;
    "Americanization" program of, 639; assem-
    bly line and, 719; five-dollar day and, 644;
    organized labor and, 765; war production
    and, 793
Ford Motor Company, 629–630, 631;
    "Americanization" program of, 639; five-
    dollar day and, 644; IWW and, 644; River
    Rouge plant, 719, 720 (illus.)
Fordney-McCumber Tariff Act (1922), 738
Foreign Miners' Tax (1850), 498
Foreign policy: approaches to (1867-1900),
    606–608; assassination and, 912–913; ex-
    pansionism and, 602–611; unilateralism in,
    993–994
Foreign trade. *See* Exports; Imports; Trade
Forestation, 494
Forest Service, 671
Formosa Straits crisis, 830, 831
Fort(s): Kearney, 492; Laramie, 492; Sheridan,
    535
Fort Bragg, North Carolina, 859
"Forty acres and a mule," 461
Fossil fuels: limitations on, 904; nuclear power
    and, 907
Foster, John W., 609
442nd Combat Team, 797
Four Power Treat, 780
Fourteen Points, 712, 713, 713 (illus.)
Fourteenth Amendment, 456, 457 (illus.),
    473, 568, 569; *Bakke* case and, 958; privacy
    rights and, 923; Scopes Trial and, 745
Fourth Armored Division, 800
France: Brussels Treaty and, 813; China and,
    623; colonies of, 786; Five Power Treaty
    and, 780; Four Power Treaty and, 780;
    German occupation of, 784; Kellogg-Briand
    Pact and, 777; League of Nations and, 714;
    Paris Peace Conference and, 713–715;
    scramble for empire and, 606; Suez Canal
    and, 830; Versailles Treaty and, 712–715;
    Vietnam and, 829–830
Franchise. *See* Voting and voting rights
Frankel, Noralee, 465
Frankfurter, Felix, 709, 772, 868
Franklin, John Hope, 476
Frasch, Herman, 522
Fraud: corporate, 987
Frawley, William, 842 (illus.)
Freedmen, 460–461; court system and, 465;
    marriage and, 464–465
Freedmen's Bureau, 456, 461, 462, 475; land
    reorganization and, 460, 461; marriage of
    freedpeople and, 464–465
Freedmen's school, 465, 465 (illus.)
Freedom 7 (spacecraft), 847

Freedom ride, 866
"Free security," 603
Free Speech movement, 880
Free trade: China and, 977; Clinton and,
    971–972; 1896 election and, 572 (illus.)
Free-trade market, U.S. as largest, 512
Frelinghuysen, Frederick T., 607
Fresh Air Fund, 547
Freud, Sigmund, 704
Frey, William, H., 908
Frick, Henry Clay, 520, 535
Friedan, Betty, 885, 885 (illus.)
Friedman, Milton, 928
Friends of the Earth, 904
Frohman, Charles, 689
Frontier: closing of, 603, 605
Frost, Robert, 650, 864 (illus.)
FSA. *See* Farm Security Administration (FSA)
Fuchs, Klaus, 824
Fuel: sources of, 904. *See also* Energy
Fuel Administration, 709
Fulbright, J. William, 861, 876, 886
Fundamentalism (religious), 928; Muslim, 895

G

Gaddy, Levonne, 968
Galbraith, John Kenneth, 866
Gale, Zona, 728
Galesburg, Illinois, 614
Gallipoli, 702 (illus.)
Gandhi, Mahatma, 853
Gardner, Lloyd, 897
Garfield, Harry A., 709
Garfield, James A., 577, 607
Garland, Hamlin, 553, 581, 590
Garland, Judy, 593
Garner, John Nance, 784
Garrett, Pat, 496
Garrison, William Lloyd, 638
Garvey, Andrew, 549
Garvey, Marcus, 730–731, 731 (illus.)
Gasoline, 903; energy crisis and, 892 (illus.),
    894, 901, 902. *See also* Energy; Oil shocks
Gauges, standardization of, 515
Gay Activist Alliance, 911
Gay Liberation Front, 911
Gay liberation movement, 907, 910–911
Gays. *See* AIDS (acquired immune deficiency
    syndrome); HIV (human immunodefi-
    ciency virus); Homosexuality
Gender. *See* Men; Women
General Electric, 631
General Federation of Women's Clubs, 589,
    660
General Motors, organized labor and, 764–765
Geneva, summit meeting in, 943
Geneva Conference: nuclear test ban and, 832;
    Vietnam and, 829
Genlitz, Theodore, 495 (illus.)
Gentlemen's Agreement (1907), 693
George, David Lloyd, 713
George, Henry, 560, 565, 582, 665
Georgetown, Virginia, 614 (illus.)
Georgia: tenant farming in, 633; voting rights
    in, 574
Gerard, James W., 694
German Americans, 538 (illus.); as immi-
    grants, 737; as Lutherans, 579; as miners,
    498; as voters, 755 (illus.); during World
    War I, 706–707

German Literary Defense Committee, 697
Germany: auto industry in, 905; Berlin
    Blockade in, 814–815; *blitzkrieg* and, 784;
    Caribbean and, 692; China and, 623;
    colonies of, 713; empire and, 606; Hitler
    and, 781; League of Nations and, 781;
    Luftwaffe, 783 (illus.); *Lusitania* and,
    689–690; and Mexico, 695; Nazi-Soviet Pact
    and, 784, 790; partition of, 808, 809; and
    Philippines, 618; prisoners of war from, 706
    (illus.); propaganda about, 706; reparations
    and, 779; Russia and, 708; Samoa and, 609;
    Tripartite Pact and, 786; and Venezuela,
    692; Versailles Treaty and, 712–715; war
    debt of, 778–779. *See also* U-boats
Germs. *See* Disease; Medicine
Geronimo (chief), 489
Gershwin, George, 729
Ghost Dances, 487
Gideon v. *Wainwright* (1963), 868
Gilbert Island, 791, 802
Gilman, Charlotte Perkins, 555
Gilman, Daniel Coit, 557
Gingrich, Newt, 973, 974
Ginsburg, Ruth Bader, 687, 910
Gladden, Washington, 562
Glasgow, Ellen, 728
Glasnost, 943, 944 (illus.)
Glass ceiling, 909
Glass-Steagall Act (1933), 772
Glavda, Anna, 909 (illus.)
Glenn, John, 846, 847 (illus.)
Global warming, 907
GNP. *See* Gross national product (GNP)
Godkin, E. L., 552, 620
Goldberg, Arthur J., 864, 868
Gold: discoveries of, 497; vs. greenbacks, 466
Golden spike, 517
Goldman, Emma, 636, 733
Goldmark, Josephine, 684–687
Gold Rush: of 1849 (California), **483,** 492,
    497; of 1875 (Black Hills), 486
Gold standard: controversy over, 578 (illus.);
    depression of 1893-1897 and, 587; election
    of 1896 and, 591, 594–595; election of 1900
    and, 622; gold supply and, 596; Hayes,
    Rutherford B., and, 577
Gold Standard Act (1900), **597**
Goldwater, Barry, 895, 927, 928; election of
    1964 and, 872; Nixon and, 888; Vietnam
    War and, 877
Gompers, Samuel, 533; AFL and, 642; Clayton
    Antitrust Act and, 677; and female workers,
    642; Philippines annexation and, 619;
    World War I and, 709
Gone with the Wind (film), 756 (illus.)
Good Housekeeping, 841
Good Neighbor policy, 693, **779**
Goodnight, Charles, 500
Goodwin, Richard, 864
Goodyear Television Playhouse, 842
GOP. *See* Republican party
Gorbachev, Mikhail, 943–944; Cold War and,
    951; Reagan and, 943–944, 944 (illus.)
Gordon, Katherine, 843
Gordon, Richard, 843
Gore, Albert, Jr., 969, 971; election of 2000
    and, 984–986, 985 (illus.)
Gotcher, Emma, 684
Gottlieb, Adolph, 844

Gould, Jay, 470, 518, 532
Government: in postwar South, 463; territorial, in West, 495. *See also* Government (U.S.)
Government (U.S.): industrial development and, 512; Nixon and, 895–897; Reagan and, 931–932
Governors: provisional, during Reconstruction, 454
Graham, Billy, 820–821, 898
Gramm, Phil, 933–936
Gramm-Rudman, 936, 949
Grand Central Station (New York), 516
"Grandfather clause," 575
Grand Old Party. *See* Republican party
Grange. *See* National Grange of the Patrons of Husbandry
Grant, Madison, 736
Grant, Ulysses S., 459; administration of, 466, 469–471; foreign policy under, 607; military intervention in South and, 468–469; scandals and, 576
Grateful Dead, 882
Great American Desert, 483
Great Britain. *See* England (Britain)
Great Comanche War Trail, 489
Great crash (stock market, 1929), 750–752
Great Depression (1930s), 750–761, 752 (illus.); African Americans and, 753, 766; bonus army and, 754; deficit spending and, 773–774; ethnocentrism during, 753; family life and, 749; food during, 749, 750 (illus.), 758; racism during, 753; recession of 1937 and, 773; voluntarism and, 754. *See also* New Deal
Greater East Asia Co-Prosperity Sphere, 786
Great Gatsby, The (Fitzgerald), 727–728
Great Lakes Naval Training Station, 535
Great Northern Railway, 517
Great Plains, 482 (illus.); Indians of, 483–485; literature about, 590; regions of, 482
Great Salt Lake region, 493
Great Society, 872, 873, 896 (illus.)
Great White Fleet, 600 (illus.)
Greece, 788, 811, 812; immigration from, 639, 644, 737
Greeley, Horace, 470, 481, 483
Green, Theodore Francis, 870 (illus.)
Greenbackers, 466
Greenback Labor party, 466, 583
Greenback party, 466
Greenbacks: vs. sound (hard) money, 466
Greenberg, Clement, 845
Green party, election of 2000 and, 985
Greensboro, North Carolina, 853 (illus.), 854
Greenspan, Alan, 961, 962, 962 (illus.), 971, 976, 980
Greenwich Village, 636, 649
Grenada, invasion of, 941–942
Grierson, Benjamin H., 489
Griffith, D. W., 476, 477 (illus.), 647
Grissom, Virgil I. "Gus," 847 (illus.)
Gromyko, Andrei, 810
Gross national product (GNP): in 1950, 839; in 1960, 840
Ground Zero, 991
Guadalcanal, 791
Guam, 622, 780; acquisition of, 618–619
Guantánamo Bay, 617, 623

Guggenheim Museum, 845
Guilbaut, Serge, 845
Guinn v. *United States,* 639
Guiteau, Charles J., 577
Gulf of Tonkin affair, 876–877
Gulf of Tonkin Resolution, 877
Gulf War. *See* Persian Gulf War (1990)
Gulf & Western, 905
Gun control, school shootings and, 982
Gunther, Max, 843
Gurkin, Michael, 544
Gutman, Herbert G., 531

H

Haeckel, Ernst, 606
Haig, Alexander, 939, 941
Hair Culturists Union of America, 681 (illus.)
Haiti, 607, 779; Carter peace mission to, 978; dollar diplomacy in, 693; intervention in, 977
Halberstam, David, 859
Haldeman, H. R., 895, 900
Haley, Jack, 593
Hall v. *DeCuir,* 475 (illus.)
Hamilton, Alice, 530, 642, 658
Hammer v. *Dagenhart,* 661
Hampton, Wade, 473
Hampton Normal and Industrial Institute, 558
Handy, W. C., 648
Hanford, Washington, 803
Hanna, Marcus A., 594, 598
Hannibal and St. Joseph Railroad, 499
Hannibal County, Missouri, 590
Hanoi, 898
Hardin, John Wesley, 500
Harding, Warren G., 716, 737–738; Latin America and, 779; Red Scare and, 734
Hard money, 466
Harlan, John Marshall, 569, 570, 868
Harlem, New York: black community of, 723, 729; rioting in, 795, 883
Harlem Renaissance, 729–732, 732 (illus.)
Harper's Weekly, 552
Harriman, Averell, 810
Harriman, Edward H., 668, 693–694
Harrington, Michael, 871
Harris, Eric, 982
Harris, Joel Chandler, 590
Harrison, Benjamin, 506; 1888 election and, 576 (illus.), 578; 1892 election and, 583, 587; foreign policy and, 607; Hawaii and, 609; Sherman Silver Purchase Act and, 579
Hart, Schaffner, and Marx, 642
Harte, Bret, 517, 590
Hartley, Marsden, 651
Harvard Club, 601
Harvard University, 558, 812 (illus.)
Harvey, Paul, 820
Harvey, William H., 594
Hastie, William H., 766
Hatch, Edward, 489
Hatch Act (1887), 504
Hate-crime legislation, 912
Haub, Carl, 968
Havana, Cuba, 612, 613 (illus.), 617
Hawaii, 609 (illus.), 787–788, 791; annexation and, 607, 608–609; foreign policy toward, 606–607; Republic of, 609; territorial status of, 622

HAWK anti-aircraft missiles, sale of, 942
Hawley-Smoot Tariff, 779
Hay, John, 614, 623–624, 691–692
Hayakawa, S. I., 915
Hay-Bunau-Varilla Treaty, 692
Hayes, Rutherford B., 471, 550; 1876 election and, 471–472, 472 (illus.), 576–577; end of Reconstruction and, 576
Hayes Valley Gang, 543
Hay-Herrán Convention (1903), 691
Haymarket Riot, 532, 535
Haynesworth, Clement, 895
Hay-Pauncefote Treaty (1901), 691
Haywood, William D. "Big Bill," 636, 643, 707
Health, Education, and Welfare Department, 848
Health and health care: Carter and, 914; Clinton and, 972; epidemiology and, 658; infant mortality and, 646; life expectancy and, 646; maternal and infant health and, 724; Medicare, Medicaid, and, 872; national health insurance and, 773, 847, 848; in Progressive Era, 635; public health and, 658, 659 (illus.). *See also* AIDS (acquired immune deficiency syndrome); Disease; HIV (human immunodeficiency virus); Medicine; Occupational safety and health; War on drugs
Health and Human Services, Department of, 923
Held, John, Jr., 725, 726
Heline, Oscar, 749
Heller, Walter, 864, 865–866
"Hello girls," 555 (illus.)
Hell's Kitchen (New York), 561
Hemingway, Ernest, 716, 727
Henri, Robert, 649, 650
Henry Street Settlement (New York), 562
Hepburn Act (1906), **669**
Herbart, Johann Friedrich, 557
Herberg, Will, 841
Herbert, Victor, 648
Herrán, Thomas, 691
Herring, George, on Vietnam War, 878
Hickok, "Wild Bill," 498, 500
Higgs, Robert, 512
"High crimes and misdemeanors," 459
Higher education: for African Americans, 966; for women, 634. *See also* Universities and colleges
Highland Park, Michigan, 630
High Plains, 482, 500
High schools, 556
High-technology industry, 905
Highway Act of 1956, 848
Hill, Anita, 948
Hill, James J., 517, 668
Hill, Joe, 643
Hillman, Sidney, 797
Hinckley, John, Jr., 931 (illus.)
Hires, Charles, 511
Hispanic Americans: draft and, 881; population of, 965–966; second great migration and, 874–875
Hiss, Alger, 823, 824 (illus.)
History and historiography: meaning of West, 507; on Reconstruction, 476–477
History of Labour in the United States (Ely), 561

"History of the Standard Oil Company" (Tarbell), 627

Hitler, Adolf, 781, 781 (illus.), 783–784, 798. *See also* Holocaust; World War II

HIV (human immunodeficiency virus), 944–946

Hoar, George F., 620

Hobby, Oveta Culp, 848

Hobson, Winslow, 624

Ho Chi Minh, 829, 830, 861

Ho Chi Minh Trail, 879, 879 (illus.)

Hoffman, Abbie, 882

Hofstadter, Richard, 565

Holbrooke, Richard, 978

Holden, William, 821

Holden v. *Hardy,* 534

Holding company, 522, 523

Hollerith, Herman, 604, 604 (illus.), 605 (illus.)

Holliday, Doc, 500

Hollings, Ernest, 933–936

Hollow Men, The (Eliot), 727

Holmes, Oliver Wendell Holmes, Jr., 667

Holocaust, 798, 800–801, 800 (illus.), 801 (illus.)

Home Insurance Building, 541

Homeland Security Department, 992, 993 (illus.)

Home Missionary Society, 606

Homestead Act (1862), 494, 575

Homesteaders, in Oklahoma District, 507

Homestead Strike, 520, **535**

Homosexuality: AIDS epidemic and, 944–946; gay liberation movement and, 910–911; gay rights movement and, 907; public attitudes toward, 912

Honduras: Contras in, 941; dollar diplomacy in, 693

Hong Kong, 616, 620

Honolulu, Hawaii, 609

Hood, Raymond, 724

Hoover, Herbert, 709, 738, 779; election of 1928 and, 740–741; election of 1932 and, 755 (illus.); Food Administration and, 709; Great Depression and, 754, 766; as secretary of commerce, 738, 739

Hoover Dam, 754

Hopi Indians, 483

Hopkins, Harry, 761, 762–763, 766, 770, 771

Hopper, Edward, 728–729

Hopwood, Cheryl, 959

Hopwood case, 959

Horses: of buffalo soldiers, 488; Plains Indians and, 483

Hospitals, 551

Hostage crises: in Iran, 916–917, 917 (illus.)

Hotel Sherman (Chicago), 727 (illus.)

"Hot line," to Soviet Union, 863

House, Edward M., 696, 713

Households: income of (1975-1995), 937 (illus.); types of (2000), 908 (illus.)

House of Mirth, The (Wharton), 728

House of Representatives (U.S.): African Americans in, 451; Unionists and, 453

House on Henry Street, The (Wald), 562

House Un-American Activities Committee (HUAC), 823, 824 (illus.)

Housing: of California tribes, 483; discrimination in, 837, 840, 868; of Indians, 483; Kennedy's executive order on, 868; for sharecroppers, 461 (illus.); in small towns, 550; social-justice movement and, 658–659; sod houses, 503; tenements, 541–542, 541 (illus.), 542 (illus.). *See also* Architecture

Housing and Urban Affairs Department, 873

Howe, Frederic C., 560, 664, 665, 696

Howells, John Mead, 724

Howells, William Dean, 512, 542, 590, 619

How the Other Half Lives (Riis), 541–542

Hubbard, Elbert, 689

Hudson, Rock, AIDS and, 945

Hudson River Railroad, 516 (illus.)

Hue, Vietnam, 886

Huerta, Victoriano, 695

Hughes, Charles Evans, 666, 699, 700, 734; as Chief Justice, 772; as secretary of state, 737–738, 780

Hughes, Langston, 729, 732 (illus.)

Hull, Cordell, 614, 779, 787, 799

Hull House (Chicago), 562–563, 563, 564, 658

Human immunodeficiency virus (HIV). *See* HIV (human immunodeficiency virus)

Human rights, Carter's policy and, 917

Humphrey, George, 848

Humphrey, Hubert, 870, 871, 872, 887–889

Hungary, 791, 809, 831, 951

Hungry Heart (Graham), 634

Hunt, E. Howard, 893, 894, 900

Huntington, Collis P., 497

Hurston, Zora Neale, 732 (illus.)

Hussein, Saddam, 954, 994 (illus.), 995; Bush, George W., and, 994; Clinton and, 977; Persian Gulf War (1990) and, 952–953

Hutchins, Robert M., 785

Hyde amendment (1978), 910

Hydrogen bomb. *See* Nuclear weapons

I

IBM (International Business Machines), 604

ICBMs. *See* Intercontinental Ballistic Missiles (ICBMs); Long-range missiles

ICC. *See* Interstate Commerce Commission (ICC)

Ickes, Harold, 761, 766, 767 (illus.), 819

Idaho, 482; woman suffrage in, 574

"I Didn't Raise My Boy to Be a Soldier" (Bryan and Piantadosi), 697 (illus.), 699

If Christ Came to Chicago (Stead), 564–565

IFOR. *See* International Force (IFOR)

"I Have a Dream" speech, 867–868, 868 (illus.)

Illegal aliens. *See* Undocumented aliens

Illinois: mining strikes in, 585–587; regulation of railroads and, 576; steel mills in, 632; as swing state in elections, 575

Illinois Factory Act (1893), 563

Illiteracy: of blacks, 557; decline in, 556

Illness. *See* Disease

I Love Lucy, 842 (illus.)

Immigrant associations, 547–548

Immigrants and immigration, 585–587; Americanization and, 639; in cities, 541, 543–548; controversy over, 964–965; cultures of, 547–548; in 1880s, 605; in 1890, 546 (illus.); Ellis Island and, 544–545; ethnocentrism and, 736–737; families and, 547, 874, 875 (illus.); during Great Depression, 753, 766–767; homeland security and, 992; Japan and, 693; Ku Klux Klan and, 735–736; labor and, 588, 639–641, 640; from Latin America and Asia, 962; legislative control of, 544, 545; literacy tests and, 641; in midwestern cities, 538 (illus.); in mining camps, 498–499; mining strikes and, 585–587; national origins system for, 874; new immigrants and, 546–547, 547 (illus.), 639; 1900-1920, 633, 639 (illus.); in 1990s, 964–965; old immigrants, 639, 736–737; political bosses and, 549–550; Populism and, 585–587; quotas and, 641, 874; racism and, 736–737; reasons for, 543; Red Scare and, 733–734; region of birth of foreign born, 2000, 875 (illus.); restrictions on, 711, 736–737, 874; second great migration and, 874–875; transcontinental railroad and, 517, 518 (illus.); undocumented, 640, 874; to U.S. (1870-1900), 543 (illus.); westward migration of, 495; in workforce, 531; World War I and, 639, 709 (illus.), 736

Immigration Act (1965), 874–875, 962

Immigration and Naturalization Service (INS), 964 (illus.), 966, 992

Immigration laws: of 1875, 545; of 1882, 545; of 1885, 545; of 1891, 545; of 1903, 545; of 1917, 545

Immigration Restriction League, 547

Impeachment: of Clinton, 983, 983 (illus.); of Johnson, Andrew, 459–460, 459 (illus.), 576; Nixon and, 900

Imperialism, 603–607; acquisition of territory and, 608–609, 617–619; anti-imperialism and, 619–620; colonial government and, 622; debate over, 619–620, 622; spirit of empire, 602–603; trade and, 603, 606–607, 619, 620; United States and, 619 (illus.), 624; world colonial empires, 621 (illus.)

Imperial Valley, 634

Imports, 904

Incandescent lamp, 524

Inchon, South Korea, 818, 819

Income: of Asian Americans, 967; disparity in, 937–938; of elderly, 964; of Hispanics, 965; household (1975-1995), 937 (illus.); inequities of, 938. *See also* Wealth

Income tax, Reagan's cuts in, 933

India: as British colony, 791; immigrants from, 967; silver and, 587

Indiana, 575, 586

Indian Bureau, 767

Indian Country, 485, 487

Indian Intercourse Act (1834), 485

Indian policy: assimilation as, 487–491; concentration as, 485; "One Big Reservation" policy, 485; Peace Commission and, 486; small reservations as, 486

Indian Reorganization Act (1934), 767

Indians. *See* Indian policy; Native Americans; Plains Indians

Indian Territory, 501, 506

Individual piecework system, 460

Indochina, 787, 829–830, 831

Industrial capitalism, immigrant families and, 547

Industrial psychology, 644

Industrial Relocation Office, 543

Industrial Revolution: second, 720–723

Industrial Workers of the World (IWW), 636, **643,** 643 (illus.), 644, 707

Industry and industrialization, 510–536, 540, 610, 840; assembly line, 631; automobile, 629–630; benefits and costs of, 536; census of 1890 and, 605; consumerism and, 633; culture of work and, 531; development in, 512; in early 1900s, 628–633; economic and social mobility and, 531; employee welfare programs and, 644–645; geographic shift of, 905; immigrant labor and, 640; impersonalization and, 531; inventions and, 519, 522–525; labor and, 531–533, 533–536; literature about, 590; marketing and advertising in, 525–529; mass production and, 629–630, 631–632, 645–646; meatpacking and, 630; in New South, 472, 473 (illus.); oil industry and, 521–522; during Progressive Era, 628–633; railroads and, 512–519; regulation of, 597; research and development in, 631; scientific management and, 631, 644, 720; steel industry and, 519–521; trends in, 905; wage earners and, 529–536; after World War II, 838, 839–840; World War II and, 792–794, 793 (illus.)

Infant mortality, 539, 551, 646. See also Children

Infant Welfare Society, 659 (illus.)

Inflation, 645–646, 896, 903; Federal Reserve and, 980; in 1970s, 904; Reagan and, 933; unemployment and, 929

Influence of Sea Power upon History, The (Mahan), 610

Injunction, 534

In re Debs, 534, 585

INS. See Immigration and Naturalization Service (INS)

Inside the Vicious Heart (Abzug), 800

Inspectors, on Ellis Island, 545

Integration: Reagan and, 932. See also Civil rights; Segregation

Intellectual thought: expansion and, 606; on poverty and wealth, 560–561; social Darwinism and, 560; on wealth, 560

Intelligence testing, 704–705

Inter-American Conference (1889), 607

Intercollegiate Athletic Association, 647

Intercontinental ballistic missiles (ICBMs), 917, 940–941, 977. See also Long-range missiles

Interest of America in Sea Power, The (Mahan), 610

Interest rates, 896, 930, 933, 987

Interlocking directorates, 677

Intermediate Nuclear Forces agreement, 944

Intermediate range missiles (IRBMs). See Long-range missiles

International Bureau of the American Republics. See Pan-American Union

International Criminal Court, 993

International Force (IFOR), in Bosnia, 978–979

International Harvester Corporation, 640

Internet. See Computers; Dot.coms

Interstate Commerce Act (1887), 576

Interstate Commerce Commission (ICC), 576; Mann-Elkins Act (1910) and, 673–674; railroads and, 669; segregation in interstate travel and, 866

Interstate highway system, 848–849, 849 (illus.)

Intervention (military). See Armed forces

Inventions and inventors: in late 19th century, 522–525. See also Technology

Investment: in dot.coms, 988–989

Invitation to the Dance (Genlitz), 495 (illus.)

Iowa, party preference in, 579

IQ testing, 704–705, 704 (illus.), 705 (illus.), 736

Iran: Big Three conference in, 799; coup of 1953, 831; fundamentalists in, 895; immigrants from, 968. See also Shah of Iran

Iran-Contra affair, 942–943

Iranian hostage crisis, 916–917, 917 (illus.), 929

Iranian Revolution, 916

Iraq: coup of 1958, 831; funds for reconstruction of, 995; invasion of, 994–996; Persian Gulf War and, 952–953, 954

IRBMs. See Long-range missiles

Ireland: immigrants from, 585–586, 644, 737

Irish Benevolent Society, 547–548

Iron Curtain, 809, 815. See also Cold War; Soviet Union

"Iron law of wages," 534

Iron ore, for steel production, 519

Irrigation, 494–495

Irvine, Alexander, 562

Isakowsky, Tillie, 556

Islam. See Muslims

Isolationism, 597, 603, 611

Israel, 941; Arab-Israeli wars and, 901; Camp David accords and, 916; Clinton and, 977; immigrants from, 968

Isthmian Canal Commission, 691

Italian Americans, 755 (illus.), 884

Italy: Five Power Treaty and, 780; immigrants and, 585–586, 639, 737; League of Nations and, 714; Mussolini in, 781; North Atlantic Treaty and, 814; Paris Peace Conference and, 713–715; Tripartite Pact and, 786; and Venezuela, 692; World War II and, 784, 791

It's Up to the Women (E. Roosevelt), 770

IWW. See Industrial Workers of the World (IWW)

J

Jackson, Andrew, 470

Jackson, Kenneth, 841

Jackson, William Henry, 538 (illus.), 540 (illus.)

Jackson State College, Mississippi, student killings at, 898

Jamaica, 730, 731

James, William, 551, 620, 662, 704

Jameson, Roscoe, 711

Japan, 693, 694; autos from, 905, 932; China and, 623, 624, 780, 781, 783, 786–787; constitution of, 816; Hawaii residents from, 609; immigration and, 634, 641, 967; imperialism of, 621; League of Nations and, 714, 781; militarists in, 781; Pearl Harbor and, 787–788, 788 (illus.); Philippines and, 618, 693; surrender of, 803; trade with, 936; Tripartite Pact and, 786; Twenty-One Demands of, 693; U.S. occupation of, 816, 817; in World War II, 792 (illus.); between World Wars I and II, 780. See also World War II

Japanese Americans: indemnity for, 797; internment of, 796–797, 796 (illus.), 797 (illus.); in military, 797; segregation and, 693;

in U.S. population (1900), 550; in workforce, 531

Jaworski, Leon, 900

Jazz age, 723–729, 732

Jazz Singers, The (Motley), 729 (illus.)

Jefferson Monument, 756 (illus.)

Jeffords, James M., 987

Jehovah's Witnesses, 737

Jewett, Sarah Orne, 590

Jews and Judaism: birth control and, 637; Brandeis and, 678; hostility toward, 641; housing discrimination and, 840; as immigrants, 639; Ku Klux Klan and, 735–736; Nazis and, 781; synagogues and religious schools of, 548; voting and, 755 (illus.); Wilson and, 678; Yiddish Theater of, 548

Jicarilla Apache Indians, 483

Jim Crow laws, 473–475, 556, 568, 569. See also Plessy v. Ferguson

Job Corps, 871

Jobs. See Employment; Labor; Workforce

John Birch Society, 869

Johns Hopkins University, 557

Johnson, Andrew, 453–454; Congress and, 455–457, 458–460; impeachment of, 459–460, 459 (illus.), 576; National Union movement and, 456; Reconstruction policy of, 454–456

Johnson, Fenton, 711

Johnson, Hiram, 666, 667, 674

Johnson, Hugh, 758

Johnson, James Weldon, 729

Johnson, Lyndon B., 869, 870, 873, 878; Civil Rights Act of 1957 and, 852; civil rights and, 852, 869, 871, 872–873, 956; Commission on Equal Employment Opportunities and, 866; Congress and, 870–871, 872–873; containment and, 876; education policy of, 872; Eisenhower and, 848, 870–871; fiscal policy of, 872; Great Society and, 872, 873; Gulf of Tonkin affair, 876–877; health policy of, 872; on Immigration Act of 1965, 874; "Johnson treatment," 870 (illus.); Kennedy, John F., and, 869, 870, 871; Latin America and, 876; leadership style of, 870–871; 1964 election and, 871–872; 1968 election and, 886–887, 887 (illus.); tax policy of, 869, 871; as vice president, 858; Vietnam War and, 876–880, 885–887; war on poverty and, 871

Johnson, Samuel, 504

Johnson, Tom L., 665

Joint Chiefs of Staff, Vietnam and, 829, 876, 877, 886

Jones, Mary Harris ("Mother"), 643

Jones, Paula, 973

Jones, Samuel M. ("Golden Rule"), 664

Jonesboro, Arkansas, school shooting in, 982

Joplin, Scott, 552

Jordan, David Starr, 496, 557

Jordan, Hamilton, 913

Jordan, Vernon, 958, 959

Joseph (Chief), 487

Journalism: Spanish-American War and, 614–615; yellow, 612

Judaism. See Jews and Judaism

Judge (magazine), 726 (illus.)

Judiciary. See Court(s)

Judson, Phoebe, 493

Julian, George, 457
Jungle, The (Sinclair), 627, 669–670, 670 (illus.)
Justice Department: civil rights division of, 850; voting rights bill and, 872
"Just say no" campaign, 946–947

K

Kaczynski, Theodore J., 981
Kael, Pauline, 749
Kaiser, Henry J., 793
Kaiser, the Beast of Berlin, The, 706
Kaiser Aluminum, affirmative action at, 966
Kalakaua (Hawaii), 608
Kallen, Horace, 969
Kandinsky, Wassily, 844
Kane, Woodbury, 601
Kansas, 482, 580, 592
Kansas-Nebraska Act (1854), 592
Kansas Pacific Railroad, 499, 500
Kaplan, John, 958, 959
Kasserine Pass, 791
Kasson, John A., 603
Kaufman, Irving, 824
Kazakhstan, 977
Kearney (ship), 785
Kearney, Fort, 492
Kearns, Doris, on Vietnam War, 878
Keating-Owen Act (1916), 661, 679
Keats, John, 842
Keene, Carolyn, 648
Kelley, Florence, 563, 564, 657, 687 (illus.); *Muller* v. *Oregon* and, 684–687; World War I and, 696
Kellogg, Frank B., 715, 777
Kellogg, John H., 555
Kellogg-Briand Pact, 777, 780
Kelly, "Honest" John, 548, 549
Kelly, William, 519
Kemp, Jack, 931
Kenna, "Hinky Dink," 548
Kennan, George, 811, 816
Kennedy, Anthony, 948
Kennedy, Edward (Ted), 913, 929, 987
Kennedy, Jacqueline, 869, 869 (illus.); Camelot and, 864; White House and, 864, 864 (illus.)
Kennedy, John F., 870, 871; assassination of, 869, 869 (illus.); Bay of Pigs and, 861–862; Berlin crisis and, 859–860; Camelot and, 864; civil rights and, 866–868, 869, 871; Cold War and, 859–864; Cuban missile crisis and, 862–864; defense spending and, 860, 865; domestic policies of, 864–869; election of 1960 and, 857–858, 858 (illus.), 865; "hot line" to Soviet Union and, 863; judicial appointments of, 866; King, Martin Luther, Jr., and, 858; New Frontier and, 858, 865; space program and, 865; Supreme Court and, 868; tax policy of, 865–866, 869, 871; voting rights and, 868
Kennedy, Robert F., 871–872, 874; assassination of, 887; as attorney general, 864; Cuban missile crisis and, 862–863; Johnson, Lyndon, and, 871–872; Meredith, James, and, 866–867; 1968 election and, 886–887
Kennedy-Nixon debate, 857–858
Kent State University, Ohio, national guard shootings in, 898

Kentucky: African American troops and, 615; school shooting in, 982
Kerosene, 521
Kerouac, Jack, 843, 843 (illus.), 846
Kerr, Clark, 927
Ketcham, Rebecca, 492
Kettle Hill, 617
Khe Sanh, Vietnam, 885–886
Khmer Rouge, 915
Khomeini, Ayatollah Ruholla, 916, 942
Khrushchev, Nikita, 833, 833 (illus.), 859–860; arms control and, 831–832; Cuban missile crisis and, 862–864; Eisenhower and, 831–833
Kickapoo Indians, 489
Killian, James R., 846
Kilrain, Jake, 553
Kim Il-Sung, 817–818
Kindergarten, 557
King, Martin Luther, Jr., 858; assassination of, 883; Black Power movement and, 883; "I Have a Dream" speech of, 867–868, 868 (illus.); March on Washington and, 867–868, 868 (illus.); Montgomery bus boycott and, 852–853; on nonviolence, 853–854; Prayer Pilgrimage to Washington, 853; Selma-to-Montgomery march and, 872; on Vietnam War, 883
King, Rodney, 966–967, 967 (illus.)
Kinsey report, 727, 911
Kinship: in Native American tribes, 484
Kiowa Indians, 483, 486, 489, 490
Kipling, Rudyard, 526
Kirkpatrick, Jeane, 940
Kissinger, Henry, 895, 897, 898 (illus.), 901, 916
Kitty Hawk, North Carolina, 598
Klamath Indians, 483
Klebold, Dylan, 982
Kline, Franz, 844
Knickerbocker Club, 601
Knights of Labor, 532, 533, 643
Knights of the White Camellia, 467
Knowland, William, 830
Know-Nothings, 823
Knox, Frank, 795
Knox, Philander, 693–694
Kodak camera, 523
Kooning, Willem de, 844
Koop, C. Everett, 945, 945 (illus.)
Korea, 693, 780, 967
Korean Americans, segregation and, 693
Korean War, 817–819, 818 (illus.); American defectors and, 820–821, 821 (illus.); desegregation of armed services and, 850; Eisenhower and, 826; "lost sheep" of, 820–821, 821 (illus.); Operation Big Switch in, 820; prosperity at home and, 839
Koresh, David, 981
Kosovo: Clinton and, 979–980; intervention in, 977
Krol, John Cardinal, 923
Krupp (Germany), 782
Kuhn, Loeb and Company, 668
Ku Klux Klan, 467–469, 468 (illus.), 469 (illus.), 476, 735 (illus.); anti-Asian attacks by, 967; Democratic party and, 739; Garvey on, 731; in 1920s, 735–736
Ku Klux Klan acts (1870-1871), 468
Kurds, 954, 995

Kuwait, 952–953, 994
Kyoto Protocol, 993

L

Labor, 533–534; absenteeism and, 644; African Americans as, 530, 531; agricultural, 634, 766; anti-imperialism and, 619; blue- and white-collar, 937; children as, 530–531; Clayton Antitrust Act and, 677; conditions in, 529–530; conflict in workplace, 641–645; culture of, 531; domestic servants and, 766, 767; eight-hour day and, 632 (illus.), 633; ethnocentrism and, 619; Fair Labor Standards Act and, 763–764; five-dollar day and, 644; health and safety of, 632–633, 635 (illus.), 665; immigrants and, 639–640; income and, 937–938; mass production and, 631–632; migrant, 634; minimum wage and, 847, 848; muckrakers and, 627; *Muller* v. *Oregon* and, 684–687; New Deal and, 763–764; in 1920s, 722; organized, 764–765; of Plains tribes, 484–485; in postwar South, 460, 461; productivity, 642; racial discrimination and, 638; "scientific" management and, 632; Wagner Act and, 763–764; War Labor Board and, 709; Wilson and, 678; women and, 530–531, 554–555, 555 (illus.); workers' compensation law and, 665; working hours and, 647, 661, 684–687, 709, 764, 840; World War I and, 709–712; World War II and, 793–794, 822. *See also* Child labor; Industry and industrialization; Labor unions; Strikes
Labor Department, 639; Division of Conciliation, 679; Red Scare and, 733–734; Women's Bureau in, 710
Labor strikes. *See* Strikes
Labor unions, 531–533; decline in, 905; in early 1900s, 642–645; membership in, 642 (illus.); social offerings of, 534; women and, 642
Labor violence. *See* Strikes
Lackawanna Railroad, 627
Ladies Anti-Beef Trust Association, 555
Ladies' Home Journal (magazine), 551 (illus.), 554, 627, 724
LaFeber, Walter, 602
La Follette, Robert M., 669, 700; election of 1924 and, 740; tariff and, 672, 673; Wisconsin Idea of, 666, 667
La Follette's Magazine, 696
Lahr, Bert, 593
Laissez-faire: in New South, 472
Lake, Anthony, 976
Lakeland, Florida, 616
Lake Shore and Michigan Southern Railway, 516 (illus.)
Lake Tahoe, growth of, 960 (illus.)
Land: as basis of wealth, 560; Dawes Act and, 490; for freedmen, 460–461; Indians and, 490; legislation concerning, 494; in postwar South, 460–461; for railroads, 495, 514–515, 514 (illus.); Reconstruction redistribution of, 457; in West, 493–495
Land-grant colleges, women in, 558, 558 (illus.)
Landing at Saipan, The (Draper), 776 (illus.)
Landon, Alfred M., 768, 769
Lange, Dorothea, 748, 759
Language(s): of Native Americans, 484

Lansing, Robert, 698, 700, 713, 715
Laos: immigrants from, 967; Vietnam War and, 879
Laramie, Fort, 492
La Raza, 968
Las Gorras Blancas ("The White Caps"), 496
Las Guasimas, 617
Latchkey children, 794
Lathrop, Julia, 642
Latin America, 779–780; Arthur, Chester A., and, 577; Carter and, 915–916; Cleveland and, 607–608; debt and, 692–693; drug trade and, 947; foreign policy toward, 607–608; Garfield and, 577, 607; Grant and, 607; Harrison, Benjamin, and, 607; immigrants from, 962, 964, 965–966; Monroe Doctrine and, 603, 606, 607–608; Roosevelt, Franklin D., and, 779–780; Roosevelt Corollary and, 692–693; second great migration and, 874–875; U.S. activities in, 695 (illus.)
Latinos. *See* Hispanic Americans; Mexicans and Mexican Americans
Law(s): of coverture, 555; evolution of, 684–687; *Muller* v. *Oregon*, 684–687; professionalization in, 658; sociological jurisprudence and, 662
Lawrence, Jacob, 796
Lawrence, Massachusetts, strike in, 643
Lazarus, Emma, 544
Leadville, Colorado, 498, 499 (illus.)
League for the Protection of the Family, 589
League of Latin American Citizens, 965
League of Nations, 713, 714; Ethiopia and, 781; Germany and, 781; Japan and, 780, 781; U.S. and, 779, 799
League of Women Voters, 770
League to Limit Armament, 696
Leahy, Patrick, anthrax scare and, 992
Lean Bear (Cheyenne chief), 481
Leary, Timothy, 882
Lease, Mary E., 582 (illus.), 633
Lebanon, 831; Israeli invasion of, 941
Lee, Alice, 551, 636
Lee, Ivy L., 644
Left wing (political), New Left and, 900
Legal codes, women and changes in, 555
Legal evidence and, 684–687
Legislative Reference Bureau, 666
Legislature. *See* specific legislative bodies
Leisure, 552–553
Lemke, William, 768
Lend-Lease, 785, 790, 810
Lenin, V. I., 708
Lesbians: gay liberation movement and, 910–911. *See also* Homosexuality
"Let's Keep the Glow in Old Glory," 688 (illus.), 697
Levitt, William, 837
Levittown, 836 (illus.), **837,** 838 (illus.)
Lewinsky, Monica, 982–983
Lewis, David, 729
Lewis, Drew, 932
Lewis, John L., 764, 765
Lewis, John Solomon, 502
Lewis, Sinclair, 728
Lewis, Wyndham, 728
Leyte Gulf, 802
Libbey-Owens-Ford Company, 631
Liberal Republicans, 470

Liberals and liberalism, in election of 1980, 930
"Liberty cabbage," 706
Liberty League, 768
Libya, 791
Lichtman, Allan J., 740
Liddy, G. Gordon, 893, 894, 900
Lieberman, Joseph, 983, 985
Life expectancy, 646
Life magazine, 627
Life on the Mississippi (Twain), 590
Lifestyle: consumer savings and, 936; of Plains Indians, 483–485; of Pueblo groups, 483; of women, 908–909. *See also* Entertainment; Housing
"Lift Ev'ry Voice and Sing," 711
Light bulb, carbon filament for, 524
Liliuokalani (Hawaii), 608–609, 608 (illus.)
Lincoln, Abraham, 481; Reconstruction initiatives of, 453
Lincoln Memorial, 766 (illus.)
Lindbergh, Charles, 726, 785
Lindsay, Vachel, 650
Lindsey, Ben, 662
Lippman, Walter, 690
Literacy: tests, 467, 545, 547; as voting requirement, 574
Literature: during depression of 1893-1897, 589–591; in Harlem Renaissance, 729–732, 732 (illus.); naturalism in, 589–591; in 1920s, 727–728; periodicals and, 726; poetry and, 650, 732; popular, 648; realism in, 589–591
Lithuanians, 585, 755 (illus.)
Little, Frank, 707
Little Bighorn, battle of, 486, 487 (illus.), 491
"Little Boxes" (Reynolds), 838
Little Rock, Arkansas, desegregation in, 851
Littleton, Colorado, school shootings in, 980, 982
Little Women (Alcott), 589
Lochner v. *New York,* 534, 685, 686, 687
Lockouts, 534, 535
Lodge, Henry Cabot, 736; League of Nations and, 714; Paris Peace Conference and, 713; Versailles Treaty and, 715
Lodge Corollary, 693
London, Jack, 590–591
Lonely Crowd, The (Riesman), 843
Long, Huey, 762, 764, 768
Long Day, The: The Story of a New York Working Girl as Told by Herself, 530–531
Long Island, 836 (illus.), 837
Long-range missiles, 831, 832–833, 859
Looking Backward, 2000-1887 (Bellamy), 561
Loomis, Samuel Lane, 540
Los Alamos, New Mexico, 803
Los Angeles: rioting in, 796, 883; smog in, 926 (illus.)
Louisiana, 469, 470; African American governor in, 615; end of Reconstruction and, 576; Ku Klux Klan in, 467, 468; segregation in, 568; Unionist government in, 453; voting rights in, 574–575
Louisville, Kentucky, segregation in, 639
Louisville & Nashville Railroad, 518
"Love Song of J. Alfred Prufrock" (Eliot), 650
Low, Seth, 664
Lowell, Amy, 650
Lowell, James Russell, 684

Loyalty oaths, 839
Loyalty Review Board, 823
Luce, Henry, 996
Ludlow, Louis, 783
Lumber industry, Timber and Stone Act and, 494
Lusitania (ship), 689–690, 690 (illus.), 698
Lutherans, 579
Luxembourg, 813
Lynchings: of African Americans, 474, 474 (illus.); antilynching efforts, 616, 681, 773, 850; Ku Klux Klan and, 736; from 1900-1914, 635, 638; of radicals, 733; after Spanish-American War, 624; of striking cotton pickers, 581; during World War I, 707, 710

M

MacArthur, Douglas, 754, 818–819, 819 (illus.); Japan and, 816; Korean War and, 818; Philippines and, 802; World War II and, 788, 791, 802
Machine gun, in World War I, 703
Machines: at Centennial Exposition, 510 (illus.), 511; farm, 504; for tabulating data, 604, 605 (illus.)
Machines (political), 451, 548–550
Mackay, John W., 497
Macon, Georgia, 615
Macune, Charles W., 581
Macy, R.H., 528
Maddox (ship), 876
Madero, Francisco I., 695
Madison Guaranty, Clinton, Hillary, and, 973
Madison Square Garden: Democratic party convention at, 739–740; labor pageant in, 643 (illus.)
Maggie: A Girl of the Streets (Crane), 590, 591 (illus.)
Magyars, 585
Mahan, Alfred Thayer, 610, 616
Maher, Bridget, 908
Mail delivery, parcel post and, 633
Mail-order business, 528–529
Maine (ship), 612, 613 (illus.), 614 (illus)
Main Street (Lewis), 728
Main-Travelled Roads (Garland), 581
Malaya, 788
Manchester, New Hampshire, 644
Manhattan Island, 542
Manhattan Project, 802–803
Manila, Philippines, 616, 618, 622
Manila Bay, 616, 617
Manker, Leslie F., 956, 957
Mann Act (1910), 660
Mann-Elkins Act (1910), 673–674
Mansfield, Arabella, 530
Manufacturing: decline in, 905, 936–937; in 1920s, 721; in 1930s, 751
Mao Tse-Tung, 816–817, 817 (illus.), 818, 830
"Maple Leaf Rag" (song), 552
Maps: physiographic map of United States, 482 (illus.)
March on the Pentagon (1967), 881–882, 881 (illus.)
March on Washington: of 1963, **867**–868, 868 (illus.); for gay rights (1987), 911
Mariana Islands, 816
Marin, John, 650
Marines (U.S.). *See also* Armed forces; Military

Market(s): Asian, 608; in late 19th century, 529; overseas expansion and, 603–606

Marketing: industrialization and, 525. *See also* Advertising

Marne, battle of, 703

Marriage: freedmen and, 464–465; of immigrants, 547; unmarried couples and, 908. *See also* Families and family life

Marsh, Reginald, 753

Marshall, George C., 812 (illus.), 815–816, 817, 825; Nobel Peace Prize for, 812; Normandy invasion and, 790–791; as secretary of state, 811. *See also* Marshall Plan

Marshall, Thurgood, 866, 948; *Brown* decision and, 850

Marshall Islands, 791, 802, 816

Marshall Plan, 812–**813**, 813 (illus.), 815, 839

Martinet, Louis A., 568

Martinique, 617

Marx, Karl, and socialism in U.S., 662

Masculine sphere of work, 554

Massachusetts: African American troops in, 615; regulation of railroads and, 576

Massachusetts Institute of Technology (MIT), 541, 557

Massillon, Ohio, 584

Massive resistance, 851

Massive retaliation, 828–**829**, 830, 859

Masson, André, 845

Mass production, 524 (illus.); of steel, 519

Mass revivals, in late 19th century, 552

Mass society, 629, 633–635, 638–641

Mass transit systems, city growth and, 541

Masters, Edgar Lee, 650

Masterson, William B. "Bat," 500

Matsu, 830

Mauser, 614

Mayaguez (ship) incident, 915

McAdoo, William G., 739

McCall's (magazine), 841

McCarthy, Eugene, 886–887

McCarthy, Joseph R., 824–825, 825 (illus.), 826–827, 827 (illus.), 839

McCarthyism, 824–827, **825**

McClure, Samuel, 627

McClure's Magazine, 627, 628 (illus.)

McCord, James, 893, 900

McCormick, Robert R., 724

McCormick Harvester works, strike at, 535

McCorvey, Norma, 920–924, 921 (illus.)

McCoy, Joseph G., 499

McDowell, Mary, 642

McFarlane, Robert, 942

McGovern, George, 899 (illus.), 900, 913, 930

McGuffey, William Holmes, 556

McGuffey's Eclectic Readers, 556

McKay, Claude, 711, 729

McKinley, William, 594, 596–598, 615, 624; assassination of, 597–598, 667; election of 1896 and, 572 (illus.), 594, 595–596, 597; election of 1900 and, 597, 622; Hawaii and, 609; Open Door Policy and, 623–624; Philippines and, 618, 619, 620, 622; Spanish-American War and, 612–614, 615, 616–618; tariff and tax policy of, 738

McKinley Tariff Act (1890), 578, 587, 607, 608

McManes, James, 548

McNamara, Robert, 859, 876, 877–878, 886

McPherson, Aimee Semple, 737

McTeague (Norris), 590

McVeigh, Timothy, 981

Meat Inspection Act (1906), 670

Meatpacking industry, 669–670; in Chicago, 526, 527; disassembly lines and, 523, 527; innovations in, 523

Media. *See* Journalism

Medicaid, 872

Medicare, 872, 930, 972, 974

Medicine: AIDS and, 944–946; medical schools and, 559; patent, 670–671; professionalization in, 658; revolution in, 551

Meese, Edwin, 943, 947–948

Mekong Delta, 879 (illus.)

Mellon, Andrew, 738, 739 (illus.)

Melting pot, 565, 875; vs. diversity, 968–969

Melting Pot, The (Zangwill), 565

Memphis, Tennessee: King assassination in, 883; lynching in, 581

Men: in mining camps, 498; in Plains tribes, 484–485; in Spanish Mexican culture, 496; Victorian era clothing of, 551, 551 (illus.); westward movement and, 492–493. *See also* Families and family life

Mencken, H. L., 542, 724, 728, 744, 747

Menominee Indians, 483

Merchant marine, 610

Meredith, James, 866–867

Merrimack River, 644

Merriwell, Frank, 648

Mesabi Range, 519

Mescalero Apache Indians, 489

Metropolitan Museum (New York), 649

Metropolitan Opera, 553

Meuse-Argonne, battle at, 706, 712

Mexicans and Mexican Americans, 481, 964 (illus.); bilingualism and, 884; in California, 496; as Chicanos, 884; as cowboys, 500; deportations of, 753, 766; ethnic nationalism of, 884; during Great Depression, 753, 766–767; as immigrants, 628, 634, 639, 640 (illus.), 711, 737, 964, 965, 966; immigration law and, 641; migration of, 711; in military, 795–796; New Deal and, 766–767; population of, 711; second great migration and, 874–875; settlement houses of, 563; in Southwest, 640; studies program for, 884; World War I and, 709; World War II and, 795–796. *See also* Hispanic Americans

Mexico: drug trade through, 947; foreign policy toward, 606; reciprocity treaty with, 607; revolution in, 640, 694–696; Roosevelt, Franklin D., and, 780; silver coinage and, 587; Zimmermann telegram and, 700

Microbiology, 551

Middle class: African Americans in, 966; blacks in Reconstruction-era, 452; family life of, 554; income of, 938; Reagan and, 937; settlement house movement and, 562; in suburbs, 541; tax burden of, 938

Middle East, 940 (illus.); Carter and, 916–917; Clinton and, 977; after Cold War, 962; Eisenhower and, 830–831; immigrants from, 968; Iran-Contra and, 942–943; Reagan and, 939, 940–941. *See also* Arab-Israeli wars

Middle West: agricultural crisis and, 580; election of 1894 and, 588; immigration and, 587; mining strikes in, 585–587; party preference in, 579; population of, 963

Midway, 607; battle of, 791

Migrants and migration: African Americans and, 539, 710, 711 (illus.), 722–723, 729, 730, 796 (illus.); agricultural workers and, 634, 767, 884 (illus.); chain migration and, 644; to cities, 723, 730; IWW and, 644; Mexican Americans and, 711, 737, 796; second great migration and, 874–875; World War I and, 710; World War II and, 794, 795, 796. *See also* Expansion and expansionism; Immigrants and immigration; Native Americans

Military: Bush, George W., on, 994; culture of, 614–615; homosexuals in, 911–912; Reagan and, 941–942; U.S. brutality in war, 620. *See also* Armed forces; Military intelligence; Navy (U.S.)

Military bases, in Britain and Germany, 939

Military districts, during Reconstruction, 458 (illus.)

Military-industrial complex, 833

Military Information Division, 616

Military intelligence, Spanish-American War and, 616

Military production, 792–794

Military rule, in Reconstruction South, 457, 458, 462

Militia: black, 462; Homestead strike and, 535; use against Klan, 468

Miller, Arthur, 529

Millis, Walter, 781

Mills, C. Wright, 843

Milosevic, Slobodan, 979–980, 979 (illus.)

Milwaukee, 538 (illus.)

Mines and mining: in Indian lands, 485; IWW and, 644; labor strikes and, 585–587; literature about, 590; Native Americans and, 483; placer mining and, 497; Roosevelt, Eleanor, and, 770; "square deal" and, 668–669; strikes in, 497–498; unions and, 586 (illus.), 643; in West, 496–499, 498 (illus.)

Minetta, Norman, 987

Minimum wage, 766, 767; Clinton and, 974

Mining camps, 498–499

Minneapolis, 513, 584, 627

Minnesota, 482

Minorities: higher education and, 558–559. *See also* Diversity; Ethnicity

Minor v. Happersett, 574

Minuteman ICBMs, 917

Miranda v. Arizona (1966), 868

MIRVs. *See* Multiple independently targeted reentry vehicles (MIRVs)

Misery index, 929

Missile gap: Eisenhower and, 832–833; Kennedy, John F., and, 859

Missiles: antiballistic (ABMs), 897; Reagan and, 939–940; Reagan-Gorbachev agreements and, 944; sale to Iran, 942–943; START I and, 951. *See also* Strategic Arms Limitation Talks (SALT)

Missions and missionaries: in city slums, 562; expansion and, 606, 608, 609, 618; Hawaii and, 608, 609; Philippines and, 618; social Darwinism and, 606

Mississippi, 468; school shooting in, 982; tenant farming in, 633; voting rights in, 574

Missouri (ship), 803

Missouri Pacific Railroad, 499, 532

Miss Zulu Bett (Gale), 728

Mitchell, John (Attorney General), 894, 895, 897, 901
Mitchell, John (union leader), 668
Mittlebau Dora (concentration camp), 800 (illus.)
Mobility: economic, 531; industrialization and, 531; social, 531
Model T Ford, 629–630
Modern Republicanism, 848–849
Moggadishu, 977
Mondale, Walter, 913, 929, 938
Mondrian, Piet, 845
Money: greenbacks vs. sound (hard) money, 466; tight-money policy and, 933
Monopolies, trusts and, 522
Monroe, Harriet, 650
Monroe Doctrine, 603, 606, 607–608; Lodge Corollary to, 693; Roosevelt Corollary to, 692–693; Versailles Treaty and, 715
Montana, 481, 482
Montgomery, Lucy M., 648
Montgomery bus boycott, 852–853
Montgomery Ward (store), 528, 528 (illus.), 529
Moody, Dwight L., 552
Moral diplomacy, 694
Morality: supervision of public, 552; Victorian, 551–552
Moral Majority, 928, 930, 934–935, 935 (illus.)
Morgan, Anne, 642
Morgan, Frank, 593
Morgan, J. P., 518–519, 520, 524, 587, 630, 642, 722, 739; Ballinger-Pinchot affair and, 673; coal mining strike and, 668; and Company, 518, 630, 668; interlocking directorates and, 677; Roosevelt, Theodore, and, 655; trustbusting and, 668
Morgan family, 696
Mormons, 491, 493
Morocco, 790, 790 (illus.), 791, 819
Morrill Land Grant Act (1862), 557
Morris, Dick, 974, 976
Morton, Ferdinand "Jelly Roll," 648
Moscow, summit in, 944
Most favored nation status, for China, 977
Mothers. See Families and family life; Women
Mothers Congress of 1896, 589
Mothers' Crusade, 786
Mother's Day, 635
Motherwell, Robert, 844
Motley, Archibald, 729
Mott, Lucretia, 885
Motto, national, 969
Movies, 821; blacklisting and, 827; early, 647; in 1920s, 721; sex in, 727; Westerns, 840 (illus.)
Muck, Karl, 706
Muckrakers, 627–628, 628 (illus.); coal mining industry and, 673; food industry and, 669–670
Mugwumps, 552
Muller, Curt, 684–687, 685 (illus.)
Muller v. *Oregon,* 534, **662,** 684–687
Multiculturalism, 968–969
Multiethnicity, 968–969
Multilingualism, in labor movement, 642
Multiple independently targeted reentry vehicles (MIRVs), 897–898

Munn v. *Illinois,* 576
Munsey's, 627
Murphy, Charles F., 548
Murrah Federal Building, bombing of, 981, 981 (illus.)
Murray, Philip, 765
Murrow, Edward R., 827
Museum(s), 756
Museum of Modern Art (New York), 844
Museum of Non-Objective Art, 844–845
Music: blues as, 648; business of, 647–648; in early 1900s, 647–648; jazz as, 648; in late 19th century, 552–553; in 1920s, 726–727, 729; of 1960s, 882; World War I and, 697 (illus.)
Muskie, Edmund, 899
Muslim Americans, anti-terrorism and, 993
Muslims: in Bosnia, 978; Cold War and, 831; in Iran, 895; in Iraq, 954; in Lebanon, 941; terrorism and, 991–992
Mussolini, Benito, 781, 791
"My Boy" (Rosenfeld), 554
My Lai massacre, 880

N

NAACP. *See* National Association for the Advancement of Colored People (NAACP)
Nader, Ralph, 913, 972; election of 2000 and, 985
NAFTA. *See* North American Free Trade Agreement (NAFTA)
Nancy Drew series, 648
NASA, 846
NASDAQ Composite Index, 984, 988–989
Nashville (ship), 692
Nasser, Gamal, 830
Nast, Thomas, 455 (illus.), 469 (illus.), 552, 631 (illus.)
Nation, The, 552, 620
National Aeronautics and Space Administration (NASA). *See* NASA
National American Woman Suffrage Association, 555, 660, 682
National Association for the Advancement of Colored People (NAACP), 476, **638,** 639, 660, 729; establishment of, 635, 638–639; funding of, 681; King and, 883; Montgomery bus boycott and, 852; National Race Commission and, 678; school desegregation and, 850–851
National Association of Colored Women, 660
National Association of Manufacturers, 658
National Birth Control League. *See* Birth Control League
National Biscuit Company, 522
National Catholic Conference, abortion and, 923
National Child Labor Committee, 657, 661
National Civic Federation, 565
National Collegiate Athletic Association (NCAA), 647
National Coming Out Day, 911
National Commission on the Conservation of Natural Resources, 671
National Conference of Charities and Corrections, 659
National Conference of Social Work, 659
National Congress of Mothers, 660
National Congress of Parents and Teachers, 589

National Conservation Congress, 671
National Consumers' League, 564, 684, 687
National Council of Jewish Women, 548, 660
National Council of Women, 589
National Defense Education Act (NDEA), 846–847
National Education Association (NEA), 658, 905
National Farm Bureau Federation, 658
National Farmers' Alliance and Industrial Union, 579–582, 583
National Farm Workers Association (NFWA), 884
National Federation of Settlements, 658
National government. *See* Government (U.S.)
National Grange of the Patrons of Husbandry, 505, 581
National Guard, Spanish-American War and, 614
Nationalist Clubs, 561
National Labor Relations Board (NLRB), 764, 773
National Labor Union, 532
National market, in late 19th century, 529
National monuments, Ellis Island as, 545
National Municipal League, 664
National Negro Business League, 680–681
National Organization for Women (NOW), 885, 910
National origins, in census, 605
National Origins Quota Act (1924), **736**–737
National parks and forests, 671 (illus.)
National parties. *See* Political parties
National Race Commission, 678
National Reclamation Act (Newlands Act) (1902), **494**–495
National Recovery Administration (NRA), 757–758, 757 (illus.), 769, 769 (illus.), 772; discrimination and, 766, 767; organized labor and, 764
National Security Act (1947), **816**
National Security Council (NSC), 816, 942
National Security League, 699
National Security Strategy (NSS), Bush, George W., on, 993–994
National Socialists. *See* Nazis
National Steel, 521
National Union movement, 456
National Urban League, 639
National Woman's party (NWP), 724, 725
National Woman Suffrage Association, 574, 660
National Women's Economic Summit, 909–910
National Youth Administration (NYA), 761, 773
Native Americans: Black Hills gold rush and, 498; end of tribal life for, 487–491; ethnic nationalism of, 884; and extermination of buffalo, 490–491; final Plains battles of, 486–487; gender division of labor tasks by, 484–485; major battles and reservations in West, 485 (illus.); New Deal and, 767, 767 (illus.); Plains Indians and, 483–485; as Rough Riders, 601; Sand Creek massacre of, 485–486; schools for, 490; transcontinental railroad and, 517; tribes and bands of, 484; in U.S. population (1900), 550; West and,

481, 482; Wounded Knee Massacre of, 487. *See also* Indian policy

Nativism: Populists and, 587. *See also* Anti-immigrant sentiment; Know-Nothings

NATO. *See* North Atlantic Treaty Organization (NATO)

Natural disasters, hurricanes as, 665 (illus.)

Natural gas, oil shocks and, 903

Natural resources: during World War II, 793

Natural selection, 606

Natzwiller-Struthof (concentration camp), 800

Navajo Indians, 483, 484, 486

Naval Advisory Board, 610

Naval Reserve, 611. *See also* Navy (U.S.)

Naval War College, 616

Navy (U.S.), 610 (illus.); Arthur, Chester A., and, 577; Great White Fleet and, 600 (illus.); growth of, 610–611, 691; Guantánamo Bay and, 623; new, 610–611; Spanish-American War and, 616

Nazis: Holocaust, 798, 800–801, 800 (illus.), 801 (illus.)

Nazi-Soviet Pact, 784, 790

NDEA. *See* National Defense Education Act (NDEA)

NEA. *See* National Education Association (NEA)

Nebraska, 482, 579, 580, 614

"Negro National Anthem," 711

Negro Silent Protest Parade, 681

Negro World, The, 730, 730 (illus.)

Neighborhood Guild, 562

Nelson, Donald, 793

Neoconservatism, 928

Netherlands, 786, 813

Netscape.com, 988

Neutrality: before World War II, 782–783

Neutrality acts, 782

Nevada, 579

Newark, New Jersey, rioting in, 883

"New Day, The" (Johnson), 711

New Deal, 749, 755; African Americans and, 766; conservatism of, 756–757, 761, 763, 764, 774; end of, 768–769, 772–774; Hundred Days and, 756–757; impact of, 764–768; labor and, 763–765; legislation of, 772–773; Mexican Americans and, 766–767; minorities and, 766–767; Native Americans and, 767; reform phase of, 761–764; relief and recovery phase of, 757–761; Roosevelt, Eleanor, and, 770–771; Supreme Court and, 769, 772–773; Truman and, 822; women and, 767, 770–771

New England: agricultural crisis and, 580; Anti-Imperialist League in, 620; literature about, 590; Republican party and, 575; after World War II, 840

New England Conservatory, 553

New Era, 722

New Freedom, 675–678, 682

New Frontier, 858, 865

New Guinea, 788, 791, 802

New Haven Railroad, 668

New immigrants, 546–547, 547 (illus.), 964

New Jersey: as swing state, 575

Newlands Act (1902), **494–495,** 634

New Left: election of 1972 and, 900; SDS and, 880–881

Newman, Barnett, 844

New Mexico, 482; Spanish-speaking citizens in, 496

New Nationalism, 675–676

New Orleans: segregation in, 568

Newport Naval War College, 610

New Republic, 629

New Right, 950 (illus.)

New South: after Civil War, 471–475; industrialization in, 472, 473 (illus.); Redeemers in, 472–473. *See also* South

Newspapers: advertising in, 525; foreign language, 548. *See also* Journalism

New Statesman, 629

Newton, Huey, 883

"New woman," 555

"New World Lessons for Old World Peoples," 640

New York (city), 540; arts in, 844; Bowery in, 591 (illus.); as finance center, 630; foreign-born population of, 546; rioting in, 795, 883; tenements in, 542; Triangle Shirtwaist Company fire in, 632–633, 632 (illus.); Tweed Ring in, 548–549; Wall Street explosion of 1920, 733 (illus.), 734. *See also* Terrorism

New York (state): Anti-Imperialist League in, 620; State Factory Investigating Commission of, 633; as swing state, 575

New York Armory art show, 649

New York Birth Control League, 637

New York Central Railroad, 516, 518

New York County Courthouse, 549

New York Daily News, 726

New York State Tenement House Commission, 659

New York Stock Exchange, 750, 882

New Zealand, 792

Nez Percé Indians, 487

NFWA. *See* National Farm Workers Association (NFWA)

Ngo Dinh Diem. *See* Diem, Ngo Dinh

Niagara Falls, New York, 638

Niagara Movement, 638

Nicaragua, 779, 915–916, 941; dollar diplomacy in, 693; Panama Canal and, 691; Sandinistas in, 895

Nichols, Jess D., 721

Nichols, Roger L., 491

Niebuhr, Reinhold, 841

Nimitz, Chester, 791, 802

Nine Power Treaty, 780

Nineteenth Amendment, 660–661, 724, 725

Ninth Cavalry. *See* Buffalo Soldiers

Ninth Ohio, 624

Nitze, Paul, 816

Nixon, Richard M., 826; Arab-Israel conflict and, 901; détente and, 897–898; economy and, 896–897; 1960 election and, 857–858, 858 (illus.); 1968 election and, 885, 888–889; 1972 election and, 899–900, 899 (illus.); pardon of, 912; *Pentagon Papers* and, 893, 894; presidency of, 895–901; resignation of, 900–901; Vietnam War and, 898–899; Watergate scandal and, 893–894, 900–901, 900 (illus.)

Nixon-Kennedy debate, 857–858

Nixonomics, 896–897

Nobel Prize: for Marshall, George C., 812; White House reception and, 864 (illus.)

Noble and Holy Order of the Knights of Labor. *See* Knights of Labor

Nonviolence, 853, 853 (illus.), 883

Nordhausen (concentration camp), 800 (illus.), 801

Noriega, Manuel, 952

Normandy invasion, 798

Norris, Frank, 590, 737

North: African Americans in, 467, 966; Reconstruction and, 576; Republican party and, 575. *See also* Civil War (U.S.)

North, Douglass C., 491–492

North, Oliver, 942–943, 943 (illus.)

North American Aviation, 793 (illus.)

North American Free Trade Agreement (NAFTA), 971–972, 972 (illus.)

North Atlantic Treaty Organization (NATO), 813–814; Balkan fighting and, 978, 979–980, 979 (illus.); expansion of, 977

North Carolina, 468; African American members of congress from, 615

North Carolina Agricultural and Technical College, 853 (illus.), 854

North Dakota, 481, 482

Northeast: population of, 963; power concentration in, 594

Northern Alliance: Farmer's Alliance and, 582

Northern Alliance (Afghanistan), 992

Northern Pacific Railroad, 517, 518, 519, 584

Northern Securities Company, 522, 668

North of Boston (Frost), 650

North Vietnam, 898, 914, 915

Northwestern Alliance, 581–582. *See also* National Farmers' Alliance and Industrial Union

Northwestern University, student protests at, 882

Northwestern University Settlement, 563

Norway, 788, 814

NOW. *See* National Organization for Women (NOW)

NRA. *See* National Recovery Administration (NRA)

NSC. *See* National Security Council (NSC)

NSC-68, 816, 819

Nuclear arms race, 810–811, 864; Cuban missile crisis and, 864; Eisenhower and, 829, 831–832; escalation of, 816, 864; origins of, 803

Nuclear dilemma, 810–811

Nuclear family: decline in, 908

Nuclear freeze movement, 940

Nuclear power: Chernobyl accident and, 906–907, 907 (illus.); Three Mile Island accident and, 904, 906–907, 906 (illus.)

Nuclear weapons: balance of terror and, 831; Clinton and, 977; Cuban missile crisis and, 862–864; first-strike capability and, 859; Hiroshima, Nagasaki, and, 803, 803 (illus.); hydrogen bomb and, 806 (illus.), 816, 829, 831; Korean War armistice and, 826; long-range missiles and, 831, 832–833; Manhattan Project and, 802–803; postwar anxiety and, 838; reduction of, 951; Soviet Union and, 816, 824; test ban and, 832, 863; testing of, 806 (illus.), 807–808, 816, 829

Number 10 (Rothko), 844 (illus.)

Nunn, Sam, 912
Nursing: schools of, 559
NWP. *See* National Woman's party (NWP)
NYA. *See* National Youth Administration (NYA)
Nye Committee, 782

O

Oak Ridge, Tennessee, 803
Oath of allegiance, for Confederates, 453
Ocala Demands, 582, 583
Occupational safety and health, 632–633, 635 (illus.). *See also* Health and health care
Occupations: Black Codes and, 462; women in, 530. *See also* Employment; Labor; Professions
O'Connor, Sandra Day, 932, 933 (illus.), 959
October War (1973), 901
Octopus (Norris), 590
Oden, Thomas G., 737
O'Donnell, Kenneth, 864
Office of Economic Opportunity (OEO), 871
Office of Economic Stabilization, 793
Office of Price Administration, 793
Oglala Sioux Indians, 485 (illus.)
Ohio: African American troops in, 615; army volunteers from, 614; mining strikes in, 585–586; as swing state, 575
Ohrdruf (concentration camp), 800
Oil and oil industry: Alaska pipeline and, 904; Clinton and, 977; October War and, 901; under Reagan, 936; rising costs and, 903; Rockefeller in, 521–522; spills and, 904; wells and, 521
Oil embargo (1973), 892 (illus.), 894, 902–903
Oil shocks, 902–903, 902 (illus.)
O'Keeffe, Georgia, 650
Okie Camp, 1935, 748 (illus.)
Okies, 766
Okinawa, Japan, 817
Oklahoma, 482; African Americans in, 502; "grandfather clause" and, 639; opening to settlers, 506
Oklahoma City, bombing in, 980, 981
Olds, Ransom E., 629
O'Leary, Hazel, 971
Oliver, James, 504
Olney, Richard, 607–608
Olson, Floyd, 762
Olympics, boycott of, 918
Omaha, Nebraska, populist convention in, 582–583
"One Big Reservation" policy, 485
101st Airborne Division, 851
O'Neill, Bucky, 601
O'Neill, Eugene, 728
On the Road (Kerouac), 843, 843 (illus.)
Onward (ship), 452 (illus.)
OPEC. *See* Organization of Petroleum Exporting Countries (OPEC)
Open Door policy, 623–624, 693–694, 780
Open range, cattle ranching on, 499
Operation Desert Shield, 952
Operation Rescue, 924
Operation Vittles, 815 (illus.)
Opportunity (magazine), 729
Orange, New Jersey, 584
Orcutt, Susan, 573
Oregon: school shooting in, 982. *See also Muller* v. *Oregon*

Oregon (ship), 609, 691
Oregon Country, 483
Organization Man, The (White), 843
Organization of Petroleum Exporting Countries (OPEC), 901–903
Origin of Species, The (Darwin), 606
Orlando, Vittorio, 713
Orpen, William, 714
Oswald, Lee Harvey, 869
Other America, The (Harrington), 871
"Other People's Money" (Brandeis), 677
Our Country: Its Possible Future and Its Present Crisis (Strong), 606
"Outcasts of Poker Flat, The" (Harte), 590
Overland Trail, 492–493
Ovington, Mary, 638

P

Pacheco, Romualdo, 496
Pacific Coast region, 482
Pacific Ocean region: acquisitions in, 619 (illus.); expansion into, 607; foreign policy toward, 606–607, 609; Hawaiian Islands in, 609 (illus.); immigrants from, 968; in World War II, 791
Pacifism and peace movements: Bryan, William Jennings, and, 690, 694, 698; and 1916 election, 699; nonviolence and, 853–854, 853 (illus.); preparedness and, 699; Vietnam War and, 880, 881–882, 881 (illus.), 886–888, 888 (illus.); vigilantism against peace figures, 706–707; World War I and, 696, 697, 701; World War II and, 781–783, 782 (illus.); youth and, 782, 782 (illus.)
Pact of Paris, 777
Pago Pago, 609
Paiute Indians, 482
Palestine Arabs, 916
Palestine Liberation Organization (PLO), 916, 941
Palmer, A. Mitchell, 733, 734
Panama: invasion of, 952; as protectorate, 693
Panama Canal, 691–692; Canal Zone and, 691–692, 691 (illus.), 876; restoration to Panama, 915
Pan-American Conference, 779
Pan-American Exposition, 597
Pan-Americanism, 606
Pan-American Union, 607
Panetta, Leon, 971
Panic(s): of 1873, 463, 466; of 1893, 518, 583–584, 587. *See also* Depression(s); Great Depression (1930s)
Panmunjom, South Korea, 820, 821 (illus.)
Parchman Farm (prison plantation), 475
Pardons, for Confederates, 453, 454, 455
Parent-Teacher Associations, 589
Paris, Treaty of: of 1898, 619–620
Paris Peace Conference, 712–715
Park Bench, The (Marsh), 753 (illus.)
Parker, Alton B., 669
Park Forest, Illinois, 843
Parks, Rosa, 852–853, 852 (illus.)
Party politics. *See* Political parties; Politics
Passion of Sacco and Vanzetti, The (Shahn), 734 (illus.)
Pasteur, Louis, 523, 551
PATCO. *See* Professional Air Traffic Controllers' Organization (PATCO)
Patent medicine, 670–671

Patents, issued from 1850-1899, 522, 523 (illus.)
Paterson, New Jersey, 636, 643, 643 (illus.)
Patriotism: after September 11, 2001, 990 (illus.)
Patten, Gilbert, 648
Patterson, Ben, 581
Patton, George, 791, 798, 800
Paul, Alice, 660, 724, 725 (illus.)
Pavlov, Ivan, 704
Pawnee Indians, 483, 490
Payne-Aldrich Act (1909), 673
Peace Commission, 486
Peace movements. *See* Pacifism and peace movements
Peale, Norman Vincent, 841
Pearl Harbor, 608, **787**–788, 788 (illus.), 791
Pease, Louis M., 562
Peña, Federico, 971
Pendleton Act (1883), 577
Penn Central Railroad, 896
Pennington, Ann, 648
Pennsylvania: mining strikes in, 586–587; terrorist attack and, 990
Pennsylvania Avenue, 614
Pennsylvania Railroad, 516, 519, 644
Pentagon: attack on (2001), 962, 984, 990–991; march on (1967), 881–882, 881 (illus.)
Pentagon Papers, 893, 894
Pentecostals, 737
People's Liberation Army (China), 817 (illus.)
People's (Populist) party, 582–583, 587, 588, 595–596
Per capita income, after World War II, 840
Perestroika, 943, 944 (illus.)
Perils of Pauline (movie), 647 (illus.)
Perkins, Frances, 768, 770, 819
Perot, H. Ross, 969, 970, 970 (illus.), 972
Perrett, Geoffrey, 719
Perry, James "Jim," 500
Pershing, John J. "Black Jack," 696, 701
Pershing II missiles, 940
Persian Gulf region: Iranian Revolution and, 916; oil from, 830, 902
Persian Gulf War (1990), 952–953, 953 (illus.)
Personal computers, 984 (illus.)
Peru, 947
Pets.com, 988, 989 (illus.)
Pettengill, Lillian, 564
Philadelphia, 540; Anti-Imperialist League in, 620; Centennial Exposition in, 511; foreign-born population of, 546
Philadelphia and Reading Railroad, 583
Philadelphia Negro, The (Du Bois), 559
Philanthropy: of Carnegie, 520; for higher education, 557; of Walker, C. J. (Madam), 681
Philippine-American War, 620–622
Philippine commission. *See* Taft Commission
Philippines, 603, 603 (illus.), 622; annexation of, 618–620, 622; Filipino insurgency in, 620, 622; Five Power Treaty and, 780; immigrants from, 967; independence and, 620, 622; Open Door policy and, 693; political cartoons and, 618 (illus.); second great migration and, 874; Spanish-American War in, 614, 616; Taft Commission in, 622; World War II and, 788, 791, 802
Phillips, David Graham, 634–635
Phillips, Kevin, 897
Phonograph, 524, 647

Photography, 759
Piantadosi, Al, 697
Picasso, Pablo, 649, 844
Piecework, 531
Pike, Zebulon, 483
Pikes Peak, 482, 485, 497
Pinchback, Pinkney B. S., 463, 615
Pinchot, Gifford, 655, 667, 671, 673
Pingree, Hazen S., 664
Pinkerton detectives, Homestead strike and, 535
Pit, The (Norris), 590
Pittsburgh, 519
Pittsburgh Pirates, 553
Placer mining, 497
Plain Facts for Old and Young (Kellogg), 555
Plain Home Talk of Love, Marriage, and Parentage (Foote), 555
Plains Indians, 484–485
Planned Parenthood Federation of America, 636
Planned Parenthood of Southeastern Pennsylvania v. *Casey,* 923–924
Plantation economy: in postwar South, 460
Planter (steamship), 451, 452 (illus.)
Planters and plantations: Johnson's Reconstruction plan and, 454
Platt Amendment, 622–623, 779
Platte River, 492
Plattsburg, New York, 699
Playhouse 90, 842
Pleiku, Vietnam, 877
Plessy, Homer A., 567, 568, 569
Plessy v. *Ferguson,* 475 (illus.), **556,** 557, 567–570, 850
PLO. *See* Palestine Liberation Organization (PLO)
Plows: chilled-iron, 504
"Plumbers" unit, 893
Plunkitt, George Washington, 549, 550
Pluralistic society, 565
Pneumonia, 551
Pocket veto, of Wade-Davis Bill, 453
Podhoretz, Norman, 928
Poetry magazine, 650
Poindexter, John, 942, 943
Poland, 713; end of Cold War and, 952 (illus.); Solidarity movement in, 951; Soviet Union and, 784, 791, 799, 808; World War II in, 783 (illus.), 784
Polaris submarine, 859
Poles and Polish Americans, 585; ethnic nationalism of, 884; immigration and, 546, 639, 640, 644, 737; as voters, 755 (illus.)
Policy Planning Staff, 811, 816
Polish National Alliance (PNA), 548
Polish Women's Alliance, 548
Political cartoons, 552; on Grant corruption, 470 (illus.); "Modern Colossus of (Rail) Roads," 516 (illus.); *Puck* cartoon "Looking Backward," 547 (illus.); *Puck* cartoon satirizing Rockefeller, 521 (illus.); on Reconstruction deadlock, 454 (illus.); "Slavery Is Dead?", 455 (illus.); "Worse Than Slavery," 469 (illus.)
Political machines. *See* Machines (political)
Political office, African Americans in, 463, 464, 473–474
Political parties: deadlock between, 575–576, 587–588; geographical distribution and,

575; realignment of, 596. *See also* Election(s); specific parties
Political power: of African Americans, 451, 452
Politicos, 470
Politics: corruption and, 738; initiative and, 666; interest groups and, 663–664; during Kennedy administration, 865; of 1920s, 737–741; realignment in, 774, 929, 930; recall, 666; referendum, 666; after Watergate, 912–914. *See also* Election(s)
Polk, Leonidas L., 582, 583
Pollack v. *Farmer's Loan and Trust Co.,* 587
Pollock, Jackson, 843, 844, 845, 845 (illus.), 846
Poll tax, 467, 574
Pollution: air, 904, 926 (illus.), 932; Chicago River and, 526; in cities, 542–543; EPA and, 903; water, 542–543
Pooling agreements, 518
Poor: studies of, 564
Poor People's March on Washington (1968), 883
Popular Mechanics, 832 (illus.)
Popular pastimes, 647–648
Population: changes in, 963–969; in cities, 539, 540, 565; elderly, 964; Hispanic, 965–966; of immigrants, 543, 543 (illus.), 546 (illus.); market growth and, 512; Native American, 491; of Plains, 502; shift in, 963–964, 963 (illus.); Spanish-speaking people in, 494; in Sunbelt, 928; urban and rural (1870-1900), 550, 550 (illus.); of U.S. (1900), 550. *See also* Census
Populists and populism, 473, 579–583, 587, 588, 595–596; vs. progressivism, 657; and Socialist party of America, 662–663
Port Huron, Michigan, 880
Portsmouth: peace conference in, 693
Potsdam Conference, 807–808, 808 (illus.), 809
Pound, Ezra, 650, 727, 728
Poverty: of Californios, 496; in depression of 1893-1897, 574, 584; distribution of wealth and, 645–646; of elderly, 964; of freedmen, 461; of Hispanics, 965; of Native Americans, 491; under Reagan, 938; as root of crime proposition, 560–561; war on, 871. *See also* Great Depression (1930s); Wealth
Powderly, Terence V., 532
Powell, Colin, 953, 986
Powell, Jody, 913
Powell, Lewis, 896; *Bakke* case and, 958
Power (political): worldwide race for, 610
Power Elite (Mills), 843
Powers, Francis Gary, 833
POWs, of Korean War, 821
Prager, Robert, 707
Pragmatism, 662
Pragmatism (James), 662
Pratt, Richard H., 490
Prayer in schools, 869
Prayer Pilgrimage to Washington, 853
Preservation of Favoured Races in the Struggle for Life, The (Darwin), 606
Presidency: authority of, 576; expansion of, 682–683, 691–692
Presidential powers. *See* Executive power
Press. *See* Journalism; Newspapers
Price, The (Miller), 529
Priceline.com, 988

Princeton Club, 601
Princeton University: pacifism and, 782
Principles of Scientific Management, The (Taylor), 632
Prioleau, George, 616
Prisoners of war. *See* POWs
Prison plantations, 475
Privacy rights, *Roe* v. *Wade* and, 923
Proclamation of Amnesty and Reconstruction (1863), 453
Professional Air Traffic Controllers' Organization (PATCO), 932, 932 (illus.)
Professions: African Americans and, 559; feminization of, 530; rise of, 657–658; social work as, 564; women in, 530
Progress and Poverty (George), 560, 665
Progressive Era, 669–671; conservation and, 671–672; farms and farming and, 633–634; health policy and, 635; industrialism and, 628–633; intellectual thought and, 662–663; labor and, 634–635, 642, 669; mass society and, 633–635, 638–641; muckrakers and, 627–628; professionalization and, 657–658, 659; purity crusade and, 659–660; race and racism and, 635, 638; railroad regulation and, 669; reform in cities and states, 663–667; social-justice movement and, 658; trustbusting and, 667–668; women's rights and, 660–662
Progressive Farmer, 581 (illus.)
Progressive party: in 1912, 656, 675–676; in 1948, 822
Progressive Republican Clubs, 674
Progressivism, 628, 656–657; census statistics and, 605; decline of, 682; and prosperity, 629; Taft and, 673–675; trusts and, 631; World War I and, 696, 699. *See also* La Follette, Robert M.; Progressive Era
Prohibition, 734, 734–735; bootlegging and, 726; Eighteenth Amendment, 660; state laws and, 579. *See also* Temperance movement
Project Mercury, 847 (illus.)
Project RACE, 968, 969 (illus.)
Prolife groups, abortion rights and, 910
Promontory, Utah, transcontinental railroad at, 517, 518 (illus.)
Property: Black Codes and, 462; in Native American tribes, 484; of Spanish-American women, 496; as voting requirement, 467
Property rights, 461
Proposition 13 (California), 927
Prostitution, 660; in mining camps, 498, 499
Protectionism, election of 1896 and, 572 (illus.)
Protective tariff: Arthur and, 577; after Civil War, 575; Cleveland and, 577–578; McKinley and, 597. *See also* Tariff(s)
Protest(s): antiwar, 880, 881–882, 881 (illus.), 886; at Columbia University, 882; SDS and, 880–881; sit-ins as, 853 (illus.), 854; at University of California at Berkeley, 880; walk-outs and, 884; against WTO, 981–982
Protestants and Protestantism: fundamentalism and, 737, 841; Ku Klux Klan and, 735; in late 19th century, 552; Prohibition and, 734; Scopes Trial and, 743–747; social thought of, 562; after World War II boom and, 841

Provisional governors, during Reconstruction, 454
Prudential Building, 541
Prussian Cur, The, 706
Psychology, 551
PTL Club, 935
Public credit. *See* Credit
Public education. *See* Education
Public facilities, equal access laws and, 462
Public schools. *See* Education
Public Works Administration (PWA), 760 (illus.), 761, 772
Pueblo Indian groups, 483
Puerperal fever, 551
Puerto Ricans, ethnic nationalism of, 884
Puerto Rico: acquisition of, 618–619; citizenship and, 622; Foraker Act of 1900 and, 622; immigrants from, 965; political cartoons and, 618 (illus.); reciprocity treaty with, 607; Spanish-American War and, 611, 615, 616, 617
Pujo Committee, 677
Pullen, Frank W., 615
Pullman, George M., 516
Pullman Palace Car Company, 585
Pullman strike, 585, 594, 662
Punched cards: to sort and tabulate data, 523; tabulator for, 604, 605 (illus.)
Pure Food and Drug Act (1906), 670–671
Pusan, South Korea, 818
Putin, Vladimir V., 977
"Putting His Foot Down," 623
PWA. *See* Public Works Administration (PWA)

Q

Qaeda, al. *See* al Qaeda
Quayle, Dan, 948
Quemoy, 830
Quotas, racial, 956–959, 966

R

Rabin, Yitzhak, 977
Race and racism: Anglo-Saxon superiority and, 606; anti-imperialism and, 619; *Birth of a Nation* and, 647; against buffalo soldiers, 488; census and, 604–605, 968; in early 1900s, 628; eugenics and, 637, 641; during Great Depression, 753; immigration and, 736–737, 874; IQ testing and, 704–705; labor unions and, 638; political cartoons and, 618 (illus.); in Progressive Era, 635, 638; after Spanish-American War, 624; views of Reconstruction and, 476; in Women's Trade Union League, 642; World War I and, 710–711, 730; World War II and, 795. *See also* Desegregation; Segregation; Slaves and slavery
Race riots: after assassination of King, Martin Luther, Jr., 883–884; in Atlanta, 638, 667; in Chicago, 710; against Chinese laborers, 498–499; in Detroit, 795, 883; in early 1900s, 638; in East St. Louis, Illinois, 681, 710; in Harlem, 883; King, Rodney, and, 966–967, 967 (illus.); in late 1960s, 883–884; in Los Angeles, 796, 883; in Newark, 883; in New York City, 710, 795, 883; in 1960s, 883; in Omaha, 710; in Rochester, 883; in South (1875), 468; during Spanish-American War, 616; in

Washington, D.C., 710, 883–884; in Watts, 883; during World War II, 795; zoot suit riots and, 796
Radcliffe College, 558
Radford, Arthur, 829
Radical Reconstruction, 457–458, 463, 470, 477; opponents of, 462, 464
Radical Republicans, 453, 454, 456, 457, 457 (illus.), 476; Black Codes and, 455
Radicals and radicalism: of African Americans, 882; on Ellis Island, 545; fear of, 732–734; Haymarket Riot and, 535, 535 (illus.); IWW and, 636, 643 (illus.), 644, 707; lynchings and, 733. *See also* Communists and communism; Red Scare
Radio, 721, 723 (illus.), 827
Ragtime music, 552
Railroad Administration, 709
Railroads: American vs. European, 513; buffalo hunting and, 491 (illus.); capital for, 514; cattle industry and, 501 (illus.); Chicago and, 526; consolidation by, 515–516, 518–519; construction of, 515 (illus.); corruption and, 515; decline of, 722; in 1870 and 1890, 517 (illus.); farmers and, 580; during Great Depression, 753; growth of, 518–519; labor and, 532, 639; land grants to, 514 (illus.); Morgan and, 519; Panic of 1893 and, 584; pooling and, 518; regulation of, 576, 669, 673–674; segregation and, 475, 568, 615; society and, 513–514; in South, 463; standardization in, 515; strikes against, 533 (illus.), 534; time zones and, 516; topography and, 513 (illus.); transcontinental, 516–518; transportation revolution and, 512; trunk lines of, 515–516; trustbusting and, 668; westward movement and, 493, 494 (illus.), 495, 515
Rainey, Gertrude "Ma," 648
Rain-in-the-Face (chief), 486
Randolph, A. Philip, 795
Rapier, James T., 464
Ratification: of ERA, 885
Rationing: during World War I, 709; during World War II, 793, 794, 794 (illus.)
Raulsten, John, 744–747
Rauschenberg, Robert, 856
Rauschenbusch, Walter, 561
Rayburn, Sam, 848, 865
RCA, 751
REA. *See* Rural Electrification Administration (REA)
Reading. *See* Literacy
Reagan, Nancy, 943, 946–947
Reagan, Ronald, 928 (illus.), 947–948; AIDS epidemic and, 945–946; assassination attempt against, 931 (illus.); budget and, 933–936; as California governor, 927; Christian Right and, 935 (illus.), 934–935; conservatism and, 927–929; election of 1984 and, 938–939, 939 (illus.); foreign policy of, 939–944; Gorbachev and, 943–944, 944 (illus.); Iran-Contra affair and, 942–943; New Right and, 950; presidency of, 929–944; social issues and, 944–947; Soviet Union and, 943–944; Supreme Court and, 946–947; wealthy and, 936–938
Reaganomics, 933–939

Real estate, inflation of, 938
Real Majority, The (Scammon and Wattenberg), 897
Rebecca of Sunnybrook Farm (Wiggins), 648
Recessions: Carter and, 929; of 1868, 466; under Nixon, 896–897; oil shocks and, 903. *See also* Economy
Reciprocity treaties: with Latin America, 607
Reclamation Service, 671
Reconstruction, 450–478; Black Codes during, 455, 456, 462; congressional, 456–458, 471; end of, 576; Ku Klux Klan and, 735; presidential (Johnson), 454–456; Radical, 457–458; retreat from, 466–471; southern society during, 460–465; state governments during, 458 (illus.); Ten Percent Plan and, 453; as "unfinished revolution," 478; views of, 476–477; wartime, 453
Reconstruction: America's Unfinished Revolution 1863-1877 (Foner), 477
Reconstruction Acts: of 1867 and 1868, 457–458, 460; First (1867), 457
Reconstruction Amendments. *See* Fifteenth Amendment; Fourteenth Amendment; Thirteenth Amendment
Reconstruction Finance Corporation (RFC), 754, 761
Records (phonograph), 524
Red Badge of Courage, The (Crane), 590
Red Cloud (chief), 485 (illus.), 486
Redeemers, in New South, **472**–473, 477
Red River Valley, 504, 504 (illus.)
Red River War, 486, 489
Red Scare, 708, 711, **732**–734, 823. *See also* Second Red Scare
Reed, John, 636
Reed, Thomas B., 578, 579, 594, 619
Reed, Walter, 623
Reform and reform movements, 847–849; of Bush, George W., 987; Johnson, Lyndon, and, 872–873; in late 19th century, 552, 560–565; political bosses and, 550; settlement houses and, 562–563; in states, 665–667; Supreme Court and, 868–869; urban, 664–665; after World War II, 847–849
Refrigerator cars, 516, 523
Regan, Donald, 947–948
Rehnquist, William, 896, 923, 948, 959, 983
Reich, Robert, 971
Religion(s): Christian fundamentalism and, 928; Christian Right and, 934–935; of new immigrants, 546; school prayer and, 927–928; Social Gospel and, 562; social justice and, 561; after World War II, 841. *See also* specific groups
Remarque, Erich Maria, 781
Remington, Frederick, 624
Reno, Janet, 971, 973
Representation: population and, 604
Republican party: "billion-dollar" Congress and, 578–579, 594; Catholics and, 579; civil rights and, 575; Civil War and, 575; Cold War and, 822–823, 825–827; Contract with America and, 973–974; energy crunch and, 904; gold standard and, 594; as Grand Old Party (GOP), 737; in Grant era, 469–470; Great Depression and, 754, 755; Ku Klux Klan and, 467–468; in 1920s, 737, 738–741; Nixon and, 897; size of government and, 739; in South, 462–464, 467; southern

blacks and, 456; after Spanish-American War, 624; split in, 655–656, 672, 673–674; voting rights and, 579. *See also* Election(s); Radical Republicans

Republic Steel, 521; strike at, 765 (illus.)

Reservations, 483; in Black Hills area, 486; in Oklahoma, 486; in West, 485 (illus.)

Resolution Trust Corporation, 950; Clintons and, 973

Reuben James (ship), 785

Reunion, after Civil War, 478

Reuther, Walter, 765

Revels, Hiram R., 463 (illus.)

Revenue Act (1916), 682

Revolution(s): in Iran, 916

Reykjavik, Iceland, summit meeting in, 944

Reynolds, Malvina, 838

RFC. *See* Reconstruction Finance Corporation (RFC)

Rhee, Syngman, 817–818

Ribicoff, Abraham, 864

Rice, Condoleezza, 986

Rice, Elmer, 728

Rice, Joseph, 556

Ridge, Tom, 992, 993 (illus.)

Riesman, David, 843

Rights. *See* Civil rights

Right wing: Christian, 934–935, 935 (illus.); Iran-Contra support from, 943; New Right and, 949 (illus.)

Riis, Jacob, 541

Riley, James Whitcomb, 540

Riley, Jim, 744

Rio Grande: Pueblo Indians and, 483

Riots. *See* Race riots

River Rouge plant (Ford), 720 (illus.)

Rivers: in Great Plains, 483

Roads and highways: Highway Act (1956) and, 848. *See also* Trails

Roaring Twenties, 726–727

Robb, Charles, 887

Roberts, Kenneth, 736

Roberts, Oral, 935

Robertson, Pat, 935

Robins, Margaret Dreier, 642

Robinson, JoAnn, 854

Rochester, New York, 883

Rochester Theological Seminary, 561

Rockefeller, John D., 521–522, 521 (illus.), 525, 557, 630, 648; interlocking directorates and, 677; labor and, 679; trustbusting and, 667–668

Rockefeller family, 696

Rockefeller Sanitary Commission, 633–634

Rocky Mountains, 482, 482 (illus.)

Roebuck, Alvah C., 529

Roe v. *Wade*, **910**, 920–924, 921 (illus.)

Rogers, William, 895

Roman Catholic Church. *See* Catholics and Catholicism

Romania, 791, 809, 951

Rommel, Erwin, 788, 791

Roosevelt, Eleanor, 767–768, 771 (illus.); African Americans and, 766, 770, 771; family planning and, 637; Roosevelt, Franklin D., and, 770; social justice and, 770–771

Roosevelt, Franklin D., 754–755, 761–762, 769, 769 (illus.), 772–774, 797–798, 802; African Americans and, 766; Casablanca meeting and, 790, 790 (illus.); cash-and-

carry and, 784, 785; China and, 789; Churchill and, 789, 790; collective security and, 779; death of, 802, 802 (illus.); Declaration of Liberated Europe, 799, 802; deficit spending and, 773–774; de Gaulle and, 789; destroyers-for-bases deal and, 784–785; on fear, 755; fireside chats of, 756; France and, 789; Germany and, 783–784; good neighbor policy of, 693, 779; as governor of New York, 755; Hundred Days and, 755–757; imperialism and, 779; Japanese Americans and, 796; on labor unrest, 765; Latin America and, 779–780; Lend-Lease and, 785; Manhattan Project and, 810; neutrality and, 783, 784–785; 1920 election and, 716, 755; 1932 election and, 755 (illus.); 1934 election and, 762; 1936 election and, 768–769; 1938 election and, 774; 1940 election and, 785; 1944 election and, 797–798; Pearl Harbor and, 787; polio of, 755, 770, 775; reform and, 761–764; road to war and, 784–788; Soviet Union and, 779, 790, 810; Supreme Court and, 769, 772–773; at Tehran, 799; women appointees of, 768; at Yalta, 799, 802. *See also* New Deal; World War II

Roosevelt, Theodore, 470, 551, 598, 602 (illus.), 654 (illus.), 655–656, 656 (illus.), 667–669, 738; and African Americans, 667; army modernization and, 691; as assistant secretary of navy, 601; on birth control, 636; conservation and, 655, 656, 671–672; consumer protection and, 669–671; election of 1904 and, 669; election of 1912 and, 656, 675–676; evolution and, 606; family life of, 636; Far East and, 693; "Gentlemen's Agreement" with Japan and, 693; as governor of New York, 624, 659; as hunter, 655, 656; at Kettle Hill, 617; *Lusitania* and, 689; and muckrakers, 627; navy expansion and, 691; New Nationalism and, 629, 675; Panama Canal and, 691–692; Portsmouth peace conference and, 693; and presidency, 682–683, 691–692; progressivism and, 667, 673, 675–676; railroad regulation and, 669; and Rough Riders, 601–602, 602 (illus.), 624; second term of, 669–672; shooting of, 675; social Darwinism and, 606; Spanish-American War and, 601–602, 612, 614; "square deal" and, 668–669, 675; Taft and, 655–656, 671–672, 672 (illus.); trustbusting and, 667–668, 668 (illus.); Turner thesis and, 605; as vice president, 597–598; World War I and, 699 (illus.)

Roosevelt Corollary, 692–**693**, 779

Root, Elihu, 667, 691, 713

Root, John, 541

Root-Takahira Agreement, 693

Rose, Reginald, 842

Rosenberg, Ethel and Julius, 824

Rosenberg, Harold, 844

Rosenberg, Sophie, 824 (illus.)

Rosenfeld, Morris, 531, 554

Ross, Edward A., 547, 666

Rostow, Walt W., 859, 861, 876

Rotary press, 525

Roth, William, 931

Rothko, Mark, 843, 844, 845, 846

Roughing It (Twain), 497

Rough Riders, 601–602, 615 (illus.), 616, 617, 624

Rover Boys series, 648

Rubin, Jerry, 882

Rubin, Robert, 971

Ruby, Jack, 869

Ruby Ridge, Idaho, shoot-out at, 981

Rudd, Lydia, 492

Rudman, Warren, 933–936

Rules Committee (Congress), 865

Rumsfeld, Donald, 986, 994

Rural areas, 759 (illus.); New Deal in, 758–759; political allegiances and, 739; in South, 557; urban "evils" and, 732–737, 739; after World War II, 840. *See also* Farms and farming

Rural Electrification Administration (REA), 764, 773

Rural Free Delivery, 646

Rusk, Dean, 817, 859, 862–863, 876

Russell, Charles M., 480 (illus.)

Russell, Richard, 870–871

Russia: Alaska purchase and, 607; Bolshevik Revolution in, 701, 708, 733; China and, 623; Clinton and, 976; Germany and, 708; immigrants from, 546, 585; IWW and, 643; Japan and, 693; Philippines and, 618; U.S. Far East policy and, 693–694; Versailles Treaty and, 712. *See also* Soviet Union

Russian Republic, 951

Rustin, Bayard, 854

Ruth, Babe, 726

S

Sacco, Nicola, 734, 734 (illus.)

Sacramento, California, 884

Sadat, Anwar, 916, 916 (illus.)

Safety standards, in workplace, 529–530

Saigon, 914; self-immolation of monks in, 861 (illus.); U.S. embassy in, 886

St. Denis, Ruth, 649

Saint-Lô, bombardment at, 798

St. Louis, 513, 627

"St. Louis Blues," 648

St. Mihiel, battle at, 703

Salisbury (Lord), 607–608

Saloons, 543

SALT. *See* Strategic Arms Limitation Talks (SALT)

Salt Lake City, 639

Salvation Army, homeless missions of, 561 (illus.)

Samoa, 609, 622

Sampson, William T., 617

Sandburg, Carl, 614, 650

Sand Creek massacre, 485–486

Sandinistas, 895, 915–916, 941

San Francisco, 497 (illus.), 693

Sanger, Margaret, 635, 636–637, 636 (illus.)

Sanger, Stuart, 636 (illus.)

Sanitation, in cities, 542–543

San Juan Hill, 617; buffalo soldiers at, 489

Sankey, Ira B., 552

Santa Fe Railroad, 584

Santiago de Cuba, 617

Santo Domingo, 607

Sarajevo, bombings of, 978

SAT. *See* Scholastic Aptitude Test (SAT)

Saudi Arabia, 819, 901, 952

Savings, personal, 936

Savings and loan industry, crisis in, 949–950
Savio, Mario, 880
Scalawags, 462, 476, 477
Scalia, Antonin, 948
Scammon, Richard, 897
Scandinavians, 737
Schiller Building, 541
Schirra, Walter M., Jr., 847 (illus.)
Schlafly, Phyllis, 910
Schlesinger, Arthur, Jr., 863
Schneiderman, Rose, 632–633, 632 (illus.)
Scholastic Aptitude Test (SAT), 705
School(s): desegregation of, 850–852,
    866–867; for freedpeople, 465, 465 (illus.);
    immigrants and, 548; in late 19th century,
    556; for Native Americans, 490, 490 (illus.);
    prayer in, 927–928; segregation in, 465;
    shootings in, 982; as training grounds, 556,
    556 (illus.)
School and Society (Dewey), 662
Schoonover, Frank, 702
Schurz, Carl, 470
Schwab, Charles M., 520
Schwarzkopf, H. Norman, 953
Science: census data and, 604; universities and,
    557
Scopes Trial, 737, 743–747, 744 (illus.)
Scott, Thomas A., 516
Scowcroft, Brent, 951
SDI. *See* Strategic Defense Initiative (SDI)
SDS. *See* Students for a Democratic Society
    (SDS)
Sears, Richard W., 529
Sears, Roebuck, 528, 528 (illus.), 529, 646 (il-
    lus.)
Seattle, 733, 980
Sea Wolf (London), 590
SEC. *See* Securities and Exchange Commission
    (SEC)
Second Child Labor Act (1919), 661
Second great migration, 874–875, 875 (illus.)
Second Industrial Revolution, Democratic
    party and, 739
Second Red Scare, 823–827, 838–839
Second World War. *See* World War II
Securities and Exchange Commission (SEC),
    773
Sedition Act (1918), **707**
Segregation: of armed forces, 702, 795–796,
    850; of Asian students, 693; Black Codes and,
    462; *Buchanan* v. *Worley* and, 639; in cities,
    647; in federal service, 678, 795; *Guinn* v.
    United States and, 639; laws allowing, 475; in
    military, 615, 616; in New South, 473; *Plessy*
    v. *Ferguson* and, 567–570; in Progressive Era,
    635; of railroads, 615; residential, 837–838,
    868; of schools, 556–557, 866–867; Southern
    Alliance and, 582; Spanish-American War
    and, 615–616, 624; of transportation, 866;
    Wilson and, 678; after World War II, 850.
    See also Civil rights; Civil rights movement;
    Desegregation
Selassie, Haile, 781
Selective Service Act (1917), **702**
Self-determination, 713
Sells Brothers, 552 (illus.)
Selma, Alabama, 872
Senate (U.S.): blacks in, 463 (illus.), 464; direct
    election of senators, 666; Unionists and,
    453

Seoul, South Korea, 819
Separate but equal doctrine, *Plessy* v. *Ferguson*
    and, 557, 567–570
Separate sphere of domesticity, 554
September 11, 2001, terrorist attacks on, 962,
    984, 990–991
Serbia: bombings of, 979; Milosevic and, 979;
    World War I and, 696
Serbs: Bosnia and, 978; as immigrants, 639
Serling, Rod, 842
Service sector, expansion of, 937
Settlement(s): of West, 481–507
Settlement houses, 539, 562–563, 658–659
700 Club, 935
Seventeenth Amendment, 666, 674
Seventh Cavalry, Wounded Knee Massacre
    and, 487
Seward, William H., 624; expansionist policy
    of, 606–607
Seward's Folly, Alaska as, 607
Sewell, Anna, 589
Sewing machine, 603 (illus.)
Sex and sexuality: AIDS epidemic and,
    944–946; Kinsey and, 727; in late 19th cen-
    tury, 555; in 1920s, 725, 726–727. *See also*
    Homosexuality
Sex in Education (Clarke), 558
Sexual harassment: Clinton and, 973; Thomas-
    Hill controversy and, 948
Shahn, Ben, 734
Shah of Iran, 895, 902
"Shame of Minneapolis" (Steffens), 627
Shame of the Cities, The (Steffens), 627, 657
Shapiro, Annie, 642
Sharecropping, 461–462, 461 (illus.)
Share the Wealth movement, 762
Shasta Indians, 483
Shaw, Anna Howard, 660
Sheik with Sheba (Held), 726 (illus.)
Shepard, Alan B., Jr., 847 (illus.)
Shepard, Matthew, 912
Sheppard-Towner Maternity and Infancy
    Protection Act (1921), 635, 724
Sheridan, Fort, 535
Sherman, James S., 672, 674
Sherman, John, 466, 619
Sherman, William Tecumseh, 460, 461
Sherman Antitrust Act (1890), **578–579,** 668,
    674
Sherman Silver Purchase Act (1890), 579, 587
Shi'ite Muslims, in Iraq, 954, 995–996
Shinn, Everett, 626
Shocking Night, A, 727
Shootings, in schools, 982
Shoshone Indians, 482, 486
Shriver, R. Sargent, 871
Shultz, George, 940, 942
Sierra Club, 904
Sierra Nevada Mountains, 482, 497
"Significance of the Frontier in American
    History, The" (Turner), 507, 605
Signing of Peace in the Hall of Mirrors, The
    (Orpen), 714 (illus.)
Signs (Rauschenberg), 856 (illus.)
Silent majority, 898
Silver: coinage of, 577, 578 (illus.), 579, 587;
    election of 1896 and, 591, 594–595; Gold
    Standard Act and, 597
Simmons, William J., 735
Simon, Theodore, 704

Simpson, Jeremiah, 582
Sims, William S., 703
Sinai region, Israel and, 940
Sinclair, Upton, 627, 669–670, 762
Singer Sewing Machine Company, 603 (illus.)
Single parent families, 908
Single-tax clubs, 560
Sink or Swim (Alger), 589
Sino-Soviet relations: split in, 860; treaty and,
    817
Sioux Indians, 483, 484–485, 489, 498
Sioux War, 486–487
Sirhan, Sirhan, 887
Sitting Bull (medicine man), 486, 487, 491
Six Day War (1967), 901
Sixteenth Amendment, 674, 677
Sixth Fleet, 831
Sixth Massachusetts Regiment, 615
Sixth Mount Zion Baptist Church (Richmond,
    Virginia), 464 (illus.)
Skilled workers, 529, 532
Skliris, Leonidas, 639
Skyscrapers, 520, 540–541, 540 (illus.)
Slaughterhouse Cases, 568
"Slavery Is Dead?" (Nast), 455 (illus.)
Slaves and slavery: Black Codes and, 455, 456,
    462. *See also* African Americans
Slayton, Donald "Deke" K., 847 (illus.)
Sloan, John, 649
Slovaks, 585
Slums, 541; missions in, 562; settlement
    houses in, 562–563
Small reservations policy, 486
Smalls, Robert, 451–452, 452 (illus.), 464, 473
Smeal, Eleanor, 910
Smith, Alfred E., 739–741, 768, 769
Smith, Bessie, 648
Smith, Gerald L. K., 768
Smith, Howard K., 857
Smith, Margaret Chase, 827
Smith and Wesson, 709
Smith college, 558
Smog, in Los Angeles, 926 (illus.)
"Smoked Yankees," 615–616
Snyder, Charles, 819
Sochen, June, 725
Social class. *See* specific classes
Social Darwinism, 560, 590, 606
Social Democratic party, 662
Social Gospel, 562
Socialism: Debs and, 585; in Progressive Era,
    662; in World War I, 707–708
Socialist Labor party, 662
Socialist party of America, 662–663; Debs and,
    585; Sanger and, 636. *See also* Debs, Eugene
    V.
Social-justice movement, 658–659;
    Progressive party and, 675; World War I
    and, 709
Social mobility. *See* Mobility
Social Security, 762–763, 763 (illus.); African
    Americans and, 766; Carter and, 914; con-
    servatives and, 872; Eisenhower and, 848;
    Fair Deal and, 847; limitations of, 766;
    Reagan and, 930, 932; Supreme Court and,
    772; tax increase for, 938. *See also* Medicaid;
    Medicare
Social Security Act (1935), 635, **762,** 773

Social thought. *See* Intellectual thought
Social welfare: crisis in, 564–565. *See also* Welfare system
Social work, 564, 659
Society: AIDS and, 944–946; and cultural change, 550–560; pluralistic, 565; railroads and, 513–514; in South, 460–465. *See also* Ethnicity; Race and racism; Women
"Society" (Howells), 590
Society for the Suppression of Vice, 552
Sociology, 559
Sod houses, 503
Soft money. *See* Greenbacks
Soldiers: buffalo, 486, 488–489, 488 (illus.); Rough Riders and, 601. *See also* Armed forces; Military
Solidarity movement, 951
Solomon Islands, 791
Somalia, Clinton and, 977
Somerset Club, 601
Somme, battle at, 703
Somoza, Anastasio, 915, 941
Son of the Middle Border (Garland), 581
Sooners (Oklahoma homesteaders), 506
Sorensen, Theodore, 864
Souls of Black Folk, The (Du Bois), 559, 638
Souter, David H., 948
South: African Americans in, 966; Black Codes in, 455, 456, 462; black political power in, 451, 452; child labor in, 589; civil rights resistance in, 851; convict-lease system in, 474–475; crop lien system in, 580; Democratic-Conservatives in, 468, 469; Democratic party and, 472, 575, 587, 594, 739; education in, 463, 556–557; election of 1894 and, 587–588; farming in, 633–634, 638; "force bill" and, 579; imperialism and, 620; Jim Crow laws in, 473–475; Ku Klux Klan in, 467–469; literature about, 590; lynchings in, 474, 474 (illus.); military rule in, 457, 458; Panic of 1873 in, 463; population of, 963; Populism and, 579, 588; race riots in, 468; railroads in, 516; Reconstruction and, 458 (illus.), 460–465, 576–577; Redeemer regimes in, 472–473; Republican party in, 462–464, 467; segregation in, 556–557; separate but equal doctrine in, 557, 567–570; silver coinage and, 591; Southern Alliance in, 581; violence against blacks in, 462; voting rights and, 458, 574–575, 588. *See also* New South; Reconstruction; Sunbelt
South America: drug trade and, 947. *See also* Central America; Latin America
South Carolina, 468, 469; after Civil War, 460; Reconstruction and, 576; tenant farming in, 633; voting rights in, 574
South Dakota, 481, 482, 592
Southeast Asia: immigrants from, 967; and Vietnam War, 877 (illus.); World War II in, 791
South End House (Boston), 563
Southern Alliance, 581–582. *See also* National Farmers' Alliance and Industrial Union
Southern Christian Leadership Conference (SCLC), 853
Southern Europe, immigrants from, 546–547
Southern Farmers' Alliance, 473
Southern Manifesto, 851
Southern Pacific Railroad, 517, 666

Southern Railway, 519
South Pass (Rockies), 493
South Vietnam, 898, 914. *See also* Vietnam; Vietnam War
Southwest: economic caste system in, 496; Spain and, 496; Spanish-speaking people in, 495–496; undocumented aliens in, 965
Soviet Union: Afghanistan and, 918; Allied victory and, 798–799; arms control and, 831–832; arms race with, 803; Axis Powers and, 781; Carter and, 917–918; Chernobyl accident and, 906, 907, 907 (illus.); China and, 816–817, 830; Cuba and, 831, 862–864; détente and, 897–898; Eastern Europe and, 791; end of, 951, 952 (illus.); espionage and, 823–824, 833, 833 (illus.); Korean War and, 817–818; Nazi-Soviet Pact and, 784, 790; nuclear weapons and, 810, 829, 832; postwar relations with U.S., 790, 810; Reagan and, 943–944; Roosevelt, Franklin D., and, 779, 790; Russia and, 939–940; Sino-Soviet relations and, 817, 830; Suez Canal and, 830; UN and, 818; on U.S. expansionism, 814 (illus.); at Yalta, 799, 802. *See also* Cold War; Russia
Space program, 832, 846–847, 847 (illus.); Kennedy and, 865
Spain: cession of territory to U.S., 618–619; Ten Years' War and, 611
Spanish-American War, 597, 611–620, 617 (illus.); African Americans in, 615–616, 617, 624; buffalo soldiers in, 489; casualties of, 617; civil rights and, 624; Hawaii and, 609; *Maine* explosion, 612; outcome of, 624, 630; reasons for, 601–602; Rough Riders and, 601–602, 617
Spanish-speaking people, in Southwest, 495–496, 495 (illus.)
Special electoral commission (1877), 471
Special Forces, Kennedy, John F., and, 859
Specie Resumption Act (1875), 466
Spectator sports, 553
Speculation, 494; Native American lands and, 490; stock market crash of 1929 and, 751
Spencer, Herbert, 560
Spending: federal, 896; oil shocks and, 903; personal, 936
Spider and the Fly, The, 581
Spies, August, 535 (illus.)
Split-Level Trap, The (Gordon, Gordon, and Gunther), 843
Spock, Benjamin, 841
Spoilsmen, 470
Spoon River Anthology (Masters), 650
Sports, 553, 647, 726
Sprague, Frank J., 525
Springfield, Illinois, rioting in, 638
Springfield, Oregon, school shooting in, 982
Springfield rifle, 614
Spring Valley, Illinois, 586
Sputnik, **832**, 846 (illus.), 858, 863; Khrushchev and, 833; reaction to, 841, 846–847
Spying. *See* Espionage
"Square deal," 668–669
Stalin, Joseph, 790, 799, 802, 826; Berlin Blockade and, 814, 815 (illus.); division of Europe and, 810; Korean War and, 818; Manhattan Project and, 810; Mao Tse-Tung and, 818; NATO and, 814; at Potsdam,

807–808, 808 (illus.); at Tehran, 799; at Yalta, 799, 802
Stalingrad, Battle of, 791
Stampp, Kenneth M., 476
Standardization, 515
Standard of living, 936. *See also* Lifestyle
Standard of Living among Working Men's Families in New York City, The, 659
Standard Oil Company, 521, 522, 627, 628, 630, 631, 644; great crash and, 751; railroad rebates and, 669; trustbusting and, 668, 674
Standish, Burt, 648
Stanford, Jane, 558
Stanford, Leland, 497, 557
Stanford University, 557, 704, 884
Stanton, Edwin, 459
Stanton, Elizabeth Cady, 467, 467 (illus.); legacy of, 885
Starr, Kenneth, 982, 983
"Star-Spangled Banner, The" (Key), 699
START I, 951
START II, 951
Star wars. *See* Strategic Defense Initiative (SDI)
State(s): with new immigrant populations, 964; readmission of, 457
State Factory Investigating Commission, 633
State governments: experiments of, 576; Ku Klux Klan and, 736
States' rights: Wilson and, 675
States' Rights party, 822, 850
Statue of Liberty, 544, 631 (illus.)
Stead, William T., 564–565
Steamboats, 512
Steel industry, 520–521; Bessemer process and, 519; economic change and, 905; international production of, 519 (illus.)
Steel Workers Organizing Committee, 765
Steffens, Lincoln, 627, 657
Stein, William, 704
Stephens, Alexander, 455
Stephens, Uriah, 532
Stereopticon, 552
Stevens, John L., 609
Stevens, Thaddeus, 457, 457 (illus.), 458, 470, 476
Stevenson, Adlai, 832, 841; election of 1952 and, 826–827; election of 1956 and, 849
Stewart, A. Thomas, 744, 747
Stewart, Jimmy, 821
Stewart, Potter, 922
Stimson, Henry L., 780, 803
Stockholm (ship), 712 (illus.)
Stock market: crash of 1893 and, 583–584; crash of 2001 and, 984; and dot.coms, 988–989; great crash of 1929 and, 751. *See also* Wall Street
Stock ticker, 523
Stone, Lucy, 467, 467 (illus.)
Stowe, Harriet Beecher, 669
Straight, Willard, 693–694
Strategic Arms Limitation Talks (SALT), 897–898; SALT I, 897–898; SALT II, 917, 918, 941
Strategic bases, 610
Strategic Defense Initiative (SDI), 939, 944
Strategy of Peace, The (Kennedy), 859
Stratemeyer Literary Syndicate, 648
Streetcars, 541; electric, 525
Street gangs, 543

Strikes, 641–644; at Coeur d'Alene, 535; from 1870-1890, 534 (illus.); from 1880 to 1900, 534; during Great Depression, 765, 765 (illus.); great railroad strike (1877), 533 (illus.), 534; at Hart, Schaffner, and Marx, 642–643; Haymarket Riot, 532, 535, 535 (illus.); Homestead, 520, 535–536; injunctions and, 534; IWW and, 643–644; at Ludlow, Colorado, 679 (illus.); of miners, 585–587; in 1919, 722, 733; by PATCO, 932 (illus.); Pullman, 534, 585, 594, 662; against railroads, 532; by silk workers, 643 (illus.); and Triangle Shirtwaist Company, 642; violence and, 643; after World War II, 822

Strong, Josiah, 606

Struggling Upward (Alger), 589

Stryker, Roy, 759

Student Nonviolent Coordinating Committee (SNCC), 854, 866, 883

Student protests: antiwar, 880, 881–882, 881 (illus.), 886; sit-ins and, 853 (illus.), 854; walk-outs, 884

Students for a Democratic Society (SDS), 880

Studio One, 842

Submarines, 611, 917. *See also* U-boats

Sub-Saharan Africa: AIDS in, 946

Subsidies: for railroads, 463, 514–515; for western economies, 481–482

Suburbs: critics of, 842–843; growth of, 541, 963–964; housing discrimination and, 837, 840; Levittowns and, 837–838; middle class in, 554; in 1920s, 721, 723; shopping centers and, 840; after World War II, 839, 840–841

Subway systems, electric, 525

Suez Canal, 788, 830

Suez crisis, 830, 831

Suffrage: black male, 453, 457; Fifteenth Amendment and, 466–467; for women, 555. *See also* Voting and voting rights; Woman suffrage

Sugar and sugar industry, 608; in Cuba, 612

Sugimoto, Henry, 797

Sullivan, John L. ("Boston Strong Boy"), 553

Sullivan, Louis H., 541

Sumner, Charles, 456, 457, 470

Sumner, William Graham, 560

Sunbelt, 963; industry in, 905; 1972 election and, 900; population shift to, 928, 963, 963 (illus.); after World War II, 839–840

Sunday, 1926 (Hopper), 728

Sunday, Billy, 733

Sunni Muslims, in Iraq, 995

Supply-side economics, 930, 933

Supreme Court (U.S.), 534; activism of, 869; *Bakke* case and, 956–959; black civil rights and, 475, 475 (illus.); Nixon and, 895–896; Reagan and, 948; Reconstruction legislation and, 567–568; reform and, 868–869; Roosevelt, Franklin D., and, 769, 772–773; on segregated schooling, 556; on separate but equal doctrine, 557, 567–570; women on, 932

Surgery, 551

Surplus, in federal budget, 980

Survival of the fittest (Spencer), 560

Sussex pledge, 698–699

Swaggart, Jimmy, 935

Swan, Joseph William, 524

Swift, Gustavus F., 523, 525, 527

Swift and Company, 631

Sylvis, William H., 532

Symphony orchestras, 553

Synagogues, 548

Syria, 830, 831, 901, 940

T

Taft, Helen H., 672

Taft, Robert A., 785, 825

Taft, William Howard, 641, 672, 673–675; dollar diplomacy of, 693; election of 1908 and, 671–672; election of 1910 and, 674; election of 1912 and, 656, 675–676; Paris Peace Conference and, 713; Philippines and, 622; and presidency, 691; Roosevelt, Theodore, and, 655–656, 667, 671–672, 672 (illus.), 693; Roosevelt Corollary and, 693; tariffs and, 672, 673; trustbusting and, 668, 674

Taft Commission, 622

Taft-Hartley Act, 822

Taft-Katsura Agreement (1905), 693

Taiwan, 817, 830

Taliban (Afghanistan), 992

Tammany Hall, 471, 548, 549 (illus.)

Tampa, Florida, 616, 617

Tanguay, Eva, 648

Tanguy, Yves, 845

Tannenberg, battle at, 702 (illus.)

Tarbell, Ida, 555, 627, 628, 706

Tariff(s): Harding and, 738; McKinley and, 738; reciprocal, 606, 607, 608; Taft and, 672, 673; Underwood tariff schedules, 738; Wilson and, 676–677, 738. *See also* specific tariffs

Tariff Commission Act (1916), 682

Taxation: Bush, George, and, 960, 961; Bush, George W. and, 987, 990; Clinton and, 971; cut in, 903; election of 2000 and, 985; income tax and, 587, 645–646, 674, 677, 682, 738–739, 793; Kennedy and, 865–866; in 1920s, 738–739; poll tax and, 574, 635, 771; Reagan's cuts in, 930–931, 933; single-tax clubs and, 560; Truman and, 822; wealthy and, 738–739, 793, 822; World War II and, 793. *See also* Tariff(s)

Tax Reform Act (1986), 948

Taylor, A. J. P., 781

Taylor, Frederick Winslow, 632, 644

Taylor, Maxwell, Vietnam and, 861

Teaching: in Freedmen's schools, 465 (illus.); training for, 557; women in, 530–531

Teapot Dome scandal, 738

Technology: for cattle ranching, 500; industry and, 512; photoengraving, 627; punch card tabulator and, 604, 605 (illus.); for railroads, 516

Teenagers: black, 966. *See also* Adolescence

Tehran, Iran, 799

Telegraph, 512, 522–523, 524

Telephone, 512, 523

Televangelists, 928, 934, 935

Television: Army-McCarthy hearings and, 827; blacklisting and, 827; early years of, 842, 842 (illus.); Kennedy-Nixon debate on, 857–858; McCarthy, Joseph R., on, 827, 827 (illus.); quiz shows and, 842; Westerns on, 840. *See also* Televangelists

Teller Amendment, 613

Temin, Peter, 519–520

Temperance movement, 552

Tenements, 541–542, 541 (illus.)

Tennessee, 468; African American troops and, 615

Tennessee Coal and Iron Company, 668, 674–675

Tennessee v. *John Thomas Scopes,* 743–747

Tennessee Valley Authority (TVA), 757, 757 (illus.), 761, 772, 872

Ten Percent Plan, 453

Tenth Cavalry. *See* Buffalo soldiers

Tenure of Office Act, 458, 459

Ten Years' War, 611

Terkel, Studs, 749, 753

Terman, Lewis M., 704

Territories: in West, 495

Terrorism, 980; anthrax scare and, 992; against blacks, 462; Homeland Security Department and, 992; immigration and, 964, 965; Ku Klux Klan and, 467–469, 468 (illus.), 469 (illus.), 736; Red Scare and, 733–734; of September 11, 2001, 962, 984, 990–991; war on, 991; World Trade Center attack (1993) and, 962

Tesla, Nikola, 525

Tet offensive, 886

Teton Sioux Indians, Ghost Dances of, 487

Texas, 482; population shift to, 963

Texas and Pacific Railroad, 532

Texas longhorns, 499, 500

Texas Rangers, 601

Textbooks, in late 19th century, 556

Textile industry: child labor and, 588–589

Thain, Howard, 718

Theater: ethnic, 548

Theory of the Leisure Class, The (Veblen), 561

Thernstrom, Stephan, 531

Third Army, 798, 800, 801

Third World, 905; AIDS in, 946

Thirteenth Amendment, 454, 457 (illus.), 569

38th parallel, 817–818

This Side of Paradise (Fitzgerald), 727–728

Tho, Le Duc, 898

Thomas, Clarence, 948

Thomas, Lorenzo, 459

Thomas, Norman, 785

Thomson, J. Edgar, 516; Steel Works of, 520

Thoreau, Henry David, 853

Thornburgh, Richard, 906

369th Infantry, 712 (illus.)

Three Mile Island, nuclear accident at, 904, 906–907, 906 (illus.)

Three Soldiers (Dos Passos), 716

Thurmond, Strom, 822, 822 (illus.)

Tiananmen Square (Beijing), demonstration in, 950–951, 951 (illus.)

Tilden, Samuel J., 471

Tillman, Benjamin F., 582, 588

Timber and Stone Act (1878), 494

Timber Culture Act (1873), 494

Times Square, 718 (illus.)

Time zones, 516

"Tin Lizzie," 629

Titanic (ship), 689

Title VII (Civil Rights Act of 1964), 871

Titusville, Pennsylvania, oil well at, 521

Tobacco and tobacco industry, 581 (illus.)

Todd, Helen, 556

Tojo, Hideki, 787

Tombstone, Arizona, 498

Tom Swift series, 648, 648 (illus.)

Torlino, Tom, 490 (illus.)

"To Secure These Rights," 850
Tougaloo College, 853
Tourgée, Albion W., 568–569, 570
TOW antitank missiles, 942, 943
Towns. *See* Cities and towns
Townsend, Francis, 762, 764
Townsend Clubs, 762
Townsend Plan, 762, 763
Toynbee Hall, 562
Tracy, Benjamin F., 610–611
Trade: with China, 977; Clinton and, 980; deficit in overseas, 936; drug, 947; expansion of, 606; Federal Trade Commission and, 678; free, 971–972; in illegal drugs, 947; imperialism and, 603, 606–607, 619, 620; Kissinger and, 897; World War I and, 697–698
Trade cards, 603 (illus.)
Trading-with-the-Enemy Act (1917), 707
Tragic Era, The, 476
Trails: cattle, 501 (illus.); Sioux War and Bozeman, 486
Transamerica Corporation, 905
Transatlantic cable, for telegraphs, 522–523
Transcontinental railroad, 516–518
Trans-Mississippi West: territories in, 495. *See also* West
Transportation: freedom ride and, 866; Highway Act of 1956, 848; interstate highway system, 848–849, 849 (illus.); revolution in, 512; segregation in, 462; trucking, 722. *See also* Railroads
Transportation, Department of, 873
Trash, of westward movement, 492
Traveler from Altruria, A (Howells), 590
Treaties: of arbitration (Great Britain), 608; Indians and, 485, 487; in Latin America, 607; after Sand Creek massacre, 486; of Washington (1871), 607
Treaty of Paris (1898), **619**–620
Treaty of Washington (1871), 607
Triangle Shirtwaist Company, 632–633, 632 (illus.), 642
"Triangulation" policy, of Clinton, 974
Tribune Tower, 724 (illus.)
Trident submarine, 917
Tripartite Pact, 786
Tripp, Linda, 982
Truman, Harry S., 822–823, 850; air force and, 816; atomic bomb and, 803; Berlin Blockade and, 814; China and, 817, 830; civil rights and, 850; defense policy of, 828; domestic policies of, 819, 822–823; election of 1944 and, 797–798; election of 1948 and, 814, 822–823, 822 (illus.), 823 (illus.); Fair Deal and, 847–848, 850; health insurance plan of, 847, 872; hydrogen bomb and, 816; idealism of, 807, 808; Korean War and, 818; labor policy of, 822; loyalty issue and, 823–824; MacArthur, Douglas, and, 818–819; Medicare law and, 872; New Deal and, 819, 822; postwar aid and, 810; at Potsdam, 807–808, 808 (illus.); Roosevelt's death and, 802; Soviet Union and, 810; tax policy of, 822. *See also* Cold War; World War II
Truman Doctrine, 811–**812**
Trunk lines, 515–516
Trusts and trustbusting, 630–631, 631 (illus.), 667–668, 674, 677; development of, **522;** Sherman Antitrust Act and, 578–579

Tuberculosis, 541 (illus.), 551
Tulane, 557
Tunisia, 791
Tunney, Gene, 726
Turkey: Cold War and, 811; Cuban missile crisis and, 862; World War I and, 696
Turner, Frederick Jackson, 507, 605
Turner, Henry McNeal, 475–478, 478 (illus.)
Turner's thesis, on American frontier, **507,** 605
Tuskegee Institute, 558–559, 559 (illus.), 681
TVA. *See* Tennessee Valley Authority (TVA)
Twain, Mark, 497, 590, 619
Tweed, William M., 548–549, 549 (illus.)
"Tweed Days in St. Louis" (Steffens), 627
Tweed Ring, 471, 548–549
Twenty-fifth Infantry, 615, 617
Twenty-fourth Infantry, 615
Twenty-one, 842
Twenty-One Demands, 693
Tyco International, 987
Tydings, Millard, 825
Typewriter, 523, 525 (illus.)
Typographical Union, 533

U

UAW. *See* United Automobile Workers (UAW)
U-boats: U.S. losses to, 701 (illus.); in World War I, 668–669, 689–690, 697, 698–699, 698 (illus.), 700; in World War II, 785, 793. *See also* Submarines
Udall, Stuart, 864
UN. *See* United Nations (UN)
Unabomber, 981
Understanding AIDS, 945 (illus.)
Underwood Tariff Act, 676–677
Undocumented aliens, 874, 965
Unemployment, 896, 969; of African Americans, 462, 966; attitudes about, 588; Bush, George W., and, 987; during depression of 1893-1897, 574, 591; in early 1900s, 628; during Great Depression, 751, 751 (illus.), 755; Native Americans and, 491; in 1980, 929; Panic of 1893 and, 584; public works projects and, 754, 760 (illus.), 761; Social Security and, 763; after World War II, 840
UNIA. *See* United Negro Improvement Association (UNIA)
Unilateralism, 993–994
Unionists, 453
Union Pacific Railroad, 470, 495, 515–516, 518, 584
Union party, 768
Unions (labor). *See* Labor unions
Union Station (Washington), 516
Union Stock Yards (Chicago), 526, 526 (illus.), 527, 527 (illus.)
United Airlines, 992
United Automobile Workers (UAW), 765, 905
United Fruit, 630
United Kingdom. *See* England (Britain)
United Mine Workers, 586–587, 586 (illus.), 668
United Nations (UN): arms control and, 831–832; Bosnia and, 978; Declaration of, 789; disarmament and, 810; Iraq invasion and, 994, 995; Korean War and, 817, 818
United Negro Improvement Association (UNIA), 730–731

United States, physiographic map of, 482 (illus.)
U.S. Army Intelligence Alpha Test, 704–705, 705 (illus.)
U.S. Chamber of Commerce, 658
U.S. Patent Office, 522
U.S. Public Health Service, 634
U.S. Reclamation Service, 634
U.S. Rubber, 630
U.S. Steel, 520–521, 630; Kennedy, John F., and, 865; organized labor and, 764; trustbusting and, 668, 674–675
U.S. Treasury: depression of 1893-1897 and, 587; Panic of 1893 and, 583
United States v. *E. C. Knight Co.,* 579
United States v. *Harris,* 475 (illus.)
Universal education, 556
Universities and colleges: coeducation in, 558; education as field of study in, 557; football at, 553; in late 19th century, 557–560; for women, 558
University of Alabama, 867
University of California: *Bakke* case and, 956–959; student protests at Berkeley, 880
University of Chicago, 557; antiwar protest at, 782 (illus.); Manhattan Project and, 803; School of Pedagogy at, 662
University of Michigan, 558 (illus.); Medical School at, 658
University of Mississippi, 866–867
University of Wisconsin, 588; reform and, 666
Unskilled workers, 529; immigrants as, 543
Urban areas: African Americans in, 966–967; immigrants in, 964. *See also* Cities and towns
Urbanization, 540, 605, 963–964; automobile and, 721; census of 1890 and, 605; Democratic party and, 739; Great Depression and, 759; migration and, 722–723; in 1900-1920, 645–648; 1920 census and, 723; segregation and, 647; urban population and, 633; World War II and, 795; zoning laws and, 646–647. *See also* Suburbs
Urban League, 729, 883
Utah, 482; Mormons in, 491; woman suffrage in, 574
Utah Copper Company, 639
Ute Indians, 482, 483, 486
U-2 (plane), 833, 833 (illus.), 862

V

Vaccines, 551
Vagrancy laws, 462
Valentino, Rudolph, 727
Values: religious and patriotic, 552
Vance, Cyrus, 913, 917
Vandenberg, Arthur, 811–812
Vanderbilt, Alfred G., 689
Vanderbilt, Cornelius, 516, 516 (illus.)
Vanderbilt University, 557
Van Devanter, Willis, 769, 772
Van Doren, Charles, 842
Van Vorst, Bessie, 535, 564
Van Vorst, Marie, 564
Vanzetti, Bartolomeo, 734, 734 (illus.)
Vaqueros, 499
Vassar, 558
Vaudeville, 648
Vaughn, Harry, 819

Veblen, Thorstein, 561

Veiller, Lawrence, 658–659

Venezuela, 607–608, 692–693

Venture capital firms, 988

Verdun, battle at, 703

Versailles Treaty, 708, 712–716, 714 (illus.); Hitler and, 781; Roosevelt, Franklin D., and, 779; Senate rejection of, 715 (illus.)

Vertical integration, 520, 522

Veterans: bonus army and, 754; of Civil War, 575, 577; Dependent Pensions Act and, 578

Veterans of Future Wars, 782

Veto: Cleveland and, 577; Johnson, Andrew, and, 456; Lincoln and, 453

Vichy regime (France), 789

Vickers (Great Britain), 782

Vicksburg, 635

Victorian morality, 551–552

Victorious Retreat Back to the Rhine (Schoonover), 702 (illus.)

Victor Talking Machine Company, 647

Vietcong, 879–880, 879 (illus.), 885–886. *See also* Vietnam War

Vietminh. *See* Vietnam War

Vietnam: Ford and, 914; immigrants from, 967; second great migration and, 874

Vietnam War, 876–880, 877 (illus.), 878 (illus.), 879 (illus.), 880, 885–889; costs of, 896, 896 (illus.); ending of, 898–899; events leading to, 829–830; Geneva conference and, 829; Kennedy and, 860–861; King, Martin Luther, Jr., on, 883; monks and, 861, 861 (illus.); road to, 829 (illus.), 831

Vigilante movement, Klan as, 467

Villa, Francisco "Pancho," 695–696, 701

Villard, Oswald Garrison, 638, 678

Violence: against blacks, 462; of Ku Klux Klan, 467–469; in 1990s, 980–982; against WTO, 981–982. *See also* Strikes

Virginia: African American troops in, 615; Ninth Cavalry in, 615

Virginia City, Nevada, 497, 498

Virgin Islands, 692

Vittum, Harriet, 539, 563

Volstead Act, 734

Voluntarism, during Great Depression, 754

Voting and voting rights: African Americans and, 473, 574–575, 579, 872–873, 873 (illus.); ballot box and, 575 (illus.); civil rights movement and, 852, 866, 867, 872–873; "eight box" law and, 574; election of 2000 and, 985; election of 1980 and, 929–930, 930 (illus.); ethnic groups and, 755 (illus.), 769; Fourteenth Amendment and, 458; "grandfather clause" and, 575, 639; Ku Klux Klan terrorism and, 467–468; literacy requirement and, 574; NAACP and, 639; in 1972, 900; participation and, 664 (illus.); poll tax and, 574, 635; reapportionment and, 868–869; secret ballot and, 575; in South, 454, 473; woman suffrage and, 660–662; women and, 574. *See also* Nineteenth Amendment; Suffrage

Voting Rights Act: of 1957, 871; **of 1965, 872,** 873 (illus.)

W

Wabash, St. Louis, & Pacific Railway Co. v. *Illinois,* 576

Waco, Texas, 980, 981

Wade, Benjamin, 459, 470

Wade, Henry, *Roe* v. *Wade* and, 920–921

Wade-Davis Bill (1864), **453**

Wage(s): differences in, 531; 1880-1914, 529; of immigrants, 964–965; of women, 530

Wage labor: freedmen and, 460, 461. *See also* Labor

Wage/price freeze, 896–897, 896 (illus.)

Wagner, Robert, 763

Wagner Act (1935), **763**–764, 765, 772, 773, 822

Wagon trains, 492–493

Wainwright Building, 541

Wald, Lillian, 562, 563, 696

Walesa, Lech, 951

Walker, Alice, 681

Walker, C. J. (Madam), 680–681, 680 (illus.), 681 (illus.)

Walker, Charles, J., 680

Walker, Martin, 970

Walking cities: transportation and, 541

Wallace, George C., 897; civil rights movement and, 867; election of 1968 and, 888–889; election of 1972 and, 899–900; as governor of Alabama, 889

Wallace, Henry A., 758, 797, 822

Wallace, Lew, 589

Walling, William E., 638

Wall Street: explosion of 1920, 733 (illus.), 734; Panic of 1893 and, 583–584. *See also* Stock market

Wall Street Journal, on illegal aliens, 965

Wanamaker, John, 528

Wang Dan, 951 (illus.)

War Committee on Labor, 709

Ward, A. H., 450 (illus.)

Ward, Aaron Montgomery, 528–529

Ward, Will J., 697 (illus.)

War Department, 614, 615, 616, 624

Ware, James E., 542

War Industries Board (WIB), 708

War Labor Board (WLB), 709

War on drugs, 946–947

War on poverty, 871

War on terrorism, 991

War Production Board (WPB), 793

Warren, Earl, 850, 868, 895

Warren Commission report, 869

Warren Court, 868–869

Wars and warfare: guerrilla warfare, 879–880; Kellogg-Briand Pact and, 777; Native Americans and, 484; U.S. brutality in, 620. *See also* specific battles and wars

War Shipping Board, 709

War Trade Board, 709

Washington (state), 481

Washington, Booker T., 558–559, 559 (illus.), 620, 639, 680, 681; Du Bois and, 638; White House visit by, 667

Washington, D.C.: antiwar movement in, 886; bonus army in, 754; Coxey's Army in, 584–585; march on Pentagon (1967) in, 881–882, 881 (illus.); March on Washington (1963) in, 867–868, 868 (illus.); Mothers' Crusade in, 786; parades in, 614; Poor People's March (1968) in, 883; Prayer Pilgrimage to, 853; Randolph's threatened march on, 795; rioting in, 883–884. *See also* Terrorism

Washington, George: foreign relations and, 602–603

Washington, Treaty of, 607

Washington Disarmament Conference, 780

Washington Monument, 520

Washington Post, 893

Waste Land, The (Eliot), 727, 728

Water, 542–543; pollution and purification of, 542–543; as western issue, 494–495. *See also* Irrigation

Watergate scandal, 893–894, **900–901**

Watson, Thomas E., 582, 595

Watt, James, 932

Wattenberg, Ben, 897

Watts: King, Rodney, riots in, 966–967, 967 (illus.); rioting in, 883

WCTU. *See* Women's Christian Temperance Union (WCTU)

Wealth: distribution of, 645–646, 723, 752, 762, 794; inequality of, 937–938; intellectual thought on, 560–561; Long, Huey, and, 762; in 1920s, 720–723; per capita income and, 720; postwar boom and, 839–841; under Reagan, 936–938; in South, 460; taxation and, 738–739; transfer of, 938; wage rates and, 722. *See also* Affluence

Wealth gap, 938

Weapons: arms race and, 917; of Hussein, Saddam, 954; naval, 611; Spanish-American War and, 614

Weapons of mass destruction (WMD), 994, 995

Weaver, James B., 577, 583, 587

Weaver, Randy, 981

Weaver, Robert, 866

Webb, Walter Prescott, 483

Weber, Max, 650

Webster's Spellers, 556

Weddington, Sarah, 921, 922, 923

Weinberger, Caspar, 940, 942

Welch, Joseph, 827

Welfare system: Clinton and, 974; Nixon and, 895

Wellesley college, 558

Wells-Barnett, Ida B., 681

West: African American troops in, 615; agriculture in, 505 (illus.); buffalo soldiers in, 488–489, 488 (illus.); cattle ranching in, 499–501, 501 (illus.); Chinese laborers in, 498–499; Democratic party and, 739; economies of, 481–482; farming in, 502–506; imperialism debate and, 620; irrigation in, 634; land in, 493–495; meaning of, 507; mining in, 496–499, 498 (illus.); Native Americans in, 481, 483–491; Northwestern Alliance in, 581–582; Oklahoma territory and, 506; population of, 928, 963; Populism and, 579, 588; railroads and, 513 (illus.); settlement of, 481–507; silver coinage and, 591; territorial government in, 495; Timber Culture Act and, 494; woman suffrage and, 574. *See also* Southwest; Sunbelt; Westward movement

West Berlin, 860 (illus.)

Western Federation of Miners, 643

Western Pacific Railroad, 639

Western-themed toys, 840 (illus.)

Western Union, 709

West Germany, Berlin Wall and, 860 (illus.)

Westinghouse Electric Company, 525, 751

Westmoreland, William, 879–880, 885–886
West Paducah, Kentucky, school shooting in, 982
Westward movement: between 1870 and 1900, 491–496
Weyler y Nicolau, Valeriano, 612, 620
Wharton, Edith, 728
"What Every Girl Should Know" (Sanger), 636
What Price Glory (Anderson), 716
What Social Classes Owe to Each Other (Sumner), 560
Wheeler, Burton, 772
"Whiskey Ring," 470
White, Byron, 923
White, George H., 473–474, 615
White, Henry, 713
White, Theodore, on election of 1980, 930
White, William Allen, 540, 551, 657, 785
White Collar (Mills), 843
White-collar jobs, Reagan and, 937
White Committee, 785
White House: Kennedys in, 864 (illus.); protection of, 588, 597; telephone in, 523; "war room" in, 617. *See also* Presidency
White League, 468
Whites: in U.S. population (1900), 550
White Shadows (McKay), 729
White supremacy, 464; lynchings of blacks and, 474, 474 (illus.); in New South, 472; Reconstruction and, 458, 476. *See also* Ku Klux Klan
Whitewater scandal, 973, 982
Whitman, Walt, 513–514, 589
Whittier, John Greenleaf, 511
Whyte, William H., 843
Wiggins, Kate Douglas, 648
Wild West Show, of Buffalo Bill Cody, 491, 498, 500 (illus.)
Wiley, Harvey W., 671
Wilhelm II (Germany), 696, 698, 706
Willard, Frances E., 552
Williamsburg: Colonial Williamsburg and, 756
Williams v. *Mississippi*, 475 (illus.), 574
Willkie, Wendell, 785
Wilson, Charles E., 848
Wilson, Edith Bolling, 715
Wilson, Luzena, 492
Wilson, William B., 679
Wilson, Woodrow, 522, 676, 677 (illus.), 708, 715, 716; African Americans and, 678, 681; on *Birth of a Nation,* 476; Colombia and, 692; Committee on Public Information and, 706; Congress and, 678; Democratic party and, 596; draft and, 701–702; election of 1912 and, 656, 675–676; election of 1914 and, 678; election of 1916 and, 699–700; election of 1920 and, 716; foreign policy under, 694–696; Fourteen Points of, 712–714, 713 (illus.); immigration and, 641, 736; labor and, 661, 678–679, 682, 709; *Lusitania* and, 689–690, 698; Mexico and, 694–696; moral diplomacy of, 694; neutrality and, 696–698, 701; New Freedom and, 629, 675–678, 708; New Nationalism and, 678–679, 682; Panama Canal and, 694; Paris Peace Conference and, 708, 712–713; "peace without victory" speech of, 700; and presidency, 682–683, 691; reform and, 666, 678–679, 682; repression and, 706–708; Roosevelt Corollary and, 693; Russia and,

712; *Sussex* pledge and, 698–699; tariffs and, 676–677; trade policy of, 678; trustbusting and, 677; Versailles Treaty and, 712–716; woman suffrage and, 682. *See also* World War I
Wilson-Gorman Tariff Act (1894), 587, 607, 611
Winfrey, Oprah, 681
Winnebago Indians, 483
Wisconsin, 482; La Follette in, 666 (illus.)
Wisconsin Idea, 666–667
Wives, 555; of middle class, 554
WLB. *See* War Labor Board (WLB)
Wobblies. *See* Industrial Workers of the World (IWW)
Woman's Peace party, 696
Woman's Political Caucus, 854
Woman suffrage, 467, 574 (illus.), 660–662; demonstrations for, 661 (illus.); *Minor* v. *Happersett* and, 574; movement, 555; National Woman Suffrage Association and, 574; before 1920, 661 (illus.); Wilson and, 682. *See also* Nineteenth Amendment; Voting and voting rights; Women
Woman Who Toils, The: Being the Experiences of Two Gentlewomen as Factory Girls (Van Vorst), 564
Women: abortion rights and, 910, 920–924; advertising to, 721 (illus.); AFL and, 533; African American, 634, 660; birth control and, 635, 636–637, 725; birthrate and, 725, 908; Civil Rights Act of 1964 and, 885; civil rights movement and, 854; divorce rate and, 725; as domestics, 589 (illus.), 634; education and, 557–558, 634; election of 1916 and, 700; employment of, 937; family life and, 554, 634, 724–725; feminism and, 660–662, 724, 885; flapper image and, 724–725; in government, 767–768, 848; Great Depression and, 767–768; in higher education, 634; household labor of, 725; as humanitarians, 724; in immigrant associations, 548; in Knights of Labor, 532, 532 (illus.), 533; in labor force, 588, 634, 709, 724, 767, 768 (illus.), 794–795, 795 (illus.), 841; labor law and, 684–687; legal codes for, 555; lifestyle of, 908–909; marital status and employment of, 634; in medical profession, 559, 634; in mining camps, 498, 499; Mother's Day and, 635; *Muller* v. *Oregon* and, 684–687; "new woman" and, 554–555; in 1920s, 724–725; in professions, 768; as reformers, 635; roles of, 794–795, 795 (illus.), 885; Seneca Falls and, 660; as settlement house workers, 562; sexuality and, 725, 727; in single parent families, 908; on strike, 642–643; study clubs of, 557–558; suburbanization and, 841; suffrage movement and, 660–662, 724; on Supreme Court, 932, 933 (illus.); Title VII of Civil Rights Act of 1964 and, 871; in unions, 632, 635, 640, 642, 905; voting and, 938; wage discrimination and, 709, 710, 767, 885; westward migration of, 492–493; in workforce, 530–531, 634; World War I and, 709–710, 710 (illus.); World War II and, 794–795, 795 (illus.). *See also* Abortion and abortion rights; Nineteenth Amendment; Wives; Woman suffrage
Women and Economics (Gilman), 555

Women and Lovers, 727
Women Rebel, 636–637, 637 (illus.)
Women's Bureau, 710
Women's Christian Temperance Union (WCTU), 465, **552,** 659–660
Women's rights: Reagan and, 932. *See also* Woman suffrage; Women
Women's rights movement, 467
Women's Trade Union League (WTUL), 632, 635, **640,** 642, 660, 770
Women Wage-Earners: Their Past, Their Present and Their Future (Campbell), 564
Wonderful Wizard of Oz, The (Baum), 592 (illus.), 593 (illus.)
Wood, Leonard, 602, 622, 733
Woodham, Luke, 982
Woodhull, Victoria Claflin, 574 (illus.)
Woods, Robert A., 562, 563
Woods, Tiger, 968, 969 (illus.)
Woodstock (music festival), 882, 883 (illus.)
Woolworth, F. W., 528
Woolworth building, 723
Woolworth's, 722; lunch counter sit-in, 853 (illus.)
Work and Win (Alger), 589
Workers. *See* Labor
Workers, The (Wyckoff), 564
Workforce: women in, 909. *See also* Employment; Labor
Working class: in cities, 541; family life of, 554; voting patterns of, 587
Workingmen's party (California), 531
Works Progress Administration (WPA), 760 (illus.), **761,** 762, 771 (illus.), 773, 844; African Americans and, 766; immigrants and, 767; women and, 770
WorldCom, Inc., 987
World Series (baseball), 553
World Trade Center: attack on (1993), 962; destruction of (2001), 962, 984, 990–991, 991 (illus.)
World Trade Organization (WTO), 981–982
World War I: African Americans and, 681, 702, 709, 710–711, 730–731; alliances in, 696–697, 702 (illus.); battlefronts in, 702 (illus.), 703 (illus.); bureaucracies and, 709; casualties in, 706, 706 (illus.); end of, 703, 706; financing of, 708; freedom of seas and, 697–698; Germany and, 714; home front during, 706–712; immigration and, 639; IQ testing and, 704; joint resolution ending, 716; labor during, 709–712; loyalty and, 707, 707 (illus.); mobilization for, 701; neutrality and, 696–697; preparedness and, 699, 701; propaganda and, 688 (illus.), 706–708; public opinion and, 696–697, 701; rationing and, 709; repression during, 706–708; size of government and, 709, 711; *Sussex* pledge and, 698–699; trench warfare in, 702–703, 706; U.S. in, 700–703, 706; before U.S. entry, 696–701; veterans of, 754; war bonds and, 681; war debt and, 778–779; war plans for, 701; women and, 709–710, 710 (illus.); World War II and, 781; Zimmermann telegram and, 700. *See also* U-boats
World War II, 776 (illus.), 783–784, 783 (illus.), 799 (illus.), 804; alliances and, 780, 781, 788–789; Allied strategy in, 790–791; anti-Comintern pact and, 781; appeasement and, 783–784, 811; arms buildups

World War II (continued): before, 780; arsenal of democracy and, 792–794; Bataan death march and, 788; Berlin-Rome-Tokyo axis in, 781; *blitzkrieg* and, 784; Casablanca meeting and, 790; cash-and-carry and, 784, 785; code breaking during, 787; Cold War origins and, 808–810; Corregidor and, 788; D-Day and, 798; destroyers-for-bases deal in, 784–785; end of, 798–799, 802–803; in Europe, 783–786, 788–792; events leading to, 784–788; family life and, 794; Free French and, 789; Greater East Asia Co-Prosperity Sphere and, 786; Holocaust and, 798, 800–801, 800 (illus.), 801 (illus.); home front during, 789 (illus.), 792–798, 804; intelligence testing and, 705; interventionism and, 785–786; isolationism and, 777–779, 780–781, 784–786, 786 (illus.); Japanese Americans during, 796–797, 796 (illus.), 797 (illus.); Japanese surrender in, 803; labor and, 793–794; Leyte Gulf and, 802; Marshall Plan and, 812–813; migration during, 794; Nazi-Soviet Pact and, 784, 790; neutrality and, 781–783; in North Africa, 788, 791; in Pacific, 781, 786–788, 791–792, 792 (illus.), 802–803; pacifism and, 781–783; Pearl Harbor and, 787–788, 788 (illus.); postwar period, 808–810, 809 (illus.); Potsdam Summit and, 807–808, 808 (illus.); rationing during, 793, 794, 794 (illus.); reparations and, 808; Russia, invasion of, and, 788; second front in, 798; service stars and, 789 (illus.); Tripartite Pact and, 786; unconditional surrender and, 790, 802; undeclared U.S. naval war in, 785–786; after U.S. entry, 788–792; Vichy regime and, 789; Yalta Conference and, 799, 802, 816. *See also* Axis Powers

"Worse Than Slavery" (Nast), 469 (illus.)

Worthington, Howard, 749

Wounded Knee Massacre, 487

Wovoka (Paiute messiah), 487

WPA. *See* Works Progress Administration (WPA)

WPB. *See* War Production Board (WPB)

Wright, Frank Lloyd, 541

Wright, Orville, 598

Wright, Wilbur, 598

Wriston, Henry W., 854

WTO. *See* World Trade Organization (WTO)

Wyckoff, Walter, 564

Wyoming, 482, 574

Wyoming Stock Growers' Association, 500

X

X ray, 598

Y

Yahoo!, 989

Yale Club, 601

Yalta Conference, 799, 802, 816, 818

Year 2000 (Y2K), 984

Yellow journalism, 612

Yeltsin, Boris, 951, 953 (illus.), 976–977

Yemen, *Cole* attack in, 991

Yergin, Daniel, 808

Yiddish (Jewish) Theater, 548

Yippies, 882

YMCA, 681

Yom Kippur War. *See* October War (1973)

Young, Charles, 615 (illus.)

Y2K problem, 984

Yugoslavia, breakup of, 978, 978 (illus.)

Yurok Indians, 483

Yzaguirre, Raul, 968

Z

Zangwill, Israel, 565, 968

Zen Buddhism, 843

Ziegfeld's Follies, 648

Ziegler, Ron, 893

Zimmermann telegram, 700

Zuni Indians, 483, 484